FROM HIRING TO FIRING

A Comparative Study
on Selected Legal Safeguards
for the Independence and Impartiality
of International Civil Servants
Serving in the United Nations Secretariat
and in the European Commission

FROM HIRING TO FIRING

A Comparative Study on Selected Legal Safeguards
for the Independence and Impartiality of International Civil Servants
Serving in the United Nations Secretariat
and in the European Commission

Iveta Alexovičová

ISBN: 978-90-5850-846-1

Cover design: Jeroen Nuissl
Cover image: 'Tug of War' by Bruno Budrovic

Published by:
Wolf Legal Publishers (WLP)
Postbus 31051
6503 CB Nijmegen
The Netherlands
E-Mail: info@wolfpublishers.nl
www.wolfpublishers.com

FROM HIRING TO FIRING

A Comparative Study
on Selected Legal Safeguards
for the Independence and Impartiality
of International Civil Servants
Serving in the United Nations Secretariat
and in the European Commission

DISSERTATION

to obtain the degree of doctor at Maastricht University,
on the authority of the Rector Magnificus,
Prof. dr. G.P.M.F. Mols,
in accordance with the decision of the Board of Deans,
to be defended in public
on Wednesday the 4th of July 2012, at 14.00 hours

by

Iveta Alexovičová

Supervisor:

Prof. dr. P.L.H. Van den Bossche

Assessment Committee:

Prof. dr. E.I.L. Vos (Chairperson)

Prof. dr. N.M. Blokker (Leiden University)

Prof. dr. S. Vanhoonacker

To Jeroen, who made it all possible,
and
to Zara Alexandra,
whom I dreamed of since the beginning of this research
and who came at the very end of it

ACKNOWLEDGEMENTS

This book has been a lengthy project, and many people have contributed to its completion. I would like to take this opportunity and express my heartfelt gratitude to them.

In particular, I owe an enormous thanks to Peter van den Bossche, my thesis supervisor. He offered me a posibility to write a PhD thesis under his supervision and left me all the space to choose and repeatedly modify and adjust the topic as I thought necessary. I am thankful to Peter also for his patience in reading endless pages of text and for his excellent and detailed comments. I am also grateful for Peter's exceptional kindness and understanding for a personal difficulty that profoundly marked the years during which I worked on this book.

I would also like to thank my doctoral assessment committee, Ellen Vos (Chairperson), Sophie Vanhoonacker and Niels Blokker, for finding the time to read the lengthy manuscript and for providing me with valuable comments. To Ellen Vos I am, in addition, thankful for her suggestion to make staff serving in the European Commission a part of this study. Her suggestion came at the very beginning of my research when I was considering comparing the situation in a number of international organizations instead. Ellen's enthousiasm and encouragement to compare an international organization with the European Commission was decisive for the final determination of the topic of this book. I also owe an additional thanks to Niels Blokker who provided me with important contacts at the Duch Ministry of Foreign Affairs. As he did, also Sophie Vanhoonacker showed a much appreciated interest in my topic, long before the book was completed. Sophie Vanhoonacker also helped with a number of specific questions with which I turned to her, for which too I am sincerely thankful.

When conducting research for this book, I have been fortunate to benefit from the experience and insights of many people. Busy as they are, they found time to speak to me extensively and/or repeatedly and to provide me with useful information. In particular, I would like to express my gratitude to the following persons (listed in alphabetic order and with the function they held at the time of our interview). In the United Nations, or related to it, I benefited from the help and advice of: Mr. M. Abelian, Secretary, Administrative and Budgetary (Fifth) Committee of the General Assembly & the Committee for Programme and Coordination; Mr. B.R.E. Coffi, Counselor, Ivory Coast Permanent Mission to the United Nations; Mr. Y. Kishimoto, First Secretary, Permanent Mission of Japan to the United Nations; Mr. J. Kramer, Member, Advisory Committee on Administrative and Budgetary Questions; Ms. M.H. Lopez, Director, Office of Human Resources Managementof the United Nations Secretariat; Ms. R. Page, First Secretary, United Kingdom Mission to the United Nations; Ms. M. Rafajová, Second Secretary, Permanent Mission of the Slovak Republic to the United Nations; Mr. K. P. Rhodes, Chairman, International Civil Service Commission; Mr. K. de Rijk, First Secretary, Permanent Mission of the Kingdom of The Netherlands to the United Nations; Mr. W. Stöckl, Vice-Chairman, International Civil Service Commission; Ms. M. Struyvenberg, Executive Secretary, United Nations

Administrative Tribunal; later Principal Registrar, Office of Administration of Justice; Ms. L. Swart, Executive Director, Center for UN Reform Education; and Mr. A. Torres Lépori, Member, Advisory Committee on Administrative and Budgetary Questions.

I am also grateful to the following persons working for, or related to, the European Commission: Mr. J. Currall, Director - Principal Legal Adviser, Legal Service; Ms. B. Eggers, Member, Legal Service; Ms. S. Jacobs, First Vice-president, Union Syndicale Fédérale; Mr. P. J. Kuijper, Professor at University of Amsterdam, former Director, Legal Service; Mr. J. Schuijt, HRM Officer, Middle and Senior Management Staff, Directorate General for Human Resources and Security; Mr. M. Šefčovič, Vice-President of the European Commission, Inter-Institutional Relations and Administration; Mr. H. Spitzer, Head of Unit, Administration and Human Resources, European Anti-fraud Office (OLAF); Mr. H. van Lier, Director, Directorate-General for Human Resources and Security; Mr. M. Will, Head of Unit, Staffing, Organisational Structure and Metrics, Directorate General for Human Resources and Security; Ms. R. Zarnauskaite, Policy Officer, Directorate General for Trade. My thanks also goes to the following persons working in the Directorate General for Human Resources and Security of the European Commission who provided me with specific information and/or documents used in this book: Mr. L. Blasig; Ms. Ch. Huguet, Ms. Ch. Judmaier, Ms. F. Salinas, Mr. Th. Andreou, Ms. M. Relich-Imbart, and Mr. T. Steiger. I also owe thanks to Ms. B. Joziasse, Coordinator International Positions, Dutch Ministry of Foreign Affairs; to Mr. T. Van Boven, Professor at Maastricht University with past experience as a senior official of the United Nations Secretariat, for sharing their experience with me.

My special thanks goes to Klaus de Rijk, mentioned above, who opened many doors for me in New York and whose persistent interest in this book, advice and assistance was invaluable. I also thank Helen Westerhuijs, who worked as intern secretary at the Dutch Permanent Mission to the United Nations. Under the supervision of Klaus de Rijk, Helen set up almost the entire programme of interviews in New York for me. Similar words of appreciation go to Beáta Podhorná, assisstant of the Vice-President of the European Commissioner Šefčovič, who helped me repeatedly in my contact with the Vice-President.

All these people have been indispensable for the completion of this book. However, none of them bears responsibility for the opinions expressed in the book or any errors; they are mine alone.

My big thanks is also due to Denise Prévost, my colleague at Maastricht University and friend, who helped me in countless ways over the past years. Her excellence and thoughtful advice were of great importance to me. I also owe such thanks to two other colleagues and friends, Elissaveth Malathouni and Arkady Kudryavtsev, who repeatedly took over some of my duties at Maastricht University, thereby allowing me to work on this book.

My thanks goes also to those who have contributed to the actual production of the book. In particular, I would like to thank Nuggehally Jayaram for proofreading the text, and Michelle Prévost for providing this book with a perfect lay-out. I am also grateful to my step-mother-in-law Tineke Van den Burg and to my husband Jeroen

Nuissl for translating the summary of this book into Dutch.

My husband Jeroen deserves an additional and very special thanks. This book would have never been completed without his gigantic help and support. As a sign of my deep gratitute, and love, I dedicate this book to him, and to our daughter Zara Alexandra.

The manuscript for this book was completed on 1 August 2011. It does not reflect changes that took place in the United Nations Secretariat and the European Commission after 1 January 2011. From this date onwards, last revisions of the manuscript took place. The subsequent delay with publication is due to the birth of my daugther and my maternity and parental leave.

TABLE OF CONTENTS

LIST OF ABBREVIATIONS

AD	Administrators
AST	Assistants
AUT	Austria
BEL	Belgium
BGR	Bulgaria
CDR	Career Development Review
CFI	Court of First Instance of the European Communities
CIE	Committee of Independent Experts of the European Parliament
CYP	Cyprus
CZE	Czech Republic
DEU	Germany
DNK	Denmark
EC	European Community
ECJ	Court of Justice of the European Union
ECR	European Court Reports
ECSC	European Coal and Steel Community
EEC	European Economic Community
EP	European Parliament
EPSO	European Personnel Selection Office
ESP	Spain
EST	Estonia
EU	European Union
EURATOM	European Atomic Energy Community
FIN	Finland
FRA	France
G-77	The Group of 77
GBR	Great Britain
GRC	Greece
HUN	Hungary
IDOC	Investigation and Disciplinary Office of the European Commission

ILOAT	Administrative Tribunal of the International Labour Organisation
IRL	Ireland
ITA	Italy
JIU	Joint Inspection Unit
LTU	Lithuania
LUX	Luxemburg
LVA	Latvia
MEP	Member of the European Parliament
MLT	Malta
MS	Member State(s)
NCRE	National Competitive Recruitment Examinations
NLD	Netherlands
OHRM	Office of Human Resources Management
OIOS	Office of Internal Oversight Services
OJ	Official Journal of the European Union
OLAF	European Anti-Fraud Office
OPAS	Operational, Executive and Administrative Services
POL	Poland
PRT	Portugal
ROM	Romania
SVK	Slovakia
SVN	Slovenia
SWE	Sweden
TAOs	Technical Assistance Officers
UK	United Kingdom
UN	United Nations
UNAT	United Nations Administrative Tribunal
UNDP	United Nations Development Programme
US	United States
WHO	World Health Organization

LIST OF TABLES

LIST OF SCHEMES

Introduction

The importance of international organizations in the contemporary world hardly needs to be emphasized. A large volume of literature has been produced by political scientists, lawyers and others explaining the impact of international organizations on our daily lives. Indeed, as Schermers and Blokker, authors of one of the classic works on international organizations, state:

> *We depend for our future on international order. Our destiny is increasingly influenced by the activities – or lack thereof – of international organizations.*[1]

Naturally, the degree to which international organizations influence world affairs depends on the scope left to them by their Member States. The latter continue to be principal elements of the contemporary international society. In the last two decades, they have even shown increased assertiveness regarding their sovereign powers, including those delegated to, or shared with, international organizations.[2] Despite this, there is general agreement that international organizations are of great importance and 'a necessary part of the system for dealing with international problems'.[3]

Broad agreement also exists with regard to the understanding that, in order to function properly, international organizations need efficient, competent and dedicated staff.[4] This is, of course, not different from any other public or private organization. Like them, international organizations need staff to perform their tasks and carry out their objectives.[5] In addition, in international organizations, it is the staff who are continuously present. Although, formally speaking, Member States constitute international organizations and decide upon their mandates and directions, the representatives of those States are not involved in the organizations' daily functioning; the staff are. For that reason it is the staff who are generally 'equated' with

[1] Schermers, H. G. and Blokker, N. M., *International Institutional Law, Unity within Diversity,* Martinus Nijhoff Publishers, Boston / Leiden, 2003, p. v.

[2] On the issue of international organizations *vis-à-vis* state sovereignty, see, for example, Martinez, M. M. M., *National Sovereignty and International Organizations,* Kluwer Law International, The Hague / Boston / London, 1996; Emadi-Coffin, B., *Rethinking International Organizations, Deregulation and Global Governance,* Routledge, London / New York, 2002 and Sarooshi, D., *International Organizations and Their Exercise of Sovereign Powers,* Oxford University Press, Oxford, 2005. See also, for example, Klabbers, J., *An Introduction to International Institutional Law,* Cambridge University Press, Cambridge, 2002, pp. 334-344; Schermers and Blokker, *International Institutional Law, Unity within Diversity,* p. vi; 1-4 and 1202-1205; and Spence, D. and Edwads, G. (eds.), *The European Commission,* John Harper Publishing, London, 2006, p. 6.

[3] Claude, I. L., Jr., *Swords Into Plowshares,* Random House, Inc.&Random House of Canada Limited, New York / Toronto, 1971, p. 6. See also, for example, Weiss, T. G., *International Bureaucracy, An Analysis of the Operation of Functional and Global International Secretariats,* Lexington Books, D.C. Health and Company, Massachusetts / Toronto / London, 1975, pp. xiii and xvi; Lemoine, J., *The International Civil Servant: An Endangered Species,* Kluwer Law International, The Hague / London / Boston, 1995, pp. 2-3; Archer, C., *International Organizations,* Routledge, London / New York, 2001, pp. 175-181; Sands, P. and Klein, P., *Bowlett's Law of International Institutions,* Sweet & Maxwell, London, 2001, p.14; Klabbers, *An Introduction to International Institutional Law,* p. 344; and Schermers and Blokker, *International Institutional Law, Unity within Diversity,* pp. 1203-1204.

[4] For example, Sands and Klein, *Bowlett's Law of International Institutions,* p. 302.

[5] Amerasinghe, C. F., *The Law of the International Civil Service, Volume I,* Claredon Press, Oxford, 1994, p. 3.

international organizations, not the Member States.[6] Claude noted in this respect the following:

> *[T]he identity of every organization ... tends to be lodged in its professional staff. Members, stockholders, or citizens may control the organization, but they cannot be it; the staff, in a fundamental sense, is the organization.*
>
> *This concept is nowhere more applicable than in the realm of international organization. The secretariat of an international agency has a peculiar importance, since it is normally the sole tangible evidence, in human form, of the continuous existence of the agency. ... The secretariat is the major organ that best expresses the permanence and vitality of the whole, as distinguished from its parts. In international organization, the member states are "organized", but the staff is the "international" component.*[7]

Naturally, the importance of staff and their influence on the actual policy and decision making of international organizations varies, depending – as with the influence of the international organizations themselves – on Member States' willingness to delegate their powers to the organization at issue, but also, for example, on the area of activity.[8] Despite the differences, it has been argued that international secretariats and their staff are 'by necessity a main source of advice and thus of influence'.[9] Lemoine believes that there are two reasons for this. First:

> *[I]n a very diverse world riven by complex conflicts of interests, [decisions of the representative bodies of the organization] may be absent or more frequently constitute compromises capable of several interpretations or again be so broad as to leave to the judgment of the Secretariat what course of action to propose or what specific action to take.*[10]

Second:

> *[T]he Secretariat is the element of continuity in the organization, whereas delegates come and go [and they] may not be familiar with precedents and procedures or lack technical grasp...*[11]

The importance of staff serving in international organizations can thus hardly be disputed. The same is true for the importance of staff quality and dedication to the international cause; they both are decisive for the success or failure of each

[6] Bulkeley, J. R., *Depoliticizing United Nations Recruitment: Establishing a Genuinly International Civil Service*, in: New York University Journal of International Law and Politics, Vol. 22, Nr. 4, pp. 749-792, pp. 749-750 and Lemoine, *The International Civil Servant: An Endangered Species*, p. 2.

[7] Claude, *Swords Into Plowshares*, p. 191.

[8] Lemoine, *The International Civil Servant: An Endangered Species*, p. 39 and Mouritzen, H., *The International Civil Service, A study of Bureaucracy: International Organizations*, Dartmouth, Aldershot / Brookfield / Hong Kong / Singapore / Sydney, 1990, p. 5. Mouritzen analyzed the sphere of influence of international bureaucracy in different policy areas. For his analysis, see ibid, Part III.

[9] Lemoine, *The International Civil Servant: An Endangered Species*, p. 39.

[10] Ibid., p. 39.

[11] Ibid., p. 39.

international organization. It is, therefore, not surprising that international organizations pay much attention to the development of policies aimed at attracting and retaining persons with the highest level of competence. Without such staff, international organizations would not be able to carry out the often complex responsibilities conferred on them by organizations' constituting instruments and/or decisions of their organs.

Similar considerations apply to the requirement of the independence and impartiality of staff serving in international secretariats. Such requirement exists in all contemporary international organizations established by States.[12] It aims at ensuring that staff employed by such organizations, and through the staff the organizations themselves, act in the manner beneficial to the common interests of all their Member States, not just one, or some, of them. It is commonly accepted that without independent and impartial staff, international organizations would not be able to operate properly. In words of Sands and Klein:

> *The effective functioning of international organizations is to a significant extent dependent on the quality of their Secretariats and in particular on their ability to be perceived as truly international – that is to say independent and impartial and not serving the particular interests of a member or a group of members.*[13]

The importance of the independence and impartiality of staff serving in international organizations was recognized already in the early years of the League of Nations.[14] There, the international civil service, a 'new human category' composed of persons distinct from States representatives having the duty to act in the interest of the entire international community, not in the interest of individual States, was

[12] See, for example, *Charter of the United Nations*, 26.06.1945, available at http://www.un.org/aboutun/charter/index.html, last visited on 30.12.2010, Article 100 and *Staff Regulations of the United Nations, ST/SGB/2009/6*, 27.05.2009, available in the Human Resources Handbook of the United Nations, available at http://www.un.org/hr_handbook/English/, last visited on 30.12.2010, Regulation 1.2(d); *Articles of Agreement of the International Monetary Fund*, Article XII, Section 4(c), available at http://www.imf.orq/external/pubs/ft/aa/aa12.htm#4, last visited on 13.12.2010; *International Labour Office, Staff Regulations*, January 2010, available at http://www.ilo.org/public/english/bureau/pers/staffreg/downloads/staff_reg_2010-compilation-en.pdf, last visited on 30.12.2010, Article 1.1 and *Regulation No 31 (EEC), 11 (EAEC), Laying down the Staff Regulations of Officials and the Conditions of Employment of Other Servants of the European Economic Community and the European Atomic Energy Community, First Part: Staff Regulations of Officials*, OJ 45, 14.06.1962, p. 1385, subsequently amended, available at http://eur-lex.europa.eu/LexUriServ/LexUriServ.do?uri=CONSLEG:1962R0031:20100101:EN:PDF (consolidated unofficial version), last visited on 30.12.2010, Articles 11 and 11a.

[13] Sands and Klein, *Bowlett's Law of International Institutions*, p. 302. See also, for example, Meron, T., *Status and Independence of the International Civil Servant*, Sijthoff & Noordhoff, Alphen aan den Rijn, 1980, p. 297. Meron stated that objective, independent and efficient staff were indispensable for the proper functioning of international organizations and for the achievement of their objectives. – Ibid.

[14] Although the League of Nations was not the first international organization whose staff had an independent and impartial status, it was the one with 'the first comprehensive and multilateral secretariat' and with the most influence on future developments in this area. – Langrod, G., *The International Civil Service, Its Origins, Its Nature, Its Evolution*, A. W. Sythoff & Oceana Publications, Inc., Leyden / New York, 1963, pp. 50 and 133-136. Examples of other organizations pre-dating the League of Nations and employing staff independent form their home countries are provided in Langrod, *The International Civil Service, Its Origins, Its Nature, Its Evolution*, pp. 39-42.

developed.[15] It was a result of a gradual evolution from early international bureaus composed of national civil servants temporarily posted to international conferences, and later international unions, by States' Governments. As the nature of the tasks entrusted to such bureaus was becoming increasingly international, so were the bureaus' composition and the mentality of their officials. The latter gradually obtained a genuine legal status as international civil servants, owing their loyalty to the international organization, not to their Governments.[16] In the League of Nations, a clear distinction was made between national delegates representing States' Governments and independent and impartial officials acting on behalf of the League.[17] This was seen as a necessary prerequisite for such an international organization becoming a more effective form of international cooperation.[18] It was, and still is, indispensable to fulfilling the function of international organizations 'to find and keep alive and to broaden whatever may be the common denominator in foreign policies of the nations', to avoid that actions taken by international organizations are compromised by short-term national interests and to ensure a collective point of view.[19] The international responsibilities of international secretariats thus require them to have an international composition and their staff to be independent and impartial. As noted by Dag Hammarskjöld, Secretary-General of the United Nations ('UN') from 1953 to 1961:

> *an international civil service of this kind [i.e. responsible only to the international organization] could not be made up of persons indirectly responsible to their national governments.*[20]

The concept of international civil service, effectively established during the League of Nations, has later been taken over by virtually all international organizations founded after the Second World War. This concept is of great importance to the present study - it is the main basis for the comparison between the organizations chosen for the study as well as for its direct connection with the requirement of independence and impartiality of these organizations' staff. It is therefore useful to discuss this concept and the requirements of independence and impartiality in some detail, before the aim, scope and structure of this study are explained.

1. International civil service, its independence and impartiality

The concept of international civil service contains two components which, in fact, define it: the 'civil service' component and the 'internationality'. The 'civil service'

---

[15] Langrod, *The International Civil Service, Its Origins, Its Nature, Its Evolution*, pp. 25, 49-50 and 74-77.

[16] Ibid., p. 40. For excellent works on the early development of the international civil service, see, for example, Langrod, *The International Civil Service, Its Origins, Its Nature, Its Evolution*, in particular Chapters 1-2, 5-7; or Lemoine, *The International Civil Servant: An Endangered Species*, Chapters 2 and 3.

[17] Lemoine, *The International Civil Servant: An Endangered Species*, p. 31.

[18] Ibid., p. 36.

[19] Ibid., p. 35.

[20] Hammarskjöld, D., *The International Civil Servant in Law and in Fact*, Oxford University Press, Oxford, 1961, p. 8.

component means, just as it does in national civil services, that staff serving in international organizations perform tasks normally found in the public sector. The service is organized in a strictly defined hierarchical system in which staff are appointed and promoted on the basis of their technical competences and administrative skills. Under the traditional concept of civil service, civil servants enjoy job security, promotion prospects, salary and social benefits, though it must be admitted that in the recent past some of these aspects, such as job security, might have become less prominent. The functioning of civil servants is based on political neutrality and prohibition from certain acts that would compromise the position of servants of the government and general public.[21]

The 'internationality' of the international civil service needs a more elaborate explanation as it is a feature unique to this service. The 'internationality' of the international civil service means, first of all, its international composition – staff serving in international organizations come from a large number of countries, preferably all countries that are members of the organization. By including nationals from different Member States, secretariats of international organizations become common to all their Member States, i.e. 'international' – not only in their composition but also in their actions. Because each individual international civil servant reflects his country of origin, its culture, mentality and attitudes, the presence of civil servants with various nationalities results in many cultures being reflected in the organizations' approach, too.[22] The international character of international secretariats generates thus an international approach to matters of interest to international organizations.[23] This would not be possible if secretariats of international organizations were composed of nationals of merely one or a few Member States. Such persons would act in the manner characteristic of, and limited to, those countries only, mirroring their specific attitudes, culture and mentality. This would inevitably result in the domination of those countries in the international organization at issue, be it cultural or political, which would diminish the confidence of the remaining Member

[21] For classic works on public administration and bureaucracy, see, for example, Weber, M., *The Theory of Social and Economis Organization, Edited with an Introdcution by Talcott Parsons,* The Free Press, A division of Macmillan Publishing Co., Inc., Collier Macmillan Publishers, New York / London, 1964, in particular pp. 329-341; and White, L. D., *Introduction to the Study of Public Administration,* MacMillan, New York, 1958. For common standards of classical type of civil service, see, for example, Coombes, D., *Politics and Bureaucracy in the European Community, A Portrait of the Commission of the E.E.C.,* George Allen and Unwin Ltd., London, 1970, p. 124.

[22] Bulkeley, *Depoliticizing United Nations Recruitment: Establishing a Genuinly International Civil Service,* pp. 759 and 761; Lemoine, *The International Civil Servant: An Endangered Species,* p. 252; Kassim, H. and Menon, A., *European Integration since the 1990s: Member States and the European Commission,* ARENA Working Papers WP 6/04, 2004, available at http://www.sv.uio.no/arena/english/research/publications/arena-publications/workingpapers/working-papers2004/wp04_6.pdf, last visited on 30.12.2010, p. 22; and Spence, D. and Stevens, A., *Staff and Personnel Policy in the Commission,* in: D. Spence and G. Edwards (eds.), The European Commission, John Harper Publishing, London, 2006, pp. 173-208, p. 197. See also *Second Report on Reform of the Commission, Analysis of Current Practice and Proposals for Tackling Mismanagement, Irregularities and Fraud, Volume II,* 10.09.1999, available at http://www.europarl.europa.eu/experts/pdf/rep2-2en.pdf, last visited on 30.12.2010, para. 6.2.20.

[23] Göttelmann and Münch, *Article 101,* in: B. Simma (ed.), The Charter of th United Nations, A Commentary, Oxford University Press, Oxford, 2002, pp. 1252-1276, p. 1273; and also Bulkeley, *Depoliticizing United Nations Recruitment: Establishing a Genuinly International Civil Service,* pp. 759 and 763-764.

States in the organization and its capability to address issues of common interest to all Member States in an independent and impartial manner. As pointed out by Langrod, the international composition of secretariats of international organizations is thus needed in order to:

> *... widen the range of intellectual and cultural contributions and at the same time so to proportion these contributions as to avoid the undue preponderance of any one civilizing influence, of one mode of action or thought, or of a single national training and tradition.*[24]

The UN General Assembly has expressed itself in a similar vein. Already in its first resolution on staff matters, adopted in 1947, the Assembly stated:

> *...in view of its international character and in order to avoid undue predominance of national practices, the policies and the administrative methods of the Secretariat should reflect, and profit to the highest degree from, assets of various cultures and the technical competence of all Member nations.*[25]

Also the European Commission noted that the requirement of broad national diversity of its staff was a guarantee of 'cultural wealth and cohesion of the European civil service.'[26] The Committee of Independent Experts ('CIE'), established by the European Parliament in 1999 in order to investigate allegations of mismanagement, irregularities and fraud in the European Commission, regarded this requirement to be a means for overcoming internal differences in international organizations occurring as a consequence of the national distinctiveness of each Member State:

> *It is only through the employment of a staff of different nationalities working together and over a lengthy period of time that the problems of cultural, linguistic and national identity in general may be minimized.*[27]

---

[24] Langrod, *The International Civil Service, Its Origins, Its Nature, Its Evolution*, p. 94. Langrod compared the situation within the international organizations to the one existing in federal states. He stated that in these states too the balance among the contributions of various constitutive parts of the federation was essential for the proper functioning of the federal states.

[25] *General Assembly Resolution 153(II), A/RES/153(III)*, 15.11.1947, available in the Official Document System of the United Nations, available at http://documents.un.org/, last visited on 30.12.2010, Preamble. In its subsequent resolutions, the General Assembly often repeated this objective, adding from time to time other attributes of individual countries which should be reflected among the international civil servants, too, for example the 'diversity of attitudes' of all Member States. - For example, *General Assembly Resolution 3417(XXX), A/RES/3417(XXX)*, 8.12.1975, available in the Official Document System of the United Nations, available at http://documents.un.org/, last visited on 30.12.2010, Preamble. See also, for example, *General Assembly Resolution 61/244, A/RES/61/244*, 22.12.2006, available in the Official Document System of the United Nations, available at http://documents.un.org/, last visited on 30.12.2010, Section II, para. 6.

[26] *Compilation Document on Senior Officials Policy, SEC(2004) 1352/2*, 25.10.2004, available in the Register of Commission Documents, available at http://ec.europa.eu/transparency/regdoc/registre.cfm?CL=en, last visited on 30.12.2010, p. 4.

[27] *Second Report on Reform of the Commission of 1999, Volume II*, para. 6.2.19.

The CIE also noted that the requirement of broad national diversity in the EU civil service was 'aimed at securing Member States a proportionate share in [the European Union's] decision-making processes'.[28]

The presence of nationals of various Member States among staff serving in international organizations thus ensures that organizations' approach to the matters of common interest to all their Member States remains free from the predominant influence of just a limited number of Member States, that it is 'international' and therefore independent and impartial.

This feature of the international civil service is of great importance. Sands and Klein even considered the international character of staff serving in international organizations to be 'the single most important characteristic' of such staff.[29] Similarly, Langrod regarded it a *sine qua non* of modern international organizations.[30] He explained:

> *The fact that the administration is effectively international – and not only intergovernmental or multinational – is part of the historic process of the drawing together of mankind. From small beginnings, it has grown unceasingly, despite troubles and dangers. The existence in the international arena of an impartial body dedicated to the general interest, to the persistent search for methods of collective action, to a "neutral" approach to world problems, thus appears indispensable. It is impossible to imagine the world of the future without such a factor; necessary in the past, it will be doubly so in the future.*[31]

Of course, the international composition of the international civil service is not the only safeguard of its international character. There are other necessary prerequisites as well, in particular those relating to the individual international civil servants, as there can be no independent and impartial international civil service without independent and impartial international civil servants. Indeed, the concept of the international civil service implies also that individual international civil servants are independent and impartial.

Naturally, as explained by Langrod, the international civil servant is not independent in the sense of being free from any orders whatsoever since, in the end, he is a civil servant and therefore subordinated to the hierarchy he belongs to, owing obedience to his supervisors. In addition, via relevant organs of the international organization, the international civil servant is responsible for his work to Member States whose representatives participate in these organs.[32] According to Langrod, the independence of the international civil servant must be understood as protection against Member States' attempts to exercise pressure on him but also as protection of his political neutrality. With regard to the latter, Langrod further explained that the international civil servant is not neutral in the sense of having no political

[28] Ibid., para. 7.5.9.

[29] Sands and Klein, *Bowlett's Law of International Institutions*, p. 309.

[30] Langrod, *The International Civil Service, Its Origins, Its Nature, Its Evolution*, p. 267.

[31] Ibid., p. 324.

[32] Ibid., p. 91.

opinions but rather in the sense of ensuring that his opinions do not interfere with the interests of the service.[33]

Langrod's understanding of neutrality of the international civil servant was based on the positions taken by the Dag Hammarskjöld, the UN Secretary-General from 1953 to 1961. In his well known speech, *The International Civil Servant in Law and in Fact*, held at the University of Oxford in 1961, Hammarskjöld put forward two definitions of neutrality, accepting one of them as a necessary characteristic of the international civil servant but rejecting the other one. According to Hammarskjöld, neutrality in the sense of not taking a stand on a political issue when needed was contrary to the *UN Charter.* On the other hand, neutrality in the sense of being 'wholly uninfluenced by national or group interests or ideologies' was essential to the concept of the international civil service.[34] Hammarskjöld further explained his understanding of this second definition of neutrality as follows:

> *[The international civil servant] is not requested to be neuter (sic) in the sense that he has to have no sympathies or antipathies, that there are no interests which are close to him in his personal capacity or that he is to have no ideas or ideals that matter to him. However, he is requested to be fully aware of those human reactions and meticulously check himself so that they are not permitted to influence his action.'*[35]

Neutrality of the international civil servant thus should not mean 'political celibacy', to use the words of the late Soviet leader Nikita Khrushchev, but the awareness of one's preferences and the control over their influence on his conduct.[36]

The fact that Hammarskjöld placed the term neutrality between the quotation marks when providing his second definition indicates that he might have realized that this definition was not the most self-evident. Indeed, this second definition of neutrality comes close to that of impartiality, generally defined as 'objectivity, lack of bias, tolerance, restraint'.[37] The two concepts – neutrality and impartiality – have been used for explaining the same characteristic of international civil servants. Graham and Jordan, for example, regarded the obligation of international civil

[33] Ibid., p. 91.

[34] Hammarskjöld, *The International Civil Servant in Law and in Fact,* p. 14.

[35] Ibid., p. 27.

[36] Interview of Mr. Khrushchev by Walter Lippmann, in *New York Herald Tribune,* 17.04.1961, quoted in Ibid., p. 1. The Soviet leader Khrushchev, quoted by Dag Hammarskjöld, stated: 'While there are neutral countries, there are no neutral men ...There can be no such thing as an impartial civil servant in this deeply divided world, and the kind of political celibacy which the British theory of the civil servant calls for is in international affairs a fiction.' See also Wass, D., *Loyality, Neutrality and Commitment in a Career Civil Service,* EGPA Leuven Conference paper, 1985, 1985, available at http://ipac.coleurop.be/ipac20/ipac.jsp?session=1312621X119B4.179112&profile=brugge&uri=link=3100006~!20462~!3100001~!3100002&aspect=power&menu=search&ri=1&source=~!horizon&term=Loyality%2C+neutrality+and+commitment+in+a+career+civil+service+%2F&index=TITLE#focus, last visited on 30.12.2010, p. 8.

[37] *Report on Standards of Conduct in the International Civil Service* prepared by the International Civil Service Advisory Board in 1954, referred to in Langrod, *The International Civil Service, Its Origins, Its Nature, Its Evolution,* p. 243 and Beigbeder, Y., *Threats to the International Civil Service: Past Presures and New Trends,* Pinter Publishers Limited, London, 1988, p. 23.

servants to be 'administrators, not politicians' and thus to refrain from taking sides in the performance of official duties to fall under the concept of impartiality.[38] They also understood impartiality as the duty to '[carry] out the orders of [one's] political masters without question'.[39] This is very similar to Hammarskjöld's definition of the neutrality of international civil service. Building on the latter, Reymond and Mailick made a clear distinction between neutrality and impartiality. In their understanding, impartiality of the international civil servant means the duty to 'prevent personal feelings and prejudices from affecting his judgment and behavior'.[40] Reymond and Mailick stressed that this did not mean that international civil servants must be neutral in the sense of not having 'ideas and ideals'.[41] The impartiality of the international civil servant is thus not about his personal opinions and feelings, but about his conduct which must be supportive to the position of the organization he serves, even if that position is in contrast with his own views.[42] In this sense impartiality is linked with loyalty towards the organization and with integrity. Loyalty of the international civil servant has been defined as:

> *[involving] willingness to try to understand and be tolerant of different viewpoints, different cultural patterns and different work habits, willingness to work without prejudice or bias with persons of all nationalities, regions and cultures. ... not the absence of personal, political or national views, but rather restraint at all times in the expression of such views.*[43]

The concept of integrity refers to 'honesty, truthfulness, fidelity, probity, freedom from corrupting influences'.[44] As noted by Loveday, integrity of international civil servants is a characteristic based on 'an understanding of and belief in the ultimate value of the work and purposes of the institution'.[45]

A distinction should also be made between impartiality and independence. The latter is an essential condition for the former; it enhances it, but it cannot guarantee it.[46] Indeed, one can hardly be impartial without being independent. However, it is

---

[38] Graham, N. A. and Jordan, R. S. (eds.), *The International Civil Service, Changing Role and Concepts*, Pergamon Press (published in cooperation with UNITAR), New York / Oxford / Toronto / Sydney / Frankfurt / Paris, 1980, p. 2.

[39] Ibid., p. 18.

[40] Reymond, H. and Mailick, S., *International Personnel Policies and Practices*, Praeger Publishers, New York, 1985, p. 15.

[41] Ibid., p. 15, citing Dag Hammarskjöld in Press Conference, 12 July 1961, *Note to Correspondents*, No. 2347, p. 11.

[42] Ibid., p. 15.

[43] Beigbeder, *Threats to the International Civil Service*, p. 23, referring to the *Report on Standards of Conduct in the International Civil Service* of the International Civil Service Advisory Board prepared in 1954. See also, for example, Lemoine, *The International Civil Servant: An Endangered Species*, p. 45.

[44] Beigbeder, *Threats to the International Civil Service*, p. 23, referring to the *Report on Standards of Conduct in the International Civil Service* of the International Civil Service Advisory Board prepared in 1954.

[45] Loveday, A., *Reflections on International Administration*, Clarendon Press, Oxford, 1956, p. 32, as cited in Ibid., p. 25.

[46] Lemoine, *The International Civil Servant: An Endangered Species*, p. 42 and Amann, D. M., *Impartiality Deficit and International Criminal Judging*, 2006, avaiable in the Social Science Research Network, available at http://ssrn.com/paper=955431, last visited on 30.12.2010, p. 9.

certainly possible to be independent but not impartial – one can be free of control and interference by outside sources while being influenced in his opinions or by his own personal prejudices and preferences.[47] In this sense, impartiality should be regarded as a subjective feature, as a 'state of mind with regard to the issue and the parties to the issue', whereas independence is more an objective state of affairs and relates to one's position towards others.[48] For the international civil servant, independence means autonomy, absence of control and interference in his official responsibilities from any authority external to the international organization in which he serves.[49]

2. Aim and scope of this study

International organizations realize that they need high quality staff in order to fulfill their increasingly complex and demanding mandates. They are also aware that, given their importance, their (potential) impact on a large number of public and private matters, and the role played in it by their staff, these staff are likely to confront pressures in the performance of their responsibilities, both from outside the organization as well as from inside. The external pressure may come from Member States, in particular the Member State of origin, which often have specific interests they wish to see realized by international organizations. Of course, Member States also have – and use – other, more formal methods, at their disposal by which they can influence actions of the organization, for example participation in the organization's organs. Nonetheless, as discussed in more detail below, experience has shown that Member States do endeavor to use informal ways broadly in order to get things done (their way), too. One of the most prominent informal ways is contacting individual international civil servants, especially those possessing their own nationality. Another source of external pressure on international staff are interest groups, be it profit or non-profit organizations and associations. Such groups often have great stakes in actions and decisions (to be) taken by international organizations which can influence their activities considerably. As far as the internal pressure is concerned that international civil servants may face, such pressure may come from other officials, especially supervisors, who too might have interest in having things done a certain way; a way which does not always need to correspond to the interests of the organization. The reasons behind such internal pressure might be the personal interest of the individual official, or of his relative or acquaintance.

---

[47] Reymond and Mailick, *International Personnel Policies and Practices*, p. 13.

[48] Impartiality was defined as 'a state of mind…' in Amann, *Impartiality Deficit and International Criminal Judging*, avaiable in the Social Science Research Network, p. 9.

[49] For example, Langrod, *The International Civil Service, Its Origins, Its Nature, Its Evolution*, pp. 78-79; Graham and Jordan (eds.), *The International Civil Service*, p 20; Reymond and Mailick, *International Personnel Policies and Practices*, p. 13; Lemoine, *The International Civil Servant: An Endangered Species*, p. 42; Cini, M., *The European Commission, Leadership, Organisation and Culture in the EU Administration*, Manchester University Press, Manchester / New York, 1996, p. 127. See also Langrod, *The International Civil Service, Its Origins, Its Nature, Its Evolution*, p. 243, referring to the *Report of the International Civil Service Advisory Board on Standards of Conduct in the International Civil Service* of 1954; and also Beigbeder, *Threats to the International Civil Service*, p. 23, also referring to this report.

However, it can also be a result of pressure such official himself is put under by, for example, his country of origin.

To offset the pressure, but also to attract persons possessing professional excellence, international organizations offer attractive pay and solid conditions of employment. They also have detailed rules on staff rights and obligations, including those on conflict of interests and on disciplinary proceedings invoked in cases in which obligations have been breached. Last but not least, international organizations have rules to ensure that the staff are appointed, placed in specific posts but also separated from service in a manner which, on the one hand, makes the two organizations an attractive employer and, on the other hand, prevents inappropriate connections between the staff and persons or institutions external to the organization they serve. The latter rules are meant to prevent individual staff members from being 'burdened by gratitude' for getting or retaining their job or a particular post in the organization. Such gratitude could, consciously or otherwise, influence the staff behavior and result in their taking into account the interests of those to whom they 'owe gratitude', rather than the interests of the organization.

Despite its vital importance, the issue of the independence and impartiality of staff serving in international secretariats has received little attention in the last two decades. Until the 1990s, a vast volume of academic writings was dedicated to the matter. One of the important reasons was the existence of special policies maintained by the then socialist countries in respect of the conditions under which their nationals could be employed in international organizations. The socialist countries exercised significant control over their nationals serving in international organizations, thereby compromising their independence and impartiality. Such policies were formally renounced in the early 1990s when most formerly socialist countries adopted new, more democratic, political systems.[50] Since that time, political and academic attention in the area of human resources has been dedicated in particular to the issues of accountability, efficiency and general management of human resources.[51] The issue of independence and impartiality of international staff has largely disappeared from political and academic debates, suggesting that the change of approach of former socialist countries inevitably removed all threats in this respect. In addition, many international organizations have gone through a thorough reform process of their human resources management, amending their rules and regulations which, as it appears, took place in many instances without a close examination of the (potential) impact of the changes on the independent and impartial status of staff. The underlining objective of the reforms has been to make international staff more efficient and less costly, while preservation or, if needed, enhancement of their independence and impartiality has been mentioned only on the side, if at all.[52] At the same time, warnings that these reforms, or their implementation, may

---

[50] For more details, see chapter 6, section 2.1.

[51] See, for example, Cooker, C. D. (ed.), *Accountability, Investigation and Due Process in International Organizations*, Martinus Nijhoff Publishers, Leiden / Boston, 2005.

[52] For example, *A More Secure World: Our Shared Responsibility, Report of the High-level Panel on Threats, Challenges and Change*, A/59/565, 02.12.2004, available in the Offical Document System of the United Nations, available at http://documents.un.org/, last visited on 30.12.2010, paras. 295-296; *Investing*

have negative consequences on the independence and impartiality of international staff have been voiced especially by the international staff themselves.[53]

This study examines whether this concern is warranted. It analyzes a number of human resources policies that are currently in place in two of the most prominent contemporary international organizations, the United Nations and the European Union ('EU'), and their potential impact on the independence and impartiality of international civil servants who work for them. The analysis is based on a detailed description of the rules in force in the UN and in the EU and their subsequent comparison.

It is not the ambition of this study to analyze all human resources policies in the UN and the EU after the reforms. Such an endeavor would require more time and resources than those available for this study. Therefore, the study focuses on a number of selected human resources policies, namely those that regulate staff appointment, placement and separation. More specifically, the study analyzes and compares rules concerning the role of nationality in staff recruitment, promotion and separation; recruitment procedures; staff promotion and mobility; the type of appointment or contract used for staff engagement; and reasons and procedures under which staff may be separated from the organization. All these issues mark the entire employment cycle of staff serving in international secretariats, starting with their recruitment and ending with their separation. At the same time, as explained

---

in People, Report of the Secretary-General, A/61/255, 09.08.2006, available in the Official Document System of the United Nations, available at http://documents.un.org/, last visited on 30.12.2010, para. 6; *Overview of Human Resources Management Reform, Report of the Secretary-General, A/65/305*, 02.09.2010, available in the Official Document System of the United Nations, available at http://documents.un.org/, last visited on 30.12.2010, para. 5; *Reforming the Commission - A White Paper - Part I, /*COM/2000/0200 final*/*, 01.03.2000, available at http://eur-lex.europa.eu/LexUriServ/LexUriServ.do?uri=CELEX:52000DC0200(01):EN:HTML, last visited on 30.12.2010, Introduction by the members of the Commission and parts I-III; *FAO Reform: A Vision for the Twenty-first Century, C 2005/INF/19*, October 2005, available at ftp://ftp.fao.org/docrep/fao/meeting/009/j6285e.pdf, last visited on 30.12.2010, paras. 65-67; *The Future of the World Trade Organization, Addressing Institutional Challenges in the New Millenium, Report by the Consultative Board to the Director-General Supachai Panitchpakdi*, 2004, available at http://www.wto.org/english/thewto_e/10anniv_e/future_wto_e.pdf, last visited on 30.12.2010, Chapter IX.

[53] For example, *Views of the Staff Representatives of the United Nations Secretariat: Staff Union (New York), Field Staff Union (Brindisi) and Staff Coordinating Council (United Nations Office in Geneva), Addendum, A/C.5/63/3/Add.2*, 15.10.2008, available in the Official Document System of the United Nations, available at http://documents.un.org/, last visited on 30.12.2010, Part I, especially para. 6; and Union Syndicale, *Activity Report of the Executive Committee for the 2004-2007 Mandate*, 16.04.2007, available at http://www.unionsyndicale.eu/usb/usb_070923_04.pdf, last visited on 30.12.2010, p. 1; and Union Syndicale, *Demolition of the European Public Service: After the Newly Imposed REC, We Are Now Faced with the "Modernisation" of Human Resources*, 18.07.2008, available at http://www.uslux.eu/articles.php?lng=en&pg=374, last visited on 30.12.2010. Concerns were also expressed at other levels. See, for example, the recommendation of the UN Secretary-General's High-level Panel on Threats, Challenges and Change of 2004 which advised UN Member States to 'recommit themselves to Articles 100 and 101 of the Charter of the United Nations'. - *A More Secure World: Our Shared Responsibility, Report of the High-level Panel on Threats, Challenges and Change, A/59/565*, available in the Offical Document System of the United Nations, para. 296. Articles 100 and 101 of the *UN Charter* prohibit UN officials seeking or receiving instructions from Member States governments or any other authority external to organization, as well as Member States seeking to influence the chief officer and the staff of the organization in the performance of their duties. - *UN Charter*, Articles 100 and 101.

in more detail below, each of these issues is of direct relevance to the independence and impartiality of staff serving in international organizations.

Although the study is limited in its scope to the selected policies, it does intend to offer an analysis of these policies in detail. To facilitate such analysis, and to provide a sufficient basis for the comparison between the UN and the EU, detailed descriptions of the relevant legal framework are included in each substantive part of this study. Given the scarcity, even absence, of relevant literature in this area, and the novelty arising from recent reforms of UN and EU human resources policies, detailed descriptions are unavoidable. Without them, proper analysis and comparison would not be possible. In addition, they provide a valuable source of information for those interested in the particularities of the relevant policy areas.

The included policies are explained and analyzed from the legal point of view and on the basis of applicable rules and regulations as well as relevant jurisprudence. The study does not intend to provide a comprehensive political evaluation of UN and EU human resources policies, or their theoretical background. Rather, it aims at clarification of the existing legal framework set up by the two organizations for the selected policies, and at assessment of its potential impact on the independence and impartiality of international civil servants working for these organizations.

The choice of comparing the UN and the EU, whose nature, structure and functions are generally regarded as dissimilar, is justified by the fact that their human resources policies are based on the same concept of international civil service. As already mentioned, both the UN and the EU adopted the concept of international civil service upon their establishment and based their human resources policies on it. In the UN, the concept is enshrined in the *Charter of the United Nations* ('*UN Charter*'). Article 100 thereof stipulates:

> *1. In the performance of their duties the Secretary-General and the staff shall not seek or receive instructions from any government or from any other authority external to the Organization. They shall refrain from any action which might reflect on their position as international officials responsible only to the Organization.*
>
> *2. Each Member of the United Nations undertakes to respect the exclusively international character of the responsibilities of the Secretary-General and the staff and not to seek to influence them in the discharge of their responsibilities.*[54]

Furthermore, in its relevant part, Article 101(3) provides:

> *Due regard shall be paid to the importance of recruiting the staff on as wide a geographical basis as possible.*[55]

These two provisions are repeated and worked out in more detail in the *Staff Regulations of the United Nations* ('*UN Staff Regulations*') which set out the basic rights and obligations of staff serving in the UN Secretariat.[56] Similar provisions

---

[54] *UN Charter*, Article 100.

[55] Ibid., Article 101(3).

[56] *UN Staff Regulations of 2009*, in particular, though not exclusively, Regulations 1.1(a) and (b), 1.2(d), (e)

can be found in the *Staff Regulations of Officials of the European Union* ('*EU Staff Regulations*'). Article 11(1) thereof stipulates:

> *An official shall carry out his duties and conduct himself solely with the interests of the [Union] in mind; he shall neither seek nor take instructions from any government, authority, organisation or person outside his institution. He shall carry out the duties assigned to him objectively, impartially and in keeping with his duty of loyalty to the [Union].*[57]

The relevant part of Article 27 of the *EU Staff Regulations* furthermore provides:

> *Recruitment shall be directed to securing for the institution the services of officials ... recruited on the broadest possible geographical basis from among nationals of Member States of the [Union].*[58]

The UN and the EU thus adhere to the same basic concept for their staff, including the same requirements for their actions. Also the implementation of these requirements in specific human resources policies of the UN and the EU shows many similarities. For example, both organizations organize competitive examinations in order to recruit staff to entry level posts; when filling posts at higher levels they both give preference to internal staff above external candidates; both have special rules for senior officials, both attempt to ensure adequate presence of nationals of each Member State at all levels etc. There are, however, also many differences between the UN and the EU human resources policies. The EU, for example, uses different recruitment methods for hiring career staff as opposed to non career staff, while the UN does not make such a distinction. The UN, on the other hand, makes a difference between various categories of staff, depending on the type of work they perform, and links its recruitment methods to it.

While some of the dissimilarities are a consequence of the disparity between the two organizations as regards their nature, structure and competences, other dissimilarities have their roots in the historical development of the staffing policies themselves. It is therefore interesting to compare the two systems and discover whether, and if so which, different experiences could be used in the other system in order to improve it. It is even more interesting to do so at present since both the UN and the EU have gone through overarching human resources management reform processes. In the UN, such reform constituted a part of the overall reform of the organization which started with the 1997 report of the then UN Secretary-General Kofi Annan on *Renewing the United Nations, A Programme for Reform*.[59] In the area

and (f), and 4.2.

[57] *EU Staff Regulations*, Article 11(1).

[58] Ibid., Article 27.

[59] *Renewing The United Nations: A Programme for Reform, Report of the Secretary-General, A/51/950*, 14.07.1997, available in the Official Document System of the United Nations, available at http://documents.un.org/, last visited on 30.12.2010. This report was followed up by a large number of subsequent reports. The key reports, supplementing the first one, include in particular *Strengthening of the United Nations: An Agenda for Further Change, Report of the Secretary-General, A/57/387*, 09.09.2002, available in the Official Document System of the United Nations, available at http://documents.un.org/, last visited on 30.12.2010; *In Larger Freedom: Towards Development, Security and Human Rights for All,*

of human resources management, the reform resulted in numerous changes, for example the adoption of a single staff selection system incorporating staff recruitment, placement, promotion and mobility policies; the introduction and afterwards suspension of mandatory mobility of staff; the adoption of a new staff appraisal system; the abolition of different series of *Staff Rules of the United Nations ('UN Staff Rules')* and some types of appointments; the replacement of permanent appointment by continuing appointment; and the introduction of a new system of internal justice.[60]

In the EU, the reform was launched by the *White Paper Reforming the Commission* issued in 2000 as a response to the 1999 reports of the Committee of Independent Experts which led to the resignation of the European Commission led by Jacques Santer in September 1999. This Committee was established by the European Parliament in order to investigate allegations of fraud, mismanagement and nepotism in the European Commission and to suggest proposals for improvement.[61] Similarly as in the UN, the reform of the European Commission too included issues of human resources management.[62] As noted by the Commission itself, during the reform 'the entire spectrum of staff policy – from recruitment to retirement – has been revised' (emphasis removed).[63] As a result, in 2004, the *EU Staff Regulations* received the biggest make-over since their first adoption in 1961.[64]

This study is further limited to the UN proper and its Secretariat, referred to as the UN Secretariat on the one hand, and to the European Commission on the other. The

Report of the Secretary-General, A/59/2005, 21.03.2005, available in the Official Document System of the United Nations, available at http://documents.un.org/, last visited on 30.12.2010; *Investing in the United Nations: For a Stronger Organization Worldwide, Report of the Secretary-General, A/60/692*, 07.03.2006, available in the Official Document System of the United Nations, available at http://documents.un.org/, last visited on 30.12.2010; and in the area of human resources management *Investing in People, Report of the Secretary-General, A/61/255*.For more information on the UN reform, see the official website of the United Nations, available at http://www.un.org/reform/index.shtml, last visited on 15.10.2010.

[60] Note that details of these issues are discussed throughout this study. See, in particular, chapter 3, section 2.2.2; chapter 5, section 2.1; chapter 4, section 2.1.2.3; chapter 6, section 2.3; chapter 7, section 2.3.2.6.

[61] See *First Report on Allegations Regarding Fraud, Mismanagement and Nepotism in the European Commission*, 15.03.1999, available at http://www.europarl.europa.eu/experts/pdf/reporten.pdf, last visited on 30.12.2010; *Second Report on Reform of the Commission, Analysis of Current practice and proposals forTackling Mismanagement, Irregularities and Fraud, Volume I*, 10.09.1999, available at http://www.europarl.europa.eu/experts/pdf/rep2-1en.pdf, last visited on 30.12.2010 and *Second Report on Reform of the Commission of 1999, Volume II*; *Reforming the Commission - A White Paper - Part I*, and *Reforming the Commission - A White Paper - Part II - Action Plan, /*COM/2000/0200 final*/*, 1.3.2000, available at http://eur-lex.europa.eu/LexUriServ/LexUriServ.do?uri=CELEX:52000DC0200(02).EN.HTML, last visited on 30.12.2010.

[62] For details, see EuropeanCommission, *Reforming the Commission, An Administration at the Service of Half a Billion Europeans*, 15.10.2010, 22.05.2006, available at http://ec.europa.eu/reform/2002/index_en.htm.

[63] Ibid.

[64] *Council Regulation (EC, EURATOM) No 723/2004 of 22 March 2004 Amending the Staff Regulations of Officials of the European Communities and the Conditions of Employment of Other Servants of the European Communities*, OJ L 124, 27.04.2004, p. 1-118. As is the case with the UN, also for the EU the relevant changes introduced by the reform are discussed throughout this study.

reason for this limitation is a pragmatic one. Both in the UN and in the EU, separate organizations and/or institutions have their own staff policies, reflecting, among others, their functional specificities but also historical background. Including other UN organizations and EU institutions in this study would go beyond the time and resources available for this study. At the same time, it could result in an unnecessary complexity caused by too many detailed differences and variations in policies and regulations. Undoubtedly, the comparison of the differences and variations within each of the two respective systems would be an interesting exercise. However, such an exercise would not serve the purpose of this study, namely the comparison of two relatively different systems which, at the same time, are based on the same basic principles.[65] The choice of the UN Secretariat and the European Commission has been made on the basis of their dominant position in the two respective systems, both of them being by far the largest staff employers in the UN and in the EU, respectively.

As explained in more detail in chapter 1, the study further focuses predominantly on professional staff engaged in the organizations' policy and decision making.[66] This is especially so for the UN Secretariat since in the European Commission differences in staff policies applicable to the so-called Administrators (i.e. professional staff) as compared to Assistants (i.e. support staff) are minimal and concern in particular remuneration, an issue which is not dealt with in this study. Therefore, with regard to the European Commission, most of the issues addressed in this study are of relevance to both the Administrators as well as Assistants.[67]

In addition to an analysis of the present state of affairs in the two organizations, this study also offers a brief historical overview for each included issue. For the EU, this historical overview includes a discussion of the High Authority of the former European Coal and Steel Community ('ECSC'), established in 1952, as well as the Commission of the European Economic Community ('EEC'), established in 1958 and renamed the European Community ('EC') by the Treaty of Maastricht in 1992. In 1967, the High Authority of the ECSC and the Commission of the EEC as well as the Commission of the European Atomic Energy Community ('EURATOM'), also established in 1958, were merged to form the Commission of the European Communities. This changed in 2009 when the *Lisbon Treaty amending the Treaty Establishing the European Community and the Treaty on European Union* came into force. Under the *Lisbon Treaty*, the European Community was merged with the European Union and the Commission became the Commission of the European Union. This Commission

[65] Note that the UN system of organizations, formally referred to as the UN common system, coordinate their staff policies, with an important role played in it by the International Civil Service Commission. – See *International Civil Service Commission, Statute and Rules of Procedure, ICSC/1/Rev.1*, May 1975, March 1987, available at http://icsc.un.org/resources/pdfs/statute/english.pdf, last visited on 30.12.2010 and, for example *Report of the International Civil Service Commission for the Year 2010, A/65/30*, August 2010, available in the Official Document System of the United Nations, available at http://documents.un.org/, last visited on 30.12.2010. As far as various EU institutions are concerned, their staff policies are even based on the single set of the *EU Staff Regulations*. - *EU Staff Regulations*, Articles 1a and 1b.

[66] See below, chapter 1, in particular section 2.1.1.

[67] For details on staff classification in both the UN Secretariat and the European Commission, see below, chapter 1.

continues to carry out the tasks of the European Atomic Energy Community too, although this Community has remained a separate legal entity distinct from the European Union. Because the European Atomic Energy Community was and still is a separate legal entity, this study does not pay special attention to the historical developments of relevant human resources policies which took place in the Commission of the European Atomic Energy Community.[68] As for the European Coal and Steel Community, it ceased to exist in 2002, in accordance with the terms of the ECSC Treaty itself. However, because the Commission of the former European Economic Community was, to a large extent, built on the example of the ECSC High Authority, the historical developments in the High Authority are briefly discussed, where relevant.

3. Structure of the study

The structure of this study follows to a great extent the employment cycle of international civil servants. It begins with defining the UN and EU civil services and continues with assessing UN and EU policies on recruitment of new staff, promotion and mobility of internal staff, and staff separation. Two issues receive separate attention. The first is the role of nationality in staff recruitment, promotion and separation; and the second is the types of appointment used in the UN and in the EU. The role of nationality in staff recruitment, promotion and separation is addressed as the very first issue in this study. This is because its predominant relevance lies at the beginning of the employment cycle of international civil servants. At the same time, it is an issue distinct from recruitment procedures, which are the subject-matter of the subsequent chapter. As for the types of appointment, while the decision on which type of appointment is granted to an individual international civil servant is often, though not exclusively, taken at the beginning of his employment cycle, its relevance for this study is closely linked to the issue of separation, rather than to recruitment. This is because the type of appointment granted to international civil servants is a decisive determinant of the level of protection of these servants against termination of their employment.

The following sections explain in detail the relevance of each of the selected human resources policies for ensuring 'the highest standards of efficiency, competence and integrity' of UN and EU staff, to use the words of the *UN Charter*.[69] They include the explanation of (potentially) problematic elements in the policies at hand that could compromise the independence and impartiality of the UN and EU staff.

---

[68] Note that before the merger of the ECSC High Authority, the EEC Commission and the Euratom Commission, the same staff regulations applied to both Commissions, though some differences in application existed due to the highly specialized nature of the work of the Euroatom Commission. - Coombes, *Politics and Bureaucracy in the European Community, A Portrait of the Commission of the E.E.C.*, p. 120.

[69] *UN Charter*, Article 101(3).

3.1. Definition of the UN and EU civil services

To facilitate proper understanding of various categories of international civil servants that exist in the UN and in the EU, chapter 1 provides an overview of all UN and EU staff categories. It also explains which of them are included in this study and why.

3.2. Role of nationality

Chapter 2 addresses the first substantive issue dealt with by this study, namely the role of nationality in the UN and EU staff selection process. Generally speaking, nationality is an important determinant in staff selection in all international organizations that have accepted the concept of international civil service, thus also in the UN and the EU. It has been explained above that the international composition of staff is one of the defining features of this concept. Its relevance lies with the reflection of the international membership of each international organization and its consequent ability to ensure that international organizations can profit from the richness and diversity of various cultures as well as from the best technical knowledge and competence available in any of their Member States.[70] It also guarantees an independent and impartial approach on the part of the international civil service towards issues dealt with by international organizations, by preventing the predominance of one or some Member States in international organizations, be it political or cultural. Such predominance would inevitably diminish confidence among the rest of the Member States in such organizations; they would consider the organizations to be a tool of the dominating Member State or States for achieving their own aims rather than a means for addressing interests common to all Member States.[71]

Problems may arise, however, when nationality becomes the decisive determinant in the individual staff selection process. When posts are filled by persons possessing the desired nationality rather than by the most meritorious, the quality of staff will inevitably suffer. In addition, while the international composition of the international civil service is of vital importance to *its* independence and impartiality, it may, at the same time, be detrimental to the independence and impartiality of individual international civil servants. Lemoine puts it as follows:

> *a balanced cultural diversity rooted in national origin in the staff of the [UN] Secretariat is both a condition for the credibility of its independence and impartiality and a source of their destruction when perverted by the urge to place one's nationals in the Secretariat.*[72]

---

[70] For example, *General Assembly Resolution 153(II)*, Preamble. See also, for example, Langrod, *The International Civil Service, Its Origins, Its Nature, Its Evolution*, p. 94.

[71] Weiss, *International Bureaucracy, An Analysis of the Operation of Functional and Global International Secretariats*, p. 57. Weiss noted that national diversity within the international civil service was necessary in order to prevent an international organization becoming 'the tool of one power or its block'.

[72] Lemoine, *The International Civil Servant: An Endangered Species*, p.239.

In this context, a clear distinction must be made between the international civil service as a body of officials on the one hand and the individual international civil servants on the other. The potential problem lies with the latter. If an individual needs to posses the 'right' nationality in order to be selected for a certain post in an international secretariat, the danger that such a person would rely on his ties with the country of origin in order to enhance his chances for appointment, promotion or other placement is great. Such a situation may then easily result in inappropriate connections between the person and the country involved once he obtains the desired position. Even where no such undue ties are developed in reality, a mere perception or a possibility of their existence compromises the independent and impartial status of the international civil servant.

As shown below, much criticism has, therefore, been expressed against the role which nationality (may) play in personnel policies of international organizations at the individual level. This criticism has derived from both the conceptual anomaly of the requirement of broad national diversity of staff serving in international secretariats, but also from problems with the application of this requirement in practice. Especially the problems with application have frequently led to questioning of the justifiability of this requirement, and the principle through which this requirement has been formalized, as such. This principle is known as the principle of geographical distribution in the UN and as the principle of geographical balance in the EU. In this study, it is referred to as the principle of broad geographical representation, unless the specific UN or EU system is discussed. The reason for such a deviation from the commonly used terminology is the intention to cover both the UN and the EU systems, while respecting the difference in the organizations' own terminology and, at the same time, pointing to the great similarity of the content of this principle in the two organizations.[73]

Turning to conceptual problems with this principle, they relate in particular to the unfortunate symbolism that the principle inevitably entails, and to its connotation of dependency of individual international civil servants. As far as unfortunate symbolism is concerned, it has been argued that, while aiming at securing international character for the international civil service, the principle of broad geographical representation accentuates the national rather than the international character of international civil servants. Thereby the principle creates an incorrect impression of the nature of the international civil service as such. According to Weiss, under the principle of broad geographical representation, it is the nationalism which is esteemed by both Member States and international organizations, not the neutrality.[74] Also in Mouritzen's view this principle, and its reflection in quotas entailing the number of nationals of individual Member States to be employed in a specific international organization, are 'symbolically unfortunate, because they express a representational way of thinking'.[75] Such a way of thinking is not only incorrect but

[73] For further explanation of this terminology, see below, chapter 2, section 1.

[74] Weiss, *International Bureaucracy, An Analysis of the Operation of Functional and Global International Secretariats*, p. 58.

[75] Mouritzen, *The International Civil Service, A study of Bureaucracy: International Organizations*, p. 41.

also undesirable as it suggests that the international civil service is composed of national representatives rather than independent and impartial international civil servants. Bulkeley noted that such a situation 'frustrates the intended benefits of a neutral multinational civil service'.[76] This was also the reason for Lemoine to condemn the principle of geographical representation and the system of national quotas existing in the UN as 'a perversion of an otherwise essential concept of an independent staff free from cultural and resultant implicit political domination.'[77]

Another conceptual difficulty with the principle of broad geographical representation, partly related to the first one, is its connotation of, and with a potential for creating, dependency of individual international civil servants on their home countries. The principle of broad geographical representation, important from the point of view of ensuring an independent and impartial *body* of international officials, inevitably means that each individual official owes his job, at least partly, to his nationality. It has been argued that a 'person who is recruited, hired, and promoted according to his origins would normally hesitate to ignore them', although the contrary has been claimed as well, especially in the EU context.[78] Egeberg, for example, argued that the great attention dedicated to the issue of nationality of European Commission staff did not necessarily correspond to its real impact on staff behavior.[79] In his view:

> *[T]here is no direct link between an official's administrative style, personal attitudes or informal contact patterns and his decision behavior in the Commission. In-between are organization roles, procedures and eyes and ears of colleagues and bosses. In fact, the DG attachment of officials seems far more important than their national background for understanding their preferences and choices in their daily work.*[80]

Also Hooghe, who studied the views of senior officials in the European Commission on the role of nationality in their institution and on their policy shaping, argued that Commission officials did not 'simply bow to the authorities that appoint them...'.[81] However, she agreed that nationality factors were highly significant and shaped professional opportunities in the European Commission profoundly.[82]

---

[76] Bulkeley, *Depoliticizing United Nations Recruitment: Establishing a Genuinly International Civil Service*, pp. 759-760.

[77] Lemoine, *The International Civil Servant: An Endangered Species*, p. 245.

[78] Weiss, *International Bureaucracy, An Analysis of the Operation of Functional and Global International Secretariats*, p. 57.

[79] Egeberg, M., *The European Commission - The Evolving EU Executive*, ARENA Working Papers WP 02/30, 2002, available at http://www.sv.uio.no/arena/english/research/publications/arena-publications/workingpapers/working-papers2002/wp02_30.htm, last visited on 30.12.2010, p. 12.

[80] Ibid., pp. 12-13.

[81] Hooghe, L., *Consociationists or Weberians? Top Commission Officials on Nationality*, ARENA Working Paper WP 98/20, 1998, available at http://www.sv.uio.no/arena/english/research/publications/arena-publications/workingpapers/working-papers1998/wp98_20.htm, last visited on 30.12.2010, p. 32.

[82] Ibid., pp. 31-32.

Clearly, the relevance of nationality for the behavior of each individual international civil servant, and also for his independence and impartiality, depends on the weight and the place given to the nationality in the hierarchy of factors significant for the officials' recruitment and career advancement. When the nationality is of high importance, the temptation to use the formal connection with the home country as a means of supporting one's career aspirations is high. If such connection is actually used, the official's professional independence and impartiality is compromised – he acquires a complicated and uneasy relationship of gratitude with his home country which results in him, knowingly or otherwise, taking the interests of this country into account in his work.

The decisive question in this respect is thus how the principle of broad geographical representation can be implemented in practice without compromising the independence and impartiality of individual international civil servants. There are a number of difficulties there. The first one is the problematic nature of the relationship between this principle and that of merit, the latter requiring that candidates with the best merits be selected for posts in international secretariats. To do justice to the principle of broad geographical representation, a criterion which is entirely ignorant of the quality of a potential candidate needs to be applied, whilst it is precisely the candidate's superior qualification which is, pursuant to relevant constituent instruments and/or staff regulations, required to be the primary consideration in staff appointment in all current international organizations. Moreover, there is also a possible inconsistency of the principle of broad geographical representation with the prohibition of discrimination. When preference is given in staff selection process to a certain candidate because he possesses a desired nationality, unsuccessful candidates can argue that they have been discriminated on the basis of their nationality.[83]

International organizations have been trying to reconcile all these different principles in practice in various ways and with varying degrees of success. They have usually approached the matter in the same manner as they have dealt with positive discrimination for women. Hence, candidates with the desired nationality are to be granted preferential treatment under generally the same conditions as those that apply for preferring women above equally qualified men. The bottom line for such action is an essential equality of qualifications of the candidates. Thus, positive discrimination favouring a national of a certain Member State may not materialize to the detriment of a better qualified candidate. Of course, in practice it is not easy to arrive at a situation in which the qualifications of two or more persons can be considered to be essentially the same. Even when one disregards differences in educational systems that exist in different countries, it is always challenging to compare people's careers, professional experiences and the skills they have acquired throughout their previous career.

---

[83] The formal contradiction between the principle of geographical representation and the principle prohibiting discrimination on the basis of nationality was emphasized, for example, in *Second Report on Reform of the Commission of 1999, Volume II*, para. 6.2.23.

Another obstacle facing the implementation of the principle of broad geographical representation in practice is the shortage of the 'right' people, i.e. people with the required qualifications and experience, from the 'right' countries, i.e. countries whose representation should be improved in a particular international organization. There are several reasons for this. One of them is the unavailability of talented and competent persons in some countries due to lack of qualifications or foreign language proficiency. This is especially the case with some developing countries. As rightly pointed out by Lemoine, scarcity of qualified persons is one of the main features of underdevelopment itself.[84] Furthermore, nationals of many developing countries who do posses necessary qualifications often prefer to stay at home to build the system and to contribute to the development of their country rather than to leave for a career in international civil service. [85] Another reason for insufficient availability of candidates from certain countries may be the fact that those countries offer more attractive employment or business opportunities than international organizations. That is, for instance, the case with the United Kingdom which is considered notoriously underrepresented in both the UN and the EU. Many British nationals find it unattractive to work for the UN or the EU because their professional prospects in the private sector in Britain are considered superior to those in Brussels or New York.[86] The importance of family and family relations and the corresponding unwillingness to move abroad, as well as a higher prestige for the career in national civil service than in the international civil service could be other plausible explanations for diminished interest among nationals of some countries in applying for employment with international organizations.

Yet another difficulty in implementing the principle of broad geographical representation in practice is the considerable interest of Member States in staff selection matters. This interest is reflected in Member States' general as well as individual interventions in staff selection policies and processes. The general interventions take the form of regulations, rules and guidelines which Member States adopt in order to ensure that the principle of broad geographical representation is sufficiently incorporated in staff policies of international organizations, resulting in an adequate number of nationals of each individual Member State in the organizations' workforce. In some organizations, notably the UN, Member States' general interventions have led to the development of special mechanisms aimed at meeting the above mentioned objective. The problem with these interventions is that, as rightly observed by Reymond and Mailick, the pressure to comply with the requirement to ensure adequate nationality representation introduces a disturbing factor in the recruitment process in that the search for suitable candidates is directed not towards candidates with the best qualifications but rather towards those who are likely to satisfy the national quotas. As legitimate as such a motive may be, the result is that the quality of selected staff is compromised by national-

[84] Lemoine, *The International Civil Servant: An Endangered Species*, p. 247.

[85] Ibid., p. 247. See also Bulkeley, *Depoliticizing United Nations Recruitment: Establishing a Genuinly International Civil Service*, p. 770.

[86] See, for example, *Britain's Costly Disdain*, in: The Economists, 3.11.2007.

ity considerations.[87] Experience shows that, for example in the UN, this indeed led to nationality becoming a *de facto* determinant in staff appointment in the past. Reymond and Mailick, for example, stated in 1985 that nationality had in practice replaced competence in the UN.[88] Similarly, a few years later Bulkeley noted that:

> *The [UN General] Assembly, in a series of resolutions over the last twenty years, has inadvertently made the geographic identity of a potential candidate for a U.N. staff position the primary basis for recruitment.* [89]

Bulkeley strongly warned against the considerable influence that UN Member States had with regard to composition of the international civil service in the Fifth Committee of the UN General Assembly which advises the Assembly on budgetary and administrative matters. He also cautioned against 'unfounded expectations' of countries in the entitlement to posts within their national quotas:

> *Many governments believe themselves entitled to the posts within their assigned ranges. They also assume a prerogative to propose candidates for their "allotted posts." These beliefs are often reinforced as same-nationality applicants are permitted to replace the fixed-term staff members to ensure that the geographic representation of the member state is not adversely affected.*[90]

Bulkeley furthermore warned that:

> *Eventually, the number of nations represented becomes more important than the asserted interest of quotas – creation of diversity within the UN system. Perpetuation of this system extends beyond the geographical distribution provisions of Article 101(3) of the Charter.'*[91]

Also Meron cautioned already in 1976 that the administrative 'obsession' with filling national quotas in the UN was detrimental to the principle of merit. The increasing emphasis on quantitative guidelines resulted, in Meron's view, in the growing reluctance of the UN Administration to exercise discretion in determining the most

---

[87] Reymond and Mailick, *International Personnel Policies and Practices*, p. 79. See also Bulkeley, *Depoliticizing United Nations Recruitment: Establishing a Genuinly International Civil Service*, p. 762.

[88] Reymond and Mailick, *International Personnel Policies and Practices*, p. 43. See also Plantey, A., *The International Civil Service, Law and Management*, MASSON Publishing USA, Inc., New York / Paris / Barcelona / Milan / Mexico City / Rio de Janeiro, 1981, p. 87.

[89] Bulkeley, *Depoliticizing United Nations Recruitment: Establishing a Genuinly International Civil Service*, pp. 758 759. See also pp. 761 762 where Bulkeley quotes a UK delegate to the Fifth Committee as stating: 'The effect of the resolutions adopted over the years had been to create an impressive set of mandates which reached far into the day-to-day work of the Office of Personnel Services... References in resolutions on personnel matters to Article 101, paragraph 3, of the Charter were all too often perfunctory, appearing in the preambular part only to be swamped in the operative paragraphs by mandates on geographical distribution...'.

[90] Ibid., p. 762.

[91] Ibid., p. 769. Besides warning against far reaching influence of the UN General Assembly in the UN recruitment process, Bulkeley has also strongly criticized the involvement of individual Member States in the recruitment of individual staff members. – See pp. 773-777.

suitable candidate in cases in which such candidate fell outside the quantitative guidelines.[92]

In this context it has been argued that Member States' interest in staff selection matters is based not only on the belief that broad national diversity of the international civil service is important for the high quality, independence and impartiality of this service. It is also based on countries' conviction that a high number of their nationals in the service of international organizations, in particular at a senior level, is a matter of prestige and national interest.[93] In the EU context, Page noted:

> *We can speculate about the reasons for this – national pride would be visibly hurt if a country had very few or no top officials, a national government might feel it would be easier to influence or even just do business with top officials who speak the same language as its representatives and share the same culture. Or governments might believe officials trained in its country are simply better than any others.*[94]

Under this approach, thus, a broad national diversity of international civil service would not suffice – what is needed is representation of each country.

It has been claimed that the principle of geographical representation has been used as a cloak for Member States' attempts to influence the staff selection process:

> *It is through the doorway of geographical distribution that government representatives enter and seek to exercise influence on a series of personnel functions: recruitment, transfer, promotion, missions, extensions of contract, terminations.*[95]

The result is Member States' interventions in specific staff selection processes. Such interventions may take place upon the initiative of an individual who wishes to be appointed to a (particular) position in the international civil service. They may, however, also occur as a result of individual governments' own political interests. They may wish to place certain individuals within the secretariat of the international organization in order to achieve their own political goals. As noted by Lemoine:

> *[S]o far as member States are concerned, the romanticism of the general interest ... never supplemented the deeper, living conviction that international organization was but another means of advancing national interest.*[96]

---

[92] Meron, T., *Staff of the United nations Secretariat: Problems and Directions*, in: The American Journal of International Law, Vol. 70, pp. 659-693, p. 666.

[93] See, for example, Langrod, *The International Civil Service, Its Origins, Its Nature, Its Evolution*, p. 97; Bulkeley, *Depoliticizing United Nations Recruitment: Establishing a Genuinly International Civil Service*, p. 762; Mouritzen, *The International Civil Service, A study of Bureaucracy: International Organizations*, p. 2; and Dinan, D., *Ever Closer Union. An Introduction to European Integration*, Palgrave, Basingstoke, 1999, p. 33, as cited in Kassim and Menon, *European Integration since the 1990s: Member States and the European Commission*, p. 22.

[94] Page, E. C., *People Who Run Europe*, Clarendon Press, Oxford, 1997, p. 41.

[95] Ali, A., *The International Civil Service: The Idea and the Reality*, in: C. De Cooker (ed.), International Administration, Law and Management Pratices in International Organizations, Martinus Nijhoff Publishers, Dordrecht / Boston / London, 1990, pp. INT.ADMIN I.1/3-20, p. INT. ADMIN I.1/8.

[96] Lemoine, *The International Civil Servant: An Endangered Species*, p. 323. Lemoine believed that the

The evidence from the past, documented in official reports and academic writings, confirms the existence of Member States' interference in international organizations, including the UN and in the EU. Although most countries have in theory accepted the importance of the freedom of each international organization to select its own staff with no external intervention, in practice they have often ignored this prerogative.[97] Javier Perez de Cuellar, the UN Secretary-General between 1982 and 1991, stated in this respect the following:

> *[W]hile all profess their dedication to the principles of independent and objective international administration, few refrain from bringing pressure to bear in favour of their particular interests. This is especially so on the personnel side.*[98]

As noted by Lemoine, such a situation existed not only in the UN, which is in essence a political organization, but also in other more technical international organizations.[99] In some organizations, and indeed especially in the UN, things have at times gone so far as to generate wide perceptions of threats to the independence of international civil service.[100] Reymond and Mailick, for example, noted in 1985 that the invasion of external political moments into staff recruitment distorted the process and, understandably, seriously affected faith in the international character of the international civil service.[101] Also Jonah regarded 'campaigning for posts' to be a heavy derogation from the basic concept of an international civil service.[102]

As in the UN, Member States of the EU too have been taking a close interest in the appointment and placement of EU staff, especially at the senior level. In 1970, Coombes observed:

> *Appointments to all policy-making posts, and even to some others, were a political matter... Especially in the higher grades, Member States governments were*

---

existence of the international community depended on the political balance between countries and that the existence of international organizations did not change this. He held that it was 'naïve to believe' that the membership in international organizations, whereby countries make political commitments, would end centuries-old political reality and practices or would lessen it. - pp. 298-299.

[97] Plantey, *The International Civil Service, Law and Management*, p. 266, para. 901. See also, for example, Hammarskjöld, *The International Civil Servant in Law and in Fact*, pp. 15-16; Langrod, *The International Civil Service, Its Origins, Its Nature, Its Evolution*, p. 97; and Spence and Stevens, *Staff and Personnel Policy in the Commission*, in, pp. p. 173.

[98] Lemoine, *The International Civil Servant: An Endangered Species*, p. 94.

[99] Ibid., pp. 94-95.

[100] For example, an attitude survey on the views of UN diplomats on the UN system of 1982 conducted by the United Nations Institute for Training and Research (UNITAR) showed that the independence of the international civil service was at the time perceived as being increasingly threatened due to political interference from Member States' governments. 83 percent of 179 respondents agreed with this statement. - Franck, T. M., Renninger, J. P. and Tikhomirov, V. B., *An Attitude Survey: Diplomat's View on the United Nations System*, UNITAR, New York, 1982, pp. 34-35, Table 18b.

[101] Reymond and Mailick, *International Personnel Policies and Practices*, p. 76.

[102] Jonah, J. O. C., *Independence and Integrity of the International Civil Service: The Role of the Executive Heads and the Role of States*, in: New York University Journal of International Law and Politics, Vol. 14, pp. 841-859, p. 850.

usually involved and appointments often required much traveling and telephoning back and forth between the various capitals.[103]

Moreover, Coombes considered it to be generally known that certain posts had been in practice reserved for nationals of particular Member States, although he admitted that providing real evidence of such practice was difficult.[104] More than a quarter of a century later, Page noted that the nationality issue was at the heart of a more general political process of senior level appointments.[105] In Page's view, at stake in this process was not so much whether the post 'belonged' to a particular nationality but whose turn it was to have another of their nationals at this level.[106]

Kassim *et al.*, who studied changes in the position and powers of the European Commission since the 1990s, came to the following conclusion:

> *[T]the inclination and ability of member states to place, and use, their nationals in the Commission as sources of information and influence varies considerably, but there is less respect for the independence of the Commission. Even in countries where Commission independence has historically been regarded as sacred, such as the Netherlands, contact with the Dutch Commissioner is no longer regarded as taboo. Not only do member states encourage officials from their national administrations to sit the concours (thereby, ensuring 'their people' are placed in that institution), but both the emphasis on sending short term secondees, and the way in which national administrations are striving to maintain close contact with fellow national in Brussels attest to the ways in which member state influence extends to inside that institution.*[107]

The EU Member States have been exercising influence on the appointment and promotion of their nationals in EU institutions usually, though not exclusively, through their permanent representations.[108] As pertinently stated by Spence, who claimed that national influence in the EU recruitment and career prospects remained pronounced, permanent representations of the EU Member States often 'do what they do' to advance the cause of their nationals.[109] An excellent work from 2001, edited by Kassim *et al.*, on the permanent representations of eleven EU Member

---

[103] Coombes, *Politics and Bureaucracy in the European Community, A Portrait of the Commission of the E.E.C.*, pp. 157-158.

[104] Coombes, D., *Towards a European Civil Service*, Chatham House, London, 1968, p. 21. Such reservations have been, in Coombes' view, existing especially at the higher levels of the administration, notably in (former) category A. Directors-General, for example, appeared to be appointed according to the same formula as the Commissioners themselves. See also Hooghe, L., *The European Commission and the Integration of Europe, Images of Governance*, Cambridge University Press, Cambridge, 2001, p. 177.

[105] Page, *People Who Run Europe*, p. 68; see also Endo, K., *The Presidency of the European Commission under Jacques Delors, The Politics of Shared Leadership*, Macmillan Press and St. Martin's Press in association with St Antony's College, Oxofrd, Basingstok / New York, 1999, p. 37.

[106] Page, *People Who Run Europe*, p. 68.

[107] Kassim and Menon, *European Integration since the 1990s: Member States and the European Commission*, pp. 22 – 23.

[108] Kassim, H., Menon, A., Peters, B. G. and Wright, V. (eds.), *The National Co-ordination of EU Policy, The European Level*, Oxford University Press, Oxford, 2001.

[109] Spence and Edwads (eds.), *The European Commission*, p. 196 and pp. 199-200.

States showed that among the main functions of these representations was acting as a point of contact for own nationals in the EU institutions, maintaining contacts with these persons as well as networking in the Commission.[110] Clearly, the extent to which a particular permanent representation exercises these functions, the methods it uses and the resources it has at its disposal vary significantly. The description provided by Kassim and Peters deserves full citation:

> *Providing a point of contact for nationals working in EU institutions is a commitment undertaken by some, but by no means all, permanent representations, and is pursued with varying degrees of vigour by the former. Some member states take a very active role, first, in trying to establish contact with their nationals, particularly in the Commission. UKREP, for example, has a special unit that offers career support and advice to UK nationals... FRANREP, meanwhile, has since the mid-1990s employed an official to maintain contact with French nationals, monitor their careers, and prompt intervention by the government to ensure that they are promoted at the appropriate stages. .... However, the officials in both missions are insistent that, while they want to make sure that the government's position on an issue is understood, the intention is not to create or mobilize national networks of filières nationals within the institution... Other missions, such as Greece's permanent representation, take a more ad hoc approach or, as in the case of Belgium, make no particular effort in this direction at all.'*[111]

Kassim and Peters continued by explaining the second concern of some EU Member States, namely the need to ensure their representation at various levels in the Commission:

> *The UK and France are particularly exercised on this point. The UK is under-represented in the middle echelons of the Commission, and UKREP, in close liaison with the Cabinet Office, is active in efforts to improve recruitment through, for example, the European fast stream programme, designed to prepare young high-fliers for the concours. France has, in the recent past, become much more concerned about its presence in the Commission bureaucracy. FRANREP is charged with responsibility for tracking upcoming vacancies in senior administrative positions – at [former] A1, A2 and A3 level – in order to alert Paris in good time. It also plays an active role in the recruitment of detached national experts. It identifies areas where secondment opportunities are likely to arise, provide assistance to French detached national experts when they arrive, and helps them find a posting in the national administration at the end of their stay in Brussels...*[112]

---

[110] Kassim, Menon, Peters and Wright (eds.), *The National Co-ordination of EU Policy, The European Level*, p. 311.

[111] Kassim, H. and Peters, B. G., *Co-ordinating National Action in Brussels - a Comparative Perspective*, in: H. Kassim, A. Menon, B. G. Peters and V. Wright (eds.), The National Co-ordination of EU Policy, The European Level, Oxford University Press, Oxford, 2001, pp. 297-339, pp. 316.

[112] Ibid.in, pp. , pp. 316-317.

The practices of the 'older' EU Member States were taken over also by countries which acceded to the EU relatively recently. A 2007 report *The Slovak Voice in Brussels, How to Make It Louder and More Coherent*, for example, stated:

> *[The Slovak Permanent Representation to the EU in Brussels] carries out activities supporting the selection of Slovaks applying for EU positions as well as manages contacts with people already employed in the EU institutions. In its actions [the permanent representation] has been inspired by countries where the systems of pursuing countrymen in the EU institutions and of finding and managing contacts with people already working in the institutions, is well established (e.g. Finland, Denmark, Ireland).*[113]

The report at issue was prepared for the Slovak Governance Institute with funding by the British Embassy in Bratislava. Its objective, as stated in the report, was to propose changes which would increase Slovakia's influence on actions and decision-making processes in the EU, mainly focused on getting more Slovaks into EU institutions.[114] This report provides interesting information not only on actions, and often inaction, of Slovakia in this respect but also on activities pursued by other (new) Member States. For example, with regard to the selection procedure of senior managers, the report stated:

> *Commissioner's intervention during senior management selection procedures is essential, being a common practice in other Member States as well. Many EU officials confirmed that the Hungarian Commissioner, Mr. László Kovács, is very active in this field, which may explain why Hungarians are extremely successful in filling the management positions.*[115]

Elsewhere the report noted and recommended:

> *The last stage of the selection procedure is filling the management position, where political support is necessary. Here the Ambassador [i.e. the Permanent Representative] and the Government of [the Slovak Republic] should intervene directly, supported by the Commissioner and his cabinet. We recommend for the Ambassador to use his network of contacts in particular institutions and prepare the ground for lobbying from the side of the relevant Minister or the Deputy Prime Minister. In case of senior management positions, if required, the direct intervention of the Prime Minister should be involved. The Ambassador should also inform the Commissioner and members of his cabinet about the process and ask for their informal intervention (as in the case of the Hungarian Commissioner).*[116]

The Slovak report demonstrates that the interest of EU Member States in obtaining important posts in the EU civil service for their nationals has not diminished with

---

113 *The Slovak Voice in Brussels, How to Make It Louder and More Coherent, Report of the Slovak Governance Institute*, July 2007, available at http://www.governance.sk/assets/files/publikacie/slovak%20voice%20in%20brussels%20web.pdf, last visited on 30.12.2010, pp. 23-24.

114 Ibid., p. 4.

115 Ibid., p. 25.

116 Ibid., p. 49.

time. This applies to new but also to old EU Member States. The government of the United Kingdom ('UK') which took its office in June 2010 admitted that it was '"determined" to increase its influence in the European Union and ... push for more top EU jobs for British officials'.[117]

3.3. Recruitment procedures

The following chapter of this study, chapter 3, explains in what manner international civil servants serving in the UN Secretariat and in the European Commission are recruited. This issue is a logical continuation of the previous one since it is generally agreed that inappropriate interference of individual Member States in the staff selection process in international organizations is only possible if this process is not sufficiently regulated by detailed, objective and transparent procedures that would prevent subjectivism and favoritism. The absence of such procedures allows interference in the selection process not only by Member States' governments but also by other actors, such as various interest groups, interested in compromising the independence and impartiality of international civil servants for their own benefit. There is broad agreement among experts that, not only in order to ensure excellence but also to protect the independent and impartial status of international civil servants, personal, political and other external considerations must be eliminated from the staff selection process, freeing it from any kind of favouritism and nepotism. There also is a consensus that one way of achieving this is by establishing and maintaining proper procedures to 'protect the integrity of the appointment and promotion process by as many safeguards, checks, and balances as possible'.[118] Without such safeguards, merit as well as staff morale would suffer and political considerations would become a 'runaway horse'.[119] The selection methods and procedures are thus of fundamental importance to the international civil service and deserve special care and attention.[120] They can ensure that both the officials involved in the staff selection process as well as officials subject to this process are protected from pressures by external sources, be they governments or other sources, but also that the best people are attracted to, and retained in, the international civil service. In that context it has been argued that 'the prestige, competence and integrity of international officials are a more effective barrier than legal formulae against States'.[121] However,

[117] Brand, C., *Hague Vows to Increase UK's EU Influence*, in: European Voice, 01.07.2010. See also Willis, A., *UK Sets Out Plan To Regain Influence in EU*, in: euobserver.com, 02.07.2010.

[118] Meron, T., *The United Nations Secretariat*, Lexington Books, Lexington, Toronto, 1977, p. 173.

[119] Ibid., p. 56.

[120] Langrod, *The International Civil Service, Its Origins, Its Nature, Its Evolution*, p. 93 and 305. See also Meron, *The United Nations Secretariat*, p. 59; Bulkeley, *Depoliticizing United Nations Recruitment: Establishing a Genuinly International Civil Service*, p. 749 and pp. 773 et seq.; Sands and Klein, *Bowlett's Law of International Institutions*, p. 302, para. 12-010; and Schermers and Blokker, *International Institutional Law, Unity within Diversity*, p. 346, para. 494. Lemoine adds that the need for increasingly detailed rules and procedures is also caused by the fact that the number of staff serving in international organizations has become large. Without detailed rules and procedures control of the process would be difficult, if not impossible. - Lemoine, *The International Civil Servant: An Endangered Species*, p. 322.

[121] Langrod, *The International Civil Service, Its Origins, Its Nature, Its Evolution*, p. 305.

as much as the independent and impartial status of staff is one of the consequences of a sound selection process, the independent and impartial character of that process is a *sine qua non* for such a consequence. As put by Plantey, 'the selection of the most promising candidates depends on impartiality being guaranteed'.[122]

The protection of officials involved in the staff selection process against undue pressures begins with the respect of Member States' governments for the exclusive competence of organizations' chief administrative officers in staff selection matters. This basic principle, contained in constitutive instruments of virtually all contemporary international organizations, must be further upheld by, and translated into, a proper legal framework, including objective and transparent procedures.[123] Their importance for the protection of the selection process from outside pressures was fittingly explained by Meron:

> *The existence of [fair and impartial procedures and safeguards] enables executive heads to resist pressures from governments because they create an unmistakable duty to conform the administration of personnel affairs to a tangible standard of propriety set out, for example, by the views of promotion bodies, various rules and regulations, or the broader requirements of due process.*[124]

Formal procedures also constitute an essential protection for candidates in recruitment (but also promotion).[125] As already mentioned, they 'defend' them against pressure groups, be they governments or other groups, thereby creating and protecting their independent status of international civil servants. In addition, proper procedures also work as safeguards for individual officials against unfair, arbitrary and/or politically motivated decisions.[126] To guarantee that appointed officials will fulfill their duties in an independent and impartial manner, decisions leading to

---

[122] Plantey, *The International Civil Service, Law and Management*, pp. 276-277, para. 942.

[123] See, for example, *UN Charter*, Article 100(2); *Articles of Agreement of the International Monetary Fund*, Article XII, Section 4(c), available at http://www.imf.org/external/pubs/ft/aa/aa12.htm#4, last visited on 13.12.2010; and *Convention Establishing the World Intellectual Property Organization*, Article 9(8), available at http://www.wipo.int/treaties/en/convention/trtdocs_wo029.html#P169_16656, last visited on 13.12.2010.

[124] Meron, T., *The Role of the Executive Heads*, in: New York University Journal of International Law and Politics, Vol. 14, pp. 861-869, p. 866-867. See also Meron, *The United Nations Secretariat*, p. 57; Meron, *Status and Independence of the International Civil Servant*, p. 308; and Bulkeley, *Depoliticizing United Nations Recruitment: Establishing a Genuinly International Civil Service*, p. 778.

[125] Plantey, *The International Civil Service, Law and Management*, p. 278, para. 946.

[126] *Case No. 1414, UNAT Judgment No. 1315 [2006]*, available at http://untreaty.un.org/UNAT/UNAT_Judgements/Judgements_E/UNAT_01315_E.pdf, last visited on 30.12.2010, para. VI. The UNAT has condemned procedural irregularities in the staff selection process on many occasions, even if it sometimes had to refrain from intervening in the substantive decision due to the discretion which the UN administration enjoys in this respect. – See, for example, *Lopes Braga v. Secretary-General of the United Nations, UNAT Judgment No. 1122 [2003]*, available at http://untreaty.un.org/UNAT/UNAT_Judgements/Judgements_E/UNAT_01122_E.pdf, last visited on 30.12.2010 and *Federchenko v. Secretary-General of the United Nations, UNAT Judgment No. 1153 [2003]*, available at http://untreaty.un.org/UNAT/UNAT_Judgements/Judgements_E/UNAT_01156_E.pdf, last visited on 30.12.2010. In the latter case, the UNAT held that procedures relating to staff career and work ought to be carefully respected and be taken up with necessary care so that suspicions that they are tailor-made are avoided. - *Federchenko, UNAT Judgment No. 1153 [2003]*, para. II.

their recruitment, promotion or other placement ought to be reached pursuant to objective and transparent criteria and procedures and without improper interventions, including those from inside of the organization in question. Also, as noted by Meron, such internal interventions by persons directly not involved in the staff selection process, including for example the UN Secretary-General himself, are usually politically motivated and, therefore, detrimental to the integrity of the process and to the interests of the civil service concerned:

> *It casts doubt on the Charter principle of merit, it weakens and even discredits bodies appointed to advice on appointments and promotions, and it sets a dangerous example for the many officials who are only too ready to exert political pressure on those bodies.*[127]

This study explains how this is done in the UN and in the EU. In chapter 3, the study analyses whether the UN and EU staff recruitment process is safeguarded by objective and transparent procedures which prevent outside influence – be it from Member States or other sources interested in compromising the independence and impartiality of the international civil service to their own benefit.[128] Chapter 3 focuses on recruitment, i.e. the process of filling posts by external candidates, not by appointment of internal candidates. The latter is the subject-matter of subsequent chapters.

3.4. Promotion

The above mentioned considerations on the importance of formal procedures for the independent and impartial status of international staff apply to all three modes of filling posts in international secretariats, not only to recruitment. Therefore, this study looks also at staff promotion and mobility, which are two other existing modes of filling posts.[129]

The relevance of promotion policies for ensuring the independence and impartiality of international civil servants is, however, broader than that. It is generally recognized that without reasonable career prospects, the best persons would stay out of the international civil service.[130] In addition, if such prospects do not exist, persons who do enter the international civil service are likely to reach out in an inappropriate manner to persons or institutions that could enhance their chances to climb up the career ladder, thereby endangering their future independent and impartial functioning.[131] The existence of adequate promotion possibilities in international secretariats is therefore of great importance for ensuring the independence and impartiality of international civil servants. It is examined in chapter 4.

---

[127] Meron, *The Role of the Executive Heads*, pp. 865-866.

[128] See chapter 3.

[129] See also below, chapter 3, section 1.

[130] For example, Meron, *The United Nations Secretariat*, pp. 123-124.

[131] For example, Lemoine, *The International Civil Servant: An Endangered Species*, p. 252.

3.5. Mobility

Staff movement is yet another way of filling posts in international secretariats. For reasons explained above, also this method of staff placement needs to occur in accordance with objective and transparent procedures. If not, it could be misused, for example, for removing an individual from a post in order to create space for another, more favoured, person. Misuse could also occur through placing a favoured person in a post which fell vacant due to an objective reason but which is of special interest to the person that wishes to exercise influence on the future occupant of this post. To prevent such situations, objective and transparent procedures are needed according to which mobility of staff serving in international secretariats is exercised.

Apart from this, mobility is relevant for the independence and impartiality of the international civil servants also because regular movement can prevent individual officials from gaining too much influence in a specific post for a long period of time. Moreover, knowledge that the successor in post in the foreseeable future will be able to access information related to the exercise of powers by his predecessor increases significant reluctance to commit undesirable or possibly questionable acts. It enhances chances that such exercise of power will occur in an objective, independent and impartial manner. This was explicitly confirmed, for example, by the European Commission which introduced mandatory mobility for its senior officials with the following phrase:

> *[The] rotation of senior officials is a way of preventing bureaucratic stasis and resisting national influence. It also acts as a safety valve for DGs administering large budgets.*
>
> *Mobility of its top management is thus important in ensuring that the Commission can play its role as the neutral guardian of the Treaties. ... Checks and balances are the order of the day: there can be no thought of sinecures. Making decisions on top appointments stick in the face of national pressures is also a matter of the Commission's credibility.*[132] (emphasis removed)

Similarly, the UN Joint Inspection Unit ('JIU') stated:

> *Mobility should also be used as a tool to improve and promote transparency in the administration of resources. Therefore, those posts, especially senior posts, involving the responsibility to administer considerable resources – for example, in procurement, finance and treasury – should be subject to special mandatory mobility requirements. Also, the Inspectors believe that posts mandated with oversight functions should be included under this mandatory approach.*[133]

---

[132] Archived website of the European Commission, *Reforming the Commission,* http://ec.europa.eu/reform/2002/chapter02_en.htm#2_2, last visited on 23.07.2010.

[133] *Staff Mobility in the United Nations, Report of the Joint Inspection Unit, JIU/REP/2006/7,* 2006, available in the Official Document System of the United Nations, available at http://documents.un.org/, last visited on 30.12.2010, Section III, Part C, para. 47.

For these reasons, the mobility policies in place in the UN Secretariat and in the European Commission are addressed in this study, too, in chapter 5.

3.6. Type of appointment

Apart from assessing the UN and EU staff selection process, including all three modes of filling vacant posts, this study also deals with issues related to staff separation. As the former, also the latter issues are relevant not only for attracting and retaining high quality staff in international secretariats, but also for their independence and impartiality. The reasons are similar to those that apply to staff appointment and placement. As it has already been mentioned, solid, long-term opportunities to build a career and an adequate protection against losing the employment are necessary for attracting and retaining persons of high quality for service in international organizations. Without them, the best candidates would stay away and realize their professional aspirations and interests elsewhere. Moreover, adequately regulated separation policies prevent international civil servants from paying regard, in the exercise of their international responsibilities, to interests of those whose goodwill they need in order to keep their job. Without sufficient protection against separation from service on grounds not related to the interests of the organization or satisfactory performance and conduct of staff, the independence and impartiality of international civil servants would be compromised, either because of their overcautiousness fearing loss of employment, or because of gratitude for keeping it. An explanation of the need to protect international officials against separation from service that was made by William Rappard, the representative of Switzerland to the League of Nations, deserves to be quoted in full:

> *If you want faithful international servants, you must surround their choice, and afterwards their work by a series of conditions... What is dangerous is that officials should be exposed to dismissal because they have too exclusively served the international community. That kind of security is an absolute duty which we owe to men whom we ask to swear an oath of fidelity to the international cause, for it would be a veritable betrayal to attract them to Geneva, to entrust them with an international task, and then to dismiss them, to "drop" them because their governments thought they had been unfaithful to it.*[134]

There are two specific issues of relevance in this respect. The first one concerns the type of appointment used for staff engagement and the second one the legal grounds and procedures for staff separation. The relevance of the type of appointment used in international organizations rests with the differences in protection against termination of employment offered by permanent as opposed to non-permanent appointments. While permanent appointments may, in principle, not be terminated, except for reasons exhaustively listed in relevant legal instruments, termination of non-permanent appointments may be influenced rather easily. Appointments of

[134] League of Nations, Official Journal, Special Supplement No, 88, Records of the Eleventh Ordinary Session of the Assembly, Minutes of the Fourth Committee, Geneva, 1930, p. 74, as cited in Lemoine, *The International Civil Servant: An Endangered Species*, p. 199.

indefinite duration may be terminated at any time and appointments concluded for a fixed-term period end upon expiry of such period, unless extended or renewed. The non-extension or non-renewal of such appointments equals in reality to termination of the employment relationship. As with the termination of appointments of indefinite duration, the non-extension and non-renewal of fixed-term appointments take place on the basis of a decision of the international organization at issue which could be – and past experience shows that it has been – influenced by external considerations compromising the independence and impartiality of the international civil service.[135]

It has been argued that permanency of employment, or tenure, is of importance to the international civil service for a number of reasons. It has also been argued by some that permanency is a condition for, and a guarantee of, professional excellence – it is needed and used to attract and retain the most competent staff.[136] The UN Preparatory Commission, for example, noticed in this regard the following:

> *Unless members of the staff can be offered assurance of being able to make their careers in the Secretariat, many of the best candidates from all countries will inevitably be kept away.*[137]

Apart from ensuring professional excellence of the international civil service, permanency also offers the benefit that the experience gained by staff during a long service and the security of continuity and institutional memory are secured for the organization.[138] It has also been noted that permanency results in the creation of 'esprit de corps' or 'sense of identification' among international civil servants which can hardly occur among staff who are but temporarily parts of the body of international staff.[139] This was recognized already in the League of Nations. A statement of the British delegate to the League deserves direct citation:

> *Immediately a man starts his work he will have in his mind that he may be dispensed with after five years. ... He will immediately start to look out for another job, and if he gets another job in a year or two he will leave. ... You will not promote international spirit by five year appointments.*[140]

---

[135] For more details, see below, chapter 6, in particular section 2.1.

[136] For example, Graham and Jordan (eds.), *The International Civil Service*, p. 17 and Meron, *The United Nations Secretariat*, p. 115.

[137] *Report of the Preparatory Commission of the United Nations, PC/20*, 23.12.1945, available in the Official Document System of the United Nations, available at http://documents.un.org/, last visited on 30.12.2010, Chapter VIII, Section 2. E, para. 59.

[138] Reymond and Mailick, *International Personnel Policies and Practices*, p. 96 and Plantey, *The International Civil Service, Law and Management*, p. 15.

[139] For example, Graham and Jordan (eds.), *The International Civil Service*, p. 3; Plantey, *The International Civil Service, Law and Management*, p. 15; and Barnes, R., *Tenure and Independence in the United Nations International Civil Service*, in: New York University Journal of International Law and Politics, Vol. 14, pp. 767-782, p. 779.

[140] The statement of the British delegate G. N. Barnes to the League of Nations, as cited in Langrod, *The International Civil Service, Its Origins, Its Nature, Its Evolution*, p. 137, note (3).

Langrod, author of one of the classic works on the international civil service, noted in this respect the following:

> *While the wheels of an international organization are set in motion by the spokesmen of the national governments represented in it, only the international civil service (apart from the International Court) is composed of persons who, by their permanence, their technical knowledge and their autonomy, can attempt to act as catalysts of the international spirit. That is the product of the process of growth and the essence of the international civil service.*[141]

Hence, permanency, together with other features of international civil service, is a warranty of an international approach to international problems, free from national attitudes and, thus, independent.[142]

It has also been argued that permanency of the international civil service creates, as well as guarantees, the loyalty of international staff towards the organization.[143] Explaining the approach with regard to the UN at the time of its establishment, Graham and Jordan noted:

> *[T]he impartiality of international officials could only be assured if their first loyalty was to the community of Member States in whose service they were employed. It was deemed essential that international officials had the independence to act in the best interest of the international community and to be protected from reprisal by individual Member States who might not approve of their actions. It was felt that such independence could only be assured if international officials had security of tenure.*[144]

This statement was made with regard to the newly established UN but the same applied also to other post-war organizations, including the EU. There, too, was a shared, though not unanimous, belief that international staff must be loyal and responsible solely to the organization in which they serve and not to their national governments or any other external entities and that such loyalty can only be generated by offering international staff tenure.[145]

The above quote also shows a close link between loyalty and yet another important effect of tenure on the independence and impartiality of international staff, namely

[141] Ibid., pp. 48-49.

[142] Meron, *The United Nations Secretariat*, p. 115, referring to the statements of the Federation of International Civil Servants' Associations. See also Graham and Jordan (eds.), *The International Civil Service*, p. 81.

[143] For example, Reymond and Mailick, *International Personnel Policies and Practices*, p. 96, but also *Human Resources Management Policies, Report of the Secretary-General, A/49/445*, 29.09.1994, available in the Official Document System of the United Nations, available at http://documents.un.org/, last visited on 30.12.2010, para. 33.

[144] Graham and Jordan (eds.), *The International Civil Service*, p. 81.

[145] France, one of the EU founding Member States, argued that the European Commission should be predominantly composed of seconded national civil servants of the Member States' governments. France, however, did not find support for this argument among the other Member States. For more details, see below, chapter 6, section 3.1.

its ability to provide protection against outside pressure and influence. Permanency of employment has always been regarded as one of the best, and by some as *the* best, means of providing protection of international staff in particular against pressures from their home countries' governments.[146] It could even be argued that protection against national governments was the predominant reason for the introduction of tenure in staff policies of post-war international organizations. To understand this view adequately, it should be noted that when these organizations were being established, a majority of their new staff came from Member States' national civil services where expertise in the relevant areas was present.[147] Unless these national civil servants were offered permanent employment, they would not leave the security of tenure existing in national civil services. In addition, as stated in 1978 by the then UN Secretary-General Kurt Waldheim:

> *[without a permanent international civil service] there would be a danger that the Secretariat would become simply a continuation in international form of the foreign services of the Members.*[148]

The UN Secretary-General made this statement in the context of discussions on the balance between permanent staff and staff seconded from national governments. Secondment, i.e. temporary posting in international organizations of (initially only) national civil servants (but later also national experts employed in other public institutions, such as science institutes and academics), has been one of the important ways in which international organizations have been meeting their temporary needs for specific expertise. It has been used from the outset in virtually all international organizations. At the same time, it has been criticized for its potentially distorting effects on the independent and impartial character of the international civil service.

Secondment of national civil servants in international organizations is a phenomenon traditionally marked by considerable controversy. On the one hand, it is generally recognized that secondment offers a number of advantages. As noted by Beigbeder, secondment is beneficial to all parties involved: the individual concerned who gains international experience and contacts, while retaining continuity of his national career; to the seconding country whose image becomes one of 'generosity towards international cooperation' and which eventually benefits from the official's new experience and contacts, too; and to the organization itself which obtains services of qualified individuals at no (or less than normal) costs.[149] The 'continuing influx of fresh blood and of updated outside experience' is an advantage of

[146] For example, Meron, *The United Nations Secretariat*, p. 103; Meron, *Status and Independence of the International Civil Servant*, p. 308; Graham and Jordan (eds.), *The International Civil Service*, p. 81; and Reymond and Mailick, *International Personnel Policies and Practices*, pp. 96-97.

[147] For details relating to the UN Secretariat and the European Commission, see below, chapter 6, sections 2.1 and 3.1.

[148] Miron, D., *Tenure, Fixed-Term Appointments and Secondment in the United Nations*, in: New York University Journal of International Law and Politics, Vol. 14, pp. 783-798, pp. 794-795, referring to a statement of the UN Secretary-General made in 1978.

[149] Beigbeder, *Threats to the International Civil Service*, p. 166.

secondment observed by Reymond and Mailick.[150] Coombes, furthermore, noted that secondment serves as means for acquiring services of persons with specific qualifications and experience.[151] Moreover, as observed by Cini, the 'intermingling' of national and international civil servants has a potential for furthering the process of Europeanization at the national as well as sub-national level.[152]

Also many official documents have emphasized the positive effects of secondment. For example, the UN Preparatory Commission stressed in 1945:

> *[I]t is important that officials from national service should be enabled to spend a short period of no longer than two years in the Secretariat, so that personal contacts between the Secretariat and national administrations may be strengthened and a body of national officials with international experience created.*[153]

The UN General Assembly expressed its support to secondment, too, and emphasized that secondment from government service was beneficial to both the UN and the Member States.[154] The UN Secretary-General noted:

> *Staff seconded from their national Governments formed the nucleus of the original United Nations Secretariat and secondment remains an important method of securing the temporary services of persons who have skills and experience in areas of particular interest to the United Nations.*[155]

Similarly, the European Commission stated in 2008:

> *Seconded national experts ... should enable the Commission to benefit from the high level of their professional knowledge and experience, in particular in areas where such expertise is not readily available.*
>
> *It is highly desirable to foster the exchange of professional experience in, and knowledge of, European policies by temporarily assigning experts from the administrations of the Member States to the Commission, even for short periods.*[156]

---

[150] Reymond and Mailick, *International Personnel Policies and Practices*, p. 96.

[151] For example, Coombes, *Towards a European Civil Service*, p. 39.

[152] Cini, *The European Commission, Leadership, Organisation and Culture in the EU Administration*, p. 121.

[153] *Report of the UN Preparatory Commission*, Chapter VIII, Section 2. E, para. 61.

[154] See, for example, *General Assembly Resolution 47/226, A/RES/47/226*, 08.04.1993, available in the Official Document System of the United Nations, available at http://documents.un.org/, last visited on 30.12.2010, Section I.A.2., para. 1; but also *General Assembly Resolution 51/226B, A/RES/51/226B*, 03.04.1997, available in the Official Document System of the United Nations, available at http://documents.un.org/, last visited on 30.12.2010, Section III.B., para. 7 and *General Assembly Resolution 55/258, A/RES/55/258*, 14.06.2001, available in the Official Document System of the United Nations, available at http://documents.un.org/, last visited on 30.12.2010, Section IV, para. 19 in which the General Assembly urged the Secretary-General to pursue secondment practices on a wider scale.

[155] *Human Resource Management Policies, Report of the Secretary-General, A/49/445*, para. 27.

[156] *Commission Decision Laying Down Rules on the Secondment to the Commission of National Experts and National Expert in Professional Training, C(2008) 6866 final*, 12.11.2008, available in the Register of Commission Documents, available at http://ec.europa.eu/transparency/regdoc/registre.cfm?CL=en, last visited on 30.12.2010, Preamble, paras. (1) and (2).

Despite all the benefits, many have expressed concern regarding secondment, and in particular secondment of national civil servants, pointed to some dangers. One of the most important dangers is the vulnerability of secondment to its abuse for political purposes. According to Lemoine, who based his conclusions on past experiences with secondment in the UN, two main abuses can take place: first, when secondment becomes in fact nothing more than government sponsorship of certain persons designated to serve in the international organization; and second, when secondment turns into a tool of political pressure on both the organization and its staff. Lemoine explained that in the UN the pressure had been exercised, in most cases, through the disapproval by the relevant government of the extension of secondment despite a clear intension of the organization and the will of the staff member concerned to continue his engagement at the UN.[157]

Another notable problem with secondment, partly related to the first, is the possible increased receptivity of the seconded officials to demands from their home governments.[158] Such receptivity is a direct result of the nature of the secondment since seconded officials remain formally employed by their original employer, in most cases the government of their home country. To this employer seconded officials also return after the period of secondment to the international organization has ended. The future career development of these officials thus depends on their governments and not so much on the international organizations to which they are temporarily attached. It is self-evident that the continuing relationship with the home government influences, consciously or otherwise, the mindset of seconded officials and, in the absence of proper safeguards, it may also have an impact on the manner in which these officials carry out their duties while staying with international organizations. As stated by Egeberg, officials serving on secondment might have 'incentives to pursue the interests of their current employer as well as the goals of those providing their future career, e.g. national governments'.[159] As a consequence, in Egeberg's view, secondment and the existence of national quotas for permanent staff are elements that might lead to the conduct of officials in an intergovernmental rather than international direction.[160]

---

[157] Lemoine, *The International Civil Servant: An Endangered Species*, p. 219 and 205. For more details, see pp. 205-219.

[158] Reymond and Mailick, *International Personnel Policies and Practices*, p. 17. See also Spence and Edwads (eds.), *The European Commission*, p. 195.

[159] Egeberg, *The European Commission - The Evolving EU Executive*, p. 13.

[160] Ibid., p. 13. In contrast, Trondal, who conducted an empirical study on the representation position of seconded national experts in the European Commission, found that these experts tended to evoke multiple representational roles. He argued that the Commission, and its organization and hierarchical structure, had a reasonably strong influence on the seconded national experts who evoked especially departmental and epistemic (an independent expert) roles, which were stronger than the supranational role. Trondal also argued that the intergovernmental role was 'barely emphasized'. However, he admitted that his analysis was based on the limited amount of data and the overall Scandinavian bias of samples which, therefore, required that his conclusions were taken with caution and that further studies were conducted. - Trondal, J., *An Institutional Perspective on Representation. Ambiguous Representation in the European Commission*, European Integration Online Papers (EIoP) Vol. 10, No. 4, 2006, available at http://eiop.or.at/eiop/texte/2006-004a.htm, last visited on 30.12.2010.

The European Commission, for example, has admitted a potential problem in using seconded national experts in cases where specific expertise is needed and the effects of such use on the 'perceived independence' of the institution in shaping its policies.[161] Also the European Parliament has been criticizing the use of seconded national experts, considering it as 'a potentially dangerous move towards the "nationalization" of the European administration – allowing its operation to become unduly influenced by member states.'[162] In 1993 a report prepared by the Committee on Institutional Affairs of the European Parliament stated that:

> *an excessive number of national experts, particularly in posts of responsibility, also calls into question the independence of the European civil service itself.*[163]

The Committee requested the European Commission to end the extensive use of such persons and the 'renationalisation' of the management of certain sectors.[164] Particularly problematic is the situation where seconded officials (continue to) receive emoluments from their original employer. As pointed out by Beigbeder, in such cases there is a clear risk that the seconded officials 'feel more "national" than "international"'.[165]

Because of all the (potential) dangers, it has been considered important to keep secondment under control, in particular with regard to the number of staff. Already in 1961, the then UN Secretary-General Dag Hammarskjöld stated:

> *To have [a large proportion] of the Secretariat staff in the seconded category would be likely to impose serious strains on its ability to function as a body dedicated exclusively to international responsibilities. Especially if there were any doubts as to the principles ruling their work in the minds of the governments on which their future might depend, this might result in a radical departure from the basic concepts of the Charter and the destruction of the international civil service as it has been developed in the League and up to now in the United Nations.*[166]

Similarly, the Court of Justice of the European Union ('ECJ'), then referred to as the Court of Justice of the European Communities, stressed that in 1969:

> *the practice of having recourse within the departments of the Community to the services of national officials does call for certain reservations if the use of such officials attains sizeable proportions and lasts a considerable time.*[167]

---

[161] *Collection and Use of Expertise by the Commission, Principles and Guidelines - "Improving the Knowledge Base for Better Policies", COM(2002) 713 final*, available in the Register of Commission Documents, available at http://ec.europa.eu/transparency/regdoc/registre.cfm?CL=en, last visited on 30.12.2010, p. 17.

[162] Page, *People Who Run Europe*, p. 60.

[163] The report is cited in Ibid., p. 60.

[164] Ibid., p. 60.

[165] Beigbeder, *Threats to the International Civil Service*, p. 167.

[166] Hammarskjöld, *The International Civil Servant in Law and in Fact*, p. 19.

[167] *Jeannette Fux v. Commission of the European Communities, Case 26/68, ECR [1969], p. 145*, para. 25.

Hence, although secondment as such may be beneficial to all parties concerned, if it occurs on a large scale, it can constitute a threat to the international character of the international civil service due to the increased vulnerability of seconded officials to pressure and influence from their governments. As noted by Meron, even though all international civil servants who are not protected by tenure are opened to outside pressures, the problem is more acute in the case of seconded officials.[168]

Because permanency of employment has traditionally been considered to be an important guarantee of the independence and impartiality of international civil servants, employment of non-permanent staff by international organizations, including secondment of national civil servants, has been generally regarded as acceptable only to a limited extent and only for the purposes of acquiring (updated) expertise not (readily) available among permanent staff or because of the political nature of the function involved.[169]

Two particular dangers of the absence of tenure in case of non-permanent staff have been identified. First, the fact that non-permanent staff, and in particular staff serving on fixed-term contracts, live in the continuous fear that their contracts will not be extended or renewed after the fixed period expires. Similarly, staff serving on indefinite appointments must cope with the knowledge that their appointment may be terminated at any time without their having any influence over it. It is self-evident that these staff will not devote all their time and energy to the exercise of their duties but will spend some of that on securing their future employment, either with the international organization at issue or elsewhere. As rightly pointed out by Beigbeder, tenure contributes to staff independence by creating space to concentrate on the core functions and tasks rather than worrying about a possible non-extension (or termination) of the employment.[170] Even more important in this respect is the danger of staff compromising their own independence and impartiality in the exercise of official duties with the aim of ensuring future employment. Vulnerability of non-permanent staff to outside pressure and influence is thus greater than in case of permanent officials who do not need to 'please' their potential future employers, with whom they inevitably come into contact during the service in international organizations. There is thus lesser sense of independence among non-permanent staff than there is among permanent staff.

The second danger of the absence of tenure in case of non-permanent staff is the inadequacy of protection for such staff against negative effects of actions carried out in the exercise of their international responsibilities. A former international civil servant stated in this regard:

---

[168] Meron, *Status and Independence of the International Civil Servant*, pp. 309-310.

[169] See, for example, *Human Resource Management Policies, Report of the Secretary-General, A/49/445*, para. 32. In the EU, for example, the so-called Spierenburg Committee of 1979 considered that the presence of more than twenty per cent of temporary staff at middle levels was potentially distorting the European character of the EU civil service. - Stevens, A. and Stevens, H., *Brussels Bureaucrats? The Administration of the European Union*, PALGRAVE, Houndmills / New York, 2001, p. 20. See also Spence and Stevens, *Staff and Personnel Policy in the Commission*, p. 194.

[170] Beigbeder, *Threats to the International Civil Service*, p. 71.

I could never have survived doing what I did in places like the Middle East [without] the knowledge that I have a career service.[171]

This former official pleaded for tenure for the core international civil servants because he believed that it offered protection against removal of staff who had become 'inconvenient' to some Member States' governments.[172] Such removal is not possible, or at least much less likely to happen, if one holds a permanent appointment.

It must be admitted that there are also those who have disagreed with the above views on the importance of tenure for the independence and impartiality of the international civil servants. Barnes, for example, analyzed the effect of fixed-term employment on international civil service in the beginning of the 1980s, i.e. at a time of deep division within the UN on this issue. He claimed that the use of fixed-term contract alone did not have any negative influence on staff's impartiality and loyalty but that the 'integrity depend[ed] upon each individual's moral attributes, not on his contractual status'.[173] Barnes did admit that the sense of identification with the international organization might come sooner and easier for staff recruited for life than for those engaged for a limited period of time. However, he believed that, despite this, there was 'no reason to conclude that fixed-term staff ... are less loyal to the organization for want of a permanent appointment.'[174]

Barnes' views are not generally shared, though. Meron, for example, strongly disagreed with them. A long quote from his work on the UN Secretariat deserves to be reproduced in full:

[S]ome Secretariat officials, on the basis of their undocumented and unresearched impressions, reject the notion that temporary, or even seconded officials, are less loyal to the Organization than permanent or long-term staff. They argue that such assertions have not been proved. But can it really be doubted that seconded civil servants ... have a different relationship with their governments from that of other staff members? And can it truly be claimed that fixed-term officials are not far more vulnerable to the pressure of their governments than tenured officials are? Will they not need the goodwill of those very governments in the context of the possible extension of their contracts, especially if they occupy the relatively senior positions, or, when they return to their home countries?[175]

Of course, Meron's statements were made at times when fixed-term contracts were given to UN staff for political reasons rather than for reasons related to the needs of the organization.[176] Nonetheless, as explained earlier, the belief that tenure is of great importance for international organizations in order to secure independence

[171] Jonah, J. O. C., *Can the United Nations Survive Without a Vital International Civil Service?, A talk to an AFICS (NY) luncheon*, 04.12.2002, available at http://www.unstaff.org/index.php?option=com_content&task=view&id=83&Itemid=8, last visited on 17.03.2009, p. 2.

[172] Ibid., p. 2.

[173] Barnes, *Tenure and Independence in the United Nations International Civil Service*, p. 778.

[174] Ibid., p. 779.

[175] Meron, *The United Nations Secretariat*, p. 114.

[176] For more details on this point, see below, chapter 6, section 2.1.

and impartiality of their staff, has long been generally shared. This study examines what place tenure has in human resources policies of the UN Secretariat and the European Commission at present. It does so in chapter 6, which also assesses whether the various types of appointments used in the two organizations ensure the independence and impartiality of their staff.[177]

3.7. Separation from service

The concerns relating to the issue of separation from service are not exhausted by the issue of tenure only. Also permanent appointments may, under certain conditions be terminated. It is possible, for example, when the international organization needs to reduce its staff numbers or when a particular post is abolished. It is also permitted to terminate employment of international civil servants whose performance or conduct is unsatisfactory.[178] The relevant question here is whether the legal grounds available for termination of permanent appointments in the UN and in the EU are such as to prevent termination for political or other external reasons. If, for example, the nationality of staff were a relevant legal ground for ending the employment relationship with the international organization in order to create space for the appointment of a national of another country, the international civil servants could be tempted to reach out to their government for help. They would attempt to ensure that other staff members with their nationality are separated instead of themselves. It is self-evident that such behavior could involve promises towards the government possibly compromising the independent and impartial exercise of the official responsibilities of international civil servants.

Another important question related to the issue of termination of permanent appointments is whether procedures pursuant to which such termination takes place are sufficiently objective and transparent as to prevent their abuse for pursuing political or other external motives. The question thus is whether procedures for separation from service of international civil servants allow for termination of employment of persons who, for various reasons, might have become unwelcome, under the guise of a formally acceptable legal ground which is available for staff separation from service.

Protection against abusive firing is of vital importance to international civil services since, as noted by Lemoine, interference with the independence and impartiality of international officials may take various forms, including not only 'pressure for the appointment of "reliable" nationals, not so say agents, [but also] pressure to terminate the appointment of officials who are not, or no longer, in the good graces of the governments'.[179] This study examines whether the legal framework which is

---

[177] See chapter 6.

[178] More details on legal grounds for separation from service available in the UN Secretariat and in the European Commission, see below, chapter 7, sections 2.2 - 2.3 and 3.2 – 3.4.

[179] Lemoine, *The International Civil Servant: An Endangered Species*, p. 103.

in place in the UN and in the EU provides adequate protection again such danger.[180] Such assessment is provided in chapter 7.

4. Terminology

For reasons of simplicity, any reference in this study to a person of the male sex includes a reference to a person of the female sex, unless the context suggests otherwise.

Similarly, references to the Director(ate)-General for Human Resources and Security of the European Commission include also, where relevant, the former Director(ate)-General for Personnel and Administration. The latter name was in use until December 2009 when the Commission under the second Presidency of José Manuel Barrosso took office. This applies equally to the Commissioner for Personnel and Administration who is currently referred to as the Commissioner for Human Resources and Security. Also the Court of First Instance of the European Communities ('CFI') has been renamed relatively recently. The *Lisbon Treaty*, which entered into force on 1 December 2009, renamed it the General Court of the European Union. However, as the judgments of the Court of First Instance carry this (former) name, this study uses it as well.

Finally, the term 'Administration' is employed in this study when the UN Secretariat and/or the European Commission are referred to as employers exercising powers conferred upon them in the area of human resources management.

[180] See chapter 7.

Chapter 1

THE UN AND EU CIVIL SERVICE DEFINED

1. Introduction

Both the UN Secretariat and the European Commission employ their personnel under various types of appointments and contracts, and classify them under a number of categories and subcategories. Most of these divisions and classifications are of great relevance to this study because they determine which rules and regulations, that constitute the basis for this study's analysis, apply in which situation. It is therefore of utmost importance to understand the classification of UN and EU personnel well. An overview of both UN and EU classifications is offered in this chapter. The chapter covers also persons not considered to be UN or EU staff members but engaged at the UN Secretariat or European Commission under various contracts. These persons fall outside the formal UN and EU personnel statutes. Although they cannot be regarded as international civil servants and are therefore not covered in this study, they are briefly described in this chapter. Its intention is to provide as complete picture of all UN and EU personnel as possible.

2. Classification of personnel employed by the UN Secretariat

Classification of all personnel working in, or for, the UN Secretariat into clear categories is a rather complex exercise. This is so not only because such classification can be made on the basis of different criteria but also because the UN personnel system is quite complicated. The *UN Staff Regulations* and the *UN Staff Rules* are not particularly helpful in this regard. They provide only for a basic definition and classification of UN staff, leaving details to be set out by the Secretary-General. Moreover, the two legal instruments provide no information on personnel engaged by the UN Secretariat but not considered UN staff members, i.e. 'non-staff' personnel. The UN Secretary-General has adopted a number of administrative issuances in which he defines various categories of such 'non-staff' personnel and sets out conditions of their employment. However, a number of these issuances date back to the 1980s and 1990s without being properly adjusted in line with subsequent developments in the UN personnel policy. Moreover, some of these issuances on 'non-staff' personnel overlap in their scope and some even include provisions on UN staff.[1]

[1] *Secretary-General's Bulletin, Policies for Obtaining the Services of Individuals on behalf of the Organization, ST/SGB/177*, 19.11.1982, available in the Human Resources Handbook of the United Nations, available at http://www.un.org/hr_handbook/English/, last visited on 30.12.2010; *Administrative Instruction, Temporary Staff and Individual Contractors, ST/AI/295*, 19.11.1982, available in the Human Resources Handbook of the United Nations, available at http://www.un.org/hr_handbook/English/, last visited on 30.12.2010 and *Administrative Instruction, Technical Co-operation Personnel and OPAS Officers, ST/AI/297*, 19.11.1982, available in the Human Resources Handbook of the United Nations, available at http://www.un.org/hr_handbook/English/, last visited on 30.12.2010 together with *Administrative Instruction, Technical Co-operation Personnel and OPAS Officers, Addendum, ST/AI/297/Add.1*, 7.12.1995, available in the Human Resources Handbook of the United Nations, available at http://www.un.org/hr_handbook/English/, last visited on 30.12.2010, both abolished in 2010 by *Administrative Instruction, Administration of Temporary Appointments, ST/AI/2010/4*, 27.04.2010, available in the Human Resources Handbook of the United Nations, available at http://www.un.org/hr_handbook/English/, last visited on 30.12.2010 and *Administrative Instruction, Staff Selection System, ST/AI/2010/3*, 21.04.2010, available in the Human Resources Handbook of the United Nations, available at http://www.un.org/hr_handbook/English/, last visited on 30.12.2010, respectively; *Administrative Instruction, Consultants and*

Before going into details on the first group of UN personnel, namely the UN staff, the following scheme provides an overview of all personnel working in, or for, the UN Secretariat at present:

Scheme 1: Types of personnel in the UN Secretariat

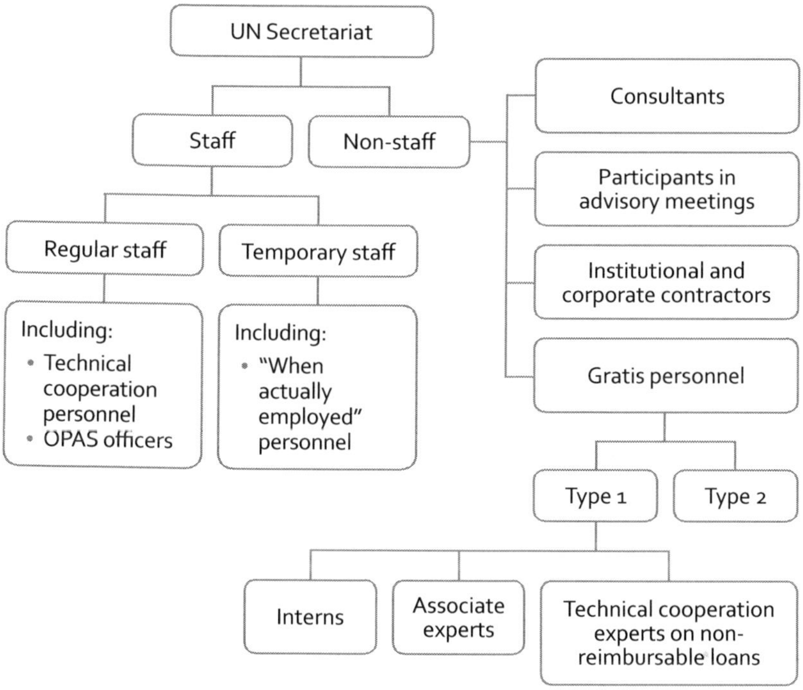

Participants in Advisory Meetings, ST/AI/296, 19.11.1982, available in the Human Resources Handbook of the United Nations, available at http://www.un.org/hr_handbook/English/, last visited on 30.12.2010; *Administrative Instruction, Consultants and Individual Contractors, consolidated text, ST/AI/1999/7, as last amended by ST/AI/1999/7/Amend.1*, 25.08.1999, available in the Human Resources Handbook of the United Nations, available at http://www.un.org/hr_handbook/English/, last visited on 30.12.2010; *Administrative Instruction, Institutional or Corporate Contractors, ST/AI/327*, 23.01.1985, available in the Human Resources Handbook of the United Nations, available at http://www.un.org/hr_handbook/English/, last visited on 30.12.2010; *Secretary-General's Bulletin, Use of "When Actually Employed" Contracts for Special Representatives, Envoys and Other Special High-level Positions, ST/SGB/283*, 29.8.1996, available in the Human Resources Handbook of the United Nations, available at http://www.un.org/hr_handbook/English/, last visited on 30.12.2010; *Administrative Instruction, Non-reimbursable Loans of Personnel Services from Sources External to the United Nations Common System, ST/AI/231/Rev.1*, 23.1.1991, available in the Human Resources Handbook of the United Nations, available at http://www.un.org/hr_handbook/English/, last visited on 30.12.2010; *Administrative Instruction, United Nations Internship Programme, ST/AI/2000/9*, 19.09.2000, consolidated text as last amended by ST/AI/2005/11 effective on 01.09.2005, available in the Human Resources Handbook of the United Nations, available at http://www.un.org/hr_handbook/English/, last visited on 30.12.2010 and *Administrative Instruction, Gratis Personnel, ST/AI/1999/6*, 28.5.1999, available in the Human Resources Handbook of the United Nations, available at http://www.un.org/hr_handbook/English/, last visited on 30.12.2010.

2.1. UN staff

The basic definition of UN staff can be found in the *UN Staff Regulations*. They stipulate:

> *For the purposes of these Regulations, the expressions "United Nations Secretariat", "staff members" or "staff" shall refer to all the staff members of the Secretariat, within the meaning of Article 97 of the Charter of the United Nations, whose employment and contractual relationship are defined by a letter of appointment subject to regulations promulgated by the General Assembly pursuant to Article 101, paragraph 1, of the Charter.*[2]

Article 97 of the *UN Charter* provides that the UN Secretariat is to 'comprise a Secretary-General and such staff as the Organization may require'.[3] Article 101(1) furthermore states that the UN staff are to be appointed by the Secretary-General under regulations established by the UN General Assembly.[4] Such 'regulations established by the General Assembly' include the *UN Staff Regulations*.

UN staff may be divided into a number of groups, and according to a number of criteria, including the duration of employment at the UN Secretariat and type of work performed. The most basic division could be made in accordance with the *Secretary-General's Bulletin, Policies for Obtaining the Services of Individuals on Behalf of the Organization ST/SGB/177*, promulgated on 19 November 1982 and still in force.[5] This bulletin makes a distinction between regular UN staff and temporary staff.

The regular UN staff carry out substantive programmes and perform support and service functions mandated by the *UN Charter* or by the UN legislative bodies as the direct responsibility of the UN Secretary-General. This group of staff includes persons appointed for a period of at least one year. Since 2010, it also includes two specific categories of staff that were previously governed by separate administrative issuances, namely the so-called technical cooperation personnel and the Operational, Executive and Administrative Services (OPAS) officers. Conditions for engagement of these staff used to be set out in the already mentioned *Secretary-General's Bulletin, Policies for Obtaining the Services of Individuals on Behalf of the Organization ST/SGB/177* of 19 November 1982 and in the *Administrative Instruction, Technical Co-operation Personnel and OPAS Officers ST/AI/297* of the same date as the Bulletin.[6] Since 2010, engagement of both technical cooperation personnel and

---

[2] *UN Staff Regulations of 2009*, Scope and Purpose.

[3] *UN Charter*, Article 97.

[4] Ibid., Article 101(1).

[5] *Secretary-General's Bulletin, Policies for Obtaining the Services of Individuals on behalf of the Organization*.

[6] Ibid., paras 11-13; and *Administrative Instruction, Technical Co-operation Personnel and OPAS Officers*, parts I and II. The technical cooperation personnel was defined as personnel 'provid[ing], or assist[ing] in providing, advisory services to Governments on their request within the framework of a technical co-operation programme, project or activity'. These personnel had to possess specific technical skills and could be engaged under various types of arrangements, such as experts on mission, or national experts. – *Secretary-General's Bulletin, Policies for Obtaining the Services of Individuals on behalf of the Organization*, para. 11. The OPAS officers were hired on the basis of an agreement with a government

OPAS officers fall under the administrative instruction that applies to most other regular UN staff.[7]

The UN temporary staff are staff engaged by the UN Secretariat for less than one year.[8] Since 2010, temporary staff also include the so-called 'when actually employed' (WAE) contractors, previously governed by a separate administrative issuance.[9] At present, engagement of WAE contractors is governed by the administrative instruction that applies to all UN temporary staff, i.e. the *Administrative Instruction, Administration of Temporary Appointments ST/AI/2010/4*.[10]

In general, when recruited for UN service, both regular and temporary staff receive a letter of appointment. Their conditions of employment are set out in the *UN Staff Regulations* and the *UN Staff Rules*, which apply to both regular and temporary staff.[11] Although the distinction between regular and temporary staff formally persists – the Secretary-General's Bulletin ST/SGB/177 of 1982 is still in force – it could be argued that this distinction has lost its importance in the meantime. Meanwhile, many different types of appointments have been introduced and subsequently abolished in the UN Secretariat, all of them distinguished not only by the appointment duration but partly also by the type of work performed. For some of these types of appointment, a separate set of *UN Staff Rules* was introduced. The original *UN Staff Rules* became the so-called 100 series of the *UN Staff Rules* and the newly introduced *UN Staff Rules* became 200 series, later complemented by 300 series and even 400 series. Each of the series contained different conditions of employment for staff falling within their scope.[12] In 2009, however, the *UN Staff Rules* were unified in a single document, as they were in the early years of the UN.[13] While temporary appointments, and temporary staff, are still possible and the administration of

---

to perform functions of an operational, executive and administrative character. The specificity of this category of personnel was that they were employees of the government, not the UN – and considered a part of the national civil service of the relevant government, accountable to it and paid by it. The UN, however, provided supplementary payments and certain allowances in order to compensate service done on behalf of the UN – *Secretary-General's Bulletin, Policies for Obtaining the Services of Individuals on behalf of the Organization*, para. 13.

[7] *UN Staff Selection System*.

[8] *Secretary-General's Bulletin, Policies for Obtaining the Services of Individuals on behalf of the Organization*, paras. 3 and 4. For details on UN temporary appointments, see below chapter 6, section 2.3.1.

[9] *Secretary-General's Bulletin, Use of "When Actually Employed" Contracts for Special Representatives, Envoys and Other Special High-level Positions*. Pursuant to this bulletin, 'when actually employed' contractors could be hired to perform work which was of an intermittent or discontinuous nature, or to carry out assignments with uncertain duration or with timing not clearly identifiable in advance; or to ensure the availability of persons with necessary special skills at short notice. When they were actually employed, i.e. performed functions specified in their contract, they had the status of UN staff members and were thus subject to the *UN Staff Regulations* and the *UN Staff Rules*. During days they were not actually working, these persons were obliged to 'continue to exercise utmost discretion in all matters concerning the Organization'. – paras. 2 and 12.

[10] Ibid., para. 13. For WAE contractors, some specificities are still provided for in the *Secretary-General's Bulletin, Use of "When Actually Employed" Contracts for Special Representatives, Envoys and Other Special High-Level Positions ST/SGB/283 of 1996*. See, for example, para. 3 on the period of employment.

[11] *UN Staff Regulations of 2009*, Regulation 1.1.

[12] For details, see below, chapter 6, section 2.2.

[13] See below, chapter 6, section 2.3.

temporary appointments has been subjected to a separate administrative instruction, no further distinction is being made between regular and temporary staff.[14] For example, the Secretary-General's annual reports on the composition of the UN Secretariat include both regular and temporary staff and provide no special data on temporary staff and staff serving under other types of appointment.[15]

It could therefore be argued that a more important classification of UN staff is that by staff categories. Initially, all (regular and temporary) UN staff were classified as a single category with no distinction related to the manner of recruitment (international or local), the duty station or tasks performed. Every person was part of a single corps of the UN staff. The situation changed in 1949 when a separate category of staff was created for clerical and lower posts – the General Service category.[16] Since then, two main distinct categories of UN staff have existed – Professional and General Service. These two categories differ not only in the type of work performed but also in the manner of recruitment, application of different remuneration principles and certain rights and obligations.

Over the years, other specific categories of staff have been created outside the two main groups. They have consisted of staff employed for special tasks, such as peace-keeping.[17] These other categories have been referred to as 'related' to the General Service category.[18] In 2009, one of these 'related' categories, namely the Field Service category, formally became a separate staff category.[19] Meanwhile, the Professional category has been extended with the so-called 'higher' categories, sometimes also referred to as the 'above' categories.[20]

---

[14] Administration of temporary appointments is governed by administrative instruction ST/AI/2010/4 - *Administrative Instruction, Administration of Temporary Appointments*. For more details, see below, chapter 6, section 2.3.1.

[15] For the most recent report, see *Composition of the Secretariat: Staff Demographics, Report of the Secretary-General, A/65/350*, 08.09.2010, available in the Official Document System of the United Nations, available at http://documents.un.org/, last visited on 30.12.2010.

[16] Reymond and Mailick, *International Personnel Policies and Practices*, p. 58-59. See also *United Nations Common System of Salaries, Allowances and Benefits*, January 2009, available at http://icsc.un.org/resources/pdfs/sal/sabeng09.pdf, last visited on 30.12.2010, p. vii.

[17] Reymond and Mailick, *International Personnel Policies and Practices*, p. 58-59. See also *United Nations Common System of Salaries, Allowances and Benefits of the ICSC*, p. vii. For more details on the development of different categories of staff and related types of appointments in the UN Secretariat, see chapter 6, section 2.2.

[18] For example, *Composition of the Secretariat, Report of the Secretary-General, A/64/352*, 15.09.2009, available in the Official Document System of the United Nations, available at http://documents.un.org/, last visited on 30.12.2010, para. 14.

[19] *Staff Rules of the United Nations, 100 Series, ST/SGB/2009/7*, 16.06.2009, available in the Human Resources Handbook of the United Nations, available at http://www.un.org/hr_handbook/English/, last visited on 30.12.2010Rule 2.1(b).

[20] The expression 'Professional and above categories' is used, for example, in the most recent version of the *UN Staff Selection System*. – *UN Staff Selection System*, for example Section 2.2. Although this system serves as one of the main legal sources in this study, especially though not exclusively in chapters III – VI, the study employs consistently the expression 'Professional and higher categories'. This is the expression used also by the most recent version of the *UN Staff Rules*, promulgated after the most recent version of the *UN Staff Selection System*. – See *Staff Rules of the United Nations, ST/SGB/2010/6*, 02.09.2010, available in the Human Resources Handbook of the United Nations, available

The situation at present is thus as follows. There are three main (groups of) categories of staff in the UN Secretariat: the Professional and higher categories; the Field Service category; and the General Service and related categories.[21] The first and the last group are further divided into separate categories that are shown in the scheme below and further explained in the following sections. Staff in each of the existing categories serve in one of four entity groups of the UN Secretariat, namely in departments and offices, regional commissions, tribunals or field operations.[22] They hold different types of appointment, including permanent, probationary, indefinite, fixed-term, temporary and continuing appointment.[23] Note that the category in which an individual staff member is classified, the entity in which he serves, and the type of appointment he holds are entirely independent of each other.

Scheme 2: Staff categories in the UN Secretariat

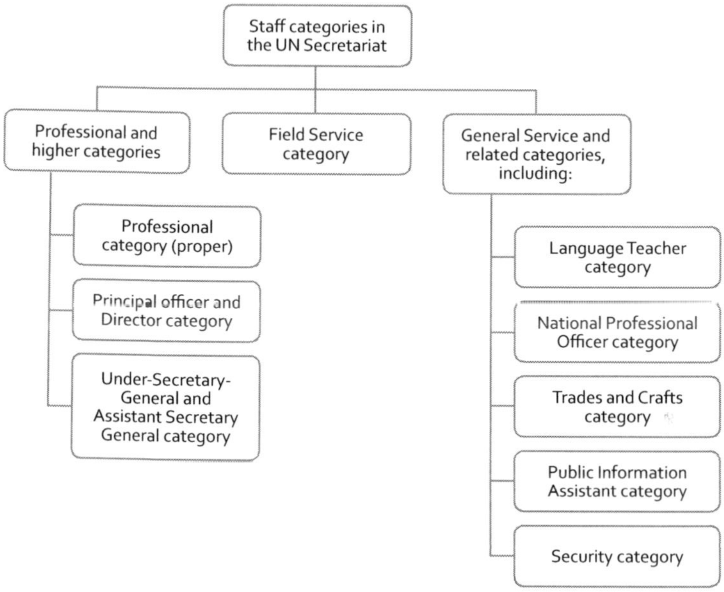

at http://www.un.org/hr_handbook/English/, last visited on 30.12.2010, Rule 2.1(b).

[21] *UN Staff Rules*, Rule 2.1(b).

[22] *Composition of the Secretariat: Staff Demographics, Report of the Secretary-General, A/65/350*, para. 11, table 7. The UN Secretariat is divided into a number of departments and offices, located in the headquarters in New York but also outside New York, in Addis Ababa, Bangkok, Beirut, Geneva, Nairobi, Santiago, Vienna and elsewhere. In addition, there are five regional commissions, namely the Economic and Social Commission for Asia and the Pacific, the Economic and Social Commission for Western Asia, the Economic Commission for Africa, the Economic Commission for Europe and the Economic Commission for Latin America and the Caribbean; as well as two international criminal tribunals, namely the International Tribunal for Rwanda and the International Tribunal for the Former Yugoslavia. – see the official website of the UN Secretariat, available at http://www.un.org/en/mainbodies/secretariat/, last visited on 29.11.2010. As far as the entity field operations are concerned, it refers to peacekeeping missions and certain special political missions. - *Composition of the Secretariat: Staff Demographics, Report of the Secretary-General, A/65/350*, para. 7; for more information see *ibid.*

[23] For details on types of appointments used in the UN Secretariat at present, see chapter 6, section 2.3.1.

According to the most recent figures, some 44.000 active staff served at the UN Secretariat as of 30 June 2010, regardless of the type and length of appointment. About 42.000 staff, i.e. 94 per cent, had a contract of one year duration or longer. Roughly 35 per cent of all staff served in departments and offices, while 55 per cent served in field operations, including peacekeeping missions and certain special political missions. The rest served in regional commissions (six per cent) and in international tribunals (four per cent).[24] The division of staff per category was as follows:

Table 1: All staff of the UN Secretariat by category and entity as on 30 June 2010

Category	Departments / Offices	Regional commissions	Tribunals	Field operations	Total
Professional and higher categories	7.689	992	639	2.839	**12.159 (28%)**
Field Service category	67	3	268	4.100	**4.438 (10%)**
General Service and related categories	7.832	1.709	942	17.054	**27.537 (62%)**
TOTAL	**15.588 (35%)**	**2.704 (6%)**	**1.849 (4%)**	**23.993 (55%)**	**44.134 (100%)**

Source: *Composition of the Secretariat: Staff Demographics, Report of the Secretary-General, A/65/350* of 8 September 2010[25]

2.1.1. Professional and higher categories

Staff serving in the Professional and higher categories are those who are of most interest to this study. Although these staff constitute less than 30 per cent of the UN human resources, they are involved in the drafting of policies subsequently submitted to the competent UN organs for decisions.[26] The International Civil Service Commission ('ICSC') defines work performed by these staff as:

> *analytical, evaluative, conceptual, interpretative and/or creative and thus require[ing] the application of the basic principles of an organized body of theoretical knowledge, such as a field of science, learning or specialized discipline. It is intricate and involves a level of difficulty and complexity requiring the identification and consideration not only of the interrelationships between its constituent elements, which are of a varied and diverse nature, but also the broader context and perspective within which it is performed, including its impact*

[24] *Composition of the Secretariat: Staff Demographics, Report of the Secretary-General, A/65/350*, Table 5, pp. 19-20.

[25] Ibid., Figure II on p. 25; Table 5 on pp. 19-20; and Table 7 on pp. 28-29.

[26] On 30 June 2010, 12.159 out of the total 44.134 staff served in Professional and higher categories. – Ibid., p. 28.

> *on, and interrelationship with, the larger objectives and programmes of the Organization. It requires judgement in analysing and evaluating problems and in decision-making involving discretionary choices between alternative courses of action.*[27]

Because of this type of work and the responsibilities staff in the Professional and higher categories have, they are generally considered to constitute the main body of the international civil service.[28] Moreover, these are staff for whom problems relating to impartiality and independence are most relevant. That is precisely the reason for which the present study pays predominant attention to staff serving in the Professional and higher categories.

The Professional and higher categories include the Professional category proper, the Principal Officer and Director category, and the Under-Secretary-General and Assistant Secretary-General category. From these categories, the last is also excluded from the present study. The reason is that Under-Secretaries-General and Assistant Secretaries-General are generally regarded as political appointees, similarly as the UN Secretary-General and his Deputy. Not only responsibilities, but also appointment, performance evaluation and other related matters concerning Under-Secretaries-General and Assistant Secretaries-General deviate strongly from those applicable to other staff in the Professional and higher categories.[29] Since

[27] International Civil Service Commission, *The Common Classification of Occupational Groups*, April 1994, available at http://icsc.un.org/resources/pdfs/ppd/ccog/ccogi_ii.pdf, last visited on 30.12.2010, Part VII, para. 1, available at http://www.un.org/Depts/icsc/ppd/job_clas/index.htm , last visited on 10.12.2007.

[28] For example, Sands and Klein, *Bowlett's Law of International Institutions*, p. 298 and Lemoine, *The International Civil Servant: An Endangered Species*, p. xi.

[29] See, for example, *A Guide to a Career with the United Nations*, available at http://esa.un.org/techcoop/associateexperts/APPLICANTS/Guide_to_employment/unpan000153.pdf, last visited on 30.12.2010, p. 33 and *Toward a New System of Performance Appraisal in the United Nations Secretariat: Requirements for Successful Implementation, Report of the Joint Inspection Unit, JIU/REP/94/5*, June 1994, available in the Official Document System of the United Nations, available at http://documents.un.org/, last visited on 30.12.2010, para. 101. Note that the post of Deputy Secretary General is an integral part of the Office of the Secretary-General. Among the main responsibilities of this post is assisting the Secretary-General to manage the Secretariat's operations and to ensure inter-sectoral and inter-institutional coherence of UN activities and programmes. - *General Assembly Resolution 52/12B, A/RES/52/12B*, 19.12.1997, available in the Official Document System of the United Nations, available at http://documents.un.org/, last visited on 30.12.2010, Part A, para. 1. Appointments to posts of Deputy Secretary-General, Under-Secretary-General and Assistant Secretary-General are, unlike in the case of other staff, made directly by the Secretary-General. There are no formal procedures for these appointments and the only practice that is followed is consultation with Member States (in the case of the Deputy Secretary-General and Under-Secretaries-General such consultations are even formally required) and sometimes with an informal group of advisers. – See *General Assembly Resolution 52/12B*, Part A, para. 2 and *Senior-Level Appointments in the United Nations, Its Programmes and Funds, Report of the Joint Inspection Unit, JIU/REP/2000/3*, 2000, available in the Official Document System of the United Nations, available at http://documents.un.org/, last visited on 30.12.2010, Part III.B. The Deputy Secretary-General, Under-Secretaries-General and Assistants Secretary-General also do not fall under the performance evaluation system applicable to all other staff. Their performance is 'subject to close personal supervision by the Secretary-General'. - *Toward a New System of Performance Appraisal in the United Nations Secretariat: Requirements for Successful Implementation, Report of the Joint Inspection Unit, JIU/REP/94/5*, para. 101. See also *Administrative Instruction, Performance Management and Development System, ST/AI/2010/5*, 30.04.2010, available in the Human Resources Handbook of the United Nations, available at http://www.un.org/hr_handbook/English/, last visited on

the present study focuses on persons engaged by the UN Secretariat because of their professional qualifications, and not on political appointees, the recruitment, placement and separation of those holding posts of Under-Secretary-General and Assistant Secretary-General are not addressed.[30]

The Principal Officer and Director category is the second highest staff category in the UN Secretariat. It has two grades: D-1 (Principal Officer) and D-2 (Director), considered the most senior career grades in the UN Secretariat.[31] As such, posts at these grades are filled in preference by staff who have climbed the career ladder from lower grades, in most cases in the Professional category proper.

The Professional category proper consists of five grades, P-1 and P-2 being the entry levels and P-5 being the highest level.[32] This category includes grades involving special language requirements, namely interpreters, revisers and translators.[33]

The classification of posts into specific grades is based on a number of criteria, such as professional knowledge, difficulty of work, independence of work, work relationships, supervisory responsibilities and impact of work.[34] This was confirmed by the United Nations Administrative Tribunal ('UNAT') which held in *Moser* that:

> *The classification of each post depends on the nature of the duties and responsibilities assigned to it and not on the personal qualifications, experience or performance of the incumbent. Therefore, posts should be classified according to their respective job descriptions, which must be presumed to set forth accurately the nature of the duties and responsibilities of the job. Classification refers to the task to be performed by the incumbent of a given post...*[35]

30.12.2010, Section 1.

[30] Note that as of 30 June 2010, the UN Secretariat included 61 persons serving as Under-Secretary-General and 67 persons in the grade of Assistant-Secretary-General. The total number of UN staff was 44.134. – *Composition of the Secretariat: Staff Demographics, Report of the Secretary-General, A/65/350*, para. 10(a), Figure III.

[31] *A Guide to a Career with the United Nations*, p. 34. See also *Administrative Instruction, System for the Classification of Posts, ST/AI/1998/9*, 6.10.1998, available in the Human Resources Handbook of the United Nations, available at http://www.un.org/hr_handbook/English/, last visited on 30.12.2010, available at http://www.un.org/hr_handbook/English/sourcedocuments_/09administrativ_/1998_/ai19989classifi/ai19989classifi.doc , visited on 10.12.2007, and also *Senior-Level Appointments in the United Nations, Its Programmes and Funds, Report of the Joint Inspection Unit, JIU/REP/2000/3*, Part II.A, para. 9 and part III.B. Note that from the total of 44.134 UN staff members serving in the UN Secretariat on 30 June 2010, 169 staff members held a post at the D-2 level and 510 at the D-1 level. - *Composition of the Secretariat: Staff Demographics, Report of the Secretary-General, A/65/350*, para. 10(a), Figure III.

[32] *UN Charter*, Annex I. The majority of professional staff serve at P-3 and P-4 levels (almost 70 per cent). The P-1 and P-2 level staff represent approximately 15 per cent of this category, like the staff at the P-5 level. - *Composition of the Secretariat: Staff Demographics, Report of the Secretary-General, A/65/350*, para. 10(a) and Figure III.

[33] On 30 June 2010, the UN Secretariat had 511 interpreters, 141 revisers and 102 translators. - *Composition of the Secretariat: Staff Demographics, Report of the Secretary-General, A/65/350*, para. 10(a) and Figure III.

[34] For details, see International Civil Service Commission, *The Common Classification of Occupational Groups*. For details on the system for the post classification in the UN Secretariat, see *Administrative Instruction, System for the Classification of Posts*.

[35] *Moser v. Secretary-General of the United Nations, UNAT Judgment No. 388 [1987]*, available at http://

Although the Secretary-General enjoys discretion in determining the classification of posts, this discretion is not absolute and must be in compliance with applicable rules and regulations.[36]

Candidates for posts at all levels, i.e. in all grades, in the Professional and higher categories require an advanced university degree. Such degree must be accompanied by professional experience, though the latter is not (extensively) required for entry level posts.[37] Of course, the type of degree required depends on the so-called occupational group to which the post at issue belongs – all posts in the UN Secretariat are divided into such occupational groups, as also those in other staff categories. The division into occupational groups depends, of course, on the type of work. Examples of occupational groups in the Professional and higher categories are personnel management specialists; economists; computer information specialists; purchasing and contracting specialists; auditors; jurists; and statisticians.

Last but not least, it should be noted that all posts in the Professional and higher categories are filled by international recruitment, as opposed to local recruitment which applies to most of the other categories of staff.[38] This also applies when staff recruited for posts in the Professional and higher categories are in practice recruited locally; such staff are also formally considered to be internationally recruited.[39] The status of 'internationally recruited staff' is linked to the entitlement for allowances and benefits, for example payment of travel expenses upon initial appointment and on separation, home leave, education grant and repatriation grant.[40] It is also linked to the manner in which staff remuneration is determined; it differs for internationally recruited staff as oppose to locally recruited staff. The remuneration of staff recruited internationally is based on what is referred to as the Noblemaire principle. According to this principle staff remuneration is set by reference to the highest paying national civil service.[41]

2.1.2. Field Service category

The Field Service category was created in 1949 for staff employed in peacekeeping missions and in special political missions.[42] From the original, more of a support type

untreaty.un.org/UNAT/UNAT_Judgements/Judgements_E/UNAT_00388_E.pdf, last visited on 30.12.2010, para. I.

[36] Ibid., para. II.

[37] Electronic Bulletin *United Nations Human Resources Management*, available at http://www.un.org/Depts/OHRM/examin/exam.htm, last visited on 10.12.2007.

[38] *UN Staff Rules*, Rules 4.4(a) and 4.5(a).

[39] Ibid., Rule 4.5(b).

[40] Ibid., Rule 4.5(a). Note that some of these allowances and benefits may not be available for locally recruited staff in the Professional and higher categories. - Rule 4.5(b).

[41] *United Nations Common System of Salaries, Allowances and Benefits of the ICSC*, p. 2. Note that the International Civil Service Commission makes a periodic review of UN Member States' national civil services in order to identify which one has the highest pay levels and is, by its size and structure, comparable to the UN civil service. Thus far, the federal civil service of the United States of America has been taken as the highest paid national civil service. – Ibid.

[42] *General Assembly Resolution 297(IV), A/RES/297(IV)*, 22.11.1949, available in the Official Document

of work carried out by staff in this category, the functions have gradually evolved towards more administrative and management ones, including budgetary, finance, human resources, procurement and similar functions. In 2006, the Secretary-General reported that 35 per cent of the Field Service staff carried out administrative and finance functions, while remaining in the peacekeeping and special political missions.[43]

The Field Service category entails seven grades, FS-1 being the lowest and FS-7 the highest. At levels 5 and above, functions and responsibilities of the Field Service staff are comparable to those of staff serving in the Professional category.[44] As with the Professional staff, those in the Field Service category are internationally recruited.[45]

2.1.3. General Service and related categories

The General Service and related categories cover most UN staff, some 60 per cent.[46] The General Service category itself constitutes the greatest part of this group, amounting to more than 95 per cent. As noted above, this category was created in 1949. It was the result of a recommendation of the Committee of Experts on Salary, Allowance, and Leave Systems which believed that locally recruited staff should be graded and paid below the level applicable to internationally recruited staff.[47] The reason was the nature of work performed by staff serving in the General Service category. It is formally defined as:

System of the United Nations, available at http://documents.un.org/, last visited on 30.12.2010.

[43] *Investing in People, Report of the Secretary-General, Addendum, Reforming the Field Service Category: Investing in Meeting the Human Resources Requirements of United Nations Peace Operations in the Twenty-First Century, A/61/255/Add.1*, 22.08.2006, available in the Official Document System of the United Nations, available at http://documents.un.org/, last visited on 30.12.2010, para. 11. For more details on the development of the Field Service category, see chapter 6, section 2.2. Note that on 30 June 2010 there were 4.438 staff members in the UN Secretariat serving in the Field Service category. – *Composition of the Secretariat: Staff Demographics, Report of the Secretary-General, A/65/350*, p. 28.

[44] *Composition of the Secretariat: Staff Demographics, Report of the Secretary-General, A/65/350*, Figure IV, p. 26 and *Reforming the Field Service Category: Investing in Meeting the Human Resources Requirements of United Nations Peace Operations in the Twenty-First Century, A/61/255/Add.1*, para. 12. See also *Personnel Statistics 2006, United Nations System, Chief Executives Board for Coordination, High-Level Committee on Management, CEB/2007/HR/15*, 15.10.2007, available at http://www.unsceb.org/ceb/stats/hr/ps/years/2006, last visited on 30.12.2010, p. vi, para. (c).

[45] *UN Staff Rules*, Rules 4.4(a) and 4.5(a). See also *Reforming the Field Service Category: Investing in Meeting the Human Resources Requirements of United Nations Peace Operations in the Twenty-First Century, A/61/255/Add.1*, para. 13.

[46] On 30 June 2010, 27.537 out of the total of 44.143 UN staff members served in the General Service and related categories. - *Composition of the Secretariat: Staff Demographics, Report of the Secretary-General, A/65/350*, Figure II, p. 25.

[47] Reymond and Mailick, *International Personnel Policies and Practices*, p. 58. As noted above, the internationally recruited staff are remunerated in accordance with the Noblemaire principle that links remuneration of international staff with the highest paid national civil service salaries. In order to decouple remuneration of locally recruited staff from this principle, the Committee on Salary, Allowance, and Leave Systems recommended that a separate category would be created for such staff. Reymnd and Mailick claim that the adoption of this recommendation resulted in a break with the initial UN doctrine of a single class of international civil servants. – Ibid.

> *procedural, operational or technical in nature and support[ing] the execution of the programmes of the organization. It ranges from simple, routine or repetitive duties based on following detailed instructions to varied and complex assignments requiring identification and consideration of alternative courses of action based on extensive and in-depth practical knowledge of a specific subject area. The assignments are generally performed on a continuing basis. The knowledge of the subject field and higher level skills are generally developed through long experience and familiarity with applicable procedures, regulations and precedents or projects of the organization in a narrow technical field or in an administrative support activity.*[48]

Staff serving in the General Service category perform thus clerical, secretarial and administrative work. This category includes, therefore, staff, such as messengers, clerks, typists, secretaries and administrative support staff.[49]

Similar type of work is performed by categories related to the General Service category. These categories include Language Teacher category; National Professional Officer category; Public Information Assistant category; Security category; and Trades and Crafts category.[50] As in the General Service category, staff in the related categories are recruited locally, not internationally. They also enjoy different conditions of employment when compared to their internationally recruited colleagues, in particular with regard to remuneration, allowances and benefits.[51] Exceptionally, staff recruited to General Service and related categories may be considered to be recruited internationally, subject to 'special circumstances and conditions determined by the Secretary-General'.[52] Such staff would, of course, be entitled to allowances and benefits available to internationally recruited staff.

One of the related categories, namely the National Professional Officer category, has a special position among them. Not only is this by far the largest of the categories related to the General Service category. Its staff are in a special position, too, somewhere in between the General Service and related categories and the Professional category.[53] As the name suggests, the National Professional Officers are 'professional' staff members recruited and engaged at the national level, i.e. locally. They are employed in situations where knowledge and experience at the national level is required by the very nature of the tasks and can, therefore, not be

---

[48] International Civil Service Commission, *The Common Classification of Occupational Groups*, Section VII, para. 2, available at http://www.un.org/Depts/icsc/ppd/job_clas/index.htm , last visited on 10.12.2007.

[49] *Personnel Statistics 2006, United Nations System, Chief Executives Board for Coordination, High-Level Committee on Management*, p. 13.

[50] *UN Staff Rules*, Rule 2.1(b); and *Composition of the Secretariat: Staff Demographics, Report of the Secretary-General, A/65/350*, Figure V, p. 27.

[51] *UN Staff Rules*, Rule 4.4(a) and (c). See also Rule 4.5 concerning internationally recruited staff.

[52] Ibid., Rule 4.5(c).

[53] On 30 June 2010, there were 1470 National Professional Officers in the UN Secretariat, while the other related categories had in total 610 staff members. - *Composition of the Secretariat: Staff Demographics, Report of the Secretary-General, A/65/350*, Figure V, p. 27. Note that in this most recent report on the composition of the UN Secretariat the National Professional Officials are referred to as National Officers.

dealt with as effectively by internationally recruited personnel. This happens normally in the areas of development assistance and public information, often in post-conflict environments. Since the National Professional Officers are locally recruited, they are paid according to the best local practices, not according to the Noblemaire principle that applies to their colleagues in the Professional category. However, the type of work the National Professional Officers perform is, in its nature, the same as that of staff serving in the Professional category. Therefore, the standards of recruitment qualifications and performance required for National Professional Officers are the same as those used for the Professional staff. So are their grades and post classification.[54]

Although the number of staff serving in the General Service and related categories is higher than the number of Professional staff, the former are not included in the present study. The reason for their exclusion is that, with the exception of the National Professional Officers, staff of the General Service and related categories do not perform functions which could be considered to constitute 'the very essence of the International Civil Service'.[55] As stated by Lemoine, the clerical and technical staff do not take a 'significant part in independent research, preparations for policy formulation and standard setting and control of their application' and are, therefore, not international civil servants in the real sense of the word.[56] This study follows the same line of reasoning. As far as the National Professional Officers are concerned, although they do perform Professional type of work, they are recruited locally, in accordance with local conditions. The UN Secretariat has no general rules in this respect. Inclusion of these staff in the present study would, therefore, not be feasible in any case.

2.2. Other ('non-staff') personnel

The *Secretary-General's Bulletin, Policies for Obtaining the Services of Individuals on behalf of the Organization ST/SGB/177* of 19 November 1982, mentioned earlier, establishes a basic legal framework in which conditions are set out for the

[54] *UN Staff Rules*, Rule 4.4 and *National Professional Officers, Report of the Secretary-General*, *A/62/762*, 25.03.2008, available in the Official Document System of the United Nations, available at http://documents.un.org/, last visited on 30.12.2010, para. 2. Note that unlike other staff in the General Service and related categories, the National Professional Officers must hold the nationality of the country in which their office is located. - *UN Staff Rules*, Rule 4.4(b). The use of National Professional Officers was approved by the General Assembly in 1994 upon recommendation of, and under the conditions established by, the ICSC. – *General Assembly Resolution 49/223*, *A/RES/49/223*, 23.12.2010, available in the Official Document System of the United Nations, available at http://documents.un.org/, last visited on 30.12.2010, Section IV, Part B; and *Report of the International Civil Service Commission for the Year 1994*, 05.08.1994, available in the Official Document System of the United Nations, available at http://documents.un.org/, last visited on 30.12.2010, para. 244 and Annex VII. The first National Professional Officers were used in the UN Secretariat in 1995 as human rights officers in the UN Verification Mission in Guatemala and then in 1997 in the Judicial System Assessment Project in the UN Mission in Bosnia and Herzegovina. They were also used, for example, in Kosovo and Afghanistan. - *National Professional Officers, Report of the Secretary-General, A/62/762*, para. 3.

[55] Lemoine, *The International Civil Servant: An Endangered Species*, p. xi.

[56] Ibid., p. xi.

engagement of individuals who are not regular UN staff members. As stipulated in this document, the UN departments and services may, besides appointing permanent staff members, engage individuals in the following capacities too: temporary staff; individual contractors; consultants; participants in advisory meetings; technical co-operation personnel; or Operational, Executive and Administrative Service (OPAS) officers.[57] In 1985 and 1996, respectively, another two categories were added to the list, namely institutional and corporate contractors and 'when actually employed' contractors.[58] There are also the so-called gratis personnel who serve in the UN Secretariat. Engagement of these additional categories of UN personnel is governed not by the *Secretary-General's Bulletin, Policies for Obtaining the Services of Individuals on behalf of the Organization ST/SGB/177* of 19 November 1982, but by separate administrative issuances, addressed in more detail in this section below.[59]

As far as the *Secretary-General's Bulletin, Policies for Obtaining the Services of Individuals on behalf of the Organization ST/SGB/177* of 1982 is concerned, it must be noted that this issuance also includes provisions relating to UN staff, both 'regular' and temporary. As explained above, employment of such staff occurs under the conditions set out in the *UN Staff Regulations* and the *UN Staff Rules*. Both regular and temporary staff, including 'when actually employed' personnel, technical cooperation personnel and OPAS officers, were addressed in the previous section.[60] This section deals with other UN personnel, not considered to be UN staff, engaged at the UN Secretariat. Unlike in the case of UN staff, engagement of non-staff personnel at the UN Secretariat does not occur on the basis of a letter of appointment, but on the basis of a contract that contains precise employment conditions as well as mutual rights and obligations. It goes without saying that these contracts must be in accordance with relevant administrative issuances.

It must also be noted that the *Secretary-General's Bulletin, Policies for Obtaining the Services of Individuals on behalf of the Organization ST/SGB/177* of 1982 is not exhaustive and is significantly outdated. The Bulletin is not exhaustive in the sense of being supplemented by a number of separate administrative issuances that regulate engagement of non-staff personnel in the UN Secretariat. Some of these issuances were promulgated together with this Bulletin, some of them later, sometimes partly abolishing and/or superseding the previous issuances.[61] The *Secretary-General's*

---

[57] *Secretary-General's Bulletin, Policies for Obtaining the Services of Individuals on behalf of the Organization*, para. 2.

[58] *Administrative Instruction, Institutional or Corporate Contractors*, and *Secretary-General's Bulletin, Use of "When Actually Employed" Contracts for Special Representatives, Envoys and Other Special High-level Positions*.

[59] See below, sections 2.2.2 and 2.2.3.

[60] See above, section 2.1.

[61] *Administrative Instruction, Temporary Staff and Individual Contractors*, for temporary staff and individual contractors; *Administrative Instruction, Consultants and Participants in Advisory Meetings*, for consultants and participants in advisory meetings; *Administrative Instruction, Technical Co-operation Personnel and OPAS Officers*, *Administrative Instruction, Consultants and Individual Contractors, consolidated text*, for consultants and individual contractors; *Administrative Instruction, Technical Co-operation Personnel and OPAS Officers, Addendum*, for technical co-operation personnel and OPAS officers; *Administrative Instruction, Institutional or Corporate Contractors*, for institutional and corporate

Bulletin, Policies for Obtaining the Services of Individuals on behalf of the Organization of 1982 does not incorporate these later developments, nor does it reflect the recent changes in the UN contractual system, adopted in 2009.[62] It is therefore important to read this Bulletin in the light of the subsequent developments.

2.2.1. Consultants and participants in advisory meetings

Consultants and participants in advisory meetings are called upon in instances in which skills, knowledge or expertise not possessed by regular staff are required but for which there is no continuing need in the UN Secretariat.[63] The engagement of consultants and participants in advisory meetings is time-limited, in the case of the former to a maximum of six months in any period of twelve consecutive months and in the case of the latter to the duration of a meeting.[64] Neither the consultants nor the participants in advisory meetings become UN staff members falling under the *UN Staff Regulations* regime.[65] Their engagement at the UN Secretariat occurs in accordance with the *Secretary-General's Bulletin, Policies for Obtaining the Services of Individuals on behalf of the Organization ST/SGB/177* of 19 November 1982, the *Administrative Instruction, Consultants and Participants in Advisory Meetings ST/AI/296* of the same date, and the *Administrative Instruction, Consultants and Individual Contractors ST/AI/1999/7* of 25 August 1999, as amended, which partly superseded the previous instruction ST/AI/296.[66]

---

contractors; and *Secretary-General's Bulletin, Use of "When Actually Employed" Contracts for Special Representatives, Envoys and Other Special High-level Positions*, for 'when actually employed' contracts.

[62] Consequent to the 2009 reform of the contractual arrangements in the UN Secretariat, addressed in detail in chapter 6 of this study, some of the old administrative instructions were abolished and replaced by the new administrative instruction regulating temporary appointments or by the most recent version of the *UN Staff Selection System*. - *Administrative Instruction, Administration of Temporary Appointments*, and *UN Staff Selection System*. The *Administrative Instruction, Administration of Temporary Appointments ST/AI/2010/4* abolished and replaced the *Administrative Instruction, Temporary Staff and Individual Contractors*, and the *UN Staff Selection System* abolished and replaced the *Administrative Instruction, Technical Co-operation Personnel and OPAS Officers*, and *Administrative Instruction, Technical Co-operation Personnel and OPAS Officers, Addendum*.

[63] *Secretary-General's Bulletin, Policies for Obtaining the Services of Individuals on behalf of the Organization*, para. 7; and *Administrative Instruction, Consultants and Individual Contractors, consolidated text*, Section 1.

[64] *Secretary-General's Bulletin, Policies for Obtaining the Services of Individuals on behalf of the Organization*, paras. 8 and 9. See also *Administrative Instruction, Consultants and Individual Contractors, consolidated text*, Section 5.3 and *Administrative Instruction, Consultants and Participants in Advisory Meetings*, para. 13.

[65] *Administrative Instruction, Consultants and Participants in Advisory Meetings*, para. 9 and *Administrative Instruction, Consultants and Individual Contractors, consolidated text*, Section 5.5.

[66] *Secretary-General's Bulletin, Policies for Obtaining the Services of Individuals on behalf of the Organization*, paras. 7-9; *Administrative Instruction, Consultants and Participants in Advisory Meetings*, and *Administrative Instruction, Consultants and Individual Contractors, consolidated text*.

2.2.2. Institutional or Corporate Contractors

Temporary services required from time to time by the UN may be obtained by engaging individual contractors but, as explained in paragraph 2 of the *Administrative Instruction, Institutional or Corporate Contractors* ST/AI/327 of 23 January 1985, also by contracting an institution or a corporation.[67] Conditions and procedures under which such action may be taken are set out in relative detail in this instruction. The instruction stipulates, for example, that institutional and corporate contractors may be hired to carry out activities similar to those of individual contractors, such as interpretation, translation, editing, library work, language training, public information, and secretarial, clerical or guidance services.[68] Furthermore, institutional and corporate contractors may also fulfill functions which require 'analyzing problems, directing seminars or training courses, preparing documents for conferences and meetings or writing reports on the matters within the area of expertise on which advice or assistance is sought'.[69] They are 'independent contractors' whose employees are not considered to be UN staff members in any respect.[70]

2.2.3. Gratis personnel

Besides the regular staff and the non-regular personnel, the UN Secretariat meets human resources needs by making use of the so-called gratis personnel too. Gratis personnel are those provided by UN Member States' governments or other entities, which remain responsible for their remuneration.[71]

There are two types of gratis personnel, type I and type II. Type I gratis personnel comprise three distinct categories: interns, associate experts and technical co-operation experts obtained on a non-reimbursable loan basis.[72] Type II gratis personnel are all others provided by a government or other entity responsible for their remuneration.[73]

Interns

The internship programme of the UN is intended for young graduate and post-graduate students who wish to gain acquaintance with the work of the UN Secretariat. Its objective is to provide students with an opportunity to enhance their education with practical experience, to expose them to the work of the UN, but also to provide

[67] *Administrative Instruction, Institutional or Corporate Contractors*, para. 2.

[68] Ibid., para. 3.

[69] Ibid., para. 3.

[70] Ibid., para. 5.

[71] *Administrative Instruction, Gratis Personnel*, available in the Human Resources Handbook of the United Nations, Section 1.

[72] *Gratis Personnel Provided by Governments and Other Entities, Report of the Secretary-General, A/59/716*, 28.02.2005, available in the Official Document System of the United Nations, available at http://documents.un.org/, last visited on 30.12.2010, para. 3.

[73] *Administrative Instruction, Gratis Personnel*, available in the Human Resources Handbook of the United Nations, Section 1.

the UN Secretariat with assistance and knowledge in different specialization fields free of charge.[74] The internship lasts in principle two months. The interns work full time and under the supervision of a regular staff member.[75]

Associate experts

Associate Experts are young graduates of universities or higher education institutions with limited or no professional experience, recruited under bilateral agreements between the UN and donor countries for the development of regional projects and activities in different fields, such as medicine, economy, political science, international relations or law. The donor countries bear all the costs related to the appointment of an Associate Expert, including salary and other allowances, insurance, travel expenses and the administrative costs of the UN itself.[76]

The Associate Experts are usually appointed for a period of one year with a possible extension. They perform their duties under the supervision of an expert who is specialized and experienced in the relevant field, as well as the chief technical adviser of the project at hand. After the expiry of the contract, the Associate Experts in principle leave the UN – there is no automatic transfer to regular positions, although such a step is not entirely excluded.[77]

Technical co-operation experts on non-reimbursable loans

Not all technical co-operation experts in the UN used to be engaged on the basis of the former Administrative Instruction *Technical Co-operation Personnel and OPAS Officers* ST/AI/297 of 19 November 1982, mentioned above.[78] Some of them provided – and still provide – their services to the UN on a non-reimbursable loan basis, i.e. 'gratis', at least from the point of view of the UN. Costs of these 'gratis' engagements (remuneration, allowances, insurance and other benefits) are borne by donor governments or other donor sources external to the UN. The engagement of personnel on a non-reimbursable loan basis is permitted and regulated by the *Administrative Instruction, Non-reimbursable Loans of Personnel Services from Sources External to the United Nations Common System*, ST/AI/231/Rev.1 of 23 January 1991.[79]

Technical co-operation experts on non-reimbursable loans are engaged in order to assist in the execution of technical co-operation activities.[80] Terms and conditions

[74] UN interns receive no remuneration and bear all expenses related to their travel to, and stay in, the place of the relevant UN office. - *Administrative Instruction, United Nations Internship Programme*, available in the Human Resources Handbook of the United Nations, Section 6.

[75] Ibid., Sections 3.

[76] *A Guide to a Career with the United Nations*, pp. 38-39. Note that 19 UN Member States participate in the Associate Expert Programme and the Associate Experts are usually nationals of these 19 countries. They may also come from other, especially developing, countries outside the programme participants but this is possible only when one of the participating countries agrees to finance their appointment.

[77] Ibid., p. 39.

[78] See above, section 2.1.

[79] *Administrative Instruction, Non-reimbursable Loans of Personnel Services from Sources External to the United Nations Common System*.

[80] Ibid., para. 4.

of such engagements are set out in special agreements concluded between the UN and the donor. The duration of the agreement is limited to three years with a possible extension, in exceptional cases, up to a maximum of five years in total.[81] 'Technical co-operation experts serving on non-reimbursable loans have the position of independent contractors.[82] They are not UN staff members and do not fall under the scope of the *UN Staff Regulations* and other general rules applicable to UN staff.[83] Furthermore, they may not be used for filling secretariat-type posts or functions normally authorized under the regular programme budget and may be employed solely in locations other than the UN Headquarters, UN Offices in Geneva and Vienna, with two narrow exceptions.[84]

Type II gratis personnel

Pursuant to *Administrative Instruction, Gratis Personnel* of 28 May 1999, type II gratis personnel may be accepted only on an exceptional basis in two pre-defined situations. The first situation concerns cases where relevant expertise is not available within the UN and is not required on a continuing basis. In this case, experts are used for very specialized functions for a specified period of time of a maximum of one year with possible extension, should the need for relevant expertise remain.[85] Secondly, gratis personnel of this type may be accepted when a new mandate is created for the UN Secretariat, or an existing one is expanded, and the level of resources required for the implementation of this mandate has not yet been decided by the General Assembly. The absence of such decision means that no recruitment of a regular staff can take place and the vacant posts need to be filled by temporary gratis personnel.[86] It follows that these personnel fulfill tasks which would otherwise be carried out by regular staff members. They do so 'under the authority and in full compliance with the instructions of the appropriate official in the United Nations department or office concerned'.[87]

3. Classification of staff working at the European Commission

Staff working in the European Commission can be divided into two main groups: officials and so-called 'other servants'. The decisive distinguishing element between the two groups is the duration of their engagement. While EU officials hold permanent appointments, 'other servants' are employed for limited periods. This division between EU officials and 'other servants' is reflected in the legal instruments regulating their employment; officials are covered by the *EU Staff Regulations*, whereas 'other servants' fall under the *EU Conditions of Employment of Other Servants*.

---

81 Ibid., para. 10.
82 Ibid., para. 6.
83 Ibid., para. 6.
84 Ibid., paras. 4 and 5.
85 *Administrative Instruction, Gratis Personnel*, para. 2.1 (a) and 6.1.
86 Ibid., para. 2.1 (b).
87 Ibid., para. 10.1.

Interestingly, both legal instruments constitute a part of the same regulation.[88] In spite of that, it must be emphasized that the two groups of staff are, in principle, exclusive.[89] An individual staff member may thus come either within the scope of the *EU Staff Regulations* or the *EU Conditions of Employment of Other Servants*.

The group of 'other servants' is further subdivided into four distinct categories: temporary staff, contract staff, local staff, and special advisers.[90] Each of these categories are defined in the *EU Conditions of Employment of Other Servants*, similarly as their conditions of employment, including many similarities but also many differences between the individual categories of 'other servants'. In this respect it must be noted that differences in status between the various categories of EU staff may not be questioned or regarded, for example, as unequal treatment. As explained by the European Court of Justice:

> *Each of those categories is defined in accordance with the legitimate requirements of the Community administration and the nature of the permanent or temporary tasks which it has to perform. The fact that some categories of persons employed by the Communities may enjoy guarantees under the Staff Regulations and social security benefits which are not given to other categories cannot, therefore, be regarded as discrimination.*[91]

---

[88] The first *EU Staff Regulations* and *EU Conditions of Employment of Other Servants* were adopted in 1961. They were modified in 1968 after the institutions of the three existing European Communities had been merged. The currently applicable *EU Staff Regulations* and *EU Conditions of Employment of Other Servants* are, legally speaking, the same document, though a major modification took place in 2004 as a result of the overall reform of the European Commission. - See *Regulation No 31 (EEC), 11 (EAEC), Laying down the Staff Regulations of Officials and the Conditions of Employment of Other Servants of the European Economic Community and the European Atomic Energy Community*, 18.12.1961, OJ 45, 14.06.1962 - Special Edition 1959-62, November 1972; *Regulation (EEC, Euroatom, ECSC) No 259/68 of the Council of 29 February 1968 laying down the Staff Regulations of Officials and the Conditions of Employment of Other Servants of the European Communities and Instituting Special Measures Temporarily Applicable to Officials of the Commission*, OJ L 56, 04.03.1968 - Special Edition 1968, 1 December 1972, and *Regulation No 723/2004 Amending the EU Staff Regulations and Conditions of Employment of Other Servants*. To simplify the referencing to the current version of the *EU Staff Regulations* and *EU Conditions of Employment of Other Servants*, they are for the purposes of this study referred simply to as *'EU Staff Regulations'* and *'EU Conditions of Employment of Other Servants'*, respectively.

[89] *Hugues Desmedt v. Commission of the European Communities, Case 105/80, ECR [1981], p. 1701*, para. 13. In this case Mr. Desmedt, a former member of the local staff, had been appointed as a probationary official but, following a negative assessment at the end of the probationary period, he was dismissed. Mr. Desmedt claimed that, instead of being dismissed, he should have been reinstated as a member of the local staff. The Court ruled that this was not the case. It noted, however, that the situation could have been different if the EU Administration had taken an explicit decision to the contrary, i.e. suspended the initial contract with Mr. Desmedt as a member of the local staff. The Court also stated that the EU Administration had been free to reinstate a member of the local staff after dismissing him from the post of a probationary official, but it had no such obligation. – para. 15.

[90] *Regulation No 31 (EEC), 11 (EAEC), Laying down the Staff Regulations of Officials and the Conditions of Employment of Other Servants of the European Economic Community and the European Atomic Energy Community, Second Part: Conditions of Employment of Other Servants*, OJ 45, 14.06.1962, p. 1442, subsequently amended, available at http://eur-lex.europa.eu/LexUriServ/LexUriServ.do?uri=CONSLEG:1962R0031:20100101:EN:PDF (consolidated unofficial version), last visited on 30.12.2010, Article 1.

[91] *Maria Grazia Celant and others v. Commission of the European Communities, Joined cases 118 to 123/82, ECR [1983], p. 2995*, para. 22.

Apart from officials and 'other servants', the European Commission also employs persons who fall outside the EU 'statutory' system created by the *EU Staff Regulations and Conditions of Employment of Other Servants*. These persons are referred to as non-statutory staff and include those contracted by the European Commission as agents recruited under national law, interns as well as persons who have an employer other than the European Commission but, for some time, work for this Commission.[92]

The overall situation in the European Commission is thus as follows:

Scheme 3: Staff employed by the European Commission

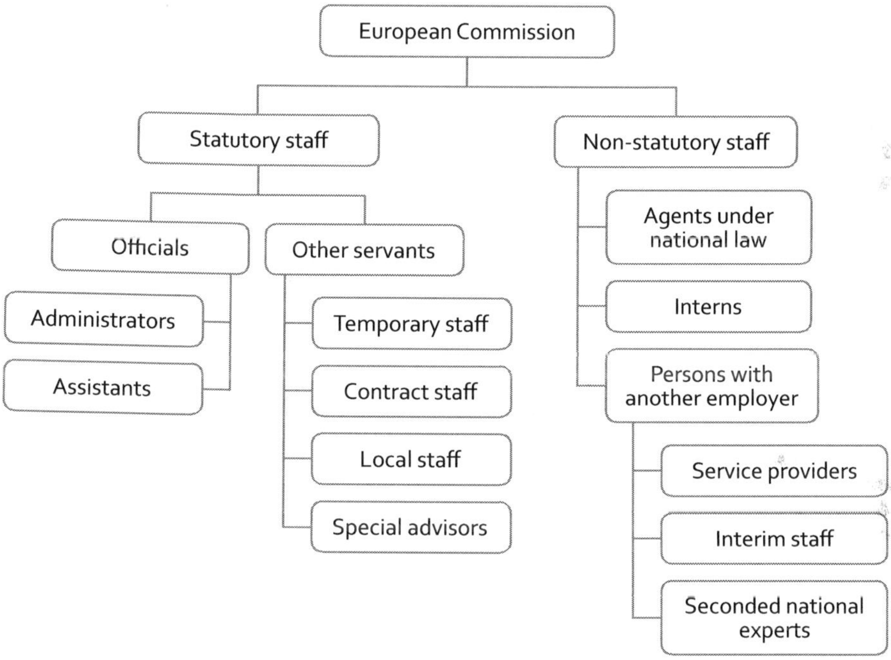

[92] *Human Resources Report 2009, Towards a Qualitative and Forward-looking Management of Staff and Competencies Through the Professionalisation of Human Resources Management*, pp. 28-29.

As for the number of staff serving in each category, the situation is as follows:

Table 2: Distribution of staff in activity in the European Commission by staff category on 31 December 2008 (most recent data available)

Member State	Staffing in 2008	In % of total staff (2008)
Officials	22829	58,9%
Temporary agents	1889	4,9%
Contract agents	5766	14,9%
Special advisers (remunerated)	28	0,1%
Special advisers (non-remunerated)	27	0,1%
Local agents	3034	7,8%
Other (non-statutory staff)	5192	13,4 %

Source: Commission's *Human Resources Report* of 2009.[93]

The following sections describe briefly all mentioned categories of European Commission staff.

3.1. Statutory staff

3.1.1. Officials

As already noted, EU officials are persons who serve in EU institutions on a permanent basis. Generally speaking, EU officials begin their career in the EU in one of the starting grades and move up the career ladder through a number of successive promotions until they retire. The rights and obligations and conditions of employment of EU officials are set out in the *EU Staff Regulations* which constitute a common framework law for officials of all EU institutions. This common framework is supplemented by more detailed provisions adopted by individual EU institutions in accordance with Article 110(1) of the *EU Staff Regulations* which stipulates that:

> *The general provisions for giving effect to these Staff Regulations shall be adopted by each institution after consulting its Staff Committee and the Staff Regulations Committee. Agencies shall adopt the appropriate implementing rules for giving effect to these Staff Regulations, after consultation of the relevant Staff Committee and in agreement with the Commission.*[94]

Each EU institution, including the European Commission which is the subject-matter of this study, has thus its own set of rules governing specific issues of personnel pol-

[93] Ibid., p. 30.

[94] *EU Staff Regulations*, Article 110(1).

icy. The Commission's internal rules constitute an important source of information for this study, in addition to the *EU Staff Regulations* and, for 'other servants', the *EU Conditions of Employment of Other Servants*.

EU officials are divided into two function groups – Administrators ('AD') and Assistants ('AST').[95] The AD function group comprises 12 grades (AD5 – AD16) corresponding to administrative, advisory, linguistic and scientific duties. The AST function group has 11 grades (AST1 – AST11) corresponding to executive, technical and clerical duties.[96] Grades in the two function groups partly overlap – grades 5 till 11 are available in both of them.[97] Moreover, grades are rather flexible – most functions can be carried out in two or more of them. For example, the function of Head of Unit can be categorized in grades AD9 up to AD14, the function of Director in grades AD14 and AD15, and the function of Director-General in grades AD15 and AD16. Similarly, a documentarist may be graded in grades AST5 and AST6 and a clerical officer in grades AST9 up to AST11.[98] Note that officials serving grades AD9 – AD14 and perform managerial functions are referred to as middle management staff. The European Commission has adopted a separate set of rules that relate to these staff. They are contained in the *Commission Decision on Middle Management Staff* C(2008) 5028/2 of 9 September 2008.[99] Similarly, a separate set of rules has been established for Commission senior officials, i.e. officials serving in grades AD14 – AD16. These

[95] Ibid., Article 5 and Annex I. On the criteria for classification in grade and step applicable on appointment in the European Commission, see *Commission Decision on General Implementing Provisions Concerning the Criteria Applicable to Classification in Grade and Step in Appointment or Engagement, C(2004)1313, Informations Administratives No 55-2004 of 4.6.2004*, 7.4.2004, available at http://europa.eu/epso/documents/decision_on_classification_en.pdf, last visited on 30.12.2010. Note that until 2004 there were 4 categories of EU officials – category A/LA responsible for policy tasks (LA included the translation staff), category B carrying out executive tasks, category C composed of secretarial and clerical staff and, finally, category D which included manual and service staff. Each category was divided into a number of grades (A1-A8, LA 3 - LA 8, B1-B5, C1 – C5 and D1 – D4). See, for example, *Staff Regulations of Officials and Conditions of Employment of Other Servants of the European Communities, consolidated version*, February 1998, Article 5 and Annex I. Note also that the number of staff performing functions of what currently falls in AST function group has stabilized since 2000, whereas the number of staff working in current AD function group has gradually increased. On 31 December 2008, the Commission had 50,7 per cent of staff classified as AD and 49,3 per cent classified as AST. In 2000, 44 per cent of the Commission staff were (current) Administrators and 56 per cent (current) Assistants. The Commission expects that due to technological progress and reductions in manual and administrative tasks, there will be greater space for more conceptual activities in future, leading to a further increase in the proportion of staff serving in AD function group. - *Commission's Human Resources Report 2009*, p. 37.

[96] *EU Staff Regulations*, Article 5(2) and Annex I.

[97] Ibid., Annex I. See also, for example, Coull, J. and Lewis, C., *The Impact of the Staff Regulations in Making the Commission a More Modern and Efficient Oragnization: an Insider's Perspective*, in: Eipascope, Vol. 2003, Nr. 3, pp. 2-9, p. 4. Coull and Lewis note that, under the new system, officials would be recruited at the lower grade compared to the former system, but they would have more possibilities to reach 'a much higher level of play and responsibility'. – Ibid.

[98] *EU Staff Regulations*, Annex I.

[99] *Commission Decision on Middle Management Staff, Consolidated Version, C(2008) 5028/2*, 09.09.2008, available in the Register of Commission Documents, available at http://ec.europa.eu/transparency/regdoc/registre.cfm?CL=en, last visited on 30.12.2010.

rules can be found in the *Compilation Document on Senior Officials Policy* SEC(2004) 1352/2 of 25 October 2004.[100]

To return to general classification of EU posts, each grade – both in function group AD and in function group AST – comprises 5 steps.[101] Newly recruited staff are, in principle, appointed at the first step in their grade.[102] Similarly, staff promoted to a higher grade are to be placed in the initial steps of their new grade.[103] Movement from one step to another, i.e. within the same grade, occurs automatically every two years.[104] On the other hand, movement from one grade to another takes place only in cases of promotion (move to a higher grade) or degrading (move to a lower grade).[105]

3.1.2. 'Other servants'

These are the second group of persons serving in the European Commission. As mentioned above, 'other servants' do not have a permanent employment status and do not fall under the regime established by the *EU Staff Regulations*; they are governed by a separate set of rules contained in the *EU Conditions of Employment of Other Servants*.

As officials, 'other servants' are included in this study since, as explained in more detail in the following sections for each category of 'other servants', they often perform tasks similar to those of officials. There is, in principle, no significant difference between officials and 'other servants' in this respect. Moreover, although conditions of employment of 'other servants' are not identical to those that apply to officials, 'other servants' have the same obligations concerning their independence and impartiality as officials.[106] In addition, as shown in the table below, 'other servants' constitute a large part of the Commission staff, amounting in total to almost 30 per cent. The influence of 'other servants' on the Commission work output is thus considerable.

From among four categories of EU 'other servants', this study pays special attention to temporary and contract staff and focuses less on local staff and special advisers. The reason for this lies with the specific status of the latter two categories of 'other servants'. Local staff are employed partly under conditions set out in national laws of the country in which they serve. Although the Commission has adopted framework rules, it is not feasible to provide an analysis of the appointment, placement and

[100] *Commission Compilation Document on Senior Officials Policy*,

[101] *EU Staff Regulations*, Article 66.

[102] Ibid., Article 32. This provision tolerates taking professional experience into account and allows additional seniority up to a maximum of two years.

[103] Ibid., Article 46. Special rules apply in case of promotion of middle and senior management. These officials are placed in the second step of the new grade.

[104] Ibid., Article 44. This provision also provides for certain specificities that may apply to staff appointed as Head of Unit, Director or Director-General.

[105] For details on the promotion process in the European Commission, see chapter 4, section 3.

[106] See, for example, *EU Conditions of Employment of Other Servants*, Article 11 or Article 54.

separation process for all local staff with their distinct legal regimes under various national rules and practices.[107] Special advisers, on the other hand, are connected to the Commission by a contract while their main employment is elsewhere. Therefore, they cannot be considered as genuine staff members of the Commission.[108] That said, where relevant and possible, this study does explain the main rules that apply to the European Commission local staff and special advisers.

The following sections explain in more detail the main differences between the four categories of 'other servants'.

3.1.2.1. Temporary staff

Article 2 of the *EC Conditions of Employment of Other Servants* defines temporary staff as follows:

> *For the purposes of these conditions of employment, 'temporary staff' means:*
>
> *(a) staff engaged to fill a post which is included in the list of posts appended to the section of the budget relating to each institution and which the budgetary authorities have classified as temporary;*
>
> *(b) staff engaged to fill temporarily a permanent post included in the list of posts appended to the section of the budget relating to each institution;*
>
> *(c) staff, other than officials of the Communities, engaged to assist either a person holding an office provided for in the Treaties establishing the Communities, or the Treaty establishing a Single Council and a Single Commission of the European Communities, or the elected President of one of the institutions or organs of the Communities, or one of the political groups in the European Parliament or the Committee of the Regions, or a group in the European Economic and Social Committee;*
>
> *(d) staff engaged to fill temporarily a permanent post paid from research and investment appropriations and included in the list of posts appended to the budget relating to the institution concerned.*[109]

There are thus four distinct subcategories of temporary staff: (a) staff engaged in temporary or highly specialized tasks, also referred to as 'Article 2(a) temporary staff' or 'temporary staff on temporary posts'; (b) staff temporarily filling a vacant (permanent) post in situations in which there is no internal candidate to fill the post and the competition reserve lists were exhausted, referred to as 'Article 2(b) temporary staff' or 'temporary staff on permanent posts'; (c) staff serving in the so-called 'cabinets', referred to as 'Article 2(c) temporary staff' or 'temporary staff in cabinets; and (d) research staff', referred to as 'Article 2(d) temporary staff' or

[107] For more details, see below, section 3.1.2.3.

[108] For more details, see below, section 3.1.2.4.

[109] *EU Conditions of Employment of Other Servants*, Article 2.

'temporary agents on permanent posts – research appropriations'.[110] All these staff serve in posts included in the list of posts provided in the budget of each relevant EU institution, classified either as permanent or as temporary posts.[111]

Temporary staff are graded in the same way as permanent officials.[112] Also the conditions of their employment are, in general, the same as those applicable to officials.[113] This is due to the fact that temporary staff do 'essentially ... the same kind of work as [permanent] officials'.[114] Although the number of temporary posts has been drastically reduced in the course of the staff reform which took place between 2000 and 2004 and many temporary posts were transformed into permanent ones, the possibility of employing staff in temporary posts has been retained in the *EU Conditions of Employment of Other Servants*. The reason for this is simple: temporary staff enable EU institutions to be flexible in reacting to their staffing needs.[115] The transformation of a large number of temporary posts into permanent ones in the early 2000s took place only because it was clear that many temporary staff members were, in fact, engaged in tasks that had in the meantime become permanent.[116]

3.1.2.2. Contract staff

Contract staff constitute a new category of EU 'other servants', introduced by the 2004 amendment of the *EU Conditions of Service of Other Servants*. The new contract staff have replaced auxiliary staff, a category that had existed since the adoption of the first *EU Staff Regulations* in 1961 until 2007.[117] As reported by the Commission, contract staff have also replaced:

---

[110] *Commission's Human Resources Report 2009*, p. 30. Note that on 31.12.2010 the distribution of temporary staff serving in the Commission in various categories was as follows: Article 2(a) temporary staff (temporary posts): 189; Article 2(b) temporary staff (permanent posts): 1283; Article 2(c) temporary staff (cabinets): 175; and Article 2(d) temporary staff (research): 242. The number of temporary staff varies significantly between different Directorates-General. Most Directorates-General have between 0,5 per cent and 16 per cent of staff serving as temporary staff. For more details, see *ibid.*

[111] *Lars Bo Rasmussen v. Commission of the European Communities, Case C-398/93 P, ECR [1994], p. I-4043*, para. 27 and *Fausta Deshormes, née La Valle v. Commission of the European Communities, Case 17/78, ECR [1979], p. 189*, para. 43.

[112] *EU Conditions of Employment of Other Servants*, Article 15(1) and *Commission Decision on General Implementing Provisions Concerning the Criteria Applicable to Classification in Grade and Step in Appointment or Engagement*, Article 1

[113] See *EU Conditions of Employment of Other Servants*, Chapters 4 -8 and information on the Commission official website, the European Commission Civil Service portal, available at http:/ec.europa.eu/civil_service/job/temp/index_en.htm, last visited on 26.11.2007.

[114] The Commission official website, the European Commission Civil Service portal, available at http:// ec.europa.eu/civil_service/job/temp/index_en.htm, last visited on 26.11.2007.

[115] See the information on the Commission archived website concerning the staff reform, available at http://ec.europa.eu/reform/2002/chapter04_en.htm, last visited on 22.1.2008.

[116] *Report from the Commission to the European Parliament and the Council - Follow-up Report on the European Parliament Resolution on 2000 Discharge for the General Budget, COM/2002/0696 final*, 10.12.2002, available at http://eur-lex.europa.eu/LexUriServ/LexUriServ.do?uri=COM:2002:0696:FIN :EN:PDF, last visited on 30.12.2010, p. 10.

[117] See *EU Conditions of Employment of Other Servants*, Article 3b and 52. See also *Commission's Human Resources Report 2009*, p. 32.

> *other staff categories employed under a national law contract, such as the Local Staff for Administrative and Technical Assistance (ALAT), the individual experts intra-muros, a number of local agents from the representations as well as staff under Belgian and Luxembourgian law. Officials and auxiliary agents from the former category D in the [Directorates-General] and services as well as officials and auxiliary agents from different categories in the offices have also been replaced.*[118]

At present, contract staff constitute the second largest category of the Commission staff, amounting to some 15 per cent. The only larger group are (permanent) officials.[119] Contract staff perform their tasks under the supervision of officials or temporary staff members.[120] They fulfill a great variety of duties and are spread over many different levels. As pointed out by Spence and Stevens, these staff may be employed at levels with the range as broad as the equivalent of the former category D up to at the middle of the former category A, covering functions such as nurses in crèches but also implementation of policy.[121] Apart from the European Commission, especially EU agencies make extensive use of contract staff. This is because of the flexibility this type of employment provides.[122]

Formally speaking, contract staff are divided into two subcategories named after the provisions in which they are defined: 'Article 3a contract staff' and 'Article 3b contract staff', the latter also referred to as 'contract staff for auxiliary tasks'.[123] Article 3a of the *EU Conditions of Employment of Other Servants* concerns the following staff:

> *staff not assigned to a post included in the list of posts appended to the section of the budget relating to the institution concerned and engaged for the performance of full-time or part-time duties:*
>
> *(a) in an institution to carry out manual or administrative support service tasks,*
>
> *(b) in the agencies referred to in Article 1a(2) of the Staff Regulations,*

---

[118] *Commission's Human Resources Report 2009*, p. 33.

[119] Ibid., p. 30. Out of the total of 5.766 contract staff serving in the Commission on 31.12.2010, 2.647 were 'Article 3(a) contract staff', employed in the administrative offices, Commission delegations outside EU, Commission representations in the EU Member States and in the Commission Directorates-General. 'Article 3(b) contract staff' comprised 3.119 persons, employed predominantly in the Commission Directorates-General. – footnote 6. The distribution by function group was as follows: function group I: 757 agents (13 per cent); function group II: 2.006 agents (35 per cent); function group III: 1.124 agents (20 per cent); function group IV: 1.879 agents (33 per cent). - p. 37.

[120] *EU Conditions of Employment of Other Servants*, Article 80.

[121] Spence and Stevens, *Staff and Personnel Policy in the Commission*, p. 193-194.

[122] Spence also noted that flexibility was precisely the intention behind creating the category of contract staff in the EU. – Ibid.in, pp. , p. 194.

[123] See the information on contract staff on the Commission official website, the European Commission civil service portal, available at: http://ec.europa.eu/civil_service/job/contract/index_en.htm, last visited on 26.11.2007.

> *(c) in other entities inside the European Union created, after consultation of the Staff Regulations Committee, by specific legal act issued by one or more institutions allowing for the use of such staff,*
>
> *(d) in Representations and Delegations of Community institutions,*
>
> *(e) in other entities situated outside the European Union.*[124]

Article 3b of the *EU Conditions of Employment of Other Servants* provides:

> *For the purposes of these Conditions of Employment, "contract staff for auxiliary tasks" means staff engaged in an institution within the time limits set in Article 88 in one of the function groups referred to in Article 89:*
>
> *(a) to perform full-time or part-time duties others than those referred to in Article 3a(1)(a), without being assigned to a post included in the list of posts appended to the section of the budget relating to the institution concerned,*
>
> *(b) to replace, after the possibilities of temporary posting of officials within the institution have been examined, certain persons who are unable for the time being to perform their duties, namely:*
>
> *(i) officials or temporary staff in the function group AST;*
>
> *(ii) exceptionally, officials or temporary staff in the function group AD occupying a highly specialised post, except Heads of Unit, Directors, Directors General and equivalent functions.*
>
> *The use of contract staff for auxiliary tasks is excluded where Article 3a applies.*[125]

This last quote also shows that EU contract staff are further divided into four function groups, depending on the duties to be performed. And each function group is divided into grades corresponding to the qualifications and experience possessed by staff concerned. Thus, function group IV relates to administrative, advisory, linguistic and equivalent technical tasks and has six grades (13 to 18). For this function group, a level of education corresponding to completed university studies of at least three years or professional training of an equivalent level is required. Function group III (with grades 8 to 12) concerns executive tasks, drafting, accountancy and other equivalent technical tasks. Function group II (comprising grades 4 to 7) corresponds to clerical and secretarial tasks and, like function group III, requires a post-secondary level of education or secondary level of education giving access to post-secondary education and appropriate professional experience. In some cases, professional training or experience of an equivalent level may suffice, too. Function group I (grades 1 to 3) covers manual and administrative support service tasks for which a successful completion of compulsory education is the only qualification needed.[126]

---

[124] *EU Conditions of Employment of Other Servants*, Article 3a.

[125] Ibid., Article 3(b).

[126] Ibid., Article 80 and Article 82(2). Note that EU institutions and agencies enjoy a wide discretion in evaluating when specific duties fall within a certain function group. - *María del Carmen de la Cruz v.*

A specificity of 'Article 3a contract staff' is that these staff may only be recruited at the lower grades of each function group. For example, in function group IV, 'Article 3a contract staff' may only enter the EU civil service in grades 13, 14 or 16, while the upper grade for function group IV as a whole is 18.[127]

3.1.2.3. Local staff

Local staff are, as the name suggests, staff recruited locally, in places in which they are to serve. The definition of local staff is provided in Article 4 of the *EU Conditions of Employment of Other Servants* and reads as follows:

> *"[L]ocal staff" means staff engaged in places outside the European Union according to local practice for manual or service duties, assigned to a post not included in the list of posts appended to the section of the budget relating to each institution and paid from the total appropriations for the purpose under that section of the budget. Staff engaged in places of employment situated outside the European Union for duties other than those mentioned above which, in the interests of the service, could not be assigned to an official or servant having another capacity within the meaning of Article 1, shall also be regarded as local staff.*[128]

It follows from this definition that local staff are exclusively employed in countries other than EU Member States. Normally, these staff would be hired to perform manual and service duties not accounted for in the regular budget of the institution at issue. However, there is a possibility of engaging local staff for other type of duties as well. The condition for such engagement is that duties in question could not have been assigned to a permanent official or a temporary or contract staff member or a special adviser.

Conditions of employment of local staff are determined by each EU institution autonomously. However, they ought to be in line with rules and practices that exist in the place in which staff are employed. This includes the manner of engagement, termination of contract, leave, remuneration, and employer's social security contributions.[129] The precise relationship between the EU rules and local law has been clarified by the ECJ. It has held that the *EU Conditions of Employment of Other Servants* confer a wide discretion on the EU institutions with regard to the local staff, allowing them to take into account various considerations in establishing their conditions of employment, including the economic and social situation within which the local

---

European Agency for Safety and Health at Work (OSHA), Case F-32/06, available at http://curia.europa.eu/jurisp/cgi-bin/form.pl?lang=en&Submit=Rechercher&alldocs=alldocs&docj=docj&docop=docop&docor=docor&docjo=docjo&numaff=F-32/06&datefs=&datefe=&nomusuel=&domaine=&mots=&resmax=100, last visited on 30.12.2010, para. 65. The Tribunal also held that the judicial review of compliance with the division of the duties between the various function groups is limited to assessing the question whether the relevant authority stayed within reasonable bounds and did not use its discretion in a manifestly incorrect way.

[127] *EU Conditions of Employment of Other Servants*, Article 86 and Article 80.

[128] Ibid., Article 4.

[129] Ibid., Articles 120 – 121.

staff members are placed.[130] Nonetheless, the EU institutions must, in establishing a contractual relationship with the local staff in a specific location, act in accordance with their own internal rules applicable to the conditions of employment of local staff which, in addition, must be drawn up pursuant to the rules and practices of the relevant country.[131] Moreover, the phrase 'current rules and practice in the place where they are to perform their duties', referred to in current Article 120 of the *EU Conditions of Employment of Other Servants* as something that needs to be taken into account when conditions of employment of local staff are being determined, does not cover all aspects of the employment relationship. It does not cover aspects others than those which are regulated in the *EU Conditions of Employment of Other Servants* for other categories of 'other servants'.[132]

In the European Commission, specific conditions of employment of local staff are adopted for each of employment. They must be in accordance with the general conditions contained in the *Framework Rules Laying Down the Conditions of Employment of Local Staff of the Commission of the European Communities Serving in Non-member Countries* (*'Commission Framework Rules on Local Staff'*) of 21 November 1989 and in force since 1 January 1990.[133] These Rules also specify that the Commission may employ local staff for posts divided into six groups, depending on the type of duties to be carried out: administrative, advisory and supervisory posts; executive posts; senior clerical posts; clerical posts; skilled manual posts; and manual posts.[134] Each group contains a number of steps. The starting step of each individual local staff member is identified on the basis of his experience. Advancement to higher steps occurs, in principle automatically every year. Advancement in two steps is excep-

---

130 *Friedrich Asmussen and others v. Commission and Council of the European Communities, Case 50/74, ECR [1975], p. 1003*, para. 34.

131 *Roberto Vitari v. European Training Foundation, Case C-126/99, ECR [2000], p. I-09425*, para. 23. Note that in *Asmussen* the Court stressed that rules adopted by EU institutions in respect of the local staff in a certain Member State, compared to the conditions of local staff employed in another Member State, may only be challenged if the EU institution in question has misused its powers. – *Asmussen and others v. Commission and Council, Case 50/74*, para. 35. For the obligation of EU institutions to respect their own internal rules, see, for example, *Tony Robinson v. European Parliament, Case T-328/01, ECR-SC [2004], p. I-A-5, II-23*, para. 50.

132 *Betriebsrat der Vertretung der Europäischen Kommission in Österreich v. European Communities, Commission of the European Communities, Case C-165/01, ECR [2003], p. I-07683*, last visited on 08.09.2010, para. 43.

133 *Framework Rules Laying Down the Conditions of Employment of Local Staff of the Commission of the European Communities Serving in Non-member Countries*, 21.11.1989, available in the Register of Commission Documents, available at http://ec.europa.eu/transparency/regdoc/registre.cfm?CL=en, last visited on 30.12.2010. Note that at the end of 2008 there were in total 3034 local staff employed by the Commission, which is almost eight per cent of the total Commission staff. - *Commission's Human Resources Report 2009*, p. 30.

134 *Commission Framework Rules on Local Staff*,, Article 4(1) and Annex I. Note that Annex I provides that it is not necessary that the group of posts should correlate with the educational requirements. Examples of posts placed in the group administrative, advisory and supervisory posts are engineers, lawyers, economists, press officers, project leaders, translators and editors. Executive posts are posts of accountants, archivists, administrative staff etc. Skilled manual posts include drivers, security officers, office assistants etc. Examples of posts falling in the remaining groups are also to be found in Annex I.

tionally possible, too, constituting promotion of a deserving staff member, with an overall maximum of such promotions being set at four.[135]

3.1.2.4. Special advisors

The last category of 'other servants' included in the *EU Conditions of Employment of Other Servants* are special advisers. They are defined in Article 5 as follows:

> *'[S]pecial adviser' means a person who, by reason of his special qualifications and notwithstanding gainful employment in some other capacity, is engaged to assist one of the institutions of the Communities either regularly or for a specified period and who is paid from the total appropriations for the purpose under the section of the budget relating to the institution which he serves.*[136]

Contrary to all the other categories of staff to whom the *EU Staff Regulations* or the *EU Conditions of Employment of Other Servants* apply, special advisers are not employed by the EU institutions as regular employees. The definition provided above clearly shows that special advisers are persons who have 'gainful employment in some other capacity'. Their engagement with EU institutions is thus of a particular nature. It is based on a contract concluded for the purposes of advising these institutions on a particular matter or matters. The Commission document C(2007)6655 of 19 December 2007, named *Rules on the Special Advisers to the Commission* (*'Commission Rules on Special Advisers'*), explains that the task of special advisers is to assist Commissioners and certain institutional bodies, such as the disciplinary board.[137] The Commission further explains that:

> *The added value of appointing special advisers to the Commission derives from their exceptional qualifications and/or the relevance, quality and level of the professional experience and expertise acquired prior to or while performing the duties of special adviser.*[138]

EU special advisers can be paid or unpaid. The latter category is normally composed of former Commission officials but, exceptionally, it may also include independent external experts whose remuneration is paid from other sources.[139] When a special adviser is paid by the Commission, the level of remuneration depends on the 'quality and level of their professional experience'.[140] All special advisers, paid and unpaid, are appointed pursuant to a procedure set out in the *Commission Rules on Special Advisers*, mentioned above. These Rules also provide for relatively detailed rules on conflict of interest of (prospective) special advisers. In addition, the *EU Conditions of Employment of Other Servants* provide which other rights and obligations of EU staff

[135] Ibid., Article 4(2)-(4).

[136] *EU Conditions of Employment of Other Servants*, Article 5.

[137] *Rules on Special Advisers to the Commission, C(2007) 6655*, 19.12.2007, available at http://ec.europa.eu/civil_service/about/who/sa_en.htm, last visited on 30.12.2010, Part 2, second paragraph.

[138] Ibid., Part 2, third paragraph.

[139] Ibid., Part 2, last paragraph.

[140] Ibid., Part 2, fourth paragraph.

apply also to special advisers. They include the prohibition of discrimination, duty to act independently, impartially and solely with the interests of the EU in mind, rules on conflict of interest, confidentiality and such others.[141]

3.2. Non-statutory staff

Since the early years, the EU institutions, but in particular the European Commission, have been meeting some of their human resources needs by engaging persons from outside the formal human resources structure. As noted earlier, since these persons do not fall under the EU 'statute', i.e. the *EU Staff Regulations* and the *EU Conditions of Employment of Other Servants*, they are referred to as 'non-statutory staff'. In the past, there was much uncertainty about the types and precise number of non-statutory staff employed by the European Commission.[142] The situation has changed only recently and the first official overview of non-statutory staff was provided by the Commission in its *Human Resources Report* of 2009.[143]

The non-statutory staff are divided into two groups. The first consists of non-statutory staff contracted by the Commission as agents recruited under national law contract and interns. The second group of non-statutory staff concerns staff who have an employer other than the Commission. This group includes service providers, interim staff but also seconded national experts.

Agents recruited under national law contract

Agents recruited under national law contract are engaged for manual tasks in the catering services, childcare centers and crèches, support tasks in the delegations and the Commission medical service. The Commission reported that, in order to simplify the procedures but also to ensure equal treatment, it strives to reduce the use of these agents and employ contract staff instead.[144]

Interns

The Commission interns are normally young university graduates engaged for an official in-service training. As stated by the Commission itself, this training is aimed at benefiting both trainees and the Commission. Trainees acquire knowledge of and practical experience in the Commission work and functioning and get an opportunity to work in a multi-national environment. The Commission, on the other hand, benefits from the fresh outlook and up-to-date academic knowledge of young graduates. It also creates potential future cooperators, collaborators and 'ambassadors' of the European Union.[145] New trainees come to the Commission twice a year for a

[141] *EU Conditions of Employment of Other Servants*, Article 124 and relevant provisions of the *EU Staff Regulations* referred to in this provision.

[142] For more details, see below, chapter 6, section 3.1.

[143] *Commission's Human Resources Report 2009*, p. 27.

[144] Ibid., p. 28.

[145] *Rules Governing the Official Traineeships Scheme of the European Commission*, *Commission Decision C(2005)458*, 02.03.2005, available at http://ec.europa.eu/stages/rules/rules_en.pdf, last visited on

period of three to five months and work under the instructions and responsibility of an adviser.[146] Details of the Commission traineeship programme are set out in the Commission Decision C(2005)458 of 2 March 2005 titled *Rules Governing the Official Traineeships Scheme of the European Commission.*[147]

Service providers

Service providers are persons hired by private companies that are contracted by the Commission for performing outsourced specialized tasks, such as those in the information technology field.[148] They constitute the largest part of non-statutory staff and amount approximately to 6 per cent of all Commission staff.[149]

Interim staff

Interim staff are hired for the Commission by an interim agency. They replace absent staff and/or perform short term duties.[150]

Seconded national experts

Seconded national experts are usually national civil servants from EU Member States who come to the Commission for a few years in order to gain practical experience about the Commission, its work and functioning, and at the same time to provide the Commission with their specific expertise.[151] Of all non-statutory staff, it is this category that is of interest to this study, although formally speaking, seconded national experts are not staff members of the European Commission. As already noted, seconded national experts are usually national civil servants who stay with the Commission for a number of years. They are temporarily posted to the Commission by national public authorities (be it central, regional or local authorities) but may also come from other public or even private or voluntary entities.

30.12.2010, Section 1.1.1.

146 Ibid., Section 5.1.1. and 5.1.2.

147 Ibid.. Note that since 2008, the Commission provides a separate training programme for freshly appointed national civil servants. Training of these national experts takes place in accordance with the Commission decision which applies to the seconded national experts. - *Commission Decision on Secondment*, Title II.

148 *Commission's Human Resources Report 2009*, p. 29.

149 On 31.12.2008, there were 2.241 service providers in the Commission which employed in total 38.765 staff members. - Ibid., p. 30.

150 Ibid., p. 29. On 31.12.2008, the Commission counted 658 interim staff members, amounting to less than 2 per cent of the total Commission staff. – p. 30.

151 Ibid., p. 29. Note that according to the most recent version of the *Commission Decision on Secondment* of 2008, there are two types of national experts in the Commission. The first type are the seconded national experts (SNEs) who come to the Commission to work for a few years and provide the Commission with their expertise. The second type are the so-called 'national experts in professional training' (NEPTs) who enter the Commission for a few months in order to receive professional training with regard to the Commission's working methods and policies. – *Commission Decision on Secondment*, Articles 1, 4, 30(1) and 33(1). These national experts in professional training are not seconded national experts in the strict sense and should be considered rather as special types of trainees.

Seconded national experts remain in the service of their employer during the whole period of secondment and continue to be paid by that employer.[152]

Seconded national experts are of interest to this study because of their role in the Commission's work output. Formally speaking, seconded national officials only 'assist' officials and temporary staff in carrying out their duties.[153] However, in practice, seconded national experts work alongside Commission officials and temporary staff on the same tasks. It has been argued that they have been often used in situations which did not allow the engaging of a sufficient number of regular staff for the existing workload because of budgetary constraints. Seconded national experts have thus often helped to '[fill] gaps within the A grades' performing exactly the same functions as regular officials.[154] The *Decision Laying down Rules on the Secondment to the Commission of National Experts and National Experts in Professional Training* ('*Commission Decision on Secondment*') C(2008) 6866 of 12 November 2008 explicitly restricts the functions and duties which may be performed by seconded national experts only with regard to middle and senior management duties and representation of the Commission with a view to entering into commitments or negotiating on behalf of the Commission. On the other hand, seconded national experts may, for example, participate in missions or external meetings, accompanied by an official or temporary staff member, or act alone as an observer or information officer. In cases where there is no potential conflict of interests, seconded national experts may even receive a specific mandate for one or more missions. They may also represent the Commission in legal proceedings, though they may only act as co-agents together with an official.[155] Because of the importance of the duties in which seconded national experts participate, their relatively extensive use (in some departments), and the possible length of their stay in the Commission, it is interesting to assess the manner in which they are appointed and placed and how their engagement with the Commission may be ended.

---

[152] *Commission Decision on Secondment*, Article 1(1) and (2) and Article 2. Note that The Commission may provide certain allowances related to the stay of seconded national experts in Brussels (or other place of secondment). - Chapter 3.

[153] Ibid., Article 6(1).

[154] Spence and Stevens, *Staff and Personnel Policy in the Commission*, p. 194. See also Page, *People Who Run Europe*, p. 60. Page and Spence also noted that although the number of seconded national experts had been rather low in the first decade of the operation of the system, after 1985 it had grown rapidly and had reached the amount accounting to about 15 per cent of the (former) A grade staff with even higher proportion in some Directorates-General. - Page, *People Who Run Europe*, p. 59 and Spence and Stevens, *Staff and Personnel Policy in the Commission*, pp. 194–195. At present, seconded national experts constitute only some 3 per cent of the total statutory and non-statutory Commission staff. However, division of seconded national experts among individual Directorates-General, services, cabinets, delegations and administrative offices ranged from 0 to 11 per cent. - *Commission's Human Resources Report 2009*, pp. 30-31. These data include both AD and AST staff and since seconded national experts are only engaged in tasks corresponding AD function group, it must be presumed that their proportion in some Directorates-General was considerably higher.

[155] *Commission Decision on Secondment*, Article 6.

4. Conclusion

The above sections show that a relatively large number of different staff categories exist both in the UN Secretariat and in the European Commission. Some of these categories even include persons who are not considered to be UN or EU staff, respectively, and are engaged by the two institutions under arrangements other than those included in the *UN Staff Regulations* or *EU Staff Regulations and Conditions of Employment of Other Servants*.

Given the topic of this study, the study does not pay attention too all persons engaged by the two relevant institutions. It focuses on staff whose work and responsibilities (may) trigger problems in relation to their status of the independent and impartial international civil servant. Other staff (and where relevant non-staff) categories are discussed only where necessary for the sufficient analysis of the situation applying to the staff addressed in the present study.

For the UN Secretariat, this means that only staff serving in the Professional and higher categories falls within the scope of this study, with the exception of Assistant Secretaries-General and Under-Secretaries-Generals considered as political appointees rather than international civil servants. Staff serving in other categories is not specifically addressed. For staff in the Professional and higher categories, it makes no difference for this study whether they serve as regular staff, or 'merely' as temporary staff engaged for a relatively short period of time. The reason for this is that also temporary staff may perform same or comparable duties to those carried out by regular UN staff.

This is similar to the situation in the European Commission. There, the main distinction among various categories of staff is made *not* on the basis of the type of work performed by staff, but on the basis of their employment duration – officials are permanent employees, while 'other servants' serve on a temporary basis. Nonetheless, both officials and 'other servants' perform comparable tasks. And as it is precisely the type of work that is decisive for the inclusion of certain staff category in this study, not the duration of appointment, both EU officials and 'other servants' are included, similarly as all UN staff serving Professional and higher categories, regardless the duration of their appointment. No difference is thus being made in this respect between the European Commission and the UN Secretariat.

On the other hand, while it is possible to exclude from this study UN staff employed for more of the support type of work, this is not possible with regard to such staff serving in the European Commission. The reason for this is that in the European Commission, same rules apply across the board, to both officials serving in AD function group as well as to officials serving in AST function group. A similar situation exists with regard to 'other servants'. In the UN Secretariat, on the contrary, different rules apply to staff serving in different staff categories, be it Professional and higher categories, Field Service category, or General Service and related categories. UN staff serving in categories created for support rather than policy formulation type of work can therefore be excluded from this study, unlike support staff serving in the European Commission. Consequently, the latter is addressed in this study together with EU staff serving in AD function group.

The present study pays attention also to UN and EU staff serving on secondment. This is in particular the case of seconded national experts temporarily posted with the European Commission. As explained in one of the previous sections, such experts are of interest to this study because of their role in, and (potential) influence on, the Commission's work output.[156] Contrary to the UN, where seconded national experts fall under the regime established by the *UN Staff Regulations* for all UN staff, engagement of seconded national experts in the European Commission occurs under a separate set of rules. It is therefore necessary that the present study pays distinct attention to these rules and assesses separately whether they are sufficient to ensure independent and impartial conduct of these experts.

Apart from seconded national experts, this study pays no attention to persons engaged with the Commission outside its statutory framework, i.e. the non-statutory staff. This applies also to special advisers, despite their subordination to the *EU Conditions of Employment of Other Servants*. Given the particular (and limited) nature of the engagement of special advisers with the European Commission, and the fact that their main employment is elsewhere, this study argues that special advisers cannot be regarded as international civil servants. Similar considerations apply to UN non-staff personnel who too are excluded from the scope of this study.

[156] See above, section 3.2.

Chapter

2

ROLE OF NATIONALITY

1. Introduction

Modern international organizations pay great attention to the nationality of people applying for posts in their secretariats. Constitutive instruments and/or staff regulations of all international organizations require that their staff be recruited on as broad a geographical basis as possible, subject to the requirement of ensuring the highest standards of quality, efficiency and integrity.[1] The requirement to recruit the best talent available is generally referred to as the principle of merit, while – as already explained in the introduction to this study - the requirement of the broadest possible geographical basis for staff recruitment has become known as the principle of geographical distribution in the UN system and the principle of geographical balance in the EU system, respectively. In order to cover both the UN and the EU systems and, at the same time, to respect the difference in the organizations' own terminology, this study refers to this principle to by a joint name: the principle of broad geographical representation, unless the specific UN or EU system is discussed. The use of term 'representation' may be regarded as inappropriate, even dangerous, since it may create an impression that staff directly or indirectly represent their country of origin. This might be the reason why this term is found neither in the constitutive instruments of international organizations nor in their staff regulations or rules. Nonetheless, the term is commonly and broadly used in other formal documents, relevant jurisprudence, political statements etc.[2] The choice to employ this term in the present study has been made in full understanding of its possible controversy, even criticism, and merely in the view of the fact that a more suitable term that could be applied commonly to both the UN and the EU system has not been found.

The principle of broad geographical representation among the staff of international organizations did not always constitute a part of international institutional law. Originally, the staff of secretariats to international conferences and bureaus of public international unions were either provided for by the foreign offices of

[1] See, for example, *The Charter of the United Nations*, Article 101(3); *Articles of Agreement of the International Monetary Fund*, Article XII, Section 4 d); *Articles of Agreement of the International Bank for Reconstruction and Development*, Article V, Section 5 d); *Articles of Agreement of the International Development Association*, Article VI, Section 5 d); *Articles of Agreement of the International Finance Corporation*, Article IV, Section 5 d); *Constitution of the International Labour Organisation*, Article 9, paragraph 2; *Agreement Establishing International Fund for Agricultural Development*, Article 6, Section 8 (e); *Constitution of the the Food and Agriculture Organization of the United Nations*, Article VIII:3; *Convention Establishing the World Intellectual Property Organization*, Article 9, paragraph 7). For the EU, see *Staff Regulations of Officials of the European Union*, Article 27.

[2] This is especially the case in the UN. See, for example, *Human Resources Management Reform, Report of the Secretary-General, A/55/253*, 01.08.2000, available in the Official Document System of the United Nations, available at http://documents.un.org/, last visited on 30.12.2010, para. 23(a); or *Composition of the Secretariat, Report of the Secretary-General, A/60/310*, 29.08.2005, available in the Official Document System of the United Nations, available at http://documents.un.org/, last visited on 30.12.2010, Section II, Part C. In the EU, the term geographical 'balance' is more often used, but the expression, 'reasonable and fair representation of Member States' has occurred in the EU policy documents as well. - See, for example, *Recruitment of Senior Managers from the New Member States - Implementation Measures, Communication from Vice-President Kinnock in Agreement with the President, SEC(2004)0252*, available at http://ec.europa.eu/reform/pdf/sec_2004_0252_en.pdf, last visited on 15.01.2008, p. 1.

the host states or recruited from within such host states. Unions' membership was neither reflected in the composition of the bureaus, nor was it sought to be.[3] The situation changed after the First World War.[4] According to Article 395 of the *Peace Treaty of Versailles*, part XIII of which contains the first *Constitution of the International Labour Organization*, the staff of the International Labour Office was to be selected, as far as possible, from among diverse nationalities. By including this requirement in the ILO Constitution, the ILO founding fathers decided for the first time in the history of international organizations to create a secretariat with a truly international composition. They empowered the ILO Director to select persons of various nationalities when recruiting staff for the organization, although – as the wording of Article 395 suggests – they did not expect him to guarantee placement of nationals from all ILO Member States but rather from 'various' Member States. The requirement to ensure diversity of nationalities in the ILO Office was also made subject to the condition that such staff selection would not jeopardize the efficiency of the Office's work.[5]

Interestingly, and in contrast to the *Constitution of the International Labour Organization*, the *Covenant of the League of Nations*, which constituted part I of the same *Treaty of Versailles*, remained silent as regards the composition of the League's future staff. Article 6 of the *Covenant* only stipulated that the staff of the League's Secretariat was to be appointed by the Secretary-General with the subsequent approval of the Council, not providing for any further guidance.[6] Once established, the Council gave a relatively free hand to the League's Secretary-General, Sir Eric Drummond, who used this discretion to a great extent and established a truly independent international civil service. One of the most important means of achieving it was the engagement of persons of various nationalities. Although the primary consideration in staff appointment was given to candidates'

---

[3] Goodrich, L. M., *Geographical Distribution of the Staff of the UN Secretariat*, in: International Organization, 1962, pp. 465-482, p. 465. For example, staff of the United Bureaux created for the 1883 Paris Convention for the Protection of the Industrial Property and the 1886 Berne Convention for the Protection of Literary and Artistic Works, succeeded in 1970 by the Secretariat of the World Intellectual Property Organizations, were appointed by the Swiss government. - Schermers and Blokker, *International Institutional Law, Unity within Diversity,* para. 434. For other examples, see Beigbeder, *Threats to the International Civil Service*, pp. 15-17; Ali, *The International Civil Service: The Idea and the Reality*, p. INT. ADMIN I.1/4 and Lemoine, *The International Civil Servant: An Endangered Species,* pp. 16-22. Note that since the Hague Conference of 1899, secretariats of international conferences increasingly acquired multinational composition. The secretariat to the Hague Conference, for example, included diplomats from Russia, the Netherlands, France and Belgium. - Beigbeder, *Threats to the International Civil Service,* p. 15.

[4] It should be noted that the International Labour Office was not the first in history whose staff acquired an international status, independent from the Member States. It was staff of the International Institute of Agriculture, established in 1905, preceding the later UN Food and Agriculture Organization, and the European Commission of the Danube created in 1856. However, as noted by Beigbeder, the transformation from national to multinational and later international secretariats reached its maturity with the organizations established by the Peace Conference of 1919. - Beigbeder, *Threats to the International Civil Service*, p. 17.

[5] *Peace Treaty of Versailles*, 28.06.1919 available in the The World War I Document Archive, available at http://net.lib.byu.edu/~rdh7/wwi/versailles.html, last visited on 30.12.2010, Part XIII, Article 395.

[6] Ibid., Part I, Article 6.

competence, Sir Drummond paid great attention to the need to ensure international character of the Secretariat. As explained in the introduction to this study, such character was considered indispensable for a secretariat expected to carry international duties and responsibilities and to act in the interests of all League's Member States.[7] Sir Drummond's approach was supported by the Balfour Report of 1920 which established the basic principles of the League's personnel policy, and which Sir Drummond admitted to have been a co-author of. The Balfour principles were confirmed by the League's Council and Assembly and later confirmed by the Noblemaire Report of 1921 and the Report of the Committee of Thirteen of 1930.[8] The last mentioned stated, for example:

> *In the interests of the State Members of the League, the Committee has endeavored to make provision for the widest possible contacts between the Secretariat and the different countries. Its desire is that the representatives of the various nationalities should be found in every grade of the Secretariat, as far as this is possible.*[9]

International organizations founded after the Second World War followed the example of the League of Nations and took over the principle of broad geographical representation in their Secretariats. This is also the case of the UN and the EU. The introduction to this study explains that both the UN and the EU have adopted the concept of an international civil service and thus also of an international composition of their staff. They have done so in order to ensure that their international civil service is independent from, and impartial vis-à-vis, individual Member States. The inevitable consequence is, however, that the independence and impartiality of each individual UN or EU staff member may be under pressure, depending on how the principle of geographical representation is applied in these organizations' staff selection process. If this principle is placed above the principle of merit, requiring that competence, efficiency and integrity of candidates be given primary consideration, the principle of geographical representation may, actually or potentially, endanger the independence and impartiality of UN and/or EU international civil

[7] See above, Introduction, section 1.

[8] Langrod, *The International Civil Service, Its Origins, Its Nature, Its Evolution*, pp. 109-110, 113-115 and 120-121. Note that the development and implementation of the principle of international character in the League's Secretariat was not without problems. For example, in early years, there was, in fact, a preponderance of British and French officials in the Secretariat, given the leading role of the two powers in the League and the longstanding tradition of their civil services and diplomacy. The absence and/or the insufficient representation of Member States other than Great Powers in the League's Secretariat caused tensions throughout the League's history. In addition, in the late 1920s, some countries, in particular fascist Italy, wished for a weaker Secretariat and more limited powers of the Secretary-General. The increased political tensions among the League's Member States resulted in stronger claims for certain posts in the Secretariat and higher involvement in staff matters. This was detrimental to the international character of the League's Secretariat. – For details, see Ibid., chapter 5. See also Goodrich, *Geographical Distribution of the Staff of the UN Secretariat*, p. 466; Weiss, *International Bureaucracy, An Analysis of the Operation of Functional and Global International Secretariats*, pp. 55-56; and Lemoine, *The International Civil Servant: An Endangered Species*, p. 239 and 242.

[9] *Report of the Committee of Enquiry into the Organization of the Secretariat, International Labour Office and the Registry of the Permanent Court of International Justice (Committee of Thirteen), A.16.1930, 11th Assembly, 4th Committee, Annex 8*, 28.06.1930, para. 12.

servants. As a consequence, it would engender the status of the UN and/or EU international civil service as such.

This chapter describes and analyzes the legal framework within which the principle of broad geographical representation is applied in these two organizations. It also assesses how this principle is reconciled with the principle of merit. Apart from staff appointment, the chapter also looks at the role the principle of broad geographical representation plays in staff promotion and separation from service. In order to facilitate better understanding of the legal framework existing in the two organizations, the chapter begins with an outline of past developments, legal as well as political.

2. The UN Secretariat

2.1. Historical overview

2.1.1. Introduction of the UN system of desirable ranges

Upon establishment of the United Nations, the principle of geographical representation and related personnel practices developed in the League of Nations were taken on board without much discussion. Meron stated in this respect:

> *The question of the future composition of the Secretariat was not one of the main preoccupations of the authors of the several drafts of the Charter... Nor was it one of the main concerns of the Dumbarton Oaks Conference or of the San Francisco Conference.*[10]

As further explained by Meron, the proposals made in Dumbarton Oaks for the establishment of what later became the UN contained no detailed provisions for staff. In San Francisco, with the exception of questions related to the deputies of the Secretary-General, the composition of staff was discussed only briefly. There was a general understanding that staff should be appointed in a manner ensuring the highest quality and truly international character of the Secretariat.[11] The UN Founding Fathers thus fully relied on the heritage from the League of Nations in this respect and included a principle of broad geographical representation in Article 101(3) of the *UN Charter*. This provision has remained unchanged to date and stipulates the following:

> *The paramount consideration in the employment of the staff and in the determination of the conditions of service shall be the necessity of securing the highest*

[10] Meron, *The United Nations Secretariat*, p. 1. The Dumbarton Oaks Conference took place in 1944 and included the Great Powers and China. This conference was the first international discussion on the aims, constitution and general structure of the future international organization later named the United Nations. The San Francisco Conference of 1945 formally established the United Nations and adopted its *Charter*. It included all founding countries. - Langrod, *The International Civil Service, Its Origins, Its Nature, Its Evolution*, pp. 153 and 155.

[11] For more details, including proposals of some individual countries, see Meron, *The United Nations Secretariat*, pp. 3-6.

> *standards of efficiency, competence, and integrity.* Due regard shall be paid to the importance of recruiting the staff on as wide a geographical basis as possible. *(emphasis added)*

The wording of this provision leaves no doubt that the UN Founding Fathers intended to establish a truly international Secretariat. Its international character had to be safeguarded by the composition of the Secretariat but, in addition, also by the staff appointment process. This can be deduced from Article 101(1) of the *UN Charter*, which gives exclusive authority to the Secretary-General to appoint all the staff. Unlike in the League of Nations, the authority of the UN Secretary-General was not even limited by consent of another body. The only formal restrictions imposed were the obligation to pursue the staffing policy in accordance with the regulations to be established by the General Assembly, with the requirement of achieving the highest possible qualification, efficiency, competence and integrity, and the already mentioned requirement of paying due regard to the importance of recruiting the staff on as wide a geographical basis as possible.[12]

At the outset, UN Member States appeared not to have been very concerned with the way the Secretary-General would recruit his staff, with the notable exception of the most senior staff, who were to be recruited in accordance with an informal agreement concluded among the Great Powers.[13] In the first General Assembly resolution on personnel matters, UN Member States empowered the Secretary-General to establish an administrative organization for discharging his responsibilities and for meeting the needs of UN organs. They reaffirmed requirements of Article 101(3) of the *UN Charter* but did not further elaborate on them and made no explicit requests as to how the Secretary-General should implement that provision.[14] Arguably, the issue of geographical representation was at that time thought to be of secondary importance.[15]

However, already at its second session, a year later, the General Assembly emphasized the need to 'attain a balanced geographical distribution in the composition of the Secretariat', thereby clearly reacting to the unsatisfactory state of affairs that had come about in the recruitment of staff during the first two years.[16] Although the Assembly recognized that this situation was a result of 'unavoidable difficulties encountered in the initial stages of organization', it requested the Secretary-General to examine his recruitment policy and to take necessary steps in order to improve the situation and to engage the staff from countries which had no nationals in the

[12] *UN Charter*, Articles 101(1) and 101(3).

[13] Such an informal agreement was made already in San Francisco and concerned a *de facto* division of senior posts among Great Powers. Each specific senior post in the Secretariat was to be occupied by a national of a certain Great Power. It was thus, in fact, 'preserved' for the country at issue. For more details, see below, section 2.3.2.

[14] *General Assembly Resolution 13(I), A/RES/13(I)*, 13.02.1946, available in the Official Document System of the United Nations, available at http://documents.un.org/, last visited on 30.12.2010, Section III.

[15] Graham and Jordan (eds.), *The International Civil Service*, p. 11.

[16] *General Assembly Resolution 153(II)*, para. 2.

Secretariat yet.[17] The Secretary-General was asked to issue necessary rules and regulations that would help achieve this goal.[18]

Indeed, due to the necessity of servicing as many as 1.600 meetings of the UN organs in 1946 alone, the first Secretary-General Trygve Lie had to recruit a large number of staff, some 2.900 officials, in a very short period of time.[19] Understandably, most of these initial recruits came primarily from countries where available candidates with the required qualifications could quickly be found, i.e. North America and West Europe.[20] As a result, in 1946, roughly two thirds of the staff were nationals of France, the UK or the USA.[21] Hence, the UN started with a heavy 'handicap' with regard to the geographic representation of its Member States in the Secretariat.[22] Responding to the General Assembly's requests, the Secretary-General Trygve Lie took numerous measures to rectify the initial situation - he replaced a large number of the early temporary recruits from over-represented countries, made no appointments from the over-represented countries unless no other suitable candidate was found, actively sought qualified people from the under-represented countries, etc.[23]

Arguably the most significant step of Trygve Lie in this area was the introduction of the system of desirable ranges in 1948. Under this system, the recruitment policy was to be led by the presumption that whenever the number of nationals of a specific Member State was within a certain range of posts, that state was adequately represented. A precise desirable range was to be established for each Member State taking into account its contribution to the UN budget.[24] Such range, as oppose to a specific number or a percentage, was to guarantee a much needed flexibility of the system:

> *Rightly understood, the cardinal principle of geographical distribution is not that nationals of a particular nation should have a specified number of posts at a particular grade or grades, or that they should receive in salary as a group a particular percentage of the total outlay in salaries, but that, in the first place, the administration should be satisfied that the Secretariat is enriched by the experience*

[17] Ibid., para. 2.

[18] Ibid., para. 2.

[19] Swift, R. N., *Personnel Problems and the United Nations Secretariat*, in: International Organization, 1956, pp. 228-247, p. 228; Langrod, *The International Civil Service, Its Origins, Its Nature, Its Evolution*, pp. 174-175. As stated by Langrod, the UN Secretariat 'had all the characteristics of a house built in a hurry'. – *ibid.*, p. 175.

[20] Swift, *Personnel Problems and the United Nations Secretariat*, p. 228; Lemoine, *The International Civil Servant: An Endangered Species*, pp. 242-243.

[21] Lemoine, *The International Civil Servant: An Endangered Species.* See also Langrod, *The International Civil Service, Its Origins, Its Nature, Its Evolution*, pp. 186-7 and Meron, T., *Charter Powers of the United Nation's Secretary-General with regard to the Secretariat and the Role of General Assembly Resolutions*, in: Heidelberg Journal of International Law, Vol. 42, pp. 731-779, p. 753.

[22] Lemoine, *The International Civil Servant: An Endangered Species*, pp. 242-243. Lemoine also notes that the specialized agencies suffered less from this handicap. The growth of their staff numbers was slower and therefore the recruitment could have been better controlled. In addition, these organizations were located in different cities, ensuring greater variety of available talent. – Ibid.

[23] Swift, *Personnel Problems and the United Nations Secretariat*, p. 231.

[24] Graham and Jordan (eds.), *The International Civil Service*, p. 12.

and culture which each Member nation can furnish and that each Member nation should, in its turn, be satisfied that its own cultures and philosophy make a full contribution to the Secretariat.

The whole problem, therefore, is that of establishing acceptable criteria which are administratively workable. Any rigid mathematical formula, to whatever yardstick it may be related, whether to national income, literacy, financial contribution to the budget of the United Nations, or any other criterion, would restrict in an impracticable fashion the flexibility on which the success of any good administration must depend, and is therefore unacceptable.

Accordingly, after a great deal of consideration, including discussion with the Staff Committee, the conclusion was reached that no single criterion would by itself be valid but that as financial contributions to the United Nations budget had been fixed in relation to a combination of pertinent criteria, it would be reasonable to take them as a basis for the flexible system.[25]

Trygve Lie thus worked with a relatively loose framework of quotas.[26] A similar flexible approach permeated the policy adopted by Lie's successor Dag Hammarskjöld.[27] Like Trygve Lie, he too rejected the idea of a stricter arithmetic rule.[28]

The 1948 system of desirable ranges institutionalized the principle of geographical distribution. It laid down the foundation to the system that has continued to exist to date, with the important difference that the original system was more relaxed than subsequent regimes. The latter were the result of continuous and increasingly insistent demands from Member States that were short of their quota to have their nationals placed in the Secretariat. In doing so, Member States ignored the warnings

---

[25] *Report of the Secretary General, Composition of the Secretariat and the Principle of Geographical Distribution*, document number A/652 of 2 September 1948, as quoted in *Comprehensive Assessment of the System of Geographical Distribution and Assessment of the Issues Relating to Possible Changes in the Number of Posts Subject to the System of Geographical Distribution, Report of the Secretary-General*, A/59/724, 04.03.2005, available in the Official Document System of the United Nations, available at http://documents.un.org/, last visited on 30.12.2010, pp. 4-5.

[26] Reymond and Mailick, *International Personnel Policies and Practices*, p. 44; Lemoine, *The International Civil Servant: An Endangered Species*, p. 244.

[27] Graham and Jordan (eds.), *The International Civil Service*, p. 12. Also Langrod, *The International Civil Service, Its Origins, Its Nature, Its Evolution*, pp. 250-251.

[28] Langrod, *The International Civil Service, Its Origins, Its Nature, Its Evolution*, p. 250. Langrod explains that Dag Hammarskjöld worked very pro-actively towards improving geographical distribution in the Secretariat and undertook a number of steps in that regard, including, for example, the conduct of a regular and detailed analysis of the Member States' representation status as well as all vacant posts in the Secretariat services; the subsequent regular invitations to inadequately represented Member States to submit suitable candidates; the building up of contacts with permanent delegates of these countries as well as regular visits to these countries aimed at consulting them about the recruitment process. According to Langrod, Hammarskjöld's close cooperation with Member States in seeking candidates from unrepresented and underrepresented countries constituted a conscious compromise between the prohibition of Member States' involvement in staff recruitment enshrined in the *UN Charter* and the political reality of rather narrow possibilities for improving the situation, given the fact that the UN Secretariat had reached a high degree of stability and the margin for changes in its composition were limited. - Langrod, *The International Civil Service, Its Origins, Its Nature, Its Evolution*, pp. 250-251.

of the International Civil Service Advisory Board on Recruitment Methods and Standards for United Nations and the Specialized Agencies, which had expressed its concerns already in 1950 and emphasized that 'no strict quota should be adopted or recognized', as it would be 'extremely harmful to an international secretariat'.[29] Clearly, the Board was aware of possible detrimental consequences of strict quotas for the independent and impartial character of the UN civil service. Obviously, such quotas would not harm the international character of the UN Secretariat; rather to the contrary, they would ensure it. It was thus the danger of strict quotas for the independent and impartial status of the UN Secretariat that the Board considered to be unacceptable.

2.1.2. The 1962 reform

In general, the original 1948 system of desirable ranges was accepted without serious criticism until 1960.[30] In 1952, it was even considered to be successful – 56 out of 60 Member States had their nationals on the UN staff.[31] The situation began to change in the mid-1950s when a number of new states acceded to the UN. These new Member States were impatient in gaining their recognition in the organization, including its Secretariat, and considered progress in achieving an adequate representation of unrepresented and underrepresented nations at all levels slow and insufficient. Nonetheless, the complaints 'did not seem to be numerous or bitter' at that time.[32]

A considerable shift occurred in the late 1950s and early 1960s. It was related to two main political developments. The first was the already mentioned accession of a rapidly growing number of newly independent states to the United Nations. The General Assembly Resolution 1097 (XI) of 27 February 1957 dealing with the issue of geographical distribution, for example, explicitly noted the admission of 20 new Member States. These – mostly African and Asian – countries were anxious to obtain full and quick acceptance of their demands and their full participation in the organization at all levels.[33] As stressed by Goodrich, these countries were 'still in the mood of revolt against colonialism, all too often identified with Western influence, and were impatient in their demands for recognition'.[34] Via General Assembly reso-

---

[29] Lemoine, *The International Civil Servant: An Endangered Species*, p. 245. See also Langrod, *The International Civil Service, Its Origins, Its Nature, Its Evolution*, pp. 188-189; and Reymond and Mailick, *International Personnel Policies and Practices*, p. 44 et seq.

[30] Goodrich, *Geographical Distribution of the Staff of the UN Secretariat*, p. 475.

[31] Swift, *Personnel Problems and the United Nations Secretariat*, p. 231.

[32] Graham and Jordan (eds.), *The International Civil Service*, p. 12. As pointed out by Swift, the debate of the General Assembly in 1956 was 'neither long nor heated'. Only 30% of Member States participated in this discussion and basically confirmed the existing practice of giving appropriate preference in staff recruitment to nationals of countries with 'disproportionate small part of the Secretariat', subject to the provisions of Article 101(3) of the *UN Charter*. - Swift, *Personnel Problems and the United Nations Secretariat*, as cited by Graham and Jordan (eds.), *The International Civil Service*, p. 12.

[33] Goodrich, *Geographical Distribution of the Staff of the UN Secretariat*, p. 470 and Graham and Jordan (eds.), *The International Civil Service*, p. 13.

[34] Goodrich, *Geographical Distribution of the Staff of the UN Secretariat*, p. 470.

lutions, the new Member States maintained that 'without an adequate regional and cultural representation at the policy-making level of the Secretariat, the purposes of the Charter cannot be duly served'.[35] Delegates from some underrepresented Member States even argued that 'a political organization such as the United Nations could not attach only a secondary importance to the principle of geographical distribution in the composition of a principal organ'.[36] This basically meant that in the recruitment process the principle of merit should be subordinated to that of geographical distribution and not *vice versa*. Moreover, some new Member States were of the view that 'while competence, efficiency, and integrity [were] prerequisites that must be satisfied, these qualifications [were] too often judged in exclusively Western terms...'.[37]

The second reason for the increased dissatisfaction of UN Member States with the original 1948 system of relatively flexible quotas was the pressure from the Soviet Union and other socialistic states of East Europe. These countries were suggesting modification of the essential character of the Secretariat and the abolition of the idea of independent career service. According to these countries, there could be no impartial person in a deeply divided world such as the prevailing one. The idea of an independent and impartial international civil service was, in their view, just a (dangerous) illusion. The Soviet bloc began to put strong emphasis on geographical representation in the Secretariat with the intention of reducing the independent influence of the Secretary-General and his staff. They held that the UN Secretariat should not be independent but rather reflect the various political tendencies of the UN members, i.e. the socialist, neutralist and capitalist orientation of the existing groups of states.[38]

At the end of the 1950s, the General Assembly, reflecting dissatisfaction with the existing practice of the system of desirable ranges, requested a Committee of Experts, established in order to review the activities and the organization of the UN Secretariat, to study the categories of posts subject to geographical distribution and the criteria for determining the desirable ranges. The Committee was to advise the General Assembly how to secure a wide geographical distribution of the Secretariat staff.[39] On the basis of the Committee's conclusions and the subsequent

---

35 *General Assembly Resolution 1436(XIV), A/RES/1436(XIV)*, 5.12.1959, available in the Official Document System of the United Nations, available at http://documents.un.org/, last visited on 30.12.2010, Preamble.

36 Meron, *The United Nations Secretariat*, p. 13 and Meron, *Charter Powers of the United Nation's Secretary-General with regard to the Secretariat and the Role of General Assembly Resolutions*, p. 755.

37 Goodrich, *Geographical Distribution of the Staff of the UN Secretariat*, p. 470.

38 Ibid., p. 469; also Meron, *The United Nations Secretariat*, p. 14-15. The change in the Soviet Union's policy in the direction of the view of the Western countries took place only at the end of the cold war. – see Cooker (ed.), *Accountability, Investigation and Due Process in International Organizations*, p. II.2/9, footnote 3.

39 *General Assembly Resolution 1559(XV), A/RES/1559(XV)*, 18.12.1960, available in the Official Document System of the United Nations, available at http://documents.un.org/, last visited on 30.12.2010, para. 1.

proposal of the Secretary-General, a reform of the system of desirable ranges took place in 1962.[40]

A number of new elements were introduced into the system. Besides the contribution to the UN budget, other factors were recognized as relevant for the calculation of the Member States' desirable ranges, namely the very fact of membership in the UN as well as the size of Member States' population. Consequently, each UN Member State received the same number of posts in its desirable range as a reflection of its membership and a different number of posts depending on its contribution to the budget and its population size. In addition, some space was given to the allocation of a certain number of posts on a regional basis.[41] Regional representation became an important tool for the strengthening of the position of some groups of countries, especially. For many years, facts and figures used to show not only which States but which world regions were inadequately represented in the UN Secretariat. A similar approach can be seen in literature which often provided only regional data. Besides, it was the ratio of the population of specific regions (not States) to the world population that was used in the calculations.[42]

Apart from the four mentioned factors used for the calculation of the Member States' desirable ranges (contribution to the budget, membership, population and regional representation), the Secretary-General was also requested to pay attention to the relative importance of posts at different levels and to ensure countries' geographical representation especially at the level of senior posts.[43] This issue became increasingly important during the 1960s and many General Assembly resolutions adopted in that period paid attention to it.[44]

---

[40] *General Assembly Resolution 1852 (XVII), A/RES/1852(XVII)*, 19.12.1962, available in the Official Document System of the United Nations, available at http://documents.un.org/, last visited on 30.12.2010. For more details on the discussions about the proposed and eventually adopted changes in the General Assembly, see Meron, *Charter Powers of the United Nation's Secretary-General with regard to the Secretariat and the Role of General Assembly Resolutions*, pp. 756-760.

[41] *General Assembly Resolution 1852 (XVII)*, paras. 1(b) and (d).

[42] For example, *General Assembly Resolution 1928(XVIII), A/RES/1928(XVIII)*, 11.12.1963, available in the Official Document System of the United Nations, available at http://documents.un.org/, last visited on 30.12.2010, para. 2 and *General Assembly Resolution 2736(XXV), A/RES/2736(XXV)*, 17.12.1970, available in the Official Document System of the United Nations, available at http://documents.un.org/, last visited on 30.12.2010, para. 2(a). The practice of indicating the representation status by major geographical regions was abolished by a General Assembly resolution in 1999. The General Assembly required the Secretary-General to report in future on the representation status of individual countries. - *General Assembly Resolution 53/221, A/RES/53/221*, 07.04.1999, available in the Official Document System of the United Nations, available at http://documents.un.org/, last visited on 30.12.2010, Section IX, para. 4.

[43] *General Assembly Resolution 1852 (XVII)*, paras. 1(c) and (d).

[44] See, for example, *General Assembly Resolution 1928(XVIII)*, Preamble and para. 2; *General Assembly Resolution 2241(XXI), A/RES/2241(XXI)*, 20.12.1966, available in the Official Document System of the United Nations, available at http://documents.un.org/, last visited on 30.12.2010, Preamble and para. 3; *General Assembly Resolution 2359 (XXII), A/RES/2359(XXII)*, 19.12.1967, available in the Official Document System of the United Nations, available at http://documents.un.org/, last visited on 30.12.2010, Preamble and para. 2; *General Assembly Resolution 2480(XXIII), A/RES/2480(XXIII)*, 21.12.1968, available in the Official Document System of the United Nations, available at http://documents.un.org/, last visited on 30.12.2010; *General Assembly Resolution 2539(XXIV), A/*

2.1.3. The 1986 reform

By 1970, the influence of the Third World Member States in the UN had increased even more. As a result, from the early 1970s, the emphasis in the General Assembly resolutions partly shifted from representation within and among various regions to representation of developing countries as such. The problem of inadequate representation of developing countries in the UN staff structure was explicitly addressed by the General Assembly in 1975 when a separate part of the resolution was dedicated to this issue.[45] The General Assembly stressed that while the developing countries constituted 73 per cent of the UN membership, 64,5 per cent of the staff occupying senior posts in the Secretariat were nationals of the developed countries.[46] The point has been repeatedly underlined ever since in a number of resolutions concerning the composition of the UN Secretariat.[47] Resolution 31/26 of 29 November 1976 even stressed that wider representation was necessary for the achievement of the objectives and goals of the United Nations 'especially with regard to the new international economic order'.[48] The dominance of Western nationals especially in the high-level posts in the Secretariat was seen as leading to 'another form of colonialism'.[49] All these concerns demonstrated the considerable global imbalance as between the industrialized and the (newly independent) developing countries at that time.

Apart from the requirements mentioned thus far (representation among and within regions; representation of developing countries; and representation at the senior level), Member States imposed in due course a number of additional criteria to guide the Secretary-General in his recruitment efforts. He had to weight factors such as the linguistic balance within the Secretariat, the need to increase the number of women, the number of young people or the number of people willing to accept a career appointment rather than a short-term appointment. As observed by the Secretary-General in 1976, all these guidelines made it necessary to assess the candidate's fitness for appointment against a great many criteria, while it was unclear what weight should be given to each of them.[50]

RES/2539(XXIV), 11.12.1969, available in the Official Document System of the United Nations, available at http://documents.un.org/, last visited on 30.12.2010, Preamble and para. 3.

[45] *General Assembly Resolution 3417(XXX)*, Part A.

[46] Ibid., Part A, Preamble.

[47] See, for example, *General Assembly Resolution 31/26, A/RES/31/26*, 29.11.1976, available in the Official Document System of the United Nations, available at http://documents.un.org/, last visited on 30.12.2010, Preamble and para. 2; *General Assembly Resolution 33/143, A/RES/33/143*, 20.12.1978, available in the Official Document System of the United Nations, available at http://documents.un.org/, last visited on 30.12.2010, Preamble and Section I, para. 4; *General Assembly Resolution 39/245, A/RES/39/245*, 18.12.1984, available in the Official Document System of the United Nations, available at http://documents.un.org/, last visited on 30.12.2010, para. 4; and *General Assembly Resolution 40/258, A/RES/40/258*, 18.12.1985, available in the Official Document System of the United Nations, available at http://documents.un.org/, last visited on 30.12.2010, Part A, para. 3.

[48] *General Assembly Resolution 31/26*, Preamble.

[49] Graham and Jordan (eds.), *The International Civil Service*, p. 14.

[50] Meron, *Staff of the United nations Secretariat: Problems and Directions*, p. 666 and Meron, *Charter Powers of the United Nation's Secretary-General with regard to the Secretariat and the Role of General*

During the 1970s and 1980s, several minor amendments of the system of desirable ranges took place. The last one was adopted in 1987, entered into force on 1 January 1988 and is still applicable. These amendments retained the basic elements of the system unaltered. The main modifications related especially to the weight given to the three factors (membership, population, contribution) used for the calculation of Member States' individual ranges. As stated by the General Assembly itself, the primary aim was to achieve a 'balanced application of all factors'.[51] The weight of each factor varied thus over the years in accordance with the successive General Assembly resolutions, with the continuous preference to the contribution factor which has always had the greatest weight. Contrary to this, the membership factor has continuously had the smallest weight, though it has gradually obtained more weight over the years. This was mostly to the detriment of the contribution factor.[52] Such developments were the result of the explicit efforts of Member States which were *not* major contributors to the budget to balance the weight of the contribution and the membership factors as much as possible.[53] Last but not least, the weight of the population factor fluctuated in both directions, first increasing, later decreasing again.[54] Until 1987, the population factor was applied to each region as a whole and

Assembly Resolutions, pp. 761-770.

[51] *General Assembly Resolution 40/258*, para. 4.

[52] The weight of the membership factor has evolved from the minimum of 6,9 per cent in 1962 to 40 per cent in 1988, while the weight of the contribution factor has dropped from the maximum of 86,4 per cent in 1962 to 55 per cent in 1988. An interesting 'intermezzo' in this gradual increase in the weight of the membership factor and decrease of the contribution factor existed in the first half of the 1980s. At that time the membership factor amounted to 25,4 per cent in 1980, but only to 7,75 per cent in 1981. By 1985 it had risen again and reached 36,8 per cent. Similarly, the contribution factor was good for 65,9 per cent in 1980 but for no less than 85 per cent in 1981 (an increase of almost 20 per cent), while dropping back down to only 56 per cent by 1985. – *Comprehensive Assessment of the System of Geographical Distribution and Assessment of the Issues Relating to Possible Changes in the Number of Posts Subject to the System of Geographical Distribution, Report of the Secretary-General, A/59/724*, p. 6, Table 1. See also *General Assembly Resolution 35/210, A/RES/35/210*, 17.12.1980, available in the Official Document System of the United Nations, available at http://documents.un.org/, last visited on 30.12.2010, Part II, para. 1.

[53] These efforts were institutionalized in 1979 when the so-called concept of parity was introduced. According to this concept, the criterion of membership should be weighted at 50 per cent or equal to the percentage used for the criterion of contribution while the existing percentage for the population factor would be maintained. - *General Assembly Resolution 34/219, A/RES/34/219*, 20.12.1979, available in the Official Document System of the United Nations, available at http://documents.un.org/, last visited on 30.12.2010, para. 1(b). The concept was very much discussed by the General Assembly at a number of its sessions as the Member States' opinions as to how fast the parity should be achieved differed sharply. Some Member States were impatient and wished to achieve parity of the membership factor with the contribution criterion as quickly as possible, whereas others preferred gradual changes in that direction. In 1986, when the General Assembly requested the Secretary-General to submit updated calculations on desirable ranges, the movement towards the establishment of parity between the two factors was set as one of four criteria that the Secretary-General had to take into account when proposing new ranges. Eventually, the General Assembly decided to grant the membership factor 40 per cent of weight. - *General Assembly Resolution 42/220A, A/RES/42/220A*, 21.12.1987, available in the Official Document System of the United Nations, available at http://documents.un.org/, last visited on 30.12.2010, Section III, para. 1. This level has been maintained until now.

[54] From 6,7 per cent in 1962 when the criterion of population was introduced, to 8,9 per cent in 1980, and then back to current 5 per cent (in force since 1988). - *Comprehensive Assessment of the System of Geographical Distribution and Assessment of the Issues Relating to Possible Changes in the Number*

not to individual Member States. This was due to the original purpose of this factor - to embrace differences in population sizes that were not given sufficient weight by the budget contributions, i.e. to correct (increase) the maximum for the region, but not for the individual states of that region. The factor itself was even referred to as 'population correction factor'.[55] Such an arrangement provided the Secretary-General with additional flexibility in allowing overrepresentation of certain Member States without a consequent under-representation of another Member State. The Secretary-General considered this arrangement to be well workable. In 1987, when the system was once again under review, he warned that any changes in the arrangement would have negative consequences, making the whole system of desirable ranges much more rigid. Despite this warning, the General Assembly decided to relate the population factor directly to the population of the individual Member States. Consequently, posts subject to the population factor had to be distributed among specific Member States in proportion to their population.[56]

2.2. Current system of desirable ranges

The following sections explain in detail the existing legal framework of the UN system of desirable ranges. The principle of geographical distribution is translated into practical terms through this system and rendered suitable for implementation in specific human resources policies. The system establishes a desirable range of each individual UN Member State and, thereby, its representation status. This representation status is the starting point for the UN Administration in order to take action in a specific human resources area and remedy a possible inadequate situation.

2.2.1. Calculation of desirable ranges

As mentioned above, the current system of desirable ranges was established by the General Assembly Resolution 42/220A of 21 December 1987. It entered into force on 1 January 1988. Pursuant to this resolution, the system is based on the following

of Posts Subject to the System of Geographical Distribution, Report of the Secretary-General, A/59/724, p. 6, Table 1.

55 Reymond and Mailick, *International Personnel Policies and Practices*, pp. 45-46; also Lemoine, *The International Civil Servant: An Endangered Species*, p. 245.

56 *General Assembly Resolution 42/220A*, Section III, para. 1(c). In this resolution, the General Assembly also decreased the weight of the population factor, which is something originally not intended. In its resolution 41/206 C of 11 December 1986, the General Assembly requested the Secretary-General to take into account the requirement of the direct allocation of posts subject to the population factor of 7,2 per cent to Member States in proportion to their population. A year later, in resolution 42/220 A of 21 December 1987, the Assembly decided however that the population factor would have a weight of 5 per cent. It did preserve the requirement of direct allocation of the posts to individual Member States according to their population, though. The Assembly also emphasized that it would consider raising the weight of the population factor in three years time again, during a review of the desirable ranges. So far, no such change has taken place. - *General Assembly Resolution 41/206B, A/RES/41/206B*, 11.12.1986, available in the Official Document System of the United Nations, available at http://documents.un.org/, last visited on 30.12.2010, para. 1(c) and *General Assembly Resolution 42/220A*, Section III, paras. 1(c) and 2.

criteria: a base figure; membership; population; contribution to the regular UN budget; and certain flexibility upward and downward from the midpoint of the desirable range.[57] The first criterion, the base figure, represents the number of posts in the Secretariat, occupied as well as vacant, which are subject to geographical distribution, i.e. are part of the system of desirable ranges. The figure is not constant; it is adjusted whenever the actual number of posts subject to geographical distribution increases or decreases by 100 – the base figure is always rounded down to the nearest hundred. At the time of adoption of the resolution 42/220A, establishing the current system of desirable ranges, the base figure amounted to 2.700 posts. In 1998, for example, the base figure was 2.600 and in 2005 it came to 2.800.[58] The most recent base figure was 3.300 posts as at 30.06.2010.[59]

Only posts meeting the following requirements are subject to the system of desirable ranges, and thus included in the base figure: they are in the Professional and higher categories; the initial appointment to these posts is made for a period of one year or longer; and the posts are funded under the regular UN budget. Staff members appointed to posts that meet these requirements obtain a 'geographical status' which they retain throughout the whole period of service, disregarding the nature of the post or functions to which they may later be assigned. In addition to the above mentioned posts, all candidates successful in a national recruitment competitive examination receive 'geographical status' as well, regardless of what post they are initially appointed to.[60]

Posts that do not match the above criteria are not subject to geographical distribution. They are thus not included in the base figure and, consequently, in the calculations of the representation status of the individual Member States. This concerns posts occupied by the following staff categories: staff appointed to the secretariats of subsidiary programmes, funds and organs with special status in matters of appointment; staff appointed to peacekeeping posts, posts specifically funded for other field mission service or posts financed under the support account for peacekeeping operations; staff appointed to posts with special language requirements; staff in the Field Service and the General Service and related categories who are locally recruited; staff appointed to posts for service limited to the United Nations Environment Programme, the United Nations Human Settlements Programme, or the United Nations Office on Drugs and Crime; staff appointed to posts financed

[57] *General Assembly Resolution 42/220A*, Section III, para. 1.

[58] *Composition of the Secretariat, Report of the Secretary-General, A/53/375*, 11.09.1998, available in the Official Document System of the United Nations, available at http://documents.un.org/, last visited on 30.12.2010, p. 18, para. 35 and *Composition of the Secretariat, Report of the Secretary-General, A/60/310*, p. 10, para. 13.

[59] *Human Resources Management Reform: Comprehensive Assessment of the System of Geographical Distribution and Assessment of the Issues Relating to Possible Changes in the Number of Posts Subject to the System of Geographical Distribution, Report of the Secretary-General, A/65/305/Add.2*, 02.09.2010, available in the Official Document System of the United Nations, available at http://documents.un.org/, last visited on 30.12.2010, para. 14. As reported by the Secretary-General, the actual number of posts subject to geographical distribution was 3.373.

[60] *UN Staff Selection System*, Section 1 (j). For details on the national recruitment competitive examinations, see below, chapter 3, section 2.2.1.2.

on an inter-agency basis; staff appointed to technical cooperation project posts; national officers at United Nations information centres.[61] Also language positions up to and including P-5 level are excluded from the system.[62]

The long list of posts excluded from the system of desirable ranges already suggests that the number of posts that *are* subject to the system is relatively low. Indeed, less than 10 per cent of all posts in the UN Secretariat have geographical status. To be more precise, in 2010 the ratio of the posts subject to the system of desirable ranges to the total number of posts in the UN Secretariat was approximately 8 per cent.[63] Naturally, these 8 per cent of posts are posts in the Professional and higher categories of duration longer than one year, i.e. posts which could, arguably, be regarded as the most influential. In addition, although all the remaining posts are excluded from the system of desirable ranges, the principle of broad geographical representation contained in Article 101(3) of the *UN Charter* applies to them as well – it applies to all staff engaged by the UN Secretariat, i.e. also to staff serving in posts which do not have geographical status. Yet, it remains the case that only a small number of posts in the UN Secretariat fall under the formalized system used to measure the adequacy of Member States' representation in the UN Secretariat, twisting the real picture to a significant extent.

The representation status of each individual Member State is measured via its desirable range. This range is calculated for each country on the basis of three substantive factors mentioned above – the membership factor (each Member State receives the same number of posts in its desirable range due to the very fact of its UN membership); the population factor (the more populated the Member State is, the more posts are allocated to it in its desirable range); and contribution factor (the higher a Member State's contribution to the regular UN budget, the most posts in its desirable range). As mentioned earlier, the weight of each of these factors in the determination of the desirable ranges differs. It depends on the decision of the General Assembly. Under the current system of desirable ranges, the weight of the

[61] *Human Resources Management Reform: Comprehensive Assessment of the System of Geographical Distribution and Assessment of the Issues Relating to Possible Changes in the Number of Posts Subject to the System of Geographical Distribution, Report of the Secretary-General, A/65/305/Add.2*, para. 22. Note also that staff on special leave without pay and staff on secondment to other organizations are not included in the total number of staff in geographic posts.

[62] *UN Staff Selection System*, Section 1(j).

[63] According to the latest available data, on 30 June 2010 the base figure was, as already mentioned, 3 300 posts, while the total number of occupied posts reached 44.134 and the number of posts with geographical status but vacant was 487. - *Composition of the Secretariat: Staff Demographics, Report of the Secretary-General, A/65/350*, para. 2 and *Human Resources Management Reform: Comprehensive Assessment of the System of Geographical Distribution and Assessment of the Issues Relating to Possible Changes in the Number of Posts Subject to the System of Geographical Distribution, Report of the Secretary-General, A/65/305/Add.2*, para. 32. The latter states that there were 2.886 staff with geographical status in the UN Secretariat on 30.06.2010. To recall, the total number of posts subject to geographical distribution on that date was 3.373. If all posts with geographical status were filled, the total number of occupied posts in the UN Secretariat in 2010 would thus have been 44.621. This means that the 2010 ratio of the posts subject to the system of desirable ranges to the total number of posts in the UN Secretariat was approximately 8 per cent (3.373 out of 44.621 posts).

membership is 40 per cent, of the population 5 per cent and of the contribution the remaining 55 per cent.

On the most recent reported date, 30.06.2010, the calculations of individual desirable ranges was thus based on the following figures:

Table 3: Determination of desirable ranges of individual UN Member States

FACTOR	WEIGHT	TOTAL NUMBER OF POSTS TO BE DIVIDED AMONG ALL MEMBER STATES	NUMBER OF POSTS TO BE ALLOCATED TO INDIVIDUAL MEMBER STATES
MEMBERSHIP	40%	40% out of 3.300 = **1.320 posts**	320 posts divided among 192 Member States = **6,9 posts per Member State**
POPULATION	5%	5% out of 3.300 = **165 posts**	Member State's population to the global population of all UN Member States
CONTRIBUTION	55%	55% out of 3.300 = **1.185 posts**	Depends on the proportion of each Member State's contribution to the UN regular budget

Source: Prepared on the basis of data provided in the report of the UN Secretary-General providing comprehensive assessment of the system of geographical distribution and assessment of the issues relating to possible changes in the number of posts subject to this system.[64]

The number of posts allotted to each Member State through the application of the above factors together constitutes the midpoint of the desirable range of posts which are to be filled by nationals of that particular state. This midpoint is an ideal figure, however. It deems to reflect a fully equitable geographical representation of all Member States. Of course, a strict adherence to this figure would render the requirement of geographical representation unachievable in practice. Therefore, the system provides for a flexible range of posts to be distributed among the Member States. They are considered to be adequately represented, i.e. *'within range'*, if the number of posts occupied by their nationals falls within the upper and lower limits of their range. These upper and lower limits are at the level of '15 per cent upward and downward from the midpoint of the desirable range, but not less than

[64] *Human Resources Management Reform: Comprehensive Assessment of the System of Geographical Distribution and Assessment of the Issues Relating to Possible Changes in the Number of Posts Subject to the System of Geographical Distribution, Report of the Secretary-General, A/65/305/Add.2*, paras. 15-17.

4,8 posts up and down, the upper limit of the range being not less than 14 posts'.[65] Consequently, when the number of nationals of a certain Member State serving at the UN at a post with geographical status exceeds the upper limit of the desirable range of that state, the state is considered to be *overrepresented*. If this number is below the lower limit, the Member State is *underrepresented*. When there are no nationals with the geographic status having nationality of a certain Member States, the relevant State is *unrepresented*. In 2010, the situation at the UN Secretariat was as follows: 12 Member States were *un*represented; 31 were *under*represented; 17 were *over*represented; and 132 were *within* their desirable range.[66]

Obviously, the representation status of the Member States can change rather easily. As pointed out by the Secretary-General, there are many factors that influence this status, in particular staff turnover, changes in the scale of assessment used for the calculations of Member States' budgetary contributions, and changes in the total number of Member States.[67] For example, in 2009, the Secretary-General explained that while the number of unrepresented Member States had been consistently decreasing during the last years, the number of underrepresented countries had increased. This increase resulted from a peak in retirements from the newly under-represented Member States during the last two years and by the increase in the number of posts subject to geographical distribution.[68]

In addition to the calculation of 'regular' desirable ranges for each Member State, the UN Secretary-General uses a separate mechanism to calculate the so-called 'weighted ranges', showing the distribution of posts among Member States at different post levels. As it has been mentioned in the overview of the historical developments of the system of desirable ranges, the UN Member States have since long been demanding their equitable representation at all levels, being especially concerned with the senior and policy-making posts.[69] In 1967, they requested the

---

[65] *General Assembly Resolution 42/220A*, Section A.III, para. 1 (e)

[66] *Composition of the Secretariat: Staff Demographics, Report of the Secretary-General, A/65/350*, para. 34 and Table 19. The 12 unrepresented Member States were: Comoros, Democratic People's Republic of Korea, Kiribati, Kuwait, Liechtenstein, Marshall Islands, Nauru, Palau, Sao Tome and Principe, Timor-Leste, United Arab Emirates and Vanuatu. The 31 underrepresented Member States were Afghanistan, Angola, Bahrain, Brunei Darussalam, Burkina Faso, Cambodia, Finland, Iran, Japan, Latvia, Libyan Arab Jamahiriya, Lithuania, Micronesia, Monaco, Montenegro, Norway, Oman, Poland, Qatar, Republic of Korea, Samoa, Saudi Arabia, Sierra Leone, Solomon Islands, Spain, Tonga, Turkey, Turkmenistan, Tuvalu, United Kingdom of Great Britain and Northern Ireland and United States of America. The 17 overrepresented Member States were: Argentina, Australia, Austria, Bulgaria, Cameroon, Egypt, Ethiopia, Italy, Kenya, Lebanon, Philippines, Russian Federation, South Africa, Trinidad and Tobago, Uganda, Ukraine and Zimbabwe. – Table 20.

[67] *Human Resources Management Reform. Comprehensive Assessment of the System of Geographical Distribution and Assessment of the Issues Relating to Possible Changes in the Number of Posts Subject to the System of Geographical Distribution, Report of the Secretary-General, A/65/305/Add.2*, para. 19.

[68] *Composition of the Secretariat, Report of the Secretary-General, A/64/352*, para. 91.

[69] These concerns are as present nowadays as they were some 40 years ago. Virtually each resolution passed by the General Assembly with respect to the human resources management which includes the issue of geographical representation contains a request to the Secretary-General 'to take all necessary measures to ensure, at the senior and policymaking levels of the Secretariat, equitable representation of Member States, especially those with inadequate representation at those levels, and to continue to include relevant information thereon in all future reports on the composition of the Secretariat'.

Secretary-General to include in his report on the composition of the Secretariat, which normally includes information on the geographical distribution of the staff and the representation status of Member States, data reflecting also the distinction between posts of various grades.[70] In reaction, and although the system of 'regular' desirable ranges formally applies to all posts, including those at higher levels, the Secretary-General has developed a special system of weighted ranges.

Over the years, different methods to calculate such weighted ranges have been used. At present, the calculation is made as follows: The percentage of total staff in each grade is applied to the base figure. The resulting figure is weighted by the gross annual salary in United States ('US') dollars divided by 1.000, which produces a weighted base figure. For example, in 2009 when such analysis was provided for the last time, the weighted average value of each post amounted to 92,17 points, leading to 121,670 points for the weighted membership factor; 15,209 points for the weighted population factor; and 167,296 points for the weighted contribution factor. All these numbers are global and separate calculations are made for each Member State resulting in individual weighted mid-points. The weighted position of each Member State consists then of the total number of posts of that state by grade multiplied by the gross annual salary by grade.[71] Naturally, the weighted position of each Member State may, and usually does, differ from its general representation status, depending on the number of posts occupied by its nationals at various levels.

2.2.2. Ongoing requests for review

Since its introduction, the system of desirable ranges has been under constant discussion and review. Although the system as such has been generally regarded by the Member States as positive and helpful for ensuring representation of all nationalities among UN staff, there have always been reasons for dissatisfaction. The initial criticism related mainly to the insufficient actual progress towards adequate representation of all Member States, later strengthened with regard to posts at higher levels. Relatively soon an additional point concerning the weight to be accorded to various factors used in calculations of desirable ranges entered the discussions.[72] While retaining both previous concerns, more recent debates also include the issue of the personal scope of the system, as only a small proportion of UN staff, some 8 per cent, is currently subject to it.[73] This situation is a result of the radical

– Most recently, *General Assembly Resolution 63/250, A/RES/63/250*, 24.12.2008, available in the Official Document System of the United Nations, available at http://documents.un.org/, last visited on 30.12.2010, Section IX, para. 7.

[70] *General Assembly Resolution 2359 (XXII)*, Part A, para. 3.

[71] *Composition of the Secretariat, Report of the Secretary-General, A/64/352*, Annex I, para. 7.

[72] See above, sections 2.1.2 and 2.1.3. See also, for example, *Personnel Questions, Composition of the Secretariat, Alternative Options for Desirable Ranges for the Geographical Distribution of Staff in the Professional Category and Above, Report of the Secretary-General, A/C.5/46/2*, 27.08.1991, available in the Official Document System of the United Nations, available at http://documents.un.org/, last visited on 30.12.2010.

[73] For example, *Towards a Compact, Proposals for Improved Governance and Management of the*

change in the staff composition caused by the change of the Secretariat's role and mandates from mostly office tasks to field tasks. A great majority of present staff serves in peacekeeping and other field locations, all of them being excluded from the system of desirable ranges.[74] The legitimacy of the system is therefore being questioned, since Article 101(3) of the *UN Charter*, used as the legal basis for the system of desirable ranges, does not make any distinction between different categories of staff.

Therefore, in 2003, the General Assembly requested the Secretary-General to conduct a comprehensive assessment of the system of geographical distribution and of the issues relating to the possible changes in the number of posts subject to this system.[75] The results of such a study were presented in the report of the Secretary-General of 2005, which offered three different scenarios for modifications of the current system.[76] The first scenario suggested five different variants for changes of the weight of existing factors, while retaining the current base figure.[77] The second scenario proposed four variants for possible change in the number of posts subject to geographical distribution through the inclusion of new categories of staff, while maintaining the current weight of the three factors.[78] The third scenario consisted of the application of the system of weighted ranges, i.e. modifying the system of desirable ranges by distinguishing between posts by their grades.[79]

United Nations Secretariat, Report of Final Proposals by the Four Nations Initiative on Governance and Management of the UN, September 2007, available at http://www.the4ni.org/images/stories/documents/towards%20a%20compact%20-%20final%20report%20by%20the%204ni.pdf, last visited on 30.12.2010, pp. 34-35.

[74] *Composition of the Secretariat, Report of the Secretary-General, A/64/352*, Table 1, Figures I and II, pp. 11-14.

[75] *General Assembly Resolution 57/305, A/RES/57/305*, 15.04.2003, available in the Official Document System of the United Nations, available at http://documents.un.org/, last visited on 30.12.2010, Section IX, para. 2.

[76] *Comprehensive Assessment of the System of Geographical Distribution and Assessment of the Issues Relating to Possible Changes in the Number of Posts Subject to the System of Geographical Distribution, Report of the Secretary-General, A/59/724*, available in the Official Document System of the United Nations.

[77] Ibid., paras. 23-26 and Table 2. Within this scenario, in the first three alternatives one of the factors is given a weight of 100 per cent and the other two 0 per cent. The fourth alternative suggests the weight of the membership factor of 75 per cent (as opposed to the present 40 per cent), the weight of the population factor of 10 per cent (at present 5 per cent) and the reduction of the contribution factor to 15 per cent (instead of the current 55 per cent). Under the fifth alternative, the weight of the contribution factor is raised to 70 per cent (currently it is 55 per cent), the membership factor drops to 25 per cent (from the present 40 per cent) and the population factor remains at a weight of 5 per cent.

[78] Ibid., para. 32. The four variants included the following staff categories: first, all staff in posts in the *Professional and higher categories* under the regular budget; second, all staff in posts in the Professional and higher categories but *also in the General Service and related categories* under the regular budget; third, all staff in posts in the Professional and higher categories under the *regular budget and extra-budgetary resources*; and fourth, all staff in posts in the Professional and higher categories and also in the General Service and related categories under the regular budget and extra-budgetary resources, i.e. basically *all staff*.

[79] Ibid., para. 41. This last scenario would in fact mean the institutionalization of the practice used by the Secretary-General for decades when providing annual information to the General Assembly on the composition of the Secretariat. In the Secretary-General's proposal, a complex mathematical formula is again employed for the calculations of the weighted position for each Member State. The result

When presenting his report to the Assembly at its sixty-first session held in 2006, the Secretary-General did not recommend any of the scenarios and variants for adoption. His main arguments were that possible changes in the weight of calculation factors did not reflect the importance of all factors attached to them by the General Assembly and that including new categories of staff in the system would fundamentally alter the scope of the existing concept of geographic distribution and would greatly modify the Member States' representation status. In addition, such changes would have regulatory and financial implications by extending the number of staff entitled to various allowances and benefits and would also affect stability and human resources planning.[80] The General Assembly took note of the report and, as recommended by the Secretary-General, it did not adopt any changes of the system.[81] However, quite soon thereafter, in 2008, the Assembly directed a new request at the Secretary-General and asked for:

> *a comprehensive review of the system of desirable ranges, with a view to establishing a more effective tool to ensure equitable geographical distribution in relation to the total number of staff of the global United Nations Secretariat.*[82]

The General Assembly explained that this request was based on the recognition of considerable changes in the composition and in the number of UN staff, which had taken place during the last two decades.[83] The wording of the resolution suggests that the Member States are in search of 'a more effective tool' than the current system of desirable ranges that would, in addition, reflect the different composition of the UN staff compared to that which existed when the system of desirable ranges was introduced.

The Secretary-General's 'comprehensive assessment of the system of geographical distribution and assessment of the issues relating to possible changes in the

of this calculation is compared with the non-weighted position of each country. The proposal also examines the impact of five variants of the first two scenarios with changing weights on the factors and with changing base figures resulting in important consequences for the representation status of a number of Member States. – Ibid., paras. 43-45.

[80] Ibid., paras. 27-31, 37-40 and 48-50.

[81] *General Assembly Resolution 61/244*, Section X, para. 16. Note that the preceding discussion in the Fifth Committee, which took place in November 2005, did not pay much attention to the report. It seems that Member States agreed with the Secretary-General that none of the proposed alternatives to the present system of calculation of desirable ranges would be feasible. Not many representatives of states present addressed the report, although most delegates did touch upon the issue of geographical representation as such. The representative of the United Kingdom, speaking on behalf of the European Union and associated states, for example, said that the system of geographical distribution worked adequately and the problems that did exist were not necessarily those of methodology, but perhaps of recruitment practices. The Chinese representative would most probably disagree with the statement that the system works adequately, considering the ongoing criticisms of China in this respect. Most other discussants too expressed dissatisfaction with the results that the system has achieved so far. The Chinese representative, however, admitted that the proposed adjustment could hardly meet the interests of interested parties and would not be practical. - *Official Records, Summary Record of the 17 Meeting, A/C.5/60/SR.17*, 01.11.2005, available in the Official Document System of the United Nations, available at http://documents.un.org/, last visited on 30.12.2010, in particular paras. 70 and 89.

[82] *General Assembly Resolution 63/250*, Section IX, para. 17.

[83] Ibid., Section IX, para. 17.

number of posts subject to the system of geographical distribution' was submitted in September 2010.[84] It entirely failed, however, to meet the request of the General Assembly and to 'review' the current system of desirable ranges, let alone to propose 'a more effective tool' guaranteeing adequate geographical representation of Member States in the global UN Secretariat. The report merely repeated the overview of the historical developments of the existing system of desirable ranges and updated scenarios developed in 2005 with new figures, illustrating possible changes in the representation status of every Member State under each of the scenarios. Unlike the previous Secretary-General Kofi Annan, who presented the 2005 report developing the different scenarios but not recommending any of them, the current Secretary-General Ban Ki-moon did not make any proposal to the General Assembly. Rather, he asked the Assembly for further guidance on the matter, emphasizing that he continued to make 'efforts to address the issues surrounding representation of Member States in the Secretariat'.[85]

The inadequacy of the Secretary's-General 2010 report was heavily criticized by the General Assembly's Advisory Committee on Administrative and Budgetary Questions.[86] The General Assembly itself repeated its previous request to the Secretary-General, and asked him to propose a comprehensive review of the existing system of desirable ranges.[87] It remains thus to be seen what changes of the system will still be proposed and eventually adopted, if any. However, the chances for any significant departure from the current system of desirable ranges appear to be rather slim. None of the past proposals succeeded and nothing suggests that any substantial developments in the Member States' approach have taken place since the last report of 2005, reviewed by the General Assembly in 2006. In addition, possible modifications relating to the weight of factors used for the calculations of Member States' desirable ranges would only be a mathematical operation under which changes in the representation status of individual Member States would occur on paper rather than in the real composition of the staff. An alternative, which is the inclusion of other categories of staff in the system can have significance only if it were to include larger categories of staff. Such a step could, however, have strong financial but also political consequences. As pointed out by the Secretary-General in his 2005 report, the newly included staff could acquire rights to some benefits and allowances unavailable to them at present.[88] At a time when financial problems

[84] *Human Resources Management Reform: Comprehensive Assessment of the System of Geographical Distribution and Assessment of the Issues Relating to Possible Changes in the Number of Posts Subject to the System of Geographical Distribution, Report of the Secretary-General, A/65/305/Add.2*, available in the Official Document System of the United Nations.

[85] Ibid., para. 43. See also para. 44.

[86] *Human Resources Management, Report of the Advisory Committee on Administrative and Budgetary Questions, A/65/537*, 22.10.2010, available in the Official Document System of the United Nations, available at http://documents.un.org/, last visited on 30.12.2010, paras. 61-62.

[87] *General Assembly Resolution 65/247, A/RES/65/247*, 24.12.2010, available in the Official Document System of the United Nations, available at http://documents.un.org/, last visited on 30.12.2010, para. 63.

[88] For details, see *Comprehensive Assessment of the System of Geographical Distribution and Assessment of the Issues Relating to Possible Changes in the Number of Posts Subject to the System of Geographical Distribution, Report of the Secretary-General, A/59/724*, paras. 34-36. In brief, the main problem is that

grip the UN, it does not appear to be a feasible option. No less important could be possible political consequences of including new large categories of staff in the system of desirable ranges. Many of such staff serve in extra-budgetary posts, often financed by Member States which provide the resources knowing their nationals will be employed through them. Some of these Member States may reconsider their financial support to the projects at issue if the system of desirable ranges, and thus national quotas for all Member States, were to apply to projects they finance. Moreover, if the number of nationals of each country serving in peacekeeping and other field missions were to count towards the desirable ranges, some countries would certainly end up with having no space for their nationals in the Professional and higher categories because they contribute disproportionately to field missions. Consequently, a significant extension of the system of desirable ranges to other categories appears rather unlikely at present. Such a reading of the situation would appear to be supported by the General Assembly's explicit reaffirmation in its last resolution that the system applied only to regular budget posts in the Professional and higher categories.[89] Furthermore, the General Assembly emphasized the need to 'continue to ensure the proper representation of troop-contributing countries'.[90] If these requirements are to be included in a future system of desirable ranges, little room would remain for any significant modification therein.

2.3. Principle of geographical distribution in the UN recruitment process

The application of the principle of geographical distribution through the system of desirable ranges has not been an unproblematic undertaking in the UN. The most challenging issue was the reconciliation of this principle with the principle of merit. As explained in the introduction to this study, the latter requires that candidates with the best merits are selected, while the application of the principle of geographical distribution means, both in theory and in practice, that preference is given to candidates possessing the 'right' nationality, a criterion which is entirely ignorant of the candidates' merits.

It must be stressed, however, that it is not the precise relationship between the two principles that has led to questions, rather the application of this relationship in practice. The two issues should be distinguished from each other, though it is not disputed that the second issue (i.e. the practical application of the two principles) depends on the first one (i.e. on the relationship between the principles). Formally, the relationship between the principle of geographical distribution and the principle

staff considered as internationally recruited (Professional and higher categories) has the right to certain allowances and benefits which are not available to staff considered as locally recruited (all other staff, including a large number of peacekeeping staff). These allowances and benefits may, depending on the type of appointment, include travel expenses upon initial appointment and on separation, removal of household effects, home leave, education grant and repatriation grant. The estimated costs of extending these allowances and benefits to other categories of staff were approximately 55,5 million US dollars. – On allowances and benefits, see also *UN Staff Rules*, Rule 4.5.

[89] *General Assembly Resolution 65/247*, para. 67.

[90] Ibid., para. 65.

of merit is clear. According to the wording of Article 101(3) of the *UN Charter*, merit is to prevail over the need for broad geographical basis for the staff recruitment. To recall, this provision stipulates:

> *The paramount consideration in the employment of the staff and in the determination of the conditions of service shall be the necessity of securing the highest standards of efficiency, competence, and integrity. Due regard shall be paid to the importance of recruiting the staff on as wide a geographical basis as possible.*[91]

The text of Article 101(3) is almost literally repeated in Regulation 4.2 of the *UN Staff Regulations* which deals with the appointment and promotion of the UN staff. It provides:

> *The paramount consideration in the appointment, transfer or promotion of the staff shall be the necessity of securing the highest standards of efficiency, competence and integrity. Due regard shall be paid to the importance of recruiting the staff on as wide a geographical basis as possible.*[92]

The necessity of securing the highest standards of efficiency, competence, and integrity is thus to be the paramount, i.e. primary, consideration in the staff employment and in the determination of the conditions of service, whereas the importance of recruiting the staff on as wide a geographical basis as possible may only be taken into account as a secondary consideration.[93] This subordination of the principle of geographical distribution to the principle of merit under Article 101(3) of the *UN Charter* and Regulation 4.2 of the *UN Staff Regulations* has two important aspects. First of all, the application of the principle of geographical distribution is, unlike in the case of the principle of merit, not a condition *sine qua non* but rather a requirement which is only to be given *due regard*. In addition, the principle of geographical distribution is to be applied only *as far as possible* and thus not in each and every case. Each individual situation must thus be judged on the basis of its specific circumstances.[94]

The superiority of the principle of merit over that of geographical distribution has been confirmed by the UNAT, which addressed this issue on several occasions. An important case in this regard is *Estabial*, decided in 1983.[95] In this case, the applicant challenged a decision of the UN Administration not to consider him for a post of

---

[91] *UN Charter*, Article 101(3).

[92] *UN Staff Regulations of 2009*, Regulation 4.2.

[93] Note that as far as the *conditions of service* are concerned, the requirement of the broadest possible geographical basis does not apply. This follows from the wording of Article 101(3) of the *UN Charter* itself as well as Regulations 4.2 and 1.1(d) of the *UN Staff Regulations*. The last mentioned provision reads as follows: 'The Secretary-General shall seek to ensure that the paramount consideration in the determination of the conditions of service shall be the necessity of securing staff of the highest standards of efficiency, competence and integrity'. The geographical factor is not mentioned in this provision. - Ibid., Regulation 1.1(d).

[94] Langrod, *The International Civil Service, Its Origins, Its Nature, Its Evolution*, p. 164.

[95] *Estabial v. Secretary-General of the United Nations, UNAT Judgment No. 310 [1983]*, available at http://untreaty.un.org/UNAT/UNAT_Judgements/Judgements_E/UNAT_00310_E.pdf, last visited on 30.12.2010.

Director of the Division of Recruitment, arguing that the post was in fact in advance reserved for nationals of French-speaking African countries. Having examined relevant documentary evidence, the UNAT agreed that, indeed, the alleged *a priori* limitation of the pool of candidates to be considered for the vacant post had been in place. Subsequently, the UNAT ruled that such limitation was in violation of *UN Staff Regulations*, which require that the paramount consideration in staff recruitment be given to the necessity of ensuring that candidates with the most superior merits are hired. The UNAT emphasized that it attached great importance to the requirements of Article 101(3), last sentence, of the *UN Charter* as well as Regulation 4.2 of the *UN Staff Regulations* on the importance of broad geographical basis for staff recruitment. It held, however, that:

> *It was not for the Secretary-General to alter [the] conditions laid down by the Charter and the Staff Regulations [with respect to the necessity of ensuring the highest standards of efficiency, competence and integrity in staff appointment, transfer and promotion] by establishing as a "paramount" condition the search, however legitimate, for "as wide a geographical basis as possible", thereby eliminating the paramount condition set by the Charter in the interests of the service.*[96]

The result of the Secretary-General's decision to limit the pool of candidates to be considered for the vacancy was that the applicant was denied any chance of success, and so the decision was declared unlawful due to error in law. The error consisted of the Administration 'binding and restricting itself by legally erroneous conditions' that caused an automatic elimination of the applicant from consideration for the vacant post, without having any regard to his merits.[97]

Similarly, in *Araim* the UNAT ruled that a decision made in advance to give preference in filling a vacant post to nationals of the Soviet Union, although only temporarily, was unfair to persons of other nationalities and was in breach with jurisprudence. The UNAT referred hereby to its judgment in *Estabial.* Such decision constituted a denial of consideration for a post and therefore entailed responsibility of the UN Administration.[98]

Thus, in theory, the relationship between the principle of geographical distribution and the principle of merit is clear – merit prevails over geographical distribution. However, the practical application thereof has too often led to 'complex, if not impossible situations'.[99] The reasons for it were the political sensitivity of the issue and the lack of any specific guidelines as to how the hierarchy between two principles should be determined in practice – neither the *UN Charter* nor the *UN Staff*

---

[96] Ibid., para. XIV.

[97] Ibid., paras. XII-XVII. As a consequence, the UN Administration was required to pay damages to the applicant for injury he had sustained. The damages amounted to the applicant's two months net base salary. – para. XXII.

[98] *Araim v. Secretary-General of the United Nations, Judgment No. 657 [1994]*, available at http://untreaty.un.org/UNAT/UNAT_Judgements/Judgements_E/UNAT_00657_E.pdf, last visited on 30.12.2010, paras. V-VIII.

[99] Langrod, *The International Civil Service, Its Origins, Its Nature, Its Evolution*, p. 185.

Regulations provide any help in this respect.[100] The UN Preparatory Commission admitted the problem already in 1945 when it stated:

> *How best to ensure the fulfillment of these two principles ... has been one of the major preoccupations of the Preparatory Commission.*[101]

Unfortunately, the Commission left this self-posed question unanswered. It did believe, though, that the two principles could be reconciled.[102] Also the General Assembly has repeatedly reaffirmed the compatibility of the principle of geographical distribution with the principle of merit.[103] Similarly, other relevant UN bodies, including UN Secretaries-General, have emphasized that no conflict exists between these principles and that the merit principle has to be given priority.[104] Yet, experience shows that simultaneous practical application of these principles has been difficult. Many scholars have argued that 'geographical considerations often run counter to a proper application of the merit'.[105] Due to considerable political pres-

---

[100] According to Meron, the precise relationship between the principle of merit and the principle of geographical distribution was one of those issues that did not receive much attention by the United Nations Founding Fathers. In Meron's view, the Charter negotiators had no precise idea about this relationship – not beyond the establishment of the paramountcy of the principle of merit. They also did not define the term 'geographical distribution'. Meron states that this term most probably meant simply the widest possible representation of nationalities and not a broad cultural or regional basis, as advanced by various interest parties later, nor weighted representation based on the assessment of the budget and population. According to Meron, the meaning of the term 'geographical basis' used in Article 101(3) of the *UN Charter* has to be distinguished from the meaning of 'equitable geographical distribution' under Article 23 of the *UN Charter*, which deals with the elections of non-permanent Members of the Security Council. Meron also points out that it was the Preparatory Commission which used the term 'equitable geographical distribution', originating in Article 23 of the *UN Charter*, to the UN staff, thereby significantly rephrasing the wording of Article 101(3), second sentence, of the *UN Charter*. - Meron, *Status and Independence of the International Civil Servant*, p. 299 and Meron, *Staff of the United nations Secretariat: Problems and Directions*, p. 662. See also Meron, *The United Nations Secretariat*, pp. 6-7 and 9.

[101] *Report of the UN Preparatory Commission*, Chapter VIII, Section II, Part A, para. 7.

[102] Ibid., Chapter VIII, Section II, Part A, para. 7. The Preparatory Commission stressed, in this context, positive experiences from the past, clearly referring to the League of Nations. – Ibid.

[103] The very first resolution dealing with the issue of geographical distribution of posts – *General Assembly Resolution 153(II)*, Preamble. See also, for example, *General Assembly Resolution 1852 (XVII)*, Preamble; *General Assembly Resolution 2359 (XXII)*, Preamble; *General Assembly Resolution 31/26*, Preamble; *General Assembly Resolution 37/235*, *A/RES/37/235*, 21.12.1982, available in the Official Document System of the United Nations, available at http://documents.un.org/, last visited on 30.12.2010, Preamble. The last mentioned resolution is also the last one to have explicitly made such a statement.

[104] See, for example, *Report of the International Civil Service Advisory Board on Recruitment Methods and Standards for United and the Specialized Agencies* of 1950, UN document COORD/CIVIL SERVICE/2/Rev.1, especially paras. 8-10, as cited in Reymond and Mailick, *International Personnel Policies and Practices*, p. 42 and in Langrod, *The International Civil Service, Its Origins, Its Nature, Its Evolution*, pp. 188-189; Report of the Secretary-General Dag Hammarskjöld for 1960-1961 to the General Assembly, *General Assembly, Official Records*, 16th session (1961), Supplement No. 1A, p. 6, as cited in Reymond and Mailick, *International Personnel Policies and Practices*, p. 42.

[105] Plantey, *The International Civil Service, Law and Management*, p. 87. See also Meron, *The United Nations Secretariat*, : '[D]espite the ritualistic reaffirmation, from time to time, of the principle of merit, that principle which according to the Charter was to be paramount has been relegated to a secondary position.' – p. 25.

sures, the Secretaries-General have often been forced to give more than just secondary consideration to the geography element. The pressure has come from two sources – individual Member States as well as the General Assembly itself.

Clearly, any direct involvement of individual Member States in the recruitment process is contrary to Articles 100 and 101 of the *UN Charter*. Especially in the past, however, such involvement was sometimes inevitable, given the absence of alternative methods for scouting suitable candidates among the nationals of certain countries outside the governmental channels.[106] In addition, individual Member States have often tried to influence the Secretary-General in his personnel decisions for the sake of securing their own political interests:

> *Under the guise of 'improving the geographical distribution' of the staff, some [governments] not only recommend or nominate candidates for employment, but they also insist on their placement in a specific post, at a specific grade. Some intervene more or less openly to facilitate contract extension and promotions. Inversely, some demand that the executive head terminate the contract of their citizens considered disloyal or unrepresentative.*[107]

Also the General Assembly has repeatedly put the Secretary-General under pressure and requested him to ensure recruitment of sufficient number of nationals from countries inadequately represented in the UN Secretariat, disregarding the practical limitations. The very same resolutions that have officially proclaimed that merit should be the primary consideration in the recruitment process have called upon the Secretary-General to give preference to nationals from inadequately represented Member States when filling a vacant post.[108] As explained in more detail below, in the past, the General Assembly even approved, and never formally revoked, the so-called replacement principle, which had to ensure that the sufficient number of nationals from socialistic countries were in certain posts, though it was clear that this replacement principle was contrary to the superiority of the principle of merit over the principle of geographical distribution enshrined in Article 101(3) of the *UN Charter*.[109] In the meantime, the political reality in many UN Member States has changed but there still – or again – seem to be two camps of Member States in the UN, each having different views on the relationship between the principle of geographical distribution and the principle of merit. The Group of 77 ('G-77'), which is an informal grouping of some developing countries, and China request a *de facto*

[106] Langrod states that the consequence of such practice was that the influence of some governments in staff recruitment was decisive in practice since they alone had a grip, for example, on the place and time of vacancy announcements. In addition, they could specify which candidates were acceptable and which ones were not. - Langrod, *The International Civil Service, Its Origins, Its Nature, Its Evolution*, p. 187.

[107] Beigbeder, *Threats to the International Civil Service*, p. 26. See also Langrod, *The International Civil Service, Its Origins, Its Nature, Its Evolution*, p. 187 and Lemoine, *The International Civil Servant: An Endangered Species*, p. 249.

[108] See, for example, *General Assembly Resolution 53/221*, Section IX, para. 10. For the extensive analysis of the role of the General Assembly and its resolutions in this regard, see Meron, *Charter Powers of the United Nation's Secretary-General with regard to the Secretariat and the Role of General Assembly Resolutions*.

[109] See above, section 2.3.2.

equality of the two principles, while mostly Western countries, since the early 1990s joined by Russia, put strong emphasis on merit.[110]

Individual UN Secretaries-General have struggled through the decades in their attempts to 'square the circle', employing various methods to help reach adequate distribution of posts among all Member States. Upon persistent requests from the General Assembly, the Secretaries-General have developed a number of specific mechanisms in this respect. They are described in the following sections, which also assess their compatibility with Article 101(3) of the *UN Charter* and Regulation 4.2 of the *UN Staff Regulations*. To recall, the UNAT has interpreted the two provisions in *Estabial* and *Araim* as providing all eligible persons wishing to apply for a vacant post with the right to be fully and fairly considered. Such persons may not be excluded from consideration purely on the basis of their nationality. On the other hand, nationals from one or more specific countries, be they unrepresented or underrepresented, may enjoy preference in the selection process only when their qualifications are equal to those of other best candidates. It is clear that this interpretation restricts the possibilities available in this respect to the Secretary-General and makes it difficult for him to remedy inadequate representation status of relevant countries promptly. In the end, '[the] availability [of talented and competent persons] for international service does not correspond to the arithmetics (*sic*) of quotas'.[111] Nonetheless, as stated by the UNAT in *Estabial*, Article 101(3) of the *UN Charter* and Regulation 42 of the *UN Staff Regulations* need to be respected.[112] In any other case, independence and impartiality of the UN staff could be in danger - individuals would be more tempted to use the formal links with their home countries with a consequence of acquiring a difficult relationship of gratitude towards them. It cannot be doubted that the higher the importance of candidates' nationality in the staff selection process, the greater the risk of such situation occurring.

The below analysis of specific mechanisms developed by the UN Secretariat with the aim of improving geographical representation of inadequately represented Member States is followed by discussion of the so-called national preserves. As these preserves are not a mechanism used in the UN recruitment process, they are addressed separately.

2.3.1. Specific mechanisms

As indicated above, while the system of desirable ranges applies only to posts made subject to it, Article 101(3) of the *UN Charter* does not make any distinction between different categories of staff. Therefore, the recruitment of *all* UN staff is to

[110] See, for example, discussions in the Fifth Committee, *Official Records, Summary Record of the 14 meeting of 1 November 2006, A/C.5/61/SR.14*, 01.11.2006, available in the Official Document System of the United Nations, available at http://documents.un.org/, last visited on 30.12.2010.

[111] Lemoine, *The International Civil Servant: An Endangered Species*, p. 247. See also Langrod, *The International Civil Service, Its Origins, Its Nature, Its Evolution*, p. 187.

[112] See above in this section.

be conducted on as broad a geographical basis as possible.[113] Despite this, there are at present no binding rules or instructions specifying in what manner the broadest possible geographical basis in recruitment of staff *not* subject to the geographical distribution should be realized. On the other hand, a number of rules and practices have been developed in order to achieve full compliance with the system of desirable ranges. As repeatedly stressed by the General Assembly, this system is 'the mechanism for recruitment of staff to posts subject to geographical distribution, in accordance with Article 101, paragraph 3, of the Charter'.[114] Posts subject to geographical distribution are thus those that have received most attention from Member States, and arguably also from the Secretariat, certainly as far as geographical representation is concerned.[115]

Initially, the efforts of the UN Secretaries-General to improve geographical representation of inadequately represented Member States were made mostly by relying on active cooperation with these Member States and by taking candidates' nationality into consideration during the staff selection process. With regard to the cooperation with the Member States, the Secretaries-General have been circulating among them all vacancy announcements. Moreover, they have been using facilities of inadequately represented countries to find potential candidates, such as information and contacts with states and possibly other institutions, as well as visiting

[113] See also *Mendez v. Secretary-General of the United Nations, UNAT Judgment No. 268 [1981]*, available at http://untreaty.un.org/UNAT/UNAT_Judgements/Judgements_E/UNAT_00268_E.pdf, last visited on 30.12.2010, paras. VII-VIII.

[114] *General Assembly Resolution 63/250*, Section IX, para. 16.

[115] It should be noted that especially in more recent years, there have been increased efforts to ensure broad geographical representation also among staff not subject to the system of desirable ranges. For example, in 2007, the Secretary-General reported that despite the fact that the system of desirable ranges did not apply to the peacekeeping and special political mission staff, the Department of Peacekeeping Operations did ensure that the issue of geographical representation was taken into account in the recruitment of such staff. He also pointed out that efforts were made to comply with the requests of the General Assembly with regard to the reflection of the contribution of troop-contributing countries in the composition of peacekeeping staff. - *Human Resources Management Reform: Recruitment and Staffing, Report of the Secretary-General, A/61/822*, 27.03.2007, available in the Official Document System of the United Nations, available at http://documents.un.org/, last visited on 30.12.2010, para. 66. With regard to the latter, see also *General Assembly Resolution 63/250*, Section IX, para. 13. Furthermore, already for some time, attention has been paid to the geographical imbalance among non-staff performing work for the UN Secretariat, in particular among consultants hired to provide outside expertise to the Secretariat in various areas. – See in particular *The Use of Consultants in the United Nations, Report of the Joint Inspection Unit, JIU/REP/2000/2*, 2000, available in the Official Document System of the United Nations, available at http://documents.un.org/, last visited on 30.12.2010, Section IV. According to Section 4.3 of the administrative instruction regulating the engagement of consultants, every effort is to be made during selection to ensure their widest possible geographical representation. - *Administrative Instruction, Consultants and Individual Contractors, consolidated text*. In practice, however, although consultants come from the majority of the Member States, the fact is that a large number of them are drawn from a small number of countries, in particular from Canada, France, the UK and the US. – For example, *Consultants and Individual Contractors, Report of the Secretary-General, A/63/310/Add.3*, 21.08.2008, available in the Official Document System of the United Nations, available at http://documents.un.org/, last visited on 30.12.2010, paras. 13 and 14. The UN Member States have been concerned about this imbalance and repeatedly require information on the measures taken for addressing it. – Most recently in *General Assembly Resolution 63/250*, Section XI, para. 2 and *General Assembly Resolution 65/247*, para. 70.

these countries in order to discuss recruitment possibilities.[116] Over the last two decades, a number of additional practices and measures have been developed, specifically aimed at increasing the chances of nationals from inadequately represented Member States to be recruited. An overview of these practices, implemented as well as planned, was presented by the Secretary-General in his report *Improvement of Equitable Geographical Representation in the United Nations Secretariat*, presented to the General Assembly, upon its request, in 2004.[117] The list of specific measures provided by the Secretary-General in his report included: recruitment through national competitive examinations; human resources action planning; requirements of the staff selection system; partnership with Member States; 'fast-track' recruitment procedure; and establishment of focal points.[118] In subsequent years, this list has been supplemented by two additional measures: special functions of the electronic staffing system; and establishment of the Outreach Unit of the Office of Human Resources Management of the UN Secretariat ('OHRM').[119] Some of these measures are specifically related to the issue of geographical distribution, others regulate a broader range of subject matters falling under human resources management, including the issue of geographical distribution. The following sections focus solely on the elements relevant to this issue.

2.3.1.1. National Competitive Recruitment Examinations

National Competitive Recruitment Examinations ('NCRE') are held annually in individual UN Member States (hence the 'national' tag) in order to recruit staff at the junior Professional level (P-1 and P-2) and occasionally also the middle Professional level (P-3). The examination is held in a number of disciplines, such as administration, economics, and information technology, depending on the expected needs of the Secretariat in a particular year. It consists of a written and an oral exam and in the case of P-3 posts also of a case presentation. Successful candidates are put on

---

[116] For example, Langrod, *The International Civil Service, Its Origins, Its Nature, Its Evolution*, p. 178 and 251.

[117] *Improvement of Equitable Geographical Representation in the United Nations Secretariat, Report of the Secretary-General*, *A/59/264*, 13.04.2004, available in the Official Document System of the United Nations, available at http://documents.un.org/, last visited on 30.12.2010.

[118] Ibid., Sections III-IV.

[119] *Investing in People, Report of the Secretary-General, A/61/255*, Section 3, para. 46; and *Human Resources Management Reform, Report of the Secretary-General, A/63/282*, 14.08.2008, available in the Official Document System of the United Nations, available at http://documents.un.org/, last visited on 30.12.2010, Section IV, Part B.3(a), para. 59 and part B.7, paras. 88-91. For specific reports on the measures aimed at the improvement of geographical representation of the staff serving in the Office of High Commissioner of Human Rights, see recently *Measures to Improve the Balance in the Geographical Distribution of the Staff in the Office of the United Nations High Commissioner for Human Rights, Report of the Secretary-General, A/62/823*, 28.03.2007, available in the Official Document System of the United Nations, available at http://documents.un.org/, last visited on 30.12.2010 and *Measures to Improve the Balance in the Geographical Distribution of the Staff in the Office of the United Nations High Commissioner for Human Rights, Report of the Secretary-General, A/63/204*, 31.07.2008, available in the Official Document System of the United Nations, available at http://documents.un.org/, last visited on 30.12.2010.

a reserve list of qualified candidates. They can subsequently be recruited to vacant posts at the appropriate level.[120]

The Secretary-General considers the NCRE to be the 'main vehicle for improving the representation of Member States'.[121] Member States too attach great importance to this examination and its possible positive impact on the recruitment of suitable candidates from inadequately represented countries.[122] There are two main reasons for this high appreciation of the NCRE: first, the fact that the competitive examinations are, in principle, the exclusive entry point to junior Professional non-language posts at the UN Secretariat; and second, the fact that the NCRE are only opened to nationals of those Member States that are inadequately represented among the Secretariat staff or are in danger of becoming so.

Regarding the first issue, Rule 4.16(b)(i) of the *UN Staff Rules* stipulates that appointments to P-1 and P-2 posts subject to the system of desirable ranges or special language requirements are to be made exclusively through a competitive examination.[123] For posts subject to the system of desirable ranges, this required competitive examination is the NCRE. No other competitions are organized for these posts at the junior or even higher levels.[124] The only exception is available to those who

---

[120] *Administrative Instruction, Conditions under which Individuals May Take National Competitive Recruitment Examinations, ST/AI/2010/8*, 01.06.2010, available in the Human Resources Handbook of the United Nations, available at http://www.un.org/hr_handbook/English/, last visited on 30.12.2010, especially Sections 1, 6 and 9. See also, for example, *2010 National Competitive Recruitment Examinations (P-2)*, 2010, available at http://www.un.org/Depts/OHRM/examin/2010e.pdf, last visited on 30.12.2010, paras. 1, 2,7 and 16. For more details on the NCRE as a recruitment tool, see below, chapter 3, section 2.2.1.2.

[121] *Investing in People, Report of the Secretary-General, A/61/255*, p. 12, para. 46.

[122] The NCRE is discussed at each meeting of the Fifth Committee dealing with human resources management and gains attention in every resolution passed by the General Assembly on staff matters. - For example, *Official Records, Summary Record of the 14 meeting of 1 November 2006*; and *General Assembly Resolution 53/221, A/RES/53/221*, 03.04.1997, available in the Official Document System of the United Nations, available at http://documents.un.org/, last visited on 30.12.2010, para. 24; *General Assembly Resolution 55/258*, para. 10 et seq.; and *General Assembly Resolution 61/244*, Section III.

[123] *UN Staff Rules*, Rule 4.16(b)(i). Note that until the large amendment of the *UN Staff Rules* that took place in 2009, this requirement applied to all P-1 and P-2 posts, not only those subject to the system of desirable ranges. - *Staff Rules of the United Nations, 100 Series, consolidated text, ST/SGB/2002/1*, 01.01.2002, as last amended by ST/SGB/2008/1, available in the Human Resources Handbook of the United Nations, available at http://www.un.org/hr_handbook/English/, last visited on 30.12.2010, Rule 104.15(b)(i). The condition of passing competitive examination under Rule 4.16(v)(i) of the *UN Staff Rules* also applies to posts requiring special language skills, referred to as language posts. A separate set of rules has been established for these examinations, namely *Administrative Instruction, Competitive Examinations for Recruitment and Placement in Posts Requiring Specific Language Skills in the Professional Category, ST/AI/1998/7*, 23.03.1998, available in the Human Resources Handbook of the United Nations, available at http://www.un.org/hr_handbook/English/, last visited on 30.12.2010. Both UN staff members, though only those at the P-3 level and below, and external candidates may participate in the examination for the language posts. - *Administrative Instruction, Competitive Examinations for Recruitment and Placement in Posts Requiring Specific Language Skills in the Professional Category*, Section 2.

[124] Recruitment at higher levels occurs according to a separate set of rules. A slight exception are P-3 posts, for which competitions should 'normally' be organized in accordance with the second sentence of the same Rule 4.16(b)(i) of the *UN Staff Rules*. However, this rule is not as strict as the rule for P-1 and P-2 posts subject to geographical distribution or special language requirements which must be filled

already are UN staff members but serve in other than Professional category. They can enter the Professional category via a competitive examination organized specifically for their category under a separate administrative instruction.[125] Of course, staff members may also participate in the NCRE, alongside external candidates, though under slightly modified conditions.[126]

Consequently, external candidates, i.e. those not yet employed at the UN Secretariat but wishing to join it at the junior Professional level in posts subject to geographical distribution, cannot do so in any way other than through passing the NCRE. However, the NCRE is opened, as pointed out above, only to persons who possess the nationality of an inadequately represented country or a country that is about to become so.[127] Hence, in 2010, for example, the NCRE was opened to nationals of 35 out of the total of 192 UN Member States.

'exclusively' via competitive examination. From P-4 level upwards, appointments occur on the basis of the *UN Staff Selection System*, which does not provide for a competitive examination. Appointments at those levels are to be made predominantly via promotions, transfers or reassignments of staff. External candidates, i.e. candidates who are not UN staff members, may be considered only if no internal candidate is suitable for the post at issue. No competitive examination for such external candidate is held, however. For more details on the UN recruitment procedures, see below, chapter 3, section 2.

[125] *Administrative Instruction, Competitive Examination for Recruitment to the Professional Category of Staff Members from Other Categories ST/AI/2010/7*, 01.06.2010, available in the Human Resources Handbook of the United Nations, available at http://www.un.org/hr_handbook/English/, last visited on 30.12.2010.

[126] *Administrative Instruction on NCRE*, Section 3.3.

[127] Website of the OHRM, http://www.un.org/Depts/OHRM/examin/ncrepage.htm, last visited on 20 February 2010 and, for example, *2009 National Competitive Recruitment Examination (P-1/P-2)*, 2008, available at http://www.un.org/Depts/OHRM/examin/2009e.doc, last visited on 30.12.2010, para. 4. See also *Review of the National Competitive Recruitment Examination as a Recruitment Tool, Report of the Joint Inspection Unit, JIU/REP/2007/9*, 2007, available in the Official Document System of the United Nations, available at http://documents.un.org/, last visited on 30.12.2010, para. 3.

The statistics for the last ten years period look as follows:

Table 4: Participation of UN Member States in the NCRE (2000-2010)

Year	Number of countries requested to participate in the NCRE	Number of countries that participated in the NCRE*
2000	27	23
2001	46	39
2002	41	33
2003	64	53
2004	71	62
2005	69	58
2006	60	46
2007	not available	38
2008	not available	55
2009	not available	44
2010	35	not available yet

** The NCRE is organized by the OHRM in close cooperation with the relevant Member States. It is up to these Member States to decide whether they will participate in the NCRE in the particular year.*

Sources: Calculated on the basis of data provided in the *Report of the Joint Inspection Unit on Review of the National Competitive Recruitment Examination as a Recruitment Tool* (for the period of 2000-2006); *Report of the Secretary-General on the Composition of the Secretariat* of 2007, 2008 and 2009; and on the internet site of the OHRM (for the 2010 NCRE).[128]

These data show that the pool of candidates permitted to participate in the NCRE in a given year is considerably restricted. Only candidates possessing the nationality of a relatively small number of the Member States may take part. In addition, in order to be eligible for the participation in the NCRE, candidates may not be older than 32 years.[129] This means that if the NCRE is not organized in a particular country

[128] *Review of the National Competitive Recruitment Examination as a Recruitment Tool, Report of the Joint Inspection Unit, JIU/REP/2007/9*, Annex II; *Composition of the Secretariat, Report of the Secretary-General, A/62/315*, 31.08.2007, available in the Official Document System of the United Nations, available at http://documents.un.org/, last visited on 30.12.2010, para. 74; *Composition of the Secretariat, Report of the Secretary-General, A/63/310*, 29.09.2008, available in the Official Document System of the United Nations, available at http://documents.un.org/, last visited on 30.12.2010, para. 76; *Composition of the Secretariat, Report of the Secretary-General, A/64/352*, para. 75; and the internet sire of the OHRM, available at http://www.un.org/Depts/OHRM/examin/ncrepage.htm, last visited on 28.09.2010.

[129] *Administrative Instruction on NCRE*, Section 3.1(b). Note that in 2010 the Secretary-General even proposed lowering the age up to which candidates may take the NCRE in the future to 28 years. - *Human Resources Management Reform: Young Professionals Programme, Report of the Secretary-General, A/65/305/Add.4*, 02.09.2010, available in the Official Document System of the United Nations,

for several years because that country's representation status is satisfactory, all potential candidates from that country are permanently barred from applying. These two limitations, combined with the fact that the NCRE is the only way of acquiring a post at junior Professional level which is subject to geographical distribution, i.e. any Professional non-language post of at least one year's duration covered by the regular UN budget, lead to the conclusion that a potentially large number of candidates are excluded from being considered for such vacant posts and that this exclusion is based purely on their nationality.

Such a situation is clearly in contradiction with Article 101(3) of the *UN Charter* and Regulation 4.2 of the *UN Staff Regulations* as well as relevant jurisprudence. Nationals of Member States which are within or above their desirable range are denied every opportunity to apply and, consequently, to be considered for vacant posts, disregarding their merits. While it is not disputed that the NCRE are a useful tool contributing to the improvement of the geographical distribution of posts to the benefit of inadequately represented countries, it cannot be denied that the potentially permanent exclusion of some candidates from participation in this examination is not in accordance with the applicable law.[130] As stated by the International Civil Service Commission already in 1982, the denial of access to the UN civil service to certain candidates frustrates both the *UN Charter* and the *UN Staff Regulations*.[131] A warning in this respect was sounded also by the Group of High Intergovernmental Experts, also referred to as G18, established by the General Assembly in 1986 in order to review the efficiency of the administrative and financial functioning of the UN Secretariat.[132] In its report, referred to as the '*G18 Report*', the G18 emphasized the importance of organizing national competitive examinations without discrimination against any Member States so that the principles of Article 101(3) of the *UN Charter* would be fully respected.[133] However, more than a decade later, the NCRE are still organized only for nationals of (potentially) inadequately represented Member States, with the door to the most important junior Professional posts remaining

available at http://documents.un.org/, last visited on 30.12.2010, para. 18. If accepted, this would have further restricted the pool of potential candidates. However, upon recommendation of the General Assembly's Advisory Committee on Administrative and Budgetary Questions, the General Assembly decided that, at least for the time being, the age limit would remain 32 years. –*Human Resources Management, Report of the Advisory Committee on Administrative and Budgetary Questions, A/65/537*, para. 75 and *General Assembly Resolution 65/247*, para. 39.

130 For the analysis of the NCRE in this respect, see *Review of the National Competitive Recruitment Examination as a Recruitment Tool, Report of the Joint Inspection Unit, JIU/REP/2007/9*, paras. 19-21 and Table 3. See also *Human Resources Management Reform, Report of the Secretary-General, A/63/282*, paras. 96-97.

131 Bulkeley, *Depoliticizing United Nations Recruitment: Establishing a Genuinly International Civil Service*, p. 763, referring to a study of the International Civil Service Commission on some personnel matters conducted upon request from the General Assembly.

132 *Report of the Group of High Intergovernmental Experts to Review the Efficiency of the Administrative and Financial Functioning of the United Nations, A/41/49*, available in the Official Document System of the United Nations, available at http://documents.un.org/, last visited on 30.12.2010.

133 Ibid., para. 43(1).

closed to candidates from the rest of the countries.[134] No change is envisaged in this respect in the future.[135]

Another problem is the direct involvement of Member States in the NCRE process. Although most of the work is done by the OHRM, the Secretary-General recently admitted that certain countries do their own screening of candidates participating in the NCRE.[136] This is clearly contrary to the *UN Charter* and the *UN Staff Regulations*, which prohibit Member States' involvement in staff matters. It also encroaches on the exclusive authority of the UN Secretary-General as chief administrative officer. It is, therefore, regrettable that the Secretary-General intends to maintain this practice for another few years. Under his new Young Professionals Programme, that includes recruitment of young talent for UN service through the NCRE, he envisages that candidates' screening by countries will only be abandoned in 2013 when phase II of this programme commences.[137] This is rather difficult to understand, especially as already since the start of the programme's first phase in 2011, screening of NCRE candidates should be automated to a large extent by employing a new information technology tool Inspira, explained in more detail below.[138] The automated screening should be followed by manual screening to review the best candidates identified by Inspira.[139] Since Inspira should be used in the NCRE process from 2011, it is rather surprising, and unfortunate, that Member States are to be involved in the screening process for another couple of years.

2.3.1.2. Human resources action plans

Human resources action planning was introduced in the UN Secretariat in 1999.[140] It involves specific biennial plans developed for each department or office of the

---

[134] The phrase 'door closing' comes from Bulkeley, *Depoliticizing United Nations Recruitment: Establishing a Genuinly International Civil Service*, p. 767 and 772.

[135] In 2010, the UN Secretary-General presented a new 'Young Professionals Programme' which includes, *inter alia*, the issues related to the NCRE. In its respect the Secretary-General retained the scope of countries to be included in the NCRE in the future. - *Human Resources Management Reform: Young Professionals Programme, Report of the Secretary-General, A/65/305/Add.4*, para. 17 and Table 1, point 2, on p. 8.

[136] Ibid., Table 1, point 3, on p. 8.

[137] Ibid., Table 1, point 3, on p. 8. The Young Professionals Programme is to integrate the outreach, recruitment, placement, career development and mobility of entry-level staff into one centrally managed process. It was proposed, and approved by the General Assembly, in 2010. Its aim is to rejuvenate the UN Secretariat and to develop 'a pool of dynamic, adaptable and diverse young professionals to their full potential and from which the Organization could draw to fill middle and senior management functions in the medium and long term'. - Ibid., para. 13. See also para. 12 and *General Assembly Resolution 65/247*, para. 35.

[138] See below, section 2.3.1.7.

[139] *Human Resources Management Reform: Young Professionals Programme, Report of the Secretary-General, A/65/305/Add.4*, Table 1, point 3, on p. 8 and paras. 27-29.

[140] The planning was introduced pursuant to the *General Assembly Resolution 53/221*, see in particular Section III, para. 2. Note that in 2007, pilot human resources action plans were developed and introduced in six peacekeeping operations with the idea of broadening this initiative to all peacekeeping operations after the evaluation of this pilot project. - *Human Resources Management Reform, Report of the Secretary-General, A/63/282*, para. 26.

UN Secretariat by the head of that department or office together with the OHRM. The purpose of the plan is to assist the department or office in 'setting goals and assessing results' in a number of key human resources management areas, such as vacancy management, female representation, mobility, performance appraisal and also geographical distribution. Each departmental plan contains specific targets and awareness indicators as well as corresponding performance indicators for each of the included areas. The achievements of each department and office are assessed twice a year and at the end of the two year cycle. The assessments are made by the OHRM and the relevant department and office and reviewed by a body established for this purpose, the Management Performance Board.[141]

Examples of targets and indicators used in the human resources action plans can be found in the report of the Secretary-General on the first year of the activities of the Management Performance Board submitted in 2006 upon a request of the General Assembly.[142] In the area of geographical distribution, two targets were set for the whole UN Secretariat: first, an increase in the number of recruitments of candidates from unrepresented and underrepresented Member States on posts subject to geographical distribution; and second, a reduction, as much as possible, in the number from overrepresented Member States. Both targets were given performance indicators. Thus, the target on the increase in the number of recruitments of candidates from unrepresented and underrepresented Member States were given two performance indicators, namely the number of geographical recruitments from these Member States and the percentage of such recruitments compared to all geographical recruitments during the relevant cycle. Similarly, the target on the reduction from overrepresented countries got two performance indicators, namely the

[141] The Management Performance Board was established by the Secretary-General in 2005. - *Secretary-General's Bulletin, Management Performance Board, ST/SGB/2005/13*, 05.05.2005, available in the Human Resources Handbook of the United Nations, available at http://www.un.org/hr_handbook/English/, last visited on 30.12.2010. See also *Measures to Strengthen Accountability at the United Nations, Report of the Secretary-General, A/60/312*, 30.08.2005, available in the Official Document System of the United Nations, available at http://documents.un.org/, last visited on 30.12.2010, especially Section II, Part A. By this action the Secretary-General reacted to the criticism from the General Assembly expressed during the first years of the human resources action planning and concerning the lack of accountability of departmental managers for the enforcement of specific targets set up in their plans. - See, for example, *General Assembly Resolution 57/305*, Section II, para. 33; *General Assembly Resolution 59/266, A/RES/59/266*, 22.12.2004, available in the Official Document System of the United Nations, available at http://documents.un.org/, last visited on 30.12.2010, Section I, para. 10. The tasks of the Board thus are, *inter alia*, to monitor and analyze how senior managers exercise their authority and whether they achieve the objectives included in their action plans. It may also recommend appropriate corrective measures. - *Secretary-General's Bulletin, Management Performance Board, ST/SGB/2010/4*, 15.04.2010, available in the Human Resources Handbook of the United Nations, available at http://www.un.org/hr_handbook/English/, last visited on 30.12.2010, Section 1. Note that the Secretary-General's Bulletin on the Management Performance Board adopted in 2010 replaced the original bulletin of 2005.

[142] *Management Performance Board, Report of the Secretary-General, A/61/319*, 09.09.2006, available in the Official Document System of the United Nations, available at http://documents.un.org/, last visited on 30.12.2010, Annex I. This report provided data for the fourth cycle of human resources action planning which took place in 2005-2006.

number of recruitments from overrepresented countries and the percentage of such recruitments compared to all geographical recruitments in the relevant cycle.[143]

In addition to the targets, each area of the human resources action plans also contained certain awareness indicators. In the area of geographical distribution, the awareness indicator for the relevant cycle was to monitor the share of developed countries, developing countries and countries with economies in transition in the geographical composition of the Secretariat in the Professional and higher categories. This was to be done by targeting the share of these groups of countries in the staff representation to their respective aggregated share in the sum of their desirable ranges. The corresponding performance indicators to these awareness indicators were the number and percentage of staff from developed, developing countries and countries with economies in transition against total number of geographical posts at the Professional and higher levels and the number of staff at these levels from each group of countries by targeting their share in the staff representation to their respective aggregated share in the sum of their desirable ranges. The awareness indicator for departments and offices was simply 'awareness'.[144]

This brief overview demonstrates that a number of objectives of the human resources management at the UN Secretariat have been quantified so that their achievement would be more stimulated and better monitored. However, it is questionable whether specific targets and performance as well as awareness indicators in the area of geographical distribution have any significant value added compared to the past. The objective of improving the geographical representation of inadequately represented countries had been a part of the human resources management objectives long before the action planning was introduced. Moreover, statistics on the achievements in this area have been provided annually in the Secretary-General's reports on the composition of the UN Secretariat and thus known also to individual departments and offices. It is thus difficult to see how these additional figures and formulas would lead to any substantive improvements. The mere fact that, for example, a specific percentage has been identified for the reduction of the inadequately represented Member States does not seem to be a tool capable of leading to the achievement of that percentage. Such targets have been set in the past as well and did not seem to result in any significant breakthrough.[145] The Secretary-General himself admitted problems in his report of 2006, stating that many departments had had 'real problems in achieving... geographic targets'.[146] Hence, it does not appear that the human resources action planning itself has significantly contributed

---

[143] Ibid., Annex I, p. 12. Note that targets set out for the whole UN Secretariat were then broken down to specific accountability targets for individual departments and offices. Accordingly, two departmental targets were set: a quarter of all geographical recruitments in the planning cycle were to be from unrepresented and underrepresented Member States (with a tolerance margin of 20 per cent) and no recruitments were to be made from overrepresented Member States.

[144] Ibid., Annex I, pp. 12 and 13.

[145] For example, *General Assembly Resolution 33/143*, Section II, para. 1. In this resolution, the General Assembly requested the Secretary-General to fill 40 per cent of all vacancies related to posts subject to geographical distribution by appointing nationals from unrepresented or underrepresented Member States.

[146] *Secretary-General's Bulletin, Management Performance Board of 2005*, para. 6.

to the achievement of the objectives of these plans thus far.[147] However, in 2008, the Secretary-General still believed that more visible availability of data would, besides enhancing transparency, empower senior officials in their efforts to achieve targets. To that end, he has also published the departmental human resources action plans on the UN intranet and introduced an online system providing regular updates on the progress of each department and office in the implementation of their action plans.[148] In 2010 the Secretary-General even announced a replacement of the human resources action plans by the human resources management scorecards in 2011, hoping the latter would improve monitoring in achieving agreed targets.[149] Although the Secretary-General did not make any explicit assessment of the success of human resources action plans in achieving specific targets, including geographical ones, concentrating instead on the insufficient monitoring capacity of these plans, it could be argued that the replacement of the human resources action plans by the human resources management scorecards indicates that the plans proved inadequate in achieving set targets.

Arguably, a more helpful tool was introduced in 2005 – senior management compacts. Such compacts used to complement each departmental or office human resources action plan and will remain in use under the system of management scorecards as well. The compacts are annual programme management plans agreed between the relevant Head of Department or Office and the Secretary-General. They are a set of indicators covering programmatic and managerial objectives for which the department head will be held accountable, including in the area of human resources management.[150] Although the indicators used in the senior management compacts are of a similar nature to those in the human resources action plans, the fact that the compacts are to be taken into account during the individual annual performance appraisal of the senior officials may be decisive for their success.

That said, an important question arises in this respect with regard to the compatibility of such strong requirements for personal accountability of senior managers for meeting their targets on geographical distribution with Article 101(3) of the *UN Charter* and the relevant *UN Staff Regulations*. The pressure created upon senior managers by the requirement of reaching specific numerical targets may result in a practice of giving preference to less qualified candidates with the 'right' nationality to the detriment of those with the best merits. This danger is more than just

[147] Similar criticism was expressed by some UN Member States. - See, for example, discussions in the Fifth Committee held on the report of the Secretary-General on the human resources action planning and the first year of the Management Performance Board in 2006 - *Official Records, Summary Record of the 14 meeting of 1 November 2006* This criticism resulted in the adoption of a resolution requesting the Secretary-General to present further proposals for enforcing the implementation of human resources policies and action plan objectives. - *General Assembly Resolution 61/244*, Section XII, para. 6. See also Section X, para. 11.

[148] *Human Resources Management Reform, Report of the Secretary-General, A/63/282*, paras. 27-28.

[149] *Overview of Human Resources Management Reform, Report of the Secretary-General, A/65/305*, paras. 145 et seq.

[150] *Management Performance Board, Report of the Secretary-General, A/61/319*, paras. 9-10 and Annex III. See also *Overview of Human Resources Management Reform, Report of the Secretary-General, A/65/305*, para. 152.

theoretical, considering that the achievement of targets on the number of officials recruited from unrepresented or underrepresented countries is easily measurable, whereas the achievement of the requirement of recruiting the best qualified officials cannot be checked.[151] While the calls for greater accountability of senior managers for their decisions are indeed understandable and should be supported, senior managers should not be forced to take decisions for the wrong reasons and block the recruitment of qualified staff. Threats of removing the delegated recruitment authority from senior managers for 'consistent non-achievement of the targets', explicitly admitted by the Secretary-General, may cross the fine line between motivation and penalization, the latter being arguably on the verge of contravening the requirement of paying only *due regard* to the geographical distribution under Article 101(3) of the *UN Charter* and Regulation 4.2 of the *UN Staff Regulations*.[152]

The General Assembly seems to have realized a possible problem in this area by stressing in its Res. 61/244 of 2006 that measures on meeting accountability targets and indicators of achievement with respect to geographical distribution, contained in human resources action plans and recruitment procedures, including selection decisions, must 'fully correspond' to the requirements of Article 101(3) of the *UN Charter* and to relevant mandates of the General Assembly.[153] On the other hand, the General Assembly simultaneously called for greater accountability of heads of department for the achievement of equitable geographical distribution.[154] In addition, it established specific targets for reducing the number of unrepresented and underrepresented Member States in the Secretariat: 20 per cent reduction by 2008 and 30 per cent reduction by 2010 compared to the 2006 level.[155] The General Assembly also requested the Secretary-General to present further measures for enforcing the implementation of human resources policies and action plan objectives as well as for the use of incentives and sanctions which should become an integral part of the human resources management system.[156] The UN Member States seem thus to attach great importance to the accountability of senior managers for achieving objectives they identified in various resolutions. Despite the formal reaffirmation of the requirements of Article 101(3) of the *UN Charter*, they appear to find these objectives more important than the *Charter* principles. During the 2006 meeting of the Fifth Committee on human resources management issues, a representative from Nigeria, speaking on behalf of the African group, for example, said the Fifth Committee should take 'a fresh look' at the measures to ensure that the managers were held accountable when they failed to meet targets, 'in particular where geographical representation was concerned'.[157] The representative of Algeria

---

[151] Szasz, P. C., *The Role of the U.N. Secretary-General: Some Legal Aspects*, in: New York University Journal of International Law and Politics, Vol. 24, pp. 161-198, pp. 182-183.

[152] On the warning of the Secretary-General with regard to the removal of the delegation authority in recruitment matters, see *Secretary-General's Bulletin, Management Performance Board of 2005*, para. 7.

[153] *General Assembly Resolution 61/244*, Section X, para. 20.

[154] Ibid., Section X, para. 6. See also *General Assembly Resolution 63/250*, Section V.

[155] *General Assembly Resolution 61/244*, Section X, para. 12.

[156] Ibid., Section XII, para. 7.

[157] *Official Records, Summary Record of the 14 meeting of 1 November 2006*, available in the Official

even suggested the establishment within the General Assembly of a mechanism 'to hold the managers accountable and to take whatever measures were necessary if the General Assembly's wishes were not implemented'.[158]

2.3.1.3. Staff selection system

The *UN Staff Selection System* integrates rules on recruitment, placement, mobility and promotion of UN staff. It covers most, though not all, Professional staff, excluding, for example, recruitment of staff to junior Professional posts for which a competitive examination is required.[159] The system was introduced in 2002 as a part of the reform programme of the human resources management, replacing previous separate systems on staff recruitment and staff placement and promotion.[160] In 2006, the system was replaced by a new one established by the administrative instruction ST/AI/2006/3 and amended in January 2010.[161] In April 2010 a revised system was set up by the administrative instruction ST/AI/2010/3, introducing important changes to the system applied previously.[162]

From 2006 till April 2010, the system included a number of important obligations for persons involved in the staff selection process in the area of geographical distribution, which were to ensure that the requirement of equitable geographical distribution of posts was actively taken into account in each selection process. First of all, programme managers must have, after conducting a pre-selection procedure and submitting a proposal for an appointment of a candidate to the Head of Department or Office, ensured - and certified - that they had taken into account the human resources planning objectives and targets, especially with regard to geography and gender.[163] The same duty applied to the actual selection of a candidate by the relevant Head of Department or Office. Moreover, when the Head of Department or Office wished to select an external candidate from an overrepresented country for

Document System of the United Nations, para. 11.

158 Ibid., para. 57.

159 *UN Staff Selection System*, Section 3.2(c). According to the same section, if a competitive examination is organized for P-3 level posts, the application of the *UN Staff Selection System* is excluded, too.

160 *Secretary-General's Bulletin, Introduction of a New Staff Selection System, ST/SGB/2002/5*, 23.4.2002, available in the Human Resources Handbook of the United Nations, available at http://www.un.org/hr_handbook/English/, last visited on 30.12.2010, Preamble and *Administrative Instruction, Staff Selection System, ST/AI/2002/4*, 23.04.2002, available in the Human Resources Handbook of the United Nations, available at http://www.un.org/hr_handbook/English/, last visited on 30.12.2010, Section 2.1. This *Administrative Instruction, Staff Selection System ST/AI/2002/4* abolished *Administrative Instruction, Recruitment Procedures for Professional Staff ST/AI/1997/7* and *Administrative Instruction, Placement and Promotion System ST/AI/1999/8*, as subsequently amended. - *UN Staff Selection System of 2002*, Section 13.2.

161 *Administrative Instruction, Staff Selection System, ST/AI/2006/3*, 15.11.2006, available in the Human Resources Handbook of the United Nations, available at http://www.un.org/hr_handbook/English/, last visited on 30.12.2010 and *Administrative Instruction, Staff Selection System, ST/AI/2006/3/Rev.1*, 11.01.2010, available in the Human Resources Handbook of the United Nations, available at http://www.un.org/hr_handbook/English/, last visited on 30.12.2010.

162 *UN Staff Selection System.*

163 *UN Staff Selection System of 2006, revised in January 2010*, Section 7.7 and Annex II, para. 1(g).

a post in the Professional or a higher category that was subject to the requirement of the geographical distribution, he must have justified his choice to the OHRM. Furthermore, the OHRM must have approved the selection of such a candidate before the actual decision by the Head of Department or Office to that effect.[164] This rule applied also to the selection of external candidates for any vacant post at the P-3 level.[165]

Interestingly, appointment of an *internal* candidate from an overrepresented country to a vacant post subject to geographical distribution did not need to be justified and approved by the OHRM. This is remarkable since such appointment could have disturbed countries' representation status as much as an appointment of an external candidate. This would be the case where the internal candidate concerned would have served in a non-geographical post before being appointed to the vacant geographical post. This discrepancy in the treatment of internal and external candidates can, however, be easily explained. While appointment of external candidates occurs via outside recruitment, appointment of internal candidates constitutes, in fact, their transfer or promotion. Pursuant to Article 101(3) of the *UN Charter* and Regulation 4.2 of the *UN Staff Regulations*, considerations related to equitable geographical distribution are only permitted in the staff initial recruitment and are not allowed in subsequent career progression. Hence, the nationality of an internal candidate must be – and according to the rule in question was – irrelevant in the staff selection process.

Since the introduction of the new *UN Staff Selection System* in April 2010, the rule according to which appointment of an external candidate from an overrepresented Member State for a geographical post in the Professional or a higher category must be justified and approved is no longer in place. It was replaced by a new requirement to justify selection of *any* external candidate, disregarding the representation status of his country of origin.[166] This new system also abolished all the above noted obligations of the programme managers (newly referred to as hiring managers and occupational group managers) and the Heads of Department or Office. Although selection decisions must still take into account the UN human resources objectives and targets, including those regarding geographical distribution, hiring managers and occupational group managers are no longer required to certify it.[167] Neither are heads of departments and offices obliged to make such certification.[168] Furthermore, the new *UN Staff Selection System* contains an explicit list of categories of candidates who are to be given due consideration in the selection process. Candidates from unrepresented and underrepresented Member States are, however, and rather surprisingly, not included in this list.[169]

---

[164] Ibid., Section 9.2 and Annex I, para. 1(d). In this regard, the relevant programme manager must have submitted a documented record to the OHRM for approval. – *ibid.*, Annex II, para. 3.

[165] Ibid., Section 7.2(b).

[166] *UN Staff Selection System*, Section 9.3.

[167] Ibid., Section 1(x).

[168] Ibid., Section 9.3.

[169] Ibid., Section 9.3. The list includes: 'staff members who are victims of malicious acts or natural disasters; serving staff members who have served under the former 200 and 300 series of the Staff Rules;

It would therefore appear that the new *UN Staff Selection System* has left out all rules designed to ensure that candidates from unrepresented and underrepresented countries are given certain priority in the staff selection process. This is not entirely the case, however. The new *UN Staff Selection System* does contain a number of provisions dealing specifically with such candidates. It still provides that UN geography targets are to be taken into account in selection decisions.[170] The system also gives authority to the OHRM to pre-screen individuals identified through an outreach strategy aimed at certain target groups, including geographical ones, and to release candidates successful in such pre-screening to the hiring managers and occupational group managers for further assessment and consideration for the job opening.[171] It is unclear, though, what value added this provision has, given the fact that all candidates successful in pre-screening, which is always conducted by the OHRM, are released to the relevant hiring manager or occupational group manager in any case.[172]

The *UN Staff Selection System* also provides now that information accompanying the shortlist of candidates recommended for job openings at the D-2 level includes statistics on relevant UN targets and candidates' nationality.[173] Such a provision existed, however, already before, though it was contained in a different document.[174] Last but not least, the new *UN Staff Selection System* contains some provisions allowing for 'placement outside normal process' of candidates who have passed a competitive examination but have not been placed in a certain P-2 post within a specified period. These provisions apply to rather specific situations, though, in which posts remain vacant for several months.[175]

When assessing the existing requirements of the *UN Staff Selection System* related to the issue of geographical distribution and their compatibility with Article 101(3) of the *UN Charter* and relevant *UN Staff Regulations*, and in particular the requirement of justification and prior approval of selection of external candidates, it should be noted that, since April 2010, this requirement applies indeed to all external candidates and not only those from inadequately represented Member States. Moreover, the requirement does not deprive external candidates from overrepresented countries of their right to be fully considered in the individual selection process and their selection remains possible. If the relevant hiring manager or occupational group manager and/or the Head of Department or Office are convinced that the merits

candidates from troop- or police-contributing countries for positions in a peacekeeping operation or Headquarters support account-funded positions in the Department of Peacekeeping Operations, the Department of Field Support and other departments with support account resources; and prior service or employment of candidates in field duty stations, for positions for which relevant field experience is highly desirable, as applicable and as stipulated in General Assembly resolution 63/250.'

170 Ibid., Section 1(x).

171 Ibid., Section 7.3.

172 Ibid., Section 7.2.

173 Ibid., Section 7.9.

174 *Secretary-General's Bulletin, Senior Review Group, ST/SGB/2009/2*, 01.01.2009, available in the Human Resources Handbook of the United Nations, available at http://www.un.org/hr_handbook/English/, last visited on 30.12.2010, Section 4.2.

175 *UN Staff Selection System*, Section 11.3-11.5.

of such a candidate warrant his appointment despite his nationality of a country already overrepresented in the UN Secretariat, they have the possibility to justify his selection and apply for approval. Subsequently, the OHRM considers the case on the basis of its individual merits, bearing in mind its obligations to ensure that the best suited candidate for the post at issue is selected.[176] Naturally, the OHRM would have to consider the geographical status of the country of nationality of the recommended candidate as well as the status of the implementation of the human resources action plan of the relevant department or office.[177] However, the OHRM too may eventually agree with the selection of an external candidate form an over-represented Member State. Therefore, compliance with Article 101(3) of the *UN Charter* and the relevant *UN Staff Regulations* is not precluded and depends on the behavior of the UN Administration in each individual case.

Before concluding this section, it must be noted that, following the General Assembly's request contained in its most recent resolution of December 2010, the requirement of justification and prior approval of selection of an external candidate will need to be removed from the *UN Staff Selection System*.[178] Such removal will mean that considerations relating to adequate geographical representation will rest solely on the shoulders of hiring managers, occupational group managers and/or Heads of Department or Office. They will remain responsible for paying due regard to this issue in staff selection but will no longer need to justify their choice of a specific candidate, include that from an adequately or overrepresented Member State, or to receive a prior approval for it.

2.3.1.4. Partnership with Member States

Another practice employed by the Secretary-General in order to achieve adequate geographical representation among staff is active co-operation or, as called by the Secretary-General in his reports, 'partnership' with the Member States.[179] It has been mentioned above that the Secretaries-General used to rely on cooperation with Member States in this respect since the early years. This practice was put into place partly because of the interest shown by Member States in recruitment matters and partly because of the unavailability of candidates or paucity of means for gathering and disseminating relevant information as well as communicating with potential candidates.[180]

---

[176] The obligation to select the best suited candidate is explicitly stipulated in the *UN Staff Selection System*. - Ibid., Section 9.3.

[177] See also *Human Resources Management Reform, Report of the Secretary-General, A/63/282*, Section IV, Part B.3(a), para. 54.

[178] *General Assembly Resolution 65/247*, para. 19. The General Assembly adopted this request upon recommendation by its Advisory Committee on Administrative and Budgetary Questions. – *Human Resources Management, Report of the Advisory Committee on Administrative and Budgetary Questions, A/65/537*, para. 13. For reasons cited by the Advisory Committee on Administrative and Budgetary Questions for the removal of the requirement at issue, see below, chapter 3, section 1.

[179] *Improvement of Equitable Geographical Representation in the United Nations Secretariat, Report of the Secretary-General, A/59/264*, Section III, Part E.

[180] See above, introduction to section 2.3.1. See also, for example, *Estabial, UNAT Judgment No. 310*

At present, the OHRM still circulates all vacancy announcements to the Member States' permanent representations to the UN and informs them about appointments made.[181] In addition, the OHRM continues holding regular annual meetings with representatives of inadequately represented countries. The purpose of these meetings is to inform the countries at issue of the measures taken to recruit their nationals, to learn about their concerns and to identify possible actions. In addition to the regular meetings, special meetings are arranged when a country requests them.[182] Furthermore, the OHRM also organizes recruitment missions to countries with no or low representation status. As reported by the Secretary-General in 2004, these missions involve various activities aimed at enhancing recruitment of possible candidates, such as recruitment campaigns and interviews. Selected candidates are then put on a list presented to the heads of the Secretariat departments or offices for consideration.[183]

The involvement of the Member States in the recruitment of their nationals has been severely criticized in the past. For example, Langrod stated that the influence of governments in finding suitable candidates from among nationals of inadequately represented countries had been significant, even decisive, as these governments alone had had access to information and to potential candidates. According to Langrod, this situation resulted in factual helplessness of the UN Secretariat and its powerlessness with regard to respecting the principles of the *UN Charter*.[184] Also Reymond and Mailick warned against involving Member States in the UN recruitment process. While they noted that there was nothing wrong in cooperating with governments in certain areas, such as promoting candidacies or providing additional data and information on applicants, they emphasized that such cooperation entailed a danger of abuse, for example, by restricting the list of candidates to those politically acceptable or by providing unfavourable information about candidates.[185] They said:

> *What is initially willingness to assist may too easily degenerate into interference. The distinction between selfless assistance and self-serving pressure often be-*

[1983], para. III.

[181] Member States even keep requiring hard copies of the announcements, next to the electronic versions. - See, for example, *General Assembly Resolution 55/258*, Section IV, paras. 3 and 4; *General Assembly Resolution 57/305*, Section II, para. 22. ; *General Assembly Resolution 59/266*, Section II, para. 5. With regard to the information on the appointments made, the Member States require the Secretary-General to inform them about these appointments 'monthly, through the Internet, through the United Nations public web site and, upon request, in printed form'. - *General Assembly Resolution 59/266*, Section II, para. 14.

[182] *Improvement of Equitable Geographical Representation in the United Nations Secretariat, Report of the Secretary-General, A/59/264*, Section III, Part E, paras. 17-18.

[183] Ibid., Section III, Part E, para. 19. Note that Member States seem to be rather enthusiastic about the recruitment missions and encourage the Secretary-General to continue this practice and even to intensify the efforts. - *General Assembly Resolution 59/266*, Section IV, para. 10.

[184] Langrod, *The International Civil Service, Its Origins, Its Nature, Its Evolution*, p. 187.

[185] Reymond and Mailick, *International Personnel Policies and Practices*, p. 77.

comes blurred, and too many governments feel that it is natural and appropriate to use their influence to promote the appointment of their own candidates.[186]

In Bulkeley's view, regular contacts of the UN with Member States' ministries, instead of national-level recruiting services, and dependence on the pool of candidates proposed by these ministries, among other things, had led to the increased role of Member States in the UN recruitment process. Supplemented by the tolerated 'parochial lobbying' from Member States, the system at the time did not provide adequate possibilities for the selection of best candidates, as required by the *UN Charter*.[187]

Clearly, general cooperation and information exchange between the Secretariat and the Member States can be advantageous to both sides, especially in creating trust among the inadequately represented countries that the problem of their inadequate representation is being taken seriously and addressed. Therefore, the organization of regular or even special briefings with Member States' representations should be supported. Nonetheless, any deeper involvement of Member States in the actual recruitment and selection process should be avoided if Articles 100 and 101 of the *UN Charter* are to be respected. It could be argued, for example, that the need to use Member States' facilities to gain access to potential candidates has diminished and has even disappeared with the emergence and wide-spread use of modern information technology tools. All vacancy announcements are nowadays published on the internet and thus accessible to any person potentially interested in and qualified for a job with the UN. Persons with no access to this information tool will most probably not be eligible for the vacancy in any case. In addition, over the years, direct contacts between the UN Secretariat and a large number of non-governmental organizations and institutions, such as universities and other specialized institutions, have been developed and can be utilized for collecting and spreading necessary information, including those on job opportunities at the UN. Therefore, there no longer seems to be a relevant justification for dissemination of all vacancy announcements to the Member States' permanent missions, other than the political interest of (some) Member States to be in control of recruitment of their nationals for UN service. Although a large majority of former socialist countries have transformed themselves into democracies in which citizens are allowed to apply for jobs in international organizations without their governments' approval, there still are countries with more or less totalitarian governments that might require such approval. They may also block their citizens' access to certain information provided on the internet or in other generally available public medium, thereby preventing them from applying for (some) positions in the UN Secretariat. Cooperation with such Member States could therefore seem necessary in order to reach potential candidates for jobs. However, it remains true that, from the legal point of view, the interest and involvement of individual Member States in the UN recruitment and se-

---

186 Ibid., p. 77.

187 Bulkeley, *Depoliticizing United Nations Recruitment: Establishing a Genuinly International Civil Service*, pp. 774 -775.

lection process should not be stimulated. Otherwise the principles of the *UN Charter* may be put at risk.

On the other hand, the organization of recruitment missions to inadequately represented countries should be encouraged. Indeed, recruitment campaigns may be very effective in raising awareness among potential candidates about the possibilities employment at the UN Secretariat offers. In some countries, this awareness may be low due to various reasons – a simple lack of information, but also a lack of visibility of the UN in the country, prejudice created by the country's past experience with the UN, fears of insecurity or expectations of unattractive pay or other working conditions at the UN Secretariat.[188] All these issues could be effectively addressed in the information campaigns. However, certain doubts could be raised about the practice of the OHRM presenting lists of specific candidates identified during the recruitment missions to the Heads of Departments and Offices. It could be argued that such practices are incompatible with an independent, impartial and transparent selection process. Although the Secretary-General explicitly stated that the candidates selected during the recruitment missions were being appointed after having gone through the regular recruitment process, the fact remains that the heads of departments and offices are presented with their candidacy in a manner not available to other candidates. This practice creates an inevitable prejudice in favour of those who have not yet proven the superiority of their merits vis-à-vis other candidates when they are presented to the heads of departments and offices. This practice could be incompatible with the principle of equal treatment. Recruitment missions should therefore remain within the borders of informing potential candidates about the possibilities and conditions of UN employment but should refrain from placing some candidates on an unequal footing with others.

2.3.1.5. 'Fast-track' recruitment procedure

The so-called 'fast-track' recruitment procedure was a pilot project that took place in the 2006-2008 period on the basis of a proposal by the Secretary-General and authorization by the General Assembly.[189] It was based on the idea of a speedy recruit-

[188] For example, it could be assumed that nationals of Japan, Norway, the UK or even the USA, all currently underrepresented Member States, could consider the UN salary as being below the level offered for comparable jobs in their own country.

[189] The project was proposed by the Secretary-General in his report on Improvement of Equitable Geographical Representation in the United Nations Secretariat A/59/264 of 2004. - *Improvement of Equitable Geographical Representation in the United Nations Secretariat, Report of the Secretary-General, A/59/264*, Section VI, Part A. The General Assembly approved the project in 2005 for an initial period of two years and extended it in 2006 for another two years. - *General Assembly Resolution 59/266*, Section IV, para. 9; *General Assembly Resolution 61/244*, Section X, para. 13. The preceding discussion in the Fifth Committee clearly showed that Member States, very much concerned over the issue of geographical representation, welcomed the introduction of fast-track rosters. - See, for example, the statement of representatives of China, Saudi Arabia and Japan - *Official Records, Summary Record of the 14 meeting of 1 November 2006*, paras. 15, 45 and 78, respectively. China even proposed an extension of this procedure to the countries currently below the mid-point of their desirable range, which were likely to become underrepresented in future. - *Official Records, Summary Record of the 14 meeting of 1 November 2006*, para. 15.

ment of candidates from unrepresented and underrepresented countries identified during a targeted recruitment campaign conducted by the OHRM in partnership with Secretariat departments and offices and concerned Member States.[190]

At the beginning of the project, a number of vacancies at the P-4 and P-5 level were specially identified and included in the project. Announcements of these vacancies were transmitted to the Member States with inadequate representation status. Countries that decided to participate in the project then publicized these special vacancy announcements and searched for candidates. Received applications were evaluated and, after having been reviewed by the relevant central review body, approved candidates were placed on a special fast-track roster. They were to remain on this roster until the representation status of their country came within the desirable range. The roster was subsequently presented to the programme managers who could select one or more candidates for their vacant posts without issuing a regular vacancy announcement. This roster included also other external candidates from inadequately represented Member States who had applied for another vacancy not included in the fast-track pilot project and who had been approved by a relevant central review body but not yet placed.[191]

In 2008, the fast-track project was discontinued. The Secretary-General reported that lessons learned from it had been incorporated into the continuation of outreach efforts already in place in order to improve the overall geographical representation.[192] From the legal point of view, however, the procedure used in this pilot project could be questioned for its compatibility with Article 101(3) of the *UN Charter* and relevant *UN Staff Regulations*. First of all, the fact that the vacancies could be filled without being published causes serious concerns as it limits the number and scope of potential candidates, thereby ignoring the requirement to ensure that the best persons available are recruited. In addition, all potential candidates from countries within or above their desirable range were *a priori* excluded from consideration for the posts included in the project. The fact that other external candidates who might have responded to specific vacancy announcements and been selected by the central review bodies but not yet placed could also be put on the fast-track roster does not remedy the situation as this rule only applied to other external candidates from inadequately represented Member States, leaving the candidates from other countries excluded. Hence, the eventual selection of a candidate for a specific post remained limited to the best person available on the fast-track roster, not the best person as such. The need to ensure that candidates with the best merits are recruited was thus sacrificed to the need to ensure adequate geographical representation. Moreover, the direct involvement of Member States in the recruitment process preceding the placement of candidates on the special fast-track roster is also a potential matter for concern.

---

[190] *Improvement of Equitable Geographical Representation in the United Nations Secretariat, Report of the Secretary-General, A/59/264*, Section IV, Part A.

[191] Ibid., Section IV, Part A ; and *Human Resources Management Reform, Report of the Secretary-General, A/61/228*, 07.08.2006, available in the Official Document System of the United Nations, available at http://documents.un.org/, last visited on 30.12.2010, para. 99.

[192] *Human Resources Management Reform, Report of the Secretary-General, A/63/282*, para. 59.

2.3.1.6. Focal points

There are two sorts of focal points relevant to the UN recruitment: national focal points and the focal point of the OHRM. The national focal points have been designed to facilitate cooperation between the UN Secretariat – in particular the OHRM – and the national representations of Member States with no or low representation status. The cooperation should relate to various aspects of activities aimed at increasing these countries' geographical representation, such as the organization of national competitive examinations and the identification of potential candidates.[193] The main role of the focal point of the OHRM is the systematic development and implementation of strategies for recruiting from unrepresented and underrepresented countries. It is to work closely with the individual departments and offices of the UN Secretariat and the concerned Member States. In addition, in cooperation with national focal points, the OHRM focal point is to organize recruitment missions.[194]

As mentioned above, general cooperation between the UN Secretariat and the Member States is welcome. Moreover, a more intensive collaboration with Member States whose representation status is not optimal should be supported so that the specific circumstances of such countries are addressed in the most appropriate manner. As long as this cooperation remains at the general rather than at the individual level, it should not constitute a source of concern. However, caution is needed. For example, the identification of potential candidates for UN service should not take place on the basis of a direct involvement of Member States, risking violation of the relevant provisions of the *UN Charter* and *UN Staff Regulations*.

2.3.1.7. Galaxy and Inspira

The electronic staffing system of the UN Secretariat called Galaxy was introduced in 2002 as a supporting electronic tool for the new *UN Staff Selection System*.[195] The Secretary-General explained its main advantages as follows:

> *For the first time in the Secretariat, Galaxy allowed the creation and advertising of vacancies electronically on a global basis; the submission, receipt and review of applications online; the tracking of the status of applications; recording of the selection process; and the generation of reports (e.g., on selection decisions, geography, gender and numbers of applicants).*[196]

Galaxy thus became available on the internet and thereby accessible to any potential candidate for a UN job.[197] In the view of the Secretary-General, the introduction

---

[193] *Improvement of Equitable Geographical Representation in the United Nations Secretariat, Report of the Secretary-General, A/59/264*, para. 23.

[194] Ibid., para. 24.

[195] *Human Resources Management Reform, Report of the Secretary-General, A/59/263*, 13.08.2004, available in the Official Document System of the United Nations, available at http://documents.un.org/, last visited on 30.12.2010, paras. 12(c) and 57.

[196] Ibid., para. 57.

[197] The Galaxy website address is available at https://jobs.un.org/Galaxy/Release3/Vacancy/Vacancy.

of Galaxy in combination with the new *UN Staff Selection System* enabled the UN to reach a much wider pool of potential candidates and improved efficiency and transparency in staff selection. Relatively soon after its introduction, however, Galaxy became a victim to its own success. The enormous increase in the volume of applications caused by the global accessibility of the vacancy announcements via Galaxy, from 50.000 to 350.000 annual average, led to the inability of programme managers to give proper consideration to all received applications. In addition, Galaxy proved not to be very user-friendly, *inter alia* by lacking integration with other technology systems used at the UN Secretariat in the area of human resources management, such as the electronic Performance Appraisal System and the Integrated Management Information System. This made the processing of data and the required reporting difficult and time-consuming.[198] Because further modification of Galaxy would be cost-ineffective, it was decided to replace it with a new software package.[199] The deployment of such a new 'e-staffing talent management support tool', named Inspira, started in April 2010 and was to continue in 2011.[200] Once fully in use, it will constitute a single platform for talent management, replacing the systems used previously for staffing and performance management support. In addition, Inspira will be a new technological support to learning management not available in the past.[201]

In the area of human resources management related to the issue of geographical distribution, Inspira is said to retain facilities introduced by Galaxy.[202] The latter provided officials in charge of staff selection with a possibility to identify candidates from countries whose representation was inadequate. Galaxy helped highlight candidates from underrepresented and unrepresented countries and allowed for search of candidates on the basis of their nationality.[203] In addition, a direct link from the websites of the United Nations Information Centres in inadequately represented countries was made to Galaxy, thereby providing an easy access to the information on existing vacancies and UN recruitment rules for nationals of these countries.[204] Inspira will retain, and improve, search facilities introduced by Galaxy and set up a new UN career portal replacing the former job website of the United Nations.[205]

---

aspx, last visited on 31.12.2010.

[198] *Investing in People, Report of the Secretary-General, A/61/255*, para. 61. See also para. 372.

[199] Ibid., paras. 374-375 and *Human Resources Management Reform, Report of the Secretary-General, A/61/228*, para. 55. See also *Human Resources Management Reform, Report of the Secretary-General, A/63/282*, para. 12(b).

[200] *Human Resources Management Reform: The Talent Management Tool, Inspira, Report of the Secretary-General, A/65/305/Add.3*, 02.09.2010, available in the Official Document System of the United Nations, available at http://documents.un.org/, last visited on 30.12.2010, para. 10.

[201] Ibid., paras. 3-4.

[202] *Human Resources Management Reform, Report of the Secretary-General, A/63/282*, para. 83.

[203] *Human Resources Management Reform, Report of the Secretary-General, A/59/263*, paras. 12(c) and 59-60 .

[204] *Human Resources Management Reform, Report of the Secretary-General, A/63/282*, para. 59.

[205] *Human Resources Management Reform: The Talent Management Tool, Inspira, Report of the Secretary-General, A/65/305/Add.3*, paras. 22(b) and 31.

In this context, it should be noted that questions have been raised with regard to possible influence of the e-staffing tool on upholding the principles of merit and transparency.[206] Although past concerns related in particular to the manageability of the large volume of applications upon the introduction of Galaxy, similar concerns could be voiced with regard to any system that will manage such volume in a more efficient manner but that will, like Galaxy, retain the possibility of pre-selecting candidates who will be considered more closely solely on the basis of their nationality. If a particular programme manager uses nationality as a starting point for his first selection from among a large pool of candidates, he inevitably deprives all other candidates, with other than the desired nationality or nationalities, from further consideration. Every programme manager is required to assess the suitability of *all* candidates for a vacant post, not only – and at the same time not in the first place – candidates from inadequately represented Member States. Therefore, a search function on the basis of candidates' nationality may lead to questionable consequences if used at the initial stage of candidates' consideration. Naturally, once candidates with equal merits have been identified, the use of the search tool for further elimination of candidates may be justified by the need to select a candidate who would improve the geographical representation of an unrepresented or underrepresented Member State. At that stage, the highlighting of candidates from inadequately represented countries does not seem to go against the need for fair and full consideration of all received applications.

2.3.1.8. Outreach

In 2008, a special Outreach Unit was established in the Strategic Planning and Staffing Division of the OHRM.[207] One of the important functions of this Unit is the identification of candidates 'who would help the Organization to meet its geographic targets'.[208] The Unit fulfills this function by developing an outreach strategy. It does so, above all, by analyzing the workforce planning and by establishing partnerships with professional associations, governmental entities and non-governmental organizations. These organizations and entities should help the unit to track down potential candidates from countries with no or low geographical representation in the Secretariat. The Outreach Unit is also the relevant UN body holding meetings with inadequately represented Member States and carrying out outreach missions, previously referred to as 'recruitment missions'.[209]

The Outreach Unit thus seeks to bring together various past and new practices aimed at improving equitable geographical distribution among the Secretariat staff.

---

[206] See, for example, a statement of a representative of Ghana in the Fifth Committee. This representative questioned how individual programme managers could handle the large numbers of applications received for specific vacancies and still adhere to the principles of merit and transparency. - *Official Records, Summary Record of the 14 meeting of 1 November 2006*, para. 22.

[207] *Human Resources Management Reform, Report of the Secretary-General, A/63/282*, paras. 59 and 88.

[208] Ibid., para. 59.

[209] Ibid., paras. 88-91 and *Overview of Human Resources Management Reform, Report of the Secretary-General, A/65/305*, paras. 61-61. For the recruitment missions, see above, section 2.3.1.4.

The past practices that came into the Unit's hands are, for example, cooperation with Member States and organization of recruitment, or outreach, missions. The addition seems to be the establishment of contacts with entities other than governmental organizations. This move has been long overdue. Professional and other non-governmental organizations are certainly the right doors to knock at. Not only do they possess valuable information and further contacts which might be helpful in approaching potential qualified candidates, they can also contribute to decreasing the UN Secretariat's dependence on governmental channels in this respect, assuming that such entities are independent from states' governments themselves. This move would undoubtedly eliminate the danger of encroaching upon Articles 100 and 101 of the *UN Charter*, which prohibit Member States' involvement in staff recruitment and selection.

2.3.2. National preserves

Apart from the mechanisms discussed in the previous section, there was, and arguably still is, yet another special arrangement in the UN Secretariat that should serve the purpose of ensuring adequate representation of Member States in certain specific posts. The arrangement concerns posts at the senior and decision-making level and the so-called national preserves.

The need for more equitable representation of all Member States at the senior and decision-making level was accentuated since the early years and has become even more so over the decades, especially as developing Member States felt that the allocation of posts on those levels to their nationals did not correspond with their share in the organization's membership.[210] The problem has its roots in the organization's history: already at the San Francisco conference establishing the United Nations, the Great Powers agreed on an unofficial division of senior posts in the Secretariat among themselves, thereby creating *de facto* 'national preserves' on these posts.[211] According to this agreement, when a post filled by a national of a

[210] Almost all General Assembly resolutions on geographical distribution, and later on human resources management, adopted since 1958. See, for example, *General Assembly Resolution 1294(XIII), A/RES/1294(XIII)*, 5.12.1958, available in the Official Document System of the United Nations, available at http://documents.un.org/, last visited on 30.12.2010, para. 1(a); *General Assembly Resolution 2241(XXI)*, Preamble and para. 3; *General Assembly Resolution 3417(XXX)*, para. 1; *General Assembly Resolution 40/258*, para. 3; *General Assembly Resolution 51/226B*, para. 3; *General Assembly Resolution 61/244*, Section X, para. 9.

[211] The post division was as follows: the USSR got the post of Assistant Secretary-General for Security Council Affairs; the US the post of Assistant Secretary-General for Administrative and Financial Services; the UK the post of Assistant Secretary-General for Economic Affairs, France the post of Assistant Secretary-General for Social Affairs; and China the post of Assistant Secretary-General for Trusteeship Council Affairs. - Langrod, *The International Civil Service, Its Origins, Its Nature, Its Evolution*, p. 176. See also Göttelmann and Münch, *Article 101*, p. 1260. As further stated in ibid, in the course of time Member States from other regional groups have been accorded a number of senior posts, too, whereby the factual recognition of 'national preserves' has not changed. For an interesting survey on the question of national preserves in the UN, see Meron, *The United Nations Secretariat*, pp. 93-101 and Meron, T., *Editorial Comment: "Exclusive Preserves" and the New Soviet Policy towards the UN Secretariat*, in: American Journal of International Law, Vol. 85, pp. 322-329.

certain country became vacant, it was to be filled by a national of the same country, mostly on the basis of that country's recommendation. Despite the lack of any binding legal nature of this agreement, the first Secretary-General Trygve Lie appeared to have been left with no choice but to accept it.[212] In addition, as noted by Langrod, the agreement proved to be a 'bad augury' for the years to come.[213] For decades the most senior posts at the UN Secretariat have been continuously and exclusively occupied by nationals of the same country, thereby precluding nationals from other states from being appointed or promoted into these positions.

This practice has become more heavily criticized since the 1970s when Member States began to explicitly emphasize that 'no post, individual department, division or unit in the Secretariat should be considered as the exclusive preserve of any individual Member State or any region'.[214] They began to request the Secretary-General to ensure that this rule was applied 'faithfully in accordance with the principle of equitable geographical distribution'.[215]

On the other hand, already in 1980 an important exception to this rule was adopted. In its Resolution 35/210, the General Assembly gave the Secretary-General full authority to:

> *continue to permit replacement by candidates of the same nationality within a reasonable time-frame in respect of posts held by staff members on fixed-term contracts, whenever this is necessary to ensure that the representation of Member States whose nationals serve primarily on fixed-term contracts is not adversely affected.*[216]

This exception became known as the replacement principle and constituted a *de facto* legalization of a practice pre-dating the resolution. Its rationale lay in the consequences of a former policy followed by the Soviet Union and other socialist countries with regard to their nationals serving in international organizations. According to this policy, nationals of the socialistic countries could have only been appointed on the basis of secondment from their countries' governments or other public institutions. They served thus on fixed-term contracts and had to leave the organization upon the contract's expiry. With each departure, however, the geographical representation status of the relevant Member States could have been endangered if the vacant post went to a national of another country. In order to prevent such a situation, a large number of posts were reserved for nationals from each socialis-

---

[212] Langrod, *The International Civil Service, Its Origins, Its Nature, Its Evolution*, p. 176. Langrod noted that the agreement had been imposed on Trygve Lie as a *fait accompli*. He also explained that the posts at issue were divided among the Great Powers expecting the appointed officials to be representatives of their countries or group of countries. – Ibid., pp. 176-177.

[213] Ibid., p. 177.

[214] *General Assembly Resolution 31/26*, Preamble.

[215] *General Assembly Resolution 33/143*, Section II, para. 2. See also, for example, *General Assembly Resolution 35/210*, Section I, para. 3; *General Assembly Resolution 41/206B*, Preamble; *General Assembly Resolution 61/244*, Section X, para. 15.

[216] *General Assembly Resolution 35/210*, para. 4.

tic country that pursued the exclusive secondment policy.[217] When a staff member with nationality of such a country left the Secretariat, the post had to be filled by a candidate with the same nationality, to the exclusion of other candidates.

Clearly, such an arrangement, as well as any other agreement on national preserves, is contrary to the spirit of the *UN Charter* and of the *UN Staff Regulations*. Although neither the *Charter* nor the *Staff Regulations* have an express provision in this regard, any limitation of the scope of possible candidates to nationals of one country severely restricts the search for the best candidate, which is explicitly required by Article 101(3) of the *UN Charter* and Regulation 4.2 of the *UN Staff Regulations*. Moreover, it clearly encroaches upon the independent and impartial character of the international civil service.

The United Nations Administrative Tribunal confirmed that national preserves were indeed contrary to two provisions mentioned above in *Estabial*, a 1983 case discussed earlier.[218] However, in 1990, in *Dauchy* the UNAT gave effect to the replacement principle. In this case, the post which was to fall vacant due to retirement had been occupied by Soviet nationals for 25 years. The applicant in this case, a French national with excellent qualifications for the job, applied for this post but a Soviet national was appointed. The applicant challenged the appointment decision as well as the replacement principle itself. In addressing the challenge, the UNAT pointed to the specific circumstances of the case, namely the prohibition by some Member States of their nationals acquiring permanent status in the UN Secretariat, the above mentioned resolution of the General Assembly and the need 'to prevent a situation which would undermine the principle of equitable geographical distribution of posts ... to the detriment of those States'.[219] Subsequently, the UNAT supported the authority of the Secretary-General to decide whether making use of the replacement principle was in the interest of the United Nations. It did recall its previous decision in *Estabial* and the duty of the Secretary-General to give full and fair considerations to all candidates applying for a vacant post and found that, by excluding *a priori* any chance for success of the applicant's candidacy, the applicant sustained a moral injury, for which the UN Administration was responsible. Therefore, the UNAT ordered the Administration to compensate the damage by a payment of a specific sum.[220] On the other hand, the UNAT rejected all other pleas of the applicant requesting condemnation of the replacement principle as incompatible with several fundamental principles of the international civil service, with Article 101(3) of the *UN Charter* and corresponding Regulations 4.2 and 4.4 of the *UN Staff Regulations* and

[217] Meron, *Editorial Comment: "Exclusive Preserves" and the New Soviet Policy towards the UN Secretariat*, p. 322.

[218] *Estabial, UNAT Judgment No. 310 [1983]*, para. XIV. For more details on this case, see above, section 2.3.1.

[219] *Dauchy v. Secretary-General of the United Nations, UNAT Judgment No. 492 [1990]*, available at http://untreaty.un.org/UNAT/UNAT_Judgements/Judgements_E/UNAT_00492_E.pdf, last visited on 30.12.2010, para. VIII. See also para. IX.

[220] Ibid., paras. XIV – XVI, XIX and XXI.3. The applicant was to be paid 5.000 US dollars in damages. – Ibid.

with specific instructions of the General Assembly.[221] Contrary to these contentions of the applicant, the UNAT explicitly upheld the replacement principle:

> *The Tribunal has ... found that in accordance with the practice followed since 1964, as confirmed by General Assembly resolution 35/210 of 17 December 1980, a Soviet national was to be appointed to the post of Director of the Division. The [UN] Legal Counsel concluded that such appointment was in the interest of the United Nations. The Tribunal does not contest his conclusion.*[222]

This controversial decision reflects, of course, the political reality of the UN in those days. By upholding the replacement principle, the UNAT in fact approved privileged treatment of countries which refused to adhere to the fundamental principles of the international civil service enshrined in the *UN Charter* and to respect the international character of this service. Regrettable though this was, it is clear, that the UN Administration had little, if any, choice other than to respect the existing political reality.

Interestingly, and despite the abolition at the end of the 1980s and beginning of the 1990s of the former policy of socialistic countries in personnel matters which led to the adoption of the replacement principle at first place, the issue of national preserves has remained on the UN agenda up to now.[223] A quote from a relatively recent report – of 2007 prepared by The Four Nations Initiative – shows that the problem is indeed still present:

> *The top jobs of the organization have tended to go predominantly to citizens of P5 states. Some jobs are thinly disguised, or even entirely undisguised, national preserves of major states, who make their own decisions about who will fill a secretariat position, to the point sometimes of not even offering the Secretary-General a list of their preferred citizens to choose from.*[224]

---

[221] Ibid., p. 5 and para. XXI.3.

[222] Ibid., para. XIV.

[223] For the change of the policy by former socialist countries, see, for example, *Personnel Questions: Other Personnel Questions, Secondment from Government Service, Report of the Secretary-General, A/C.5/46/9*, 23.09.1991, available in the Official Document System of the United Nations, available at http://documents.un.org/, last visited on 30.12.2010, paras. 6 and 7. Note that, as pointed out by Meron, the replacement principle has not been explicitly renounced by the UN General Assembly. However, the change of the above mentioned policy should, in Meron's view, automatically lead to the termination of this principle. In the end, this principle was intended as a specific exception to the general prohibition of national preserves in the UN. - Meron, *Editorial Comment. "Exclusive Preserves" and the New Soviet Policy towards the UN Secretariat*, p. 325.

[224] *Towards a Compact, Appendices to the Report of Final Proposals by the Four Nations Initiative on Governance and Management of the UN*, September 2007, available at http://www.the4ni.org/images/stories/documents/towards%20a%20compact%20-%20appendices.pdf, last visited on 30.12.2010, p. 10. The Four Nations Initiative was an initiative of the governments of Chile, South Africa, Sweden and Thailand, launched in 2005 with the purpose of providing 'new ideas and perspectives on governance and management of the UN Secretariat'. - *Towards a Compact, Proposals for Improved Governance and Management of the United Nations Secretariat, Report of Final Proposals by the Four Nations Initiative on Governance and Management of the UN*, p. 5.

Naturally, this state of affairs has been broadly criticized, by both the UN Member States as well as by the UN staff. Representatives of the latter pointed out in 2008 that 39 per cent of senior and policy-making posts were held by nationals from the 'big five' Member States, namely France, Germany, Russia, the UK and the US.[225] In 2010, for which the last statistical data are available, the proportion of these five countries in senior level posts was 37 per cent.[226]

The UN Member States themselves have been expressing their concerns in this regard regularly – and in a more pressing manner than in the past. Through General Assembly resolutions, they have been requiring the Secretary-General to ensure that there is 'no monopoly on senior posts by nationals of any State or group of States' but also that 'as a general rule, no national of a Member State succeeds a national of that State in a senior post'.[227] Compared to earlier resolutions, in which the Assembly required the Secretary-General to *strive* to appoint nationals of a country other than that of the incumbent to a vacant post, the latest resolutions establish a general rule which, in principle, *prohibits* the succession of a departing national by a person with the same nationality.[228] Although this prohibition is to be regarded as a 'general' rule, thus providing for certain latitude, the language of these last resolutions is considerably stronger than that of earlier ones. The continuous dissatisfaction of the General Assembly with the Secretary-General's failure to comply with its requests has led the Assembly to request a separate report on this issue. The report was to be submitted during the sixty-third session of the General Assembly, i.e. in 2008, but it was not.[229] No such report has been presented thus far.

From a legal point of view, even though national preserves as such are clearly contrary to the *UN Charter* and *UN Staff Regulations*, it is questionable whether the general prohibition of a succession in post incumbency by two persons of the same nationality does not also go beyond what is permissible. It could be argued that such general prohibition leads to *a priory* exclusion of persons of certain nationality from eligibility for a post that becomes vacant. Naturally, it is the Secretary-General who has the final responsibility and the final say in each specific case. However, if he indeed disregarded a candidate solely on the basis of his 'unfortunate' nationality, he would be in clear violation of the *Charter*. The ruling of the UNAT in *Estabial*, mentioned above, would apply in such situations *a contrario* in that not candidates

[225] *Views of the Staff Representatives of the United Nations Secretariat: Staff Union (New York), Field Staff Union (Brindisi) and Staff Coordinating Council (United Nations Office in Geneva), Addendum, A/C.5/63/3/ Add.2*, para. 25.

[226] ***Composition of the Secretariat: Staff Demographics, Report of the Secretary-General, A/65/350,*** Annex, Table 2.C. The division of posts was as follows: 20 posts were held by French nationals, 24 by Germans, 18 by Russians, 25 by UK nationals and 49 by nationals of the US. In total, these countries held 136 out of 368 posts under consideration.

[227] See *General Assembly Resolution 53/221*, Section IX, para. 6; *General Assembly Resolution 55/258*, Section X, para. 1; *General Assembly Resolution 57/305*, Section II, para. 37; *General Assembly Resolution 59/266*, Section IV, para. 13; *General Assembly Resolution 61/244*, Section X, para. 15.

[228] For the comparison, see, for example, *General Assembly Resolution 41/206B*, para. 2.

[229] *General Assembly Resolution 61/244*, Section X, para. 15 and *General Assembly Resolution 63/250*, Section IX, para. 19.

of all but one nationality but candidates of a specific nationality would be deprived full and fair consideration for the vacant post at issue.

2.4. Role of nationality in staff promotion

In a 2005 staff survey titled *A Picture of the UN Staff*, approximately 17 per cent of all responses cited the geographical distribution principle and/or support from governments as the main factors which conditioned promotion in the UN Secretariat. Another 40 per cent of all answers cited 'having "connections"', including 'connections' in one's government or permanent representation. Competence was considered the main factor only in 16 per cent of all responses, and seniority in 10 per cent.[230] These results indicate that the staff perception is that nationality plays a relatively important role in the promotion process, much more than competence. Unsurprisingly, contradictory results have been delivered by another survey conducted among programme managers in 2008. The Secretary-General reported that programme managers, who possess decisive competences in staff promotion process, unanimously identified merit, and not nationality or gender, as the primary concern in the selection process.[231]

Legally speaking, nationality may be taken into account only in the staff recruitment. As explained above, the principle of geographical distribution as enunciated in Article 101(3) of the *UN Charter* and in Regulation 4.2 of the *UN Staff Regulations* does not apply to promotion or any other movement of staff. According to the wording of both provisions, due regard is to be paid 'to the importance of *recruiting* the staff on as wide a geographical basis as possible' (emphasis added).[232] Moreover, both provisions explicitly stipulate that the *appointments, transfer or promotion of the staff* must be guided above all by the need of securing as competent, efficient and loyal staff as possible. Regulation 1.1(d) of the *UN Staff Regulations*, dealing with the determination of the *conditions of service*, contains the very same obligation and does not mention the principle of geographical distribution at all.

This view was confirmed by the UN Legal Counsel in his opinion as early as in 1957, as well as by the various UN Secretaries-General.[233] Nonetheless, in practice, political pressures from Member States have been considerable. In many resolutions, the UN General Assembly Member States urged the Secretary-General to ensure adequate geographical representation at all levels of the Organization, especially

[230] *A Picture of the UN Staff*, 2005, available at http://www.unspecial.org/StaffPictures/report_p2a.html, last visited on 30.12.2010, question 10. The remaining percentages went to gender, productivity, training, mobility and other factors.

[231] *Human Resources Management Reform, Report of the Secretary-General, A/63/282*, para. 73. The Secretary-General did not state whether programme managers had indicated whether nationality had been taken into account in the promotion process at all.

[232] *UN Charter*, Article 100(3) and *UN Staff Regulations of 2009*, Regulation 4.2.

[233] Meron, *Status and Independence of the International Civil Servant*, p. 306. As pointed out by Meron, for example, U Thant, the UN Secretary-General from 1961 to 1971, declared that his intention was to ensure that the principle of geographical distribution remained relevant only to recruitment of the staff and would play no role in the promotion or placement processes. – Ibid., p. 307.

at the senior and policy-making level.[234] Evidence that nationality has indeed been a relevant factor in staff promotion is provided in the case law dealt with by the UNAT. For example, in the already mentioned *Estabial* the applicant claimed, and the UNAT accepted, that he had been disregarded in a promotion exercise due to his nationality.[235]

The demands of the General Assembly with regard to equitable representation at the senior and policy-making level continue to be present and are expressed in virtually every resolution dealing with human resources management.[236] At the same time, posts at the D-level remain career posts. This means that appointments to these posts should be made, as a matter of priority, by internal promotions.[237] While it is true that the appointment process for D-level posts does provide certain space for external candidates, and in their case nationality may be of relevance, it is difficult to imagine how this criterion would be disregarded for internal candidates, especially since the end result should be to the improvement of geographical distribution of an inadequately represented Member State.

It could be argued that the situation is different above the D-level, i.e. at the levels of Assistant Secretary-General and Under Secretary-General. Posts at these levels are regarded to be political and so is the appointment to them. Clearly, in these cases nationality is one of the important considerations, especially if the appointment process entails recruitment from outside, as it regularly happens, where the principle of geographical distribution is applicable. As far as career posts are concerned, however, no regard should be paid to nationality when the recruitment to such posts involves promotion. As stressed by many authors, any considerations of staff nationality in the promotion process may lead to undue influence on staff independence and impartiality. Lemoine, for example, strongly points out that:

> *Where promotions appear to be due to considerations of nationality and delegations' intervention, this is not only discouraging but leads the qualified officials who have been passed over into the temptation to forget their obligations as*

[234] For example, *General Assembly Resolution 1436(XIV)*, para. 1(b); *General Assembly Resolution 1928(XVIII)*, para. 2; *General Assembly Resolution 39/245*, para. 4. See also, for example, Cameron, H., *Establishment of the European Union Civil Service Tribunal*, in: The Law and Practice of International Courts and Tribunals, Vol. 5, Nr. 2, pp. 273-283, p. 307. Sometimes, specific demands for promoting nationals of certain countries have even been made. - Meron, *Staff of the United nations Secretariat: Problems and Directions*, p. 671.

[235] *Estabial, UNAT Judgment No. 310 [1983]*, especially paras. XII-XIII and XVI. In this case, the UNAT did not address the question whether nationality could play a role in staff promotion since it found that the post at issue had been a priori reserved to nationals of certain countries. This situation alone was found to be a violation of both the *UN Charter* and the *UN Staff Regulations* because the applicant could not be given any fair consideration for the vacant post, being excluded on the basis of his nationality in any case.

[236] For example, *General Assembly Resolution 57/305*, Section II, para. 38; *General Assembly Resolution 59/266*, Section IV, para. 5 and 6; *General Assembly Resolution 61/244*, Section X, para. 9 and especially para. 14; *Human Resources Management Reform, Report of the Secretary-General, A/63/282*, Section IX, paras. 2 and 7.

[237] For details on the main principles concerning appointment procedures in the UN Secretariat, see below, chapter 3, section 1 and section 2.2.

> *international civil servant and to seek their country's delegation's intervention on their behalf.*[238]

Mouritzen also warns:

> *Quotas in connection with promotions may demoralize the civil servants who feel passed over due to their nationality, in favour of a demonstrably less qualified candidate ... [A]n international civil service with less qualified and demoralized civil servants, even though only a minority, will not be able to function creatively, or to further proposals that can win adherence by member countries.*[239]

These warnings are undoubtedly as valid now as they were in the past. On the other hand, denying geographical considerations any role in staff promotions raises an important question of how can adequate geographical distribution be achieved at all levels in the UN Secretariat. The problem is that, as a rule, vacant posts at all levels above the entry level are to be filled in preference by transfer or promotion of staff already in UN service.

2.5. Role of nationality in staff separation

The issue of separation from service is addressed in more detail in the last chapter of this study, which explains what legal grounds and procedures are in place in the UN in this respect. In this section, attention is only paid to the relevance of the principle of geographical distribution, and thus nationality of individual staff members, in their possible separation from service. The main question this section attempts to answer is whether UN staff members can be separated in order to create a vacancy to be filled by a national from an unrepresented or inadequately represented Member State.

Unsurprisingly, the need to ensure equitable geographical representation of UN Member States does not appear among the legal grounds listed in the *UN Staff Regulations* and the *UN Staff Rules* on the basis of which an appointment of an individual staff member could be terminated. Moreover, legal grounds available for termination do not provide much room for the interpretation in the sense of including the issue of geographical representation. They relate to the following situations: abolition of posts or reduction of staff; unsatisfactory service; incapability for service due to health reasons; disciplinary reasons; and the *post ante* discovery of facts relevant to the appointment decision but unknown at the time of appointment.[240] The only possible leeway in this respect could be the legal ground not yet mentioned,

---

[238] Lemoine, *The International Civil Servant: An Endangered Species*, p. 252.

[239] Mouritzen, *The International Civil Service, A study of Bureaucracy: International Organizations*, p. 42

[240] *UN Staff Regulations of 2009*, Regulation 9.3(a) and *UN Staff Rules*, Rule 9.6. Note that UN staff may be separated also for other reasons, in particular resignation, abandonment of post, expiration of appointment, retirement and death. These reasons for separation are, however, not regarded as termination initiated by the Secretary-General. – *ibid.*, Rules 9.1 and 9.6(a) and (b). See also *UN Staff Regulations of 2009*, Article IX.

namely 'the interest of the good administration of the Organization'.[241] Of course, the important question is whether the need to ensure adequate geographical representation of UN Member States among staff could be regarded as falling within the scope of the concept, 'the interest of the good administration of the Organization'.

2.5.1. Geographical distribution as interest of the good administration of the organization

Although the *UN Staff Regulations* and the *UN Staff Rules* have undergone a major amendment due to the reform of the contractual arrangements in the UN in 2009, the concept 'the interest of the good administration of the Organization' is not new. It was available for termination of both permanent and non-permanent appointments. However, in order to provide an increased protection of permanent appointments, the consent of the staff member concerned was required for termination of such an appointment on this legal ground. The same applied to termination of fixed-term appointments in the interest of the good administration of the organization before the expiry of their term. Only probationary appointments and appointments of indefinite duration could be terminated on this legal ground without the staff member's consent.[242] This is not surprising given the nature of these appointments, the first one being 'merely' probationary and the second having no expiry date and thus open-ended.

At present, all three types of existing appointments, i.e. temporary, fixed-term and continuing appointments, may be terminated in the interest of the good administration of the organization as long as the staff member concerned agrees. However, continuing appointments, which have replaced the former permanent appointments, may also be terminated on this legal ground without such consent.[243] It is rather unlikely that an individual staff member would consent to termination of his appointment because his nationality has become 'undesired' or 'less desired' for the time being. Termination of appointments other than continuing ones on the grounds that it is in the interest of the good administration of the organization is therefore highly improbable. The question remains whether such termination could take place in the case of a staff member serving on a continuing appointment.

---

[241] *UN Staff Regulations of 2009*, Regulation 9.3(a)(vi) and (b); and *UN Staff Rules*, Rule 9.6(c)(vi) and (d).

[242] *Staff Regulations of the United Nations, ST/SG/2007/4*, 01.01.2007, available in the Human Resources Handbook of the United Nations, available at http://www.un.org/hr_handbook/English/, last visited on 30.12.2010, Regulation 9.1. Note that there was a small difference in the wording of the concept applicable to permanent and fixed-term appointments on the one hand and the rest of the non-permanent appointments on the other hand. The former could have been terminated 'in the interest of the good administration of the Organization', whereas the latter 'in the interests of the United Nations'. – Ibid., Regulations 9.1(a), last paragraph and 9.1(c). It does not appear, however, that the difference in the wording was intended to have legal consequences.

[243] *UN Staff Regulations of 2009*, Regulation 9.3(a)(vi) and (b); and *UN Staff Rules*, Rule 9.6(c)(vi) and (d), referred to before.

Thus far, the concept of 'the interest of the good administration of the Organization' has not been interpreted by the UNAT.[244] Furthermore, the need to ensure equitable geographical distribution has never been invoked in relation to this concept. Therefore, the UNAT has not yet had an opportunity to clarify whether concerns regarding geographical distribution could fall within the scope of the concept at issue.[245] Nonetheless, it could be argued that continuing appointments could not be terminated on this basis due to the fact that for the purpose of termination of these appointments on this legal basis, the concept is to be 'principally interpreted as a change or termination of a mandate'.[246] Although the word 'principally' leaves the door opened to other possible interpretations as well, it could be argued that the interpretation should not be extensive but rather restrictive. The rationale behind this reasoning is the mere fact that the General Assembly has indicated only one reason for terminating continuing appointments in this manner: that reason in fact equates to the ultimate impossibility of retaining staff in employment because of the termination of the need for it. Moreover, the use of the rather instructive word 'principally' instead of another, more neutral phrase, such as 'among others' or 'for example', support this line of argumentation. Had the General Assembly wished to leave space for a broad interpretation of the concept 'in the interests of the good administration of the Organization', it is very likely that it would have employed less restrictive wording.[247]

It could perhaps be argued that the replacement of permanent appointment by continuing appointment could be interpreted as diminishing the importance of career

---

[244] This provision was at stake in several cases but the focus of most of these cases was not on the interpretation of the concept of the 'interest of the good administration of the Organization' but on the question whether mutual consent to the termination of the applicants' appointment, also required by the provision in question, existed. – For example, *Bernard v. Secretary-General of the United Nations, UNAT Judgment No. 244 [1979]*, available at http://untreaty.un.org/UNAT/UNAT_Judgements/Judgements_E/UNAT_00244_E.pdf, last visited on 30.12.2010 or *Salinas v. Secretary-General of the United Nations, UNAT Judgment No. 530 [1991]*, available at http://untreaty.un.org/UNAT/UNAT_Judgements/Judgements_E/UNAT_00530_E.pdf, last visited on 30.12.2010.

[245] According to the pre-2009 case law, the Secretary-General enjoys a broad discretion in deciding what constitutes 'interests of the Organization' under former Regulation 9.1(c) of the *UN Staff Regulations* and whether to terminate an appointment on this ground. However, the UNAT would review whether the reasons characterized as interest of the organization indeed could fall within the scope of this concept. *Crawford v. Secretary-General of the United Nations, UNAT Judgment No. 18 [1953]*, available at http://untreaty.un.org/UNAT/UNAT_Judgements/Judgements_E/UNAT_00018_E.pdf, last visited on 30.12.2010, para. 1 and *Cooperman v. Secretary-General of the United Nations, UNAT Judgment No. 93 [1965]*, available at http://untreaty.un.org/UNAT/UNAT_Judgements/Judgements_E/UNAT_00093_E.pdf, last visited on 30.12.2010, para. VI. It is feasible to argue that similar approach would be taken also with regard to the application of former Regulation 9.1(a) of the *UN Staff Regulations* and present Regulation 9.3(a)(vi) and 9.3(b) of the *UN Staff Regulations* and corresponding *UN Staff Rules*

[246] *UN Staff Regulations of 2009*, Regulation 9.3(b); and *UN Staff Rules*, Rule 9.6(d). See also *General Assembly Resolution 63/250*, Section II, para. 22.

[247] Note that the General Assembly's Advisory Committee on Budgetary and Administrative Questions has explicitly stated that the principal interpretation of the phrase 'in the interest of the Organization' should not include other legitimate considerations, such as those put forward by the Secretary-General in his proposal stipulating the conditions for implementing the new type of UN appointment, the continuing appointment. The Committee has warned against interpretation going beyond that provided by the General Assembly. – *Human Resources Management, Report of the Advisory Committee on Administrative and Budgetary Questions, A/65/537*, para. 54.

service, stressed by the UNAT in *Gordon* as the main reason for greater protection of permanent appointments against their termination.[248] However, the fact that different types of appointment have been retained demonstrates that there still is the intention to maintain a certain proportion of staff on career bases. When approving the new system of contracts at the UN Secretariat, the General Assembly explicitly confirmed this approach by prescribing:

> *a judicious mix of career and fixed-term appointments, so as to have an appropriate balance between institutional memory, long-term commitment and independence and the ability to bring in fresh insight and expertise, and to dismiss non-performing staff.*[249]

Last but not least, it could be argued that the principle of geographical distribution has never had a place in areas of human resources management other than recruitment and that this has not been changed by the recent modification of the types of appointment, adopted in 2009. Both Article 101(3) of the *UN Charter* as well as Regulation 4.2 of the *UN Staff Regulations* have remained unchanged, clearly stipulating that due regard is to be paid to the principle of geographical distribution in staff *recruitment*. In addition, pursuant to Regulation 1.1(d) of the *UN Staff Regulations*, the *conditions of service* are to be determined solely by the need of securing as efficient, competent and loyal staff as possible.[250] Consequently, the principle of geographical distribution should not be associated with the concept 'the interest of the good administration of the Organization' in the context of the termination of staff appointments.

2.5.2. Nationality as a reason for contract non-renewal

There are two types of appointments in the UN Secretariat that end upon expiry of a term stated in the letter of appointment – temporary and fixed-term appointments. Both these types of appointment can, however, be extended or renewed, subject to certain conditions.[251] Of course, non-extension or non-renewal of an appointment cannot, strictly speaking, be regarded as its termination; the termination of such appointment occurs due to the expiry of the agreed term, not due to non-extension or non-renewal of the appointment. Nonetheless, the denial of an available extension or renewal has the same practical effect as termination by ending the employment relationship between the UN and the relevant staff member. The question is whether considerations relating to the geographical representation status of UN Member States could be a legitimate reason for a non-extension or a non-renewal of an appointment made for a fixed-term period.

---

[248] *Gordon v. Secretary-General of the United Nations, UNAT Judgment No. 29 [1953]*, available at http://untreaty.un.org/UNAT/UNAT_Judgements/Judgements_E/UNAT_00029_E.pdf, last visited on 30.12.2010, p. 123, para. 2.

[249] *General Assembly Resolution 63/250*, Section II, para. 16.

[250] *UN Staff Regulations of 2009*, Regulation 1.1(d).

[251] *UN Staff Rules*, Rules 4.12 and 4.13.

To begin with, it should be noted that, according to settled case law, the UN Administration enjoys a broad discretion with regard to extension and renewal of fixed-term appointments.[252] This means that non-extension and non-renewal of such appointments may be based on any legitimate reason, including that relating to the need to ensure equitable geographical distribution in the UN Secretariat. Moreover, it is possible to argue that an extension or a renewal of an individual appointment leads, in fact, to a new appointment. Therefore, considerations connected to making new appointments should apply, including those relating to the principle of geographical distribution. In situations in which the geographical representation status of certain Member State(s) needs to be improved, the non-extension or non-renewal of an appointment could even be considered as being 'in the best interests of the Organization', as required by the jurisprudence, opening up a possibility to improve the representation status of countries that need it.[253]

2.5.3. Termination of appointment due to change of nationality

Although the change in staff members' nationality may lead to the modification of the representation status of their country, such change is irrelevant for the continuation of staff members' appointment. While UN staff are required to inform the Secretary-General about any intention to change their nationality, that information is not intended to serve purposes related to the continuation of service but rather those related to possible changes in staff member's rights to certain allowances.[254]

3. The European Commission

3.1. The principle of geographical balance in the past and present

Unlike the *UN Charter*, neither the *Treaty on European Union* nor the *Treaty on the Functioning of the European Union* deal with the issue of geographical balance of the EU staff. The same was true for the founding treaties of the European Communities, which preceded the European Union. The only relevant provision in this respect was Article 246(3) of the former *EEC Treaty* which provided that, until staff regulations would be adopted, each institution could recruit staff it needed by concluding contracts of limited duration. This provision also stipulated that questions concerning

---

[252] *Rau v. Secretary-General of the United Nations, UNAT Judgment No. 101 [1966]*, available at http://untreaty.un.org/UNAT/UNAT_Judgements/Judgements_E/UNAT_00101_E.pdf, last visited on 30.12.2010, para. III. Note that in some instances, staff may have acquired legal expectancy of extension or renewal of their appointment. In such instances, discretion of the UN Administration does not exist. If the appointment at issue is not extended or renewed, the staff member concerned must be compensated for damage suffered. For more on the concept of legal expectancy in the UN, see below, chapter 6, section 2.4.2.

[253] For example, *Karmoul v. Secretary-General of the United Nations, UNAT Judgment No. 791 [1996]*, available at http://untreaty.un.org/UNAT/UNAT_Judgements/Judgements_E/UNAT_00791_E.pdf, last visited on 30.12.2010, paras. II and VI.

[254] *UN Staff Rules*, Rule 1.5(c). See also Rule 4.3(b) on the discretion of the Secretary-General to decide which nationality is to be used for the UN purposes in case a staff member possesses more than one nationality.

the 'number, remuneration and distribution of posts' were to be arranged by the institutions with the Council of Ministers.[255] As far as the 'distribution of posts' is concerned, this arrangement took the form of an informal gentleman's agreement concluded among the Member States, based on which the posts in the future Commission, which needed to be filled in 1958, were to be distributed among Member States' nationals in a proportion equivalent to the countries' individual contributions to the budget.[256] Helped by national Administrations, friends and assistants involved in the negotiations of the EEC Treaty, each Commissioner drew up a list of potential candidates for Commission employment of their nationality.[257] This practice was similar to that which had existed in the ECSC High Authority in the early 1950s before formal recruitment procedures were adopted. There, candidates were nominated by the Directors of the High Authority's divisions and approved by a member of the High Authority of the candidate's own nationality.[258]

A partial formalisation of the early practice in the EEC took place in 1961 when the first *EEC Staff Regulations* were adopted. Article 27 thereof stipulated that Community officials were to be recruited on the widest possible geographical basis among nationals of the EEC countries.[259] The relevant part of this provision has remained unchanged and its current version reads as follows:

> *Recruitment shall be directed to ensuring for the institution the service of officials of the highest standard of ability, efficiency and integrity, recruited on the broadest possible geographical basis from among nationals of Member States of the Communities.*
>
> *No posts shall be reserved for nationals of any specific Member State.*[260]

The requirement to recruit Community staff on the broadest possible geographical basis has come to be known as 'the principle of geographical balance'. Although Article 27 itself does not use the term 'balance', the European Court of Justice explained in one of the very first staff cases that by including the requirement of recruiting staff on the broadest possible geographical basis in Article 27, 'geographical balance among the [EU] staff' was meant to be ensured:

[255] *Treaty Establishing the European Economic Community*, 25.03.1957, available at http://eur-lex.europa.eu/en/treaties/index.htm#founding, last visited on 30.12.2010, Article 246(3). Note that an identical provision existed in the Euratom Treaty, too. - *Treaty Establishing the European Atomic Energy Community*, 25.03.1957, available at http://eur-lex.europa.eu/en/treaties/index.htm#founding, last visited on 30.12.2010, Article 213(3).

[256] Coombes, *Politics and Bureaucracy in the European Community, A Portrait of the Commission of the E.E.C.*, pp. 141-142. In specific figures, it meant that 28 per cent of posts must have been filled by nationals of France, Germany and Italy, respectively; 7,9 per cent of posts were reserved for Dutch and Belgian nationals, respectively; and 0,2 per cent for nationals of Luxembourg. See Article 200(1) of the original EEC Treaty stipulating Member States' financial contributions.

[257] Ibid., pp. 141-142.

[258] Stevens and Stevens, *Brussels Bureaucrats? The Administration of the European Union*, pp. 72-74.

[259] *EU Staff Regulations of 1961*, Article 27.

[260] *EU Staff Regulations*, Article 27.

> *... [R]ecruitment on the broadest possible* geographical basis*... mean[s] that it is a factor to be taken into consideration ... in order to secure the best possible* geographical balance. *(emphasis added)*

and:

> *... [W]here the qualifications of the various candidates are approximately equal, the administration should allow nationality to play a decisive role when it is necessary to maintain or to re-establish a* geographical balance *among its staff.*[261] *(emphasis added)*

Despite this formalization of the principle of geographical balance in the *EEC Staff Regulations*, neither these initial *Regulations*, nor the current *EU Staff Regulations*, have institutionalized the informal gentleman's agreement between the Member States on national quotas. Nonetheless, it has been argued that national quotas have existed in the European Commission in practice for decades. The quotas, as well as other reflections of the principle of geographical balance, are addressed in more detail in a section below. Before turning to that, however, attention is first paid to the relationship between the principle of geographical balance and the principle of merit. As the wording of Article 27 of the *EU Staff Regulations*, quoted above, stipulates, both merit and geographical considerations have their place in EU staff policy, as they do in the UN. A proper understanding of the relationship between the two principles in the EU system is necessary for the subsequent assessment of the manner in which the EU has tried to translate the principle of geographical balance into practice.

3.2. Relationship between geographical balance and merit

The ECJ addressed the issue of the precise relationship between the principle of geographical balance and the principle of merit and the manner in which they may be applied in its early case law. In its 1964 judgment in *Lassalle*, the applicant challenged the legality of a requirement of a perfect knowledge of the Italian language contained in the notice of vacancy.[262] The applicant claimed that such requirement was a disguised method of reserving the post at hand to a person of Italian nationality and made any considerations of merit of all other eligible candidates impossible. The European Parliament, respondent in this case, confirmed that the purpose of the clause was, indeed, to impose a condition of nationality. Therefore, the ECJ first examined whether the notice of vacancy could include a nationality requirement. The ECJ stated that '[i]f this were the case, the aims of Articles 7 and 27 of the Staff Regulations would be incapable of being realized' as these provisions were aimed to ensure that treatment of staff was in line with the interest of the service and with no regard to nationality.[263] The ECJ further emphasized that pursuant to Article 27, no posts might be reserved for nationals of any specific Member State. It held that

[261] *Claude Lassalle v. European Parliament, Case 15/63, ECR [1964], p. 36*, p.38
[262] Ibid..
[263] Ibid., p. 37.

even though the same provision referred to recruitment on as broad a geographical basis as possible, this factor had to be taken into consideration at a later stage of the recruitment process. The ECJ also decided that:

> *where the qualifications of the various candidates are approximately equal, the administration should allow nationality to play a decisive role when it is necessary to maintain or to re-establish a geographical balance among its staff. Such a possibility is not incompatible with the prohibition in Article 7(1) of the Staff Regulations.*[264]

In the case at hand, however, the purpose of the language clause was to reserve the vacant post to a national of a particular Member State – without any chance of prior considerations of the merit. Consequently, candidates of other than required nationalities were *a priori* deprived of a possibility to have their candidature considered, a situation the ECJ found to be incompatible with, *inter alia*, Articles 7 and 27 of the *EU Staff Regulations*.[265] In this case, the ECJ thus gave full effect to the principle of geographical balance included in Article 27(3) of the *EU Staff Regulations* but clearly subordinated this principle to merit which must be the decisive criterion in the recruitment process. Nationality may play a role, and even an important one, but only when examination of candidates' qualifications has led to very similar results.

This approach was upheld a few years later in *Reinarz*. In that case the ECJ confirmed that both merit and geographical balance were relevant in the process of recruitment, promotion and assignment of EU staff to posts, with nationality being 'the overriding criterion' only in cases where the qualifications of the candidates were substantially the same.[266] Some time later, in *Schloh*, the ECJ held that only when the qualifications of the various candidates for a vacant post, assessed first, proved to be clearly the same, might nationality become decisive. The ECJ emphasized once again that:

> *in any other circumstances, the need to redress a geographical imbalance must be subordinated to the requirement of the interest of the service and the consideration of the personal merits of the candidates.*[267]

In this respect it must be noted that the ECJ has been rather inconsistent in using terms related to the level of equality of the candidates' qualifications required in order for nationality to come into play. It has been using expressions, such as: 'approximately equal' in *Lassalle*;[268] 'substantially the same' in *Reinarz*;[269] 'equal' in

[264] Ibid., p. 38.
[265] Ibid., p. 38.
[266] *Andreas Reinarz v. Commission of the European Communities, Case 17/68, ECR [1969], p. 61*, para. 35
[267] *Bernhard Schloh v. Council of the European Communities, Case 85/82, ECR [1983], p. 2105*, para. 26.
[268] *Lassalle v. European Parliament, Case 15/63*, para. 38.
[269] *Reinarz v. Commission, Case 17/68*, para. 35.

Ragusa;[270] 'clearly the same' in *Schloh*;[271] 'essentially the same' in *Kalavros*[272] and in *Kotzovis*.[273] There is no doubt that an important difference exists between the phrases 'clearly the same' and 'essentially the same'. The first expression leaves no room for any difference between the qualifications whatsoever, while the second one allows for a certain degree of differentiation. It could be argued that the latter should be regarded as correct. This view is supported by the fact that it is, in practice, close to impossible to find two persons with identical qualifications. If not in the education degree itself, any two individuals would differ in experience and capabilities acquired in the course of their respective professional careers.

Regarding the assessment of merit and candidates' qualifications, according to the established case law, it is for the appointing authority to assess whether a candidate fulfils required conditions. The appointing authority has a wide discretion in this assessment and the ECJ will not substitute or question its assessment, unless a manifest error has occurred.[274] Hence, as long as the Administration remains 'within reasonable bounds and does not use its power in a manifestly incorrect way or for the purposes other than those for which it was conferred upon it', the ECJ will decline to verify the merit assessment.[275] It will, however, require evidence proving that a comparative examination of the candidates' qualification has taken place.[276]

The ECJ has thus generally accepted the simultaneous use of both principles – merit and geographical balance – in the EU recruitment process. It has agreed with the relevance of the nationality criterion because it leads to the establishment and/or maintenance of overall geographical balance in the EU civil service envisaged, in the ECJ's view, by Article 27 of the *EU Staff Regulations*. Nonetheless, the ECJ has declared illegal any direct ways of achieving such balance. It has refused to approve practices of giving preference to nationals of certain Member States without considering their qualifications first, or instances of reserving posts for candidates of a specific nationality.

The question that necessarily arises in this respect is how the principle of geographical balance has been translated into practical terms suitable for application in the actual staff selection process as well as compatible with the above-mentioned legal requirements. The following two sections provide an answer to this question. They

[270] *Salvatore Ragusa v. Commission of the European Communities, Case 282/81, ECR [1983], p. 1245*, para. 14.

[271] *Schloh v. Council, Case 85/82*, para. 26.

[272] *Gregoris Evangelos Kalavros v. Court of Justice of the European Communities, Joined cases T-160/89 and T-161/89, ECR [1990], p. II-871*, para. 41.

[273] *Petros Kotzonis v. Economic and Social Committee, Case T-586/93, ECR [1995], p. II-665, ECR-SC [1995], p. I-A-61, II-203*, para. 86.

[274] See, especially, *Ragusa v. Commission, Case 282/81*, para. 13; *Santo Picciolo v. European Parliament, Case 111/83, ECR [1984], p. 2323*, para. 16; *G. B. C. Echternach and A. Moritz v. Minister van Onderwijs en Wetenschappen, Joined cases 389/87 and 390/87, ECR [1989], p. 723*, para. 29; *Kotzonis v. Economic and Social Committee, Case T-586/93*, para. 81.

[275] *Kotzonis v. Economic and Social Committee, Case T-586/93*, para. 81.

[276] *Ragusa v. Commission, Case 282/81*, para. 13; *Kalavros v. ECJ, Joined cases T-160/89 and T-161/89*, para. 31.

do this first, by analysing the systems of national quotas, flags, diversity and colonies, the existence of which has been observed and, on an exceptional basis, also officially admitted; and second, by explaining which mechanisms have been used in order to advance the placement of nationals of individual Member States.

3.3. National quotas, flags and colonies

The system of national quotas and national flags, the colonization of certain administrative units and, according to some authors, also the existence of the policy of national diversity are all practical reflections of the principle of geographical balance in EU staff policy. Although their existence has always been unofficial, and from time to time denied by relevant bodies, many political scientists who have conducted empirical studies on the European Commission have concluded that these systems have formed an important part of EU staff selection process for decades. The following sections explain what these systems entail and assess their compatibility with Article 27 of the *EU Staff Regulations*, as interpreted by the ECJ. With regard to the factual assessment of the existence of the systems, the sections rely considerably on the empirical studies conducted by political scientists, adding some more recent data.

3.3.1. National quotas

In its *Compilation Document on Senior Officials Policy* of 2004, the European Commission expressly declares that it does not apply national quotas at any level of posts for its officials. At the same time, the Commission affirms that it 'will respect an adequate balance of nationalities represented in the Commission's service', subject to the prevailing criterion of merit.[277] The Commission also puts forward an objective of each nationality having at least one function corresponding to the basic post of Director-General.[278] Furthermore, it expresses an obligation to ensure that:

> *during the entire procedure for filling vacancies [for senior posts], the principles and objectives decided on by the Commission on geographical balance ... are respected.*[279]

Further elaboration on these 'principles and objectives' which should lead to securing geographical balance in the recruitment process is not included in the document, neither is such specification to be found elsewhere.

It follows that there are no formal arrangements to ensure geographical balance in the European Commission civil service. The situation in the European Commission, therefore, considerably differs from that in the UN Secretariat where the issue of geographical distribution of posts and calculation of national quotas, referred to as desirable ranges, has been the subject-matter of extensive discussions from the

---

[277] *Commission Compilation Document on Senior Officials Policy*, p. 3.

[278] Ibid., p. 4.

[279] Ibid., p. 5.

early years of the UN until now. The UN Secretary-General is obliged to conform to these national quotas by recruiting sufficient number of candidates from each individual country that does not reach its desirable range and he is regularly held accountable for it.[280]

In the European Commission, no such formal system of national quotas exists. Its absence, however, does not necessarily mean that quotas did not or do not exist in reality. As mentioned above, when the original EEC was established, Member States concluded an informal gentleman's agreement according to which the posts that needed to be filled in the first year of the organization's functioning were to be distributed among nationals of all six Member States on the basis of their share in the budget contribution.[281] In the 1960s, the nationality was still taken into account in the staff appointment policy, although it became less important when compared to the early years.[282] Certain features of the initial informal approach continued to exist, however, especially in the process of recruitment and appointment to senior posts.[283] Many authors have observed that there was a strong norm in the Commission staff policy to ensure proportionate national representation especially at the top echelons. Thus, while in theory the Commission's senior officials were appointed on the basis of merit, in practice they did need to have the right nationality to fit within the quota of their country.[284] It has also been argued that the considerations relating to geographical balance have not been limited to the Commission's higher echelons only. Page, for example, claimed that, although there was more emphasis on merit in posts down to former category A8 and geographical balance was less even, nevertheless, this balance was still much more even than in former grades B, C and D.[285] Page compared the nationality of people who had applied for the EU competition and of those who were subsequently employed and concluded that the geographical balance factor played a role in deciding which candidates successful in the competition would actually be appointed.[286]

Since national quotas have never been formalized, it is not entirely clear how the individual quota for each Member State was established. According to Hooghe, national quotas were calculated in approximately the same manner as the distribution of votes in the Council of Ministers.[287] Bodiguel claimed that the division of seats in

---

280 See above, section 2.2.

281 See above, section 3.1.

282 Coombes, *Politics and Bureaucracy in the European Community, A Portrait of the Commission of the E.E.C.*, p. 163.

283 Stevens and Stevens, *Brussels Bureaucrats? The Administration of the European Union*, pp. 72-74.

284 Hooghe, *The European Commission and the Integration of Europe, Images of Governance*, pp. 59 and 177. See also, for example, Page, *People Who Run Europe*, p. 46; Endo, *The Presidency of the European Commission under Jacques Delors, The Politics of Shared Leadership*, p. 37.

285 See also Stevens and Stevens, *Brussels Bureaucrats? The Administration of the European Union*, pp. 92-94.

286 Page, *People Who Run Europe*, p. 46.

287 Hooghe, *The European Commission and the Integration of Europe, Images of Governance*, p. 177

the European Parliament was used as a guideline.[288] Kassim *et al.* have mentioned the share of Member States in the EU population as the decisive criterion.[289]

The Commission itself used to firmly deny the existence of any such formula, except in cases when the existing geographical balance needed adjusting for the benefit of nationals from Member States which had newly acceded to the EU. In those instances, the Commission calculated specific quotas reflecting the relative weight of the new Member States in the enlarged Union and that were to be filled within a certain transitional period. For the enlargements prior to 2004, the calculations were established mostly on the basis of negotiation and comparison between old and new Member States. Occasionally, a reference was made to objective criteria, such as population and gross domestic product. Due to the specific nature of the 2004 and 2007 enlargements, the Commission used a different approach there and established three firm criteria which were taken into consideration in calculations of national quotas for new Member States: the population, the weighting of votes in the Council and the number of seats in the European Parliament.[290] A slightly different approach applied to senior positions. At the level of Director-General, for example, the objective was to recruit at least one national from each new Member State.[291]

Despite the formal denial of national quotas, their existence was occasionally admitted. Perhaps the most important instance, in which the quotas were explicitly addressed, was the second report of the Committee of Independent Experts prepared in 1999.[292] In Chapter 6 dealing with personnel matters, the report stated:

> *Nationality as a general criterion for appointment, though aimed at securing Member States a proportionate share in Community decision-making processes, inevitably gives rise to informal quota provisions.*[293]

Furthermore, the Committee noted that among actions that should be taken in order to improve the existing state of affairs, a certain flexibility should be introduced within the system of national quotas:

---

288 Bodiguel, J.-L., *Les Fonctions Publiques dans l'Europe Des Douze*, Librairie Général de Driot et de Jurisprudence, Paris, 1994, p. 159, as cited in Stevens and Stevens, *Brussels Bureaucrats? The Administration of the European Union*, p. 93.

289 Kassim and Peters, *Co-ordinating National Action in Brussels - a Comparative Perspective*, p. 316.

290 *Communication Relative au Recruitement de Fonctionnaires de la Commission des Nouveaux Etats Membres, Communication de M. Kinnock, C(2003)436/5*, 14.02.2003, available at http://ec.europa.eu/reform/pdf/sec_2003_0436_en.pdf, last visited on 15.01.2008, p. 4. The specific nature of the 2004 and 2007 enlargements resulted especially from the low Gross Domestic Product (GDP) of the new Member States. For example, the combined GDP of the countries that acceded to the EU in 2004 was only 4,4 per cent of the total GDP of the enlarged Union. Consequently, GDP could not have been used as an objective criterion for calculating the geographical factor because it would result in an unfair situation.

291 *Recruitment of Senior Managers from the New Member States - Implementation Measures, Communication from Vice-President Kinnock in Agreement with the President, SEC(2004)0252*, p.2.

292 *Second Report on Reform of the Commission of 1999, Volume II.*

293 Ibid., para. 7.5.9.

We might also think about the development of flexibility in the current system of 'national quotas', which would enable ability and professional experience to play a more decisive role in the appointments procedure (see below, section on 'Appointment of the most senior officials'). At all events, that criterion should be applied with respect to the – somewhat 'atypical' – post of Secretary-General of the Commission.[294]

Moreover, with regard to the recruitment of senior officials, the Committee recommended:

A set of rules, or at least a code of conduct, laying down a number of objective and transparent criteria should therefore be drawn up to cover the recruitment of such officials, so as to reduce the risk of problems arising and to start to reverse the current trend. Thus, with regard to the significance of national balances, the flexibility of the current 'quota' system could be progressively increased, a time limit could be place on the length of service in such posts, the appointment of a successor of the same nationality could be prohibited, and so on. As regards recruitment procedures, more thorough selection criteria should be introduced, as should more transparent procedures.[295]

According to some observers, the strict quota system in place in the Commission previously has indeed been abandoned.[296] However, when comparing recent data on the number of officials serving in the Commission to the weight of the individual Member States in the European Parliament and in the Council of Ministers, a clear correlation can still be detected. This trend is particularly visible in senior positions. Although formally the Commission's policy on this point is merely to have at least one national of each Member State, available data suggest otherwise. This is in particular the case of the 15 older Member States.

[294] Ibid., para. 6.2.32.

[295] Ibid., para. 6.5.47.

[296] Egeberg, M., *Organising Institutional Autonomy in a Political Context: Enduring Tensions in the European Commission's Development*, ARENA Working Papers WP 02/2004, 2004, available at http://www.sv.uio.no/arena/english/research/publications/arena-publications/workingpapers/working-papers2004/wp04_2.pdf, last visited on 30.12.2010, p. 11.

Table 5: Combined weight of individual EU Member States in the European Parliament and Council of Ministers

Member State	No. of MEP*	% of all MEP	No. of votes in the Council**	% of all votes in the Council	Combined weight in the EP and Council (%)
AUT	17	2,31	10	2,82	**2,565**
BEL	22	2,99	12	3,38	**3,185**
BGR	17	2,31	10	2,82	**2,565**
CYP	6	0,82	4	1,13	**0,975**
CZE	22	2,99	12	3,38	**3,185**
DEU	99	13,47	29	8,17	**10,82**
DNK	13	1,77	7	1,97	**1,87**
ESP	50	6,8	27	7,6	**7,2**
EST	6	0,82	4	1,13	**0,975**
FIN	13	1,77	7	1,97	**1,87**
FRA	72	9,8	29	8,17	**8,99**
GBR	72	9,8	29	8,17	**8,99**
GRC	22	2,99	12	3,38	**3,185**
HUN	22	2,99	12	3,38	**3,185**
IRL	12	1,63	17	4,79	**3,21**
ITA	72	9,8	29	8,17	**8,99**
LTU	12	1,63	7	1,97	**1,8**
LUX	6	0,82	4	1,13	**0,975**
LVA	8	1,09	4	1,13	**1,11**
MLT	5	0,68	3	0,85	**1,53**
NLD	25	3,4	13	3,66	**3,53**
POL	49	6,67	27	7,6	**7,135**
PRT	22	2,99	12	3,38	**3,185**
ROM	33	1,49	14	3,94	**2,715**
SVK	13	1,77	7	1,97	**1,87**
SVN	7	0,95	4	1,13	**1,04**
SWE	18	2,45	10	2,81	**2,63**
TOTAL	*735*	*97*	*355*	*100*	***99,28***

Sources: * Retrieved from the official *EU website*.

** *Treaty of Lisbon*, Protocol No. 36, para. 3.[297]

[297] Relevant data on the Europa internet site are available at http://www.europarl.europa.eu/members/expert/groupAndCountry.do?language=EN, last visited on 05.03.2010;

Table 6: Nationality of European Commission senior officials – all 27 Member States

(February 2010)

Member State	No. AD16*	No. AD15*	No. AD14*	Total No. AD16-14	% of total AD16-14	Member State weight
AUT	1	4	15	20	**2,74**	**2,565**
BEL	1	22	65	88	**12,05**	**3,185**
BGR			2	2	**0,27**	**2,565**
CYP		1	3	4	**0,55**	**0,975**
CZE		2	3	5	**0,68**	**3,185**
DEU	5	27	46	78	**10,68**	**10,82**
DNK	1	6	10	17	**2,33**	**1,87**
ESP	5	27	31	63	**4,6**	**7,2**
EST		1	3	4	**0,55**	**0,975**
FIN	1	4	8	13	**1,78**	**1,87**
FRA	5	32	77	114	**15,62**	**8,99**
GBR	6	27	43	76	**10,41**	**8,99**
GRC		13	29	42	**5,75**	**3,185**
HUN		3	7	10	**1,37**	**3,185**
IRL	2	9	15	26	**3,56**	**3,21**
ITA	5	21	29	55	**7,53**	**8,99**
LTU			2	2	**0,27**	**1,8**
LUX		2	5	7	**0,96**	**0,975**
LVA			2	2	**0,27**	**1,11**
MLT			1	1	**0,14**	**1,53**
NLD	1	12	21	34	**4,66**	**3,53**
POL		2	11	13	**1,78**	**7,135**
PRT	1	10	11	22	**3,01**	**3,185**
ROM			5	5	**0,68**	**2,715**
SVK		1	3	4	**0,55**	**1,87**
SVN		1	3	4	**0,55**	**1,04**
SWE	1	4	14	19	**2,6**	**2,63**
TOTAL	*35*	*231*	*464*	*730*	*95,94*	*99,28*

Table 7: Nationality of European Commission senior officials – 15 old Member States
(February 2010)

Member State	No. AD16*	No. AD15*	No. AD14*	Total No. AD16-14	% of total AD16-14	Member State weight
AUT	1	4	15	20	2,74	2,565
BEL	1	22	65	88	12,05	3,185
DEU	5	27	46	78	10,68	10,82
DNK	1	6	10	17	2,33	1,87
ESP	5	27	31	63	4,6	7,2
FIN	1	4	8	13	1,78	1,87
FRA	5	32	77	114	15,62	8,99
GBR	6	27	43	76	10,41	8,99
GRC		13	29	42	5,75	3,185
IRL	2	9	15	26	3,56	3,21
ITA	5	21	29	55	7,53	8,99
LUX		2	5	7	0,96	0,975
NLD	1	12	21	34	4,66	3,53
PRT	1	10	11	22	3,01	3,185
SVN		1	3	4	0,55	1,04
SWE	1	4	14	19	2,6	2,63

***Source:** *Distribution of Officials and Temporary Agents by Genders, Nationalities, Function Groups and Grades (All Budgets)*, as on 01.02.2010.[298]

A similar, though considerably less strong, trend can be seen in the figures relating to all AD staff. Especially in the case of the 15 older Member States (in no less than ten out of 15 older Member States), the number of AD positions held by their nationals manifestly corresponds to the combined weight of these countries in the European Parliament and Council of Ministers.

[298] *Distribution of Officials and Temporary Agents by Genders, Nationalities, Function Groups and Grades (All Budgets)*, Sysper2, 01.02.2010, p. 1, available at http://ec.europa.eu/civil_service/docs/europa_sp2_bs_nat_x_grade_en.pdf, visited on 05.03.2010.

Table 8: Number of European Commission officials in AD posts per nationality and the average weight of individual EU Member States in the European Parliament and Council of Ministers – all 27 Member States

(February 2010)

Member State	No. of AD*	% of AD	AD % MS weight
AUT	178	2,26	2,565
BEL	949	12,03	3,185
BGR	67	0,85	2,565
CYP	39	0,49	0,975
CZE	134	1,7	3,185
DEU	949	12,03	10,82
DNK	177	2,24	1,87
ESP	664	8,42	7,2
EST	38	0,48	0,975
FIN	141	1,79	1,87
FRA	954	12,1	8,99
GBR	621	7,87	8,99
GRC	365	4,63	3,185
HUN	171	2,17	3,185
IRL	175	2,22	3,21
ITA	803	10,18	8,99
LTU	66	0,84	1,8
LUX	33	0,42	0,975
LVA	30	0,38	1,11
MLT	51	0,65	1,53
NLD	351	4,45	3,53
POL	288	3,65	7,135
PRT	245	3,11	3,185
ROM	70	0,89	2,715
SVK	85	1,08	1,87
SVN	54	0,68	1,04
SWE	188	2,38	2,63

Table 9: Number of European Commission officials in AD posts per nationality and the average weight of individual EU Member States in the European Parliament and the Council of Ministers – 15 old Member States

(February 2010)

Member State	No. of AD*	% in all AD	AD % MS weight
AUT	178	2,26	2,565
BEL	949	12,03	3,185
DEU	949	12,03	10,82
DNK	177	2,24	1,87
ESP	664	8,42	7,2
FIN	141	1,79	1,87
FRA	954	12,1	8,99
GBR	621	7,87	8,99
GRC	365	4,63	3,185
IRL	175	2,22	3,21
ITA	803	10,18	8,99
LUX	33	0,42	0,975
NLD	351	4,45	3,53
PRT	245	3,11	3,185
SWE	188	2,38	2,63

Sources: **Distribution of Officials and Temporary Agents by Genders, Nationalities, Function Groups and Grades (All Budgets)*, as on 01.02.2010.[299]

As the data demonstrate, there is one sharp exception, Belgium, which has traditionally been heavily overrepresented in the Commission given its headquarters location. As far as the new Member States are concerned, the figures are rather different and the number of their AD officials, including senior officials, is considerably lower than their weight in the European Parliament and Council of Ministers. It could be argued that this is because the quotas of the new Member States have not yet been filled, given the relatively short period of time which has passed since their accession to the EU.

If it is indeed accepted that informally national quotas exist in the European Commission, a question that arises is why their existence is formally denied. It would be only reasonable to expect that the appointing authority, making a choice

[299] *Distribution of Officials and Temporary Agents by Genders, Nationalities, Function Groups and Grades (All Budgets)*, Sysper2, 01.02.2010, p. 1; available at http://ec.europa.eu/civil_service/docs/europa_sp2_bs_nat_x_grade_en.pdf, visited on 05.03.2010.

between candidates for a vacant post, may pay regard to their nationality when their qualifications are essentially the same, and that it would be aware of the desirable and the actual state of affairs. If there were no quotas, no figures, no precise data, the appointing authority could not know which nationality is overrepresented or underrepresented. Consequently, it could not know which candidate should be given preference in order to restore geographical balance, if needed.

It appears that the Commission's denial of national quotas is rooted in its fear of possible incompatibility of national quotas with the *EU Staff Regulations*.[300] The Committee of Independent Experts of 1999 explicitly acknowledged such doubts:

> *Whether this system [of national quotas] is consistent with Community law is doubtful, given that the ECJ has held that job allocation should not be predetermined and should be decided on merit...*[301]

The Commission itself stated the following:

> *National "quotas" for posts are not an acceptable tool of personnel policy and not permissible unde (sic) the Staff Regulations. Maintaining broad geographical balance is, however, a valid objective in a multinational public administration like the Commission.*[302]

The Commission thus seems to understand Article 27 of the *EU Staff Regulations* as envisaging geographical balance in a general rather than in a strict numerical sense. This is interesting since the wording of the relevant part of Article 27 of the *EU Staff Regulations* is fairly identical to the wording of Article 101(3), second sentence, of the *UN Charter*. The latter has been worked out in the system of desirable ranges, which entails the number of posts considered as adequate for a fair representation

---

[300] The possible incompatibility of the transitional national quotas and other measures aimed at their direct implementation through a preferential recruitment of nationals of new Member States with Article 7(1) and then Article 27(3) of the *EU Staff Regulations* has been resolved by the Council's adoption of time-limited derogations from the two provisions. See, for example, *Regulation (Euratom, ECSC, EEC) No 2530/72 of the Council of 4 December 1972 Introducing Special and Temporary Measures Applicable to the Recruitment of Officials of the European Communities in Consequence of the Accession of New Member States, and for the Termination of Service of Officials of Those Communities*, OJ L 272, 05.12.1972, p. 1-5, p. 1; *Council Regulation (ECSC/EEC/Euratom) No 662/82 of 22 March 1982 Introducing Special and Temporary Measures Applicable to the Recruitment of Officials of the European Communities in Consequence of the Accession of the Hellenic Republic to the Communities*, OJ L 78, 24.03.1982, p. 1, p. 1; *Council Regulation (ECSC, EEC, Euratom) No 3517/85 of 12 December 1985 Introducing Special and Temporary Measures Applicable to the Recruitment of Officials of the European Communities as a Result of the Accession of Spain and Portugal*, OJ L 335, 13.12.1985, p. 55, p. 55; *Council Regulation (EC) No 626/95 of 20 March 1995 Introducing Special and Temporary Measures Applicable to the Recruitment of Officials of the European Communities as a Result of the Accession of Austria, Finland and Sweden*, OJ L 66, 24.03.1995, p. 1, p. 1. Note that at the time of the EU enlargements (except of the 2007 enlargement) it was paragraph 3 that prohibited reservation of posts for nationals of a certain Member State. In the meantime, the second paragraph of Article 27 was deleted and paragraph 3 has become paragraph 2.

[301] *Second Report on Reform of the Commission of 1999, Volume II*, para. 7.5.9., footnote 100.

[302] *European Commission Announces Next Steps in Implementing New Senior Staff Policy*, Press Release, IP/02/124, 23.01.2002, available at http://europa.eu/rapid/pressReleasesAction.do?reference=IP/02/124&format=HTML&aged=0&language=EN&guiLanguage=en, last visited on 30.12.2010.

of each UN Member State in the UN civil service.[303] The legality of this system of desirable ranges has never been challenged before the UN Administrative Tribunal. Also the ECJ has never been asked to rule on the legality of national quotas in the EU institutions. Of course, the absence of a challenge could be due to the difficulties the applicant faces in presenting positive evidence of the existence of the quotas. In addition, the absence of a challenge of the system of desirable ranges or national quotas does not prove its legality. Nonetheless, at least for the UN, this absence does indicate it is unlikely that the system of desirable ranges as such is incompatible with the requirement of ensuring broad geographical balance among international staff. In fact, the system could be seen as reflecting this requirement.

When assessing the possible (in)compatibility of national quotas with the *EU Staff Regulations*, it should be borne in mind that neither Article 27 nor any other provision thereof explicitly outlaws any sort of quotas. Article 27 lays down an obligation to put the candidates' qualifications and the interest of the service before nationality when filling a vacant post. On the other hand, it does not exclude nationality from being considered, rather the contrary. The candidates' nationality may play even a decisive role in cases where their merits are essentially the same. It could be argued that the mere existence of quotas would not contravene the superiority of the principle of merit over that of geographical balance, although its application could. If the quotas were applied in a manner undermining or disregarding the supremacy of the principle of merit, Articles 27 of the *EU Staff Regulations* would be violated. But if the quotas serve a sole purpose of informing the authorities about the desirable number of nationals from each Member State, and thus about the desirable level of each Member State's representation for the purposes of reaching or maintaining an adequate geographical balance within the EU civil service, no such violation necessarily occurs, especially not when candidates' merits are assessed first.

Naturally, in reality there might be other, less legal, reasons for the Commission's formal denial of the existence of national quotas. The experience in the UN has shown that the existence of formal quotas inevitably results in Member States' understanding that they have the right to the number of posts indicated in their quota, and that whenever the quota is not reached, the upcoming appointments should remedy the situation by giving preference in the selection process to their nationals.[304] It is only reasonable to presume that the Commission does not wish

[303] See above, sections 2.1 and 2.2.

[304] This argument is supported by the relatively recent developments surrounding the establishment of the European External Action Service ('EEAS'). The recruitment of the first pool of staff for this Service was severely criticized, in particular by the newer Member States and their representatives in the European Parliament. They pointed out their gross underrepresentation among the newly recruited EEAS staff. However, calls for more or less soft national quotas were eventually not adopted. On the other hand, the EU High Representative for Foreign Affairs and Security Policy is required to ensure an 'appropriate and meaningful presence of nationals from all the Member States' in the EEAS. In a joint press statement issued by the European Parliament rapporteurs shortly before the adoption of the modalities of the EEAS functioning by the European Parliament, it has been explicitly noted that: 'Any further provisions and/or quotas overemphasizing EEAS staff nationality would in our view be detrimental to the communitarian nature of the Service.' - *EU Diplomatic Service: Accountability and Balanced Recruitment*, Press Release, 20101020IPR88408, 20.10.2010, available at http://www.

to tie its hands in staff appointment matters in such a manner. Formal quotas thus remove flexibility in the management of staff matters.

Another, more political, reason for the denial of the existence of national quotas might be an inevitable consequence of quotas admission, namely the need to reveal the method of their calculation. In the UN, there is a strict formula approved by the General Assembly.[305] In the EU, there seems to be a political agreement leading to, as demonstrated above, a certain division of the number of posts among nationals of each Member State. Nonetheless, the particularities of this agreement are not formally known, although the most plausible assumptions suggest that the number of votes in the Council of Ministers and seats in the European Parliament constitute (one of) the bases for calculations. If these two factors are indeed of relevance, the question is whether this should be formally admitted, given the political character of the agreements concerning the number of seats and votes in these institutions and also their inadequate reflection of the real status of each EU Member State. For example, it is generally known that the number of seats of some Member States in the European Parliament do not fully correspond to their population size.[306] Certain discrepancy has also been observed in the division of the votes in the Council of Ministers.[307] Obviously, it is one thing to conclude a political agreement among the EU Member States on the division of their power within EU institutions but quite another to admit that such agreement applies to the number of officials of each nationality to be engaged in the European institutions.

3.3.2. National flags

Similarly to the UN notion 'national preserves', the expression 'national flag' used in the EU refers to informal agreements between EU Member States according to which certain positions at high echelons of the EU civil service are successively filled

europarl.europa.eu/pdfs/news/expert/infopress/20101020IPR88408/20101020IPR88408_en.pdf, last visited on 30.12.2010 and *EEAS: Joint Press Statement by Parliament Rapporteurs*, Press Release, 20101019IPR88330, 19.10.2010, available at http://www.europarl.europa.eu/pdfs/news/expert/infopress/20101019IPR88330/20101019IPR88330_en.pdf, last visited on 30.12.2010. See also Rettman, A., *Old Boys Club Dominates EU Diplomacy*, in: euobserver.com, 25.08.2010; Rettman, A., *EU Parliament to Arm-Twist Ashton on Appointments*, in: euobserver.com, 01.09.2010; *EEAS: Staff Rules to Ensure Geographical and Gender Balance*, Press Release, 20101018IPR87689, 18.10.2010, available at http://www.europarl.europa.eu/pdfs/news/expert/infopress/20101018IPR87689/20101018IPR87689_en.pdf, last visited on 30.12.2010, p. 2; and Rettman, A., *MEPs Drop Idea of Soft Quotas for EU Diplomatic Staff*, in: euobserver.com, 19.10.2010.

305 See above, section 2.2.

306 For example, Luxemburg has 6 seats in the European Parliament, whereas Slovenia 7 while the latter's population is four times as large as the population of the former (2 million compared to 0,5 million inhabitants). On the other hand, the number of seats of Malta with 0,4 million inhabitants, comparable to that of Luxemburg, is only 5 while Luxemburg has 6 seats. – For Member States' population sizes, see information on the Europa website on EU Member States, available at http://europa.eu/about-eu/member-countries/index_en.htm, last visited on 29.09.2010.

307 For example, Germany has 29 votes which equals the number of votes of France, the UK and Italy, while in the European Parliament Germany has 99 seats compared to 72 seats each for the other three Member States.

by nationals of the same Member State.[308] Such agreement seemed to operate rather rigidly in the early years of the EU and, though diminished in its extent, continued to exist for decades.[309] In 1994, for example, Grant observed that:

> *the Director General of financial services is always a Briton, that of agriculture a Frenchman, that of competition policy a German, that of regional policy a Spaniard and that of economic and monetary policy an Italian.*[310]

A number of political scientists have studied this phenomenon. For example, Page examined nationality of Directors-General serving in the course of 1975-1995 and found that most Directorates-General were headed by persons of more than one nationality, although five Directorates-General had officials of the same nationality throughout the whole 20 year period, namely Directors-General for Economic and Financial Affairs; Competition; Agriculture; Credit and Investment; and Budgets.[311] Page also noted that national flags were more strongly connected to the posts at the level of Directors-General and Deputy Directors-General than to other levels, such as the level of Directors. In the case of the former, around one in three changes were between officials of the same nationality, while in the latter case it was around one in four changes.[312] Page, furthermore, observed that not much evidence indicated that below the level of Director-General 'more than a minority of even the top positions is filled on [the basis of national flags]'.[313] He concluded, however, that 'this does not mean that nationalities within the Directorates General are not consciously balanced' but that 'the balance is generally achieved by somewhat more subtle means than passing on the national flag'.[314]

According to Hooghe, even though certain positions were reserved for a particular nationality, such reservations were not always permanent. She stated that 'the bulk [of positions] regularly changes "ownership"' and that nationalities engage from time to time in a strong competition in order to plant their flag on a vacated position.[315]

Another broad analysis by Georgakakis and De Lassalle, conducted in 2007, confirmed the results of the previous studies by Page and Hooghe. Georgakakis and De Lassalle analyzed the background of persons who held a post of Director-General or Deputy Director-General in the European Commission between 1960 and 2000 and found, for example, that 43 out of 46 heads of the Directorate-General for Agriculture had been French, 35 out of 45 Directors-General for Competition had been German, 26 out of 32 Directors-General for Employment had had the Belgian nationality,

[308] For details on the issue of national preserves in the UN Secretariat, see above, section 2.3.2.

[309] Coombes, *Politics and Bureaucracy in the European Community, A Portrait of the Commission of the E.E.C.*, p. 131-132; Page, *People Who Run Europe*, p. 52.

[310] Grant, C., *Delors: Inside the House that Jack Built*, Nicholas Brealy Publishing, London, 1994, as cited in Page, *People Who Run Europe*, p. 52.

[311] Page, *People Who Run Europe*, p. 52.

[312] Ibid., pp. 54-55.

[313] Ibid., p. 54.

[314] Ibid., p. 55.

[315] Hooghe, *The European Commission and the Integration of Europe, Images of Governance*, p. 183

13 Spaniards had held the post of Director-General for Regional Policy and 23 out of 40 Directors-General for Transport had been British nationals. Georgakakis and De Lassalle further claimed that the same could be said about Deputy Directors-General. For example, if a post carried the French flag (e.g. Directorate-General for Agriculture), the deputies in the same Directorate-General were German – 37 out of 106, British – 31 out of 106 or Italian – 33 out of 106, i.e. in total 101 out of 106 instances.[316]

All these studies thus confirmed a *de facto* existence of national flags in the meaning of a longstanding reservation of certain jobs to nationals of specific Member States. However, Page claimed that the direct importance of national flags was exaggerated and that the system did not dominate the Commission.[317] Moreover, a clear distinction between the exercise of national flags and the more widely accepted principle of geographical balance was, according to Page, a difficult one because, in order to maintain the balance, senior positions especially were likely to be filled by nationals of the same Member State.[318] Also Hooghe claimed that the real effect of national flags was exaggerated. In her opinion, in daily work it did not make much difference whose flag fluttered where.[319] Nevertheless, the perception of negative effects of such practice on the independence and impartiality of the senior officials is understandable. The *Second Report of the Committee of Independent Experts*, prepared after the fall of the Santer Commission in 1999, listed 'a form of "nationalisation" of posts (and even of services, as a result of posts being reserved for a given nationality) resulting from one or more people of a given nationality holding a post for a long period of time'. The Commission cited this as one of the important risks in the recruitment of senior officials that needed to be eliminated.[320]

Legally speaking, the system of national flags has always been explicitly outlawed by the *EU Staff Regulations*. Since the adoption of the first Staff Regulations in 1961, Article 27 stipulates in its relevant part that '[n]o post shall be reserved for nationals of any specific Member State.' This provision has not been altered and has been the subject matter of a number of judicial staff cases. Besides the above mentioned *Lasalle* case, illegality of national flags was, for example, highlighted in *Fischer*.[321] In that case, the Court of First Instance condemned the Commission's decision to appoint to the positions of Director two candidates who had the same nationality as the departing officials (the post previously held by a Spaniard was given to another Spanish national and the post previously held by an Italian went to another Italian),

[316] Georgakakis, D. and De Lassalle, M., *Who Are the Directors-General? European Construction and Administrative Careers in the Commission*, Paper based on EU-CONSENT WORKSHOP The Commission and the European Civil Service, Paris, 21-22.6.2006 (Deliverable No. '17'), 2007, available at http://www.eu-consent.net/library/deliverables/D17_Team7_georgakakis-delassalle.pdf, last visited on 30.12.2010, pp. 7-8, see especially Table 2 and Table 3.

[317] Page, *People Who Run Europe*, p. 52

[318] Ibid., p. 54

[319] Hooghe, *The European Commission and the Integration of Europe, Images of Governance*, p. 190

[320] *Second Report on Reform of the Commission of 1999, Volume II*, para. 6.5.46.

[321] *Dierk Booss and Robert Caspar Fischer v. Commission of the European Communities, Case T-58/91, ECR [1993], p. II-147.*

because these appointments were based on the 'matching' nationality rather than on the qualification of the candidates. The Commission's argument that 'certain political realities' exist at the level of Director that should not be ignored, namely the importance of the posts for Member States involved and the relevance of the geographical aspect at that level, was rejected.[322] The CFI did accept the existence and objectives of the principle of geographical balance but disapproved of the system of national flags. The CFI first ruled that the requirement of the (then) third paragraph of Article 27, prohibiting the reservation of posts for the nationals of certain specific Member States, must be observed in all recruitment procedures, including the special procedure provided for the appointment of senior officials.[323] The CFI further emphasized that the proper functioning of the service was the only possible justification for any deviation from Article 27(3). It held that such justification was not present in the case at hand:

> *[The] decision [under consideration] was motivated by the "political reality" pleaded before the Court, whilst considerations concerning the proper functioning of the service, which might have justified the "broadest possible geographical basis" within the meaning of the first paragraph of Article 27 of the Staff Regulations, played no part.*[324]

Therefore, the CFI annulled the contested appointments, thereby rejecting the argument that, at least at certain levels, the reservation of posts and the attendant national flags practice should be tolerated.

Attempts to prevent national flags being put over senior posts in the European Commission civil service, following the fall of the Santer Commission in 1999, confirm that concerns over the effect of the existence of national flags on the independence and impartiality of the EU staff are not unfounded. The Committee of Independent Experts recommended that 'nationalization of posts' should be avoided and suggested that increased staff mobility at all levels be introduced in order to combat it.[325] The Prodi Commission acknowledged the problem of national flags and expressed its determination to put a definite stop to it. In its Press Statement of 29 September 1999, the Commission Vice President Kinnock stated:

> *[W]hile the Commission will maintain a broad geographical balance as is obviously necessary and right in this multinational Community administration, nationality will no longer be the determinant in appointing a new occupant to a specific post. The application of this principle means an end to the* convention of attaching national flags to senior position.[326] *(emphasis added)*

---

[322] Ibid., para. 94 and para. 100.

[323] Ibid., para. 85.

[324] Ibid., para. 96 and similarly para. 100.

[325] *Second Report on Reform of the Commission of 1999, Volume II*, para. 6.2.33.

[326] *Mr. Niel Kinnock, Vice President of the European Commission, Press Statement, Brussels, 29 September 1999*, SPEECH/99/118, 29.09.1999, available at http://europa.eu/rapid/pressReleasesAction.do?reference=SPEECH/99/118&format=HTML&aged=1&language=EN&guiLanguage=en, last visited on 30.12.2010. The Commission decision that 'the nationality of an outgoing post-holder may not be a factor in the appointment of a new occupant of a post' was incorporated into the new Commission

The Commission followed the recommendation of the Committee of Independent Experts and introduced a stronger mobility system. For senior officials mobility has become mandatory. Under the new rules, they are required to change their posts at regular intervals.[327] This decision, one of the first taken in the framework of the 2000 staff reform, was put in practice immediately. During the period from 1999 until 2003 a big reshuffle took place in most senior posts, leaving no Director-General in his position for more than 5 years.[328] The subsequent reshuffles, or 'mobility packages' as the Commission calls them, were announced in November 2005, November 2006 and December 2008.[329]

Reflecting on these developments, Egeberg stated in 2004 that 'the tendency to attach national flags to top posts at the Commission almost has come to an end'.[330] Indeed, regular mobility has helped prevent any Member State from planting its national flag on any senior position in future. Repeated changes in all senior posts contribute to avoiding their occupation by people of certain nationalities while leaving the overall balance of nationalities undisturbed as most officials remain in service, only in different positions.

3.3.3. National diversity and colonization

According to Hooghe, a policy of national diversity exists in all Directorates-General, Directorates, units and task forces of the European Commission: each division should seek variety of nationalities among its staff as well as a balance between north and south.[331] However, there are no official documents directly or indirectly confirming the existence of this policy. This is not surprising, given that the ECJ decided already in 1969 that 'the fulfilment of the obligation to secure the recruitment of officials on the broadest possible geographical basis must not be limited to a small number of posts within a single Directorate-General'.[332] Consequently, the policy of national diversity within each organizational unit could be legally problematic as the ECJ explicitly confirmed that the need to ensure geographical balance in the Commission should be regarded as comprising the whole institution, not just its

policy on senior officials - see *Commission Compilation Document on Senior Officials Policy*, p. 4.

[327] *Commission Compilation Document on Senior Officials Policy*, Section 9.1.

[328] Spence and Edwads (eds.), *The European Commission*, p. 477. See also *European Commission Announces Next Steps in Implementing New Senior Staff Policy*.

[329] *New Faces in Top Management Posts: Commission Reshuffles its Directors General and Deputy Directors General Teams*, Press Release, IP/05/1399, 09.11.2005, available at http://europa.eu/rapid/pressReleasesAction.do?reference=IP/05/1399&format=HTML&aged=1&language=EN&guiLanguage=tr, last visited on 30.12.2010; *Commission Adopts Mobility Package for Directors-General, Directors and Principal Advisers*, Press Release, IP/06/1610, 22.11.2006, available at http://europa.eu/rapid/pressReleasesAction.do?reference=IP/06/1610&format=HTML&aged=0&language=EN&guiLanguage=en, last visited on 30.12.2010; and *Commission Reshuffles Senior Managers*, Press Release, IP/08/1881, 03.12.2008, available at http://europa.eu/rapid/pressReleasesAction.do?reference=IP/08/1881&format=HTML&aged=0&language=EN&guiLanguage=en, last visited on 30.12.2010.

[330] Egeberg, *Organising Institutional Autonomy in a Political Context: Enduring Tensions in the European Commission's Development*, p. 11.

[331] Hooghe, *The European Commission and the Integration of Europe, Images of Governance*, p. 178.

[332] *Reinarz v. Commission, Case 17/68*, paras. 34-37.

part. On the other hand, organizational units should not be dominated by nationals of one particular Member State, an alleged practice in the Commission referred to as colonization.[333] Although there is no specific provision in the *EU Staff Regulations* explicitly prohibiting such practice, a prevalence of people of the same nationality in one department would indisputably lead to doubts about independence and impartiality of that department and about its objectivity.

Allegations of colonization in some departments have not been uncommon. Hooghe, for example, found that 39 per cent of Commission senior officials considered national colonization to be a problem, even though 59 per cent did not.[334] Hooghe asked whether national colonization was a problem, not whether it existed. But the responses suggest that the practice was indeed in place. If it were not, it would not be considered problematic.[335] On the other hand, a study of Page did not confirm that colonization existed. While lacking sufficient numbers in each unit for a statistical comparison, Page was able to broadly indicate the situation in the European Commission, finding little evidence in support of the above assertions. On the contrary, he observed that attempts were made to ensure as much as possible that no two links in the hierarchical chain of command within the senior levels of the Commission were occupied by people of the same nationality.[336]

More recent data confirm Page's findings, although only at the level of Directorates-General as no staff statistics are available for lower levels. The comparison of the nationality of the Directors-General and of their staff disproves the allegation of systematic colonization in the Commission Directorates-General.

---

[333] Page, *People Who Run Europe*, p. 55.

[334] Hooghe, *The European Commission and the Integration of Europe, Images of Governance*, p. 179.

[335] The question Hooghe posed reads: 'It hurts the Commission's legitimacy that certain [Directorates-General] tend to be dominated by particular nationalities, such as agriculture by the French, competition by the Germans, regional policy by the Spanish, environment by the north...'. - Ibid., p. 179.

[336] Page, *People Who Run Europe*, pp. 58-59.

Table 10: Comparison of nationalities of AD and AST officials and temporary agents in the European Commission Directorates-General, excluding Commission offices

(October 2010)

Directorate-General*	Nationality of current Director-General (or equivalent)*	Nationality of Director-General during the previous Commission term (2004-2009)**	Number of officials and temporary agents with the same nationality as the current Director-General)***	Most represented nationality***	Second most represented nationality***	Total number of officials and temporary agents in the Directorate-General***
Secretariat-General	Irish	Irish - since 1/2005	8	117 - Belgian	49 - Italian	481
Legal Service	Spanish	French - 12/2008–06/2009	34	63 - Belgian	34 - Spanish	376
Communication	Danish	Danish - since 1/2006	22	89 - Belgian	50 - French	581
Bureau of European Policy Advisers	French	Italian - 03/2007–2010	5	7 - Portuguese	5 - Belgian and 5 - French and 5 - Italian	33
Economic and Financial Affairs	Italian	Italian - since 2/2008	45	97 - Belgian	50 - German	499
Enterprise and Industry	Austrian	Austrian - since 1/2005	19	167 - Belgian	99 - French	770
Competition	Dutch	British - 09/2002–09/2009	26	136 - Belgian	87 - German	755
Employment, Social Affairs and Equal Opportunities	French	German 06/2006–06/2009	59	118 - Belgian	64 - Italian	645
Agriculture and Rural Development	French	French - since 2006	83	244 - Belgian	105 - Italian	981

Mobility and Transport	German	German - since 2006	41	99 - Belgian	54 - French	452
Energy	British	German - 2006–02/2010	28	93 - Belgian	75 - French	498
Environment	German	German - since 01/2009	33	81 - Belgian	42 - French	463
Climate Action	Belgian	NEW DG	18	18 - Belgian	11 - British	109
Research	Dutch	Spanish - 01/2006–06/2010	33	285 - Belgian	157 - French	1217
Joint Research Centre	German	German - since 1/2005	248	474 - Italian	248 - German	1794
Information Society and Media	British	Italian - 01/2005–03/2010	39	206 - Belgian	93 - French	814
Maritime Affairs and Fisheries	British	Greek - 2007–06/2010	16	60 - Belgian	31 - French and 31 - Spanish	296
Internal Market and services	British	Swedish - 2007–06/2010	23	85 - Belgian	47 - French	466
Regional Policy	German	German - since 1/2007	42	94 - Belgian	57 - Spanish	579
Taxation and Customs Union	German	French - 07/2002–06/2009	33	117 - Belgian	33 - German and 33 - French	432
Education and Culture	Polish	French - 1/2006–2010	24	135 - Belgian	54 - Italian	502
Health and Consumers	Italian	British - 2004–03/2010	61	120 - Belgian	79 - French	754
Home Affairs	Italian	British - 3/2003–06/2010	26	39 - Belgian	32 - Polish	244
Justice	French	British - 3/2003–06/2010	14	34 - Belgian	23 - German	249
External Relations	Czech	Spanish - 2003–08/2009 Portuguese - 08/2009–2010	11	126 - Belgian	74 - Spanish	647

Trade	Irish	Irish - since 01/2005	11	84 - Belgian	47 - French	466
Development and Relations with ACP States	Greek	Italian - 2004–06/2010	5	55 - Belgian	37 - Italian	280
Enlargement	British	British - since 2006	17	29 - Belgian	28 - German	229
EuropeAid Cooperation Office	Dutch	Dutch - since 2004	14	171 - Belgian	85 - French	595
Humanitarian Aid	German	German - since 2008	12	57 - Belgian	20 - French and 20 - Italian	197
Eurostat	German	German - since 04/2008	84	84 - German and 84 - French	68 - Belgian	604
Human Resources and Security	Greek	French - 2004–05/2009	11	202 - Belgian	75 - French	634
Informatics	Spanish	Spanish - since 01/2005	29	169 - Belgian	48 - French	432
Budget	French	Spanish - 06/2002–06/2009	39	149 - Belgian	39 - French	409
Internal audit service	British	German - 2004–06/2009	6	16 - Belgian and 16 - Spanish	13 - French	89
European Anti-Fraud Office	British	German- 02/2000–01/2010	21	72 - Belgian	39 - German	358
Interpretation	Italian	Italian - since 01/2004	76	108 - Belgian	65 - Spanish	772
Translation	Belgian	Finish - 2004–04/2010	236	236 - Belgian	156 - German	2314

Table 11: Comparison of nationalities of permanent AD officials in the European Commission Directorates-General, excluding Commission offices

(October 2010)

Directorate-General*	Nationality of current Director-General (or equivalent)*	Nationality of Director-General during the previous Commission term (2004-2009)**	Number of AD permanent officials with the same nationality as the current Director-General)****	Most represented nationality***	Second most represented nationality***	Total number of AD permanent officials in the Directorate-General)****
Secretariat-General	Irish	Irish - since 1/2005	3	29 - French	19 - Belgian	196
Legal Service	Spanish	French - 12/2008–06/2009	17	25 - German	20 - Italian	211
Communication	Danish	Danish - since 1/2006	8	22 - French	19 - Spanish	214
Bureau of European Policy Advisers	French	Italian - 03/2007–2010	3	3 - French	2 - Spanish and 2 - Italian	11
Economic and Financial Affairs	Italian	Italian - since 2/2008	25	41 - German	29 - Belgian	274
Enterprise and Industry	Austrian	Austrian - since 1/2005	10	60 - German	58 - French	392
Competition	Dutch	British - 09/2002–09/2009	23	62 - German	54 - French	341
Employment, Social Affairs and Equal Opportunities	French	German - 06/2006–06/2009	37	42 - German	37 - French	347
Agriculture and Rural Development	French	French - since 2006	50	56 - Belgian	50 - French	475

Mobility and Transport	German	German - since 2006	25	36 - French	26 - Belgian	215
Energy	British	German - 2006–02/2010	14	34 - German	25 - Belgian	216
Environment	German	German - since 01/2009	3	25 - French	24 - British	245
Climate Action	Belgian	NEW DG	8	11 - German and 11 - British	8 - Belgian	73
Research	Dutch	Spanish - 01/2006–06/2010	25	101 - French	74 - Belgian	659
Joint Research Centre	German	German - since 1/2005	132	160 - Italian	132 - German	784
Information Society and Media	British	Italian - 01/2005–03/2010	23	51 - French	46 - Belgian	421
Maritime Affairs and Fisheries	British	Greek - 2007–06/2010	6	23 - Spanish	19 - French	144
Internal Market and services	British	Swedish - 2007–06/2010	17	32 - German and 32 - French	25 - Polish	278
Regional Policy	German	German - since 1/2007	24	32 - Spanish	31 - French	308
Taxation and Customs Union	German	French - 07/2002–06/2009	20	42 - Belgian	26 - French	204
Education and Culture	Polish	French - 1/2006 2010	16	22 - French	21 - Italian	211
Health and Consumers	Italian	British - 2004–03/2010	37	58 - French	44 - German	387
Home Affairs	Italian	British - 3/2003 – 06/2010	18	18 – Italian	17 – Polish	142

Justice	French	British - 3/2003 – 06/2010	12	17 - German	12 – French and 12 - Italian	121
External Relations	Czech	Spanish - 2003-08/2009 Portuguese – 08/2009 - 2010	5	45 - Spanish	42 – French	307
Trade	Irish	Irish - since 01/2005	2	31 - German	28 – French	247
Development and Relations with ACP States	Greek	Italian - 2004 – 06/2010	5	23 - Italian	21 – German	155
Enlargement	British	British - since 2006	10	16 - German	15 – Italian	116
EuropeAid Cooperation Office	Dutch	Dutch - since 2004	11	55 - French	39 – Italian	271
Humanitarian Aid	German	German - since 2008	10	15 - Belgian	12 – French	84
Eurostat	German	German - since 04/2008	49	49 - German	27 – French	257
Human Resources and Security	Greek	French - 2004-05/2009	3	23 - French	22 – Belgian and 22 - Italian	155
Informatics	Spanish	Spanish - since 01/2005	14	39 - Belgian	14 – Spanish	110
Budget	French	Spanish - 06/2002-06/2009	22	32 - Belgian	22 – French	161
Internal audit service	British	German - 2004 - 06/2009	4	14 - Belgian	9 – French	56
European Anti-Fraud Office	British	German-02/2000-01/2010	5	16 - Italian	11 – Belgian and 11 – German	119
Interpretation	Italian	Italian - since 01/2004	64	64 - Italian	55 - British	563

Translation	Belgian	Finish - 2004 – 04/2010	124	130 –German	124 - Belgian	1696

Sources: * *Commission Directory*

** *Musical Chairs: Officials Take Turns at European Commission*; the internet page of the European Commission civil service and of the individual Directorates-General.

*** *Distribution of Officials and Temporary Agents by Directorate-General and Nationality (All Budgets)*, dated 01.10.2010.

**** *Distribution of Officials and Temporary Agents by Directorate General and Nationality (All Budgets)*, separate data for AD permanent officials, AD temporary agents, AST permanent officials and AST temporary agents, dated 01.10.2010.[337]

337 *Commission Directory*, available at http://ec.europa.eu/staffdir/plsql/gsys_page.display_index?pLang=EN , visited on 14.10.2010; *Musical Chairs: Officials Take Turns at European Commission*, available at http://www.euractiv.com/en/future-eu/musical-chairs-officials-take-turns-european-commission; the internet page of the European Commission civil service and of the individual Directorates-General, available at http://ec.europa.eu/civil_service/docs/directors_general/day_en.pdf; http://ec.europa.eu/dgs/legal_service/pdf/romero_en.pdf; http://ec.europa.eu/civil_service/docs/directors_general/sorensen_en.pdf; http://ec.europa.eu/bepa/docs/cv/jean_claude_thebault_fr.pdf; http://ec.europa.eu/civil_service/docs/directors_general/buti_en.pdf; http://ec.europa.eu/enterprise/dg/files/cv_zourek_en.pdf; http://ec.europa.eu/civil_service/docs/directors_general/italianer_en.pdf; http://ec.europa.eu/civil_service/docs/directors_general/verrue_en.pdf; http://ec.europa.eu/civil_service/docs/directors_general/demarty_en.pdf; http://ec.europa.eu/dgs/energy_transport/wcm/career_dg_matthias_ruete.pdf; http://ec.europa.eu/commission_2010-2014/potocnik/about/cv/index_en.htm; http://ec.europa.eu/civil_service/docs/directors_general/lowe_en.pdf; http://ec.europa.eu/civil_service/docs/directors_general/delbeke_en.pdf; http://ec.europa.eu/research/press/2007/pdf/pr_150107_cv_smits_en.pdf; http://ec.europa.eu/civil_service/docs/directors_general/schenkel_en.pdf; http://ec.europa.eu/civil_service/docs/directors_general/madelin_en.pdf; http://ec.europa.eu/civil_service/docs/directors_general/evans_en.pdf; http://ec.europa.eu/civil_service/docs/directors_general/faull_en.pdf; http://ec.europa.eu/civil_service/docs/directors_general/ahner_en.pdf; http://ec.europa.eu/civil_service/docs/directors_general/deffaa_en.pdf; http://ec.europa.eu/civil_service/docs/directors_general/truszczynsken.pdf; http://ec.europa.eu/civil_service/docs/directors_general/testori_en.pdf; http://ec.europa.eu/civil_service/docs/directors_general/lebail_en.pdf; http://ec.europa.eu/civil_service/docs/directors_general/kovanda_en.pdf; http://ec.europa.eu/trade/about/organisation/director-general/; http://ec.europa.eu/civil_service/docs/directors_general/fotiadis_en.pdf; http://ec.europa.eu/civil_service/docs/directors_general/leigh_en.pdf; http://ec.europa.eu/civil_service/docs/directors_general/richelle_en.pdf; http://ec.europa.eu/civil_service/docs/directors_general/zangl_en.pdf; http://ec.europa.eu/civil_service/docs/directors_general/radermacher_en.pdf; http://ec.europa.eu/dgs/human-resources/documents/cv/souka_en.pdf; http://ec.europa.eu/civil_service/docs/directors_general/garcia_moran_en.pdf; http://ec.europa.eu/civil_service/docs/directors_general/jouanjean_en.pdf; http://ec.europa.eu/civil_service/docs/directors_general/gray_en.pdf; http://ec.europa.eu/dgs/olaf/directory/Senior-Management/cv-ilett-en.html; http://ec.europa.eu/civil_service/docs/directors_general/benedetti_en.pdf; http://ec.europa.eu/dgs/translation/whoweare/director/index_en.htm; http://ec.europa.eu/civil_service/docs/directors_general/reicherts_en.pdf; http://europa.eu/rapid/pressReleasesAction.do?reference=IP/08/230&type=HTML;http://www.europolitics.info/institutions/cabinet-appointments-art259456-36.html; http://europa.eu/rapid/pressReleasesAction.do?reference=IP/08/1337&type=HTML; and http://europa.eu/rapid/pressReleasesAction.do?reference=IP/07/1125&type=HTML&aged=0&language=EN&guiLanguage=en, all visited on 14.10.2010; *Distribution of Officials and Temporary Agents by Directorate-General and Nationality (All Budgets)*, Sysper2, 01.10.2010, available at http://ec.europa.eu/civil_service/docs/europa_sp2_bs_nat_x_dg_en.pdf, visited on 14.10.2010; *Distribution of Officials and Temporary Agents by Directorate General and Nationality (All Budgets)*, data for AD permanent officials, Sysper2, 01.10.2010, received from the Directorate-General for Human Resources and Security.

As the first table above shows, out of 38 Directorates-General in the European Commission, only three have the largest proportion of staff of the same nationality as the current and/or last Director-General. (Data relating to previous Directors-General were included in order to reflect the fact that the new Commission, and consequently also a number of new Directors-General, have been appointed relatively recently.) The number of Directorates-General with the second largest proportion of the same nationals as the current and/or former Director-General is higher – nine. This is still relatively low when compared to the total number of the current Directorates-General, i.e. 38.

Of course, it could be argued that the number of all permanent officials and temporary agents is not sufficiently representative as it is the permanent officials serving in the AD function group who are decisive for the Directorates-General's policy and decision making. The second table above shows, indeed, that the number of Directorates-General where the nationality of the current and/or former Director-General is identical to the largest group of permanent AD officials is higher and amounts to 10. In addition, in 11 Directorates-General, the number of permanent AD officials with the same nationality as the current and/or former Director-General is the second largest. Two Directorates-General fall under both categories, i.e. the largest and the second largest nationality there is the same as the nationality of the current and former Director-General. In total thus, 19 out of 38 Directorates-General, i.e. a half of them, are composed of the officials whose nationality is the largest or the second largest in the Directorate-General and at the same time the same as the nationality of the current and/or former Director-General.

Even though these figures could be considered relatively high, they still do not prove the existence of colonization in the Commission Directorates-General. The main reason for this assertion is that the number of officials with the relevant nationality is relatively low when compared to the total number of all permanent AD officials serving in the Directorates-General at issue. If the Bureau of European Policy Advisers is disregarded as being too small with its 11 officials to be sufficiently representative, the largest proportion of the same nationals as the current and/or former Director-General is in Eurostat. Since 2008 Eurostat is headed by a German national and 19 per cent of its personnel are German nationals. The second largest instance can be found in the Joint Research Centre headed also by a German national, since 2005, with about 17 per cent of permanent AD officials of German nationality. Most of other Directorates-General where the most or second most common nationality is the same as that of the current and/or former Director-General make up between ten and 15 per cent of permanent AD officials possessing the nationality at issue. In addition, it must be noted that in almost all instances the nationalities at hand are those of the large 'old' Member States, namely France, Germany, Italy and Spain, barring the UK. The only exception is Belgium but this is understandable, given the location of the Commission seat.[338] The absence of the UK is also unsurprising

[338] There are eight Directorates-General in which French nationals are the most or the second most populous; five where this is the case with German nationals; four with Italian nationals; two with Spanish nationals and two with Belgian nationals.

since it has been in general long underrepresented among Commission officials. The large proportion of the French, Germans, Italians and Spanish in the Commission Directorate-Generals is certainly due, at least partially, to their size, not necessarily to the fact that the Director-General is of the same nationality. No real colonization thus appears to be currently at work in the European Commission.

It could be argued that this situation is, certainly in part, a result of a policy adopted during the 2000 reform requesting regular mobility of Directors-General. According to this policy, no Director-General should stay in his post longer than five years, and in exceptional circumstances, seven years.[339] In addition, Directors-General should not have the same nationality as their portfolio Commissioner.[340] This also means that there might be further moves of Directors-General when new Commissioners are appointed. In effect thus the Directors-General do not remain in the same post long enough to build up a 'colony'. Even if in the recruitment of new staff (undue) preference was often given to the Director-General's compatriots, staff turn-over is arguably not high enough to ensure any considerable success in a short time frame since the majority of staff usually have permanent contracts.[341]

One reservation must be made, however, to the foregoing about the non-existence of colonization in the European Commission. It concerns private offices of individual Commissioners, known as cabinets. In the past, cabinets used to be composed largely of people from the same Member State as the Commissioner. Although there has always been a requirement for at least one outsider in each cabinet, Commissioner's private offices were generally considered to be sites of national affiliations and interests.[342] This was severely criticized by the Committee of Independent Experts of 1999:

> *It is unacceptable that cabinets – which are involved in policy making in the Commission... – should be composed exclusively or predominantly of persons of the same nationality as the commissioner. That would put the Community character of the commissioner's work too much at risk.*[343]

Since the 2000 staff reform, each cabinet must be composed of at least three different nationalities, with the maximum number of cabinet members being six for the Commissioners and 11 for the Commission President. Moreover, the Head of the Cabinet or his Deputy 'should preferably' have a nationality different from the Commissioner's.[344]

---

339 *Commission Compilation Document on Senior Officials Policy*, Section 9.1.

340 Ibid., Section 9.1.

341 For recent statistics on the contractual status of Commission staff, see *Distribution of Staff by Statutory Links and DGs*, 01.03.2010, available at http://ec.europa.eu/civil_service/docs/bs_fonct_ext_dg_en.pdf, last visited on 05.03.2010.

342 McDonald, M., *Identities in the European Commission*, in: N. Nugent (ed.), At the Heart of the Union, Studies of the European Commission, Macmillan Press Ltd, Houndmills / Basingstoke / Hampshire / London, 1997, pp. 49-70, pp. 50-51.

343 *Second Report on Reform of the Commission of 1999, Volume II*, para. 7.5.9.

344 *Rules Governing the Composition of the Members' Cabinets and the Spokespersons, SEC(2008) 2602*, 08.10.2008, available in the Register of Commission Documents, available at http://ec.europa.

Although these rules aimed at ensuring that no colonization takes place in the Commissioners' cabinet, in practice the majority of cabinet staff are still of the same nationality as the Commissioner who appointed them.[345] Certainly, the combination of a restriction on the number of cabinet members and of the requirement of a minimum number of different nationalities contributes to differentiation within each cabinet. If three out of six members should have different nationalities, including the Head of Cabinet and his Deputy, no more than four persons in each cabinet should be compatriots. On the other hand, four out of six is still a relatively large proportion and can lead to colonization and 'nationalization' of cabinets.[346] In January 2010, when the new Commission was going to be appointed, a clear trend in this direction was detected by the Commission President Barroso himself. An online periodical reported:

> *The internal note distributed by Barroso's services underlines that ... many cabinets are too nationally-oriented, with an all-too-evident predominance of officials from the same country as the commissioner who selected them.*
>
> ...
>
> *Antonio Tajani (Industry; Italy), has five Italians and only three other nationals in his team. Karel De Gucht (Trade; Belgium), László Andor (Social Affairs; Hungary) John Dalli (Health; Malta) and Johannes Hahn (Regional Policy; Austria) have all picked half of their assistants from their own countries.*[347]

As for the Heads of Cabinet, a majority of them are still of the same nationality as their Commissioner, although in all such cases the Deputy Heads are indeed of a different nationality, as required. However, when the Head of Cabinet is of a nationality other than the Commissioner's, the Deputy Head is almost always the Commissioner's compatriot. The recent data shows that in the Commission appointed in late 2009, only one Commissioner had both the Head of the Cabinet and his Deputy of a nationality other than his own.

---

eu/transparency/regdoc/registre.cfm?CL=en, last visited on 30.12.2010, Section A.3.1. See also *Commissioners Meet Prodi's Targets for Better Gender Balance and Multinational Mix in Cabinets*, Press Release, IP/99/703, 28.09.1999, available at http://europa.eu/rapid/pressReleasesAction.do?reference =IP/99/703&format=HTML&aged=0&language=EN&guiLanuage=en, last visited on 30.12.2010.

[345] Stevens and Stevens, *Brussels Bureaucrats? The Administration of the European Union*, pp. 84-87. According to data available on the internet sites of individual Commissioners with regard to their cabinets, this is still the case in 2010. For details, see below, section 3.4.2.2.

[346] In 1999, relatively shortly after the introduction of the 'maximum six members' and 'at least three nationalities' rules, the Commission reported that all cabinets had complied: all cabinets had a maximum of 6 staff members, and 9 cabinets had 3 nationalities, 6 cabinet 4 nationalities, 3 cabinets 5 nationalities and 1 cabinet had 6 nationalities. The President's cabinet counted 7 nationalities. - *Commissioners Meet Prodi's Targets for Better Gender Balance and Multinational Mix in Cabinets.*

[347] *Barroso Urges Reshuffle of Top EU Officials* in: EurActiv Network, 21.01.2010.

Table 12: Nationality of the Commissioners, Heads of Cabinet and Deputy Heads of Cabinet in the European Commission (2010-2014)

(March 2010)

Commissioner	Head of the Cabinet	Deputy Head of the Cabinet
Austrian	Austrian	Italian
Belgian	Belgian	German
British	British	*UNAVAILABLE**
Bulgarian	*UNAVAILABLE**	*UNAVAILABLE**
Cypriot	French	Cypriot
Czech	British	Czech
Danish	Dutch	Danish
Dutch	Irish	Spanish
Estonian	Estonian	*UNKNOWN***
Finish	Finish	French
French	French	German
German	German	*UNKNOWN***
Greek	Greek	Austrian
Hungarian	Portuguese	Hungarian
Irish	Irish	Spanish
Italian	Italian	Spanish
Latvian	British	Latvian
Lithuanian	British	*UNKNOWN***
Luxembourgish	German	Luxembourgish
Maltese	Maltese	German
Polish	Luxembourgish	Polish
Portuguese	German	Portuguese
Romanian	Austrian	Romanian
Slovak	Slovak	German
Slovenian	*UNAVAILABLE**	*UNAVAILABLE**
Spanish	Spanish	French
Swedish	Swedish	French

* *data on the post incumbent unavailable on the Commissioners' internet websites*[348]
** *nationality of the post incumbent unknown*

[348] See the following websites:
http://ec.europa.eu/commission_2010-2014/president/about/team/index_en.htm; http://www.eeas.europa.eu/ashton/team/index_en.htm; http://ec.europa.eu/commission_2010-2014/reding/about/team/index_en.htm; http://ec.europa.eu/commission_2010-2014/almunia/about/team/index_en.htm; http://ec.europa.eu/commission_2010-2014/kallas/about/team/index_en.htm; http://ec.europa.eu/commission_2010-2014/kroes/about/team/index_en.htm; http://ec.europa.eu/commission_2010-2014/tajani/about/team/index_en.htm; http://ec.europa.eu/

These data show that out of the total of 27, as many as 14 Heads of Cabinet and nine Deputy Heads of Cabinet are of the same nationality as their Commissioner, while the nationality of three Deputy Heads is unknown. Two Commissioners do not provide information on their cabinet members on their websites (Bulgaria and Slovenia). Finally, only the Dutch Commissioner has both the Head of Cabinet and his Deputy with a nationality other than his own. Even though these arrangements are not contrary to the Commission's internal rules, the data suggests that the Commissioners still attach great importance to having their compatriots in charge of their cabinets.

3.4. Implementation of the principle of geographical balance in the Commission recruitment process

As mentioned earlier, the first European Commission staff were hired on the basis of lists prepared by individual members of the High Authority or the Commission recommending nationals of their home countries.[349] During the 1960s, nationality was still taken into account in staff recruitment but was less important compared to the early years.[350] Even though the *EU Staff Regulations* were already at that time based on the presumption that recruitment should be aimed at, and ensure, that appointed officials join an independent and structured career service, some features of the initial informal approach continued to exist, especially in the process of recruitment and appointment to senior posts. Selection to these positions continued to be heavily influenced by individual Commissioners and their senior cabinet staff.[351] The

commission_2010-2014/sefcovic/about/team/index_en.htm; http://ec.europa.eu/commission_2010-2014/potocnik/about/team/index_en.htm;http://ec.europa.eu/commission_2010-2014/rehn/about/team/index_en.htm;http://ec.europa.eu/commission_2010-2014/piebalgs/about/team/index_en.htm;http://ec.europa.eu/commission_2010-2014/barnier/about/team/index_en.htm; http://ec.europa.eu/commission_2010-2014/vassiliou/about/team/index_en.htm; http://ec.europa.eu/commission_2010-2014/semeta/about/team/index_en.htm; http://ec.europa.eu/commission_2010-2014/degucht/about/team/; http://ec.europa.eu/commission_2010-2014/dalli/cabinet_en.htm; http://ec.europa.eu/commission_2010-2014/geoghegan-quinn/about/team/index_en.htm; http://ec.europa.eu/commission_2010-2014/lewandowski/about/team/index_en.htm; http://ec.europa.eu/commission_2010-2014/damanaki/about/team/index_en.htm; http://ec.europa.eu/commission_2010-2014/georgieva/about/team/index_en.htm; http://ec.europa.eu/commission_2010-2014/oettinger/contact/myteam/index_en.htm; http://ec.europa.eu/commission_2010-2014/hahn/about/team/index_en.cfm; http://ec.europa.eu/commissiron_2010-2014/hedegaard/my_team/my_team_en.htm; http://ec.europa.eu/commission_2010-2014/fule/about/team/index_en.htm; http://ec.europa.eu/commission_2010-2014/andor/about/team/index_en.htm; http://ec.europa.eu/commission_2010-2014/malmstrom/aboutme/myteam/default_en.htm; http://ec.europa.eu/commission_2010-2014/ciolos/about/team/index_en.htm, all visited on 25.03.2010. In case of unavailability of information on nationality of the (Deputy) Head of Cabinet, other internet sites were consulted, such as the European Commission civil service website providing curricula vitae of senior officials, available at http://ec.europa.eu/civil_service/about/who/dg_en.htm, visited on 25.03.2010.

[349] See above, section 3.1.

[350] Coombes, *Politics and Bureaucracy in the European Community, A Portrait of the Commission of the E.E.C.*, p. 163.

[351] Stevens and Stevens, *Brussels Bureaucrats? The Administration of the European Union*, pp. 72-74.

situation did not change dramatically until the late 1990s. No major changes occurred in personnel policy, including in practices employed to ensure geographical balance among the Commission staff. A few attempts at personnel and budgetary reform between the 1970s and 1990s were in most parts unsuccessful and had no direct consequences for the application of the principle of geographical balance.[352]

After the fall of the Santer Commission in 1999, internal reform of the Commission, including the human resources policies, became one of the Commission's priorities. The issue of geographical balance appeared among the recruitment policy objectives listed in the *White Paper on Reforming the Commission* of 2000.[353] Action 26, which was to be implemented in the course of the reform process, concerned measures to ensure a reasonable geographical balance among staff in accordance with Article 27 of the *EU Staff Regulations*. The *White Paper* envisaged in this respect the following actions: first, wide publication of notices announcing competitions, and second, ensuring that the tests used in competitions took account of the multicultural dimension of the EU. Competitions organized by nationality, national quotas or a general move towards competitions by language were explicitly mentioned as inappropriate. This relatively poor list, with only two specific measures, was complemented by an undertaking to reflect on further means of ensuring reasonable geographical balance.[354] However, no further specific measures seem to have been adopted thus far.

Understandably, legal constrains, represented by the superiority of the principle of merit over that of geographical balance and by the prohibition of national flags, as well as the Commission's belief that national quotas are incompatible with the *EU Staff Regulations*, all make it difficult to develop specific mechanisms which could be directly used in the staff recruitment process. As direct ways of applying the principle of geographical balance have been declared illegal by the ECJ, various methods potentially circumventing the superiority of the principle of merit had found their ways into the EU recruitment policy. In addition, a close cooperation between the EU Member States and the Commission can be detected in this area. The Member States have always been keen to ensure that their individual interests in EU matters are secured at each possible level, a desire often leading to attempts to influence and enhance the appointment chances of their nationals in the Commission. The Commission, on the other hand, is obliged to secure geographical balance within its staff, a task difficult to reconcile with the hierarchically prevailing merit principle. Political scientists claim that the Commission has not always been very eager to suppress Member States' pressures in this respect. On the contrary, the Commission has often been seen as 'adept in finding ways around its own rules'.[355]

---

[352] For an overview of the EU staff reform see, for example, Stevens, H. and Stevens, A., *The Internal Reform of the Commission*, in: D. Spence and G. Edwards (eds.), The European Commission, John Harper Publishing, London, 2006, pp. 454-480 , pp. 457-463 or Coull and Lewis, *The Impact of the Staff Regulations in Making the Commission a More Modern and Efficient Oragnization: an Insider's Perspective*.

[353] *Reforming the Commission - A White Paper - Part II - Action Plan*, Part XII, Section 1.

[354] Ibid., Part XII, Action 26.

[355] Stevens and Stevens, *Brussels Bureaucrats? The Administration of the European Union*, p. 87.

This section examines past and present practices designed to secure appointments of nationals of particular Member States, with special attention to their legal status.

3.4.1. Officials

European Commission staff below the senior level serving on permanent appointments are recruited via competitive examinations and a subsequent selection process in which the predominant consideration is to be given to qualification and experience.[356] In this process, there is no official mechanism aimed at ensuring a broad geographical balance of candidates other than wide publication of vacancies. It appears thus that candidates' nationality is not taken into account, not until the very last stage of the selection process involving the actual selection of a successful candidate who will be appointed. As explained in more detail below, in that last stage candidates' nationality would become relevant where geographical balance would need to be corrected and where candidates with the same level of merit would be available. The remainder of the recruitment process is thus, at least formally, largely ignorant of candidates' nationality, relying on the presumption that vacancies in the European Commission attract sufficient number of suitable candidates from all Member States. There seems to be a belief that the only permitted, but also effective, way of attracting people from all Member States is to pay them more than they can receive elsewhere. This 'strategy' has a fair success, though there are some 'problematic' Member States in this respect. For example, it has been relatively difficult to attract a sufficient pool of people from the United Kingdom, an EU Member State that has been underrepresented in the European Commission for decades.[357]

To influence geographical balance, which might have been disturbed for various reasons, but also to placate individual Member States, the European Commission has employed a number of more or less official mechanisms in the past and at present. Some of them relate to the eligibility criteria for vacant posts, others to the competition process, and yet others to practices of granting permanent appointment to persons who have never passed a competition.

3.4.1.1. Linguistic and other nationality related eligibility requirements

In the early years, the EU Administration used language requirements as a disguised method of ensuring that vacant posts were filled by persons of the desired nationality.[358] This was declared illegal by the ECJ in the 1964 case *Lassalle*. As mentioned above, the applicant in this case challenged the requirement of a perfect knowledge of Italian, included in the vacancy notice as an eligibility condition for the post con-

---

[356] For details on recruitment procedures of the European Commission officials, see below, chapter 3, section 3.2.

[357] See tables with staff statistics above, section 3.3.1. See also *Britain's Costly Disdain*.

[358] Coombes, *Politics and Bureaucracy in the European Community, A Portrait of the Commission of the E.E.C.*, p. 156.

cerned. The respondent, the European Parliament, admitted that the real purpose of this requirement was to impose a condition of nationality and argued that it was necessary in order to secure geographical balance of the staff. The ECJ agreed that the Administration was entitled to take geographical balance into account when filling vacant posts but held that nationality might only be considered at a later stage in the recruitment process. Imposing a condition of nationality in advance amounts to a violation of, *inter alia*, Article 27 of the *EU Staff Regulations* for two reasons: firstly, it gives preference to geographical distribution before considering merit; and secondly, it amounts to reserving a post to a national of a particular Member State. Consequently, linguistic requirements, which are in fact conditions of nationality in disguise, are not permitted because they automatically deprive those not of the required nationality of an opportunity to have their candidature considered.[359]

On the other hand, instances in which it is proven that linguistic requirements are in the interest of the service are allowed, especially if the requirements include 'thorough knowledge' of a certain language and not 'mother tongue'. Thus, when the level of the required linguistic knowledge corresponds with the actual requirements of the post at issue, the ECJ will approve it. Such was the case in *Küster* where the applicant contested the requirement of thorough knowledge of English in a vacancy notice. The ECJ ruled that in the present case the special nature of the tasks in the secretariat of the parliamentary committees might justify the requirement since English was one of the languages used by members of these committees.[360]

A similar approach was taken with regard to the requirement of knowledge of a particular national legal system. In *Kurrer* the ECJ found that the efficient running of the legal department of the Council required a balanced composition of staff. It explained:

> *In a Community composed of States, each of which retains its own national legal system, it is essential that a well organized legal department should include, as far as possible, officials possessing, apart from their knowledge of international law and of the actual law of the Communities, a theoretical training and practical experience in one or other of the national legal systems.*[361]

Since it was not shown that the specific requirement in this case, namely the knowledge of the legal system of a certain Member State, in fact served other purposes than the proper functioning of the relevant department of the Council secretariat, the ECJ dismissed the challenge. The ECJ did not base its decision only on the failure of the applicant to demonstrate that other purposes were served by the requirement of the knowledge of the specific legal system, but also on the evidence put forward by the Council positively proving its intention to make the choice dependent not on the nationality of the candidate but on the knowledge and experience of a given legal system.[362]

---

[359] *Lassalle v. European Parliament, Case 15/63*, pp. 37-38.

[360] *Berthold Küster v. European Parliament, Case 22/75, ECR [1975], p. 1267*, para. 14.

[361] *Dietrich Kurrer v. Council of the European Communities, Case 33/67, ECR [1968], p. 127*, p. 135.

[362] Ibid., p. 135.

The existing jurisprudence thus clearly allows the inclusion of nationality related requirements as eligibility criteria for vacant posts, but only under the condition that these requirements are necessary for the proper performance of duties in the posts in question. In such instances, candidates' nationality has a greater weight than their merits; it is even decisive - it constitutes the starting point in the relevant recruitment process. Nonetheless, such situation cannot be regarded as problematic or detrimental to the independent and impartial status of the future staff member as it is necessary for his ability to perform his new function.

3.4.1.2. Restrictions in competition

Competition is the most pronounced demonstration of the merit principle, serving its goal, namely the identification of persons with best qualities. Success in competitions is based solely on one's qualities and abilities disregarding any other personal characteristics, including nationality. This also means, however, that competition as such is not an effective tool for ensuring adequate geographical balance among recruited staff. Candidates successful in competitions do not necessarily have to reflect diversity of nationalities, let alone in the desired proportion.

This problem has been recognized for many years. The *Spierenburg Report* of 1979 made several observations on this point. It suggested, for example, that competitions would be publicized in a broader and more effective manner in various Member States. It also called for more regular contacts with universities and public authorities, proposed greater decentralization of the places in which tests were conducted as well as involvement of external evaluators to enhance representation of diverse national cultures.[363]

The Committee of Independent Experts of 1999 identified the failure of the system of competitions to ensure adequate representation of different nationalities in the European Commission civil service as a serious problem. The Committee stated in its *Second Report on the Reform of the Commission* that this was because there was a discrepancy between the number and diversity of nationalities of those who took part in and those who succeeded. This discrepancy was, according to the Committee, a result of the diversity of the educational systems in individual Member States. In some Member States, multinational oriented education is developed more than in others.[364] The Committee of Independent Experts recommended that this diversity should be better reflected in the competitions and that they should be organized separately for different languages.[365] The Committee explained that such calibrated competitions, organized in the past for posts in the Council and in the European Parliament, had certain undeniable advantages, such as taking account of cultural

[363] Stevens and Stevens, *Brussels Bureaucrats? The Administration of the European Union*, pp. 90-91, quoting the so-called *Spierenburg Report*.

[364] *Second Report on Reform of the Commission of 1999, Volume II*, para. 6.5.7.

[365] Ibid., para. 6.5.18.

and professional differences among Member States, and they were also capable of dealing with existing or possible deficits of the system.[366]

In addition to the reasons identified by the Committee, namely the levels of multinational orientation of education in various Member States, there is another important factor, namely a great variety in national educational cultures. As noted by Stevens, detailed specific and memorized knowledge is appreciated in France, for instance, whereas in the UK the assessment of general qualities, skills and personality is preferred.[367] In the Netherlands, to take another example, education is focused on developing broad knowledge and skills rather than on encyclopedic memorization of data. Dutch students are used to consulting documents even during examinations rather than having to memorize them. The EU competitions, especially the written tests, have always been based on detailed and precise knowledge of very specific data, which is why Dutch nationals in general do poorly in these competitions. Other nationalities, with a similar handicap, may be even discouraged from participation.

The Commission *White Paper* of 2000 reflected on the comments made by the Committee of Independent Experts but did not accept the suggestion of organizing competitions by language. The Commission explicitly stated that competitions by nationality were an inappropriate means of addressing the matter of geographical balance.[368] Nonetheless, it did admit the need to take full account of the multicultural dimension of the EU in developing new tests.[369] It took another decade, though, for new tests to be introduced. In March 2010 the European Personnel Selection Office ('EPSO') finally unveiled the new exam and said it was, among other things, 'shifting the emphasis from knowledge to competency-based assessment'.[370] The EPSO explained that the new tests were a more objective, reliable and fair testing tool, a good predictor of future work performance, and, in addition, 'largely unaffected by differences in ethnicity, education, gender, and cultural background'.[371] It remains to be seen whether this shift will contribute to a greater balance of nationalities among competition participants and, eventually, among successful candidates.

The new tests for competitive examinations are not the EU Administration's only tools designed to 'correct' results in favour of candidates of a certain nationality, if at all. The most important tools in this respect are the specific use of reserve lists and the organization of targeted competitions for newly acceded Member States.

---

366 Ibid., para. 6.5.12.

367 Stevens and Stevens, *Brussels Bureaucrats? The Administration of the European Union*, p. 90.

368 *Reforming the Commission - A White Paper - Part II - Action Plan*, Part XII, Action 26.

369 *Reforming the Commission - A White Paper - Part I*, Section IV.2.

370 *Better, Faster, Stronger: Launch of New Selection Procedure for EU Officials*, Press Release, IP/10/262, 11.03.2010, available at http://europa.eu/rapid/pressReleasesAction.do?reference=IP/10/262&format=HTML&aged=1&language=EN&guiLanguage=en, last visited on 30.12.2010. See also Pop, V., *New EU Exam to Axe Dreaded Quiz on Union Trivia*, in: *euobserver*.com, 03.03.2010.

371 European Personnel Selection Office, *New Administration Tests - The Re-designed Computer-Based Testing (CBT)*, 29.01.2010, available at http://europa.eu/discover/news/news15_en.htm, last visited on 10.03.2010.

3.4.1.2.1. Reserve lists

Reserve lists are lists of candidates successful in competitions and considered by relevant selection boards as suitable for appointment. Candidates who pass a competition do not receive an appointment in an EU institution directly after the competition results are known. They are first considered by the relevant selection board which draws up a list of candidates suitable for future vacant posts – the reserve list. This list is made available to individual departments that decide autonomously which of the candidates placed on the list they will eventually appoint. The reserve list does not contain ranking of individual candidates but some of them do include division in a few merit groups (usually 1-3), through which a distinction is made among candidates in accordance with their performance in the competition.[372]

In making the choice from a specific reserve list, the relevant appointing authority enjoys broad discretion. The ECJ has confirmed this prerogative of the EU Administration on a number of occasions. It has done so by interpreting Article 30 of the *EU Staff Regulations* and, in particular by focusing on its wording. Article 30 stipulates that the appointing authority 'decides' which of the candidates placed on the reserve list by the selection board to appoint to the vacant posts. The ECJ has pointed out that this provision needs to be read together with Article 29 requiring the appointing authority to follow the procedure of competition before filling a vacant post or construing a reserve list. The ECJ has concluded that the appointing authority is thus entitled to ignore the precise order of merit in the competition as provided in the reserve lists, if it could objectively justify it. However, the ECJ has also warned that the Administration does not enjoy 'complete freedom of choice' – it may not 'destroy the very concept of competition by departing substantially from the results of the competition without serious reasons'.[373]

An interesting case in this respect is *Kotsonis*. The applicant in this case argued that an appointment had been made to the post of Head of the Greek Division of the Language Service without having taken into account, firstly, his qualification which he claimed to be superior to that of the appointed candidate and, secondly, his own higher position on the reserve list compared to that of the appointed candidate – the applicant had been placed first, the appointed candidate second. The ECJ considered that, with regard to the first argument, the qualification of candidates successful in the competition could be ignored in the subsequent selection process. It explained that the fulfilment of the (minimum) qualification requirements was taken into account when deciding whether candidates were to be admitted to the competition but became irrelevant with regard to the success of the candidates in the competition. The placement on the reserve lists was based on the results of the competition, not on the qualifications anymore.

[372] *EU Staff Regulations*, Article 30. For more details on the EU competition and reserve lists, see below, chapter 3, section 3.2.1.

[373] *Manlio Serio v. Commission of the EAEC, Case 62/65, ECR [1966], p. 561,* pp. 570-571.

On the second argument, namely that the applicant's higher position on the reserve list should have led to his appointment instead of a candidate whose results in the competition were less good, the ECJ recalled its standing jurisprudence and ruled:

> *The appointing authority is entitled in making its selection to ignore the precise order of merit in the competition for reasons which it is incumbent upon the administration to determine and to justify before the court, provided that it does not destroy the very essence of the competition by departing substantially from the results of the competition without serious reasons. It follows that the administration is not in all circumstances bound to appoint the candidate placed first but may give preference to another candidate listed as suitable if it has reasons for doing so which serve the interests of the service.*[374]

In the case at hand, the ECJ accepted the reasoning of the Council to appoint the second placed candidate who, in the Council's view, possessed better organization and administration abilities and natural authority than the applicant. The appointed candidate had demonstrated such abilities during his temporary assignment in the relevant division as well as in the oral test in the competition, in which he scored better than the applicant.[375]

In another important case, *Serio*, the ECJ even accepted that nationality could be a valid reason for a deviation from the order in the reserve list. In this case, the ECJ dismissed the applicant's argument that such action constituted a violation of Article 27 of the then *EU Staff Regulations* and explained that:

> *the practical requirements of the post [of the Director in the DG Administration and Personnel] may well have made it necessary to avoid the appointment of a fourth servant with the same legal and administrative training in a Directorate whose staff comprises six persons in all.*[376]

In that case, two out of four posts of Head of Department and the post of Director were already occupied by Italians. Therefore, it was for the appointing authority 'not possible ... to select the applicant, who was also Italian, for fear of further aggravating the geographical imbalance of posts in the Directorate in question'.[377] The ECJ thus accepted that in such a situation a preference could be given to a candidate of a nationality other than that of the applicant.

It follows from this case law that the reserve lists may be used in a flexible manner. The appointing authority may, when deciding which candidate to appoint, take into account various factors as long as they constitute 'the interests of the service'. Clearly, this phrase is open to potentially broad interpretation and, as confirmed by the case law, it may even include the need to ensure or restore adequate geographical representation among the staff.

[374] *Vassilios Kotsonis v. Council of the European Communities, Case 246/84, ECR [1986], p. 3989*, para. 9.

[375] Ibid., para. 10.

[376] *Serio v. EAEC Commission, Case 62/65*, p. 569.

[377] Ibid., p. 568.

Some authors have observed that the use of the reserve lists might lead to inappropriate adjustments of competition results. It could, for instance, provide a means for dealing with a high number of successful candidates from one nationality.[378] These authors claim that such adjustments might frustrate the requirement of the highest standard of ability, efficiency and integrity and compromise it for the sake of other criteria which, according to Article 27 of the *EU Staff Regulations*, must play only a secondary role in the staff selection process. In addition, it has also been argued that, in the actual selection of candidates from the reserve lists, much depends on the initiative of the candidates themselves and their contacts in the Commission or in their national permanent representation in Brussels.[379] The flexibility enjoyed by the appointing authorities in using the reserve lists provides sufficient space for such practices. Moreover, any challenge of an undue use of the Administration's discretion before the ECJ, for example for employing mentioned practices, would have to cope with the serious problem of providing sufficient evidence to support the claim of misuse of power by the Administration which would need to be provided by the applicant.

Since the actual limits of the discretion of the appointing authorities in the selection process can only be determined on a case-by-case basis, it is important that the decisions they take are transparent. The Committee of Independent Experts in its *Second Report* of 1999 expressed some concern in this regard. The Committee criticized, in particular, the then existing practice of the European Commission to publish reserve lists in alphabetical order of candidates, not indicating how successful specific candidates were in competitions.[380] The Committee emphasized that such practice, combined with the absence of publicity and the motivation of the appointment decision, was questionable, far from transparent and not necessarily respecting the rights of the candidates 'who, despite having got through a difficult competition, are obliged to roam the Commission corridors for months – and perhaps even years – in the hope of hearing something useful or (even better for them) finding what they are looking for'.[381] Such a practice leading to 'total uncertainty' was considered unacceptable by this Committee.[382] The Committee even suggested that, if necessary for the improvement of the system, Article 30 of the then *EU Staff Regulations* should be amended so as to ensure greater transparency. The Committee further called for making public the list of suitable candidates, the choices made in each case and the reasons for those choices.[383] Some improvements have taken place since then. The reserve lists are made public on the internet site of the European Personnel Selection Office but they are still in alphabetic order and contain no individual ranking of candidates. In addition, although some reserve

---

[378] Bodiguel, *Les Fonctions Publiques dans l'Europe Des Douze*, as cited in Stevens and Stevens, *Brussels Bureaucrats? The Administration of the European Union*, p. 79.

[379] For example, Stevens and Stevens, *Brussels Bureaucrats? The Administration of the European Union*, p. 80.

[380] *Second Report on Reform of the Commission of 1999, Volume II*, para. 6.5.15.

[381] Ibid., para. 6.5.16.

[382] Ibid., para. 6.5.16.

[383] Ibid., para. 6.5.21.

lists provide for merit groups which indicate the difference in candidates' quality at least to some extent, not all of them do so.[384] Moreover, Article 30 of the *EU Staff Regulations* has remained unchanged, and the full decision on actual selection of a candidate for a vacant post, including the motivation, is still not publicly available.

3.4.1.2.2. Competitions for new Member States

The successive accessions of new countries to the European Union have necessitated adjustment to the existing geographical balance among the EU staff. Unlike the UN, the EU has approached this problem by organizing a series of specific competitions, also referred to as 'national waves', opened only to nationals from newly acceded Member States. Such national waves have taken place on the occasion of each EU enlargement during an agreed transitional period.

There is no doubt that with each enlargement the principle of geographical balance is thus temporarily put above the principle of merit. Such action would, in principle, be incompatible with, *inter alia*, Article 7 and Article 27 of the *EU Staff Regulations* which prohibit paying regard to nationality in the recruitment process and the reservation of posts for nationals of specific Member States. The EU has addressed this legal problem by adopting explicit derogations from the mentioned provisions on the occasion of each enlargement.[385] Based on these derogations, special and temporary measures could be taken in order to secure the appointment of a sufficient number of officials from new Member States. Unsurprisingly, such special and temporary measures usually took the form of a series of national competitions organized over several years.[386]

As long as the eventual appointments from among nationals of newly acceded Member States are made on the basis of merit, not affiliation with national governments, and follow the general recruitment procedures, or the procedures adopted specially for the purposes of recruitment from among nationals of new Member States, closed competitions are not problematic from a legal point of view. However, while acknowledging the legitimate purpose of these competitions, some observers have pointed to their negative effect on the overall EU staff policy. According to Stevens, the link between recruitment and EU enlargements is one of the major recruitment problems in the European Union. The preferential recruitment from among nationals from newly acceded countries as well as the temporary block over any openings for nationals of Member States other than the acceding ones leads,

384 See European Personnel Selection Office, *Reserve Lists. Administrators (A A* AD)*, 2010, available at http://europa.eu/epso/success/list/admin/index_en.htm, last visited on 10.03.2010.

385 For example, *Regulation No 2530/72*, p. 1; *Regulation No 662/82*, p. 1; *Regulation No 3517/85*, p. 55; *Regulation No 626/95*, p. 1.

386 For example, in the case of the biggest enlargement of 2004, special and temporary measures adopted for the recruitment of nationals of the ten new Member States were to be taken within a period of seven years (2004-2010) – see *Communication Relative au Recruitement de Fonctionnaires de la Commission des Nouveaux Etats Membres, Communication de M. Kinnock, C(2003)436/5*, p. 3 and *Recruitment of Senior Managers from the New Member States - Implementation Measures, Communication from Vice-President Kinnock in Agreement with the President, SEC(2004)0252*, p. 2.

in her view, to an uneven age profile, with undesirable consequences for promotion prospects and career development.[387]

These concerns are indeed serious. However, an alternative, namely the abandonment of competitions organized specially for nationals of new EU Member States, could cause perhaps an even greater problem. As the UN experience has shown, it could take a long time to restore the geographical balance among the staff disturbed upon accession of each new country. Political pressure that would inevitably accompany this imbalance could result in the Administration reaching towards practices less transparent than competitions in order to restore the balance and satisfy new Member States. The unfortunate negative consequences of the closed competitions organized after the 2004 and 2007 accession waves, referred to by Stevens, might also be caused by the exceptional nature of these enlargements involving no less than ten new Member States acceding simultaneously, followed by another two Member States in less than three years time. It is very unlikely that such a situation will present itself again. An accession of just one country and competitions organized specifically for nationals of this country should not disturb the state of affairs among the Commission staff to such a great extent as the 2004 and 2007 accessions undoubtedly did.[388]

3.4.1.3. Submarine approach

The 'submarine approach' is an expression related to a specific career advancement practice in the European Commission under which an initially non-permanent contract is converted into a permanent one. By taking several steps over a certain period of time, an originally temporary servant could acquire a permanent position while having to face no or only limited competition.[389] For example, a person originally appointed as a consultant, later acquired a status of auxiliary agent, afterwards classified as a full temporary agent who, eventually, became eligible for an internal competition for a permanent post.[390]

According to Stevens, the submarine approach once constituted one of the three main routes of entry to a permanent appointment in the European Commission: the first being the classic route via external competition; the second being the so-called *parachutage*, which allows for recruitment to senior positions without

[387] Stevens and Stevens, *Brussels Bureaucrats? The Administration of the European Union*, pp. 92-95.

[388] Note that in March 2010, upon the introduction of new selection procedures, the European Personnel Selection Office announced that country specific competitions would no longer be organized. This announcement was made in relation to competitions to be organized in 2010 and it is not clear whether it will apply when a new country accedes to the European Union. – European Personnel Selection Office, *New Selection Procedures - Your Questions Answered*, 20.01.2010, available at http://europa.eu/discover/news/news14_en.htm, last visited on 10.03.2010.

[389] Stevens and Stevens, *Brussels Bureaucrats? The Administration of the European Union*, p. 87.

[390] Spence, D., *Staff and Personnel Policy in the Commission*, in: G. Edwards and D. Spence (eds.), The European Commission, Longman, London, 1997, pp. 97-114, p. 80, cited in Stevens and Stevens, *Brussels Bureaucrats? The Administration of the European Union*, p. 87. Note that this example predates the new structure of the EU civil service, based on which one category of temporary staff, namely auxiliary staff, no longer exists.

having recourse to a competition; and the third being the submarine approach.[391] With regard to the last one, Stevens observed that such entry into the European Commission 'by the back door' was 'by no means unusual'.[392] Page, moreover, listed the submarine approach as one of the 'immediate and direct ways of ensuring the nationals of a Member State reach senior positions'.[393]

The use of the submarine practice has been severely criticized, on two counts mainly: first, a less regulated access to the status of 'other servant'; and second, a difference between external and internal competitions. As for the first issue, recruitment of non-permanent staff was largely unregulated in the past. Only some of the temporary staff and some of the auxiliary staff had to undergo a sort of a preselection process. Engagement of the remaining non-permanent staff, thus most of it, occurred on the basis of no rules of general application.[394] Although the *EU Staff Regulations* contained a number of provisions imposing general conditions for the employment of other servants, there was no established procedural framework. Getting a non-permanent contract with the European Commission thus largely depended on personal knowledge of the system and of the right people, thereby lacking any transparency and objectivity. In this manner, the process was (potentially) open to pressure by various interested parties, including not only those who wished to join the EU staff but also other stakeholders who had interest in getting certain persons in.

The second reason for criticising the submarine practices was the difference between external and internal competitions. As pointed out by the European Parliament in one of the staff cases in which internal competitions were at issue, 'results of an external open competition cannot be seriously compared with those of an internal competition' because of the number of candidates competing in the respective competitions and the consequent degree of difficulty of the competitions and subsequent selection. The Parliament stressed that the nature and level of the tests were different in the two competitions. The candidates who were to become officials needed to show 'competence justifying benefits of the public service', whereas those with temporary appointments no longer needed to prove they had the merits to become officials.[395] Also the 1999 Committee of Independent Experts condemned practices using internal competitions for giving non-permanent staff access to permanent appointment:

> *The general comment that should be made here is that in such [internal] competitions there is always a risk of there being a tendency to 'keep things in the family', given that candidates may be known personally to the examiners. Consideration should thus be given to their abolition, or at least to the introduction of*

[391] Stevens and Stevens, *Brussels Bureaucrats? The Administration of the European Union*, p. 72. Note that *parachutage* is addressed in the following section dealing with the EU senior officials – see below, section 3.4.2.1.

[392] Ibid., p. 89.

[393] Page, *People Who Run Europe*, p. 49.

[394] *Second Report on Reform of the Commission of 1999, Volume II*, para. 6.4.11.

[395] *Brigitte Bataille and others v. European Parliament, Case T-56/89, ECR [1990], p. II-597*, para. 56.

mechanisms which ensure genuine transparency and selectivity, thus guarding against this unwanted tendency.[396]

Legally speaking, the conversion of non-permanent contracts into permanent ones through a series of subsequent steps was in conformity with the *EU Staff Regulations* and *EU Conditions of Employment of Other Servants* which allowed engagement of persons under various types of non-permanent contract and their eventual recruitment into permanent posts through internal competition. As for internal competitions, although the *EU Staff Regulations* did not mention temporary staff or other categories of 'other servants' in their context, the ECJ recognized the right of such staff to participate in the internal competition in a number of cases.[397] It also recognized the right of non-permanent staff to take legal proceedings and defend their right to be admitted to internal competitions.[398] Furthermore, it found that internal rules restricting access of non-permanent staff to internal competitions were incompatible with the *EU Staff Regulations*.[399]

In 2000, reacting to the criticism of the use of internal competitions for regularization of non-permanent staff, the Commission promised that it would no longer organize them.[400] Despite this intention, expressed in the framework of the overall Commission reform, internal competitions have remained possible under the amended *EU Staff Regulations* and still – or again – take place. There is, however, an important difference with the past regime. At present, only officials and temporary staff have access to internal competitions.[401] At the same time, the number of temporary staff in the Commission is significantly lower than it was before the reform and also lower than the number of other non-permanent staff, especially contract staff. This amendment of Article 29 of the *EU Staff Regulations* thus means that the access of non-permanent staff to permanent appointment through internal competitions has been reduced significantly.

3.4.2. Senior officials

An adequate geographical balance at the senior level has been a constant concern of the European Commission. Officially, the Commission has always been committed to choosing the 'best' qualified candidate for its senior positions. At the same time, it has acknowledged that such commitment sometimes resulted in imbalances of nationalities at the senior level and in under-representation of a number of nationalities.[402] The Commission has employed a number of practices in order to correct

[396] *Second Report on Reform of the Commission of 1999, Volume II*. paras. 6.5.23 and 6.5.25.

[397] For example, *Gertrud Rauch v. Commission of the EEC, Case 16/64, ECR [1965], p. 135*, p. 142 and *Bataille v. Parliament, Case T-56/89*, para. 41. For more details, see below, chapter 3, section 3.2.1.2.

[398] *Antonio Giannini v. Commission of the European Communities, Case 265/81, ECR [1982], p. 3865*, para. 8.

[399] *Bataille v. Parliament, Case T-56/89*, paras. 45-48.

[400] *Second Report on Reform of the Commission of 1999, Volume II*, para. 6.5.24.

[401] *EU Staff Regulations*, Article 29(1)(b).

[402] *European Commission Announces Next Steps in Implementing New Senior Staff Policy.*

these imbalances, most notably the so-called practice of *parachutage*. In addition, it has also allowed active involvement of Commissioners' top cabinet members in the selection process. This involvement was a reflection of great interest cherished by EU Member States in the appointment of their nationals into senior positions in the European Commission. Given the fact that senior officials assume a major role in framing Commission policy and in decision-making, Member States have always regarded these positions as being of great significance. Both *parachutage* and the involvement of Commissioners' cabinets in choosing senior officials are addressed in the following sections. The last section provides an overview of other specific principles and measures employed by the Commission in order to ensure geographical balance at the senior level.

3.4.2.1. *Parachutage*

Parachutage is a common name for a special route of entry to a permanent appointment in the European Commission, allowing for direct appointments into senior positions of persons who have not gone through a competition. It is considered the best known way of making an immediate and direct impact ensuring that nationals of a particular Member State reached senior positions.[403] It has also been used for filling senior posts reserved for nationals of newly acceded Member States.[404] In addition, *parachutage* has served as a means by which members of cabinets have moved into permanent posts after their Commissioner's term of office expired.[405] It must be noted, though, that other considerations, such as extraordinary personal skills or political closeness of the *parachutists* to a Commissioner, have also been important considerations.[406]

Studies show that a significant number of Commission senior officials are *parachutists*. Data collected by Page in 1997 suggest one third, while Hooghe's research published in 2001 estimates almost a half, the latter noting that the practice has declined since the mid-1980s.[407] While *parachutage* has been explicitly permitted by the *EU Staff Regulations*, the practice has been much contested for its (potential)

---

403 Page has observed a direct link between *parachutage* and the system of national flags. He has claimed that when a position had to be filled by a person of certain nationality based on the system of national flags,, *parachutage* often came into the play. - Page, *People Who Run Europe*, p. 49. On the continuing use of parachutage for the purposes of improving geographical balance among senior officials, see, for example, *European Commission Announces Next Steps in Implementing New Senior Staff Policy*, Annex, Part 3.2.

404 Hooghe, *The European Commission and the Integration of Europe, Images of Governance*, p. 60. Hooghe explains that the use of *parachutage* in these cases was caused by the absence of internal candidates who could be promoted into these posts at the time of accession. – Ibid.

405 Stevens and Stevens, *Brussels Bureaucrats? The Administration of the European Union*, p. 85. For recent examples of placement of former cabinet staff in new posts, see, for example, King, T., *Staff Reforms that Failed to Make the Grade*, in: EuropeanVoice.com, 26.07.2007, last paragraph; or Rettman, A., *Sweden Complains about EU Appointment to US*, in: euobserver.com, 22.02.2010 and Pop, V., *Sweden Continues Attack on US Appointment*, in: euobserver.com, 23.02.2010.

406 Page, *People Who Run Europe*, p. 50.

407 Ibid., p. 51; Hooghe, *The European Commission and the Integration of Europe, Images of Governance*, p. 177.

negative effects on the independence and impartiality of officials who have entered the EU civil service by using ties with their Member States. As noted by Hooghe, many *parachutists* have connections with their national governments. Her research showed that 55 per cent of *parachutists* had, prior to their appointment in the European Commission, been national civil servants or diplomats, while for officials who had got their senior position by internal promotion this was only the case for 27 per cent.[408]

In addition, Page has claimed that *parachutage* has always involved 'a highly contentious struggle among Member States for an important new position' or it had constituted 'a routine replacement of a retiring official who [was] expected to be replaced by a fellow countryman'.[409] According to Page, the negotiation process leading to a *parachutist's* appointment normally involved a variety of individual and groups of individuals, including very prominent ones: senior officials of the Directorate-General responsible for personnel matters, the Permanent Representatives, the Council, the Commissioner responsible for the Directorate-General in which the appointment is sought, Commissioners from the home state of the applicants, the President of the Commission, and the Vice-President of the Commission.[410] Clearly, a number of these actors should have had no place in the Commission staff selection process, most notably the Permanent Representatives, the Council, Commissioners from the home state of the applicants, and, arguably, also the President and a Vice-President of the Commission.

On the other hand, there are those who claim that the negative effects of *parachutage* on senior officials' independence and impartially are limited. For example, according to Hooghe, her research demonstrates that most *parachutists* are not alleged 'Trojan horses'. She claims that *parachutage* gives national governments an illusion of control but no more than that. In the end, Member States do not have the final say over appointments, the EU Administration does. Furthermore, all officials, including *parachutists*, are protected against potential national pressure by the tenure of their appointments. Hooghe concludes that national governments' interest in *parachuting* persons into the Commission is driven by habit and status rather than by concerns about ensuring that their national interests will be protected.[411]

Be that as it may, it could be argued that even a perception of a negative influence of *parachutage* on the independence and impartiality of senior Commission officials is unacceptable. The fact is that this negative perception, be it well founded or not considering its real effects on the behaviour of individual senior officials, has led to modification of the recruitment procedures of these officials in the framework of the 2000 reform process. *Parachutage* as such has been maintained in the *EU Staff Regulations* in Article 28(d) in conjunction with Article 29(2) but new rules for the appointment of senior officials have been adopted.[412]

---

408 Hooghe, *The European Commission and the Integration of Europe, Images of Governance*, p. 184.

409 Page, *People Who Run Europe*, p. 50.

410 Ibid., p. 50.

411 Hooghe, *The European Commission and the Integration of Europe, Images of Governance*, p. 190.

412 Article 29(2) has not been substantially modified since its adoption in the *Staff Regulations* of 1961.

According to Article 28(d) of the *EU Staff Regulations*, an official can be appointed on the condition that he passes open competition, with an exception provided for in Article 29(2) thereof. Pursuant to the relevant part of Article 29(2):

> *A procedure other than the competition procedure may be adopted by the Appointing Authority for the recruitment of senior officials (Directors-General or their equivalent in grade AD 16 or AD 15 and Directors or their equivalent in grade AD 15 or AD 14).*[413]

The relevant appointing authority may thus adopt a procedure other than open competition in case a senior official is to be recruited. No further specification of this 'other' procedure is provided in the *EU Staff Regulations* and no conditions are set out there. In general, recourse to Article 29(2) does not even need to be published.[414] As explained by the ECJ, the purpose of Article 29(2) of the *EU Staff Regulations* is to let the appointing authority include the greatest possible number of potential candidates in the selection process for senior posts.[415]

The wording of Article 29(2) of the *EU Staff Regulations* has not been substantially modified since its adoption in 1961. What has changed under the 2000 staff reform is the practical implementation of this provision. Following the recommendations of the Committee of Independent Experts of 1999, which had pleaded for the introduction of more rigorous criteria for the selection of senior officials and for more transparent procedures, new rules have been adopted.[416] They can be found in the *Commission Compilation Document of Senior Officials Policy SEC(2004) 1352/2*.[417] It has been argued that the new rules had been introduced in order to 'internalise' the recruitment process of senior officials in the sense of excluding external actors.[418] As noted by Egeberg, under the new rules neither the governments of the EU Member States nor the Permanent Representations in Brussels have a formal point of access to the recruitment process. As far as informal interventions are concerned, the Member States could, of course, make attempts through contacting 'their' Commissioners or his cabinet members since these actors have indeed retained some role in the appointment of senior officials.[419]

As for Commissioners, they are involved in creating the vacancies related to their portfolios and the profile of these vacancies; they can influence the decision whether to publish the vacancy notice internally or externally; they must be consulted by

New rules for the appointment of senior officials can be found in *Commission Compilation Document on Senior Officials Policy*.

413 *EU Staff Regulations*, Article 29(2)

414 *Giuliano Marenco and others v. Commission of the European Communities*, *Joined cases 81 to 88/74, ECR [1975], p. 1247*, para. 23.

415 *Kotzonis v. Economic and Social Committee, Case T-586/93*, para. 95.

416 *Second Report on Reform of the Commission of 1999, Volume II*, Recommendation 71, see also paras. 6.5.43-6.5.47.

417 *Commission Compilation Document on Senior Officials Policy*, Parts 4 and 5.

418 Egeberg, *Organising Institutional Autonomy in a Political Context: Enduring Tensions in the European Commission's Development*, p. 8.

419 Ibid., p. 10.

the rapporteur when making an evaluation of candidates who are recommended to the Consultative Committee of Appointments for the interviews; and, eventually, they take the final decision on the appointment. The Commissioners may also decide to appoint a candidate who was not short-listed by the Consultative Committee of Appointments or to repeat the whole recruitment process.[420] With regard to the latter, it seems, however, a great majority of the appointments have been made from among the short-listed candidates.[421]

Turning to cabinet members, the Head of the Cabinet of the Commissioner for Human Resources and Security and the Head of the Cabinet of the Commission President are members of the Consultative Committee of Appointments in choosing a Director-General; and the former also in the appointment of a Director.[422] However, there are another five persons in the Committee, thus diminishing the influence of the concerned Heads of Cabinet.[423] Moreover, it is always the heads of the cabinets of the Commissioner for Personnel and Administration and the head of the cabinet of the Commission President who are involved in all appointment cases. The number of nationalities that could receive any advantage from such involvement is thereby limited to a minimum.

According to Egeberg, the new rules for the recruitment of Commission senior officials have led to the 'insulation' of the recruitment of these officials from pressure that could be applied by governments as well as the political level of the Commission itself.[424] In Egeberg's view, the Commission has enhanced its control of the appointment of senior officials through more transparent procedures, clearly specified requirements that need to be met by the candidates, 'technical' pre-selection (specific requirements related to qualifications and experience) which candidates need to pass before being interviewed and the newly introduced role of Permanent Rapporteur who assists in the recruitment procedures on a full-time basis. On the basis of these elements, Egeberg has concluded that the new system 'generate[s]

[420] *Commission Compilation Document on Senior Officials Policy*, Parts 4 and 5. See also Egeberg, *Organising Institutional Autonomy in a Political Context: Enduring Tensions in the European Commission's Development*, pp. 9-10. For more details on the appointment procedures of senior officials, see below, chapter 3, section 3.2.3.

[421] Egeberg, *Organising Institutional Autonomy in a Political Context: Enduring Tensions in the European Commission's Development*, p. 11.

[422] *Commission Compilation Document on Senior Officials Policy*, para. 5.1.2.

[423] The members of the Consultative Committee of Appointments for the appointment of senior officials to occupy the post of director are: the Director-General for Human Resources and Security (chair), a Deputy Secretary-General, the recruiting Director-General, the Head of Cabinet of the Commissioner for Human Resources and Security, the Permanent Rapporteur and the Rapporteur for the case. For appointment to the post of Director-General, the Consultative Committee of Appointments is composed of the Secretary-General (chair), the Director-General for the Human Resources and Security, the Head of Cabinet of the President, the Head of Cabinet of the Commissioner for Human Resources and Security, the Permanent Rapporteur and the Rapporteur for the case. - Ibid., Article 5.1.2.

[424] Egeberg, *Organising Institutional Autonomy in a Political Context: Enduring Tensions in the European Commission's Development*, p. 11.

more focused attention and capacity at the administrative level to deal with top appointments.'[425]

Hence, despite the fact that *parachutage* – a practice heavily criticized in the past for allowing external parties to be involved in the selection process of Commission senior staff – is still possible under the current *EU Staff Regulations*, the adoption of a clear internal procedure seems to have eliminated at least a direct access of such parties. This departure from past practices does not mean, however, that the Commission has abandoned its goal of ensuring geographical balance among its senior staff. In its *Compilation Document on Senior Officials Policy* the Commission explicitly states that the principles and objectives decided on by the Commission on geographical balance must be ensured during the entire appointment procedure.[426]

3.4.2.2. Role of cabinets

In the past, Commissioners' cabinets, considered to be sites of national affiliations and interests and even outposts for Member States' governments, were often accused of exercising undue influence on appointments in the European Commission. McDonald observed, for example, that cabinets:

> *readily recruit[ed] people directly from national context, by-passing the services, and they [had] regular contacts with national administrations, national lobbyists and the permanent representations. They also notoriously "parachute[d]" their chosen national recruits directly into key service jobs, over the heads of well-qualified and experienced officials in the services. ...*[427]

According to Hooghe, negotiations for top appointments in the Commission took place among three cabinets: first, the cabinet of the Commissioner under whose functional responsibility the vacant position fell; second, the cabinet of the Commissioner for human resources and security, and in case of most important positions this would be the cabinet of the President of the Commission instead; and third, the cabinet of the Commissioner of the applicants' nationality.[428] Spence and Stevens pointed out in this respect that the Heads of Cabinet were traditionally well acquainted with the staff, 'know[ing] the people and the vacant posts and keep[ing] it all pretty much in their hands'.[429]

This demonstrates the importance of the role of Commissioners' cabinets in appointment matters in the past. Hooghe even noted that this importance seemed to have increased during the 1980s and 1990s.[430] As recently as in 2001, Stevens claimed that, even though the recruitment procedures in the EU had become more

[425] Ibid., p. 12.

[426] *Commission Compilation Document on Senior Officials Policy*, Section 5, first paragraph.

[427] McDonald, *Identities in the European Commission*, p. 51. See also Endo, *The Presidency of the European Commission under Jacques Delors, The Politics of Shared Leadership*, p. 45.

[428] Hooghe, *The European Commission and the Integration of Europe, Images of Governance*, p. 177.

[429] Spence and Stevens, *Staff and Personnel Policy in the Commission*, p. 200, quoting a cabinet member.

[430] Hooghe, *The European Commission and the Integration of Europe, Images of Governance*, p. 177.

transparent and professional than in the past, there still was sufficient room for flexibility. This flexibility, together with the importance of senior appointments, meant, in Stevens' view, that Heads of Cabinet were likely to continue to invest up to 20 per cent of their time in activities related to filling vacancies at the top level.[431] On the other hand, a few years later, Egeberg concluded that the adoption of new rules on the appointment of senior officials and on the composition of the cabinets had resulted in more independent appointments at the senior level.[432]

To assess the current situation from a legal perspective, attention needs to be paid to two important changes that have taken place during the 2000 reform. The first change, mentioned in the previous section, is the adoption of new rules of procedure for the appointments of Commission senior officials. These rules have reduced, if not eliminated, cabinets' influence in this respect. As stated above, formally, only Heads of Cabinet of the President and of the Commissioner for the Human Resources and Security are members of the Consultative Committees of Appointments of Directors-General and/or Directors. In addition, these Heads of Cabinet are in the minority in the Consultative Committee composed of six members.[433] Furthermore, other cabinets have no formal role in the recruitment of senior officials.

The second important change relates to the composition of the cabinets, also addressed in one of the previous sections. First of all, each cabinet must be composed of persons of at least three different nationalities. Secondly, heads or Deputy Heads of the Cabinets should preferably be of a different nationality than that of their Commissioners.[434] These decisions are clearly aimed at eliminating national influence in the individual cabinets, including their often contested role in the appointment procedures of senior officials. As noted by Egeberg, due to the 'multinational chain of command' within each cabinet and Directorate-General, it has become rather difficult for Commissioners' cabinets to exercise any relevant influence.[435] Evaluating possible consequences of multi-national composition of the cabinets on the appointment of Commission senior staff, Egeberg has observed that new rules have probably changed the cabinets' role.[436] Also Kassim and Menon have admitted that, as a consequence of this decision on cabinets' composition, as well as placing the cabinets in the same building as the Directorate-General of their portfolio,

> *there seems to be some evidence that the Commissioner cabinets have been less ready since 1999 to act as spokesperson for the national capital.*[437]

---

[431] Stevens and Stevens, *Brussels Bureaucrats? The Administration of the European Union*, p. 83.

[432] Egeberg, *Organising Institutional Autonomy in a Political Context: Enduring Tensions in the European Commission's Development*, p. 19.

[433] See above, section 3.4.2.1.

[434] *Commission Rules on the Composition of Cabinets and the Spokespersons*, Section A.3.1.

[435] Egeberg, *The European Commission - The Evolving EU Executive*, p. 12.

[436] Egeberg, *Organising Institutional Autonomy in a Political Context: Enduring Tensions in the European Commission's Development*, p. 7. Two years earlier Egeberg stated: 'It is indeed hard to imagine that the role of cabinets as liaison units between national governments and the Commission will not be profoundly redefined in the future.'- Egeberg, *The European Commission - The Evolving EU Executive*, p. 9.

[437] Kassim and Menon, *European Integration since the 1990s: Member States and the European Commission*,

Last but not least, it should be noted that the *Commission Rules Governing the Composition of the Members' Cabinets and the Spokespersons SEC(2008) 2602* explicitly spell out the obligation of cabinets staff to respect overall professional ethics:

> *In performing their duties Cabinet staff must only have the interest of the institution in mind. Cabinet staff is subject to the same rules of professional ethics as all Commission staff.*[438]

Similarly, the *Code of Conduct for Commissioners SEC(2004) 1487/2* stipulates:

> *The Cabinet shall act solely in the interests of the institution in performing its tasks.*[439]

The *Code of Conduct for Commissioners* also stresses that relations between cabinets and Commission departments should be 'based first and foremost on loyalty, trust and transparency'.[440] The Code sets out more or less precise lines along which cooperation between these two different actors should take place.[441] All these requirements on the expected behaviour of cabinet members, so explicitly elucidated, demonstrate that, at least formally, the Commission wishes to part with the past practice of cabinets being sites of national interests.

3.4.2.3. Other specific principles and measures

As mentioned above, the *Compilation Document on Senior Officials Policy* stipulates that during the entire appointment procedure, the principles and objectives decided on by the Commission on geographical balance must be observed. It is not entirely clear, however, what exactly these 'principles and objectives' are and where they can be found. It appears that they include those announced in the Commission's press release of 2002 entitled *European Commission Announces Next Steps in Implementing New Senior Staff Policy*.[442] This press release presented a number of specific measures and principles relating specifically to the issue of geographical balance.

Firstly, Commissioners making proposals for appointments into senior posts are required to pay special attention to candidates of under-represented nationalities, especially those short-listed by the Consultative Committee on Appointments. However, priority to a person of an under-represented nationality can only be given when he possess required merit. Because merit is explicitly confirmed as paramount, the requirement to 'pay special attention' to persons from under-represented Member States is therefore in line with Article 27 of the *EU Staff Regulations*.

---

p. 22.

438 *Commission Rules on the Composition of Cabinets and the Spokespersons*, Section A.2.

439 *Code of Conduct for Commissioners, SEC(2004)1487/2*, available in the Register of Commission Documents, available at http://ec.europa.eu/transparency/regdoc/registre.cfm?CL=en, last visited on 30.12.2010, Section 2.2., para. 5.

440 Ibid., Section 2.1.

441 Ibid., Section 2.2.

442 *European Commission Announces Next Steps in Implementing New Senior Staff Policy*.

The second specific principle is a possibility to prefer external appointments if they are necessary for improving geographical balance, even though as a general rule, priority in all staff appointments in the European Commission is to be given to internal candidates.[443] The inclusion of external candidates in senior officials' selection procedure is compatible with the *EU Staff Regulations* and, in particular, its Articles 28 and 29, addressed above. They mandate the Commission to adopt 'other procedure', i.e. other than competition, for the appointment of senior officials, opening the scope of potential candidates to outsiders. In addition, such a move broadens the pool of potential candidates. That in itself increases the chances of recruiting the best qualified candidate, which is the primary objective of Article 27 of the *EU Staff Regulations*.

The third specific principle is that in cases in which new appointments would worsen the existing geographical imbalance, the Administration would examine how future movements (departures, retirement, etc.) could contribute to remedying the situation. As long as the Commission does not violate Article 7 of the *EU Staff Regulations* while implementing the suggested remedies, this requirement should not be problematic either. Article 7 prohibits discrimination on the basis of, *inter alia*, nationality in the assignment of officials to particular posts. Thus, in taking specific decisions on staff appointment or transfer, the EU Administration should act solely in the interest of the service and without regard to nationality.

The fourth specific measure announced with regard to the issue of geographical balance at the senior level is a bi-annual review of the existing state of affairs and adoption of necessary recommendations.[444] The Commissioner for Human Resources and Security is required to submit to the College of Commissioners twice a year a note about the geographical balance of senior officials.[445] Clearly, a mere regular collection and analysis of relevant data is not a problem. Even if followed by actions that would be contrary to the *EU Staff Regulations*, the legality of the data review itself cannot be disputed. Illegal actions, of course, could be, but on their own grounds.

3.4.3. Other servants

Provisions equivalent to Article 27 of the *EC Staff Regulations*, addressed above, apply to some categories of 'other servants' too. In particular, temporary and contract staff also are expected to reflect the geographical diversity of the organization. No such requirement applies to local staff or special advisers. In the case of the former, of course, the very nature of this staff excludes any such prerequisite. As for the latter, the geographical balance among its members is perhaps not as important because their involvement with the EU is only limited and their main employment rests elsewhere.

[443] *EU Staff Regulations*, Article 29(1).

[444] *European Commission Announces Next Steps in Implementing New Senior Staff Policy*, Annex.

[445] *Commission Compilation Document on Senior Officials Policy*, Section 3.3.

The following section examines how the principle of geographical balance has been applied in relation to temporary and contract staff where relevant.

3.4.3.1. Temporary staff

Article 12 of the *EU Conditions of Employment of Other Servants* is an equivalent of Article 27 of the *EU Staff Regulations*. It requires in its relevant part that:

> *The engagement of temporary staff shall be directed to secure the services of persons of the highest standards of ability, efficiency and integrity, recruited on the broadest possible geographical basis from among the nationals of the Member States of the Communities.*[446]

However, the *Commission Decision on a New Policy for the Engagement and Use of Temporary Agents C(2004) 1597* of 2004 does not provide any guidance in how these two requirements of merit and geographical balance should be applied. For most temporary staff, it does not even provide details on selection procedures to be followed. A rather general framework for selection of temporary staff falling under the scope of Article 2(a) of the *EU Conditions of Employment of Other Servants* is available in Article 2, paragraph (c) of this Decision. This provision stipulates that the selection takes place on the basis of a profile of the vacant post established by the relevant Directorate-General or service and approved by the Directorate-General for Human Resources and Security and a consideration by a three-member selection committee. After having considered candidates, the committee sets up a list of successful candidates from which temporary staff is eventually chosen.[447] The same procedure is to be followed for the engagement of 'Article 2(b) temporary staff' and in particular those engaged in case of need for specialists where no temporary post is available and the organization of an external competition for the occupation of a single post would not be justified, or for meeting a temporary need.[448] Research staff are to be selected by a committee from a database of spontaneous applications.[449] No formal selection procedure exists for the rest of temporary staff.[450] The Commission states on its internet site that these posts are filled through selection from a list of candidates who submitted their spontaneous application in an online database created for this purpose.[451]

---

[446] *EU Conditions of Employment of Other Servants*, Article 12.

[447] *Commission Decision on a New Policy for the Engagement and Use of Temporary Agents, C(2004)1597, Informations Administratives No 74-2004 of 23.4.2004*, 28.4.2004, available at http://europa.eu/epso/documents/decision_new_policy_for_at_en.pdf, last visited on 30.12.2010, Article 2(c).

[448] Ibid., Article 3(b).

[449] Ibid., Article 5.

[450] Ibid., Articles 3(a) and 4.

[451] Internet site of the European Commission Civil Service, available at http://ec.europa.eu/civil_service/job/cvonline/index_en.htm#3, last visited on 15.03.2010. The Commission explains: 'This online database is the source of choice for our managers looking for candidates for specific job openings which do not require a special selection procedure. You simply register. Nothing else needs to be done. If we are interested in you, we will contact you by e-mail or by telephone.' – Ibid.

Since there are no or only very general formal rules on the selection of Commission temporary staff, it is not possible to establish how the need to ensure geographical balance among them is implemented. Moreover, there seem to be no published statistical data on the nationality of actually recruited temporary staff – available statistics include data on both permanent officials and temporary staff.[452] It appears therefore that officials involved in choosing temporary staff would not even be able to know which nationality is over-represented or under-represented. The only information they could possess would relate to the individual department or service of the Commission but not to the Commission as a whole. Such information should, however, not play any role in the selection process. As mentioned above, the ECJ has ruled that the requirement of geographical balance may not be restricted to individual Directorates-General.[453]

3.4.3.2. Contract staff

Article 82 of the *EC Conditions of Employment of Other Servants* requires in its relevant part the following:

> *Contract staff shall be engaged on the broadest possible geographical basis from among the nationals of the Member States of the Communities...*[454]

The *Commission Decision on Contractual Agents C(2004)1313* of 2004, as subsequently amended, specifies the procedure for the selection of contract staff, separately for both types of this staff ('Article 3a contract staff' and 'Article 3b contract staff').[455] Although these procedures are more elaborate than those for temporary staff, none of their parts seem to be concerned with the issue of geographical balance. In general, candidates who respond to a call for expression of interest and who meet the conditions set out therein are invited to sit tests. Those who are successful in all the tests are then listed in a database which constitutes the basis on which individual institutions recruit staff for specific job vacancies.[456] Clearly, officials involved in the last phase of the selection process could take the requirement to ensure broad geographical balance among contract agents into account when making the final choice. To be able to do so, they could use information on the factual situation with

---

[452] For example, *Distribution of Officials and Temporary Agents by Genders, Nationalities, Function Groups and Grades (All Budgets)*, 01.02.2010, available at http://ec.europa.eu/civil_service/docs/bs_sexe_nat_grade_en.pdf, last visited on 05.03.2010; *Distribution of Officials and Temporary Agents by Directorate General and Nationality (All Budgets)*, 01.02.2010, available at http://ec.europa.eu/civil_service/docs/bs_dg_nat_en.pdf, last visited on 05.03.2010; and *Distribution of Staff by Statutory Links and DGs*.

[453] *Reinarz v. Commission, Case 17/68*, p. 34-37. See also above, section 3.3.3.

[454] *EU Conditions of Employment of Other Servants*, Article 82.

[455] *Commission Decision C(2004)1313 of 7 April 2004 on General Implementing Provisions on the Procedures Governing the Engagement and the Use of Contract Staff at the Commission, as amended by Commission Decision C(2004)2862 of 27 February 2004, Commission Decision C(2004)4952 of 17 December 2004, and Commission Decision C(2005)5411 of 16 December 2005*, available in the Register of Commission Documents, available at http://ec.europa.eu/transparency/regdoc/registre.cfm?CL=en, last visited on 30.12.2010, Articles 5 and 8. For more details, see chapter 3, section 3.3.2.

[456] The internet site of the EPSO, available at http://europa.eu/epso/discover/selection_proced/selection/index_en.htm#chapter3, visited on 15.03.2010.

respect to the composition of contract staff which the Commission is required to present in its yearly report on the use of contract staff, including the geographical balance.[457]

3.4.4. Seconded national experts

It has been argued that the engagement of staff under the terms of secondment constitutes one way around the limitations imposed by the need to maintain geographical balance among the EU staff. The argument was that since the seconded national experts did not fall under the definition of EU staff member, they were excluded from official calculations of geographical balance.[458]

Indeed, people serving in the European institutions under the terms of secondments do not constitute a part of the EU civil service and are not covered by the *EU Staff Regulations*. Neither do they fall under the regime established by the *EU Conditions of Employment of Other Servants*. However, since 2008, seconded national experts are, next to other categories of external staff engaged by the European Commission, systematically registered in the Commission human resources information system called Sysper2. Therefore, the Commission is now able to provide statistical data on the seconded national experts too. It did so for the first time in its second annual *Human Resources Report* issued in 2009.[459] This included information on the distribution of seconded national experts by nationality.[460]

As for the particular issue of geographical balance, pursuant to Article 1(4) of the *Commission Decision Laying Down Rules on the Secondment of National Experts and National Experts in Professional Training* (*'Commission Decision on Secondment'*), the Commission is obliged to ensure geographical balance when accepting seconded national experts into its departments.[461] The obligation to take account of geographical balance among the seconded national experts existed also in the previous versions of the *Commission Decision on Secondment*.[462] However, in 2008, this obligation seems to have been given greater emphasis. First of all, the wording has been changed from 'the Commission shall *take account of*' to 'the Commission shall *ensure*' geographical balance. Secondly, it has been stressed that when the Director-General of Human

[457] *EU Conditions of Employment of Other Servants*, Article 79(3).

[458] Page, *People Who Run Europe*, p. 59. The Commission confirmed in its *Human Resources Report* of 2009 that the staff categories for which statistical data had usually been provided were officials, temporary agents and (what now are) contract agents. - *Commission's Human Resources Report 2009*, p. 26.

[459] *Commission's Human Resources Report 2009*, p. 26. On 31.12.2008, there were 1139 seconded national experts in the Commission, which amounted to 2,9 per cent of the Commission staff. *ibid.*, p. 30.

[460] Ibid., pp. 46-47.

[461] *Commission Decision on Secondment*, Article 1(4).

[462] *Commission Decision C(2006)2033 Laying Down Rules on the Secondment of National Experts to the Commission*, C(2006)2033, 01.06.2006, available at http://ec.europa.eu/reform/human_resources/regime_end_2006_en.pdf, last visited on 30.12.2010 and *Commission Decision Concerning the Amendment of Decision C(2002) 1559 of 30 April 2002 Amended by Decision C(2003)406 of 31 January Laying Down Rules on the Secondment of National Experts to the Commission*, C(2004) 577, 27.02.2004, available in the Register of Commission Documents, available at http://ec.europa.eu/transparency/regdoc/registre.cfm?CL=en, last visited on 30.12.2010, in both cases Article 1(3).

Resources and Security authorizes secondment outside an agreement and/or exchange programme concluded between the Commission and individual Member States, thus on a case-by-case basis, he must take the existing geographical balance into consideration.[463] Thirdly, a new obligation was introduced for the Directorate-General for Human Resources and Security, namely to monitor compliance with the obligation to ensure geographical balance among the seconded national experts and to take necessary corrective measures in case of serious imbalance at the level of the whole Commission or at the level of individual Directorate-General.[464] It is therefore rather surprising that a possibility existing in Article 19 of the previous version of the *Commission Decision on Secondment* to reimburse all or a part of the seconded national experts' salaries to their employers was abolished in 2008. Article 19(2) of the pre-2008 *Commission Decision on Secondment* explicitly stated that the authorization of such reimbursement should take account of the need to use seconded national experts from all Member States.[465] The new *Commission Decision on Secondment* of 2008 does not allow for such reimbursement.[466]

At present, there is thus no possibility to correct inadequate geographical balance among seconded national experts by using financial means, while it is clear that the actual number of seconded national experts of a particular nationality could depend on the resources individual Member States are able and/or willing to spend for the secondment of their officials to the Commission. The economically stronger Member States can afford to second more officials than the weaker ones. Said that, available data suggest that although there might be a certain correlation between the number of national experts seconded to the Commission and the wealth of the country, a greater connection seems to exist with the size of the individual Member State, with some exceptions.[467] This fact, combined with the publication by the Commission of the precise number of seconded national experts in the annual *Human Resources Report*, including their nationality, leads to the conclusion that the use of seconded national experts for modifying figures on geographical balance of staff no longer seems to occur.

[463] *Commission Decision on Secondment*, Article 2(3). An agreement or exchange programme concluded between the Commission and individual Member States is the regular basis for secondment. – Ibid., Article 2(2).

[464] Ibid., Article 1(4).

[465] *Commission Decision on Secondment of 2006*, Article 19. Pursuant to the second paragraph of Article 19, the reimbursement is authorized on a case-by-case basis by the Director-General for Personnel and Administration. In case of national experts seconded to Commission delegations, the powers of the Director-General for Personnel and Administration are vested in the Director-General for External Relations – Article 31.

[466] *Commission Decision on Secondment*, Article 2(1).

[467] According to the data provided in the Commission's *Human Resources Report* of 2009, the most seconded national experts came from France (155), Germany (135), Italy (95), the Netherlands (77) and the UK (76). The lowest numbers were from Luxemburg (4) and Cyprus, Lithuania, Malta and Slovenia (5 in each case). An interesting case is Hungary which belongs neither among the most wealthy nor among the most populated Member States, yet the number of its national experts seconded to the Commission in 2008 was relatively high. There were 48 experts from Hungary, compared, for example, to 17 from the Czech Republic, with a similar economic and population situation as Hungary's; or 28 from Belgium which has the same population size as Hungary. - *Commission's Human Resources Report 2009*, p. 47.

3.5. The principle of geographical balance and promotion

Many observers have claimed that the nationality of candidates seeking promotion and their connections with their national governments have played an important, if not a decisive, role in the careers of many EU staff. According to Hooghe, nationality has been 'a central criterion for promotion in the Commission, and this is likely to make it a critical resource – or handicap.'[468] Stevens has stated that arrangements for the career developments of Commission officials have been open to national patronage.[469] McDonald has pointed out the following:

> *It is often claimed that promotion comes about through the support of the national context of the candidate, through the cabinets, the national politicians and the permanent representations, rather than through merit or any "European" propriety. Moments of anger and disillusionment are rife on these points – to the extent that one senior official explained: "One certain way to failure is to be European."*[470]

As explained above, it has also been argued that national quotas have existed in the European Commission for posts in higher echelons, reflecting the political reality in the EU where, like in the UN, Member States have been demanding their share in senior level appointments. Observers have noted that this quota system has led to problems in staff promotion because it has regularly put a hold on further promotion of staff not possessing the 'right' nationality, especially since senior level posts have been, in reality, filled more on the basis of nationality than on the basis of merit.[471]

Legally speaking, Article 45(1) of the *EU Staff Regulations*, dealing with the promotion of EU officials, provides in its relevant part that promotion is to be based on officials' merit:

> *Promotion shall be exclusively by selection from among officials who have completed a minimum of two years in their grade after consideration of the comparative merits of the officials eligible for the promotion.*[472]

---

[468] Hooghe, *The European Commission and the Integration of Europe, Images of Governance*, p. 29.

[469] Stevens and Stevens, *Brussels Bureaucrats? The Administration of the European Union*, p. 115.

[470] McDonald, *Identities in the European Commission*, p. 62.

[471] For example, Hooghe, *Consociationists or Weberians? Top Commission Officials on Nationality*; Cini, *The European Commission, Leadership, Organisation and Culture in the EU Administration*, p. 126; Nugent, N. (ed.), *At the Heart of the Union, Studies of the European Commission*, Macmillan Press Ltd, Houndmills / Basingstoke / Hampshire / London, 1997, pp. 61-62; Nugent, N., *The European Commission*, Palgrave, Houndmills / Basingstoke / Hampshire / New York, 2001, pp. 173-174; Stevens and Stevens, *Brussels Bureaucrats? The Administration of the European Union*, p. 98 and pp. 102 103; Hooghe, *The European Commission and the Integration of Europe, Images of Governance*, p. 191; Spence and Stevens, *Staff and Personnel Policy in the Commission*, p. 189. Nugent, for example, studied precise figures related to the Commission's senior officials and found that the 'entitlement' of each Member State for a senior level post was proportionate to its size. He showed that the larger Member States had had the largest proportion of A-grade staff and A1 posts (e.g. A-grade staff / A1 posts: France 15% / 8 posts, Germany 12% / 8 posts, UK 11% / 8 posts), while the smaller states were being guaranteed a presence (e.g. Denmark 3% / 1 post, Finland 2% / 1 post, Luxembourg 1% / 2 posts). - Nugent, *The European Commission*, pp. 174-175, Tables 7.2 and 7.3.

[472] *EU Staff Regulations*, Article 45(1). This legal situation exists since the adoption of the first *EU Staff*

This provision also sets out eligibility requirements for promotion. They are rather straightforward: officials aspiring for promotion must have occupied a post classified in the same function group for a minimum of two years, demonstrated their merit and have second language proficiency.[473] Before the first promotion, an additional condition regarding the ability to work in a third language is imposed.[474]

As explained in more detail in chapter 4, promotion of Commission officials who meet the above mentioned eligibility requirements can take place in two ways. Firstly, they can be promoted in the course of an annual promotion exercise; and secondly, they can be appointed into a vacant post classified at a level higher than their current post. Promotion via appointment into a vacant post occurs in accordance with Article 29(1)(a) of the *EU Staff Regulations* which stipulates that before a vacant post is filled by an external candidate, the appointment authority must first consider whether it could be filled by transfer, appointment of an official serving in function group AST to a post in function group AD or promotion. Promotion via the annual promotion exercise is regulated by an internal Commission decision. It occurs when officials accumulate a sufficient number of promotion points, thereby reaching promotion thresholds established on the basis of relevant budgetary appropriations, and are subsequently included by the relevant appointing authority in the list of promoted officials. Promotion points are granted in accordance with allocation criteria established by each Directorate-General, paying regard to the individual performance appraisal of officials contained in the relevant staff report; the use of languages in the performance of duties; the level of exercised responsibilities; and the work done in the interest of the institution (for example, membership of a selection board or marker of competition papers). A separate set of rules applies to promotion via the annual promotion exercise of senior officials and to promotion of officials serving in the assistant (AST) function group to the administrator (AD) function group.[475] The latter type of promotion does not fall under Article 45 of the *EU Staff Regulations* but under Article 45a thereof.

Regulations in 1961 – the merits of candidates eligible for promotion are to be compared and the better candidate will get promoted. - *EU Staff Regulations of 1961*, Article 45(1).

[473] *EU Staff Regulations*, Article 45(1). Note that in the case of first promotion, the minimum period of two years runs from the date of the official's establishment. - *Detlef Brüggemann v. Economic and Social Committee of the European Communities, Case 248/86, ECR [1987], p. 3946*, paras. 7-8. This applies also to officials who have to serve a probationary period before being established since the probationary period does not count for promotion purposes. A former probationary official must thus complete the full minimum period required by Article 45 of the *EU Staff Regulations*, too. - *Aristides Vlachos v. Court of Justice of the European Communities, Joined cases 20 and 21/83, ECR [1984], p. 4149*, para. 17. Similarly, the period during which an official served in his institution as a temporary agent before being established as official may not be taken into account in calculating the minimum period required for promotion. - *Wolfdietrich Zoder v. European Parliament, Case T-30/90, ECR [1991], p. II-207*, para. 22.

[474] *EU Staff Regulations*, Article 45(2).

[475] Relevant internal Commission documents are: *Commission Decision on General Provisions for Implementing Article 45 of the Staff Regulations, C(2008) 3028*, 18.06.2008, available in the Register of Commission Documents, available at http://ec.europa.eu/transparency/regdoc/registre.cfm?CL=en, last visited on 30.12.2010; *Promotion of Commission Senior Officials, Principles and Procedure, SEC(2007)605*, 04.05.2007, available in the Register of Commission Documents, available at http://ec.europa.eu/transparency/regdoc/registre.cfm?CL=en, last visited on 30.12.2010 and *Commission Decision Laying Down the General Provisions for Implementing Article 45a of the Staff Regulations,*

None of the two provisions of the *EU Staff Regulations*, neither their implementing provisions adopted by the European Commission, provide for nationality – or the need to ensure geographical balance at all levels – as a relevant consideration in decisions on promotion. Moreover, Article 27 of the *EU Staff Regulations*, which is the only provision containing the requirement of broad geographical balance among the EU staff, clearly relates to staff recruitment, not to promotion. It stipulates that staff *recruitment* is to be conducted on the broadest possible geographical basis from among nationals of Member States.

Despite this, the ECJ has approved taking nationality into account in the promotion process when the promotion is a means of filling a vacant post pursuant to Article 29(1)(a)(iii) of the *EU Staff Regulations*. In deciding upon such appointment, the appointing authority is, of course, required to consider first of all the comparative merits of the candidates, as provided for in Article 45(1) of the *EU Staff Regulations.*[476] However, according to the ECJ, the appointing authority must also observe principles laid down in Article 27 of the *EU Staff Regulations*. The ECJ has emphasized that Article 27, as a general provision, applies to all the recruitment procedures provided for in Article 29 (i.e. to transfer; appointment of an official in function group AST to a post in function group AD; promotion; internal competition and *parachutage*).[477] Consequently, both principles laid down in Article 27 – the principle of merit and that of geographical balance – must be observed also in the procedure of filling a vacant position through promotion. In such instances, the process of recruitment and the process of promotion are, to a certain extent, blurred and both Article 45 and Article 27 of the *EU Staff Regulations* apply simultaneously. Nationality of the officials applying for a vacant post through promotion can thus play a role in the consideration of their candidatures.[478]

Despite the ECJ's green light, the Commission itself has stressed in the *White Paper* of 2000, which addressed the issue of promotion of European Commission staff to a considerable extent, that promotions are to be based on performance and its formal appraisal. The Commission has promised to put more weight on merit and less on seniority or other concerns, such as nationality.[479] This promise includes promotions into senior level posts. In its *Compilation Document on Senior Officials Policy*, the Commission states:

> *Since 1999 the Commission has reviewed the procedures for appointing staff to senior management positions with a view to selecting the candidates who are the most deserving and the best qualified. According to the principles underlying*

C(2007) 5694, 20.11.2007, available in the Register of Commission Documents, available at http://ec.europa.eu/transparency/regdoc/registre.cfm?CL=en, last visited on 30.12.2010. For details on promotion in the European Commission, see below, chapter 4, section 3.

476 *Fischer v. Commission, Case T-58/91*, para. 67.

477 Ibid., para. 85.

478 See, for example, cases *Lassalle v. European Parliament, Case 15/63*, *Kurrer v. Council, Case 33/67*, *Küster v. Parliament, Case 22/75*, *Ragusa v. Commission, Case 282/81*, *Fischer v. Commission, Case T-58/91*.

479 *Reforming the Commission - A White Paper - Part II - Action Plan*, Action 33.

> *the Staff Regulations, such appointments must target "officials of the highest standard of ability, efficiency and integrity".*
>
> *The primary criterion for the appointment of senior officials is merit and competence relevant to the function. The emphasis placed on relevant qualifications and experience seeks to guarantee that officials who are appointed have an adequate knowledge and skills in the policy area in which they are to be working. The selection shall therefore be primarily based on the comparison of the respective merits of the candidates...*[480]

Merit is thus strongly emphasized. Nonetheless, subject to the primacy of the principle of merit, 'respect [for] an adequate balance of nationalities represented in the Commission's services' has made its place into general principles on which the appointment into senior posts is to be based.[481] The Commission has explained its intentions in this regard as follows:

> *The Commission aims to maintain a broad geographical balance in order to ensure a fair spread of all the nationalities of the EU within the staff at all grades and in all departments of the Institution, thereby guaranteeing the cultural wealth and cohesion of the European civil service.*[482]

Therefore, the Commission has declared that it will ensure that during the entire appointment procedure for senior posts 'the principles and objectives decided on by the Commission on geographical balance ... [will be] respected.'[483] Although the Commission has not elaborated on how this is to be done, the available statistics on nationality of senior officials, provided in one of the previous sections, reveal that the Commission has indeed been rather successful in this regard and that geographical balance among top level officials is a fact.[484] As mentioned above, from the legal point of view, the Commission may pay attention to nationality of officials applying for a senior post by promotion under the condition established by the jurisprudence, namely that merits of candidates at issue are essentially the same. When this condition is met, nationality may play even a decisive role in promotions that occurs via appointment to a vacant post.

3.6. The principle of geographical balance and termination of service

As in the UN, so in the EU, the question is whether there is a sound legal basis for a possible termination of an appointment for the purposes of creating space for a national of another Member State. Unlike in the UN, the list of legal grounds for termination of appointments of EU officials has not changed since the adoption of the first *EU Staff Regulations*. This list can be found in Article 47 and includes:

---

480 *Commission Compilation Document on Senior Officials Policy*, Section 3.1.

481 Ibid., Section 3, introductory paragraph.

482 Ibid., Section 3.3.

483 Ibid., Section 5., introductory paragraph.

484 See above, pp. ##.

resignation; compulsory resignation; retirement in the interests of the service; dismissal for incompetence; removal from post; retirement; and death. An additional legal ground is provided in Article 34 of the *EU Staff Regulations*, dealing with probation, namely dismissal during or at the end of the probationary period.

As far as termination of non-permanent appointments is concerned, appointments concluded for a fixed term end upon the expiry of that term. This termination takes place automatically and does not require any action on the side of the EU Administration or the staff member concerned. When a non-permanent staff member holds an indefinite appointment, the EU Administration must take action to end it and give a notice of termination to the person at issue. In principle, the EU Administration enjoys wide discretion in deciding whether and when to terminate appointments of indefinite duration.[485]

An analysis of the list of legal grounds available for termination of appointments in the EU indicates that there could be two possibilities for separation of permanent officials on the basis of their nationality: compulsory resignation and retirement in the interests of the service. With regard to non-permanent staff, fixed-term appointments may be 'left' to expire without being renewed and indefinite appointments may be terminated upon giving notice. The question is whether the nationality of another servant can be the reason behind a decision not to renew a fixed-term appointment or to terminate an indefinite appointment.

3.6.1. Compulsory resignation

Pursuant to Article 49 in conjunction with Article 28 of the *EU Staff Regulations*, an official who has lost the nationality of an EU Member State without having acquired that of another EU Member State no longer fulfills conditions for appointment in the EU civil service and should therefore resign.[486] However, resignation is not an inevitable consequence of the loss of nationality. The appointing authority may grant an official whose nationality has changed an exception on the basis of which such official could remain in service.[487] The appointing authority enjoys a broad discretion to decide, after having heard the official concerned and having consulted the Joint Committee, whether it grants an exception or whether it requests the official's resignation.[488]

Compulsory resignation on grounds of change of officials' nationality can thus occur only under very limited circumstances, the loss of nationality of an EU Member State in itself not being sufficient for it. First, an exception to remain in service may be granted to an official who has lost the nationality of an EU Member State without acquiring that of another Member State. Second, when, at the time of losing

[485] For example, *Alain de Briey v. Commission of the European Communities, Case 25/80, ECR [1981], p. 637*, para. 16. For more details on termination of appointments in the European Commission, see chapter 7, section 3.

[486] *EU Staff Regulations*, Article 49, first paragraph and Article 28(a).

[487] Ibid., Article 49, first paragraph.

[488] Ibid., Article 49, second paragraph.

the nationality of one EU Member States, the official concerned acquires that of another Member State, he may not be required to resign. Although the balance of nationalities of different Member States would change, this cannot be 'corrected' by separating the official at issue.

3.6.2. Retirement in the interests of the service

Article 50 of the *EU Staff Regulations* is the second legal ground on the basis of which some Commission officials could, arguably, be separated because of their nationality. According to this provision, senior officials may be retired in the interests of the service at any time following a decision of the appointing authority. The reasons for the retirement are not further defined and according to the relevant jurisprudence they may relate to both the objective requirements of the service as well as to the assessment of specific qualities of the officials concerned in relation to such objective requirements.[489] In principle, the Commission enjoys a considerable discretion in deciding whether and when it uses Article 50, although it has been argued that it is difficult to do so when the senior official at issue disagrees.[490]

The question is whether the need to ensure (or to correct) geographical balance among (senior) officials would be accepted as an interest or an objective requirement of the service falling under Article 50 of the *EU Staff Regulations*. So far, this question has not presented itself in any staff case dealt with by the ECJ and arguments could feasibly be made in both directions.

On the one hand, it could be argued that Article 27 of the *EU Staff Regulations* – the only legal provision containing the requirement of broad geographical balance – could hardly be extended to termination of appointments. This would be in clear contradiction of the letter and spirit of Article 27 as it relates exclusively to staff recruitment. It is true that, as explained above, the ECJ has extended the application of the requirements contained in Article 27 to staff promotions. However, the ECJ has done so only with regard to promotions as means of filling vacant posts in accordance with Article 29 of the *EU Staff Regulations* explicitly referring to promotions.[491] Clearly, no such link exists between Article 27 and Article 50 of the *EU Staff Regulations*.

On the one hand, the ECJ regards discretion of the EU Administration under Article 50 of the *EU Staff Regulations* to be 'a corollary' to the discretion granted by Article 29(2) thereof relating to the appointment of senior officials.[492] Because of the existence of special provisions for both recruitment and termination of appointments to senior positions, the ECJ appears to believe that senior positions are of a specific nature, distinct from other positions. Therefore, it is of the opinion that the wide discretionary powers conferred on the EU Administration in the recruitment and

[489] *Canzio Almini v. Commission of the European Communities, Case 19/70, ECR [1971], p. 623*, para. 10.

[490] Spence and Stevens, *Staff and Personnel Policy in the Commission*, p. 190.

[491] See above, section 3.5.

[492] *Almini v. Commission, Case 19/70*, para. 9.

separation of senior officials 'assume a considerable freedom to take decisions, as regards both the objective requirements of the service and the assessment of the specific qualities of the officials concerned'.[493] In addition, the ECJ has explicitly stated that the *EU Staff Regulations* 'do not limit the reasons which may justify a retirement under Article 50'.[494] The only restriction placed by the ECJ on the EU Administration is the obligation to exercise its discretion in full knowledge of all relevant factors and to give the official at issue opportunity to state his case if the reasons for separation are linked to his personal qualities.[495] In addition, in cases dealing specifically with the issue of geographical balance in the EU, the ECJ has acknowledged the importance of the need to ensure such balance. In the ECJ's view, broad geographical balance among the EU staff is 'required by the Community spirit'.[496] It could be argued that this is even more so in case of senior officials, given their distinct position. However, it could also be argued that broad geographical balance among these officials can be ensured by means others than retirement of an individual official, for example by the appointment of an official with a desired nationality to a post which will become vacant in the future. Retiring an individual senior official solely for the purpose of replacing him by another with a more desired nationality could therefore be questionable.

Said that, there certainly are instances in which the nationality of an individual senior official would be regarded as an acceptable justification for retirement in the interests of the service. This would particularly be the case when the official at issue would hold a post of Director-General and his nationality would be the same as that of the relevant portfolio Commissioner. As explained in more detail above, in order to ensure the objectivity, independence and impartiality of its actions, the Commission has adopted a policy by which individual Commissioners and their Directors-General should have different nationalities. To implement this policy, the Commission regularly reshuffles Directors-General each time (a) new Commissioner(s) take(s) office.[497] It could be argued that this approach is in line with the requirements of the ECJ which has always linked the interests of the service to the proper functioning of the service, departments and similar.[498]

Thus, it is likely that the requirement of a broad geographical balance among EU staff could, in certain circumstances, play a role in terminating appointments of senior officials on the basis of Article 50 of the *EU Staff Regulations*. Of course, as Article 50 only applies to senior officials, i.e. (Deputy) Directors-General and Directors, termination of appointments other than at the senior level through retirement in the interests of the service would not be legal.

493 *Jozef Oslizlok v. Commission of the European Communities, Case 34/77, ECR [1978], p. 1099*, para. 18. See also paras. 16-17.

494 *Almini v. Commission, Case 19/70*, para. 10. See also *Oslizlok v. Commission, Case 34/77*, para. 17.

495 *Almini v. Commission, Case 19/70*, paras. 9-11 and *Oslizlok v. Commission, Case 34/77*, para. 18.

496 *Lassalle v. European Parliament, Case 15/63*, p. 38.

497 See above, section 3.3.2.

498 Already the early case *Lassalle v. European Parliament, Case 15/63*, p. 38.

3.6.3. Termination of non-permanent appointments

The question posed above with regard to termination of non-permanent appointments in the EU was whether the nationality of an individual 'other servant' could be a reason behind a decision not to renew or extend a fixed-term appointment or to terminate indefinite appointment. In principle, the decision not to renew or extend a fixed-term appointment lies within a broad discretion of the authority authorized to conclude the contract. Even if the conditions for renewal or extension set out in the contract itself and/or in the *EU Conditions of Employment of Other Servants* are met, the person at issue does not have a legal right to have his contract renewed or extended, unless the relevant authority limited its discretion in this respect.[499] Consequently, it could be argued that when no limitation of the discretion exists, non-renewal or non-extension of a fixed-term contract may be based on any reason.

The situation with appointments of indefinite duration appears to be more complex, especially in the light of relatively recent case law. In 2006, the European Union Civil Service Tribunal held in *Landgren* that appointment for an indefinite duration guarantees a certain degree of job security, even though it is less than that for permanent appointment. Therefore, the Tribunal ruled, the termination of an appointment of indefinite duration must also be properly justified.[500] This ruling was a significant departure from previous case law, pursuant to which, no reasons needed to be given for ending an appointment of indefinite duration.[501] Thus, if termination of an appointment of indefinite duration was to be caused by staff member's nationality, termination could have taken place with no formal reasons being provided. Since *Landgren*, this is no longer possible. On the other hand, the European Union Civil Service Tribunal also stressed in that case that the fact that the Administration must explain the reasons on which it based its decision to terminate an indefinite appointment did not prevent it from enjoying broad discretion with regard to the reasons. The only limitation in this respect is that the Administration may not make a manifest error or misuse its powers.[502] Here the question arises whether reasons related to nationality considerations would be regarded as misuse of powers by the EU Administration. It is quite likely that they would since, as in the case of permanent

---

[499] *Stefano Cocchi et Evi Hainz v. Commission of the European Communities, Case T-330/00 and T-114/01, ECR-SC [2002], p. I-A-193, II-987*, para. 83; *Norman Pyres v. Commission of the European Communities, Case T-7/01, ECR-SC [2003], p. IA-37, II-239*, paras. 38-40; and *Rainer Wenning v. European Police Office (Europol), Case F-114/07*, available at http://curia.europa.eu/jurisp/cgi-bin/form.pl?lang=en&Submit=Rechercher&alldocs=alldocs&docj=docj&docop=docop&docor=docor&docjo=docjo&numaff=F-114/07&datefs=&datefe=&nomusuel=&domaine=&mots=&resmax=100, last visited on 30.12.2010, paras. 144-147. See also jurisprudence and its analysis on the principle of protection of legitimate expectations, chapter 6, section 3.2.3.

[500] *Pia Landgren v. European Training Foundation, Case F-1/05, ECR-SC [2006], p. I-A-1-123, II-A-1-459*, paras. 68-72.

[501] For more details, see below, chapter 6, section 3.2.3.

[502] *Landgren v. ETF, Case F-1/05*, para. 75. Note that the same reasoning regarding the statement of reasons was applied by the Tribunal to the termination of fixed-term appointments before the expiry of their fixed term. – *ibid.*, paras. 74-75.

staff, also in the case of non-permanent staff, the need to ensure broad geographical balance relates to staff recruitment, not to their separation.[503]

It is, however, quite unlikely that termination of an indefinite appointment on the basis of the staff member's nationality would occur in practice. There are only two categories of staff who hold indefinite appointments in the European Commission: first, staff serving in the Commissioners' cabinets and, second, contract staff performing manual and administrative support service tasks hired under Article 3a of the *EU Conditions of Employment of Other Servants*.[504] Given the type of duties performed by the latter category of staff, it is unlikely that their nationality would be considered sufficiently relevant for an action such as appointment termination. As far as the former category of staff, i.e. cabinet staff, is concerned, they may be freely hired and fired by individual Commissioners who do not need to justify their decisions. Therefore, even if they separated a staff member because of his nationality, it would be within their broad discretion to do so.[505]

4. The UN and the EU compared

The previous sections discuss the relevance of, and the problems with, the principle of geographical representation in the UN and in the EU appointment process. They explain in detail how the two respective organizations have been approaching this principle in theory and how they have translated it into practice. In this respect, a number of commonalities between the UN and the EU approach can be discerned. They relate to the following four elements: first, the legal base; second, the relationship between the principle of geographical representation and the principle of merit; third, post reservation; and fourth, the situation with regard to separation from service. Despite these important commonalities, which go to the very heart of the principle of broad geographical representation, there are differences in the manner in which the two respective organizations have been approaching it in theory and, more importantly, the way they have been applying it in their staff appointment processes. The most important differences are discussed in the following section, after the common features of the two systems are outlined.

4.1. Commonalities

The first common ground is the incorporation of the principle of geographical representation in both organizations' staff policies. Core documents on the UN and EU personnel policies contain almost identical provisions in this respect. Article 101(3) of the *UN Charter* as well as Regulation 4.2 of the *UN Staff Regulations* require that due

[503] *EU Conditions of Employment of Other Servants*, Articles 12(1) and 82(1).

[504] Ibid., Articles 8 and 85. See also *Commission Decision on Temporary Agents*, Article 4 and *Commission Decision on Contract Staff*, Article 6. For more detail on duration of appointments of non-permanent staff serving in the European Commission, see below, chapter 6, section 3.2.2.

[505] Note that the broad discretion of Commissioners in 'hiring' and 'firing' of their cabinet staff was fully recognized by the judiciary. For more details, see below, chapter 3, section 3.3.1.

regard be paid to the importance of recruiting the staff on 'as wide a geographical basis as possible'. Similarly, Article 27 of the *EU Staff Regulations* envisages recruitment on 'the broadest possible geographical basis', although this requirement is not included in the *EU Treaty* itself.[506] From the legal perspective, both organizations have thus the same starting point.

Similarly, neither in the UN nor in the EU may specific posts be *a priori* reserved for nationals of particular Member States. While the illegality of post reservation in the EU is explicit and incorporated in the *EU Staff Regulations* since their first adoption in 1961, no such explicit prohibition can be found in the UN. Nonetheless, the UN General Assembly has been emphasizing, and requiring, for years that no post is (to be) considered a preserve of any particular country. Moreover, like the ECJ, the UN Administrative Tribunal has also explicitly outlawed post reservation.[507]

The UN and the EU have a very similar position with regard to the relationship between the principle of geographical representation and that of merit. The wording of the provisions representing the legal bases in the UN and in the EU as well as the relevant UN and EU jurisprudence clearly provide that nationality may play a role in the recruitment process in these organizations but only in instances in which the merits of the candidates under consideration are similar. Candidates from inadequately represented countries may thus be given preference in the appointment process when their qualifications are, in essence, equal to those of the best candidate. A clear legal subordination of the principle of geographical representation to that of merit is thus at work in both organizations.[508]

Equally, both the UN and the EU appear to have a similar approach to the role of nationality in termination of appointments. Despite a lack of jurisprudence on this point, it could be argued that neither UN nor EU civil servants can be separated from service solely on the basis of their nationality, with an exception available in the EU for officials who lose their nationality without acquiring the nationality of another EU Member States and a possible exception for EU senior officials who could, certainly in some circumstances, be retired in the interests of the service.[509]

4.2. Differences

Despite the above mentioned similarities on basic issues related to the principle of broad geographical representation, there are a number of differences in its practical application in the UN and EU staff selection processes. In addition, the two organizations approach this principle with a different theoretical mind-set.

---

[506] See above, sections 2.1.1., 2.3.1 and 3.1.

[507] See above, sections 2.3.2 and 3.3.2.

[508] See above, sections 2.3.1 and 3.2.

[509] See above, sections 2.5 and 3.6.

4.2.1. Theoretical differences

The analysis of the UN and EU sets of rules and practices set out in the previous sections clearly demonstrates that the principle of geographical representation is interpreted differently in the two organizations. In the UN, the requirement to recruit staff on 'as wide a geographical basis as possible' is considered to be a legal basis for a numerical distribution of posts among the Member States. It is reflected in the UN system of desirable ranges, which are calculated in great detail for each individual Member State. The fact that one or more Member States fall outside the desirable range is considered to be a severe problem that needs fixing as soon as possible. This 'numerical' approach of the UN to the principle of broad geographical representation also demonstrates itself in the name which has been given to this principle quite early on, namely the principle of geographical 'distribution' (of posts).[510]

In contrast, in the EU, the same principle is referred to as the principle of geographical 'balance'. This name reflects the requirement of Article 27 of the *EU Staff Regulations* in a more general rather than in a numerical way. The EU appears to be more concerned with situations in which there is a clear underrepresentation or overrepresentation of a certain Member State rather than with the precise quotas allocated in advance for each individual country. In the EU, national quotas are – at least officially – considered to be inappropriate and even incompatible with Article 27 of the *EU Staff Regulations*.[511] In the UN, on the other hand, the quotas, which take the form of precisely calculated desirable ranges, are openly acknowledged as a reflection of the letter and spirit of Article 101(3) of the *UN Charter*. They are even used as the main instrument for the fulfillment of this provision. Interestingly enough, there has been no decision of either the UN Administrative Tribunal or the European Court of Justice on the possible (in)compatibility of national quotas with the requirements set in the two UN and EU provisions respectively, containing almost identical wording.

Another important difference between the UN and EU lies in their theoretical approach to the role nationality may play in staff promotion. In the UN, promotions must be, at least formally, based solely on the candidates' qualifications and performance. Nationality considerations have thus no formal place in the promotion of staff serving in the UN Secretariat.[512] In the European Commission, however, due regard may be paid to nationality of staff eligible for promotion when promotion takes place through appointment into a vacant post at a higher level.[513] Given that a fair representation of nationalities is sought at all levels in both organizations, the EU approach appears to be better suited compared to the UN approach. Since in the UN promotion occurs exclusively via appointment to a vacant post at a higher level and all vacant posts are to be filled by internal candidates before external can-

[510] See above, sections 2.1.1 and 2.2.1.
[511] See above, section 3.3.1.
[512] See above, section 2.4.
[513] See above, section 3.5.

didates may be considered, there is no other manner of ensuring broad national diversity at all levels without taking nationality of internal candidates into account. Clearly, although formally not possible, this would need to be the case in reality. The internal inconsistency of two UN policies, the one on the principle of geographical distribution and other one on staff promotion, is therefore regrettable.

4.2.2. Differences in application

Despite the almost identical wording of Article 101(3) of the *UN Charter* and Article 27 of the *EU Staff Regulations*, the application of the requirements contained in these provisions in practice differs in the two organizations considerably. Arguably, the roots of this difference lie in the developments in their early years. In the European Commission, the first appointments were based on a gentleman's agreement about the division of the available posts among nationals of Member States. Thus, the desired geographical balance among the EU Member States was reflected in the staff composition right away.[514] Initial recruitment in the UN Secretariat, on the other had, met with two severe problems. First, a large number of staff had to be recruited within a very short period of time. Second, qualified persons were at that time available only in a limited number of the original UN Member States. Thirdly, political domination of, mostly the same, few countries was significant.[515] As a result, the UN started with a heavy handicap in the geographic representation of its Member States, a situation that did not present itself in the EU.

In addition, the initial imbalance in the UN Secretariat worsened badly upon the accession of numerous new countries to the UN in the 1950s and 1960s. Unlike the EU, the UN did not take measures specially designed to adjust staff composition to the new situation.[516] In the EU, a series of national recruitment waves specifically for the recruitment of nationals from the acceding countries were organized at the time of each accession. Temporary derogations from the provisions and regulations prohibiting preferential treatment of nationals of a particular Member States were adopted for a transitional period set in advance.[517] No such action took place in the UN. There, the incorporation of nationals of new Member States happened gradually and often resulted in a long lasting set-back for the newly acceded countries which was difficult to remedy.

The attempts to restore the initial handicap in the UN led to the establishment of the system of desirable ranges in 1948 and a strict adherence to it during subsequent years. Even in times when the distribution of posts in the UN Secretariat almost corresponded with the official desirable ranges, requests for full compliance were continuously put on the table by UN Member States whose representation was, in their view, not entirely adequate. The UN Secretary-General was, and still is,

---

[514] See above, section 3.1.

[515] See above, sections 2.1.1. and 2.1.2.

[516] See above, section 2.1.2.

[517] See above, section 3.3.1.

constantly asked to present additional mechanisms specifically aimed at achieving full representation of each and every Member State.[518]

No such developments occurred in the European Commission. There, the system has always been more flexible. This is not to say that the interest of the Member States with adequate representation within the European Commission staff was or is less strong. As explained in the introduction to this study, many EU Member States have been using their power to influence the organization's staff policy as much as many UN Member States have.[519] However, the necessity to maintain balance in the composition of the European Commission civil service has since early on been approached in a more general and informal way. Formally, no quotas and no specific mechanisms were developed. Quotas that existed in the past especially at the level of senior positions were strictly unofficial. The current officially admitted quotas for senior posts are only a minimum requirement of one post per Member State.[520] The requirement to ensure geographical balance among the staff in the European Commission appears thus to be considered as a broad guideline rather than a strict numerical rule. This requirement is taken into account especially in situations of considerable discrepancy in the composition of the staff arising because the number of officials with a certain nationality has, for various reasons, increased. In such cases, the managers are asked, as far as possible, not to appoint nationals of the Member State in question for the time being, unless their merits are superior to those of other candidates. However, unlike in the UN Secretariat, no personal accountability on the side of the managers responsible for the fulfillment of such requirement exists, or is demanded, in the European Commission.[521] The requirement to ensure broad geographical balance is deemed more an invitation to attempt, rather than a strict obligation to actually achieve, the desirable result.

Naturally, also in the European Commission various mechanisms and practices were used in the past in order to help achieve adequate representation of all nationalities, among others linguistic and other nationality related eligibility requirements for vacant posts; competitions restricted to nationals of newly acceded Member States; the involvement of cabinet staff with strong national links in the appointment of senior officials; or the appointment of external candidates with the desirable nationality into senior posts (*parachutage*). Besides, as in the UN Secretariat, also in the European Commission, temporary and external appointments, including the use of seconded national experts, were sometimes used as a means of circumventing or 'correcting' the official statistics on staff composition.[522] Some of these practices were declared illegal. Most of those which had a solid basis in applicable law are still in use, such as the above mentioned *parachutage*. It could be argued, however, that a series of measures adopted under the framework of the 2000 re-

[518] See above, sections 2.2 and introduction to section 2.3.1.

[519] See above, Introduction, section 3.2.

[520] See above, section 3.3.1.

[521] See above, sections 2.3.1.2. and section 3.4.

[522] See above, section 3.4.

form of the European Commission have eliminated the use of practices which used to have undue influence on staff appointment based on nationality considerations.

In comparison, in the UN Secretariat, a strict and sometimes rather extreme adherence to the system of desirable ranges has led to the adoption of many formal measures aimed at combating the non-representation and under-representation of countries not reaching the minimum figure of their desirable range. Most of these measures are still in use. National competitive recruitment examinations are organized for inadequately represented countries only. The biennial human resources action plans of each department and office of the UN Secretariat include specific objectives and targets aimed at improving the geographical representation among staff. Responsible officials are obliged to take account of these objectives and targets during the recruitment process in which they play a role. They are being held personally accountable for fulfilling targets set in the departmental human resources action plans and their individual senior officials' compacts, though the specific obligation previously existing under the *UN Staff Selection System* to certify that the geographical targets have been taken into account in each specific appointment proposal were recently, in 2010, abolished. The UN electronic staffing system is equipped with special functions for searching and identifying candidates from unrepresented and underrepresented countries. Regular and special information meetings with the concerned Member States are organized, as well as special recruitment missions. National focal points exist in the unrepresented and underrepresented countries as well as a full time focal point of the OHRM. Relatively recently, a special Outreach Unit was established in the OHRM as well.[523]

All these measures prove that the UN approach to the fulfillment of the requirement of adequate geographical representation among its staff is a very proactive one. Unlike in the EU, in the UN much effort is expected and spent to ensure that nationals of each individual Member State receives the number of posts considered adequate for the position of that state within the UN. Detailed calculations of a desirable range of posts for each UN Member State and the long list of specific measures designed ensuring their realization is the greatest difference between the approaches of the UN and the EU to the requirement of broad geographical representation of Member States within their respective civil services.

5. Conclusions

As in the past, both the UN and the EU are and will remain bound by the requirement to ensure broad national diversity among their staff, while at the same time being obliged to guarantee the presence of the best, most efficient and most loyal work force. There seems to be no alternative to this. A broad national diversity of staff is indeed needed in both the UN Secretariat and the European Commission in order for them to fulfil the function of institutions independent from cultural and political predominance of some Member States to the detriment of others. No inde-

[523] See above, section 2.3.1.

pendent and impartial international civil service serving the common interests of all countries participating in the organization would otherwise be possible.

The difficulties of reconciling the principle of broad geographical representation with that of merit will, most probably, also remain a part of the UN and EU human resources policies. Besides the uneasy relationship between the two principles, requiring application in the staff selection process of criteria which are difficult to combine, even more troubling is the interest of countries to ensure that a high number of their nationals serve in the UN Secretariat and the European Commission. The UN, in particular, copes in this respect with significant challenges. The reasons for it are, to a large extent, of a political nature, including in particular the considerable lack of mutual trust among (groups of) countries as well as in the UN Secretariat.[524] This lack of trust results in the strong emphasis that many UN Member States place and will continue to place on the employment of a sufficient number of their nationals in the UN Secretariat. The countries are also likely to continue their attempts to influence the staff appointment process in individual cases. The UN Administration should, however, ensure that such attempts are resisted and that the appointment process is objective, transparent, and free from nepotism. To guarantee independent and impartial staff, the UN Secretariat should part with practices allowing any unnecessary involvement of Member States in staff appointment. Of course, the UN Secretariat should continue and even enhance its campaign efforts aimed at raising awareness about the employment possibilities in the UN in countries less likely to produce a sufficient number of applicants. It should also continue providing a possibility to all applicants to sit recruitment examinations in their own countries, thereby enhancing chances that applicants with limited means are also able to prove their merits. However, the UN Secretariat should put a stop to the exclusion of a large number of potential candidates from participation in recruitment examinations solely on the grounds that their country is adequately represented among the UN staff at present. This exclusion clearly contradicts the requirements of the *UN Charter* and the relevant *UN Staff Regulations* and presents the danger of decreasing quality of newly recruited staff.

The UN Secretariat, and perhaps even more the Member States, should also discontinue placing too much emphasis on a problem that, in fact, does not exist. Figures shows that a great majority of countries have been adequately represented among the UN staff for decades, although it is indeed regrettable that not every UN Member State has as yet (a sufficient number of) its nationals on board.[525] Nonetheless, it could be argued that the requirement of the *UN Charter* to ensure that staff recruitment occurs on 'as broad a geographical basis as possible', seen in the light of its objectives, is satisfied. The UN should therefore stop accentuating the geographical representation status of every individual country at every given moment. It should refrain from practices such as 'punishing' senior officials who do not succeed in fully

[524] See, for example, *Results-based Management in the United Nations in the Context of the Reform Process, Report of the Joint Inspection Unit, JIU/REP/2006/6*, 2006, available in the Official Document System of the United Nations, available at http://documents.un.org/, last visited on 30.12.2010, paras. 33-34.

[525] For the most recent statistics, see *Composition of the Secretariat, Report of the Secretary-General, A/64/352*, p. 37, Figure XVI.

filling national quotas of each Member State since, otherwise, they might do so to the detriment of not only staff quality and efficiency, but also their independence and impartiality. Rather, the UN should address the real problem in this area, namely the fact that the current system of desirable ranges no longer reflects the reality of UN human resources. Apart from the political problems existing in the UN, this appears to be an issue deserving, but lacking, sufficient attention by both the UN Secretariat and Member States.

The massive change in the composition and role of a great majority of the UN staff over the last two decades requires fundamental adjustments of the system of desirable ranges developed for implementing the principle of broad geographical representation at times marked by an entirely different, more headquarters-oriented, UN Secretariat. The elimination of the system, often criticized for its rigidity and counter-productiveness, or a development of completely new arrangements, for example a 'desirable minimum' instead of the current 'desirable ranges', will most probably still not be politically acceptable for a majority of UN Member States.[526] However, it is clear that the current system of desirable ranges needs to be modified in order to reflect the reality in a more adequate fashion. Most importantly, sufficient thought must be given to extending the system to at least some categories of staff that are currently not included. It is unsustainable to retain less than ten per cent of staff subject to the formal system and claim that, despite the lack of any other arrangements, all staff be recruited on a broad geographical basis so that the UN Secretariat benefits from the diversity of culture, approaches, and expertise of all Member States.

Furthermore, the UN system needs to be made more flexible than it currently is. It is true that a certain flexibility already exists since the system is based on desirable 'ranges' rather than on strict numbers of nationals to be engaged from each Member State. However, the assessment of the representation status of UN Member States should be more relaxed. The question whether an individual country falls within its desirable range should not be judged at every given point in time since the status of each country can easily change at any moment, for example, by a number of retirements of its nationals. This should, of course, not mean that a national of that country should be recruited when the next vacancy occurs. Legally speaking, this is not the case at present either, but there is a clear tendency in that direction in practice, at least in policy terms. It would be more appropriate to approach the matter by evaluating the representation status of each Member State over a longer period

---

[526] The idea of a desirable minimum comes from Bulkeley. Twenty years ago he recommended the replacement of the UN system of desirable ranges by a system of 'desired minimum' under which each UN Member State would be entitled to a certain minimum number of staff calculated on the basis of the equality of sovereign states. This minimum would be definite, i.e. it would not be subject to any future changes, and it would represent a sort of a minimum threshold for each country. Bulkeley also recommended that compliance with this desired minimum should be assessed against an averaged number of staff from each country during a specified period of time, not at any given moment. Such assessment would, in Bulkeley's view, be more appropriate as it would prevent 'hereditary' practices as well as 'door closing' for well-represented nationalities. – Bulkeley, *Depoliticizing United Nations Recruitment: Establishing a Genuinly International Civil Service*, p. 770-773.

of time.[527] Another possibility could be to return to the former approach and look, at least in part, at the representation status of regions or groups of countries which are culturally or politically close.[528] Of course, every individual country is unique and the more variety of nationalities in the UN Secretariat, the better. However, it is unfeasible to expect and to guarantee that all of almost 200 UN Member States can be continuously fully represented. Moreover, UN Member States do group with others to pursue their interests in the UN, testifying to the political closeness of certain groups of countries, more often than not caused by cultural and/or ideological proximity. Reflecting this feature in the composition of UN staff could make the current system of desirable ranges more flexible.

Flexibility and a longer-term approach are perhaps something the UN could learn from the EU. Naturally, the UN and the EU are different organizations, in many aspects that are of relevance to the issue of broad geographical representation. Clearly, the number of EU Member States is considerably smaller than in the UN. Also the diversity of Member States is of a lesser degree, even though North-South, and since recently also West-East, differences exist in the EU too. The same is true for differences in Member States' educational systems and their magnitude of involvement in EU staff policies. However, the power struggle between the EU Member States and the European Commission, demonstrated, for example, by recent developments around the establishment of the European External Action Service, does not appear to be caused by, or to cause, mutual distrust, clearly detectable in the UN. It seems to be more a question of Member States' prestige. Another important difference between the UN and the EU relevant for the issue of broad geographical representation is the presence and visibility of the EU among Europeans, which is undoubtedly greater than that of the UN among the world population, though there certainly are important exceptions. Also the availability of qualified candidates and the geographical proximity of the Commission offices to nationals of EU countries are different when compared to the UN. Due to these and certainly also other reasons, the getting of (a sufficient number of) nationals of each Member State on board is less of a problem in the European Commission than it is in the UN Secretariat. Therefore, there seems to be smaller need for a more formal approach and formulas in the European Commission.

Nonetheless, like in the UN, also in the EU individual Member States do pay considerable attention to the number of their nationals employed in the European Commission, especially at the senior level. Figures confirm that so does the European Commission Administration itself.[529] The reluctance to admit the existence of formal arrangements in this respect is, to some extent, understandable, given the negative experiences in the UN. However, the EU should provide more transparency in its

[527] See Bulkeley's suggestions in Ibid., p. 770-773.

[528] Already in 1963, Langrod explained that application of the principle of geographical distribution on regional or continental basis would mitigate negative harmful consequences of rigid national formulas since it would place more emphasis on cultural affinities and intellectual training rather than on nationality of candidates for posts in international secretariats. – Langrod, *The International Civil Service, Its Origins, Its Nature, Its Evolution*, p. 96.

[529] See above, section 3.3.1.

approach towards the issue of broad geographical representation. While in the UN it is evident and publicly known what the position of each individual Member State is, secrecy is the rule in the EU. Despite the official denial by the Commission of the existence of any national quotas, it is difficult to believe that no formal or informal indications exist on the desired number of nationals who should be employed from each Member State. The suspicions become even stronger when the number of nationals of each Member State serving in the Commission is compared to the position of the individual Member States in the EU institutions.[530] The Commission's denial may lead to perhaps unsubstantiated suspicions with regard to the real state of affairs in the Commission as well as methods used to address nationality considerations. Of course, because of the differences between the UN and the EU, there indeed seems to be a greater need for a more formal system for the implementation of the principle of broad geographical representation in the UN than it is in the EU. However, the Commission should be more open on the existing, albeit less formal, arrangements in this respect.

That said, perhaps the most challenging question in both organizations is how they cope with Member States' interest in, and pressure over, individual staff appointments. There, as explained in the introduction to this study, procedures for appointment and placement of staff are of vital importance. The following chapters explain details of such procedures, including those that apply to recruitment of external candidates and promotion and mobility of internal candidates.

[530] See above, section 3.3.1.

Chapter 3

RECRUITMENT

1. Introduction

The previous chapter explains the role of nationality in the relevant UN and EU staffing policies. It analyses how the principle of broad geographical representation is implemented in the UN Secretariat and in the European Commission and whether this implementation is as such as not to impede independence and impartiality of UN and EU staff. In order to explain the role of nationality in staff recruitment, promotion and separation, the previous chapter regularly refers to specific procedures set up in the UN Secretariat and European Commission. For reasons of clarity, however, that chapter does not offer a comprehensive analysis of the entire process of staff selection. Such analysis is offered in this and the following two chapters.

This chapter explains and assesses procedures in place for recruitment of the UN and EU staff from outside. As mentioned briefly earlier, such recruitment constitutes one of the three modes of staff appointment to specific posts, next to promotion and transfer of internal candidates.[1] Procedures used for all three modes of appointment are of great importance to this study. As explained in its introduction, precise, objective and transparent procedures, precluding subjectivism and favoritism, must be in place in international organizations in order to prevent that their staff selection process is directly or indirectly influenced by Member States or other subjects with stakes in the organizations' work and therefore possibly interested in compromising the independence and impartiality of international civil servants for their own benefit. An adequate procedural framework for staff appointment must thus be in place in such organizations ensuring that both the officials involved in the staff selection process as well as officials subject to it are sufficiently protected from outside pressures.

Before turning to the procedural set up existing in the UN Secretariat and in the European Commission, it is important to understand each mode of staff appointment as well as the mutual relationship between them. In both aspects, the situation in the UN Secretariat and the European Commission is similar. With regard to definitions, there is, in principle, no difference between the UN and the EU. The present study therefore follows the commonly understood definitions: recruitment being regarded as appointment of a person from outside of the organization; promotion as appointment of a person who is already employed by the organization in another post classified at a lower level to a post at a higher level; and mobility as transfer of a person employed by the organization to another post classified at the same level as his current post.[2]

---

[1] See above, Introduction, section 3.3.

[2] For the distinction between recruitment and promotion, see for example *Vlachos v. ECJ, Joined cases 20 and 21/83*, para. 20. In this case the ECJ explained that recruitment implies entry of a person into a category or a service of the Community institutions, whereas promotion covers the advancement of the career that has started by the recruitment within the category or service within which the candidate has entered the Community institutions. Note that the terminology used for other ways of staff placement is sometimes confusing. For example, in the UN the following terms are being employed: appointment, recruitment, selection, placement, mobility, reassignment, transfer, lateral move, redeployment, promotion. The UN *Administrative Instruction, Staff Selection System* which integrates staff recruitment, placement, promotion and mobility, uses most of the above mentioned terms but defines only the

As regards the relationship between recruitment from outside on the one hand and promotion and mobility of internal candidates on the other, in both the UN and the EU, appointment of an internal candidate has, in principle, priority before appointment of an external candidate. Regulation 4.4 of the *UN Staff Regulations* stipulates in this respect:

> *Subject to the provisions of Article 101, paragraph 3, of the Charter, and without prejudice to the recruitment of fresh talent at all levels, the fullest regard shall be had, in filling vacancies, to the requisite qualifications and experience of persons already in the service of the United Nations. ... The Secretary-General may limit eligibility to apply for vacant posts to internal candidates, as defined by the Secretary-General. If so, other candidates shall be allowed to apply, under conditions to be defined by the Secretary-General, when no internal candidate meets the requirements of Article 101, paragraph 3, of the Charter as well as the requirements of the post.*[3]

Rule 4.10 of the *UN Staff Rules* furthermore stipulates, in a relevant part, the following:

> *Vacancies for which eligibility to apply is restricted to such internal candidates shall be referred to as "internal vacancies". The conditions under which persons other than internal candidates may apply for vacancies shall be defined by the Secretary-General.*[4]

Interestingly, it appears that the Secretary-General has not (yet) determined in which situations vacancies could be restricted to internal candidates. The *UN Staff Selection System*, which sets out conditions and procedures for appointment of almost all (non-junior) staff in the UN Secretariat, contains no such specification, while it does define who internal candidates are, referring to them as 'internal applicants':

> *Internal applicants: serving staff members holding an appointment under the Staff Rules, other than a temporary appointment, who have been recruited after a competitive process under staff rule 4.15 (review by a central review body) or staff rule 4.16 (competitive recruitment examination). Staff members of the separately administered United Nations funds and programmes are not considered internal applicants. However, women who are serving with the separately administered United Nations funds and programmes or any specialized agency or organization of the United Nations common system holding a current appointment at the P-3 or P-4 levels and who have been in service for a continuous period of 12 months and whose appointments have been reviewed by a review body or*

---

lateral move. – *UN Staff Selection System*, Section 1. The notion of mobility was defined in another administrative instruction, but this instruction was suspended in 2010. – *Administrative Instruction, Managed Reassignment Programme, ST/AI/2007/2*, 23.05.2007, available in the Human Resources Handbook of the United Nations, available at http://www.un.org/hr_handbook/English/, last visited on 30.12.2010, Section 1.

[3] *UN Staff Regulations of 2009*, Regulation 4.4.

[4] *UN Staff Rules*, Rule 4.10.

equivalent in their organization are considered internal applicants for positions at the P-4 or P-5 levels, respectively. Associate experts (Junior Professional Officers) are not considered internal applicants.[5]

This definition is in line with Rule 4.10 of the *UN Staff Rules*. It defines 'internal candidates' as follows:

For the purpose of staff regulation 4.4, the expression "internal candidates" means staff members recruited under staff rules 4.15 and 4.16.[6]

Rules 4.15 and 4.16 of the *UN Staff Rules* concern UN Professional staff and staff in General service and related categories recruited either via competitive examination or via the *UN Staff Selection System*, both explained in more detail later on in this chapter.[7]

Turning to the relationship between external recruitment and internal promotion and mobility further, the *UN Staff Selection System*, which incorporates appointment, promotion and mobility of many UN staff, used to stipulate that, in filling vacant posts, internal candidates had to be considered before external ones and no external candidate could have been appointed if an internal candidate meeting post requirements was available. This means that recruitment from outside could only take place if no staff member could be transferred or promoted to the vacant post at issue. Further hierarchy existed between transfer and promotion, the former having

---

[5] *UN Staff Selection System*, Section 1(o).

[6] *UN Staff Rules*, Rule 4.10. Note that, in the past, the notions 'internal candidates' and 'internal vacancies' were not used in the *UN Staff Regulations*, only the notion 'persons already in the service of the United Nations' which still appears in Regulation 4.4 of the *UN Staff Regulations*, quoted in the text above. This latter notion was interpreted broadly by the UNAT in *Balogun*. The applicant in that case challenged his exclusion from consideration for a vacant posts opened to 'internal candidates' on the basis that he held a contract under the former 200 series of the *UN Staff Rules* and not under the former 100 series. After stating that the words 'internal candidate' did not appear in the *UN Staff Regulations* and could therefore not be of relevance, the UNAT interpreted the concept 'persons already in the service of the United Nations' and ruled that it also included staff serving under the former 200 series of the *UN Staff Rules*. It argued that like staff falling under the former 100 series, the former 200 series personnel are also employed in the exclusive service of the UN, have also taken an oath to the UN, and are also obliged to abide by the terms and conditions of the *UN Staff Regulations* and *Rules*. Since all these persons had the same legal obligations towards the UN, they should have had the same rights as well. In addition, the choice among possible candidates for a vacant post should be as wide as possible so that the person possessing the 'highest standards', as required by Article 101(3) of the *UN Charter* and Regulation 4.4 of the *UN Staff Regulations*, can be selected. The UNAT disregarded arguments put forward by the UN Administration, such as the fact that the employment conditions under the former 200 series are less stringent than those under the former 100 series or that there was different sources of funding for the two categories of staff. It held that neither the employment conditions, nor the source of funding, but the capacity to perform required tasks are relevant for the selection of the best candidate and that the appointment and promotions bodies should have been 'perfectly capable' to determine on the basis of individual files of each candidates which of them was the most qualified. The argument that only staff serving under the former 100 series performed 'core functions' of the UN Secretariat was also struck down. The UNAT stressed that such a concept was nowhere defined and could therefore constitute no appropriate benchmark for determination of staff members' careers. - *Balogun v. Secretary-General of the United Nations, UNAT Judgment No. 852 [1997]*, available at http://untreaty.un.org/UNAT/UNAT_Judgements/Judgements_E/UNAT_00852_E.pdf, last visited on 30.12.2010, paras. III-VIII.

[7] See below, sections 2.2.1 and 2.2.2.

in general preference over the latter.[8] This strict priority rule was abandoned in April 2010 when the new *UN Staff Selection System* replaced the previous one. Under the new system, the 'only' relevant requirement to be respected in staff selection is prior justification in writing to, and approval by, the OHRM of the selection of an external candidate.[9] Hence, unlike before April 2010, currently, external candidates are considered alongside internal ones and may be selected above internal candidates if proper justification for such a choice is provided.

That said, even this recent, less stringent, requirement of justification and prior approval for selecting an external candidate is likely to be removed from the *UN Staff Selection System* soon. Such removal is explicitly required by the General Assembly in its most recent resolution on human resources management, adopted in December 2010.[10] The General Assembly acted in this respect upon recommendation of its Advisory Committee on Budgetary and Administrative Questions. This Committee's reason for recommending removal of the relevant provision was explained as follows:

> *The new procedure fosters the impression that selection of external candidates is not desirable and presents onerous requirements that would discourage managers from selecting external candidates. In the Committee's view, all candidates should be assessed on the basis of the requirements of the post. In evaluating candidates, managers should adhere to the Charter of the United Nations, General Assembly mandates and relevant staff regulations, giving due regard to the qualifications and experience of persons already in the service of the United Nations, as well as to the principle of geographical diversity and gender parity in the staffing of the Organization.*[11]

The Committee's statement is rather surprising given that, as explained above, 'binding' priority to internal over external candidates had existed in the *UN Staff Selection System* since its first adoption in 2002, while the new 2010 system made the requirement to give such priority less stringent and made it possible, as long as written justification is provided by the selecting officer and an approval is granted by the OHRM. Until 2010, external candidates could not even have been considered for a vacant post before all suitable internal candidates had been assessed and rejected as not suitable. The 2010 system thus places consideration of both internal and external candidates on equal footing, though the actual selection of an external candidate requires an additional formality. On this basis, it appears that the Advisory Committee – and the General Assembly by following Committee's

---

[8] *UN Staff Selection System of 2002*; *UN Staff Selection System of 2006*, and *UN Staff Selection System of 2006, revised in January 2010*, in all cases Sections 5.4-5.6.

[9] *UN Staff Selection System*, Section 9.3. See also *Overview of Human Resources Management Reform, Report of the Secretary-General, A/65/305*, para. 52. Note that there are some other, specific, priority rules in the *UN Staff Selection System*, relating to certain special circumstances. For details, see below, section 2.2.2.2.

[10] *General Assembly Resolution 65/247*, para. 19.

[11] *Human Resources Management, Report of the Advisory Committee on Administrative and Budgetary Questions, A/65/537*, para. 13.

recommendation – were not aware of the pre-2010 situation, though it is also possible they have simply changed their approach in this regard. The latter would be a better, and less embarrassing, scenario.

In the EU, the hierarchy between various methods of filling a specific vacant post is set out in Article 29(1) of the *EU Staff Regulations*. A relevant part of this provision stipulates:

> *Before filling a vacant post in an institution, the Appointing Authority shall first consider:*
>
> *(a) whether the post can be filled by:*
>
> *(i) transfer, or*
> *(ii) appointment in accordance with Article 45a, or*
> *(iii) promotion*
>
> *within the institution;*
>
> *(b) whether requests for transfer have been received from officials of the same grade in other institutions, and/or whether to hold a competition internal to the institution, which shall be open only to officials and temporary staff...;*
>
> *and then follow the procedure for competitions on the basis either of qualifications or of tests, or of both qualifications and tests...*[12]

Article 29(1) of the *EU Staff Regulations* thus sets out the order in which the relevant EU authorities must examine various possibilities of filling a vacant post. As emphasized by the ECJ, this provision gives priority to the staff of EU institutions, including non-permanent staff, over external candidates and its main purpose is to protect the interests of the staff already employed by the EU institutions and to give them possibilities to advance their careers.[13] With regard to the specific methods related to filling a specific vacant post by an internal candidate, Article 4 of the *EU Staff Regulations* further provides that:

> *If the vacancy cannot be filled by transfer, appointment to a post in accordance with Article 45a or promotion, it shall be notified to the staff of the other institutions, and/or an internal competition shall be organized.*[14]

As explained by the ECJ in its early case law, this provision lays down 'a single rule of priority' between transfer, promotion or internal competition on the one hand

---

[12] *EU Staff Regulations*, Article 29(1). Article 45a deals with officials in function group Assistant (AST) who may, under certain conditions, be promoted to a post in function group Administrator (AD). For more details on this type of promotion, see below, chapter 4, section 3.2.2.

[13] *V. R. v. Commission of the European Communities, Case 75/85, ECR [1986], p. 2775*, para. 18. In this case the ECJ also held that, as a consequence of the hierarchy established by Article 29(1) and the purpose thereof, external candidates may not challenge breach of this provision. – Ibid. Note that permanent officials may be considered in priority to the non-permanent staff members. As pointed out by the Court in *Cocchi v. Commission*, the two types of staff (permanent and non-permanent) have different status and may therefore be treated differently. - *Cocchi et Hainz v. Commission, Case T-330/00 and T-114/01*, paras. 40 and 45.

[14] *EU Staff Regulations*, para. Article 4, third indent.

and an open competition on the other hand. The former were thus 'being put on an equal footing among themselves', followed by the latter.[15] Interestingly, later case law recognized certain further priority order, namely that between promotion and transfer on the one hand and internal competition on the other. In *Belle* the ECJ ruled:

> *... examination shall be made, in order of preference, first of the possibilities of filling the post by promotion or transfer within the institution where the vacancy has occurred, next of the possibility of holding competitions internal to that institution, and, thirdly, of applications for transfer made by officials of other institutions.*[16]

This quote clearly shows not only that promotion and transfer must be preferred to internal competition, but also that internal candidates serving in the institution where a specific vacant post is to be filled are to be considered before candidates serving in other EU institutions. With regard to the last mentioned, in *Volger* the CFI ruled:

> *Article 29(1)(a) of the Staff Regulations requires the appointing authority to consider as a priority the possibilities of promotion and transfer within the institution, before proceeding to one of the subsequent stages laid down by that article, that is to say, in order, consideration of the possibility of organizing an internal competition, reviewing requests for inter-institutional transfer and, if necessary, organizing an open competition. Accordingly, the appointing authority may only consider requests for transfer by officials of other institutions if it is of the opinion, following a proper review of candidatures for promotion or internal transfer, that none of them fits the requirements of the vacant post, and it has considered the possibility of organizing an internal competition.*[17]

Thus, in the EU, hierarchy exists not only between internal *versus* external recruitment but also among the various methods of appointment of internal candidates: direct transfer and promotion have priority over internal competition organized in the relevant institution, which, furthermore, must be preferred over inter-institutional transfer.

---

[15] *Eva Rittweger v. Commission of the European Communities, Case 21/70, ECR [1971], p. 7*, para. 5. See also *Claudette van Belle v. Council of the European Communities, Case 176/73, ECR [1974], p. 1361*, paras. 4-6 and *Fernando Carbajo Ferrero v. European Parliament, Case C-304/97 P, ECR [1999], p. I-1749*, paras. 29-30. With regard to the relationship between transfer and promotion only, the ECJ held in *Reinarz* that 'Article 29 of the Staff Regulations treats transfer on a par with promotion...' - *Andreas Reinarz v. Commission of the European Communities, Case 55/70, ECR [1971], p. 379*, para. 4. Furthermore, in *Rittwerger* the ECJ held that the EU Administration is free to choose for promotion alone, and not, for example, for transfer or internal competition. - *Rittweger v. Commission, Case 21/70*, para. 6. Note that Article 45a of the *EU Staff Regulations*, also referred to in Article 29(1) under consideration here, was only added in the *EU Staff Regulations* in 2004 and it, therefore, does not appear in the ECJ's consideration.

[16] *Van Belle v. Council, Case 176/73*, para. 5.

[17] *Cornelis Volger v. European Parliament, Case T-52/90, ECR [1992], p. II-121*, para. 19.

It must be stressed, however, that the hierarchy of both Article 4 and Article 29(1) of the *EU Staff Regulations* does not require the EU Administration to actually *follow* the order among the various methods of filling a vacancy but merely to *consider* these methods in that order. In *Ley* the applicant argued that by not having organized an internal competition in order to fill the post at issue the Commission had infringed Article 29(1) of the *EU Staff Regulations.* The infringement was, in the applicant's view, based on the omission to follow the hierarchy of various appointment procedures established by the above mentioned provision. The ECJ disagreed with the applicant and noted that the Administration was not obliged to follow the order but merely 'to consider in each case whether they [were] capable of resulting in the appointment of an official of the highest standard of ability, efficiency and integrity'.[18] Consequently, the EU Administration may proceed with the method of appointment listed as later even where there are one or more candidates who satisfy all the conditions and requirements of the vacancy notice under the mode of appointment listed as earlier. The objective of this broad margin of appreciation of the EU Administration is to widen its choice in order to find the best candidate.[19]

In this respect, the EU approach used to be very different from the former UN approach. As explained above, until April 2010, in the UN the established order of priority among various means of filling vacant posts was to be followed by actual consideration of eligible candidates in this order, not just by considering which method would be the most appropriate. Hence, a UN staff member aspiring promotion, for example, could not even have been considered for a vacant post before it was certain that there was no staff member who could be transferred.[20] At present, the UN and EU approaches are closer to each other, although differences persist. Most importantly, in the UN, all (internal and external) candidates must be considered towards the vacant post at issue, while in the EU it is up to the Administration to decide whether it opens up the vacancy to external candidates or keep it restricted to internal candidates only.

Detailed description and analysis of the appointment process of external candidates existing in the UN Secretariat and European Commission at present is the subject-matter of this chapter, while the appointment of internal candidates via their promotion or transfer are dealt with in the following two chapters.[21]

---

[18] *Ernest Ley v. Commission of the EEC, Joined cases 12/64 and 29/64, ECR [1965], p. 107,* p. 121. See also *Dimitrios Coussios v. Commission of the European Communities, Case C-119/94 P, ECR [1995], p. I-1439*, para. 98; *Kotzonis v. Economic and Social Committee, Case T-586/93*, para. 43; and *European Parliament v. Pierre Richard, Case C-174/99 P, ECR [2000], p. I-6189*, para. 38.

[19] *Parliament v. Richard, Case C-174/99 P*, para. 40-41. See also *Eoghan O'Hannrachain v. European Parliament, Case C-121/01 P, ECR [2003], p. I-05539*, para. 16.

[20] See above, pp. ££.

[21] See chapter 4 concerning promotion and chapter 5 concerning mobility.

2. Recruitment in the UN Secretariat

2.1. Historical overview

In 1945, when the UN was being established, the Preparatory Commission recommended that 'appropriate methods of recruitment' would be set up, methods which would lead to the creation of staff possessing the highest standards of efficiency, competency and integrity, as required by Article 101(3) of the *UN Charter*, with due regard being paid to the need to ensure broad geographical diversity among such staff.[22] The Preparatory Commission made a number of general suggestions on how the staff selection should be arranged, including organization of written examinations for most posts in the UN Secretariat and the establishment of machinery for participation of staff in matters of appointment and promotion.[23] The Preparatory Commission also proposed that an international civil service commission would be established in order to advise the Secretary-General, *inter alia*, on the methods of recruitment of the Secretariat staff.[24]

The recommendations of the Preparatory Commission were adopted by the General Assembly *en bloc* in its Resolution 13(I) of 1946.[25] Their practical application required more time, however, not always resulting in measures envisaged by the Preparatory Commission.[26] In addition, the recruitment of the initial large pool of staff was done on an *ad hoc* basis, without any methodology or guiding principles. This was due to the need to engage a great number of staff in a short period of time, explained in more detail in the previous chapter.[27] Only after this initial 'emergency' had passed, Trygve Lie, the first UN Secretary-General, developed a number of methods for staff recruitment with the intention to search actively for persons suitable for the UN service. For example, he set up field recruiting offices outside the United States, used recruiting representatives and volunteer committees, made special recruitment trips to areas with no or little staff at the Secretariat, and organized first examinations for language posts and for junior administrative posts. Attempts were also made to hold examinations for recruiting some junior professional staff but that

---

[22] *Report of the UN Preparatory Commission*, Chapter VIII, Section 1, para. 1.

[23] Ibid., Chapter VIII, Section 1, para. 17; Section 2, paras. 50-57.

[24] Ibid., Chapter VIII, Section 1, para. 19 and Section 2, para. 58.

[25] *General Assembly Resolution 13(I)*, Section III.

[26] For example, with regard to the establishment of the international civil service commission, after further discussions in committees of the General Assembly and other UN organs, the International Civil Service Advisory Board (ICSAB) was established instead. It was set up in 1948 as a subsidiary advisory body of the Administrative Committee on Coordination. It has been argued that the mandate of the ICSAB was more limited when compared to the recommendation of the Preparatory Commission, thereby restricting its possible positive impact on the UN staff recruitment process. - Lengyel, P., *Some Trends in the International Civil Service*, in: International Organization, 1959, pp. 520-537, p. 524-525 and Reymond and Mailick, *International Personnel Policies and Practices*, p. 80. The ICSAB ceased to exist on 31 December 1974. The ICSAB was replaced by the International Civil Service Commission established by the General Assembly Resolution in 1972 as a subsidiary organ of the UN General Assembly itself. –*General Assembly Resolution 3042(XXVII)*, *A/RES/3042(XXVII)*, available in the Official Document System of the United Nations, available at http://documents.un.org/, last visited on 30.12.2010, especially paras. 1 and 6.

[27] See above, chapter 2, section 2.1.1.

proved to be impractical and the attempts were therefore abandoned. The main problem was a small number of job openings at that time and a large geographical area which needed to be covered. Moreover, those few vacancies which did become available needed to be filled with nationals from new Member States. In addition, the suitability of examinations for adequate assessment of candidates was much doubted at that time. Partly for this reason, senior posts were filled on the basis of interviews only.[28]

Further steps aimed at the improvement of the UN recruitment were taken by Dag Hammarskjöld, the second Secretary-General of the UN, who partially and gradually reformed recruitment process. His objective was to move from 'a series of isolated operations [organized in a haphazard manner]' to a continuous process.[29] Actions taken by Dag Hammarskjöld included effective search for candidates, while ensuring the independence of recruiting offices; organization of competitive examinations when possible; review of the vacancy announcement methods; thorough examination of qualifications; and improvement of the system of tests and interviews.[30]

Despite efforts made by the successive Secretaries-General, the UN recruitment was considered largely unsatisfactory for a long time. Two main causes of this disappointing situation were identified: first, a lack of guiding principles and adequate methodology; and second, undue involvement of Member States in staff recruitment.[31] Regarding the first issue, for more than two decades, the UN Secretary-General was receiving no instructions from the General Assembly on staff recruitment other than those related to the issue of geographical distribution of posts and to the proportion of temporary contracts.[32] Beyond this, the recruitment procedures were not addressed by the General Assembly until 1970, when the following statement was made:

> *In the interest of long-term recruitment planning policies, special efforts should be made to recruit qualified young men and women for service with the United Nations through the development of more objective selection methods such as,*

---

[28] Swift, *Personnel Problems and the United Nations Secretariat*, pp. 229-230. See also Lengyel, *Some Trends in the International Civil Service*, pp. 523-524.

[29] Langrod, *The International Civil Service, Its Origins, Its Nature, Its Evolution*, p. 246.

[30] Ibid., p. 246.

[31] For example, Graham and Jordan (eds.), *The International Civil Service*, p. 49; Bertrand, M., *The Recruitment Policy of the United Nations Staff*, in: C. De Cooker (ed.), International Administration, Law and Management Practices in International Organizations, Martinus Nijhoff Publishers, Dordrecht / Boston / London, 1990, pp. INT.ADMIN II.2/1-9, p. 1; Reymond and Mailick, *International Personnel Policies and Practices*, pp. 76-77; Bulkeley, *Depoliticizing United Nations Recruitment: Establishing a Genuinly International Civil Service*, pp. 773-775. Langrod also pointed out to yet another problem in this regard, namely a lack of qualified candidates. He referred to the report of the ICSAB of 1961 which had stated the following: 'Experience in all the larger organizations since 1956 leaves no doubt that the recruiting position which was "marginally satisfactory" in 1956 is now quite unsatisfactory. No organization has ever sought to do more than ensure that "all the staff should be of a high level of competence" while obtaining a "fair share of brilliant staff", but the point has been reached where even that cannot be achieved ad where, all too often, the choice is between accepting unsatisfactory standards or leaving posts unfilled...' – Langrod, *The International Civil Service, Its Origins, Its Nature, Its Evolution*, p. 304.

[32] Graham and Jordan (eds.), *The International Civil Service*, p. 48.

wherever appropriate, open competitive examinations, special allowance being made for candidates whose mother tongue is not one of the working languages of the Secretariat.[33]

In 1978, the General Assembly adopted the first formal set of guidelines for the recruitment of UN Professional staff. These guidelines included requirements related to the publicity of vacancies, composition of the roster of candidates, definition of occupational groups, national competitive examinations and similar.[34] Despite the adoption of these guidelines, it was argued that the formal framework as well as the practice of UN recruitment had remained insufficient. Graham and Jordan, for example, noted inadequacy and irrationality of used selection methods, slowness and cumbersome nature of various administrative operations, as well as difficulties in relations between substantive departments and personnel services.[35] Bulkeley criticized the 'chaotic system of recruitment guidelines' and called for equality of access for a wide pool of potential candidates, special programmes for the 'disadvantaged' ones, a common roster, and objective methods with would bring more accountability and objectivity.[36] Bertrand stressed the ambiguity of the role of the UN Secretariat and insufficient specificity of countless mandates given to it by the General Assembly, leading to insecurity about the kind of personnel actually needed.[37] The lack of formal rules for recruitment, but also for advancement, career development or training of UN officials led, according to Bertrand, to filling the vacuum by:

practices characterised by an unspoken consensus on a number of principles that are diametrically opposed to the spirit of the Charter and by a power struggle to gain control of the allocation of posts.[38]

Disappointment with policies and practices concerning staff selection was expressed also by the Group of High Level Intergovernmental Experts, also referred to as G18, established by the General Assembly in 1986 with a mandate to review efficiency of the administrative and financial functioning of the UN. The G18 recommended, for example, organization of competitive examinations for posts at the P-1 to P-3 levels and suggested that the standards and criteria governing the internal and external

---

33 *General Assembly Resolution 2736(XXV)*, para. 2(d).

34 *General Assembly Resolution 33/143*, Section I, para. 1. More specific rules were established in the Resolution 35/210 of 1980 and its Annex on Recruitment Procedures for Posts Subject to Geographical Distribution in the United Nations Secretariat. - *General Assembly Resolution 35/210*, Section III and Annex.

35 Graham and Jordan (eds.), *The International Civil Service*, pp. 48-49. Graham and Jordan stressed that 'great process could be made in this field if more rational methods were applied'. – p. 49.

36 Bulkeley, *Depoliticizing United Nations Recruitment: Establishing a Genuinly International Civil Service*, pp. 777-782.

37 Bertrand, *The Recruitment Policy of the United Nations Staff*, p. 1.

38 Ibid.in, pp. , p. 3. Despite severe criticism, Bertrand admitted that some progress had been made and mentioned in particular the establishment of a system of recruitment by competition, the use of a recruitment rooster made up of list of qualified and available candidates of all nationalities, and the adoption of resolutions which have stressed the need to adopt objective recruitment methods for grade at all levels. – Ibid., pp. 4-6.

examinations would be alike. It also recommended that the staff selection to P-4 and P-5 posts was based on 'objective methods and clear criteria' and that tests or individual examinations were designed in order to assess candidates adequately.[39]

The second main problem of the UN recruitment system in the past was the inappropriate involvement of Member States in the staff selection process.[40] According to Meron, for example, the problem was the insufficiency of the position of the Secretary-General and his power to resist pressures for the appointment of particular individuals exercised by Member States' governments. He explained that the position of the Secretary-General – who aspires re-election once his term of office expires and who needs to seek support of Member States in many other policy areas – was rather weak.[41] Also the G18 expressed its concern in this regard:

> *Personnel policy and management in the United Nations has suffered as a result of the considerable political and other pressures that have influenced the selection of staff. The Secretary-General should exercise greater leadership in personnel matters and ensure that the selection of staff is done strictly in accordance with the principles of the Charter.*[42]

The G18 recommended protection of the authority of the official and office responsible for personnel matters.[43]

Member States' practices to influence recruitment of UN staff were broadly criticized as being one of the causes of insufficiently established recruitment system. According to Bulkeley:

> *States have exploited their role within the recruitment process by taking the initiative to dominate hiring. They have effectively identified, approved or disapproved, and then offered up candidates for the international civil service. Consequently, the personnel system has been unable to formulate reliable selection and recruitment methods.*[44]

Similarly, Bertrand was of the opinion that 'purely political considerations' relating to the issue of geographical distribution of posts and the appropriate status of international civil servants, about which Member States had had rather divergent ideas, prevented these countries from taking real interest in the establishment of 'rational' recruitment methods.[45] Bertrand noted:

---

[39] *G18 Report*, Recommendation 43.

[40] A study conducted in 1971 showed that out of 46 appointments in New York assessed in a sample survey, 19 candidates, i.e. 41,3 per cent, were appointed on the recommendation of their government. - Reymond and Mailick, *International Personnel Policies and Practices*, p. 77.

[41] Meron, *The United Nations Secretariat*, p. 59. See also, for example, Reymond and Mailick, *International Personnel Policies and Practices*, p. 76.

[42] *G18 Report*, Recommendation 41.

[43] Ibid., Recommendation 41.

[44] Bulkeley, *Depoliticizing United Nations Recruitment: Establishing a Genuinly International Civil Service*, p. 773.

[45] Bertrand, *The Recruitment Policy of the United Nations Staff*, pp. 1-2.

> ... *in the struggle of getting posts, scant regard to paid to principles unless they serve the interests that one is seeking to advance.*[46]

Bertrand also stressed that the UN Secretariat was very dependent on national diplomatic bureaucracies. In his view, the General Assembly, through its Fifth Committee, was the only true employer of UN staff because it, the General Assembly, not the Secretary-General, was the body fixing staff salaries and determining terms of employment as well as career arrangements.[47]

The most severe reflection of the Member States' involvement in staff recruitment was clearance of individuals by the government of the Member State of their nationality before they could be appointed. The aim of such clearance was to ensure that only persons selected by the government for their 'true and tried devotion' would be appointed and, should that devotion wane, that such persons could easily be dismissed.[48]

For the sake of clarity, it should be noted that clearance practices pre-date the United Nations. Clearance was, for example, required by an Italian law of 1927, according to which Italian nationals who wished to serve in an international organization needed to obtain the permission of the Italian Ministry of Foreign Affairs or a competent diplomatic authority, under the threat of heavy punishment for a violation of this obligation.[49] In the United Nations, when the organization was being established, Yugoslavia proposed that the appointment of UN staff members would be made only if the government of the state of their nationality would consent to it. This proposal was, however, largely rejected.[50] The UN Founding Fathers agreed instead to include the following two provisions in the *UN Charter*: Article 100(2) stipulating:

> *Each Member of the United Nations undertakes to respect the exclusively international character of the responsibilities of the Secretary-General and the staff and not to seek to influence them in the discharge of their responsibilities.*[51]

and Article 101(2) providing:

> *The staff shall be appointed by the Secretary-General under regulations established by the General Assembly.*[52]

It was thus agreed that there would be no role for UN Member States' governments in staff recruitment outside the framework of the General Assembly. Consequently, any clearance practices were, and still are, contrary to the *UN Charter*.[53]

---

[46] Ibid.in, pp. , p. 2.

[47] Ibid.in, pp. , p. 2.

[48] Lemoine, *The International Civil Servant: An Endangered Species*, p. 194.

[49] Schermers and Blokker, *International Institutional Law, Unity within Diversity*, p. 368, para. 527.

[50] Meron, *The United Nations Secretariat*, pp. 9-10; Reymond and Mailick, *International Personnel Policies and Practices*, p. 78; Lemoine, *The International Civil Servant: An Endangered Species*, pp. 111-112; Schermers and Blokker, *International Institutional Law, Unity within Diversity*, p. 368, para. 527.

[51] *UN Charter*, Article 100(2).

[52] Ibid., Article 101(2).

[53] See also Meron, *The United Nations Secretariat*, p. 67 and Reymond and Mailick, *International Personnel*

Despite the theoretical rejection of clearance, however, it was often argued that the actual practice had been different, especially before 1990. As noted by Meron, demands for clearance were not infrequent.[54] According to Beigbeder, the first UN Secretary-General Trygve Lie started this unfortunate practice himself when he asked the United States' government for assistance in search of well-qualified individuals of the US nationality. Moreover, in 1948, Lie even concluded a highly confidential agreement with the US pursuant which the US was allowed to identify candidates of the US nationality as well as US officials already serving at the UN who appeared to be members of the Communist Party or under communist influence.[55] As a result, as pointed out by Schermers and Blokker, the US government exercised great influence on the secretariats of the UN organizations in the period between 1949 and 1954 with regard to the (no)-nomination and expulsion of staff members who might have had communist sympathies.[56]

Dag Hammarskjöld, the second UN Secretary-General, seemed to have had a firmer position on the issue of clearance. His predecessor Lie admitted that 'it [had] often been necessary for [him] to seek the assistance of governments of Member States in checking the character and record of applicants and staff members'.[57] Hammarskjöld recognized the need for a relationship of mutual confidence and trust between the officials and their governments, too. Therefore, he was willing to accept information from governments regarding suitability of their nationals for the UN service. However, he explicitly refused to accept any instructions from Member States' governments.[58]

The subsequent Secretaries-General consulted Member States' governments with regard to staff recruitment as well, although, as pointed out by Meron, this had always been unofficial. Meron explained that, formally, no information or consultation with the governments was taking place prior to offering a specific position to a candidate. Only when an offer of appointment was despatched to the candidate, a note was sent to the permanent mission of the Member State whose nationality the

Policies and Practices, pp. 77-78. Reymond also noted that clearance practices had been explicitly refused by the ICSAB. In its report of 1969, the ICSAB defined the limits of government assistance in providing information on candidates. It emphasized that merely communication of individual applications of own nationals, if requested by them, possibly including government comments or support of the candidacy would be acceptable. Putting more serious value on these candidacies than on those of other sources would, however, not be in line with the *UN Charter*. – Ibid.

[54] Meron, *The United Nations Secretariat*, pp. 70-71.

[55] Beigbeder, *Threats to the International Civil Service*, pp. 48-49.

[56] Schermers and Blokker, *International Institutional Law, Unity within Diversity*, p. 368, para. 527. On practices of clearance of US nationals, see also Weiss, *International Bureaucracy, An Analysis of the Operation of Functional and Global International Secretariats*, pp. 65-67 and Meron, *The United Nations Secretariat*, pp. 68-70. These practices continued to exist as long as until 1986 when they were terminated on the basis of a judgment of a US district court in Pennsylvania which had declared the US law (on which the clearance procedure was based) unconstitutional. –Beigbeder, *Threats to the International Civil Service*, p. 56.

[57] *Repertory of Practice of United Nations Organs*, available at http://www.un.org/law/repertory/, last visited on 30.12.2010, Article 100, p. 207. See also Beigbeder, *Threats to the International Civil Service*, p. 48.

[58] Beigbeder, *Threats to the International Civil Service*, p. 50.

candidate possessed. This note did not request or sought any comments or reaction from the Member State at issue, unless the candidate was a national civil servant or, in order to avoid a brain drain, unless the candidate had recently studied abroad on government scholarship. In practice, however, written communications were sometimes sent to relevant Member States' governments which went further than a mere information on an offer of appointment.[59] In addition, a growing number of candidates were recruited on secondment basis and on basis of the referral by the governments.[60] As mentioned in the previous chapter, especially nationals of the former Soviet Union and other socialistic countries were employed by the UN on the basis of a time-limited secondment. Schermers and Blokker noted that rules governing appointment and functioning of Soviet nationals in the UN Secretariat had been defined in detail in a special document.[61]

The existence of 'special procedures' for 'accommodating' some Member States' requests to be informed and consulted about the employment of their nationals by the UN was explicitly admitted by the legal counsel of the Secretary-General in case *Levcik* heard by the UNAT.[62] As pointed out by Lemoine, legal proceedings before the UNAT offer scarce, if not the only, evidence available about various practices of governments' involvement in staff recruitment.[63] A rather recent example of such case is Case No. 1358 of 2006, concerning the United Nations Development Programme ('UNDP'), in which the UNAT stated:

59 Meron, *The United Nations Secretariat*, p. 68.

60 Ibid., p. 68.

61 Schermers and Blokker, *International Institutional Law, Unity within Diversity*, pp. 368-369, para. 527. Schermers and Blokker also noted that, in addition to clearance practices, each month Soviet employees had to hand over money they earned at the UN to the USSR mission. They were then paid their 'salary' according to the scale established by the Soviet government which could be less than half of the official UN salary. – Ibid.

62 Meron, *The United Nations Secretariat*, p. 72.

63 Lemoine, *The International Civil Servant: An Endangered Species*, p. 195. Lemoine noted that most of these proceedings concerned above all the non-renewal of the fixed-term appointments of officials seconded from the national civil service because of the disapproval of their home Member State's government. Lemoine tried to identify reasons why clearance practices, being officially recognized as contrary to the UN Charter, were nonetheless ignored by the rest of UN Member States and 'submitted to, if not actually condoned' by the UN Secretariat. – Ibid., p. 156. In Lemoine's view, the first reason was that it was the price to be paid in order to ensure at least some degree of cooperation of concerned Member States necessary to secure reasonably smooth functioning of the United Nations. The second reason was, according to Lemoine, the high vulnerability of UN Secretariat to violent attacks for failure to ensure adequate geographical distribution of posts 'and thus exhibiting bias against the Socialist countries, while satisfying the demand for the recruitment of nationals of those states otherwise than through the appointment of government-sponsored candidates meets with virtually insuperable difficulties.' – Ibid., p. 196. Lemoine stressed a narrow scope of the relevant labour market in the socialistic countries caused by limited possibilities of advertising of the vacancies and seeking candidates outside official channels. He also noted that individuals interested in a job at the UN would be cautious to actually apply without official support. – Ibid., p. 196. As many others, Lemoine condemned the clearance practices because of their negative consequences for the officials and the organization involved. In his view, because of 'total ideological reliability and single-minded devotion to State and Party', officials appointed on the basis of their governments' nomination were 'fundamentally ill-adapted to work in international secretariats operating in a divided, pluralistic environment'. – Ibid., p. 197.

The record makes clear that the [United Arab Emirates'] Government specifically directed the hiring and termination of staff members in the UNDP Office in Abu Dhabi based solely on their national origin, and that it also tried to interfere with already-approved salary increases. The Tribunal concludes that UNDP's implementation of such directions was a clear violation of international law, the United Nations Charter, the Basic Agreement between the UAE Government and UNDP, as well as a violation of the Staff Regulations and Rules. By allowing the UAE Government to interfere in personnel decisions such as those involving the Applicant, UNDP abdicated its duty not to allow outside forces, including member states, to make such decisions.[64]

The UNAT further stressed:

In reaching its decision, the Tribunal is not unmindful of the inherent complexities that UNDP faces with member states in matters such as these. Member States, because they are contributors to the budget of UNDP, may consider they are entitled to pressure UNDP in respect of personnel and budget decisions. The Tribunal, however, reminds that the independent functioning of the Organization requires that such pressures be resisted and the fundamental tenets upon which the United Nations was founded be upheld.

The UNAT also recalled its earlier judgment in case *Stepczynski* where a Member State's interference in UN staffing process was found, too:

The Tribunal sorely regrets that the Administration, which was aware of these machinations, which are incompatible with the requirements of Article 100 of the Charter regarding the independence of the staff, did absolutely nothing to put a stop to them. The Tribunal believes that the repetition of such an attitude on the part of the Secretary-General would discredit not only the Organization but would also seriously compromise its proper functioning.[65]

It is not possible to say in how much UN Member States are informally involved in actual staff selection process at present. It is however certain that they are, be it on an *ad hoc* basis at least. The fact that they continue requesting dissemination of all vacancy announcements, both external and internal ones, to their permanent representations confirms their interest in this area.[66] The General Assembly also

---

[64] *Case No. 1358, UNAT Judgment No. 1275 [2005]*, available at http://untreaty.un.org/UNAT/UNAT_Judgements/Judgements_E/UNAT_01275_E.pdf, last visited on 30.12.2010, para. X.

[65] Ibid., para. XI. See also *Stepczynski v. Secretary-General of the United Nations, UNAT Judgment No. 774 [1996]*, available at http://untreaty.un.org/UNAT/UNAT_Judgements/Judgements_E/UNAT_00774_E.pdf, last visited on 30.12.2010, para. VII. In the latter case, the UNAT explained: 'The file reveals that the President of INCB had himself highly recommended and strongly supported the Applicant's candidature for promotion .... However, a change in the attitude of [International Narcotics Control Board ('INCB')] occurred as a result of the very negative influence of a representative of a permanent mission of a Member State. It becomes clear from the file that the representative of that country had held great animosity towards the Applicant owing to the latter's refusal to yield to external pressure to appoint as Deputy Secretary of INCB a person whose candidature was supported by this representative, while the Applicant, exercising his independence, preferred another candidate.'- para. VI.

[66] For example, *General Assembly Resolution 53/221*, Section V, para. 5; *General Assembly Resolution*

requests the Secretary-General to 'inform member states smoothly, through the United Nations web site, and upon request in hardcopy, of appointments made'.[67] In addition, in 1997, when the Secretary-General announced in its report *Renewing the United Nations: A Programme for Reform A/51/950* that he planned to start consulting an informal group of independent advisers on the appointment of senior officials, the group of UN Member States known as G-77 and China reacted as follows:

> *In the implementation of this Action, the Secretary-General should ensure that the principles of transparency and equitable geographical representation, as well as* consultations with member states *on these appointments are fully adhered to.*[68] *(emphasis added)*

This is a clear signal that, at least some countries, are not prepared to give up their involvement in the area of staff recruitment.

The above mentioned report *Renewing the United Nations: A Programme for Reform A/51/950* of 1997 started the overall UN reform process, including a reform of the human resources management. In this respect, the Secretary-General announced that a 'fundamental review' of the existing policies would involve identification and conduct of specific steps in, *inter alia*, staff recruitment.[69] One of the key elements of the intended change was a 'simplified, flexible, timely and cost-effective system of recruitment and placement'.[70] In the subsequent years, a number of actions took place, with the emphasis on putting more responsibility for staff selection in the hands of specific hiring managers rather than several advisory bodies that had existed in the past.[71] The main goal of these changes was:

> *to introduce a system that: is based on predicted staffing needs as determined through effective human resources planning; is timely, that is, posts will be filled within a maximum of 120 days; holds managers accountable for making selection decisions based on objective, job-related criteria; facilitates mobility throughout the Secretariat; provides placement and advancement opportunities for staff based on merit; and complies with the Organization's policies of appointment on the basis of merit, paying due regard to the principles of geographical representation and gender balance.*[72]

55/258, Section IV, paras. 3 and 4; *General Assembly Resolution 57/305*, Section II, para. 22; *General Assembly Resolution 59/266*, Section II, para. 5.

[67] *General Assembly Resolution 57/305*, Section II, para. 18.

[68] *Renewing The United Nations: A Programme for Reform, Report of the Secretary-General, A/51/950*, Action 20, p. 75 and *Preliminary Position of the Group of 77 and China on Actions Contained in the Report of the Secretary-General: Renewing the United Nations: A Programme for Reform (A/51/950)*, 29.10.1997, available at http://www.g77.org/doc/reform2.htm, last visited on 30.12.2010, Action 20.

[69] *Renewing The United Nations: A Programme for Reform, Report of the Secretary-General, A/51/950*, Action 18, p. 74.

[70] *Human Resources Management Reform, Report of the Secretary-General, A/53/414*, 13.10.1998, available in the Official Document System of the United Nations, available at http://documents.un.org/, last visited on 30.12.2010, Section I, Part C, para. 9(f). For more details on actions to be taken, see Section III, Part B.

[71] Ibid., Section III, Part B, paras. 21(a) and 23.

[72] *Human Resources Management Reform, Report of the Secretary-General, A/55/253*, Section II, Part C,

In 2002, the most important achievements of the reform in the area of staff recruitment, placement and promotion thus far, identified by the Secretary-General, included adoption of a new staff selection system integrating recruitment, placement, mobility and promotion; adoption of a number of administrative issuances governing the new system; establishment of central review bodies, development of generic job profiles; development of a global web-based tool for the staff selection system named Galaxy; implementation of learning and communication programme; and setting up an electronic help desk for staff.[73]

A few years later, however, the Secretary-General had to admit that in spite of the achievements, the UN approach to recruitment remained 'reactive and slow'.[74] In the report *Investing in People A/61/255* of 2006, the Secretary-General emphasized, in addition, that there was an increasingly serious problem in the UN caused by the differences in approach towards the headquarters staff on the one hand and towards the field and peacekeeping staff on the other hand. While all staff were considered to be international civil servants, different contractual arrangements, different benefits and conditions of service, and different recruitment policies were applied to these two groups. The Secretary-General considered such state of affairs to be 'complex, outmoded and fragmented' and pled for a fundamental change.[75]

In this context, the report *Investing in People* presented a long list of proposals envisaged to deal with the outstanding or new challenges not addressed by the previous reforms. The proposals contained issues, such as more extensive outreach based on strategic workforce planning; use of rosters of pre-screened candidates; establishment of a recruitment and staffing centre; and revision of examinations and job profiles.[76] Despite the efforts, the UN recruitment system has remained a subject of concerns and criticism of various stakeholders, including the Office of Internal Oversight Services and the UN Member States.[77] The OIOS expressed its view

para. 34.

[73] *Human Resources Management Reform, Report of the Secretary-General, A/57/293*, 08.08.2002, available in the Official Document System of the United Nations, available at http://documents.un.org/, last visited on 30.12.2010, Section III, Part C, paras. 27-33. See also *Human Resources Management Reform, Report of the Secretary-General, A/59/263*, Section III, Part C; *Investing in People, Report of the Secretary-General, A/61/255*, Section III, paras. 34-66; *Human Resources Management Reform, Report of the Secretary-General, A/61/228*, Section IV, Part C.

[74] *Investing in People, Report of the Secretary-General, A/61/255*, Section II, para. 18.

[75] Ibid., Section II, para. 16. Detailed discussion on the change in contractual arrangements in the UN is provided in chapter 6, section 2.3.

[76] Ibid., Section III, paras. 67-121. For the follow-up, see *Human Resources Management Reform: Recruitment and Staffing, Report of the Secretary-General, A/61/822*; and *Human Resources Management Reform, Report of the Secretary-General, A/63/282*, Section IV, parts B and C.

[77] See, for example, recent discussions in the Fifth Committee. - *Official Records, Fifth Committee, Summary Record of the 18th Meeting of 14 November 2008, A/C.5/63/SR.18*, 20.01.2009, available in the Official Document System of the United Nations, available at http://documents.un.org/, last visited on 30.12.2010. The representative of Japan, for example, criticized 'arbitrary selection, sometimes reflecting nepotism, apparent in the current system'. – Ibid., para. 59. The representative of Cameroon called for better oversight measures which would monitor hiring managers' exercise and possible abuse of their delegated authority in staff recruitment. – Ibid., para. 67. Similarly, the representative of the Russian Federation expressed 'serious concerns' about the system. – Ibid., para. 84.

in a relatively recent report *In-depth Evaluation of the Office of Human Resources Management A/63/221* of 2008.[78] The OIOS was of the opinion that, despite recent improvements, the current staff selection process still did not facilitate strategic 'talent management', introduced by the Secretary-General in his 2006 report *Investing in People*.[79] The OIOS has identified a number of reasons for its dissatisfaction, in particular too long staff selection time frames; shortcomings associated with Galaxy tools, the Integrated Management Information System and peacekeeping mission information technology systems; as well as low credibility of the staff selection system.[80]

The following section explains many of these issues in more detail, focusing on procedural questions.

2.2. Current recruitment procedures

Before going into details on specific recruitment procedures used in the UN at present, a few general remarks should be made. Firstly, recruitment of all UN Professional staff is conducted internationally. There is only one exception, namely that relating to National Professional Officers whose recruitment is local.[81] Local recruitment is also conducted for all non-Professional staff, i.e. staff serving in the General Service and related categories, not specifically addressed in this study.[82] International recruitment means that candidates for posts are sought internationally, disregarding the place of the vacant post's location.

Secondly, UN staff recruitment is based on two main principles: first, explained in the introductory section to this chapter, filling vacancies by internal candidates is to be preferred to the external recruitment; and second, staff selection is to be made 'so far as practicable... on a competitive basis'.[83] The latter requirement, relevant for this chapter, is reflected in the manner in which staff recruitment is conducted, in particular in the organization of competitive examination for certain categories of staff.[84] For staff who are not recruited through competitive examination, elements of competitiveness are incorporated in the *UN Staff Selection System*, the system that applies to recruitment of staff hired for at least one year who, as explained in detail below, are not selected through competitive examinations.[85] The UN recruitment occurs thus either by means of competitive examination or under the pro-

[78] *In-depth Evaluation of the Office of Human Resources Management, Report of the Office of Internal Oversight Services, A/63/221*, 22.09.2008, available in the Official Document System of the United Nations, available at http://documents.un.org/, last visited on 30.12.2010.

[79] *Investing in People, Report of the Secretary-General, A/61/255*, para. 22.

[80] *In-depth Evaluation of the Office of Human Resources Management, Report of the Office of Internal Oversight Services, A/63/221*, Summary.

[81] *UN Staff Rules of 2009*, Rules 4.5 and 4.4.(b). For the definition of this category of staff, see above, chapter 1, section 2.1.3.

[82] Ibid., Rule 4.4(a).

[83] *UN Staff Regulations of 2009*, Regulations 4.3. and 4.4. See also above, section 1.

[84] See below, section 2.2.1.

[85] See below, section 2.2.2.

visions of the *UN Staff Selection System*, with special rules applying to temporary positions, i.e. positions with duration shorter than one year.[86] This section follows the distinction between the three mentioned systems and addresses them one by one. Moreover, it pays separate attention to recruitment to senior posts.[87]

Thirdly, a general remark that applies to all three systems is that disregarding the level of the post or the recruitment method, there is no right to be appointed or selected for a particular post in the UN.[88] The UN Administration enjoys a broad discretion in appointment matters, although it must exercise this discretion in accordance with established procedures. As stated by the UNAT, such procedures contain important safeguards aimed at ensuring fairness and objectivity of the appointment process.[89] This is important for external but also for internal recruitments:

> *It is especially important ... to ensure the right of staff members to an equitable procedure when discretionary decisions are taken by the Administration, in order not to leave them entirely to the mercy of caprice.*[90]

There, of course, the role of the judicial review is essential:

> *The Tribunal has many times affirmed the imperative need for oversight of the discretionary decisions of the Administration, in which it seeks a delicate balance between the need to allow the Secretary-General of the Organization room to exercise judgment and the need to provide an essential protection to the staff members working in the service of the Organization.*[91]

The review by the UNAT focuses on the assessment of possible abuse of discretion, procedural irregularities, bias, prejudice or discrimination.[92] In addition, the UNAT examines whether candidates have been given full and fair consideration in the appointment process. The burden of proving that such consideration has been accorded falls, in case of a dispute, upon the Administration.[93] On the other hand, the burden of proof with regard to the abuse of discretion, discrimination and similar allegations rests on the staff member.[94]

[86] See below, sections 2.2.2. and 2.2.3.

[87] See below, section 2.2.2.5.

[88] *Case No. 1447, UNAT Judgment No. 1369 [2007]*, available at http://untreaty.un.org/UNAT/UNAT_Judgements/Judgements_E/UNAT_01369_E.pdf, last visited on 30.12.2010, para. V.

[89] *Case No. 1414, UNAT Judgment No. 1315 [2006]*, para. VI

[90] *Bonder v. Secretary-General of the United Nations, UNAT Judgment No. 1052 [2002]*, available at http://untreaty.un.org/UNAT/UNAT_Judgements/Judgements_E/UNAT_01052_E.pdf, last visited on 30.12.2010, para. IV.

[91] Ibid., para. IV.

[92] *Lopes Braga, UNAT Judgment No. 1122 [2003]*, para. III.

[93] *Williamson v. Secretary-General of the United Nations, UNAT Judgment No. 362 [1986]*, available at http://untreaty.un.org/UNAT/UNAT_Judgements/Judgements_E/UNAT_00362_E.pdf, last visited on 30.12.2010, para. VII.

[94] *Cooperman, UNAT Judgment No. 93 [1965]*, para. XII.

2.2.1. Recruitment through competitive examinations

As noted earlier in this study, given their very nature, competitions – or, to use the UN terminology, competitive examinations - are the most evident mechanism to be used for ensuring that persons with the best merits are selected for vacant posts. Because competitive examinations are ignorant of other individual characteristics of potential candidates, focusing solely on their knowledge and experience, they are best suited for the identification of candidates of superior quality. Moreover, since such examinations assess all candidates in the same manner, they leave no space for subjectivism or possible pressure from unauthorized sources. It could therefore be argued that the more competitive examinations are being used in the organizations' recruitment process, the better. At the same time, however, it must be admitted that in order to do honour to this statement, competitive examinations must be conducted in an objective, transparent and non-discriminatory manner. This section discusses whether the legal framework that exists for the conduct of competitive examinations organized in the UN Secretariat meets these requirements.

2.2.1.1. Scope

Until 2009, all junior positions in the Professional category (P-1 and P-2 posts) in the UN Secretariat were to be filled exclusively through competitive examinations.[95] At present, however, a distinction is made between, on the one side, between P-1 and P-2 posts which are subject to the system of desirable ranges or are language posts and, on the other side, the remaining P-1 and P-2 posts. Only the former are to be filled via competitive examinations. Since 2009, Rule 4.16 of the *UN Staff Rules* provides, in its relevant part, the following:

> *Appointment: appointment to P-1 and P-2 posts that are subject to the system of desirable ranges and to posts requiring special language competence at the United Nations Secretariat shall be made exclusively through competitive examination.*[96]

The 2009 change of the relevant Regulation of the *UN Staff Regulations* appears to have been initiated in the context of addressing the issue of geographical imbalance in the Office of High Commissioner for Human Rights. In 2006, upon proposal of the Secretary-General, the General Assembly decided:

> *To allow, in the effort to redress the specific geographical imbalance of the Office of the United Nations High Commissioner for Human Rights, the establishment of a temporary mechanism whereby recruitment of staff in the Office at the P-2 level would not be restricted to successful candidates from the national competitive examination.*[97]

---

[95] *UN Staff Rules of 2002*, Rule 104.15(b)(i).

[96] *UN Staff Rules of 2009* and *UN Staff Rules*, Rule 4.16(b)(i).

[97] *General Assembly Resolution 61/159, A/RES/61/159*, 19.12.2006, available in the Official Document System of the United Nations, available at http://documents.un.org/, last visited on 30.12.2010, para. 1(b).

Elsewhere the General Assembly stated that the national competitive examinations were 'the source of recruitment for P-2 posts subject to geographical distribution in order to reduce non-representation and underrepresentation'.[98] The Secretary-General interpreted these two statements as qualifying the requirement of former resolutions to conduct appointment to P-1 and P-2 posts exclusively through competitive examination. On that basis, he amended the relevant staff rule and excluded P-1 and P-2 posts which are not subject to geographical distribution or special language requirements from the obligation to hold competitive examinations.[99] Notably, and unlike the above quoted decision of the General Assembly, this amendment did not include only P-2 posts in the OHCHR but all P-1 and P-2 posts in the entire UN Secretariat. Despite this, the General Assembly took note of the amendment without addressing its discrepancy with the Assembly's previous decision.[100]

The result of the 2009 change of Rule 4.16 of the *UN Staff Regulations* is that P-1 and P-2 posts that are not subject to geographical distribution or special language requirements are no longer to be filled through competitive examinations. As there is no provision in UN administrative issuances explicitly determining how these posts are to be filled, this study presumes that they fall under the *UN Staff Selection System* which also applies to appointment to non-junior Professional posts. Arguments for applying the *UN Staff Selection System* to P-1 and P-2 posts that are not filled through competitive examinations are provided in the section explaining the scope of that system.[101]

Apart from the junior level posts subject to geographical distribution or special language requirements, also posts at the P-3 level are to be filled by means of competitive examination. This rule applies, however, as a matter of principle but it is not exclusive – the *UN Staff Rules* require that appointments at the P-3 level are made *normally* through competitive examination, not *exclusively* as it is with P-1 and P-2 posts subject to geographical distribution or special language requirements.[102]

The need to base selection of staff for posts below the higher level on written examinations was recommended already by the UN Preparatory Commission in its report of 1945. The Commission considered such examination to be suitable to reveal 'specialized ability' of candidates.[103] This recommendation most probably followed the experience of the League of Nations were staff recruitment by competition had

[98] *General Assembly Resolution 61/244*, Section III, para. 1.

[99] *Measures to Address the Imbalance in the Geographical Distribution of the Staff in the Office of the United Nations High Commissioner for Human Rights, Report of the Secretary-General, A/61/823*, 28.03.2007, available in the Official Document System of the United Nations, available at http://documents.un.org/, last visited on 30.12.2010, Section III, para. 8 and Annex.

[100] *General Assembly Resolution 63/250*, Section XIII, para. 6.

[101] See below, section 2.2.2.1.

[102] *UN Staff Rules of 2009*, Rule 4.16(b)(i).

[103] *Report of the UN Preparatory Commission*, paras. 50-53. The Preparatory Commission also recommended that written examinations should be supplemented by further assessment 'the temperament, character and general capacity of candidates'. – Ibid., para. 52.

been a principal rule as well.[104] Despite the recommendation of the Preparatory Commission, however, it was not until 1980 that the competitive examination was formally established for junior posts.[105] During the following decade, a possibility of expanding the system to P-3 posts was discussed and eventually approved by the General Assembly in 1989.[106] After postponing the actual organization of P-3 examinations for a couple of times, mostly due to financial difficulties in the UN and consequent personnel freeze, first P-3 examinations were held in the 1990s.[107] Currently, competitive examinations for P-3 posts are organized when a specific need arises.[108] If no examination is held, appointment to a vacant P-3 post occurs in accordance with the *UN Staff Selection System*, discussed below.[109]

Competitive examinations organized by the UN take several forms, depending on the type of posts they relate to. Competitive examinations for geographical posts take form of the National Competitive Recruitment Examinations (NCRE). Since June 2010, these examinations are regulated by the *Administrative Instruction, Conditions under which Individuals May Take National Competitive Recruitment Examinations ST/AI/2010/8*.[110] The competitive examinations for language posts ('competitive language examinations') fall under the *Administrative Instruction, Competitive Examinations for Recruitment and Placement in Posts Requiring Specific Language Skills in the Professional Category ST/AI/1998/7* and *Administrative Instruction, Special Conditions for Recruitment or Placement of Candidates Successful in a Competitive*

---

[104] Langrod, *The International Civil Service, Its Origins, Its Nature, Its Evolution*, p. 114.

[105] *General Assembly Resolution 35/210*, Annex, para. 10. This resolution formally established the competitive examination as rule for recruitment of junior Professional staff. The process that preceded this decision was 'long and difficult'. - Bertrand, *The Recruitment Policy of the United Nations Staff*, p. 4; see also p. 5. The first suggestions were made already in 1970. - *General Assembly Resolution 2736(XXV)*, para. 2(d). The first competitive examinations were organized on an experimental basis in Italy and Germany in 1974. – *Review of the National Competitive Recruitment Examination as a Recruitment Tool, Report of the Joint Inspection Unit, JIU/REP/2007/9*, para. 4. See also Bertrand, *The Recruitment Policy of the United Nations Staff*, p. 5. Bertrand noted that the establishment of such competitive examinations was the most significant reform in the UN recruitment policies until that time. – Ibid., p. 4.

[106] *General Assembly Resolution 44/185 A*, 18.12.1989, available in the Official Document System of the United Nations, available at http://documents.un.org/, last visited on 30.12.2010, Part A, para. 6. See also *General Assembly Resolution 39/245*, Section I, para. 6(c). Also the High-Level Group of Intergovernmental Experts (G18) recommended that such examinations should be held for posts of the P-1 through P-3 level. - *Human Resource Management Policies, Report of the Secretary-General, A/49/445*, Recommendation 43.

[107] See *Human Resource Management Policies, Report of the Secretary-General, A/49/445*, para. 46.

[108] *Administrative Instruction on NCRE*, Section 1 and *NCRE Frequently Asked Questions*, available in the Human Resources Handbook of the United Nations, available at http://www.un.org/hr_handbook/English/, last visited on 30.12.2010.

[109] See below, section 2.2.2.

[110] *Administrative Instruction on NCRE*. Note that, very recently, a possible extension of the NCRE to other posts has been considered. - See, for example, *Human Resources Management, Report of the Advisory Committee on Administrative and Budgetary Questions, A/63/526*, 07.11.2008, available in the Official Document System of the United Nations, available at http://documents.un.org/, last visited on 30.12.2010, para. 62; and *General Assembly Resolution 63/250*, Part IV, para. 2. A rather limited extension was eventually approved in December 2010, including 15 per cent of P-1 and P-2 posts in field operations financed through both the regular budget and voluntary contributions. – *General Assembly Resolution 65/247*, para, 37.

Examination for Posts Requiring Special Language Skills ST/AI/2000/1, as amended.[111] The following sections address the two types of competitive examinations in turn.

2.2.1.2. NCRE

Before discussing the main procedural rules applicable to the NCRE process, it should be first noted that the adoption of the *Administrative Instruction ST/AI/2010/8* was an important step forward towards objectivity, transparency and legal certainty of the NCRE. Until June 2010, there was no proper administrative issuance or other formal set of rules that would govern the NCRE process as such. There was an administrative instruction of 1997 establishing conditions under which UN staff could participate in the NCRE. There was also an outdated bulletin of the Secretary-General of 1985 which stipulated that the external recruitment into P-1 and P-2 posts subject to geographical distribution must have been conducted through the national competitive examinations, subject to limited exceptions authorized by the OHRM.[112] This bulletin provided for a number of ground rules to be followed in the organization of the NCRE but was very general and missed necessary detail.[113] As reported by the Joint Inspection Unit in its *Review of the National Competitive Recruitment Examination as a Recruitment Tool JIU/REP/2007/9* of 2007, specific rules actually used for different individual aspects of the NCRE had their basis in a set of measures set up through case-by-case managerial decisions adopted in the course of years. The Joint Inspection Unit also noted, and criticized, that the NCRE process was based on individual managerial decisions and informally established practices and recommended that the entire process of the NCRE was regulated by an administrative instruction.[114] As mentioned above, such instruction was finally adopted in June 2010. It was a long due step towards greater transparency, and arguably also objectivity, of the NCRE.

Objectives and scope

As noted by the Joint Inspection Unit in its 2007 report, the NCRE pursue three main objectives: first, providing highly qualified candidates for Professional posts in the UN Secretariat at the entry level; second, improving geographical representation among the Secretariat's staff; and third, improving staff's gender balance.[115] These

[111] *Administrative Instruction, Competitive Examinations for Recruitment and Placement in Posts Requiring Specific Language Skills in the Professional Category*, and *Administrative Instruction, Special Conditions for Recruitment or Placement of Candidates Successful in a Competitive Examination for Posts Requiring Special Language Skills*, ST/AI/2000/1, 12.01.2000, as amended by ST/AI/2003/1, available in the Human Resources Handbook of the United Nations, available at http://www.un.org/hr_handbook/English/, last visited on 30.12.2010.

[112] *Secretary-General's Bulletin, National Competitive Examinations, ST/SGB/210*, 22.01.1985, available in the Human Resources Handbook of the United Nations, available at http://www.un.org/hr_handbook/English/, last visited on 30.12.2010, para. 2.

[113] Ibid., paras. 3-6.

[114] *Review of the National Competitive Recruitment Examination as a Recruitment Tool, Report of the Joint Inspection Unit, JIU/REP/2007/9*, paras. 32-35.

[115] Ibid., para. 14.

objectives are reflected in a number of features of the NCRE, in particular in their scope.

First of all, the NCRE are in principle held only for junior level posts. They should be held for posts at both the P-1 and P-2 level but, in practice, they are only organized for P-2 posts given the fact that posts are in practice seldom, if ever, filled at the P-1 level.[116] The only exception are P-3 posts, for which the NCRE are organized when a specific need arise.[117] In all instances, the NCRE are held annually, for a number of specific occupational groups, depending on actual needs of the UN Secretariat for the upcoming year.[118]

Secondly, the NCRE are generally open to external candidates, although UN staff members serving in General Service and related categories are eligible to participate as well, though they must comply with a few additional eligibility requirements relating to the duration of the appointment held and past performance.

Thirdly, as explained in chapter 2, dealing with the issue of geographical representation, the NCRE are only opened to nationals of those UN Member States whose representation in the UN Secretariat is missing, inadequate or about to become such.[119] Member States who are adequately represented or overrepresented are not listed in the notice of NCRE for the particular year and their nationals are thus 'not qualified to apply', with no exception possible.[120] For example, in 2009 44 countries participated in the NCRE.[121] Consequently, nationals of the remaining 149 Member States fell outside the NCRE scope, though it must be noted that the number of countries that actually participate in the NCRE in a given year does not necessarily corresponds to the number of unrepresented or underrepresented countries

[116] *Administrative Instruction on NCRE*, Section 1. See also *General Assembly Resolution 35/210*, Annex, para. 10 and *Review of the National Competitive Recruitment Examination as a Recruitment Tool, Report of the Joint Inspection Unit, JIU/REP/2007/9*, para. 3.

[117] *Administrative Instruction on NCRE*, Section 1 and *NCRE Frequently Asked Questions*.

[118] *Administrative Instruction on NCRE*, Section 1. See also *Human Resources Management Reform, Report of the Secretary-General, A/59/263*, para. 65; *Review of the National Competitive Recruitment Examination as a Recruitment Tool, Report of the Joint Inspection Unit, JIU/REP/2007/9*, para. 36; and *2009 National Competitive Recruitment Examination (P-1/P-2)*, para. 2. Note that in its 2007 report the Joint Inspection Unit criticized the NCRE planning process, considering it unreliable and non-proactive. - *Review of the National Competitive Recruitment Examination as a Recruitment Tool, Report of the Joint Inspection Unit, JIU/REP/2007/9*, Part III. B. The JIU stated that the forecasting of organization's needs was 'more or less a static reproduction of the previous year's recruitment figures' and that the situation in planning process of the NCRE is unsatisfactory because it is 'a result of earlier practice followed year after year from the time when labour force planning did not exist in the [UN]'. - *Review of the National Competitive Recruitment Examination as a Recruitment Tool, Report of the Joint Inspection Unit, JIU/REP/2007/9*, paras. 37-38. Together with an excessively long waiting period for placement of candidates from the roster, poor labour force planning was considered by the JIU to be major difficulties of the NCRE process. – *Review of the National Competitive Recruitment Examination as a Recruitment Tool, Report of the Joint Inspection Unit, JIU/REP/2007/9*, para. 52. The new 2010 administrative instruction on the NCRE requires the OHRM to conduct a workforce planning exercise for the purpose of establishing the occupational groups for which examinations is needed and projected vacancies. - *Administrative Instruction on NCRE*, Section 2.

[119] *Administrative Instruction on NCRE*, Section 2. See above, chapter 2, section 2.3.1.1.

[120] *NCRE Frequently Asked Questions*.

[121] *Composition of the Secretariat, Report of the Secretary-General, A/64/352*, para. 75.

or those who are in danger of becoming so. Not all, though most, countries with such geographical status do organize the NCRE in the relevant year; each country is invited by the OHRM to take part in the NCRE but decides for itself whether it does or does not wish to do so. Only if it does, the OHRM will facilitate the NCRE process.[122]

As argued in the previous chapter dealing with the role of nationality in the UN recruitment process, the total *a priory* exclusion of a large number of Member States from the NCRE scope is contrary to the relevant provisions of the *UN Charter* and *UN Staff Regulations* because it places a greater weight on the nationality of potential candidates than on their merits.

Procedure

Each NCRE formally begins with a formal notice publish on the internet site of the OHRM and an announcement to internal staff published in information circulars. The notice includes information, such as the occupational groups for which the examinations are held in the particular year, participating countries, eligibility requirements, procedural aspects, application procedure etc. The notice, published at least on the internet site of the OHRM, also includes the application form and indicates the deadline for its submission.[123]

Once submitted, applications are reviewed by the Central Recruitment Examination Board which, in instances of a large number of applications from individuals of the same nationality in the same occupational group that exceeds the operational capacity, decides which candidates are to be admitted to the tests. This admission decision is made on the basis of qualifications exceeding the minimum entrance criteria.[124] The fact that elimination of some candidates takes place already at this stage of the examinations is understandable; it provides a possibility to bring examinations with a large number of applicants to manageable terms from the organizational point of view.

Admitted candidates are invited to sit written tests, which entail a specialized paper (testing substantive knowledge of the discipline for which the candidate applies) and a general paper (testing drafting skills).[125] The examinations for all occupational groups are held simultaneously in different locations worldwide and follow a similar format.[126] Candidates who succeed in the written part are further invited to oral examinations which consist of an interview aimed at testing whether candidates

[122] *Administrative Instruction on NCRE*, Section 2.3. See also *Review of the National Competitive Recruitment Examination as a Recruitment Tool, Report of the Joint Inspection Unit, JIU/REP/2007/9*, paras. 47-51.

[123] *Administrative Instruction on NCRE*, Sections 1 and 4. The last available notice is for the 2010 NCRE - *2010 National Competitive Recruitment Examinations (P-2)*, available at http://www.un.org/Depts/OHRM/examin/2010e.pdf, lastly visited on 03.07.2010.

[124] *Administrative Instruction on NCRE*, Section 5.

[125] Ibid., Sections 6.2(a). and 6.3(a).

[126] Ibid., Sections 6.4 and 6.5. In 2004, the UN Secretary-General reported that there were some 45 examination centers worldwide. - *Human Resources Management Reform, Report of the Secretary-General, A/59/263*, para. 65.

possess UN core values and competences and whether they have sufficient general knowledge of international affairs. In P-3 examinations, the oral examinations are preceded by a written and oral case presentation to which candidates successful in written examinations are invited. Alike written examinations, all oral examinations normally follow a similar format in all occupational groups.[127]

Both written and oral examinations are marked by specialized boards of examiners. These boards also conduct oral examinations and recommend to the Central Recruitment Examination Board the list of candidates to be invited to oral examinations and, for P-3 posts, case presentations. The Central Recruitment Examination Board decides how many candidates will be invited. The specialized boards of examiners also prepare ranking of successful candidates at the end of the examinations and make recommendations to the Central Recruitment Examination Board on the passing thresholds for the determination of candidates who should be included in the roster of successful candidates. These thresholds depend on the level of difficulty of the examinations. The Central Recruitment Examination Board makes final recommendations to the Secretary-General, who takes final decisions. The ranking of successful candidates, the recommendations and the final decisions are all confidential and must fully respect anonymity.[128]

The above description of the NCRE procedure shows that this procedure is fairly transparent and objective. All eligible candidates, both external and internal, have access to information on the organization of the NCRE. All admitted applicants in each occupational group sit the same written tests and they all are subject to interviews before the same board. Throughout the whole process, different collective bodies are involved, which ensures that decisions taken in the process are not wronged by subjectivity. However, the fact that the ranking of successful candidates and the final decisions are confidential is unfortunate. It deprives candidates of a possibility to make their own assessment of the overall results and to make an informed decision whether they should challenge the results or not. This is harmful to this otherwise fairly transparent process.

NCRE roster

Candidates successful in the particular NCRE are placed on a reserve list of suitable candidates, referred to as NCRE roster.[129] The establishment of this roster is the main purpose of the NCRE. The actual selection of a particular candidate takes place when a specific post becomes available at any duty station of the UN worldwide. It is carried out by relevant hiring managers on the basis of candidates' profiles and further interviews.

The NCRE roster is not time-limited. In principle, candidates remain on the roster until it is cleared. Their removal from the roster is only possible upon a second re-

[127] *Administrative Instruction on NCRE*, Sections 6.2(b), 6.3(b) and (c), 6.4 and 6.6.
[128] Ibid., Sections 9.1 and 9.3.
[129] Ibid., Section 9.

fusal of a formal offer of employment.[130] However, not all candidates included in the roster actually do receive an appointment. Because the number of candidates on the roster is notoriously higher than the number of available posts, the waiting period since the placement on the roster is long (between six months and three years and in some instances even longer).[131] As reported by the Joint Inspection Unit in 2007, this period usually does not depend on the skills or quality of the candidates but on UN internal matters which are outside candidates' influence.[132] The Unit criticized this practice noting that, together with general planning problems, the lack of time limit leads to the continuous surplus of candidates on the roster. The very high number of candidates, many of which are no longer available for a UN position after not having been placed for several years, makes the roster management non-transparent and burdensome.[133] Such lack of transparency in the last stage of the NCRE process is unfortunate. The situation also puts doubts on the process' objectivity, since it is by no means certain that relevant hiring managers are able to make an objective choice when having to select a candidate for appointment from a list which includes so many names.

130 Ibid., Section 9.6. Note that under the recently approved Young Professionals Programme, the NCRE roster should be limited to one year from 2011 onwards. –*Human Resources Management Reform: Young Professionals Programme, Report of the Secretary-General, A/65/305/Add.4,* Table 1 on p. 8, point 4; and *General Assembly Resolution 65/247,* paras. 35-40.

131 *Review of the National Competitive Recruitment Examination as a Recruitment Tool, Report of the Joint Inspection Unit, JIU/REP/2007/9,* paras. 74 and 76 and Table 6. On 31 December 2006, 25 percent of candidates on the roster have bee waiting for more than two and 30 percent for more than three years. This time should be added to on average two years that are needed for the NCRE cycle, i.e. time from planning to placing candidates on the roster. - *Review of the National Competitive Recruitment Examination as a Recruitment Tool, Report of the Joint Inspection Unit, JIU/REP/2007/9,* para. 52.

132 *Review of the National Competitive Recruitment Examination as a Recruitment Tool, Report of the Joint Inspection Unit, JIU/REP/2007/9,* para. 98. The Unit mentioned the following causes of the long waiting period on the NCRE roster: inadequate labour force planning; changed geographic representation status of countries; different language requirements of specific vacant posts; but also changed personal circumstances of the candidates.

133 Ibid., para. 74. Besides the high number of candidates on the roster, other problems with roster management identified by the Joint Inspection Unit include issues, such as long waiting periods on the roster, insufficient and delayed update of the database, difficult access of the roster database by hiring managers, lack of possibilities for candidates placed on the roster to play a proactive role in recruitment, as well as communication problems. - paras. 74-91.

For better understanding, the NCRE process could be illustrated as follows:

Scheme 4: NCRE process

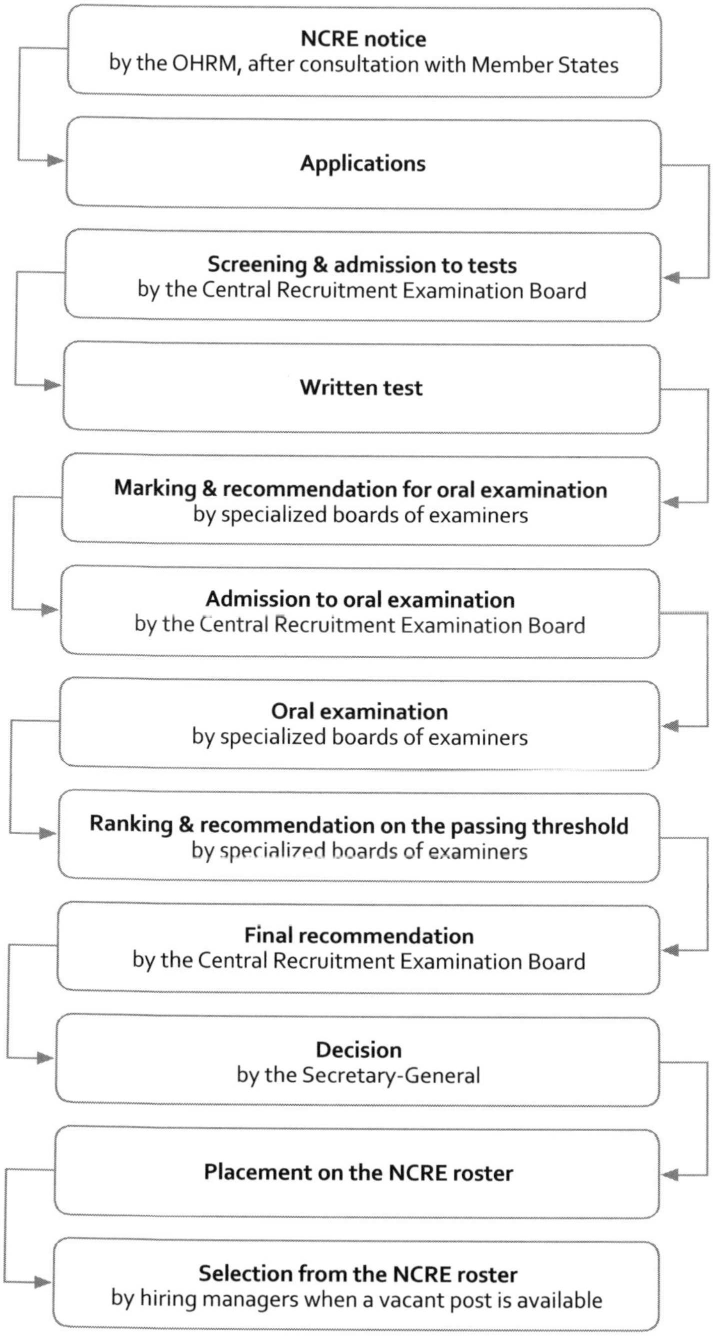

Authorities involved in the NCRE

There are two main authorities involved in the NCRE: the specialized boards of examiners and the Central Recruitment and Examinations Board.[134] The specialized board of examiners consists in principle of UN staff members but it may include also staff members of specialized agencies, consultants, outside experts and retirees.[135] All members of the board are nominated by the Assistant Secretary-General for Human Resources Management and appointed by the Secretary-General.[136] Unfortunately, and rather surprisingly, there are no specific criteria for the selection of board members. Such criteria did not exist in the past and the new administrative instruction on the NCRE did not remedy the situation – the instruction contains no conditions or requirements for board membership, not even the level of the post held. It also does not indicate the required number of board members. At least formally, the composition and membership of the specialized boards of examiners is thus entirely unregulated, which is regrettable since it diminishes transparency of the NCRE process. In practice, the board normally consists of three till eleven members, depending on the number of applications, who are staff members at P-3 level and above and volunteer to sit on the boards.[137] In addition, each specialized board of examiners also has a non-voting *ex officio* member who represents the Assistant Secretary-General for Human Resources Management. This is explicitly required by the administrative instruction at issue.[138] The presence of a representative of the Assistant Secretary-General for Human Resources Management in the specialized boards of examiners is remarkable, and arguably also questionable, as it suggests that the UN Administration wishes to maintain some kind of control over the boards' work. This could raise concerns about the independent nature of the specialized boards of examiners.

The same applies to the second body involved in the NCRE, namely the Central Recruitment Examination Board which also include such a non-voting *ex officio*

---

[134] *Secretary-General's Bulletin, National Competitive Examinations*, para. 4. Note that boards of examiners are envisaged in Rule 4.16(a) of the *UN Staff Rules* which provides, very generally, that such boards are to ensure the regularity of the competitive examinations administered pursuant to conditions established by the Secretary-General. - *UN Staff Rules of 2009*, Rule 4.16(a).

[135] *Administrative Instruction on NCRE*, Section 8.1.

[136] Ibid., Section 8.1.

[137] *Review of the National Competitive Recruitment Examination as a Recruitment Tool, Report of the Joint Inspection Unit, JIU/REP/2007/9*, para. 62. See also para. 63. Note that the Joint Inspection Unit criticized the absence of selection criteria for appointment of boards' members in this report of 2007. It is therefore surprising that the new administrative instruction did not remedy the situation. The Joint Inspection Unit also drew attention to difficulties in finding timely a sufficient number and/or quality of staff who would volunteer to sit on the board and a lack of adequate support for their functioning as board members. The latter related in particular to difficulties in combining the board work with routine tasks the board members have in their regular posts. – paras. 62-65. These last concerns have been addressed in the new administrative instruction dealing with the NCRE. The instruction stipulates now that staff serving on the specialized boards of examiners are to be released by their departments on a full time basis for the time sufficient for the completion of their tasks as board members and that these tasks are to be part of the staff's work plan and reflected in their performance evaluation. - *Administrative Instruction on NCRE*, Section 8.2.

[138] *Administrative Instruction on NCRE*, Section 8.1.

member representing the Assistant Secretary-General for Human Resources Management. Next to this representative of the Assistant Secretary-General for Human Resources Management, the Central Recruitment Examination Board includes a chair, at least four other members, each from a different department of the UN, and a secretary.[139] Alike with the specialized boards of examiners, there are no selection criteria on basis of which the Secretary-General is to appoint the members of this Board. The Joint Inspection Unit reported in 2007 that the board normally comprised staff members at the P-5 level and/or above who had previously served as members of a specialized board of examiners.[140]

The Central Recruitment Examination Board is entrusted with the 'overall responsibility' for the NCRE overseeing the examination procedures and arrangements.[141] Its main role is to consider recommendations of the specialized boards of examiners concerning the arrangements for the marking of papers, which candidates are to be invited to the oral examinations and, when relevant, case presentation, the threshold for the inclusion in the roster and the final ranking of candidates. Under the new administrative instruction, the Board also conducts prescreening of all applications and decides on eligibility of candidates who will be admitted to the examinations. It also makes recommendations to the Secretary-General on possible improvements of the future NCRE.[142]

In 2007, thus before the adoption of the present administrative instruction on the NCRE, the functioning of the Central Recruitment Examination Board was criticized by the Joint Inspection Unit which considered that the board was 'poorly regulated' and amounted to following practices established in the past years.[143] The Joint Inspection Unit's criticism was clear and strong:

> *in many aspects [the Central Recruitment Examination Board] acts as a rubber stamping administrative body, and plays no role in substantial evaluation or oversight of the examination process.*[144]

The Unit recommended that this Board should be reorganized and its mandate strengthened so that it in future plays a meaningful oversight role in the NCRE process.[145] The new administrative instruction has brought some improvements in this respect, although it is questionable whether the changes go far enough. The tasks of the Central Recruitment Examination Board have remained broadly the same, perhaps with the exception of the initial review of applications and decision on

139 Ibid., Section 7.1.

140 *Review of the National Competitive Recruitment Examination as a Recruitment Tool, Report of the Joint Inspection Unit, JIU/REP/2007/9*, para. 67.

141 *Administrative Instruction on NCRE*, Section 7.2(a). See also *Secretary-General's Bulletin, National Competitive Examinations*, para. 4.

142 *Administrative Instruction on NCRE*, Section 7.2. See also *Review of the National Competitive Recruitment Examination as a Recruitment Tool, Report of the Joint Inspection Unit, JIU/REP/2007/9*, para. 67.

143 *Review of the National Competitive Recruitment Examination as a Recruitment Tool, Report of the Joint Inspection Unit, JIU/REP/2007/9*, para. 67.

144 Ibid., para. 67.

145 Ibid., para. 68, Recommandation 7.

candidates' admissibility which were previously fulfilled by the specialized boards of examiners. An additional mandate, called for by the Joint Inspection Unit, has, however, been bestowed upon the Central Recruitment Examination Board, namely the initiation of changes to the examination process. The Board may make recommendation to that effect to the Secretary-General.[146] It remains to be seen whether this additional mandate makes the Board a more meaningful body than it was in the past.

Last authority involved in the NCRE process is the OHRM, in particular by its Examination and Test Section and Staff Development Service, which carries out the operational implementation of the NCRE.[147] The OHRM also assists the UN Member States that participate in the NCRE. It does so by, for example, organizing briefings and providing information and examination material.[148]

The UN Member States participating in the NCRE are much involved in the NCRE process, too. They organize publicity of the examination and arrange the actual conduct of the examinations. Some Member States are even involved in candidates' screening. Especially the latter is a matter of concern to this study. The fact that (some) Member States have the right to decide which candidates are admitted to the examinations and which are not runs counter the provisions of the *UN Charter* and the *UN Staff Regulations* that prohibit Member States' involvement in the staff selection process. While there is no doubt that Member States receive instructions and criteria on the basis of which they are to conduct candidates' screening, there is also little doubt that the proper use of this power can be checked in all cases. There is therefore scope for its misuse or abuse, to the detriment of NCRE candidates and their independence and impartiality once becoming UN staff members.

2.2.1.3. Competitive language examinations

As explained above, P-1 and P-2 posts subject to special language requirements are filled through competitive language examinations which are regulated by a separate set of rules contained in two administrative instructions ST/AI/1998/7 and ST/AI/2000/1. Similarly as with the NCRE, both external and internal candidates may take part in the examinations. However, the examinations are not organized annually but 'from time to time', depending on the organization's needs.[149] The ex-

[146] *Administrative Instruction on NCRE*, Section 7.2(d).

[147] *Review of the National Competitive Recruitment Examination as a Recruitment Tool, Report of the Joint Inspection Unit, JIU/REP/2007/9*, para. 67 and Box I: NCRE flow chart on p. 2. See also *Secretary-General's Bulletin, Organization of the Office of Human Resources Management, ST/SGB/2004/8*, 07.04.2004, available in the Human Resources Handbook of the United Nations, available at http://www.un.org/hr_handbook/English/, last visited on 30.12.2010, Section 6.4(a).

[148] *Improvement of Equitable Geographical Representation in the United Nations Secretariat, Report of the Secretary-General, A/59/264*, para. 9; *Review of the National Competitive Recruitment Examination as a Recruitment Tool, Report of the Joint Inspection Unit, JIU/REP/2007/9*, Annex I; and *Human Resources Management Reform: Young Professionals Programme, Report of the Secretary-General, A/65/305/Add.4*, p. 8, Table 1, point 3.

[149] *Administrative Instruction, Competitive Examinations for Recruitment and Placement in Posts Requiring Specific Language Skills in the Professional Category*, Sections 1 and 2.

aminations process involves steps similar to those in the NCRE, namely a notice, applications, their review for meeting eligibility requirements, tests, placement on a roster, and selection from the roster and appointment as vacancies occur.[150] The roster is not time-limited, alike the NCRE roster, and candidates thus remain on it until appointed. Their removal from the roster is only possible upon a second refusal of a formal offer of employment.[151] Since the process of these examinations is similar to that of the NCRE, comments made above with regard to the latter apply to these examinations, too.

Unlike the administrative instruction dealing the NCRE, the two instructions regulating the competitive language examinations do not provide any detail on tests to be used. Their attention is more focused on eligibility requirements for external as well as internal candidates and conditions of employment applicable to successful candidates, such as probationary period.[152] This is regrettable – for the same reasons as the absence of an administrative issuance for the NCRE in the past, namely the lack of transparency and possibly also objectivity of this formally unregulated process. That said, from a notice of a specific examination held in 2010 for Russian language translators, for example, it can be understood that tests used in the competitive language examinations consist in practice of a written test, comprising a number of papers requiring translation of a provided text and/or preparation of its summary, and an competency-based interview. During this interview, candidates may be asked to take another test, for example a computer skills test.[153]

From the relevant administrative instruction, and from a 2010 competition notice for Russian language translators taken as an example, it appears that the only board involved in the competitive language examinations is the specialized board of examiners which reviews the applications for meeting eligibility requirements. No further competences of this board are set out in the relevant administrative instruction, although in practice the board conducts other tasks as well, in particular marking of the tests, deciding on which candidates will be invited to the oral tests and recommending to the Assistant Secretary-General for Human Resources Management which candidates are to be placed on the roster. The absence of an adequate legal regulation for the functions of the specialized boards of examiners is, once again, detrimental to the examinations' transparency and objectivity. The composition of the specialized board of examiners is comparable to that of a

[150] Ibid., Sections 3 and 4 and *Administrative Instruction, Special Conditions for Recruitment or Placement of Candidates Successful in a Competitive Examination for Posts Requiring Special Language Skills*, Section 2.

[151] *2010 Competitive Examinations for Russian-language Translators/Precis-writers (Russian main language), Notice*, 2010, available at http://www.un.org/Depts/OHRM/examin/languageexam.htm, last visited on 30.12.2010, para. 12, available at http://www.un.org/Depts/OHRM/examin/languageexam.htm, last visited on 04.07.2010.

[152] *Administrative Instruction, Special Conditions for Recruitment or Placement of Candidates Successful in a Competitive Examination for Posts Requiring Special Language Skills*, Sections 3 and 4.

[153] *2010 Competitive Examinations for Russian-language Translators/Precis-writers (Russian main language), Notice*, paras. 8 and 10, available at http://www.un.org/Depts/OHRM/examin/languageexam.htm, last visited on 04.07.2010.

NCRE board, and so are thus the remarks made with regard to the NCRE boards.[154] It should also be noted that board's decisions are final and may not be appealed.[155] As far as the Central Recruitment Examination Board is concerned, no such a board is involved in the process. This is yet another difference between the competitive language examinations and the NCRE. It would be preferable if both types of examinations followed a similar legal framework, making understanding thereof by potential candidates less complex.

2.2.2. Recruitment through the *UN Staff Selection System*

As noted in the previous chapter, the *UN Staff Selection System* was firstly introduced in April 2002, integrating staff recruitment, placement, promotion and mobility in one system.[156] The 2002 system was replaced by a new staff selection system in November 2006 which was amended in January 2010, just to be replaced by a new system three months later, in April 2010.[157]

Upon its first introduction, the system aspired, *inter alia*, to create a regime that would lead to a faster and more transparent appointment process. It was to ensure that selection decisions would occur through a competitive process and would have their basis in objective and job-related criteria and in candidates' merits. The ultimate objective of the system was the development of a 'more versatile, multi-skilled and experienced international civil service'.[158] Compared to the previous system, the *UN Staff Selection System* has introduced novelties in the UN staff appointment process, such as the establishment of central review bodies, delegation of decision-making authority in the selection process to hiring managers and Heads of Department or Office, development of generic formats for vacancy announcements for similar jobs, and rostering of qualified shortlisted candidates for similar jobs.[159]

One of the important novelties of the *UN Staff Selection System* was the already noted integration of staff recruitment, placement, promotion and mobility into one system.[160] This meant that all mentioned processes were to be conducted pursuant one set of rules contained in one administrative instruction. This was, however, not entirely the case since a number of relevant issues were further worked out in

[154] *Administrative Instruction, Competitive Examinations for Recruitment and Placement in Posts Requiring Specific Language Skills in the Professional Category*, Section 4.

[155] *2010 Competitive Examinations for Russian-language Translators/Precis-writers (Russian main language), Notice*, paras. 7 and 12, available at http://www.un.org/Depts/OHRM/examin/languageexam.htm, last visited on 04.07.2010.

[156] *Secretary-General's Bulletin, Introduction of a New Staff Selection System*, and *UN Staff Selection System of 2002*.

[157] *UN Staff Selection System of 2006*; *UN Staff Selection System of 2006, revised in January 2010*; and *UN Staff Selection System*.

[158] *Secretary-General's Bulletin, Introduction of a New Staff Selection System*.

[159] *Investing in People, Report of the Secretary-General, A/61/255*, paras. 34 and 37.

[160] *UN Staff Selection System of 2002*; *UN Staff Selection System of 2006*; *UN Staff Selection System of 2006, revised in January 2010*; and *UN Staff Selection System*; in all three cases Section 2.1.

separate guidelines.[161] Referral to such guidelines - or manuals - is included also in the latest version of the *UN Staff Selection System* of April 2010.[162] Also, since 2009, certain matters concerning appointment to posts at the D-2 level are regulated by a specific set of rules contained in the *Secretary's-General Bulletin, Senior Review Group.*[163] In addition, since the beginning, the administrative instruction regulating the *UN Staff Selection System* did not – and still does not - apply to selection of all UN staff. To facilitate better understanding of the system, the following section explains in detail its scope as well as its limitations.

2.2.2.1. Scope

The scope of the *UN Staff Selection System* is set out in Section 3 of the relevant administrative instruction ST/AI/2010/3. First of all, the system applies only to staff members to whom the UN has granted or proposes to grant an appointment of at least one year.[164] Appointment of duration below one year occurs outside this system, through temporary vacancy announcement governed by a separate administrative instruction, addressed in a separate section below.[165]

Secondly, a number of staff and/or situations are explicitly excluded from the scope of the system. To begin with, the system does not apply to appointment of staff selected through competitive examination, i.e. junior Professionals at the P-1 and P-2 level subject to geographical distribution or special language conditions, and sometimes also at the P-3 level.[166] The *UN Staff Selection System* explicitly excludes from its scope appointment of staff selected through competitive examination, though the reference in the administrative instruction covers only P-1 and P-2 level posts subject to geographical distribution and P-3 posts, omitting P-1 and P-2 language posts.[167] Nonetheless, since the *UN Staff Rules* require that also junior language

[161] Until 2010, for example, such guidelines included: *Guidelines for Programme Case Officers on Building Vacancy Announcements and Evaluation Criteria under ST/AI/2006/3/Rev1*, available in the Human Resources Handbook of the United Nations, available at http://www.un.org/hr_handbook/English/, last visited on 30.12.2010; *Evaluation and Selection Guidelines for Action by Programme Case Officers and Heads of Department under ST/AI/2006/3/Rev1*, available in the Human Resources Handbook of the United Nations, available at http://www.un.org/hr_handbook/English/, last visited on 30.12.2010; and *Roster Management Guidelines*, 16.09.2005, available in the Human Resources Handbook of the United Nations, available at http://www.un.org/hr_handbook/English/, last visited on 30.12.2010. It is expected that some, if not all, of these guidelines will be replaced by new manuals in order to reflect changes introduced by the new *UN Staff Selection System* adopted in April 2010.

[162] *UN Staff Selection System*, Section 2.6.

[163] *Secretary-General's Bulletin, Senior Review Group of 2009*.

[164] *UN Staff Selection System*, Section 3.1.

[165] *Administrative Instruction, Administration of Temporary Appointments*. For details, see below, section 2.2.3.

[166] *UN Staff Selection System*, Section 3.2(c). As explained above, appointment of staff to P-3 posts can also occur via competitive examination, similarly as appointment to P-1 and P-2 posts. – See above, section 2.2.1.1. If indeed such examination is applied at the P-3 level, the *UN Staff Selection System* does not apply. On competitive examinations for P-1 and P-2 posts subject to geographical distribution or special language requirements, see above, sections 2.2.1.2 and 2.2.1.3.

[167] Ibid., Section 3.2(c).

posts are to be filled via competitive examination, it can be argued that these posts too, together with P-1 and P-2 posts subject to geographical distribution and P-3 posts which are filled through competitive examination, fall outside the scope of the *UN Staff Selection System*.

As far as P-1 and P-2 posts which are *not* filled through competitive examination are concerned, i.e. those that are *not* subject to geographical distribution or special language requirements, appointment to these posts appears to fall within the *UN Staff Selection System*. This is nowhere stated explicitly. Nonetheless, the administrative instruction ST/AI/2010/3 establishing the *UN Staff Selection System* provides that the system applies, *inter alia*, to 'staff in the Professional and higher categories ... for positions established for one year or longer, irrespective of the functions or source of funding'.[168] Since only appointment to P-1 and P-2 posts which are to be filled through competitive examination are excluded, it could be argued *in contrario* that appointment to all other P-1 and P-2 posts should fall within the system. The same applies to P-3 posts that are not filled through competitive examination. To recall, the *UN Staff Rules* require that P-3 posts are 'normally' (not exclusively) filled through such examination.[169] As explained above, in practice, examinations for P-3 posts are only organized when a specific need arises.[170]

Apart from appointment of junior staff specified above, the *UN Staff Selection System* also does not apply to recruitment to Professional posts of staff serving in General Service and related categories.[171] Staff serving in these categories may, under certain conditions, apply for Professional posts but, in such cases, the appointment occurs through the so-called G to P examination. Since appointment of staff already in the UN service constitutes promotion rather than recruitment from outside, details on this G to P examination are provided in the chapter of this study dealing with staff promotion.[172]

As far as the General Service and related categories are concerned, all entry level posts are filled outside the *UN Staff Selection System*. Appointment to, and promotion at, middle and higher levels in these categories (up to and including the G-4, TC-3 and S-2 levels), however, do fall within the scope of the system.[173] The one existing exception is appointment of staff in the General Service category in peacekeeping operations and special political missions, which is excluded from the scope of the *UN Staff Selection System*.[174] The same applies to appointment to the National Professional Officer category in peacekeeping operations and special political missions, as well as to appointment of staff selected to serve in the Executive Office of the Secretary-General or as his special envoys.[175]

---

168 Ibid., Section 3.1.

169 *UN Staff Rules*, Rule 4.16(a)(i).

170 See above, sections 2.2.1.1. and 2.2.1.2.

171 *UN Staff Selection System*, Section 3.2(f).

172 See below, chapter 4, section 2.2.

173 *UN Staff Selection System*, Section 3.2(g).

174 Ibid., Section 3.2(h).

175 Ibid., Section 3.2(i)-(j).

As far as movement of staff is concerned, the *UN Staff Selection System* does not apply to mobility of junior Professional staff, including language staff. As explained in detail in chapter dealing with staff mobility, movement of junior staff that follows after the recruitment is regulated by separate administrative instructions.[176] Furthermore, the *UN Staff Selection System* does not apply to movement of other than junior staff who participate in voluntary reassignment programmes and to lateral moves decided upon by the heads of department, office or mission.[177]

Despite all these limitations, it must be admitted that the *UN Staff Selection System* covers appointment, promotion and mobility of a great number of UN staff. Since April 2010, when the new system was introduced, it even covers selection of UN field staff, including staff serving in humanitarian operations. The UN Secretary-General has explained that this novel policy integration is aimed at ensuring application of the same recruitment standards to all UN staff, disregarding whether their duty station is located at a headquarters or in the filed.[178] This development is a result of the overall contractual reform in the UN approved in 2009. As explained in more detail in chapter 6, the reform attempted to simplify the UN system of appointments but also to remove differences in approach to, and conditions of service of, in particular non-headquarters staff.[179]

2.2.2.2. Procedures up to the D-1 level

Job opening

The recruitment process under the *UN Staff Selection System* begins with a job opening, be it position-specific or generic, anticipated or immediate. Job opening is defined as 'vacancy announcement issued for one particular position or for a set of job openings'.[180] Where the job opening relates to one position at a specific duty station, it is referred to as 'position-specific job opening', and where it relates to a set of positions, it is referred to as 'generic job opening'.[181] Generic job openings are always based on the so-called 'generic job profiles' which are classified standard job description encompassing a large group of related jobs with similar characteristics, i.e. similar duties, responsibilities, required education, skills, competences and work experience.[182] As stressed by the *UN Staff Selection System*, generic job openings are used:

---

176 Ibid., Section 3.2(d) and (e). For mobility of UN junior staff, see below, chapter 5, section 2.2.2.

177 Ibid., Section 3.2(k)-(l).

178 See *Overview of Human Resources Management Reform, Report of the Secretary-General, A/65/305*, paras. 37 and 41. For information on recruitment to field missions before 2010, see *Comprehensive Report on the Staffing of Field Missions, Including the Use of 300 and 100 Series Appointments, Report of the Secretary-General, A/59/291*, 23.08.2004, available in the Official Document System of the United Nations, available at http://documents.un.org/, last visited on 30.12.2010, in particular paras. 9 and 19-24.

179 For details on the UN contractual reform of 2009, see below chapter 6, section 2.3.

180 *UN Staff Selection System*, Section 1(p).

181 Ibid., Section 1(v) and (i). See also Sections 4.2 and 4.3.

182 Ibid., Section 1(i) and (h).

> *for the purpose of creating and maintaining viable rosters of qualified and available candidates for immediate and anticipated job openings identified through workforce planning in entities with approval to use roster-based recruitment, peacekeeping operations, special political missions and other field operations.*[183]

Last but not least, job openings are anticipated if they concern a position or positions that are expected to become available in accordance with the workforce planning or forecasting. They are immediate if the position or positions they relate to have become available unexpectedly. For example, an anticipated job opening could be a result of a retirement, while an immediate job opening could be caused by separation from service for disciplinary reasons.[184]

All job openings, position-specific, generic, anticipated or immediate, are advertised through the so-called compendium of job openings.[185] This compendium is an official register of available posts of duration of at least 1 year.[186] Until April 2010, compendium was published both electronically (with a daily update) as well as in print (once a month).[187] At present, the publication takes place only electronically and should be updated regularly.[188] The fact that all vacancies are published is an important safeguard of the transparency of the whole selection process. It also ensures equality of all potential candidates who can access necessary information under the same conditions. Clearly, any restrictions on vacancy publications could lead to subjectivism in the process, even nepotism; a situation that could have negative consequences for the independent and impartial status of future staff members selected through such process.

Job openings are posted in the compendium upon request of the relevant hiring manager or occupational group manager.[189] The hiring manager is the official responsible for filling the vacant post. He is responsible to his Head of Department or Office for effective and efficient management of staff and resources that are under his supervision, thereby ensuring the delivery of the mandated activities.[190] If the job opening relates to a peacekeeping operation or a special political mission, it may be placed in the compendium of job openings upon request of the occupational group manager. The occupational group manager is 'an official responsible for managing the supply of available candidates ... to meet the staffing requirements identified through workforce planning for a specific occupational group or groups in peacekeeping operations and special political missions'.[191] 'Occupational groups' are

---

183 Ibid., Section 1(i).

184 Ibid., Sections 1(a) and (n).

185 Ibid., Section 4.1.

186 Ibid., Section 4.1.

187 *UN Staff Selection System of 2006, revised in January 2010*, Section 4.1.

188 *UN Staff Selection System*, Section 4.1. The electronic version of the compendium of vacancies is available on the OHRM website: https://jobs.un.org/elearn/production/home.html, last visited on 30.12.2010, though the active link provided for access to the compendium regularly fails to work.

189 Ibid., Section 4.4.

190 Ibid., Section 1(m).

191 Ibid., Section 1(t).

occupations and sub-occupations that are grouped into work categories because of their functional similarity.[192]

Job openings must reflect the functions and the location of the post and include information on required qualifications, skills and competencies of the candidates as well as the date of posting of the job opening and the deadline for filling applications.[193] They should be based, as much as possible, on the generic job profiles approved by the OHRM, on job opening previously published, or on a previously classified individual job description that reflects the actual functions of the position at issue. If a job opening is based on an individually classified job description, the evaluation criteria that will be used for the assessment of candidates must be approved in advance by the relevant central review body. Moreover, before posting in the compendium, all job openings – based on generic or individually classified job descriptions - must be approved by the OHRM, the relevant local human resources office or the Department of Field Support, depending on the position to be filled.[194] The use of generic job profiles, previously published job openings, or previously classified job descriptions contributes to the transparency and to objectivity of the selection process, as it prevents that job openings are tailor-made on favored candidates. The fact that individual classified job descriptions are also permitted is understandable, though; there may be situations in which an entirely specific job needs to be filled. In such instances, the approvals by the human resources department of the evaluation criteria and of the job opening, mentioned above, compensate the 'individuality' of the situation to a certain extent. Caution has its place here, however. The relevant human resources department must be able to ensure that tailor-making by responsible programme managers is prevented.

Pre-screening

Pre-screening of applications who have reacted on the vacancy announcement occurs on the basis of pre-screening questions which should determine applicants' suitability for the relevant job opening. These questions must relate to the responsibilities of the position at issue and the required experience and professionalism, as reflected in the job opening.[195] The fact that the pre-screening questions are to be prepared as a part of job opening contributes to the transparency and objectivity of the process as it prevents a possibility of their subsequent tailor-making on certain (favorite) candidates.

---

[192] Ibid., Section 1(s).

[193] Ibid., Sections 4.5 and 4.6. For positions-specific job openings at the Professional level and above, the application deadline is, in principle, 60 days, and in the peacekeeping operations and special political missions, in principle, 30 days. The latter applies also to some other position-specific job openings. In case of generic job openings, the application deadline depends on what is deemed sufficient in order to attract a sufficient number of candidates. – Section 4.8.

[194] Ibid., Sections 4.5 and 4.6. The ORHM has apparently spent a considerable effort on producing generic job profiles. Its aim was to simplify the job classification and to reach 'greater standardization, efficiency, speed and transparency in creating vacancy announcements and in clarifying job expectations'. *Human Resources Management Reform, Report of the Secretary-General, A/59/263*, para. 55. See also *Investing in People, Report of the Secretary-General, A/61/255*, para. 54.

[195] *UN Staff Selection System*, Section 4.7.

The pre-screening is conducted by the ORHM, the relevant local human resources office or the Field Personnel Division of the Department of Field Support on the basis of information provided by applicants in their application form.[196] It occurs through the Secretariat's e-staffing system. Until very recently, this was rather problematic due to the very large number of applications. As mentioned in the chapter 2, dealing with the issue of geographical representation, the original e-staffing system called Galaxy became a victim to its own success.[197] One of the consequences of this was that proper screening of all candidates became practically impossible and it could even be argued that it was, at least to a certain extent, a matter of chance. Concerns in this respect were voiced even by the UN General Assembly, which explicitly required the Secretary-General to ensure fair treatment of all applicants and requested development of a screening system which would not exclude well qualified candidates from consideration merely on the basis of not matching search keywords used in the pre-screening stage of the selection process.[198] Eventually, a new e-tool called Inspira, replacing Galaxy (and some other e-systems existing in other areas of UN staffing policy), was developed.[199] Its deployment started in April 2010 and continued through 2011.[200] Adequate evaluation of this new e-tool, and its impact on objectivity and transparency of candidates' pre-screening, is therefore not yet possible. Nonetheless, as Inspira should bring automaticity of the pre-screening process and Boolean types of searches for various factors (i.e. and/or, inclusive, exclusive, etc.), it could improve the situation considerably – it could reduce the number of candidates to be viewed by the relevant hiring or occupational group manager as well as to narrow down the number of indicated candidates during their further screening.[201] One of the inevitable conditions in this respect is, however, that the automaticity of pre-screening will concern only the eligibility criteria, while substantive screening and actual evaluation of candidates will continue to be conducted 'manually' by persons capable to assess and compare candidates' suitability for the post under consideration. Any other situation would raise concerns with regard to the objectivity and impartiality of the process.

[196] Ibid., Sections 7.1.

[197] See above, chapter 2, section 2.3.1.7.

[198] *General Assembly Resolution 59/266*, Section III, para. 12.

[199] A/65/305, Part I, Section C; and *Human Resources Management Reform: The Talent Management Tool, Inspira, Report of the Secretary-General, A/65/305/Add.3*.Note that the General Assembly 'underlined' in its resolution of 2008 once again that the new e-staffing system, which was at that time being developed, must, *inter alia*, ensure transparency and non-discrimination. It also requested the Secretary-General to report to the matter on its next session dealing with human resources management issues. - *General Assembly Resolution 63/253, A/RES/63/253*, 24.12.2008, available in the Official Document System of the United Nations, available at http://documents.un.org/, last visited on 30.12.2010, Section III, para. 11. The Secretary-General did so by issuing a report in September 2010. –*Human Resources Management Reform: The Talent Management Tool, Inspira, Report of the Secretary-General, A/65/305/Add.3*, available in the Official Document System of the United Nations.

[200] *Human Resources Management Reform: The Talent Management Tool, Inspira, Report of the Secretary-General, A/65/305/Add.3*, para. 10.

[201] For Inspira's functionalities in the area of staffing, see Ibid., para 22. See also *Overview of Human Resources Management Reform, Report of the Secretary-General, A/65/305*, para. 46.

Assessment

The results of the pre-screening are released electronically to the hiring or the occupational group manager, depending whether the job opening is position-specific or generic.[202] The hiring or the occupational group manager subsequently further evaluates candidates who have passed the pre-screening process and prepares a shortlist of those who seem most qualified. This shortlisting occurs on the basis of the documents at the manager's disposal. Further assessment of the shortlisted candidates, aimed at evaluating their technical requirements and competences, is conducted by the hiring or the occupational group manager, too, this time by using various evaluation mechanisms. They may include a competency-based interview, written tests, work sample tests, assessment centers or other assessment techniques.[203] None of these mechanisms is, however, mandatory; the choice of what is the appropriate evaluation mechanism in an individual case lies entirely in the hands of the relevant hiring or occupational group manager. Even the obligation to hold in all cases a competency-based interview, existing until April 2010 as a guarantee for the quality of the selected candidates, is no longer present.[204] The only exception are job openings for positions at the D-2 level, for which interviews by an interdepartmental panel are required.[205] Another interesting, and rather surprising, detail is that the actual evaluation of candidates is to be made against the pre-approved evaluation criteria, not against other candidates.[206]

The above description of the candidates' assessment process leaves no doubts about the position of the relevant hiring or occupational group manager in it. This manager possesses all powers in the process, needing to share it with no other authority. The manager is limited only by the pre-approved evaluation criteria that he must follow in candidates' evaluation and by the obligation to document the results of the evaluation by a reasoned and documented record.[207] The latter facilitates taking the final selection decision by the Head of Department or Office and allows central review bodies as well as judiciary to review the evaluation process in case of any doubts or challenges.[208] Interestingly, however, the requirement to record candidates' evaluation only applies to 'proposed' candidates. This means that evaluation of candidates

---

[202] *UN Staff Selection System*, Sections 7.2.

[203] Ibid., Section 7.5.

[204] See *UN Staff Selection System of 2006, revised in January 2010*, Section 7.5 and *Human Resources Management Reform, Report of the Secretary-General, A/59/263*, para. 55. Note that if an interview is employed, it is conducted by a panel that should normally be composed of three or more members, one of them being female and one being from outside the relevant work unit. - *UN Staff Selection System*, Section 1(c).

[205] *UN Staff Selection System*, Section 7.9; and *Secretary-General's Bulletin, Senior Review Group of 2009*, Section 4.1. See also below, section 2.2.2.5.

[206] *OHRM Evaluation and Selection Guidelines*, Section II., paras. 9 and 10. Although this document predates the currently applicable *UN Staff Selection System*, the requirement to evaluate candidates against pre-approved criteria, explained in the document, has not changed when compared to the previous version(s) of the *UN Staff Selection System*.

[207] *UN Staff Selection System*, Section 7.6. See also *OHRM Evaluation and Selection Guidelines*, Section II., paras. 9 and 10.

[208] *UN Staff Selection System*, Section 7.6.

who are eventually not proposed for selection is not recorded, and thus also not reviewed by either the central review body or the Head of Department or Office. This is also rather surprising, and regrettable. It provides further evidence that the hiring or the occupational group manager possess broad powers in the candidates' evaluation process with just a few restrictions and a limited administrative review.

With regard to possible judicial review of candidates' evaluation, it should be noted that even though the evaluation of candidates' qualifications, experience, past performance etc. is a discretionary competence of the relevant programme managers (and thus the UN Administration), the judiciary may perform its scrutiny in cases of its abuse, procedural irregularities, bias, prejudice or discrimination.[209] The judiciary also reviews whether all candidates have received full and fair consideration in the selection process. Since it is for the Administration to provide evidence that this obligation has been met, the UNAT has emphasized the importance of keeping proper records.[210]

Interestingly, when a staff member claims that his qualifications are superior to those of a selected candidate, the burden of proof is 'neutral'. The UNAT explained in one of its recent cases decided in 2006 that, although normally the party making an allegation must prove that the allegation is true, in cases such as this, where the relevant evidence is solely in the hands of the Administration, the Administration:

> *should place [the evidence] where possible before the body carrying out the review [so that] the review body [can] decide for itself from the evidence if the process was fair and regular, without reference to which of the parties might be seen as carrying the onus of proof.*[211]

Said that, and despite the availability of judicial review in this respect, current rules contained in the *UN Staff Selection System* with regard to candidates' evaluations do not guarantee sufficiently objectivity and impartiality of the evaluation process, placing too much power in the hands of just one person. As discussed in more detail below, strong criticism has been voiced in this respect, for example by the UN staff unions, which put into question the legitimacy of the whole *UN Staff Selection System* which, in their view, does not provide sufficient guarantees against abuse of authority by hiring managers.[212] Because the criticism is inseparably connected to the overall position of the hiring or the occupational group managers under the *UN Staff Selection System*, not only to their role in the candidates' evaluation process,

---

[209] *Lopes Braga, UNAT Judgment No. 1122 [2003]*, para. III. The review by the central review body entails an assessment whether the pre-approved criteria were satisfied and whether applicable procedures were followed. - *UN Staff Selection System of 2006*, Section 8. For more details, see below in this section.

[210] *Williamson, UNAT Judgment No. 362 [1986]*, para. VII.

[211] *Case No. 1386, UNAT Judgment No. 1302 [2006]*, available at http://untreaty.un.org/UNAT/UNAT_Judgements/Judgements_E/UNAT_01302_E.pdf, last visited on 30.12.2010, para. III. The UNAT stressed that any other approach would deprive the applicant with a possibility to challenge the Administration's decision. – see also para IV.

[212] *Views of the Staff Representatives of the United Nations Secretariat, A/C.5/63/3/Add.2*, 11.10.2006, available in the Official Document System of the United Nations, available at http://documents.un.org/, last visited on 30.12.2010, p. 46.

it is further elaborated on below, taking into account the complete picture of the managers' position under the system.[213]

Proposal

To continue with the selection procedures under the *UN Staff Selection System*, steps following the final evaluation of candidates depend on whether the job opening is position-specific or generic. In the case of a position-specific job opening, the hiring or the occupational group manager prepares a proposal with candidates suitable for the position at issue. This proposal includes a list of one, or preferably more, candidate(s), unranked, and including at least one female. The hiring or occupational programme manager submits the list to the relevant central review body, described in more detail below, via the OHRM, relevant local human resources office or the Field Personnel Division of the Department of Field Support.[214] When the job opening at issue is a generic one, involving posts in peacekeeping operations and/or special political missions, a proposal of qualified, unranked candidates, among whom at least one female, is submitted to the Director of the Field Personnel Division of the Department of Field Support. When the Director satisfies himself that the process has been complied with and that Secretariat's target and objectives have been taken into consideration, he forwards the proposal to the field central review body, further explained below in this section.[215]

The explicit prohibition of ranking of candidates included in the list of proposed candidates has also been strongly criticized, also by the UN staff unions.[216] Concerns of the UN staff unions in this area were partly caused by the fact that there was no substantive involvement of the OHRM in the staff selection process and by the fact that, as explained in more detail below, central review bodies, which review hiring managers' recommendation of suitable candidate or candidates before the final selection is made, have no mandate to review the recommendation of the relevant hiring manager from the substantive but only from the procedural point of view.[217] This concern has, arguably, partly been solved by the recent introduction of the obligation for hiring managers to submit the proposal of candidates suitable for appointment via the OHRM, relevant local human resources office or the Field Personnel Division of the Department of Field Support. Such obligation was introduced in the new *UN Staff Selection System* adopted in April 2010 for all positions up to and including D-1 level.[218] Before that time, the hiring manager had to submit his

---

213 See below, section 2.2.2.4.

214 *UN Staff Selection System*, Sections 7.6 and 7.7.

215 Ibid., Section 7.8.

216 *Views of the Staff Representatives of the United Nations Secretariat*, *A/C.5/63/3/Add.2*, p. 46.

217 *Views of the Staff Representatives of the United Nations Secretariat: Staff Union (New York), Field Staff Union (Brindisi) and Staff Coordinating Council (United Nations Office in Geneva), Addendum, A/C.5/63/3/Add.2*, paras. 15 and 23. See also para. 74 in which the staff unions state that the delegation of authority to perform human resources functions to managers has led to increased and above all 'disproportionate subjectivity in performing those functions'. Note also *Views of the Staff Representatives of the United Nations Secretariat, A/C.5/63/3/Add.2*, paras. 29-34 and para. 39. For competence of central review bodies, see below, section 2.2.2.4.

218 *UN Staff Selection System*, Section 8.1.

proposal to the central review body through the Head of Department or Office.[219] Under the new *UN Staff Selection System*, the OHRM, relevant local human resources office and the Field Personnel Division of the Department of Field Support have thus acquired competence to check whether the hiring manager complied with the required process.[220] Further – procedural - check is conducted by the relevant (field) central review body to which the proposal of the hiring manager is submitted by the OHRM, the local resources office and the Field Personnel Division of the Department of Field Support.[221]

Despite the fact that the list of proposed candidates is to be presented to the central review body through the relevant human resources office at present, it could be maintained that the absence of candidates' ranking on this list contributes neither to the transparency nor to the objectivity and impartiality of the selection process. It is without much doubt that inclusion of such ranking would enable central review bodies to form a more accurate opinion on the proposal made by the hiring or occupational group manager. It would also ensure that Heads of Departments and Offices, who are responsible for making the final selection, would be in a better position to judge candidates' suitability for the posts at issue and, consequently, to take a more objective and impartial decision. The statement of the UN Secretary-General made in this respect only confirms this view. The Secretary-General has explained that the absence of ranking in the list of proposed candidates should guarantee discretion of the Heads of Departments and Offices in making selection decisions and facilitate taking UN policies on geography and gender into account when the selection decision is made.[222] As legitimate as these concerns may be, the absence of ranking deprives involved candidates, or any other person concerned, of a possibility to verify which considerations were decisive for the final selection. Transparency and objectivity of this stage of the staff selection process is hereby suppressed to a significant extent.

Review

The description above already suggests that before the relevant Head of Department or Office takes the final decision, the list of proposed candidates is reviewed by a (field) central review body. This body checks whether candidates were assessed in accordance with the relevant evaluation criteria and whether applicable procedures have been properly applied.[223] It is indeed so that, pursuant the *UN Staff Selection System*, the central review body does not make any substantive review of the proposed candidate(s) and their evaluation, despite the fact that the *UN Staff Rules* give central review bodies authority to 'offer recommendations on the appoint-

---

[219] *UN Staff Selection System of 2006*, and *UN Staff Selection System of 2006, revised in January 2010*, Section 7.7.

[220] *UN Staff Selection System*, Section 8.1.

[221] Ibid., Sections 7.7 and 8.

[222] *Human Resources Management Reform, Report of the Secretary-General, A/61/228*, Section IV, Part C.4(b), para. 80.

[223] *UN Staff Selection System*, Section 8.1.

ment, selection and promotion of candidates'.[224] The relevant rule of the *UN Staff Rules* further stipulates that:

> *Where these recommendations are not in line with those of the relevant manager, they shall transmit their recommendations for final decision to the Secretary-General, who shall give due consideration to the recommendations of the central review bodies.* [225]

This provision could arguably be interpreted as giving mandate to the central review bodies to make own recommendations on suitable candidates. However, no such reading of the central review bodies' mandate is possible under the *UN Staff Selection System.* This system clearly limits the terms of reference of central review bodies to the procedural review of the individual selection process.

It is briefly mentioned above that the absence of a possibility of central review bodies to review the substantive evaluation of candidates proposed by the relevant manager has been severely criticized, for example, by the UN staff unions. The unions have been pleading for a change and, until an adequate change takes place, they boycott the central review bodies and refuse to appoint members who need to be designated by the staff representatives.[226] The unions require that central review bodies' mandate is made comparable to that of the Senior Review Group which is involved in the selection for posts at the D-2 level. As explained in more detail below, this body reviews not only compliance with procedural rules but, in addition, it also makes proposal on appointment of the most suitable candidate for the post at issue.[227]

The UN staff unions are not the only critics of the mandate of the central review bodies. Some deficiencies in the function of these bodies were found also by the Office of Internal Oversight Services (OIOS), although the OIOS believed that functions which central review bodies had constituted in theory appropriate checks and balances to the delegation of authority in selection system. The problems found related, among others, to the lack of access of central review bodies to information relevant for reviewing evaluations and proposals and the lack of uniformity in key aspects of the evaluation process. For example, central review bodies have no access to questions asked to, and answers provided by, candidates screened and are thus unable to verify whether criteria used to screen applicants are objective and related to the post. The OIOS also reported instances in which central review bodies recommended managers to review applicants they had personally knowledge of, given the fact that managers are not obliged to interview (all) candidates. The OIOS stressed the problematic nature of such practices and its possible contradiction with the principle of equal and fair treatment of those candidates who are not in a posi-

---

[224] *UN Staff Rules of 2009*, Rule 4.16(i)(ii).

[225] Ibid., Rule 4.16(i)(ii).

[226] *Views of the Staff Representatives of the United Nations Secretariat, A/C.5/63/3/Add.2*, para. 30.

[227] *Views of the Staff Representatives of the United Nations Secretariat: Staff Union (New York), Field Staff Union (Brindisi) and Staff Coordinating Council (United Nations Office in Geneva), Addendum, A/C.5/63/3/Add.2*, para. 132.

tion to make central review bodies aware of their applications.[228] It does not appear that since the issuance of the OIOS report in 2004 much has changed, especially with regard to the last mentioned issue since managers are still free to choose whether, and if so, which candidates they interview and which not. In the light of the OIOS report, the General Assembly has requested the UN Secretary-General to propose an appropriate amendment the terms of reference of these bodies but this does not seem to have happened.[229] The direct consequence of this is that the mandate of the central review bodies remains limited to procedural review. The question that needs to be posed in this respect is whether such state of affairs is beneficial to the transparency, objectivity and impartiality of the selection process, in particular in the view of concentration of significant powers in the hands of hiring (or occupational group) managers, noted earlier and discussed in more detail below.[230]

Selection decision

Upon clearance by the central review body, a final decision on which candidate will be appointed to the specific vacant post is taken. This decision is made by the Head of Department or Office.[231] When the appointment concerns a post involving significant functions in financial management, the decision is also subject to a positive review of the proposal by personnel management or general service administration.[232] In case that the review by the central review body does not end with positive findings, i.e. when the body finds that either pre-approved evaluation criteria or procedures were not followed, the Head of Department or Office may not proceed with taking the final selection decision. The decision would, in such an instance, be made by the official who has authority to make decisions on behalf of the Secretary-General, namely the Under-Secretary-General for Management for appointments to P-5 posts and the Assistant Secretary-General for Human Resources Management for all other posts.[233] Surprisingly, the *UN Staff Selection System* provides no further guidance or requirements in this respect. The latest version of the *UN Staff Selection System*, in force since April 2010, even removed the previously existing obligation to give due regard to recommendations of the central review body in such cases.[234] It appears thus that the official designated to decide upon the matter enjoys absolute discretion, including the option to appoint the candidate proposed by the hiring manager despite the existing procedural flaws. Naturally, one could argue that the

---

[228] *Impact of the Human Resources Management Reform, Report of the Office of Internal Oversight Services, A/59/253*, 24.09.2004, available in the Official Document System of the United Nations, available at http://documents.un.org/, last visited on 30.12.2010, Section III, Part B, especially paras. 30-31, 34-39.

[229] *General Assembly Resolution 59/266*, Section III, para. 13. See also *Views of the Staff Representatives of the United Nations Secretariat, A/C.5/63/3/Add.2*, para. 31.

[230] See below, section 2.2.2.4.

[231] *UN Staff Selection System*, Section 9.2.

[232] Ibid., Section 9.2.

[233] Ibid., Section 8.2 and *Secretary-General's Bulletin, Central Review Bodies, ST/SGB/2002/6*, 23.04.2002, available in the Human Resources Handbook of the United Nations, available at http://www.un.org/hr_handbook/English/, last visited on 30.12.2010, Section 5.6.

[234] *UN Staff Selection System*, Section 8.2 and *UN Staff Selection System of 2006, revised in January 2010*, Section 9.1.

Under-Secretary-General for Management and the Assistant Secretary-General for Human Resources Management are unlikely to proceed in this manner. However, the mere fact that such a possibility exists puts the system, its objectivity, transparency and impartiality, into question.

Returning to the Head of Department or Office, he also enjoys broad discretion in making the final selection of the candidate to be appointed. This discretion was confirmed by the UNAT in a recent case decided in 2008. In that case the UNAT also noted the difference with the past procedure where the list of proposed candidates included candidates' ranking and a clear identification of one recommended candidate. As mentioned above, at present, the recommended candidates are unranked. Therefore, the final choice is fully in the hands of the Head of Department or Office.[235]

Despite this broad discretion, the Head of Department or Office must follow a number of principles. The starting point is that the candidate best suited for the function should be chosen.[236] Until April 2010, there was also an explicit obligation of the Head of Department or Office to take account, when making selection, of the departmental human resources action plan, especially regarding issues of gender and geographical balance.[237] This obligation still appears in the *UN Staff Selection System*, but it is no longer spelled out in section concerning selection decision. On the other hand, the definition of the term 'selection decision' refers to the need to take UN human resources objectives, including those on geography and gender, into account, though it could be argued that it is not clearly indicated as the duty of the Head of Department or Office.[238]

In April 210, the general duty to pay regard to the UN human resources objectives in taking the selection decision was furthermore supplemented by the duty to give due consideration to certain (groups of) candidates who hereby acquired special status in the process. As the list of these candidates is relatively complex, it deserves to be reproduced in full. The list includes:

> *staff members who are victims of malicious acts or natural disasters; serving staff members who have served under the former 200 and 300 series of the Staff Rules; candidates from troop- or police-contributing countries for positions in a peacekeeping operation or Headquarters support account-funded positions in the Department of Peacekeeping Operations, the Department of Field Support and other departments with support account resources; and prior service or employment of candidates in field duty stations, for positions for which relevant field experience is highly desirable....*[239]

[235] *Case No. 1477, UNAT Judgment No. 1407 [2008]*, available at http://untreaty.un.org/UNAT/UNAT_Judgements/Judgements_E/UNAT_01407_E.pdf, last visited on 30.12.2010, para. V.

[236] *UN Staff Selection System*, Section 9.3.

[237] *UN Staff Selection System of 2006, revised in January 2010*, Section 9.2.

[238] *UN Staff Selection System*, Section 1(x).

[239] Ibid., Section 9.3.

Another 'priority' rule which currently needs to be taken into account when selection decision is being made relates to internal *versus* external candidates. The *UN Staff Selection System* requires that 'candidates already in the service of the Organization as well as those encumbering posts that are slated for abolition or are serving in secretariat entities undergoing downsizing and/or liquidation' are to be given the fullest regard.[240] This general duty is worked out in the obligation imposed on the Head of Department or Office to justify in writing selection of any external candidate. Such selection must, furthermore, be approved by the OHRM before the decision is taken.[241] Said that, it should be recalled that this obligation (to justify in writing and to receive a prior approval for selection of an external candidate) should soon be removed from *the UN Staff Selection System*, in accordance with the General Assembly resolution adopted in December 2010.[242]

It is important to note that the compliance with rules on, what could arguably be called, positive discrimination of, for example, female candidates, nationals of unrepresented or underrepresented Member States, or internal candidates is subject to judicial review. In a rather recent case decided in 2006, such review took place in the context of a challenge of a decision to select a male candidate and not, as alleged, equally qualified female candidate.[243] The approach adopted in this case by the UNAT could apply to other instances of positive discrimination as well, as the basis principle behind all these instances is the same, namely that when qualifications are substantially equal, preference us to be given to the member of positively discriminated group of candidates, be it female or a national of an unrepresented or underrepresented country, or an internal candidate.

The applicant in the case claimed that she had been entitled to be selected to the post at issue because she had possessed all the required qualifications and, in addition, as a female candidate had to have been given preference in accordance with rules on positive discrimination of women adopted by the General Assembly as well as the UN Administration itself. The Administration argued, to the contrary, that the selected male candidate had been chosen on basis to his superior qualifications when compared to those of the applicant. The UNAT held that it was essential that the examination and comparison of the candidates' qualifications was conducted in a transparent manner in order to provide sufficient material for its review. The UNAT stated that it was desirable to:

> *identify in a similar, clearly visible and measurable way the manner in which [the evaluating authority] carried out its evaluation and how it concluded that the qualifications and experience of the recommended male candidate were substantially superior to those of the top female candidate, when a male candidate*

[240] Ibid., Section 1(x).

[241] Ibid., Section 9.3. Note that until April 2010, justification and approval of the selection of an external candidate was only required when the posts at issue as in the Professional or a higher category, was subject to geographical distribution and the candidate had a nationality of an overrepresented Member State, or when it was at the P-3 level. - *UN Staff Selection System of 2006, revised in January 2010*, Section 9.2.

[242] See above, section 1.

[243] *Case No. 1386, UNAT Judgment No. 1302 [2006].*

> *is recommended for the post. This is so that when, in turn, its evaluations and conclusions are being reviewed, it can be determined on an evidentiary basis if the policy of affirmative action [to select a female candidate] has been honoured, and the factual basis for the decision can be readily ascertained.*[244]

After examining the evidence, the UNAT concluded that the Administration's judgment that qualifications of the selected male candidate were superior was not supported by any 'demonstrable or measurable evidence' and that, therefore, the applicant had to have been given preference.[245] This case illustrates that, despite the broad discretion of the Administration, the judiciary may and will scrutinize how the qualifications of various candidates are assessed. This is an important guarantee for the objectivity and impartiality of this stage of the selection process.

Rosters

When a certain candidate is selected and appointed to the vacant post at issue, other candidates who were also approved by the hiring or the occupational group manager and endorsed by the central review body but who are *not* selected are placed on a roster of candidates pre-approved for similar functions. This roster is drawn for candidates from all duty stations for vacancies in the Professional and higher categories. It is valid for two years for male candidates and three years for female candidates. Candidates included in the roster may be chosen and appointed to a post that becomes vacant directly by the Head of Department or Office, without any further reference of the matter to the central review body.[246] Naturally, candidates' qualifications must correspond to those required for the post to which they are appointed. Their suitability for a job opening is considered already in the pre-screening stage of the selection process. The OHRM, the local human resources office or the Field Personnel Division of the Department of Field Support that conduct pre-screening consider also candidates on the roster and release them together with new applicants who passed the pre-screening to the hiring manager.[247] The hiring manager then considers eligible pre-approved candidates side by side with new applicants successful in the pre-screening.

Also candidates for generic job openings who were endorsed by the central review body are placed on a roster, set up separately for each relevant occupation, and valid for two years for male candidates and three years for female candidates. Similarly as their counterparts on the pre-approved roster mentioned above, candidates placed on the occupational rosters may be proposed by the hiring manager and selected by the Head of Department or Office for suitable job openings without further reference to the central review body.[248]

---

[244] Ibid., para. VI.

[245] Ibid., para. VII.

[246] *UN Staff Selection System*, Section 9.4.

[247] Ibid., Section 7.2.

[248] Ibid., Section 9.5.

When properly managed, the use of pre-approved rosters in staff selection process does not seem to raise questions with regard to the transparency and objectivity of the process. The absence of ranking does. As was the case with the lists of proposed candidates, which also contain no ranking of candidates, the absence of ranking of candidates placed on a specific roster not only deprives candidates of a possibility to distinguish themselves from candidates whose merits were considered to be lower than their merits. It also time makes this stage of the selection process less transparent and more vulnerable to subjectivism and partiality on the side of hiring and occupational group managers.

Summary

To sum up, the staff selection process that takes place in under the *UN Staff Selection System* works as follows:

Scheme 5: Staff selection process under the ***UN Staff Selection System***

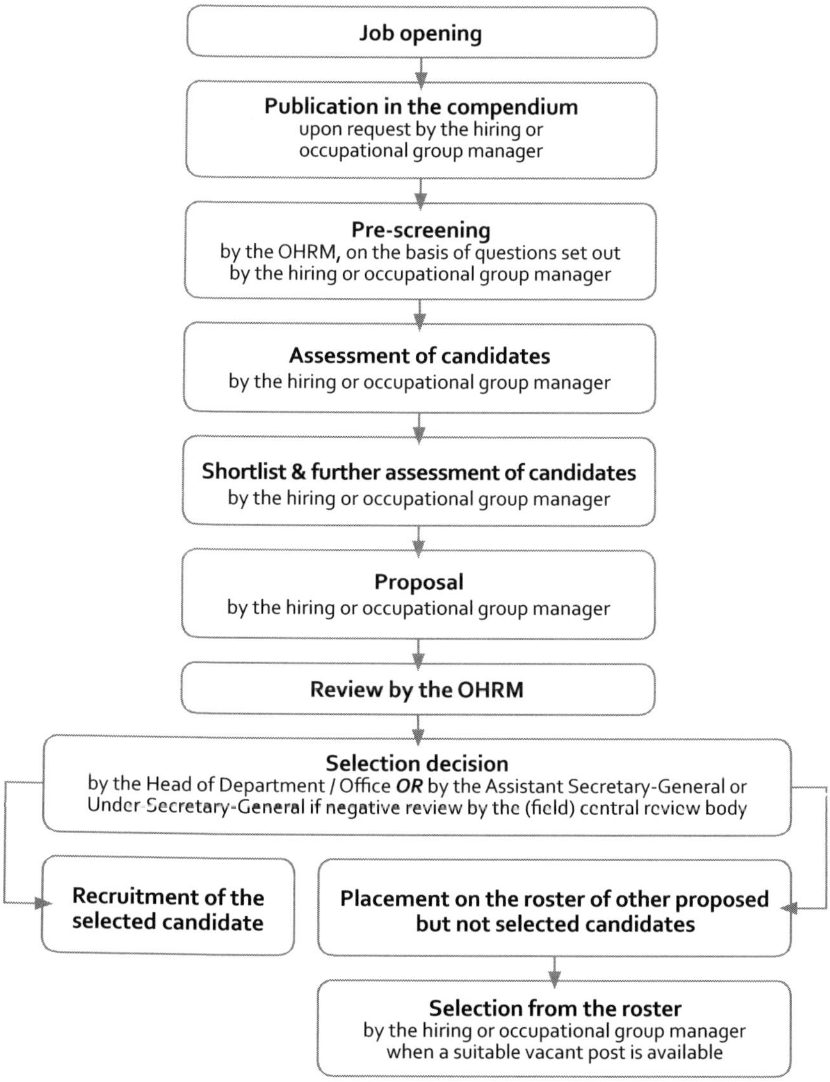

2.2.2.3. Placement outside normal process

The staff selection process described until this point is a regular process which is to be followed under normal circumstances. Certain positions may, however, be filled outside such normal process. Section 11 of the *UN Staff Selection System* gives authority to the Assistant Secretary-General for Human Resources Management to place the following staff in vacant posts outside the normal process: staff whose posts were reclassified upward if another applicant has been selected; staff affected by post abolition or funding cutbacks; and staff returning from secondment lasting more than two years when his placement in the original department has failed.[249]

Furthermore, the Under-Secretary-General for Field Support may transfer staff members who hold appointments not limited to a specific missions or department between activities administered by the Department of Field Support and/or Departments of Peacekeeping Operations, Political Affairs and Field Support. In these cases, staff members maybe transferred outside normal process to job openings classified at the same level. Such transfers do not require advertisement or referral to the central review body. Before taking decision, however, the Under-Secretary-General for Field Support must consult the heads of Departments of Peacekeeping Operations and Political Affairs, the head(s) of the missions concerned and the staff member concerned.[250]

In addition, despite the fact that the *UN Staff Selection System* in principle does not apply to recruitment of staff to P-2 posts, Section 11.3 thereof provides that candidates successful in the NCRE or examinations held for staff from other categories applying for post in the Professional category may be placed to P-2 posts subject to geographical distribution outside the normal process if those posts have not been filled within three months with candidates successful in a competitive examination.[251] Moreover, the Assistant Secretary-General may, at any time, select candidates from the roster of the national competitive examinations or examinations held for staff from other categories applying for post in the Professional category in order to fill P-2 positions in peacekeeping operations and special political missions.[252]

Decisions on placement outside the normal process which are taken by the Assistant Secretary-General for Human Resources Management do not need to follow any additional procedures. Unlike in the past, the Assistant Secretary-General is not even required to inform *ad post* about such placements the appropriate central review body.[253]

In most noted situations, placement outside normal staff selection process should not be regarded as problematic. It is understandable and so is related limitation on its transparency. However, it is regrettable that decisions are not announced to central review bodies or other authority capable of reviewing whether specific placement does not raise possible questions with regard to its objectivity and impartiality. As things stand now, too much room is left for possible misuse or abuse of power vested in this respect on the UN Administration.

[249] Ibid., Section 11.1.

[250] Ibid., Section 11.2.

[251] Ibid., Section 11.3.

[252] Ibid., Section 11.5.

[253] Ibid., Section 11.1 and *UN Staff Selection System of 2006, revised in January 2010*, Section 11.2.

2.2.2.4. Authorities involved up to the D-1 level

The previous two sections explain step-by-step procedures taken in the selection process under the *UN Staff Selection System*. As those sections shows, a number of authorities are involved in the process. For the sake of clarity, and for facilitation of better analysis of these authorities' position, they are further discussed in this section. The section briefly recapitulates the mandate of each of the involved authorities and evaluates whether this mandate contributes to transparency, objectivity and impartiality of the selection process. Where relevant, the section also explains and evaluates the composition of the authority at issue. The discussion begins with the authorities at the top of the administrative hierarchy and finishes with the hiring and occupational programme managers whose position in the staff selection process has been subject to most criticism. This, arguably less usual, order is also due to the fact that assessment of managers' position depends partly on that of other involved authorities, in particular the central review bodies. The latter must therefore be explained before the former.

Under-Secretary-General for Management and Assistant Secretary-General for Human Resources Management

The Under-Secretary-General for Management and Assistant Secretary-General for Human Resources Management are involved in the staff selection process only to a limited extent, and in situations which cannot be regarded as usual. First, they take final decisions in cases in which central review bodies find that required procedures were not followed. Secondly, they decide on staff placement outside normal process. The actual involvement of each of the two officers depends on the type and/or level of the post at issue.

As noted earlier, the *UN Staff Selection System* provides no real guidance on the manner in which the power vested upon the two officers in the situations at hand are to be exercised. It may therefore be safely concluded that these officers enjoy very broad, if not absolute, discretion here. As understandable as the need for certain flexibility in staff selection process is, it is clear that this state of affairs does not add positively to the perception of the UN selection process as being fully transparent, objective and impartial.

OHRM, local human resources office and Field Personnel Division of the Department of Field Support

The human resources offices have a number of tasks under the *UN Staff Selection System*. As explained in more detail in the previous section, they approve all job openings; conduct candidates' prescreening; receive proposals from managers which they subsequently send for review to the relevant central review body. The OHRM, in addition, also approves generic job profiles.

The involvement of the human resources offices in the selection process is thus more than just a formality, though a more substantial involvement in individual selection procedures seems to be missing. This is rather surprising, given that in most other (public or private) organizations human resources experts play an important role in the actual selection of organizations' future staff. Normally, they even form a part of the team which performs candidates' assessment. This enhances chances that the selected candidates match not only organizations' professional requirements but also their general culture. Considerations such as these are, however, of no relevance to this study. What is relevant is the fact that the UN human resources offices *are* involved in the selection process, even though they merely oversee tasks conducted by the hiring and occupational group managers. As limited as it is, involvement of the human resources offices does reduce a danger of these managers misusing or abusing their broad powers.

Heads of Department or Office

Heads of Department or Office have only one task under the *UN Staff Selection System*, namely to take final decisions on appointment. They do so on the basis of a proposal proposed by the manager and endorsed by the relevant central review body. If such proposal contains more than one name, Heads of Department or Office make an actual selection of the candidate who will receive appointment. As explained in the previous section, they enjoy broad discretion in this respect. Where the proposal includes only one candidate, though, which is permitted under this system, there is no choice to be made. It appears therefore that in such a case the Head of Department or Office concerned merely rubberstamps the choice made by the relevant manager. The choice on the number of names included in the proposal rests also with the manager.

The role of Heads of Department or Office in the staff selection process is thus, in practice, rather limited. This is, however, not necessarily a negative conclusion. Since Heads of Department or Office are not directly involved in the specific programmes' delivery, they indeed do not appear to be in the best position to assess what personnel are needed. On the other hand, since they have been made a part of the staff selection process, they should be able to perform their role in a manner which involves more than just formal rubberstamping of decisions taken by the hiring managers. Proposals put in front of Heads of Department or Office should, therefore, always include more than just one name, offering them a choice. In addition, proposals should rank candidates in accordance with their merits proven in the selection process. Only under such conditions, Heads of Department or Office will be able to give a meaning to their role in each individual selection process and to increase its objectivity and impartiality.

Central review bodies

As explained in the previous two sections, central review bodies fulfil a relatively limited number of the tasks in the staff selection process. First, they approve evaluation criteria, ensuring that these criteria are objective, relate to the functions of the post and reflect relevant competencies.[254] Second, they review specific proposals for filling vacant posts and assess whether the evaluation criteria were applied and

[254] *UN Staff Rules of 2009*, Rule 4.15(i)(ii) and *Secretary-General's Bulletin, Central Review Bodies*, Section 5.1.

whether applicable procedures were adhered to.[255] Central review bodies cannot, however, make a substantive assessment of the proposal or to propose another candidate, not even in cases in which they find that relevant evaluation criteria were *not* applied or that applicable procedures were *not* followed.[256]

As it is noted above, the current mandate of central review bodies has been regarded as largely inadequate, in particular by the UN staff unions, which have been very critical in this respect. Their main argument relates to the lack of control central review bodies are able to exercise over hiring and occupational programme managers. As discussed in more detail below in this section, staff unions' criticism is not unfounded and should be seriously considered by the relevant UN organs so that any subjectivity and nepotism in the staff selection process, or a perception thereof, are limited to a minimum.

As far as the type and composition of central review bodies are concerned, all these bodies are established in accordance with Rule 4.15 of the *UN Staff Rules* and further defined in the *Secretary-General's Bulletin, Central Review Bodies* ST/SGB/2002/6 of 2002, *Secretary-General's Bulletin, Field Central Review Bodies ST/SGB/2009/5* of 2009 and *Secretary-General's Bulletin, Senior Review Group* ST/SGB/2009/2 of 2009.[257] For the appointments at the Professional level, there are in principle three types of central review bodies involved: central review committees, central review boards and the Senior Review Group, depending on the level on which the vacant post is classified.[258] A further distinction is made between central review bodies for 'regular' Professional posts on the one side and for Professional posts administered by the Department of Field Support on the other side.[259] This Department also administers posts in the Field Service category, in peacekeeping missions and special political missions, for which distinct central review bodies (namely field central review panels) are established.[260] However, as non-Professional posts are not included in this study, the field central review panels are not further elaborated on.

To begin with (regular) central review committees, they are set up in all major duty stations (New York, Geneva, Vienna, Nairobi, Addis Ababa, Bangkok, Beirut and Santiago) and involved in selection process for posts in the Professional category up to P-4 level. The exception is appointment of candidates who have passed competitive examination, such as the NCRE. As discussed above, advices on such ap-

---

[255] *UN Staff Rules of 2009*, Rule 4.15(i)(ii) and *Secretary-General's Bulletin, Central Review Bodies*, Section 5.2. Note that in case of questions or doubts, central review bodies may request necessary information from a relevant authority. – Ibid., Section 5.5.

[256] See above, section 2.2.2.2.

[257] *Secretary-General's Bulletin, Central Review Bodies*; *Secretary-General's Bulletin, Field Central Review Bodies, ST/SGB/2009/5*, 01.05.2009, available in the Human Resources Handbook of the United Nations, available at http://www.un.org/hr_handbook/English/, last visited on 30.12.2010; and *Secretary-General's Bulletin, Senior Review Group of 2009*.

[258] *Secretary-General's Bulletin, Central Review Bodies*, Section 1.1 and 1.2.

[259] For the latter, see *Secretary-General's Bulletin, Field Central Review Bodies*, and below in this section.

[260] Ibid., Section 1.3 and Section 4.

pointments are given by boards of examiners, defined in Rule 4.16 of the *UN Staff Rules*.[261]

Central review committees are composed of seven staff members at the level P-3 and above with rank not below that of the level of the post to be filled. They are selected by the Secretary-General (three members and an appropriate number of alternates) and by the staff representative body at the relevant duty station (three members and the same number of alternates as those selected by the Secretary-General). One additional member is chosen jointly by the rest of the committees' members who were selected by the Secretary-General and by the staff representatives.[262] The appointment to the committee membership is made for a period of two years, with a maximum of four continuous years.[263] There is also an *ex officio* non-voting member of the central review committee – the Assistant Secretary-General for Human Resources Management or his authorized representative.[264]

The appointment in P-5 and D-1 posts is assisted by central review boards established at all four headquarters of the UN (New York, Geneva, Vienna and Nairobi) and, if needed, also elsewhere.[265] These boards are composed of staff members at the P-5 level and above with rank not below that of the level of the post to be filled, selected in the same manner as the members of the central review committees. Hence, three members (and a number of alternates) are selected by the Secretary-General, three members (and a number of alternates) are chosen by the relevant staff representative body, and one member is selected jointly by the members chosen by the Secretary-General and members chosen by the staff representatives.[266] The *ex officio* non-voting member attends the boards' meetings in the same capacity as in the central review committees.[267] Terms of office of the central review boards are also the same as the term of office of the central review committees.[268]

---

[261] *UN Staff Rules of 2009*, Rule 4.15(b)(ii) and (i)(i), and Rule 4.16; also *Secretary-General's Bulletin, Central Review Bodies*, Section 1.2. See also *Human Resources Management Reform: Recruitment and Staffing, Report of the Secretary-General, A/61/822*, Part II, para. 6.

[262] *Secretary-General's Bulletin, Central Review Bodies*, Section 3.1.

[263] *UN Staff Rules of 2009*, Rule 4.15(g), (d) and (e); and *Secretary-General's Bulletin, Central Review Bodies*, Section 3.4.

[264] *UN Staff Rules of 2009*, Rule 4.15(d)(iv). Note that until the adoption of the 2009 *UN Staff Rules*, two additional persons were taking part in the central review committees' meetings. First, a representative of the OHRM (in New York) or of the local personnel office (in other duty stations) who served as an *ex officio* non-voting member. Second, a representative of the Office of the Special Adviser on Gender Issues and Advancement of Women (in New York) or a departmental focal point for women (in other duty stations) who attended the committee's meetings in an advisory capacity. *Secretary-General's Bulletin, Central Review Bodies*, Sections 3.5 and 3.6. Interestingly, this *Secretary's General Bulletin* has not yet been amended in order to correspond to the new *UN Staff Rules*.

[265] *UN Staff Rules of 2009*, Rule 4.15(i) and *Secretary-General's Bulletin, Central Review Bodies*, Section 1.1.

[266] *UN Staff Rules of 2009*, Rule 4.15(d) and *Secretary-General's Bulletin, Central Review Bodies*, Section 2.1.

[267] *UN Staff Rules of 2009*, Rule 4.15(d)(iv) and *Secretary-General's Bulletin, Central Review Bodies*, Sections 2.5 and 2.6.

[268] *UN Staff Rules of 2009*, Rule 4.15(e) and *Secretary-General's Bulletin, Central Review Bodies*, Section 2.4.

Functions of central review bodies for staff serving in field are performed by field central review bodies. The latter perform the same functions as 'regular' central review bodies, although the Secretary-General's Bulletin ST/SGB/2009/5 on field central review bodies, promulgated in May 2009, has separate provisions on these bodies' functions.[269] Nonetheless, since in April 2010 recruitment to field posts was integrated in the *UN Staff Selection System*, provisions of the administrative instruction ST/AI/2010/3 establishing the system apply to field central review bodies, too.[270]

There are two types of field central review bodies involved in selection process for Professional posts in the field. Depending on the level of the post, either a field central review committee or a field central review board is involved. The former are established for posts up to and including the P-4 level and the latter for posts at the P-5 and D-1 levels.[271] This is thus identical with the situation with 'regular' central review bodies.

Also composition of field central review committee and boards is similar to that of 'regular' central review committees and boards. For Professional posts, field central review committees are composed of staff members at the P-4 and above level. In central review boards, participating staff members must hold appointments at the D-1 level and above.[272] Both field central review committees and field central review boards, each of them, consist of three members and seven alternates selected by the Secretary-General or his representative; three members and seven alternates selected by the Field Staff Union; and a chairperson. The chairperson is a member selected from among and by the members selected by the Secretary-General and those selected by the field staff representatives. If a need arises, additional members and/or alternates are selected by the Secretary-General and/or the Field Staff Union. Both members and alternates of field central review committees and of field central review boards are selected in a manner ensuring balance representation of nationalities, genders and the peacekeeping operations and special political missions administered by the Department of Field Support. They all are appointed for two years and may serve for a maximum of four years.[273] Apart from members and alternates, field central review committees and field central review boards also include a non-voting member - a secretary selected by the Department of Field Support, as well as an *ex officio* non-voting member – a representative of the Field Personnel Division designated by its Director. Lastly, meetings of each field central review committee and field central review board are also to be attended, in an advi-

[269] *Secretary-General's Bulletin, Field Central Review Bodies*, Section 5.

[270] See *UN Staff Selection System*, in particular Sections 1(d), 2.3 and 13.3. The latter explicitly states that provisions of this administrative instruction prevail over inconsistent provisions of other administrative issuances in force at the time of the adoption of this instruction. Clearly, this applies to the Secretary-General's Bulletin concerning field central review bodies, too.

[271] *Secretary-General's Bulletin, Field Central Review Bodies*, Sections 1.1 and 1.2.

[272] Ibid., Sections 2.1 and 3.1.

[273] Ibid., Sections 2.1, 2.5, 3.1 and 3.5.

sory capacity, by a representative of the Departmental Focal Point for Women in the Department of Field Support.[274]

The description of central review bodies' composition clearly shows that, despite their limited mandate, attention has been paid to ensuring that these bodies perform their functions in an objective and impartial manner. Involvement of equal number of persons designated by staff representatives when compared to those appointed by the UN Administration constitutes an important safeguard in this respect. The only regrettable fact is the involvement of *ex officio* non-voting members who represent the Assistant Secretary-General for Human Resources Management or, in the case of field central review bodies, the Director of the Field Personnel Division of the Department of Field Support. Although the *ex officio* members do not have voting rights, their involvement in central review bodies' work creates a perception that the UN Administration desires to maintain at least some control over the selection process in every stage, including this one.

Note that the importance of the bodies involved in the staff selection process has often been emphasized in the UNAT's case law. Despite their advisory function, the UNAT has been of the view that irregularities in composition or work of these bodies may lead to denial of due process. For example, in *Choudhury and Ramchandani* the UNAT stated that such bodies must have been properly constituted so that justice was not only done but also seen to be done.[275] In that case the relevant advisory body had no member from the staff representation. The UNAT ruled that this was an irregularity for which the applicant had to be compensated, without having to prove that he would have had been promoted if the body in question was composed properly. It also did not matter that the relevant body played merely an advisory role.[276] This ruling demonstrates that (currently) central review bodies should be regarded as an important safeguard of an objective and transparent selection process.

Hiring and occupational group managers

From the above description is it clear that the role of hiring and occupational group managers in the staff selection process conducted under the *UN Staff Selection System* is significant. To briefly recapitulate, these managers request posting of job openings in the compendium; prepare evaluation guidelines; evaluate candidates, including those who were placed on the roster in previous selection procedures; shortlist candidates who appear most qualified; decide which assessment mechanisms will be used for further evaluation of shortlisted candidates and conduct this evaluation; and prepare proposals from which Heads of Department or Office select candidates who will receive appointment.

UN hiring managers possess these broad powers since the introduction of the *UN Staff Selection System* in 2002. Before that time, collective bodies had been involved

[274] Ibid., Sections 2.2, 2.3, 3.2 and 3.3.

[275] *Choudhury and Ramchandani v. Secretary-General of the United Nations, UNAT Judgment No. 870 [1998]*, available at http://untreaty.un.org/UNAT/UNAT_Judgements/Judgements_E/UNAT_00870_E.pdf, last visited on 30.12.2010, para. VII.

[276] Ibid., para. VII.

in the process and performed tasks now done by the hiring manager. The pre-2002 system was changed as a part of the overall human resources management reform in the UN Secretariat. The underlining idea was to provide hiring managers, who are responsible for delivery of their programmes, with competences needed for successful programme delivery, including the ability to choose staff working on it. The Secretary-General explained that the system existing before the reform was 'cumbersome and slow, with decision-making diffused among several parties – programme managers, staff representatives, appointment and promotion bodies and the Department of Management'.[277] Supporting the delivery of the programmes by providing programme managers (now referred to as hiring managers) with greater flexibility as well and simplifying the staff selection process were among the key elements of the reform.[278]

As noted earlier, the delegation of large powers to hiring managers in the UN staff selection has been severely criticized by the UN staff unions. Besides accusations of misuse of these powers and lack of transparency, the staff unions also criticize the 'disproportionate subjectivity in performing these functions'.[279] They point out that delegation of authority to individual hiring managers leads to recruitment on a subjective basis so as to optimalize specific programme delivery for which hiring managers are responsible. According to the UN staff unions:

> *It is a stretch to assume that even as managers recruit personnel for the needs of specific programme delivery, they will also contemplate the big picture encompassing generalists for a "more versatile, multi-skilled and experienced international civil service, based on the predicted needs of the Organization" [as envisaged by the UN Administration].* [280]

In the unions' view:

> *... Insofar as personnel are recruited to serve a wider interest and perform their functions that require multiple skills, their recruitment is too important to delegate to individual [hiring] managers.*[281]

The unions stress the insufficiency of accountability mechanisms for decisions related to human resources management, a concern also admitted by the Office of Internal Oversight Services, the Joint Inspection Unit and the UN General Assembly, too.[282] The Joint Inspection Unit, for example, stated in 2006:

---

[277] *Human Resources Management Reform, Report of the Secretary-General, A/55/253*, Annex II, para. 6.

[278] See, in particular, *Renewing The United Nations: A Programme for Reform, Report of the Secretary-General, A/51/950*, Action 18 on p. 74, and Strategy 3 and 4 on p. 77; *Human Resources Management Reform, Report of the Secretary-General, A/53/414*, paras. 9(f), 10, 21 and 23; and *Human Resources Management Reform, Report of the Secretary-General, A/55/253*, para. 35(c) and Annex II, paras. 4 and 6.

[279] *Views of the Staff Representatives of the United Nations Secretariat: Staff Union (New York), Field Staff Union (Brindisi) and Staff Coordinating Council (United Nations Office in Geneva), Addendum, A/C.5/63/3/Add.2*, para. 76.

[280] Ibid., para. 20. See also paras. 22 and 23.

[281] Ibid., para. 20.

[282] *Views of the Staff Representatives of the United Nations Secretariat, A/C.5/63/3/Add.2*, paras. 81-86;

> *The new [UN Staff Selection System] launched within the Secretariat (ST/AI/2002/4) has given higher flexibility to managers to recruit staff...*
>
> *It is difficult to understand the rationale behind the increased delegated authority granted to managers in the current staff selection system given the serious managerial problems identified by the Secretary-General himself within the Secretariat and extensively discussed in this review. The recruitment of the right individuals is crucial for the Organization to fulfil (sic) its mandate; it is hard to understand why the fundamental issue of weak management has not been solved in a first instance and then enough authority delegated to improved management to recruit according to the Secretariat's needs. The consequences of this arrangement are difficult to determine at this stage.*[283]

In the same report, the Joint Inspection Unit recommended that the staff selection system be reviewed in order to make it 'more objective, measurable and acceptable'.[284] One of the specific actions to be taken was to enable central review bodies to play a more active advisory role in this process.[285] Despite an amendment of the *UN Staff Selection System* in 2006, the Office of Internal Oversight Services (OIOS) reported in 2008 a continuing existence of weaknesses in delegation of authority structure, including 'a significant lack of sufficient OHRM monitoring of the human resources authority delegated to other departments' and inadequacy of existing accountability tools, namely the human resources action plans and senior management compacts.[286] The OIOS reported that credibility of the *UN Staff Selection System* was still low. Its findings deserve full quotation:

> *Key stakeholders, including staff and managers, perceive a lack of transparency and question the fairness of staff selection outcomes. Over half of Secretariat staff rated transparency of the selection process as "very poor" or "poor" and only 2 per cent as "excellent". Staff ratings on the application of competency-based interviews were only slightly more favourable, with most respondents*

Views of the Staff Representatives of the United Nations Secretariat: Staff Union (New York), Field Staff Union (Brindisi) and Staff Coordinating Council (United Nations Office in Geneva), Addendum, A/C.5/63/3/Add.2, para. 23; *Impact of the Human Resources Management Reform, Report of the Office of Internal Oversight Services, A/59/253*, para. 15 and 26; *Results-based Management in the United Nations in the Context of the Reform Process, Report of the Joint Inspection Unit, JIU/REP/2006/6*, paras. 82-84 and 146-147; and *General Assembly Resolution 59/266*, Section I, para. 10. The General Assembly requested the Secretary-General to make proposals to amend the terms of reference of the central review bodies in the light of past experience but the Secretary-General was of the opinion that no change was needed and that continuing the training of the hiring managers and the central review bodies was sufficient to facilitate proper and effective selection process. – *Human Resources Management Reform, Report of the Secretary-General, A/61/228*, Section IV, Part C.4(b), paras. 79-81.

283 *Results-based Management in the United Nations in the Context of the Reform Process, Report of the Joint Inspection Unit, JIU/REP/2006/6*, paras. 146-147. The 'serious managerial problems', referred to by the Join Inspection Unit, relate in particular to the lack of skilled managers capable of performing tasks they are entrusted with well. – paras. 82-84 and 95-96.

284 Ibid., Recommendation 17, p. 36.

285 Ibid., Recommendation 17(d), p. 36.

286 *In-depth Evaluation of the Office of Human Resources Management, Report of the Office of Internal Oversight Services, A/63/221*, Section III, Part C.

> *rating this as only "fair" and the remainder equally split between negative and positive perceptions. The majority of Secretariat staff reported that they did not perceive the selection process resulting in selection of the most qualified candidate. Twenty-seven per cent of managers rated transparency as "fair", with the remaining respondents split equally between negative and positive perceptions. OIOS notes that, despite OHRM initiatives such as the promotion of competency-based interviewing, desired outcomes are not being fully achieved.*[287]

Also UN Member States remain concerned over transparency of the selection process. For example, during the meeting of the Fifth Committee in 2009, Japan's representative called for eliminating 'arbitrary selection, sometimes reflecting nepotism, apparent in the current system'.[288] Similarly, the representative of Cameroon requested that control mechanisms be developed to monitor exercise delegated authority by hiring managers and that sanctions, including a removal of the authority, be applied in cases of abuse.[289]

In spite of all the deficiencies, there appears to be a general belief in the UN that the delegation of authority in staff recruitment to hiring (and occupational group) managers is appropriate, subject to the existence of sufficient checks and balances.[290] Nonetheless, concerns are understandable. It is indeed true that hiring managers know best what personnel they need for the successful delivery of their programme. It is also true that, if interviews are held, each candidate faces a panel, not just the hiring manager, and that each proposal for appointment must be substantiated in writing. It is also the fact that, unlike in the past when the former appointment and promotion boards – predecessors of current central review bodies – had to make judgments on the basis of often insufficient information they received, at present the central review bodies have direct access to all data they wish to consult via the electronic staffing system. They are thus better able to make their judgments. However, it is equally true that there is a strong negative perception of this state of affairs by the UN staff unions. Moreover, almost the entire selection process, and the substantive evaluation of candidates, is in the hands of hiring managers who, as much as they wish to be, can never be as objective and as unbiased as a collective body. In addition, the proposals of hiring managers not only lead to the appointment of one candidate they need for filling a vacant post in their programme, they also result in placement of proposed but not appointed candidates on the roster. This opens the door to the possibility of appointing such candidates to other available posts in the UN Secretariat in future, i.e. possibly in other programmes. It is questionable whether individual hiring managers are indeed capable of judging future needs of other programmes well. Central review bodies, which are better placed to form an opinion on the overall picture of the UN Secretariat, not limited to one

---

[287] Ibid., Section IV., Part A.1(d), para. 27.

[288] *Official Records, Fifth Committee, Summary Record of the 18th Meeting of 14 November 2008*, para. 59.

[289] Ibid., para. 67. See also a statement of the Representative of the Russian delegation – Ibid., para. 84.

[290] See, for example, *Delegation of Authority for the Management of Human and Financial Resources in the United Nations Secretariat, Report of the Joint Inspection Unit, JIU/REP/2000/6*, 2000, available in the Official Document System of the United Nations, available at http://documents.un.org/, last visited on 30.12.2010.

programme, lack powers necessary to substantially influence the selection process for vacant posts in cases in which procedures are properly followed. The broadening of the mandate of central review bodies either in the direction of the Senior Review Group or at least in the sense envisaged by the *UN Staff Rules* would, therefore, be desirable. The Senior Review Group substantially reviews a short list of candidates prepared by the relevant department and puts forward one candidate who is subsequently appointed by the Secretary-General. A similar regime could be used across the whole Secretariat. Proposals for appointment could be made by central review bodies on the basis of files prepared by the hiring managers who could make their views on individual candidates known to the relevant central review body. Alternatively, the *UN Staff Rules* grant central review bodies competence to make their own recommendation in cases of disagreement with the proposal submitted by the hiring manager. This competence should be incorporated in the *UN Staff Selection System.* This is not the case at present, although it could be argued that the presence of the rule in the *UN Staff Rules* is sufficient considering its higher legal value when compared to the *UN Staff Selection System*. However, it is difficult to imagine that central review bodies would go beyond their mandate as set out in the *UN Staff Selection System*.

2.2.2.5. Posts at the D-2 level

The *UN Staff Selection System* applies, in principle, also to appointment to positions at the D-2 level. However, certain steps in the procedure outlined above differ. First of all, as already mentioned, all candidates who have been successful in the pre-screening process must be interviewed by an interdepartmental assessment panel before they may appear on the short list.[291] This assessment panel should include at least three members, two of whom should be from outside the department or office concerned. At least one member of the assessment panel should be a female.[292] To recall, the assessment process for posts up to an including D-1 level may but does not need to include an interview, the decision depending fully on the hiring or occupational group manager.[293] The fact that an interview by a collective body must be conducted for filling any D-2 post must be praised. It ensures a more objective and impartial assessment of candidates.

Secondly, the submission of the proposal for the selection decision follows a different process – there are different actors involved, different supportive documentation that need to be submitted, different number of candidates who must be recommended, with additional considerations that need to be taken into consideration during their selection. The process takes places as follows: The Head of the Department or Office submits a proposal with three shortlisted candidates, among them at least one female, to the central review body established for advising the

[291] *UN Staff Selection System*, Section 7.9 and *Secretary-General's Bulletin, Senior Review Group of 2009*, Section 4.1.

[292] *UN Staff Selection System*, Section 1(c).

[293] See above, section 2.2.2.2.

Secretary-General on appointment into D-2 posts, described in the following paragraph. The proposal is accompanied by a comprehensive evaluation and justification of the shortlisted candidates, their personal history profile and statistics on D-1 and D-2 staff in the relevant department or office, including information on nationality and gender. In making the proposal, due regard should be given to candidates' diversity of experience and career mobility.[294] Once the shortlist is submitted, the relevant central review body reviews it and makes a final recommendation for appointment.[295]

The obligation to normally include three candidates in the proposal submitted to the central review body is a welcome difference with the requirement that applies in the selection process concerning posts up to and including the D-1 level. Formally speaking, a proposal containing just one name is sufficient there. The fact that for D-2 posts normally three names are to be proposed is clearly related to the next difference between the selection process for posts up to and including D-1 level on the one hand and that at the D-2 level on the other, namely to a different mandate of the involved central review body.

As already noted, responsibilities of the central review body involved in the selection process concerning posts at the D-2 level are carried out by the Senior Review Group.[296] This body was established in 1991 with the following objectives:

- *to provide the Secretary-General with more structured advice in the consideration of candidates;*
- *to ensure consistent implementation of personnel policies and recruitment guidelines;*
- *to satisfy members aspiring to such posts that their candidacies are given adequate consideration.*[297]

Currently, the functions and the composition of the Senior Review Group are set out in the *Secretary-General's Bulletin, Senior Review Group ST/SGB/2009/2*, mentioned above. According to this document, the Senior Review Group is a standing advisory body whose task is to make recommendations to the Secretary-General on appointment and promotion to D-2 posts.[298] The body is composed of a chairperson and eight members appointed by the Secretary-General. They all are UN officials serving at the Under-Secretary-General or Assistant Secretary-General level. They are

---

[294] *UN Staff Selection System*, Section 7.9 and *Secretary-General's Bulletin, Senior Review Group of 2009*, Sections 4.1-4.2.

[295] *UN Staff Selection System*, Section 7.9 and *Secretary-General's Bulletin, Senior Review Group of 2009*, Section 5.

[296] *UN Staff Selection System*, Sections 7.9 and 3.1.

[297] *Senior-Level Appointments in the United Nations, Its Programmes and Funds, Report of the Joint Inspection Unit, JIU/REP/2000/3*, para. 46. The UNAT has explained that the phrase 'more structured advice', mentioned in the quote in the text above, means that the Senior Review Group is to 'provide an independent and impartial evaluation of the suitability of all short-listed candidates, along the lines more clearly set out for appointments at levels below D-2 in section 6 of [the relevant] administrative instruction'. - *Case No. 1414, UNAT Judgment No. 1315 [2006]*, para. II.

[298] *Secretary-General's Bulletin, Senior Review Group of 2009*, Section 1.

assisted by a secretary (i.e. the Assistant Secretary-General for Human Resources Management) and an *ex officio* adviser for gender issues (i.e. the Special Adviser on Gender Issues and Advancement of Women).[299] The internal functioning of the Senior Review Group is governed by rules of procedures adopted by the Senior Review Group itself.[300]

The fact that all members of the Senior Review Group are selected and appointed by the Secretary-General is regrettable. It could be argued that this manner of selection of members of the Senior Review Group contains a risk of appointing persons favorable to a candidate pre-selected by the Secretary-General in advance. Fortunately, this is, at least to a certain extent, prevented by the fact that the Senior Review Group is a standing body. Therefore, its composition does not change with each individual selection procedure. In addition, the Senior Review Group comprises as many as nine officials. Unfortunately, there is no formal rule indicating the duration of office of (members of) the Senior Review Group. It, therefore, appears that the Secretary-General is free to dismiss a member or members of this advisory body and appoint new ones whenever he considers it appropriate. It is also regrettable that the staff representatives are not involved in the process at all since such involvement would increase transparency of this process.

Turning to the functions of the Senior Review Group, they are twofold. Firstly, the Senior Review Group reviews proposals for appointment into vacant D-2 posts made by the relevant department or office. Similarly as central review committees and central review boards, the Senior Review Group is required to ensure that the evaluation of the candidates corresponds to the job opening announcement and that appropriate procedures were complied with. To that effect, the Senior Review Group may request information it considers necessary from either the relevant department or office or from the OHRM. Secondly, the Senior Review Group makes recommendation to the Secretary-General in respect of the final decision. This is the case when the Senior Review Group finds that the evaluation criteria and applicable procedures were properly applied.[301] It is unclear, however, how the matter would proceed if the Senior Review Group found a flaw in the candidates' evaluation or followed procedures. The *Secretary-General's Bulletin, Senior Review Group* has no provision to that effect. Legally speaking, the *UN Staff Selection System*, which applies to recruitment process of D-2 posts subject to special arrangements under the *Secretary-General's Bulletin, Senior Review Group* could not apply in such a case as the relevant provision requiring referral of the matter to the Secretary-General explicitly refers to posts up to and including D-1 level.[302] The *Secretary-General's Bulletin, Senior Review Group* also does not provide which body approves the evaluation criteria for job openings at the D-2 level created on the basis of individually classified job descriptions as oppose to generic job profiles, compliance with which

[299] Ibid., Section 2.

[300] Ibid., Section 3. For the most recent rules of procedure, see *Senior Review Group, Rules of Procedure*, 31.07.2008, available at http://www.un.org/hr_handbook/English/sourcedocuments_/topics_/appointment2adv/appointment2adv.doc#ICTaskToolsAdvisoryBodies, last visited on 30.12.2010.

[301] *Secretary-General's Bulletin, Senior Review Group of 2009*, Section 5.

[302] *UN Staff Selection System*, Section 8.2.

the Senior Review Group oversees. Contrary to the central review committee and central review boards, the Senior Review Group has not been granted such mandate. This is, of course, rather surprising, and difficult to explain. It might be an unintended omission or the intention of leaving the two matters in the hands of the Secretary-General himself. As there are no other provisions, it appears it would be him who needs to approve the evaluation criteria for job openings at D-2 level created on the basis of individually classified job descriptions and who would take a final decision in cases in which the Senior Review Group would find that the evaluation criteria and applicable procedures were not properly applied. Such situation can hardly be regarded as supporting transparency and impartiality of the selection process. Suspicions that (may) arise here are, in themselves, harmful and unnecessary. When the Senior Review Group finds that the evaluation criteria and applicable procedures were not properly applied, the process should not proceed and the Secretary-Genera should not be permitted to select a candidate before the flows are adequately remedied or the whole process is repeated.

Returning to differences between the selection process for posts up to and including D-1 level and those at the D-2 level, the last two specificities of the latter that should be noted are: first, the final decision on appointments in vacant posts at the D-2 level is taken by the Secretary-General; and second, candidates who were shortlisted but not appointed to the specific job opening at the D-2 level do not have a possibility to be placed on a roster of pre-approved candidates since such roster is only available for posts up to and including D-1 level.[303] Shortlisted but not selected candidates for D-2 posts thus need to apply to a new job opening and undergo the whole process again.

2.2.3. Recruitment to temporary posts

Differently from posts of duration of at least one year, addressed in the previous sections, posts of shorter duration, i.e. the so-called temporary posts, are filled in accordance with a separate set of rules. They are contained in the *Administrative Instruction, Administration of Temporary Appointments ST/AI/2010/4* of 27 April 2010.[304] The recent adoption of this instruction constitutes an important step forward towards greater objectivity and transparency of the recruitment process for the positions in question. The reason for this is that two issuances regulating, *inter alia*, appointments of such limited duration previously regulated only conditions under which such appointments could have been concluded and contained no procedural arrangements with regard to the staff selection.[305] The new administrative instruction remedies this problem, albeit only to a certain, and rather limited, extent.

---

[303] Ibid., Sections 9.2 and 9.3; and *Secretary-General's Bulletin, Senior Review Group of 2009*, Section 5.3. See also above, section 2.2.2.2.

[304] *Administrative Instruction, Administration of Temporary Appointments*.

[305] *Administrative Instruction, Temporary Staff and Individual Contractors*, and *Administrative Instruction, Appointment, Extension and Conversion of Contractual Status of Staff in the General Service, Security Service and Manual Workers Categories, ST/AI/274*, 30.06.1980, available in the Human Resources Handbook of the United Nations, available at http://www.un.org/hr_handbook/English/.

Pursuant to the new instruction, recruitment process for temporary posts depends on the duration of the future appointment. Posts of duration of less than three months may be filled without issuance of a temporary vacancy announcement. Appointment into such posts is within absolute discretion of the relevant hiring manager. If such appointment is to be extended for three or more months, the extension is subject to the issuance of an announcement.[306]

Vacancies for temporary posts for more than three but less than twelve months must be announced by issuing a so-called temporary vacancy announcement. Such announcement must be posted internally and may be advertised internally, if deemed necessary and appropriate.[307] The assessment of candidates' suitability is made by the hiring manager who may choose one or more assessment techniques which he considers to be appropriate. They may include written tests, interviews and similar selection techniques, none of them being compulsory. The final decision is taken by the Head of Department or Office on the basis of 'a competitive process', the latter not being further defined or explained.[308]

It follows that the power vested in the hands of hiring managers is, once again, relatively broad. It is virtually unlimited for all posts of duration less than three months. For posts lasting more than three but less than twelve months, discretion of hiring managers is only limited by the requirement to prepare a vacancy announcement in each case and to publish it at least internally, and by the fact that the final decision is left in the hands of Heads of Department or Office, not of the hiring managers themselves. Since the relevant administrative instruction does not specify what it means by requiring that selections are to be made as a result of 'a competitive process', it appears that as long as more than one candidate is considered and the best one is selected, this requirement is satisfied. It is regrettable that no real safeguards for a more transparent, objective and impartial selection process exist. There is, for example, no selection or review committee involved, neither for posts of duration shorter than three months, nor for those between three and twelve months.

In this respect it should be noted that great flexibility of hiring managers in the selection process concerning temporary posts was severely criticized in the past. In particular the UN staff unions accused hiring managers of abuse and favoritism and requested adoption of rigorous recruitment procedures.[309] Unfortunately, the new administrative instruction on temporary appointments has not improved the situation substantially. Although it sets out the procedure to be followed for temporary appointments lasting longer than three months, it preserves the broad discretion of hiring managers. A few improvements have taken place, but their practical effect is

[306] *Administrative Instruction, Administration of Temporary Appointments*, Section 3.2.

[307] Ibid., Sections 3.1. and 3.3.

[308] Ibid., Section 3.6.

[309] *Views of the Staff Representatives of the United Nations Secretariat, A/C.5/63/3/Add.2*, para. 42; *Views of the Staff Representatives of the United Nations Secretariat: Staff Union (New York), Field Staff Union (Brindisi) and Staff Coordinating Council (United Nations Office in Geneva), Addendum, A/C.5/63/3/Add.2*, paras. 23 and 134. The staff unions claimed that hiring managers hired candidates of their choice under the temporary vacancy announcement system for a period of 3-11 months and after a break of one month rehired them again and again.

uncertain. One of the improvements is the introduction of a restriction on the possibility to re-appoint the same person by imposing mandatory breaks between each new appointment. The new instruction also provides a list of situations in which extension of temporary appointments beyond one year is possible, establishing an overall maximum duration of appointments without a mandatory break.[310] This clearly enhances the transparency and predictability of the process. It also addresses at least some past concerns related to the abuse of the former system (referred to as system of temporary vacancy announcement) by hiring managers who reappointed staff initially engaged under such temporary vacancy announcement either under a succession of new temporary contracts or, even more worryingly, 'regularized' such staff.[311] The mandatory breaks in temporary staff employment introduced by the new administrative instruction do prevent, or at least render more difficult, the abuse of granting repetitive temporary appointments to the same persons. It could be argued, however, that a break of three months is not sufficient. This period is in many countries covered by unemployment support, not forcing former temporary staff to look for another employment but rather to hope, and lobby, for new temporary contract with the UN. Moreover, the new administrative instruction is silent about succession between a temporary and a fixed-term appointment. The newly introduced mandatory break only concerns new temporary appointments and appointments as consultants and individual contractors. This means that, as in the past, hiring managers may still consider staff serving under temporary appointment for fixed-term posts, eventually leading to continuing appointment. Given the fact that hiring managers are the decisive actors in the selection process for such fixed-term posts through the *UN Staff Selection System*, the objectivity and impartiality of the process could be questioned once again.

3. Recruitment in the European Commission

3.1. Brief historical overview

The previous chapter noted that the first European Commission staff had been recruited in a rather informal manner and on a temporary basis. For posts to be filled directly after the *Treaty Establishing the European Economic Community* had come into force, lists of potential candidates of each nationality were drawn up by the Commissioners from the relevant Member States, helped by friends and assistants who had been involved in the negotiations of the *EEC Treaty*.[312] This practice was similar to that existing in the High Authority of European Coal and Steel Community, operational since 1952. Also there, there were no formal recruitment procedures for several years; candidates for jobs at the ECSC High Authority were nominated by the

---

[310] See above, section 2.2.3.

[311] See, for example, *Inspection of the Application of United Nations Recruitment, Placement, and Promotion Policies, Part II – Placement and Promotions, Report of the Joint Inspection Unit, JIU/REP/96/6*, 1996, available in the Official Document System of the United Nations, available at http://documents.un.org/, last visited on 30.12.2010, paras. 21-23.

[312] Coombes, *Politics and Bureaucracy in the European Community, A Portrait of the Commission of the E.E.C.*, pp. 141-142.

Directors of relevant divisions and approved by the member of the High Authority who had the same nationality as the candidate at issue.[313]

The initial recruitment system at the European Commission was thus relatively 'subjective and clientilistic'.[314] This state of affairs was softened, although not entirely banished, by the adoption of the first *Staff Regulations* in 1961, and later in 1968 by the consolidation of *Staff Regulations* of all three European Communities into one document made because of the merger of the executives of these Communities. The newly adopted *Staff Regulations* linked the staff recruitment with the establishment of an independent career service. They both were based on the presumption that the recruitment process had to ensure that appointed officials joined an independent and structured service providing full career possibilities. Despite this, a number of features of the initial informal approach continued to exist also after the adoption of the *Staff Regulations*. This was especially the case with the recruitment for senior posts, which remained heavily influenced by the individual Commissioners and their senior cabinet staff for decades.[315]

The 1961, and later the consolidated 1968, version of the *Staff Regulations* provided a number of provisions relating to staff recruitment and establishing a number of principles on which this recruitment was to be based. Articles 4 and 29 provided for manners in which vacant posts were to be filled, establishing priority for the appointment of internal candidates over external ones. Article 7 established an obligation to act solely in the interest of the service in assigning staff to particular posts. It also explicitly outlawed prohibition of discrimination on the basis of nationality in staff assignment. Article 27 set up two principles which were to guide staff recruitment, namely the principle of merit and the principle of geographical balance. Article 28 fixed the substantive conditions that needed to be met for becoming an EU official and the need to pass a competition. Article 29 also set up the possibility to adopt a different procedure for recruitment of staff to posts requiring special qualifications or senior posts. Article 30 granted discretionary power to the appointment authority to decide on staff appointment. Lastly, Annex III to the *Staff Regulations* set up more detailed rules on the conduct of competitions.[316]

All of the above mentioned provisions have remained relevant and most of them unchanged till now. Consequently, the Commission staff has been, in principle, recruited in the same manner since the 1960s, subject to some minor changes regarding, for example, competition tests. This is rather surprising, giving in particular the considerable increase in the Commission size and responsibilities over the past five decades.[317] The few reports which attempted to review the internal functioning of

[313] Stevens and Stevens, *Brussels Bureaucrats? The Administration of the European Union*, pp. 72-74.

[314] Ibid., pp. 72-74.

[315] Ibid., pp. 72-74.

[316] *EU Staff Regulations of 1961*, and *EU Staff Regulations of 1968*, Articles 4, 7, 27, 28, 29, 30 and Annex III.

[317] Coull and Lewis, *The Impact of the Staff Regulations in Making the Commission a More Modern and Efficient Oragnization: an Insider's Perspective*, p. 2; Schon-Quinlivan, E., *Administrative Reform in the European Commission: From Rethoric to Re-legitimisation*, Paper based on EU-CONSENT WORKSHOP The Commission and the European Civil Service, Paris, 21-22.6.2006 (Deliverable No. '17'), 2006,

the Commission, such as the *Spierenburg Report* of 1979 or the *Williamson Report* of 1998, did not pay much attention to the recruitment issues as such.[318] Even the *Second Report* prepared by the Committee of Independent Experts in 1999 devoted relatively modest attention to the issue of staff recruitment when compared to other issues, such as geographical balance or career development, perhaps with the exception of the issue of recruitment into senior posts.[319] It appears thus that the recruitment system as such has been generally considered to be rather satisfactory. One of the important reasons of this satisfaction could be that competitions, regarded as the best and the most objective and transparent manner of staff recruitment, has been used to the exclusion of other recruitment methods since early years, with just a few clearly defined exceptions.

In spite of the general satisfaction with the system, a number of specific problems in staff recruitment were nonetheless identified. Some of these problems have been successfully addressed during the 2000 overall staff reform. The Committee of Independent Experts, whose report provided the basis for the 2000 reform, highlighted in particular problems with the lack of human resources planning in the sense of tasks and priority setting and correspondent staff deployment, leading to an excessive and non-transparent use of external staff.[320] The Committee also stressed problems with manageability of competitions caused by the considerable increase in the number of candidates. It noted that such high numbers of candidates, as many as 56.000 in 1994 and 31.000 in 1998, had resulted in, *inter alia*, enormous organizational problems, too long time of the processing and increased expenditure. The Committee concluded that, as a result of these problems, it was impossible to make a proper and effective selection.[321] Another difficulty with competitions was their lack of transparency, objectivity and certainty in the eventual selection and placement of candidates from the reserve list on which all candidates successful in the competition are placed before they are selected by individual Directorates-General.[322] Moreover, the Committee observed the insufficient suitability of competitions to ensure adequate geographical balance among staff, explained in the previous chapter.[323] Another criticism of the Committee of Independent Experts related to internal competitions – they were considered to lack transparency and impartiality in final decision making, often leading to hiring persons personally known to the examiners.[324] Last but not least, the Committee criticized recruitment into senior posts, in particular the absence of formal or even informal set of rules containing objective and transparent selection criteria.[325]

---

available at http://www.eu-consent.net/library/deliverables/D17_Team7_Schon1.pdf, last visited on 30.12.2010, p. 1.

[318] Coull and Lewis, *The Impact of the Staff Regulations in Making the Commission a More Modern and Efficient Oragnization: an Insider's Perspective*, p. 2.

[319] See *Second Report on Reform of the Commission of 1999, Volume II*, Section 6.5.

[320] Ibid., paras. 6.4.28.-6.4.36.

[321] Ibid., paras. 6.5.4.-6.5.6.

[322] Ibid., paras. 6.5.13.-6.5.21. For details on reserve lists and selection, see below, section 3.2.1.3.

[323] Ibid., para. 6.5.7. See also above, chapter 2, section 3.4.1.2.

[324] Ibid., paras. 6.5.22.-6.5.23.

[325] Ibid., paras. 6.5.43-6.5.47.

Many problems identified by the Committee of Independent Experts were admitted by the Commission in its *White Paper* of 2000. In this document, the Commission also announced a number of measures that it planned to adopt in order to improve the situation. The action plan contained measures relating to better identification of the Commission needs, such as improvement of the organization of competitions, improvements with regard to competition selection boards, as well as to the increase in transparency for candidates.[326] The following sections explain how the legal framework for staff recruitment in the European Commission works at present, after the changes of the 2000 staff reform have been put in place.

3.2. Recruitment of permanent officials

Article 28 of the *EU Staff Regulations* stipulates that, as a matter of principle, no one becomes EU civil servant without passing a competition.[327] The only two possible exceptions are provided in Article 29(2) of the *EU Staff Regulations;* they concern appointments to posts requiring special qualifications and appointments of senior officials. In such instances, the EU Administration may use 'procedure other than competition' if it considers that such other procedure would be more appropriate.[328] If Article 29(2) of the *EU Staff Regulations* cannot be applied, recruitment to permanent posts may occur only by means of competition.

The following sections explain in detail the organization of competitions in the European Commission. They are followed by a detailed analysis of procedures employed for the recruitment of officials engaged in posts requiring special qualifications and, subsequently, for the recruitment of senior managers. As already noted, recruitment to these two categories of posts may, and often is, conducted by means others than competition.[329]

---

[326] *Reforming the Commission - A White Paper - Part I*, Section IV.2 and *Reforming the Commission - A White Paper - Part II - Action Plan*, Actions 24-29.

[327] *EU Staff Regulations*, Article 28(d).

[328] Ibid., Article 28(d) in conjunction with Article 29(2). For more details, see below, section 3.2.2 for posts requiring special qualifications and section 3.2.3. for senior posts. Note that Article 29(2) of the *EU Staff Regulations* does not apply to posts at the middle management level, only to senior posts, i.e. those equivalent to the basic post of Director and Director-General (and posts requiring special qualifications). Therefore, unless a specific middle management post is a post requiring special qualifications, it is filled by a transfer or promotion of an official who have passed competition when first recruited to the EU civil service. - *Commission Decision on Middle Management Staff*, Articles 6, 7(1) and (2), 9(1) and (2). One important exception exists, however, in this respect. It relates to appointment of middle managers from among nationals of Member States that newly accede to the EU. Since there are, at the time of accession, no or almost no nationals of the new Member State serving in the EU civil service, there is no possibility of transfer or promotion. To ensure the new geographical balance at all levels, middle management posts are thus initially filled by outside recruitment. However, this recruitment happens on the basis of competitions organized for middle management posts reserved for nationals from the newly acceded country. These competitions are similar to those used for regular recruitment of officials at lower levels. As explained above, special regime for the recruitment of nationals in an enlargement situation is legally possible due to derogations from certain provisions of the *EU Staff Regulations* adopted by the Council for each enlargement. – For details, see above, chapter 2, section 3.4.1.2.2.

[329] Since, as explained above, middle management posts are in principle filled by transfer or promotion,

3.2.1. Competition

As emphasized above, competition is the main vehicle for recruitment of permanent officials in the European Commission. Generally speaking, using competition is aimed at ensuring that best people available are hired. The main objective of competition is thus to offer relevant authorities the broadest choice possible guaranteeing that the best candidate is eventually appointed. If conducted properly, competition also contributes to the objectivity of the staff selection process, as it leaves little scope for partiality and favouritism.

In the EU, two types of competition are used - open and internal.[330] Open competition is organized for the purpose of establishing a reserve list from which candidates may be selected in case of a vacancy arising in future. While this type of competition includes external candidates as well as all internal staff, internal competition is restricted only to internal candidates, i.e. officials who wish to move to another post, for example via transfer or promotion, or non-permanent staff who wish to become permanent officials. Such internal competition may be organized either for the establishment of a reserve list or for filling a specific vacancy or vacancies.[331] As mentioned in the introduction to this chapter, the *EU Staff Regulations* require that the possibility to organize internal competition be considered in each case in which a vacant post is to be filled before an external candidate may be recruited.[332]

The *EU Staff Regulations* contain a set of general rules which are to be applied when a competition is organized, including eligibility conditions and applicable procedures. The general eligibility conditions are provided in Article 28. They include requirements related to the issues of nationality, full citizen rights, obligation concerning military service, character references, physical fitness and language proficiency.[333] Article 29(1)(b), (3) and (4) set additional eligibility conditions for internal competi-

---

appointment to these posts is discussed in the following chapters of this study.

[330] *EU Staff Regulations*, Annex III, Article 1(a). Note that internal competitions may be held for the institution having a vacancy but also to more institutions. Similarly, open competition may also be common to two or more institutions. Ibid.

[331] Ibid., Article 29(1), last sentence. See also, for example, European Commission, *Notice of Internal Competition, Heads of Unit AD12 (COM/INT/EU27/09/AD12)*, No 29-2009, 20.04.2009, available at http://www.cc.cec/guide/publications/infoadm/2009/ia09029_en.html, last visited on 07.05.2010, Section VII.

[332] *EU Staff Regulations*, Articles 4 and 29(1). See also above, section 1.

[333] Article 28 of the *EU Staff Regulations* reads as follows:
'An official may be appointed only on condition that:
(a) he is a national of one of the member states of the Communities, unless an exception is authorized by the appointing authority, and enjoys his full rights as a citizen;
(b) he has fulfilled any obligations imposed on him by the laws concerning military service;
(c) he produces the appropriate character references as to his suitability for the performance of his duties;
(d) he has, subject to Article 29(2), passed a competition based on either qualifications or tests, or both qualifications and tests, as provided for in Annex III;
(e) he is physically fit to perform his duties; and
(f) he produces evidence of a thorough knowledge of one of the languages of the Communities and of a satisfactory knowledge of another language of the Communities to the extent necessary for the performance of his duties.'

tions. They relate especially to the type of appointment which needs to be held by potential candidates and are discussed in more detail below.[334]

Both open and internal competitions are conducted under the same set of procedural rules. They are set out in Annex III to the *EU Staff Regulations*, although the EU Administration may adopt further rules and conditions which govern a specific competition.[335] The Administration enjoys a wide discretion in this regard, subject to the condition that it stays within the limits of the criteria of ability required for the posts to be filled, as set out in the vacancy notice, and within the limits of the interest of the service.[336]

Both internal as well as open competitions can be held either on basis of qualifications or on basis of tests, or on basis of both, qualifications and tests.[337] They involve a number of steps and a number of bodies that play a role in the competition and in the subsequent selection process.

3.2.1.1. Authorities involved in competition

There are three main authorities involved in EU competitions: the appointing authority, the Joint Committee and a selection board.

Appointing authority

The appointing authority is the body which decides that there is a post which needs to be filled, establishes the criteria of ability required for the such a post, decides which method of recruitment is to be applied (competition or other method, such as internal promotion), and, after suitable candidates have been selected, it decides which of them will eventually be appointed. In exercising these powers, the appointing authority enjoys wide discretion.[338]

Since the appointing authority is free to decide which recruitment method is best suitable and capable of leading to the appointment of a candidate of highest stan-

---

[334] See below, section 3.2.1.2.

[335] Note that, pursuant Article 110(1) of the *EU Staff Regulations*, EU institutions may adopt further provisions which would address certain points relating to competitions more specifically than the *EU Staff Regulations*. However, as pointed out by the ECJ in, for example, *Rauch*, rules contained in the *EU Staff Regulations* and in Annex III are sufficiently clear and the EU institutions, therefore, do not necessarily need to adopt other rules for giving effect to them. - *Rauch v. Commission, Case 16/64*, p. 146; also *Thérèse Marie-Louise Vandevyvere v. European Parliament, Case 23/64, ECR [1965], p. 157*, p. 165.

[336] *Francine Deboeck v. Commission of the European Communities, Case 90/74, ECR [1975], p. 1123*, para. 29; *Marie Hélène Ruske v. Commission of the European Communities, Case 67/81, ECR [1982], p. 661*, para. 9; *Cornelis Henrick Fabius v. Commission of the European Communities, Case 39/83, ECR [1984], p. 627*, para. 7.

[337] *EU Staff Regulations*, Annex III, Article 1(b).

[338] *Gijsbertus van Reenen v. Commission of the European Communities, Case 189/73, ECR [1975], p. 445*, para. 5. The ECJ has emphasized that the purpose of this discretion is to find a candidate with the highest standard of ability, efficiency and integrity. – Ibid. See also *Sven-Ole Mogensen and others v. Commission of the European Communities, Case 10/82, ECR [1983], p. 2397*, paras. 9-10 and *Androniki Vlachou v. Court of Auditors of the European Communities, Case 135/87, ECR [1988], p. 2901*, para. 23.

dard of ability, efficiency and integrity, it is for its own consideration to choose whether, for example, to hold a competition.[339] It may also decide whether to hold an internal competition, for example instead of promoting an official.[340] Moreover, the appointing authority is not obliged to pursue recruitment procedures already started or to actually fill the vacant post under all circumstances.[341] As stated by the ECJ, there might be 'weighty reasons' justifying departure from the recruitment which has already been commenced. Such a 'weighty reason' could, for example, be an abolition of the relevant post.[342] The appointing authority has thus freedom of choice with regard to the decision to begin a recruitment procedure as well as to cancel it, though in the latter case this freedom is not unlimited. Therefore, in absence of important reasons, the appointing authority must proceed and fill the vacant post in accordance with the started procedure and its results.[343] This is an important safeguard of the objectivity of the selection process. In its absence, the EU Administration could annul competition, or its results, whenever it would suit it. It could, for example, do so when certain candidates would – or would not – be successful in the competition.

As already mentioned, the appointing authority is also free to decide upon the criteria of ability required for the post to be filled and, in the light of those criteria and in the interest of service, also upon the actual rules governing the specific competition.[344] The appointing authority, furthermore, has discretion in assessing comparative merits of candidates, suitability of each candidate for the vacant post,

---

339 *Domenico Morina v. European Parliament, Case 11/65, ECR [1965], p. 1017*, p. 1024 and *Morina v. Parliament, Case 11/65*, p. 1039. In both cases, decided on the same day, the ECJ held that: 'Assessment of the expediency or necessity of organizing a competition lies within the exclusive domain of the Appointing Authority. In these circumstances, the Court cannot order a competition to be held or reheld without encroaching upon the prerogatives of the administrative authority.'

340 *Berthold Küster v. European Parliament, Case 123/75, ECR [1976], p. 1701*, para. 13.

341 *Fux v. Commission, Case 26/68*, para. 11; *Vlachou v. Court of Auditors, Case 135/87*, para. 24; *Ingfried Hochbaum v. Commission of the European Communities, Case T-38/89, ECR [1990], p. II-43*, para. 15; *Kotzonis v. Economic and Social Committee, Case T-586/93*, para. 44.

342 In *Fux*, for example, the post for which the competition had been held was abolished due to the merger of the European executives. The ECJ considered that, in those circumstances, the decision to abolish the post at issue was justified and, consequently, no infringement of the *EU Staff Regulations* had taken place by the discontinuation of the recruitment procedure. - *Fux v. Commission, Case 26/68*, para. 11-15. On the other hand, Irregularities which occur during the competition have been found insufficient for cancellation of the entire recruitment procedure, especially when there are other possible solutions of resolving the problem. In *Hanning*, certain persons were illegally admitted to the reserve list. The CFI considered this to be an insufficient reason for cancellation of the competition. It observed that a possible solution to this problem was to consider and appoint one of those persons who were included on the reserve list legally. The CFI stressed wide discretion of the appointing authority to disregard the precise order of the reserve list for the reasons connected with the interest of service. - *Jack Hanning v. European Parliament, Case T-37/89, ECR [1990], p. II-463*, paras. 70-75.

343 *Nelly Kohler v. Court of Auditors of the European Communities, Joined cases 316/82 and 40/83, ECR [1984], p. 641*, para. 22. See also *Hanning v. Parliament, Case T-37/89*, paras. 46-48, 55-56 and 70-75.

344 *Deboeck v. Commission, Case 90/74*, para. 29; *Ruske v. Commission, Case 67/81*, para. 9; *Fabius v. Commission, Case 39/83*, para. 7. In these cases the ECJ emphasized that the discretion of appointing authority in establishing the criteria of ability required for the posts to be filled and in determining the rules and conditions governing the competitions must stay within the limits of the set criteria and the interest of the service.

and, eventually, in choosing which candidate will be appointed.[345] With regard to the last mentioned, the appointing authority may ignore the precise order of the results of the competition. It may do so 'for reasons which it is incumbent upon to the Administration to evaluate and justify before the Court'.[346] On the other hand, the EU Administration must keep in mind that it may not 'destroy the very concept of competition by departing substantially from the results of the competition without serious reasons.'[347] Another limitation of the discretion of the appointing authority in the assessment of comparative merits of the candidates is the requirement to comply with the conditions laid down in the vacancy notice - the discretion of the appointing authority must thus in all circumstances be exercised within the self-imposed limits contained in the vacancy notice - as well as the requirement of careful examination of the personal files of candidates.[348]

Despite limitations, it is clear that discretion of the appointing authority in the staff selection process based on competition is broad. This is not surprising. It is a result of the fact that certain powers exercised by the appointing authority, such as assessment of candidates' comparative merits, involve 'judgment calls' and can therefore never be precisely regulated. Discretion is an inevitable part of such powers. In other cases, involving for example selection from the reserve lists disrespecting the precise order of the competition results, discretion conferred upon the appointing authority reflects the need for certain flexibility which exists in each selection methods. In such cases, however, it is important that adequate safeguards are in place so that possible abuse or misuse of discretion can be detected and challenged. It appears that the EU case law has developed a number of such safeguards, mentioned in the previous paragraph.

Last but not least, it must be noted that competences conferred upon the appointing authority by the *EU Staff Regulations* are, pursuant Article 2(1) thereof exercised by a person or authority determined by each EU institution itself.[349] In case of the European Commission, the relevant appointing authority is defined in the *Commission Decision C(2007)5730 on the on the Exercise of Powers Conferred by the Staff Regulations on the Appointing Authority and by the Conditions of Employment of Other Servants on the Authority Responsible for Concluding Contracts of Employment.*[350] Specific competences of the appointing authority in the recruit-

---

[345] *Daniele Grassi v. Council of the European Communities, Case 188/73, ECR [1974], p. 1099*, para. 26 and *Henri Brasseur v. European Parliament, Case 88/71, ECR [1972], p. 499*, paras. 16-17.

[346] *Serio v. EAEC Commission, Case 62/65*, p. 570.

[347] Ibid., p. 570. See also *Kotsonis v. Council, Case 246/84*, p. 4005 et seq. and *Gloria Pérez-Mínguez Casariego v. Commission of the European Communities, Case T-1/90, ECR [1991], p. II-143*, paras. 74 and 80.

[348] *Grassi v. Council, Case 188/73*, paras. 26, see also para. 38-40. More on vacancy notice, see below, section 3.2.1.3.

[349] Note that the exercise of some or all of the powers conferred on the Appointing Authority by the *EU Staff Regulations* may be entrusted to another EU institution or even to an inter-institutional body, except of decisions relating to appointments, promotions or transfers of EC officials. See *EU Staff Regulations*, Article 2(2).

[350] *Commission Decision on the Exercise of Powers Conferred by the Staff Regulations on the Appointing Authority and by the Conditions of Employment of Other Servants on the Authority Responsible for Concluding Contracts of Employment, C(2007)5730*, 30.11.2007, available in the Register of Commission

ment process are exercised by different actors. For example, the vacancy notice is prepared by the Director-General concerned, the internal or open competition notice by the Director-General for Human Resources, the latter also exercising the power to appoint a successful candidate following a competition. Some specific competences of the appointing authority in the competition process are exercised by the European Personnel Selection Office which is responsible for the organization of all competitions for the EU institutions.[351] Both the Director-General for Human Resources and the Directors-General concerned may delegate their competences to other officials in their Directorate-General.[352] The division of competences of the appointing authority in the European Commission is thus not that simple. It reflects the complexity of an institution of the Commission's size and can hardly be avoided. The fact that a number of actors are involved can, in fact, be regarded as positive as it (may) prevent concentration of too much power in the hands of just one person. The more persons involved in the process, the less chance of them exercising their competence in an inappropriate manner.

Joint Committee

The second body which is involved in the EU competition procedure is the Joint Committee. Depending on the number of officials at the place of employment, one or more Joint Committee(s) are established within each EU institution.[353] Each institution also determines the composition and procedure of the Joint Committee, subject to the provisions of Annex II of the *EU Staff Regulations*. Pursuant to Article

---

Documents, available at http://ec.europa.eu/transparency/regdoc/recherche.cfm?CL=en, last visited on 30.12.2010, as amended by subsequent decisions *Commission Decision Amending Decision C(2007) 5730 of 30 November on the Exercise of Powers Conferred by the Staff Regulations on the Appointing Authority and by the Conditions of Employment of Other Servants on teh Authority Responsible for Concluding Contracts of Employment*, C(2008) 5085, 10.09.2008, available in the Register of Commission Documents, available at http://ec.europa.eu/transparency/regdoc/registre.cfm?CL=en, last visited on 30.12.2010, *Commission Decision Amending Decision C(2007)5730 of 30 November on the Exercise of Powers Conferred by the Staff Regulations on the Appointing Authority and by the Conditions of Employment of Other Servants on teh Authority Responsible for Concluding Contracts of Employment, C(2009)3074 final*, 29.04.2009, available in the Register of Commission Documents, available at http://ec.europa.eu/transparency/regdoc/recherche.cfm?CL=en, last visited on 30.12.2010 and *Commission Decision Amending Decision C(2007)5730 of 30 November on the Exercise of Powers Conferred by the Staff Regulations on the Appointing Authority and by the Conditions of Employment of Other Servants on teh Authority Responsible for Concluding Contracts of Employment, C(2010)184 final*, 19.01.2010, available in the Register of Commission Documents, available at http://ec.europa.eu/transparency/regdoc/recherche.cfm?CL=en, last visited on 30.12.2010, Annex, AA Table, I. Filling Vacant Posts.

[351] *Commission Decision on the Appointing Authority*, as amended, Annex, AA Table, see especially points 1., 3.-7. Note that special provisions apply to staff of the Joint Research Center and OLAF. – Ibid., Annex I and III.

[352] Ibid., as amended, Article 5. The Directors-General may delegate their powers to Deputy Directors-General, Directors, Heads of Unit and Heads of Sector. The delegation of authority within the Directorate-General for Human Resources and Security is regulated by the *Decision of the Director-General for Human Resources and Security on the Exercise of the Powers Conferred on the Appointed Authority and the Authority Responsible for Concluding Contracts of Employment* and its Annex. - *Decision of the Director-General for Human Resources and Security on the Exercise of the Powers Conferred on the Appointment Authority and the Authority Responsible for Concluding Contracts of Employment*, 03.02.2010.

[353] *EU Staff Regulations*, Article 9(1)(a), second indent.

2 of that Annex, the Joint Committee consists of a chairman, appointed each year by the appointing authority, and members and their alternates who are appointed at the same time in equal numbers by the appointing authority and by the Staff Committee. The Staff Committee, also established within each EU institution, is a committee representing the interests of the staff of that institution vis-à-vis the Administration.[354]

The Joint Committee does not have many tasks in the recruitment process of EU officials. To be precise, it only has one task. It is to be consulted by the appointing authority when the notice of a specific competition is drawn up. The appointing authority may, however, consult the Joint Committee on questions of a general nature, too, if it considers that such consultation is needed or useful.[355]

Selection board

The third and the last body involved in the competitions is a selection board. The selection board is a board appointed by the appointing authority for each specific competition. Article 30 of the *EU Staff Regulations* stipulates that the main task of this board is to draw a list of candidates suitable for the appointment, while the actual appointment rests with the appointing authority itself.[356] It is, however, not the only activity of the selection board. It has a number of tasks which may be divided into two separate stages. The first stage consists of the examination of the candidates' applications and their compatibility whit the requirements of the competition notice in order to select candidates who will be admitted to the competition and those who will not.[357] The second stage of the tasks of the selection board consists of an examination of abilities of the candidates for the posts to be filled and, indeed, in drawing up a list of those candidates who are considered suitable for the post. As pointed out by the ECJ in *Casariego*, this second stage of the selection boards' tasks entails:

> *making a selection from the candidates admitted to the competition by means of either a comparative scrutiny of their diplomas, other qualifications and relevant*

[354] Ibid., Article 9(3).

[355] Ibid., Annex III, Article 1 and *EU Staff Regulations*, Article 9(4). The Join Committee fulfills tasks in other areas of personnel policy, too, for example the one related to the remuneration of EC officials and 'other servants'. In all cases, the Join Committee is a body where EU staff takes part in the discussion of issues of common interests to it as well as to the institution that employs them.

[356] *EU Staff Regulations*, Article 30

[357] See *Mario Costacurta v. Commission of the European Communities, Case 31/75, ECR [1975], p. 1563*, para. 10 and *Casariego v. Commission, Case T-1/90*, para. 74. Note also a recent judgment in which the European Civil Service Tribunal annulled a decision excluding the applicant from the competition as a result of failing pre-selection tests. These tests had been defined by the EPSO, not by the selection board. The Tribunal's ruled that that only the selection board and not the EPSO may establish the content of all competition tests, including pre-selection ones. - *Pachtitis v. Commission, Case F-35/08, available at http://curia.europa.eu/jurisp/cgi-bin/form.pl?lang=en&Submit=Rechercher&alldocs=alldocs&docj=docj&docop=docop&docor=docor&docjo=docjo&numaff=F-35/08&datefs=&datefe=&nomusuel=&domaine=&mots=&resmax=100, last visited on 30.12.2010*, available at http://curia.europa.eu/jurisp/cgi-bin/form.pl?lang=en&Submit=Rechercher&alldocs=alldocs&docj=docj&docop=docop&docor=docor&docjo=docjo&numaff=F-35/08&datefs=&datefe=&nomusuel=&domaine=&mots=&resmax=100, last visited on 30.12.2010, paras. 64-65.

experience, or reference to the marks obtained in test, or finally, the application of both those selection criteria, depending on the nature of the competition in question.[358]

As is the case with the appointing authority, also the selection board enjoys a wide discretion in exercising its competences, namely: in deciding upon the arrangements for and the detailed content of the tests;[359] in assessing certificates produced by the candidates;[360] in determination whether the documents justify admission of a candidate to the competition;[361] in allowing only a limited number of candidates admitted to the competition to take tests;[362] in making final assessment where marking of the tests is the same;[363] in determination that a candidate failed a test;[364] in evaluation of candidates' knowledge and abilities.[365]

This broad discretion of selection boards is, however, not unlimited. This constitutes an important safeguard of the objectivity and impartiality of the selection process. First of all, the selection board is bound by the notice of competition.[366] This notice forms the legal basis as well as the basis for assessment for the selection board.[367] So, for example, in assessing certificates produced by the candidates, the relevant selection board may not exceed the requirements laid down by the notice of competition.[368] As pointed out by the CFI in *Van Hecken*:

---

358 *Casariego v. Commission, Case T-1/90*, para. 74.

359 *Vincenzo Gallone v. Council of the European Communities, Case T-132/89, ECR [1990], p. II-549*, para. 27. See also *Protocol on the Statute of the Court of Justice annexed to the Treaty on European Union, to the Treaty Establishing the European Community and to the Treaty Establishing the European Atomic Energy Community*, in accordance with Article 7 of the Treaty of Nice, amending the Treaty on European Union, the Treaties establishing the European Communities and certain related acts, signed at Nice on 26 February 2001 (OJ C 80 of 10 March 2001), as amended by Council Decision of 15 July 2003 (OJ L 188 of 26 July 2003, p. 1), by Article 13(2) of the Act concerning the conditions of accession of 16 April 2003 (OJ L 236 of 23 September 2003, p. 37), Council Decisions of 19 and 26 April 2004 (OJ L 132 of 29 April 2004, pp 1 and 5, and OJ L 194 of 2 June 2004, p. 3 (corrigendum)), Council Decision of 2 November 2004 establishing the European Union Civil Service Tribunal (OJ L 333 of 9 November 2004, p. 7 and OJ L 103 of 20 April 2007, p. 54), by Council Decision of 3 October 2005 (OJ L 266 of 11 October 2005, p. 60), by Article 11 of the Act concerning the conditions of accession of 25 April 2005 (OJ L 157 of 21 June 2005, p. 203) and by Council Decision of 20 December 2007 (OJ L 24 of 29 January 2008, p. 42), paras. 41 and 64; *Íñigo Valverde Mordt v. Court of Justice of the European Communities, Case T-156/89, ECR [1991], p. II-407*, paras. 121 and 123; and *Pachtitis v Commission, Case F-35/08*, para. 64-65.

360 *Guido van Hecken v. Economic and Social Committee, Case T-158/89, ECR [1991], p. II-1341*, paras. 22-25.

361 *Magdalena Allgayer née Parzinger v. European Parliament, Case 74/77, ECR [1978], p. 977*, para. 7.

362 *Vandevyvere v. Parliament, Case 23/64*, p. 166.

363 *Georges Kolivas v. Commission of the European Communities, Case 40/86, ECR [1987], p. 2643*, para. 15; *Gallone v. Council, Case T-132/89*, para. 28.

364 *ECJ Statute*, para. 102.

365 *Vincenzo Le Voci v. Council of the European Union, Case T-371/03, ECR-SC [2005], p. I-A-209, II-957*, para. 102.

366 For more on the notice of competition, see below, section 3.2.1.3.

367 *Le Voci v. Council, Case T-371/03*, para. 50.

368 *Van Hecken v. ESC, Case T-158/89*, paras. 22-25.

> *The system laid down in ... the Staff Regulations would be deprived of its substance if the Selection Board could ... apply requirements which do not appear in the notice of competition and, therefore, go beyond a comparative examination of the candidates on the basis of the qualifications required. Moreover, such an interpretation would be incompatible with the division which exists, between the powers of the appointing authority, on the one hand, and those of the Selection Board, on the other, whereby the Appointing Authority has a broad discretion in drawing up the requirements of the competition whilst the Selection Board is bound by these requirements in carrying out its task under ... the Staff Regulations.*[369]

The division of power between the appointing authority and the selection board contributes to the objectivity of the competition process.

The relevant selection board must also in advance establish criteria based on which the assessment of candidates and their qualifications will take place so that the objectivity and non-arbitrariness of the assessment is ensured.[370] Furthermore, the assessment of candidates may not be based on information unknown to the candidate (from his personal file, if relevant, or otherwise brought to the candidate's attention), otherwise the relevant selection board would act in contradiction to Article 26, concerning the personal file of an official, as well as Article 43, concerning periodical reports which must be communicated to the official who is entitled to make comments on it.[371] An assessment based on information unknown to the candidate may constitute a reason for annulment of such assessment, as happened, for example, in *Rittweger*. In that case, the relevant decisions were adopted on basis of assessments which were contained, in respect of each internal candidate, in a telex messages sent by the Commission departments in Luxemburg. These assessments, which in the applicant's case contained unfavorable assessments strikingly different from the assessments included in her periodical report, were not included in her personal file and neither were they brought to her attention. The ECJ considered such procedure to be vitiated by illegality and annulled the decision at issue.[372] The role of personal files and the fact that factors on which the assessment of the selection board is based must be known to the candidates were confirmed in a number of other cases brought before the ECJ which consistently emphasized the candidates' right to defend themselves.[373]

Another important limitation of the discretion of the selection board, safeguarding the transparency, objectivity and impartiality of the process, is of a procedural nature. The selection board is obliged to give reasons for most of their decisions, be it in some instances only in a summary form. As stated by the ECJ in *Marenco*:

---

[369] Ibid., para. 24.

[370] *Morina v. Parliament, Case 11/65*, p. 1040.

[371] *Rittweger v. Commission, Case 21/70*, paras. 36-40.

[372] Ibid., paras. 29-41.

[373] See, for example, *Brasseur v. Parliament, Case 88/71*, paras. 16-17; *Sorani and others v. Commission of the European Communities, Case 293/84, ECR [1986], p. 967*, paras. 17-20 and *Hermanus Adams and others v. Commission of the European Communities, Case 294/84, ECR [1986], p. 977*, paras. 22-25.

[T]he proceedings of a Selection Board involve at least two distinct stages, that is, first consideration of the applications, in order to sort out the candidates allowed to enter the competition and, secondly, considerations of the abilities of the candidates for the post in order to draw up a list of those suitable.

If the second stage above all consists of making comparison and is, therefore, governed by the principle of secrecy inherent in the proceedings of a Selection Board, the first consists, in particular in a competition on the basis of qualifications, of a comparison of the qualifications proceeded by the candidates with those required by the notice of competition.

As this comparison is carried out on the basis of information which is objective and, moreover, known to each of the candidates in so far as it concerns his case, sufficient reasons must be given for the results arrived at.[374]

Purpose of this duty is, on the one hand, to enable the judiciary to review the legality of the decision at issue and, on the other hand, to provide the person concerned with information necessary to recognize whether or not the decision in question is well founded.[375]

The duty of the selection board to state reasons exists in both stages of their involvement in the selection process: first, in rejecting candidates' applications which do not fulfill the conditions of the notice of competition, and second, in the stage involving the consideration of abilities of candidates leading to drawing up a reserve list.[376] In principle, the statement of reasons must be notified to the person adversely affected by the decision together with this decision, i.e. at the same time.[377] Although the absence of a statement of reasons cannot be remedied by the fact that a candidate gets acquainted with the reasons during the Court proceedings, the situation is different in cases of an *adequate* statement of reasons. In such cases, the ECJ ruled that if the details provided during the proceedings enable the ECJ to exercise its power of judicial review (which, as mentioned above, is one of the functions of the duty to state reasons) and the reasons are correct and they do not exceed discretion of the authorities in their value judgments, the ECJ will not annul the decision at hand.[378] On the other hand, a total absence of a statement of reasons cannot be remedied by explanations provided after a legal action has started before

[374] *Antonio Marcato v. Commission of the European Communities, Case 44-71, ECR [1972], p. 427*, paras. 19-21.

[375] *Bernard Michel v. European Parliament, Case 195/80, ECR [1981], p. 2861*, para. 22; *Picciolo v. European Parliament, Case 111/83*, para. 20; *Hanning v. Parliament, Case T-37/89*, para. 39; *Volger v. Parliament, Case T-52/90*, para. 40.

[376] *Marcato v. Commission, Case 44-71*, para. 19; *Kalavros v. ECJ, Joined cases T-160/89 and T-161/89*,para. 68; and*Marcato v. Commission, Case 44-71*, paras. 19 -21; *Armelle Detti v. Court of Justice of the European Communities, Case 144/82, ECR [1983], p. 2421*, para. 27; *Kalavros v. ECJ, Joined cases T-160/89 and T-161/89*, para. 68.

[377] *Michel v. Parliament, Case 195/80*, para. 22.

[378] *Hanning v. Parliament, Case T-37/89*, para. 42.

the Court because such explanation no longer fulfills its function.[379] As stated by the CFI in *Volger*:

> *The commencement of proceedings ... puts an end to the possibility of the appointing authority' s regularizing its decision by a reasoned reply rejecting the complaint.*[380]

In proceedings with a large number of candidates the selection board is permitted to use summarized statements of reasons for the refusal to admit a candidate to a competition. However, it is not allowed to make a mere reference to the condition which was not met. Such reference is inadequate since it is 'not capable of providing the person concerned with a sufficient indication to allow him to know whether the refusal is well founded or on the other hand whether it is vitiated by a defect which would make it possible to contest its legality'.[381] On the other hand, the selection board may take into account the different levels and types of competition, and more particularly the number of candidates, when considering in how far the statement of reasons must be provided, otherwise it could be left with an 'intolerable burden' on itself and on the personnel offices.[382] In cases of a 'very large number of applications', the selection board may initially provide merely information on the criteria for selection and the result thereof and leave individual explanations until later for those candidates who expressly request them.[383]

Decisions of the selection board cannot be annulled, amended or revoked by the appointing authority. This is a consequence of the division of power between the two authorities, which is an important safeguard of the objectivity of the competition process, as mentioned above. Nonetheless, the appointing authority may - and is even required to - review the legality of the admission of a candidate to the competition. If it finds that the admission was illegal, the appointing authority may not appoint such candidate.[384] This ensures that illegalities caused by the selection

---

379 *Volger v. Parliament, Case T-52/90*, para. 40.

380 Ibid., para. 40.

381 *Enrico M. Salerno, Xavier Authié and Giuseppe Massangioli v. Commission of the European Communities, Joined cases 4, 19 and 28/78, ECR [1978], p. 2403*, para. 29. See also, for example, *Dorothea Kobor, née Sonne, v. Commission of the European Communities, Case 112/78, ECR [1979], p. 1573*, para. 16; *John Szemerey v. Commission of the European Communities, Case 178/78, ECR [1979], p. 2855*, para. 8; *Francesco Bonu v. Council of the European Communities, Case 89/79, ECR [1980], p. 553*, paras. 5-6; *Juan Jaenicke Cendoya v. Commission of the European Communities, Case 108/88, ECR [1989], p. 2711*, para. 10.

382 *Bonu v. Council, Case 89/79*, para. 6. See also, for example, *Michel v. Parliament, Case 195/80*, para. 25; *Rudy Verzyck v. Commission of the European Communities, Case 225/82, ECR [1983], p. 1991*, para. 16; *Giovanni Sergio and others v. Commission of the European Communities, Joined cases 64, 71 to 73 and 78/86, ECR [1988], p. 1399*, para. 50.

383 *Michel v. Parliament, Case 195/80*, para. 27. See also *Verzyck v. Commission, Case 225/82*, para. 16; *Sergio and others v. Commission, Joined cases 64, 71 to 73 and 78/86*, para. 50. Note that the selection board is not obliged to state reasons when the requests of the candidates do not seek additional individual explanations but rather a reconsideration of the selection board's decision not to admit the candidates at issue to the competition. - *Patricia Belardinelli and others v. Court of Justice of the European Communities, Case 225/87, ECR [1989], p. 2353*, para. 10.

384 *Claudia Delloye and others v. Commission of the European Communities, Case T-44/92, ECR [1993], p. II-221*, para. 23; *Salerno and others v. Commission, Joined cases 4, 19 and 28/78*, summary point 1.; and

board are remedied during the competition process and do not lead to illegal overall results. This, in itself a useful rule, may however result in the appointing authority 'correcting' inconvenient decisions taken by the selection board. Clearly, this should not be permitted.

The proceedings of the selection board as such are also unchallengeable before the ECJ. As ruled by the ECJ in *Morina*, the selection board is not a body empowered to take decisions binding upon officials and its proceedings are merely preparatory acts. The legality of such acts may therefore be questioned only in applications against decisions to which these acts of the selection board were preliminary.[385] Also, the deliberations, for example the examination of candidates' ability, of the selection board are 'covered by the cloak of secrecy' and cannot, in principle, be subjected to control by the ECJ, except of cases of obvious infringements of the rules governing the proceedings of the selection board.[386] The ECJ emphasized on several occasions that the secrecy of the proceedings of the selection board was introduced in order to guarantee the independence of this body and the objectivity of its work by 'protecting [it] from all external interference and pressures whether these come from the Community Administration itself or the candidates concerned or third parties'.[387] Consequently, there is no obligation to reveal attitudes of individual members of the selection board or details relating to individual or comparative assessment of candidates.[388] However, disclosure of objective facts, and especially the criteria which constituted the basis for the assessment of candidates, falls outside the scope of the secrecy of the selection board.[389] This enables the judiciary to asses whether the rules governing the proceedings of the selection board were not breached or whether a manifest error or misuse of powers has not occurred. These are the exceptions recognized as capable of leading to the annulment of decisions of the selection board by the ECJ.[390]

Regarding the composition of the selection board, it consists of a chairman, appointed by the appointing authority, and of members designated by the appointing authority and by the Staff Committee, each of them appointing the same number of members. Members of the selection board are chosen from among the officials with function group and the grade at least equal to that of the post which is to be filled.[391] The involvement of staff representatives in the selection board is one of the important safeguards of the objectivity and independence of the selection process.

Hartmut Schwiering v. Court of Auditors of the European Communities, Case 142/85, ECR [1986], p. 3177, paras. 19-20.

385 *Morina v. Parliament, Case 11/65*, p. 1039.

386 *Anna-Maria Campogrande and others v. Commission of the European Communities, Joined cases 112, 144 and 145-73, ECR [1974], p. 957*, para. 53.

387 *Bonu v. Council, Case 89/79*, para. 5. See also, for example, *Kolivas v. Commission, Case 40/86*, para. 18 and *Le Voci v. Council, Case T-371/03*, para. 123.

388 *Kolivas v. Commission, Case 40/86*, para. 11.

389 *Bonu v. Council, Case 89/79*, para. 5.

390 *Campogrande and others v. Commission, Joined cases 112, 144 and 145-73*, para. 53; *Kolivas v. Commission, Case 40/86*, para. 11.

391 *EU Staff Regulations*, Annex III, Article 3. See also *Deboeck v. Commission, Case 90/74*, para. 34; *Valverde Mordt v. ECJ, Case T-156/89*, para. 109. In these cases the ECJ emphasized that members of a Selection

Many other safeguards can be deducted from rather extensive case law which relates to the composition of EU selection boards. Its importance has been often stressed by the ECJ which noted that the composition of these boards must ensure objective assessment of the candidates. Therefore, for example, the members of the relevant selection board must possess certain specific abilities which enable them to judge professional qualities of the candidates.[392] Naturally, which abilities are required from the members of a particular selection board will depend on the post for which the competition is held. For example, in *Valverde Modrt*, where a post of a reviser was at issue, the CFI considered that the members of the selection board at issue had to have a good understanding of the language in which the candidate would be required to revise, some legal knowledge and experience of the revision of legal texts. However, the CFI noted that it did not mean that *each member* of the selection board must have had a perfect knowledge of the relevant language. Furthermore, it was sufficient that the experience of the revision of legal texts existed 'within the selection board'.[393] In *Gallone* the CFI approved the selection board at issue even though not all of its members knew the language of certain candidates since the candidates' papers had been translated and the selection board had the translation at its disposal. The CFI did not consider the fact that the papers had been translated before they were marked to be a violation of the principle of equal treatment of the candidates.[394]

The ECJ is also of the opinion that composition of the selection board is not unlawful when its member happens to be a superior of one of the candidates or to be acquainted with him. In *Burban* it ruled that even in such a situation the selection board was not allowed to act contrary to the clear requirements of the competition notice binding upon all members of the selection board, including the candidate's superior and/or acquaintance.[395] Furthermore, the mere possibility that a member of the selection board might have been able to identify the various candidates, for example from their handwriting and language combination, as was alleged in *Valverde Mordt*, is in itself not sufficient to conclude that the composition of the selection board at hand was unlawful or that it did not guarantee an objective assessment of the candidates' abilities.[396]

The appointment of a member of the selection board is in itself not challengeable before the ECJ since it is merely a preparatory measure.[397] The ECJ held in *Weighardt* that, in staff cases, preparatory acts were not capable of being annulled and could not be contested as such. One may effectively file a complaint against such preparatory measure only in an action directed against a final measure, which is capable of

Board do not need to be officials and only if they are, they must be chosen from officials whose grade is at least equal to that of the post to be filled.

392 *Georges Marcopoulos v. Court of Justice of the European Communities, Joined cases T-32/89 and T-39/89, ECR [1990], p. II-281*, para. 37; *Valverde Mordt v. ECJ, Case T-156/89*, para. 105-106.

393 *Valverde Mordt v. ECJ, Case T-156/89*, para. 106.

394 *Gallone v. Council, Case T-132/89*, paras. 35 and 36.

395 *Jean-Louis Burban v. European Parliament, Case C-255/90 P, ECR [1992], p. I-2253*, para. 15.

396 *Valverde Mordt v. ECJ, Case T-156/89*, para. 110.

397 *Marcopoulos v. ECJ, Joined cases T-32/89 and T-39/89*, para. 22.

being annulled.[398] This means that a decision on the appointment of members of the selection board may be contested only in an action against the decision concluding the recruitment procedure.[399]

In carrying out its duties, the selection board may be assisted by one or more examiners who in such cases serve in an advisory capacity.[400] As noted by the ECJ, an intervention of private undertakings in the organization of practical tests does not put the legality of the competition in question. The ECJ stressed that such intervention was authorized by the *EU Staff Regulations*, an in particular its Annex III, subject to the condition that the intervention is 'in an advisory capacity and that the Selection Board regains ultimate control over the procedure and its discretionary power'.[401] Furthermore, as stressed by the ECJ, the cases listed in Annex III of the *EU Staff Regulations* are not exhaustively enumerating situation in which the selection board may have recourse to examiners to assist it. Especially when there are a large number of candidates, the selection board could face problems with completing its work within reasonable time if it could not employ examiners serving in an advisory capacity.[402]

3.2.1.2. Internal competition

Having explained which bodies are involved in the competition proceedings, this section devotes its attention to the analysis of the first type of competitions held for the recruitment of EU staff, namely the internal competition. As explained above, internal competition is a competition open only to persons who already are in EU service as permanent officials or as temporary staff.[403] Before 2004, there was no explicit referral to temporary staff in this respect in the *EU Staff Regulations*.[404] It was the ECJ who recognized the right of this staff to participate in internal competitions. In *Rauch*, where a challenge of the legality of the admission of non-permanent staff to the internal competition was made for the first time, the ECJ ruled that:

> *The expression "competition internal to the institution", taken as it stands, means any persons employed by the institution, in whatever capacity.*
>
> *This interpretation is confirmed by the aim assigned to the recruitment procedure by Article 27 of the Staff Regulations namely "securing for the institution the serv-*

---

[398] *Kurt Weighardt v. Commission of the EAEC, Case 11/64, ECR [1965], p. 285*, p. 298.

[399] *Marcopoulos v. ECJ, Joined cases T-32/89 and T-39/89*, paras. 21-22.

[400] *EU Staff Regulations*, Annex III, Article 3

[401] *Deboeck v. Commission, Case 90/74*, para. 38. See also *Augusta Agneessens and others v. Commission of the European Communities, Case 122/77, ECR [1978], p. 2085*, ', paras. 8-9; *Salerno and others v. Commission, Joined cases 4, 19 and 28/78*, paras. 14-15 and *Le Voci v. Council, Case T-371/03*, paras. 100-101.

[402] *Agneessens v. Commission, Case 122/77*, para. 8; *Salerno and others v. Commission, Joined cases 4, 19 and 28/78*, paras. 14-15; *Gallone v. Council, Case T-132/89*, para. 28, *Le Voci v. Council, Case T-371/03*, para. 101.

[403] *EU Staff Regulations*, Article 29(1)(b).

[404] See *EU Staff Regulations and Conditions of Employment of Other Servants of 1998*, Article 29(1)(b).

> *ices of officials of the highest standard of ability, efficiency and integrity". This aim involves the necessity of recruiting officials on as broad a basis as possible.*[405]

Hence, persons employed by the European institutions had to be admitted to the internal competitions, subject to the condition that they are employed by the relevant institution at the time when the competition is initiated.[406]

In another important case *Bataille* the CFI decided, in addition, that internal rules restricting access of temporary staff to the internal competition were incompatible with the *EU Staff Regulations*.[407] The applicants in this case were all temporary agents employed at the European Parliament. They challenged Parliament's decisions prohibiting them from taking part in an internal competition opened for the recruitment of a number of permanent posts. Parliament's decisions were based on internal rules adopted by the Bureau of the Parliament which stipulated that, in principle, no one could be appointed a permanent official without appearing on a reserve list that would be a result of an external open competition. The internal rules of the European Parliament, furthermore, provided that temporary staff who had been recruited otherwise than from such reserve lists could not participate in internal competitions, unless they obtained a special authorizing decision.[408] Contracts of temporary staff contained a clause based on which these staff had to acknowledge that they would not take part in internal competitions taking place in future.[409] The applicants argued that both the internal rules and the relevant parts of their contracts of employment were incompatible with the *EU Staff Regulations* and, therefore, unlawful. The CFI confirmed the previous case law and stated that, in principle, temporary staff were entitled to take part in competitions that were internal to their institutions and that no distinction could be made among various categories of temporary staff.[410] The CFI acknowledged the Parliament's claim that the institutions enjoyed a wide discretion with regard to the organization of competitions but stressed that the decision at issue to refuse the access of temporary staff to internal competition had been taken not as a result of the exercise of such discretion in the organization of a specific competition, but that it had been taken on a general basis by adopting rules concerning all competitions within the Parliament. Such general rules were, according to the CFI, incompatible with the *EU Staff Regulations* as they did not comply with the conditions of Annex III thereof requiring appointing authorities, when organizing internal competitions, to specify diplomas and other evidence of formal qualifications required for the vacant posts. The requirement included in the internal rules of the European Parliament was, in the view of the CFI, not necessarily linked with the possession of certain diplomas

[405] *Rauch v. Commission, Case 16/64*, page 142. See also *Giannini v. Commission, Case 265/81*, para. 7 and *Bataille v. Parliament, Case T-56/89*.

[406] *Rauch v. Commission, Case 16/64*, p. 144. The ECJ also held that it was irrelevant whether the employment had continued or expired during the competition proceedings. The decisive moment was the time of initiation of the competition. – Ibid.

[407] *Bataille v. Parliament, Case T-56/89*.

[408] Ibid., paras. 3 and 4.

[409] Ibid., para. 6.

[410] Ibid., para. 41.

or other evidence of formal qualifications but aimed at exclusion of the possibility of establishment of temporary staff on the basis of an internal competition. In the view of the CFI, such exclusion did not correspond to the objective of internal competitions - an increase in the number of possible applications enhancing the appointment of officials of the highest standards of ability as envisaged in Article 27 of the *EU Staff Regulations*, but could rather work to the contrary to this objective - by excluding candidates with the same or possibly better qualifications than those of other candidates admitted to the competition.[411]

The ECJ has thus interpreted the scope of internal competitions very broadly. Its clear purpose was to include as many potential candidates as possible, thereby enhancing chances that the best available person was eventually selected. As important as it was, this broad interpretation lost its relevance under the 2004 amendment of the *EU Staff Regulations*. Pursuant to the present version of Article 29(1)(b), internal competitions are opened only to officials and temporary staff engaged under Article 2 of the *EU Conditions of Employment of Other Servants*, i.e. not to other categories of other servants, such as contract or local staff.[412] Given the fact that temporary staff constitute a relatively small proportion of the Commission staff, some five per cent, the amendment of the *EU Staff Regulations* of 2004 has limited the pool of persons who may gain permanent appointment through internal competition to a significant extent.[413]

Said that, it must be stressed that the used of internal competition for recruitment of permanent staff is not unproblematic. Although internal competition is a competition, it is less competitive than open competition. This is due to the limited number of persons eligible to participate in internal competition. The position of temporary staff in internal competition is thus necessarily easier than it would be in an open competition. Further, while the general procedure and tests used in internal competition are similar to those in open competitions, it can hardly be denied that at least some part(s) of the selection process is aimed at eliminating extremely large numbers of participants, something that is not needed in the case of internal competitions where the number of participants is significantly lower. The position of candidates in internal competition is thus more advantageous compared to candidates who needed to go through open competition.

An additional, and arguably more important, argument against the practice of granting permanent appointments through internal competition is the problem of candidates being personally acquainted with selecting officials. This has been severely criticized in the past. For example, the EU Committee of Independent Experts of 1999 stated:

---

[411] Ibid., paras. 45–48.

[412] *EU Staff Regulations*, Article 29(1)(b). Note also special provisions for internal competition organized solely for cabinet staff in Article 29(3) and (4).

[413] According to the last available data, in 2008, there were 1889 temporary staff members serving in the European Commission. The total number of staff was 38.765. - *Commission's Human Resources Report 2009*, p. 30.

> *in such competitions there is always a risk of there being a tendency to 'keep things in the family', given that candidates may be known personally to the examiners. Consideration should thus be given to their abolition, or at least to the introduction of mechanisms which ensure genuine transparency and selectivity, thus guarding against this unwanted tendency.*[414]

Recruitment of non-permanent staff to permanent posts through internal competition has thus generally been considered not only as less fair but also less transparent and impartial than recruitment through open competition. This conclusion stands despite the opinion of the ECJ in *Rauch* where the Court considered that internal competition needed to be open to all non-permanent staff, not only to permanent officials. The Court's reasoning was based on the idea of broadening up the pool of potential candidates for a specific vacant post and on the fact that the then relevant version of the *EU Staff Regulations* did not exclude non-permanent staff from internal competition but referred to 'staff' in general'.[415] Concerns as to the fairness vis-à-vis external candidates and transparency of the selection process where selecting officials personally know some of the candidates remain thus important arguments against allowing non-permanent staff to acquire permanent appointment in the European Commission. In the end, non-permanent staff seeking permanent position can always take open competitions.

In 1999, at the time of the issuance of the report of the Committee of Independent Experts, the European Commission declared it would not hold internal competitions for granting permanent appointments to non-permanent staff in future. The Committee of Independent Experts took note of this Commission decision and recommended amendment of the *EU Staff Regulations* in this sense. Unfortunately, this has not happened and the possibility of organizing internal competitions for one category of non-permanent staff, namely temporary staff, remained in the *EU Staff Regulations*, adding two new specific provisions for temporary staff serving in cabinets and in the European Parliament.[416] At present, internal competitions are also being organized in practice.[417]

With regard to the situations in which internal competition may be held, it has been already explained that when internal competition is organized in order to fill a specific vacancy, it may only be held if the vacant post cannot be filled by transfer, appointment of an official serving in AST function group to an AD post, promotion or by a transfer of a staff member from another institution.[418] This priority rule is, to a

[414] *Second Report on Reform of the Commission of 1999, Volume II*, para. 6.5.23.

[415] See above, section 3.2.1.2.

[416] *EU Staff Regulations*, Article 29(1)(b), (3) and (4). Note that neither the Explanatory Memorandum to the new *EU Staff Regulations*, nor its Preamble, provide explanation with regard to the retention of internal competition or the introduction of the limitation of the pool of staff eligible to take part in internal competition. - *Proposal for a Council Regulation Amending the Staff Regulations of Officials and the Conditions of Employment of Other Servants of the European Communities, COM(2002) 213 final* 24.04.2002, OJ C 291E , 26.11.2002, p. 33-135, and *EU Staff Regulations*, Preamble.

[417] See, for example, European Commission, *Notice of Internal Competition, Heads of Unit AD12 (COM/INT/EU27/09/AD12)*, Section III.2.

[418] *EU Staff Regulations*, Article 4.

certain extent softened by the fact that it is up to the appointing authority to decide which method will be used in each specific case. This authority has, once again, a wide discretion in deciding whether to hold internal competition or whether to employ another method, such as promotion or transfer. Even where there is only one candidate suitable for promotion, who could be directly appointed to the vacant post, i.e. without the need to conduct any selection process, the appointing authority may still decide to hold an internal competition.[419] As stated by the ECJ:

> *In such a case the Appointing Authority, since it had available for consideration only one candidate suitable for promotion, may have all the more reason for holding an internal competition since it may rightly consider that it does not have a sufficiently wide choice to ensure recruitment in accordance as far as possible with the requirements of the post to be filled.*[420]

On the other hand, when the appointing authority decides to fill a vacant post by promotion or transfer, it is under no obligation to consider candidates who would be eligible to enter the internal competition if it were held.[421]

As also already noted, internal competitions may be organized for one EU institution or for more institutions.[422] All internal competitions must be advertised within the institutions of both existing European Communities with the same time-limits.[423] As most procedural rules applicable to internal competitions are the same as those that apply to open competitions, they are further discussed in the following section dealing with open competition.

3.2.1.3. Open competition

Competition notice

The open competition, also referred to as *concours*, is opened to every one who meets the requirements set in the competition notice, which is a notice containing all necessary specifications of the relevant competition, including all the conditions the potential candidates need to comply with, such as degrees, expertise or language proficiency. The competition notice is drawn by the relevant appointing authority after consultation with the Joint Committee.[424] It is a legally binding document which must be obeyed by all persons and authorities involved in the competition procedure.

When competition is held to fill a specific vacancy (i.e. when it is internal competition), the competition notice must correspond with the vacancy notice, which pre-

---

[419] *Küster v. Parliament, Case 123/75*, paras. 13 and 16.

[420] Ibid., para. 17.

[421] *Giannini v. Commission, Case 265/81*, para. 11 and para. 2 of the summary.

[422] *EU Staff Regulations*, Article 29(3) and Annex III, Article 1(b).

[423] Ibid., Annex III, Article 1(3).

[424] Ibid., Annex III, Article 1(1).

cedes the competition notice.[425] The vacancy notice sets up the framework for the recruitment procedure, especially by defining the nature of the vacant post and by setting out the qualifications and knowledge which will, in the interest of service, be required from the candidates. The vacancy notice is drawn up before the first stage of the recruitment procedure begins, i.e. before consideration is given to the type of recruitment procedure which would be the most suitable for finding a candidate with a highest standard of efficiency, ability and integrity.[426] As noted by the ECJ, the vacancy notice, as well as the notice of competition, 'constitutes the legal framework which the appointing authority imposes on itself'.[427] Any special conditions of eligibility for the post must therefore be taken into account when the vacancy notice is drawn.[428]

According to the ECJ, both the vacancy notice and the notice of competition have the same function, namely 'to give those interested the most accurate information possible about the conditions of eligibility for the post to enable them to judge whether they should apply for it'.[429] The competition notice constitutes furthermore 'the legal and final form for the decision on the organization of a competition'.[430] It is also 'the legal basis and the basis for assessment by the selection board'.[431] The relevant selection board is bound by the competition notice and its wording as published.[432] Hence, although relevant authorities - the selection board, the appointing

---

425 As held by the ECJ, the objective of the requirement concerning the sequence of the two notices is to enable the appointing authority to examine, before the competition procedure begins, whether the post should be filled by transfer or promotion. - *Deboeck v. Commission, Case 90/74*, para. 13.

426 *Ferrero v. Parliament, Case C-304/97 P*, para. 31.

427 *Erik Dan Frederiksen v. European Parliament, Case T-169/89, ECR [1991], p. II-1403*, para. 67.

428 *Ferrero v. Parliament, Case C-304/97 P*, para. 32. In *Grassi* the ECJ has ruled that the conditions of eligibility for the post to be filled may not be decided upon by the relevant authority after the vacancy notice was published. When the appointing authority finds, after the publication of the vacancy notice, that the conditions of eligibility included in that notice differ from those needed by the service, it may only withdraw the original vacancy notice and publish a new, amended one instead. - *Grassi v. Council, Case 188/73*, paras. 39 and 43. See also *Erik van der Stijl and Geoffrey Cullington v. Commission of the European Communities, Joined cases 341/85, 251, 258, 259, 262 and 266/86, 222 and 232/87, ECR [1989], p. 511*, para. 51 and *Frederiksen v. Parliament, Case T-169/89*, para. 67; *Ferrero v. Parliament, Case C-304/97 P*, para. 33. Furthermore, when the appointing authority decides to change the recruitment procedure and proceed, for example, from an internal procedure to one open to external candidates and to include automatically candidates who have applied in the internal procedure, regard must be paid to the conditions laid down by the vacancy notice and those in the recruitment notice, too. - *Kotzonis v. Economic and Social Committee, Case T-586/93*, para. 45.

429 *Grassi v. Council, Case 188/73*, para. 40. See also *Van der Stijl and Cullington v. Commission, Joined cases 341/85, 251, 258, 259, 262 and 266/86, 222 and 232/87*, para. 51. For the function of the notice of competition, see for example *Andrée Anselme, née Heirwegh and Roger Constant v. Commission of the European Communities, Case 255/78, ECR [1979], p. 2323*, para. 9, *Ruske v. Commission, Case 67/81*, para. 9; *Willy Seghers v. Council of the European Communities, Case T-69/92, ECR [1993], p. II-651*, para. 34.

430 *Campogrande and others v. Commission, Joined cases 112, 144 and 145-73*, para. 66.

431 *Le Voci v. Council, Case T-371/03*, para. 50.

432 *Ruske v. Commission, Case 67/81*, para. 9, *Vassilis Mavridis v. European Parliament, Case 289/81, ECR [1983], p. 1731*, para. 21; *Delloye and others v. Commission, Case T-44/92*, para. 22. Note that the relevant selection board may not act contrary to the wording in the competition notice even in a situation when different but erroneous information on the conditions included in the competition notice was given to candidates by an official who was not authorized to change the provisions of the competition notice. Such situation occurred, for example, in *Burban* where the applicant claimed that he had been

authority - have a wide discretion in comparing the candidates' merits, this discretion must be exercised 'within the self-imposed limits contained in the notice...'.[433] This means, for example, that the selection board may not exclude a candidate for the competition arguing that he does not satisfy a condition which was not stated in the notice.[434] As noted by the CFI in *Van Hecken*:

> *The system... would be deprived of its substance if the Selection Board could... apply requirements which do not appear in the notice of competition and, therefore, go beyond a comparative examination of the candidates... Moreover, such an interpretation would be incompatible with the division which exists between the powers of the appointing authority, on the one hand, and those of the Selection Board, on the other, whereby the Appointing Authority has a broad discretion in drawing up the requirements of the competition whilst the Selection Board is bound by these requirements in carrying out its task under Article 30 of the Staff Regulations.*[435]

The requirement to comply with the (wording of the) competition (and vacancy) notice, which is imposed on the authorities involved in the competition, is one of the guarantees of the transparency and objectivity of this type of selection process. Its importance is proven also by the relatively large number of staff cases in which it has been discussed and further clarified.[436]

---

given incorrect information with regard to the submission of documents relevant to his application for a vacant post. The CFI, and in the appeal also the ECJ, considered that the conditions laid down in the competition notice had been clear, precise and unconditional and that the applicant had had duty to 'read carefully the conditions in question', especially since the notice of competition was entirely unambiguous. - *Jean-Louis Burban v. European Parliament, Case T-133/89, ECR [1990], p. II-245*, para. 36 and *Burban v. Parliament, Case C-255/90 P*, paras. 10 and 12. Furthermore, in cases where it does not appear from a 'careful reading' of the notice that, for example, a theoretical training constitutes one of the conditions of eligibility for the post to be filled, such condition may not be imposed on the candidates in the course of the selection procedure. - *Ruske v. Commission, Case 67/81*, paras. 10-12 (in case of a notice of competition).

433 *Grassi v. Council, Case 188/73*, para. 38. See also *Ruske v. Commission, Case 67/81*, paras. 9-12; *Fischer v. Commission, Case T-58/91*, para. 67.

434 *Van Hecken v. ESC, Case T-158/89*, para. 25.

435 Ibid., para. 24.

436 For example, with regard to the conditions for admission to the competition and, in particular, the conditions concerning professional qualifications and experience, the competition notice may use a general formula, such as the one contained in Article 5 of the *EU Staff Regulations* which sets out qualification requirements for each function group and each grade, or even just repeat the wording of that provision, and leave it to the selection board to judge in each individual case whether the qualifications and experience of the candidate, as evidenced by provided documents, correspond to the level required by the *EU Staff Regulations* for the vacant post. - *Marcato v. Commission, Case 44-71*, para. 14. See also *Belardinelli and others v. ECJ, Case 225/87*, para. 13. Both the vacancy notice and the notice of competition may also include special details of specific qualifications required for the posts to be filled and add them to the general requirements laid down by the relevant institution. - *Kurrer v. Council, Case 33/67*, p. 135. The notices may also impose more rigorous conditions than those corresponding to the minimum requirements for post laid down by the *EU Staff Regulations*. As held by the ECJ, Article 5 of the *EU Staff Regulations* provides only a general definition of the minimum level which is required for an official of a specific category and drawn up according to the nature of the duties corresponding to the post, and it does not concern conditions of recruitment. The conditions of recruitment are established in Article 29 of the *EU Staff Regulations* and in Annex III thereto. These

It should be noted, however, that the competition notice does not need to prove that all the rules which concern the competition procedure have been complied with. It only needs to ensure that the competition is sufficiently publicized. It, therefore, cannot be argued that, for example, the competition notice is void because it did not state whether consideration was given to filling post by other means, such as promotion or transfer.[437]

Any irregularities in the competition notice may be challenged before the ECJ but legal actions must be brought in 'good time'. The ECJ is of the opinion that it would be contrary to the principles of legal certainty, legitimate expectation and sound administration to allow challenges of a competition notice 'long after it had been published and after most or all of the operation carried our in connection with the competition had already taken place'.[438] On the other hand, if one fails to challenge the notice of competition within the set time-limits, one can still contest irregularities that have occurred during the competition, even if the origin of such irregularities could be found in the wording of the competition notice.[439]

Each notice of competition is published in the Official Journal of the European Union.[440] In practice, the notice is also published in press and on the internet site of the EPSO which organizes all competitions. It goes without saying that broad publication of all competitions contributes directly to the transparency of this type of selection process. All open competitions are also advertised internally, within the EU institutions, since staff already employed by the institutions may participate in the open competition, too.[441] Obviously, this is especially the case of either non-permanent staff who wishes to acquire a permanent position in the EU civil service or permanent staff who aspire promotion.

Screening

Candidates who submit the application form for an open competition are first scrutinized by the relevant appointing authority. This authority subsequently draws a

---

provisions do not prevent the notice of competition from setting out conditions more demanding than those corresponding to the minimum requirements resulting from the classification of posts disregarding whether such conditions are established in order to fill a specific vacancy or to constitute a reserve for posts in a certain category.- *Willy Orlandi v. Commission of the European Communities, Case 117/78, ECR [1979], p. 1613*, para. 21 and *Szemerey v. Commission, Case 178/78*, para. 3. See also *David Lipman v. Commission of the European Communities, Case 143/82, ECR [1983], p. 1301*, para. 7; *Cendoya v. Commission, Case 108/88*, para. 25 and *Ana Fernandes Ferreira de Freitas v Commission of the European Communities, Case T-2/90, ECR [1991], p. II-103*, para. 54. In addition, Article 1(1)(d) of the Annex III only specifies the headings which each notice of competition must contain, namely the diplomas and other evidence of formal qualifications or the degree of experience, and not the content of these headings. - *Lipman v. Commission, Case 143/82*, para. 7. Consequently, the ECJ was also able to hold that the notice might require possession of a university degree or diploma *in addition to* experience and not only instead of it. - *Szemerey v. Commission, Case 178/78*, para. 5.

[437] *Cesare Alfieri v. European Parliament, Case 35/64, ECR [1965], p. 261*, p. 267.

[438] *Adams and others v. Commission, Case 294/84*, para. 17. See also *Sergio and others v. Commission, Joined cases 64, 71 to 73 and 78/86*, para. 13; *Burban v. Parliament, Case T-133/89*, para. 48.

[439] *Sergio and others v. Commission, Joined cases 64, 71 to 73 and 78/86*, para. 15.

[440] *EU Staff Regulations*, Annex III, Article 1(1) and (2).

[441] Ibid., Annex III, Article 1(3) and *EU Staff Regulations*, Article 4.

list of candidates satisfying the basis conditions for the appointment into the EU civil service set up in Article 28(a), (b) and (c) of the *EU Staff Regulations*. As mentioned above, requirements of Article 28 relate to the nationality of one of the EU Member States, military service and character references, but do not include any age limit.[442]

The list drawn by the appointing authority is subsequently examined by the relevant selection board who, afterwards, prepares a list of candidates meeting the requirements of the competition which had been announced in the notice of competition. Only these candidates are then admitted to the competition.[443] Selection boards enjoy a broad discretion with regard to the admission of candidates to the competition. Their assessment of whether a candidate meets the requirements of the vacancy notice, and of the notice of competition, may only be questioned in the event of manifest error. The ECJ held that it 'cannot substitute itself for the appointing authority and review the latter's assessment of the professional abilities of the candidates, except in so far as it finds a manifest error of assessment'.[444] As already mentioned above, the appointing authority also cannot review the decisions of selection boards. However, if it finds that the admission of a candidate by the relevant selection board was illegal, the appointing authority may, in the later stage of the procedure, not appoint such candidate.[445]

In assessing whether candidates meet the condition set out in the competition notice, the selection board may merely examine whether candidates meet those condition 'prima facie and as a whole'.[446] When the competition is based on the tests and qualifications or only on qualifications, the relevant selection board first determines how the qualifications are to be assessed.[447] The ECJ stressed that the examination of the 'matching' of the qualifications with the requirements of the competition notice must be based on the objective facts which must be known to the candidates and the results of the 'matching' must be backed by sufficiently clear reasons.[448] Furthermore, the ECJ ruled that 'the difficulty inherent in such comparison cannot justify the lack of any attempt to make a more precise analysis or the lack of any additional criterion of selection'.[449]

The whole examination by, first, the appointing authority and, subsequently, by the selection board takes place on basis of facts, information, documents provided by the candidates together with their application. The candidates are responsible for providing sufficient documents and information without being requested to do so

[442] *EU Staff Regulations*, Annex III, Article 4. See above, introductory part to section 3.2.1.

[443] Ibid., Annex III, Article 5.

[444] *Picciolo v. European Parliament, Case 111/83*, para. 16 and *Kalavros v. ECJ, Joined cases T-160/89 and T-161/89*, para. 29.

[445] *Schwiering v. Court of Auditors, Case 142/85*, paras. 19-20. See above, p. ##.

[446] *Allgayer v. Parliament, Case 74/77*, para. 7; *Xavier Authié v. Commission of the European Communities, Case 34/80, ECR [1981], p. 665*, para. 16.

[447] *EU Staff Regulations*, Annex III, Article 5.

[448] *Costacurta v. Commission, Case 31/75*, para. 12.

[449] Ibid., para. 14.

by the selection board.[450] The selection board may, but is under no obligation to, require additional information from candidates if it considers it necessary or fit.[451] Same rule applies to candidates who are officials. These candidates may not rely on the institutions' personnel services to submit to the selection board at issue documents which might be available in their personal files and relevant for the competition.[452]

Evaluation of candidates

Candidates admitted to the competition, i.e. included in the list prepared by the relevant selection board, are subsequently admitted to the tests, if the competition is based on the tests or on the tests and qualifications.[453] If the competition is based on qualifications only, the selection board proceeds with the examination of candidate's abilities, based on their qualifications and professional experience, if relevant. It also conducts interviews. This means that qualifications and experience are taken into account in more than just one stage of the selection process, especially in the competition which is not based solely on the tests. Firstly, they are relevant for the decision which candidates meet the requirements set out in the competition notice and are thus admitted to take part in the competition; and secondly, they come into play when, after the results of the competition have been considered, the list of suitable candidates is drawn.[454] This increases the objectivity of the process.

The examination of candidates' abilities by the relevant selection board is above all comparative in nature and is not subjected to control by the judiciary, except of the cases where rules governing the proceedings of the selection board are infringed.[455] As mentioned above, selection boards enjoy a broad discretion on this point, although they must base their assessments on objective criteria known to each candidate and they must state adequately the grounds for their value judgments.[456] Moreover, the comparison must also remain within the limits imposed by the vacancy notice and the notice of competition. This means that, for example, when the relevant authority becomes aware of conditions which are specially needed to fill the vacant post but which were not included in the vacancy notice, it may not interpret the vacancy notice in a manner which would be in the best interest of service but not corresponding with wording of the vacancy notice.[457]

---

[450] *Allgayer v. Parliament, Case 74/77*, para. 9; *Picciolo v. European Parliament, Case 111/83*, para. 13; *Henri Maurissen v. Court of Auditors of the European Communities, Case 417/85, ECR [1987], p. 551*, para. 13; *Burban v. Parliament, Case T-133/89*, para. 34.

[451] *Maurissen v. Court of Auditors, Case 417/85*, para. 13. See also *Burban v. Parliament, Case T-133/89*, para. 35, upheld in the appeal proceedings – *Burban v. Parliament, Case C-255/90 P*, paras. 16-20.

[452] *Burban v. Parliament, Case T-133/89*, para. 31.

[453] *EU Staff Regulations*, Annex III, Article 5.

[454] *Manlio Serio v. Commission of the European Communities, Case 115/73, ECR [1974], p. 341*, para. 7.

[455] *Campogrande and others v. Commission, Joined cases 112, 144 and 145-73*, para. 53. See also *Helmut Müllers v. Economic and Social Committee of the European Communities, Case C-81/88, ECR [1990], p. I-249*, para. 3 of the summary.

[456] *Detti v. ECJ, Case 144/82*, para. 27.

[457] *Fischer v. Commission, Case T-58/91*, para. 67.

When the competition is based on the tests or on the tests and qualifications, the candidates first sit a written test and those who succeed in the written test then continue with an oral test. Since 2010, when a new format of competition tests was introduced, testing is divided into two stages – the admission test stage and an assessment stage.[458] The admission testing takes place in individual EU Member States and even some non-EU countries so that a wide pool of candidates is reached.[459] It involves computer-based tests, the type depending on the type of posts at issue, i.e. administrators, linguists, or assistants.[460] The second stage of the competition, namely the assessment stage, occurs normally in Brussels. In this stage, the emphasis is placed on specific professional skills and knowledge and on job related competencies, such as analysis and problem solving, communicating, prioritizing and organizing and working with others, not on factual knowledge. These competencies are assessed by way of a full or half day of case studies, group exercises, oral presentations, interviews and/or similar methods designed to test the desired skills. The choice of the methods depends on the competition and on the type of posts at issue (administrators, linguists, assistants or specialists). In any case, each of them is assessed by at least two assessors.[461]

Formally speaking, the content of the competition test is established by the relevant selection board that has, once again, a broad discretion on this point.[462] The board must, however, act consistently with information provided in the competition

[458] Until 2010, there were two staqes in the written tests. The first one was the so-called 'pre-selection' stage where three tests were held with multiple choice questions evaluating candidates' general knowledge of the EU institutions and policies, specific knowledge in their field of expertise, such as law or economics, and their general administrative skills. To pass this stage of the written tests, candidates must have passed in each of the three subjects. The next stage of the written examinations took form of three open questions - general essay, essay on a specialized topic and a dossier exercise. The subsequent oral test, attended only by candidates who had succeeded in the written examinations, took form of an interview before a relevant selection board. During this interview, the candidates were further tested with regard to their knowledge, ability to make clear oral statements and second language proficiency. - Stevens and Stevens, *Brussels Bureaucrats? The Administration of the European Union*, pp. 78-79. See also *General Rules Governing Open Competitions*, 2009/C 47 A/01, 26.02.2009, available at http://eur-lex.europa.eu/LexUriServ/LexUriServ.do?uri=OJ:C:2009:047A:0001:0017:EN:PDF, last visited on 30.12.2010, sections 4-6.

[459] According to information provided by the EPSO, there are 35 testing locations in the EU Member States and five locations outside the EU (Australia, Canada, China, Switzerland and United States). – see *Frequently Asked Questions*, pp. 6-7, available at http://europa.eu/epso/doc/faq_as_pdf_en.pdf, last visited on 09.07.2010.

[460] For administrators, for example, there are four tests - the first three test cognitive abilities, meaning verbal, numerical and abstract reasoning, the fourth test being a situational judgment test. A distinct admission testing is used for competitions organized for specialist profiles. There, candidates are, in principle, selected on the basis of qualifications and professional experience. - European Personnel Selection Office, *Selection Procedure*, 2010, available at http://europa.eu/epso/discover/selection_proced/selection/index_en.htm, last visited on 10.03.2010 and European Personnel Selection Office, *New Adminission Tests - The Re-designed Computer-Based Testing (CBT)*.

[461] European Personnel Selection Office, *Selection Procedure*, and European Personnel Selection Office, *New Admінission Tests - The Re-designed Computer-Based Testing (CBT)*. See also *Better, Faster, Stronger: Launch of New Selection Procedure for EU Officials*, and European Personnel Selection Office, *Guide to Open Competitions*, 2010/C 184 A/01, 08.07.2010, available at http://eur-lex.europa.eu/LexUriServ/LexUriServ.do?uri=OJ:C:2010:184A:0001:0014:EN:PDF, last visited on 30.12.2010, sections 4 and 5.

[462] *Gallone v. Council, Case T-132/89*, para. 27. See also *Valverde Mordt v. ECJ, Case T-156/89*, para. 121.

notice which must always specify what kind of tests will be used and how they will be graded.[463] When the content of actual tests is not confined within the limits laid down by the competition notice, or is not consonant with the purposes of the test or of the competition, the ECJ could review the content of the tests.[464] The possibility of such review constitutes an important limitation of the broad discretion that selection boards enjoy in establishing the detailed content of the competition tests.

Choice of the subject of the written tests must be such as not to put into unfair advantage a candidate who could profit from a special experience acquired in the performance of duties in the post which is put up for competition. Such situation occurred in *Martin* where the subject of the written tests was 'Community relations with the Mediterranean countries: Association or non-preferential system'. One of the candidates who was admitted to the test served as a member of the temporary staff in the post to be filled and was responsible for matters connected with Turkey and Yugoslavia. The ECJ considered these two countries to be typical examples of those falling within the scope of the subject of the test and found that such situation was in breach of the principle of equality of treatment of the candidates in the relevant competition. Consequently, the ECJ annulled decisions and procedures which were subsequent to the tests.[465] On the other hand, in *Guglielmi* the ECJ did not accept the existence of special advantage to one of the candidates who had made special studies on the subject-matter in the past. The Court considered that the subject at issue – describing in the form of an article for magazine with broad circulation the advantages or disadvantages of candidates' country's belonging to the community - was of a sufficiently general nature and did not require any special knowledge or specific experience.[466] It could be argued that the distinction between these two cases is relatively small. This suggests that the permissibility of the subject of the written tests would depend heavily on the individual circumstances of each case. It is questionable, however, whether it is possible to avoid a correlation between the tests' subject and the individual position of all candidates, especially if they are not known at the time when the content of the tests is set.

The written tests must be held on the same conditions for all candidates, otherwise the principle of equality would be breached. No exception from this rule is possible. The ECJ held in *Prais* that any interest of participants not to have the test on a certain date must be balanced with the necessity of equal treatment, and in case of written test, also with the practical difficulties of comparison. In that case the applicant could not take part in the written test on the set date due to religious reasons. The ECJ did accept that the authorities should take such difficulties of candidates into account when deciding on the date of the tests and to take reasonable steps to avoid fixing an unsuitable date. However, the ECJ recognized that the authorities need to be informed about such difficulties in good time so that they have a possibility set a

[463] *EU Staff Regulations*, Annex III, Article 1(1)(e). See also *Le Voci v. Council, Case T-371/03*, para. 40.

[464] *Gallone v. Council, Case T-132/89*, para. 27.

[465] *Hélène Martin v. Commission of the European Communities, Case 24/78, ECR [1979], p. 603*, para. 20-21.

[466] *Anna Guglielmi v. European Parliament, Case 268/80, ECR [1981], p. 2295*, paras. 11-13. See also judgment in *Sergio - Sergio and others v. Commission, Joined cases 64, 71 to 73 and 78/86*, paras. 26-28.

date which would reflect the difficulties. In any case, the date must be the same for all candidates.[467] This condition is not imposed on the oral tests. As stated by the CFI in *Gallone*, the very nature of the oral tests precludes them from being conducted at the same time for all candidates.[468] With regard to the place of the written tests, tests may be, and as explained above also are, held in more places but it must be simultaneously and the content of such tests must be identical.[469] This is clearly to ensure the highest possible objectivity of the competition process.

Irregularities which occur during the tests cannot be remedied by a repetition of the tests. That means that the only alternative is an application of a corrective factor in the assessment of the tests. Such corrective factor must be applied unequivocally and the candidate concerned must be informed of the criteria adopted.[470] In *Detti*, for example, the tests organized in Brussels and in Luxemburg were not entirely identical. As a consequence, the selection board decided that the tests taken in Luxemburg would be marked 'more severely' than those taken in Brussels. However, the selection board did not explain which specific criteria had been used in the marking and the ECJ could not check whether the criteria applied were of an objective nature and whether the candidates were treated equally. Therefore, the ECJ annulled the decision at issue.[471]

It must be noted that not all irregularities that occur during the competition tests lead to the annulment of the tests. Only irregularities which are 'substantive in nature and capable of distorting the results of the tests' are considered to affect the tests' lawfulness.[472] In *Albani* the CFI ruled that an irregularity in an intermediate stage of the competition is a ground for the annulment of the contested decision only if it distorts the outcome of the competition. In that case the word limit of the written tests was not observed and it was not possible to determine whether the candidates were treated equally in the marking of the tests - the tests were in the meantime destroyed - or whether that irregularity may have distorted the final outcome of the competition. The CFI therefore annulled the marking of the tests and all subsequent acts.[473]

Reserve list

After the tests and/or the assessment of qualifications are completed, the relevant selection board draws a list of candidates suitable for the appointment and sends it

---

[467] *Vivien Prais v. Council of the European Communities, Case 130/75, ECR [1976], p. 1589*, paras. 13-19.

[468] *Gallone v. Council, Case T-132/89*, para. 36. In this case the CFI also accepted differences in the content of the oral tests. – Ibid.

[469] *Detti v. ECJ, Case 144/82*, para. 28.

[470] Ibid., para. 29.

[471] Ibid., paras. 29-32.

[472] *Carmen Jiménez v. Office for Harmonisation in the Internal Market (Trade Marks and Designs) (OHIM), Case T-200/97, ECR-SC [1999], p. I-A-19; II-73*, para. 55. See also *Le Voci v. Council, Case T-371/03*, para. 65 and 79; and *Neophytos Neophytou v. Commission of the European Communities, Case F-22/05, ECR-SC [2006], p. I-A-1-159, II-A-1-617*, para. 60.

[473] *Alessandro Albani and others v. Commission of the European Communities, Case T-35/89, ECR [1990], p. II-395*, paras. 52-53. See also paras. 25 and 33.

to the relevant appointing authority.[474] This list is also known as 'reserve list' since it contains candidates who are in a 'reserve' position. This means that the successful candidates do not receive an immediate appointment but wait until an EU institution is in need of a person with their qualification. The selection process does not end with the reserve lists thus. It continues with when a specific vacancy occurs. The relevant institution identifies a potential candidate from the reserve list and invites him for an interview. Only when the interview is successful and the institution at hand is satisfied with the candidate, it offers him an appointment. In other instances, the candidate remains on the reserve list until the expiry date of this list. Naturally, this stage of the competition does not apply to internal competition which is held for a specific vacancy or vacancies. There, no reserve lists are prepared and the selection process ends with the decision of the appointing authority selecting an individual candidate for the post at issue.

It is important to note that the reserve lists are time-limited. They are in principle in force just for one year, although a prolongation for another year or more is not uncommon.[475] The CFI has accepted the 'common practice' of limiting the duration of reserve list as consistent with the purpose of Article 27(1) and Article 29(1) of the *EU Staff Regulations*. These provisions stipulate the main objective of the recruitment process, namely the appointment of persons of the highest standards of ability. The CFI explained that limited duration of the validity of reserve lists gives the opportunity to new candidates to make 'an attempt after a certain period of time has lapsed'.[476]

A possible consequence of this situation is that there might be candidates on the reserve list who will not receive an appointment before the expiry of the relevant reserve list. The ECJ noted on a number of occasions that candidates do not have the right to be appointed.[477] This applies equally to candidates listed in the reserve list in the first place due to their best results in the competition.[478] As already mentioned above, the appointing authority enjoys a wide discretion in making selection from reserve lists as long as it does not 'destroy the very concept of competition by departing substantially from the results of the competition without serious reasons'.[479] In making its choice, the appointing authority does not need to provide reasons for not appointing candidates who appeared on the lower places, if the reserve list was drawn according to the order of merit, i.e. candidates' results in the competition. But if the reserve list is set out in alphabetical order, which is also permissible, the candidates who were not appointed have the right to know reasons why.[480] The CFI stated in *Casariego* the following:

---

[474] *EU Staff Regulations*, Annex III, Article 5.

[475] European Personnel Selection Office, *Reserve Lists: Administrators (A-A*-AD)*.

[476] *Valverde Mordt v. ECJ, Case T-156/89*, para. 63.

[477] See, for example, *Casariego v. Commission, Case T-1/90*, para. 80.

[478] *Fux v. Commission, Case 26/68*, paras. 8-11.

[479] *Serio v. EAEC Commission, Case 62/65*, p. 570. For details on limits of the discretion of the appointing authority, see above, section 3.2.1.1.

[480] *Casariego v. Commission, Case T-1/90*, para. 76. See also para. 77.

> *It would be truly unreasonable, unfair and contrary to the very letter and spirit of the second paragraph of Article 25 of the Staff Regulations if candidates rejected in the first two stages of the procedure were entitled to receive decisions relating to them together with a statement of the reasons on which they were based and were thus able fully to enforce their rights, as has consistently been held by the Court of Justice... whereas better candidates who had succeeded in reaching the third stage of the competition procedure and appeared on a list of suitable candidates drawn up irrespective of order of merit could be excluded from the recruitment procedure without being given any statement of grounds whatsoever that might enable them to find out the reasons for which they were not ultimately selected by the appointing authority and to determine whether or not such reasons were sound.*[481]

Clearly, the requirement to provide reasons to candidates listed in the reserve list but not appointed contributes to the transparency of the selection process. It also helps to prevent nepotism which would be otherwise more likely to occur. The fact that the appointing authority enjoys broad discretion in making the final choice is not surprising. As noted earlier, this fact reflects the need for a certain flexibility existing in each selection process. Fortunately, it is counterbalanced by the duty to state reasons to unsuccessful candidates who can exercise some control over the use of discretion by the appointing authority in this manner.

To guarantee sufficiently a broad choice for the appointing authority, reserve lists contain, in principle, at least twice as many names as the number of posts which are, on the basis of the human resources and budgetary planning, to be filled.[482] This is not an absolute rule, however. As held by the ECJ, it is merely a recommendation to the selection board aiming at facilitation of the decision of the appointing authority. Whether this recommendation is followed depends on the nature of the competition, relevant circumstances, number and qualifications of the candidates.[483] In *Agneessens*, for example, the ECJ accepted that the reserve list contained only 114 names, while 109 posts were eventually filled. The ECJ held that the nature of the competition and the very large number of the posts to which the competition was related justified the manner in which the selection board drew up the reserve list.[484]

[481] Ibid., para. 77

[482] *EU Staff Regulations*, Annex III, Article 5.

[483] *Agneessens v. Commission, Case 122/77*, para. 22

[484] Ibid., paras. 6, 22 and 23.

Summary

To sum up, the EU competition process proceeds as follows:

Scheme 6: EU competition process

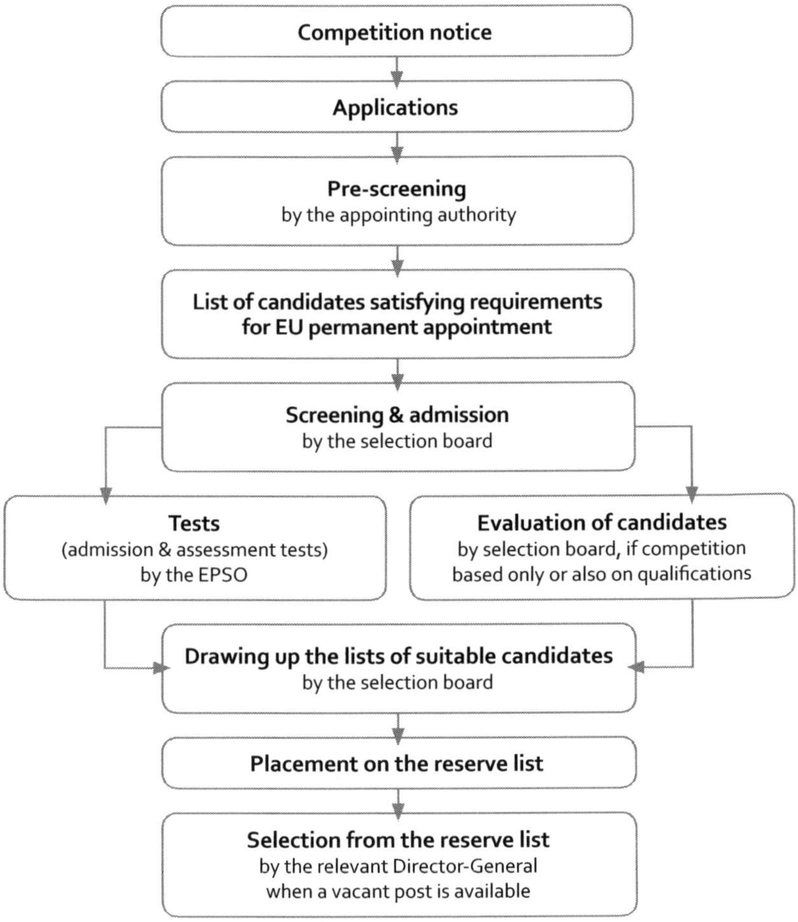

3.2.2. Posts requiring special qualifications

It has been mentioned earlier that the competition is the primary entry door to the permanent appointment in the European Commission below the managerial level. It has also been noted, however, that an exception to this rule exists for posts requiring special qualifications. This exception has its legal base in Article 29(2) of the *EU Staff Regulations*, which stipulates in its relevant part the following:

> *A procedure other than the competition procedure may be adopted by the Appointing Authority ... in exceptional cases ... for recruitment to posts which require special qualifications.*[485]

As the wording of this provision indicates, the possibility to have recourse to this provision in cases involving posts which require special qualifications is very limited. The ECJ held in *Bode* that the use of the expression 'exceptional cases' in Article 29(2) of the *EU Staff Regulations* demonstrates that:

> *the application of this provision is subject to very strict conditions as to form and substance, which moreover is in accordance with both the requirements of the service and the legitimate interest of officials. Therefore the institutions may only have recourse to the special procedure laid down in Article 29(2) when they have examined with the greatest care whether the conditions for the application of that provision are fulfilled. Moreover, the decision to have recourse to that procedure must state the reasons on which it is based so that the Court may, if necessary, review the legality of that decision.*[486]

In another important case *Van der Stijl*, the ECJ further explained that the extraordinary procedure of Article 29(2) for recruitment to posts requiring special qualifications, which might be employed only exceptionally, may be relied on when the appointing authority is faced with 'circumstances of such a nature as to render inappropriate the ordinary procedures laid down in Article 29(1)'.[487] In that case, for example, the ECJ did not agree that such circumstances had existed. The Commission made recourse to Article 29(2) of the *EU Staff Regulations* in order to fill a post of head of division arguing that qualifications required for that post were special because they related to the nuclear production cycle, management of fissile materials and safeguards. The Commission claimed that the choice of candidates available to it under Article 29(1) of the *EU Staff Regulations*, which had been followed before recourse was made to Article 29(2), had been inadequate. However, the ECJ noted that the minutes of the relevant Commission meeting had not contained any statement of reasons why the inadequacy of the choice under Article 29(1) would have been the case. In addition, the Commission admitted that the wish to preserve geographical balance within the relevant Directorate-General, in particular via appointment of a French national, had played an important role in taking the decision

---

485 *EU Staff Regulations*, Article 29(2). Note that the procedure under Article 29(2) can be used not only in situations when the post at issue is to be filled by external candidates, i.e. candidates outside the EU institutions, but also in cases where the recruitment process is limited to internal candidates. In *Van Belle*, the ECJ held: '... although it may be accepted that an open competition may, in certain circumstances, appear inappropriate for the purpose of filling a vacant post, there is no reason why the same might not possibly be true in the case of an internal competition, especially as the detailed rules for these two types of competition are identical.' - *Van Belle v. Council, Case 176/73*, paras. 13-15. See also *Marenco v. Commission, Joined cases 81 to 88/74*, para. 17; *Schloh v. Council, Case 85/82*, para. 25 and *Kotzonis v. Economic and Social Committee, Case T-586/93*, para. 95.

486 *Fritz-August Bode v. Commission of the European Communities, Joined cases 45 and 49-70, ECR [1971], p. 465*, para. 15.

487 *Erik van der Stijl v. Commission of the European Communities, Case 128/84, ECR [1985], p. 3281*, para. 21.

at issue. The ECJ noted that the procedure of Article 29(1) had produced at least three candidates who satisfied the requirements of special qualifications and that one of them had even been considered very competent and particularly suitable for the relevant post. Therefore, the ECJ ruled that the even special nature of the post had not satisfied the treatment of the case as exceptional under Article 29(2) of the *EU Staff Regulations.*[488] The fact that the ECJ interprets this provision strictly, and reviews its use, constitutes an important safeguard preventing its possible abuse or misuse by the appointing authority. In absence of such safeguard, the appointing authority could (be tempted to) make recourse to Article 29(2), for example, in cases in which it would wish to give preference to considerations other than candidates' merits, just as it did with geographical balance in *Van der Stijl*, or where it would have a particular – favoured –candidate in mind. It goes without saying that such course of action would be detrimental to the objectivity and impartiality of the selection process.

When Article 29(2) procedure is used, it replaces the competition procedure in all respects.[489] The EU Administration has, in general, a rather broad discretion is deciding in which manner it will arrange the actual organization of the procedure. This means, among others, that the Administration does not need to follow rules of Annex III to the *EU Staff Regulations* which concerns competitions and is, therefore, not applicable. Because of the special nature of the procedure under Article 29(2), the Administration may even, for example, introduce additional criteria which candidates need to meet and which did not appear in the vacancy notice. In addition, such additional criteria do not need to be published in the Official Journal. The same applies to the selection committee to which the relevant appointing authority may delegate its right to make the selection.[490]

The existence of broad discretion of the EU Administration in this special procedure is understandable; it results from its very nature. It could be argued, however, that at least general guidelines should be in place here, outlining steps to be taken by the Administration and safeguarding that the selection process is conducted in a transparent and objective manner. It is true that the EU judiciary has developed a number of safeguards. For example, all involved authorities must respect the principle of the protection of legitimate expectation in applying the procedure of Article 29(2).[491] In addition, as in all cases of filling a vacant post, disregarding which method is eventually employed, the Administration has duty to have regard to the interest of the staff. This duty reflects 'the balance of reciprocal rights and obligations established by the Staff Regulations in relations between the public authority and civil service

[488] Ibid., in particular paras. 5-8, 14, 17-20 and 22.

[489] *Kotzonis v. Economic and Social Committee, Case T-586/93*, para. 94. Note that the commencement of this procedure does not prevent the Administration from considering also candidates who could have participated in the competition if it were chosen for. Moreover, Article 29(2) may also be employed in cases of transfer and promotion. - paras. 98-99.

[490] *Mavridis v. Parliament, Case 289/81*, para. 16 and *Constantin Verros v. European Parliament, Case 306/81, ECR [1983], p. 1755*, para. 16.

[491] *Mavridis v. Parliament, Case 289/81*, para. 21.

employees.'[492] These are indeed important limitations of the Administration's discretion which could otherwise be more easily misused or abused, given the unregulated nature of the procedure. Yet, they do not provide for sufficient specificity that would permit candidates to exercise any control over the manner in which the Administration proceeds in an individual selection procedure. This is currently the case when the same Article 29(2) of the *EU Staff Regulations* is used for filling senior posts in the European Commission, discussed in the following section.

3.2.3. Senior posts

Although the general regime of the recruitment in the EU civil service through competition is, in principle, applicable to the appointments into the senior posts, too, in practice competition is never used at that level.[493] Usually, the special procedure provided for in Article 29(2) of the *EU Staff Regulations* is followed. As already mentioned above, Article 29(2) stipulates that a procedure other than competition may be adopted also for the recruitment of senior officials, i.e. Directors-General or their equivalent in grade AD 16 or AD 15 and Directors or their equivalent in grade AD 15 or AD 14.[494]

The European Commission has worked out Article 29(2) of the *EU Staff Regulations* in its *Commission Compilation Document on Senior Officials Policy* of 25 October 2004.[495] Section 4 of this document explains that there are a number of possible ways in which vacant senior posts may be filled, including transfer, promotion, internal competition and inter-institutional transfer in accordance with Article 19(1) of the *EU Staff Regulations*, as well as external procedure under Article 29(2) thereof. This section further stresses that, as a general rule, senior posts are to be filled from among the internal staff of the Commission and other EU institutions serving in management grades, and by preference by way of promotion. In some instances, however, 'a case can be made for recruiting from the outside'.[496] In all instances, i.e. of internal, inter-institutional as well as external recruitment, however, the same procedure and the same methodology for candidates' assessment applies.[497] They are set out in detail in Section 5.2. of the *Commission Compilation Document on Senior Officials Policy* and are as follows.

---

[492] *Heinz-Jörg Moritz v. Commission of the European Communities, Case T-20/89, ECR [1990], p. II-769*, para. 39. See also *Schwiering v. Court of Auditors, Case 142/85*, para. 16.

[493] Stevens and Stevens, *Brussels Bureaucrats? The Administration of the European Union*, p. 84. Stevens has argued, though, that the fact that a special procedure is used for recruitment into senior posts does not mean that the process of selection of the most suitable candidate for a vacant post is not highly competitive. – Ibid.

[494] *EU Staff Regulations*, Article 29(2). For a more elaborate explanation, see *Commission Compilation Document on Senior Officials Policy*, Section 2.

[495] *Commission Compilation Document on Senior Officials Policy*.

[496] Ibid., Section 4.2.

[497] Ibid., Section 5.2., introductory paragraph.

Vacancy notice

As soon as it is clear that there is a vacancy, the recruiting Directorate-General prepares a draft vacancy notice which is consulted with the Rapporteur appointed for this particular appointment procedure ('Rapporteur for the Case', referred in this study also as 'designated Rapporteur'). The draft vacancy is then sent to the appointing authority which needs to approve it. After the approval, the vacancy notice is in most cases published, either internally or externally. Since senior posts should be, in principle, filled internally, the internal publication of vacancies is the general rule. The additional external publication takes place only when a need to recruit from outside occurs.[498] If the vacancy is published also externally, it must be done in a manner ensuring that all interested parties receive an equal opportunity of appointment to the vacant post.[499]

Despite the fact that the Commission appears to attach great importance to the publication of vacancies as a means of guaranteeing transparency of the procedure, it is possible that a certain vacancy is not made public. This is regarded as an exception, though, with a clearly defined scope – a vacancy does not need to be published only when an official is transferred to a vacant senior post which is at his existing grade.[500] The fact that all (other) vacancies must be published constitutes an important guarantee for transparency and objectivity of the entire selection process and must, therefore, be praised.

Application and assessment

Applications for the vacant posts are examined first by a pre-selection panel established by the Directorate-General at issue. On the basis of evaluation grids and, if appropriate, interviews, a report on the pre-selection is submitted to the Consultative Committee on Appointments, an advisory body in the procedure for the appointment of senior officials. This report is drawn by the recruiting Director-General in agreement with the designated Rapporteur. If the vacant post is at the level of Director-General, the report is drawn by the designated Rapporteur after consultations with the portfolio Commissioner and agreement with the chair of the pre-selection panel.[501]

Having received the report with details on the pre-selection, the Consultative Committee on Appointments identifies the most suitable applicants and invites them for interview.[502] The interview involves a wide-ranging meeting with the Committee itself, assisted by external experts in the relevant field and/or in recruiting to high-level positions. In appropriate cases, and always when the vacancy is

---

[498] Ibid., pp. 4-5.

[499] Ibid., Sections 5.2.1. and 5.2.2.

[500] Ibid., Section 4.1. and *EU Staff Regulations*, Article 7(1).

[501] *Commission Compilation Document on Senior Officials Policy*, Section 5.2.4.

[502] Ibid., Section 5.2.5.

published also externally, the interviews also involve individual and/or group exercises and in-depth discussions focused on management skills.[503]

The assessment of candidates for senior posts in the European Commission occurs thus on a number of occasions, by a number of actors and by using a number of different assessment techniques. This ensures not only better, but also more objective, assessment of candidates' merits. Consequently, it enhances the objectivity and impartiality of the whole selection process.

Selection

After the interviews, the Consultative Committee on Appointments draws a shortlist of most suitable candidates accompanied by evaluation sheets on each candidate. The shortlist is submitted to the relevant Commissioner or Commissioners, depending on the level of vacancy.[504] Having further interviewed candidates of his or their potential choice, the relevant Commissioner or Commissioners make a proposal to the College of Commissioners which is the final appointing authority for senior posts appointments.[505] However, if the portfolio Commissioner is not satisfied with the candidates who have been interviewed, he may either re-publish the vacancy notice, with a possibility to add external publication, or decide to interview candidates who were not shortlisted by the Consultative Committee on Appointments.[506]

The proposal submitted to the College of Commissioners includes also a reasoned opinion from the Consultative Committee on Appointments, with attached assessment scale and curriculums vitae, and a reasoned proposal from the Commissioner responsible for administration. Furthermore, the proposal for the appointment of Directors-General must be in agreement with the President of the Commission and the portfolio Commissioner and, in all other cases, of the portfolio Commissioner and the Director-General concerned. All these requirements are important guarantees for the proposal's objectivity, together with the involvement of a relatively large number of actors.

The Commission takes its decision by oral procedure.[507] The final decision is announced internally as well as externally to the press, including the justification of

503 Ibid., Section 5.2.6.

504 Ibid., Section 5.2.7. The relevant Commissioners are: for the posts of Director-General, Head of Service or equivalent – the Commissioner responsible for administration, the portfolio Commissioner and the President of the Commission; for posts of Deputy Director-General – the Commissioner responsible for administration and the portfolio Commissioner; and for all other senior posts – portfolio Commissioner. – Ibid.

505 Ibid., Section 5.2.8.

506 Ibid., Section 5.2.7.

507 Ibid., Section 5.2.8. Oral procedure is the standard manner in which the College of Commissioners takes decisions, though it may also use written, empowerment and delegation procedures. For details on the Commission decision making, see *Rules of Procedure of the Commission, C(2000) 3614*, 08.12.2010, OJ L 308, 08.12.2000, p. 26, as amended by Commission Decision 2010/138/EU of 24.02.2010, OJ L 55, 05.03.2010, p. 60, Articles 4, 8 and Articles 13-16.

the choice of candidate.[508] This is a welcome contribution to the transparency of the entire selection process, adding to its objectivity and impartiality as well.

Scheme 7: European Commission selection process for senior posts

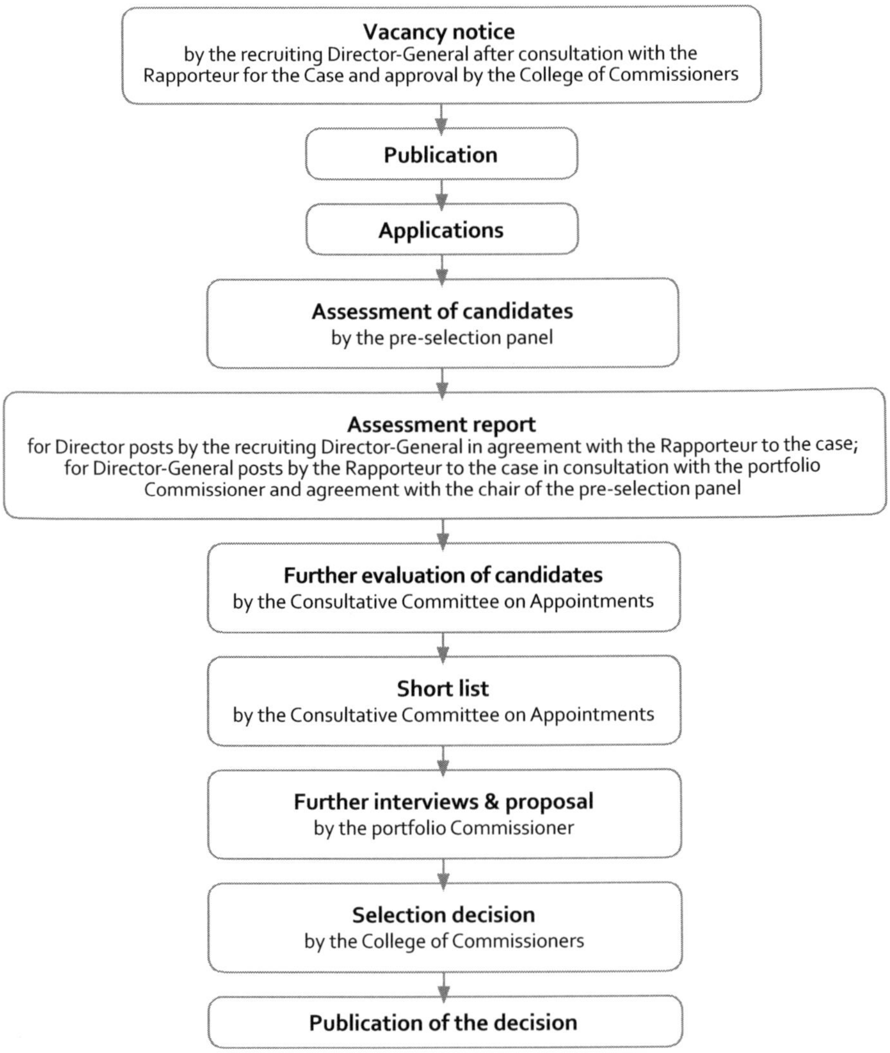

Authorities involved in the process

As can be seen from the above description, a number of authorities take part in the selection process of senior officials. They are different than those involved in the regular competition. In case of the latter, there is an appointing authority,

[508] *Commission Compilation Document on Senior Officials Policy*, Section 5.2.9.

the Joint Committee and a selection board. In the appointment process for senior positions, the following authorities are involved: the recruiting Director-General, the pre-selection panel, Rapporteur for the Case, the Consultative Committee on Appointments, including the Permanent Rapporteur to the Consultative Committee on Appointments, individual Commissioners and the College of Commissioners. In some instances, external consultants may be used as well, as 'supporting actors' in the selection process.

The role of the recruiting Director-General in the senior officials' selection process is limited to the preparation of a draft vacancy notice and of a report on the first assessment of candidates by the pre-selection panel. The fact that the draft vacancy notice must be consulted with the designated Rapporteur and approved by the appointing authority, and that it is not him but the pre-selection panel which assesses candidates, reduces a danger of the Director's-General possible subjectivism and partiality that could harm the entire selection process already at its outset. It is therefore unfortunate that the pre-selection panel itself is nowhere defined. Considering that this panel's assessment constitute the starting point for candidates' further evaluation, clear rules on its composition should be in place in order to guarantee the panel's objectivity as well as the transparency of the process.

The Rapporteur for the Case is the next authority involved in the selection process for senior posts. This post was established in 2000 in the course of the overall reform of the human resources management in the European Commission. The function of the Rapporteur for the Case is fulfilled for each particular case by one of the Directors-General of Directors appointed by the chair of the Consultative Committee on Appointments. The appointment is made from among a pool of serving Directors-General or Directors designated by the Commission for a period of a minimum of two years, renewable. The Rappoteur for the Case appointed for a specific selection procedure should hold at least the same grade and occupy a function of at least the same level as the one for which the selection procedure is applicable.[509]

The Rapporteur for the Case fulfills several tasks throughout the whole selection procedure of senior officials. He is personally responsible to follow the selection procedure from the beginning (initial publication of a vacancy notice) until the very end (final decision of the Commission on the appointment of a particular person into the post at issue). Main duties of the Rapporteur to the Case are set out in the *Commission Compilation Decision on Senior Officials Policy* and include:

> *(1) to approve the vacancy notice;*
>
> *(2) for functions of director-general, Head of Service or equivalent to consult the portfolio Commissioner on the candidacies received, to prepare a presentation to the [Consultative Committee on Appointments] as well as a recommendation on which candidates should be interviewed by the Committee as well as to participate in the [Consultative Committee on Appointments] as a member;*

[509] Ibid., Section 5.1.4.

(3) for all other senior management functions to consult the director-general and the portfolio Commissioner on the candidacies received and to monitor the preliminary assessment made of them, to inform the [Consultative Committee on Appointments] of their views before the Committee decides on the list of candidates to be interviewed as well as to participate in the [Consultative Committee on Appointments] as a member;

(4) to assist, where necessary, the Chair of the [Consultative Committee on Appointments] in debriefing the portfolio Commissioner.[510]

The Rapporteur to the Case must be distinguished from the Permanent Rapporteur to the Consultative Committee on Appointments. This post was also created in the framework of the 2000 reform with the aim of improving the career development of all senior officials. The Permanent Rapporteur, an official at the D-level with 'confirmed skills and experience in human resources management', is responsible for promoting successful career development of senior officials, including mobility across several posts and using the 'particular talents of officials' in the best possible manner.[511] Involvement of the Permanent Rapporteur in individual selection procedures for senior posts takes place through his membership in the Consultative Committee on Appointments.

The Consultative Committee on Appointments is an advisory body in this process. It was established in 1980 and its main task is to function as an interviewing and evaluation board recommending a shortlist of candidates to the Commissioners who make the appointment proposals.[512] The composition of the Consultative Committee on Appointments depends on the level of the senior post which is to be filled. For the posts of Director-General, the Committee consists of: the Secretary-General (chair); the Director-General for Human Resources and Security; the Head of Cabinet of the Commission President; the Head of Cabinet of the Commissioner for Human Resources and Security; the Permanent Rapporteur; and the Rapporteur for the Case. For the posts of Director, the Consultative Committee on Appointments consists of: the Director-General for Human Resources and Security (chair); a Deputy Secretary-General; the recruiting Director-General; the Head of Cabinet of the Commissioner for Human Resources and Security; the Permanent Rapporteur; and the Rapporteur for the Case. Moreover, the Director-General for Budget participates as observer in the Committees interviews with candidates for posts of the so-called Resource Directors. Furthermore, the Committee may be at any time assisted by human resources experts or other independent experts or other persons.[513]

As already noted, the *Commission Compilation Document on Senior Officials Policy* permits use of professional external experts by the standing authorities. It lists, by way of an example, several occasions on which the assistance of such persons may be sought:

---

[510] Ibid., Section 5.1.4.

[511] Ibid., Section 5.1.3.

[512] Ibid., p. 5.

[513] Ibid., Section 5.1.1., 5.1.2. and 5.1.5.

– *an external human resources consultant assists the [Consultative Committee on Appointments] in the examination*

of candidacies and during interviews with candidates;

– *where applicable, the results of the tests run in the assessment centers will be made available to the [Consultative Committee on Appointments] before it carries out the interviews;*

– *where appropriate, the Commission will appoint independent experts with specialized knowledge and of international reputation to advise the [Consultative Committee on Appointments] on the pre-selection of candidates and/or during the interviews.*[514]

In all instances, the external consultants work on a confidential basis and under a framework contract with the Commission. They are obliged to consult extensively the precise remit for the search for candidates with the relevant Commissioner and Director-General. The *Commission Compilation Document on Senior Officials Policy* also stresses that the pre-selection of candidates for interview as well as the final assessment of the candidates remains in the hands of the Commission itself.[515]

The Commission itself is involved in the selection process both through its individual Commissioners and as the College of Commissioners, the latter acting as the appointing authority for all senior posts in the European Commission. Individual Commissioners who are involved in the process are the portfolio Commissioner and the Commissioner responsible for the Commission's human resources management. The latter is responsible for submitting a proposal on the basis of which the College takes the final decision. It is however the former, i.e. the portfolio Commissioner, who further interviews candidates and prepares that proposal. The portfolio Commissioner does so after he has interviewed candidates he chose from the shortlist drawn up by the Consultative Committee on Appointments. He may, however, also interview candidates not included on this shortlist, or to decide not to continue with the selection procedure but to re-publish the vacancy notice instead, and to publish it externally. It could be argued that the discretion of the portfolio Commissioner is too broad and could be abused, for example when the shortlist does not include a person favoured by the Commissioner. This would mean, in fact, clear circumvention of the decisions taken by the Consultative Committee on Appointments. However, it must be admitted that any final proposal for appointment is made not by the portfolio Commissioner himself but by the Commissioner for Human Resources and Security. In addition, this proposal needs to be made in agreement with the Commission President (for Director-General positions) or the relevant Director-General (for Director positions). Moreover, the appointment must be approved by the whole College of Commissioners. All this could be regarded as an additional safeguard ensuring objectivity of the selection process for the European Commission's senior positions.

[514] Ibid., Section 5.1.5.

[515] Ibid., Section 5.1.5.

3.3. Recruitment of 'other servants'

Recruitment of the European Commission's 'other servants' occurs on the basis of the legal framework set out in internal Commission decisions. This is in particular the case for temporary and contract staff, and less for local staff. Although employment of the latter is also subject to an internal Commission decision, namely the *Commission Framework Rules on Local Staff* of 1989, this decision contains no precise rules on recruitment of such staff. As explained in chapter 1, appointment of local staff is conducted in accordance with rules and practices which exist in the place of employment of such staff.[516] As these rules and practices vary, so does the relevant recruitment process. Recruitment of local staff is, therefore, not further addressed in the following sections. They focus on temporary and local staff whose recruitment is regulated by internal Commission decisions.

3.3.1. Temporary staff

Procedures concerning the recruitment of temporary staff vary almost as much as the categories of these staff. As explained above, there are four distinct categories of temporary staff, namely (a) staff filling posts of a specialized nature or meeting temporary needs; (b) staff engaged in cases where the reserve lists are not available or are insufficient; (c) cabinets staff; (d) research staff.[517] The Commission policy on all four types of temporary staff, including the recruitment procedures, is set up in the *Commission Decision on Temporary Agents* of 2004.[518]

Type (a) temporary staff is selected on basis of a profile laying down the requirements concerning the education, professional training and experience, and the linguistic proficiency. Such profile is established by the relevant Directorate-General or Commission service and approved by the Directorate-General for Human Resources and Security after informing the Joint Committee. The profile is transmitted to the permanent representations of the EU Member States. It is also published at the EPSO's website and possibly also at the internet site of the Directorate-General concerned and/or elsewhere. The actual selection is conducted by a selection committee. This committee assesses candidates who have applied on the basis of qualifications and professional experience, as stated in the application forms and motivation letters. The pre-selected candidates are then invited for an interview with the selection committee which subsequently, having evaluated interviewed candidates, establishes a list of successful candidates. Persons who are to be engaged as temporary agents of type (a) are drawn from this list. The selection committee is composed of three persons: one from the Directorate-General or service concerned, one appointed by the Staff Committee and one from the Directorate General or service not concerned with the profile at issue. The latter member of the selection committee acts also as its chair.[519]

---

[516] See above, chapter 1, section 3.1.2.3.

[517] For details, see above, chapter 1, section 3.1.2.1.

[518] *Commission Decision on Temporary Agents.*

[519] Ibid., Articles 2, 3 and 5 and, for example, European Commission, *Selection of Temporary Staff for*

Scheme 8: Selection process of European Commission temporary staff filling posts of a specialized nature or meeting temporary needs

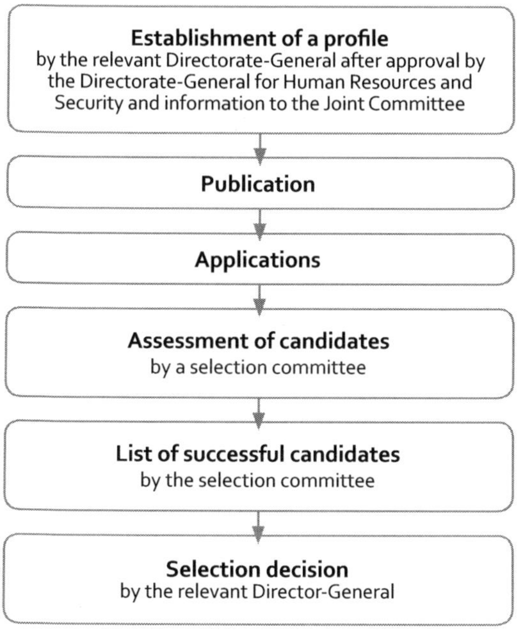

In case of temporary staff of type (b), the *Commission Decision on Temporary Agents* makes distinction between two instances in which engagements of such staff may occur. The first instance concerns the use of temporary staff for permanent posts for which reserve lists of successful candidates of internal or external competition are unavailable or insufficient. The second situation occurs where there is a need for the engagement of a specialist and no temporary post is available and where the organization of an external competition for filling just one vacancy cannot be justified or for meeting a temporary need.

The selection procedure differs in the two mentioned instances and depends also on the duration of the employment of the staff. In case of unavailable or exhausted reserve lists and the employment for a maximum initial period of three years, the recruitment is authorized and notified by the Directorate-General responsible for human resources management. The candidates are then drawn from the database of spontaneous applications which is established by the European Personnel Selection Office. There is no formal selection procedure for this. The only formal requirement laid down by the *Commission Decision on Temporary Agents* is that the conditions of the vacancy which is to be filled must be met. The absence of any selection procedure, or guidelines, is regrettable; it harms the overall transparency of the process

the Directorate-General Regional Policy, Vacancy Announcement, COM/TA/REGIO/10/01, available at http://ec.europa.eu/dgs/regional_policy/communication/doc/vacancy_1001_en.pdf, last visited on 30.12.2010.

and, on the individual level, it may be detrimental to its objectivity and impartiality. For the posts of an initial duration longer than three years or for extensions of contract beyond the three years period, the selection procedure is the same as in case of the recruitment of the temporary staff of type (b) in situations where there is a need for the engagement of a specialist and no temporary post is available. For the selection in those cases the same rules apply as for the selection of temporary staff of type (a), described above, including publications of a profile setting out requirements of the post and a selection by a selection committee which draws up a list of successful candidates from which the future temporary staff member is selected by the relevant Directorate-General.[520]

There is no formal procedure for the selection procedure for the employment of the temporary staff of type (c), i.e. the cabinet staff.[521] The selection and the appointment of these staff are entirely in the hands of the individual Commissioners. Note that the CFI has upheld the existence of a wide discretion of the relevant authorities in setting up not only the modalities but also the application of the organization of the selection procedure of the cabinet staff. In the context of the cabinet staff serving in the European Parliament (i.e. in the office of the Parliament's President or in the Parliament's political groups), the CFI has ruled that the margin of discretion is not exceeded by giving an opportunity to national delegations to meet candidates for a vacant post under consideration. The CFI has explained that this might be needed for ensuring a link of mutual confidence between the cabinet staff and their employer, in case at hand a political group of the Parliament. On the other hand, the opinion of an involved national delegation may not substitute the final comparative examination of the candidates which must be done by the relevant authority in line with the applicable internal rules.[522] In another recent case decided in 2006, the CFI emphasized the importance of the link of mutual trust as an essential element of the employment contract for the cabinet staff, including staff in functions with technical nature. The absence or the loss of the mutual confidence is regarded as sufficient justification for non-recruitment of a particular candidate and also for the termination of contract already existing. In addition, judicial review of such cases is very limited and comprises issue of the regularity of the internal procedure, statement of reasons, preciseness of facts on which the decision is based and misuse of powers. With regard to the issue of mutual trust, EU judges may assess whether the absence or the loss of it is effectively invoked and whether the motive used in this regard does not violate fundamental rights of the person concerned.[523]

For type (d) of the temporary staff, i.e. the research staff, the appointing authorities make use of existing general databases or the specific database of spontaneous applications established by the Directorate-General for Research. Furthermore, the composition of the selection committee must take account of the decentral-

520 *Commission Decision on Temporary Agents*, Article 3.

521 Ibid., Article 4.

522 *Chantal Hectors v. European Parliament, Case T-181/01, ECR-SC [2003[, p. I-A-19, II-103*, paras. 94 and 102-104.

523 *André Bonnet v. Court of Justice of the European Communities, Case T-406/04, ECR-SC [2006], p. I-A-2-213, II-A-2-1097*, paras. 47-49, 50-52 and 93.

ized nature of the Joint Research Centre. The President of the selection committee may furthermore be designated from the administrative services of this Centre.[524] It goes without saying that the involvement of the selection committee in this process contributes to its objectivity and impartiality.

Before moving to the next category of non-permanent staff, it should be noted that the ECJ has recognized a wide discretion of the appointing authorities in filling posts by temporary staff. In *Van der Stijl*, for example, the ECJ ruled that even if a post was permanent, the appointing authority could decide to engage a temporary agent in accordance with Article 2(b) of the *EU Conditions of Employment of Other Servants* before employing a permanent official. This was seen as a result of a broad discretion which the EC institutions have in choosing the most appropriate means for meeting their personnel needs. Despite this, the discretion is not unlimited. The ECJ emphasized that it was subject to the limitations imposed by the *EU Staff Regulations* and *Conditions of Service of Other Servants*, for example the applicable legal procedures.[525] The authorities authorized to conclude engagement contracts with temporary agents have also a wide discretion in comparing the merits of candidates. On the other hand, as is the case with permanent officials, the relevant authorities may disregard neither internal rules adopted by the relevant institution, nor the vacancy notice.[526] This proves importance of rules and procedures in each selection process. Their absence should therefore be remedied, perhaps with an exception of posts in the Commissioners' cabinets where mutual trust between the Commissioner and his cabinet staff is regarded as more important.

3.3.2. Contract staff

The selection procedure of the contract staff is set out in the *Commission Decision on Contract Staff* of 7 April 2004, as subsequently amended.[527] As explained in chapter 1, there are two categories of contract staff, namely 'contract staff 3a' (defined in Article 3a of the *EU Conditions of Employment of Other Servants*) and 'contract staff 3b' (defined in Article 3b of the *EU Conditions of Employment of Other Servants*).[528] The *Commission Decision on Contract Staff* reflects this categorization and contains different provisions for each of the two categories of contract staff.

The selection process of the 'contract staff 3a' begins with the publication of a general call for expression of interest for specific profiles. Such publication is done

---

[524] *Commission Decision on Temporary Agents*, Article 5.

[525] *Van der Stijl and Cullington v. Commission, Joined cases 341/85, 251, 258, 259, 262 and 266/86, 222 and 232/87*, paras. 11 and 33.

[526] *Robinson v. Parliament, Case T-328/01*, para. 73 and *Oreste Montalto v. Council of the European Union, Case T-116/03, ECR-SC [2004], p. I-A-339, II-1541*, paras. 63-68. For a more recent case see, for example, *Risto Suvikas v. Council of the European Union, Case F-6/07*, available at http://curia.europa.eu/jurisp/cgi-bin/form.pl?lang=en&Submit=Rechercher&alldocs=alldocs&docj=docj&docop=docop&docor=docor&docjo=docjo&numaff=F-6/07&datefs=&datefe=&nomusuel=&domaine=&mots=&resmax=100, last visited on 30.12.2010, paras. 88 and 101-102.

[527] *Commission Decision on Contract Staff.*

[528] See above, chapter 1, section 3.1.2.2.

by the EPSO and usually takes place on the EPSO website. In response, interested candidates may fill in on-line applications which are then stored in a database set up for this purpose. The applicants who match specific competency profiles and have required qualifications are invited to sit tests. Pursuant to the *Commission Decision on Contract Staff*, the tests are to assess general aptitudes and linguistic ability of the candidates. Candidates successful in these first tests are then listed in a database for a period of two years. A joint committee established for the purpose of an evaluation of applications listed in the database further assesses these applications and invites selected candidates to further tests concerning also knowledge of European integration and the institutions and professional competence. Successful candidates are 'validated' in the database for a period of three years, with a possible extension. Validated candidates who are considered by a hiring service to be suitable to their specific requirements are to be invited to an interview by a selection committee which adopts the final decision on the employment of a specific contract agent.[529]

Scheme 9: Selection process of the European Commission 'contract staff 3a'

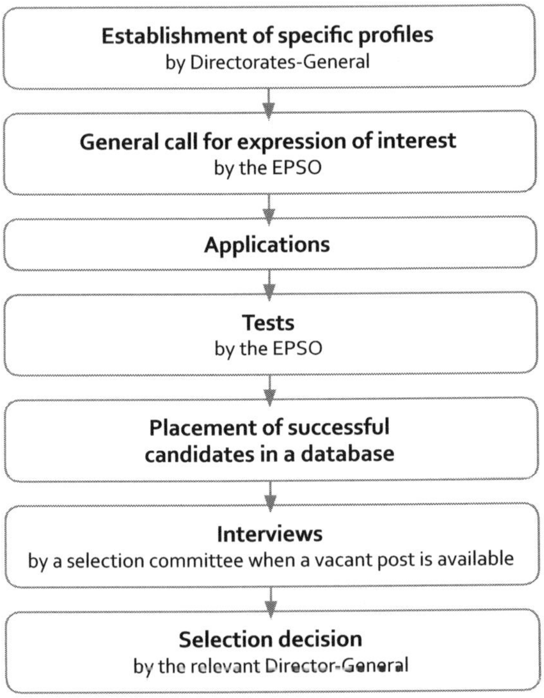

[529] *Commission Decision on Contract Staff*, Article 5.

The 'contract staff 3b' is also engaged on the basis of validation lists, unless no suitable candidates are available. In the latter case, the hiring Commission service identifies suitable candidates from the two-year database which has been established after the first tests on general aptitutes and linguistic abilities. So identified candidates are invited to sit further tests and/or interviews as follows:

> *- In function group II: tests, organized by EPSO, of the candidates' competences relevant to that job and interviews with the candidates who have passed these tests; these interviews shall be conducted by a committee established for this purpose and shall focus on the personal competencies of the candidates; in the case of selection procedures for functions where no appropriate test is available the tests may be replaced by extending the interviews to include the professional competencies of the candidates;*
>
> *- In function groups III and IV: interviews with the candidates conducted by a committee established for this purpose. These interviews shall focus on the professional and personal competencies of the candidates.*[530]

Said that, it must be noted that in 2010 the EPSO announced the launch of new selection procedure for contract agents, together with the new types of tests for open competitions held for recruitment of officials. The first set of tests to be used for contract agents are computer based, and are aimed at assessing general aptitudes of candidates, in particular verbal and numerical reasoning capacity, and knowledge of European affairs. These tests should be conducted in the candidates' second language in order to assess, in addition, language proficiency. Candidates successful in the first set of tests should further be tested more specifically with regard to their competence. These tests may be conducted in an oral form. Successful candidates will be listed in a database from which EU institutions will recruit staff for specific vacant posts. The database should be time limited and valid for three years. Like now, there will be no legal guarantee that candidates placed in the database will actually be recruited as contract agent.[531] This new selection procedure for contract agents announced by the EPSO in 2010 has, however, not (yet) been reflected in the *Commission Decision on Contract Staff*. Since procedures contained therein, explained above, differ in several respects when compared to the EPSO new procedures, it is to be expected that the *Commission Decision on Contract Staff* will be amended.

3.4. Recruitment of seconded national experts

The European Commission normally recruits seconded national experts from EU countries via their permanent representations to the EU. In case of non-EU nationals, applications are forwarded to the Commission by the diplomatic missions of the relevant non-Member States. When secondment takes place from the EFTA

[530] Ibid., Article 8(2)(b). For details on various function groups in which 'contract staff 3a' serve, see above, chapter 1, section 3.1.2.2.

[531] European Personnel Selection Office, *Selection Procedure*.

Secretariat or from a secretariat of an international organization, the applications are submitted via their relevant bodies.[532] After an agreement on the secondment of a specific person is reached and authorized by the Directorate-General for Human Resources and Security, it is effectuated by a formal exchange of letters between the Director-General for Human Resources and Security and the relevant office of the permanent representation of the Member State, diplomatic mission of the non-Member State, EFTA or other international secretariat.[533]

The most recent version of the *Commission Decision on Secondment* adopted in 2008 stipulates that the selection of seconded national experts is to be conducted according to an open and transparent procedure, details of which are to be decided by the Directorate-General for Human Resources and Security.[534] To date, no formal set of rules have been developed, though. The selection process of seconded national experts appears therefore to be conducted solely on the basis of informal rules and practices rather than on a formal procedure, which is regrettable, for obvious reasons. In this respect it should also be noted that vacancy notices for positions of seconded national experts do not seem to be published in any official medium of the EU and persons interested in working as an seconded national expert are selected through Permanent Representations of EU Member States.[535] Since most seconded national experts do indeed come from Member States' national civil services, this is, to a certain extent, understandable. It is indeed not surprising that governments wish to maintain certain control over who is temporarily posted with the Commission. In the end, they are one of the three parties to each individual agreement on secondment. Also, Member States' governments have the best access to potential candidates and can easily spread information on existing vacancies. However, it could be argued that the exclusivity of the competence of Member States' governments to propose future seconded national experts goes too far and that national civil servants should be able to apply for secondment positions in the European Commission also directly. If they succeed in the selection process, they should have a fair opportunity to make appropriate arrangements for the period of absence with their superiors at

[532] *Commission Decision on Secondment*, Article 3(3). See also Commission information on the European Commission Civil Service portal, available at http://ec.europa.eu/civil_service/job/sne/index_en.htm, last visited on 22.1.2008.

[533] Ibid., Article 3(4).

[534] Ibid., Article 3(1).

[535] Neither the EUR-Lex, official internet portal for access to all published EU documents, nor the official on-line Register of Commission Documents, reveal any vacancy notices for seconded national experts. Many vacancy notices can, however, be found on the internet, through a general search function. These notices provide no information on the selection procedure, though, only substantive requirements that need to be met by potential candidates. See, for example, European Commission, *Notice of Vacancy, Seconded National Experts*, available at http://www.mof.gov.cy/mof/papd/papd.nsf/all/C5D7B9006BE32327C225770E0038D474/$file/EN%20rectificatif%2029.pdf?openelement, last visited on 30.12.2010. The official European Commission Civil Service website states in this regard the following: 'The Commission recruits Seconded National Experts from EU countries via their Permanent Representations to the EU. If you are interested in working as an SNE, you should initially enquire at your Permanent Representation to the EU. There you should be put in touch with the person responsible for managing SNE recruitment from your Member State who can deal with your request.' – available at http://ec.europa.eu/civil_service/job/sne/index_en.htm, last visited on 30.12.2010.

home. Only in such cases one can be certain that seconded national experts are fully independent and impartial from their governments.

4. The UN and the EU compared

4.1. General observations

As explained in the introductory section to this chapter, the independence and impartiality of international civil service and international civil servants are, among others, guaranteed by an objective and transparent recruitment process free from extraneous influence and adhering by clear and sufficiently precise rules. The previous two sections of this chapter describe and analyses legal framework established in the UN Secretariat and in the European Commission, respectively, for their staff recruitment. This section compares both legal frameworks and further assesses their objectivity and transparency.

To begin with, there are many similarities in the approach as well as in the procedural framework used in the UN Secretariat and in the European Commission for recruitment of staff from outside. Nonetheless, a number of differences can be identified, conceptual as well as concrete ones in specific procedures. The most important conceptual difference relates to the basis on which a specific recruitment method is employed in a certain type of situation. In the EU, the main distinction on the basis of which a certain recruitment method is to be used is the type of appointment of the future staff member. Thus, permanent officials are recruited according to a set of rules different from that for non-permanent staff. In addition, different categories, or even subcategories, of non-permanent staff are recruited by using different methods of recruitment. Apart from the distinction in the basis of the type of future contract, another differentiation between recruitment methods to be used is made on the basis of the level of the vacant post. While the same recruitment method applies to the great majority of posts, a specific set of rules apply to senior posts.

Contrary to the EU, in the UN the method of recruitment is not necessarily linked to the type of future contract but depends partly on the level of the post to be filled, partly on the category in which the future staff will serve and partly on other considerations, such as the need to ensure equitable geographical distribution. Thus, for example, Professional staff at entry level subject to the geographical distribution are recruited by employing one method, while Professional staff at entry level not subject to the geographical distribution are recruited using other methods, much like Professional staff above the entry level, with an additional distinction for senior staff. Furthermore, staff in different non-Professional categories are selected via various different means, some via the same means as certain categories of Professional staff, others not.

The UN approach is thus fairly complex. This complexity renders a comparison between the two systems rather difficult. In order to overcome this difficulty, four distinct comparisons are made. The first comparison is between the UN and EU competition systems, as both respective organizations use this method of outside recruitment, albeit to a different extent. The second comparison is between the *UN*

Staff Selection System and the EU competitions. The reason for this comparison is that the former is used for recruiting staff to posts comparable with those for which EU officials need to pass a competition. The third comparison is between respective UN and EU procedures used for recruiting temporary and other non-permanent staff (or non-quasi-permanent ones, as explained in more detail below). The fourth and the last comparison concerns recruitment to senior posts, given their special regime in both the UN Secretariat and the European Commission.

4.2. UN and EU competitions

In both the UN Secretariat and in the European Commission, competition is considered to be the most appropriate means of recruiting external staff. 'Written examinations', supported by further appraisal of general capacities of candidates, were recommended already by the UN Preparatory Committee of 1945 as the appropriate means of selecting future UN staff, with the exception of staff who were to fill specialized or senior posts.[536] Also the 1986 Group of High-Level Intergovernmental Experts referred to as G-18 recommended the use of tests or individual examinations for selection of candidates for posts at the P-4 ad P-5 level, for which no competitive examinations were organized.[537] In the EU, the Committee of Independent Experts of 1999 noted the 'obvious merits' of a system of competition, ensuring that recruitment leads to appointment of persons with highest standards of ability, efficiency and integrity.[538] If properly administered, competition guarantees transparency, objectivity, independence of the process as well as equality of treatment of all candidates. In that sense, both the UN and the EU staff regulations provide for competition as the principal method for staff recruitment. However, the extent to, and the level of posts for, which competition is mandatory differs.

In the European Commission, passing a competition is the exclusive route to becoming a permanent official. Few and very limited exceptions to this rule are explicitly provided for in the *EU Staff Regulations* – they relate to posts requiring special qualifications and senior posts.[539] The competition requirement also does not apply to non-permanent posts, although in some categories of non-permanent staff candidates need to sit one or more tests before they may be engaged. This is the case of future contract staff, who constitute by far the largest category of non-permanent staff serving in the European Commission, amounting to some 15 per cent of all Commission employees.[540] Other non-permanent employees, notably temporary staff, are recruited without any tests, and some subcategories of temporary staff even without going through any formal selection process, while the type of work performed by temporary staff is in essence the same as that of permanent staff.[541]

---

536 *Report of the UN Preparatory Commission*, Chapter VIII, Section 2, paras. 50-53.

537 *G18 Report*, Recommendation 43(2), p. 20.

538 *Second Report on Reform of the Commission of 1999, Volume II*, para. 6.5.4. See also paras. 6.5.1.-6.5.3.

539 See above, sections 3.1, 3.2.2 and 3.3.3.

540 *Commission's Human Resources Report 2009*, p. 30. For details on tests used for the recruitment of the European Commission contract staff, see above, section 3.3.2.

541 See above, section 3.3.1.

Although the number of temporary staff serving in the Commission is relatively low, amounting to about 5 per cent of all staff, in absolute terms there are almost 2.000 temporary agents in the Commission who do not need to pass any test before being engaged.[542] The entire group of non-permanent staff other than contract staff, who are thus not subject to competition or tests, constitutes as much as 25 per cent of all Commission staff.[543]

In the UN Secretariat, competition is compulsory only for entry level posts at the P-1 and P-2 level which are subject to geographical distribution or require special language competence. Other P-1 and P-2 posts and posts above the P-2 level are not subject to the competition requirement, although competition normally should, and sometimes is, used at the P-3 level, too.[544] At present, the number of posts for which a competition needs to be passed is thus rather limited, although it is not entirely clear what it means in quantitative terms – data concerning the composition of the UN Secretariat, provided in the Secretary-General's latest report, are not sufficient for making a precise assessment. The Secretary-General reported that on 30 June 2010 there were 53 staff members at the P-1 level and 1737 staff members at the P-2 level.[545] Of the latter 426 had geographical status, representing less than one per cent of all Secretariat staff.[546] Since no data were provided for geographical staff at the P-1 level, it must be presumed that there were no such staff at the reported date. Furthermore, in total 754 staff members served in posts classified as language ones, though the report does not specify how many of them were at the junior level.[547] Now, even if all these language staff were added to 426 geographical staff serving at the P-2 level, the total proportion of these staff would be about 2,5 per cent of all Secretariat staff. But since not language staff were junior staff, it must be concluded that less than 2,5 per cent of all staff in the UN Secretariat are subject to competition before being appointed. Recent considerations towards broadening the scope of one type of UN competitions, namely the national competitive recruitment examination (NCRE), have not led to any significant change.[548] The proportion of UN staff recruited through competition will thus remain, at least for the time being, very low, certainly compared to the European Commission.

The *UN Staff Regulations* are thus considerably less strict in imposing competition as a requirement for becoming international civil servant than the *EU Staff Regulations*. While the latter considers competition as a mandatory condition for all permanent officials and some non-permanent staff, the former only calls for recruitment 'on a competitive basis' and 'so far as practicable'.[549] As explained above, the phrase 'so

[542] For the number of the European Commission temporary staff, see *Commission's Human Resources Report 2009*, p. 30.

[543] For the total number of the European Commission non-permanent staff, see Ibid., p. 30.

[544] See above, section 2.2.1.

[545] *Composition of the Secretariat: Staff Demographics, Report of the Secretary-General, A/65/350*, p. 28, Table 7.

[546] Ibid., p. 51, Table 21.

[547] Ibid., p. 28, Table 7.

[548] See above, chapter 2, section 2.3.1.1.

[549] *EU Staff Regulations*, Articles 28(d) and *UN Staff Regulations of 2009*, Regulation 4.3.

far as practicable' has been implemented in the UN by imposing competition only for recruitments to P-1 and P-2 geographical and language posts.[550] On the other hand, it could be argued that the requirement 'on a competitive basis' is not identical to the requirement to hold a competition and that there are other methods of recruitment containing competitive elements without being regarded as competition. Some competitive elements are indeed present in the recruitment method used for filling UN posts above the entry level – many of them are filled via the *UN Staff Selection System* which does not involve competition proper but allows for the use of selection tests. The problem is that such tests may but do not necessarily need to be employed – it is up to the relevant hiring manager to decide which evaluating mechanism he deems appropriate – and thus whether tests are 'practicable' in a particular recruitment case or not. Of course, it could be argued that even where no recourse is made to tests in a specific selection procedure, the mere fact that a number of candidates are considered and evaluated contains an element of competitiveness. Regrettably, such competitiveness is in all these instances reduced to a certain extent by the obligation to evaluate candidates against the vacancy requirements, not against other candidates. This approach is thus different from that typically employed in competitions and has been criticized, for example, by the UN Joint Inspection Unit. Its statement, made in 2006 but still relevant, deserves to be cited in full:

> *The current recruitment and promotion process gives to managers latitude to choose among those candidates who meet "the minimum requirements". This approach is far from ideal and can easily lead to unfairness, favouritism and discrimination. It goes against the statements made by the Secretary-General in several papers indicating that the Organization should attract the best available candidates. Furthermore, it goes against regulations established by the General Assembly...*[551]

The Unit continued:

> *Thus, the correct approach should be to choose "the best candidate" among those who meet the minimum requirements. This could be done easily if quantifiable and/or verifiable criteria are pre-established, made known to the candidates and spelled out through a comparative evaluation, the results of which should be recorded for demonstrating the fairness and objectivity of the selection process in the event of cases of appeal.*
>
> *In support of such a system of transparent recruitment, tools and mechanisms should be developed - for instance tests, competency-based interviews and "assessment centres" - to assist managers in discharging their responsibilities. Predefined, quantitative and qualitative, clear and verifiable criteria should be*

[550] See above, introductory part to section 2.2.

[551] *Results-based Management in the United Nations in the Context of the Reform Process, Report of the Joint Inspection Unit, JIU/REP/2006/6*, para. 153.

> *used in the selection of candidates, and the respective weights of these criteria should be clearly determined.*[552]

It is clear that the existing *UN Staff Selection System* has not reflected these recommendations.

The EU approach is stricter than that in the UN. Unlike UN civil servants, all EU civil servants are required to have passed a competition in the real sense of the word, though this statement needs to be qualified in several respects. First, as already mentioned, recruitment to non-permanent posts in the European Commission occurs without holding a competition, even if some categories of non-permanent staff need to pass one or more tests before being engaged. Still, some 25 per cent of European Commission staff are hired without any competition or tests, while at least some of these staff, namely temporary staff and seconded national experts, are in charge of issues comparable with those dealt with by permanent officials.[553]

The second necessary qualification, partly related to the first one, is that it is not always and necessarily open (i.e. external) competition that needs to be passed before a permanent appointment is granted in the European Commission. As explained above, when a vacant post occurs, the EU Administration may decide to fill it by means of internal competition, which it may open to temporary staff, too.[554] Having passed such internal competition, such non-permanent staff can become permanent, without having to pass open (i.e. external) competition. This possibility softens, to a certain extent, the rather strict competition requirement for granting permanent appointments in the European Commission. As stated earlier, the use of internal competitions for recruitment of permanent staff is less desirable, not only because its fairness vis-à-vis external candidates can be questioned, but also because it may result in personal acquaintances playing a too important, even decisive, role. This (may) make(s) the selection process less transparent, less objective and less impartial than open competition.

The third and last necessary qualification to the statement that the EU requirement to hold competitions is stricter that the UN requirement to conduct staff recruitment on a competitive basis is that in the EU passing a competition leads to a permanent

---

552 Ibid., paras. 153-154.

553 See above, section 3.3 and chapter 1, section 3.1.2. Note that temporary staff and seconded national experts represent about eight per cent of all Commission staff. – *Commission's Human Resources Report 2009*, p. 30.

554 There are no data available on how many posts are filled by internal competition. In its most recent *Human Resources Report* of 2009, the Commission reported merely on internal competitions organized specifically for nationals of new Member States. - Ibid., p. 110. Elsewhere it did note, however, that 30 per cent of newly recruited officials were working in the Commission at the time of recruitment as temporary or contract staff members. Another 0,8 per cent of new recruits were working in other EU institutions when appointed by the Commission. In absolute terms, this amounts to 1367 recruitments of former temporary and contract staff members and 38 recruitments from other institutions. – *Commission's Human Resources Report 2009*, p. 104. Of course, this information does not necessarily mean that all mentioned temporary staff members were recruited to permanent posts via internal competition; some of them might have passed an open competition and been recruited under that procedure. Moreover, contract staff are not eligible to take internal competition.

appointment, whereas in the UN such appointments are no longer granted. As explained in chapter 6, which addresses the issue of different types of appointments employed in the two organizations, in 2009 the UN replaced permanent appointment with continuing appointment. The latter provides no security of tenure and is granted only by way of conversion of a probationary or a fixed-term appointment, after a number of years of satisfactory service with the UN. Such continuing appointment lasts until it is terminated, although termination is only possible under relatively strict conditions.[555]

The comparison of the EU and UN competition requirement means thus comparing different situations. In the EU, when a candidate passes an open competition, he may receive permanent appointment with the European Commission, after serving a probationary period of several months. In the UN, passing a competition, where provided, never leads to granting permanent appointment. It may only result in a fixed-term appointment, with the possibility of converting this appointment into a continuing one later.

Despite this difference, and despite the formally open-ended character of the UN's continuing appointment, this study argues that the new type of continuing appointment is not as dissimilar to the past permanent appointment as it seems to be claimed by the UN Administration.[556] Therefore, for the purposes of this study and for facilitating comparison of the UN recruitment process with that of the EU, the UN continuing appointment is considered to be a (quasi) permanent appointment, unless otherwise specified. Since it is expected that many of the UN staff members recruited initially for a fixed-term period will eventually be granted continuing appointments, their status is comparable to that of permanent EU civil servants. Because of the less strict requirement in the UN regarding the need to pass a competition before receiving UN appointment, many of these eventually (quasi) permanent UN staff will have never passed competition, whereas the EU permanent officials always do. The initial statement that the UN system is less strict than the EU system thus stands, although it is subject to the refinements explained earlier.

It is not easy to explain the difference in the UN and EU approaches with regard to the (non) exclusivity of competition for recruitment to (quasi) permanent posts. As noted earlier in this section, the importance of competition in staff selection was recognized already in early years in both organizations. However, unlike the EU, the UN has never adopted it as an exclusive means. Moreover, the establishment of the existing systems of competitive examinations in the UN took place gradually, at different points in time for different types and levels of posts.[557] In the meantime, staff were selected through other methods which, perhaps unintentionally to start with, have remained in use until now. In the EU, competition was introduced *en bloc* for all permanent posts with the adoption of the first *EU Staff Regulations*.[558]

[555] For details on types of appointment used in the UN Secretariat, see below, chapter 6, section 2.3.

[556] For details, see chapter 6, section 2.4.

[557] See above, section 2.2.1.1.

[558] See above, section 3.1.

Another possible explanation of the divergence between the UN and the EU in this respect might be their different approaches to the idea of career service. In the EU, career service has been regarded as the basis for the employment of a large majority of staff performing core functions. All such staff are, in principle, to be recruited for their entire career and move from lower to higher levels. The need to bring in external staff is considered to exist only at the most senior level. As a result, in the EU, permanent staff are normally recruited at the junior level and are expected to stay in the EU civil service until their retirement.[559] In the UN, external staff enter the organization at all levels. The greater variety of posts, especially with regard to the type of work performed and its (expected) duration, might be the reason behind this, together with the need for flexibility and/or for continuous refreshment of the organization's workforce by outside expertise at all levels. In such a situation, competitive examination is perhaps not the most suitable method of recruitment, as it would need to be organized separately for each type and level of post. Be it as it may, the fact remains that, if conducted properly, competition is the most objective manner of staff recruitment.

Comparing the UN and EU competitions themselves, there are two types of competitions in both organizations. As already mentioned, in the EU, they take the form of open or internal competitions, depending on the status of persons eligible to take part in them. In the UN, a distinction is made on the basis of the type of posts for which competition is organized, be it either non-language or language posts. Since 2010, competitions for generalist posts are organized on an annual basis in both the UN and the EU. Before 2010, the EU competitions were organized when needed, which often led to unpredictable timing for both the candidates and the EU institutions. Currently, competitions for generalists are organized annually and only competitions for specialist profiles take place *ad hoc*, thus when a need arises. Similarly, the UN NCRE are organized annually but the competitive language examinations are prepared in accordance with specific needs.[560] The introduction of annual organization of EU competitions for generalists in 2010 must be praised for it brings predictability to the system which is of an obvious value to potential candidates. It could even be argued that this predictability increases the transparency of the system as such. For the UN, the NCRE have been organized annually for some time, though the competitions' predictability is decreased there by the fact that not all UN Member States organize them each year. It depends on their representation status, which is indeed not so unpredictable, but also on the autonomous decision of each Member State whether it organizes the competition in a certain year or not. Potential candidates for junior Professional posts in the UN Secretariat thus never know whether they have access to the, in principle, exclusive entry point or not, and if they do, when (i.e. in which year to come).

Turning to the legal basis for EU competitions and UN competitive examinations, it has been explained above that until June 2010 there was no proper administrative issuance comparable to Annex III to the *EU Staff Regulations* setting out rules

559 For details on EU career system, see chapter 6, section 3.

560 See above, sections 2.2.1 and 3.2.1.

according to which the UN NCRE were to be conducted. In addition, two administrative instructions related to the UN competitive language examinations did not, and still do not, possess sufficient detail, for example with regard to the content of the tests.[561] Although the latter is also the case with Annex III to the *EU Staff Regulations* – they refer in this regard to the EPSO, an EU agency administering EU competitions – the EPSO adopts general rules governing competitions where all the details are provided. The promulgation of a long due administrative instruction on the UN NCRE is thus an important improvement of the UN competitions system, providing a clear and detailed guidance to all persons and authorities involved, contributing thereby to the overall transparency of this system.[562]

Procedural steps to be taken in the UN and EU competitions are fairly comparable. In both, the process begins with a formal notice of competition. Received applications are checked for their admissibility by a relevant board that decides which applicants will be admitted to the competition. The admitted candidates then sit written and oral tests and are subsequently considered by a relevant board. After individual consideration of candidates successful in the tests, a decision is taken as to which candidates are suitable for appointment and are therefore to be placed on a list referred to as roster of suitable candidates in the UN and as reserve list in the EU. When a relevant post becomes vacant, a candidate is selected from the list and appointed. The selection of the candidates to be appointed is made in the UN by the relevant Head of Department or Office and in the EU by the Director-General, unless this authority is delegated to another official.[563]

Despite all these similarities, there are a number of notable differences. The first one is that EU competitions may be based not only on tests and qualifications but also on qualifications only. In the latter case, no tests are organized and candidates are assessed only through a comparison of their merits by the relevant selection board. The UN competitions, both the NCRE and the competitive language examinations, always include tests, both written and oral.[564] The EU competition based only on qualifications appears to be similar to recruitment under the *UN Staff Selection System* where selection occurs solely on the basis of the evaluation of candidates' qualifications. An important difference between the two situations is, however, that EU competitions based only on qualifications are in practice never used for recruitment of external candidates, while the *UN Staff Selection System* includes such a possibility. Clearly, the use of tests for assessing candidates' knowledge and suitability for international civil service is a more objective manner than a mere comparison of qualifications, in particular given the sometimes significant differences between various education systems in place in different countries. This is especially the case in the UN where, arguably, differences between Member States are greater than in the EU. Yet, tests, being the more objective method of assessing candidates' exper-

[561] See above, sections 2.2.1.2. and 2.2.1.3.

[562] See above, section 2.2.1.2.

[563] See above, sections 2.2.1.2 and 3.2.1.3.

[564] See above, sections 2.2.1.2 and 3.2.1.3.

tise and suitability for employment, are not required under the *UN Staff Selection System*.[565]

The next two important differences between the UN and EU competitions concern EU reserve lists and UN rosters. Firstly, the EU reserve lists are time limited, whereas UN rosters are not – neither the NCRE roster nor the roster for language posts – though this seems to change for the NCRE roster in future.[566] At present, UN candidates who succeed in the competition are added to those who have been placed on the relevant roster in the past and have not yet received an appointment. This leads to the accumulation of a large number of candidates waiting for an appointment, sometimes for years without having any real objective and transparent possibility to influence the outcome.[567] Although in the EU the actual appointment may take some time, too, for most, if not all, candidates on the reserve list this time is reasonable. In the UN, the commonly known uncertainty about the actual placement and the length of the waiting time may tempt candidates to take recourse to practices that would enhance their chances but, inevitably, compromise their independence and impartiality once appointed.

The second difference between the EU reserve lists and the UN rosters concerns candidates' ranking. Although ranking of candidates is provided neither on the EU reserve lists nor on the UN rosters, candidates who make it to the EU reserve lists are usually divided into different merit groups. These indicate how well candidates did in the competition – candidates in merit group I did better than candidates in merit group II and so on.[568] This allows for a certain degree of comparison of the quality of candidates by the official making final selection, even though it must be admitted that full comparison between individual candidates is not possible due to the absence of individual ranking. In the UN, there is no ranking at all of candidates placed on the relevant roster or other classification that could inform hiring managers how well individual candidates did in the competitive examinations. Clearly, this does not support the transparency and impartiality of the final stage of the selection process. Since the length (and lack of update) of UN rosters makes objective selection close to impossible, it directly or indirectly forces the hiring managers to rely on information on individual candidates who are on the roster from other sources who may thereby (wish to) influence the final selection. Moreover, the absence of ranking and the fact that no individual results are released make it difficult for UN candidates placed on the NCRE roster to assess whether selection of another can-

[565] See above, section 2.2.2.2.

[566] See above, sections 2.2.1.2 and 3.2.1.3. See also the Secretary-General's outline of the new Young Professionals Programme to be introduced from 2011 onwards, according to which the NCRE roster will be valid for one year. - *Human Resources Management Reform: Young Professionals Programme, Report of the Secretary-General, A/65/305/Add.4*, p. 8, Table 1, point 5. The Young Professionals Programme was approved by the UN General Assembly in its most recent resolution adopted in December 2010. - *General Assembly Resolution 65/247*, Section III.

[567] For example, in October 2009 there were 521 candidates on the NCRE roster. The Secretary-General admitted that candidates who stay on the roster for more years have significantly smaller chance of being appointed. - *Human Resources Management Reform: Young Professionals Programme, Report of the Secretary-General, A/65/305/Add.4*, paras. 55 and 56.

[568] See above, section 3.2.1.3.

didate was indeed objective or whether they might have a case objecting to it.[569] To compare, EU candidates who are not appointed into an individual post not only have the right to request reasons of their non-selection.[570] They might be more encouraged to challenge the decision if they are aware, for example, of the fact that a candidate from a lower merit group was appointed.

It could thus be argued that objectivity and transparency of the recruitment and selection process is better guaranteed in the European Commission than in the UN Secretariat. An additional argument supporting this view is the fact that in the UN the decision on the placement on the roster of suitable candidates is, at least formally, taken by the Secretary-General (for the NCRE) or by the Assistant Secretary-General for Human Resources Management (for the competitive language examinations), and not by the board of examiners. This creates an impression of a less objective and transparent system. In the end, it is the board of examiners which examines and evaluates individual candidates.[571] This board is thus better qualified to judge which candidates are suitable for appointment with the UN than the Secretary-General or the Assistant Secretary-General for Human Resources Management. In addition, the board of examiners is a collective body, which is another factor contributing to a more objective and impartial decision. An additional layer in the process of decision making on the placement of successful candidates on the roster seems thus to be unnecessary. In the EU competitions, the decision on the placement on the reserve list is taken by the relevant selection board which forwards the list to the appointing authority.[572]

Arguably, UN boards of examiners and EU selection boards are the most important authorities involved in the UN competitive examinations and in the EU competitions, respectively. In general terms, these boards decide on applicants' admissibility to competition, conduct candidates' assessment and prepare the list of candidates suitable for appointment. EU selection boards also decide on the placement of candidates on the reserve lists.[573] When comparing composition of the UN and EU boards, the most striking difference is the involvement of a non-voting *ex officio* member in the UN boards, representing the Assistant Secretary-General for Human Resources Management. Such a member sits on all boards – the NCRE board of examiners, the board of examiners for the competitive language examinations and the Central Recruitment Examination Board.[574] The presence of such official in the UN boards clearly indicates the interest of the UN Administration in being involved in, or at least informed of, details of the work of these boards. Although the *ex officio* member has no voting rights, his involvement raises concerns about the independent nature of these boards, especially because all members of the UN boards of examiners as well as of the Central Recruitment Examination Board are also appointed

[569] See above, section 2.2.2.2.

[570] See above, section 3.2.1.3.

[571] See above, section 2.2.2.2.

[572] See above, section 3.2.1.3.

[573] See above, sections 2.2.1 and 3.2.1.

[574] See above, sections 2.2.1.2 and 2.2.1.3.

by the UN Administration.[575] In the EU, half of the members of the selection board are appointed by the staff representatives and even of the members appointed by the EU Administration. None of them directly represents the Administration. In addition, the chair of the selection board is appointed jointly by the Administration and the staff representatives. EU staff representatives are also present in the Joint Committee which must be consulted by the Administration when drawing up the notice of a specific competition.[576] Given the importance of the involvement of staff representatives in the selection process, noted above, also their absence from UN boards is regrettable. The same hold true for the fact that the relevant UN administrative instructions provide no requirements or criteria to be used for selection of the boards' members, except that members of the Central Recruitment Examination Board, involved in the NCRE, must belong to different departments of the UN Secretariat. They also allow consultants, outside experts and retirees to become members of the specialized boards of examiners.[577] For the EU, a set of clear and detailed rules on the selection of board's members are included in the Annex III to the *EU Staff Regulations*. They provide that the function group and the grade of officials serving on the selection board may be not lower than that of the post to be filled.[578] It is regrettable that the recently adopted administrative instruction of 2010 concerning the NCRE does not include formal rules on the selection criteria of the members of the boards involved in this competition. The reasons for the absence of formal rules is unclear but it is possible that the UN Secretary-General wished to retain maximum flexibility, considering the difficulties in finding volunteers to do the work. Having said that, the mere fact that both the specialized boards of examiners and the Central Recruitment Examination Board now have clear legal basis for their mandate and tasks is already an important step in the right direction.

Another important difference in the authorities involved in the UN and EU competitions is the participation of the UN and EU Member States. Given the fact that the UN competition takes the form of national examinations, UN Member States are closely associated with the whole process. They first of all decide whether they wish to participate in the competition in a particular year and, if so, provide necessary facilities, including approaching and sometimes even screening potential candidates. Most of the organization work is done by the OHRM, similarly as it is with the EPSO in EU competitions.[579] In the EU, Member States have not been involved thus far, though this could change with the introduction of the new EPSO tests. When launching the new system in 2010, the EPSO announced that the first stage of the competition, the admission testing, will be held in individual EU Member States in order to reach a wider pool of potential candidates.[580] It appears, however, that even in such a case EU Member States will only provide technical facilities and have no say in the organization or administration of the competition at any stage. Their only

575 See above, sections 2.2.1.2 and 2.2.1.3.

576 See above, section 3.2.1.1.

577 See above, sections 2.2.1.2 and 2.2.1.3.

578 See above, section 3.2.1.1.

579 See above, sections 2.2.1.2. and 3.2.1.1.

580 See above, section 3.2.1.3.

remaining involvement is, and will be, organization of training courses for potential applicants with the aim of preparing them for the tests. This has been done by a number of EU Member States for decades, although the degree of involvement has differed greatly among individual countries.[581] In the UN, such training is not common but the Member States participating in the NCRE are relied on with regard to the active search of potential candidates. Some Member States are even involved in screening candidates who have decided to participate in the NCRE.[582] This could be questioned from the point of view of an objective and independent conduct of the competition. On the other hand, the mere fact that an administrative instruction with precise and detailed rules on the organization of the NCRE has finally been adopted is a positive step in this respect – any kind of involvement of participating UN Member States must respect the limits provided by this instruction. This enhances objectivity and transparency of the conduct of the competition process – one of the essential prerequisites for independence and impartiality of newly hired international civil servants. An immediate stop should, however, be put to Member States' screening of NCRE candidates.

4.3. *UN Staff Selection System* versus EU competitions

It has been explained earlier that UN competitions are only used for recruitment to entry level posts subject to geographical distribution or special language requirements. Most of the remaining posts in the UN Secretariat are filled by using procedures set out in the *UN Staff Selection System*. This includes entry level P-1 and P-2 posts which are *not* subject to geographical distribution or special language requirements, P-3 level posts which are *not* filled by competition, all Professional posts above this level as well as posts in General Service and related categories above the entry level.[583] Staff in these posts, recruited via the *UN Staff Selection System*, often hold functions and perform duties comparable to those of EU officials recruited via a competition. Therefore, it is reasonable to compare recruitment procedures under the *UN Staff Selection System* with those applicable to EU competitions. Such comparison is of special relevance in regards to middle level posts. Although in both the UN and EU posts above the entry level are to be filled by preference by internal candidates, in the UN such posts may be filled by an external candidate as well. Such appointment would follow the rules of the *UN Staff Selection System*, without resorting to any kind of competition.[584] Middle level positions in the UN Secretariat may thus be occupied by persons who have never passed a competition. This is not possible in the European Commission where middle level posts are filled by people who have been promoted from lower ranks, to which they have been appointed through a competition procedure, or, exceptionally, who have been recruited directly at a middle level but, again, through a competition. The only available exception in the EU are posts requiring special qualifications, for which a special recruitment proce-

[581] See above, Introduction, section 3.2.
[582] See above, chapter 2, section 2.3.1.1.
[583] See above, section 2.2.2.1.
[584] See above, section 2.2.2, in particular 2.2.2.1.

dure may be organized other than competition.[585] Any other method of recruitment to middle level posts would result in a non-permanent appointment. As explained above, all EU non-permanent appointments are made outside the competition process, using different sets of rules.[586] Permanent appointment at the middle level can, however, only be obtained by passing a competition, with the already mentioned exception of posts requiring special qualifications.

Briefly recalling the procedural steps to be taken under the *UN Staff Selection System* on the one hand and in the EU competition on the other, they both begin with a notice on the vacancy or competition, setting out specificities of the post or posts for which recruitment is organized and eligibility conditions. In the UN, this notice is issued when the vacancy arises, whereas in the EU, competitions are organized once a year now. In the UN, vacancy announcement is followed by the preparation of evaluation criteria which either follow pre-approved standards or are approved specifically for the vacancy by the relevant central review body, involving staff representatives. In the EU, competition notice is consulted with the Joint Committee, also involving staff representatives, before it is issued. This EU Joint Committee has no further role in the competition process in any way, whereas the UN central review body does. As mentioned above, when the proposal for a suitable candidate to be appointed is made, the relevant central review body checks whether evaluation criteria and appropriate procedures were properly followed and if they were not it passes the matter to the official designated by the Secretary-General instead of allowing the Head of Department or Office to proceed with the selection.[587]

Applications received upon publication of the notice of vacancy or competition notice are first scrutinized for their admissibility. Such initial scrutiny is done by the OHRM in the UN and by the appointing authority and selection board in the EU. The EU appointing authority checks only the general eligibility criteria for appointment with the EU, while the compliance with specific requirements of the competition are subsequently considered by the selection board. In the UN, the OHRM may, upon request by the hiring manager, also conduct qualitative screening of applicants and indicate to the hiring manager which candidates are suitable and are likely to qualify for the vacant post. The EU Administration has no such power, all qualitative assessment of candidates is strictly done by the selection board.[588] This latter arrangement seems to be more appropriate from the point of view of the objectivity and impartiality of the process as the EU selection board involves staff representatives while the OHRM does not. The qualitative screening of candidates by the UN Administration has greater susceptibility to being influenced than if such screening is conducted by the relevant selection board.

The next step in the proceedings differs in the UN and EU. In the UN, the relevant hiring manager proceeds with the evaluation of candidates. He uses evaluation mechanisms he deems appropriate. Since 2010, he is not even required to conduct

---

585 See above, introductory part to section 3.2.

586 See above, section 3.3.

587 See above, sections 2.2.2.2 and 3.2.1.3.

588 See above, sections 2.2.2.2 and 3.2.1.3.

an interview. If an interview is employed, it is always conducted by a panel he sets up. The hiring manager may also use written tests but, once again, the choice of appropriate evaluation mechanisms is within his broad discretion.[589] In contrast, in the EU competition, both written and oral examinations are held in every case, unless competition is conducted on the basis of qualifications only which, however, does not happen in cases of open competition. Formally, the content of the tests is established by the selection boards but, in practice, tests are prepared and managed by the EPSO.[590]

The final evaluation of candidates is conducted by the hiring manager in the UN and by the selection board in the EU. The proposal of a candidate or candidates recommended for appointment, made by the UN hiring manager, is reviewed by the central review body which, as explained above, may only assess whether evaluation criteria and required procedures were properly applied. The final decision on appointment is taken by the Head of Department or Office or, in case of a negative result of the review by the central review body, by an official designated by the Secretary-General. Candidates who were also recommended by the hiring manager and endorsed by the central review body but not appointed are placed on a roster and may be selected directly to fill a vacancy for which they possess required qualifications. In the EU, the selection board prepares a list of suitable candidates who are put in a reserve position and appointed when a specific vacancy becomes effective. The appointment is made by the appointing authority, i.e. by the relevant Director-General.[591]

It should also be recalled that while candidates included in the EU reserve list are divided into different merit groups, depending on how well they performed in the competition, no ranking is provided for candidates proposed for UN appointment or later placed on the UN roster.[592] This situation is similar to that in UN competitions where no ranking of successful candidates takes place either.[593] As argued earlier, the lack of any ranking of candidates means less transparency in the final step of the UN selection process, also when compared to the EU. An individual candidate placed on the UN roster and not selected for a specific vacant post has little possibility to check criterion on which the selection from the roster was made.

From the description of the respective UN and EU process of staff selection for the middle level posts it follows that much of the role of the EU selection board is fulfilled by the individual hiring manager under the *UN Staff Selection System*. It has been noted earlier that dangers of this situation have been emphasized, for example, by the UN staff unions, Joint Inspection Unit, the Office of Internal Oversight Services and even some UM Member States.[594] This is not surprising. This study also argues that the concentration of power in the hands of individual hiring managers

[589] See above, section 2.2.2.2.

[590] See above, sections 3.2.1.1 and 3.2.1.3.

[591] See above, sections 2.2.2.2 and 3.2.1.3.

[592] See above, sections 2.2.2.2 and 3.2.1.3.

[593] See above, section 2.2.1.2 and 2.2.1.3.

[594] See above, section 2.2.2.4.

constitutes potentially a greater threat to the objectivity and impartiality of the selection process under the *UN Staff Selection System* than, for example, EU competitions. There, most substantive work is done by selection boards which, firstly, are collective bodies and, secondly, have balanced composition. Powers vested upon the UN hiring managers should be thus restricted. Alternatively, limited powers of UN central review bodies involved in the selection process under the *UN Staff Selection System* should be reviewed and extended. Mandate of the Senior Review Group could serve as an example here. Competence of central review bodies should also be reviewed with regard to the situations in which they find that applicable rules and procedures were not followed in a particular selection process. Clear rules should regulate such instances. At present, the case is submitted to the Assistant Secretary-General or Under-Secretary-General, depending on the level of post at issue, who enjoy absolute discretion in deciding how to proceed with the matter. This appears to include the option to appoint the candidate proposed by the hiring manager despite the existing procedural flaws. This is clearly an unacceptable state of affairs, putting the entire system, its objectivity, transparency and impartiality, into question.

The last but not the least concern, applying to both the *UN Staff Selection System* and the EU competitions, relates to the actual selection from the UN roster established under the *UN Staff Selection System* and EU reserve list, respectively. The two instruments are comparable as they provide for lists from which eventually appointed candidates are selected, though there is an important difference between the UN roster and EU reserve list. Candidates listed on the UN roster should be considered in the selection process but may be disregarded to the advantage of a new candidate applying for the (subsequently occurring) vacant post, but the EU reserve list provides an exclusive instrument from which officials must be selected, without the possibility of looking for a suitable candidate elsewhere. In both organizations, however, the official making the selection from the roster or the reserve list enjoys discretion and large flexibility. As pointed out by Cini, in the EU context:

> *Once on the reserve list, finding an interesting job depends much more on who you know than what you know.*[595]

Transparency and impartiality in the last stage of the staff selection seem to be absent in both the UN and the EU. The current procedures do not appear to provide safeguards in this respect, which is regrettable.

4.4. Recruitment to non-(quasi)-permanent posts

Having compared the recruitment process leading to the appointment of external candidates to permanent – and in case of the UN (quasi) permanent – posts, it is time to address recruitment to posts which are, and will remain during their whole duration, of a temporary nature. This includes EU temporary and contract posts and

---

[595] Cini, *The European Commission, Leadership, Organisation and Culture in the EU Administration*, p. 119. For details on the current UN contractual arrangements, see below, chapter 6, section 2.3.

UN temporary posts. Although the latter are of a maximum one year's duration, while the former may last longer, and in some cases even indefinitely, the comparison is justified by the fact that recruitment to all these posts occurs pursuant to a set of rules distinct from those for recruitment to posts which are, at least potentially, (quasi) permanent. As explained earlier, the *UN Staff Selection System* applies, with some exceptions, to all posts of a duration of more than one year. According to the UN contractual arrangements adopted in 2009, all these posts are formally for fixed term periods. However, many of them stand chances of being converted into continuing appointments after five years.[596] This makes them comparable to the EU permanent appointment. The remaining UN posts, i.e. those of a duration shorter than one year, cannot be converted into continuing appointments and will thus remain temporary for their entire duration, as is the case with non-permanent posts in the EU.

When comparing the UN and EU regimes, it should be noted that recruitment procedures for both UN temporary posts and EU non-permanent positions do not depend on the level of the post. The same procedures apply to the UN temporary posts classified at the entry level as well as for temporary posts at all other levels. Similarly, the same procedures are used to a certain type of EU non-permanent posts, regardless of whether the relevant post is at the entry or middle level. Senior posts have their own regime in both organizations and are therefore addressed separately.[597]

To being with the UN temporary posts, since April 2010, the recruitment for these posts is regulated by the *Administrative Instruction, Administration of Temporary Appointment ST/AI/2001/4*. Until then the selection process for such jobs in the UN was unregulated, although there did exist administrative issuances setting out conditions under which engagements for these jobs could take place.[598] The adoption of the new administrative instruction is thus a positive step towards transparency of the selection process. Unfortunately, as explained above, this new instruction does not contain any specific rules that would regulate selection for temporary posts for less than three months, giving full competence to hiring managers. It follows that UN hiring managers may hire a person for such positions in any way they see fit. UN hiring managers enjoy broad discretion also in the selection process for temporary posts that are to last longer than three months, conducting most relevant work with little restrictions.[599]

In the European Commission, recruitment to non-permanent positions occurs outside a formal competition process, too, though it is, to a certain extent, formalized in case of some categories of non-permanent staff. In those instances, a selection committee is involved. Its composition and mandate is not addressed by the *EU Conditions of Employment of Other Servants*, which apply to the engagement of EU non-permanent staff, but relevant Commission decisions pay attention to it. They provide that selection committees are composed of officials appointed by both the

[596] See below, chapter 6, in particular section 2.4.2.

[597] See below, section 4.5.

[598] See above, section 2.2.3.

[599] See above, section 2.2.3.

Administration and the staff representatives, respectively. The main responsibility of committees involved in the selection process for the European Commission non-permanent staff is to establish a list of suitable candidates, while appointment to specific vacant posts is in the hands of the authority authorized to conclude contracts, i.e. the EU Administration, usually a Director-General or a Director.[600]

The fact that no selection committee is involved in the recruitment of UN temporary staff is, to a certain extent, understandable. Temporary posts are, by their very nature, of a relatively short duration and engagement of a selection committee could be considered too burdensome, unnecessarily prolonging the recruitment process, in particular when considering the relatively low number of such recruitments.[601] However, some of the EU non-permanent jobs are of a few months duration, too.[602] Nonetheless, a collective organ is involved, for most types of non-permanent appointment. From the point of view of objectivity and impartiality of the selection process, the EU regime provides more adequate guarantees than the UN process that places all the authority in the hands of individual hiring managers.

4.5. Recruitment to senior posts

Appointment of senior officials follows special procedures in both the UN and the EU. In the European Commission it occurs pursuant to a specific set of rules contained in the *Commission Compilation Document on Senior Officials Policy* which establishes a distinct procedure to be followed for all senior posts, including both the level of Director-General and the level of Director and equivalent.[603] In the UN, the *UN Staff Selection System*, applying to most UN Professional posts above the level for which competitions are organized, covers D-level posts as well, even though a number of specific rules for appointment to D-2 posts (i.e. level of Director, functioning as head of division) are contained in the *Secretary-General's Bulletin, Senior Review Group*, in force since 2009. These specific rules relate in particular to the procedure to be followed by the departments when making recommendations for filling a D-2 position and to the composition and functions of the review body involved in the selection process.[604] They result in a slight modification of the appointment procedure for D-2

[600] See above, section 3.3.

[601] As at 30 June 2010, 2.437 out of the total of 44.134 appointments in the UN Secretariat were temporary appointments. – *Composition of the Secretariat: Staff Demographics, Report of the Secretary-General, A/65/350*, p. 29. Although the proportion of temporary appointments is thus relatively low, constituting only 6 per cent of the total number of appointments, the absolute number is not small – almost two and a half thousand persons were employed on a temporary basis.

[602] In 2009, the total number of non-permanent staff serving under the *EU Conditions of Employment of Other Servants* amounted to 10.744, i.e. 27,8 per cent of all Commission staff, although it must be noted that the duration of non-permanent appointments varies in the EU between different (sub-) categories of staff. Therefore, not all non-permanent appointments in the European Commission are of only a few months duration, with no official statistics available for each of the (sub-)categories. For details on duration of different types of contracts in the European Commission, see chapter 6, section 3.2.2.

[603] See above, section 3.2.3.

[604] See above, sections 2.2.1.1 and 2.2.2.5.

posts when compared to D-1 posts (i.e. level of Principal Officer, functioning as head of service).[605]

Unlike in the UN, only minor disparities exist in the EU between procedures applicable to the level of Director on the one hand and to the level of Director-General on the other. A difference exists, for example, in the composition of the Consultative Committee on Appointments, an advisory body involved in the appointment procedure for all senior posts.[606] However, the procedure as such is in principle the same, including the same underlining principles and the same steps.

When comparing the UN and the EU, there are many similarities between the two organizations, especially between the procedure applicable to the UN D-2 posts and that for all senior appointments in the EU. The most striking parallels are: first, all vacancies must be published, subject to specific exceptions explicitly set out in the UN *Secretary's-General Bulletin, Senior Review Group* and the European Commission *Compilation Document*, respectively; second, the selection process can be limited to internal candidates only but, when it is open to external candidates, there is no obligation to give priority to internal candidates over external ones; third, an advi-

[605] There are four most notable differences between procedures for D-1 posts on the one hand and for D-2 posts on the other hand. The first relates to the final proposal for appointment of an individual candidate for a vacant D-post made to the appointing authority. While the proposal for D-1 position is made by the relevant hiring manager, in case of a D-2 position it is done by the Senior Review Group, functioning as the central review body for all D-2 appointments. The central review body for D-1 appointment is the central review board but this board has no power to propose a suitable candidate, it only reviews the proposal made by the hiring manager and checks whether relevant evaluation criteria and applicable procedures were respected. In addition, the proposal prepared by the hiring manager for a D-1 position may contain one but preferably more names from which the appointing authority will choose, whereas the proposal of the Senior Review Group is for a single candidate regarded the most suitable. On the other hand, it should be noted that the proposal of the Senior Review Group is made on the basis of a preceding proposal from the relevant department or office listing three candidates short-listed by that department or office. It should also be noted that the proposal of the Senior Review Group is based on the review of files and data provided by or requested from the relevant department or office. In case of D-1 posts, the hiring manager prepares the proposal on the basis of his own personal evaluation of candidates made, *inter alia*, by interviewing them. The Senior Review Group conducts no interviews and evaluates the short-listed candidates on the basis of the files received from the relevant department or office (and prepared by the hiring manager). The second notable difference between appointment procedures for D-1 and D-2 posts concerns the composition of the review body involved. The Senior Review Group is composed of persons appointed by the Secretary-General only, with no involvement of staff representatives. That is, however, the case with the central review board involved in the selection process for D-1 posts. The central review board is composed of members selected by the Secretary-General and by the staff representatives, respectively, each of them designating half of the members, while one member is selected jointly by both the Secretary-General and the staff representatives. The fact that the Senior Review Group comprises only members selected by the Secretary-General suggests that the Secretary General does not want any role for the Secretariat staff in the selection of their Directors. The third important difference between appointments for D-1 and D-2 posts concerns the authority taking the final decision. For D-2 posts the decision is taken by the Secretary-General himself, whereas for D-1 posts it is the Head of Department or Office who does so. The fourth and last notable difference is that candidates for D-1 posts who have been short-listed but not appointed are placed on a roster from which they can be directly appointed to a future vacant post. This is not possible with candidates for D-2 posts – these candidates would need to go through the whole procedure for filling a future D-2 vacancy from the beginning. – See above, sections 2.2.2.2, 2.2.2.4 and 2.2.2.5.

[606] See above, section 3.2.3.

sory body composed of most senior officials is involved in the process of making a recommendation or a proposal to the appointing authority; and fourth, the final decision is taken by the Secretary-General or by the College of Commissioners, i.e. by the highest administrative authority.[607] In particular the publication of vacancies and the involvement of an advisory body in the selection process for both UN and EU senior posts are important safeguards for this process' transparency and objectivity. Unfortunately, extent to which the relevant advisory body, and in fact also other bodies and authorities, are involved in the UN selection process leaves much to be desired, for example in comparison with the EU.

Indeed, most of the dissimilarities between the UN, as far as D-2 positions are concerned, and the EU relate to the actors involved in the process, their composition and their precise competences. To begin with, considerably more persons are involved in the EU procedure than in the UN. In the European Commission, there is a preselection panel established by the relevant Directorate-General, the Consultative Committee on Appointments, the portfolio Commissioner and for some posts also other relevant Commissioner(s), the College of Commissioners and, under precisely specified rules, external experts in the relevant field and/or in recruitment to high level posts and/or officials responsible for financial management matters. In addition, throughout the whole procedure in the European Commission a Rapporteur to the Case is involved.[608] In the UN Secretariat, most work throughout the procedure is done by a single person, namely the hiring manager. The Senior Review Group and eventually the Secretary-General get involved only in the final stage of the selection process.[609]

The great concentration of competence in the hands of the hiring manager in the UN Secretariat is striking when compared to the situation in the European Commission. There, each of the persons involved has different tasks, although the most 'substantive' work is conducted by the Consultative Committee on Appointments. It is also this Committee that decides which candidates will be interviewed and conducts the interviews as well. The Committee also decides whether and which external experts should participate in the process. Subsequently, the Committee decides which candidates will be shortlisted and prepares such a shortlist for the relevant Commissioner who proceeds with the selection process further.[610] The functions of the European Commission's Consultative Committee on Appointments are thus incomparable with the functions of the Senior Review Group in the UN Secretariat which only steps in the selection process after a shortlist of candidates has been made by the relevant department or office, in practice by the relevant hiring manager. In addition, as mentioned above, the Senior Review Group makes its recommendations for the appointment on the basis of files received from the department or office at issue, without itself having interviewed the candidates. That competence rests, once again, with the individual hiring manager, although he is obliged to

[607] See above, sections 2.2.2.2, 2.2.2.4, 2.2.2.5 and 3.2.3.
[608] See above, section 3.2.3.
[609] See above, sections 2.2.2.2, 2.2.2.4 and 2.2.2.5.
[610] See above, section 3.2.3.

employ an interdepartmental panel for conducting interviews for D-2 positions.[611] In the European Commission, the Consultative Committee on Appointments itself interviews candidates suggested by the departmental pre-selection panel. Moreover, the portfolio Commissioner, who makes the final proposal of one candidate to the appointing authority, also interviews candidates short listed for him by the Consultative Committee on Appointments.[612] The final candidate proposed to the appointing authority has thus in the European Commission been interviewed by many persons and at several stages of the selection process, including by the person who makes the final proposal. In contrast, in the UN Secretariat the final candidate proposed for appointment is interviewed only once and not by the body making the final proposal.

On the basis of this comparison, it could be argued that the EU system contains more guarantees that selection of senior officials is conducted in an objective and impartial manner than the UN system does. An argument challenging this view could be made with regard to the fact that in the European Commission the portfolio Commissioner can decide that none of the candidates proposed by the Consultative Committee on Appointments suits him and to either interview another candidate or to re-advertise the vacancy.[613] In the UN Secretariat, neither the relevant hiring manager nor the Senior Review Group has such mandate. The discretion of an individual portfolio Commissioner in the European Commission is thus broad and involves a danger of it being abused or misused. However, as explained earlier, all proposals for appointment to senior posts must be agreed upon by the portfolio Commissioner, the Commissioner for Human Resources and Security, as well as the Commission President (for Director-General positions) or the relevant Director-General (for Director positions). The appointment itself must, furthermore, be approved by the entire College of Commissioners.[614] Arguably, these safeguards reduce the danger of the portfolio Commissioner using his discretion in an inappropriate or questionable manner, even though it cannot be denied that the danger is not eliminated entirely.

Comparing with the UN Secretariat, the fact that the final proposal is prepared by a collective organ composed of as many as nine persons guarantees, to a certain extent, an objective and unbiased process, arguably more adequately than the safeguards just mentioned with regard to the process in the European Commission. Unfortunately, the Senior Review Group in the UN Secretariat can only make its choice from among three candidates proposed by the department or office at issue, without having interviewed any of these candidates. [615] Contrary to this, the European Commissioner may choose from a longer shortlist prepared by the

[611] See above, section 2.2.2.5.
[612] See above, section 3.2.3.
[613] See above, section 3.2.3.
[614] See above, section 3.2.3.
[615] See above, section 2.2.2.5.

Consultative Committee on Appointments or, as already noted, even go beyond the list and choose a candidate he considers the best.[616]

The European Commission's rules on procedures for filling senior posts also require that the shortlist prepared by the Consultative Committee on Appointments offers the Commissioner as wide a choice of candidates as possible but takes into account the need to avoid too heavy a burden of comparative assessment of a large number of candidates. The number of shortlisted candidates should thus not be too large but also not too small, unlike in the case with the UN short list which comprises just three names of suitable candidates.[617] It could be argued that the flexibility provided in this respect in the EU better serves the objectivity of the selection process as it allows for adjustments depending on each individual procedure, some of which might have more than three candidates highly suitable for the post at issue. Authorities advising the appointing authority should therefore be able to assess all these candidates.

Also the membership and the composition of the advisory authority involved in the selection process for senior posts in the European Commission appear more appropriate than that in the UN Secretariat, better safeguarding the objectivity and impartiality of this process. Members of the European Commission's Consultative Committee on Appointments are not appointed but become members *ex officio* due to their function (such as (Deputy) Secretary-General, Director-General for Human Resources, Head of Cabinet of the Commission President or of the Commissioner for Human Resources, Permanent Rapporteur). The only exception is the Rapporteur to the Case appointed by the chair of the Consultative Committee on Appointments from among serving Commission Directors or Directors-General.[618] In contrast, members of the Senior Review Group existing in the UN Secretariat are all selected and appointed by the Secretary-General. The only exceptions are the secretary and the Special Adviser on Gender Issues and Advancement of Women who are *ex officio* members and whose role is limited.[619] In addition, as explained above, there appear to be no requirements other than officials' rank which the UN Secretary-General would need to follow when choosing individual officials for the membership of the Senior Review Group. Only the fact that this Group is a standing body limits, to a certain extent, Secretary-General's powers here, preventing their abuse in individual cases. Unfortunately, also this statement must be qualified. The absence of formal rules on the duration of office of (members of) the Senior Review Group means that the Secretary-General may dismiss a member or members of this advisory body and appoint new ones whenever he considers it appropriate. It is also regrettable that the staff representatives are not involved in the process at all, although this is also the case with the European Commission's Consultative Committee on Appointments. The involvement of staff representatives in the selection process of senior officials is thus not considered appropriate in both organizations.

---

[616] See above, sections 2.2.2.5 and 3.2.3.

[617] See above, sections 2.2.2.5 and 3.2.3.

[618] See above, section 3.2.3.

[619] See above, section 2.2.2.5.

Last but not least, the composition of the Senior Review Group illustrates its political nature – the Group is composed of UN officials at the Under-Secretary-General and Assistant Secretary-General levels who are generally considered to be political appointees.[620] The Senior Review Group includes no officials below this political level, though the D-2 posts are career and not political posts. It appears that political considerations are relevant also for appointments at the D-2 level.[621] Senior positions in the European Commission are considered to be at least partly political, although formally speaking they are career positions. The political interest in senior appointments is reflected in the composition of the Consultative Committee on Appointments, in particular by the involvement of the (Deputy) Secretary-General and especially of Heads of Cabinet of the Commission President and of the Commissioner for Human Resources. The latter are political appointees themselves recruited without any formal procedure and at full discretion of the Commission President and Commissioner for Human Resources and Security, respectively. On the other hand, the presence of other members of the Consultative Committee and the existence of fairly detailed rules on the procedure to be followed enhance objectivity and transparency of the selection process.

5. Conclusions

Current procedures for recruitment of both the UN and the EU staff are more elaborate than they used to be in the past. The UN Secretariat has taken several important steps forward in this respect, adopting a number of new administrative issuances. The most notable examples are the instructions on the NCRE, on staff selection and on temporary posts, covering the recruitment process of most UN staff. By placing this process in a legal framework, the UN Secretariat has enhanced its transparency and facilitated greater objectivity of the recruitment process. The European Commission too shows progress on this front. Detailed rules, often more detailed than in the UN Secretariat, are in place for each method of recruitment. This includes rules relating to senior officials, bringing thereby more transparency into the process, characterized by considerable secrecy and overriding political concerns in the past.

There are many features in the respective UN and EU recruitment procedures ensuring their objectivity and transparency. Apart from the existence of relevant formal legal instruments, they include the use of competitions, the obligation to publish vacancy announcements, the involvement of collective bodies and in many instances, of staff representatives in the process, especially in the EU, and the possibility of review, including judicial review.

Nonetheless, it appears that the current state of affairs is ideal in neither organization. In the UN Secretariat, one of the most worrying concerns is that many staff

[620] See above, section 2.2.2.5 and also chapter 1, section 2.1.1.

[621] See, for example, *Views of the Staff Representatives of the United Nations Secretariat: Staff Union (New York), Field Staff Union (Brindisi) and Staff Coordinating Council (United Nations Office in Geneva), Addendum, A/C.5/63/3/Add.2*, para. 28.

serve in (quasi) permanent posts without having passed a competition, possibly without even having gone through tests which would assess their expertise and suitability for the service with the UN Secretariat. Another concern is the broad discretion of hiring managers, virtually unlimited in the case of temporary appointments of maximum three months' duration, in staff selection, including external staff, and the lack of competence of central review bodies to review the selection process substantively. As for competitions, there are no staff representatives involved in the UN competition boards. Moreover, it is regrettable that human resources management experts are not present in these boards as a matter of course, although the possibility of including them in the competition boards exists. This applies to both the UN and the EU. Further, in both organizations, the final selection for appointment from a roster or reserve list lacks all transparency, often depending considerably on direct or indirect personal links with the official responsible for making the choice. For senior posts in both organizations, political considerations play a role even though the posts in question are formally considered to be career jobs. In the UN Secretariat, in addition, the limited involvement of the Senior Review Group in the process, when compared to the European Commission's Consultative Committee on Appointments, reduces transparency and objectivity, placing, once again, most power in the hands of hiring managers.

Last but not least, the relatively large number of relevant legal instruments regulating the UN recruitment process is rather confusing and diminishes transparency of the recruitment system for outside candidates. Some rules can be found in the *UN Staff Regulations*, some in the *UN Staff Rules*, some in the *UN Staff Selection System*, some in the Secretary-General's bulletins, and some in a number of administrative instructions (some of which are of almost identical wording). Clearly, this multiplicity of legal instruments partly reflects differences in the approach to the various types of posts and corresponding recruitment process. Nonetheless, such a situation also leads to an impression that a piecemeal approach continues to be present in the UN human resources management. Some consolidation of legal instruments would therefore be advisable. For example, there is no reason why rules on central review bodies and those on Senior Review Group – which, in the end, exercises competence of a central review body for D-2 posts – could not be contained in one legal instrument. Similarly, specific rules applicable to recruitment to D-2 posts could also be incorporated in the *UN Staff Selection System*, which generally applies to recruitment to these posts. Also, various types of competition could be regulated by one set of rules, clearly listing necessary specificities for each type of competition.

The EU recruitment system is less complex in this regard, reflecting the fact that most permanent posts are filled by using a sole recruitment method, namely competition. Separate rules apply only to senior posts and possibly to posts requiring specialized knowledge. On the other hand, there are also a number of different regimes for different categories and even subcategories of non-permanent staff. Also here a single set of rules would better serve transparency for outside candidates who are often not familiar with the complexities of the overall human resources framework of the organization in question. Even more worrying in the European Commission is, however, that some staff are selected without a proper selection process. For some staff categories, rules are very general and lack necessary detail, and for others they are even non-existent. It is perhaps understandable, and even endorsed by the judiciary, for staff serving in private cabinets. However, such a state of affairs does not promote transparency in the EU staff recruitment process. In fact, many of these staff, recruited without a formal and transparent selection process, eventually remain in the European Commission after their posting in a cabinet ends, often becoming (highly placed) permanent officials. This is possible when such non-permanent staff pass internal competition. Also the fact that some non-permanent staff are permitted to participate in internal competitions has been criticized in the past. The European Commission had taken note of this criticism, but the possibility of organizing internal competitions, including for such staff, has been retained in the *EU Staff Regulations* and is used in practice, too. This is highly unfortunate and should be changed.

Chapter 4

PROMOTION

1. Introduction

To recall, the relevance of the UN and EU promotion policies to this study is twofold. First, promotion is a way of filling vacant posts in the UN Secretariat and in the European Commission. Without addressing it, the picture on the appointment processes in the two organizations provided in this study would be incomplete. Second, adequate promotion prospects are a prerequisite without which international organizations would succeed not only in attracting and retaining the best staff possible, but also in securing their independence and impartiality. It can hardly be disputed that the independence and impartiality of staff serving in international secretariats would be compromised if these staff were compelled, or even just tempted, to reach out to certain individuals or institutions in order to enhance their promotion chances because they are otherwise objectively too limited or because the procedural framework for promotion does not guarantee a fair and transparent process but, rather, leaves room to subjectivity and favouritism.[1]

This chapter explains, analyses and compares legal frameworks regulating the promotion process in the UN Secretariat and the European Commission. It also assesses whether the two legal frameworks are sufficiently transparent, objective and impartial so that staff serving in the UN Secretariat and the European Commission do not feel the need to turn to inappropriate channels in order to safeguard their career advancement. This would, actually or potentially, jeopardize the independent and impartial status of such staff.

2. Promotion in the UN Secretariat

There are two types of promotion in the UN Secretariat – promotion to a higher level post within the same staff category and promotion to the professional category from other categories. The latter is sometimes regarded as recruitment, not promotion, because it normally takes place at the entry level. For example, some UN administrative issuances refer to this procedure as recruitment. However, there are also documents referring to it as promotion.[2] Since this process involves movement of staff already in service to a post with higher classification, rather than engagement of an outsider, it appears to be more appropriate to consider it as promotion, not recruitment.[3]

---

[1] See also above, Introduction, section 3.4.

[2] See *Administrative Instruction on G to P examination*; but see also *Administrative Instruction, Movement of Staff from the Field Service Category to the Professional Category*, 15.11.1993, available in the Human Resources Handbook of the United Nations, available at http://www.un.org/hr_handbook/English/, last visited on 30.12.2010, Section I. dealing with 'promotion' to the Professional category through the competitive examination. Although the latter administrative issuance is no longer in use, it illustrates the inconsistency in the terminology used by the UN Secretariat in respect of the movement of staff from other categories to the Professional category.

[3] See, for example, *Capio v. Secretary-General of the United Nations, UNAT Judgment No. 266 [1980]*, available at http://untreaty.un.org/UNAT/UNAT_Judgements/Judgements_E/UNAT_00266_E.pdf, last visited on 30.12.2010; *Knight et al v. Secretary-General of the United Nations, UNAT Judgment No. 722 [1995]*, available at http://untreaty.un.org/UNAT/UNAT_Judgements/Judgements_E/UNAT_00722_E.pdf, last visited on 30.12.2010 or *Gurun v. Secretary-General of the United Nations, UNAT Judgment*

It must be admitted, however, that the two types of promotion do not have much in common. They are, therefore, addressed in this section separately. The section first describes the promotion process within the same staff category, including a brief overview of past promotion systems used in the UN. The second part of this section contains explanation of the procedures used for placement of staff in the professional category from other categories.

2.1. Promotion within the staff category

2.1.1. Historical overview

The past and present UN systems of promotion have always been based on placement against a vacant post. Contrary to some national administrations and to the EU, the UN Secretariat has never used a system of in-post promotion, with the exception of promotion of a staff member to a post at a higher level which he already occupies on a temporary basis.[4] This means that, in principle, promotion in the UN Secretariat has only been possible when a vacant post exists, for which the staff member to be promoted is qualified and selected through a staff selection process.

Through the years, three different systems have been developed in the UN on the basis of which individual promotions have been carried out. The initial system was a system of annual review, applied from the late 1950s until the mid-1980s. This system was temporarily replaced by a 'vacancy management and staff redeployment programme' between 1987 and 1991. Since the early 1990s, promotions take place under a 'placement and promotion system'. Many similarities exist between these systems – they all require(d) good performance, comparison of merits between eligible staff members and a vacancy to which staff deserving promotion could be placed. Unsurprisingly, the role that each of these, and other relevant, elements have played in the particular promotion system differed. The most important difference between the annual review promotion system on the one hand and the vacancy management and staff deployment and placement and promotion systems on the other is their connection to the specific vacancy. Although in all three systems, a vacant post to which an individual staff member could be appointed must have been available before promotion could take place, the order in which the consideration for promotion and the existence of vacancy were considered differed. The following parts of this section briefly explain how each of the promotion systems worked.

No. 851 [1997], available at http://untreaty.un.org/UNAT/UNAT_Judgements/Judgements_E/UNAT_00851_E.pdf, last visited on 30.12.2010; and *Inspection of the Application of United Nations Recruitment, Placement, and Promotion Policies, Part II - Placement and Promotions, Report of the Joint Inspection Unit, JIU/REP/96/6*, para. 21.

[4] *Inspection of the Application of United Nations Recruitment, Placement, and Promotion Policies, Part II - Placement and Promotions, Report of the Joint Inspection Unit, JIU/REP/96/6*, para. 16.

2.1.1.1. Annual review promotion system

The annual promotion system was in use between 1958 and 1986, i.e. for more than three decades. The system was provided for by Rule 104.14(f)(iii) of the *UN Staff Rules* and entailed an annual grade-by-grade review of all staff. The review was based on recommendations of Heads of Departments and on comparative analysis of the merits of the staff members recommended or not recommended but eligible for promotion. To be eligible, a staff member had to have a minimum number of years of service in the relevant grade. Factors considered in deciding which eligible staff would be promoted, i.e. in comparing merits, included demonstrated efficiency, integrity and competence; ability to perform at the higher level; acquired training; second official language proficiency; as well as mobility between headquarters and the field offices.[5]

The review was conducted by departmental panels which conducted comparative analysis of all staff eligible for promotion. Such analysis was based on the personnel record and on the recommendations of the supervisors. Recommendations of the departmental panels were submitted to the Heads of Department who reviewed them and prepared their own recommendations. Such recommendations were subsequently considered by appointment and promotion bodies which could disagree with the Heads of Department on individual recommendations, even when the Heads of Department insisted. Final recommendations of the appointment and promotion bodies were submitted to the Secretary-General for approval. Approved staff members, i.e. those recommended for promotion, were placed on a list known as promotion register. They were promoted when a budgetary post with matching classification became vacant.[6]

The most characteristic feature of the annual review promotion system was its profound reliance on seniority.[7] In addition, the system was not clearly linked to the recommendation of the involved supervisor and Head of Department – they could be overruled by the appointment and promotion bodies and, in the final stage of the process, also by the Secretary-General.[8] Furthermore, promotion took place after a vacancy become available though the consideration for promotion was conducted beforehand.

---

[5] *Review of the National Competitive Recruitment Examination as a Recruitment Tool, Report of the Joint Inspection Unit, JIU/REP/2007/9*, paras. 37-39. Formally speaking, mobility between duty stations was not a condition for promotion, although it could eventually help. There was, however, no systematic means of encouraging staff mobility besides the rotation of the language staff and junior economists and statisticians. – see Graham and Jordan (eds.), *The International Civil Service*, pp. 111-112.

[6] *Review of the National Competitive Recruitment Examination as a Recruitment Tool, Report of the Joint Inspection Unit, JIU/REP/2007/9*, paras. 38-40.

[7] The minimum number of years required for promotion depended on the level of the post and type of promotion. In case of a regular promotion, the minimum number of years was 5 years for promotion to posts at the P-5 level and above, and 3 years for all other levels and categories. In case of accelerated promotion, the minimum periods were 3 and 2 years, respectively. In case of a special measure available for promotion of women (since 1986) flexibility was used in applying the above mentioned rules. – Ibid., paras. 38-39.

[8] *Inspection of the Application of United Nations Recruitment, Placement, and Promotion Policies, Part II - Placement and Promotions, Report of the Joint Inspection Unit, JIU/REP/96/6*, para. 48.

This promotion system was often heavily criticized, perhaps not so much for its own set up but rather for the manner in which it was implemented in practice. A number of criticisms were put forward. One of the most important critiques was related to the actual 'non-existence' of a proper comprehensive career development system. In 1977, Meron, for example, wrote:

> *[C]areer development and planning remains still in the realm of theory and rather unclear plans for the future. It is unfortunate that as of now talented members of the staff, especially those who have been recruited pursuant to a competitive examination, have no way of anticipating their promotional ladders, their future mobility, and assignments in the Secretariat, and so forth.*[9]

Also Graham noted in 1980 that the UN Secretariat had had

> *neither a formal nor an informal career policy on an organization-wide basis. Career development, up to now, has been undertaken principally at the initiative of staff members themselves and certain supervisors.*[10]

Graham continued:

> *It is not possible for a staff member entering the service of the Secretariat at the P.1/P.2 level to know with any degree of certainty what his or her career might be like.*[11]

Similarly, in 1985, Reymond and Mailick stressed:

> *Too often development of a career is a random and unplanned occurrence, left to individual staff members who possess the necessary initiative and ability to promote their own progress, with the occasional help of an enlightened supervisor.*[12]

Not only academics criticized the UN promotion and career policy. A number of internal studies and reports were dedicated to the problem, too. For example, the Joint Inspection Unit stated in its 1971 report that 'under the present system... career organization for Professional staff members is left to chance'.[13]

Besides the absence of a comprehensive career policy, there were other reasons for criticism of the UN promotion system as well, especially the politicization of promotions to more senior posts, including D-1 and D-2 levels. It was argued that, in practice, not seniority and merit but political considerations were decisive for

---

[9] Meron, *The United Nations Secretariat*, p. 127.

[10] Graham and Jordan (eds.), *The International Civil Service*, p. 110.

[11] Ibid., p. 111. Graham estimates that a junior staff member may expect to achieve at least P-5 level, while prospects to achieve D-1 level are still 'quite good'. However, the chances of a position at the D-2 level are 'very small', in particular in view of limited number of such posts. – *Ibid.*

[12] Reymond and Mailick, *International Personnel Policies and Practices*, pp. 106-107.

[13] Ibid., p. 109.

promotions at those levels, and for the choice of external candidates rather than promotion of eligible internal staff.[14]

The politicization of the UN promotion process was partly related to the issue of geographical distribution of posts among nationals of all Member States, or at least all regional groups. As explained in the chapter dealing with the issue of geographical representation, in theory, in the UN geographical distribution may be taken into account only in the recruitment process, not in promotions.[15] Nonetheless, in practice, there was considerable political pressure from Member States in this respect, individually or through resolutions of the General Assembly. They were urging the Secretary-General to ensure adequate geographical representation at all levels of the organization, especially at the senior and policy-making level.[16] Naturally, since positions in higher echelons were to be filled by internal candidates in the first place, the nationality of staff must have been taken into account when deciding on promotion. A clear evidence of this is provided, for example, in the UNAT case law.[17]

The practice of taking candidates' nationality into account in staff promotions has been heavily criticized. Lemoine, for example, considered the demands of balance of nationalities in middle and high level posts to be one of the obstacles for an efficient career planning and development.[18] Miron pointed to the negative consequences of this practice:

> *Governments regularly addressed notes to the Secretary-General at the beginning of each year, drawing his attention not only to the candidates they had proposed for appointment, but also to those already in service who awaited promotion. Promotions arising from contract renegotiation, and not through the*

[14] Meron, *The United Nations Secretariat,* p. 125. Meron provides a number of figures to support his allegations. He claims that appointments to the D-2 level, and above all to the D-1 level, from outside, i.e. from among candidates who were not UN staff members, had increased considerably – 43 percent of outside appointments in D-1 level in 1975 compared to 28 percent in 1972. – Ibid.

[15] *UN Charter*, Article 101(3). As explained in the chapter devoted to the issue of geographical representation in the UN and EU, Article 101(3) of the *UN Charter* stipulates that due regard is to be paid to the importance of *recruiting* the staff on the widest possible geographical basis. The same was and still is provided in the Regulation 4.2 of the *UN Staff Regulations*. - *UN Staff Regulations of 2009*, Regulation 4.2. This view was confirmed by the Legal Counsel in his opinion as early as in 1957, as well as by the various UN Secretaries-General. See, for example, Meron, *Status and Independence of the International Civil Servant*, p. 306. As pointed out by Meron, for example, U Thant, one of the first Secretaries-General, declared that his intention was to ensure that the principle of geographical distribution remains relevant only to recruitment of the staff and would play no role in the promotion or placement processes. – Ibid., p. 307.

[16] For example, *General Assembly Resolution 1436(XIV)*, Preamble; *General Assembly Resolution 1928(XVIII)*, Preamble and para. 2; and *General Assembly Resolution 2241(XXI)*, Preamble. See also, for example, Cameron, *Establishment of the European Union Civil Service Tribunal*, p. 307.

[17] For example, in *Estabial* the applicant claimed, and the UNAT accepted, that he had been disregarded in a promotion exercise due to his nationality since the position he had sought had been in advance reserved for nationals of French-speaking African countries. The reason for this was the need to ensure adequate geographical representation of French-speaking African countries in the UN Secretariat. -*Estabial, UNAT Judgment No. 310 [1983]*, especially paras. XII-XIII and XVI. See also above, chapter 2, introduction to section 2.3.

[18] Lemoine, *The International Civil Servant: An Endangered Species*, p. 274.

> *procedure of comparative evaluation governing the advancement of career staff, soon emerged as a point of contention in staff-management relations.*[19]

In the framework of the comprehensive review of the efficiency of the administrative and financial functioning of the UN conducted in 1986 by the group of high-level intergovernmental experts, also referred to as G-18, it was emphasized that political and other pressures should be excluded from UN staff selection. More specifically on promotions, the G-18 recommended that in order to secure fairness and objectivity in the management of appointments and promotions, strict and clear criteria should be developed for promotions at all levels. The group also called for review of the functions and composition of appointment and promotion bodies, providing them with sufficient ability to assess the technical expertise of individual candidates.[20]

On the basis of these and other recommendations of the G-18, as well as the financial emergency situation which emerged in the UN in the mid-1980s, the annual review promotion system was discontinued in December 1986 and the application of Rule 104.14(f) of the *UN Staff Rules* was temporarily suspended.[21] A number of measures were introduced, including freeze in recruitment and a six-month delay in implementing promotions due in 1987. The new vacancy management and staff redeployment programme was developed, replacing the annual review promotion system. The objective of this vacancy management and staff redeployment programme was to alleviate the impact of these measures on the delivery of UN programmes by deploying staff where they were most needed.[22]

2.1.1.2. Vacancy management and staff redeployment programme

The vacancy management and staff redeployment programme was applied between 1987 and 1991. As its name suggests, it was based on a system of redeployment, i.e. relocation, of staff in the Professional category and above and in the General Service (latter within the same duty station) where it was most needed.[23] The main

---

[19] Miron, *Tenure, Fixed-Term Appointments and Secondment in the United Nations*, p. 786.

[20] *G18 Report*, Recommendations 41 and 51, pp. 20-21. See also *Inspection of the Application of United Nations Recruitment, Placement, and Promotion Policies, Part II - Placement and Promotions, Report of the Joint Inspection Unit, JIU/REP/96/6*, para. 15.

[21] See to that respect *Upadhya v. Secretary-General of the United Nations, UNAT Judgment No. 537 [1991]*, available at http://untreaty.un.org/UNAT/UNAT_Judgements/Judgements_E/UNAT_00537_E.pdf, last visited on 30.12.2010, especially paras. III-V. The UNAT held in this case that even though there had been no formal suspension of the relevant staff rules on promotion, it had had to be understood as such temporary suspension as an emergency measure. – Ibid. (Are some words missing or superfluous in the last sentence? Pl chek)

[22] *Inspection of the Application of United Nations Recruitment, Placement, and Promotion Policies, Part II - Placement and Promotions, Report of the Joint Inspection Unit, JIU/REP/96/6*, paras. 42 and 43. See also *Secretary-General's Bulletin, The Financial Situation of the Organization, ST/SGB/222*, 22.12.1986, available in the Human Resources Handbook of the United Nations, available at http://www.un.org/hr_handbook/English/, last visited on 30.12.2010, para. 2(c) and para. 4. The UNAT approved the system as being within the discretion of the Secretary-General and in no violation of *UN Staff Regulations*. – *Upadhya, UNAT Judgment No. 537 [1991]*, paras. XII-XIII.

[23] *Inspection of the Application of United Nations Recruitment, Placement, and Promotion Policies, Part II -*

objectives of this system were explained by the Secretary-General in his 1987 report to the General Assembly as follows:

> *There are two main objectives: to identify existing current vacancies which it is essential to fill in order to fulfill key programme mandates; and to redeploy to those essential posts staff occupying posts considered of less vital importance in the present contingency.*[24]

The system was thus meant to ensure that reduced human resources of the UN Secretariat were distributed in the most optimal manner, taking into account the needs of individual UN programmes. It was, however, also meant to 'build the foundations of a more equitable and effective system of career development'.[25]

The criteria for promotion and the eligibility factors for individual staff members under this system were similar to those used previously under the annual review promotion system, although different minimum periods of service were established.[26] An important change when compared to the previous system was that the promotion register was abolished. Under the new system, staff could be promoted only after application for a vacant post. If eligible for promotion at the time of application, as pre-screened by the Office of Personnel Services, candidates were considered by the Redeployment Committee. This committee recommended a shortlist of best qualified staff members for each vacancy to the relevant Heads of Department or Office who took the final decision.[27]

As stated by the Joint Inspection Unit in its report on staff placement and promotion of 1996, the vacancy management and staff redeployment programme introduced 'the principle of open job-bidding for vacancies', regarded as the most important feature of this programme.[28] This feature was taken over in the placement and promotion system which succeeded the vacancy management and staff redeployment programme and is still in use. The former was introduced after the latter had to be terminated in December 1991 following a judgment of the UNAT. In *Upadhya* the UNAT ruled that because the financial emergency situation of the UN no longer existed, the temporary suspension of Rule 104.14 of the *UN Staff Rules* had to be ended.[29] The actual introduction of the new placement and promotion system was proceeded by temporary transitional reinstatement of the original annual grade-by-

---

Placement and Promotions, Report of the Joint Inspection Unit, JIU/REP/96/6, para. 44.

[24] *Reform and Renewal in the United Nations: Progress Report of the Secretary-General on the Implementation of the General Assembly Resolution 41/213, A/42/234*, 23.04.1987, available in the Official Document System of the United Nations, available at http://documents.un.org/, last visited on 30.12.2010, para. 57.

[25] Ibid., para. 66(2)(g).

[26] For promotion from posts at P-1 to P-2 level - two years; from P-2 to P-3 and from P-3 to P-4 - three years; from P-4 to P-5 and from P-5 to D-1 - five years. - *Inspection of the Application of United Nations Recruitment, Placement, and Promotion Policies, Part II - Placement and Promotions, Report of the Joint Inspection Unit, JIU/REP/96/6*, para. 44.

[27] Ibid., paras. 42, 45-46.

[28] Ibid., para. 48.

[29] Ibid., para. 49. See also *Upadhya, UNAT Judgment No. 537 [1991]*, paras. XIV-XVI.

grade review promotion system, used in the first three decades of the UN history, but slightly adjusted. The transitional period time lasted from December 1991 till November 1993, when the new promotion system was launched.[30]

2.1.1.3. Placement and promotion system

Similar to the vacancy management and staff redeployment programme in use between 1987 and 1991, the new placement and promotion system also provided for announcement of vacancies as a pre-requisite for any possible promotion. The system included a continuous and comprehensive review of staff for the purposes of identifying staff to be placed or promoted in the identified vacant posts.[31] As noted by the Secretary-General in his bulletin introducing the system, its purpose was to 'increase the transparency of the placement and promotion processes, which should reward staff for competence, creativity, versatility and, increasingly, mobility'.[32]

The main features of the procedure leading to promotion were the regular announcement of vacancies, review by the OHRM of the eligibility of all staff who applied, consideration by the Heads of Departments assisted by departmental panels, review of recommendations of the Heads of Departments by the appointment and promotion bodies, submission of the recommendation of the appointment and promotion bodies to the Secretary-General for decision, together with comments made by the heads of departments on the recommendation of the appointment and promotion bodies, and the final decision by the Secretary-General. Elements to be taken into account when considering candidates included past performance, efficiency, demonstrated ability to perform at a higher level, integrity, experience, seniority, supervisory abilities if relevant, mobility and linguistic proficiency.[33]

Despite its praiseworthy intentions, the new placement and promotion system soon became the object of criticism. Lemoine, for example, noted in 1995 that 'an orderly progression in the hierarchies of responsibilities and rank remains at best an elusive goal'.[34] He pointed out that a decade old statement of Reymond and Mailick that the career development in the UN is a 'random and unplanned occurrence' was still 'largely true'.[35]

---

[30] *Inspection of the Application of United Nations Recruitment, Placement, and Promotion Policies, Part II - Placement and Promotions, Report of the Joint Inspection Unit, JIU/REP/96/6*, para. 50.

[31] *Secretary-General's Bulletin, Placement and Promotion, ST/SGB/267*, 15.11.1993, available in the Human Resources Handbook of the United Nations, available at http://www.un.org/hr_handbook/English/, last visited on 30.12.2010, para. 2. The specific rules of the new system were set out in administrative instruction ST/AI/390 of 15 November 1993. - *Administrative Instruction, Placement and Promotion, ST/AI/390*, 15.11.1993, available in the Human Resources Handbook of the United Nations, available at http://www.un.org/hr_handbook/English/, last visited on 30.12.2010.

[32] *Secretary-General's Bulletin, Placement and Promotion*, para. 2.

[33] *Administrative Instruction, Placement and Promotion*, paras. 4-17. See also *Inspection of the Application of United Nations Recruitment, Placement, and Promotion Policies, Part II - Placement and Promotions, Report of the Joint Inspection Unit, JIU/REP/96/6*, paras. 57-61.

[34] Lemoine, *The International Civil Servant: An Endangered Species*, p. 272.

[35] Ibid., p. 274. For the quote of Reymond and Mailick, see above, section 2.1.1.1.

Also the Joint Inspection Unit concluded in a report of 1996 that the new system 'suffer[ed] from most of the flaws and deficiencies which [had been] characteristic of the previous systems'.[36] It pointed to the very limited promotion possibilities for UN staff, caused by the need for vacancy to exist before promotion can take place, but also by the restructuring and downsizing of the UN Secretariat in the previous years, by circumvention of UN recruitment policies through the use of short-term appointments, by 'regularization' of temporary staff and by placements on higher level posts without internal vacancy announcement.[37]

The Joint Inspection Unit noted that the new placement and promotion system still lacked objective criteria and was regarded as largely dissatisfactory by the UN staff. The Unit reported that many staff members believed there were no promotion opportunities in the UN and that 'having friends higher up' was regarded by staff to be the most important factor in the promotion process (65,9 per cent), followed by government support (26 per cent) and only then by competence (20,8 per cent) and seniority (20,1 per cent). Moreover, mobility, productivity and training were considered by staff as largely irrelevant for their promotion.[38] On the other hand, the Joint Inspection Unit identified cases of 'sky-rocketing careers', despite the absence of general policy or rules for accelerated promotion. The Unit warned that such a situation 'open[ed] the door to all kinds of abuses'.[39] It also cautioned against inappropriate involvement of the UN Secretary-General in individual cases, which was detected in a number of instances.[40]

Ten years after the issuance of its 1996 report on placements and promotions, the Joint Inspection Unit had to repeat that 'there [was] no effective managed career development within the Secretariat'.[41] The JIU pointed out that this situation existed despite great efforts made to enhance staff career development programmes.[42] The lack of career and promotion prospects were also identified as the most important demotivating factor for UN staff in a survey conducted in 2005. This survey also confirmed the staff belief, existing in the past, that 'having connections' was by far the main factor conditioning promotion in the UN, followed by competence, support from governments, seniority, geographical distribution and other factors. As many

[36] *Inspection of the Application of United Nations Recruitment, Placement, and Promotion Policies, Part II - Placement and Promotions, Report of the Joint Inspection Unit, JIU/REP/96/6*, p. iv.

[37] Ibid., p. iv and para. 67. The findings of the Joint Inspection Unit confirmed that there were at the time more than one thousand Professional staff who have remained at the same level for more than five years and over six hundred of staff who have not passed to another level for more than ten years. Furthermore, almost one hundred Professional staff have remained at the same level for more than fifteen years. - Ibid., para. 66.

[38] Ibid., p. iv-v and paras. 64-66. Note that respondents to the survey, on which the JIU based its data, could indicate more than one factor. That is why the sum of the percentages given to individual factors exceeds 100 per cent.

[39] Ibid., para. 77.

[40] Ibid., paras. 79-80.

[41] *Staff Mobility in the United Nations, Report of the Joint Inspection Unit, JIU/REP/2006/7*, para. 57. It must be stressed that the statement of the Joint Inspection Unit concerned the career development system as such, not only the system of promotion.

[42] Ibid., para. 57.

as 66,4 per cent of all respondents agreed about primacy of 'having connections'. Moreover, staff who considered competence to be the key to promotion stated that the existing performance appraisal system, through which competence was regularly assessed, was counterproductive.[43]

It appears thus that the current state of affairs in the UN Secretariat is still not ideal. This is despite – or perhaps due to – further changes of the UN promotion system that have taken place in the last decade. The following sections explain how this system works and assess whether it contributes to the independence and impartiality of UN staff by offering them a transparent and objective process of promotion.

2.1.2. Current system

As explained earlier, the placement and promotion system introduced in 1993 continues to be used at present, albeit with some modifications. The legal basis of the system is to be found in the already mentioned administrative instruction ST/AI/2010/3 which provides the most recent version of the *UN Staff Selection System*. To recall, this system integrates recruitment, placement, promotion and mobility of the UN staff.[44] As explained by the Secretary-General in his bulletin introducing the system, one of the system's goals is 'to provide more career opportunities and career development for staff'.[45]

The previous chapter explains that the *UN Staff Selection System* – and thus also the placement and promotion system integrated therein – is based on vacancy announcement.[46] In that sense the promotion system is very much connected to the recruitment system – vacancies in the UN Secretariat are normally opened to internal as well as external candidates. Although both categories of candidates may be allowed to apply for a specific vacancy, consideration of internal candidates is granted priority over the external ones. Regulation 4.4 of the *UN Staff Regulations* provides in its relevant part the following:

> *Subject to the provisions of Article 101, paragraph 3, of the Charter, and without prejudice to the recruitment of fresh talent at all levels, the fullest regard shall be had, in filling vacancies, to the requisite qualifications and experience of* persons already in the service of the United Nations. ... *The Secretary-General* may limit eligibility to apply for vacant posts to internal candidates, *as defined by the Secretary-General. If so, other candidates shall be allowed to apply, under conditions to be defined by the Secretary-General, when no internal candidate meets the requirements of Article 101, paragraph 3, of the Charter as well as the requirements of the post. (emphasis added)*[47]

---

[43] *A Picture of the UN Staff*, questions 7 and 10.

[44] *UN Staff Selection System*, Section 2.1.

[45] *Secretary-General's Bulletin, Introduction of a New Staff Selection System.*

[46] See above, chapter 3, section 2.2.2.2.

[47] *UN Staff Regulations of 2009*, Regulation 4.4.

Until its modification in April 2010, the *UN Staff Selection System* furthermore stipulated that vacancies were available to other (i.e. external) candidates only after internal candidates had been considered.[48] The system also provided for a priority order in which various groups of internal candidates could be considered. This priority order needed to be respected in each individual selection process and meant that UN staff must have complied not only with substantive eligibility criteria for promotion but also with procedural eligibility criteria before they could be considered.[49] The most recent *UN Staff Selection System*, adopted in April 2010, modified these rules. While it still requires priority consideration for internal over external candidates, it no longer requires different deadlines for application for vacant posts by different categories of internal candidates and an order in which such applications should be considered in a specific selection process. All procedural eligibility criteria, existing under the previous versions of the *UN Staff Selection System*, have been abolished. The substantive eligibility criteria for promotion have been retained and some of them modified. They are briefly explained in the following section, and followed by an explanation of procedures that apply to staff promotion in the UN Secretariat.

2.1.2.1. Eligibility criteria

Since the UN staff members may be promoted only when there is a vacant post, obviously, the first substantive eligibility criterion for promotion is the fulfillment of the requirements of the vacant post at issue, such as qualification, skills and professional experience. Although not explicitly mentioned in Section 6 of the *UN Staff Selection System*, this requirement is a logical consequence of the essential feature of the UN promotion system, being the existence of a vacant post to which a staff member

[48] *UN Staff Selection System of 2006, revised in January 2010*, Sections 2.2, 5.4, 5.5 and 7.1. Note that the notion 'external candidate' was defined in *Case No. 1387, UNAT Judgment No. 1303 [2006]*, available at http://untreaty.un.org/UNAT/UNAT_Judgements/Judgements_E/UNAT_01303_E.pdf, last visited on 30.12.2010. In this case the UNAT held that UN staff members are, by definition, not external candidates. – Ibid., para. II.

[49] Section 5.5 of the 2006 *UN Staff Selection System* stipulated in detail which staff needed to be considered at what stage of the procedure. The rules were rather complicated, making a distinction between eligibility for lateral move (i.e. movement to a vacant post at the same level as the occupied post) or promotion (i.e. movement to a vacant post at a higher level) under regular circumstances and those applicable in certain specified instances. The specificity related to issues such as the limitation of the appointment of the staff member concerned to a particular office, appointment in mission service, appointment in field service category, geographical status, gender etc. – See *UN Staff Selection System of 2006, revised in January 2010*, Sections 5.4-5.6. Without going into specificities, in principle, lateral move had priority before promotion, while promotion had priority before appointment of an external candidate. This means that staff members eligible for lateral move were to be considered against the vacant post in question before a chance was given to staff members eligible for promotion. Staff promotion was thus clearly subordinated to staff mobility, limiting opportunities for the former. An exceptional situation which deserves to be mentioned existed with regard to vacancies at the P-3 level. There, candidates eligible for promotion competed with candidates eligible for lateral move as well as candidates who have passed the National Recruitment Competitive Examinations. There was thus no priority for lateral move vis-à-vis promotion at the P-3 level, and also no priority for promotion compared to the external candidates placed on the NCRE roster. - *UN Staff Selection System of 2006*, Section 7.2.

may be promoted. The substantive requirements of the post, set out in the vacancy announcement, are binding for the applicants but also for the UN Administration. The latter may not select a candidate who, for example, does not possess required qualifications or experience.[50] As stressed by the UNAT, the vacancy announcement sets out 'objective criteria of evaluation' and the Administration is obliged to follow them, especially since it set out these criteria itself.[51] In addition, the Administration must pay full regard to *all* the criteria included in the vacancy announcement and may not disregard one or some of them claiming that they are just one out of many requirements. Such an approach would, in the UNAT's view, harm all prospective candidates who would not respond to the vacancy announcement because they do not meet certain requirement or requirements.[52] Clearly, such situation would also be detrimental to the transparency and objectivity of the process, allowing the authority making the selection to pay regard to, or to put disproportional weight on, a criterion that would place a certain (favoured) candidate in a more advantageous position.

The second substantive eligibility requirement for promotion is the occupancy of a post which is classified precisely one level lower than the vacant post. Pursuant to Section 6.1 of the *UN Staff Selection System*, staff members are not eligible for consideration for promotion to posts that are more than one level higher than their personal grade.[53] Promotion must thus be gradual and may involve just one grade at a time.

The third substantive eligibility requirement for promotion in the UN is mobility. At least two prior lateral moves, i.e. (generally speaking) moves to a different position at the same level for a duration of at least one year, must take place before a staff member is eligible for promotion. However, this requirement applies only to promotions to the P-5 level and is subject to a number of refinements.[54] Promotion to levels P-3 and P-4 does not involve prior mobility as a necessary condition.

The role of seniority, i.e. number of years of service in a given grade, as an eligibility requirement for UN promotions has been modified several times. This traditional requirement had existed since the adoption of the first promotion system until 2006, when an amended version of the original *UN Staff Selection System* came into

---

[50] For example, *Lopes Braga, UNAT Judgment No. 1122 [2003]*, para. X; and *Case No. 1475, UNAT Judgment No. 1405 [2008]*, available at http://untreaty.un.org/UNAT/UNAT_Judgements/Judgements_E/UNAT_01405_E.pdf, last visited on 30.12.2010, para. IX. It should be noted, though, that an express exception to this rule exists for staff who were promoted to the Professional and above categories after having passed the G to P examination when they applied for job openings in these categories. – *UN Staff Selection System*, Section 6.8.

[51] *Case No. 1402, UNAT Judgment No. 1326 [2007]*, available at http://untreaty.un.org/UNAT/UNAT_Judgements/Judgements_E/UNAT_01326_E.pdf, last visited on 30.12.2010, para. V.

[52] *Lopes Braga, UNAT Judgment No. 1122 [2003]*, para. V.

[53] *UN Staff Selection System*, Section 6.1. Note that also here, two exceptions exists. The first one relates to the possibility of temporary promotion in a peacekeeping mission or special political mission. The second exception concerns staff serving in General Service and related categories who may apply for posts in the Field Service category at any level, irrespective of their current grade, if they meet the requirements of the post at issue. For details, see Sections 6.5 and 6.6; and Section 6.1.

[54] Ibid., Section 6.3 and, for the definition of lateral move, Section 1.

force.[55] The 2006 version of the *UN Staff Selection System* no longer included the minimum period of post occupancy, though it retained a clause stressing that:

> *experience, knowledge and institutional memory relevant to the functions must be considered as the personal contribution of the candidate to the achievement of the goals of the Organization and as such are an important element of the selection process.*[56]

The most recent version of the *UN Staff Selection System*, in force since April 2010, has reintroduced the seniority requirement for some staff serving in the Field Service category. Staff who occupy a post at the FS-6 level may apply for a post at the P-3 or P-4 level only after they have served in their current grade for at least one year. The same applies to staff serving in grade FS-7 and applying for a post at the P-4 or P-5 level.[57] Apart from these two instances, the seniority requirement applies to no other UN staff.

Formally irrelevant in the UN promotion system is also the requirement of geographical distribution of posts among nationals of all UN Member States. As explained earlier, in practice, however, the Secretary-General has been repeatedly requested by Member States to ensure geographical balance at all levels of the Secretariat. It follows that nationality of applicants, while formally irrelevant, plays a more or less important role in the UN promotion process in case of posts subject to geographical distribution.[58]

Last but not the least, it should be noted that the *UN Staff Selection System* adopted in April 2010 introduced explicit age limits for applying for any post in the UN Secretariat, and thus also for promotion. The minimum limit is 18 years of age, while the maximum limit corresponds to the mandatory retirement age in the UN, which is 60 years for staff appointed before 1 January 1990 and 62 years for staff appointed after that date.[59]

2.1.2.2. Procedures

Similarly to the eligibility criteria for promotion, procedures under which individual staff members may be appointed to a post at a higher level can be found in the *UN Staff Selection System*. The *UN Staff Regulations* and the *UN Staff Rules* do not contain any provisions in this respect, besides listing central review bodies and their

---

[55] The original 2002 version of the *UN Staff Selection System* still provided for seniority as a condition for promotion. It required two years in post before any promotion to a higher level could take place, with special rules for staff who had exercised mobility and with a possibility for the OHRM and local personnel offices to waive the seniority requirement where the needs of service could justify it. - See *UN Staff Selection System of 2002*, Section 5.1.

[56] Ibid., Section 5.3 and *UN Staff Selection System of 2006*, Section 5.1.

[57] *UN Staff Selection System*, Section 6.4. Note that FS-7 staff must also comply with the mobility requirement before they may be promoted to the P-5 level.

[58] For details, see above, chapter 2, section 2.4.

[59] *UN Staff Selection System*, , Section 6.2. For details on mandatory retirement in the UN Secretariat, see chapter 7, section 2.2.4.

competence in Rule 104.14 of the *UN Staff Rules*.[60] As explained in the previous chapter, central review bodies are those involved in the staff selection process, including all forms of filling vacant posts.[61] Since the UN system of staff selection is integrated into one 'staff selection system', procedures relevant for the promotion of staff are identical to those applicable to the recruitment. They both fall within the scope of the same administrative instruction. In addition, although appointment of staff at the entry level posts (P-1 and P-2) subject to geographical distribution or to special language requirements is excluded from the scope of this instruction, promotion of such staff falls within it.[62]

One of the consequences of integrating staff recruitment, placement, promotion and mobility into one system is that procedures described in the previous section of this study dealing with the UN recruitment are equally relevant to this section, too. To recall, the process begins with a job opening which is placed in the compendium of job openings published regularly. The placement of the job opening is done upon request by the hiring or occupational group manager and approval by the OHRM, the local human resources officers or the Department of Field Support. The hiring and the occupational group managers also conduct evaluation of candidates who have been pre-screened by the OHRM, the local human resources officers or the Department of Field Support and prepare a shortlist of candidates who appear most suitable for the post at issue. Shortlisted candidates are further assessed through evaluation mechanisms chosen by the hiring or occupational group manager. The final selection decision is made by the Head of Department or Office upon proposal by the hiring or occupational group manager, subject to a positive examination of the proposal by the (field) central review body. A number of special rules apply to appointments to positions involving significant functions in the management of financial, human and physical resources and/or information and communication technology as well as to posts at the D-2 level.[63]

While UN staff members do not have the right to be promoted, they do have the right to have their candidature for a vacant post to which they apply fully and fairly considered.[64] The burden of proving that such regard has indeed been granted in an individual case rests with the Administration, not with the staff member concerned:

---

[60] See *UN Staff Regulations of 2007*, Article IV named 'Appointment and Promotion' and similarly *UN Staff Rules of 2002*, Chapter 4.

[61] See above, chapter 3, section 2.2.2.2.

[62] *UN Staff Selection System*, Sections 2.1 and 3.2(c).

[63] For details, see chapter 3, section 2.2.2.

[64] *Williamson, UNAT Judgment No. 362 [1986]*, para. VII ; and *Case No. 1309, UNAT Judgment No. 1258 [2005]*, available at http://untreaty.un.org/UNAT/UNAT_Judgements/Judgements_E/UNAT_01258_E.pdf, last visited on 30.12.2010, para. IV. In the latter case the UNAT also held that the determination whether a particular staff member has been given full and fair consideration for promotion and whether that process has been transparent is a matter that often needs to be considered on the basis of surrounding circumstances. – Ibid.

If once called seriously into question, the Administration must be able to make at least a minimal showing that the staff member's statutory right was honoured in good faith in that the Administration gave "the fullest regard" to it.[65]

Nonetheless, the UN Administration enjoys wide discretion in deciding which candidate is to be promoted. It has a free hand in evaluating candidates' qualifications, experience and performance, not compromised by the existence of any expectancy or right of promotion on the side of UN staff members. As long as this discretion is exercised objectively, without bias, prejudice, discrimination or procedural irregularities, it will not be subject to judicial review.[66]

A number of limitations to the discretion of the UN Administration in promotion matters do exist, though. One of them relates to promises made to individual staff members with regard to their promotion. When the Administration makes such a promise, it should adhere to it. The Administration does retain its discretion to promote the staff member in question or not, since promotion decisions remain its sole prerogative, but when it the staff member is not promoted, the UNAT may hold the Administration responsible and order it to compensate for the injury caused to the staff member.[67] Making commitments with regard to promotion of individual staff members may, in addition, cause discrimination against those staff members who do not receive such promises. The UNAT stressed in *Gomez* that, in general, the UN Administration was not supposed to enter into legally binding arrangements with

---

[65] *Williamson, UNAT Judgment No. 362 [1986]*, para. VII. See also *Klein v. Secretary-General of the United Nations, UNAT Judgment No. 1031 [2001]*, available at http://untreaty.un.org/UNAT/UNAT_Judgements/Judgements_E/UNAT_01031_E.pdf, last visited on 30.12.2010, paras. VII-VIII.

[66] For example, *Noll-Wagenfeld v. Secretary-General of the United Nations, UNAT Judgment No. 636 [1994]*, available at http://untreaty.un.org/UNAT/UNAT_Judgements/Judgements_E/UNAT_00636_E.pdf, last visited on 30.12.2010, para. II; *Lopes Braga, UNAT Judgment No. 1122 [2003]*, para. III ; and *Case No. 1398, UNAT Judgment No. 1324 [2007]*, available at http://untreaty.un.org/UNAT/UNAT_Judgements/Judgements_E/UNAT_01324_E.pdf, last visited on 30.12.2010, para. VIII. Note that discrimination is also not allowed in instances in which the policy of enhancing equal opportunities for women is involved. In *Grinblat*, the applicant, a male staff member, was found to be discriminated against since he had been illegally excluded from a short list of candidates to be considered for promotion on the basis of his gender. The UNAT ruled that because the applicant's merits were equal to those of the shortlisted candidates, he should have been included in the short list as well. The priority to female candidates could have been given but only in further steps of the promotion process where the choice was to be made from among the shortlisted candidates. - *Grinblat v. Secretary-General of the United Nations, UNAT Judgment No. 671 [1994]*, available at http://untreaty.un.org/UNAT/UNAT_Judgements/Judgements_E/UNAT_00671_E.pdf, last visited on 30.12.2010, paras. XVII-XIX. The latter was affirmed in *Anderson Bieler* where the applicant was declared by the UNAT to have had a right to promotion since she had been the only female candidate who was shortlisted. - *Anderson Bieler v. Secretary-General of the United Nations, UNAT Judgment No. 765 [1996]*, available at http://untreaty.un.org/UNAT/UNAT_Judgements/Judgements_E/UNAT_00765_E.pdf, last visited on 30.12.2010, para. V.

[67] *Warner v. Secretary-General of the United Nations, UNAT Judgment No. 418 [1988]*, available at http://untreaty.un.org/UNAT/UNAT_Judgements/Judgements_E/UNAT_00418_E.pdf, last visited on 30.12.2010, paras. XXI and XXIV. Note that a simple recommendation for promotion of an individual staff member does not amount to a legally binding commitment. – *Khan v. Secretary-General of the United Nations, UNAT Judgment No. 848 [1997]*, available at http://untreaty.un.org/UNAT/UNAT_Judgements/Judgements_E/UNAT_00848_E.pdf, last visited on 30.12.2010, para. IV. On the issue of expectancy of promotion, see also Amerasinghe, C. F., *The Law of the International Civil Service, Volume II*, Clarendon Press, Oxford, 1988, pp. 912-913.

its staff members on their career development and was to refrain from expressing false hopes.[68] In *Tortel* the UNAT added in this respect that the UN staff members were entitled to expect that the organization would honour its commitments on which they relied in good faith.[69]

Another important limitation to the UN Administration's discretion is the obligation to observe its own rules when exercising discretion. In *Lopes Braga*, for example, the Administration advertised a vacant post, including certain qualification requirements, in particular an undergraduate degree, as one of the criteria for the selection. Eventually, a candidate who did not possess such a degree was promoted to the post. The UNAT held that the Administration had failed to apply objective criteria for evaluating the candidates in a consistent way and thereby failed to give full and fair consideration to the applicant, but also harmed the prospects of other potential candidates who might have not applied for the post because they did not possess the required qualification. The UNAT stressed that it was within the discretion of the Administration to establish evaluation criteria. However, once the criteria were set up, they must be observed.[70]

The obligation to consider fairly and fully all candidates for appointment, i.e. also those who seek promotion, has been reflected in many – more specific – obligations 'imposed' by the UNAT on the UN Administration. One of them is the obligation to select the best qualified candidate, as stipulated by Article 101(3) of the *UN Charter* and Regulation 4.2 of the *UN Staff Regulations*. In order to be able to make such selection, the Administration is obliged to give full and fair consideration to all candidates.[71] This is linked to another important limitation of the discretion of the Administration, namely the obligation to justify the decision, especially if it departs from the recommendations of the advisory bodies involved in the promotion process. In his discretion, the Secretary-General is not bound by the recommendation of such bodies as they only act in an advisory capacity.[72]

---

[68] *Gomez v. Secretary-General of the United Nations, UNAT Judgment No. 342 [1985]*, available at http://untreaty.un.org/UNAT/UNAT_Judgements/Judgements_E/UNAT_00342_E.pdf, last visited on 30.12.2010, para. V

[69] *Tortel v. Secretary-General of the United Nations, UNAT Judgment No. 444 [1989]*, available at http://untreaty.un.org/UNAT/UNAT_Judgements/Judgements_E/UNAT_00444_E.pdf, last visited on 30.12.2010, para. VIII. See also *Salama v. Secretary-General of the United Nations, UNAT Judgment No. 936 [1999]*, available at http://untreaty.un.org/UNAT/UNAT_Judgements/Judgements_E/UNAT_00936_E.pdf, last visited on 30.12.2010, para. III.

[70] *Lopes Braga, UNAT Judgment No. 1122 [2003]*, para. V.

[71] *Klein, UNAT Judgment No. 1031 [2001]*, paras. VII-VIII.

[72] *Walter v. Secretary-General of the United Nations, UNAT Jugment no. 390 [1987]*, available at http://untreaty.un.org/UNAT/UNAT_Judgements/Judgements_E/UNAT_00390_E.pdf, last visited on 30.12.2010, para. VIII. See also *Salama, UNAT Judgment No. 936 [1999]*, para. II ; and *Klein, UNAT Judgment No. 1031 [2001]*, paras. VII-VIII. In the latter case, the formerly existing appointment and promotion board rejected a candidate proposed by the Administration, arguing that that candidate was not qualified for the post at issue, and advised that the post be re-advertised. Nonetheless, the Administration appointed the candidate, providing no proper grounds or reasons for its decision. When the decision was challenged by another candidate, the UNAT held the Administration had violated due process and the applicant's rights to full and fair consideration. It stated that the Administration's discretion in promotion matters was subject to the requirement of selecting the best

The obligation to give full and fair consideration to all candidates is also connected to yet another limitation of the Administration's discretion in promotion matters, namely the requirement to base the evaluation of the candidates' qualifications on the official appraisal of their performance recorded in the performance evaluation reports.[73] This requirement is justified by the need to ensure staff members' rights to be aware of, and have an opportunity to comment on, clarify, or contradict any adverse information that may eventually be taken into account in their evaluation.[74] The failure to prepare a staff member's performance evaluation report (in time) and/or failure to take the relevant report into consideration in the promotion process violates staff members' right to fair and full consideration and is, to use the words of the UNAT, 'inexcusable'.[75] Similarly, the Administration must pay regard to the rebuttal report, if relevant.[76] In addition, it should await the outcome of a rebuttal process before starting selections for promotion.[77]

Given the importance of the performance appraisal of the UN staff members for their possible promotion, the next part pays more detailed attention to it.

2.1.2.3. Performance appraisal

The appraisal of staff members' performance is of great importance in the decision making process for promotions since it provides indispensable information on staff members' merits, the decisive criterion in each promotion exercise. Without an adequate and effective performance evaluation system, there can thus be no well-functioning promotion system. On the contrary, a good system of performance evaluation recognizes staff competence and efficiency and rewards them by advantageous career progression, leading to greater personal satisfaction and motivation and, consequently, even better performance.

Performance appraisal is not a simple exercise, though:

---

qualified candidate, as stipulated by Article 101(3) of the UN Charter and Regulation 4.2 of the UN Staff Regulations. In order to be able to make such a selection, the Administration is obliged to give full and fair consideration to all candidates.

73 *Case No. 1475, UNAT Judgment No. 1405 [2008]*, para. VI.

74 *Case No. 1379, UNAT Judgment No. 1297 [2006]*, available at http://untreaty.un.org/UNAT/UNAT_Judgements/Judgements_E/UNAT_01297_E.pdf, last visited on 30.12.2010, para. V. See also *Case No. 1498, UNAT Judgment No. 1430 [2008]*, available at http://untreaty.un.org/UNAT/UNAT_Judgements/Judgements_E/UNAT_01430_E.pdf, last visited on 30.12.2010, para. IV. In the latter case the UNAT stressed the importance of timely and properly conducted performance evaluation as means for informing staff of possible shortcomings of their performance, as well as of providing staff with an opportunity for improvement before using such shortcomings in decisions on staff career development.

75 *Case No. 1408, UNAT Judgment No. 1331 [2007]*, available at http://untreaty.un.org/UNAT/UNAT_Judgements/Judgements_E/UNAT_01331_E.pdf, last visited on 30.12.2010, para. XXIX.

76 Ibid., paras. XXVI-XXVII.

77 Ibid., para. XVII.

> *Hiring is the most important decision made by the manager of professional activities, firing and disciplining are the most painful, but performance evaluation may be the most difficult.*[78]

The complex nature as well as the importance of performance evaluation has been emphasized by the UNAT already in the early years:

> *All methods of annual report upon staff are difficult both in conception and in application. But such markings serve a double purpose. Firstly, they enable the essential appraisal of efficiency to be reached. Secondly, they afford the staff the opportunity of knowing critical comments made about them, with a view both to offering their observations thereon and to correcting any lack of efficiency.*[79]

Through the years, the UN has struggled considerably in its quest for a well-functioning system of performance evaluation. In the past, evaluation systems were criticized by both the managers and the staff for their unfairness, inefficiency and meaninglessness caused by the fact that a gross majority of staff – above 90 per cent – were rated as performing very well or outstandingly. A number of attempts to reform the system failed.[80]

In 1995, a new system of performance appraisal was introduced. In its revised version, this system applied until April 2010 when it was replaced by another called Performance Management and Development System.[81] The most important improvements of the Performance Appraisal System introduced in 1995, noted by the Office of Internal Oversight Services, were the inclusion of competences and career aspirations of staff and of the link between individual work planning and departmental work plans.[82] However, the OIOS criticized the functioning of this system and its impact on career development of UN staff:

---

78 Shapero, A., *Managing Professional People: Understanding Creative Performance*, The Free Press, New York, 1985, as cited in *Toward a New System of Performance Appraisal in the United Nations Secretariat. Requirements for Successful Implementation, Report of the Joint Inspection Unit, JIU/REP/94/5*, p. 1.

79 *De Pojidaeff v. Secretary-General of the United Nations, UNAT Judgment No. 17 [1952]*, available at http://untreaty.un.org/UNAT/UNAT_Judgements/Judgements_E/UNAT_00017_E.pdf, last visited on 30.12.2010, para. 18. Similarly, see a recent decision in *Case No. 1498, UNAT Judgment No. 1430 [2008]*, para. IV. In the latter case the UNAT stated: 'the Tribunal is not satisfied that the Applicant's performance evaluation was completed in a reasoned, cautious and proper manner. Rather, it appears that the Applicant's supervisors avoided the prescribed evaluation process, using e-mail and informal meetings rather than the mid-year review to express dissatisfaction. Thus, depriving the Applicant of an opportunity to be properly advised of his shortcomings and also depriving him of an opportunity for improvement.' – Ibid.

80 *Toward a New System of Performance Appraisal in the United Nations Secretariat: Requirements for Successful Implementation, Report of the Joint Inspection Unit, JIU/REP/94/5*, pp. 9-16.

81 *Administrative Instruction, Performance Appraisal System, ST/AI/2002/3*, 20.03.2002, available in the Human Resources Handbook of the United Nations, available at http://www.un.org/hr_handbook/English/, last visited on 30.12.2010 and *Administrative Instruction, Performance Management and Development System*.

82 *Impact of the Human Resources Management Reform, Report of the Office of Internal Oversight Services, A/59/253*, Part III, Section D, para. 58.

a strong link between the Secretariat Performance Appraisal System (e-PAS), participation in learning programmes and strategic development of staff skills and career paths has not yet been fully established. For example, staff performance appraisal information is not consistently considered during the staff selection process, and almost half of staff respondents reported that they do not see the e-PAS as an effective tool for career development. In addition, more than half do not see any relationship between their performance appraisal and promotion opportunities. More than half of Secretariat managers either "disagree" or "strongly disagree" that e-PAS is being used effectively to support departmental efforts to promote the most qualified candidate.[83]

In addition, the system was perceived by both the staff and the management as lacking fairness and as not reflecting staff performance accurately. Moreover, many managers had indicated that the system was not used effectively for assessing staff performance.[84] Consequently, the OIOS recommended that the system be reviewed.[85] The result of such review was the introduction of a new Performance Management and Development System in April 2010, whose overall objective is identical to that of the previous performance appraisal system. It aims at improving programme delivery by optimizing staff performance. This objective, and instruments for its achievement, are set out in the *Administrative Instruction, Performance Management and Development System ST/AI/2010/5*.[86] This administrative instruction also lays down detailed rules on the basis of which annual performance review for all UN staff members with a contract duration longer than one year, including the most senior ones, should be conducted. This is in line with Rule 1.3 of the *UN Staff Rules* envisaging annual performance evaluation of UN staff.[87]

The annual review is conducted for a performance cycle of twelve months, starting each year on 1 April.[88] It involves a number of players: staff members, first and

[83] *In-depth Evaluation of the Office of Human Resources Management, Report of the Office of Internal Oversight Services, A/63/221*, Part IV, Section A.3.(c), para. 48.

[84] Ibid., Part IV, Section A.3.(e), para. 51. The credibility of the Performance Appraisal System, in which ninety-nine per cent of staff was rated as fully meeting or frequently or consistently exceeding expectations, was questioned also by the Advisory Committee on Administrative and Budgetary Questions. The Committee also called for strengthening the links between performance and future career prospects. - *Human Resources Management, Report of the Advisory Committee on Administrative and Budgetary Questions, A/63/526*, Part II, paras. 26-27.

[85] *In-depth Evaluation of the Office of Human Resources Management, Report of the Office of Internal Oversight Services, A/63/221*, Part VI, Recommendation 1, para. 80. See also, for example, *Towards a Compact, Proposals for Improved Governance and Management of the United Nations Secretariat, Report of Final Proposals by the Four Nations Initiative on Governance and Management of the UN*, pp. 35-36

[86] *Administrative Instruction, Performance Management and Development System*. The relevant instruments include: '(a) Promoting a culture of high performance, personal development and continuous learning; (b) Empowering managers and holding them responsible and accountable for managing their staff; (c) Encouraging a high level of staff participation in the planning, delivery and evaluation of work; (d) Recognizing successful performance and addressing underperformance in a fair and equitable manner.'- Section 2.1.

[87] *UN Staff Rules*, Rule 1.3.

[88] *Administrative Instruction, Performance Management and Development System*, Section 3.1. Special rules apply to appraisal in situations in which a staff members takes up new duties upon recruitment,

second reporting officers, heads of departments and offices, possibly members of rebuttal panels, but also two monitoring committees. The first reporting officers are designated for each staff member at the start of the performance cycle. Normally, the direct supervisor of each staff member serves as his first reporting officer. If a staff member works under more than one supervisor, either for an important assignment or for a longer period of time, additional supervisors may be designated to take part in the appraisal process. The main tasks of the first reporting officers are to develop the individual work plan of staff under their responsibility, to provide on-going feedback on and conduct evaluation of their work, to advise, support and coach staff members in their professional development, to develop a performance improvement plan, if needed, and to ensure timely completion of the evaluation documents.[89] The second reporting officer is the supervisor of the first reporting officer. The second reporting officer is responsible especially for ensuring that the Performance Management and Development System is applied consistently and fairly across units and for holding the first reporting officers accountable for tasks under this system.[90]

The consistency across the department is to be ensured by the Head of Department or Office, who is assisted by a Joint Monitoring Group established in each department and office. The Group is a standing body composed of two members nominated by the management, two nominated by the staff and a chairperson selected by the Head of Department or Office in consultation with the staff, all appointed by the Head of Department for a two year renewable term. The Group monitors and reviews implementation of the Performance Management and Development System by the department or office with regard to timeliness of the process and compliance with its purpose and procedures.[91] Besides the Joint Monitoring Groups of each department or office, there is also a Global Joint Monitoring Group which is a subsidiary organ of the Staff-Management Coordination Committee. This Global Joint Monitoring Group is responsible for examining the policy issues related to implementation of the Performance Management and Development System across the UN. Members of this group are nominated and appointed in the same manner as those of the departmental monitoring groups and their term of office is one year, also renewable.[92]

It follows that the annual performance review of UN staff involves a relatively large number of actors placed in a hierarchical structure that should ensure that review of individual staff members is as objective and impartial as possible. This structure also includes staff representatives who, as noted in this study earlier, constitute an important element increasing the transparency and objectivity of the process.

transfer or assignment during the performance year, or in which a staff member or his supervisor is reassigned or transferred from a department or office, or when either of them is separated from service. – Ibid., Sections 3.2. and 3.3.

[89] Ibid., Section 5.1.

[90] Ibid., Sections 5.2.-5.3.

[91] Ibid., Sections 11-12.

[92] Ibid., Sections 6.1-6.2.

Regarding the annual evaluation procedure itself, before each annual performance cycle begins, work plans are developed for the entire Secretariat, for each department and office, for each work unit and eventually also individual work plans. The individual plans are prepared together by the supervisors and individual staff members.[93] The plans are important, even decisive, for later performance evaluation of individual staff members, setting performance benchmarks for each individual.

The actual performance review is conducted in two steps. A midpoint review takes place, as its name suggests, in the middle of each performance cycle. During this review the progress made thus far is indicated, after discussion with the staff member at issue, and, if need be, the individual work plan is updated. In cases of disagreement, both sides are required to make efforts to resolve the disagreement, if need be with the assistance of the second reporting officer.[94]

The final appraisal takes place at the end of the performance cycle. It begins with a meeting between the first reporting officer and the individual staff member at which overall progress is discussed. Before this meeting, the staff member may (be encouraged) to conduct self-appraisal which may be later commented on by the first reporting officer. The first reporting officer conducts the actual appraisal of the staff member's performance during the relevant cycle against the goals and expectations set out in the staff member's individual work plan. He also gives an overall rating on this performance. The appraisal prepared by the first reporting officer is reviewed by a second officer who may add his own comments. The appraisal exercise ends with the signature of the appraisal report by all three persons involved.[95]

[93] *Administrative Instruction, Performance Appraisal System of 2002*, Section 5 and 6.1. Individual work plans contain three parts: first, an actual work plan, including results-oriented elements such as key results and actions to take to achieve them; second competences, i.e. a performance standard against which staff member at issue will be evaluated; and third personal development plan, indicating staff members' wishes with regard to other competencies and skills they wish to acquire and their future career aspirations. - Section 6.3.

[94] *Administrative Instruction, Performance Management and Development System*, Section 7.

[95] Ibid., Section 8. Note that staff may receive four performance ratings: outstanding (exceeding performance expectations); fully competent (successfully meeting performance expectations); requires development (partially meeting performance expectations) and unsatisfactory (not meeting performance expectations). These ratings establish the level to which individual staff members demonstrated core values and competences during the performance cycle and serve as important information taken into account when decisions are made on staff member's career development, including promotion. General definition of each performance level is since 2010 provided in the relevant administrative instruction. - *Administrative Instruction, Performance Management and Development System*, Section 9.

Scheme 10: Performance appraisal procedure in the UN Secretariat

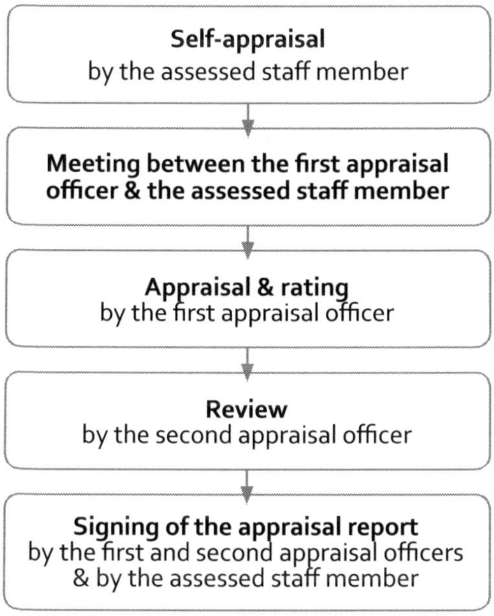

Before turning to the next (possible) step in the performance evaluation, it should be noted that the performance of each individual staff member should be observed, mutually discussed and evaluated during the whole performance cycle, not only at the point of formal review. The first reporting officer and the staff member should 'address recognition for good performance and any shortcomings as they become apparent at any time during the cycle'.[96] Identified shortcomings should be remedied, using assistance of the first reporting officer, in consultation with the second reporting officer, and employing appropriate remedial measures, such as counselling, transfer to more suitable function, coaching and supervision. If the problem is not rectified in this manner, a written performance improvement plan must be prepared by the first reporting officer in consultation with the staff member concerned and the second reporting officer. Further measures and/or sanctions, including non-renewal or termination of appointment due to unsatisfactory service may only follow after these steps have taken place.[97]

When a staff member does not agree with the rating he has received in an annual performance review, he may start a rebuttal process by submitting a written statement to the Executive Office at Headquarters (or to the Chief of Administration or Mission Support outside Headquarters) and specifying reasons. Such rebuttal is possible when the received rating is the worst or the second worst possible (i.e. when the staff member is considered not meeting performance expectations or meeting

[96] *Administrative Instruction, Performance Management and Development System*, Section 7.1.

[97] Ibid., Section 10.

them only partially). The best and the second best rating (received by staff members exceeding performance expectations or successfully meeting performance expectations) cannot be rebutted.[98] The question is the denial of a possibility to rebut the second best rating is in line with existing jurisprudence. In a relatively recent case of 2007, the UNAT held that staff members were entitled to rebut the correctness of their evaluation, as well as to have their due process rights respected in the rebuttal process.[99] The emphasis in this case was on the due process rights, not on the right to the rebuttal, as the latter was not disputed. However, it would be difficult to argue that the second best rating cannot have adverse effects on the staff members' chances in future promotion process. It is namely rather likely that in a specific selection procedure staff members ranked in the second category will compete with those who have been rated higher. Since the promotion process depends heavily on candidates' merits, and merits are evidenced also by performance evaluation, candidates with the second best rating are disadvantaged when compared to those with the best rating. If the rating is not correct, and there is no possibility to challenge it, the objectivity of the entirely selection process is inevitably compromised. It could even be argued that the performance evaluation system could be abused for underrating certain staff members in order to restrict their promotion chances or to favour other staff members.

Returning to the rebuttal procedure, each rebuttal is dealt with by a panel whose members are chosen by the staff member at issue from a list composed of three groups of staff from the relevant department or office appointed for two years. One group contains members designated by the Head of Department or Office, one members designated by the staff representatives of that department or office, and one chairpersons selected by the Head of Department or Office after consultation with the staff representatives. The rebutting staff member must choose one person from each group to compose his rebuttal panel.[100] It can hardly be disputed that the involvement of staff representatives in rebuttal panels and the fact that the rebutting staff member has a choice with regard to all members of his rebuttal panel enhance the objectivity and impartiality of the rebuttal process to a significant extent. Further guarantees of such process are provided by the procedure which must be followed by each rebuttal panel. The panel first reviews the original appraisal in the light of the rebuttal statement of the staff member concerned and the reply to this statement prepared by the Head of Department or Office or his representative and submitted to the panel before it takes up its tasks. The rebuttal panel may hear persons it considers relevant. It always hears the staff member concerned and the first and second reporting officers, unless it is impractical due to the geographical location in which case telephone statements may be taken. In its report, the panel states reasons for which the original appraisal report should be maintained or modified and, if relevant, it designates the new rating. The performance rating estab-

---

[98] Ibid., Section 15.1.

[99] *Case No. 1403, UNAT Judgment No. 1327 [2007]*, available at http://untreaty.un.org/UNAT/UNAT_Judgements/Judgements_E/UNAT_01327_E.pdf, last visited on 30.12.2010, para. V.

[100] *Administrative Instruction, Performance Management and Development System*, Sections 14 and 15.1.-15.2.

lished by the report is binding on both the staff member at issue and the Head of Department or Office. It is however not binding on the Secretary-General who may further review the case, if he wishes. As indicated in the administrative instruction, such power rests with the Secretary-General as UN Chief Administrative Officer.[101] This is, in itself, not surprising, but it is regrettable. It cannot be denied that the UN Secretary-General is indeed the highest administrative officer of the UN Secretariat, responsible for all its personnel. He should however not stand above the rules and procedures adopted after broad and careful consideration by many involved stakeholders. The very adoption of such rules and procedures is aimed at ensuring that the process takes place in a fair, objective and transparent manner. Ignoring results of the rebuttal process in individual cases would deprive it of such character.

Scheme 11: Rebuttal process of the performance appraisal in the UN Secretariat

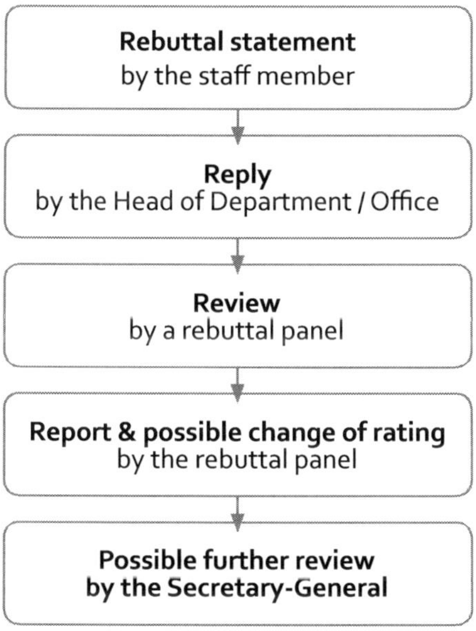

The report of the rebuttal panel is placed in the official file of the staff member concerned.[102] The final rating (established by the rebuttal panel, or where no change took place by relevant reporting officers) may not be further appealed. However, any decision which is based on the rating and which affects conditions of service of the staff member at issue, for example a (non)promotion decision, may be subject to a regular administrative appeal provided for by the *UN Staff Regulations* and *Rules*,

[101] Ibid., Section 15. Note that the rebuttal panel is allowed but not obliged to hear witnesses. - *Case No. 1403, UNAT Judgment No. 1327 [2007]*, para. V. Also, while due process rights of the staff member rebutting his appraisal must be respected and protected, the rebuttal process should not be compared to disciplinary proceedings. Therefore, the UNAT recognizes a more nuanced approach to the staff members' right in the rebuttal process. – *Case No. 1403, UNAT Judgment No. 1327 [2007]*, para. V.

[102] *Administrative Instruction, Performance Management and Development System*, Section 15.4.

i.e. in the first instance to the United Nations Dispute Tribunal and in the second instance to the United Nations Appeals Tribunal.[103] An appeal against any decision based on the performance rating constitutes an indirect means of appeal against the rating itself.

The competence of the United Nations Administrative Tribunal, replaced in 2009 by the UNDP and UNAT, to review the staff performance evaluation report was confirmed, for example, in *Ho* case.[104] As expressly stated by the UNAT, the review of staff members' evaluation is necessary because it provides 'a vital insight into the [staff members'] treatment during the promotion exercises'.[105]

The UNAT has consistently recognized that staff performance evaluation is within the discretionary authority of the UN Administration and that it could not substitute its opinion for that of the officer making the appraisal.[106] However, the UNAT could, in its own view, interfere with that opinion in cases of inadequate or erroneous information, bias, prejudice, discrimination or another extraneous consideration.[107] For example, in *Ibañez* the UNAT found that the report did not present an accurate picture of the applicant's performance because it had granted the applicant the lowest rating while his performance in respect of his main duties was generally satisfactory; only the performance regarding other (than main) duties was not satisfactory.[108] On the other hand, in *Anderson* the UNAT dismissed pleas because no discrimination, prejudice or other extraneous considerations were proven, even though the Administration had not acted in the most advisable manner. In this case, the applicant's performance was assessed as 'very good' in the first evaluation report but as 'not fully meeting standards' in the second report, while the performance itself was the same during both evaluated periods. When challenged, the UN Administration explained that the second evaluation exercise had been conducted according to tightened criteria in order to provide more accurate and honest evalu-

[103] Ibid., Section 15.7. The same applies also to decisions to withhold salary increments which may be a result of unsatisfactory ratings granted in the annual appraisal process. Such decisions are not reviewable by the rebuttal panels at all as they are only empowered to deal with rebuttals of the performance ratings. - Section 16. For detailed rules on appeals, see *UN Staff Regulations of 2009*, Article XI and *UN Staff Rules*, Chapter XI.

[104] *Ho v. Secretary-General of the United Nations, UNAT Judgment No. 122 [1968]*, available at http://untreaty.un.org/UNAT/UNAT_Judgements/Judgements_E/UNAT_00122_E.pdf, last visited on 30.12.2010, para. II. See also, for example, *Anderson v. Secretary-General of the United Nations, UNAT Judgment No. 457 [1989]*, available at http://untreaty.un.org/UNAT/UNAT_Judgements/Judgements_E/UNAT_00457_E.pdf, last visited on 30.12.2010, para. I.

[105] *Case No. 1408, UNAT Judgment No. 1331 [2007]*, para. IX.

[106] *De Pojidaeff, UNAT Judgment No. 17 [1952]*, para. 20; *Ho, UNAT Judgment No. 122 [1968]*, para. II; *Adler v. Secretary-General of the United Nations, UNAT Judgment No. 267 [1980]*, available at http://untreaty.un.org/UNAT/UNAT_Judgements/Judgements_E/UNAT_00267_E.pdf, last visited on 30.12.2010, para. XXIV; and more recently *Case No. 1355, UNAT Judgment No. 1272 [2005]*, available at http://untreaty.un.org/UNAT/UNAT_Judgements/Judgements_E/UNAT_01272_E.pdf, last visited on 30.12.2010, para. V.

[107] *Ho, UNAT Judgment No. 122 [1968]*, para. II.; *Adler, UNAT Judgment No. 267 [1980]*, para. XXIV; *Anderson, UNAT Judgment No. 457 [1989]*, para. II; or *Lopes Braga, UNAT Judgment No. 1122 [2003]*, para. III.

[108] *Ibañez v. Secretary-General of the United Nations, UNAT Judgment No. 223 [1977]*, available at http://untreaty.un.org/UNAT/UNAT_Judgements/Judgements_E/UNAT_00223_E.pdf, last visited on 30.12.2010, paras. VIII-X.

ation of staff members' performance. In the UNAT's view, it was regrettable that the applicant had never been warned about the deficiencies which constituted the basis for her negative assessment but as the new criteria had been applied to all staff and no prejudice against the applicant was found, her pleas were rejected.[109]

In a 2006 case, the UNAT held that the mere fact that a staff member had after years of excellent evaluation received a bad evaluation in a specific year was not, in itself, an exceptionally significant matter or a sign of discrimination. The UNAT added, however, that such development did call for an explanation, requiring a closer focus on the 'facts, figures, and evidence' which had been the basis for the negative evaluation.[110] The UNAT confirmed its previous case law that the performance evaluation falls within the discretionary powers of the Administration but stressed that:

> *when the manner in which this undoubtedly discretionary power is exercised comes under serious attack, claiming abuse thereof as being motivated by extraneous factors, in such cases it is imperative that a clear explanation and justification of the assessment be forthcoming for scrutiny. Such a process will not lead to any substitution of the Respondent's judgment regarding performance evaluation; but such a process does become a necessary step to refute a charge of discrimination, prejudice or bias.*[111]

Besides the existence of inadequate or erroneous information, bias, prejudice, discrimination or another extraneous consideration, the UNAT would also review whether applicable procedures have been followed in the performance evaluation process and whether due process has been adhered to. The UNAT has ruled that the Administration is obliged to conduct timely evaluations of staff performance so that the records, relevant for the promotion process, are complete, accurate and up-to-date.[112] Absence of an up-to-date appraisal report amounts to a violation of due process, especially if the promotion is denied as a result of incomplete and inaccurate information on the performance of the staff member under consideration.[113]

---

[109] *Anderson, UNAT Judgment No. 457 [1989]*, para. III.

[110] *Case No. 1355, UNAT Judgment No. 1272 [2005]*, para. IV.

[111] Ibid., para. V.

[112] *Khan, UNAT Judgment No. 848 [1997]*, para. VII.

[113] *Monteleone-Gilfillian v. Secretary-General of the United Nations, UNAT Judgment No. 814 [1997]*, available at http://untreaty.un.org/UNAT/UNAT_Judgements/Judgements_E/UNAT_00814_E.pdf, last visited on 30.12.2010, para. IV and more recently, for example, *Case No. 1392, UNAT Judgment No. 1285 [2006]*, available at http://untreaty.un.org/UNAT/UNAT_Judgements/Judgements_E/UNAT_01285_E.pdf, last visited on 30.12.2010, para. III or *Case No. 1455, UNAT Judgment No. 1390 [2008]*, available at http://untreaty.un.org/UNAT/UNAT_Judgements/Judgements_E/UNAT_01390_E.pdf, last visited on 30.12.2010, para. VI. See also *Case No. 1408, UNAT Judgment No. 1331 [2007]*, where the UNAT condemned the Administration for not having awaited the outcome of the rebuttal process as this had clearly been relevant for proper assessment of the applicant's past performance. - para. XVII.

2.2. Promotion to the Professional Category from Other Categories ('G to P')

At the beginning of this section it is explained that there are two different types of promotion in the UN Secretariat, one within the category and another from other categories to the Professional category. Although the terminology sometimes used in UN documents refers to the latter as recruitment, this study follows the opinion of the UNAT and considers it to be promotion.

The movement of staff from General Service categories to the Professional category by way of competitive examinations occurred already in the late 1940s.[114] Formally, however, the competitive examination for such movement was established only in 1978 by the General Assembly resolution 33/143. The resolution set out the main principles by which the movement was to be governed, including the limitation of the movement to P-1 and P-2 level posts, the number of posts that could be filled by such movement out of the total of recruitments at the relevant levels, the obligation to pass competitive examinations, and the minimum education and experience requirements.[115]

The legality of examinations as the sole way of promotion of staff of the General Service category to the Professional category was contested in a number of staff cases lodged before the UNAT. The UNAT, however, upheld the system. In *Capio*, the applicant argued, *inter alia*, that the competitive examinations as a new method of deciding promotions from the General Service category to the Professional category as well as the ceiling of possible annual promotions in this manner was inconsistent with the *UN Charter* and relevant *UN Staff Regulations*, requiring that the merit principle be accorded paramount consideration in the appointment, transfer or promotion decisions relating to UN staff.[116] The applicant argued that the resolution of the UN General Assembly 33/143 establishing the system of competitive examinations and the subsequent administrative instruction adopted by the Secretary-General in order to implement that resolution were incompatible with the *UN Charter* and *UN Staff Regulations*. The UNAT rejected these claims and held that:

> *the General Assembly was entitled to demand the introduction of a new system to govern such promotions and that the Secretary-General has exercised his discretion in setting up a system of selection by competitive examination...*[117]

In a later case, *Knight et al.* the applicants claimed, *inter alia*, that the system of promotion from General Service to the Professional category based on competitive

[114] Swift, *Personnel Problems and the United Nations Secretariat*, p. 229
[115] *General Assembly Resolution 33/143*, Section I, para. 1(g).
[116] *Capio, UNAT Judgment No. 266 [1980]*, p. 345.
[117] Ibid., para. IV. Note that in *Abebe* the UNAT ruled that the requirement of passing the G to P examination, which is the normal procedure, had had to be waived in the case of the applicant, a General Service category staff member, because the Administration had created exceptional situation in her case by improperly having allowed her to occupy a post in the Professional category for six years. - *Abebe v. Secretary-General of the United Nations, UNAT Judgment No. 1169 [2004]*, available at http://untreaty.un.org/UNAT/UNAT_Judgements/Judgements_E/UNAT_01169_E.pdf, last visited on 30.12.2010, para. XX.

examinations violated their right to be considered for promotion to the Professional category on the basis of equity and merit. They claimed that the system was discriminatory towards the staff of the General Service category who were not treated equally alongside candidates from other categories and external candidates.[118] The reaction of the UNAT on these claims deserves full citation:

> *In furtherance of their general objective, the Applicants advance arguments of a policy nature. These aim at showing that the competitive examination is unfair or discriminatory in certain respects and that it is not in the best interests of the Organization. Such arguments are addressed to the wrong forum. The specific requirements of the examination, such as the choice of occupational groups, or age requirements in national competitive examinations, are policy decisions by the Secretary-General made in the reasonable exercise of his discretion, based on his assessment of the staffing needs and objectives of the Organization. The Tribunal's function, as defined by its Statute, is to determine whether there has been non-observance of the terms of the employment contracts, which include the competitive examination. In these cases, the Tribunal can find no such non-observance since the competitive examination, as a whole, which is being challenged by the Applicants, is based on General Assembly resolutions and implementing administrative instructions. The goal of the Applicants is not to redress alleged violations of the system affecting them individually. They seek a fundamental change in the system as a whole, i.e. in the terms of their employment. But it is not the function of the Tribunal to substitute its views for those of the General Assembly or the Respondent on how best to manage the Organization.*[119]

The UNAT continued:

> *Quite clearly, the General Assembly had a rational basis for requiring a competitive examination procedure for promotion from the General Service to the Professional category. Equally, the differentiation between various categories of staff, such as Professional, Field Service categories and General Service, has a rational basis.*[120]

The UNAT concluded:

> *The General Assembly has the power to promulgate conditions of service for the staff. The International Court of Justice has so held in its advisory opinion of 20 July 1982, Application for Review of Judgement No. 273 of the United Nations Administrative Tribunal, Advisory Opinion, I.C.J. Reports 1982, p. 325, paragraph 68. The view of the [International Court of Justice] is entirely consistent with that previously indicated by the Tribunal in Capio. The Tribunal has also held that General Assembly Resolutions are part of the conditions of service that bind the staff. The Tribunal considers that, since the competitive examination places no*

[118] *Knight, UNAT Judgment No. 722 [1995]*, paras. III and VI.
[119] Ibid., para. VII.
[120] Ibid., para. VIII.

improper restriction on the eligibility of any staff member for the competitive examination, it raises no questions under Article 8 of the Charter. The Tribunal likewise sees no conflict between the competitive examination system and Article 101 of the Charter since the obvious purpose of a competitive examination is to seek the best qualified of the candidates being examined.[121]

In *Gurun*, the UNAT further held that there was no discrimination between staff of the General Service category and external candidates. The UNAT explained that while General Service staff must pass examinations for movement to the Professional category, external candidates need to pass a national competitive examination, which is in form as well as content identical to the examination for movement from the General Service to the Professional category. Consequently, both internal and external candidates need to take the same examinations in order to enter the Professional category at the P-1 and P-2 levels. In the UNAT's view, this showed that both pools of candidates were treated 'evenhandedly'.[122]

In the more recent Judgment No. 1303 of 2006, the UNAT explained that movement of staff in the General Service category to the Professional category was limited to P-1 and P-2 levels and that it was not possible for such a staff member to be appointed to a P-3 level post unless he no longer served in the General Service category and applied as an external candidate. Hence, while serving in the General Service category, the staff may only access the Professional category at P-1 or P-2 level and exclusively through the competitive examinations. P-3 level would then follow through an internal promotion.[123]

In the meantime, as with the staff serving in the General Service category, staff from other categories related to the General Service category, such as Trades and Crafts and Security Service, may also make use of the competitive examination to get promoted to the Professional level. The current version of Rule 4.16 of the *UN Staff Rules* provides, in its relevant part, the following:

Recruitment to the Professional category of staff from the General Service and related categories in the United Nations Secretariat: recruitment to the Professional category at the United Nations Secretariat of staff from the General Service and related categories having successfully passed the appropriate competitive examinations shall be made within the limits established by the General Assembly. Such recruitment shall be made exclusively through competitive examination.[124]

Details are worked out in the *Administrative Instruction, Competitive Examination for Recruitment to the Professional Category of Staff Members from Other Categories ST/AI/2010/7* adopted in June 2010.[125] This instruction replaces the former ST/AI/2003/7

---

[121] Ibid., para. X. See also *Gurun, UNAT Judgment No. 851 [1997]*, para. IV.

[122] *Capio, UNAT Judgment No. 266 [1980]*, para. V.

[123] *Case No. 1387, UNAT Judgment No. 1303 [2006]*, paras. IV-V.

[124] *UN Staff Rules*, Rule 4.16(b)(ii).

[125] *Administrative Instruction on G to P examination.*

with the same title.[126] However, the new instruction does not introduce any dramatic changes when compared to the previous one. In fact the two instructions, the former and the current one, are very similar, including many identical provisions. The only exception is the incorporation of rules in the new instruction on the establishment and management of the roster of candidates successful in the competitive examinations. Previously too, such roster was used but had no legal basis in the relevant administrative instruction. Its management occurred pursuant to *Guidelines on G to P Roster* adopted by the OHRM in 2006.[127] At this point it should be noted that, for reasons of simplicity, the phrase 'G to P' has been used in the UN for decades to refer to the movement from General Service ('G') to the Professional ('P') category. This abbreviation has remained in use even after other categories related to the General Service category were included in the system. As it is a helpful and commonly used abbreviation, this study employs it, too, when appropriate.

The conditions and procedures under which the G to P competitive examinations is held are very similar to those for the UN National Competitive Recruitment Examinations (NCRE).[128] The format of both types of examinations has been realigned in order to place all persons entering junior Professional positions in the UN Secretariat on equal footing. As explained above in this section, this correspondence between the two types of competitive examinations was also used by the UNAT for finding non-discrimination and even-handedness in treatment of external and internal applicants for junior Professional jobs with the UN Secretariat.

Like the NCRE, also the G to P examinations are organized annually for a number of occupational groups, such as economists, auditors, jurists, and statisticians, in accordance with the needs identified during the workforce planning conducted by the OHRM. An important limitation exists in this respect - the total number of posts made available for the G to P examinations may not exceed ten percent of the number of staff, other than language staff, recruited at the junior Professional level by means of competition in the previous calendar year. Additionally, up to seven

[126] *Administrative Instruction, Competitive Examination for Recruitment to the Professional Category of Staff Members from Other Categories*, ST/AI/2003/7, 30.10.2003, as amended by ST/AI/2005/9 of 01.08.2005, available in the Human Resources Handbook of the United Nations, available at http://www.un.org/hr_handbook/English/, last visited on 30.12.2010. See *Administrative Instruction on G to P examination*, Section 10.3. It also appears that the *Administrative Instruction, Movement of Staff from the Field Service Category to the Professional Category ST/AI/360/Rev.1* of 15 November 1993 no longer applies, even though there is no explicit abolition of this instruction in the *Administrative Instruction, Competitive Examination for Recruitment to the Professional Category of Staff Members from Other Categories ST/AI/2010/7*. However, the ST/AI/360/Rev.1 has been removed from the UN Human Resources Handbook available on the internet.

[127] *G to P Roster: Guidelines*, available in the Human Resources Handbook of the United Nations, available at http://www.un.org/hr_handbook/English/, last visited on 30.12.2010.

[128] Administrative instructions concerning the two types of the competitive examinations were adopted at the same time, and even on the same day – 1 June 2010. From the wording of the *former* administrative instruction on the G to P competitive examinations it is clear that this instruction served as the basis for both new instructions. They contain many identical provisions. Naturally, there are a number of specificities in each instruction related to the fact that one forms the basis for external recruitment and the other for internal promotion. However, authorities involved and procedures to be followed are identical. For details on NCRE, see above, chapter 3, section 2.2.1.2.

vacant posts, other than language posts, not subject to geographical distribution, may be filled, as well as up to three posts in duty stations with chronically high vacancy rates when no successful candidates from the NCRE are available.[129]

The G to P competitive examinations are open to all staff members in the General Service and related categories, including the Field Service category up to and including FS-5 level, meeting the following conditions: holding an appointment valid until at least six months after the date scheduled for written examinations; a minimum of five years of continuous service; positive performance evaluation in the last two performance assessments; and satisfying the minimum educational criteria.[130] The G to P examinations are not open to National Professional Officers. As explained in the administrative instruction, the reason for this is that National Professional Officers already perform functions in the Professional category. To enter it, the National Professional Officers need to take the NCRE like any other external candidates.[131] The eligibility of staff applying for the G to P competitive examinations is assessed by the Central Examinations Board in consultation with the OHRM. Candidates found ineligible are informed of the reasons and may appeal to the same Board.[132]

The actual examination consists of a written and an oral part. The written part is held simultaneously for all occupational groups at all duty stations. Applicants whose performance in the written exam reached the required standard, as assessed by the relevant board of examiners, are invited for an interview.[133] The results of the examination are communicated to all candidates in writing, including candidates' ranking and a note on whether they have reached a mark of 30 percent or higher in the written part. Candidates who have participated in the oral part of the examination also receive information on their ranking there. The overall ranking is made on the basis of the combined scores in the relevant parts of the examination. It is done by the relevant board of examiners. This board also prepares a recommendation for the Central Examination Board as to the level above which the candidates are considered to be qualified to perform at the junior Professional level. The recommendation takes into account the level of difficulty of the examinations and the requirement to follow the same performance standard as the NCRE. The recom-

[129] *Administrative Instruction on G to P examination*, Section 2.2. Note that until 1999 the ceiling for the total number of Professional posts which may be made available for candidates from the G to P examinations was thirty per cent. - *General Assembly Resolution 33/143*, Section I, para. 1(g) and *General Assembly Resolution 55/258*, Section IV, para. 17.

[130] *Administrative Instruction on G to P examination*, Section 3.1. For minimum educational criteria, see Sections 3.4-3.5. Additional eligibility criteria are set for staff who have taken the G to P competitive examinations in the past but have not passed it. – Section 3.6.

[131] Ibid., Section 3.3. More on the UN staff category National Professional Officers in chapter 1, section 2.1.3.

[132] Ibid., Sections 3.7-3.8. The written examination amounts to 80 percent of the mark and includes a specialized paper testing substantive knowledge of the specific occupation and a general paper testing drafting skills. The oral part of the examination, which amounts to 20 percent of the marks, entails an interview designed to test the candidate's general knowledge of international affairs and of the United Nations and whether he possesses core values and competencies needed for the position in the relevant occupational group.

[133] Ibid., Section 5.

mendations of the board of examiners as well as the final ranking are made confidentially and anonymously.[134]

The final recommendations are made by the Central Examination Board and approved by the Secretary-General.[135] On their basis successful candidates are placed on a roster from which they may be selected by a hiring or occupational group manager looking for a candidate suitable for a vacant post at the P-2 level. In addition, the first ranked candidate in a specific occupational group is automatically placed in the first vacant post in that occupational group if no candidates have been selected in that occupational group by 1 January of the second year after the G to P examination was completed. All candidates successful in the G to P competitive examinations and placed on the roster remain on this roster until they are placed, unless they refuse a second formal job offer.[136]

As the above description clearly shows, a number of authorities are involved in the G to P competitive examinations process: the Central Examination Board, the boards of examiners, the Secretary-General, and the OHRM. To begin with the last, the OHRM conducts the workforce planning preceding the examinations and establishes the occupational groups for which the examination is to be held in the particular year. It also assists the Central Examination Board in assessing the eligibility of applicants, monitors the appointment of successful candidates in specific posts and informs the Central Examination Board of reaching the maximum number of appointments allowed in the specific year.[137]

The Central Examination Board oversees the examinations and recommends possible improvements. In each individual G to P examination, it also performs a number of specific functions, such as screening applications for determining eligibility, reviewing appeals and complaints, and reviewing and deciding on recommendations made by the boards of examiners.[138] The last mentioned function concerns especially the following recommendations:

> *the arrangements for the marking of papers; recommendations on which examinees are to be convoked to the oral examination, based on results of the written examination; and recommendations on the minimum professional standards required for recruitment, and to establish the final ranking of candidates.*[139]

The composition of the Central Examination Board is defined in Section 6.1 of the administrative instruction ST/AI/2010/7:

> *The Central Examinations Board is composed of five members appointed by the Secretary-General: a chairperson selected from among staff serving at Headquarters, with the concurrence of the representatives of the staff; two*

[134] Ibid., Section 8.

[135] Ibid., Section 8.3.

[136] Ibid., Sections 8.3 and 9.

[137] Ibid., Sections 2.1, 3.7 and 9.3.

[138] Ibid., Section 6.2.

[139] Ibid., Section 6.2(d).

members nominated by the representatives of the staff, one of whom will be from a duty station away from Headquarters; and two members nominated by the Assistant Secretary-General for Human Resources Management, one of whom will be from a third duty station. The Board will have a non-voting ex officio member representing the Assistant Secretary-General for Human Resources Management and a secretary. The Secretary-General will also appoint alternates to all of these positions.[140]

The boards of examiners are composed of persons appointed by the Secretary-General and nominated in equal numbers by the Assistant Secretary-General for Human Resources Management and by the staff representatives, respectively. They also involve a non-voting *ex officio* member representing the Assistant Secretary-General for Human Resources Management. Apart from the staff of the UN Secretariat, those of specialized agencies and outside experts may also be included, if both the representatives of the Secretary-General and of the staff agree.[141] A board of examiners is established for each occupational group and has the following tasks:

(a) To mark the written examination. A board of examiners will be established to mark the specialized paper of the written examination, and another board of examiners will be established to mark the general paper of the written examination;

(b) To report to the Central Examinations Board the results of the written examination;

(c) To recommend to the Central Examinations Board the minimum standard required in the written and oral parts of the examination;

(d) To recommend to the Central Examinations Board a list of examinees (who are not identified by name), in ranking order, to be convoked to the oral examination for each occupational group, based on the results of the written examination;

(e) To conduct and mark the oral examination;

(f) To recommend to the Central Examinations Board the final ranking of examinees (who are not identified by name) by occupational group, based on the total of the combined results of the written and oral examinations.[142]

Finally, the UN Secretary-General appoints members of both the Central Examination Board and boards of examiners. He also formally approves the list of successful candidates who are subsequently placed on the roster.[143]

---

[140] Ibid., Section 6.1.

[141] Ibid., Sections 7.1.-7.2.

[142] Ibid., Section 7.3.

[143] Ibid., Sections 6.1, 7.1 and 8.3.

Since both the procedures and the authorities involved in the G to P examinations show great similarities with those of the NCRE, comments made in the previous chapter with regard to the latter apply equally to the former.[144]

3. Promotion in the European Commission

In general, career progression in the EU civil service may involve three distinct movements: first, movement through the steps within the same grade; second, movement to a higher grade; and third, movement from one category to another.[145] Only the second and third type of movement is considered to be promotion. The first type of movement, i.e. through the steps within the same grade, occurs, in principle, automatically and is based exclusively on the officials' seniority, i.e. on the length of his service with the EU. According to Article 44 of the *EU Staff Regulations*, all EU officials who have been at one step in their grade for two years advance automatically to the next step in that grade.[146]

Promotion to a higher grade is regulated by Article 45 of *EU Staff Regulations*. This provision sets out eligibility criteria for promotion within the same function group, either AST or AD. Such promotion is not automatic and requires a decision of the appointing authority. The decision concerning an individual official can be taken on two occasions: either when appointing this official to a vacant post classified at a higher grade, or during the annual promotion exercise. In both instances, the official gets promoted, but in the second instance he will remain in his incumbent post. Promotion from one function group (formerly called staff category) to another function group, i.e. from AST to AD, falls under Article 45a of the *EU Staff Regulations*. Such movement is considered to be promotion as it entails a progression to a higher level.[147]

In the EU civil service, promotion to a certain level is a 'normal expectation'.[148] Nonetheless, like in most national and international civil services, EU officials do not have any legal right to promotion.[149] Nor can they claim the right to a particular post – it is for the appointing authority to assign officials in the interest of the service to

---

[144] See above, chapter 3, section 2.2.1.2.

[145] *Second Report on Reform of the Commission of 1999, Volume II*, para. 6.5.26.

[146] *EU Staff Regulations*, Article 44. The view that this type of career progression cannot be seen as promotion is also supported by the fact that Chapter 3 of the *EU Staff Regulations*, in which Article 44 can be found, carries a title 'Reports, advancement to a higher step and promotion'. This clearly indicates that advancement to a higher step must be distinguished from promotion.

[147] See, for example, *Deboeck v. Commission, Case 90/74*, Summary point 3. The title of the relevant Chapter 3 of the *EU Staff Regulations* also reflects this categorization - since movement from AST to AD function group cannot be seen as 'advancement to a higher step', it must fall under 'promotion'.

[148] Spence and Stevens, *Staff and Personnel Policy in the Commission*, p. 185. See also Stevens and Stevens, *Brussels Bureaucrats? The Administration of the European Union*, p. 7. Stevens explains that most EU officials who enter the EU service at the starting grade can expect to reach senior grade if they remain in service for approximately twenty years. – Ibid.

[149] *Mathilde Becker and Josyane Starquit v. European Parliament, Case C-41/88 and C-178/88, ECR [1989], p. 3807*, Summary point 4.

any post that corresponds to their grade, and also to promote them.[150] This section explains how the decisions on promotion of EU officials are taken and what conditions need to be satisfied.

3.1. Brief historical overview

The original career system in the European Commission was introduced with the first *EU Staff Regulations* which entered into force in 1962. The system was drawn up according the same lines as the traditional (national) civil services that existed at that time in most EU Member States. It included division of staff into four categories (A to D), each category consisting of eight grades and each grade having eight steps; and an automatic move up of all staff every two years.[151] Promotion was used to fill posts above the entry level, together with transfer and internal competition.[152] It was based on the same eligibility requirements and basic principle as now – Articles 4 and 43-46 of the *EU Staff Regulations*, relevant for staff promotion, have not changed substantially since their first adoption in the 1962, although some modifications and clarifications did take place especially during the overall amendment of the *EU Staff Regulations* of 2004.

In the first years of the Commission's existence, promotions were all but a complex exercise. Given the relatively small size of the Commission at that time, decisions concerning promotions were taken in a rather informal manner. Commission officials knew each other well and it was therefore not difficult to 'lay one's hand on the right person to fill a particular post'.[153] Nonetheless, already at that time the EU promotion system suffered from shortcomings, especially from slowness. Promotions

[150] *André Huybrechts v. Commission of the European Communities, Case 21/68, ECR [1969], p. 85*, para. 8 and *M. Goffredo Raponi v. Commission of the European Economic Community, Case 27/63, European Court Reports, English special edition, p. 129*, p. 137,

[151] Coull and Lewis, *The Impact of the Staff Regulations in Making the Commission a More Modern and Efficient Oragnization: an Insider's Perspective*, p. 3.

[152] Coombes, *Politics and Bureaucracy in the European Community, A Portrait of the Commission of the E.E.C.*, p. 142. Coombes reported that most posts above the entry level had been filled by transfer, promotion or internal competition and only a small share of them went to outsiders – between 1962 and 1967 promotions and transfers amounted to 43 per cent of all appointments in category A and internal competitions to 46 per cent. Internal competitions, however, included not only promotions but also appointments of auxiliary staff (i.e. non-permanent staff who was permitted to take part in internal competition) and/or candidates who did not meet requirements for promotion, such as seniority. – *ibid*, p. 145. See also Coombes, *Towards a European Civil Service*, p. 35. With regard to the auxiliary staff and its participation in internal competition, Coombes noted that this practice had caused serious concerns with staff and staff representatives who had argued that auxiliary staff had not entered the Commission service through normal external competition. Therefore, appointment of such staff into permanent posts via internal competition must have been seen as incompatible with the *EU Staff Regulations*. Another concern of permanent staff related to the auxiliary staff related to threats to career progression possibilities of many officials of B-category, restricted by appointment of auxiliary staff into permanent posts. As a result of this criticism, by 1967 recruitment of auxiliary staff was limited. Coombes regarded this development to be 'an important concession towards the supporters of a career service' in the EU. - Coombes, *Politics and Bureaucracy in the European Community, A Portrait of the Commission of the E.E.C.*, p. 144.

[153] Stevens and Stevens, *Brussels Bureaucrats? The Administration of the European Union*, p. 96, citing Spierenburg report of 1979, p. 79.

at the highest levels were regarded to be even slower – and very limited. A partial solution was found in the system of automatic promotion within one's career, introduced in 1965, providing for promotion without a change of function. According to some, this improved the situation at lower levels.[154] A significant problem remained, however. Due to the fact that the number of positions above A4 grade was limited and many of these positions were filled by outsiders, only a small number of staff could hope for promotion above A4 grade. The main reasons for reaching out to outsiders were, according to Coombes, the stress on specialization, the need to maintain geographical balance and the reservation of posts for particular types of candidates.[155] The result of these limitations was that promotion to the top level grades was not a 'reasonable possibility' in the Commission, something that was regarded as a standard feature of a career civil service.[156]

By the end of the 1970s it became clear that the initial, relatively informal, promotion process no longer corresponded with the Commission size and needs and that more formal procedures were needed.[157] They were introduced in the 1980s, but also they left some old problems unsolved, in particular those regarding top level posts. The pyramidal structure of the Commission remained and continued to limit the number of posts at senior levels available for promotion, even though most of them were filled by internal candidates, thus also by promotion.[158] Further reduction of the already small number of these posts was caused by the continuing practice of filling some of them by external candidates. Under strong political and national influences, external candidates were often preferred even if suitable internal candidates were available.[159] In 2001, Stevens noted:

---

[154] Coombes, *Politics and Bureaucracy in the European Community, A Portrait of the Commission of the E.E.C.*, p. 146. Coombes explained that promotions within one's career had been made from a list prepared by a joint committee which took into account seniority, competence, performance and good conduct. – *ibid.* See also Coombes, *Towards a European Civil Service*, p. 36.

[155] Coombes, *Politics and Bureaucracy in the European Community, A Portrait of the Commission of the E.E.C.*, pp. 146-147. Coombes noted that most posts at the director level had gone to 'outsiders' and fewer than 25 per cent had been filled by the Commission's own staff, including in many cases through promotion from Commissioner's cabinets rather than from Directorates-General. - *ibid.* See also Coombes, *Towards a European Civil Service*, pp. 35-36.

[156] Coombes, *Politics and Bureaucracy in the European Community, A Portrait of the Commission of the E.E.C.*, p. 146; and Coombes, *Towards a European Civil Service*, p. 36. Coombes also noted that there had been no shortage of posts compared to the number of candidates but rather a lack of compatibility between the immediate needs of the Commission and the normal criteria of a career service. - Coombes, *Politics and Bureaucracy in the European Community, A Portrait of the Commission of the E.E.C.*, p. 147; and Coombes, *Towards a European Civil Service*, pp. 36-37.

[157] Stevens and Stevens, *Brussels Bureaucrats? The Administration of the European Union*, p. 96.

[158] Spence and Stevens, *Staff and Personnel Policy in the Commission*, p. 185. See also, for example, Stevens and Stevens, *Brussels Bureaucrats? The Administration of the European Union*, pp. 97-98; and Coull and Lewis, *The Impact of the Staff Regulations in Making the Commission a More Modern and Efficient Oragnization: an Insider's Perspective*, p. 4.

[159] For example, Cini, *The European Commission, Leadership, Organisation and Culture in the EU Administration*, p. 126; Nugent (ed.), *At the Heart of the Union, Studies of the European Commission*, pp. 61-62; Nugent, *The European Commission*, pp. 173-174; Stevens and Stevens, *Brussels Bureaucrats? The Administration of the European Union*, p. 98 and pp. 102-103; Hooghe, *The European Commission and the Integration of Europe, Images of Governance*, p. 191; Spence and Stevens, *Staff and Personnel Policy in the Commission*, p. 189.

> *As a result, internal appointments in all the institutions, especially at the more senior level, remain a battle-field on which the interest of the Community and its own permanent staff are in continuous tension with those of the member states.*[160]

At lower levels, the main problem with promotions was their striking automaticity. The system worked as follows: All newly recruited permanent staff were placed in the starting grade of their category (e.g. A category) and moved every year automatically one step higher. Having reached the highest step in his grade, staff remained there until they were promoted to the next grade. The promotion occurred on the basis of points accumulated for age, length of service and merit, and a subsequent placement on a list of staff eligible for promotion, which included ranking. The points awarded for age, seniority and merit were granted formally by the Directors-General, in practice by the Directors, from the total amount of points available for all promotions to take place in that year in accordance with relevant budgetary coverage of the Commission. The annual distribution of available points among Directorates-General depended on the number of staff they had. The decision on promotion was taken by a promotion board, composed of representatives of the Directorate-General for Personnel and Administration, the home Directorate-General of the staff member under consideration, and the Directorate-General in which the post to be filled was based. In this way, promotion from A8 to A7 took approximately 6 years, while promotion from a starting to a senior (but not managerial) level post took in total some 15 to 20 years.[161] Promotion did not always imply a change of a position, but could also take place through a change of grade only.

The result of this system was the absence of any real incentives for staff to perform well. The only space available to staff to influence the number of points to be earned, and thus to speed up their promotion, was related to the merit criterion – age and seniority could, for obvious reasons, not be influenced at all. Points for merit were, however, awarded on the basis of bi-annual staff reports, which were 'too bland to produce meaningful distinctions between candidates'.[162] As a result, in practice, the most important factor influencing promotion at the levels below the senior level was not merit but seniority, or various political considerations.

These problems led to great dissatisfaction among staff.[163] A staff survey conducted in 1988 showed that perceptions on the best way in which promotion could be ensured had been: right connections, seniority, luck, the right nationality, service in a cabinet, the will to succeed, ability, qualification, knowing when to keep quiet.

160 Stevens and Stevens, *Brussels Bureaucrats? The Administration of the European Union*, p. 96.

161 Page, *People Who Run Europe*, pp. 26-27; Nugent, *The European Commission*, pp. 172-173; Stevens and Stevens, *Brussels Bureaucrats? The Administration of the European Union*, pp. 97-98; Spence and Stevens, *Staff and Personnel Policy in the Commission*, pp. 185-186.

162 Spence and Stevens, *Staff and Personnel Policy in the Commission*, p. 185. See also Stevens and Stevens, *Brussels Bureaucrats? The Administration of the European Union*, pp. 101-102. Stevens explained that all Commission officials had been receiving the two highest (out of five available) ratings.

163 Nugent, *The European Commission*, p. 174; also Stevens and Stevens, *Brussels Bureaucrats? The Administration of the European Union*, p. 97.

Producing results and hard work were considered to be least important. Moreover, a considerable number of staff said they had no influence on their promotion.[164]

The problems were recognized by the first comprehensive review of the personnel policies of the European Commission prepared by Spiereburg as early as in 1979.[165] However, no significant changes were adopted or planned until the Santer Commission took office.[166] The Santer Commission was the first to propose modification of the old Commission career structure along merit lines. It also suggested simplifying the structure and reducing the existing four categories into two.[167] After the fall of the Santer Commission in 1999, the Committee of Independent Experts of the European Parliament took over some conclusions and recommendations of the past reports, including those prepared under the Santer Commission.

The Committee of Independent Experts was of the opinion that the promotion system in the European Commission was not (seen as) fair and reliable due to a number of shortcomings.[168] Among others, the CIE criticized especially the non-existence of a real performance assessment culture, resulting in poorly drawn and imperfect staff reports, as well as a common tendency of giving an excessive number of points in staff assessment to all staff, leading to a general impossibility of making distinction among individual staff members for promotion purposes.[169] The CIE confirmed that, in reality, promotions within the Commission were automatic, based on seniority rather than on genuine assessment of staff and recognition of the principle of merit.[170] Furthermore, the CIE noted that the general principles set out in the EU *Staff Regulations*, such as the merit principle, might be in some instances jeopardized by the discretionary component of the merit assessment process which carries a certain risk of favouritism.[171] Consequently, the CIE pleaded for a revision of the staff reports and promotion system and recommended a number of more or less radical solutions. One of them was the introduction of internal competitions

---

164 Stevens and Stevens, *Brussels Bureaucrats? The Administration of the European Union*, p. 103. See also Spence and Stevens, *Staff and Personnel Policy in the Commission*, p. 186.

165 Stevens and Stevens, *Brussels Bureaucrats? The Administration of the European Union*, p. 102.

166 In its study of the European Commission of 1997, McDonald, for example, stated: 'For better or worse, national identity is seen to be encouraged in the Commission not only by external pressures, but also by some features of the modes of recruitment and promotion, by the *cabinet* system, the national officials on secondment, and *parachutage*. These aspects structure important contradictions into the heart of the organization. ... People who came in through the *concours* (examination) system, who have been in the Commission for years, who feel they have struggled to build something called Europe, can suddenly find themselves passed over for promotion – ostensibly on national lines. It is often claimed that promotion comes about through the support of national context of the candidate..., rather than through merit or any 'European' propriety. Moments of anger and disillusionment are rife on these points – to the extent that one senior official explained: "One certain way to failure here is to be European."' - McDonald, *Identities in the European Commission*, pp. 61-62.

167 Coull and Lewis, *The Impact of the Staff Regulations in Making the Commission a More Modern and Efficient Oragnization: an Insider's Perspective*, p. 2.

168 *Second Report on Reform of the Commission of 1999, Volume II*, para. 6.5.39.

169 Ibid., paras. 6.5.35-6.5.38.

170 Ibid., para. 6.3.27.

171 Ibid., paras. 6.5.34 and 6.5.41.

for available posts based on qualifications and tests and on selection conducted by external selection boards.[172]

Inevitably, the reform of the promotion system was one of the key elements of the overall personnel reform introduced by the Commission *White Paper* of 2000. In this document, the Commission recognized the inadequacy of the existing career structure based on qualifications and experience of staff at the time of their recruitment and not reflecting subsequent evolution of staff capacities. It admitted that this led to bottlenecks at the higher level and little incentive to good performance. Accordingly, the *White Paper* of 2000 proposed a new linear career structure, including more grades and no differentiation of staff in different categories. Promotion from one grade to another was to depend solely on merit, while movement from one step to another within the same grade would be based on seniority. Promotion to higher posts should no longer be necessarily linked to managerial function, thereby creating better career possibilities for staff who did not wish and/or qualify to become managers. In order to achieve these aims, a number of prerequisites were to be put in place, in particular a new annual performance appraisal system with precise job descriptions and task assignment as the starting point. A specific appraisal system was to be developed for (senior) managers, including peer review and/or assessment by managerial staff. The performance appraisal was to be linked to promotion and help in detecting underperformance. The latter was to be dealt with by employing specific procedures and remedies, distinct from the disciplinary ones.[173]

Most of the above mentioned was implemented by the Commission's decisions but some changes required amendment of the *EU Staff Regulations*, which took legal effect in 2004. An important modification of the initial intentions presented in the 2000 *White Paper* took place, though. The new career structure was eventually based on two categories of staff (or 'function groups', as officially named in the EU *Staff Regulations*), namely Administrators (AD) and Assistants (AST).[174] Despite this modification of the initial intention of the 2000 *White Paper*, it has been argued that the acceptance of the decisive importance of merit in career development of the staff, and not just seniority, reflects a 'significant modernizing shift for the Commission'.[175] The following parts describe how the new Commission promotion system functions at present.

[172] Ibid., paras. 6.5.40-6.5.42.

[173] *Reforming the Commission - A White Paper - Part I*, Section IV.2, Part Career Structure. See also *Reforming the Commission - A White Paper - Part II - Action Plan*, Chapter IV, Section XIII, Parts 1 and 2; and Section XIV, Parts 1 and 2. In addition, see Schon-Quinlivan, *Administrative Reform in the European Commission: From Rethoric to Re-legitimisation*, p. 13.

[174] *EU Staff Regulations*, Article 5(1). New AD function group replaced former A category, while new AST function group took the place of formal categories B and C. Former category D was gradually phased out. See *EU Staff Regulations*, Annex XIII. See also Commission' archived website *Reforming the Commission*, http://ec.europa.eu/reform/2002/chapter02_en.htm#3, visited on 22 June 2009.

[175] Coull and Lewis, *The Impact of the Staff Regulations in Making the Commission a More Modern and Efficient Oragnization: an Insider's Perspective*, p. 3. Coull and Lewis further note that this radical psychological break with the old system and the old culture was to be symbolized by the large amendment of the *EU Staff Regulations*, even though the new career system could have been implemented under the

3.2. Current legal framework for promotion of officials

As mentioned earlier, besides the introduction of the new, more linear, career structure, the main principles of the Commission career development system have not changed in comparison with the past system. The current system still includes an automatic move to a higher step within the same grade every two years, promotion to a higher level on the basis of comparison of merits of all eligible officials, and a promotion from one function group to another.

The legal framework within which the Commission promotion system continues to function is composed of relevant provisions of the *EU Staff Regulations*, namely Articles 4, 29 and 43-46, and Commission decisions implementing some of these provisions. In particular, Article 4 of the *EU Staff Regulation* subjects all promotions to the existence of a vacant post classified in the next higher grade. In case such a vacancy exists, promotion within the same function group – together with transfer, promotion from AST to AD function group and internal competition – enjoys priority in filling the vacancy, in accordance with Article 29 of the *EU Staff Regulations*.[176] The decision on the most appropriate means for filling the vacant post is left to the broad discretion of the appointing authority.[177] The latter may thus decide whether the post is to be filled by promoting an eligible official, by transferring an official from another post or whether internal competition is to be organized. The discretion of the EU Administration in promotion cases is considerable and, as explained in more detail below, judicial review is rather limited.[178]

The core legal base for promotions within the same function group can be found in Article 45 of the *EU Staff Regulations*, while rules setting out conditions for promotion from AST to AD function group are contained in Article 45a thereof. Related provisions are Article 43 concerning staff reports, as well as Articles 44 and 46 comprising special rules for promotion into senior posts. Articles 43, 45 and 45a are further worked out in three Commission decisions, namely *Decision on General Provisions for Implementing Article 43 of the Staff Regulations* C(2008) 3026 ('*Decision on Article 43*'); *Decision on General Provisions for Implementing Article 45 of the Staff Regulations* C(2008) 3028 ('*Decision on Article 45*'), both adopted on 18 June 2008; and *Commission Decision Laying Down the General Provisions for Implementing Article 45a of the Staff Regulations* C(2007)5694 ('*Decision on Article 45a*') of 20 November 2007.[179]

---

original regulations as well. – Ibid.

176 *EU Staff Regulations*, Article 4 and Article 29(1)(a).

177 *Franco Colussi v. European Parliament, Case 298/81, ECR [1983], p. 1131*, para. 17. The Administration is thus entitled to, for example, give preference to a candidate who can be appointed by means of promotion, if it considers that this candidate is more suitable than others who could be transferred to the vacant post at issue. - *Rittweger v. Commission, Case 21/70*, para. 6.

178 *Raponi v. Commission, Case 27/63*, p. 137. For details on judicial review, see below, section 3.2.3.

179 *Commission Decision on General Provisions for Implementing Article 43 of the Staff Regulations, C(2008) 3026*, 18.06.2008, available in the Register of Commission Documents, available at http://ec.europa.eu/transparency/regdoc/registre.cfm?CL=en, last visited on 30.12.2010; *Commission Decision on Article 45*; and *Commission Decision on Article 45a*.

The following parts explain first the legal framework for promotion within the same function group, including both ways of such promotion – through appointment into a vacant post and through annual promotion exercise; and subsequently the legal framework for promotion from AST function group to AD function group.

3.2.1. Promotion within the same function group

3.2.1.1. Eligibility conditions

As mentioned above, there is no right to promotion in the EU civil service, not even in case of officials who meet all the conditions for promotion.[180] The decision to promote an individual official rests exclusively in the hands of the relevant appointing authority. Before being considered for promotion, however, an official must be eligible, i.e. he must meet a number of requirements set out in Article 45 of the *UN Staff Regulations*. This provision provides, in a relevant part, the following:

> 1. *...[Promotion] shall be effected by appointment of the official to the next higher grade in the function group to which he belongs. [It] shall be exclusively by selection from among officials who have completed a minimum of two years in their grade after consideration of the comparative merits of the officials eligible for promotion. ...*
>
> 2. *Officials shall be required to demonstrate before their first promotion after recruitment the ability to work in a third language...*[181]

There are thus three eligibility conditions for promotion in the EU. First, the official concerned must occupy a post classified in the same function group and in the next lower grade. Second, the occupancy of such a post must have lasted for at least two years.[182] Third, the ability to work in a third language must be established before the first promotion takes place.

The *Commission Decision on Article 45* sets out two additional conditions for Commission officials. To be considered for promotion, Commission officials must be in active employment, on parental or family leave, leave for military service or on secondment in the interest of the service. Other administrative status, for example leave on personal grounds, does not lead to eligibility for promotion. Last but not least, past performance of official duties carried out by the Commission officials seeking promotion must have at least partly met expectations. Staff whose perform-

---

[180] *Becker and Starquit v. Parliament, Case C-41/88 and C-178/88*, Summary point 4.

[181] *EU Staff Regulations*, Article 45(1).

[182] Note that in case of first promotion, the minimum period of two years runs from the date of the official's establishment. - *Brüggemann v. ESC, Case 248/86*, paras. 7-8. This applies also to officials who have to serve probationary period before being established since the probationary period does not count for the promotion purposes. Former probationary official must thus complete the full minimum period required by Article 45 of the EU Staff Regulations, too. - *Vlachos v. ECJ, Joined cases 20 and 21/83*, para. 17. Similarly, the period during which an official served in his institution as a temporary agent before being established as official may not be taken into account in the calculations of the minimum period required for the promotion. - *Zoder v. Parliament, Case T-30/90*, para. 22.

ance did not meet expectations are not eligible for promotion.[183] As explained in more detail below, the evaluation of the officials' performance takes place annually through a Commission performance appraisal system called Career Development Review ('CDR').[184]

Officials meeting all eligibility conditions are considered for promotion either when they apply for a vacant post at one level higher than the post they hold or during the annual promotion exercise. In both situations, promotion should, pursuant to Article 45 of the *EU Staff Regulations*, take place after consideration of the comparative merits of all eligible officials.[185] When promotion occurs via appointment to a vacant post at a higher level, the comparison of merits involves all candidates who have applied for the post and is conducted by the authority responsible for selection of the new incumbent to the vacant post during the selection process. When promotion occurs via annual promotion exercises, however, the comparison of merits takes place at the moment of allocation of promotion points which each official can receive depending on the results of the appraisal of his performance. Since the total number of promotion points which can be awarded is limited, the decision on the number of points awarded to each individual official inevitably involves an indirect comparison between officials – a distinction is made among those who have performed well, those who have performed even better, those who have performed less well. Over the years, a considerable volume of case law has been developed on the issue of consideration of comparative merits. The most important conclusions are presented in the following part of this section.

3.2.1.2. Consideration of comparative merits

The assessment of candidates' merit is, once again, within the broad discretion of the appointing authority. This authority is also free to decide on the manner in which it will compare candidates' merits.[186] However, the discretion of the appointing authority is not unlimited. There are a number of restrictions to it. They help to prevent a misuse or abuse of this discretion by the appointing authority, which could do so, for example, to the benefit of a favoured candidate for the post to be filled.

Perhaps the most important limitation of the discretion of the appointing authority is the obligation to conduct the comparative consideration of candidatures 'with

---

[183] *Commission Decision on Article 45*, Article 8(1).

[184] See below, section 3.2.1.3.

[185] See also, for example, *Aristotelis Perakis v. European Parliament*, Case T-78/92, ECR [1993], p. II-1299, para. 17.

[186] *Jan Eliza de Wind v. Commission of the European Communities, Case 62/75, ECR [1976], p. 1167*, para. 17. Note that the Curt has ruled that, because of the broad discretion, there is, for example, no obligation on the side of the Administration to adopt specific rules addressing the situation of officials who have exercised mobility in order to safeguard the interests of these officials in the promotion process. – *Jacques Hinderyckx v. Council of the European Union, Case F-57/06*, available at http://curia.europa.eu/jurisp/cgi-bin/form.pl?lang=en&Submit=Rechercher&alldocs=alldocs&docj=docj&docop=docop&docor=docor&docjo=docjo&numaff=F-57/06&datefs=&datefe=&nomusuel=&domaine=&mots=&resmax=100, last visited on 30.12.2010, para. 59.

care and impartiality, in the interest of the service and in accordance with the principle of equal treatment'.[187] In order to ensure such an assessment, the Administration is required to guarantee 'scrupulous consideration' of personal files of eligible candidates, using comparable information. The candidates' merits must be evaluated on the basis of equality and the evaluation must pay regard to information originating from comparable sources and having comparable content.[188] Moreover, since promotion decisions must be reached with full knowledge of facts, the Administration is obliged, at each stage of the examination of the candidates' merits, to evaluate whether further information should be obtained or whether additional assessments should be made, for example on the basis of interviews with all the candidates or just with some of them.[189] The assessing authority is allowed, and even required, to request any additional documents and clarifications which it regards appropriate or necessary, so that the assessment of merits is conducted objectively and accurately.[190]

Although the interests of the service are not explicitly mentioned in Article 45 of the *EU Staff Regulations*, the Court has held that the interests of the service are the decisive criterion in determining the choice of candidates to be promoted.[191] As with the candidates' merits themselves, however, the actual evaluation of what the interests of the service are is within the discretion of the appointing authority.[192]

Another restriction of the Administration's discretion in the comparative assessment of candidates' merits is the obligation to obey any internal decision that might be adopted by the relevant institution for the purposes of implementing provisions of the *EU Staff Regulations* in accordance with Article 110 thereof. Such internal decision would, for example, be the *Commission Decision on Article 43* or the *Commission Decision on Article 45*, mentioned above. The obligation includes

---

[187] *Perakis v. Parliament, Case T-78/92*, para. 16.

[188] *Raponi v. Commission, Case 27/63*, p. 137.

[189] *Perakis v. Parliament, Case T-78/92*, para. 15.

[190] *Georges Caravelis v. European Parliament, Case T-197/02, ECR-SC [2004], p. I-A-33, II-133*, para. 31. For the purposes of gathering all necessary information, the appointing authority may use assistance of the administrative services at various levels. Therefore, applications for promotion may, for example, be preliminary examined within the individual Directorates-General. The Court has upheld such procedure as a reflection of the principle of sound administration. It has also ruled that the involvement of the directors-general in the promotion procedure is legal, even necessary, as it ensures that regard is paid to factors specific to their Directorates-General and that the staff reports of the various officials drawn by different assessors are viewed in a uniform manner. - *Prodromos Mavridis v. Commission of the European Communities, Case T-97/02, ECR-SC [2004], p. I-A-9, II-45*, paras. 76-77. See also *Mario Paulo Tenreiro v. Commission of the European Communities, Case T-216/03, ECR-SC [2004], p. I-A-245, II-1087*. In this case the Court held that the comparison of the average analytical assessment of officials belonging to two different Directorates-General with the average analytical assessments of these respective Directorates-General was lawful since it counteracted the subjectivity of the assessments made by various assessors. – para. 97. On the other hand, it should be noted that the Court has rejected legality of the practice of considering merits only of officials placed at the top of the list prepared by various Directorates-General. - *Georges Caravelis v. European Parliament, Case T-182/99, ECR [2001], p. II-1313, ECR-SC [2001], IA-113, II-523*, para. 34.

[191] *Andre Huybrechts v. Commission of the European Communities, Case 306/85, ECR [1987], p. 629*, para. 10.

[192] *Colussi v. Parliament, Case 298/81*, para. 17.

also other internal directives, which do not have the status of internal decisions as envisaged by Article 110, but by which the Administration imposes on itself rules of conduct indicating the practice to be followed in certain situations or matters. When the Administration wishes to disregard such internal rules, it must specify the reasons for doing so, otherwise it infringes the principle of equal treatment.[193] For example, if an internal directive of an institution, such as a guide to staff reports, requires that officials are given an opportunity to present their views on all the information on the basis of which decisions of appeal assessors are adopted, but the actual procedure in a specific case disregards this rule, that procedure is irregular and the relevant staff report can be, if challenged, annulled.[194] Similarly, where an institution sets up an internal advisory committee, not envisaged by the *EU Staff Regulations*, in order to receive an opinion on appointments to certain posts with regard to the qualifications, abilities and aptitudes of candidates, the appointing authority of that institution is obliged to consider opinions of such a committee in making its assessment of the candidates, even if it does not consider itself to be bound by it.[195]

Where promotion occurs via filling a vacant post at a higher level, an important factor that further limits the discretion of the Administration in the assessment of merits is the vacancy notice which includes conditions for eligibility for the post concerned.[196] As held by the Court, each vacancy notice constitutes a legal framework for the evaluation of officials who apply for the vacancy, which the appointing authority establishes by itself and for itself.[197] During the actual comparison of candidates' merits, the authorities assess candidates' qualifications for the vacant post. In doing so, they are required to consider candidates' knowledge and professional experience, but also other factors, such as the quality of the work performed in their past duties.[198] In addition, the evaluation of the knowledge should not be conducted as an abstract assessment of the level of one's training evidenced by diplomas but as a specific assessment in view of the relevant post.[199] The number and the nature

[193] In general, see *Adam P.H. Blomefield v. Commission of the European Communities, Case 190/82, ECR [1983], p. 3981*, para. 20. For promotion cases, see, for example, *Robert Adam and others v Commission of the European Communities, Joined cases 80 to 83/81 and 182 to 185/82, ECR [1984], p. 3411*, para. 22 or *Edward Patrick Latham v. Commission of the European Communities, Case T-63/89, ECR [1991], p. II-19*, para. 25.

[194] *Calvin E. Williams v. Court of Auditors of the European Communities, Case T-33/91, ECR [1992], p. II-2499*, paras. 66-71.

[195] *Richard Schönherr v.Richard Schönherr v Economic and Social Committee Economic and Social Committee, Case T-25/90, ECR [1992], p. II-63*, paras. 27-28.

[196] *Grassi v. Council, Case 188/73*, para. 26.

[197] *Helen Mc Avoy v. European Parliament, Case T-45/91, ECR [1993], p. II-83*, para. 48.

[198] *Christiane Hoffmann v. Commission of the European Communities, Case 280/81, ECR [1983], p. 889*, para. 9. The Court explained that an official can thus not dispute promotion of another official possessing qualifications regarded by the former as inferior to his own. The promotion exercise is based on a broader assessment of officials merits than, e.g., recruitment in case of which qualifications may be of bigger significance than in case of promotion. – Ibid., paras. 9-10.

[199] *Williams v. Court of Auditors, Case T-33/91*, para. 37. The applicant in this case claimed that another official who held a post comparable to his own had received the same assessment under the heading 'knowledge required for post occupied' as him, while that other official had had no specific relevant training and he had. The Court ruled that, in the absence of other reasons, such a situation did not

of the degrees held by candidates are to be seen as one of the factors to be considered, alongside competence and efficiency proven in the service, especially in cases where candidates possess long experience.[200] In addition, the appointing authority is competent to evaluate whether professional experience is equivalent to university education as evidenced by a degree.[201] Furthermore, the Administration may base its assessment of merits on other aspects, such as information on the administrative and personal position of candidates. Consideration of these other aspects may qualify assessments made exclusively on the basis of staff reports. [202]

Unsurprisingly, periodic staff reports, and personal files of EU officials in general, are of great importance in the consideration of officials' merits. The EU Administration is required to base its assessments for promotion purposes on such personal files.[203] A decision based on a document containing candidate's evaluation that has not been included into the candidate's personal file and has not been brought to his knowledge is, as ruled by the Court, in violation of the *EU Staff Regulations*, namely of Article 26 concerning personal files and Article 43 relating to periodical staff reports.[204] The two provisions aim at guaranteeing officials' right of defense in the sense that they allow the officials to comment on any information that appears in the included documents or to challenge them. A promotion decision infringing the official's right of defense by using information or assessment that has not been available to the official for commenting is unlawful and can as such be annulled.[205]

---

constitute discrimination since the assessment of the knowledge required does not include only qualifications and diplomas. – Ibid.

[200] *Colussi v. Parliament, Case 298/81*, para. 22.

[201] *J. Mulcahy v. Commission of the European Communities, Case 110/77, ECR [1978], p. 1287*, summary.

[202] *Mrs X. v. Commission of the European Communities, Joined cases T-89/91, T-21/92 and T-89/92, ECR [1993], p. II-1235*, para. 49.

[203] *Luigi de Pascale v. Commission of the European Economic Community, Case 97/63, European Court Reports, English special edition, p. 515*, Part 2.

[204] *Rittweger v. Commission, Case 21/70*, paras. 39-41. Note that Article 26 concerns officials' personal files and provides that the personal file of each official must contain all documents related to the official's administrative status, all his periodical staff reports as well as his comments on these documents. It also stipulates that officials have the right to acquaint themselves with all the documents in their personal file and to take their copies, even after they have left the EU service. Article 43 provides, in short, for the obligation to prepare periodic reports on each official and to communicate these reports to him, and for the right of the officials to comment on their reports and to appeal against the reporting procedure.

[205] *Anna Bonino v. Commission of the European Communities, Case 233/85, ECR [1987], p. 739*, Para. 11. In this case, an official was promoted because, other merits being equal to those of the applicant, he was regarded to have greater managerial skills than the applicant. This was concluded on the basis of an internal memorandum in which the results of the trial periods undergone by both candidates were included and compared. This memorandum was not brought to the attention of the applicant and was not placed in her personal file. The Court held that although the comparative assessment of candidates should not have been included in the personal file of the two candidates, as it was a part of the appointment procedure, the report on the results of the applicant's trial period itself should. Since the memorandum included both assessments (results of the trail period as well as comparison between the two candidates) and had decisive influence on the appointment decision, the decision was declared unlawful. – Paras. 10-14. In another case the Court has ruled that an oral evaluation of an official expressed during a meeting of a promotion committee, against which the official in question did not have an opportunity to exercise right to a fair hearing, is incompatible with the EU *Staff Regulations* and must therefore be annulled. - *Ralph Loebisch v. Council of the European Communities,*

The obligation to base the assessment of candidates' merits on periodical staff reports constitutes another important restriction on the discretion of the EU Administration in considering comparative merits of candidates for promotion.[206] As explained by the Court in one of its early staff cases, Article 45 of the *EU Staff Regulations* concerning promotions refers by implication to Article 43 on staff reports and requires for the application of Article 45 measures envisaged by Article 43, i.e. adoption of repots on the ability, efficiency and conduct in the service of officials. Such reports are to be one of the factors in the consideration of comparative merits of candidates for promotion.[207]

3.2.1.3. Staff reports

The periodical staff reports prepared under Article 43 of the *EU Staff Regulations* are internal documents intended to provide regular information to the EU Administration on the performance of duties by its officials.[208] Article 43 of the *EU Staff Regulations* stipulates that these reports concern the assessment of the ability, efficiency and conduct of each official. Hence, along with the description of the tasks carried out by officials in the relevant period, reports must also include an evaluation of the qualities demonstrated by the evaluated official in the performance of his tasks. As emphasized by the Court, the reports are formal evidence of the quality of officials' work.[209] They constitute an essential criterion of officials' assessment each time their career is being considered by the Administration. Therefore, the preparation of the staff reports is compulsory: this includes both the prescribed periodicity of the reports as well as the required form.[210]

As for periodicity, according to Article 43 of the *EU Staff Regulations*, the reports for each official are to be drawn up at least once every two years, but in the European Commission the reports are prepared annually.[211] It should be noted that, in principle, a delay in drawing up staff reports may in itself be prejudicial to EU officials since their career progress may be affected by the absence of the reports existing at the time of the adoption of a decision affecting them.[212] The Court has held that an appointment procedure is vitiated by irregularity where the relevant authority was

---

Case 14/79, ECR [1979], p. 3679, para. 8.

206 *Perakis v. Parliament, Case T-78/92*, para. 17.

207 *Pierre Bernusset v. Commission of the European Economic Community*, Joined cases 94/63 and 96/63, ECR [1964], p. 297, Part 1.

208 *Daniele Grassi v. Council of the European Communities, Joined cases 6/79 and 97/79, ECR [1980], p. 2141*, para. 20.

209 *Donal Gordon v. Commission of the European Communities, Case C-198/07 P, ECR [2008], p. I-10701*, para. 44. The Court has also held that officials have the right to have their work recognized by an appraisal prepared in a just and equitable manner and, in case of the contrary, the right to challenge reports – either with regard to their content or with regard to the procedures that failed to be followed. - para. 45.

210 *Jean-Jacques Geist v. Commission of the European Communities, Case 61/76, ECR [1977], p. 1419*, paras. 44-45.

211 *EU Staff Regulations*, Article 43 and *Commission Decision on Article 43*, Article 2.

212 *Moritz v. Commission, Case T-20/89*, para. 47.

not able to consider the comparative merits of the candidates due to substantial delay in the preparation of staff reports on one or more of these candidates which was caused by the Administration.[213] Justifications of such delays based on internal administrative organization, absence of a director or reorganization of a department have all been rejected by the Court. The Court has held that considerable delays are incompatible with the principle of sound administration and constitute maladministration causing non-material damage to the officials who have been put in an uncertain and anxious state of mind by the fact that their personal files are irregular and incomplete.[214] On the other hand, it is not necessary that periodic reports of all candidates for promotion be at the same stage when the appointment decision is adopted. Neither is it required that the appointing authority postpones its decision because, for example, the most recent report on one candidate is not final due to its referral to an appeal assessor.[215]

In addition, the absence of the staff report of an individual candidate for promotion in itself is not sufficient for the annulment of promotions, unless it can be proved that such absence was capable of having a decisive effect on the promotion procedure.[216] That would be the case, for example, where the merits of a candidate were evaluated on the basis of a promotion proposal which was not included in the candidate's personal file and which contained a less favourable assessment than a periodical staff report prepared subsequently.[217] In exceptional circumstances, the existence of other information on the officials' merits may compensate the absence of the periodical reports.[218] However, this is only possible when the Administration is able to prove the existence of special circumstances of such nature that justifies the delay.[219]

3.2.1.3.1. Performance appraisal below the senior level

The detailed rules according to which staff reports are currently drawn up in the European Commission can be found in the latest *Commission Decision on Article 43,*

---

[213] *Harald List v. Commission of the European Communities, Case 263/81, ECR [1983], p. 103*, para. 26.

[214] *Pierre Gratreau v. Commission of the European Communities, Joint cases 156/79 and 51/80, ECR [1980], p. 3943*, para. 15 and *Giovanni Barbi v. Commission of the European Communities, Case T-73/89, ECR [1990], p. II-619*, paras. 35 and 41.

[215] *List v. Commission, Case 263/81*, para. 27.

[216] Ibid., para. 27 or *Malcolm Bevan v. Commission of the European Communities, Case 140/87, ECR [1989], p. 701*, summary point 4.

[217] *Giovanni Barbi v. Commission of the European Communities, Case T-68/91, ECR [1992], p. II-2127*, para. 27.

[218] *Gratreau v. Commission, Joint cases 156/79 and 51/80*, para. 22.

[219] *Kuno Ditterich v. Commission of the European Communities, Case 207/81, ECR [1983], p. 1359*, paras. 26-27. Note that officials cannot successfully complain of a delay in the preparation of staff reports if they contributed to it or it is attributable to them at least partially. The Court has explained that all officials have a duty of loyalty and cooperation to the authority they belong to. The Court held in *Moritz* that since the applicant had waited almost four months before replying on the proposal of his superior to extend his periodic report, the applicant was in breach of his duty of loyalty and cooperation to his institution and could not claim non-material damage. - *Moritz v. Commission, Case T-20/89*, paras. 46 and 49.

adopted on 18 June 2008 and applicable to the reports established from 1 January 2009 onwards.[220] This decision applies to staff below the senior level. It is based on the same appraisal system, named Career Development Review (CDR), as its predecessor introduced in 2003 in the framework of the staff reform initiated by the Commission *White Paper* of 2000.[221] This initial system has been modified twice – in 2004 and lastly in 2008.[222] The last modification of 2008 constitutes a significant departure from the division of points to be awarded in the assessment and subsequent promotion procedure. While previously there was a possibility to earn promotion but also the so-called priority points which could speed up one's promotion, currently there are only promotion points. The Commission explains in its 2008 *Decision on Article 43* that this modification aims at simplification of the appraisal system, making it less time consuming and more transparent and strengthening the link between performance evaluation and promotion.[223]

Each annual appraisal is based on evaluation of three key indicators: efficiency, ability and conduct in the service during the given reporting period, which is, in principle, the calendar year preceding the year in which the assessment takes place.[224] Efficiency

---

[220] *Commission Decision on Article 43*. This decision applies to officials and, with some exceptions, also to temporary staff. It does not apply to officials and temporary agents who occupy a position of senior manager. – Ibid., Article 1.

[221] Commission's archived website *Reforming the Commission*, available at http://ec.europa.eu/reform/2002/chapter02_en.htm#3, visited on 22 June 2009. The initial regime adopted in 2003 involved an annual appraisal leading to the awarding of up to 20 merit points which then counted towards promotion, together with the so-called priority points which could have been awarded in the subsequent annual promotion procedure. The merit points were divided among three criteria on the basis of which the assessment took place: up to ten points could have been granted for performance, up to six points for ability and up to four points for conduct. The appraisal was conducted by the line manager and was based on the agreed job description, task assignment and objectives, established at the start of the year preceding the actual appraisal year. Individual job descriptions for each official were prepared by his line managers (starting with the Head of Unit and ending with Director-General) and entailed three parts: job profile (definition of functions and duties); job environment (factors and circumstances barring upon the working conditions of the official); and job requirements (education, training, knowledge, experience and skills). In the Commission's view, the job descriptions made staff assessment more objective. To further ensure greater objectivity, all appraisal reports had to be countersigned by the assessor's superior.

[222] *Commission Decision on General Provisions for Implementing Article 43 of the Staff Regulations*, 23.12.2004, available in the Register of Commission Documents, available at http://ec.europa.eu/transparency/regdoc/registre.cfm?CL=en, last visited on 30.12.2010 and *Commission Decision on Article 43*.

[223] *Commission Decision on Article 43*, Preamble, para. (3). The new system has been, however, severely criticized by some EU staff unions. For example, the *Union Syndicale* has stressed that the new CDR system slows down average career speed for the 70 per cent of EU officials in order to pay for the 30 per cent of those who receive faster promotions. – Union Syndicale, *Assessment and Careers "From VERY BAD to EVEN WORSE"*, 08-09, 23.03.2009, available at http://www.unionsyndicale.eu/public/t_090420_03.pdf, last visited on 30.12.2010. The *Union Syndicalle* noted that in 2009 48,2 per cent of staff received notes below the 6-point average. – Union Syndicale, *The Career ReDucer Has Arrived*, 16-09, 26.05.2009, available at http://www.unionsyndicale.eu/public/t_090601_08.pdf, last visited on 30.12.2010.

[224] *Commission Decision on Article 43*, Preamble and Article 2. Note that Annex I to this Decision specifies specific appraisal situations in which the assessment takes place for a different period or in a different manner than normally. These situations include cases in which employment ceased or has been terminated or in which the official concerned was on leave on personal grounds, parental leave, leave

is assessed on the basis of objectives established either when the official enters the service or during the previous appraisal exercise. Achievement of these objectives and the quality of the work performed are then assessed against common standards adopted by the Directorate-General for Human Resources. Common standards are developed also for evaluating ability and conduct, the two remaining key indicators for officials' appraisal. The common standards of the Directorate-General for Human Resources may be supplemented by additional standards developed for the following periods by Directors-General for staff serving in their Directorate-General. The adoption of such additional standards is, however, subject to a consultation with staff members fulfilling the function of reporting and countersigning officers and an approval by the Directorate-General for Human Resources.[225]

The actual appraisal procedure is set out in Article 7 of the *Commission Decision on Article 43*. It involves several steps, beginning with an administrative notice issued by the Directorate-General for Human Resources and a discussion between each Director-General and his senior managers and officials acting as reporting and countersigning officers. They discuss 'the general overall picture of performances demonstrated across the Directorate-General in each grade during the reporting period'.[226] Subsequently, the appraisal report is electronically launched and the assessed official is requested to produce a self-assessment. This is followed by a formal dialogue between the reporting officer – a direct supervisor of the assessed official, usually Head of Unit – and the assessed official, including the assessment of the official's performance during the reporting period, the establishment of objectives for the year following the reporting period, and an update of the training map.[227] After the dialogue has been held, the reporting officer prepares an individual qualitative appraisal of the official's efficiency, ability and conduct in the service and transmits it to the countersigning officer – usually a direct superior of the reporting officer.[228] The countersigning officer verifies whether appraisal standards have been applied consistently. He may confirm, complete or modify the appraisal. Subsequently, the appraisal is sent to the assessed official who may comment on it to the countersigning officer. The latter will confirm, complete or modify the appraisal after having

for military service etc.

[225] Ibid., Article 5.

[226] Ibid., Article 7(2).

[227] Ibid. Article 3(1). Note that, following the previous case law, the European Union Civil Service Tribunal has held that possible disagreements between the assessed official and his supervisor and the consequent irritation between them does not, in itself, imply that the superior is not capable of assessing the merits of the official concerned objectively. - *Wenning v. Europol, Case F-114/07*, para. 174.

[228] *Commission Decision on Article 43*, Article 3(2). Note that official conducting individual appraisal enjoys wide discretion in this respect. The Court has consistently emphasized that reporting officers must be allowed freedom of assessment and that the Court itself cannot substitute personal judgments made by these officers, such as marks awarded, by its own assessments. Due to the wide discretion of the assessing officials, the Court's interference with their assessments is only possible in cases of misuse of discretion, error or manifest exaggeration. Such defects could, in the Court's view, made staff reports unlawful. - *Grassi v. Council, Joined cases 6/79 and 97/79*, para. 20 and *Charlotte von Bonkewitz-Lindner v. European Parliament, Case T-33/90, ECR [1991], p. II-1251*, para. 62, *Seton v. Commission, Joined cases 36/81, 37/81, 218/81*, para. 23; *Küster v. Parliament, Case 123/75*, paras. 8-10.

viewed these comments. Before the appraisal is finalized by the countersigning officer, statistics on the appraisal and overall distribution of performance levels by function group and by grade are submitted by the Directorate-General for Human Resources to the Joint Appraisal and Promotion Committee which may give recommendations to the Directorates-General and to the Directorate-General for Human Resources. The final appraisal report is communicated to the assessed official who may accept it with or without adding comments or reject it, stating the reasons.[229]

Rejection automatically triggers the launch of an appeal procedure, set out in Article 8 of the *Commission Decision on Article 43*. The matter is referred to the Joint Appraisal and Promotion Committee. This Committee delivers its opinion after having considered an opinion of the countersigning officer. The latter is first made available to the assessed official who may comment on it. The countersigning officer may also hold a meeting with the assessed official, upon the official's request, possibly in the presence of the reporting officer. The minutes of this meeting are attached to the appraisal report.

The opinion of the Joint Appraisal and Promotion Committee is transmitted to the assessed official, the reporting and countersigning officers and to the appeal assessor. The latter is, in principle, the relevant Director-General who may, however, delegate the role to his Deputy Director-General.[230] His task is to check the assessment made by the previous assessor. If he considers that the initial assessment is right, he may confirm it.[231] The appeal assessor may also amend the appraisal report. In both cases he is required to take the opinions of the countersigning officer and of the Joint Appraisal and Promotion Committee into account. If the appeal assessor does not follow the opinion of the Committee to amend the report and confirms it, he must state substantive reasons for doing so. The decision of the appeal assessor must be based solely on the facts on which the assessed official had an opportunity to comment. The last step of the appeal procedure is communication of the final report to the assessed official.

[229] Performance of each official during the reporting period is summarized by one of the five existing performance levels: IA (the performance consistently exceeded expectations); IB (the performance frequently exceeded expectations); II (the performance fully met expectations); III (the performance partly met expectations); and IV (the performance did not meet expectations). Only a maximum of 8 per cent of all performances may be classified at level IA and 22 per cent at level IB, with a possibility to add the proportion to level IB if less than 8 per cent of performances are classified at level IA. The overall maximum for levels IA and IB together may not exceed 30 per cent of all performances, though. These maxima apply to each Directorate-General and each grade separately and compliance with them is compulsory. An adjustment is possible when the application of the maximum percentages would lead to a structurally disadvantageous situation of officials in a certain Directorate-General compared to officials with the same profile of another Directorate-General. The adjustment is made by a decision of the appointing authority after consultation with the Joint Appraisal and Promotion Committee. - *Commission Decision on Article 43*, Article 6.

[230] Ibid., Article 3(3).

[231] See also *Pieter Willem Seton v. Commission of the European Communities*, Joined cases 36/81, 37/81, 218/81, ECR [1983], p. 1789, para. 20.

Scheme 12: European Commission performance appraisal process below senior level

As can be seen in the above description of the appraisal and appeal procedure, they are regulated in a great detail. This is not surprising, considering their importance for career development of staff serving in the European Commission, including their promotion. Detailed regulation of the performance evaluation process ensures its transparency but also its objectivity since it limits the discretion of officials who conduct actual evaluation. Another notable safeguard of the objectivity and impartiality of this process is the involvement of not just one but a number of persons, even a collective body, that conduct staff assessment and/or watch over it. As the description above shows, the process involves reporting officer, countersigning officer, appeal assessor, and the Joint Appraisal and Promotion Committee.[232] The first three mentioned are defined in Article 3 of the *Commission Decision on Article 43*, while the composition of the Joint Appraisal and Promotion Committee can be found in Annex II to this Decision. With regard to the latter, there are actually two separate Joint Appraisal and Promotion Committees – one for officials in AD function group and one for officials in AST function group. The former is composed of Directors-General of the Commission services and 15 members designated by the Central Staff Committee and chaired by the Director-General for Human Resources. The Joint Appraisal and Promotion Committee for officials in AST function group is chaired by a Director designated by the Director-General for Human Resources and is composed of 15 Directors also designated by the Director-General for Human Resources and 15 members designated by the Central Staff Committee.[233] As noted earlier in this study, involvement of staff representatives in committees such as these contributes to the greater objectivity and impartiality of the entire process, in this case performance appraisal process. The same applies to the explicit rule which requires replacement of the chairpersons or members of the two Joint Appraisal and Promotion Committees in situations in which the independence of the involved person is likely to be impaired due to a conflict of interest. Such a conflict is deemed to arise in three instances: when the person in question has been involved in the appraisal or appeal procedure as reporting or countersigning officer or appeal assessor; when the appealing official has had contact with the person in question on behalf of the staff representation; and when the person in question belongs to the same grade and to the same Directorate-General as the appealing official.[234]

Each annual appraisal exercise is followed by an annual promotion exercise through which EU officials who have accumulated a required number of points get promoted. As explained earlier, this is one of the two ways in which EU officials can get promoted, the other being promotion through appointment to a vacant post at a

[232] Note that, apart from the Joint Appraisal and Promotion Committee, the *Commission Decision on Article 43* also establishes a Joint Monitoring Committee. This is an *ad hoc* Committee set up for each appraisal exercise, composed of a chair and four members of the Joint Appraisal and Promotion Committee, designated by the Director-General for Human Resources or the Staff Committee, respectively. The Joint Monitoring Committee meets twice, at the beginning and the end of the relevant exercise. Its main task is to evaluate the management of the appraisal exercise. On the basis of information submitted to it by Directorates-General, the Joint Monitoring Committee prepares a report which it transmits to the Directorate-General for Human Resources, to the Directorates-General and to the Staff Committee. Apart from the relevant appraisal exercise, this Joint Monitoring Committee evaluates the promotion exercise as well. - *Commission Decision on Article 43*, Article 10 and *Commission Decision on Article 45*, Article 10.

[233] *Commission Decision on Article 43*, Annex II, Article 1. Note that each of the two Committees is assisted by joint working groups which prepare deliberations of the Committees and draft opinions on appeals lodged against appraisal reports. Deliberations and documents of the Committees are confidential. – *ibid.*, Articles 2 and 4.

[234] Ibid., Annex II, Article 3. Note that a possibility to conduct staff assessment by an senior official having the same grade as the assessed official has been upheld by the Court. - *Loebisch v. Council, Case 14/79*, para. 8.

higher level. Obviously, the two ways of promotion occur pursuant to different sets of rules. They are both explained below.[235]

Before that, however, it should be noted that the appraisal system for middle managers, i.e. Heads of Unit, (Deputy) Heads of Delegation and Heads of an Office or Representation in the EU Member States (grades AD9 – AD14), is similar to that applicable to other staff. Yet, it includes particular criteria linked to special job requirements of middle managers. They reflect the importance of quality control function for the areas of their responsibility which the appraisal of middle managers fulfills. They also include assessment of communication, interpersonal and negotiating skills.[236] Special rules apply to the assessment of middle managers during and at the end of the trial period. They are set out in the *Commission Decision on Middle Management Staff*.[237]

3.2.1.3.2. Performance appraisal at the senior level

Appraisal of Commission senior officials follows a separate set of rules contained in Section 7 of, and Annex III to, the *Commission Compilation Document on Senior Officials Policy,* not pursuant to the *Commission Decision on Article 43*. The appraisal system for senior officials is new; it was introduced in 2004 under the overall staff reform. Its objective is 'to assist senior officials in their career development, providing feedback on their performance, training needs and possible future postings'.[238] Moreover, as stressed by the Commission, the new appraisal system of senior officials is, in addition, aimed at providing further information needed for decisions on senior staff appointment, promotion and mobility.[239]

As is the case with other Commission officials, senior officials are, in principle, appraised annually.[240] The appraisal is based on a 360-degree feedback system, which means that officials' competence, efficiency and conduct are assessed by different groups of internal stakeholders, collaborators, as well as other persons, if appro-

[235] See below, section 3.2.1.4.

[236] Commission's archived website *Reforming the Commission*, http://ec.europa.eu/reform/2002/chapter02_en.htm#3, visited on 22 June 2009.

[237] *Commission Decision on Middle Management Staff*, Section 4.

[238] *Commission Compilation Document on Senior Officials Policy*, Section 7(2).

[239] Ibid., Section 5.1.5. See also Commission's archived website *Reforming the Commission*, section on Top Officials, http://ec.europa.eu/reform/2002/selection/chapter7_en.htm#7, visited on 13 July 2009.

[240] Ibid., Section 7(1). There are a few exceptions, though. First, officials in senior posts who have been recruited externally and therefore serve a probationary period of nine months are assessed in an earlier stage, in two phases. The first phase involves an interim assessment after five months of service; and the second a probation report drawn one month before the expiry of the probationary period. The probation report replaces the appraisal report that would otherwise be drawn for the period of probation. Details on the procedure to be followed in this assessment exercise can be found in Annex II to this *Compilation Document*. The second exception to the rule of annual appraisal relates to senior officials newly appointed to a higher function. Such officials are also assessed after the first nine months, followed by subsequent regular annual assessments. Last but not least, senior officials who are about to retire, whose appointment is to be definitely terminated, or who are granted an invalidity pension are not subject to the annual appraisal at all. – Sections 6, 7(5) and (6).

priate, and the assessed senior officials themselves. Internal stakeholders are staff members with no hierarchical links to the assessed official and are chosen to participate in the evaluation exercise by random selection. Collaborators are staff members working closely with the assessed official, as identified pursuant to Annex III to the *Commission Compilation Document on Senior Officials Policy*. Other persons are interlocutors of the appraised official outside the Commission who may be asked to participate in the assessment exercise.

Persons who participate in the evaluation exercise (five internal stakeholders and ten collaborators, plus possibly other persons) are requested to fill in an electronic questionnaire which automatically aggregates data needed for a comprehensive assessment of the official. These data are subsequently made available and can be analyzed and commented upon by both the reporting officer and the assessed senior official. The final result takes the form of a table with average scores reached and is sent to the assessed official and the reporting officer. Also the assessed official is required to fill in a self-assessment form; this form constitutes an integral part of the Career Development Review. The reporting officer subsequently holds a formal dialogue with the assessed official and draws up the final appraisal report. In doing so, the reporting officer takes opinions received from the evaluating stakeholders into account but is, in principle, free to decide how the feedback is reflected in the final appraisal. The reporting officer must assess the official at issue on the basis of a number of elements, including the realization of job objectives agreed upon between the assessed official and his superior; accepted standards of good human resources management; and, if relevant, sound financial management. The reporting officer must pay particular attention to assessing core competences that have been developed in the European Commission and are expected from senior officials.[241] Having assessed the official at issue, the reporting officer may award up to a maximum of 20 points for three elements evaluated: performance, competence and conduct. The assessed official may comment before the appraisal report is finalized and appeal the final report if he disagrees with it.

[241] The Competency Model for senior officials involves the following competences: information management (developing vision; conceptualizing); task management (managing the organization; organizing; deciding); people management (inspiring; directing teams; building teams); people management (inspiring); and personal management (achieving objectives). - Ibid., Annex III.

Scheme 13: European Commission performance appraisal process for senior officials

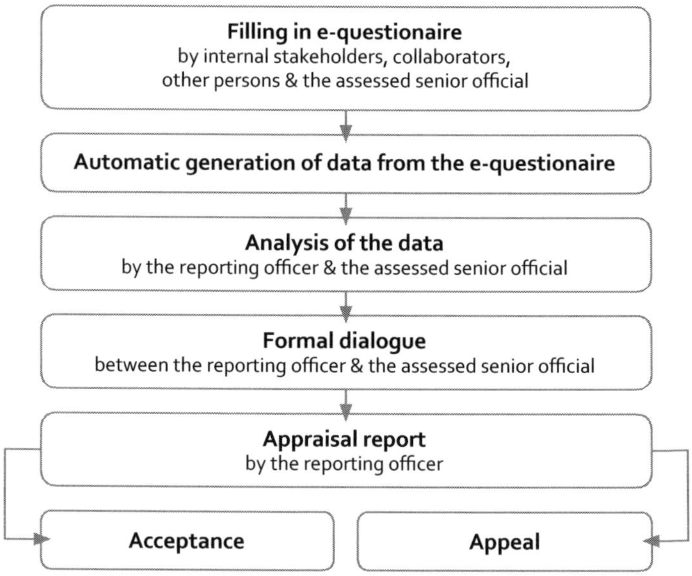

With regard to the authorities involved in the senior officials' appraisal process, the function of reporting officer is fulfilled by the portfolio Commissioners for the assessment of Directors-General, Heads of Service and Heads of Cabinet, and by the Director-Generals for Deputy Directors-General and Heads of Delegation. The Deputy Directors-General are the reporting officers for Directors who are under their responsibility. In discharging their responsibility of reporting officer, the Commissioners may be assisted by the Permanent Rapporteur of the Consultative Committee on Appointments or an external consultant. Appeals are dealt with by the portfolio Commissioners, except when they act as reporting officer (i.e. in cases of Directors-General, Heads of Service and Heads of Cabinet). In such instances, there is no appeal officer. In appeal cases that do take place the Commissioners are assisted by the Joint Evaluation Committee, which is a specific function performed by the Consultative Committee on Appointments. This Committee assesses whether the appraisal by the reporting officer was produced in a fair and objective manner and whether it followed required procedures. The opinion reached by the Joint Evaluation Committee is not binding upon the relevant Commissioner. However, if the Commissioner departs from the Committee's opinion, he must state reasons.[242] This is an important safeguard against misuse or abuse of power vested in the Commissioner. Interestingly, another usual guarantee of the objectivity and impartiality of the process, namely the involvement of staff representatives in the

[242] Ibid., Section 7 and Annex III. See also Commission's archived website *Reforming the Commission*, section on Top Officials, http://ec.europa.eu/reform/2002/selection/chapter7_en.htm#7, visited on 13 July 2009.

committee dealing with appeals, is missing in this procedure that concerns senior officials' appraisal.

As mentioned above, positive assessment is important for senior officials' further promotion (and/or move to another function under the Commission mobility scheme). Similarly, negative assessment, especially if repeated, may lead to a reassignment of the official at issue to another post, including a lower and/or non-managerial post. The Commission may also decide to retire senior officials serving at AD 15 and 16 levels, using Article 50 of the *EU Staff Regulations*, i.e. in the interests of the service.[243]

3.2.1.4. Promotion procedures

3.2.1.4.1. Promotion through appointment to a vacant post

As mentioned earlier, the *EU Staff Regulations* subject promotion to the existence of a vacant post.[244] This requirement does not mean, however, that there must be an actual vacant position, but rather that there must be a budgetary coverage for each promotion. The notion 'vacant post' in Article 4 is thus meant in the budgetary sense, as vacant posts in the establishment plan, not in the functional sense. This is important since, as it has already been noted, EU officials may also be promoted during an annual promotion exercise, while remaining in the same post. In practice, this is indeed the case in most instances, as long as the highest level in the career bracket has not been reached. When that happens, further promotion can only take place through appointment to a vacant post, leading automatically to a change of the career bracket.[245] Hence, an official serving below the middle management level and reaching the top of his career bracket can be further promoted only by becoming a Head of Unit, a Head of Unit by being appointed a Director, and a Director by being made a Director-General. Promotions such as these, i.e. from one career

[243] Commission's archived website *Reforming the Commission*, section on Top Officials, http://ec.europa.eu/reform/2002/selection/chapter7_en.htm#7, visited on 13 July 2009. For details on retirement of senior officials in the interests of the service, see below, chapter 6, section 3.2.1 and chapter 7, section 3.2.5.

[244] *EU Staff Regulations*, Article 4. See also *Miguel Vicente-Nuñez v. Commission of the European Communities, Case T-294/02, ECR-SC [2004], p. I-A-283, II-1279*, paras 54. In this case the Court stressed the necessity of a vacancy for promotions. It ruled that even in situations in which an official is to be promoted as a result of his success in legal proceedings, such promotion may not be retrospective. On the other hand, the Administration is obliged to ensure that the delay in promotion to which the successful applicant was subject does not harm his subsequent career since seniority in grade is a factor to be taken into account when adopting promotion decisions. – *ibid.*, paras. 54, 63, 86-91.

[245] See, for example, Spence and Stevens, *Staff and Personnel Policy in the Commission*, p. 189; and *Commission's Human Resources Report 2009*, p. 140. To recall, the EU has several career brackets for officials serving in the function group AD: a career bracket involving grades below the middle management level AD5 – AD13 and exceptionally AD14 (normal entry grades are AD5 - AD8, with AD5 being the lowest existing grade in AD function group); a career bracket for middle management level involving grades AD9 – AD14; a career bracket for directors involving grades AD14 - AD15; and finally a career bracket for directors-general with grades AD15 - AD16. The AST function group has a single career bracket with grades AST1 – AST11 (normal entry grades are AST1 - AST4). For more details, see above, chapter 1, section 3.1.1.

bracket to another, are not (also) possible via an annual promotion exercise. As already noted, such promotions (via an annual promotion exercise) are only possible until the highest grade in the relevant career bracket is reached.

This means that when an official joins the European Commission at one of the entry levels AD5 – AD8 (depending on his qualifications), he may be promoted via annual promotion exercises up to the level AD13 and exceptionally AD14 but his further promotion is linked to appointment to a middle management post. Such a post must become vacant and the relevant official must apply and succeed in the selection process. Similarly, once a Head of Unit, who may be appointed at levels AD9 – AD14, reaches the highest level in his career bracket, namely AD14, he may no longer be promoted to a higher level unless he successfully applies for appointment to a Director post which is classified in a higher career bracket, either AD14 or AD15. The same holds for a Director who has reached the top grade in his career bracket, namely AD15. On the other hand, a Head of Unit serving at the level AD14 and promoted by being appointed to a vacant post of Director would be promoted with regard to his function but not with regard to his grade – he would remain in grade AD14 and could be promoted to AD15 later via an annual promotion exercise. Similarly, a Director serving at the level AD15 and promoted to a post of Director-General would stay in the same grade until his later promotion to grade AD16 via an annual promotion exercise.

Promotion via appointment to a vacant post classified at the middle management level is not necessarily linked to the occupancy of a post in a certain grade. Under the EU post-2004 grade system, middle management posts may be classified anywhere between AD9 and AD14. It means that, at least in theory, staff in grade AD8 can apply for a vacant post of Head of Unit and, if appointed, be thereby promoted to grade AD9. Further promotion of such staff would occur via annual promotion exercises until grade AD13 and exceptionally AD14 is reached. From that grade onwards, promotion would only happen via appointment to a vacant post of Director, whose classification starts at grade AD14. Thus only Heads of Unit serving at AD13 or exceptionally AD14 could apply to such a Director post. As for posts of Director-General, because they are classified at grades AD15 and AD16 and all Directors are at least in grade AD14, they all could apply for a vacancy at AD15 level which would involve a post of a Director-General.

To sum up the general rules on promotion via appointment to a vacant post, although formally speaking such promotion is possible at any grade, it only happens in cases of appointment to a post in a higher career bracket. Promotion within the same career bracket occurs via annual promotion exercises as long as the top grade of the relevant career bracket is not reached – or until promotion via appointment to a vacant post in the next career bracket. Once a top grade in the relevant career bracket is achieved, no further promotion occurs without a change of the career bracket and thus without appointment to a vacant post classified in a higher career bracket.

Since in reality no promotions occur by appointment to a vacant post below the middle management level, there are no rules according to which such action would take place, although formally such promotions are possible at any grade. Promotion through appointment to a vacant post in the higher career bracket, i.e. at the middle management or senior level, is governed by rules and procedures applicable to appointments at these levels. They can be found in the *Commission Decision on Middle Management Staff* and the *Commission Compilation Document on Senior Officials Policy*.[246] As appointment to senior posts regularly involves both internal and external candidates, procedures according to which they take place are discussed in chapter 3 of this study dealing with staff recruitment. At this point it therefore suffices to refer to that chapter.[247]

As for procedures governing appointment to middle management posts, it should be stressed again that appointment to such posts occurs, indeed, mostly through promotion of staff serving in lower grades. That said, it needs to be recalled that middle management posts may be exceptionally filled also by external candidates. The latter could – and does - occur in cases in which specific qualifications are required for the middle management post at issue and in cases in which a number of middle management posts are to be filled by nationals of (a) Member State(s) that has or have recently joined the EU. As explained in chapter 3, appointments to posts requiring special qualifications, thus also middle management posts of such a nature, occur in accordance with Article 29(2) of the *EU Staff Regulations*.[248] And as explained in chapter 2, selection of middle managers from among external candidates possessing the nationality of (a) newly acceded EU Member State(s) takes place through an open competition organized specifically for that purpose.[249] In all other cases of appointment to middle management posts, procedures envisaged in the *Commission Decision on Middle Management Staff* of 2008 apply.[250] They result in appointment of internal candidates promoted to middle management posts.[251]

Appointment procedure set up in the *Commission Decision on Middle Management Staff* of 2008 involves a number of actors: candidates for the vacant post, a preselection board, a rapporteur for the procedure, the appointing authority, the Director-General responsible for human resources, the portfolio Commissioner, the Commission's Secretary-General, and sometimes also the Consultative Committee for Appointments that plays an important role in the appointment procedures for senior posts.[252] To begin with candidates applying for a vacant middle management

---

[246] *Commission Decision on Middle Management Staff*, Sections 2-3 and *Commission Compilation Document on Senior Officials Policy*, Sections 3-5.

[247] See above, chapter 3, section 3.2.3.

[248] See above, chapter 3, section 3.2.2.

[249] See above, chapter 2, section 3.4.1.2.2.

[250] *Commission Decision on Middle Management Staff*.

[251] Note that the process under the *Commission Decision on Middle Management Staff* may also lead to the appointment of an internal candidate who already serves at the middle management level in another post and moves to the vacant post at issue in order to exercise mobility. As explained in more detail in chapter 5, all middle managers serving in the European Commission are, in principle, subject to mandatory mobility policy. This means they must regularly move to other posts classified at the same (i.e middle management) level after they have reached the maximum period of post occupancy. - For details, see below, chapter 5, section 3.2.2.

[252] For details on the Consultative Committee on Appointments, see above, chapter 3, section 3.2.3.

post, they must be permanent officials, have seniority of minimum two years in the same post required by Article 45 of the *EU Staff Regulations*, and serve in a grade eligible for appointment to the middle management posts. Here, a difference exists between posts classified below grade AD 13 and those classified in grade AD 13 or AD 14. Applications for the latter are only accepted from officials serving in AD 12 grade and having at least two years' experience in middle management in EU institutions.[253] All candidates applying for a vacant middle management post must, of course, possess the qualifications required for the post as specified in the vacancy notice.[254] In addition, the *Commission Decision on Middle Management Staff* requires that they also possess three types of competences are required: core competences, technical qualifications and specialist knowledge.[255] The last eligibility condition for candidates applying to a vacant middle management post concerns training for management functions. To be eligible to apply to a middle management post in the European Commission, candidates must certify that they have completed the management preparation course before the deadline for submission of applications or have acquired such skills by completing other courses of training for management functions.[256]

To continue with actors involved in appointment process for middle management posts, the pre-selection board is appointed by the portfolio Director-General, i.e. the Director-General of the Directorate-General to which the post at issue is attached.[257] This Director-General fulfills the function of the appointing authority for all middle management posts, with the exception of those classified in grade AD13 / AD 14. For these posts, the portfolio Director-General acts as appointing authority in agreement with the Commission President, the Commissioner responsible for human resources and the relevant portfolio Commissioner.[258] The pre-selection board has a minimum of three members serving in a grade and management function equal to or higher than that of the vacant post at issue. One member of the pre-selection board is to be from another Directorate-General.[259] Unlike in the case of posts below the middle management level, the pre-selection board does not include any staff representatives, which is regrettable. It diminishes the transparency and objectivity of the process, especially considering that the main task of the pre-selection board

[253] *Commission Decision on Middle Management Staff*, Articles 7.2 and 9.2, and Annex.

[254] Ibid., Articles 7.2 and 9.2, in both instances forth indent point.

[255] Ibid., Articles 7.2 and 9.2, in both instances fifth indent point, and Annex II. Core competences required for appointment to the Commission middle management level include general management skills, communication skills, interpersonal skills, negotiation skills and preferably also proven ability to carry out the functions in different environments and overall knowledge of the institution acquired by previous mobility. The technical qualifications relate to familiarity with administrative, financial and oversight issues. Lastly, the required specialist knowledge refers to knowledge of the European Union policies, languages, legislation and programmes, in particular those relevant to the vacant post at issue. – Ibid.

[256] Ibid., Article 7.3.

[257] Ibid., Article 2.3.

[258] Ibid., Article 3.

[259] Ibid., Article 2.3.

is to assess applications and curriculum vitae of all candidates and to draw up a reasoned shortlist of the most suitable ones.[260]

Shortlisted candidates are (further) interviewed by the relevant portfolio Director-General and the rapporteur for the procedure, but not by a collective body.[261] As far as the rapporteur for the procedure is concerned, he is appointed by the Director-General responsible for human recourses in agreement with the Commission's Secretary-General. The rapporteur is chosen from a list of 20 officials serving in grade AD14 or AD 15 (i.e. Directors and (Deputy) Directors-General). The list of these 20 rapporteurs is drawn up by the same Director-General responsible for human resources and by the Secretary-General. They designate 10 rapporteurs from a list of 15 officials proposed by the Administration and 10 rapporteurs from a list of 15 officials proposed by the staff representatives.[262] It should be noted here that proposing officials for the list of 20 rapporteurs is the only involvement of staff representatives in the appointment process to middle management posts; most functions are performed by individual senior officials and/or Commissioners, which is a situation more vulnerable to subjectivism and favouritism.[263] This is further strengthened by the fact that the portfolio Director-General (but not the rapporteur for the procedure) may decide to interview not only applicants shortlisted by the pre-selection board but also other eligible applicants of his choice.[264] This Director-General also takes the final decision and appoints the successful candidate. Powers of the portfolio Director-General are thus broad and could easily be misused or abused. Fortunately, before taking the next step, the portfolio Director-General is required to inform and consult his choice with the portfolio Commissioner, as well as to inform about his intended action the Director-General responsible for human resources and the Secretary-General.[265] The two last mentioned officials, i.e. the Director-General responsible for human resources and the Secretary-General, may require that the intended appointment is referred to the Consultative Committee on Appointments. This would normally take place upon recommendation of the rapporteur for the procedure. If a referral to the Consultative Committee on Appointments is made, the portfolio Director-General no longer serves as appointing authority in the case at hand. That function is in such a case taken over by the Commissioner for Human

[260] Ibid., Article 8.1.2. The assessment is done by using assessment checklists and possibly by conducting interviews.

[261] Ibid., Article 8.1.3.

[262] Ibid., Article 2.7.

[263] Note that appointments to middle management posts are monitored by a Joint Committee for the Appointment of Middle Management Staff which does involve staff representatives. This Committee is established by the *Commission Decision on Middle Management Staff* and has five members: two designated by the staff representatives and two by the Administration. The chairman of the committee is appointed jointly. All members are serving Directors or Principal Advisers. However, the *Commission Decision on Middle Management Staff* expressly stipulates that the Joint Committee for the Appointment of Middle Management Staff has no competence to alter the outcome of the procedures it considers. Its main responsibilities are monitoring and assessing the operation of the system set up for selection and appointment of middle management staff and making recommendations for improvements, if needed. - Ibid., Article 15.

[264] Ibid., Article 8.1.3.

[265] Ibid., Articles 8.2.1 and 8.2.2.

Resources and Security and the portfolio Commissioner who act in agreement with the Commission President.[266] This appears to serve as a final safeguard that appointment to each middle management post is objective and impartial. Since no other collective body is involved in this stage of the selection process, referral to the Consultative Committee on Appointments can indeed prevent the final decision being marked by subjectivism of the portfolio Director-General who possess broad mandate in this process.

Although to the selection procedure is, in principle, the same for all Commission middle management posts, a number of specific rules apply to posts classified in grade AD13 and AD14. There are also a few special provisions relating to selection and appointment to middle management functions in Commission delegations and to selection and appointment of Heads of Offices and Representations in EU Member States. The latter set out in particular who fulfills certain functions or takes certain steps in the selection and appointment process.[267] As for the specific rules for posts classified in grade AD13 and AD14, as mentioned earlier in this section, the portfolio Director-General who acts as appointing authority also in such cases must act in agreement with the Commission President, the Commissioner responsible for human resources and the relevant portfolio Commissioner.[268] Further, the portfolio Director-General, who has conducted interviews of candidates shortlisted by the pre-selection board and possibly also other candidates of his choice, is required to send a full report to the Director-General responsible for human resources. In this report, the portfolio Director-General should indicate which candidate(s) should be considered. The matter is then always referred to the Consultative Committee on Appointments, which may suggest that the portfolio Director-General makes a broader choice.[269] These additional safeguards incorporated in the selection procedure for AD 13 and AD 14 posts must indeed be praised for their contribution to the objectivity of the appointment process.

This is even more so due to the fact that judicial review in this area is rather limited. It is so that, in cases of promotion via appointment to a vacant post at a higher level, the EU officials cannot complain if they are not appointed. However, they may dispute a decision to promote another official to a grade to which they themselves are eligible.[270] Although the EU Administration is, in principle, not obliged to provide reasons for promotion decisions with regard to officials not promoted, when such an official files a complaint against a promotion decision of another official and the Administration rejects the complaint, it must provide reasons. The duty to state reasons is not difficult to fulfill, though, it is met as soon as it allows for the review of legality of the decision – by the complaining official and/or by the judiciary.[271] No

[266] Ibid., Article 8.2.3.

[267] Ibid., Article 14.

[268] Ibid., Article 3, second paragraph. See also Articles 10.2.3 and 10.2.4.

[269] Ibid., Articles 10.2.1 and 10.2.2.

[270] *Robinson v. Parliament, Case T-328/01*, para. 32.

[271] *Hinderyckx v. Council, Case F-57/06*, paras. 25-27.

extensive explanation of reasons why the complaining official was not promoted is thus needed.

3.2.1.4.2. Promotion through annual promotion exercise

Below the senior level

Like the appraisal procedure, the promotion procedure currently in force has also been modified when compared to the initial reform regime adopted in 2003. Under that regime, officials could accumulate up to a maximum of 20 *merit points*, allocated in the course of the annual appraisal, and up to 12 *priority points*, awarded in the annual promotion procedure. The promotion procedure began after the formal appraisal evaluation for the previous year had been completed. The priority points were granted either for special services to the Directorate-General or for activities performed in the interest of the Commission. The former were given by the Director-General from a quota of points available to him that year in accordance with the number of staff. Half of these points went to officials with high rating in their appraisal evaluation and the second half to the rest of the staff. Priority points for activities performed in the interest of the Commission could have been granted by the Promotion Committee in each Directorate-General for different *extra curriculum* activities, such as participation in selection boards. Also the Promotion Committee received a share of points it could grant, a share which was based on the number of staff in the relevant Directorate-General. All in all, under the 2003 regime, officials could have obtained in total 32 (merit and priority) points each year. In the course of several years, they could reach the threshold needed for their next promotion. The threshold was set annually and depended on the Commission budget planning. In order to avoid inflation of points and to reach consistency throughout the whole Commission, the officials conducting evaluation and allocation of points received necessary training. In addition, the Promotion Committee reduced the quota of priority points in those Directorates-General whose average score was in the previous year above the Commission overall average.[272]

The existence of a quota for priority points within each DG and of the target average for merit points have been criticized as potentially unfair. However, when legally challenged in *Buendía Sierra*, the Court upheld both elements of the promotion system as compatible with Article 45 of the *EU Staff Regulations*, with the principle of equal treatment and with the principle of career progression. The Court held that none of the elements of the system limited the discretion of the appointing authority to an extent contrary to Article 45. The opposite was considered to be the case by the Court:

> *[These elements] favour the effective expression of an appraisal which is representative of the merits of the officials by ensuring the highest level of com-*

[272] Commission's archived website *Reforming the Commission*, http://ec.europa.eu/reform/2002/chapter02_en.htm#3, visited on 22 June 2009.

parability of appraisals in all the directorates-general of the Commission and, consequently, equal treatment for those officials.[273]

The judgment in *Buendía Sierra* was generally very important for the new promotion system based on the quantification of merits by an annual award of points. The applicant in this case challenged not only the existence of the quotas and target averages but many other decisive aspects of the new promotion system as set up by the *Commission Decision on Article 45*, such as the non-decisiveness of merit points, the absence of any obligation to state reasons for granting priority points, the limitation of discretion of the appointing authority, overvaluation of certain duties, and favouritism of officials employed in smaller Directorates-General.[274] The Court, however, upheld the system as such, including the existence of two different types of points.[275]

The initial 2003 regime was modified together with the appraisal system in 2004 and in 2008.[276] Under the last version of the *Commission Decision on Article 45*, officials are awarded only one type of points, namely *promotion* points – as opposed to the former *merit* and *priority* points granted during the appraisal and the promotion procedures, respectively. All promotion points are awarded in the course of the annual promotion exercise, which comprises points allocation and the drawing up of a list of promoted officials.[277] The promotion points received during the promotion exercise as well as the overall number of accumulated promotion points are recorded in a personal promotion file of each official. This file forms an integral part of the officials' personal files which contain also the annual appraisal reports.[278]

---

[273] *José Luis Buendía Sierra v. Commission of the European Communities, Case T-311/04, ECR [2006], p. II-4137, ECR-SC [2006], p. I-A-2-221, II-A-2-1135*, para. 172. For the whole analysis of the legality of the two elements of the previous promotion system, see paras. 168-190.

[274] Ibid., para. 125.

[275] Ibid., paras. 129-138, 143-148, 151-158, 168-190, 225-227, 233-241, 245-250, and 252-258. The Court did accept the applicant's challenge with regard to the application of the promotion system in the 2003 promotion exercise and declared illegal the Commission's decision granting the applicant a certain number of promotion points. – Ibid., paras. 286-303.

[276] The previous versions of the *Commission Decision on Article 45* and the system of allocation of the merit and priority points was reviewed by the Court, for example, in *Martial Ott and others v. Commission of the European Communities, Case T-250/06 P*, available at http://curia.europa.eu/jurisp/cgi-bin/form.pl?lang=en&Submit=Rechercher&alldocs=alldocs&docj=docj&docop=docop&docor=docor&docjo=docjo&numaff=T-250/06%20P&datefs=&datefe=&nomusuel=&domaine=&mots=&resmax=100,, last visited on 30.12.2010 and in *Buendía Sierra v. Commission, Case T-311/04*. Claims related to the compatibility of the system with Article 45 of the *EU Staff Regulations* were rejected. – *Martial Ott and others v. Commission, Case T-250/06 P*, paras. 109-125 and *Buendia Sierra v. Commission, Case T-311/04*, especially paras. 129-138. However, some perceived especially the existence of priority points as leading to (potentially) unfair situations. It was argued that allocation of the points was unclear, inconsistent across different Directorates-General, and lacking transparency. As a result, the CDR system was seen as having 'even less to do with merit and transparency than does voting in the Eurovision song festival'. – King, *Staff Reforms that Failed to Make the Grade*. The author of this article has concluded that, despite its intention to eliminate favouritism and create meritocracy in the EU staff evaluation and promotion system, the CDR system has not achieved this goal.

[277] *Commission Decision on Article 45*, Article 3.

[278] Ibid., Article 2.

The allocation of promotion points in the annual promotion procedure is conducted on the basis of the appraisal report prepared for the relevant reporting period. Article 4 of the *Commission Decision on Article 45* establishes detailed rules on the number of points that may be allocated.[279] Points that may be granted to an individual official is limited not only by the result of his performance appraisal, but also by an overall number of points which each Directorate-General has at its disposal. The latter depends on the performance level and the number of officials whose performance corresponds to that particular level.[280] If such overall number for a certain performance level does not suffice for allocation to at least one official of the highest number of points possible for the relevant level, the appropriate Directorate-General may request the Joint Appraisal and Promotion Committee for an increase of the overall number of promotion points by way of an exemption.[281]

The precise criteria for the allocation of points for each performance level are established by each Director-General, after consulting the Heads of Units, and made known to the staff at the beginning of the relevant promotion exercise. The allocation criteria must pay regard to a number of factors listed in Article 4(6) of the *Commission Decision on Article 45*, namely the individual appraisal of officials contained in the relevant staff report; the use of languages in the performance of duties; the level of exercised responsibilities; and the work done in the interest of the institution (for example, membership of a selection board or marker of competition papers). Note that, with the exception of the last criterion, all the remaining factors must be considered for the promotion purposes already on the basis of Article 45 of the *EU Staff Regulations* itself.[282]

A proposal for the so-called 'formal intentions' concerning the allocation of promotion points is prepared by the Directors and Deputy Directors-General in each Directorate-General. On their basis, provisional formal intentions are made by the relevant Director-General, followed by a review of statistics from all Directorates-General on the distribution of the provisional formal intensions by the Joint Appraisal and Promotion Committee and, possibly, by the Committee's recommendations. The last mentioned steps take place together with the corresponding annual appraisal exercise, explained in more detail above.[283] Similarly, the final formal intentions regarding the points allocation, set out by the Director-General, are announced to each official together with the relevant appraisal report.[284]

---

[279] When the officials' performance was assessed as reaching level IA, they may be allocated between 10 and 12 promotion points. Furthermore, performance level IB equals 7-9 points, performance level II gives right to 4-6 points, and performance level III to 1-3 points. No promotion points are granted if officials' performance level is evaluated as IV, i.e. when officials' performance did not meet expectations. - Ibid., Article 4.

[280] For performance level IA, the overall total number of promotion points is 10,5 times the number of officials whose performance corresponds to this level; for performance level IB – 7,5 times; for performance level II – 5,1 times; and for performance level III – 2 times. - Ibid., Article 4.

[281] Ibid., Article 4.

[282] Ibid., Article 4(6).

[283] See above, section 3.2.1.3.1.

[284] *Commission Decision on Article 45*, Article 5.

The official concerned may appeal against the formal intentions to the Joint Appraisal and Promotion Committee. After the Committee delivers a reasoned opinion on the appeal, and possibly also on the appeal against the appraisal report, if lodged, and on the increase of the overall number of promotion points for certain performance level, if requested, the appointing authority decides on the allocation of the final number of promotion points to each official.[285] The actual promotion decision is also taken by the appointing authority. According to Article 8 of the *Commission Decision on Article 45*:

> *All officials with a number of accumulated promotion points equal to or above the relevant promotion threshold shall be promoted.*[286]

Promotion thresholds are established for each grade in accordance with the so-called 'convergence plan' and available budgetary posts.[287] The convergence plan defines an average career, i.e. the average time spent in a given grade and in an administrative status before promotion.[288] The available budgetary posts are set out in the annual establishment plan of the Commission which is appended to the section of its budget indicating the number of posts in each grade and function group.[289] Details on the establishment of promotion thresholds are set out in Article 2 of Annex II to the *Commission Decision on Article 45*. Promotion thresholds are announced to all staff at the beginning of the promotion exercise.[290] Similarly, the list of promoted officials is published to the attention of all officials.[291]

It should be noted that promotion points accumulate over successive promotion exercises. When an official, promoted in a certain promotion exercise, has more promotion points than the promotion threshold required for that exercise, the remaining promotion points are carried over to the next promotion exercise.[292] Similarly, when an official is promoted in an appointing procedure following the publication of a vacancy notice and the number of his promotion points is higher than the threshold established for that year, he carries over the balance between his promotion points and the threshold to the subsequent promotion exercise. If such official's promotion points are lower than the threshold, there is nothing to carry over.[293]

---

[285] Ibid., Article 7.

[286] Ibid., Article 8(3). Note that only officials eligible for promotion, i.e. meeting the conditions set out in Article 45 of the *EU Staff Regulations* and Article 8(1) of the *Commission Decision on Article 45*, as explained above, may be promoted. All promotions are effective, in principle, as of 1 January of the year of the promotion exercise or as of the first day of the month following the month in which the official in question acquires the minimum seniority required by Article 45 of the *EU Staff Regulations*. – Ibid., Article 8(5).

[287] Ibid., Annex II, Article 2(1).

[288] Ibid., Annex II, Article 1(2).

[289] Ibid., Annex II, Article 2(1) and *EU Staff Regulations*, Article 6(1). Note that there are certain arrangements for the transition from the old pre-2004 career structure to the new career structure. These arrangements are also reflected in the convergence plan as specified in Article 1 of Annex II to the *Commission Decision on Article 45*.

[290] *Commission Decision on Article 45*, Annex II, Article 2(3).

[291] Ibid., Article 8(4).

[292] Ibid., Article 9(1) and (2).

[293] Ibid., Article 9(3).

The above description shows that each annual promotion exercise comprises a number of steps, some of which are of a rather complex and/or technical nature. For the sake of clarity, the following scheme provides their brief summary.

Scheme 14: European Commission annual promotion exercise below the senior level

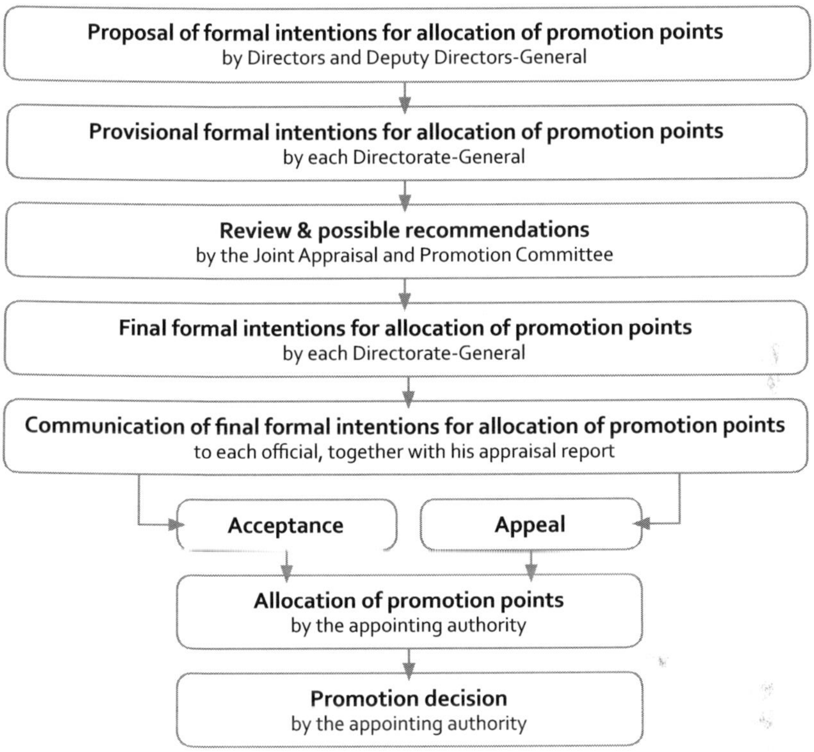

When analyzing this technical process, it must be noted that its objectivity and transparency is guaranteed by a number of features. To begin with, the relevant Commission decision contains precise rules on the number of promotion points to be allocated for each performance level, as well as a detailed list of factors which need to be taken into account by individual Directorates-General that wish to adopt additional rules for points allocation. In addition, such additional rules must be announced in advance to all staff concerned. Unfortunately, this information is provided at the beginning of the promotion exercise, thus after the year for which promotion points are awarded has passed, thereby depriving staff of a possibility to adjust their conduct accordingly. The obligation to inform staff in advance relates also to the promotion thresholds established for each grade. Moreover, the list of promoted officials is published for the attention of all Commission officials. Staff are thus sufficiently informed about all matters relevant to the promotion exercise. The allocation of points itself occurs on the basis of past performance and, although it inevitably involves exercise of discretion, this is later on limited by the fact that once the promotion threshold is reached, the official concerned is, in practice, automatically promoted. Formally, there must be a decision of the appointing authority on promotion but that depends on reaching the threshold. There is no discretion at this point, the decision is a result of an objective fact of reaching the threshold.

The objectivity and transparency of the process is further enhanced by the involvement of a joint committee as well by a possibility of appeal. Regrettably, all appeals are dealt with by just two committees – one for officials in AD function group and one for officials in AST group. This means that each of the two committees handles potentially a large number of appeals.[294] Such a situation raises questions as to the actual ability of the two committees to conduct the appellate review properly. Another problematic issue in this regard is the fact that the committees are not the final instances in which appeals are formally decided on. The committees only adopt 'reasoned opinions' and it is the appointing authority which takes the final decision.

Fortunately, Commission staff may challenge decisions taken by the appointing authority in annual promotion exercises by filing a legal action to the Court. As held in *Buendía Sierra,* a case decided in 2006 and mentioned earlier, following actions are possible: An official included on the list of promoted officials may challenge the decision determining the number of awarded points. Such an official could challenge the decision because the points not used in the relevant promotion exercise could be carried over to the following years and thus to the following promotion exercise(s). In this way, the effect of the decision at issue goes beyond the particular promotion exercise. An official not included on the list of promoted officials has three courses of action. First, he may challenge only the decision determining the number of awarded points, if he does not wish to challenge the decision establishing the list of officials to be promoted. Second, he may challenge both the decision determining the number of awarded points and the decision establishing the list of officials to be promoted. This possibility exists when he was not promoted because the number of points awarded to him was below the threshold set for the relevant promotion exercise. Third, he may challenge only the decision establishing the list of officials to be promoted. This could happen when the official was not promoted for reasons others than not reaching the required threshold, such as lesser seniority in grade. This would only be possible when the number of officials on the list is greater than the actual promotion possibilities under the relevant budget.[295]

Senior level

The *Commission Compilation Document on Senior Officials Policy* contains a one-paragraph short provision on promotion within the senior management function group, setting out two substantive requirements for promotion, namely the 'comparison of merits based on the available staff reports and the level of responsibil-

[294] For example, in 2007, 1209 appeals were filed before the committees and in 2008 729 appeals. - *Commission's Human Resources Report 2009*, p. 144.

[295] *Buendía Sierra v. Commission, Case T-311/04*, paras. 88-94.

ity of the functions held', and brief procedures.[296] In 2007, a separate Commission document entitled *Promotion for Commission Senior Officials, Principles and Procedure ('Commission Principles and Procedure for Promotion of Senior Officials')* was adopted, detailing procedural matters.[297] The document also outlines the main principles and general rules on promotion of senior officials. This 2007 document slightly modifies procedures outlined in the *Commission Compilation Document on Senior Officials Policy*. It is regrettable that the Commission did not choose to amend the latter but rather to adopt a separate document which, in addition, does not make any reference to the *Commission Compilation Document on Senior Officials Policy*. This does not contribute to the transparency of the overall senior officials policy, the importance of which was stressed by the Commission itself.

The main principles on which promotion of senior officials is to be based, are fairness and transparency, to be implemented through a simple and clear procedure and through a comparative analysis of merits evaluated through objective criteria.[298] With regard to the general rules, the document refers to Article 45 of the *EU Staff Regulations* and repeats the requirement of completing at least two years in the grade and of demonstrating ability to work in a third language.[299] In addition, as under the *Commission Decision on Article 45* applicable to promotions below the senior level, the senior official must be in active employment or be seconded in the interest of the service in order to be eligible for promotion.[300]

The annual promotion exercise consists of several steps and actors. It begins with a timetable containing the number of promotion possibilities per grade allowed by the Commission establishment plan, i.e by the relevant part of the Commission budget. The timetable is prepared by the Commissioner responsible for Human Resources in agreement with the Commission President and is disseminated to all senior officials. It includes the list of officials eligible for promotion in that particular year. Not all eligible officials will be promoted, though, only as many as permitted under the establishment plan. Which senior officials will be promoted is decided by comparing their merits.[301] Besides the qualitative assessment contained in the annual appraisal report, the comparison of merits includes also the level of responsibilities exercised by the officials concerned and their use of languages. Other factors may be taken into account as well, namely the wider contribution to the Commission work, for example by participating in a task force; seniority; the temporary exercise of a higher function; but also gender and geographical balance.[302]

The initial assessment of all eligible senior officials on their suitability for promotion is prepared by the portfolio Commissioner (for Directors-General, Deputy Directors-General and Advisers *Hors-Classe*) or by the Director-General (for Directors and

---

[296] *Commission Compilation Document on Senior Officials Policy*, Section 8.

[297] *Commission Principles and Procedure for Promotion of Senior Officials*.

[298] Ibid., Section 2.

[299] Ibid., Section 3.

[300] Ibid., Section 3.1.

[301] Ibid., Sections 4.1-4.3 and 3.2.

[302] Ibid., Section 3.2.

Principal Advisers), respectively. This assessment is discussed with the Consultative Committee on Promotion for Senior Officials, a committee established by the 2007 Commission document on promotion of senior officials. The Committee consists of the Secretary-General, the Director-General for Human Resources, the Head of Cabinet of the Commission President and the Head of Cabinet of the Commissioner in charge of Human Resources. After the consultation with the Committee, the Directorate-General for Human Resources prepares an alphabetical list of officials considered suitable for promotion and sends it to all senior officials. Objections to the list may be expressed within ten working days to the Directorate-General for Human Resources. The final list of officials proposed for promotion is prepared by the Commissioner in charge of Human Resources, after he has received the summary of assessment from the Consultative Committee. The list is submitted in agreement with Commission President to the College of Commissioners who takes the final decision on the list of senior officials who are promoted.[303]

Scheme 15: European Commission annual promotion exercise for senior officials

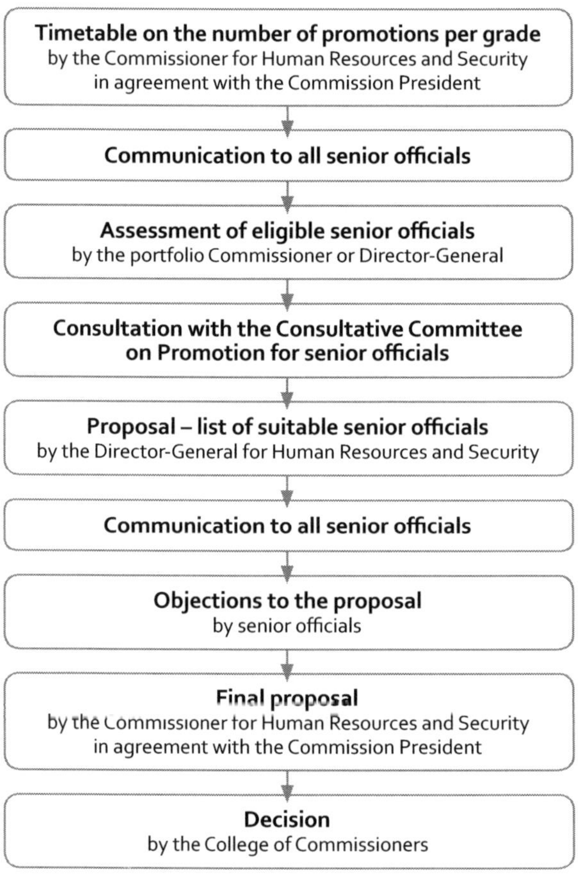

[303] Ibid., Sections 4.3 – 4.6.

The above description of the rather detailed rules on annual promotion of Commission senior officials shows that objectivity and transparency of the process constituted one of the objectives behind their adoption. Indeed, there are a number of important elements there. To be more precise, transparency of annual promotion exercises is guaranteed especially by the obligation to inform all senior officials – not only senior officials eligible for promotion in a relevant year but all Commission senior officials – of each decision taken during the annual exercise. In this sense, all senior officials receive the timetable with the number of possible promotions, the list with names of senior officials recommended for promotion and the final list of promoted senior officials. The objectivity and transparency of the process is also enhanced by the involvement of a Consultative Committee established for annual promotion exercises and by the fact that the final decision is taken by the entire College of Commissioners. It is regrettable, though, that the Consultative Committee is composed only of four persons, half of whom are, in fact, political appointees – the Head of Cabinet of the Commission President and the Head of Cabinet of the Commissioner for Human Resources and Security. Participation of another member, whose position would be comparable to that of the Permanent Rapporteur of the Consultative Committee on Appointments, would be desirable as it could help to avoid possible politicization of the promotion process.[304]

Apart form the partly political composition of the Consultative Committee on Promotion for Senior Officials, it could be argued that the requirement to pay regard to the need to ensure geographical balance at all levels may politicize the promotion process of the Commission senior officials, too. Besides being a potential cause for politicization of the promotion process, this requirement may also result in decreased transparency of the process because it is not clear from the list of promoted officials what was the decisive reason for promotion of an individual senior official, his merits or his nationality and/or gender.

The overall transparency of the, otherwise rather clear, promotion process of Commission senior officials is, to a certain extent, diminished also by the absence of clear rules on how the objections made by senior officials are to be handled. The relevant Commission Decision stipulates only that objections are to be expressed to the Directorate-General for Human Resources and Security and that the final list of officials recommended for promotion is prepared after a summary of assessment has been received by the Consultative Committee. The Commission Decision thus does not specify to what extent the summary of the assessment by the Consultative Committee is to be respected.

304 To recall, the Permanent Rapporteur of the Consultative Committee on Appointments is a function fulfilled by a person with proven skills and experience in human resources management, acting under the joint authority of the Chair of the Consultative Committee on Appointments and the Director-General for Human Resources and Security. He is responsible for promoting career development of all senior officials. - See above, chapter 3, section 3.2.3.

3.2.2. Promotion from AST to AD function group

Under the 2004 reform, a specific procedure has been adopted in order to bridge two new function groups and to provide possibilities for officials serving as Assistants (AST), from grade 5 upwards, to become Administrators (AD). Pursuant to this procedure, each year up to 20 per cent of all new appointments in AD function group may be made by appointing AST officials.[305] Naturally, to be promoted, AST officials needs to meet a number of conditions. They are set out in Article 45a of the *UN Staff Regulations* and, for Commission officials, worked out in the *Commission Decision on Article 45a*.[306]

Article 45a of the *EU Staff Regulations* stipulates in general that only AST staff who have successfully participated in a training programme and afterwards passed oral and written examinations can be promoted to AD level.[307] Participation in the training programme is not based on self-selection, though, but is decided upon by the appointing authority.[308] Such a decision depends on the evaluation of AST officials in their staff reports, as provided for in Article 43(2) of the *EU Staff Regulations*:

> *As of grade 4, for officials in function group AST, the [staff] report may also contain an opinion as to whether, on the basis of performance, he has the potential to carry out an administrator's function.*[309]

The appointing authority also takes into account the level of education and training of the AST officials, as well as needs of the service. The list of staff who have been selected by the appointing authority to participate in the training programme is reviewed by a joint committee which delivers a reasoned opinion. The final decision is taken by the appointing authority.[310]

The whole process of the selection of AST officials who will be allowed to participate in the training programme, the conditions for participation, and the appointment of successful staff to a post in the AD function group is set out in the *Commission Decision on Article 45a*. It is referred to as certification procedure and involves seven separate stages.

The first stage of the certification procedure is the determination of the number of officials authorized to participate in the training programme and the publication of

[305] *EU Staff Regulations*, Article 43(4). According to the Commission's *Human Resources Report* of 2009, in 2007 there were 48 promotions from AST to AD function group and in 2008 46 promotions, while the number of new recruitments to AD function group was 858 in 2007 and 694 in 2008. - *Commission's Human Resources Report 2009*, pp. 148 and 103, respectively. These figures show that the number of promotions from AST to AD function group is far below the 20% level permitted by the *EU Staff Regulations*.

[306] *Commission Decision on Article 45a*.

[307] *EU Staff Regulations*, Article 43(1).

[308] Ibid., Article 43(2).

[309] Ibid., Article 43(2). In the European Commission, only AST officials in active employment, on parental or family leave may apply for participation in the programme in a given year. Officials who, in the relevant year, are to be retired, separated from service or whose invalidity allowance becomes effective are excluded. - *Commission Decision on Article 45a*, Article 1(2).

[310] *EU Staff Regulations*, Article 43(2).

a call for applications, both conducted by the appointing authority. For determining the number of officials to be admitted, the appointing authority must consult a joint committee established by the Commission decision in question.[311] This committee has several other tasks under the certification procedure, mentioned below. It is composed of the following persons:

> *a chairperson and alternate both with the function of Director who are appointed by the Director-General for [Human Resources and Security]; five members and five alternate members belonging to function group AD who are appointed by the Director-General for [Human Resources and Security], at least one member being an official paid from appropriations entered in the research budget, and five members and five alternate members belonging to function group AD who are appointed by the Staff Committee.*[312]

The second stage of the certification procedure is the establishment of two different lists. The first list contains AST officials who have replied to the call for applications and have been admitted by the appointing authority to participate in the programme on the basis of their compliance with the eligibility requirements and the needs of the service. All admitted applicants are then ranked in accordance with the merit criterion, the demonstrated level of education and recent professional experience. The highest ranked applicants are 'pre-selected' and placed on the second list, referred to as list of pre-selected applicants. The precise criteria for ranking and the number of applicants to be pre-selected on each ranking list are determined by the appointing authority in consultation with the joint committee. Both lists prepared in this stage, i.e. the list of admitted applicants and the list of pre-selected applicants, are published and applicants are informed. Dissatisfied applicants may appeal to the joint committee which delivers an opinion. The final decision is taken by the appointing authority.[313]

The third stage of the procedure is the establishment of another list, of officials authorized to participate in the training programme. This list is prepared, once again, by the appointing authority. It is done, however, on the basis of an opinion of each Directorate-General on each pre-selected official. The opinions, accompanied by statement of reasons, take the form of points for pre-selected applicants, allocated on the basis of criteria specified in the present Commission Decision and common evaluation grids and guidelines prepared by the appointing authority after consulting the joint committee. They may be adjusted for each certification procedure, i.e. every year. Applicants who receive a sufficient number of points and reach the threshold are placed on yet another list, this one of officials authorized to participate in the training programme. Once again, dissatisfied applicants may appeal to the joint committee which delivers opinion and the appointing authority decides.[314]

---

[311] *Commission Decision on Article 45a*, Article 4.

[312] Ibid., Article 11(2). Article 11 contains also rules on alternates; voting, including a required quorum; adoption of rules of procedure; and an opinion which the committee adopts each year on the results of the certification exercise of the previous year.

[313] Ibid., Article 5.

[314] Ibid., Article 6.

The fourth stage of the certification procedure is the actual training programme organized by the European Administrative School. This School is established by a common decision of the EU institutions of 2005. After the programme is completed, its participants, certified by the School, take written and oral tests prepared by the EPSO and the School. The tests constitute the fifth stage of the certification procedure and are followed by the sixth stage, namely publication of the (final) list of officials who have passed the tests. This list is established by the EPSO and published by the appointing authority.[315]

The last and seventh stage of the certification procedure is the actual appointment to a post in function group AD once such a post becomes vacant. AST officials who are on the 'waiting' list remain on it, in principle, until they are appointed. It should be recalled, however, that a maximum of 20 per cent of the total number of appointments in function group AD may be made by appointing an AST official. This quota is, on the other hand, only checked once in five years, and available statistics indicate that the number of officials who have passed the certification process is consistently lower than this quota.[316]

The certification procedure for the promotion of AST officials to AD function group is thus rather complex, containing many details and many different stages.

[315] Ibid., Articles 7-9.

[316] Ibid., Article 10. According to the Commission's *Human Resources Report* of 2009, 78 AST officials were certified for appointment in AD function group in 2007 and 99 officials in 2008. As noted in a note above, the number of actual appointments of certified AST officials in AD function group was 48 in 2007 and 46 in 2008, while the total number of recruitments in AD function group was 858 in 2007 and 694 in 2008. – See above, footnote 285; and *Commission's Human Resources Report 2009*, p. 148.

It could be illustrated by the following scheme:

Scheme 16: European Commission certification process for promotion from AST to AD function group

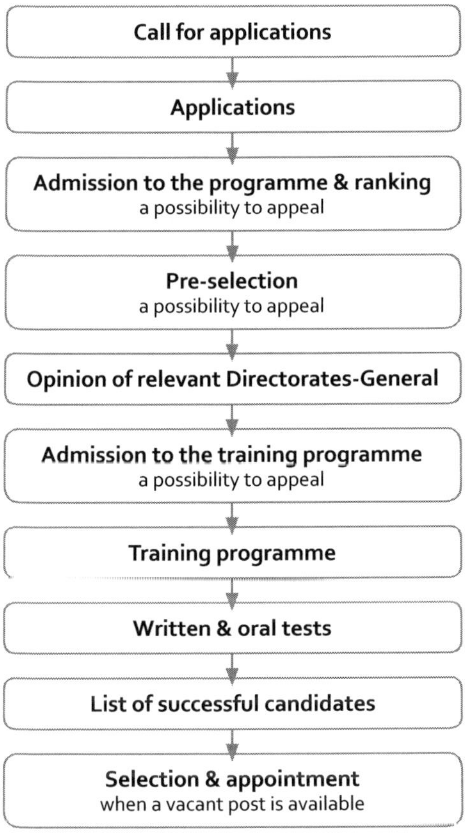

It appears that the intention of such detailed procedure is to set up a fair and transparent system providing for objective assessment of, and selection from among, eligible officials.

3.3. Promotion of other than permanent staff

3.3.1. Temporary staff

Temporary staff do not get promoted. The *EU Conditions of Employment of Other Servants* do not include such a possibility. On the other hand, performance of these staff is as regularly assessed as that of permanent officials. Both Article 43 of the *EU Staff Regulations* and the *Commission Decision on Article 43* apply to temporary staff, the latter subject to a few exceptions.[317] Temporary staff serving at the senior level are covered by the *Commission Compilation Document on Senior Officials Policy*.[318] Consequently, the analysis of appraisal of permanent staff, below the senior level and at the senior level, provided above, applies to temporary staff, too.

3.3.2. Contract staff

There is an important difference between contract staff engaged under Article 3a *EU Conditions of Employment of Other Servants*, also referred to as 'contact staff 3a' and that serving under Article 3b of the same regulation, commonly referred to as 'contract staff 3b'. To begin with the latter, 'contract staff 3b' have no promotion possibility. They do advance automatically every two years to the next step in their grade but cannot move to a higher grade or to the next function group.[319] Since each function group has seven steps, 'contract staff 3b' could move to a higher step six times at the most.[320] However, as the actual period of engagement of these staff within an EU institution may not exceed three years, including renewals, the advancement would, in practice, only occur once.[321]

Unlike 'contract staff 3b', 'contract staff 3a' can get promoted. Appraisal and promotion of these 'contract staff 3a' is governed by Article 87 of the *EU Conditions of Employment of Other Servants*. When compared to the appraisal and promotion system in use for permanent officials, the system applicable to contract staff 3a shows a number of similarities and/or commonalities. First of all, Article 43 of the *EU Staff Regulations* concerning officials' staff reports applies by analogy to the 'contract staff 3a'.[322] Second, all 'contract staff 3a' advance automatically to the next step in their grade after two years.[323] Third, promotion to the next higher grade in the same function group occurs by a decision of the authority authorized to conclude contracts by selection based on the consideration of comparative merits, taking into account the same elements as it is with officials, namely staff performance, use of languages and the level of exercised responsibilities.[324]

With regard to the last mentioned point, i.e. promotion to the next higher grade in the same function group, Article 87(3) of the *EU Conditions of Employment of*

---

[317] *EU Conditions of Employment of Other Servants*, Article 15 and *Commission Decision on Article 43*, Article 1(2). Article 15 of the EU Conditions of Employment of Other Servants stipulates that Article 43 of the *EU Staff Regulations* on staff reports applies by analogy to temporary staff. Article 1(2) of the *Commission Decision on Article 43* states that general provisions of the decision apply to temporary staff other than senior staff. It also lists three provisions that do not apply to temporary staff, all of them relating to the maximum number of officials who may be placed in performance levels IA and IB.

[318] *Commission Decision on Article 43*, Article 1(2).

[319] *EU Conditions of Employment of Other Servants*, Article 89(2).

[320] Ibid., Article 93.

[321] Ibid., Article 88(b).

[322] Ibid., Article 87(1). Understandably, this does not apply to staff whose contract is of duration shorter than one year.

[323] Ibid., Article 87(2.

[324] Ibid., Article 87(3), referring also to the last sentence of Article 45(1) of the *EU Staff Regulations*.

Other Servants stipulates that such promotion is to be effected by classifying the contract of an individual member of the 'contract staff 3a' in the first step of the next higher grade. The possibility of such reclassification is, however, only provided for staff who have a contract of at least three years and who have completed at least two years in their grade. 'Contract staff 3a' with a contract of shorter duration thus cannot be promoted to a higher grade and remain at the same grade during the whole duration of their engagement with the EU. This is not surprising given that, as in the case of permanent officials, 'contract staff 3a' must have been employed in the same grade for at least two years before becoming eligible for promotion to the next higher grade. Possible reclassification of staff whose contract duration is shorter than three years would therefore be only effective for a few months, which is apparently not considered worth the administrative burden linked to the need to follow prescribed procedures.

For 'contract staff 3a' engaged with the European Commission under a contract for at least three years, applicable procedures are set out in a Commission decision adopted for a reclassification exercise of a particular year. According to the *Register of Commission Documents* available on the internet, there have been two decisions on this matter thus far, one adopted in 2007 and another in 2008.[325] The more recent decision applied to the reclassification exercise conducted in 2008 and contained rules on performance appraisal of 'contract staff 3a' falling within its scope for the year of 2007 and their possible reclassification in 2008. The main principles and procedures contained in the decision are comparable to those that apply to permanent officials. They include: appraisal of efficiency, ability and conduct in the service; mandatory self-assessment; a formal dialogue between the staff member and the reporting officer; evaluation on the basis of the objectives established beforehand or otherwise on the job description; an appraisal report prepared pursuant to the common appraisal standards published by the Directorate-General for Human Resources and Security; review by the countersigning officer; acceptance of the report by the staff member concerned or its refusal leading to an appeal; in the case of the latter a possible meeting of all involved persons; an opinion of the countersigning officer and a decision by the authority authorized to conclude contracts, a possible appeal to the Joint Reclassification Committee established by the decision at hand on either the appraisal report or a preliminary decision of the authority authorized to conclude contracts of staff who are to be reclassified or both these documents; an opinion of the Joint Reclassification Committee; and a final decision by the authority authorized to conclude contracts.[326]

---

[325] *Commission Decision on General Provisions for Implementing Article 87(3) of the Conditions of Employment of Other Servants of the European Communities, C(2007)3714*, 01.08.2007, available in the Register of Commission Documents available at http://ec.europa.eu/transparency/regdoc/registre.cfm?CL=en, last visited on 30.12.2010 and *Commission Decision on General Provisions for Implementing Article 87(3) of the Conditions of Employment of Other Servants of the European Communities, C(2008)3933*, 29.07.2008, available in the Register of Commission Documents, available at http://ec.europa.eu/transparency/regdoc/registre.cfm?CL=en, last visited on 30.12.2010. The *Register of Commission Documents* is available at http://ec.europa.eu/transparency/regdoc/registre.cfm?CL=en, last visited on 16.08.2010. It provides access to Commission documents adopted since 2001.

[326] *Commission Decision on Reclassification of Contract Staff of 2008*, Articles 2, 5 and 9-12. Note that the

Scheme 17: European Commission reclassification procedure of 2008 for 'contract staff 3a'

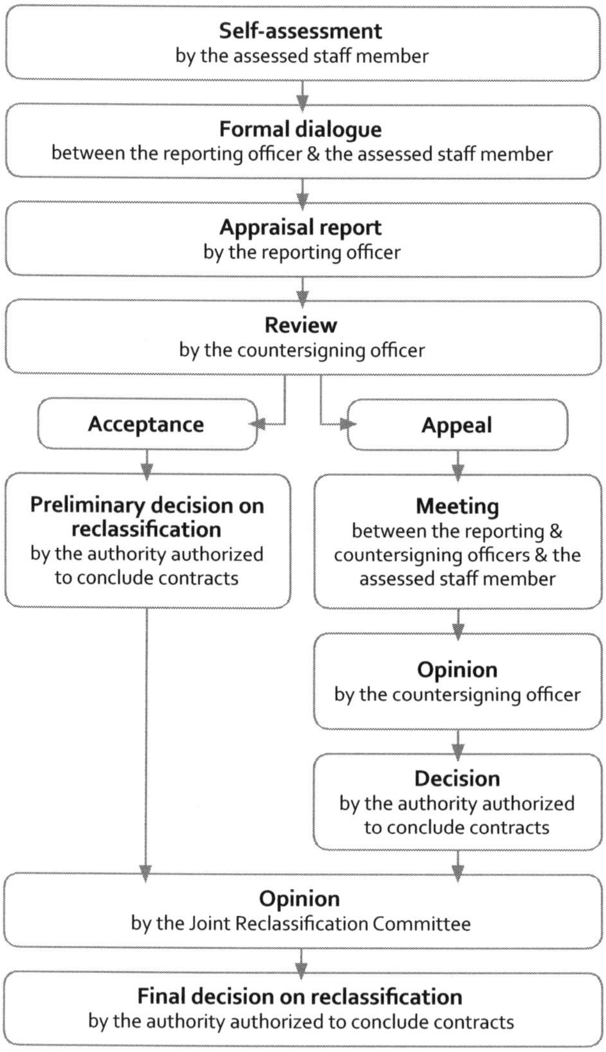

staff members' reclassification is always based on their past performance which could have been assessed as outstanding (i.e. constantly exceeding expectations), very good (i.e. frequently exceeding expectations), good (i.e. fully meeting expectations), poor (i.e. partly meeting expectations) or insufficient (i.e. not meeting expectations). A quota of five per cent of all assessments was established for outstanding performances, while very good performance could have been recognized for no more than twenty-two per cent of staff. The percentage of very good performance could be increased when the percentage of outstanding performance did not reached the established quota, while maintaining the overall maximum of twenty-seven percent for both performance levels. Moreover, the maximum percentages must have been complied with for each Commission department, each function group and, where possible, for each grade. On an exceptional basis, derogations could have been granted. – *Commission Decision on Reclassification of Contract Staff of 2008*, Article 6.

This brief overview shows that procedures for performance evaluation and promotion of 'contract staff 3a' are comparable to those used for permanent officials, including the involvement of a joint committee of representatives of both the Administration and the staff. This feature guarantees that the procedures are objective and transparent. On the other hand, the same comments could be made here as those mentioned earlier with regard to the appraisal and annual promotion exercises for permanent staff.

As far as differences between the promotion possibilities of 'contract staff 3a' and permanent officials are concerned, an interesting difference relates to the possibility to move from one function group to another. While movement of the 'contract staff 3a' to a higher function group may occur solely through participation in a general selection procedure, movement of permanent officials from the AST function group to the AD function group is facilitated by a special procedure established for this very purpose.[327] As explained above, permanent staff serving in the AST function group may be selected to participate in a special training programme followed by an exam and possible appointment to an AD position. 'Contract staff 3a' who seek engagement in a higher function group must however take part in the regular selection process which is also open to external candidates. Clearly, it is more difficult to succeed in an open selection procedure than it is in an exam conducted at the end of a training programme. This is, however, not a consideration that would be of relevance to this study.

3.3.3. Other staff

There are no provisions for appraisal or promotion of other staff employed at the European Commission, such as seconded national experts, with one exception. The *Commission Framework Rules on Local Staff* stipulate that 'particularly deserving member of local staff' may be granted promotion by being advanced in their group by two steps instead of one. As explained in chapter 1, advancement of local staff by one step at a time occurs annually and automatically, subject to satisfactory performance, and the number of such promotions is limited to four.[328]

4. The UN and the EU compared

4.1. General approach

There is a considerable difference in the possibilities for promotion available to UN and EU civil servants. In the UN, the only way in which staff can achieve promotion is by being appointed to a vacant post at a higher level. Without such a vacant post, no promotion can take place.[329] In the EU, on the other hand, as long as officials perform well, they have a *de facto* guarantee of promotion, sooner or later. Such pro-

[327] *EU Conditions of Employment of Other Servants*, Article 87(4).

[328] *Commission Framework Rules on Local Staff*, Article 4(3) and (4).

[329] See above, section 2.1.1.

motion takes place during an annual exercise when EU officials reach the promotion threshold established for each such exercise in line with budgetary possibilities of the relevant EU institution.[330]

Promotion in the EU via annual promotion exercises can take place at all levels, the only limitation being that officials who have reached the highest grade in their career bracket can no longer be promoted in this manner. Officials below the middle management level can thus be promoted this way up to grade AD13 and exceptionally AD14, middle managers up to AD14, senior officials serving at the Director level up to AD15 and senior officials serving at the Director-General level up to AD16. Given the range of the first career bracket, i.e. AD5 - AD13, this bracket sees the most movement upwards via annual promotion exercises. At the managerial levels, the relevant brackets contain a smaller number of grades, which results in fewer possibilities for such promotion. This is in particular the case at the senior level where promotion via the annual exercise can only occur once for both Directors and Directors-General.[331]

Apart from promotion through an annual exercise, EU permanent officials can, similarly as UN staff, also be promoted through appointment to a vacant post classified at one level higher than their current post.[332] The latter, however, occurs in practice only for posts at the managerial level and, unlike promotion via an annual promotion exercise, involves a change of function. This way of promotion, i.e. through appointment to a vacant post at a higher level, further extends promotion opportunities of EU officials, including those who cannot be further promoted via annual promotion exercises because they have reached the highest grade in their career bracket. When these officials apply for, and succeed in, appointment to a vacant post in a higher career bracket, they get promoted. Further promotion of such officials can occur via either an annual promotion exercise within the new career bracket or, again, via appointment to another vacant post at one level higher.

One of the important consequences of the above mentioned difference between the UN and EU promotion systems is that while in the European Commission promotion prospects until certain levels are genuinely present for all officials who do their job well, in the UN Secretariat no such guarantee exists, including for staff who perform satisfactorily. In the UN Secretariat, even though vacancies occur regularly, theoretically there always can be a candidate with better – or for other reasons more suitable – references for the vacant post concerned, halting the promotion of other staff members who have been performing well too. Moreover, in the UN Secretariat, considerations other than merit play an important role in staff selection and thus also in the process possibly leading to promotion. Such considerations include the requirement to ensure adequate geographical and gender balance at all levels.[333] Consequently, even if an individual staff member applying for promotion via appointment can prove best merits of all candidates for the vacant post

[330] See above, section 3.2.1.4.2.

[331] See above, section 3.2.1.4.2.

[332] See above, section 3.2.1.4.1.

[333] See above, chapter 3, sections 2.2.2.2 and 2.2.2.5.

at issue, another candidate may eventually be chosen because, for instance, apart from satisfying requirements for the post at issue, he also possesses the 'right' nationality or is of the 'right' gender. The merits of such a candidate with the 'right' nationality or gender do not even need to be superior to those of other candidates – under the UN staff selection process all candidates are, at least formally, to be compared against the requirements of the vacant post and not against each other.[334] This approach allows for appointing candidates on the basis of criteria other than merit, as long as they meet the requirements of the post at issue. To compare, in the European Commission, promotion is conditioned by the requirement to consider the comparative merits of candidates eligible for promotion. This condition is included in the relevant provision of the *EU Staff Regulations*.[335] Similar requirement is contained in the UN *Staff Regulations* with regard to all appointments, i.e. also those through which staff get promoted – all UN staff appointments are be to conducted on a competitive basis as far as it is practicable.[336] Despite this, the *UN Staff Selection System* requires that candidates be evaluated and thus compared against the requirements of the vacant post and not against each other.[337] This creates space for considering other issues in staff selection as well and thus further limits the already slim promotion opportunities of UN staff. Formally speaking, it could even be argued that the more limited requirement of considering candidates' merit against the requirements of the vacant post under the *UN Staff Selection System* is contrary to the *UN Staff Regulations* requiring their consideration on a competitive basis, as the latter appears to have a broader meaning than the former.

A further limitation of promotion possibilities in the UN relates to staff mobility, though its importance was significantly reduced in April 2010 when the new *UN Staff Selection System* was adopted. Until then, candidates who applied for a vacant post in order to exercise mobility must have been considered before candidates applying for promotion. As explained above, in the UN, mobility had preference over promotion for all posts except those at the P-3 level. Comparing this situation to that in the European Commission, there mobility and promotion are at the same priority level. In the Commission, candidates applying for a vacant post because they want to exercise mobility and those who seek promotion may apply and be considered simultaneously, whereas in the UN Secretariat candidates hoping for promotion were not even reviewed before it was certain that no candidate applying for lateral move was suitable for the post at issue. The new *UN Staff Selection System* adopted in April 2010 abolished this priority order in which candidates for vacant posts had to be considered, equalizing the situation to that in the European Commission.[338] Nonetheless, one limitation of promotion possibilities in the UN Secretariat relating to mobility has remained in place. To be eligible for promotion to the P-5 level, UN staff must have previously laterally moved two times, with some specific exceptions

[334] See above, chapter 3, section 2.2.2.2.

[335] See above, 3.2.1.3.

[336] See above, chapter 3, introductory part to section 2.2.

[337] See above, section 2.2.2.2.

[338] See above, chapter 3, section 1.

providing for just one or even no lateral move.[339] This means that although mobility in the UN Secretariat is no longer procedurally preferred to promotion, it still constitutes one of its substantive conditions. In the European Commission, mobility is not a formal condition for promotion at any level. Naturally, in practice, positive effects of mobility on one's professional development can bring advantage to staff serving in the European Commission, too, by increasing their chances for promotion via appointment to a vacant post at a higher level, but also by improving their work performance. The latter may be reflected in the performance evaluation and result in higher promotion points, possibly leading to faster promotion. Nonetheless, formally speaking, unlike in the UN Secretariat, mobility is not a condition for promotion in the European Commission at any level.

Promotion in the European Commission can thus occur under less strict conditions than in the UN Secretariat. The only requirement limiting promotion possibilities that exists in the European Commission and not in the UN Secretariat is that relating to seniority. To recall, to be eligible for promotion at any level, the European Commission staff must have served in the previous post for at least two years.[340] Such seniority requirement is not present in the UN Secretariat, with one particular exception relating to staff serving in the Field Service category and applying for promotion to posts in the Professional category.[341] In general, however, the seniority requirement no longer exists in the UN Secretariat.[342]

Apart from the seniority requirement, however, the situation in the European Commission is more favourable to staff promotions than in the UN Secretariat. There, as shown in this section, promotion expectations are uncertain and limited. As explained in the introductory part to this section, this may be problematic from the point of view of ensuring independence and impartiality of the UN staff, as these staff may, in order to increase their chances for promotion, be tempted to take recourse to outside sources and practices which could lead to an uneasy relationship of gratitude and, consequently, imperil staff independence and impartiality.[343] Fair and reasonable chances of promotion should be a normal part of the personnel policy of an organization such as the UN but, arguably, they are not. EU officials are, in this regard, better off than UN staff. Although UN staff performing well receive yearly salary increases, their promotion prospects are uncertain. It could be argued that for many staff members personal recognition and status is of a greater importance than a modest increase in salary.

---

[339] See above, section 2.1.2.1.

[340] See above, section 3.2.1.1.

[341] See above, section 2.1.2.1.

[342] A remark needs to be made here, though. It is so that UN staff applying for promotion to the P-5 level must have had a prior lateral movement for a duration of at least one year. This means, in fact, that staff must spend a certain amount of time in some post(s) before they can be promoted. It could be argued that this equals to the seniority requirement. However, the required movement may take place at any level below P-5. Therefore, formally speaking, holding a post for a certain period of time before becoming eligible for promotion to the P-5 level, is not a direct condition for promotion in the UN Secretariat.

[343] See above, section 1.

4.2. Procedures

Neither the *EU* nor the *UN Staff Regulations* contain detailed provisions on procedures to be followed when a UN or EU staff member is to be promoted, although the *EU Staff Regulations* do include some general requirements, for example that promotion must be done by considering comparative merits of eligible staff. The *EU Staff Regulations* also contain precise eligibility conditions under which officials can be promoted, with some additional refinements for staff serving in the European Commission to be found in a relevant internal Commission decision. Similarly, conditions for promotion of non-permanent staff for whom such a possibility exists are included in the *EU Conditions of Employment of Other Servants*. In both instances, detailed procedural rules are contained in internal Commission decisions.[344]

Similar is the case in the UN Secretariat where procedures are set out in an administrative instruction, namely the *UN Staff Selection System*, with some special rules for D-2 posts in the *Secretary-General's Bulletin, Senior Review Group*. The *UN Staff Selection System* also provides all eligibility criteria for promotion.[345] Unlike the *EU Staff Regulations*, the *UN Staff Regulations* and even the *UN Staff Rules* contain no rules in this respect, except that all appointments, thus also promotion, should take place, as far as possible, on a competitive basis, and that internal candidates are to be given priority before external ones when vacant posts are being filled.[346]

The fact that in the UN all conditions for eligibility for promotion as well as procedures to be followed are contained in an administrative instruction promulgated by the UN Secretary-General is rather surprising, especially with regard to the eligibility requirements for promotion. This state of affairs is regrettable because it provides insufficient security and predictability for staff. The relevant administrative instruction(s) may be changed at any time by a decision of the Secretary-General, whereas change of the *UN Staff Regulations* and/or *Rules* would need to be presented to the General Assembly for approval or note, respectively. At present, thus, the UN Secretary-General may modify even the most basic conditions for promotion of all UN staff, though it is true that, in practice, the General Assembly pays close attention to the Secretary-General's actions. This includes the area of human resources management, where the General Assembly acts through its Fifth Committee which often discusses actions taken by the Secretary-General in great detail. The General Assembly could thus request the Secretary-General (not) to act in a certain way or to modify conditions established by him for staff promotion. Formally speaking, however, conditions for promotion of UN staff remain to be set by the Secretary-General in an internal administrative document, not in a document approved by the General Assembly beforehand.

As far as the procedures are concerned, because promotion in the UN occurs solely via appointment to a vacant post, procedures used for filling vacant posts, addressed in chapter 3 on staff recruitment, apply to promotion as well. Similar note is

[344] See above, sections 3.2.1.1, 3.3.1 and 3.3.2.

[345] See above, sections 2.1.2.1 and 2.1.2.2.

[346] See above, chapter 3, section 1 and sections 2.2.2.2 and 2.2.2.5.

to be made for the European Commission for cases in which promotions take place through appointment to a vacant post, although this only holds for posts in a higher career bracket, not for appointment to vacant posts classified in a higher grade in the same career bracket. This is so because the latter, i.e. promotion through appointment to a vacant post in a higher grade in the same career bracket, never takes place. When promotion occurs through appointment to a vacant post classified in a higher career bracket, procedures described in chapter 3 (for Commission senior posts) and chapter 4 (for Commission middle management posts) apply.

Since most promotions in the European Commission within the same career bracket occur via annual promotion exercises, a detailed and elaborate set of rules has been developed for this type of promotion, with a distinction made between staff below and at the senior level.[347] This differentiation is not surprising considering that senior officials are subject to a distinct set of rules in most, if not all, areas of human resources management. These rules on senior officials are contained in a separate legal instrument, namely the *Commission Compilation Document on Senior Officials Policy*. It is unfortunate that rules on annual promotion of senior officials are to be searched elsewhere, in a document which deals with this one issue only and is referred to as the *Commission Principles and Procedure for Promotion of Senior Officials*. It would be more appropriate to incorporate this document into the *Commission Compilation Document on Senior Officials Policy*.

As noted above, the Commission rules on annual promotion of senior officials are rather detailed and aimed at ensuring objectivity and transparency of the process. These characteristics are guaranteed by a number of elements, such as the obligation to inform all senior officials of each decision taken during the annual exercise, by the involvement of a special committee established for annual promotion exercises, and by the fact that the final decision is taken by the entire College of Commissioners not by an individual. A few problematic issues potentially politicizing promotion process of the Commission senior officials and/or decreasing its transparency can be identified, too, These issues include involvement of political appointees in the Consultative Committee, the requirement to pay regard to the need to ensure geographical balance at all levels, and the absence of clear rules on how objections made by senior officials in a particular annual promotion exercise are to be handled.[348]

Below the senior level, objectivity and transparency during annual promotion exercises are ensured, to begin with, by the very existence of detailed rules on many aspects of this procedure, by the publication requirements, by the involvement of a joint committee as well by a possibility of appeal.[349] It is regrettable, however, that all appeals lodged the Commission officials are dealt with by just two committees

[347] See above, section 3.2.1.4.2. Note that no separate procedures have been developed for annual promotion exercises of middle management staff. Annual exercises for promotion of these staff follow the general procedural set up contained in the Commission decision that applies to all other (non-senior) staff.

[348] See above, section 3.2.1.4.2.

[349] See above, section 3.2.1.4.2.

whose capacity to properly assess a potentially large number of cases can be questioned. It could even be argued that such situation may easily result in arbitrariness of the assessment. Moreover, the fact that the result of the committees' assessment is not binding upon the EU Administration is also an element that lessens objectivity and impartiality of the process.

4.3. Promotion from one category or function group to another

Both the UN and the EU provide for a possibility of promotion of their staff serving in one category or function group via appointment to a post classified in another, higher, category or function group. Such a promotion may occur in both organizations only when there is a vacant post to which the promoted staff member at issue can be appointed. Moreover, in both organizations a maximum number of such promotions is set. This number is higher in the European Commission – 20 per cent of all appointments made in the AD function group, whereas in the UN Secretariat it is 10 per cent of all appointments in the Professional category.[350] Another difference between the UN Secretariat and the European Commission is that in the former the quota must be complied with each year, while in the latter it is only checked once in five years.[351] In this respect, the EU approach is more flexible than the UN approach. Also, in the UN Secretariat only staff with the two highest rankings of performance evaluation may eventually be promoted in this way, whereas in the European Commission the level of satisfaction with past performance is, at least formally, irrelevant.

The statement that the EU approach is more flexible than the UN approach is, however, true only to a certain extent. There are certain elements in the EU approach that make it less flexible than the UN approach. For example, with regard to performance evaluation, although in the European Commission the level of rating is formally not decisive (as long as it is positive), in reality it plays an important role in providing access of Commission staff to promotion. This is because, unlike in the UN Secretariat, only a limited number of staff may participate in the training programme and subsequent tests that may eventually lead to promotion. This admission depends on the decision of the appointing authority which, clearly, takes staff past performance into account. In addition, only staff who have been recognized as having potential to perform an administrator's function can be admitted.[352]

In the UN Secretariat, staff participation in the promotion exercise is based not on admission but on a self-selection. All staff with satisfactory past performance can apply for promotion.[353] There is no assessment of the capacity of UN staff to function in a Professional post and no competition among staff for their admissibility. Access of UN staff to the this type of promotion is thus less limited than access of EU staff, the former providing equal chances to all staff who satisfy required eligibil-

---

[350] See above, sections 2.2 and 3.2.2.

[351] See above, sections 2.2 and 3.2.2.

[352] See above, section 3.2.2.

[353] See above, section 2.2.

ity criteria. The European Commission staff who, despite meeting such criteria, are not admitted to the training programme and subsequent tests, have no access to promotion in that year. This disadvantage is compensated to a certain extent by the fact that all admitted Commission staff receive training whereby they can prepare for the required tests better than staff serving in the UN Secretariat who receive no assistance in this respect.[354] Moreover, the number of European Commission staff members who have passed the tests and are placed on the relevant reserve list is arguably significantly lower than the number of UN staff placed on the roster after having passed the G to P examinations. Although both EU and UN staff on the reserve list and roster, respectively, remain there without a time limit, i.e. until appointed, the waiting time for appointment is longer in the UN Secretariat.[355] In this regard it should be remembered that the actual selection from the UN roster or EU reserve list, conducted during the selection for a specific vacant post, lacks sufficient objectivity and transparency in both organizations, in particular when compared to the process employed in the EU for the selection from among eligible officials who are to be admitted to the programme.[356] It could be thus argued that the pre-selection, which occurs in the European Commission in an early stage of the process pursuant to clear and detailed rules, including a possibility of appeals at several stages and the involvement of a collective body (joint committee), is a more adequate guarantee of an objective and transparent process than a mere selection in the UN Secretariat from a long list of names added each year.

As regards tests possibly leading to placement on the roster or reserve list, some fundamental differences between the UN and the EU can be detected. The UN examinations used for this purpose are, in principle, the same as the examinations taken by external candidates for entry level non-language posts.[357] In this sense, UN external and internal candidates get equal treatment. No such alignment of tests exists in the European Commission, at least not formally, although tests for promotion from AST to AD function group are prepared by the EPSO, which is also in charge of tests used in open competitions. In setting up the former, however, the European Administrative School is involved as well, as this School conducts the training programme preparing AST officials for the examinations.[358] In this regard it could be argued that AST officials who are eventually promoted to the AD function group are treated more favourably than others who need to pass examinations without any help. In addition, the content of the tests may differ. However, it should be born in mind that all AST officials have already gone through a competition before being appointed as AST officials. Therefore, they have already passed a hurdle comparable to that all other candidates have faced. The situation in the UN Secretariat is specific in that staff members serving in the General Service and related categories, who take G to P examinations in order to be promoted to the Professional category, may not necessarily have passed any examinations when they were recruited to in

[354] See above, section 3.2.2.

[355] See above, section 2.2.

[356] See above, chapter 3, section 4.2.

[357] See above, section 2.2.

[358] See above, section 3.2.2.

their current category. Therefore, it is necessary that their position be equalized with that of staff directly appointed to the Professional category by passing relevant and comparable examinations. On this basis, it could be concluded that both organizations provide comparable safeguards for the objectivity of the process at hand.

A final important note in this respect must be made. In principle, in both the UN Secretariat and the European Commission, staff from another category or function group are promoted by appointment to a post in a higher category or function group which is classified at the entry level. In the UN Secretariat this means P-2 level and in the European Commission grades AD5 - AD8, depending on the level of education and professional experience. In the UN Secretariat, however, field staff serving at the levels FS-6 and FS-7 may be promoted to P-3, P-4 and even P-5 level. Moreover, such promotion would occur via the *UN Staff Selection System* and not through G to P examinations.[359] The concerned field staff thus do not need to pass any examinations for becoming Professionals. The express objective of this notable exception, stated in the *UN Staff Selection System* itself, is to 'recognize and encourage mission service'.[360] This exception places field staff in an advantageous position when compared to other staff serving in the General and other related categories, who do need to pass examinations before becoming eligible for appointment in the Professional category. However, the concerned field staff serve at higher levels than staff from the General Service and other related categories to whom the G to P examinations apply. At such higher levels, the *UN Staff Selection System* applies, allowing for direct appointment without an examination of all candidates, including external ones.[361] The field staff can be promoted to the Professional category under this system, just the way external staff can be recruited. The only difference is that the concerned field staff have a priority over external candidates, for the reasons just mentioned. There is thus no obvious discrepancy in the system in this respect. Compared with the EU, no appointment in the AD function group of AST officials at higher levels takes place.

4.4. Performance appraisal

The importance of performance evaluation for staff promotion in both the UN Secretariat and European Commission is self-evident, although in the UN Secretariat the emphasis is on accountability of staff and managers for the performance of their duties and the improvement of this performance rather than on the need for evaluation for promotion purposes.[362] In reality, however, promotion of UN staff, too, depends on how successful they are in carrying out their duties compared to other staff members who have applied for the same vacant post. On the other hand, in the European Commission it appears that the annual promotion exercises are the sole *raison d'être* of performance evaluation. The annual appraisal seems

[359] See above, section 2.1.2.2.

[360] *UN Staff Selection System*, Section 5.4(b).

[361] See above, chapter 3, section 2.2.2.2.

[362] See, for example, *UN Staff Rules*, Rule 1.3(a).

to be generally regarded by the Commission officials as a 'promotion game', the objective of which is to give sufficient evaluation and a corresponding number of promotion points to staff who are 'due' for promotion because of their seniority in the same grade. Seniority seems thus to continue to be the golden rule in the Commission promotion process – there is a general understanding that each official will be regularly promoted and that most promotions will take place in a certain average period of time.[363] Accordingly, the performance evaluation serves as a means of enforcing this informal rule. It is therefore questionable whether the introduction of a new performance evaluation system (the so-called CDR system) in the course of the Commission's overall reform launched in 2000 has contributed to a change in the culture of Commission officials. Experts argue that a decade is needed to see whether the Commission CDR system is a success.[364] Similar observation could be made with regard to the new Performance Management and Development System introduced in the UN Secretariat in 2010, although this new system builds greatly upon the previous Performance Appraisal System.[365] The latter was severely criticized in the past and it, therefore, remains to be seen whether the new system will function better.

Regarding the objectivity and transparency of procedures used for staff evaluation, both the UN Secretariat and European Commission have developed detailed sets of rules and included them in separate internal legal instruments.[366] Moreover, in the European Commission, unlike in the UN Secretariat, special rules have been established for evaluation of senior staff.[367] In the UN Secretariat, performance evaluation takes place for all staff according to the same regime, despite the fact that a more comprehensive assessment regime for senior staff was promised long ago and that many UN staff have expressed a wish to be able to evaluate their supervisors.[368]

As in other areas, in performance evaluation too a number of similarities as well as differences between the UN Secretariat and the European Commission can be detected. To begin with a similarity, evaluation is based on objectives and plans identified for each individual staff member during the preceding evaluation cycle. In the UN Secretariat, the setting out of the objectives receives much attention and occurs at several levels from the top down to individual staff members.[369] In the European Commission, the objectives are simply included in the previous evaluation exercise for each individual. There, however, common standards are adopted

---

[363] To that effect, see, for example, *Commission Decision on Article 45a*, Article 10.

[364] Spence and Stevens, *Staff and Personnel Policy in the Commission*, p. 186. The argument was made in relation to the initial CDR system introduced in 2003 but could perhaps be applied to the present system as well. Note that effects of the most recent changes of the system introduced in 2008 should be formally evaluated in 2011. - *Commission Decision on Article 45a*, Article 10(3).

[365] See above, section 2.1.2.3.

[366] See above, sections 2.1.2.3 and 3.2.1.3.1.

[367] See above, section 3.2.1.3.2.

[368] *A Picture of the UN Staff*, question 13. More than 80 per cent of staff said they would like to have the possibility of evaluating the performance of their supervisors, 10 per cent more than during the last survey ten years earlier.

[369] See above, section 2.1.2.3.

by the Directorate-General for Human Resources against which the achievement of objectives is to be measured. Additional standards may even be adopted by each Directorate-General, subject to consultation with evaluating officers and approval by the Directorate-General for Human Resources. The adoption of such standards serves an important purpose, namely the objectivity of the evaluation conducted by a relatively large number of officers, given the size of the European Commission.[370]

The staff evaluation itself takes place annually in both organizations, although in the UN Secretariat two specificities exist in this respect – first, staff and their supervisors are obliged to observe, discuss and evaluate performance throughout the year as well and, if needed, to take steps in order to secure improvements, and, second, in the middle of each performance cycle a midpoint review takes place.[371] In the European Commission, formally speaking, there is only one evaluation at the end of the evaluation cycle. It is followed by the annual promotion exercise.[372] This feature indicates a close, and perhaps a too close, connection between performance evaluation and annual promotion in the European Commission. It could indeed be argued that the sole purpose of performance evaluation is to facilitate the subsequent division of promotion points. In the UN Secretariat, on the contrary, emphasis appears to be on facilitating better performance and addressing shortcomings detected throughout the year, which is a praiseworthy development.

In both the UN Secretariat and the European Commission evaluation is conducted through a number of similar steps. It begins with a self-assessment, although in the UN Secretariat this is no longer mandatory. Staff members are encouraged to do a self-appraisal but are not obliged to do so. After the self-assessment, a meeting between the assessed staff member and the assessor takes place in both the UN Secretariat and the European Commission, in both instances followed by an appraisal by the assessing officer. In the UN Secretariat, this appraisal is reviewed by the so-called second reporting officer who may add his own comments. In the European Commission, the review by a second officer, the so-called countersigning officer, only entails verifying whether evaluation standards have been applied consistently by the first evaluating officers, but does not include the possibility of substantially reassessing individual appraisals. On the other hand, in the European Commission, the assessed official may comment on the appraisal report before it is finalized by the second reporting official who also needs to take into account statistical recommendations from the joint committee, if made. In the UN Secretariat, the assessed staff member may formally rebut only the final report. An appeal is, of course, possible also in the European Commission. An important difference here is that European Commission officials may always appeal, whereas in the UN Secretariat appeal is not possible against the first two best performance ratings.[373] It is highly questionable whether this situation is legally sustainable – the second best rating, although in itself largely satisfactory, may be prejudicial to the interests

[370] See above, section 3.2.1.3.1.

[371] See above, section 2.1.2.3.

[372] See above, sections 3.2.1.3.1 and 3.2.1.3.2.

[373] See above, sections 2.1.2.3 and 3.2.1.3.1.

of an individual staff member when he finds himself competing for a post, to which he could be promoted, with a staff member who has received the first best rating. This situation may even result in staff members who fear receiving the second best rating reaching out to inappropriate means in order to prevent it. The knowledge that the second best rating cannot be appealed while it may make a decisive difference in one's promotion prospects may facilitate such temptation, thereby being detrimental to the objectivity and impartiality of the performance evaluation process and, consequently, of the selection process which leads to promotion through appointment into a vacant post.

The appeal, or rebuttal, as it is called in the UN, is dealt with by a collective body in both the UN Secretariat and the European Commission. This is an important safeguard of the objectivity of the appeal procedure. In the UN Secretariat, the appealing staff member may even choose the members of the rebuttal panel. In the European Commission, appeals are handled by joint committees which also look into appeals lodged in the promotion process.[374] Another important difference is that the UN rebuttal panel delivers a final decision, possibly with new performance rating. This decision of the rebuttal panel is binding upon both the assessed staff member as well as on the head of his department or office, even though the Secretary-General may overrule it.[375] European Commission's joint committees only deliver an opinion the appointing authority must take into account but not necessarily follow.[376] The result of the appeal process therefore seems to be more objective and transparent in the UN Secretariat than in the European Commission, where the appointing authority has the final word without having to respect the opinion of the relevant joint committee. This is despite the fact that EU joint committees consist of a large number of persons, more than thirty, while the UN rebuttal panel has only three.[377] The objectivity of the rebuttal process in the UN Secretariat is further enhanced by the fact that the rebuttal panel always hears the appealing official as well as both the first and the second reporting officers.[378] The European Commission's joint committees may hear involved persons, too, but, in principle, they may also deliver their opinion on the basis of the written appeal, an opinion on it provided by the countersigning officer and subsequent comments by the appealing official. The committees do not even need to have a statement from, or hear, the official who made the assessment, i.e. the reporting officer.[379] This arrangement is understandable from the point of view of the potentially large number of appeals the joint committee needs to handle – as it is with appeals lodged in the course of the annual promotion exercise, all appeals against appraisal reports too are dealt with by just two committees, one for officials serving in function group AD and one for officials in function group AST. These two committees have thus little room for maneuver in each individual appeal case, which does not add to the objectivity of the process. UN rebuttals, in

[374] See above, sections 2.1.2.3 and 3.2.1.3.1.

[375] See above, section 2.1.2.3.

[376] See above, section 3.2.1.3.1.

[377] See above, sections 2.1.2.3 and 3.2.1.3.1.

[378] See above, section 2.1.2.3.

[379] See above, section 3.2.1.3.1.

contrast, are handled by rebuttal panels established for each individual case. Having just one case under consideration, UN rebuttal panels have inevitably more space to assess all the details of the case before them than European Commission's joint committees do.

As for performance evaluation of senior officials, it has been mentioned earlier that the European Commission has a separate set of rules according to which appraisal of senior officials takes place.[380] No such special rules have been developed in the UN Secretariat, meaning also that, unlike European Commission staff, staff serving in the UN Secretariat have no possibility of evaluating their supervisors. In the European Commission, 360 degree evaluation is a fact. Performance of Commission senior officials is evaluated by fifteen different persons, although the final formal appraisal is prepared by an assessing officer who has full discretion to decide in what manner he will reflect the feedback from these fifteen persons in it.[381] In any case, the broad evaluation of senior officials certainly contributes to the objectivity and impartiality of the process. Also senior officials may comment on their formal appraisal before it is completed and lodge an appeal later. The appeals are dealt with by a collective body, namely the Consultative Committee on Appointments established by the *Commission Compilation Document on Senior Officials Policy* where all rules on performance evaluation of senior officials can be found, too.[382]

5. Conclusions

Fair and reasonable opportunities for promotion constitute an inevitable part of sound human resources policy of every employer interested in attracting and keeping qualified and enthusiastic staff. In international organizations, there is an additional reason for having such policy – the need to ensure that staff has no reason to take recourse to inappropriate sources which could help them achieve promotion that would otherwise not, or only hardly, come.

Without attempting to estimate the real effects of the current UN promotion policy on the Secretariat staff, it is clear that the policy does not provide adequate promotion possibilities for all UN employees. An overwhelming majority of UN staff experience few promotions during their whole career, just two or three, while no other reward mechanisms are in place, save for regular salary increase. Already some time ago it was recognized that '[t]he system of promotion against a vacant post worked relatively well over a long period when the United Nations was expanding' but that in the meantime promotion opportunities in the UN have shrunk.[383] Nonetheless, no effective change of the policy has taken place, rather to the contrary – from 2002 till April 2010, promotion was even formally subordinated to staff mobility.

[380] See above, section 3.2.1.3.2.

[381] See above, section 3.2.1.3.2.

[382] See above, section 3.2.1.3.2.

[383] *Inspection of the Application of United Nations Recruitment, Placement, and Promotion Policies, Part II - Placement and Promotions, Report of the Joint Inspection Unit, JIU/REP/96/6*, para. 67.

The position of European Commission staff appears to be more adequate in this respect. Commission officials are promoted regularly through annual promotion exercises as long as their performance is satisfactory and until they reach the top grade in their career bracket. Even then Commission officials may be further promoted through appointment to a vacant post at a higher level, which can occur several times – via appointment as Head of Unit, Director, Deputy Director-General or Director-General. In the meantime, promotion via annual exercises continues to be a possibility at the higher levels, too, albeit to a more limited extent than at the lower levels. Moreover, in the European Commission, officials who do not qualify, aspire for or succeed in being promoted into the managerial level may also be promoted several times. From the starting grade AD5, promotion can take place until grade AD13 and exceptionally AD14, one grade at a time, and thus eight or nine times. This is possible as promotion has been partly decoupled from managerial functions. In the past, no Commission official could be promoted above a relatively low grade without necessarily accepting corresponding management functions. At the same time, the number of management functions was inevitably limited by the size and responsibilities of the Commission as a whole, inevitably halting the careers of a large majority of officials at a lower level. Due to the unchanged pyramidal structure of the EU and UN civil services, the limited number of management functions is of course still the case in both the European Commission and in the UN Secretariat. However, the European Commission has found a solution to this limitation by allowing promotion not linked to an appointment to a managerial function.

Besides broadening promotion opportunities, the European Commission has also established a detailed set of rules according to which promotion takes place in all possible instances – annual promotion exercise, appointment to a vacant post at higher level, appointment of an AST official in the AD function group and reclassification of contract staff. All these sets of rules provide for procedures to be followed; rights and obligations of both officials and the Administration; involvement, composition and competences of committees or advisory bodies; as well as possibilities of review of decisions taken at several stages of the process. Although all these sets of rules provide for a broad discretion of the EU Administration in promotion matters, this discretion is limited by a number of requirements and basic principles the EU Administration needs to keep in mind.

The foregoing illustrates that the situation in the European Commission has improved as compared to the past. However, problems remain. Arguably the most important problem is the fact that promotion via annual promotion exercises appears, in practice, to be commonly regarded as a right of all officials. It is broadly expected that, sooner or later, all Commission officials are to be promoted to the next grade. This must be consciously or subconsciously considered by all involved persons, including those who conduct performance evaluation. Officials who are 'due' for promotion can thus in practice be granted one or two promotion points more than those who still 'can wait'. If this is indeed the case, the performance evaluation loses its value and does not necessarily and fully reflect the real quality of work of European Commission officials. Rather, it is used as a tool for ensuring regular promotion of all staff. In effect, promotion occurring in this manner loses its principal feature, namely the recognition of, and reward for, good performance. Of course, such a system does not force individual staff members to reach out to inappropriate sources for help in their promotion because promotion is, in practice, more or less guaranteed in the system. From the point of view of ensuring the independence and impartiality of staff this is thus not a problem. Nevertheless, the effect of the system on staff performance could be seriously questioned, while it is precisely this effect that is to be ensured by good performance evaluation.

In comparison, the UN Secretariat still needs to find a way in which effective promotion opportunities will be provided for all staff so that they do not seek out possibilities of influence on their career prospects by external sources, such as governments that would attempt to influence promotion decisions. The existing annual salary increases, resulting from satisfactory performance, can compensate stagnation at the same career level only to some, and arguably limited, extent. Another recommendation to be made for the UN Secretariat relates to the existing legal framework for promotions. Eligibility and other conditions for promotion should be guaranteed not only by an administrative instruction, which can be changed at any time by the Secretary-General himself, but (also) by the *UN Staff Regulations* and/or *Rules*, thereby enhancing predictability and legal certainty for all UN staff.

In both the UN Secretariat and the European Commission promotion needs to have a better linkage to staff merit than is the case at present. It is true that both the UN Secretariat and the European Commission claim that promotion of their respective staff occurs solely on the basis of merit. However, this could be disputed for both organizations: In the UN Secretariat, this is because there are other criteria that must be taken into account when a specific post is being filled, such as the need to ensure equitable geographical distribution at all levels. And the same applies for the European Commission, where promotion of senior officials to a higher grade partly depends on factors, such as the need to ensure geographical and gender balance at all levels. Furthermore, in the European Commission, eligibility of all staff for promotion is also determined by taking into account their seniority, both *de jure* and *de facto*.[384] It could be argued that if staff promotion is linked solely to their merits, staff will have no option but to perform well. It will also eliminate the incentive to seek external help to advance their chances of climbing higher on the career ladder. Although it appears that in both the UN Secretariat and the European Commission possibilities for such influences from outside have been limited by the adoption and enforcement of more precise and transparent rules, where there is a will, there is a way. No chances should therefore be taken.

---

[384] *De jure* importance of seniority in the Commission promotion policy is reflected in the requirement of minimum two years in grade prior to the promotion, regardless of the manner in which promotion takes place. Moreover, seniority is a formal factor that must be taken into account in the promotion of senior officials through annual exercises. *De facto* importance of seniority in promotion in the European Commission can be seen in cases of promotion of staff below senior level through annual promotion exercises – it takes time to accumulate sufficient points and reach the promotion threshold. In addition, the averaging of points throughout the Commission limits the possible positive consequences of excellent performance by those officials who happen to serve in a directorate-general performing above the Commission's overall average, although there is a possibility of increasing the number of points by granting an exception to the relevant Directorate-General.

Chapter

5

MOBILITY

1. Introduction

Staff mobility is the last method through which vacant posts maybe filled both in the UN Secretariat and in the European Commission. It comprises a broad range of possible moves, including not only those within the same organizational unit but also those involving a change in duty station.

As explained in the introduction to this study, regular mobility of staff is important for individual professional development, providing the staff members with an opportunity to acquire new knowledge and/or skills they can then use to the benefit of the organization they serve in. At the same time, mobility allows international secretariats to deploy their human resources in a flexible manner, thereby responding effectively to the needs of the day. Regular mobility also helps to ensure that no individual staff member 'owns' the post he holds and that his decisions and work are open to scrutiny by his successor. This enhances the chances that each staff member's performance is of the highest possible quality and free of nepotism.

The following sections show how mobility is managed in the UN Secretariat and in the European Commission.

2. Mobility in the UN Secretariat

2.1. Development of the UN mobility policy

The *UN Staff Regulations* do not contain an explicit legal basis for either mandatory or voluntary mobility of staff. The only relevant regulation in this context is Regulation 1.2(c) of the *UN Staff Regulations* stipulating in its relevant part:

> *Staff members are subject to the authority of the Secretary-General and to assignment by him or her to any of the activities or offices of the United Nations...*[1]

The Secretary-General is thus equipped with the right to place staff where needed, which includes a possibility to remove an individual staff member from one position and assign him elsewhere. As pointed out by the UNAT:

> *... [I]t is obvious [from Regulation 1.2] that the Secretary-General may relieve a staff member of certain duties or invest the staff member with other duties according to the exigencies of the service, of which he is the sole judge.*[2]

---

[1] *UN Staff Regulations of 2009*, Regulation 1.2(c).

[2] *Kahale v. Secretary-General of the United Nations, UNAT Judgment No. 165 [1972]*, available at http://untreaty.un.org/UNAT/UNAT_Judgements/Judgements_E/UNAT_00165_E.pdf, last visited on 30.12.2010, para. XIII. Note that UNAT made a legal distinction between staff transfer and staff reassignment in this case. While transfer involves a move from one organizational unit to another, reassignment refers to a move within the same organizational unit involving only a change of duties. Nonetheless, both transfer and reassignment fall under Regulation 1.2 of the *UN Staff Regulations* – para. XIV., p. 419.

The idea behind this broad authority granted to the Secretary-General is to provide him with tools needed in order to ensure the proper operation of the UN.[3]

Nonetheless, regular mobility – voluntary or mandatory – is neither envisaged by the *UN Staff Regulations* or *Rules*, nor practiced. In the past, the UN staff were not expected at all to move from one post to another in any systematic manner. Once employed, staff members remained, in principle, in their post until eventual promotion, save for special cases, such as post abolition. If any other staff movement occurred, it was on an *ad hoc* and voluntary basis.[4] In 1986, the Group of High Intergovernmental Experts referred to as G-18 recommended, however, that a job rotation system among various duty stations should be developed for all UN Professional staff, constituting a part of their career development plans.[5] In reaction, the Secretary-General reported in 1987 to the General Assembly that mobility was now 'encouraged as part of the [recently initiated] vacancy management and staff redeployment system', on the basis of which all staff assignment, including promotion, was regulated, and that a rotation and mobility system were worked on.[6] The idea of introducing systematic mobility has become a part of the human resources reform ever since.

In the 1990s, a number of resolutions were adopted by the UN General Assembly calling for increased mobility of internationally recruited staff.[7] In resolution 53/221 the General Assembly even stressed that mobility of internationally recruited staff was to be 'an integral part' of their employment obligations.[8] Responding to these

[3] See, for example, *Detière v. Secretary-General of the Civil Aviation Organization, UNAT Judgment No. 136 [1970]*, available at http://untreaty.un.org/UNAT/UNAT_Judgements/Judgements_E/UNAT_00136_E.pdf, last visited on 30.12.2010, para. V. The authority of the Secretary-General to transfer UN staff members is, though broad, not unlimited. In the present case the UNAT admitted, by implication, that the conditions of employment, stipulated in the letter of appointment, could restrict the right of the UN Administration to transfer staff. – *ibid.*, para. III, p. 212. See also Amerasinghe, *The Law of the International Civil Service, Volume II*, p. 884. In addition, in case of a legal challenge, the UNAT would examine whether a decision to transfer a staff member has paid regard to all relevant considerations, including the interest of the service and the interests of the staff member concerned. – For example, *Furst v. Secretary-General of the United Nations, UNAT Judgment No. 241 [1979]*, available at http://untreaty.un.org/UNAT/UNAT_Judgements/Judgements_E/UNAT_00241_E.pdf, last visited on 30.12.2010, para. V, p. 108. The UNAT would also examine whether the Administration has exercised its discretion to assign staff to a specific activity in good faith and whether this discretion has not been tainted by some extraneous factors, such as prejudice, arbitrariness, improper motive, or discrimination. – *Case No. 1415, UNAT Judgment No. 1313 [2006]*, available at http://untreaty.un.org/UNAT/UNAT_Judgements/Judgements_E/UNAT_01313_E.pdf, last visited on 30.12.2010, paras. V-VI and *Case No. 1479, UNAT Judgment No. 1408 [2008]*, available at http://untreaty.un.org/UNAT/UNAT_Judgements/Judgements_E/UNAT_01408_E.pdf, last visited on 30.12.2010, para. III.

[4] *Human Resources Management Reform, Report of the Secretary-General, A/55/253*, Section II, Part D, para. 38. See also Annex III, para. 2.

[5] *G18 Report*, Recommendation 49, p. 21.

[6] *Reform and Renewal in the United Nations: Progress Report of the Secretary-General on the Implementation of the General Assembly Resolution 41/213*, para. 46.

[7] See, e.g., *General Assembly Resolution 49/222, A/RES/49/222*, 15.02.1995, available in the Official Document System of the United Nations, available at http://documents.un.org/, last visited on 30.12.2010, Part I, para. 9; and *General Assembly Resolution 51/226B*, Section III, Part D, paras. 6 and 7.

[8] *General Assembly Resolution 53/221*, Section III, para. 7. See also para. 8 calling for mechanisms towards enhanced mobility across the functions, department, duty stations and, if possible, even among

calls, the Secretary-General developed a new mobility policy under which 'mobility would be encouraged, valued and rewarded'.[9] Main elements of the new mobility policy were set out in the Secretary-General's report A/55/253 on *Human Resources Management Reform* of 2000.[10] In this document, mobility was defined broadly as 'the ability of staff to move within and between functions, departments, occupations, duty stations and organization of the United Nations common system'.[11] The policy cornerstones were: an actively managed approach; staff not owning specific posts; and managers not owning specific staff members.[12]

Although the 2000 report of the Secretary-General envisaged 'encouraged' mobility, the eventually adopted system set up in fact mandatory mobility for all UN Professional staff and some staff in the General Service category. The system became effective in 2002 when the first *UN Staff Selection System* entered into force. As explained above, this system incorporated for the first time recruitment, placement, promotion as well as mobility of staff. As far as mobility is concerned, it covered, and still covers, all Professional staff, except of junior staff, and some staff from other categories.[13] The junior Professional staff are covered by a special reassignment programme which was set up two years earlier, in 2000.[14]

The main reasons for the increased efforts to incorporate systematic mobility in the UN human recourses policy were, in particular, the dramatic expansion and modification of UN mandates. As reported by the Secretary-General in his 2000 report, the activities of the UN Secretariat have expended over the past few decades radically and include now a large portion of field activities in technical cooperation, peacekeeping and peace building as well as humanitarian operations. These new mandates required more flexible and more versatile staff capable of being deployed where needed. Nonetheless, the staff of the UN Secretariat remained largely the same as at times when the UN was more static.[15] To cope with the problems of persistently high vacancy rates in some duty stations, more mobility was needed. The Secretary-General had to emphasize, though, that there was no single and straightforward manner to increase mobility in the UN and that simple rotation

organizations of the UN system.

[9] *Human Resources Management Reform, Report of the Secretary-General, A/55/253*, Annex III, para. 1. See also *Human Resources Management Reform, Report of the Secretary-General, A/53/414*, Section III, Part D, para. 40.

[10] *Human Resources Management Reform, Report of the Secretary-General, A/55/253*, Section II, Part D and Annex III.

[11] Ibid., Annex III, para. 11. See also Section II, Part D, para. 40.

[12] Ibid., Annex III, para. 11.

[13] *UN Staff Selection System of 2002, UN Staff Selection System of 2006, revised in January 2010*, and currently *UN Staff Selection System*, in all instances Sections 2.1 an 3.2.

[14] Currently *Administrative Instruction, Managed Reassignment Programme for Junior Professional Staff, ST/AI/2001/7*, 28.08.2001, available in the Human Resources Handbook of the United Nations, available at http://www.un.org/hr_handbook/English/, last visited on 30.12.2010. See also *Implementation of the Mobility Policy, Report of the Secretary-General, A/62/215*, 08.08.2007, available in the Official Document System of the United Nations, available at http://documents.un.org/, last visited on 30.12.2010, para. 18.

[15] *Human Resources Management Reform, Report of the Secretary-General, A/55/253*, Annex III, para. 2.

would not work in the UN Secretariat.[16] Therefore, he attempted to set up a system that would reflect the scope and nature of the UN work, which differs considerably from the other international organizations. The Secretary-General explained that the number of Professional staff and the number of different occupational groups was large and differed among various duty stations, some of the staff even being highly specialized and serving only in certain locations. The Secretary-General's conclusion was that mobility in the UN Secretariat must differ from that in other organizations, including UN funds and programmes, and that straightforward rotation was unfeasible.[17]

As a result, a number of mechanisms were developed for implementation of and campaigning for active mobility in the UN Secretariat, including introduction of time-limited post occupancy; priority issuance of compendium of all vacancies for lateral moves; a condition of prior mobility for promotions; encouragement and facilitation of mission service; establishment of occupational networks between departments with closely linked mandates and/or common interests; and attention to work/life issues.[18] In addition, as mentioned earlier, a system of managed reassignment programme for junior Professional staff was set up.[19] The proposed policy was approved by the UN General Assembly in its resolution 55/258 of 2001.[20] Subsequently, the policy was fully developed and integrated into the new *UN Staff Selection System* effective since 2002. Section 2.2 of this system provided:

> *All staff, up to and including those at the D-2 level, are expected to move periodically to new functions throughout their careers. To facilitate and regulate mobility, the system provides for the circulation of all vacancies and anticipated mission needs through a compendium, defines maximum periods of occupancy of posts, requires that vacancies be made available in the first instance for lateral*

[16] Ibid., Annex III, para. 22.

[17] *Implementation of the Mobility Policy, Report of the Secretary-General, A/62/215*, para. 14.

[18] *Human Resources Management Reform, Report of the Secretary-General, A/55/253*, Section II, Part D, para. 41. Details on each of the proposed mechanisms can be found in Annex III of the present report.

[19] Ibid., Section II, Part D, para. 41. For details, see Annex III of this report. See also below, section 2.2.2.2.

[20] *General Assembly Resolution 55/258*, Section V. See also Section VI for the corresponding amendment of the relevant provision of the *UN Staff Rules* concerning central review bodies. Note that the General Assembly established a number of guidelines and principles on which the policy had to be based, including that mobility should be one of the essential elements of UN staff contractual status; it should be encouraged at all levels of the Professional and higher categories of posts; criteria need to be developed to ensure that staff are treated in a fair and equitable manner and that mobility is not used as an instrument of coercion against staff; mobility should not negatively affect the continuity and the quality of services and the institutional memory and capacity of the UN; mobility should not lead to the transfer or abolition of posts as a result of vacancies; there should be a clear differentiation between mobility within duty stations and mobility across duty stations, the latter being a more important factor in career advancement; mobility should have a positive impact in filling existing high vacancy rates at some duty stations and regional commissions; it should be supported by improving conditions of life and work at various duty stations; incentives should be developed in order to encourage staff to move to duty stations with chronically high vacancy rates; and appropriate monitoring and accountability measures should be in place. - *General Assembly Resolution 55/258*, Section V, Preamble and paras. 1-6 ; *General Assembly Resolution 57/305*, Section II, paras. 49-52 ; and *General Assembly Resolution 59/266*, Section VIII, paras. 2, 4, 8 and 10-12.

> *moves of eligible staff before other candidates may be considered for selection and specifies the lateral mobility requirement applicable before a staff member may be promoted to the P-5 level.*[21]

Furthermore, Section 6.4 of the *UN Staff Selection System* stipulated:

> *Staff members are encouraged to consider carefully all suitable vacancies in the compendium, as they are expected to move periodically to new positions. This is especially important for staff nearing the maximum occupancy period of the post they encumber.*[22]

These two provisions remained unaffected by the adoption of the new *UN Staff Selection System* in November 2006 and its subsequent amendment that took place in January 2010.[23]

Despite the fact that Section 6.4 of the *UN Staff Selection System* merely 'encouraged' staff falling within its scope, the establishment of the time-limited of post occupancy, one of the above mentioned mechanisms developed for the implementation of the new UN mobility policy, resulted in mobility becoming in fact mandatory. The time-limited post occupancy meant that staff could serve in a particular post only for a limited period of time, which was set generally at five years for posts up to and including the P-5 level and six years for posts above that level.[24] Hence, in principle, all posts in the Professional category became rotational, although a limited number of posts with highly specialized and/or location-specific functions could be designed by the OHRM to be non-rotational. In addition, a delay in the placement of a rotational post in the compendium of vacancies could be, in exceptional cases, requested by either the staff member or the manager concerned. Such request would be subject to legitimate reasons related to personal hardship or organizational interests and it would be examined by the OHRM. Furthermore, in certain special situations, staff members could be exempted from mobility for a specified period of time, normally not longer than one year.[25] Lastly, special rules applied

---

[21] *UN Staff Selection System of 2002*, Section 2.2.

[22] Ibid., Section 6.4.

[23] *UN Staff Selection System of 2006*, and *UN Staff Selection System of 2006, revised in January 2010*, in both instances Section 2.2 and 6.4.

[24] *UN Staff Selection System of 2002*, *UN Staff Selection System of 2006*, and *UN Staff Selection System of 2006, revised in January 2010*, in all instances Sections 1 and 4.2(d). Note that the Assistant Secretary-General for Human Resources Management could set longer or shorter maximum periods. This could be done for certain specific posts and in consultation with the head of the department or office concerned. – Ibid. Note also that the initial proposal of the Secretary-General, outlined in his introduction of the new mobility policy in 2000, intended to give competence to establish 'a normal range of minimum/maximum years for occupancy of each post or set of posts' to managers of the relevant occupational network in consultation with the OHRM. The Secretary-General provided in his policy outline a guideline of 'normally two to five years' of post occupancy. - *Human Resources Management Reform, Report of the Secretary-General, A/55/253*, Annex III, para. 26. In the end, however, the maximum post occupancy period was firmly fixed in the *UN Staff Selection System* itself. Moreover, the first version of this system contained also a minimum period of post occupancy which was two years. Before the expiry of such minimum period, staff were not eligible to apply for another post, subject to some exceptions. - *UN Staff Selection System of 2002*, Section 5.1. This provision was abolished in 2006.

[25] *Investing in People, Report of the Secretary-General, A/61/255*, Section IV, paras. 142-143. See also

– and still apply – to junior staff at the P-2 level who are subject to the Managed Reassignment Programme for Junior Professional Staff. As explained in more detail below, these staff must move to other functions already within the first five years of UN service.[26]

The significance of the maximum period of post occupancy for staff mobility was straightforward – when the post occupancy period expired, staff must have moved to another post. This rule was the starting point from which the active mobility policy had to be carried out.[27] It also meant that movement to another post was not an option, but an obligation – hence the mandatory nature of the UN mobility policy, mentioned above, though it must be noted that the UN Secretary-General preferred the term 'managed'. This term was also used for the programme set up for the first organized movement of staff that took place in 2007, i.e. five years after the introduction of the original *UN Staff Selection System*. It concerned all staff who had reached their maximum post occupancy period envisaged in that system.[28] The 'managed' movement of such staff took place in a phased manner and in accordance with the *Administrative Instruction, Managed Reassignment Programme* ST/AI/2007/2.[29] This instruction covered almost all staff up to D-2 level who were appointed for at least one year and, as already noted, reached a maximum of five years in post.[30] The instruction was based on the idea of managing mandatory staff reassignment 'level by level, in a gradual and phased manner'.[31] The obvious reason

Administrative Instruction, Managed Reassignment Programme, Section 2.4.

[26] See below, section 2.2.2.

[27] The UN Secretary-General explained that the time limit of the post occupancy was to end the practice of 'post ownership', according to which a staff member could be required to free his post only in a limited number of situations, such as in cases of a non-renewal of the personal contract, application for another post, retirement, resignation or dismissal. Such inflexible state of affairs did not correspond, in view of the Secretary-General, to the increasingly changing operational needs of the UN. - *Human Resources Management Reform, Report of the Secretary-General, A/55/253*, Annex III, para. 26.

[28] Note that, in order to prepare staff for future mandatory mobility, several pilot reassignment exercises took place prior to 2007. Professional staff at the P-3, P-4 and P-5 levels could participate in these pilot exercises on a voluntary basis. - *Human Resources Management Reform, Report of the Secretary-General, A/59/263*, Section III, Part D.2(b), para. 79; and *Investing in People, Report of the Secretary-General, A/61/255*, Section IV, para. 126.

[29] *Administrative Instruction, Managed Reassignment Programme.*

[30] Excluded from the programme were junior Professional staff, whose managed mobility was regulated by a separate administrative instruction, as well as some other categories of staff, such as some mission and language staff, staff appointed for a particular office or programme, as well as staff reaching their retirement within a three years period. - Ibid., Sections 2.1 and 2.3; and *Administrative Instruction, Managed Reassignment Programme for Junior Professional Staff*. The exclusion of some categories of staff from the managed reassignment programme under the administrative instruction in question did not mean, however, that these staff would not fall under the UN mandatory mobility policy. All staff to whom the UN Staff Selection System applied were subject to this policy as they all could remain in their post only until the maximum period of the post occupancy expires. The exclusion from the managed reassignment programme thus only meant that movement of these excluded staff was to take place under a different set of rules, some of them identified, others not. - For more details, see *Administrative Instruction, Managed Reassignment Programme*, Section 2.3.

[31] *Implementation of the Mobility Policy, Report of the Secretary-General, A/63/208*, 01.08.2008, available in the Official Document System of the United Nations, available at http://documents.un.org/, last visited on 30.12.2010, Section V, para. 41. See also *Administrative Instruction, Managed Reassignment Programme*, Section 3.1.

for such an approach was the need to spread the reassignment of a great number of staff over a longer period of time, thereby making the workload related to the reassignment exercise more manageable. Moreover, a simultaneous expiration of many post occupancy periods in future could to be avoided in this way.

As a result, four managed reassignment exercises were scheduled for a number of grades from May 2007 until November 2008, to be followed by further exercises in future.[32] For each exercise a compendium of post announcements was issued, including only posts that were included in the exercise at issue. The compendium was circulated to all staff members who served at the same level and whose post occupancy periods had expired.[33] It was also made available to the staff participating in the exercise via a special module of the Galaxy, the UN electronic staffing system.[34] All these staff were required to apply for one or, preferably, more posts listed in the compendium and accept the post for which they were subsequently selected.[35] If staff due to move did not apply and express preference for any post included in the compendium, they were automatically reviewed against posts corresponding to their competences, qualifications and skills.[36]

The selection process itself was comparable to that applicable under the *UN Staff Selection System*. It included programme managers who evaluated candidates and indicated those of them who would be suitable for posts in their department or office; the OHRM (or the local human resources office, if relevant) who conducted the matching exercise, paying regard to the preferences of individual candidates, choices made by the programme managers and the needs of the UN; and finally the Assistant Secretary-General for Human Resources Management who took the final decision on the placement of staff.[37]

There were two striking differences of the selection process under the *Managed Reassignment Programme* with the *UN Staff Selection System* which was in force at that time. First, under the *Managed Reassignment Programme*, the actual matching between available posts and candidates was done by the OHRM and decision was taken by the Assistant Secretary-General for Human Resources Management for all posts and staff members involved. Under the *UN Staff Selection System*, it was the relevant programme manager who, in fact, decided which candidate was the most suitable for 'his' vacant post, subject to the final decision by the Head of Department or Office. Naturally, since each managed reassignment exercise involved a relatively large number of posts and staff members, it would be difficult, if not impossible,

[32] The planning was as flows: May 2007: staff members at the P-3 and GS-7 levels; November 2007: staff members at the P-4 and GS-6 levels; May 2008: staff members at the P-5 and GS-5 levels; and November 2008: staff members at the D-1 and D-2 levels. - *Administrative Instruction, Managed Reassignment Programme*, Section 3.1.

[33] Ibid., Section 3.3.

[34] *Staff Mobility in the United Nations, Report of the Joint Inspection Unit, JIU/REP/2006/7*, Part III, para. 33(a).

[35] *Administrative Instruction, Managed Reassignment Programme*, Section 3.4.

[36] *Staff Mobility in the United Nations, Report of the Joint Inspection Unit, JIU/REP/2006/7*, Part III, para. 33(b).

[37] *Administrative Instruction, Managed Reassignment Programme*, Sections 3.7-3.9.

to let programme managers to make the choices. However, the adopted approach could result in some programme managers getting assigned into their units staff they were not necessarily satisfied with.

The second striking difference between the *Managed Reassignment Programme* and the *UN Staff Selection System* was the total absence of central review bodies under the former. Under the *UN Staff Selection System*, these bodies reviewed the evaluation criteria established and employed by programme managers in assessing candidates and adherence to applicable procedures.[38] No such oversight existed under the *Managed Reassignment Programme*. The Secretary-General reported that there was a working group which monitored the implementation of the mobility policy, consisting of representatives of staff as well as management, similar to the central review bodies.[39] However, the precise competences of this working group were not specified in the Secretary-General's report and, since the group was not envisaged in the administrative instruction governing the reassignment exercises itself, its competences cannot be found there either.[40]

It should also be noted that it is unclear what the precise relationship between the *Administrative Instruction on Managed Reassignment Programme* and the *UN Staff Selection System* was. As explained earlier, the *UN Staff Selection System* integrated – and still integrates – the recruitment, placement, promotion and mobility of UN staff.[41] Hence, it governed staff mobility as well, providing for procedures to be used, including the issuance of a compendium of vacancies. This compendium contained, *inter alia*, also posts whose incumbents have completed the maximum period of post occupancy.[42] Such posts were thus advertised as vacant and all relevant staff could apply for them. If staff whose post occupancy period had expired did apply, they had to be considered before any other candidate could be selected.[43] And if such staff were not selected for any vacancy, the Assistant Secretary-General for Human Resources Management could decide on their placement outside the normal process.[44] This was confirmed by a provision in the *Administrative Instruction on Managed Reassignment Programme* itself:

> *Staff members included in the managed reassignment programme retain the right to apply and be considered for vacant posts under the regular staff selection*

---

[38] *UN Staff Selection System of 2006*, Section 8. See also Sections 4.4, 7.4 and 9.1.

[39] *Implementation of the Mobility Policy, Report of the Secretary-General, A/62/215*, Part IV, Section D, para. 52.

[40] Ibid., Part IV, Section D, para. 52.

[41] Note that the *UN Staff Selection System* excluded and still excludes certain staff from its scope with regard to appointment, such as junior Professional staff recruited via competitive examinations and staff appointed through the 'G to P' examinations. However, mobility of these staff falls within the scope of the *UN Staff Selection System*, with the notable exception of junior Professional staff at P-2 level whose initial mobility is subject to a separate set of rules contained in a different administrative instruction- *UN Staff Selection System*, Sections 3.2(c), (d) and (f); and *Administrative Instruction, Managed Reassignment Programme for Junior Professional Staff*, Section 2.1

[42] *UN Staff Selection System of 2006, revised in January 2010*, Section 4.2(d).

[43] Ibid., Sections 5.4(a) and 7.2(a).

[44] Ibid., Section 11.1(a).

system governed by administrative instruction ST/AI/2006/3 [UN Staff Selection System]. Should a staff member be selected for a vacancy under that system before the conclusion of the managed reassignment programme, upon acceptance of the offer that staff member should immediately inform the executive or administrative office of his or her current department or office, which will inform the Office of Human Resources Management. In that event, the staff member would no longer be included in the managed reassignment programme but the post vacated would remain available for the placement of other staff participating in the programme.[45]

The reason behind the issuance of a separate administrative instruction for the reassignment exercises of 2007 and 2008 could have been the intention to limit the pool of candidates to be considered for posts that became vacant due to the expiry of the maximum period of post occupancy only to staff due to move, i.e. excluding other possible candidates, such as those eligible for promotion or external candidates. As legitimate a reason as it may be, the ambiguity of applicability of different legal regimes and their possible overlap did not contribute to their transparency and user-friendliness.

Already before the last phase of the first managed reassignment programme began, it had become clear that the programme was not a big success, rather the opposite. In his report *Implementation of the Mobility Policy* of 2008, the Secretary-General admitted that:

in light of the experience of the managed reassignment programme thus far, it would be prudent to explore other means of achieving the objectives, especially in light of the low percentage of staff who reached their maximum post occupancies and who needed to participate in a managed reassignment programme.[46]

and that:

many areas [were identified] that required further clarification and/or review in determining the way forward.[47]

[45] *Administrative Instruction, Managed Reassignment Programme*, Section 3.6.

[46] *Implementation of the Mobility Policy, Report of the Secretary-General, A/63/208*, Section V, Part B, para. 51. The total number of staff in all levels (from P-3 up to and including D-2) who reached the maximum post occupancy and thus became subject to managed reassignment was very low, or, as explicitly admitted by the Secretary-General, minimal – out of 4594 staff members only 141 reached the maximum post occupancy period. This constitutes approximately 3% of the relevant staff. Moreover, the percentage of staff members who have actually moved is negligible – according to the available statistics, only 28,6% of eligible staff at the P-3 level and only 6,67% at the P-4 level have actually moved to another function. Statistics for staff at the remaining P-5 up to D-2 levels were not available at the time when the Secretary-General's report was issued. - *Implementation of the Mobility Policy, Report of the Secretary-General, A/63/208*, Section V, paras. 42 and part B, paras. 46-48. On the other hand, the mobility index has increased from 10, 8% of staff in 2002 to 27, 6% in 2008. The mobility index indicates the annual ratio of the combined number of staff who had moved compared to the total number of staff in the relevant department at the beginning of the year under consideration. - *Implementation of the Mobility Policy, Report of the Secretary-General, A/63/208*, Section V, Part C, para. 54.

[47] *Implementation of the Mobility Policy, Report of the Secretary-General, A/63/208*, Section V, Part C, para. 58.

There were many problems that accompanied the mobility policy set developed by the UN Secretary-General in 2000. One of the immediate complications was the lack of support for systematic mobility among staff. Initially, both programme managers and staff were rather skeptical, though the skepticism was more notable in the headquarter offices in New York, Geneva and Vienna and less so in Nairobi, in regional commissions and field duty stations.[48] In 2006, the Secretary-General claimed, however, that this initial reluctance had been phasing out and acceptance and willingness to participate in the mobility programmes had been increasing. He believed that a new organization culture was being created and mobility was being accepted as an indispensable component of international civil service, although full acceptance remained a considerable challenge.[49] A number of initiatives to promote the mobility policy among the staff and managers and to prepare them for its implementation were undertaken. First of all, various information campaigns, workshops and information sessions, career counseling and enhanced training opportunities have been organized for all staff.[50] In addition, career resource centres were established first in New York and later in all offices away from the Headquarters and regional commissions in order to support and assist staff in planning their career

[48] The Advisory Committee on the Administrative and Budgetary Questions noted in 2000 that there was 'overwhelming support' for the policy from staff representatives in all offices of the UN Secretariat, but not in the Secretariat office in New York. Staff serving in other duty stations appeared to be more enthusiastic about the new mobility policy and about the increased access which they would gain to posts at the UN Headquarters. - *Human Resources Management Reform, Accountability and Responsibility, Personnel Practices and Policies and Management Irregularities, Report of the Advisory Committee on Administrative and Budgetary Questions, A/55/499*, 19.10.2000, available in the Official Document System of the United Nations, available at http://documents.un.org/, last visited on 30.12.2010, Annex VI, Part B, para. (f). The Joint Inspection Unit considered it to be 'interesting, indeed, thought-provoking' that staff serving at the headquarters in New York, Geneva and Vienna were in general more negative towards mandatory mobility, while staff serving in Nairobi and most of regional commissions and field duty stations, like Addis Ababa, were more positive. - *Staff Mobility in the United Nations, Report of the Joint Inspection Unit, JIU/REP/2006/7*, para. 18. Note that a staff survey of 2005 showed that, overall, only about 30 per cent of the UN Secretariat staff believed that the new mobility policy was necessary (and only 22 % of staff serving in New York and 26% of staff serving in Geneva). On the other hand, 26,64 % of staff were of the opinion that the policy was difficult to implement and less than 15% of staff believed that it was helpful in fulfilling their potential. - *A Picture of the UN Staff*, Question 22.

[49] *Investing in People, Report of the Secretary-General, A/61/255*, Part IV, paras. 133-134. See also *Staff Mobility in the United Nations, Note by the Secretary-General, Addendum, Comments of the Secretary-General on the Report of the Joint Inspection Unit, A/61/806/Add.1*, 02.04.2007, available in the Official Document System of the United Nations, available at http://documents.un.org/, last visited on 30.12.2010, para. 10.

[50] *Human Resources Management Reform, Report of the Secretary-General, A/59/263*, Part III, Section D.2(b), para. 85. See also *Investing in People, Report of the Secretary-General, A/61/255*, Part IV, para. 130 and *Implementation of the Mobility Policy, Report of the Secretary-General, A/62/215*, Part IV, Section A, paras. 21-24. Note that the Joint Inspection Unit expressed its dissatisfaction with a lack of prior consultations with staff and management before the new mobility policy was launched, resulting in misgivings about the policy and in inadequate reflection of staff concerns in the policy. - *Staff Mobility in the United Nations, Report of the Joint Inspection Unit, JIU/REP/2006/7*, para. 26-27. The Secretary-General disagreed with these findings. – see *Staff Mobility in the United Nations, Note by the Secretary-General, Addendum, Comments of the Secretary-General on the Report of the Joint Inspection Unit, A/61/806/Add.1*, paras. 6-10.

development, including mobility, and preparing for it.[51] Better career planning was to be ensured also by an improved electronic performance appraisal system which comprised a database with information useful for career planning and training needs assessment. Data provided in the system included career development goals, learning goals and indication of staff members' interest in mission assignments. By making the relevant data available to both staff and managers, the system was supposed to support mutual dialogue on career aspirations and needed competences and help to plan future career moves.[52] Another initiative aimed at better preparation of staff for mandatory mobility was the use of generic job profiles which, *inter alia*, help staff to identify more easily vacancies that suit their wishes and competences.[53]

Another problem with the UN mobility scheme was the unwillingness of staff, notably those serving in the headquarters in New York or in Geneva or Vienna, to relocate to the so-called hardship duty stations, e.g. the UN Office in Nairobi. Such duty stations have been coping with high vacancy rates due to factors like security problems or more difficult life conditions in the country at issue. The Secretary-General has been trying to create incentives for staff in order to enhance mobility to such hardship duty stations and one of these incentives has been incorporated also in the

---

[51] *Human Resources Management Reform, Report of the Secretary-General, A/59/263*, para. 93; *Human Resources Management Reform, Report of the Secretary-General, A/61/228*, para. 130; *Implementation of the Mobility Policy, Report of the Secretary-General, A/62/215*, Section IV, Part B.2, paras. 27-28 ; and *Implementation of the Mobility Policy, Report of the Secretary-General, A/63/208*, Section IV, Part B.2, paras. 28-29. The centres provide opportunities to staff to develop skills, knowledge and competencies which are need for meeting mobility requirements. Besides individual counseling and group (mini) workshops on issue like networking or preparation of job application, the career resource centres also provide other services, such as books, articles, internet-based materials and videos for self-study. - *Human Resources Management Reform, Report of the Secretary-General, A/61/228*, Section IV, para. 130 and *Implementation of the Mobility Policy, Report of the Secretary-General, A/62/215*, Part IV, Section B.2, paras. 27-29. The Secretary-General reported in 2006 that in New York alone there are over 2.400 users of the career resource centre. - *Human Resources Management Reform, Report of the Secretary-General, A/61/228*, Part IV, para. 130. In 2007 he noticed that since the opening of the New York centre in 2002 over 5.200 staff members had used it for workshops and individual counseling. - *Implementation of the Mobility Policy, Report of the Secretary-General, A/62/215*, Section IV, Part B.2, para. 28. In 2008, the figure comprised 5.600 staff members. - *Implementation of the Mobility Policy, Report of the Secretary-General, A/63/208*, Section IV, Part B.2, para. 29.

[52] *Human Resources Management Reform, Report of the Secretary-General, A/61/228*, Section IV, para. 131; *Implementation of the Mobility Policy, Report of the Secretary-General, A/62/215*, Section IV, Part B.3, para. 30; and *Implementation of the Mobility Policy, Report of the Secretary-General, A/63/208*, Section IV, Part B.3, para. 31.

[53] The generic job profiles were developed in 2002 in order to make the classification process more efficient and thereby to facilitate the first stage of the staffing process in the UN by reducing time otherwise spent on drafting and classifying each individual job description. Job profiles have thus been generalized and provide now standard job descriptions for a large group of related jobs with similar duties and responsibilities and with similar education, experience and skill requirements. They are available online and accessible to all UN staff as well as to potential outside candidates. One of the aims of the standardization of job profiles was to increase transparency and consistency in creating vacancy announcements and to enhance clarity in job expectations. Especially the latter was believed be beneficial from the mobility point of view. - *Human Resources Management Reform, Report of the Secretary-General, A/61/228*, Section IV, para. 132; *Implementation of the Mobility Policy, Report of the Secretary-General, A/62/215*, Section IV, Part B.3, para. 31 and part B.4, para. 31; *Implementation of the Mobility Policy, Report of the Secretary-General, A/63/208*, Section IV, Part B.4, para. 32.

UN mobility policy.[54] However, the usefulness of the mobility programme applied in 2007 and 2008 in addressing high vacancy rates in hardship duty stations is not clear.[55]

Encouragement and facilitation of mission service was another issue which required special attention in the UN mobility policy. As already mentioned, the number and the scope of missions conducted under the UN mandate have increased considerably in the last few decades. Consequently, the number of staff needed in these missions has grown accordingly. Unfortunately, many of the posts are filled only with difficulty or remain vacant often and/or for long. The Secretary-General therefore promised that the new mobility policy would be used to address this issue, too. Again, a number of incentives for staff to apply for posts in missions were developed but their effect in practice is not known.[56]

An additional problem which became apparent early during the development of the mobility policy was that increased mobility would inevitably lead to problems with maintaining continuity, quality of work and institutional memory of the UN

---

[54] The existing incentive is considering one lateral move to, or promotion to the P-5 level in, a hardship duty station from another duty station, and a waiver of lateral movement for promotion to the P-5 level in case of service in a non-family mission or duty station. Such service is sufficient for satisfying an existing eligibility criterion for promotion to the P-5 level. Normally, to be eligible for promotion to a P-5 position, at least two prior lateral moves are required. - *UN Staff Selection System*, Section 6.3(a) and (c). Other incentives were proposed by the Secretary-General in his report *Investing in People* of 2006. One of them concerned shorter post occupancy limits in the hardship duty stations. Moreover, staff who would serve in a hardship duty station would be given priority consideration in the selection process for future vacancies coming up in other (i.e. non-hardship) duty stations, enabling staff to move to such non-hardship duty stations more easily. Preferences expressed by staff serving in hardship duty stations in their application for a vacant post elsewhere would receive greater weight during the matching exercise by way of which staff interests and needs of the organization would be compared in the selection process for filling a particular vacancy. - *Investing in People, Report of the Secretary-General, A/61/255*, Part IV, paras. 148 and 150. These measures have, however, not been incorporated in the *UN Staff Selection System* or any other legal instrument. Consequently, they have not been applied in practice thus far.

[55] In resolution 61/244 adopted at the sixty-first session of the UN General Assembly, the Secretary-General was requested to provide such analysis in the framework of the overall analysis of the managed mobility policy. - *General Assembly Resolution 61/244*, Section IV, para. 7. However, the subsequent report of the Secretary-General on the implementation of the mobility policy presented in 2008 did not address this issue. It is possible that such analysis will be provided in the next report, due for the sixty-fifth session of the General Assembly, i.e. in 2010, containing the overall review of the policy in light of its failure admitted in 2008.

[56] Under the previous version of the *UN Staff Selection System*, applicable until April 2010, mission service was stimulated by the recognition of the cumulative service for a total period of at least one year as one later move for promotion purposes. In addition, certain internal candidates on mission were eligible to be considered for a lateral move to a non-mission post at the 15-day mark, i.e. in the very first stream of candidates considered in the selection process. Another incentive concerned promotion possibilities of some staff recruited at the P-3 level for a field mission. Such staff could be considered for vacancies at the P-4 level at the 30-day mark, together with other internal candidates eligible for promotion. Similar position had mission staff appointed at the P-4 level (under the same conditions as the previous category) who was eligible for vacancies at the P-4 or P-5 levels, if they had served a continuous period of 12 months. These staff were also to be considered at the 30-day mark. - *UN Staff Selection System of 2006, revised in January 2010*, Sections 5.3(c), 5.4(b)(i) and 5.5(b)(i).

Secretariat and its specific departments and offices.[57] 'Knowledge management practices' were therefore developed and put into practice.[58]

Arguably the most severe problem the mobility policy had to cope with was, and arguably still is, finding the right balance between the need for increased staff mobility across different duty stations all over the world on the one hand and personal and family life requirements on the other hand. As explained by the Secretary-General, factors like the availability and quality of medical care and schooling, possibilities of spouse employment and security issues do influence staff willingness and ability to move to other duty stations.[59] Therefore, the UN Secretariat developed some initiatives in order to address mentioned concerns. For example, programmes were set up aimed at helping spouses find work in new duty stations.[60] Also the problem

---

[57] *Human Resources Management Reform, Report of the Secretary-General, A/59/263*, Section III, Part D.2(c), para. 87; and *Human Resources Management Reform, Report of the Secretary-General, A/61/228*, Section IV, Part D.2(c), para. 135.

[58] Such practices included cross-training of the staff and their rotation through various assignment so that the knowledge base and institutional memory would be more spread and widely shared. Furthermore, knowledge management techniques and practices have become a part of the campaign promoting mobility policy and, due to the importance of the information technology in this respect, they were also included in courses on information technology training. - *Human Resources Management Reform, Report of the Secretary-General, A/59/263*, Section III, Part D.2(c), paras. 87-88; *Human Resources Management Reform, Report of the Secretary-General, A/61/228*, Section IV, Part D.2(c), para. 135-138; and *Implementation of the Mobility Policy, Report of the Secretary-General, A/62/215*, Section IV, Part D, para. 37. In 2006 the Secretary-General reported on the establishment of a several new initiatives and task forces, such as an electronic content management platform which will include e-management, knowledge sharing and services to intergovernmental bodies; the newly set-up Secretariat Task Force on Knowledge Sharing led by the Dag Hammarskjöld Library working on a Secretariat knowledge-sharing agenda; and the United Nations System Chief Executives Board for Coordination (CEB) Task Force on Knowledge Sharing developing a knowledge-sharing strategy for the whole UN common system. Other initiatives were undertaken by specific departments of the UN Secretariat or UN specialized programmes or agencies, for example the knowledge management tool kit of the Department of Peacekeeping Operations or the mission rooster of the United Nations Human Settlement Programme (UN-Habitat). - *Human Resources Management Reform, Report of the Secretary-General, A/61/228*, Part IV, Section D.2(c), paras. 136 -139.

[59] *Human Resources Management Reform, Report of the Secretary-General, A/55/253*, Annex III, para. 35. A couple of years later the Secretary-General reported that a staff survey showed that the most important barrier related to the difficulties for staff spouses in finding suitable employment at a new duty station or acquiring work permits. Concerns about security and adequate medical facilities had great impact on staff's decisions to move to another duty station, too. - *Human Resources Management Reform, Report of the Secretary-General, A/59/263*, Section III, Part D.2(d), para. 91. Another staff survey from 2005 confirmed that family situation had been or would be the reason preventing 35 per cent of staff from going on mission in the field, supplemented by approximately 13 per cent for other personal reasons and another roughly 13 per cent for recruitment procedures. On the other hand, the impact for those who have been on mission in the field on their career, personal development and professional competence was largely seen as positive – almost 65 % for impact on career; 86% for impact on personal development; and 83% for impact on professional competence. - *A Picture of the UN Staff*, Questions 8(b) and 9.

[60] As reported by the Secretary-General, links were established with an association of companies and organizations with mobile employees, Partnerjob.com, and an association of international companies, Permits Foundation, lobbying governments to relax work permit regulations. In 2004, a separate Spouse Support Programme was set up, comprising creation of a spousal database. This database should enable spouses to become mutually acquainted and to develop useful networks. Further, spouse support networks and focal points for spouse employment had been developed at many duty

related to the obligation of staff moving to another duty station having to renounce their permanent residence status in a country other than the country of their nationality was addressed.[61] However, other work/life issues did not receive attention, such as availability and adequacy of schooling and health care.

As a result, the mobility programme applied in 2007 and 2008 failed and, after the last phase of the programme had been completed, the programme was suspended, pending further review. Many of the issues referred to above were identified as being in need of further reflection and improvement, including the effective transfer of knowledge, work/life issues, and incentives for mobility and hardship.[62] Results of the review were to be presented for the sixty-fifth session of the General-Assembly, i.e. in 2010.[63] This, however, did not happen. The General Assembly therefore re-

stations, the latter at all main duty stations. Additionally, semi-annual job search workshops were introduced by the OHRM with the purpose of assisting spouses in finding employment, managing interviews and developing an information network. A number of other options were being explored, such as telecommuting for spouses or priority consideration of spouses for consulting opportunities. - *Human Resources Management Reform, Report of the Secretary-General, A/59/263*, Section III, Part D.2(d), para. 92; and *Human Resources Management Reform, Report of the Secretary-General, A/61/228*, Section IV, Part D.2(d), paras. 140-143 and 150. See also *Implementation of the Mobility Policy, Report of the Secretary-General, A/62/215*, Section IV, Part C, para. 34; and *Implementation of the Mobility Policy, Report of the Secretary-General, A/63/208*, Section IV, Part C, para. 35.

[61] As explained by the Secretary-General, there was a long-standing policy in the UN, existing since 1954, requiring newly recruited staff members to renounce their permanent resident status in a country other than the country of their nationality. Moreover, the acquisition or retention of such a status after recruitment for UN service was very restricted and possible only in exceptional circumstances. The reason behind this was the general believe that UN officials should be true representatives of the country of their nationality and those who loosen ties with that country should not be employed by the UN. The practice has been consistently applied for decades. In 2006, the Secretary-General proposed its modification in order to, among others, remove an additional 'substantial' obstacle to staff mobility. - *Human Resources Management Reform, Report of the Secretary-General, A/61/228*, Section IV, Part D.3, para. 145 and Annex. This proposal has been discussed by relevant UN organs but no final decision has been taken thus far. – For the most recent discussion, see *Human Resources Management, Report of the Advisory Committee on Administrative and Budgetary Questions, A/65/537*, paras. 81-86 and *General Assembly Resolution 65/247*, Section X.

[62] *Implementation of the Mobility Policy, Report of the Secretary-General, A/63/208*, Section V, Part D, para. 58. See also para. 69. Note that the Office of Internal Oversight Services identified three main problems with the UN mobility policy: first, very low participation in the managed assignment programs; second, negative experiences expressed by many participants in these programmes; and third, questioning of effectiveness of the mobility policy by other stakeholders, in particular staff in the managerial posts. - *In-depth Evaluation of the Office of Human Resources Management, Report of the Office of Internal Oversight Services, A/63/221*, Part IV, Section 2. The OIOS found that the overall satisfaction of staff participating in the mobility programs had been negative, in some cases even deeply disappointing or traumatic. Many staff members reported that their participation in the mobility programmes had had negative impact on their carriers and some claimed negative impact on their productivity. Moreover, almost 70% of managers who have made their views known considered the overall effectiveness of the mobility policy negatively, while being positive about the principles behind the policy at the same time. – Ibid., para. 37-40. The data collected by the OIOS in 2008 are in sharp contradiction with the results of the staff survey of 2005, referred to above, in which most staff who had moved in the past was positive about the change and its impact on their careers and personal as well as professional development. – See above, footnote 59.

[63] *Implementation of the Mobility Policy, Report of the Secretary-General, A/63/208*, Section V, Part C, para. 58. See also *General Assembly Resolution 63/250*, Section VII, para. 5. Note also that the General Assembly decided to review the UN regulations and rules concerning the exercise of authority by

quested the submission of a proposal at its sixty-seventh session that will take place in 2012.[64]

2.2. Current mobility policy in the UN Secretariat

Since the mandatory mobility policy introduced in the early 2000s but suspended in 2008 has not yet been replaced by a new policy, it is rather difficult to determine how mobility is to work in the UN Secretariat at present. The only exception is mobility of the junior Professional staff, regulated separately since 2000. This policy has remained unaffected by the suspension of the policy existing under the *UN Staff Selection System* and the managed reassignment programme. It is described in detail below.[65]

For staff whose mobility was – and still is – to be regulated by the *UN Staff Selection System*, it can only be noted that all elements ensuring the mandatory nature of the policy were removed from the system when its new version was adopted in April 2010. This last version of the *UN Staff Selection System* still provides for an encouragement for staff to move periodically, but it no longer obliges them to move. Section 5.3, which is an equivalent provision to Section 6.4 of the former versions of the *UN Staff Selection System* quoted above, states:

> *Staff members are encouraged to consider carefully all suitable job openings as they are expected to move periodically between positions.*[66]

Furthermore, the new version of Section 2.2 stipulates:

> *Staff in the Professional and above categories, up to and including those at the D-2 level, are expected to move periodically to different organizational units, duty stations, missions or occupational groups throughout their careers. This system provides for the circulation of job openings, including anticipated staffing needs in missions through a compendium of job openings and specifies the lateral mobility requirement applicable for promotions to the P-5 level.*[67]

the Secretary-General to assign and redeploy staff in accordance to the operational needs of the organization and requested the Secretary-General to submit relevant proposals in 2010. - *General Assembly Resolution 63/250*, Section VII, para. 3.

[64] *General Assembly Resolution 65/247*, para. 34. The UN Secretary-General reported in 2010 that 'broad principles on mobility' were being developed, including mobility models that would address 'the variety of needs in this area' and career models which would facilitate career planning . - *Overview of Human Resources Management Reform, Report of the Secretary-General, A/65/305*, paras. 114, 117 and 125-127. He also reported that a voluntary mobility pilot exercise, that had been held in a number of job networks in the meantime, attracted 130 applicants from across the UN and resulted in a mobility rate of 20 per cent (it involved 14 departments/offices and four duty stations). In comparison, the managed reassignment programmes held in 2007 and 2008 resulted in nine per cent mobility rate. – paras. 118-119.

[65] See below, section 2.2.2.

[66] *UN Staff Selection System*, Section 5.3.

[67] Ibid., Section 2.2

The latter provision shows that some mechanisms, developed under the now suspended mandatory mobility policy for its implementation, are still relevant. In fact, they are the only demonstration of the mobility policy for UN non-junior Professional staff at present. However, one of the defining features of the suspended policy that in fact made it mandatory, namely the time-limited post occupancy, was abolished. Moreover, as noted in the previous two chapters, under the current *UN Staff Selection System*, mobility no longer has formal priority before promotion or even before appointment of an external candidate.[68] The position of the mobility policy of UN non-junior Professional staff has thus changed considerably. The following section explains which mechanisms for the implementation of this policy still exist in the UN Secretariat. It focuses on the current state of affairs but, in order to provide a full picture, it also briefly explains how these existing mechanisms changed in comparison to the previous situation. It is then followed by a section describing the UN mobility policy applicable to junior Professional staff.

2.2.1. Mechanisms for implementing UN mobility policy for non-junior Professional staff

As explained above, following the introduction of mobility policy in the UN Secretariat in the early 2000s, the mechanisms developed for its implementation and campaigning included introduction of time-limited post occupancy; priority issuance of a compendium of all vacancies for lateral moves; a condition of prior mobility for promotions; encouragement and facilitation of mission service; establishment of occupational networks between departments with closely linked mandates and/or common interests; and attention to work/life issues.[69] Under the new 2010 *UN Staff Selection System*, only the compendium of vacancies, now referred to as compendium of job openings, and the condition of prior mobility for promotion have been retained. With regard to the occupational networks, now referred to as occupational groups, it is unclear whether they are to play a role in the UN mobility policy envisaged for non-junior Professional staff.[70]

2.2.1.1. Compendium of job openings

Under the previous versions of the *UN Staff Selection System*, the very first objective of the compendiums of vacancies was to encourage staff mobility by informing staff, but also outside candidates, of vacancies and field mission needs.[71] Accordingly, the compendium listed all existing and anticipated vacancies for posts for one year or longer, including both new and abandoned posts, but also posts whose occupants have completed the maximum period of post occupancy.[72] All staff falling within the

---

68 See above, chapter 3, section 1.

69 See above, section 2.1.

70 See below, section 2.2.1.3.

71 *UN Staff Selection System of 2002*, *UN Staff Selection System of 2006*, and *UN Staff Selection System of 2006, revised in January 2010*, in all instances Section 4.1.

72 For the last version, see *UN Staff Selection System of 2006, revised in January 2010*, Section 4.2.

UN Staff Selection System were 'expected' to review the compendium of vacancies on a regular basis, with an emphasis for staff whose maximum period of post occupancy was approaching its end.[73] Staff who had applied in order to exercise mobility through a so-called lateral move were then considered before other internal or external candidates, including internal candidates applying for promotion.[74] Lateral move, defined as move to a different position at the same level for a minimum period of one year, was regarded by the UN Secretary-General as the principal means of increasing staff mobility.[75] In this respect, the compendium of vacancies was seen as the key mechanism for implementing lateral mobility in the UN Secretariat.[76] It was considered to be 'a comprehensive monitoring tool, a clearing-house mechanism that promotes transparency by providing staff with information on all vacancies and matches openings with skills'.[77]

At present, the *UN Staff Selection System* still encourages staff to consider suitable job openings carefully, with a view of moving periodically to other suitable positions.[78] However, since the time-limited post occupancy was abolished, the system no longer *requires* any staff member to apply. In addition, mobility lost its priority status vis-à-vis other means of filling vacant posts, such as promotion of another internal candidate or appointment of an external candidate.[79] Moreover, mobility is in fact not very much emphasized by the current *UN Staff Selection System*, and the encouragement of mobility is no longer explicitly regarded as an objective of the compendium of job openings. Actually, the current *UN Staff Selection System* does not expressly provide for any objectives of the compendium of job openings. It only stipulates what job openings are to be included in it and when it is to be published. When a staff member applies for such a job opening, for example because he wishes to move to another position at the same level, his application is considered in accordance with the general procedure for staff selection, explained in detail in chapter 3 of this study.[80] Unlike in the past, there are no special provisions that would need to be borne in mind in such instances. Not only is there no priority for lateral movement when compared to promotion of other internal candidates or appointment of external candidates, there is also no possibility to place staff members who applied for a job opening but were not selected outside the normal process. Such

[73] Ibid., Annex III, para. 2.

[74] For the last version, see Ibid., Section 5.4. Such staff were considered at the 15-day mark, i.e. within 15 calendar days after posting the vacancy in the compendium, with some exceptions. – Sections 4.5 and 5.6. Staff applying for promotion, i.e. move to a post one level higher than the level of the current post, were considered at the 30-day mark, i.e. after candidates applying for lateral move. - Section 5.5.

[75] For the definition of lateral move under the previous *UN Staff Selection System*, see Ibid., Section 1. The notion 'different position' was interpreted broadly, including e.g. a new position in the same or different department or office, duty station, or UN organization, involving a change of place, function, supervisor or responsibilities. – Ibid. For details on the current definition of lateral move, and existing exceptions, see below, section 2.2.1.2.

[76] *Human Resources Management Reform, Report of the Secretary-General, A/55/253*, Annex III, para. 27.

[77] Ibid., Annex III, para. 41.

[78] *UN Staff Selection System*, Section 5.3.

[79] See also above, chapter 3, section 1.

[80] See above chapter 3, section 2.2.2.2.

a possibility existed under the past systems with regard to staff members whose maximum period of post occupancy had expired. The decision on the placement was taken by the Assistant Secretary-General for Human resources Management after having determined the availability of a suitable position in consultation with the Head of Department/Office and the staff member concerned. The central review body was subsequently informed of the matter.[81]

2.2.1.2. Promotion eligibility requirement of a prior lateral move

Despite the fact that UN non-junior Professional staff are no longer subject to mandatory mobility, if they wish to be promoted to the P-5 level they must have moved between different positions. First of all, staff who had entered the UN Secretariat at the junior or middle level must have gone through a promotion from one level to another. This is due to the fact that, as explained in the previous chapter, promotions in the UN Secretariat are, in principle, only possible through movement exactly one level up.[82] Given that promotion in the UN always means appointment to a new position, staff would have changed positions one or more times before reaching the P-4 level from which they may apply for promotion to the P-5 level. The number of moves would then depend on the level at which each individual staff member joined the UN Secretariat.

The second reason for UN non-junior Professional staff movement between different positions before being eligible for promotion to the P-5 level is the requirement set out in Section 6.3 of the *UN Staff Selection System*. This provision requires that before promotion to the P-5 level staff laterally moves at least two times, though, as explained in more detail below, a number of exceptions exist in this respect.[83] What exactly should be understood under lateral move is provided in Section 1 of the *UN Staff Selection System*. There lateral move is defined as:

> *movement of a staff member to a different position at the same level for the duration of at least one year.*[84]

It follows that the definition of lateral move has three elements: first, movement needs to be to 'a different position'; second, it must occur at the same level; and third, appointment in this different position must last at least one year. While the second and the third element of the definition are self-evident, the first one needed further elaboration and was provided in the same section of the *UN Staff Selection System*:

---

[81] See *UN Staff Selection System of 2006, revised in January 2010*, Sections 11.1(a) and 11.2. This placement outside the normal process was based on Regulation 1.2(c) the *UN Staff Regulations*, explicitly referred to in the *UN Staff Selection System*, which provided – and still provides - that UN staff members are subject to the authority of the Secretary-General to assign them to any activity or office of the UN. - *UN Staff Regulations of 2009*, Regulation 1.2(c).

[82] For details, see above, chapter 4, section 2.1.2.1.

[83] *UN Staff Selection System*, Section 6.3. For the exceptions to this rule, see below in this section.

[84] Ibid., Section 1(q).

> *The new position may be in the same or a different department or office, in the same or a different duty station and in the same or a different occupational group. Inter-agency loans or other movements to and from other organizations of the United Nations common system are recognized as "lateral moves".*[85]

The different (or new) position that counts towards a lateral move is thus defined broadly. It includes positions in the same department or office, in the same duty station and in the same occupational group. The *UN Staff Selection System*, however, also provides that if the move occurs in the same department or office, it must involve a change in functions. In cases in which the supervisor remains the same, the move must involve a substantial change in the staff member's responsibilities or a change in the department or office in which the staff member concerned serves. The *UN Staff Selection System* explicitly stipulated that no lateral move takes place if only the supervisor changes without a change in functions.[86]

It should be noted that the broad definition of lateral move under the *UN Staff Selection System* seems to be contrary to one of the principles for staff mobility set out by the General Assembly in number of its resolutions, in which the General Assembly required a difference be made between mobility within and mobility across duty stations, with more importance attached to the latter. It also required the development of incentives for mobility between duty stations.[87] The UN Secretary-General did state in one of his reports that movement across various duty stations was encouraged and considered to be a more important factor in one's career advancement than a move within the same duty station.[88] This is, however, not sufficiently reflected in the *UN Staff Selection System*, neither in its current version nor in the previous ones. As noted by the Joint Inspection Unit in 2006, the UN mobility policy does not require staff to move across the duty stations, only to move laterally.[89] Indeed, as mentioned above, the definition of lateral move is rather broad and includes a move to another post at the same level that can occur also within or between different functions, departments or occupations, not necessarily between various duty stations.[90] Not much has changed in this respect since 2006 when the

---

[85] Ibid., Section 1(q). Note that this section also provides that temporary assignments shorter than one year qualify as a lateral move if they last at least three months and if their cumulative duration reaches one year.

[86] Ibid., Section 1(q).

[87] *General Assembly Resolution 55/258*, Section V, paras. 3 and 4; *General Assembly Resolution 57/305*, Section II, para. 49(d); *General Assembly Resolution 59/266*, Section VIII, para. 2(d).

[88] See *Staff Mobility in the United Nations, Note by the Secretary-General, Addendum, Comments of the Secretary-General on the Report of the Joint Inspection Unit, A/61/806/Add.1*, para. 23.

[89] *Staff Mobility in the United Nations, Report of the Joint Inspection Unit, JIU/REP/2006/7*, Part III, Section E, para. 56.

[90] This has been severely criticized by the Joint Inspection Unit. The Unit has stated that such an approach, which does not necessarily lead to the acquisition of a diverse background, 'limits the value of mobility' and results in the policy being perceived as a purely bureaucratic exercise. A survey conducted by the Joint Inspection Unit showed that staff regarded mobility requirement for promotion as one more bureaucratic requirement that needed to be fulfilled but which benefited neither the staff nor the UN. The Joint Inspection Unit concluded that, under such an approach, mobility had become an end in itself rather than a way of improving UN efficiency, clearly contradicting the purposes of the policy sought by its introduction. - Ibid., Section III, Part E, para. 56.

Joint Inspection Unit made the statement referred to above, although the *UN Staff Selection System* does indeed provide for a certain relaxation of the requirement of two prior lateral moves before promotion to the P-5 level in cases in which staff have laterally moved to certain duty stations. According to Section 6.3(a) of the *UN Staff Selection System*, the requirement of two prior lateral moves is reduced to only one prior lateral move for staff who have served for at least one year in the duty station in Nairobi, in a regional economic commission other than that for Europe, or in a field duty station with hardship classification. The same holds for staff who apply for a P-5 position in these duty stations.[91] Furthermore, pursuant to Section 6.3(c) of the *UN Staff Selection System*, the requirement of a prior lateral move is completely waived for staff who have served in a non-family mission or non-family duty station for at least one year.[92] Non-family missions and duty stations are those designated as such by the UN Secretary-General. The designation is based on security considerations not permitting the presence of the family of UN staff at such duty stations.[93]

Although this arrangement could promote mobility between different duty stations, it is questionable whether staff would not rather move laterally two times in order to comply with the eligibility requirement for the P-5 posts than to expose themselves to more difficult conditions of work and/or life in the duty stations at hand, especially if they have no guarantee of moving to a 'more attractive' duty station afterwards. It should also be noted that this less stringent requirement of lateral move from and/or to hardship and non-family duty stations and missions was not introduced in order to encourage mobility across different duty stations. Rather, as explicitly stated in the provision relating to the hardship duty stations itself, it was introduced with a view to meeting concerns about high job opening rates in such stations.[94] The Secretary-General considers this arrangement to demonstrate the existence of a clear differentiation between mobility within duty stations on the one hand and mobility across various duty stations on the other, as consistently required by the General Assembly. However, the two rules at issue relate only to some duty stations, in fact those with chronically high vacancy rates, while the request of the General Assembly is broader and includes movement across any duty station. The idea behind the General Assembly's request for differentiation between the move within and the move across various duty stations is to broaden staff background, which should be the underlining rationale for the whole mobility policy. At present, there is neither an obligation for staff to move across duty stations, nor is there any incentive. The only existing incentive concerns hardship duty stations and non-family duty stations and missions. In 2007, the Secretary-General announced the introduction of a precondition for promotion to P-5 level and above, according to which 'geographical mobility or service at a field mission or another agency, for at

[91] *UN Staff Selection System*, Section 6.3(a). Hardship classification of a duty stations follows standards established by the International Civil Service Commission and depends on the overall quality of life at that duty station as assessed by the Commission, taking into account factors such as local conditions of safety and security, health care, education, housing, climate, isolation etc. – See Ibid., footnote 13.

[92] Ibid., Section 6.3(c).

[93] See *UN Staff Rules*, Rule 3.19.

[94] *UN Staff Selection System*, Section 6.3(a). See also a specific request of the General Assembly in this respect - *General Assembly Resolution 59/266*, Section VIII, para. 8.

least one year in the same or a different duty station' will have to take place before promotion.[95] However, thus far, no such measure has been adopted and, as explained above, promotion to the P-5 level can take place also after prior lateral moves that took place within the same duty station, even the same department or office.

The relaxation of the requirement of two prior lateral moves to just one if the move was to a hardship duty station and its waiver if the move was to a non-family mission or duty station are two exceptions to the general rule for eligibility for promotion to the P-5 level. Apart from them, there are two more exceptions. First, staff who join the UN Secretariat at the P-4 level need to laterally move just once before becoming eligible for a P-5 position.[96] This clearly reflects the fact that such staff enter the UN at the later stage of their career, having gone through a previous career development already. It would be rather uncommon if the relatively long experience acquired before joining the UN would not have been accompanied by sufficient career progress. If that were the case, the applicant for a job at the UN would most probably not have been successful in the selection process in the first place. Lastly, this requirement does not apply to language staff, which is also unsurprising, given the fact that such staff are subject to a distinct mobility policy, described below, while they serve at the junior level.[97]

2.2.1.3. Occupational groups

Occupational groups are:

> *occupations and sub-occupations grouped into categories of work on the basis of similarity of function.*[98]

Under the previous versions of the *UN Staff Selection System*, occupational groups were referred to as occupational networks, defined as 'a grouping of departments/offices with closely linked mandates or programmes and a common interest in collaborating in areas such as human resources planning, staff development and mobility'.[99] The occupational networks were one of the mechanisms developed by the UN Secretary-General in order to promote and implement staff mobility. Under the past versions of the *UN Staff Selection System*, Heads of Departments and Offices of the UN Secretariat were bestowed with an obligation to work together with other heads of departments and offices belonging to the same occupational network, thereby encouraging multidisciplinary approaches and the accomplishment of human resources management plans.[100] The underlying idea was that such

---

[95] *Staff Mobility in the United Nations, Note by the Secretary-General, Addendum, Comments of the Secretary-General on the Report of the Joint Inspection Unit, A/61/806/Add.1*, para. 23.

[96] *UN Staff Selection System*, Section 6.3(b).

[97] Ibid., Section 6.3(d). See also below, section 2.2.2.1.

[98] Ibid., Section 1(s).

[99] See *UN Staff Selection System of 2002*, *UN Staff Selection System of 2006*, and *UN Staff Selection System of 2006, revised in January 2010*, in all instances Section 1.

[100] For the latest version, see *UN Staff Selection System of 2006, revised in January 2010*, Annex I, para. 4.

collaboration would help staff move to other functions by, among others, providing cross-functional training or by establishing network websites providing staff as well as managers with information necessary for their (career) planning.[101] The expectation was thus that the occupational networks would enable a more systematic development of substantive multidisciplinary skills of staff needed for moving within and across different occupations.[102] The networks were thus designed to utilize affinities between various functions, to divide departmental 'silos' and to promote multidisciplinary approaches.[103] In addition, they were to enable managers to fall back on a larger pool of staff to fill vacancies.[104] Examples of envisaged occupational networks were a network called Peace and Security, Humanitarian Affairs and Human Rights, a network referred to as Economic and Social Development and a network named Resource Management.[105]

The actual establishment of occupational networks took some time. In 2004, i.e. four years after the first introduction of this mechanism, the Secretary-General reported that initial work on a pilot project of a network for managerial and administrative staff had begun.[106] In 2006, the Joint Inspection Unit noted that departmental occupational networks were actually being established.[107] In April 2010, however, when the new *UN Staff Selection System* was adopted, the occupational networks were renamed and redefined, in the sense mentioned earlier in this section. The definition of new occupational groups is more limited when compared to the definition of

Note that the Office of Human Resources Management was originally responsible and accountable for supporting the occupational networks. - *UN Staff Selection System of 2002.*, Annex IV, para. 1(q). This responsibility was not retained under the later version of the *UN Staff Selection System* of 2006, as amended in 2010.

[101] *Human Resources Management Reform, Report of the Secretary-General, A/59/263*, Section III, Part G, para. 120.

[102] Ibid., Section III, Part G, para. 125.

[103] *Human Resources Management Reform, Report of the Secretary-General, A/55/253*, Annex III, para. 23.

[104] Ibid., Annex III, para. 25. The idea was that regular meetings of the managers of each occupational network would lead, *inter alia*, to the alignment of human resources plans of involved departments/ offices; discussions of staff succession programmes; addressing vacancies; developing occupation-wide job descriptions; and carrying out joint trainings. – Ibid.

[105] Ibid., Annex III, para. 23. In this report, the Secretary-General named the three examples of possible future occupational networks that could be established in the UN Secretariat, mentioned in the main text above. The first occupational network Peace and Security, Humanitarian Affairs and Human Rights would include the Department of Political Affairs, Department of Peacekeeping Operations, Office for the Coordination of Humanitarian Affairs, Office of the United Nations High Commissioner for Human Rights, Department for Disarmament Affairs). The second proposed network Economic and Social Development would include the Department of Economic and Social Affairs, regional commissions, United Nations Conference for Trade and Development, United Nations Office of Drug Control and Crime Prevention, United Nations Environment Programme, Habitat). The third proposed network Resource Management would include the Office of Programme Planning, Budget and Accounts, Office of Human Resources Management, OCSS (including Information Technology Services Division), executive offices and administrative offices at offices away from Headquarters. *Human Resources Management Reform, Report of the Secretary-General, A/55/253*, Annex III, para. 24.

[106] *Human Resources Management Reform, Report of the Secretary-General, A/59/263*, Section III, Part D, para. 77

[107] *Staff Mobility in the United Nations, Report of the Joint Inspection Unit, JIU/REP/2006/7*, Section III, Part B, para. 31.

the former occupational networks – it no longer links the new occupational groups to staff mobility. Similarly, obligations of occupational group managers that can be found in the present *UN Staff Selection System* do not seem to relate to issues relevant for the implementation of active mobility policy. It is therefore not entirely clear what role, if any, new occupational groups are to play in supporting mobility of non-junior Professional staff in the UN Secretariat. At present, the *UN Staff Selection System* does not seem to grant occupational groups any direct role in promoting and/or implementing staff mobility. The most probable explanation of this state of affairs is that no new mobility policy for such staff has been established thus far.

2.2.2. Mobility of junior Professional staff

The overall approach to mobility of junior Professional staff differs from that applying to staff at higher levels. While staff serving in posts above the entry level are expected but no longer obliged to move regularly and in, principle, at least two times before being promoted to the P-5 level, junior staff must move – and even to move several times during the first years of their service in the UN Secretariat. The legal basis for this mobility is contained in the *UN Staff Rules* themselves. Rule 4.16(c) thereof provides:

> *Staff members appointed to the Professional category after a competitive examination shall be subject to mandatory reassignment, under conditions established by the Secretary-General.*[108]

As explained in the chapter of this study on the recruitment procedures in the UN Secretariat, competitive examinations are used for the appointment of P-1 and P-2 posts, and sometimes also P-3 posts, which are subject to the geographical distribution or special language requirements and for the appointment of staff from General Service and related categories to the P-2 posts in the Professional category.[109] Hence, all entry level staff appointed via the NCRE, competitive language examinations or 'G to P' examinations are subject to mandatory reassignment, as stipulated by the provision of the *UN Staff Rules* quoted above. No such provision can be found in the *UN Staff Rules* for staff above the entry level. As explained above, mobility at these higher levels is regulated by the *UN Staff Selection System*. That system excludes from its scope junior Professional staff – not only with regard to appointment, but also with regard to mobility. The relevant part of Section 3.2 of the *UN Staff Selection System* stipulates:

> *The system shall not apply to the following:*
>
> ...
>
> *(c) Appointment of staff selected through a competitive examination under staff rule 4.16, in accordance with the principle that staff are recruited exclusively through competitive examination at the P-1 and P-2 levels for positions subject*

[108] *UN Staff Rules*, Rule 4.16(c).

[109] See above, chapter 3, section 2.2.1.

to geographic distribution and normally through competitive examination at the P-3 level;

(d) Movement of staff subsequent to recruitment under the provisions of the administrative instruction on managed reassignment for junior Professionals;

(e) Movement during the first five years of service of staff serving against a P-2 or P-3 language position who are subject to the provisions of the administrative instruction setting out special conditions for recruitment or placement of candidates successful in a competitive examination for positions requiring special language skills;

(f) Recruitment of staff from the General Service and related categories to the Professional category; ...[110]

Hence, junior Professionals in P-1 and P-2 posts subject to geographical distribution or special language skills recruited exclusively through the NCRE or competitive language examination in accordance with Rule 4.16 of the *UN Staff Rules*, or junior Professional staff at P-2 level recruited through 'G to P' examinations fall outside the scope of the *UN Staff Selection System* – with regard to both appointment and subsequent movements. The movement of language staff at P-3 level too falls outside the system.

As stipulated by the provision of the *UN Staff Rules* mentioned above, all junior staff recruited via competitive examinations are subject to mandatory reassignment, i.e. compulsory movement. Such movement takes place under conditions set out in separate administrative instructions. For non-language staff at P-2 level recruited through the NCRE or 'G to P' examinations, it is the *Administrative Instruction Managed Reassignment Programme for Junior Professional Staff ST/AI/2001/7*, mentioned earlier.[111] For language staff at P-2 and P-3 level, it is the *Administrative Instruction Special Conditions for Recruitment or Placement of Candidates Successful in a Competitive Examination for Posts Requiring Special Language Skills ST/AI/2000/1*, as amended.[112] P-1 staff are not covered by these two instructions, the reasons for it probably being that, in practice, appointments at P-1 level no longer take place in the UN Secretariat.

In this respect it should be noted that it is not clear what the position is of externally recruited junior Professional staff who are *not* subject to geographical distribution or special languages requirements. As explained in the section of this study dealing with recruitment procedures in the UN Secretariat, since 2009 such staff may be recruited outside the system of competitive examinations. Therefore, their appointment should, in principle, fall within the scope of the *UN Staff Selection System*.[113]

---

[110] *UN Staff Selection System*, Section 3.2. Rule 4.15 of the *UN Staff Rules* concerns central review bodies and Rule 4.16 competitive examinations.

[111] *Administrative Instruction, Managed Reassignment Programme for Junior Professional Staff*. It should be noted that P-1 staff is not

[112] *Administrative Instruction, Special Conditions for Recruitment or Placement of Candidates Successful in a Competitive Examination for Posts Requiring Special Language Skills*.

[113] See above, chapter 3, sections 2.2.1.1 and 2.2.2.1.

As far as mobility of these staff is concerned, they are not covered by either of the two administrative instructions ST/AI/2001/7 and ST/AI/200/1 – the former covers only P-2 staff appointed through a competitive examination, i.e. staff subject to geographical distribution recruited via the NCRE or staff recruited from General Service and related categories via 'G to P' examination, and the latter applies only to language staff.[114] Therefore, mobility of externally recruited P-2 staff not subject to geographical distribution or special language requirements should fall under the *UN Staff Selection System*. Section 3.2 of this system, quoted above, only excludes junior Professional staff subject to the managed reassignment programme for junior Professional staff, i.e. P-2 staff subject to geographical distribution and therefore recruited through the NCRE and staff recruited through 'G to P' examinations, or P-2 staff appointed to language posts. As for the *Administrative Instruction Managed Reassignment Programme*, it was adopted, and the programme implemented, before the change of the *UN Staff Rules* in 2009 was adopted, introducing a differentiation in the manner of external appointment between junior Professional staff subject to geographical distribution or special language requirements and junior Professional staff not subject to either of the two. Consequently, the managed reassignment programme of 2007-2008 did not cover any junior Professional staff, disregarding its status. It remains to be seen whether this changes after the current review of the UN mobility policy.

One more note needs to be made with regard to non-language junior Professional staff appointed through a competitive examination, i.e. staff subject to geographical distribution and recruited via the NCRE and staff recruited via the 'G to P' examinations. Such staff appointed before 1 January 2000 are not covered by the managed reassignment programme for junior Professional staff.[115] Movement of these staff should thus fall within the scope of the *UN Staff Selection System*. However, this is the case only for staff who have *not* agreed to participate in voluntary reassignment programmes.[116] Staff agreeing to do so are reassigned in accordance with rules applicable to these programmes. This provision has become less important over time since most junior Professional staff appointed before 2000 have in the interim moved on and most probably got promoted to a higher level. They will therefore fall within the mobility programme envisaged for staff above the junior level.

To sum up, the following regimes apply to movement of various categories of UN junior Professional staff:

- language staff – placement under the *Administrative Instruction Special Conditions for Recruitment or Placement of Candidates Successful in a Competitive Examination for Posts Requiring Special Language Skills ST/AI/2000/1* – includes P-3 language staff;

[114] *Administrative Instruction, Managed Reassignment Programme for Junior Professional Staff*, Section 2.1 and *Administrative Instruction, Special Conditions for Recruitment or Placement of Candidates Successful in a Competitive Examination for Posts Requiring Special Language Skills*, Section 1.

[115] *Administrative Instruction, Managed Reassignment Programme for Junior Professional Staff*, Section 2.1.

[116] *UN Staff Selection System*, Section 3.2(k).

- staff subject to geographical distribution and therefore recruited via the NCRE and appointed *after* 1 January 2000 – movement under the *Administrative Instruction Managed Reassignment Programme for Junior Professional Staff ST/AI/2001/7*;
- staff subject to geographical distribution and therefore recruited via the NCRE and appointed *before* 1 January 2000 – movement under voluntary reassignment programmes, referred to in the *UN Staff Selection System*;
- staff appointed through 'G to P' examination *after* 1 January 2000 - movement under the *Administrative Instruction Managed Reassignment Programme for Junior Professional Staff ST/AI/2001/7*;
- staff appointed through 'G to P' examination *before* 1 January 2000 - movement under voluntary reassignment programmes, referred to in the *UN Staff Selection System*;
- other staff – movement under the *UN Staff Selection System*.

Having clarified the scope of different regimes applicable to movement of junior Professional staff, the main features of each of these regimes is now explained.

2.2.2.1. Mobility of junior language staff

Although the *Administrative Instruction Special Conditions for Recruitment or Placement of Candidates Successful in a Competitive Examination for Posts Requiring Special Language Skills ST/AI/2000/1* is considered as the appropriate legal instrument governing movement of junior language staff, there are only two provisions in this instruction relating to mobility. One provision requires that staff appointed to a post in a duty station other than headquarters spends the first six months of their appointment in the headquarters service for the purposes of training, before moving to the duty station outside headquarters.[117]

The second relevant provision stipulates that staff recruited for language posts are expected to serve, after completing successfully the trial period, at least five years in language posts before they may move to non-language posts. Such a move includes both assignment to and selection for such a non-language post. On the other hand, during this period, when the language staff must stay in language-posts, they may be assigned to any language post in the UN, in accordance with its needs, and disregarding the duty station.[118] This means that how often and how far language staff move depends solely on the decision by the UN Administration. No further requirements are set out. There is thus no expected regularity or periodicity of staff movement either. This differs considerably from non-language staff who are subject to the managed reassignment programme for junior Professional staff under the administrative instruction ST/AI/2001/7, discussed below.

[117] *Administrative Instruction, Special Conditions for Recruitment or Placement of Candidates Successful in a Competitive Examination for Posts Requiring Special Language Skills*, Section 2.3.

[118] Ibid., Section 2.2.

2.2.2.2. Managed reassignment programme for junior Professional staff

All P-2 staff appointed since 2000 through the NCRE or 'G to P' examinations are expected, and even obliged, to move during the first five years of service to another function. Under the *Managed Reassignment Programme for Junior Professional Staff*, as set out in the administrative instruction ST/AI/2001/7, these staff are considered for a new post after they complete just two years in their first post. The rationale behind this lies in the idea that junior staff should receive enhanced orientation and training in order to 'facilitate their adjustment and to accelerate the learning period leading to productive work and job satisfaction as international civil servants'.[119]

The *Managed Reassignment Programme for Junior Professional Staff* was established in 2000. It was first proposed by the Secretary-General in his report *Renewing the United Nations: A Programme for Reform A/51/950* and subsequently endorsed by the General Assembly in its resolution 51/226 of 1997.[120] This initial proposal was rather general and included not only junior but all UN staff. However, in developing a comprehensive Secretariat-wide mobility policy the emphasis was put in the first instance on entry-level Professional staff.[121] A few years later, the experience with the programme for junior staff constituted the basis for establishing a comprehensive mobility system for all staff.[122]

As already explained, the programme is mandatory for all Professional staff serving at the P-2 level who were appointed after 1 January 2000 either via the NCRE or via the examination available to staff of General Service and related categories for recruitment into the Professional category.[123] The programme does not apply to P-2 staff who have moved in the meantime to a post with different functions or were promoted.[124] All staff subject to the mandatory reassignment are informed about their obligation to follow the programme in their job offers as well as letters of appointment. In particular, the staff are informed that they will be expected to serve in two different functions during the first five years of their employment at the UN and that they will be required to move for the first time sometime between the second and third year of service.[125]

---

[119] *Administrative Instruction, Managed Reassignment Programme for Junior Professional Staff*, Section 1.1.

[120] *General Assembly Resolution 51/226B*, Section III, Part D, para. 6. See also *Human Resources Management Reform, Report of the Secretary-General, A/53/414*, Section III, Part D, para. 45.

[121] *Human Resources Management Reform, Report of the Secretary-General, A/53/414*, Section III, Part D, para. 40. See also *Human Resources Management Reform, Report of the Secretary General, A/55/253*, Annex III, para. 37. Details of the initial approach to the *Managed Reassignment Programme for Junior Professional Staff* can be found in *Human Resources Management Reform, Report of the Secretary-General, A/53/414*, para. 45.

[122] *Investing in People, Report of the Secretary-General, A/61/255*, para. 126.

[123] *Administrative Instruction, Managed Reassignment Programme for Junior Professional Staff*, Section 2.1.

[124] Ibid., Section 2.2.

[125] For example, *Implementation of the Mobility Policy, Report of the Secretary-General, A/62/215*, Section III, para. 18.

With regard to the procedure, it is very similar to that applied in 2007 and 2008 in the managed reassignment programme involving staff above the junior level. It begins with a compendium of job opportunities issued by the OHRM. Such a compendium is issued once a year for all P-2 posts that are either vacant or occupied for at least 2 years by P-2 staff falling within the scope of the programme. It includes all occupational groups and all duty stations.[126] After the compendium is released, all P-2 staff falling under the programme and who have been in the same post for two to three years are informed by the OHRM that they are obliged to apply for one or more posts listed in the compendium. Staff members may apply for more than one and less than six posts and, if so, they may indicate their order of preference. Apart from the application form, they must also hand in the last performance appraisal report, their curriculum vitae and information on their contractual status.[127] The ORHM submits all applications to the programme managers who review them, evaluate candidates and rank them as qualified for service in their department or office. The OHRM then conducts the matching exercise of all candidates. The matching exercise involves comparison of the qualifications and preferences of the candidates and the needs and preferences of specific departments and offices. The final decision on the reassignment of each candidate is made by the Assistant Secretary-General for Human Resources Management.[128]

Scheme 18: Managed reassignment programme procedure for junior Professional staff in the UN Secretariat

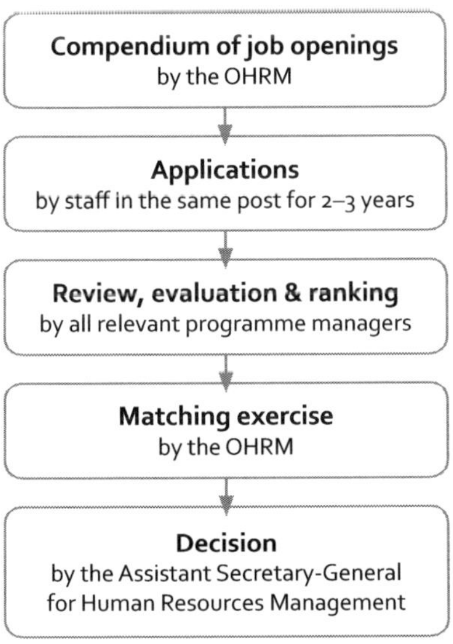

[126] *Administrative Instruction, Managed Reassignment Programme for Junior Professional Staff*, Section 3.
[127] Ibid., Section 4.
[128] Ibid., Section 5.

As under the managed reassignment programme for staff above the junior level, so also in this process no additional – review or advisory – bodies take part. No reference is made to the relevant central review body to check adherence to the advertised evaluation criteria or consistency of the selection with the procedural requirements.

In 2006, the UN Secretary-General reported that since the introduction of the reassignment programmes for junior Professional staff, in total 182 staff at the P-2 level moved within the first five years of their service. That constituted 83 per cent of all P-2 staff. Approximately 25 per cent of staff who moved were promoted and 37 per cent moved laterally on their own, while another 38 per cent moved through managed reassignment.[129] In the 2008 report on the implementation of the mobility policy, the last available report in this respect, the Secretary-General stated that the P-2 staff had acted proactively since the introduction of mobility policy and sought to comply with it even before being required to do so. The Secretary-General reported that more than half of P-2 staff eligible for mobility had changed jobs outside of the management reassignment programme by means of promotion, lateral move or temporary reassignment. The remaining staff members were to be moved through the managed reassignment program by the OHRM.[130] In his most recent report of 2010, the Secretary-General declared the managed reassignment programme for junior Professional staff to be 'quite successful'.[131] He reported that mobility rates of these staff were between 57 and 82 per cent. For 2009, the figures were as follows: 37 staff members participated in the programme, 96 per cent of them changed department, 68 per cent changed duty station and 72 per cent changed occupational group.[132]

2.2.2.3. Voluntary reassignment programmes

Although the distinction between staff appointed before and after 2000 is no longer relevant as all staff at the P-2 level appointed before 2000 have moved by now one way or another, in order to complete the picture it should be clarified that voluntary movement of staff appointed before 2000 occurred under procedures similar to the managed reassignment programme for junior Professional staff. The procedures of the voluntary reassignment programmes included a compendium of all vacant P-2 posts, circulated to all eligible staff, an invitation – not a requirement – to apply, applications accompanied by the relevant documents, reviews by the programme managers, a matching exercise by the OHRM and a decision by the Assistant Secretary-General for Human Resource Management.[133]

---

[129] *Human Resources Management Reform, Report of the Secretary-General, Corrigendum, A/61/228/Corr.1*, available in the Official Document System of the United Nations, available at http://documents.un.org/, last visited on 30.12.2010, para. 128.

[130] *Implementation of the Mobility Policy, Report of the Secretary-General, A/62/215*, Section III, para. 19.

[131] *Overview of Human Resources Management Reform, Report of the Secretary-General, A/65/305*, para. 109.

[132] Ibid., para. 109.

[133] *Human Resources Management Reform, Report of the Secretary-General, A/55/253*, Annex III, para.39

Scheme 19: Voluntary reassignment programme procedure for junior Professional staff in the UN Secretariat

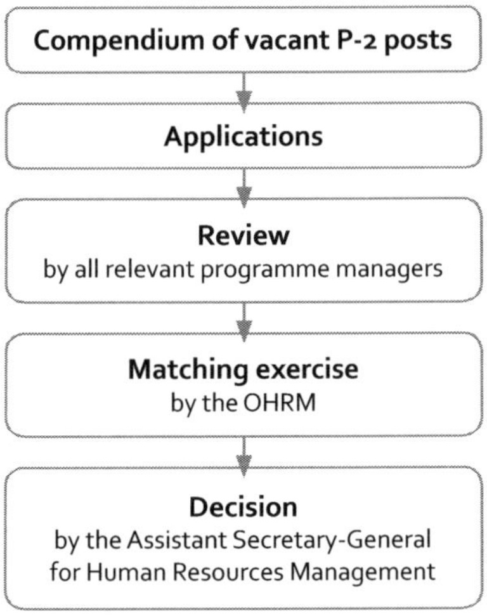

2.2.2.4. Mobility of other junior staff

Junior Professional staff outside the categories falling under the managed or voluntary reassignment, described above, should be subject to the mobility policy applicable to the rest of the staff. Consequently, the *UN Staff Selection System*, which also incorporates staff mobility, should be applicable to movement of all other junior staff who are within the scope of this system. To recall, these staff are no longer subject to mandatory mobility but are expected to consider suitable job openings with a view to moving regularly. If they apply for a specific job opening listed in the compendium, procedures for filling vacant posts under the *UN Staff Selection System* will be followed, including submission of applications, eligibility check, consideration and selection by the relevant programme manager, review by the central review body in question and final decision on appointment into a specific post by the Head of Department or Office.[134]

3. Mobility in the European Commission

The rationale behind the mobility policy in the European Commission is explained in the *Commission Guidelines on Mobility* of 2002 as follows:

> *Mobility has two basic aims: the first is to satisfy the requirements of the Institution in terms of performance, efficiency and quality of service, enabling the organization to adapt to an ever-changing environment. The second is to*

---

and *UN Staff Selection System of 2006*, Section 3.2(h).

[134] For details, see above chapter 3, section 2.2.2.2.

meet the needs of the individual in terms of interest, challenge, achievement and career development. When properly managed, mobility can thus be beneficial to both the Institution and the individual.[135]

In the *Commission Compilation Document on Senior Officials Policy*, the mobility objectives are explained as follows:

Mobility is an important management tool which is in the interest of both the Institution and the staff concerned. This applies in particular to senior officials. Mobility offers professional enrichment by widening experience and skills and fosters motivation for new management and policy challenges. It also tends to stimulate new thinking and improved performance within the services. Regular mobility of officials is also an additional safeguard for the Commission in policy areas where substantial budgets are managed.[136]

The Commission has also stressed that the changes of the last decades in many policy fields, such as external policy, biotechnology or economics, confront it with many 'unexpected political challenges' requiring swift and competent responses.[137] It is therefore essential that the institution is and remains equipped with highly competent and inventive staff and research has shown that regular change of functions fosters creativity and innovativeness.[138] The following parts show how the mobility policy has been applied in the European Commission in the past and is being observed at present.

3.1. Brief historical overview

In theory, mobility in the European Commission is not a new phenomenon. As in the UN, also in the EU there has always been a possibility of transferring officials to other posts at the same level or, under certain circumstances and on a temporary basis, even to a higher level. Article 7 of the *EU Staff Regulations*, which constitutes the legal basis for such transfers, has not been substantially altered since the first staff regulations were adopted in 1961.[139] Similarly, Article 4, third paragraph of the *EU Staff Regulations*, providing for priority of transfer of staff when filling a vacant post, and Article 8 thereof, providing for a possibility of transfer of an official temporarily

[135] *Communication from Vice-President KINNOCK to the Commission, Guidelines on Mobility, SEC(2002)146*, 05.02.2002, available in the Register of Commission Documents, available at http://ec.europa.eu/transparency/regdoc/rep/2/2002/EN/2-2002-146-EN-1-0.Pdf, last visited on 30.12.2010, Section 2.

[136] *Commission Compilation Document on Senior Officials Policy*, Section 9.1., first paragraph.

[137] Commission's archived website *Reforming the Commission*, available at http://ec.europa.eu/reform/2002/chapter02_en.htm , last visited on 24.11.2008.

[138] Ibid.

[139] *EU Staff Regulations of 1961*, Article 7. The only exception is introduction of a possibility for EC officials to apply for a transfer within their institution, i.e. to take an active step rather than waiting for another placement. This possibility was created in 1972. - *Regulation (Euratom, ECSC, EEC) No 1473/72 of the Council of 30 June 1972 Amending Regulation (EEC, Euratom, ECSC) No 259/68 Laying Down the Staff Regulations of Officials and the Conditions of Employment of Other Servants of the European Communities*, OJ L 160, 16.07.1972, p. 1-16, English special edition: Series I Chapter 1972(III), p. 703, Article 7.

serving in another institution to that institution, have not been altered since the adoption of the first *Staff Regulations* in 1961.[140]

Hence, a clear legal basis for staff mobility has always been available in the EU, involving a wide discretion on the side of EU institutions to dispose of their respective staff in accordance with their needs and tasks. The ECJ even explicitly approved a system of rotation that formally existed in the European Commission at some point. In *Carbognani* the ECJ stated:

> *... the rotation system is intended to achieve a number of objectives such as the mobility of departments, diversification and optimum use of officials' experience, closer ties between the central administration and its external offices and the securing of balanced careers for the officials concerned.*[141]

Therefore, an institution adopting a decision transferring an official under a system of rotation cannot be regarded as exceeding its powers of administration and management.[142]

Despite the availability of legal tools, mobility in the European Commission appeared to be limited in the past. In 1968, Coombes, for example, noted:

> *[T]here is still no European civil service in the sense of easy movement from one part of the administration to another; even movement between Divisions of the same Directorate General is often difficult.*[143]

On the other hand, there are those who claim that the situation was perhaps not that bad. According to Page, for example, the widely held view that there is little mobility within the EU is not necessarily correct, given the relative lack of systematic data about careers of national civil servants and of criteria to be used for determining the 'normal' or desirable degree of mobility. Page did admit that there was indeed not much mobility between major European institutions. In his view, this was due to the dominance of the Commission, not often recruiting officials serving in other institutions on the one hand, and not many officials leaving the Commission for other EU institutions on the other. However, Page believed that mobility within the Commission itself was in fact not that limited. In this context, he referred to a study conducted in the 1980s, according to which approximately 40 per cent of officials who had been in the Commission for ten to 12 years and reached the A4 and A5 level moved to another Directorate-General one or two times. In case of senior officials who had joined the Commission at the junior level, 61 per cent worked in another Directorate-General.[144]

---

[140] For details on these provisions, see below, introductory part to section 3.2.

[141] *Maria Grazia Carbognani and Marisa Coda Zabetta v. Commission of the European Communities*, Joined cases 161/80 and 162/80, ECR [1981], p. 543, para. 30.

[142] Ibid., para. 30.

[143] Coombes, *Towards a European Civil Service*, p. 39.

[144] Page, *People Who Run Europe*, p. 34-35.

According to Stevens, the situation was considerably less flattering and 'the obstacles to mobility within the Commission [were] abnormally severe', though.[145] As a result, the Commission 'has suffered from a culture of immobility'.[146] Indeed, between 1990 and 1997, only four per cent of all Commission staff moved across the Directorates-General per year, while moves between the Commission and other EU institutions were even rarer.[147] Arguably, data used by Stevens in her assessment of Commission mobility rate are more adequate than that Page used. While Page considered a number of officials who have moved over a relatively long period of time – ten to 12 years for officials at the middle level and the long-life career of senior officials, Stevens focused on the annual rate of moves. Note that the Commission itself considered mobility of its officials to be satisfactory. In 2002 it reported that between 1990 and 1999, i.e. in a ten-year period, 8.669 officials changed posts between departments. This amounted, in the Commission's view, to about a thousand moves per year, not including movement within Directorates-General for which reliable data were not available.[148] Percentage-wise, however, a thousand moves a year amount only to about 6 per cent of all permanent Commission staff.[149]

Returning to Stevens, she criticized the non-existence of an organisation in the EU institutions responsible for systematic career planning of EU staff, including mobility. She noted that the initiative for mobility rested usually with officials themselves, who were often reluctant to change their post and regarded mobility more as a threat rather than a positive contribution to their career development. In addition, the management was also reluctant to give up officials whose knowledge and experience might be difficult to replace. These were, according to Stevens, the main reasons behind limited voluntary mobility in the European Commission. Although possible, an enforced move of a particular official by management was, in Stevens view, 'extremely difficult' because almost all staff had satisfactory performance reports, a point strengthening officials' position of refusing to move. As a result, enforced mobility was infrequent.[150]

Such limited mobility leads to two main difficulties, Stevens and Spence note. The first difficulty is the limited capability of the Commission to adjust to changing staff level requirements, resulting in over- and under-staffed areas. The second problem is an increased danger of mismanagement and corruption in some 'sensitive' posts, such as those dealing with personnel and finance.[151]

---

[145] Stevens and Stevens, *The Internal Reform of the Commission*, p. 459.

[146] Ibid.in, pp. , p. 460.

[147] Stevens and Stevens, *Brussels Bureaucrats? The Administration of the European Union*, p. 103. The data come from the *Williamson Report* of 1998. See also Spence and Stevens, *Staff and Personnel Policy in the Commission*, p. 184.

[148] *Commission Guidelines on Mobility*, Section 2.

[149] The calculation was based on the staff figures for 1999 and included permanent staff only. According to date provided in the 1999 second report of the Committee of Independent Experts, there were 16.511 permanent staff serving in the European Commission in 1999. - *Second Report on Reform of the Commission of 1999, Volume II*, Annex IV.

[150] Stevens and Stevens, *Brussels Bureaucrats? The Administration of the European Union*, pp. 103-104. See also Spence and Stevens, *Staff and Personnel Policy in the Commission*, pp. 184-185.

[151] Spence and Stevens, *Staff and Personnel Policy in the Commission*, p. 185.

The problem of insufficient staff mobility was recognized by the Committee of Independent Experts assessing the functioning of the Commission in 1999. The Committee reported that even though the *EU Staff Regulations* allowed and provided means for mobility, its use in practice was inadequate – it neither encouraged staff enough to move, nor did staff aspire to do so. The Committee emphasized long-term benefits of mobility for both the organization and the staff involved and recommended compulsory change of posts with no exceptions. It noted that while setting up maximum lengths of service for all grades and functions might be desirable, the incorporation of mobility as a precondition for promotion and for appointment into leadership or managerial positions was inevitable.[152]

Following the report of the Committee of Independent Experts, the newly appointed Commission saw increased mobility of staff as one of the key objectives of the reform process. In its *White Paper* of 2000 the Commission accepted most recommendations made by the Committee of Independent Experts in this respect but did not consider mandatory mobility to be an adequate solution. The Commission explained its different approach as follows:

> *[I]t would be counterproductive to lay down generally binding rules for mobility. In particular, such rules might lead to a loss of specific expertise that is often acquired after years of "training on the job". Other disruptive effects also need to be avoided, including those provoked by the often too long period of vacancy after a mobility. Efforts to speed up the publication and filling of vacancies will continue. A variety of actions are nevertheless needed to facilitate mobility.*[153]

Among the 'variety of actions' proposed by the Commission were: development of clear and transparent guidelines for mobility; incorporation of mobility as a positive factor in staff appraisal, appointments and promotions; improvements to the existing promotion system and removal of barriers to mobility resulting from this system; development of special training possibilities; and the establishment of special measures for the Commission External Service. Furthermore, each Directorate-General was to be responsible for organizing and monitoring mobility as well as for improving the organization of passing on of relevant responsibilities between officials involved in a mobility exercise. Last but not least, possibilities and specific terms for mobility within EU institutions and for mobility between the Commission and national public and possibly even private sectors were to be explored and developed.[154]

---

[152] *Second Report on Reform of the Commission of 1999, Volume II*, Chapter 6, paras. 6.3.15-6.3.18. Note that this was not the first official call for greater mobility of the Commission staff. In 1979, an independent body who conducted the 'first comprehensive analysis of the European Commission as an administration', identified in its report – known as Spierenburg Report – that insufficient staff mobility was one of the failures which needed to be addressed in the framework of a possible Commission reform. Most of the Spierenburg reform proposals were, however, not taken over by the Commission due to opposition in the Council and in the staff unions. - Dimitrakopoulos, D. G. (ed.), *The Changing European Commission*, Manchester University Press, Manchester / New York, 2004, p. 34.

[153] *Reforming the Commission - A White Paper - Part II - Action Plan*, Chapter IV, Part XIV, Action 36.

[154] *Reforming the Commission - A White Paper - Part I*, Part IV.2. and *Reforming the Commission - A White Paper - Part II - Action Plan*, Chapter IV, Part XIV, Action 36.

Since for most of the parts of the new mobility policy no change of *EU Staff Regulations* was needed, much of it was implemented in a relatively short period of time. The first steps were taken in respect of senior officials as far back as in 1999-2000. Then, in 2002, guidelines on mobility of other than senior officials were adopted. In 2003, the new appraisal and promotions system became operative. Issues for which an amendment of the *EU Staff Regulations* was required, such as secondment, became effective in May 2004.[155]

The policy was based on the following principles: voluntarily mobility for all officials after a minimum of two and a maximum of five years of occupancy of the same post; mandatory mobility for 'sensitive' jobs; facilitation of secondment to other institutions or organisations devoted to furthering the EU's interests, and of staff exchanges between the Commission and Member States; implementation of structured mobility programmes by the Directorates-General, support on mobility matters by a Central Career Guidance Function and local careers officers in the individual Directorates-General; and greater transparency and objectivity in filling vacant posts.[156] Although not explicitly mentioned among the above stated principles, mandatory mobility for middle managers and senior officials should be added to the list of main principles as well.[157] The following parts discuss in more detail how these principles have been reflected in legal rules currently in place in the European Commission.

3.2. Mobility of permanent officials

The Commission makes an explicit distinction between internal and external mobility. Internal mobility refers to transfer to another post within the EU structure, whereas external mobility means temporary posting at a national ministry of a Member State or other organization, i.e. secondment outside the EU structure.[158] Internal mobility is defined as follows:

> *...changing your job or your working environment. It may be a change in the type of work you do (new tasks, implying a new job description), either within the same unit or in another unit, directorate or directorate-general, or even a post outside the Institution. But it may also involve changing unit, directorate or directorate-general while continuing to do the same kind of job.*[159]

[155] Commission's archived website *Reforming the Commission*, available at http://ec.europa.eu/reform/2002/index_en.htm , last visited on 24.11.2008.

[156] Ibid.

[157] Note that the mandatory nature of mobility of middle managers was not originally envisaged. Initially, middle management staff was encouraged to change functions, but not required to do so. – See *An Administration at the Service of Half a Billion Europeans, Staff Reforms at the European Commission, State of Play: Spring 2002*, available at http://ec.europa.eu/reform/2002/documents/staff_reform_2002_en.pdf, last visited on 30.12.2010, Section 2.4.1., p.19.

[158] Commission's archived website *Reforming the Commission*, available at http://ec.europa.eu/reform/2002/chapter07_en.htm, last visited on 24.11.2008.

[159] *Commission Guidelines on Mobility*, Section 1.

Hence, any change, either of the type of work or in the place of work, is considered to fall under this definition. Such change may be either voluntary or mandatory. The latter applies to three groups of officials: first, officials occupying 'sensitive' jobs, such as posts dealing with the award of contracts or subsidies, or determining rights and obligations; second, middle managers, e.g. a Head of Unit or a Head of Delegation; and third, senior officials, i.e. Directors and (Deputy) Directors-General.[160] All other Commission officials are subject to voluntary mobility.

A number of legal provisions contained in the *EU Staff Regulations* are relevant in this respect. First of all, Article 7 gives a large discretion to the EU Administration to assign officials to any post that corresponds to their category and grade. Article 7 reads, in a relevant part, as follows:

> 1. *The Appointing Authority shall, acting solely in the interest of the service and without regard to nationality, assign each official by appointment or transfer to a post in his function group which corresponds to his grade.*
>
>   *An official may apply for a transfer within his institution.*
>
> 2. *An official may be called upon to occupy temporarily a post in a grade in his function group which is higher than his substantive grade. ...*[161]

EU officials are thus assigned to specific posts by either appointment or transfer. Further, each official may himself apply for a transfer to another post within his institution. He may also be transferred to a post of a higher grade without being promoted.[162]

Interpreting Article 7 and the power of EU institutions to move their officials to other posts, the European Court of Justice ruled in *Labeyerie* that the institutions were free in organizing their offices and assigning their staff as suited to the tasks they were required to carry out.[163] The reason behind this is the necessity to create sufficient

---

[160] Note that EU officials serving in a third country are subject to regular mobility, too. Article 2 of the Annex X of the *EU Staff Regulations* concerning *Special and Exceptional Provisions Applicable to Officials Serving in a Third Country* provides that: 'By decision of the appointing authority in the interests of the service, officials [serving in a third country] shall be transferred periodically, if necessary without regard to vacant posts. The Appointing Authority shall make such transfers by a specific procedure referred to as the 'mobility procedure', for which it shall lay down detailed implementing rules, after consulting the Staff Committee.' - *EU Staff Regulations*, Annex X, Article 2.

[161] Ibid., Article 7.

[162] Such transfer is only possible for a limited period with a maximum duration of one year, subject to a few exceptions listed in Article 7(2) of the *EU Staff Regulations*. Note that transfer of an official needs to be distinguished from (re)assignment. Transfer takes place when an official is moved to another post which was vacant, whereas (re)assignment does not require an existence of a vacant post. While reassignment is not subject to any formalities, transfer entails that requirements of Articles 4 and 29 of the *EU Staff Regulations* are complied with. - *Carbognani v. Commission, Joined cases 161/80 and 162/80*, para. 19.

[163] See judgments in *Henri Labeyrie v. Commission of the European Communities, Case 16/67, ECR [1968], p. 293*, and *Geist v. Commission, Case 61/76*. For a recent case on staff mobility, see *Alberto Toronjo Benitez v. Commission of the European Communities, Case F-33/07*, available at http://curia.europa.eu/jurisp/cgi-bin/form.pl?lang=en&Submit=Rechercher&alldocs=alldocs&docj=docj&docop=docop&docor=docor&docjo=docjo&numaff=F-33/07&datefs=&datefe=&nomusuel=&domaine=&mots=&resmax=100, last visited on 30.12.2010.

flexibility for each institution to adapt to changing requirements. Therefore, institutions must be able to reassign staff as they see fit and not need to acquire consent of the staff concerned. In the Court's view, expressed in *Carbognani*, requiring any consent of the staff for their move to another post would impose an intolerable restriction on the institution's discretion.[164] Naturally, the institutions must exercise their discretion with the interest of the service in mind and respect the right of officials to be assigned to a post with the matching grade. On the other hand, the officials are obliged to accept 'any assignment in accordance with the requirements of the service, anywhere in the [Union], in any place of employment within the institution which he serves'.[165] The interest of the service may even override particular personal and/or family circumstances of officials.[166] In *Geist*, for example, the Court noted that a transfer of an official to another place of employment could not be regarded as 'an abnormal and unforeseeable event' in such official's career, even though it could cause the official family or financial difficulties.[167]

Other relevant provisions of the *EU Staff Regulations* related to the issue of staff mobility – or transfer, to use the term employed by the regulations – are Articles 4 and 29 (for movement within and between EU institutions) and Articles 8 and 37-39 (for movement outside the home institution). To begin with Article 4, this provision stipulates in its relevant part the following:

> *If the vacancy cannot be filled by transfer, appointment to a post in accordance with Article 45a or promotion, it shall be notified to the staff of the other institutions, and/or an internal competition shall be organised.*[168]

Similarly, Article 29(1) requires that before a vacant post is filled, transfer, promotion from AST to AD function group and promotion within the institution, transfer from other institution and internal competition are considered first, i.e. before internal or open competition is organized.[169]

As explained earlier, there is no priority rule between transfer and promotion within the institution, but these two means of filling vacant posts are to be considered before the other means mentioned in Articles 4 and 29(1) may be employed. On the other hand, the Administration is only required to consider these various means in the required order but not necessarily to actually use them in that order. It is within the broad discretion of the appointing authority to make the judgment as to which means are the most appropriate to find the most suitable candidate.[170]

---

164 *Carbognani v. Commission, Joined cases 161/80 and 162/80*, para. 28. Note that due to the discretionary nature of a decision reassigning an official to another post, such decision is not subject to judicial review, provided it is not a disguised penalty, is not discriminatory and does not involve misuse of powers. - *Seghers v. Council, Case T-69/92*, para. 38.

165 *Lars Bo Rasmussen v. Commission of the European Communities, Case 173/84, ECR [1986], p. 197*, paras. 24-25. See also *Carbognani v. Commission, Joined cases 161/80 and 162/80*, para. 29.

166 *Carbognani v. Commission, Joined cases 161/80 and 162/80*, para. 37.

167 *Geist v. Commission, Case 61/76*, para. 34.

168 *EU Staff Regulations*, Article 4, third paragraph.

169 Ibid., Article 29(1).

170 See above, chapter 3, section 1.

Another legal provision relevant for staff mobility is Article 8, first paragraph of the *EU Staff Regulations*. It provides for a possibility for officials seconded to other EU institutions to apply for a transfer to those institutions after a period of six months.[171] Secondment within but also outside the EU institutions, i.e. to an organization 'devoted to furthering the [Union's] interests', is governed by Articles 37-39 of the *EU Staff Regulations*.[172] Various possibilities of secondment and conditions related thereto are addressed in more detail below.[173]

The last legal basis related to the issue of staff mobility that should be noted are Commission guidelines and decisions containing more specific rules. Internal mobility of most Commission officials is governed by the *Commission Guidelines on Mobility* adopted in the course of the staff reform in 2002.[174] Rules on mobility for senior officials had been adopted before that time, at the end of 1999, and were subsequently amended. The current regime is set out in the *Commission Compilation Document on Senior Officials Policy*.[175] Last but not least, mobility of middle management staff is addressed at present in the *Commission Decision on Middle Management Staff* of 2008.[176] These three documents are used as the main sources for analysis of the Commission mobility policy in the following parts.

3.2.1. Officials below the middle management level

The *Commission Guidelines on Mobility* repeatedly emphasize that mobility of Commission officials is in principle voluntary.[177] This means that officials do not have to move to another post during their whole career in the European Commission, if they do not wish to, as long as they continue to fulfil the requirements of the post occupy. However, one may not assume that there is no active mobility policy in the European Commission. There is now indeed a clear expectation that officials *will* change positions from time to time.[178] Specific benchmarks have been established for all Commission officials, indicating a minimum and maximum time period an official should spend in one specific post. At the end of that period, officials are assisted in finding another post, if they so wish. Once again, the benchmarks are in principle voluntary and 'may not be imposed on officials', subject to an exception relating to 'sensitive' jobs, addressed below.[179]

The duration of benchmark periods as well as consequences of the expiry of these periods are different for generalists, specialists and for officials in sensitive posts.

---

[171] *EU Staff Regulations*, Article 8, first paragraph.

[172] Ibid., Article 37(b), second indent.

[173] See below, section 3.2.4.

[174] *Commission Guidelines on Mobility*.

[175] *Commission Compilation Document on Senior Officials Policy*, Section 9.

[176] *Commission Decision on Middle Management Staff*, Article 12.

[177] *Commission Guidelines on Mobility*, Section 1, last paragraph; Section 2.1., second indent; Section 2.3, first paragraph; Section 2.3.1.(1); and Section 2.4., second paragraph.

[178] Stevens and Stevens, *The Internal Reform of the Commission*, p. 477.

[179] *Commission Guidelines on Mobility*, Section 2.3. Note that Directorates-General may establish their own arrangements on mobility and career development. – Ibid.

Generalists are not defined in the *Commission Guidelines on Mobility* but, clearly, they are officials who are not specialized in a specific area but possess knowledge in various fields. In case of generalists, there is a minimum of two and a maximum of five years in post, with two exceptions. First, newly recruited generalists should not occupy the same position for more than three years; and second, officials of 55 years of age or older do not fall under the benchmarks, although they may change posts, if they wish. The latter may be asked to take on other activities, though, such as coaching of newcomers.[180]

Once the benchmark period of a generalist approaches the end, he is informed about this fact by the personnel services of his Directorate-General. Such information is provided one year before the end of the period. Each official concerned then needs to decide whether to look for another job or not. In case of an affirmative, personnel services of his current Directorate-General will advise him on available possibilities. Later in the process, if the official concerned applies for a new post, the same personnel services provide him with relevant assistance and possibly also with specific training.[181]

The second group of officials with slightly different benchmarks than generalists are specialists. They occupy posts requiring specific qualifications, i.e. education, expertise or both. Which posts have such requirements is established by each Directorate-General which, in cooperation with the Directorate-General for Human Resources and Security, draws up a list of all such posts, including suggestions on appropriate course of action for each post.[182]

Due to valuable expertise of specialists as well as due to difficulties the Commission sees in finding a balance between the need to ensure good career prospects to all its officials on the one hand and the costs for replacing specialists moving to a more general field of activities on the other, the specialists do not fall under the regular mobility policy. There are no minimum and maximum benchmarks for this group of officials. Specialists can thus, in principle, expect to stay in their professional field.[183] Nonetheless, they do not fall outside the mobility policy entirely. To certain, albeit more limited, extent specialists should change posts from time to time, too. Several means for such moves are suggested in the *Commission Guidelines on Mobility*. For example, Commission departments employing large numbers of specialists can establish arrangements for cross-mobility or rotation in order to facilitate mobility of this staff. Another possibility is temporary posting of officials to another area, for example by way of short-term assignments, such as participation in special projects.[184]

The third group of officials with different benchmarks are those occupying sensitive posts. Such posts are defined as:

[180] Ibid., Section 2.3.1.(2).

[181] Ibid., Section 2.3.1.(3).

[182] Ibid., Section 2.3.2., first paragraph and 2.3.2.(3).

[183] Ibid., Section 2.3.2.(1).

[184] Ibid., Section 2.3.2.(1) and (2).

> *[those] where, through the nature and/or context of the activity involved, there is judged to be an enhanced risk of financial impropriety or potential conflict of interest which could be detrimental to the Commission.*[185]

The 'nature ... of the activity involved' means activities with a high degree of personal judgement in decisions with financial implications, such as decisions in the area of procurement. The 'context' relates to posts with policy-making responsibilities, in which officials might be put under external pressure to reveal sensitive information, thereby endangering the Commission's interests.[186]

Based on this definition and in accordance with the guidelines prepared by the Directorate-General for Budget in this respect, each Directorate-General draws up a list with all sensitive posts in their departments.[187] It is thus clear in each case whether a specific post is considered to be sensitive or not, with relevant consequences for the mobility obligations of the post holder. In order to protect the independence and impartiality of officials in sensitive posts, all these officials are subject to mandatory mobility after a maximum of five years of the occupancy of the specific post. Hence, unlike with other officials, the benchmark periods for those holding sensitive posts are thus compulsory, with a maximum duration of five years.[188]

Also in the case of sensitive posts, one year before the end of the benchmark period the post holder is informed by the personnel services of his Directorate-General that he will be required to move to another post. This information does not come as a surprise. Before taking up the appointment to a sensitive post, officials are informed that the post at hand is classified as sensitive and that they will have to move to another post at the end of the benchmark period.[189]

The compulsory nature of mobility in case of sensitive posts constitutes one of the two existing exceptions from the rule of voluntary mobility in the European Commission. The second exception is transfer in the interest of service under Article 7(1) of the *EU Staff Regulations*. Such transfer may occur without the consent of the official concerned, although he must be informed and consulted in advance, save in exceptional cases. In its *Guidelines on Mobility*, the Commission identifies four situations, in which transfers in the interest of service may take place. First, when an official occupying a sensitive post has not moved at the end of the benchmark period. Second, when an official's performance no longer meets the high standard normally expected. Third, when an official no longer meets qualifications and/or skills required by the function he occupies. And fourth, when there is an urgent need in another department to fulfil an assignment for which the official concerned has matching profile.[190] The four indicated cases of a possible transfer in the interest

---

[185] Ibid., Section 2.3.3.(1).

[186] Ibid., Section 2.3.3.(1), first and second bullet points.

[187] Ibid., Section 2.3.3.(1). In March 2009, 3,109 posts in the European Commission, i.e. 9,4 per cent, were classified as sensitive. The proportion of posts per Directorate-General classified as sensitive varies from 1% to 47%. – *Commission's Human Resources Report 2009*, pp. 7 and 134.

[188] *Commission Guidelines on Mobility*, Section 2.3.3., first paragraph and 2.3.3.(2).

[189] Ibid., Section 2.3.3.(1).

[190] Ibid., Section 2.4. Note that all 'sensitive' posts that are due to become vacant in the near future

of service without a necessary consent of the official in question do not constitute an exhaustive list. There could be other instances in which a 'forced' transfer could take place. Pursuant to Article 7(1) of the *EU Staff Regulations*, it is up to the appointing authority of each EU institution to assign staff members to any post that corresponds to their profile.

Returning to the voluntary or mandatory move to another post after the expiry of the benchmark period, it must be noted that the Commission has tried to improve its organizational framework and to set up procedures helping officials in searching and applying for a new post. Section 2.2. of the *Commission Guideline on Mobility* lists a number of measures announced with a view to enhancing fairness and transparency in the procedures leading to filling vacant posts. The first set of measures related to the publication of vacant posts: systematic and central publication of all vacant posts on the Commission intranet and, where needed, on paper; publication as soon as the vacancy opening is known and no later than its occurrence; and a clear job description and specification of all the requirements for the post. The second set of improvements concerned notifications: no notification of an official's application for the department of origin, unless the official agrees otherwise; and compulsory notification to unsuccessful applicants on the reasons for not being selected. The last group of measures involved the application, selection and the actual move, notably: evaluation of candidates solely on the basis of merit, seeking the best match possible between the official's profile and requirements of the post; a face-to-face interview of all eligible candidates; a period of notice of 20 working days within which the department of origin must release the official selected to another post; compulsory preparation of a briefing file by the departing official for his successor; and full preparation of the new working place, including possible coaching and training, if needed.[191]

The European Commission appears thus to take the mobility of its staff seriously. Emphasizing the importance of mobility and its benefits for both the staff and the institution, the Commission has declared its preparedness to create space for mobility of all officials who wish or must change their posts, but also to hold managers responsible for promoting and implementing the policy within their departments. For example, the evaluation of managers under the career development review (CDR) system should include an assessment of managers' commitment to the mobility policy, although it is not certain whether that indeed is the case – neither the *Commission Decision on Article 43*, which governs the CDR of middle managers, nor the *Commission Compilation Document on Senior Officials Policy*, on the basis of which the CDR of senior officials is conducted, have an express provision to that effect.[192] In addition, personnel services of each Directorate-General have been endowed with the overall responsibility for organizing and monitoring mobility, detecting and solving potential problems, as well as ensuring that managers abide

because of the expiry of the benchmark periods are published on the Commission intranet. Each such post is included in the vacancy announcements one year in advance. – *Ibid.*, Section 2.3.3.(3).

[191] Ibid., Section 2.4.

[192] Ibid., Section 3.2., last paragraph.

by the mobility rules and guidelines.[193] Further, a Central Career Guidance Service, a unit in the Directorate-General for Human Resources and Security, and a network of local career guidance officers were created in order to assist individual officials in their career development.[194]

On the other hand, the promise made in the *White Paper* of 2000 that mobility would be actively encouraged and that there would be a clear link between mobility and promotion has remained unfulfilled. The encouragement of mobility is formally proclaimed in the Commission document but there it stops. There are no identifiable incentives for staff to move, besides their own interest to change jobs once in while. If such interest is present, possibilities exist and movement is facilitated. However, if an individual staff member wishes to remain at the same post for a long period of time, he may do so. In addition, due to the existing promotion scheme in the Commission, he will be regularly promoted as long as his performance is satisfactory. It has even been argued that mobility is in no way advantageous for Commission staff and that it is detrimental to their promotion prospects. When changing jobs, staff may be confronted with the unwillingness of both the former and the new supervisor to award a higher number of promotion points to them. The former supervisor has no interest in 'wasting' points on a leaving staff member, whereas the new supervisor has no interest to award 'unnecessary' points to a staff member who has not yet proven useful to his unit. Due to the fact that both supervisors have a limited number of points they may divide among their staff, they rather use them for staff who will be or have been in their unit longer. It should also be noted that mobility is not a precondition for promotion in the EU at any level, although at the management level it may be an advantage proving one's more extensive and diverse experience. Below the management level, however, no formal or informal link between mobility and promotion is present.

3.2.2. Middle managers

The mobility rules for middle managers were set out first in the Commission Communication of 30 October 2001 and later in the *Commission Decision on Middle Management Staff*.[195] According to this decision, mobility of middle managers is 'not only encouraged and regarded as a determining factor for promotion, but also *compulsory* for all middle management functions (sensitive or not)' (emphasis added).[196] Middle managers are thus obliged to change post five years after they have taken up their duties. They may move to another post earlier but must serve in one post for at least two years. A later move may take place, too. The Director-General of the relevant Directorate-General may decide that an official remains in post for more than five years, if there is a valid reason for such prolongation of the post occupancy

[193] Ibid., Section 3.3. Monitoring and some implementing responsibilities in the area of staff mobility rests with the Directorate-General for Human Resources and Security, overseeing the whole European Commission.

[194] *Commission's Human Resources Report 2009*, pp. 135-136.

[195] Currently, *Commission Decision on Middle Management Staff*.

[196] Ibid., Article 12.1.

and the decision is duly justified. An example of such a postponement, provided in the *Commission Decision on Middle Management Staff* itself, is the completion of a certain specific task or an approaching retirement of the official at hand. In exceptional cases, middle managers may be authorized to stay in the post for a period longer than seven years, or not to move at all.[197] As explained by the Commission, mandatory mobility for officials possessing 'very specific aptitudes' or carrying out 'very specific functions' is not possible and such officials may be granted derogation from compulsory mobility by the Director-General for Human Resources and Security, based on a duly reasoned request of the relevant Director-General.[198]

The actual move of middle managers may occur either within the same Directorate-General or between different Directorates-General. If it takes place within the same Directorate-General, middle management staff are encouraged to move from horizontal to operational functions and vice versa. Similarly, moves from horizontal Directorates-General to vertical or operational Directorates-General and vice versa are also strongly recommended.[199] Horizontal Directorates-General are those that serve all other Directorates-General and Services, for example, the Directorate-General for Human Resources and Security, the Commission Secretariat General or the Legal Service of the Commission. Vertical Directorates-General are policy Directorates-General, such as those dealing with competition, energy, environment or justice. Similar factors are arguably relevant for a distinction between horizontal and vertical functions, though it is not entirely clear – and nowhere defined – what exactly horizontal, vertical or operational functions, or operational Directorates-General, mean.

As far as procedures are concerned, selection and appointment of middle managers to another post at the same level follows the general legal framework for appointment procedures set out in the *Commission Decision on Middle Management Staff* and explained in chapter 4.[200] There are thus no special procedures or rules for cases in which middle managers exercise their mobility.

In some instances, middle managers may be reassigned to a non-managerial function, while retaining their grade. This can happen either when the official concerned has insufficient managerial ability; or when due to certain policy changes in the Commission, its organization chart, and thus the post division and classification, is revised; or at the own request of the official concerned. Procedures to be followed in each of the three mentioned cases are set out in Article 13 of the *Commission Decision on Middle Management Staff*.[201] Since reassignment under this provision is not an exercise of mobility, it is not further addressed in this section.

[197] Ibid., Article 12.3-12.4.

[198] Ibid., Article 12.4. An example of a position entailing a 'very specific aptitude' is a position of a specialized researcher in the Commission Joint Research Centre.

[199] Ibid., Article 12.2.

[200] See above, chapter 4, section 3.2.1.4.1. See also Ibid., Sections 1-3.

[201] Ibid., Article 13.

3.2.3. Senior officials

As already mentioned, the policy on Commission senior officials' mobility was adopted already in 1999, followed by formal decisions confirming and detailing the policy guidelines taken in 1999 and 2000.[202] Adoption of this policy was one of the very first steps in reforming the Commission after the report of the Committee of Independent Experts came out and the new Commission under the presidency of Romano Prodi took office. The core principle of the policy was mandatory mobility for all former A1 and A2 officials after five years and no later than after seven years in post. The policy was implemented right away, leading to a large reshuffle among the senior officials between 1999 and 2003.[203]

Currently, mobility of senior officials is governed by the *Commission Compilation Document on Senior Officials Policy*.[204] According to this document, vacancies at the senior level are generally opened up to competition and are published.[205] However, there are two exceptions to this rule. First, some posts can be published only internally and opened up only for transfer in the context of annual mobility of senior officials. Second, if a specific official has the necessary skills and experience, he may be transferred to another post directly, i.e. without publication.[206]

When a vacancy is published, there are two possibilities for proceeding. First, an internal and inter-institutional procedure provided for in Article 29(1) of the *EU Staff Regulations*, may be used, according to which the vacancy is filled by transfer, appointment of an official serving in AST function group, or by promotion.[207] Second, an external procedure provided for in Article 29(2) of the *EU Staff Regulations* may be used, whereby a new official may be recruited from outside the Commission.[208] In the latter case, however, the possibilities under Article 29(1) of the *EU Staff Regulations* must be explored first.[209] If a vacancy is not published, it is filled, as mentioned above, by transfer of an official who possesses skills and experience needed for the post at hand. Formally, such transfer occurs on the basis of Article 7 of the *EU Staff Regulations*, i.e. in the interests of the service.[210]

All transfers of Commission senior officials, whether occurring on the basis of a direct transfer under Article 7 or on the basis of internal competition under Article 29(1)(a) of the *EU Staff Regulations*, are a means of implementing the Commission mobility policy for senior officials. Before going into the details of this policy, it should first be

---

[202] *European Commission Announces Next Steps in Implementing New Senior Staff Policy*, p. 1.

[203] Stevens and Stevens, *The Internal Reform of the Commission*, p. 477. In 2002 it was reported that since 1999 most senior officials made moves to other posts. - *European Commission Announces Next Steps in Implementing New Senior Staff Policy*, p. 1. By the end of 2003, no Director-General remained on the post for longer than five years. - Stevens and Stevens, *The Internal Reform of the Commission*, p. 477.

[204] *Commission Compilation Document on Senior Officials Policy*, Section 9.

[205] Ibid., Section 4.1. and 4.2., last paragraph.

[206] Ibid., Section 4.1. See also IP/02/124, Annex, para. 1.

[207] Ibid., Section 4.2.(1).

[208] Ibid., Section 4.2.(2).

[209] Ibid., Section 4.2., last paragraph.

[210] Ibid., Sections 4.1. and 9.3. See also SR, Article 7.

stressed that, like middle managers, senior managers too are, in principle, obliged to move regularly. The general rule is that all senior officials serve a minimum of two and a maximum of five years in the same function, with an exceptional possibility to remain in that function for seven years. The length of incumbency of the specific function does not depend on the administrative position of this function, i.e. on its formal categorization, but rather on its substantive content, and therefore, functions that are being performed and corresponding responsibilities.[211] After the expiry of the five-year period, the official at hand is due to move to another function. As already noted, in exceptional circumstances, the maximum period can be extended for an additional two years and thus last up to seven years. Such additional period cannot be extended any further and the concerned official is reassigned to another function at the end of that period.[212]

This obligation to move to another post applies not only to senior officials who have reached the maximum period of post incumbency but also to the following officials: those who have no specific or a provisional assignment, for example because of the restructuring of some services; officials identified by their hierarchy as a potential candidate for mobility for specific reasons; officials on leave on personal grounds wishing to reintegrate the services.[213] An example of a specific reason for which a senior official might need to move before the maximum period of post incumbency expires could be that the newly appointed Commissioner is of the same nationality as his Director-General. As explained in the chapter dealing with the issue of geographical balance in the European Commission, such combination is to be prevented and each Commissioner should have Directors-General with nationality different from his.[214]

Some senior officials are exempted from the obligation to move after five years in function. First of all, senior officials of 62 years of age or more do not fall under the mandatory mobility scheme, although they may request to move.[215] Furthermore, senior officials who serve at the Commission Legal Service and in research areas are subject to special mobility rules outside the general policy.[216] On the other hand, senior officials who have not yet passed five years in the same function may volunteer for mobility.[217]

The 'practical modalities' for implementing the mobility system differ for officials occupying the basic post of Director-General on the one hand and officials holding the basic post of Director on the other hand.[218] With regard to the basic post of Director-General, there are just three rules. First, all posts that are held by those Directors-General who are due to move to another function in a particular year are published.

[211] Ibid., Section 9.2., para. (1)(a).

[212] Ibid., Section 9.1., second paragraph.

[213] Ibid., Section 9.2.

[214] See above, chapter 2, section 3.3.3.

[215] *Commission Compilation Document on Senior Officials Policy*, Section 9.2., para. (1)(b).

[216] Ibid., Section 9.2., para. (1)(c) and (d).

[217] Ibid., Section 9.2., para. (3).

[218] Ibid., Sections 9.3. and 9.4., in both instances the first sentence.

The publication is simultaneous for all the included posts, which are then open to all officials who possess required seniority in grade and function. Subsequently, the Directors-General due for mobility may apply for posts they are interested in.[219]

Second, even though the publication of posts of Directors-General due for mobility is the main rule, there is an exception. Commissioners involved in the selection procedure for a specific vacant post may agree that a certain Director-General who is due for mobility has the necessary skills and experience and should therefore be appointed to the vacant post directly. Such placement would then take place as a transfer in application of Article 7 of the *EU Staff Regulations* and would not include publication.[220]

The third specific rule relating to the mobility of Directors-General concerns those who are due to move but have not (yet) been placed in any post. At the request of the portfolio Commissioner, the Commission may appoint such a Director-General as Advisor *Hors Classe*, giving him a specific work assignment for a maximum and nonrenewable period of six months. If, after the foreseen moves of all due Directors-General are completed, the Director-General in question, serving for the time being as Advisor *Hors Classe*, has no future foreseeable work assignment, the Commission will retire him in the interests of the service under the provision of Article 50 of the *EU Staff Regulations*.[221] The appointment of such a Director-General will thus come to an end.

With regard to senior officials serving in the basic post of Director, rules slightly differ from those applicable to Directors-General. Each year an annual mobility exercise takes place in respect of Directors who are due to move to another function that year. The exercise begins with a list of officials due for mobility. Such a list is drawn up by the Directorate-General for Human Resources in consultation with the supervisors of the Directors in question. If relevant, the exercise includes also vacant posts. Each Director placed on the list is informed about this fact and is invited to make his views and preferences known. They may indicate three preferences for a possible reassignment. Afterwards, they are invited to an interview with either the Director-General of the Directorate-General for Human Resources and Security or the Permanent Rapporteur to the Consultative Committee on Appointments. The reassignment decision is taken by the College of Commissioners *en bloc*, i.e. for all moves at the same time. The decision is taken in agreement with the Directors-General concerned and should to take into account preferences indicated by the involved Directors as much as possible.[222]

In some specific circumstances, the move of a Director who is due for one may be postponed. However, such circumstances must involve either exceptional policy

[219] Ibid., Section 9.3., para. (1).

[220] Ibid., Section 9.3., introductory paragraph and para. (2).

[221] For details on the use and conditions of Article 50 of the *EU Staff Regulations*, see below, chapter 7, section 3.2.5.

[222] *Commission Compilation Document on Senior Officials Policy*, Section 9.4., paras. (1)-(5).

considerations or workload constraints. Moreover, the move to another function may be postponed only once.[223]

If a Director due for mobility is not reassigned because no suitable solution has been found, he is informed when he is nevertheless expected to change functions. He is then automatically included in the following mobility exercise, i.e. the one of the next year, unless the function of the official involved has changed in the meantime.[224]

As with the posts of Directors-General, so in the case of Directors the Commission may appoint an official concerned as, in this case, Principal Adviser. Such official receives a specific work assignment for a limited period of six months. After this period expires, those officials who neither have a foreseeable work assignment as Director (or its equivalent), nor a further specific assignment in the interest of the service as Principal Adviser are retired in the interests of the service under Article 50 of the *EU Staff Regulations*.[225]

3.2.4. Officials' secondment

Apart from regular mobility within the Commission, Commission officials may also move or be moved temporarily to other EU institutions or even other organizations 'devoted to furthering the [Union's] interests'.[226] Such a move is referred to as secondment. It can occur on the initiative of both the Commission, which may move an official in the interests of the service, or the official in question himself.

Secondment in the interests of service includes transfer of an official to a temporary post in the EU structure – a post in another institution, in a cabinet or in the research area. Since the Commission may not send its officials to serve outside the EU structure, secondment in the interests of the service is always an internal move in the sense of staying within the EU structure and EU institutions. Any official in active employment or on personal leave may be seconded in this manner.[227] Conditions of secondment in the interests of the service are set out in Article 38 of the *EU Staff Regulations*. They include competence of the appointing authority to take the decision to second an individual official and to determine the duration of secondment.[228] They also require that the official in question be heard before the decision to second him is taken and set out a number of other rights, such as entitlement to receive a differential payment in his remuneration, if relevant, and reimbursement of all additional expenses; the right to request termination of secondment every six months; the right to retain his post, advancement to a higher step and eligibility for promotion; and the right to be reinstated in his post after his secondment ends.[229]

---

[223] Ibid., Section 9.4., para. (6).

[224] Ibid., Section 9.4., para. (7).

[225] Ibid., Section 9.4., para. (8).

[226] *EU Staff Regulations*, Article 37(b), second indent.

[227] Ibid., Article 37, last paragraph.

[228] Ibid., Article 38(a) and (b).

[229] Ibid., Article 38(c)-(g).

Secondment at the request of the official in question is governed by Article 39 of the *EU Staff Regulations*. As with secondment in the interest of the service, the decision is taken by the relevant appointing authority which also determines the duration of secondment.[230] The official retains his right to advancement to a higher step and to return to his post within the first six months after leaving for secondment if he decides to terminate it.[231] During secondment, however, the official in question loses his eligibility for promotion and the right to return to his post, if secondment is not terminated within the first six months. The seconded official only has the right to be reinstated in another post which corresponds to his grade.[232] These restrictions clearly reflect the fact that this type of secondment takes place upon request of the official. Even though the relevant appointing authority must agree with it and take the formal decision on secondment, it is in principle the will of the official concerned to temporarily change the job, not necessarily the interests of the service. Therefore, the official must be prepared to bear a few negative consequences of his choice to leave the post, including losing the right to return to the same post which can be filled by another official after the first six months period of secondment expires.[233]

3.3. Mobility of 'other servants' and seconded national experts

As is the case with permanent officials, temporary staff too may be assigned, i.e. transferred, to another post when it is in the interest of the institution. In *Tziovas and Schettini*, the ECJ decided that transfer of temporary staff was within the discretion of the EU institutions.[234] Similarly, in *Plug* the ECJ ruled that, on the basis of Article 10(1) of the *EU Conditions of Employment of Other Servants* read together with Article 7(2) of the *EU Staff Regulations*, temporary staff may be called upon to occupy temporarily a post in a higher career bracket. Such temporary posting may not be refused by the staff member concerned.[235]

Article 7 of the *EU Staff Regulations* does not apply by analogy to any other category of 'other servants' – there is no provision to this effect in the *EU Conditions of Employment of Other Servants*. The same applies to national experts seconded to the Commission. Therefore, in principle, other categories of 'other servants' and the seconded national experts should serve all the period of their engagement with the Commission in the post for which they were initially placed.

As for mobility of 'other servants' and seconded national experts initiated by themselves, neither the *EU Conditions of Employment of Other Servants*, nor the Commission decisions on temporary, contract and local staff and on secondment, respectively, contain any provision. Consequently, there is no legal basis for such

---

[230] Ibid., Article 39(a).

[231] Ibid., Article 39(b) and (e).

[232] Ibid., Article 39(f).

[233] Ibid., Article 39(c).

[234] *Mareile Tziovas, née Aldinger, and Gabriella Schettini, née Virgili, v. European Parliament, Joined cases 23 and 24/87, ECR [1988], p. 4395*, paras. 17-19.

[235] *Onno Plug v. Commission of the European Communities, Case 191/81, ECR [1982], p. 4229*, para. 18.

mobility. The only movement of 'other servants' and seconded national experts can thus take place by changing their contract into another contract relating to another job. In case of temporary and contract staff, such changes are subject to limitations with regard to the maximum period during which such a staff member may be engaged, discussed in more detail in the chapter concerning types of appointments used in the European Commission.[236]

4. The UN and the EU compared

4.1. Basic principles

Staff mobility can play an important role in ensuring an independent and impartial civil service. As explained in the introduction to this chapter, mobility helps to ensure that no individual 'owns' the post he holds and that his performance and decisions are free of nepotism that could be, sooner or later, detected by a future holder of this post. The question therefore is not whether, but what kind of, mobility is needed and feasible. Naturally, the answer to this question is not the same for the UN and the EU, since it greatly depends on the structure of the UN and EU respective civil services, reflecting their mandates and, to a certain extent, past developments.

It is therefore interesting to see that the UN Secretariat, whose mandates are much more diverse than those of the European Commission, including not only administrative but also many peacekeeping and other field tasks spread over duty stations with very different work and life conditions, opted for a more rigid mobility scheme than the European Commission. When initially favouring mandatory mobility for, in principle, all staff, the UN Secretary-General intended to create a new culture where broad and regular mobility would be a natural part of employment with the UN. However, the negligible number of staff who moved to another post during the first and so far last managed mobility programme of 2007 and 2008, shows there is no mobility culture in the UN Secretariat despite the mandatory nature of mobility. On the contrary, it appears that voluntary mobility in the European Commission leads to more regular moves, be it within or between various Directorates-General.

Undoubtedly, it is much easier to move to another job in the same city, often even in the same building, than to move to another duty station often located in another country which is not always able to offer comparable or at least adequate working and living conditions. As self-evident as this is, it does not seem to have been sufficiently reflected in the UN mobility policy existing until its suspension in late 2008. For example, there was no guarantee that staff who moved to a more difficult duty station would be able to return to their previous place of employment or to move to a more attractive duty station after having served in a difficult one.[237] Thus the reluctance to move to a less attractive duty station was – and arguably still is – high, and is understandable. For staff from countries with a lower standard of living than that in their duty station, moving to another duty station could mean

[236] See below, chapter 6, section 3.2.

[237] See above, section 2.1.

losing (the prospect of) a better life and much of what these staff have built up for themselves and their families. Furthermore, few staff from countries with a high standard of living are prepared to give up their post without some assurance that it is only temporary. In addition, there is an increasing number of staff living in dual career families. The possibility of spouse employment in countries where UN duty stations are located is, therefore, another important issue in this respect. Indeed, it should be recalled that staff surveys show that family situation and, to a lesser degree, personal reasons are factors preventing UN staff from going on field missions in almost half of the cases, despite the positive effects of such movement reported by staff who did go.[238]

Therefore, serious incentives and effective solutions for work and family life issues are needed before staff mobility becomes a reality in the UN Secretariat. At present, there is only one incentive intended to 'seduce' staff to move to difficult duty stations, namely the acquisition of eligibility for promotion to the P-5 level under more lenient conditions than normally, i.e. after one instead of two prior lateral moves if such a move involves a hardship duty station, and a waiver of the requirement of prior lateral move if the mission or duty station in which staff serve is classified as non-family one.[239] This is, however, a largely insufficient incentive as staff may also move within the same department or duty stations in order to comply with the eligibility requirement for the P-5 level. It is not hard to imagine that most staff move more willingly twice within the same department or the same duty station to gain eligibility for promotion to the P-5 level in this manner rather than moving once to a difficult duty station with no guarantees of a better placement in the future.[240] Other, more effective, incentives are thus needed in order to move UN staff to less attractive duty stations – or to other duty stations in general. The fact that many staff have dual career families requires more effective recognition. Despite a fairly long list of initiatives undertaken in order to help spouse employment in new duty stations, repeatedly reported by the Secretary-General, no analysis has been provided on the effect of these initiatives in practice.[241] The Secretary-General's reports are thus neither very convincing nor motivating for staff at large. Concerns related to personal and family situations are too important, touching upon the most vital issues of peoples' lives, to be satisfied by a list of initiatives whose effectiveness in practice is not demonstrated in any way.

An important question that needs to be answered in analyzing the UN mandatory mobility policy is whether it can truly be expected of all Professional staff to be as

[238] See above, section 2.1.

[239] See above, section 2.2.1.2.

[240] The UN Secretary-General promised in 2007 an introduction of geographical mobility as a precondition for promotion to the P-5 level posts and above in order to ensure that staff acquire diverse background, skills and experience before reaching the P-5 level. - *Staff Mobility in the United Nations, Note by the Secretary-General, Addendum, Comments of the Secretary-General on the Report of the Joint Inspection Unit, A/61/806/Add.1*, Section II, para. 23. However, this was not reflected in the mobility policy and rules according to which the managed mobility programme of 2007 and 2008 was implemented. Neither was – or is – such a rule to be found in the *UN Staff Selection System*.

[241] See above, section 2.1.

mobile as the UN Secretary-General seems to wish. As much as staff believe in the UN and its mission, to the majority of UN staff, professional satisfaction and growth, and personal life, appear to be more important than UN goals. Recent staff surveys, referred to previously, show that while many staff join the UN for idealistic reasons and belief in the UN, more staff join for other reasons, including interesting work and career prospects.[242] The feeling that one's skills are being used and the work is stimulating and satisfying, motivate staff far more than belief in the principles and ideas of the *UN Charter*.[243] This should be borne in mind when forcing – formally or otherwise - staff, many of whom joined the UN before mandatory mobility across the board was introduced, to move to another job, or even to another country, especially if movement is more for its own sake than for professional and personal development or the organization's needs. If not, staff shortages in the UN Secretariat might well spread to duty stations which have not had problems in filling vacancies thus far.[244]

Better linkage to career development and more flexibility are thus needed in future UN mobility policy. The Secretary-General himself stressed that due to the complexity of the UN as an organization, a straightforward rotation would not work and, therefore, differentiation between posts with different job and location requirements was necessary. Nonetheless, the mandatory policy existing until recently could have hardly been more rigid, making no distinction between different type of jobs – with a small and unclear exception for highly specialized jobs which could be declared non-rotational – or between different locations. In principle, mandatory mobility applied to all staff obliged to move every five or six years.[245] Future UN mobility policy will need to be watched. After the suspension of the mobility policy adopted in 2000 and implemented in 2007 and 2008, the UN Secretary-General has

---

[242] *A Picture of the UN Staff*, question 1. The idealistic reasons amounted in 2005 to almost 33 per cent of answers, while doing interesting work and career prospects together amounted to more than 40 per cent of answers. Other indicated reasons were chance, salary, lack of employment prospects elsewhere, wish to remain in the country of the duty station and other. All these other reasons represented above 20 per cent of responses.

[243] Ibid., question 7(a). The factors relating to the feeling that skills are being used and to stimulating and satisfying work were indicated in half of the answer to the question on staff motivation, while belief in the principles and ideals of the *UN Charter* was checked in less than ten percent of answers.

[244] Already in 2006 the Joint Inspection Unit expressed its concerns over the mandatory nature of UN mobility policy, saying it had negative effect on staff morale. However, the Unit admitted that voluntary mobility could make the achievement of its objectives in the UN Secretariat impossible. It therefore recommended managed mobility, where voluntary schemes and attractive incentives would be used and mandatory mobility employed only for sensitive posts (incl. senior posts) or as 'the last resort ... in very special cases and after careful evaluation of previous voluntary mobility incentives'. *Staff Mobility in the United Nations, Report of the Joint Inspection Unit, JIU/REP/2006/7*, Section III, Part C, para. 47. See also para. 46. The Joint Inspection Unit also stressed that mobility should not be a goal in itself, which it found to be the case with the policy then in place in the UN. Instead of being an administrative and bureaucratic exercise, mobility must be managerial and result-based. – Ibid., Section III, Part D, paras. 48 and 52-53; and part E, para. 58..

[245] For the statement of the Secretary-General, see above, section 2.1. See also Ibid., Section III, Part G, paras. 63-64. The Joint Inspection Unit recommended that, in order to ensure transparency in the management of mobility, a list of non-rotational posts should be prepared with clear identification by specialization and location. - *Staff Mobility in the United Nations, Report of the Joint Inspection Unit, JIU/REP/2006/7*, Section III, Part G, para. 66.

not yet presented new proposals in this respect. Although he did remove from the new *UN Staff Selection System* all elements rendering mobility in the UN Secretariat mandatory, it is not certain whether this means a final or a provisional departure from the idea of mandatory mobility. In the end, after a new policy is developed, the *UN Staff Selection System* may be modified again.

The European Commission's approach to staff mobility has been more flexible. First of all, although there is a maximum period during which staff should remain in one post, most staff are 'encouraged', not obliged, to regularly move to another post. Moreover, the European Commission makes a clear distinction between different types of posts. For some, mobility is encouraged, for others it is required and for yet others it is not expected at all. Only sensitive and managerial permanent posts require regular movement of staff.[246] One of the reasons is, as explained earlier, the need to ensure full independence and impartiality of officials occupying such posts because of their increased vulnerability to outside influences – either because of the kind of job they do or because of the level of their responsibilities. On the other hand, the exclusion of posts requiring specialized expertise from regular mobility recognizes the need to preserve and further develop such expertise. In the UN Secretariat, efforts have been made to maintain knowledge and institutional memory by employing various techniques, such as staff training, while in principle all staff had to move. According to the suspended mandatory mobility policy, a limited number of posts of highly specialized nature could be designed as non-rotational, subject to a decision of the OHRM. However, this possibility appears to have been an exception rather than a rule. It was within the full discretion of the OHRM, with no involvement of individual departments or offices that were arguably better capable of judging which posts should not be subject to regular rotation.[247] In the European Commission, it is indeed each individual Directorate-General that draws up a list of posts which, due to their specialized nature, fall outside the scope of voluntary mobility. It is presumed that such list is prepared in each Directorate-General where it is needed. Moreover, the list is not subject to approval by the Directorate-General for Human Resources and Security, only its consultation.[248]

Although mobility of permanent staff in the European Commission for posts for which it is relevant, is voluntary (though 'encouraged'), staff are, in fact, expected to move after their benchmark period has expired. On the other hand, there are no visible incentives for such expected regular movement.[249] For example, there is no link between mobility and promotion possibilities, promised in the *White Paper* of 2000 as one of the means for increasing staff mobility. In the UN Secretariat, mobility was not only mandatory, it was – still is – also a necessary pre-requisite for promotion to the P-5 level, though it can be satisfied by mere movement 'across the corridor'.[250] No such requirement, or incentive, exists in the European Commission.

246 See above, sections 3.2.1-3.2.3.

247 See above, section 2.1.

248 See above, section 3.2.1.

249 See above, section 3.2.1.

250 See above, section 2.2.1.2. Note that the expression 'mobility across the corridor' has been used by

In theory, at least, Commission officials can be promoted to the most senior level without having exercised mobility within or outside their Directorate-General. In reality, Commission officials do appear to move regularly. In 2009, the Commission reported that its foreseen average mobility rate was 20 per cent of the workforce and that this rate was reached in both 2006 and 2007, with data for 2008 being temporarily unavailable. The data for 2006 and 2007 included only moves within and between various Directorates-General. Other entries to, and exits from, the Commission, including those from and to other EU institutions, were excluded.[251] On the basis of these figures, it could be argued that, in the absence of formal incentives for mobility, the relatively high rate of actual moves in the Commission is due to staff perception that regular change of position contributes to their professional and personal development.

4.2. UN and EU mobility procedures compared

Until the suspension of the mandatory mobility policy in the UN Secretariat in late 2008, in both the UN Secretariat and the European Commission, staff movement could occur by a direct transfer of an individual staff member to another post at the same level and/or by simultaneous movement of a number of staff members during a regular mobility exercise. A direct transfer would occur as a result of the selection process initiated in order to fill a specific post at the relevant level which has become vacant, while a mobility exercise would be organized for all staff due to move because of the expiry of a certain specified period. At present, these two ways are still available in the European Commission. In the UN Secretariat, mobility exercises only take place for junior staff, at least for the time being, until a new UN policy is adopted.[252]

The maximum period after which staff are expected to move to another post was, in general, five years in both the UN Secretariat as well as in the European Commission, with a few exceptions in both organizations. First, in the UN Secretariat, longer or shorter maxima could be established by the Administration for specific posts. Longer periods could, for example, be used where required by the nature of the function or the scarcity of posts. Second, UN senior staff had a longer maximum period of post occupancy, namely six years.[253] This means senior staff were subject to a less strict mobility requirement than the rest of the UN staff. This was criticized, for example, by the Joint Inspection Unit which noted that 'staff at [the senior] level should be exemplary by leading the way in implementing the mobility policy' rather than being treated more favourably.[254] Indeed, compared to the European Commission, there senior officials (as well as middle managers) are subject to a stricter – mandatory –

the Joint Inspection Unit in its report on UN mobility policy. – Section III, Part G, para. 68.

[251] *Commission's Human Resources Report 2009*, p. 133.

[252] See above, sections 2.1, 2.2.1.1, 2.2.2.1- 2.2.2.4 and 3.2.1-3.2.3.

[253] See above, section 2.1.

[254] *Staff Mobility in the United Nations, Report of the Joint Inspection Unit, JIU/REP/2006/7*, Section III, Part C, para. 41.

mobility policy, while most of other staff are only subject to voluntary mobility.[255] It is difficult to understand why UN senior staff used to receive preferential treatment compared to other staff. This is even more so considering the level of responsibilities of senior staff, requiring more rather than less strict guarantees that these responsibilities are exercised in an independent and impartial manner, free from inappropriate outside interference. There is more danger of such interference in situations in which one person occupies the same post for a longer period of time. That said, it must be recalled that the time-limited post occupancy was abolished in the UN Secretariat in April 2010, though this may change again when a new mobility policy is adopted. At present, thus, both senior and other UN staff may stay in their posts as long as they wish, even though they are, formally speaking, still encouraged and even expected to move regularly, like the European Commission staff are.[256]

As for UN junior staff appointed via competitive examinations, they were – and still are – subject to a shorter period after which they should move to another post.[257] This was thus another exception to the main five-year rule for the maximum post period occupancy that existed in the UN Secretariat.

There are other exceptions to the 'maximum five years in post' rule, still present in the European Commission. One of them relates to newly recruited staff who should move after three years in their first post with the Commission. Another, arguably more important, exception concerns specialized posts. Staff serving in specialized posts have no maximum period and are thus not subject to the Commission mobility scheme. The same applies to staff of 55 years of age or older, regardless of whether they are generalists or specialists, as well as to senior staff of 62 age or older.[258] This last rule reflects the fact that movement of staff who are close to their retirement would not be efficient. A similar provision could be found in the UN Secretariat. There, the managed reassignment programme of 2007 and 2008 that implemented mandatory mobility for non-junior Professional staff, did not apply to staff reaching their retirement age within a three years period, although the *UN Staff Selection System*, which incorporated rules on staff mobility, was silent on this issue.[259] No change has taken place in this respect upon introduction of the new *UN Staff Selection System* in April 2010.

While listing exceptions to the main rule that the benchmark period in the European Commission is, in principle, five years, it should also be noted that this may be extended or shortened. The former is possible for middle and senior management staff, on an exceptional and a case-by-case basis, if the conditions specified in the relevant legal instrument are met. The latter can occur in case of European Commission senior officials who may be required to move before their five-year benchmark period expires, for example, when their nationality collides with that of their new portfolio

[255] See above, sections 3.2.2 and 3.2.3.

[256] See above, sections 2.2.1.1 and 3.2.1.

[257] See above, section 2.2.2.

[258] See above, section 3.2.1.

[259] See above, section 2.1.

Commissioner. Mobility is used in such cases to ensure independent and impartial functioning of all involved.[260]

As regards procedures through which staff members may move or be moved to another post, the transfer of an individual upon the initiative of the relevant appointing authority itself is possible in both the UN Secretariat and European Commission for all their staff. This authority enjoys discretion in this regard in both organizations and may assign staff, in principle, when and where needed.[261] Transfers may, however, also take place on the basis of the initiative of individual staff members themselves through applying for a vacant post at their level. In the UN Secretariat , such transfers occur under the *UN Staff Selection System* for all posts falling within its scope.[262] In case of posts outside the *UN Staff Selection System*, it is not clear how transfers work and what procedures apply. It appears that a decision to transfer an individual staff member is taken by the UN Administration only on the basis of Rule 1.2(c) of the *UN Staff Rules*, which gives the UN Secretary-General the authority to assign staff in accordance with the organization's needs, and without following any formal procedure.

A similar situation exists in the European Commission. There, transfers of officials to vacant posts classified at the same level are possible under Article 29(1) of the *UN Staff Regulations* but no formal procedures have been developed for it, with the exception of managerial posts at both the middle and the senior levels where selection for vacant posts occurs under the normal procedural framework established for appointment to posts at these levels.[263] Below the management levels, however, suitability of staff for a vacant post for which they apply because they must or would like to move is considered under the full discretion of the Administration and no formal procedural framework. This is so despite the fact that, informally, selection panels consisting of four relatively senior persons appear to be involved if the vacant post concerns the AD function group or is at a higher level in the AST function group. The panels seem to be in charge, in particular, of interviewing candidates identified by the EU Administration as the most matching with the job requirements.

The absence of formal procedures in the European Commission for appointment of staff applying to a vacant post below the management levels in order to exercise mobility is a striking difference compared to the UN Secretariat. There, the *UN Staff Selection System* with clear and precise rules applies to selection of staff for all vacant posts which fall within its scope, i.e most non-junior Professional posts as well as some posts in other categories.

Besides direct transfer of an individual staff member to a vacant post at the same level, staff movement may also occur under the framework of mobility exercises organized for staff who is due to move. Such exercises are known in both the UN Secretariat and the European Commission, although in the UN Secretariat they

[260] See above, sections 3.2.2 and 3.2.3.
[261] See above, sections 2.1 and 3.1.
[262] See above, section 2.2.1.1.
[263] See above, sections 3.2.2 and 3.2.3.

are no longer organized for all staff, due to the abolition of time-limited post occupancy. At present, mobility exercises in the UN Secretariat are thus only held for junior Professional staff who are subject to a separately administered mobility policy.[264] In the European Commission too, mobility exercises are only held for some staff, namely for senior officials who must move either because their benchmark period has expired or for other reasons.[265] Interestingly, despite the fact that some other Commission staff are also obliged to regularly change posts, namely staff in sensitive posts and middle managers, no mobility exercises are organized for them. These staff need to apply for another post at their level when it becomes vacant.[266] Clearly, this arrangement is not very mobility-supportive, leaving most of the burden of finding another suitable post on the individual staff members themselves.

Comparing the UN and the EU regular mobility exercises, it may be noted that in the UN Secretariat different regimes used to apply to (various types of) junior staff on the one hand and to other staff on the other hand, whereas in the European Commission a distinction has been made between senior staff at the level of the Director-General and senior staff at the level of Director. Despite different legal regimes, procedures applied to managed reassignment of UN junior Professional staff and those that used to be in place for non-junior Professional staff were almost identical. In both cases they involved – and in case of junior Professional staff still do – a compendium of vacancies created by the expiry of the maximum post occupancy of staff at the same level; applications for one or more posts; evaluation of candidates by programme managers indicating their preferences; matching exercise by the OHRM; and final decision by the Assistant Secretary-General for Human Management Resources.[267] Regrettably, under neither of the two managed reassignment programmes central review bodies were involved in any part of the process. This is still the case for exercises held for junior Professional staff.

In the European Commission, the differences between mobility exercises for posts at the level of Director-General compared to posts at the level of Director are greater. The annual mobility exercise for Directors-General involves simultaneous internal publication of all posts subject to the exercise, application by officials due to move, and a decision by the College of Commissioners. On the contrary, the annual exercise for Directors involves drawing up of a list of officials due to move by the Directorate-General for Human Resources and Security, including other vacant posts at the relevant level as well, if appropriate; information and invitation to the officials due to move to indicate three preferences, interview by the Director-General for Human Resources and Security or by the Permanent Rapporteur to the Consultative Committee on Appointments, and final decision by the College of Commissioners for all moves simultaneously.[268]

---

[264] See above, section 2.2.2.

[265] See above, section 3.2.3.

[266] See above, sections 3.2.1 and 3.2.2.

[267] See above, sections 2.1 and 2.2.2.1-2.2.2.2.

[268] See above, section 3.2.3.

The most remarkable difference between the UN and the EU used to be that there were no regular mobility exercises organized for European Commission staff other than senior officials, whereas in the UN Secretariat such exercises were held for all staff. This difference has, however, partly disappeared with the suspension of the mandatory mobility policy for non-junior Professional staff in the UN Secretariat. Similarly as in the European Commission, in the UN Secretariat too the exercises are currently only held for staff who are (still) subject to mandatory mobility, though in the European Commission no exercises take place for officials serving in sensitive or middle management posts even though these officials too are subject to mandatory mobility.[269] Exercises in both organizations are centrally managed. In the UN Secretariat, it is the OHRM which conducts matching exercises, searching for the best possible combination of the preferences of individual staff members and the needs of the Secretariat, and in the European Commission it is the Directorate-General for Human Resources and Security and/or the College of Commissioners itself.[270] Another notable similarity is that neither in the UN Secretariat nor in the European Commission an advisory, consultative or review body is involved. The UN central review bodies as well as the European Commission's Consultative Committee on Appointments are left completely outside the door when staff is moved to another post at the same level. This is regrettable since appointment of staff to another post always involves selection and appreciation of individual merits of all candidates and in many cases consideration of other, sometimes purely political, questions. A review by a collective body, preferably composed of representatives of both the Administration and the staff representatives, would contribute to a more objective and transparent process.

An even more serious concern, relating to the European Commission, is that mobility of staff serving below the managerial levels occurs without any formal procedure. Such process lacks transparency and possibility of control. This is, in fact, quite similar to a situation which could occur in the UN Secretariat under the now suspended mandatory mobility policy. There, staff members who were due to move but were not placed in any available post during the normal selection process, could be placed outside normal process by the decision of the Assistant Secretary-General for Human Resources Management who, it seems, enjoyed full discretion in these instances.[271] It is true that the UN judiciary has recognized a broad discretion of the UN Administration in staff assignment as a necessary pre-requisite for proper functioning of the organization.[272] Nonetheless, it could be argued that in cases in which staff whose maximum period of post occupancy had expired were placed in another post outside normal process, such placement occurred not with the view of ensuring that a specific post be filled, but rather for the sole purpose of movement. Although, in general, there is no doubt that mobility is beneficial both for individual staff members and for the organization, this is arguably not the case when movements do not occur with predominant regard to the actual need of specific posts

[269] See above, sections 2.2.2, 3.2.1-3.2.3.

[270] See above sections 2.2.2 and 3.2.3.

[271] See above, section 2.1.

[272] See above, section 2.1.

but are forced in order to satisfy an administrative policy. Transfer of an individual staff member who is obliged to move but does not get placed by the decision of the Administration is also possible in the European Commission. It is so in case of sensitive posts, for which mobility is mandatory.[273] Unlike in the case of the UN placement outside normal process, however, the interest in moving the European Commission official occupying a sensitive post has a clear reason, namely the sensitivity of the post at issue and the need to eliminate the risk of financial impropriety or potential conflict of interest. It is questionable whether such motives could be linked to the placement of staff in the UN who could be moved merely for the sake of mobility itself. It could, therefore, be argued that postponing movement of an individual staff member until the next adequate opportunity presents itself would be a more appropriate reaction than placement outside normal process. Fortunately, because of the suspension (or – as is possible – the abolition) of the mandatory mobility for non-junior Professional staff serving in the UN Secretariat, the possibility of placing staff outside the normal process for the purpose of exercising mobility of such staff has been removed from the *UN Staff Selection System*.[274]

In cases in which mobility is still mandatory, there used to be a possibility to relax the requirement in individual cases, both in the UN Secretariat and the European Commission. At present, this possibility only exists in the European Commission, although that it is only provided for most managerial posts and not for sensitive posts, and mobility is mandatory for both. European Commission officials occupying sensitive posts must thus move in all cases once their benchmark period expires, whereas movement of senior officials may be postponed.[275] As far as the Commission middle managers are concerned, they may remain in the post longer – up to seven years, if there is a sound and clearly justified reason; in exceptional cases even longer. Moreover, individual middle managers possessing specific aptitudes or performing specific functions, need not move at all, subject to a formal derogation granted upon duly reasoned request.[276] Movement of European Commission senior officials serving at the basic post of Director may be postponed once if specific circumstances, exceptional policy or workload constrains requires so. No such a possibility exists in case of Commission Directors-General who, if not moved, may be temporarily appointed as Advisor *Hors Classe* and eventually retired in the interests of the service.[277]

In the UN Secretariat, under the managed reassignment programme of 2007 and 2008, individual staff members could have requested an exemption from participation in a specific mobility exercise. Such exemption would have been granted on a case-by-case basis upon approval by the Assistant Secretary-General for Human Resources Management. It had to be based on precisely defined criteria, although

[273] See above, section 3.1.

[274] For the reasons for such placement that are still available, see above, chapter 3, section 2.2.2.2.

[275] See above, sections 3.2.1 and 3.2.3.

[276] See above, section 3.2.2.

[277] See above, section 3.2.3.

no such criteria seem to have been developed.[278] Moreover, the *UN Staff Selection System*, which provided for the general legal basis for compulsory mobility, contained no provision of granting individual exemptions at that time. The same is still true for administrative instructions regulating mobility of junior Professional staff. These staff do not benefit from any exceptions.[279]

5. Conclusions

The introductory part to this chapter explains that the greater the mobility among staff of an international organization, the better – for both the staff, who can acquire diverse knowledge and experience, and the organization, which can dispose of more versatile staff and, in addition, be better protected with regard to independent and impartial exercise of its mandates. A good mobility policy must, however, be flexible and reflect the internal diversity of the organization and its functions. Regular movement of *all* staff seems neither necessary nor advisable – it is extremely complex and burdensome for both the staff and the organization in question, with benefits that do not correspond to the burden. A distinction is therefore needed between different types of functions with precise identification of posts subject to regular mobility, either due to the nature and/or due to the level of the function. Staff in posts in areas or at levels that are vulnerable to risks of undue influence should be protected by regular and mandatory mobility facilitated by an objective, clear and transparent, substantive as well as procedural legal framework.

On this basis it seems that the European Commission mobility scheme more adequately responds to the needs of both the staff and the organization than the scheme formerly and currently in place in the UN Secretariat. Despite understandable reasons for introducing mandatory mobility for, in principle, all staff, namely the creation of a mobility culture as inseparable part of conditions of employment with the UN, the rigidity of the UN policy led to many problems, frustration of both the staff and the Administration and, eventually, to the overall failure of the policy. Arguably, one of the main reasons was the absence of proper differentiation between various types of posts with no clear identification of posts which would or could be excused from mandatory mobility. In addition, the great internal diversity of the organization itself, its mandates and locations of duty stations, was not sufficiently reflected in the policy. Many related problems, such as work and family life issues, remained unresolved or inadequately resolved when the policy was implemented.

While the UN Administration has, at least for the time being, departed from the failed mandatory mobility policy, it has not (yet) developed a new policy. At present, mobility is no more than 'encouraged' for all but junior Professional staff, with no real incentives that would contribute to the development of the mobility culture

[278] See, for example, *Staff Mobility in the United Nations, Report of the Joint Inspection Unit, JIU/REP/2006/7*, Section III, Part C, para. 43. The Join Inspection Unit considered the absence of clear criteria for granting exemptions, on personal or organizational grounds, to be 'one of the major weaknesses of the current scheme'. – Ibid.

[279] See above, section 2.2.2.

sought by the UN Secretary-General. In addition, any distinction between various types of posts (with the exception of junior Professional posts), which was arguably one of the reasons for the failure of the former mandatory policy in the UN Secretariat, is still absent. In that respect, there is thus no protection in place for the independent and impartial exercise of functions related to posts more vulnerable to outside pressures or to misuse. For such posts, regular mobility is essential, but lacking.

The European Commission mobility policy is in this respect more of a success, since many staff members appear to move gladly to another post from time to time. Clearly, this is so for two main reasons. First, the policy clearly defines which posts are subject to mandatory movement, obliging only staff members who occupy sensitive or managerial posts to move regularly. The rationale of such policy is easier for the staff to accept and thus easier to implement. The second important reason is the presence of many possibilities to move within the institution with a large number of relatively diverse job opportunities, while remaining in the same or a similar location. Certainly, the fact that a change of post has no or only a limited influence on staff members' personal and family lives contributes greatly to their readiness to move. On the other hand, the relative success of the Commission mobility policy in case of staff members who are subject to voluntary policy is not so much due to the incentives the policy provides for but, arguably, to the fact that staff seem to regard regular change of jobs as positive for their personal development. In fact, the European Commission mobility policy contains fewer incentives to mobility than the UN policy. While in the UN Secretariat at least one incentive exists, namely the requirement of prior lateral movement before staff become eligible for promotion to higher levels, in the European Commission there are no incentives and no link to career development or promotion. This is regrettable. With good incentives, arguably (even) more staff would be prepared to move in both organizations.

The European Commission mobility policy appears to be also more amenable to ensuring independence and impartiality of the Commission senior officials. Unlike in the past, all senior officials move regularly now, although certain flexibility has remained. As understandable as it may be, it is questionable whether this flexibility is justified for managers when it is not available to staff occupying sensitive posts. Regular movement of managers, dealing with matters of high importance, vulnerable to inappropriate outside interference, is at least as necessary as movement of staff in sensitive posts.

As far as procedures are concerned, the situation in the UN Secretariat is more adequate than that in the European Commission for the majority of their staff. The total absence of formal rules for staff transfer in the European Commission below the managerial level is disappointing. Although staff members move at the same career level, a process of selection for a specific job takes place each time mobility is exercised. Each selection should thus occur under objective, clear and transparent procedures in order to avoid (any appearance of) undue influences in the process. Procedures developed in the UN Secretariat provide, from that point of view, a more adequate legal framework for implementing staff mobility. Regrettably, the transparency of this framework is reduced by the multiplicity of administrative issuances that apply – and sometimes overlap – to different UN staff. It is, for example, unclear why separate sets of rules are needed for junior and other non-language Professional staff, when both sets of rules provide, in principle, for the same approach, basic principles and identical procedures. Also, since the *UN Staff Selection System* is said to incorporate staff mobility as well, it would be advisable to use this system and include all necessary rules on staff movement in it instead of adopting yet another administrative instruction, especially since the general procedural legal framework contained in the *UN Staff Selection System* is highly comparable to that introduced by an additional administrative instruction. Furthermore, procedures employed for assignment of UN staff to individual posts during the mobility exercises themselves would be improved if central review bodies were included in the process. They do play a role in the selection process if movement of an individual staff member takes place under the *UN Staff Selection System.* It is difficult to understand why these bodies are excluded in other instances, including placement outside the normal process. The involvement of the central review bodies in each selection process would enhance its objectivity, impartiality and transparency. This conclusion stands for both the UN Secretariat and the European Commission.

Chapter 6

TYPES OF APPOINTMENT

1. Introduction

Most international organizations, including the UN and the EU, use various types of appointment or contract for engaging their staff, with only a certain proportion of staff members who may expect to spend most of their career in the (same) organization. The main reason for this is the need for flexibility which exists in international organizations just as it does in national public administrations and in the private sphere, though the extent of such flexibility may differ. The question arising in this respect is whether the use of (certain types of) non-career appointments and contracts in international organizations does not compromise independence and impartiality of their staff. As explained in the introductory chapter to this study, the use of non-career appointments and contracts may lead not only to many persons with high professional expertise staying away from an organization incapable of offering, or willing to offer, reasonable security of employment. It may also result in fear of losing employment adversely affecting international civil servants' independent and impartial performance of their duties. It is therefore of utmost importance that the contractual set up in international organizations ensures that the employment of non-career staff does not have such negative effects.

The following sections describe, assess and compare what types of appointment and/or contracts the UN Secretariat and the European Commission offer to their (potential) staff and under which conditions.

2. Types of appointment in the UN Secretariat

Together with the issue of geographical distribution, the question of temporary *versus* career appointment has been marked by great sensitivity in the UN. Both issues have been partly inter-related, certainly in the past, though perhaps less so at present. The interconnection between the two issues rested with the fact that the use of temporary appointments was one of the means of correcting inadequate geographical representation of unrepresented or underrepresented Member States. This was also the main reason for the sensitivity over which type of appointment should be used, career or temporary. Another important reason for the sensitivity was the use, or misuse, by Member States of temporary appointments for exercising influence over decisions regarding the retention of individual international civil servants in the UN Secretariat. This was done by forcing the UN Administration either not to renew contracts concluded for fixed-term periods or to terminate contracts of indefinite duration. The relatively large use of temporary appointments permitted such practices, challenging the concept of the UN career service at its very core.

Before assessing the current status of this concept, it is important to understand how it has developed. The following sections offer an overview of the most important developments in this regard and explain what types of appointment have been employed in the UN Secretariat over the years and how they have been recently modified.

2.1. Development of the UN career service

Like the international composition of UN staff, so too the idea of staff spending their entire career in the Secretariat was accepted at the time of its formation. It was taken over from the League of Nations together with several other basic principles on which the concept of the international civil service was founded. Despite the formal acceptance, in practice, however, the concept itself, including the idea of a career service, has been severely challenged by many UN Member States in the past. In fact, the concept became generally accepted only at the beginning of the 1990s when the former socialist countries reversed their policy concerning the employment of their nationals in international organizations and allowed them to accept permanent appointments. The road to the UN career service was thus long and thorny.

When considering the origins of the concept of an international career service, the League of Nations must indeed be seen as a pioneer. Its staffing was established on a career basis since the early 1930s upon recommendations of the Committee of Thirteen, mentioned above.[1] This Committee proposed in its report that the professional and clerical staff be appointed for life, i.e. until they reached the retirement age. Only posts at higher levels, considered to be political, should receive indeterminate appointments which could be terminated, among others, by a decision of the Secretary-General. Other posts, such as those requiring technical knowledge or special political or other qualifications, and posts with urgent or exceptional needs, should, according to the Committee of Thirteen, continue to be filled on temporary basis.[2] At the time the Committee of Thirteen delivered its report, all appointments were in practice limited to seven years, although they were almost automatically renewed.[3] The proposal of the Committee of Thirteen was approved by the Assembly of the League of Nations and, even though the actual practice was more flexible, the principle of career service was thereby firmly established.[4]

When the new United Nations was being formed, the first staff members were recruited on short-term contracts. This was done as a temporary solution awaiting the establishment of a permanent classification and recruitment plan.[5] In this regard the UN Preparatory Commission recommended that the 'bulk of staff should con-

---

[1] See chapter 2, section 1.

[2] *Report of the Committee of Thirteen*, Part II, Chapter 2, paras. 16-19.

[3] Ibid., Part II, Chapter 2, para. 16, third sub-paragraph. Note that the *Covenant of League of Nations* was silent on the point of type of appointment to be used for the organization staff. The idea of contracts of somehow longer duration was envisaged by the *Noblemaire Report* of 1921. The Noblemaire Commission had suggested a combination of short-term and long-term contracts, the latter applicable to international staff other than high-level officials. – *ibid.*, second sub-paragraph.

[4] Reymond and Mailick, *International Personnel Policies and Practices*, p. 98. See also, for example, Langrod, *The International Civil Service, Its Origins, Its Nature, Its Evolution*, pp. 114-115; Reymond and Mailick, *International Personnel Policies and Practices*, p. 114-115; p. 98; Beigbeder, *Threats to the International Civil Service*, p. 19; and Lemoine, *The International Civil Servant: An Endangered Species*, p. 266.

[5] *Report of the UN Preparatory Commission*, Chapter VIII, Section 1, para. 20.

sist of persons who will make their career in the Secretariat'.[6] It advised that, after the probationary period, staff members should be engaged for an indeterminate period, subject to review every five years by supervisors on the basis of performance reports and a possibility of termination in cases of post abolition, reduction of staff, unsatisfactory service or misconduct. The Commission also stressed that termination of appointments should not be provided for clearing a path for the appointment of persons with certain nationality or for other reasons not related to the staff members' work.[7]

While considering that a life-time career at the UN would be the main rule for a majority of staff, the Preparatory Commission also recognized that it was 'neither possible nor desirable' to employ the entire staff of the UN Secretariat on a permanent basis.[8] The Commission listed a number of situations in which temporary appointments should or could be granted instead of permanent ones. In the Commission's view, principal higher officers should be appointed under contracts of a maximum duration of five years with a possibility of renewal. Furthermore, the Secretary-General should have a possibility to grant temporary appointments to specialists in technical fields, to persons with special political qualifications needed for the performance of urgent and exceptional duties, and to persons from inadequately represented geographical regions if no suitable persons for permanent appointments were available. In addition, the Commission pleaded for the secondment of national civil servants for a period not longer than 2 years.[9]

The recommendations of the Preparatory Commission were fully accepted by the General Assembly in its Resolution 13(I) of 1946.[10] The concept of a career service was thereby established in the UN, leaving certain space for temporary appointments open under clearly specified conditions. Accordingly, in the first half of the 1950s more permanent appointments were granted and the initial predominance of temporary contracts was corrected.[11] Unfortunately, the situation deteriorated again in the second half of the 1950s and in the 1960s when a large number of (newly formed) countries acceded to the UN. As mentioned in the chapter addressing the issue of geographical representation, the new UN Member States immediately demanded a fair share among the Secretariat staff. Given a limited number of job openings, one of the main means of achieving appointments from these countries quickly was to use fixed-term contracts to a larger extent. Such contracts provided the flexibility and the opportunity to react to gaps in the geographical balance in a relatively prompt manner.[12] As a result, the ratio of fixed-term appointments dou-

[6] Ibid., Chapter VIII, Section 2.E, para. 60.

[7] Ibid., Chapter VIII, Section 1, paras. 21 and 23 and Section 2.E, paras. 60 and 65.

[8] Ibid., Chapter VIII, Section 2.E, para. 61.

[9] Ibid., Chapter VIII, Section 1, paras. 20 and 22 and Section 2.E, para. 61.

[10] *General Assembly Resolution 13(I)*, paras. 24-26.

[11] While in 1951 less than 35 per cent of the Secretariat staff served on permanent appointments and 65 per cent on temporary appointments, in 1956 89 per cent of all UN staff were reported as having permanent appointments. - Langrod, *The International Civil Service, Its Origins, Its Nature, Its Evolution*, pp. 205, note 7 and 241. See also Beigbeder, *Threats to the International Civil Service*, p. 32.

[12] See, for example, Langrod, *The International Civil Service, Its Origins, Its Nature, Its Evolution*, p. 192;

bled during the period between 1957 and 1962 – from below 13 per cent to 25 per cent of all appointments.[13] This increase was officially supported by the UN Member States – the General Assembly encouraged the use of fixed-term appointments in its Resolution 1436 (XIV) of 1959.[14]

The use of fixed-term appointments at that time did not fully correspond to the conditions suggested by the Preparatory Commission of 1945. The Commission advised that filling posts by persons from inadequately represented geographical regions on a temporary basis should be used if 'suitable candidates from that region are not readily available for permanent appointment'.[15] What was happening, however, was that staff from adequately represented or overrepresented Member States were given temporary contracts. After such contracts expired, the UN Administration could easily fill the posts that fell vacant with persons from inadequately represented countries.[16] The Preparatory Commission also suggested that secondment, which was considered by the Commission to be a positive and enriching element in the UN personnel policy, should not last longer than two years.[17] In reality, however, seconded national experts from inadequately represented countries, who were ready and available to serve in the UN Secretariat at short notice, often remained there for a longer period of time.[18]

It has been argued that the use of fixed-term appointments for ensuring adequate geographical representation in the UN was based at that time on a number of implicit assumptions. One was that the career development of permanent staff would remain unaffected as the fixed-term staff would serve at the level specified in the contract during the whole time of their appointment. Another important assumption was that competent persons would only be willing to accept an appointment for a relatively short period of time.[19] In reality, however, many temporary staff members sought extensions of their appointments, sometimes supported by their own governments. And as they often served for more than five years, they sought promotion, too.[20] Therefore, in the 1960s, when the proportion of fixed-term staff

---

Meron, *The United Nations Secretariat*, pp. 107 and 121 and, for some statistics, pp. 118-121; and Miron, *Tenure, Fixed-Term Appointments and Secondment in the United Nations*, p. 783.

[13] Miron, *Tenure, Fixed-Term Appointments and Secondment in the United Nations*, p. 787.

[14] *General Assembly Resolution 1436(XIV)*, para. 1(d). Note that the Fifth Committee even suggested in 1956 that the proportion of seconded officials should rise to about 20 per cent and the ratio of the fixed-term staff should be at least 25 per cent and should be increased to 35 to 40 per cent. - *Repertory of Practice of United Nations Organs*, Article 101, Supplement 2 (1955-1959), para. 26.

[15] *Report of the UN Preparatory Commission*, Chapter VIII. Section 2. E, para. 61.

[16] Meron, *The United Nations Secretariat*, p. 108. Meron noted: '[T]here is greater willingness to award permanent contracts to persons from underrepresented countries. Correspondingly, there is lesser willingness to award permanent contracts to persons from overrepresented countries.' Also Graham and Jordan reported in 1980 that in posts funded from the regular UN budget which were normally filled by junior level staff on a career basis, this was not done when the staff member to be recruited came from an overrepresented Member State. In such a case, a fixed-term appointment was usually offered instead of a permanent one. - Graham and Jordan (eds.), *The International Civil Service*, p. 113.

[17] *Report of the UN Preparatory Commission*, Chapter VIII. Section 2. E, para. 61.

[18] See, for example, Meron, *The United Nations Secretariat*, p. 122.

[19] Miron, *Tenure, Fixed-Term Appointments and Secondment in the United Nations*, pp. 784-785.

[20] Ibid., p. 786.

in the UN Secretariat continued to rise, various adjustments of the status of such staff took place. Their main objective was to eliminate differences between career and temporary staff, the latter gradually obtaining a status comparable to that of the former.[21]

By the mid-1960s it started to become clear that, in order to ensure stability and efficiency of the UN Secretariat, a higher proportion of permanent contracts and fixed-term contracts of longer duration was needed.[22] The UN General Assembly still believed that increased recruitment of staff on fixed-term basis could contribute to the improvement of geographical distribution, especially in case of developing countries, but it stressed that this should be seen as a temporary measure only.[23] Therefore, in its recruitment guidelines of 1970 the General Assembly established that, for posts involving complex duties and responsibilities, preference should be given to candidates 'willing to accept a career appointment or fixed-term appointment of no less than 5 years'.[24]

During the 1970s, the volume of fixed-term appointments rose to almost 40 percent of the total staff.[25] As pointed out by Reymond and Mailick, the concept of career service had been continuously deteriorating and the trend away from permanent appointments at the time was undeniable.[26] Miron explained that this situation had been mainly a result of the pressures of geographical distribution as well as of different attitudes of Member States.[27] Also Barnes regarded the opposition of certain countries to permanent appointments and the need for flexibilities in order to improve geographical balance among the staff as the main causes of the increased proportion of temporary appointments by the end of 1970s.[28]

The 'divergent views' of the UN Member States on the issue of career *versus* temporary appointments were explicitly admitted by the General Assembly in 1980.[29] While many, especially Western, countries considered career service as the predominant type of appointment in the UN ensuring independent and efficient staff, there were two groups of states strongly opposed to this view. The first consisted of the already mentioned newly independent States admitted to the UN in 1950s

[21] For details, see Ibid., pp. 788 et seq.

[22] *General Assembly Resolution 2241(XXI)*, Preamble. See also *General Assembly Resolution 2539(XXIV)*, Preamble.

[23] *General Assembly Resolution 2241(XXI)*, para. 1.

[24] *General Assembly Resolution 2736(XXV)*, para. 2(b). Interestingly, no such requirement can be found the recruitment guidelines adopted later, in 1978. - See *General Assembly Resolution 33/143*, available in the Official Document System of the United Nations.

[25] Miron, *Tenure, Fixed-Term Appointments and Secondment in the United Nations*, p. 792.

[26] Reymond and Mailick, *International Personnel Policies and Practices*, pp. 101 and 102. See also p. 110.

[27] Miron, *Tenure, Fixed-Term Appointments and Secondment in the United Nations*, p. 792. See also Reymond and Mailick, *International Personnel Policies and Practices*, pp. 102-105.

[28] Barnes, *Tenure and Independence in the United Nations International Civil Service*, pp. 771-777. It must be noted that Barnes added to these two causes another one, namely the functional need of the UN organizations for fixed-term appointments. This last reason was, in Barnes' view, the most important cause of the increased ratio of non-permanent staff in the UN. However, Barnes assessed the situation of the UN common system as a whole, not only the UN Secretariat.

[29] *General Assembly Resolution 35/210*, Section IV .

and 1960s. These counties saw the existing system of permanent appointments as an inflexible obstacle to their goal of gaining more influence in the UN via appointment of their nationals.[30] In addition, many of the newly independent States experienced severe scarcity of sufficiently qualified persons who they needed at the national level for the building of their own state system. Therefore, these countries were not willing to permanently dispense with such scarce personnel.[31] The second group opposed to permanent appointments as a matter of principle consisted of the socialistic countries of Central and Eastern Europe. As partly explained in the chapter dealing with geographical representation, socialist countries feared that if their nationals served in an international organization for a longer period of time, their loyalty to the organization would prevail over that towards the home country. Moreover, these states maintained that staff who had lived abroad and lost touch with their home country could no longer be true representatives of their countries and, therefore, had lost their value as international civil servants.[32] Nationals of socialist countries were, therefore, allowed to serve in international organizations, including the UN, exclusively on a fixed-term basis. Most of them were seconded national civil servants. After their term of office expired, they were replaced by another person from the same country employed under the same conditions.

The problem of high ratio of fixed-term appointments in the UN persisted in the 1980s. The proportion of permanent appointments in the UN Secretariat continued to be low, reaching a mere 61 per cent of the total staff in 1982 and 63 per cent in 1986.[33] Many UN diplomats whose views on the UN system were surveyed by the United Nations Institute for Training and Research in 1982 said the increasing pro portion of international civil servants with fixed-term appointments was impeding the Secretariat's efficiency.[34]

In 1986, the Group of High-Level Intergovernmental Experts, known as G18, requested by the General Assembly to review efficiency of the administrative and financial functioning of the United Nations, expressed its concern over the high number of temporary staff in the UN Secretariat and over the practice of socialist countries placing their nationals in the same posts on fixed-term basis. The G18 recommended that the ratio between permanent and fixed-term appointments should be reviewed in order to ensure that no post was an exclusive preserve of any Member State. It suggested that no more than 50 per cent of the nationals of any one Member State should be employed on the basis of a fixed-term contract and

[30] Barnes, *Tenure and Independence in the United Nations International Civil Service*, p. 772-773.

[31] For example, Lemoine, *The International Civil Servant: An Endangered Species*, p. 268.

[32] Barnes, *Tenure and Independence in the United Nations International Civil Service*, p. 772. For a detailed analysis of the socialist countries' view on the concept of the international civil service, including their attitude towards a career service, see especially Beigbeder, *Threats to the International Civil Service*, Chapter 4. See also above, chapter 2, section 2.1.2.

[33] Beigbeder, *Threats to the International Civil Service*, p. 155, Table 8.1. Reflecting on these figures, Beigbeder noted that the large proportion of non-career appointments do not match with the concept of career service. He claimed that this traditional concept had been eroded and even breached in recent years. - Beigbeder, *Threats to the International Civil Service*, p. 154.

[34] Franck, Renninger and Tikhomirov, *An Attitude Survey: Diplomat's View on the United Nations System*, p. 35, Table 18c.

that no less than 50 per cent of the staff of each particular Member State should hold permanent appointment.[35] The G18 understood the need for flexibility in the UN personnel policy. At the same time, it worried about the 'faithful' reflection of the principle of geographical distribution among the staff holding permanent appointments.[36] Unsurprisingly, these views (and the recommendations) were not shared by all members of the G18. Members from socialist countries adopted a dissenting opinion and referred to the so-called 'national preserve exception' adopted by the General Assembly in its resolution 35/210 of 1980, and allowing replacement of a temporary staff member of certain nationality by another person of the same nationality in case of Member States whose nationals serve mainly on temporary basis.[37]

At the end of the 1980s and the beginning of the 1990s came the fall of socialist regimes in most countries of Central and Eastern Europe, including the former Soviet Union. One of the consequences of these developments was a land-mark decision of the former socialist countries' governments to change their approach to the issue of the international character of staff serving in international organizations. Subsequently, nationals of these countries could be employed under the terms of a career appointment.[38] Fixed-term staff, including those on secondment from national civil services, continued to be present in the UN Secretariat but under a different political framework no longer influenced by the *a priori* disapproval of the concept of an international civil service as such.[39]

During the 1990s, an overall reform of the UN human resources management was initiated. This reform also concerned the issue of the appropriate ratio between permanent and non-permanent appointments. Unlike in the past, however, the need for a certain proportion of non-permanent appointments was now dictated by the needs of the organization and its increasingly expanding mandates of a different

[35] *G18 Report*, Recommendations 55 and 57.

[36] Ibid., Recommendation 57.

[37] Ibid., Recommendation 55 and 57. For the national preserve exception, see *General Assembly Resolution 35/210*, para. 4. See also above, chapter 2, section 2.3.2.

[38] The USSR abrogated the provisions which conformed Soviet nationals serving in international organizations to national civil servants on secondment by an ordinance, No. 1280 of 15 December 1990. - Lemoine, *The International Civil Servant: An Endangered Species*, p. 220. See also *Personnel Questions: Other Personnel Questions, Secondment from Government Service, Report of the Secretary-General*, para. 7.

[39] Note that secondment has never been defined by the *UN Staff Regulations* or the *UN Staff Rules*, except the mention that seconded officials must receive a fixed-term appointment and that in their letter of appointment it must be explicitly stated that they are on secondment. – *UN Staff Regulations of 2009*, Rule 4.13(a) and Annex II, para. (c). There is, however, a considerable amount of jurisprudence dealing with cases of seconded officials, the most important ones being *Higgins* and *Levcik*. - *Higgins v. Secretary-General of the Inter-Governmental Maritime Consultative Organization, UNAT Judgment No. 92 [1964]*, available at http://untreaty.un.org/UNAT/UNAT_Judgements/Judgements_E/UNAT_00092_E.pdf, last visited on 30.12.2010 and *Levcik v. Secretary-General of the United Nations, UNAT Judgment No. 192 [1974]*, available at http://untreaty.un.org/UNAT/UNAT_Judgements/Judgements_E/UNAT_00192_E.pdf, last visited on 30.12.2010. In the former the UNAT defined secondment and its conditions, most significantly the need for agreement of all three involved parties, i.e. the UN, the government of the relevant Member States and the seconded staff member, for extension or any other change of the agreement. - *Higgins, UNAT Judgment No. 92 [1964]*, paras. IV, VI-VII.

nature, in particular in peacekeeping operations. Accordingly, in 1994, the General Assembly requested the Secretary-General to 'examine or review the possibility and desirability of achieving an appropriate flexibility between career and fixed-term appointments, taking into account the functional and structural needs of the Organization as well as the requirements of an international career service.'[40] The Secretary-General himself admitted the importance of permanent appointments for the independence and efficiency of the UN staff but, at the same time, he noted the need for flexibility for ensuring that fresh talent and skills are brought into the organization.[41] He considered that the ratio of 30 percent for non-permanent appointments compared to 70 per cent for permanent appointments was optimal for securing both these interests.[42] The General Assembly approved this ratio and maintained it in the following years.[43]

At the beginning of the new millennium, a comprehensive reform of contractual arrangements was put forward. Discussions on the modalities of such new arrangements marked the developments in the last decade. The reform was launched by a proposal submitted by the UN Secretary-General to the General Assembly in 2000. This proposal was approved partly in December 2008 and partly in December 2010, modifying the type of both permanent and non-permanent contracts existing in the UN previously.[44] The following sections explain in more detail the evolution of various types of UN appointments and recent changes therein.

2.2. Evolution of various types of UN appointments

The UN Secretariat started with two, rather soon extended to three, main types of appointment. Over the years, this number has increased to eleven in total, rendering the administration of appointments complex and conditions of service of many UN staff doing basically the same work unequal. The reform of 2008 reduced the types of appointment back to three. This number reflects the need for differentiation between shorter and longer lasting service.

Two basic types of appointment in the UN Secretariat in early years were permanent and temporary appointment. In 1954, a third type was added: the regular appointment. These three types were distinguishable from each other above all by the nature of the appointment, i.e. scope of situation in which staff could be employed, and the possibilities to terminate them.[45]

[40] *Human Resource Management Policies, Report of the Secretary-General, A/49/445*, para. 32.

[41] Ibid., paras. 32 – 35.

[42] Ibid., para. 35. The Secretary-General noted that the optimum ratio varied among different sectors.

[43] *General Assembly Resolution 51/226B*, Section V, para. 1. See also *General Assembly Resolution 53/221*, Section V., para. 23.

[44] *Human Resources Management Reform, Report of the Secretary-General, A/55/253*, para. 47; *General Assembly Resolution 63/250*, Section II; and *General Assembly Resolution 65/247*, Section VI.

[45] *Repertory of Practice of United Nations Organs*, Article 101, para. 77.

Permanent appointments were granted to those earmarked for a career service. They entailed employment in the UN until, in principle, retirement.[46] The staff member thus served for a long period of time, developing his career within the organization. This type of appointment was granted only when a preceding probationary appointment was successfully completed.

Temporary appointments were, as their name suggests, time limited. The nature of the limitation varied depending on the category of temporary appointment used in a specific case. There were three different categories of temporary appointments: probationary appointments, fixed-term appointments and indefinite appointments. The first of them, probationary appointments, lasted for a maximum period of two years, exceptionally extended by one more year, after which the staff member was either granted a permanent (or regular) appointment or separated from service. The choice between the two options depended to a large extent on the satisfactory performance of the staff member concerned.[47] Fixed-term appointments were granted for an agreed duration as well as to persons seconded from national governments or other institutions to serve temporarily at the UN Secretariat. The set fixed-term period could not exceed five years.[48] The last category of temporary appointments, namely indefinite appointments had no expiration date and lasted until termination or conversion into another type of appointment. They were used exclusively for the Field Service or mission service; or for persons who due to medical reasons were not granted fixed-term appointment.[49]

The third type of appointment in the early UN Secretariat was the regular appointment. It was introduced in 1954 and was related to specific circumstances, in particular of a local nature. It was granted to staff members in the General Service and Manual Worker categories who had probationary appointments and had shown high standards of efficiency, competence and integrity. Regular appointments were given for an indefinite period of time and could last until retirement, subject to a review after the first five years.[50] The use of this type of appointment was later discontinued.

In the same year that regular appointment was introduced, a separate set of *UN Staff Rules* was developed for specialist project personnel employed in technical assistance projects.[51] This set of the *UN Staff Rules* was, until abolition in 2009, re-

---

[46] Ibid., Article 101, para. 79.

[47] Ibid., Article 101, para. 99.

[48] Ibid., Article 101, para. 96.

[49] Ibid., Article 101, para. 87.

[50] Ibid., Article 101, para. 102.

[51] *Detailed Proposals for Streamlining United Nations Contractual Arrangements, Report of the Secretary-General, A/62/274*, 17.08.2007, available in the Official Document System of the United Nations, available at http://documents.un.org/, last visited on 30.12.2010, Section II, para. 13. For a definition of the project personnel, see *Staff Rules of the United Nations, 200 Series, ST/SGB/2002/2*, 01.01.2002, as amended by ST/SGB/2008/2 of 01.01.2008, ST/SGB/2007/2 of 01.01.2007, ST/SGB/2006/2 of 01.01.2006, ST/SGB/2005/2 of 01.01.2005, ST/SGB/2004/2 of 01.01.2004 and ST/SGB/2003/2 of 01.01.2003, available in the Human Resources Handbook of the United Nations, available at http://www.un.org/hr_handbook/English/, last visited on 30.12.2010, Rule 200.2(b).

ferred to as the 200 series, while the initial set was referred to as the 100 series. Both series were covered by the same *UN Staff Regulations* but included some differences in the conditions of service, although with regard to staff benefits in particular the differences were not significant.[52] The project personnel engaged under the 200 series used to be divided into three sub-categories, namely project personnel with short-term status (less than one year); project personnel with intermediate-term status (duration of appointment of minimum one year and maximum five years); and project personnel of long-term status (appointment of five years or longer).[53]

In 1955, i.e. a year after the introduction of the 200 series of the *UN Staff Rules*, two additional series were established: the 300 series, used for staff hired for short-term employment not exceeding six months, such as conference services during the sessions of the UN General Assembly; and the 400 series covering dispatchers and guides in the Visitors Service at Headquarters. The last series was, however, abolished in 1978 and staff governed by it were placed under the 100 series.[54] Until 2009, thus, there were three series of the *UN Staff Rules*, all covered by a single set of the *UN Staff Regulations*.

The developments in this area did not stop in 1978 when the 400 series of the *UN Staff Rules* was abolished, though. In 1994, the existing 300 series of the *UN Staff Rules* was extended to staff engaged for peacekeeping and other missions, technical cooperation in the field and other emergency situations, all of which had an expected duration limited to up to three and exceptionally four years.[55] Since 1994, there were thus two types of appointment under 300 series: short-term appointments (maximum of six months) and appointments of limited duration (maximum of three years, with a possibility of prolongation for an additional year). The conditions of service under this 300 series were significantly different compared to the 100 and 200 series, especially with regard to benefits.

In the course of the 1990s, the proportion of staff with appointments of limited duration serving under the 300 series of the *UN Staff Rules* had increased considerably, in particular due to the increase in peacekeeping activities pursued by the UN. In the mid-2000s, more than half of the staff served in the field – and under less favourable conditions than their counterparts in the headquarters. As dissatisfaction with the conditions of service under the 300 series of *UN Staff Rules* grew, gradual changes were introduced, improving the situation of the staff serving under contracts of limited duration.[56] Despite the changes, at the end of the 1990s it became clear that a comprehensive reform of the UN contractual arrangements was needed in order to eliminate significant differences which still existed between different types of appointment while their holders often performed the same or comparable tasks.

[52] *Investing in People, Report of the Secretary-General, A/61/255*, para. 224.

[53] *200 Series of the UN Staff Rules of 2002*, Rule 200.2(f).

[54] *Detailed Proposals for Streamlining United Nations Contractual Arrangements, Report of the Secretary-General, A/62/274*, Section II, para. 13.

[55] Ibid., Section II, para. 13.

[56] *Investing in People, Report of the Secretary-General, A/61/255*, paras. 224-228.

It was also necessary to bring back the simplicity of the administration of various types of appointment, initially present but lost by later developments.[57]

The inadequate staffing situation in the UN peacekeeping operations and special political missions was the main driving force behind the reform of the UN contractual arrangements. These operations and missions were initially realized by employing staff classified in a category specially created for this purpose in 1949, namely the Field Service category. Staff in this category, originally about 300 physically fit young men with field and technical background deployable on short notice anywhere in the world, were hired to provide auxiliary support services in occupational groups, such as land transport and incidental air transport, radio communication and security of UN premises and staff. They were recruited under the 100 series of the *UN Staff Rules* on fixed-term contracts not limited to a specific mission. Upon recruitment, they were first placed in long-established missions and later deployed where needed, including non-family duty stations, while retaining allowances and benefits of the established, family, duty stations. As with all other staff, performance of the Field Service staff was regularly assessed and, on the basis of such performance assessment, they could be promoted and their fixed-term appointments converted into permanent ones. Until the early 1990s, the Field Service officers enabled the UN to meet its rapid deployment and staffing needs in peacekeeping operations.[58]

In the early 1990s, the number and complexity of mandates of the UN peacekeeping operations expended dramatically, however, requiring significantly more (civilian) staff with more diverse skills. The UN could no longer meet the requirements of these operations by relying only on the Field Service officers with relatively limited occupational background and had to hire many additional staff, especially civilian ones. As it was expected that new missions, regarded as special, were of short-term, the newly hired staff were not given the same appointment as the Field Service officers. As already mentioned, a new type of appointment of limited duration was introduced for this purpose under the 300 series of the *UN Staff Rules*, which were established for short-term appointments. This new type of appointment had a maximum duration of three years with a possibility of extension in exceptional situations for another year. It was given to all staff hired for special missions, irrespective of the nature of the function to be performed and including Professional staff. Recruitment to the Field Service category was suspended.[59]

---

[57] Ibid., para. 228.

[58] *Reforming the Field Service Category: Investing in Meeting the Human Resources Requirements of United Nations Peace Operations in the Twenty-First Century, A/61/255/Add.1*, Section II. Note that the conversion of fixed-term appointments in permanent ones was only possible until the freeze on permanent appointments was introduced in 1995.

[59] Ibid., Section I, para. 5 and Section III, paras. 14-15. See also *Comprehensive Report on the Staffing of Field Missions, Including the Use of 300 and 100 Series Appointments, Report of the Secretary-General, A/59/291*, Section V, Parts A, C and D. Note that there are two types of UN peacekeeping missions: seven established missions of a long-term duration and other missions designated as special missions for security, political and operational reasons. While the former are usually family duty stations, the latter are not. - *Comprehensive Report on the Staffing of Field Missions, Including the Use of 300 and 100 Series Appointments, Report of the Secretary-General, A/59/291*, Annex , Section II.2.

Contrary to expectations, however, the post-1990 peacekeeping operations turned out to be of longer duration than the envisaged three to four years. The need for a large number of mission staff was, therefore, of a more continuing nature. In addition, the character of the operations had changed. The then Secretary-General Kofi Annan noted:

> *since late 2003, the peacekeeping doctrine has evolved to incorporate the concept of integrated peace operations, which represent a holistic response to observing and keeping the peace, establishing or re-establishing the rule of law and good governance and undertaking post-conflict reconstruction and development efforts critical to addressing the root causes of the conflict and building a sustainable peace. United Nations peace operations therefore require staff from virtually all areas of the Secretariat, as well as qualified staff for specialist functions that are not traditionally found in the Secretariat, including in the areas of civil affairs, disarmament, demobilization and reintegration, air operations, movement control and other specialist logistics functions.*[60]

However, the UN human resources strategy had not adapted to these developments. Competing for staff with other international organizations and non-governmental entities involved in comparable activities, and not offering attractive conditions of service by granting time-limited appointments with no career prospects and with inadequate and unequal compensation and benefits, the UN ended up with a staff high turnover and persistently high vacancy rates.[61] By suspending recruitment to the Field Service category, the UN had even lost its capability to rapidly deploy highly qualified and experienced staff and to support the broader needs of its peacekeeping operations which had evolved in the meantime.[62] To regain this capacity and to attract and retain sufficient number of (civilian) staff with the required qualifications and experience, the UN had to reform its contractual arrangements and offer more fair and equal conditions of service to all staff. As stated by the UN Secretary-General, the UN could no longer do with contractual arrangements designed for constant and mainly headquarters-based personnel, not fitting the operational requirements of the UN Secretariat in changed circumstances where more than half of the staff serve in the field. In addition, the then existing system of contractual arrangements had to change due to its labor-intensiveness, complexity and non-transparency.[63]

---

[60] *Reforming the Field Service Category: Investing in Meeting the Human Resources Requirements of United Nations Peace Operations in the Twenty-First Century, A/61/255/Add.1*, Section III, para. 18.

[61] Ibid., Section VI, para. 39. See also *Comprehensive Report on the Staffing of Field Missions, Including the Use of 300 and 100 Series Appointments, Report of the Secretary-General, A/59/291*, Section II, paras. 3-5; Section IV, paras. 17-19. For details on differences in the conditions of service of staff appointed under the 300 series of the UN Staff Rules, compared to the 100 series, see Section IV, Part F and Table 6 on pp. 37-38.

[62] *Reforming the Field Service Category: Investing in Meeting the Human Resources Requirements of United Nations Peace Operations in the Twenty-First Century, A/61/255/Add.1*, Section III, para. 20.

[63] *Investing in People, Report of the Secretary-General, A/61/255*, para. 235.

Before the reform, the different types of appointments used in the UN Secretariat were as follows:

Table 13: Types of appointment in the UN Secretariat before 1 July 2009

100 series	*200 series*	*300 series*
Probationary (normally for two years, leading to permanent appointments)	**Short-term status** (for project personnel with appointments of less than one year)	**Short-term** (for a period not exceeding six consecutive months)
Fixed-term (for a specified period, usually between six months and two years, which may be renewed or extended as necessary)	**Intermediate status** (for project personnel with appointments or continuous service of one to five years)	**Limited duration** (for activities not expected to exceed three years)
Indefinite (currently used by UNHCR and, rarely, by the Secretariat in special situations)	**Long-term status** (for project personnel with appointments or continuous service of five years or more)	
Permanent (for persons who have completed a probationary period. Since 1995, there has been a freeze on the granting of permanent appointments, except for candidates recruited through competitive examinations)		

Source: *Investing in People, Report of the Secretary-General,* A/61/255 of 2006[64]

In addition, the UN Secretariat was also employing consultants and individual contractors as well as persons under the so-called 'when actually employed' contract.[65]

As mentioned earlier, the proposal for the UN contractual reform was initially submitted in 2000 but had to be refined and modified several times before the UN General Assembly gave it the green light in December 2008.[66] The reform took effect as of 1 July 2009 when new *UN Staff Regulations* and new *UN Staff Rules* came into force.[67]

---

64 Ibid., p. 49.

65 See *Administrative Instruction, Consultants and Individual Contractors, consolidated text*, and *Secretary-General's Bulletin, Use of "When Actually Employed" Contracts for Special Representatives, Envoys and Other Special High-level Positions*.

66 For the overview, see *Detailed Proposals for Streamlining United Nations Contractual Arrangements: A Way Forward, Report of the Secretary-General, A/63/298*, 15.08. 2008, available in the Official Document System of the United Nations, available at http://documents.un.org/, last visited on 30.12.2010. For the General Assembly's decision, see *General Assembly Resolution 63/250*, Section II, para. 2.

67 *UN Staff Regulations of 2009*, and *UN Staff Rules of 2009*. See also *General Assembly Resolution 63/250*,

The latter were, however, referred to as 'provisional'. The reason for this was that a number of specific issues related to the reform of contractual arrangements were postponed by the General Assembly when approving the reform in December 2008, pending further clarification by the Secretary-General and subsequent approval by the General Assembly to take place in 2009.[68] These specific issues related to the conditions under which continuing appointments could be granted. It was envisaged that the whole system, including the granting of continuing appointments, would be applicable as of 1 January 2010 but this deadline was not met. Dissatisfied with inability of the UN Secretary-General to provide satisfactory details on issues relating to the granting of continuing appointments, the General Assembly decided in December 2009 to further postpone the matter and deal with it at its next, sixty-fifth, session that took place in late 2010.[69] In December 2010, the General Assembly finally approved the granting of continuing appointments as of 1 January 2011 and established a detailed list of conditions to be respected.[70] The General Assembly also took note of new *UN Staff Rules* which the Secretary-General had, once again provisionally, promulgated in September 2010, thus before the final decision of the General Assembly on the issue of continuing appointments was adopted. The Secretary-General promulgated these provisional *UN Staff Rules* in accordance with the relevant provisions of the *UN Staff Regulations* which allow for the preparation of provisional staff rules implementing *UN Staff Regulations*, subject to the notification to the General Assembly.[71] Since the General Assembly did not indicate otherwise, the provisional *UN Staff Rules* promulgated in September 2010 – and applied since then on a provisional basis – were to come into full force on 1 January

Section II, para. 2.

[68] *General Assembly Resolution 63/250*, Section II, para. 3.

[69] *Draft Decision Submitted by the Chairman of the Committee following Informal Consultations, Provisional Staff Rules, A/C.5/64/L.9*, 02.12.2009, available in the Official Document System of the United Nations, available at http://documents.un.org/, last visited on 30.12.2010; *Human Resources Management, Report of the Fifth Committee, A/64/550*, 03.12.2010, available in the Official Document System of the United Nations, available at http://documents.un.org/, last visited on 30.12.2010, Section II, paras. 4-6; *Official Records, General Assembly, Sixty-fourth Session, 67th Plenary Meeting A/64/PV.67*, 22.12.2009, available in the Official Document System of the United Nations, available at http://documents.un.org, last visited on 30.12.2010; and *General Assembly Calls for Urgent Implementation of Proposals to Assist Survivors of 1994 Rwandan Genocide, including Medical Care, Skills Training, Victim Support*, Press Release, GA/10908, 22.12.2009, available at http://www.un.org/News/Press/docs//2009/ga10908.doc.htm, last visited on 30.12.2010.

[70] *General Assembly Resolution 65/247*, Section VI.

[71] *UN Staff Regulations of 2009*, Regulations 12.2. and 12.3. Note that the Secretary-General explained that the new provisional *UN Staff Rules* were promulgated in order to implement the new contractual arrangements approved by the General Assembly in December 2008. – *Provisional Staff Rules, Report of the Secretary-General, A/65/202*, 20.08.2010, available in the Official Document System of the United Nations, available at http://documents.un.org/, last visited on 30.12.2010, Summary. It is, however, not clear why these Rules did not await a decision of the General Assembly with regard to the granting of continuing appointments, which was left for further decision. This is in particular so considering the fact that in 2009 a new set of the *UN Staff Rules* was adopted together with the new *UN Staff Regulations*, both of them implementing the new contractual arrangements approved by the General Assembly in December 2008. After that date, no further decisions of the General Assembly were taken in this respect until December 2010, thus after the promulgation of the provisional *UN Staff Rules* in question.

2011, as determined by the Secretary-General.[72] As explained above, these *UN Staff Rules* are therefore referred to in this study as the *UN Staff Rules*, not as *Provisional UN Staff Rules*. That said, these Rules must be read in conjunction with the General Assembly's resolution adopted in December 2010 establishing conditions for granting continuing appointments, which were not yet included in the Rules on the date on this study was concluded, i.e. on 1 January 2011.

The *UN Staff Regulations* of 2009, the *UN Staff Rules* of 2010 and the relevant General Assembly resolutions, in particular the resolution adopted in December 2010, are the basis on which the following section explains the contractual framework in the UN Secretariat at present.

2.3. New contractual arrangements in the UN Secretariat

There is a single set of *UN Staff Regulations*, a single set of *UN Staff Rules* and three types of appointment that may be granted in the UN Secretariat at present. The new *UN Staff Rules* are based on the former 100 series and apply to all three new types of appointment.[73] The three new types of appointment are: temporary, fixed-term and continuing appointment. Compared to the previous contractual framework, the new temporary appointments replace the appointments given for short terms, namely the fixed-term appointments of duration shorter than one year governed by the 100 series of the *UN Staff Rules*; short-term appointments governed by the 200 and 300 series of the *UN Staff Rules*; and appointments of limited duration under the 300 series if the appointment duration was less than one year. The new fixed-term appointment replaces the previous fixed-term appointment of duration up to five years governed by the 100 series of the *UN Staff Rules*; the probationary appointment also governed by the 100 series; the fixed-term appointment of project personnel with intermediate status governed by the 200 series; and the appointment of limited duration under the 300 series. The remaining former types of appointment, namely permanent appointments, indefinite appointments and fixed-term appointments of duration longer than five years, all three formerly governed by the 100 series of the *UN Staff Rules*, as well as the appointment of project personnel with long-term status governed by the 200 series, are replaced by the third and the last new type of appointment, the continuing appointment.[74]

Staff members who enter the UN Secretariat after 1 July 2009 receive either temporary or fixed-term appointment, depending on the duration of the service. When that duration is less than one year, it results in a temporary appointment, and when it is one year or more, a fixed-term appointment is used. Continuing appointments are to be granted only after a number of years of continuing service, thus never to new recruits.

[72] This is in accordance with Regulation 12.4 of the *UN Staff Regulations*.

[73] *UN Staff Regulations of 2009*, Regulation 4.5 and *UN Staff Rules*.

[74] See *Investing in People, Report of the Secretary-General, A/61/255*, para. 240.

Before going into details with regard to the three new types of appointment, it should be noted that a number of transitional arrangements were approved by the UN General Assembly together with the new contracts. Arguably the most important transitional arrangement relates to permanent appointments that existed until 2009. On the basis of these transitional arrangements, a large number of staff will continue to serve under such permanent appointments, alongside staff who will be granted continuing appointments. This concerns staff who held permanent appointments before the effective date of the contractual reform, i.e. on 30 June 2009, and staff who acquired a right to be considered for granting permanent appointment before or on that date.[75] Although as of 1 July 2009 permanent appointments are governed by the terms and conditions which now apply to continuing appointments, there are some exceptions relating to the termination of permanent appointments. Arguably the most important exception is the inapplicability of the right of the Secretary-General to terminate an appointment in the interest of good administration of the organization without staff consent.[76] All transitional arrangements, including those that apply to former indefinite, probationary, fixed-term and mission appointments as well as 200-series and 300-series appointments can be found in Chapter XIII of the *UN Staff Rules*.[77]

2.3.1. New types of appointment

Temporary appointments

Temporary appointments may be used to meet seasonal and peak workloads and specific short-term requirements. As already mentioned, these appointments may last less than one year, although there is an exception. In case of operational needs in the field and in case of special projects with finite mandates, temporary appointments may be extended by a year, not exceeding two years in total. The expiry date of each temporary appointment is precisely specified in the letter of appointment.[78] Temporary appointments may be extended or renewed, though the *UN Staff Rules* explicitly stipulate that there is no expectancy of appointment renewal, legal or

[75] *UN Staff Rules*, Rule 13.1(a) and 13.4(b). See also *Secretary-General's Bulletin, Consideration for Conversion to Permanent Appointment of Staff Members of the Secretariat Eligible to be Considered by 30 June 2009, ST/SGB/2009/10*, 23.06.2009, available in the Human Resources Handbook of the United Nations, available at http://www.un.org/hr_handbook/English/, last visited on 30.12.2010.

[76] *UN Staff Rules*, Chapter XIII, in particular Rule 13.1(c).

[77] Ibid.,, Chapter XIII. See also *Human Resources Management Reform: Contractual Arrangements and Harmonization of Conditions of Service, Report of the Secretary-General, A/65/305/Add.1*, 07.09.2010, available in the Official Document System of the United Nations, available at http://documents.un.org/, last visited on 30.12.2010, Section I.

[78] *UN Staff Rules*, Rule 4.12. Further explanation of the operational needs in the field and special projects, which could justify an extension of a temporary appointment for an additional year, can be found in the Secretary-General's report of 2009 which introduced the 2009 *UN Staff Rules*. – *Provisional Staff Rules, Report of the Secretary-General, A/64/230*, 05.08.2009, available in the Official Document System of the United Nations, available at http://documents.un.org/, last visited on 30.12.2010, Section V, para. 26. This is further formalized in an administrative instruction dealing with administration of temporary appointments. - *Administrative Instruction, Administration of Temporary Appointments*, Section 15.

other. They also state that a temporary appointment may not be converted to any other type of appointment.[79]

On the basis of the modalities for temporary appointments approved by the UN General Assembly, the Secretary-General adopted an administrative instruction on administering them.[80] This instruction repeats that temporary appointments may only be granted for service expected to last less than one year, including extensions or successive appointments of the same person in the same or in a different office.[81] It also provides that when the set time limit is reached, the same staff may not be engaged again under a new temporary appointment or as a consultant or individual contractor in the same duty station without a break of at least three months or in a different duty station without a break of at least 31 days.[82] The precise conditions for the extension of temporary appointments for up to two years in cases of operational needs in the field and special projects with finite duration are set out in the instruction as well.[83] The instruction also lists examples of short-term needs for which temporary appointments may be granted – unexpected and/or temporary emergency or surge demand involving a natural disaster, conflict, violence or similar circumstance; seasonal or peak work which cannot be carried out by existing staff members; filling a position of staff on leave or on assignment; filling a position pending the finalization of the regular selection process, and special project with finite duration.[84]

Fixed-term appointments

The second new type of appointment is the fixed-term appointment. Such appointment may be used for engaging staff in cases of service of a prescribed duration, including staff on secondment. It may be concluded for a period of one to five years, not including possible renewals, each of which may be for any period up to five years. Similarly as with temporary appointments, the expiration date of each individual fixed-term appointment must be set out in the letter of appointment.[85] Also as with temporary appointments, fixed-term appointments carry no expectancy of renewal or conversion, except for staff members recruited via a competitive examination who have successfully completed two years of service under a fixed-term appointment. Their fixed-term appointment is, in principle, always to be converted to a continuing appointment after these two years.

Conversion to a continuing appointment is also possible for other fixed-term appointments, subject to conditions set out by the UN General Assembly and explained in more detail below.[86] However, unlike staff recruited via a competitive

[79] *UN Staff Rules*, Rule 4.12(c).

[80] *Administrative Instruction, Administration of Temporary Appointments*.

[81] Ibid., Section 2.2-2.3 and 2.5.

[82] Ibid., Section 14.1.

[83] Ibid., Section 15.

[84] Ibid., Section 2.2.

[85] *UN Staff Rules*, Rules 4.13(a) and 4.14(b)..

[86] See below, section 3.2.3.

examination, other staff have no formal legal right to a conversion, or to contract renewal for that matter.[87]

The possibility of conversion to a continuing appointment distinguishes fixed-term appointments from temporary ones – the latter may not be converted to any other appointment and they end when the period of appointment set out in the letter of appointment expires. Contrarily, fixed-term appointments may end upon the expiry of the period of appointment set out in the letter of appointment, but they may also be extended or renewed for another period of appointment, or converted into a continuing appointment. This is similar to the former regime of fixed-term appointments concluded under the 100 series of the *UN Staff Rules*. Those appointments could also end upon expiry of the set fixed term, be extended or renewed, or be converted to a permanent appointment. Renewals could also be repeated several times since there also was no time limit on the total duration of this type of appointment.[88]

Continuing appointments

The third new type of appointment is the continuing appointment. The new *UN Staff Regulations* and the *UN Staff Rules* do not contain many details on this type of appointment, though they stipulate that continuing appointments are open-ended and that their award is subject to conditions to be specified by the Secretary-General.[89] The current lack of details on this type of appointment in the formal legal instruments is most probably due to the fact that the modalities of implementation of continuing appointments were not yet worked out sufficiently enough for approval by the General Assembly at the time when the *UN Staff Regulations* and the *UN Staff Rules* were promulgated. In the meantime, however, the General Assembly approved these modalities in its resolution of December 2010. It established a number of eligibility criteria and other conditions under which continuing appointments may from 1 January 2011 onwards be granted.[90]

On the basis of the conditions set out by the General Assembly it can be argued that the continuing appointment has two defining features. First, the continuing appointment may only be granted to staff who have first served on a fixed-term appointment, thus never directly to new recruits; and second, the continuing appointment is open-ended. The latter means that, although the continuing appointment has no expiry period, it does not provide (a guarantee) for permanency as it may be terminated at any time in the interest of the good administration of the

---

[87] *UN Staff Rules*, Rule 4.13 and 4.14(c).

[88] *UN Staff Rules of 2002*, Rule 104.12(b). Initially, a possibility of extension of new fixed-term appointments was to be more limited than eventually adopted. While possible extensions in case of staff serving in UN funds and programmes were not be to time-limited, extensions in case of the peacekeeping staff was to be limited to a maximum of two years and subject to the operational needs of the peacekeeping operations, though no longer limited to a particular mission. All other extensions beyond five years were to be limited to a maximum of one year. - *Detailed Proposals for Streamlining United Nations Contractual Arrangements: A Way Forward, Report of the Secretary-General, A/63/298*, para. 13.

[89] *UN Staff Rules*, Rule 4.14 (a) and (c).

[90] *General Assembly Resolution 65/247*, Section VI.

organization, subject to a number of conditions. Given their extreme importance for the status of UN staff, both main features of the new continuing appointments – their acquisition and their possible termination in the interest of the good administration of the organization – are explained in more detail in the following two sections. The latter issue is discussed also in a broader context, i.e. also in relation to the other types of appointment. This is necessary in order to explain the differences between the former and the current system of contractual arrangements in the UN Secretariat.

2.3.2. Conversion of fixed-term appointments to continuing appointments

Under the new contractual framework of the UN Secretariat, most staff holding fixed-term appointments are eligible for conversion into continuing appointments, subject to a number criteria and conditions. Before explaining each of them, it must be noted that they do not apply to staff recruited via the NCRE and language staff who are to be granted continuing appointments after two years of successful probationary service.[91] This – clearly more favourable – treatment of staff recruited through the NCRE and language staff was adopted by the General Assembly against the wish of the Secretary-General to maintain a common threshold of five years for all staff. The Secretary-General emphasized that the elimination of inequalities and inconsistencies in treatment between different categories of staff and the simplification of administration of various types of contracts was one of the fundamental objectives of the whole reform of the contractual arrangements.[92] Nonetheless, the General Assembly considered it important not to disadvantage staff recruited via competitive examinations under the new system of contractual arrangements when compared to the former one.[93]

Turning to the eligibility criteria for granting continuing appointment to the rest of UN staff, the first criterion is a minimum of five years of continuing service under the *UN Staff Regulations* and *UN Staff Rules*, including periods of service in an entity applying these sets of rules.[94] This means staff members whose fixed-term appointment ends before the required five years, for example because the appointment was concluded for a shorter period of time and was not extended or renewed, or because the appointment was terminated, are not be eligible for continuing appointment. The same applies to staff who have served at the UN for five years but their service has not been continuous. Thus, a series of separate fixed-term appointments with

[91] Ibid., para. 50.

[92] *Detailed Proposals for Streamlining United Nations Contractual Arrangements: A Way Forward, Report of the Secretary-General, A/63/298*, Section III, paras. 20-22.

[93] See *General Assembly Resolution 63/250*, Section II, paras. 4(f) and 23. See also *Implementation of Continuing Appointments, Report of the Secretary-General, A/64/267*, 07.08.2009, available in the Official Document System of the United Nations, available at http://documents.un.org/, last visited on 30.12.2010, Section III, Part 6.

[94] *General Assembly Resolution 65/247*, available in the Official Document System of the United Nations,para. 53(a). Note that this includes staff who were previously appointed under the 100, 200 or 300 series of the *UN Staff Rules* and who have been appointed on a fixed-term appointment through a competitive process since 1 July 2009, if they have served continuously for five years.

breaks in between does not count for the purposes of eligibility for continuing appointment. Also service on a temporary appointment does not count. Moreover, as expressly stated by the General Assembly, periods of service of Junior Professional Officers are not to be taken into account when calculating the five-year period.[95]

The next few criteria can be grouped together since they exclude certain staff from eligibility for granting of continuing appointments, even if these staff have served in the UN continuously for five years or more. They concern those serving as national staff recruited for field missions; international or national staff recruited for service in the International Tribunal for Rwanda or International Tribunal for Former Yugoslavia; and staff having less than seven years of service left before reaching the mandatory age of separation.[96] No such staff may be granted continuing appointment.

The third, and last, eligibility criterion for consideration for a continuing appointment relates to the quality of past performance and conduct. To be eligible, staff members must have received performance ratings of at least 'meets expectations' or equivalent in their four most recent performance appraisal reports. In addition, staff must not have been subject to a disciplinary measure during the five years prior to consideration for the granting of a continuing appointment.[97]

Staff satisfying all the above mentioned eligibility criteria are eligible for the granting of a continuing appointment. However, this does not mean all of them will eventually be granted such appointment. That depends on an additional condition which needs to be met, namely the existence of a continuing need in the UN for the service of the staff member concerned. The existence of continuing needs is to be determined on the basis of established and temporary posts of a duration of more than five years and general temporary assistance in special political missions. Excluded are posts for local staff in field missions and posts in the International Tribunal for Rwanda or International Tribunal for Former Yugoslavia. All included posts are then divided into two post envelopes, one for international staff in the Professional and above categories and in the Field Service category and one for staff in the General Service and other locally recruited categories. These post envelopes are to be reviewed by the General Assembly regularly and expanded or contracted, depending on the UN activities. The initial level of the post envelopes, set in December 2010, was 75 per cent of the total number of posts, including existing permanent contracts.[98]

It is interesting to note that before the General Assembly established the system of post envelopes for determining the organization's continuing needs, the Secretary-General had had a different assessment of such needs in mind. He had proposed that the continuing need for the services of the staff member concerned, either at the same department or elsewhere in the UN, would be determined on the basis of

[95] Ibid., para. 59.

[96] Ibid., para. 53(b), (c) and (e). For details on the mandatory age for separation, see below, chapter 7, section 2.2.4.

[97] Ibid., para. 53(d), For details on staff performance appraisal, including ratings, see above, chapter 4, section 2.1.2.3.

[98] Ibid., paras. 51 and 52.

medium- to long-term needs of the UN and on the qualifications, experience and training of each individual considered. A staff member who would have demonstrated that he possesses 'transferable skills' with a potential to carry out long-term functions possibly differing from those of the post he holds at the time of review would be granted continuing appointments despite the 'un-continuing' character of his current post.[99] The assessment of the continuing need of services in the entire UN would be based on a thorough workforce planning. In 2009, when this issue was discussed as one of the elements that needed further clarification before continuing appointments could be implemented, it became clear, that the UN Secretariat was not ready to make such planning yet. As pointed out by the Advisory Committee on Administrative and Budgetary Questions, there was no data on the types of function for which there would be a continuing need and on the number of posts needed in each occupational group. The Committee concluded that because of the absence of such data, there was no proper basis on which continuing appointments could be awarded.[100] The Committee also pointed out that clear and transparent criteria had to be developed for assessing whether individual staff members had transferable skills in order to be granted a continuing appointment. It stressed the need to ensure that this assessment process was objective and transparent.[101] The Committee agreed with the Secretary-General that the whole process had to be centrally managed in order to retain the global picture of the workforce needs in the Secretariat but considered that the procedures proposed so far were inadequate. In the Committee's view, the procedures envisaged by the Secretary-General would be time-consuming, especially in view of the large number of staff who would be eligible for consideration for a continuing appointment in due course. The Committee was also of the opinion that these procedures did not guarantee sufficiently that an organization-wide view would be taken into account and that there was knowledge and capacity present in the relevant bodies to assess future workforce requirements and staff potential.[102] Indeed, as with most other procedures in personnel matters, here too the main work would be done by individual programme managers and/or heads of specific departments, although reviews by other authorities would also take place.[103] All these reasons led the Committee, and subsequently the General Assembly, to postpone implementation of continuing appointments in 2009 and to

[99] *Implementation of Continuing Appointments, Report of the Secretary-General, A/64/267*, Section III, Part D, para. 12(b).

[100] *Human Resources Management, Report of the Advisory Committee on Administrative and Budgetary Questions, A/64/518*, 06.11.2009, available in the Official Document System of the United Nations, available at http://documents.un.org/, last visited on 30.12.2010, Section I, para. 21. See also paras. 7-13 providing information on the number of staff who would be eligible for consideration for a continuing appointment (and as a transitional measure also for a permanent appointment) in the five year period from 2009. The total potential number of such staff was over ten thousand staff members for permanent appointments and almost 23,5 thousand staff members for continuing appointments (four and a half thousand at headquarters and almost nineteen thousand in missions).

[101] Ibid., Section I, para. 22.

[102] Ibid., Section I, paras. 32-33. For details on the proposed procedures, see *Implementation of Continuing Appointments, Report of the Secretary-General, A/64/267*, Section III, Part E.3.

[103] *Implementation of Continuing Appointments, Report of the Secretary-General, A/64/267*, Section III, Part E.3.

adopt a different system for determining the UN's continuing needs in 2010, namely the system of post envelopes.

Under this system (of post envelopes), the granting of individual continuing appointments is linked to the availability of contracts within the appropriate post envelop, which is to be assessed on an annual basis. The decision on which staff members will actually receive continuing appointments is to be made on the basis of their ranking in the number of points they have received through a mechanism set up by the General Assembly in its 2010 resolution.[104] This mechanism entails allocation of a certain number of points to each staff member eligible for the granting of a continuing appointment for the following criteria:

Table 14: Point system to assess the eligibility of staff for conversion from fixed-term to continuing appointments

Criteria	***Number of points***
Rating for the past four performance reports	
Exceeds performance expectations	7 points for each report (for at least a one-year period)
Frequently exceeds performance expectations	5 points for each report (for at least a one-year period)
Service of at least one year (continuous) in a hardship duty station:	
Categories A and B	1 point per tour of duty
Category C	3 points per tour of duty
Category D	5 points per tour of duty
Category E	7 points per tour of duty
Service in a non-family duty station for at least one year (continuous)	2 points per tour of duty
Geographic mobility for at least one year (continuous)	3 points per tour of duty
Functional mobility for at least one year (continuous)	2 points per tour of duty
Proficiency in one official language of the United Nations other than one's mother tongue	2 points
Each additional year of service beyond five years	1 point for each year

Source: *General Assembly Resolution 65/247* of 24.12.2010[105]

All seven mentioned criteria are to be regarded for internationally recruited staff in the Professional and above categories and for staff in the Field Service category

[104] *General Assembly Resolution 65/247*, paras. 54 and 56.

[105] Ibid., Annex.

who are eligible for the granting of continuing appointments. For staff serving in the General Service category and other locally recruited eligible staff, only criteria concerning performance rating, functional mobility, language proficiency and additional years of service are to be taken into account.[106] In case of equally of the number of points, the decision between staff members concerned is to be made on the basis of their seniority, i.e. the length of service.[107]

A direct consequence of this system is that some staff members who satisfy all eligibility criteria for the granting a continuing appointment will nonetheless not receive it if they fall, on the basis of their ranking, outside the appropriate post envelope. In practice, this means that there is a ceiling for the number of continuing appointments to be granted each year. The introduction of such a ceiling was the subject of intense discussions during deliberations over the new system of contractual arrangements. The UN Secretary-General on the one hand and the Member States on the other hand had a different opinion on this matter, both basing themselves on legitimate concerns. The UN Member States were especially concerned about a possible automaticity of conversion of all eligible fixed-term appointments into continuing ones, leading to a large number of staff eventually holding continuing appointments, in addition to a still rather significant number of permanent appointments continuing to exist for the next few decades. UN Member States feared that termination of so many continuing (and permanent) appointments in the case of a change or reduction of operational needs of the UN would represent a too high liability for the UN with regard to the payment of termination indemnity to staff serving on such appointments. The indemnity would not be due for termination of fixed-term appointments.[108] Member States therefore wished to limit the access of staff to continuing appointments by an annual ceiling for conversions. They were of the opinion that staff serving on fixed-term who met requirements for conversion to continuing appointment should be 'eligible – rather than entitled – for continuing contracts'.[109]

The UN Secretary-General, on the other hand, repeatedly expressed himself against the annual ceiling for granting of continuing appointments. In his view, the exclusion of staff eligible for conversion of their appointment to a continuing one

[106] Ibid., paras. 54 and 55.

[107] Ibid., para. 57.

[108] *Implementation of Continuing Appointments, Report of the Secretary-General, A/64/267*, paras. 13-14 and *Human Resources Management, Report of the Advisory Committee on Administrative and Budgetary Questions, A/64/518*, paras. 20-29. According to the most recent data provided by the Secretary-General in September 2010, without a ceiling, there would be in total 27.630 staff members who would become eligible for continuing appointment during the period 2011-2015. – *Human Resources Management Reform: Contractual Arrangements and Harmonization of Conditions of Service, Report of the Secretary-General, A/65/305/Add.1*, para. 40.

[109] From a statement of the Representative of the United States in the Fifth Committee. See *Budget Committee Takes up Reports on Staff Rules for New Contractual Arrangements, Secretariat Make-up, Ethics Office, Disciplinary Matters, Continuing Contracts*, Press Release, GA/AB/3931, 17.11.2009, available at http://www.un.org/News/Press/docs/2009/gaab3931.doc.htm, last visited on 30.12.2010, p. 16.

from receiving it would be against the interest of the UN and unfair to staff.[110] He warned that such action would 'very likely expose the Organization to appeals in the internal justice system based on claims of arbitrariness and inequitable treatment of staff'.[111] The Secretary-General also considered that a ceiling would be administratively burdensome because it would require constant monitoring and thus significant resources.[112] Unlike the General Assembly, the Secretary-General seemed thus inclined to grant continuing appointments in principle to all well performing staff for whose services there would be continuing needs in the UN Secretariat. He held that the eligibility criteria for granting continuing appointments would sufficiently guarantee that such appointments would not be automatic and that a reasonable proportion of staff would remain on fixed-term appointments at any given time.[113]

Despite the strong opposition by the Secretary-General, the General Assembly eventually did introduce a ceiling for the granting of continuing appointments in the form of post envelopes and the corresponding requirement of the availability of posts in the appropriate post envelop.

2.3.3. Termination of appointments in the interest of the good administration

One of the most important novelties of the new contractual framework of the UN Secretariat is the change in the conditions under which termination of appointments in the interest (of the good administration) of the organization may occur. Under the old system, appointments concluded for indefinite period, i.e. with no expiry period specified in the letter of appointment, could have been unilaterally terminated by the UN Secretary-General on this legal ground at any time. On the contrary, fixed-

[110] *Detailed Proposals for Streamlining United Nations Contractual Arrangements: A Way Forward, Report of the Secretary-General, A/63/298*, Section III, para. 30.

[111] *Implementation of Continuing Appointments, Report of the Secretary-General, A/64/267*, Section III, Part E.1, para. 15. See also *Human Resources Management, Report of the Advisory Committee on Administrative and Budgetary Questions, A/65/537*, para. 48.

[112] *Human Resources Management Reform: Contractual Arrangements and Harmonization of Conditions of Service, Report of the Secretary-General, A/65/305/Add.1*, paras. 36 and 44.

[113] Ibid., paras. 38 and 43. The Secretary-General was supported in this matter by the Advisory Committee on Administrative and Budgetary Questions which also disagreed with the introduction of a ceiling. On the other hand, the Committee was against 'awarding continuing appointments to virtually all staff over time'. – *Human Resources Management, Report of the Advisory Committee on Administrative and Budgetary Questions, A/65/537*, para. 55. The Committee's suggestion was that, rather than introducing a ceiling for conversions, the eligibility criteria for granting continuing appointments should be adjusted. - *Human Resources Management, Report of the Advisory Committee on Administrative and Budgetary Questions, A/64/518*, Section I, para. 29. For more details on the discussion concerning the introduction of a ceiling for granting continuing appointments, see for example *Detailed Proposals for Streamlining United Nations Contractual Arrangements: A Way Forward, Report of the Secretary-General, A/63/298*, Section III, para. 30; *Implementation of Continuing Appointments, Report of the Secretary-General, A/64/267*, Section III, Part E.1; *Human Resources Management, Report of the Advisory Committee on Administrative and Budgetary Questions, A/64/518*, Section I, paras. 26-30; *Human Resources Management Reform: Contractual Arrangements and Harmonization of Conditions of Service, Report of the Secretary-General, A/65/305/Add.1*, Section III, Part C.3(a); and *Human Resources Management, Report of the Advisory Committee on Administrative and Budgetary Questions, A/65/537*, paras. 48 and 55-58.

term appointments could have been terminated on this ground before the expiry of the fixed period only with the consent of the staff member concerned. The same condition applied to permanent appointments.[114] Termination in the interest of the good administration in the two last instances was thus not possible when the staff member contested it.

According to the current *UN Staff Regulations*, termination in the interest of the good administration of the UN is still possible for all types of appointment: temporary, fixed-term and continuing one. The important difference is that termination of the first two mentioned types is subject to consent by the staff member concerned, whereas termination of the last one is not.[115] Hence, while under the former system of contractual arrangements, permanent appointments could not be terminated in this manner without staff members' consent, the new continuing appointments can. This possibility reflects the open-endedness of the continuing appointment, mentioned above as one of the two most important features of this type of appointment.[116] Its importance for the status of UN staff who will hold continuing appointment is self-evident. Unlike holders of permanent appointments, holders of continuing appointments will have no formal security of tenure.

Realizing the possible consequences of this change, the UN General Assembly has been very strict on the UN Secretary-General in this particular matter. In an attempt to limit the danger of an overly broad interpretation of the concept of 'in the interest of the good administration', the Assembly included its own interpretation of this concept in the resolution in which it approved the new contractual arrangements. This interpretation contains only one specific reason that would allow termination on this legal ground, namely 'a change or termination of a mandate'.[117] Said that, this interpretation was characterized by the General Assembly itself as 'principal', which appears to have left certain space to the UN Secretary-General to add other interpretations.[118] This seems at least to have been the perception by the UN Secretary-General who noted in his report of 2010 that this legal ground for termination of continuing appointments covered 'a number of legitimate considerations, such as changing needs, functions and mandates of the United Nations, the reori-

[114] *UN Staff Regulations of 2007*, Regulation 9.1(a) and (c). There was a difference in the wording used in the two provisions: 'the interest of the good administration of the Organization' used in Regulation 9.1(a) applicable to termination of permanent appointments and fixed-term appointment prior to the expiry of the fixed-term period; and 'the interests of the United Nations' used in Regulation 9.1 (c) applicable to termination of appointments of indefinite duration, respectively. Despite this difference in wording, however, both provisions in fact related to the same situation, the situation in which interest of the UN was at stake. This conclusion is also supported by the fact that the current *UN Staff Regulations* unified the wording in both provisions in which it uses it. - *UN Staff Regulations of 2009*, Regulation 9.3(a)(vi) and (b).

[115] *UN Staff Regulations of 2009*, Regulation 9.6(c)(vi) and (d).

[116] Other grounds for termination of permanent appointment will remain applicable to the continuing appointment as they stand at present. They are discussed in the chapter dealing with the issue of separation from service. See below, chapter 7, section 2.3.

[117] *General Assembly Resolution 63/250*, Section II, para. 22.

[118] Ibid., Section II, para. 22.

entation of its programmes or funding cuts'.[119] It should be noted, however, that the Advisory Committee on Administrative and Budgetary Questions disagreed with the Secretary-General's interpretation and noted that it went beyond the definition adopted by the General Assembly.[120]

The importance given to this matter by the General Assembly is also demonstrated by its request to the Secretary-General on detailed information on the procedures to be used for reviewing staff performance and of the continuing need for staff services, both relevant for granting and terminating future continuing appointments. The Assembly wished to be informed how accountability for granting and terminating continuing appointments would be ensured, so that both actions would be taken 'in a fair and transparent manner, with full regard to due process and the rights of staff'.[121] Since such information on procedures had been provided in the Secretary-General's report on the basis of which the new contractual arrangements were approved by the General Assembly, it appears that the Assembly did not consider the proposed procedures as sufficient to safeguard the objectivity and transparency of the process. The Secretary-General's proposal was therefore modified, first in 2009 and then again in 2010. Since this last proposal submitted in 2010 was not further discussed or commented on and the granting of continuing appointment was approved, it can be expected that it will be implemented.

2.3.4. Procedures for granting continuing appointments

The procedures initially proposed by the Secretary-General included a recommendation by the relevant programme manager, a possibility for review by the staff member concerned, a decision by the OHRM; and a possibility of appeal by the staff member.[122] As already mentioned, in a subsequent report, submitted upon request of the General Assembly in 2009, the Secretary-General made some important modifications, in particular a review of the recommendation of the OHRM by joint review bodies together with the recommendations of the relevant programme manager and comments thereon by the staff member concerned. The advice of the joint review bodies would not be binding upon the Assistant Secretary-General, and in case of D-2 posts upon the Secretary-General, who would take the final decision. However, the advice of the joint review body would need to be taken into account.[123]

The final proposal, presented by the Secretary-General in 2010, contained the following procedure for granting continuing appointments. It is to begin with the

[119] *Human Resources Management Reform: Contractual Arrangements and Harmonization of Conditions of Service, Report of the Secretary-General, A/65/305/Add.1*, para. 39.

[120] *Human Resources Management, Report of the Advisory Committee on Administrative and Budgetary Questions, A/65/537*, para. 54.

[121] *General Assembly Resolution 63/250*, Section II, para. 4(e).

[122] See *Detailed Proposals for Streamlining United Nations Contractual Arrangements: A Way Forward, Report of the Secretary-General, A/63/298*, para. 28.

[123] *Implementation of Continuing Appointments, Report of the Secretary-General, A/64/267*, Section III, Part E.4.

regular submission of departmental lists of staff who have reached five years of continuing service and become eligible for consideration for continuing appointment. For field staff, the lists are to be submitted by the local human resources office or the Department of Field Support to the relevant programme manager. For other internationally recruited staff and staff at the Headquarters in New York, the lists are to be submitted by the relevant executive offices at Headquarters to the relevant Head of Department. The programme manager or the Head of Department is to undertake the first review of eligible staff, performance and disciplinary record, and prepare a recommendation which he is to submit to the local human resources office or the Department of Field Support or to the OHRM, respectively. There a second review is to take place, relating to the performance and disciplinary record of staff under consideration as well as to the need for his services. The second review conducted in the field is to be sent to the OHRM which is to act as the central point for all final reviews. In case of a joint positive recommendation from the first and the second review, the staff member concerned is to be granted a continuing appointment. In case of a positive recommendation from the first review but a negative opinion of the OHRM, the case may be submitted to the central review body. This is, however, to be at discretion of the OHRM, which is rather surprising and difficult to explain. When there is no joint positive recommendation, the case is to be submitted to the appropriate advisory body for review and advice, followed by a final decision by the Assistant Secretary-General for Human Resources Management on behalf of the Secretary-General. The final (negative) decision can be appealed through the system of internal justice, in accordance with the relevant provisions of the *UN Staff Regulations* and the *UN Staff Rules*. Note that authority to grant continuing appointments to locally recruited staff in the field is to be delegated to offices away from the Headquarters. These offices are to follow a procedure similar to the one just described.[124] The fact that two different instances are to review the proposal for (non)granting of continuing appointments is to be praised as it increases the objectivity of the process and helps to prevent favouritism and nepotism in it. It is, however, unfortunate that where the first and the second reviewer disagree, it is up to the latter to decide whether the case is sent to the central review body or not. Clearly, in order to ensure the objectivity and transparency of this process, such action should be an automatic consequence of any disagreement between the first and the second reviewer. The fact that the final decision not to grant a continuing appointment is subject to further judicial review does not change this conclusion, given the fact that initiation of legal proceedings is not always an (easy) step to take for the staff member concerned.

[124] *Human Resources Management Reform: Contractual Arrangements and Harmonization of Conditions of Service, Report of the Secretary-General, A/65/305/Add.1*, para. 51.

Scheme 20: Procedure for granting continuing appointments in the UN Secretariat

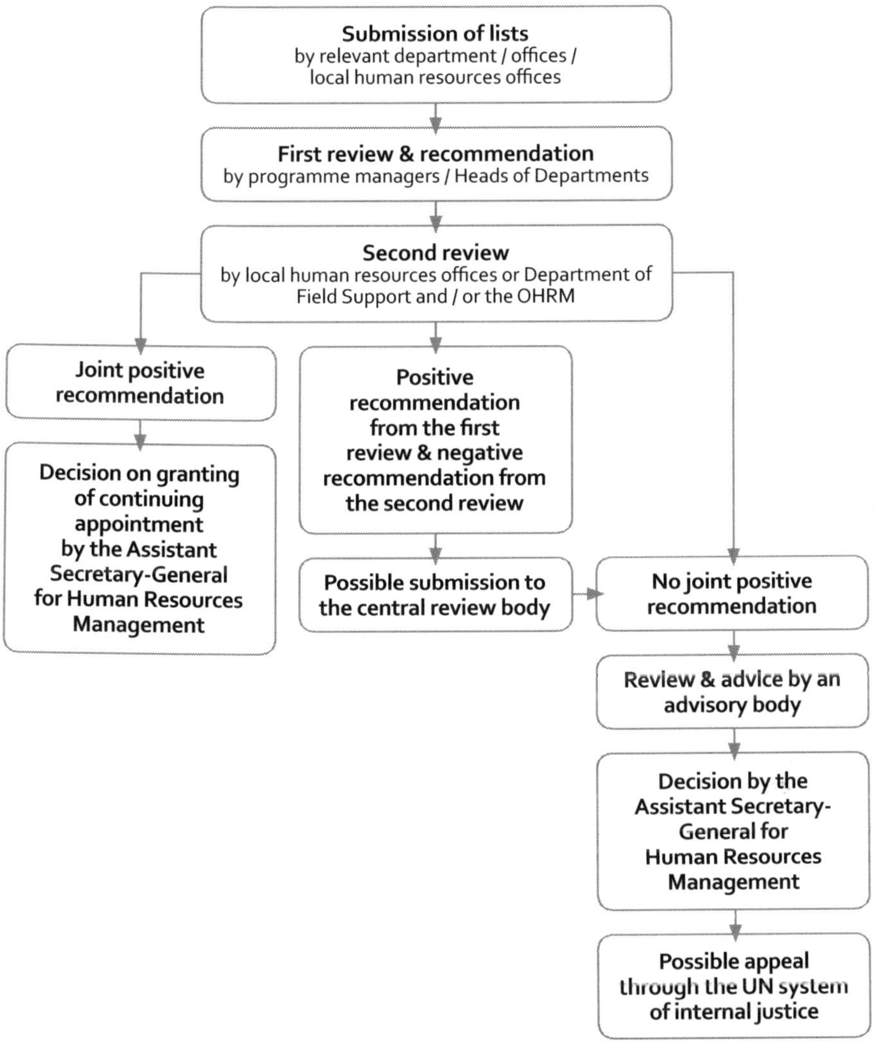

2.4. UN career service at present

The aim of this chapter is to discuss the issue of security of tenure regarded for almost a century as one of the most important conditions enduring the independence and impartiality of the international civil service. Until 2009, permanent appointments were the tool implementing this security of tenure in the UN Secretariat. In 2009, however, this type of appointment was abolished. Consequently, it appears, surely at first sight, that a significant change took place in the UN, removing the security of tenure for international civil servants serving in the UN Secretariat, thereby endangering their independence and impartiality. This certainly was the opinion of the UN staff unions. In 2008 the unions presented their views to the

General Assembly stressing their fear that the replacement of permanent appointments with continuing ones would compromise the integrity, loyalty, independence and impartiality of the international civil service.[125] The unions recalled a well-known 1961 lecture by Dag Hammarskjöld in which he discussed the importance of tenure for the existence of an independent international civil service. On that basis the unions concluded that:

> *A change from permanent contracts to a less secure form of contractual status would lead to an "intergovernmental civil service" where allegiance would shift from the Organization to individuals or Governments.*[126]

This study disagrees with the unions' view and argues that, as far as the existence of an independent career service is concerned, in fact, not much has changed in the UN. It argues that the replacement of permanent appointments by continuing ones does not mean the end of such career service – for at least two reasons: first, a large number of staff will continue to serve under permanent appointments for decades and, second, staff serving on continuing appointments will be protected against possible improper or abusive separation from service by a number of legal safeguards, similarly as permanent staff were under the previous system. In addition, a possibility for most staff engaged on a non-permanent (other than merely a short-term) basis to gain eligibility for conversion of their appointment to continuing ones could in fact enhance protection of many non-permanent staff who previously served on appointments which did not provide a possibility of conversion. Under the previous system, such staff had to fear non-extension or non-renewal of their appointments each time the expiry period was approaching, having no guarantees for future, also not when their mission or project was clearly to continue for years. This situation inevitably created unwanted incentives for a recourse to sources which could influence appointments' extension or renewal. Under the new contractual framework, many of the staff concerned should acquire an equal chance to obtain a continuing status and if so, they would thus no longer need to fear the regular expiry of their contract.

In order to assess changes introduced by the reform of contractual arrangements in more detail as well as their possible influence on the protection of the independent and impartial status of the international civil servants, it must be first recalled that there are three main elements to be looked at. The first concerns the existence of an adequate ratio of career versus non-career staff. The second element relates to the protection of non-career staff with regard to the possibility of extension of

---

[125] *Views of the Staff Representatives of the United Nations Secretariat, A/C.5/63/3/Add.2*, para. 69 and *Views of the Staff Representatives of the United Nations Secretariat: Staff Union (New York), Field Staff Union (Brindisi) and Staff Coordinating Council (United Nations Office in Geneva), Addendum, A/C.5/63/3/Add.2*, para. 6.

[126] *Views of the Staff Representatives of the United Nations Secretariat, A/C.5/63/3/Add.2*, para. 69. Staff unions feared that the termination of appointments in the interest of good administration of the organization, which was not yet defined at the time of their report, would be 'wide open to abuse by a management that has a tract record if abuse'. - *Views of the Staff Representatives of the United Nations Secretariat: Staff Union (New York), Field Staff Union (Brindisi) and Staff Coordinating Council (United Nations Office in Geneva), Addendum, A/C.5/63/3/Add.2*, para. 7.

their appointments and/or their conversion into career appointments. The third concerns the protection of career staff against improper or abusive termination of their appointment.

2.4.1. Ratio of career *versus* non-career staff

As for the first mentioned element, not much seems to have changed as a result of the 2009 reform. When approving the new contractual framework, the General Assembly explicitly stated in its resolution that:

> *a judicious mix of career and fixed-term appointments [is to be ensured by the Secretary-General], so as to have an appropriate balance between institutional memory, long-term commitments and independence and the ability to bring in fresh insight and expertise, and to dismiss non-performing staff.*[127]

This request clearly shows that the Assembly attaches significant importance to maintaining a proper balance between the number of career and non-career staff, thereby willing to contribute to safeguarding the independence of the international civil service. The precise proportion of the career staff has not been established, except for staff in posts subject to geographical distribution where 70 per cent should be on permanent contracts.[128] For other posts, however, the General Assembly has provided no indication of the ratio, only requiring 'a judicious mix'. Theoretically, this does not necessarily entail that the proportion of all career staff should be larger than that of non-career staff. Nonetheless, the express reference to the need to safeguard independence of the international civil service clearly points in this direction. It remains to be seen how the Secretary-General will implement the General Assembly's request.

2.4.2. Protection of non-career staff

With regard to the protection of non-career staff, the second element to be assessed in the evaluation of the UN reform of contractual arrangements, two partly inter-related aspects are relevant. The first relates to access of (future) UN staff to a career appointment. At the initial stage of employment, future staff needs to be protected against receiving a non-career rather than a career appointment for reasons other than the interests of the UN service, such as political goals of Member States or other extraneous factors. Later, after having served for a longer period of time at the UN Secretariat, staff need to be protected against a denial of conversion of their non-career appointments into career ones if the denial would be based on such improper reasons. The relevant second aspect here is the protection of non-career staff against non-extension or non-renewal of their appointments for such reasons.

[127] *General Assembly Resolution 63/250*, Section II, para. 16.
[128] Ibid., Section II, para. 15.

As explained earlier, in the past, the type of appointment granted to staff, their eventual conversion as well as the extension and/or renewal of non-permanent appointments were often politically influenced. In case of former socialist countries, the situation was further complicated by the fact that their nationals were permitted to serve in international organizations only with the government's consent and, in order for them to retain a genuine connection with the country of origin, for a limited period of time. For other staff, considerations relating to the issue of geographical balance were often more decisive than the requirements of the post at hand or merits of its holder. Good and effective links with Member States' governments could thus have been of great use to staff who wished to remain on appointment with the UN Secretariat and/or to build career there.

This state of affairs was clearly not beneficial to the independent and impartial status of UN staff, rather the contrary. In the meantime, the political situation in former socialist countries changed but, arguably, considerations regarding the issue of geographical distribution have remained largely the same across the UN membership. Although formally the General Assembly has retained a ratio of 70 to 30 per cent for permanent *versus* non-permanent appointments in posts subject to geographical distribution, in specific cases a decision on what type of appointment should be given to an individual could still be influenced by political considerations rather than by the interest of the UN and/or its staff. Therefore, the reform of the contractual arrangements could, arguably, be regarded as a step forward. Under the new contractual arrangements, all staff engaged for jobs of duration of at least one year are to be given the same type of appointment, namely fixed-term appointment. It is no longer possible for the UN Administration to take a different decision and grant, for example, directly a continuing appointment. The exclusion of any discretion on this point removes an opportunity and danger of influencing decisions in individual cases. Similarly, and save for precisely defined exceptions, all staff recruited on the new fixed-term contracts can under the new system become eligible for conversion of their appointment to a continuing one after five years of continuing service.[129] This study argues that the establishment of precise criteria for such conversions has limited, if not completely removed, the UN Administration's discretion in the conversion cases. The difference in the margin of discretion enjoyed by the UN Administration in the past and at present constitutes one of the most important consequences of the UN reform of contractual arrangements for the protection of non-career staff.

Discretion of the UN Administration in matters concerning granting a particular type of appointment, conversion of non-career into career appointments, as well as renewal or extension of non-career appointments has been consistently recognized and supported by the UN judiciary.[130] Of course, and as explained in more detail

[129] For exceptions, see above, section 2.3.2.

[130] On discretion of the UN Administration with regard to the type of appointment to be granted, see *El-Naggar v. Secretary-General of the United Nations, UNAT Judgment No. 205 [1975]*, available at http://untreaty.un.org/UNAT/UNAT_Judgements/Judgements_E/UNAT_00205_E.pdf, last visited on 30.12.2010, para. IV. In this case the UNAT also held that 'its competence [did] not extend to an examination of the reasons for the issue or refusal of a particular type of appointment to a staff

below, discretion of the UN Administration could be limited, for example because of its abuse or because of the Administration's own action or behavior. As summarized by the UNAT in a 2005 case:

> *Exceptions to this rule [regarding discretion of the UN Administration] may be found in countervailing circumstances, such as an express promise or an abuse of discretion including bias, prejudice or other discrimination against the staff member, or any extraneous or improper motivation on the part of the Administration.*[131]

In the absence of such circumstances, however, discretion of the UN Administration has always been regarded as broad, leaving considerable margin of appreciation in each individual case. This study argues that the new contractual arrangements may result in reconsideration of this state of affairs in the future in two instances – first, when decisions are being taken on the type of appointment to be granted to new incoming staff; and second, when decisions are being made on which staff will receive conversion of their fixed-term appointment into a continuing one. As far as the renewal and/or extension of non-career appointments are concerned, the study argues that, despite the original intensions, the new contractual arrangements do not bring about a significant change in the level of protection of non-career staff when compared to the past system.

Type of appointment to be granted & their conversion

With regard to the choice of the type of appointment the UN Administration may grant to the incoming staff, this study argues that the new contractual arrangements

member in the absence of entitlements in this regard'. – Ibid. On the discretion in contract renewal matters, see, for example, *Rau, UNAT Judgment No. 101 [1966]*, para. III; *Belas-Gianou v. Secretary-General of the United Nations, UNAT Judgment No. 707 [1995]*, available at http://untreaty.un.org/UNAT/UNAT_Judgements/Judgements_E/UNAT_00707_E.pdf, last visited on 30.12.2010, para. XVI; and *Case No. 1379, UNAT Judgment No. 1297 [2006]*, para. IV. On the discretion of the UN Administration in conversion matters, see *Mizuno v. Secretary-General of the United Nations, UNAT Judgment No. 415 [1988]*, available at http://untreaty.un.org/UNAT/UNAT_Judgements/Judgements_E/UNAT_00415_E.pdf, last visited on 30.12.2010, para. X. This case concerned in fact a non-renewal of a fixed-term appointment concluded under the former 100 series of the *UN Staff Rules* but is relevant to the issue of contract conversion, too. The applicant in this case challenged the non-extension of his fixed-term contract arguing that he had right to continuing employment, *inter alia*, on the basis of the provision of the *UN Staff Rules* providing at that time that staff on fixed-term contracts had to be given every reasonable consideration for a permanent appointment after five years of service. Due to the non-extension of his contract the applicant had not reached five years. The UNAT ruled that although staff on fixed-term contracts had indeed a right to receive 'every reasonable consideration' for contract conversion, there was no automatic right to, or reasonable expectation for, continuing employment. - *Mizuno, UNAT Judgment No. 415 [1988]*, para. X.

[131] *Applicant v. Secretary-General of the United Nations, UNAT Judgment No. 1234 [2005]*, available at http://untreaty.un.org/UNAT/UNAT_Judgements/Judgements_E/UNAT_01234_E.pdf, last visited on 30.12.2010, para. II. See also *Handelsman v. Secretary-General of the United Nations, UNAT Judgment No. 885 [1998]*, available at http://untreaty.un.org/UNAT/UNAT_Judgements/Judgements_E/UNAT_00885_E.pdf, last visited on 30.12.2010, para. III. Note that burden of proof with regard to the abuse of discretion rests on the staff member alleging the abuse. – *Case No. 1457, UNAT Judgment No. 1392 [2008]*, available at http://untreaty.un.org/UNAT/UNAT_Judgements/Judgements_E/UNAT_01392_E.pdf, last visited on 30.12.2010, para. VI.

of the UN Secretariat have limited the UN Administration's discretion to a significant extent. This is so because under the new contractual framework clear criteria have been established to determine which appointment is to be used in which type of situation, with no overlap possible. Thus, appointments of duration shorter than one year should occur under temporary contracts; appointments of duration longer than one year but of 'prescribed duration' under fixed-term contracts; and appointments for continuing service under continuing appointments. The anomaly of this set up is that no type of appointment has been made available for service which is from the outset of continuing, or at least 'un-prescribed', duration. Continuing appointments, which should in fact cover such situations, cannot initially be granted. Such service (of duration longer than one year and of 'un-prescribed' duration) is thus first to be covered by fixed-term appointment. Despite this anomaly, it can be argued that the new system of contractual arrangement does not leave any margin of appreciation to the UN Administration to decide which type of contract to use and when. The removal of any discretion here strengthens the position of new staff since the Administration has virtually no space to pay regard to any extraneous considerations when deciding which type of appointment to use.

This conclusion stands despite the fact that not all staff eligible for continuing appointment will actually be granted one. In this sense, it could be argued that the UN Administration has retained discretion to decide which type of appointment it will grant at that point of time, i.e. whether it will grant a continuing appointment to an individual staff member eligible for such appointment or rather leave him to continue to serve under a fixed-term appointment. However, here too precise criteria have been established in order to determine which eligible staff will receive a continuing appointment and which eligible staff will not. With the exception of performance evaluation, all these criteria concern an objective occurrence, existence of which cannot be disputed – for example, a continuous service in a hardship duty station of at least one year duration. Even for the criterion relating to performance evaluation, a specific system exists in the UN Secretariat under which such evaluation takes place and may be challenged. It could thus be presumed that the results of the evaluation process will be as objective as possible. Consequently, the UN Administration has in fact no discretion in deciding which eligible individual will be granted continuing appointment and which not – it has to follow the criteria established for this purpose and the consequent ranking of staff that will result from the application of these criteria. The position of UN staff is thus, once again, stronger than it was under the former system. There, staff serving on fixed-term appointments concluded under the 100 series of the *UN Staff Rules* had explicit right to be given every reasonable consideration for a permanent appointment after five years of service. Yet, no precise eligibility criteria existed, only a (rather general) rule allowing for conversions. In addition, the consideration of possible conversion of fixed-term appointments into permanent ones was subject to the requirement of 'taking into account all the interest of the Organization'.[132] Under the new system

[132] *UN Staff Rules of 2002*, Rule 104.12(b)(iii). This provision was invoked for example in cases *Alba et al and Fernandez-Amon et al.* There, the UNAT accepted a defense argument of the UN administration that it could, and even had to, take interests of the organization into account and that financial

of contractual arrangements, no such requirement exists. Moreover, it could be argued that the new UN contractual framework has a different overall set up when compared to the previous one. Continuing appointments can only be granted – and thus received – by way of conversion of fixed-term appointments. This was not the case previously. Under the former system, permanent appointments were normally granted to staff on the basis of their successful completion of probationary appointment. These staff were recruited with the expectation that they would spend their whole career in the UN Secretariat. Conversion of fixed-term appointments to permanent ones was only meant for staff who, although initially recruited for a fixed-term, eventually spent a relatively long time in the Secretariat. The conversion of such appointments was a way of rectifying the situation. It was thus not meant as the main manner of granting permanent appointments. Under the new system, however, this is precisely the intention – no other manner of acquiring continuing appointments is envisaged besides the conversion of fixed-term appointments. Therefore, precise criteria for conversion have been established, removing the UN Administration's discretion in this respect.

This conclusion is also not affected by the existence of the above noted explicit provision in the *UN Staff Rules* providing that there is no legal or other expectancy of conversion of fixed-term appointments into continuing ones. Legal expectancy for contract conversion (or its extension) was explicitly ruled out also under the former *UN Staff Rules.*[133] Yet, and despite repeated recognition of broad discretion of the UN Administration in conversion and renewal matters and the explicit exclusion of legal expectancy in such situations, the UNAT developed a principle of legal expectancy, granting protection for some staff serving on fixed-term against non-renewal or non-conversion of their appointment.

The principle of legal expectancy was developed by the UNAT in order to offer a judicial remedy to UN staff who served under fixed-term appointments in increasingly large numbers. As noted by Amerasinghe, this principle could not be found in the written law of the UN, neither could it be based on the interpretation of such law – as already mentioned, the *UN Staff Rules* explicitly excluded any expectancy of continued employment for staff on fixed-term contracts. Amerasinghe also noted

constrains could have been regarded as such. - *Alba et al and Fernandez-Amon et al v. Secretary-General of the United Nations, UNAT Judgment No. 712 [1995]*, available at http://untreaty.un.org/UNAT/UNAT_Judgements/Judgements_E/UNAT_00712_E.pdf, last visited on 30.12.2010, paras. IV-V. In *Khawaja* the UNAT stressed that 'all the interests of the Organization' were one of the necessary considerations that made a part of 'every reasonable consideration'. - *Khawaja v. Secretary-General of the United Nations, UNAT Judgment No. 930 [1999]*, available at http://untreaty.un.org/UNAT/UNAT_Judgements/Judgements_E/UNAT_00930_E.pdf, last visited on 30.12.2010, para. VII. On the other hand, in *Uspensky* it ruled that all factors relevant for conversion must be considered, not only those that constitute interests of the UN. In that case, the UN administration invoked the financial situation of the UN as reason for non-conversion of the applicant's contract. The UNAT stated that such action had amounted only to 'an illusory consideration' of the applicant's eligibility for permanent appointment because his performance and the length of his service had not been given any consideration. - *Uspensky v. Secretary-General of the United Nations, UNAT Judgment No. 1040 [2001]*, available at http://untreaty.un.org/UNAT/UNAT_Judgements/Judgements_E/UNAT_01040_E.pdf, last visited on 30.12.2010, paras. IV and VI.

[133] *UN Staff Rules of 2002*, Rule 104.12(b)(ii).

that the principle of legitimate expectancy also had no equivalent in national administrative laws.[134] In spite of that, the UNAT developed the principle and applied it in a number of specific cases. It is possible that it will do so in the future, too, although it would be difficult to argue that this principle could provide sufficient protection to all staff on fixed-term whose appointments will not be converted into continuing ones. In addition, because precise criteria exist for determining which eligible staff members should receive continuing appointments and which not, it can be expected that there will be fewer problems in this area and thus no need to invoke the principle of legal expectancy for situations involving conversions of fixed-term appointments into continuing ones.

Renewal/extension of appointments

The above conclusion may be very different for renewals and/or extensions of fixed-term appointments – either before the expiry of the five-year period necessary to acquire eligibility for a continuing appointment, or afterwards in case of staff whose contracts have not been converted because of the insufficient availability of posts in the appropriate post envelope. To begin with the latter, it must be recalled that not all eligible staff will receive a continuing appointment – their number will depend on the number of available posts in the appropriate post envelope established by the General Assembly.[135] It is so that the General Assembly expressly 'urged' the UN Secretary-General to grant five-year fixed-term appointments to all staff who would be eligible for a continuing appointment but who would not receive it because of the limitations of the post envelopes.[136] Nonetheless, this call has not been expressed in the form of a binding rule. Therefore, it will be up to the UN Administration to decide whether it grants further fixed-term appointment to each individual staff member eligible for but not receiving a continuing appointment. In this respect it could therefore be argued that the new contractual arrangements of the UN Secretariat did not bring much of a change. Similarly as in the past, a potentially large number of UN staff will continue to serve on the basis of non-career appointments for a potentially long period of time, without ever receiving career appointments. The only difference is that, in the past, only fixed-term staff serving under the 100 series of the *UN Staff Rules* could be retained in service in this manner, while fixed-term staff under the 200 and 300 series were eventually separated due to the expiry of the maximum period of employment. Under the new system, there is a single series of *UN Staff Rules* and a single type of fixed-term appointment. Therefore, in principle all fixed-term staff, disregarding the details of the type of service, could be held on repeated fixed-term appointments with no overall time maximum, not only the former 100 series staff.

This situation is in sharp contradiction with the intentions of the UN Secretary-General. As noted above, the Secretary-General was of the opinion that all UN staff

---

134 Amerasinghe, *The Law of the International Civil Service, Volume II*, p. 749. See also Plantey, *The International Civil Service, Law and Management*, p. 580.

135 See above, section 2.3.2.

136 *General Assembly Resolution 65/247*, para. 58.

satisfying criteria for continuing appointments should be awarded such appointment. This would bring equality and fairness into the system. Moreover, as stressed in one of the Secretary-General's reports, staff serving on fixed-term appointments would no longer need to worry about their prolongation as the conversion into continuing appointments would always take place always when the conditions are met.[137] According to the original proposal of the Secretary-General, staff whose fixed-term appointment would not be converted in this manner would be separated – non-conversion would inevitably mean that either there is no continuing need for staff service or there is no need for the services of the particular staff member because of his insufficient performance standard. Later, upon a recommendation of the International Civil Service Commission, the Secretary-General modified his proposal and included a few specific instances in which limited extensions or renewals of fixed-term contracts should remain possible.[138] However, as already noted, the eventually adopted system of contractual arrangements retained the possibility of repeated renewals for all fixed-term appointments as well as their non-conversion to continuing ones even if all eligibility criteria are met. For staff who will not be granted continuing appointments, the uncertainty about their further employment at the UN Secretariat will thus continue to be present, as it was in the past. The above mentioned statement of the Secretary-General, emphasizing that staff serving on fixed-term appointment will no longer need to worry about prolongation of their appointments because they will receive continuing ones, thus lost its meaning on the way to the final set up of the new contractual arrangements. It is clear that the Secretary-General's intentions were overruled by the General Assembly, which wished to avoid automaticity of granting of continuing appointments and to limit the number of staff serving on such appointments.[139] As a result, the UN Administration has retained a broad margin of discretion in deciding when and whether it extends or renews fixed-term appointments at the time of their non-conversion into continuing ones.

The same applies to extensions and renewals of fixed-term appointments at the time of their expiry, irrespective of whether such expiry takes place before or after the five-year period (established for acquiring eligibility for conversion into a continuing appointment) has passed. As explained above, all fixed-term appointments may – but do not have to – be extended or renewed, even repeatedly.[140] The new *UN Staff Rules* provide similar conditions for the fixed-term appointments as the former ones. Firstly, Rule 4.13(b) stipulates:

> *A fixed-term appointment may be renewed for any period up to five years at a time.*[141]

[137] *Human Resources Management Reform, Report of the Secretary-General, Addendum, Contractual Arrangements, A/59/263/Add.1*, 09.09.2004, available in the Official Document System of the United Nations, available at http://documents.un.org/, last visited on 30.12.2010, Section III, para. 13.

[138] See *Detailed Proposals for Streamlining United Nations Contractual Arrangements, Report of the Secretary-General, A/62/274*, Section III, paras. 31-35.

[139] See also above, section 2.3.2.

[140] See above, section 2.3.1.

[141] *UN Staff Rules*, Rule 4.13(b). For the relevant provision of the *UN Staff Rules* applicable before the

In addition, Rule 4.13(c) states:

> *A fixed-term appointment does not carry any expectancy, legal or otherwise, of renewal or conversion, irrespective of the length of service, except as provided under staff rule 4.14(b).*[142]

Rule 4.14(b) concerns staff recruited via a competitive examination who, as explained above, are always to be granted continuing appointments after two years in service, subject only to satisfactory performance.[143]

The exclusion of legal or other expectancy of renewal (or conversion) of fixed-term appointments was incorporated into the *UN Staff Rules* upon the General Assembly's explicit request.[144] Clearly, the Assembly intended to reiterate that UN staff could expect no automatic renewal (or conversion) of their appointments and that the UN Administration retained its discretion in this respect. As noted above, this study argues that despite this provision the margin of discretion of the UN Administration regarding conversion of fixed-term appointments into continuing ones has been removed, or at least limited, by the establishment of clear criteria on the basis of which conversions are to take place. However, with regard to extension and renewal of fixed-term appointments, the study argues that the situation of staff serving on such appointments has not improved. Therefore, the principle of legal expectancy, developed by the UN judiciary in the past, could continue to help to protect these staff.

The principle of legal expectancy

The principle of legal expectancy is based on a legal right of the holder of a fixed-term appointment in respect of his contract renewal (and in the past also contract conversion) deriving from an expectancy created in the mind of the staff member at issue by certain circumstances, surrounding factors, and/or behavior of the relevant administrative authority. The intention of the Administration is, in this context, of little or no relevance. What is decisive is the state of mind of the staff member concerned, his belief that he has a legal right to renewal of his appointment. The staff member's belief may, however, not be just an unsubstantiated impression. It also must be more than mere hope – hope alone cannot create a legal right.[145] To create such a right, the belief must be supported by some kind of action or behavior on the side of the Administration:

> *any factor that may have misled the staff member into believing that his or her contract of employment might be extended or converted into more*

adoption of the new contractual arrangements, see *UN Staff Rules of 2002*, Rule 104.12(b)(i).

[142] *UN Staff Rules*, Rule 4.13(c). For the relevant provision of the *UN Staff Rules* applicable before the adoption of the new contractual arrangements, see *UN Staff Rules of 2002*, Rule 104.12(b)(ii) and (iii).

[143] *UN Staff Rules*, Rule 4.14(b). See also above, section 2.3.2.

[144] *General Assembly Resolution 63/250*, Section II, para. 21.

[145] *Boelen v. Secretary-General of the United Nations, UNAT Judgment No. 261 [1980]*, available at http://untreaty.un.org/UNAT/UNAT_Judgements/Judgements_E/UNAT_00261_E.pdf, last visited on 30.12.2010, para. IV.

> *permanent employment must be weighed to determine whether it was the [UN Administration] who was responsible for causing the misapprehension.*[146]

If so, by acting in a way which has caused a staff member to believe in his continuing employment, the UN Administration limits its own discretion and makes a commitment.[147] Such commitment, express or implied, results in creating legal expectancy on the side of the staff member concerned and a corresponding legal obligation on the side of the Administration to provide further employment.[148]

The existence of legal expectancy must be deducted from the 'totality of circumstances surrounding the case'.[149] The UNAT has consistently held that terms and conditions of one's employment with the UN do not only depend on his contract of employment and on the *UN Staff Regulations* and *Rules* but that they may also be expressed or implied and that they may be collected from correspondence and surrounding facts and circumstances.[150] In each individual case brought before it, the UNAT thus investigates the history of the contractual relationship between the staff member concerned and the UN, and of all relevant facts and circumstances. On the basis thereof it establishes whether the concerned staff member could have believed that he had a legal right to his contract renewal or conversion. In a 2005 case, the UNAT even accepted that the staff member's expectancy could relate not to the specific contracts but be more general and relate to a right of further employment with the UN as such. The UNAT held in that case that although the applicant might not have had a legal expectancy as to his last appointment of limited duration, he had had a legitimate expectation of continued employment with the UN because he had been given an express promise of a new position in another duty station.[151]

It should be noted, however, that the existence of legal expectancy has been recognized only exceptionally. The UNAT held in this respect that:

---

146 *El-Sharkawi v. Secretary-General of the United Nations, UNAT Judgment No. 795 [1996]*, available at http://untreaty.un.org/UNAT/UNAT_Judgements/Judgements_E/UNAT_00795_E.pdf, last visited on 30.12.2010, para. IV.

147 *Rau, UNAT Judgment No. 101 [1966]*, para. III.

148 *Al-Abed v. Secretary-General of the United Nations, UNAT Judgment No. 128 [1969]*, available at http://untreaty.un.org/UNAT/UNAT_Judgements/Judgements_E/UNAT_00128_E.pdf, last visited on 30.12.2010, para. IV; *Dale v. Secretary General of the International Civil Aviation Organization, UNAT Judgment No. 132 [1969]*, available at http://untreaty.un.org/UNAT/UNAT_Judgements/Judgements_E/UNAT_00132_E.pdf, last visited on 30.12.2010, para. VIII; and *Bhattacharyya v. Secretary-General of the United Nations, UNAT Judgment No. 142 [1971]*, available at http://untreaty.un.org/UNAT/UNAT_Judgements/Judgements_E/UNAT_00142_E.pdf, last visited on 30.12.2010, para. X.

149 *Case No. 1360, UNAT Judgment No. 1277*, available at http://untreaty.un.org/UNAT/UNAT_Judgements/Judgements_E/UNAT_01277_E.pdf, last visited on 30.12.2010, para. IV.

150 *Sikand v. Secretary-General of the United Nations, UNAT Judgment No. 95 [1965]*, available at http://untreaty.un.org/UNAT/UNAT_Judgements/Judgements_E/UNAT_00095_E.pdf, last visited on 30.12.2010, para. III.

151 *Applicant v. Secretary-General of the United Nations, UNAT Judgment No. 1234 [2005]*, para. III.

> *there must be a combination of specific and clear factors which leave no doubt as to the nature and content of the expectations that an applicant could rely upon to plan his or her career in the future.*[152]

Besides an express promise,[153] other examples of such countervailing circumstances leading to the creation of legal expectancy recognized by the UNAT so far are: information in the offer of employment that there would be opportunities for further employment after the expiry of the initial contract;[154] practice of the UN Administration to renew contracts which contained a clause envisaging such possibility;[155] or a memorandum in which the UN Administration informed staff members that it would renew contracts of those staff members who would reach certain performance levels.[156]

On the other hand, and by way of example, the following circumstances have not been recognized as capable of creating legal expectancy: an oral promise emanating from an authority not competent to conclude contracts of employment;[157] placement on a roster of suitable candidates after passing an examination for a certain function;[158] recognition of qualifications and abilities, however high;[159] the length

---

[152] *Case No. 1500, UNAT Judgment No. 1423 [2008]*, available at http://untreaty.un.org/UNAT/UNAT_Judgements/Judgements_E/UNAT_01423_E.pdf, last visited on 30.12.2010, para. XI.

[153] *Applicant v. Secretary-General of the United Nations, UNAT Judgment No. 1234 [2005]*, para. I. See also *Case No. 1500, UNAT Judgment No. 1423 [2008]*, para. XIII. In the latter case the UNAT emphasized that a promise must be clear and certain in order to create the right of legal expectancy. – Ibid. On the other hand, the promise may be made subject to conditions, such as the availability of financing and satisfactory performance. – *Case No. 1389, UNAT Judgment No. 1305 [2006]*, available at http://untreaty.un.org/UNAT/UNAT_Judgements/Judgements_E/UNAT_01305_E.pdf, last visited on 30.12.2010, para. II.

[154] *Bhattacharyya, UNAT Judgment No. 142 [1971]*, paras. VIII and X. In order to trigger legal expectancy, such information may not be made conditional on future mutual consent since the administration may always decide to withhold its consent, even if other conditions for the contract renewal would be met. – Ibid.

[155] *Dale, UNAT Judgment No. 132 [1969]*, para. V. Such practice could lead to the creation of legitimate expectancy even if the possibility of renewal in the contract is made subject to a mutual consent. – Ibid.

[156] *Al-Fahoum v. Secretary-General of the United Nations, UNAT Judgment No. 1018 [2001]*, available at http://untreaty.un.org/UNAT/UNAT_Judgements/Judgements_E/UNAT_01018_E.pdf, last visited on 30.12.2010, para. III.

[157] *Al-Abed, UNAT Judgment No. 128 [1969]*, para. VI.

[158] *Seraphides v. Secretary-General of the United Nations, UNAT Judgment No. 140 [1971]*, available at http://untreaty.un.org/UNAT/UNAT_Judgements/Judgements_E/UNAT_00140_E.pdf, last visited on 30.12.2010, paras. VIII-IX. The UNAT held that, by having been placed on the roster, the applicant could have expected to remain in UN employment but that this expectation could not have raised any legal obligation on the side of the administration as the applicant's status of UN staff member had expired in the meantime. - Ibid.

[159] *El-Naggar, UNAT Judgment No. 205 [1975]*, para. III. In this case, the applicant claimed that his 'exceptional qualifications and performance, his accelerated promotions from P-5 to D-2 in less than six years and the repeated recommendations for conversion of his fixed-term appointment into a permanent appointment' granted him a reasonable expectancy of further employment with the UN. The UNAT, however, ruled that the mentioned factors could not by themselves create a legal right. – Ibid. See also *Case No. 1470, UNAT Judgment No. 1402 [2008]*, available at http://untreaty.un.org/UNAT/UNAT_Judgements/Judgements_E/UNAT_01402_E.pdf, last visited on 30.12.2010, para. V. On the other hand, in *Pereyra v. Secretary-General of the United Nations, UNAT Judgment No. 647 [1994]*,

of the period served with the UN;[160] early indications of the probable length of the project for which the staff member is recruited;[161] the continuation of duties beyond the duration of a staff member's fixed-term appointment;[162] an encumbrance of a budgeted post;[163] an inquiry by a supervisor on the wishes of the staff member concerned to continue his involvement in the project beyond the date of expiry of his contract;[164] request of a Member State's government to extend the staff member's contract;[165] the fact that aspects of the project on which the staff member concerned has been working are unfinished at the time of the staff member's separation;[166] opinions expressed by some representatives of the UN Administration about what the policy should be with regard to certain category of staff;[167] a memorandum from the personnel office to all staff members, intended to identify staff members interested in reassignment;[168] assurances of supervisors that they will do their utmost to obtain financing needed to maintain the staff member's employment;[169] and a recommendation of a supervisor.[170]

available at http://untreaty.un.org/UNAT/UNAT_Judgements/Judgements_E/UNAT_00647_E.pdf, last visited on 30.12.2010 the UNAT accepted that, in certain cases, staff members, serving under fixed term contracts which had been extended over a long period of time, and whose performance had been evaluated positively, might have had a reasonable expectancy that their contracts would be renewed. The applicant in this case had served with the UN for six year under 12 consecutive contracts when her post was abolished and the last contract not renewed. The UNAT ruled that the applicant had a reasonable expectancy of further renewal of her contract and a right to compensation for its non-renewal. - para. III. Arguably, the decisive element in this case was the fact that the post on which the applicant served had been abolished. If it were not for the abolition of the post, the contract would have been renewed, considering that the applicant's performance evaluation had always been positive and her contract had continuously been renewed.

160 *Jabbour v. Secretary-General of the United Nations, UNAT Judgment No. 305 [1983]*, available at http://untreaty.un.org/UNAT/UNAT_Judgements/Judgements_E/UNAT_00305_E.pdf, last visited on 30.12.2010, paras. I and VI. The UNAT held in this case that the reasonable expectations of the applicant for the continuation of his 15 years long employment with the UN under a series of successive fixed-term appointments did not amount to a legal right and, consequently, to a legal obligation on the side of the UN administration to reinstate him. – Ibid.

161 *Safavi v. Secretary-General of the United Nations, UNAT Judgment No. 465 [1989]*, available at http://untreaty.un.org/UNAT/UNAT_Judgements/Judgements_E/UNAT_00465_E.pdf, last visited on 30.12.2010, paras. II-III.

162 *Case No. 1500, UNAT Judgment No. 1423 [2008]*, para. XIV.

163 *Case No. 1470, UNAT Judgment No. 1402 [2008]*, para. V. The UNAT stated that while the encumbrance of a budgeted post may be relevant or at least convenient for the administration when deciding upon a contract renewal, it does not give rise to any right. – Ibid.

164 *Safavi, UNAT Judgment No. 465 [1989]*, p. 9 and paras. II-III.

165 Ibid., p. 11 and paras. II-III.

166 Ibid., para. III.

167 *Handelsman, UNAT Judgment No. 885 [1998]*, para. IV.

168 Ibid., para. IV.

169 *Seaforth v. Secretary-General of the United Nations, UNAT Judgment No. 1163 [2003]*, available at http://untreaty.un.org/UNAT/UNAT_Judgements/Judgements_E/UNAT_01163_E.pdf, last visited on 30.12.2010, para. VI.

170 *Case No. 1470, UNAT Judgment No. 1402 [2008]*, para. V. The UNAT stressed that a supervisor's recommendation may be fundamental for a contract renewal but that it is not more than an opinion which will be taken into account when the decision on the contract renewal will be taken. – Ibid.

All these factors, taken individually, have not been considered by the UNAT as sufficient to create a legal right. However, in some instances, a cumulative effect of a number of such factors, have led to the creation of legal expectancy:

> *The Tribunal finds that the cumulative effect of these factors ... is that the Applicant - who had every reason to believe his performance was not only satisfactory but was "good"; who was aware of his supervisor's recommendation; and, who knew his post was not subject to budgetary concerns - was entitled to rely upon the practice of renewal and, therefore, had a legal expectancy of renewal of his contract.*[171]

Similarly:

> *In the case before it, the Tribunal finds several actions by the [UN Administration] that may have misled the Applicant into believing that his contract would be renewed. Firstly, the Applicant was hired to work on an undertaking which was considered a long-term project of the United Nations. Secondly, the Applicant received repeated assurances from his supervisor that his presence was essential to the success of the project. Thirdly, there were repeated interventions by the substantive department, insisting on the Applicant's continued employment in order to finalize the project on which he was working. These factors together may have created the reasonable impression that the Applicant's employment would be continued. Therefore, based on these circumstances, the Tribunal agrees with the [recommendation of the Joint Appeals Board] that the Applicant be compensated.*[172]

In this case, the UNAT thus accepted that a combination of certain circumstances had led to the applicant's legitimate belief in his contract renewal, despite the fact that the individual circumstances had been previously rejected as a possible source of legal expectancy. As mentioned above, for example, the anticipated length of the project for which the staff member had initially been recruited was rejected in another case.[173]

The judgment on the existence of legal expectancy is thus not always easy and clear-cut. Neither is the UNAT jurisprudence:

> *The Tribunal first recalls its traditional approach, whereby even if the Applicant did not, in principle, have any right to renewal of her fixed-term contract under staff rule 104.12 (b) (ii), it ought to consider whether the prospects for renewal were greater because of certain circumstances specific to the case and whether procedural irregularities were committed during the procedure that culminated in nonrenewal and, if so, whether those irregularities are sufficiently serious to be deemed to have vitiated the non-renewal decision, in which case that decision*

[171] Ibid., para. V.

[172] *El-Sharkawi, UNAT Judgment No. 795 [1996]*, para. V.

[173] *Safavi, UNAT Judgment No. 465 [1989]*, paras. II-III.

> *should be considered null and void, or whether they simply give rise to a right to compensation for procedural irregularities.*[174]

In should be noted that in this case the UNAT mentions 'solid prospects for renewal', not the right to renewal.[175]

There have also been instances in which the UNAT awarded compensation to staff members who had no legal expectancy of contract renewal but who had been employed by the UN for a long time. It appears that, alongside the principle of legal expectancy, the UNAT has developed yet another principle, namely that even if no legal expectancy can be proven, staff should be compensated for lack of goodwill on the side of the UN Administration to find another position for staff facing the expiry of their fixed-term contract if such staff has had a long-lasting employment relationship with the UN.[176] In *Jabbour* the UNAT explicitly stated that the applicant could not have any legal expectancy of the continuation of his contract but that:

> *after a staff member has been retained in service by a series of short-term contracts for many years and has rendered satisfactory services to the United Nations he can reasonably expect a measure of accommodation either in the form of extension or renewal of short-term contracts or by the [UN Administration] trying in good faith and earnestly to find him some alternative employment.*[177]

Following this reasoning, the UNAT concluded:

> *(a) The [UN Administration] had no legal obligations either to renew the Applicant's contract or to find him another employment even if the Applicant had some reasonable expectation of such accommodation because of his service of about 15 years with the [Administration]. In view of this the Applicant's plea for reinstatement fails.*
>
> *(b) In a variety of ways the [Administration] has been negligent as an employer in failing to extend to the Applicant fair and just treatment, and as a consequence the Applicant has suffered. The Tribunal considers that the Applicant is entitled to some compensation. ...*[178]

Similarly, in *Ortega, Hernandez, Canales and Garcia* the UNAT held that despite the non-existence of legal expectancy, the UN Administration had 'at the very least' to have given every reasonable consideration for further employment of an applicant because he had served at the UN for 22 years.[179]

---

[174] *Case No. 1449, UNAT Judgment No. 1371 [2007]*, available at http://untreaty.un.org/UNAT/UNAT_Judgements/Judgements_E/UNAT_01371_E.pdf, last visited on 30.12.2010, para. IX.

[175] Ibid., para. IX. See also *Bonder, UNAT Judgment No. 1052 [2002]*, para. VI.

[176] See Amerasinghe, *The Law of the International Civil Service, Volume II*, especially pp. 758-760.

[177] *Jabbour, UNAT Judgment No. 305 [1983]*, para. I.

[178] Ibid., para. VI.

[179] *Ortega, Hernandez, Canales and Garcia v. Secretary-General of the United Nations, UNAT Judgment No. 610 [1993]*, available at http://untreaty.un.org/UNAT/UNAT_Judgements/Judgements_E/UNAT_00610_E.pdf, last visited on 30.12.2010, para. VII.

All this case law illustrates that the UNAT has taken non-extension, non-renewal or non-conversion of fixed-term appointments seriously. Although it has rejected many claims, it has accepted some, despite the fact that *UN Staff Rules* precluded legal expectancy of contract renewal or conversion. It could be argued that despite the change of the overall contractual framework of the UN Secretariat, the UNAT is likely to continue to protect staff from non-renewal of their appointment. As far as conversions are concerned, as noted earlier in this section, it appears that protection through the application of the principle of legal expectancy will not be as necessary due to the fact that the UN Administration seems to have lost its discretion in this respect.

2.4.3. Protection of career staff

The protection of career staff against separation from service is the third element to be assessed in the process of evaluating the new contractual arrangements in the UN Secretariat and their possible effect on staff independence and impartiality. It is perhaps the most obvious element in this context considering that the security of tenure has long been regarded as one of the most important safeguards of the independent and impartial status of the international civil servants. The fact that permanent appointments have been replaced by continuing ones might, at first sight, lead to an impression that this security has been removed. However, this is only partly so.

Between the former permanent and the new continuing appointment, there is only one difference with regard to their possible termination. It relates to termination in the interest (of good administration) of the organization. While permanent appointments could – and still can – be terminated on the basis of this legal ground only when the staff member concerned does not contest it, continuing appointments may be terminated in this way without the staff member's consent. Formally speaking, this is indeed a significant difference between the two types of appointment. In reality, however, there seems to be an understanding that this legal ground only encompasses situations in which 'change or termination of a mandate' is at stake. This is the principal interpretation of the concept 'in the interests of the good administration of the Organization', explicitly included in the resolution of the General Assembly approving the reform of contractual arrangements.[180] Even though the Assembly qualified its interpretation by characterizing it as 'principal', it is clear that it did not intend to allow a broad interpretation. Besides, the very fact that the Assembly considered it necessary to include the interpretation of this legal ground for termination of continuing appointments in its resolution demonstrates the importance attached to it and the intention to limit it. In that regard it should be noted that the Assembly did not accept the interpretation proposed by the Secretary-General which was only a little broader than that adopted. The Secretary-General suggested that the concept should 'include grounds such as change or completion

[180] *General Assembly Resolution 63/250*, Section II, para. 21.

of mandate, reorientation of programme or reduction in funding or activities'.[181] The General Assembly accepted the first part of the proposal only. It is true that none of the two (proposed) interpretations is exhaustive. However, they leave no doubt that the interest of the good administration of the organization will not be used lightly for terminating continuing appointments. In fact, it is very likely that when termination needs to take place, it will be based on other legal grounds which have remained available, such as post abolition or reduction of staff. These legal grounds are more precise and therefore less open to different and possibly uncertain interpretations. Their use would prevent much litigation which could undoubtedly follow terminations based on the interest of the good administration of the organization.

It appears thus that the inclusion of the possibility of contract termination in the interest of the good administration without staff consent serves more a symbolic than any other purpose. When reforming the overall contractual arrangements in the UN, the Secretary-General and the General Assembly clearly intended to simplify and modernize the system, providing for more flexibility and mobility of all UN staff. They apparently also intended to send a strong signal to staff emphasizing that their contractual status may not be considered as fixed but that they all need to be more reactive to the operational needs of the organization. Both the Secretary-General and the General Assembly undoubtedly realize that using the interest of the good administration of the organization as the ground for termination of a continuing appointment will be subject to close scrutiny by the UN judiciary. Even more so if the interest of the good administration of the organization used in an individual case will be outside the principal interpretation explicitly provided in the General Assembly's resolution. As already mentioned, the power to terminate appointments in the interest (of the good administration) of the organization existed under the previous contractual framework, too, and the UNAT has recognized it as discretionary.[182] However, the UNAT has also emphasized that this power is not unlimited and, therefore, subject to judicial review:

> *The discretion of the [Organization] to terminate employment in its interest is not unlimited or unfettered. Its exercise is subject to review by the Tribunal and can be declared invalid because it has been abused. The abuse may arise not only from improper motive, prejudice or improper purpose but also from any substantive irregularity such as error of fact or erreur d'appréciation (mistaken conclusions), or procedural irregularity.*[183]

[181] *Detailed Proposals for Streamlining United Nations Contractual Arrangements: A Way Forward, Report of the Secretary-General, A/63/298*, Section III, para. 29.

[182] *Crawford, UNAT Judgment No. 18 [1953]*, paras. 1 and 10-13. This case concerned termination of appointment of indefinite duration in the interest of the organization under the former *UN Staff Regulation 9.1(c)*. See also *Fayemiwo v. Secretary-General of the United Nations, UNAT Judgment No. 246 [1979]*, available at http://untreaty.un.org/UNAT/UNAT_Judgements/Judgements_E/UNAT_00246_E.pdf, last visited on 30.12.2010, para. I.

[183] *Shahrour v. Commissioner-General of the United nations Relief and Works Agency for Palestine Refugees in the Near East, UNAT Judgment No. 939 [1999]*, available at http://untreaty.un.org/UNAT/UNAT_Judgements/Judgements_E/UNAT_00939_E.pdf, last visited on 30.12.2010, para. V. See also *Crawford, UNAT Judgment No. 18 [1953]*, para. 2.

The abuse of the discretion would also occur if the Administration terminated appointment in the interest of the organization without having and stating the reasons for it.[184] The reasons must be specified sufficiently precisely so that the UNAT is put in a position to review the decision and to verify whether the facts relied on are correct and whether no misuse of power or arbitrariness occurred.[185] In each case it must be clear that the action to terminate the appointment is taken in the interest of the United Nations and is not, for example, a disguised disciplinary measure.[186]

On this basis it could be argued that the position of the international civil servants has, in reality, not changed dramatically under the new contractual arrangements, if at all. First of all, for a still relatively long time, a large number of staff have continued to serve on permanent appointments, protected by the prohibition of termination of their appointment in the interest of service without their consent. Second, staff who receive continuing appointments will be sufficiently protected against termination of their appointment in the interest of the good administration of the organization. The protection will come from a rather strict interpretation of this concept adopted by the General Assembly as well as from the system of internal justice, which has recently also been reformed, becoming more professional and including a possibility of appeal.[187]

Hence, although formally protection of tenure as we have known it previously is no longer offered in the UN Secretariat, separation of staff serving on continuing appointments is still subject to rather strict conditions. In addition, it could be argued that tenure does not necessarily mean that staff must hold permanent appointments and that these appointments may never be terminated. Rather, tenure means that appointments at issue are not merely temporary in nature and that their termination is subject to rigorous requirements. In this context it should be recalled that the UN Preparatory Commission of 1945 recommended that career staff were given 'indefinite' appointments, thus not 'permanent' ones, and that these indefinite appointments were subject to review after five years and a possibility to terminate them in cases of post abolition, reduction of staff or unsatisfactory service.[188] The new continuing appointments should in fact have all these features. The Preparatory Commission of 1945 also stressed that no termination of appointment should be allowed for 'clearing a way for the appointment of a person with certain nationality' or for other reasons not related to the staff member's work.[189] As long as these last

---

184 *Shahrour, UNAT Judgment No. 939 [1999]*, para. VI.

185 *Zafari v. Commissioner-General of the United Nations Relief and Works Agency for Palestine Refugees in the Near East, UNAT Judgment No. 461 [1989]*, available at http://untreaty.un.org/UNAT/UNAT_Judgements/Judgements_E/UNAT_00461_E.pdf, last visited on 30.12.2010, para. XXI. In this case, the administration only stated as a reason for separation that the confidence in the applicant had been lost. This was considered insufficient by the UNAT. – Ibid.

186 Amerasinghe, *The Law of the International Civil Service, Volume II*, p. 715. For very early cases where the issue of disguised disciplinary measures was at stake, see, e.g. *Crawford, UNAT Judgment No. 18 [1953]*, or *Gordon, UNAT Judgment No. 29 [1953]*.

187 On the reform of the UN system of internal justice, see also below, chapter 7, section 2.3.6.2.

188 *Report of the UN Preparatory Commission*, Chapter VIII, Section 1, paras. 21 and 23 ; and Section 2.E, para. 60.

189 Ibid., Chapter VIII, Section 1, para. 23 ; and Section 2.E, para. 60.

conditions are observed, too, UN staff serving on continuing appointments should not fear insufficient protection against arbitrary or abusive separation.

3. Types of appointment in the European Commission

3.1. Historical overview

Although the first staff of the High Authority of the ECSC consisted of national civil servants temporarily posted with the institution, the situation changed relatively soon. In the mid-1950s, the wave of the 'supranational ethos' that had underlined the very establishment of the ECSC led to the introduction of the notion of a European civil service, based on the idea of majority staff serving on a career basis.[190] This approach was taken over by the other two Communities established in 1958. According to the first *Staff Regulations* of these two Communities, the newly established Commission was to be staffed, to a significant extent, by permanent officials who were to fill the so-called 'established posts'. Established posts were, and still are, posts included in the Commission establishment plan appended to its section of the EU budget. It indicates the number of posts in each grade and function group.[191] Naturally, the establishment plan should include all posts necessary for the proper exercise of the Commission tasks in the long-term perspective but, as explained in more detail below, this has not always been the case. As far as the non-permanent tasks are concerned, they should be carried out by non-permanent staff, subject to conditions set out in the *Conditions of Employment of Other Servants*. As explained in the introductory chapter to this study, the *Conditions of Employment of Other Servants* constitute a part of the same Council Regulation as the *EU Staff Regulations* since its first adoption in 1961.[192]

Despite the general acceptance of the idea that the European Commission should be predominantly composed of career staff, the establishment of a body of such staff did not occur immediately. First of all, France, one of the large founding Member States, was opposed to this idea for a long time. In the 1950s and 1960s, the French government argued that the Commission should be composed exclusively of temporarily seconded national officials. As explained by Cini, the French wished for:

> *a fluid, non-permanent Commission whose staff would owe their allegiance to national governments rather than to some European ideal, institution or embryonic state. As such, the Commission would be as nationally-oriented an institution as the Council of Ministers.*[193]

Even though the French government lost its case and the idea of an independent European civil service was eventually accepted across the board, secondment from

---

[190] Cini, *The European Commission, Leadership, Organisation and Culture in the EU Administration*, p. 121.

[191] *EU Staff Regulations of 1961*, and *EU Staff Regulations*, in both instances Article 1 and 6. The relevant parts of these two provisions have not changed since their inception.

[192] See *EU Staff Regulations of 1961*.

[193] Cini, *The European Commission, Leadership, Organisation and Culture in the EU Administration*, pp. 120-121.

national civil services was not abolished. Rather, 'a balance has since been struck between the permanent established officials and the temporary national staff'.[194] Some observers have even noted in this respect that a 'parallel administration' existed in the European Commission consisting of seconded national civil servants.[195]

It is not surprising that the first permanent officials hired by the European Commission came from Member States' national civil services, similarly as temporarily posted staff had. Being civil servants themselves, national officials were obviously best qualified to perform the tasks of a new civil service, in particular since this new service was established on the basis of the Member States' civil services. As a consequence, there were two distinct groups of 'national' officials in the European Commission in the early years. The first group consisted of national civil servants who left the civil service of their home country because they were committed to the idea of European integration. These officials settled in Brussels, expected to make their career in the Commission, and after a few years in the Commission cut most formal connections with their home country public administration. According to Coombes, at the end of the 1960s, this group represented most of the Commission officials.[196] The second group of national officials who served in the European Commission at that time were those temporarily seconded by their governments. The nature of this kind of service varied, depending on the Member State's attitude. The French, for example, used a formal type of secondment, known as *roulement*. Under this system, the government actively encouraged short-term service with the Commission and, unsurprisingly, did not facilitate departure for permanent European service. The seconded officials retained their posts at home and often even enjoyed promotion by echelon during their absence. The Germans, on the other hand, practiced the so-called 'lending' of officials for the European service, leaving it up to the officials themselves to decide whether they would remain in Brussels or return home. No formal assurances were granted to the returning officials with regard to reinstatement in their previous post. The Dutch seemed to have been the most disinterested in getting their seconded national officials back, actively discouraging their return from Brussels.[197]

Despite the differences in the Member States' approaches, quite a number of officials who had entered the Commission on the basis of secondment from their Member States' governments remained there and, like their colleagues directly hired as permanent officials, eventually acquired permanent status. There were various ways in which this could take place. For example, a temporary agent could first be contracted by the Commission as auxiliary, thereby getting access to internal

[194] Ibid., p. 121.

[195] Ibid., p. 121.

[196] Coombes, *Towards a European Civil Service*, p. 37.

[197] Ibid., p. 38. See also Coombes, *Politics and Bureaucracy in the European Community, A Portrait of the Commission of the E.E.C.*, pp. 148-149. Coombes noted that regardless of the nature and type of secondment used, the Member States had always formally emphasized that all officials had been prohibited to receive instructions from their home governments. - Coombes, *Politics and Bureaucracy in the European Community, A Portrait of the Commission of the E.E.C.*, p. 149.

competition which, if passed, eventually led to a permanent position.[198] Coombes stressed, however, that the number of persons who had become officials in such a manner was not more than 20 per cent of the whole (former) A category at any time. This was considerably less than the number of national officials directly established as permanent.[199] In addition, in the course of the 1960s, an increasingly large number of newly appointed staff came originally from the private sector and academia. Coombes noted that such a development had simplified matters in two important ways. First of all, there was no longer a need to encourage national officials to leave good career prospects available at home. Secondly, true independence of Commission staff who had no previous ties with Member States' governments could be better guaranteed.[200]

Nonetheless, the use of short-term secondment from national civil service remained an important manner in which service of persons with sought specification and experience could have been acquired.[201] Indeed, the Commission often experienced gaps in its in-house expertise. It was caused especially by the expansion of the Commission's activities into new policy areas, but also by difficulties with attracting persons with specific technical knowledge for a permanent service. Temporary engagement of national experts was thus an important means for closing these gaps.[202] In addition, it has also been argued that employment of seconded national experts was a deliberate policy of the Commission allowing it to circumvent restrictions on staff recruitment imposed by the requirement of geographical balance, as the national experts were not included in official staff calculations.[203] Another alleged reason for engaging seconded officials was continuing budgetary constraints, not providing for a sufficient number of established posts needed by the Commission for carrying out its increasingly expanding duties.[204] As a consequence, the relatively low number of seconded national officials employed by the Commission rapidly expanded after the mid-1980s and reached a peak in 1992. Following demands by the European Parliament to stabilize the number of such officials, it decreased after-

[198] Coombes, *Towards a European Civil Service*, pp. 38-39; and Coombes, *Politics and Bureaucracy in the European Community, A Portrait of the Commission of the E.E.C.*, p. 149.

[199] Coombes, *Towards a European Civil Service*, p. 39; and Coombes, *Politics and Bureaucracy in the European Community, A Portrait of the Commission of the E.E.C.*, p. 149.

[200] Coombes, *Politics and Bureaucracy in the European Community, A Portrait of the Commission of the E.E.C.*, p. 150.

[201] Coombes, *Towards a European Civil Service*, p. 39. The use of national experts has been regarded as justified also by the Court of Justice, although the Court has expressed certain reservations if the use of such experts 'attains sizeable proportions and lasts a considerable time'. - *Fux v. Commission, Case 26/68*, para. 25.

[202] Page, *People Who Run Europe*, p. 60. See also Cini, *The European Commission, Leadership, Organisation and Culture in the EU Administration*, p. 121.

[203] Page, *People Who Run Europe*, p. 59.

[204] Ibid., p. 60; Nugent, *The European Commission*, pp. 165-166; and Stevens and Stevens, *Brussels Bureaucrats? The Administration of the European Union*, p. 23. Stevens, for example, stated: 'It is by no means clear that its administrative resources have been allowed to grow at the same pace as its membership and responsibilities. The Commission in particular started out with a culture which preferred small size and unbureaucratic procedures; and even when it could bring itself to demand more staff, the Council of Ministers was reluctant to approve more than minimal increases.' – *Ibid.*

wards.[205] The European Parliament criticized the extensive use of national experts on secondment, fearing a potentially dangerous 'nationalization' of the EU civil service, improperly influenced by Member States. It was noted that the very independence of the EU civil service could be put into question.[206]

According to Nugent, there were between 700 and 800 seconded officials in the Commission at any one time, which corresponded to 11 per cent of all (former) A-grade staff and to about 25 per cent of staff at middle levels A4 – A6 staff.[207] The A grade was the grade at which most of these officials worked, usually filling middle management posts and often carrying out policy and managerial duties, similar to those of permanent staff.[208] Stevens noted that the absolute numbers of seconded staff were not that high but that their significance lay in their concentration. According to her data, seconded officials accounted for about 15 per cent of all (former) A grade staff and 30 per cent of staff at the (former) A4 and A5 levels. In some Directorates-General, most notably those with more technical portfolios, such as statistics, nuclear safety, customs and taxation, the proportions were even higher.[209]

Apart from the seconded national experts, other categories of non-permanent staff – temporary staff, auxiliary staff, local staff and special advisers – have been serving in the European Commission since its inception. These staff have formally been known as 'other servants' and their engagement has been, as mentioned earlier, regulated since the early years by a separate set of rules – the *EU Conditions of Employment of Other Servants*. Together with permanent staff, whose employment at the Commission is regulated by the *EU Staff Regulations*, 'other servants' form the so-called statutory staff of the European Commission. Apart from the statutory staff, the European Commission has also been employing so-called non-statutory staff. They include persons who are covered neither by the *EU Staff Regulations*, nor by the *EU Conditions of Employment of Other Servants*, for example, agents recruited under national law contracts; service providers hired by a private company which is contracted by the Commission; or the so-called interim staff hired by an interim agency and employed to replace absent staff or sometimes to execute short term duties.[210]

---

205 Page, *People Who Run Europe*, p. 60 and Stevens and Stevens, *Brussels Bureaucrats? The Administration of the European Union*, p. 20. Page observed one more reason for the considerable expansion of the number of the seconded national experts in the Commission by the mid-1980s, namely the 'reservation' of the posts for Spanish and Portugal nationals caused by the approaching accession of these two countries to the EU in 1986.

206 Page, *People Who Run Europe*, pp. 60-61. See also Stevens and Stevens, *Brussels Bureaucrats? The Administration of the European Union*, p. 22.

207 Nugent, *The European Commission*, p. 165. Page noted that in 1995 around twelve per cent of staff at A4-A8 level were officials serving on the secondment basis. - Page, *People Who Run Europe*, p. 60. Stevens pointed out that the annual number the seconded officials had generally been thought to be around 600 – 650 since 1991, but that the DECODE report came with a figure of 750 in 1998. - Stevens and Stevens, *Brussels Bureaucrats? The Administration of the European Union*, p. 20.

208 Page, *People Who Run Europe*, p. 60 and Nugent, *The European Commission*, p. 164.

209 Stevens and Stevens, *Brussels Bureaucrats? The Administration of the European Union*, p. 20.

210 *Commission's Human Resources Report 2009*, pp. 28-29. Also, seconded national experts belong to

The Commission's reliance on non-permanent and non-statutory staff was relatively high in the past. In the first decades, especially the so-called auxiliary staff were employed in great numbers. Coombes reported that in 1963 as many as a quarter of the entire Commission personnel were auxiliaries, a considerable number of whom carried out duties of permanent and continuing nature that should rather have been performed by permanent staff.[211] Formally, auxiliary staff could have been engaged only for two purposes: first, fulfilling tasks for which no post was included in the budget; and second, replacement of regular (other than senior) staff temporarily unable to work. Coombes noted, however, that in reality the Commission employed auxiliaries when it quickly needed specialists who were not available in-house, or when it had to compensate for the budgetary restrictions for staff expenditure, or to circumvent recruitment procedures for regular posts.[212] Over time, the use of auxiliaries in large numbers began to constitute a (potential) threat to career progress of established officials. This was due to the decision of the ECJ which recognized the right of these and all other non-permanent staff to participate in internal competitions which led to permanent appointment.[213] Under the pressure of staff unions, the engagement of auxiliaries therefore became more restricted by the end of 1966. Coombes considered this development to be 'an important concession towards the supporters of a career service'.[214]

Another important category of non-permanent staff extensively used by the European Commission in the past were temporary agents, carrying out specific duties or working in specific areas. A high concentration of temporary agents could have been seen in areas requiring scientific research, in technology areas and in new policy fields. Services providing horizontal support to the Commission Directorates-General, such as those for budget or personnel matters, did not employ many temporary staff.[215] A large group of temporary agents was, however, employed in the Commissioners' cabinets, allowing Commissioners to bring in staff they had to work with on a close day-to-day basis without having to go through a lengthy recruit-

non-statutory staff.

[211] Coombes, *Politics and Bureaucracy in the European Community, A Portrait of the Commission of the E.E.C.*, p. 144.

[212] Ibid., pp. 143-144.

[213] *Rauch v. Commission, Case 16/64*, pp. 143-144.

[214] Coombes, *Politics and Bureaucracy in the European Community, A Portrait of the Commission of the E.E.C.*, p. 144.

[215] Nugent, *The European Commission*, p. 166. See also Stevens and Stevens, *Brussels Bureaucrats? The Administration of the European Union*, p. 19. The use of temporary contracts for research staff dated back to 1976. In that year a new policy was adopted in order to increase adjustment capacity of the Commission research programmes to changing requirements and in order to encourage exchange of the Commission research staff, internally as well as externally with national research institutions. - Stevens and Stevens, *Brussels Bureaucrats? The Administration of the European Union*, pp. 19-20. Indeed, Article 2 of the *EU Conditions of Employment of Other Servants*, defining temporary staff, was amended in 1976, explicitly adding research staff to this category. – *Council Regulation (ECSC, EEC, Euratom) No 2615/76 of 21 October 1976 Amending Regulation (EEC, Euratom, ECSC) No 259/68 as Regards the Conditions of Employment of Other Servants of the European Communities*, OJ L 299, 29.10.1976, p. 1 - 3, Article 1.2.

ment process applicable to permanent staff.[216] Even though the temporary status of cabinet members was linked to the presumption that these staff would leave the Commission together with their Commissioner, many cabinet staff remained after their Commissioner had left the Commission and even saw their appointments converted into permanent ones.[217]

The number of non-permanent and/or non-statutory staff employed by the European Commission at any given time has always been somewhat of a mystery. Many observers but also official committees experienced difficulties in establishing the precise number of staff working for the European Commission, both permanent and other.[218] With regard to the latter, Cini reported in 1996 that approximately 25 per cent of all Commission staff served in posts other than permanent. She also emphasized, however, that this was an official figure but that the real proportion of such staff was most probably higher since the official figure did not include staff recruited by individual services and Directorates-General.[219] Page noted a similar figure. He observed that this was an average and that the concentration of staff serving on other than permanent basis was greater in some Directorates-General. Page stated that in 1992 four Directorates-General had more than 30 per cent of non-permanent, including external, staff and two Directorates-General over 50 per cent.[220] Page also observed that the figures most probably underestimated the importance of such staff and concluded that they '[played] a large and important role in major segments of EU Administration'.[221] One of the few official figures on the number of other than permanent staff serving in the European Commission was provided in the DECODE report in 1998. This report stated that around 40 per cent of the Commission staff served as temporary agents 'broadly defined'.[222]

The difficulty with finding precise numbers of staff employed by the European Commission was a result of various types of contracts being used over the years

[216] Stevens and Stevens, *Brussels Bureaucrats? The Administration of the European Union*, p. 20.

[217] Ibid., p. 20.

[218] Ibid., p. 17. Stevens noted that official figures for all Commission staff serving in 1999 were 20.674 for permanent staff and 764 for temporary staff, i.e. 21.438 in total. However, a year earlier the DECODE report had found some 31.013 people working for the Commission, i.e. almost 10.000 more than the official figures indicated for the subsequent year. Stevens observed that it was unlikely that the staff numbers had decreased in one year. - Stevens and Stevens, *Brussels Bureaucrats? The Administration of the European Union*, p. 17 and Tables 1.2 and 1.3. See also Spence and Stevens, *Staff and Personnel Policy in the Commission*, p. 178.

[219] Cini, *The European Commission, Leadership, Organisation and Culture in the EU Administration*, p. 120. Cini made a distinction between permanent posts on the one hand and other posts on the other hand. In the latter she included external positions, but also temporary positions, including those occupied by seconded national experts and auxiliary staff.

[220] Page, *People Who Run Europe*, pp. 61-62 and Table 3.10. According to Page, in seven Directorates-General the proportion of staff serving on other than permanent basis was below 10 per cent, including staff in all grades (A-D), although these staff were disproportionately serving as former A grade officials. Note also that Page uses the term 'non-establishment' staff that includes auxiliary staff, seconded national experts as well as external staff.

[221] Ibid., p. 68.

[222] Nugent, *The European Commission*, p. 166. See also Stevens and Stevens, *Brussels Bureaucrats? The Administration of the European Union*, p. 23.

by the Commission and sometimes even a deliberate intention of the Commission to hide the true numbers in order to avoid criticism.[223] As for other than permanent staff, the situation was further complicated by the fact that there was no central register of such staff.[224] Especially contracts not covered by the *EU Staff Regulations and Conditions of Employment of Other Servants* were decided upon by the holders of, and financed from, different budgets and sub-budgets, often falling under the EU operation expenditure, i.e. Part B of the EU budget. Formally, costs connected with human resources fell under Part A of the EU budget, i.e. its administrative expenditure. This part of the budget provided for a number of temporary posts to be filled by non-statutory staff, leaving a certain degree of flexibility to the European Commission for meeting specific staffing requirements which could not be easily or adequately satisfied with established officials. However, while the Commission's tasks had been expanding considerably over the years, no corresponding increase in the number of posts was provided for in Part A of the EU budget. Therefore, the European Commission financed staff it needed from the operational part of the budget, i.e. Part B. As each programme had its own budget line, costs related to staff engaged to carry out duties in that specific programme were financed – and thus also registered – under these separate budget lines. The commonly used name for these separate budgets was 'mini-budgets'.[225]

It has been claimed that the Commission 'mini-budgets' covered thousands of staff at times, e.g. almost one third of all official staff in 1992 and nearly a quarter in 1994, with heavy dependence on such staff by some Commission departments. Some Directorates-General had even more 'mini-budget' staff in their service than statutory staff.[226] This situation was largely criticized, in particular for its striking lack of budgetary transparency, although this was not the only problem noted. Spence and Stevens, for example, observed that the employment by the European Commission of a large number of temporary staff under various 'mini-budgets' was in line with its 'carrot and stick management ethics', a convenient manner of hiring and firing staff. A threat of non-renewal of the contract was used as an incentive for better

[223] See, for example, Nugent, *The European Commission*, p. 166. Nuggent noted that criticism had been coming from the European Parliament, the Court of Auditors, but also from the Commission's own Directorate-General for Human Resources and Security. Nuggent also stated that the Commission had been 'less than transparent with its staffing figures' and that different queries had ended up with different figures – some categories of staff had or had not reported and others had never been reported. – Ibid., p. 162. See also Stevens and Stevens, *Brussels Bureaucrats? The Administration of the European Union*, p. 23.

[224] This has changed. Since 2008, all categories of staff, including seconded national experts, service providers, interim workers, local agents, agents under national law contract, special advisers and trainees are registered in the Commission human resources information system called Sysper2. Some years before Sysper1 was used. – *Commission's Human Resources Report 2009*, p. 26.

[225] Stevens and Stevens, *Brussels Bureaucrats? The Administration of the European Union*, p. 22; Dimitrakopoulos (ed.), *The Changing European Commission*, p. 35; Spence and Stevens, *Staff and Personnel Policy in the Commission*, p. 193; and Stevens and Stevens, *The Internal Reform of the Commission*, p. 470. See also *Second Report on Reform of the Commission of 1999, Volume II*, Section 6.4.35. where the Committee of Independent Experts condemns the practice of using the 'mini-budgets' for covering administrative expenditure as one of 'rather unorthodox practices'.

[226] Stevens and Stevens, *Brussels Bureaucrats? The Administration of the European Union*, pp. 22-23; and Spence and Stevens, *Staff and Personnel Policy in the Commission*, p. 193.

results, though Spence and Stevens doubted the effectiveness of such measures. They also stressed a large discretionary character of the recruitment process for 'mini-budgets' posts which lacked any central control over it.[227] Furthermore, with regard to the duties performed by the staff contracted under the 'mini-budgets', Stevens observed:

> *many of the 'experts' hired under mini-budgets found themselves managing expenditure programmes for the Commission, committing the Commission in contracts with outside firms, and generally performing tasks of a public service nature which should be performed by the Commission's own staff. In certain areas of the Commission, this practice created quasi-private personal administrations. Between 1993 and 1998, some 1,830 posts were created to absorb the additional staff hired this way.*[228]

Following the criticism, the 'mini-budgets' were put under control, but a similar device called Technical Assistance Officers ('TAOs') was subsequently introduced, with similar consequences.[229] Stevens observed in this respect:

> *TAOs could take many different forms. In practice there were simply a name given to the Commission's contractors. There was inadequate control over the contracts. As with mini-budgets, TAOs were sometimes entrusted with tasks, such as assessing tenders, managing contracts, supervision and payment of work done, which should properly have been carried out by the Commission's own staff, if the Commission were to provide assurance that Community resources had been used with die regularity and propriety.* [230]

Stevens concluded:

> *If the mini-budgets did much to undermine the integrity of the Commission's formal recruitment policies, the TAOs must bear a similar responsibility for undermining the integrity of the Commission's financial management.*[231]

The financial mismanagement in the European Commission was exposed in the first report of the Committee of Independent Experts presented in 1999, leading to the resignation of the Santer Commission and to the launch of an overall reform process of the European Commission. In its report, the Committee of Independent Experts condemned the use of Technical Assistance Officers, as well as the general complexity of the Commission staffing system, difficulties with control and other serious shortcomings.[232] While recognizing the need to compensate for the increase in the Commission tasks by making use of external human resources, the Committee of Independent Experts warned for disadvantages of the use of such staff:

---

227 Spence and Stevens, *Staff and Personnel Policy in the Commission*, p. 193.

228 Stevens and Stevens, *The Internal Reform of the Commission*, p. 470.

229 See, for example, *Second Report on Reform of the Commission of 1999, Volume II*, paras. 6.4.35.- 6.4.36; and Chapter 2.

230 Stevens and Stevens, *The Internal Reform of the Commission*, p. 470.

231 Ibid.in, pp. , p. 470.

232 *Second Report on Reform of the Commission of 1999, Volume II*, paras. 6.4.36.-6.4.37.

> *[I]t should be remembered that the use of external staff is not as advantageous as one might think. It has many drawbacks: it does not guarantee that the powers of civil servants are exercised only by staff employed under the Staff Regulations; it favours a lack of transparency, as well as abuses and nepotism in recruitment; it leads to temporary staff costing nearly as much to employ as officials, sometimes more; and it leads to unorthodox practices (with the Commission awarding several successive contracts to the same person); but most of all, the use of external staff is tending more and more to be used to meet structural needs, with the result that the Commission is becoming excessively dependent on these staff.*[233]

The Committee criticized the Commission's failure to conduct a proper analysis of its staffing needs and priorities in order to cope with its increasing tasks, but also the failure to use all the human resources offered to it by the budgetary authorities while leaving an 'abnormally high number' of available posts vacant.[234] Further, the Committee observed an excessive use of temporary agents and lack of transparency in their hiring and contract renewal. While acknowledging that steps have already been taken in order to restore the balance between permanent and non-permanent staff, the Committee called for more transparency and for 'return to the Staff Regulations and the Conditions of Employment of Other Servants', leading to simplification and rationalization of the Commission's staffing structure.[235] It emphasized that the civil service duties must be clearly identified and remain a sole responsibility of the in-house Commission staff, and that strict limits must be set out on the use of other staff.[236]

The recommendations of the Committee of Independent Experts were taken over by the Prodi Commission. In its 2000 *White Paper Reforming the Commission*, the Commission admitted that a high reliance on the non-permanent staff:

> *[brings] risks for departments in maintaining continuity in the performance of activities in the face of a high turnover of staff. This, together with the variety of contracts under which these staff are employed, is confusing for the staff concerned and for the departments which manage their work. Moreover there is an insufficient guarantee that core public service tasks are performed only by staff subject to the standards laid down in the Staff Regulations. Finally, the cost of employing non-permanent staff can be close to, or even above, that of employing a permanent official: while non-permanent staff will always be needed to fill*

---

233 Ibid., para. 6.4.34. See also paras. 6.4.7. and 6.4.29. In para. 6.4.30. the Committee illustrated the complexity of the system of external staffing in the Commission by listing different types of such staff used: 'auxiliaries and local staff..., consultants, researchers, detached national experts, visiting scientists, freelance interpreters, interim staff (having a contract with an interim agency which has concluded a framework contract with the Commission), staff of companies providing services, hostesses, doctors, social workers, language teachers, etc.'

234 Ibid., para. 6.4.32.

235 Ibid., paras. 6.4.20., 6.4.21, 6.4.23., 6.4.27 and 6.4.40.

236 Ibid., paras. 6.4.37. and 6.4.39. The Committee also stressed that external staff may only be engaged for *ad hoc* or specialist tasks, must be temporary, and supportive to tasks involving the exercise of the civil service powers. – ibid, para. 6.4.29.

> *short-term gaps or to bring specialist skills, the high percentage of non-permanent officials in the Commission cannot be justified.*[237]

The Commission, therefore, decided to 'address the degree to which the Commission relies on contractual staff and to rationalise the rules on which tasks they may perform'.[238] The objectives of the *White Paper* were realized between 2000 and 2004.[239] A great number of non-permanent posts were transformed into permanent ones. In addition, a number of decisions were adopted establishing rules on the engagement and use of temporary staff, including rules on the maximum proportion of such staff who may be engaged at any given moment; as well as rules on the maximum duration for recourse to non-permanent staff.[240]

A strong emphasis in this process was put on developing a system of Strategic Planning and Programming to help overcome shortages in the Commission's human resources in comparison to its tasks.[241] In addition, the Commission systematized its approach to externalization of its work, by creating executive agencies (a new type of body for the implementation of Community programmes); decentralizing tasks to a network of national public agencies (the Commission adopted guidelines on management of Community programmes by a network of national public agencies); and by contracting out administrative and technical assistance to the private sector (it developed guidelines for programme managers, including a standard contract).[242] The Technical Assistance Officers were gradually eliminated and a new category of non-permanent staff, contract staff, was introduced. The latter were intended to work on non-core tasks in Community agencies and executive offices, to replace local staff in EU delegations and representations as well as abolished aux-

---

[237] *Reforming the Commission - A White Paper - Part II - Action Plan*, Chapter IV, Section XVI, Part 1.

[238] Ibid., Chapter IV, Section XVI, Part 1.

[239] For details, see for example, Stevens and Stevens, *The Internal Reform of the Commission*, in, pp. ; or Dimitrakopoulos (ed.), *The Changing European Commission*; or Schon-Quinlivan, *Administrative Reform in the European Commission: From Rethoric to Re-legitimisation*.

[240] *Commission Decision on Temporary Agents*, and *Commission Decision on the Maximum Duration for the Recourse to Non-permanent Staff in the Commission Services, C(2004)1597, Informations Administratives No 75-2004 of 24.6.2004*, 26.4.2004, available at http://europa.eu/epso/documents/regle_des_six_ans_en.pdf, last visited on 30.12.2010.

[241] See, for example, Dimitrakopoulos (ed.), *The Changing European Commission*, p. 45; and Stevens and Stevens, *The Internal Reform of the Commission*, p. 465. At present, the Commission planning system consists of the Annual Policy Strategy (APS) adopted by the College for the coming year; ; annual Commission Work Programme; annual management programmes for each Commission service; and annual activity reports of each Directorate-General. – Dimitrakopoulos (ed.), *The Changing European Commission*, p. 48. In connection with these strategic planning and reporting, Schön-Quinlivan interestingly noted that 'the line between the public and private sector [had] been blurred in the Commission'. She observed that these were tools taken from the private sector, helping to structure the Commission's work but potentially dangerous for a long term perspective for reference. - Schon-Quinlivan, *Administrative Reform in the European Commission: From Rethoric to Re-legitimisation*, pp. 12-13.

[242] Dimitrakopoulos (ed.), *The Changing European Commission*, p. 49.

iliary staff.[243] The Commission claims that the core functions of the EU civil service are to be the exclusive domain of its permanent staff.[244]

3.2. Current system

When describing the current system of contracts used in the European Commission, it should first be explained that the type of contract is always linked to the staff category. As for contract duration, non-permanent contracts are usually fixed-term but some can also be indefinite contracts. The following parts explain the details of the contractual set up for each staff category, both permanent and non-permanent.

3.2.1. Permanent appointments

Permanent appointments are granted to persons who are to serve in established posts and who are expected to spend their entire career with the European Commission. In principle, duties that are reserved for civil servants, i.e. duties 'linked to the functions of the institutions which derive from the powers conferred on that institution by the Treaties or by acts adopted in pursuance of the Treaties', are to be carried out by permanent officials only.[245]

Appointment and separation from service under the system of permanent appointments in the EU is quite straightforward. Appointment takes place via an open or internal competition, unless the post in question entails special qualifications or is at a senior level which may be filled pursuant to a special procedure under Article 29(2) of the *EU Staff Regulations*.[246] Separation from service is only possible in accordance with legal grounds expressly provided in the *EU Staff Regulations*. Separation 'in the interests of the service' is possible as well but only in case of senior officials. Moreover, formally speaking, such separation does not constitute separation in the narrow sense of the word, but retirement.[247] Officials below the senior level may not be separated in the interests of the service, although their service may be terminated when, for example, staff reduction or post abolition is needed.[248]

3.2.2. Non-permanent appointments

The post-2004 system of non-permanent appointments in the EU is based on four categories of non-permanent statutory staff who may be engaged by the EU institu-

243 Ibid., pp. 49 and 54.

244 *Reforming the Commission - A White Paper - Part II - Action Plan*, Chapter IV, Section XVI, Part 1.

245 *Second Report on Reform of the Commission of 1999, Volume II*, para. 6.4.6.

246 For more details, see chapter 3 dealing with recruitment of the European Commission staff, section 3.2.

247 *EU Staff Regulations*, Article 50. For more details, see below, chapter 7, section 2.2.4.1.

248 For more details, see chapter 7 dealing with separation of the European Commission staff, section 3.2.

tions: temporary staff, contract staff, local staff and special advisors.[249] They may be engaged for a fixed-term or indefinite period, depending on the staff category and the institution's needs.

The maximum duration of any non-permanent employment in the EU institutions is laid down in the *EU Conditions of Employment of Other Servants* for each category of staff separately.[250] For Commission staff, further rules are contained in decisions concerning the engagement of each specific category of staff.[251] There is also the *Commission Decision on the Maximum Duration for the Recourse to Non-permanent Staff in the Commission Services C(2004)1597*.[252] The former contains, *inter alia*, detailed provisions on duration and termination of individual contracts in each specific case, while the latter sets out a maximum duration of employment occurring under the same or various types of successive contracts, even if they are not concluded on a continuous basis. This maximum is six years measured over a 12-year period.[253] However, it only applies to non-permanent staff covered by the decision, i.e. temporary staff other than those serving in cabinets; contract staff for auxiliary tasks, referred to as 'contract staff 3b'; seconded national experts; employment agency staff; and individuals engaged under private service contracts.[254] The maximum duration of (successive) engagement thus does not apply to temporary staff serving in cabinets or to 'contract staff 3a'. The latter instance is justified by the fact that these contract staff may eventually be granted indefinite appointments. Such appointments have no expiry date and it is, therefore, logical that there is no overall maximum for their duration. The justification for the absence of an overall maximum period for engaging cabinet staff is purely political. The entire set up of these staff's engagement is, in general, free of restrictions and is left to the discretion of each individual Commissioner.

The *Commission Decision on the Maximum Duration for the Recourse to Non-permanent Staff in the Commission Services* also does not apply to local staff (and special advisers, not covered by this study) who serve under specific legal regimes.[255] Conditions of employment of local staff are based not only on the Commission's legal framework but also on the local employment law.[256]

---

[249] *EU Conditions of Employment of Other Servants*, Article 1.

[250] Ibid., Articles 8, 85, 88 and 123. No such provision exists for local staff.

[251] *Commission Decision on Temporary Agents*, and *Commission Decision on Contract Staff*. See also *Commission Framework Rules on Local Staff*. Note that rules regarding the duration of engagement of seconded national experts can be found in *Commission Decision on Secondment*.

[252] *Commission Decision on the Maximum Duration for the Recourse to Non-permanent Staff in the Commission Services*.

[253] Ibid., Articles 2 and 3.

[254] Ibid., Article 1(2). Until 2007, the maximum also applied to auxiliary staff. – Ibid. The reason for it is that the category of auxiliary staff existed and was used until the end of 2007. The 2004 amendment of the *EU Conditions of Employment of Other Servants* abolished this category as of 1 January 2007, providing for a transitional period of one year for contracts concluded before that date. - *EU Conditions of Employment of Other Servants*, Article 52.

[255] *EU Conditions of Employment of Other Servants*, Titles V and VI.

[256] Ibid., Article 120. For more details, see above, chapter 1, section 3.1.2.3.

The following parts provide more details on the type of appointments and their duration which may be used for each specific category of non-permanent staff serving in the European Commission.

3.2.2.1. Temporary staff

The European Commission may engage temporary agents in a relatively broad range of situations. It may hire them for filling both permanent and temporary posts, generalist as well as specialists posts, posts which are of short but also of longer duration. The variety of situations in which these staff may be employed is reflected in the types of contracts which are used in each of these situations. To recall, there are four distinct types of temporary staff, some further subdivided. The first type is 'Article 2(a) temporary staff' or 'temporary staff in temporary employment' engaged in specialized posts or in case of temporary needs. The second type is 'Article 2(b) temporary staff' or 'temporary staff in permanent employment', exceptionally engaged when reserve lists are not available or are insufficient, or when a specialist is needed and no temporary post is available, or for meeting temporary needs. The third type, 'Article 2(c) temporary staff', are staff engaged in Commissioners' cabinets. The last and fourth type is 'Article 2(d) temporary staff', engaged in research budget permanent posts, i.e. 'temporary staff in permanent employment (research)'.[257]

In principle, there are no restrictions on the number of (a certain type of) temporary agents who may be employed in the Commission at one time, with two notable exceptions. The first involves 'Article 2(b) temporary staff', i.e. temporary staff serving in permanent positions. The total number of all temporary agents of this type may not exceed three per cent of the total number of authorized permanent posts in the Commission. The Commission explains the reason for this restriction - permanent positions should be held by permanent officials and the engagement of temporary staff in such positions must be seen as exceptional.[258] The second exception concerns temporary agents engaged in managerial posts. The maximum number of such contracts lies at two per cent of the total of managerial positions in the Commission. The *Commission Decision on Temporary Agents* explicitly states with regard to the engagement of temporary staff in managerial posts that it may occur on an exceptional basis only.[259] The same applies to temporary staff engaged in advisory positions, although no maximum number of such staff is set.[260] Temporary staff engaged under Article 2(a) and (d) and under Article 2(c) of the *EU Conditions of*

---

[257] Ibid., Article 2; *Commission Decision on Temporary Agents*, Articles 2-5; and *Second Report on Reform of the Commission of 1999, Volume II*, p. 3, Annex V.

[258] *Commission Decision on Temporary Agents*, Article 3. Note that according to the last available data, the number of authorized posts n the Commission in 2008 was 26.013, while the number of 'Article 2(b) temporary staff' in that year was 1.283. - *Commission's Human Resources Report 2009*, p. 30, footnote 5; and p. 35. This amounts to almost 5 per cent of staff in 'Article 2(b) temporary posts'. The Commission explained that there had been a temporary increase of temporary staff in 2007 and 2008 due to the objective of rapidly hiring staff from 12 new Member States. – Ibid., p. 31.

[259] *Commission Decision on Temporary Agents*, Article 6(1).

[260] Ibid., Article 6(2).

Employment of Other Servants, i.e. staff who fill posts of a specialized nature or posts with temporary needs, research staff and cabinets staff, may be employed by the Commission with no restrictions other than the purpose of the engagement and/or the maximum duration of the contract.

The duration of employment of temporary staff differs among various types of these staff. Some of them may be contracted for indefinite periods, but a majority of temporary staff may only serve on fixed-term basis. In some instances, the Commission's own rules are stricter in this regard than the possibilities offered by the *EU Conditions of Employment of Other Servants*. This is so, in particular, in case of temporary staff serving in temporary posts, i.e. 'Article 2(a) temporary staff'. Pursuant to the *EU Conditions of Employment of Other Servants*, such staff may be engaged for a fixed-term or indefinite period, while according the *Commission Decision on Temporary Agents* they may only be given fixed-term appointments. Moreover, the *EU Conditions of Employment of Other Servants* do not provide any maximum duration of fixed-term appointments of this type of temporary staff, whereas the *Commission Decision on Temporary Agents* does.[261]

Pursuant to both the *EU Conditions of Employment of Other Servants* and the *Commission Decision on Temporary Agents*, most temporary staff with fixed-term appointment may be given a contract of maximum four years' duration, once renewable for a maximum of two years, unless it is known in advance that the duration of the task for which the staff is engaged will be shorter.[262] A notable exception in this regard are Commission 'Article 2(b) temporary staff', i.e. temporary staff in permanent posts who may be engaged when reserve lists are not available or are insufficient. The initial appointment of these staff should be for at least three years.[263] Another exception are Commission 'Article 2(a) temporary staff' and 'Article 2(b) temporary staff' who are engaged for meeting temporary needs. Such staff may only be engaged for the duration of the relevant task.[264] Last but not least, temporary appointments are not subject to a required minimum contract duration.

Only one type of temporary staff serving in the European Commission may be engaged for indefinite periods, namely the cabinet staff.[265] Formally, these staff are thus subject to no maximum duration of their contracts. In practice, however, it is presumed that their engagement is limited to the duration of office of their Commissioner. Naturally, any such indefinite appointment may be terminated at any time, i.e. also before the term of office of the relevant Commissioner has ex-

[261] *EU Conditions of Employment of Other Servants*, Article 8 and *Commission Decision on Temporary Agents*, Article 2(a).

[262] *EU Conditions of Employment of Other Servants*, Article 8 and *Commission Decision on Temporary Agents*, Articles 2, 3, 6 and 7.

[263] *Commission Decision on Temporary Agents*, Article 3(a).

[264] Ibid., Articles 2(b) and 3(b).

[265] *EU Conditions of Employment of Other Servants*, Article 8 and *Commission Decision on Temporary Agents*, Article 4.

pired, if the Commissioner so wishes.[266] The appointment may also continue beyond that date if (another) Commissioner re-employs such staff in the next term.

Given the number of types of temporary staff and the diversity of rules applicable to each of these types, details on the possible duration of appointments are set out in the table below. For comparison purposes, the table includes the regime set out by the *EU Conditions of Employment of Other Servants* as well as the system that applies to Commission staff pursuant to the *Commission Decision on Temporary Agents*.

Table 15: Types and duration of appointments of the European Commission temporary staff

Staff category	Under *EU Conditions of Employment of Other Servants*			Under Commission decision		
	Provision	*Type*	*Duration*	*Provision*	*Type*	*Duration*
'Article 2(a) temporary staff' engaged for specialist posts	Article 8	- fixed-term, one renewal for fixed-term, further renewal for indefinite; OR - indefinite	- no restrictions	Article 2(a)	- fixed-term, one renewal for fixed-term	- initial max. 4 years; - one renewal max. 2 years; - in total max. for the duration of the task if need for specialist also temporary
'Article 2(a) temporary staff' engaged to meet temporary needs	Article 8	- fixed-term, one renewal for fixed-term, further renewal for indefinite; OR - indefinite	- no restrictions	Article 2(b)	- fixed-term	- task duration; - max. 4 years; - one renewal max. 2 years
'Article 2(a) temporary staff' engaged in managerial positions or advisory functions	- no special provision	- no special provision	- no special provision	Articles 6 and 7	- fixed-term	- max. 4 years; - one renewal max. 2 years
'Article 2(b) temporary staff' engaged when reserve lists are not available or are insufficient	Article 8	- fixed-term, renewal for fixed-term	- max. 4 years; - one renewal max. 2 years	Article 3(a)	- fixed-term, renewal for fixed-term	- initial max. 3 years; - renewal up to max. 4 years incl. initial

[266] As explained in chapter 3 dealing with recruitment procedures, recruitment of cabinet staff is within full discretion of each individual Commissioner, subject to the Commissioners' Code of Conduct. For details, see above, chapter 3, section 3.3.1.

'Article 2(b) temporary staff' engaged when a specialist is needed and no temporary post is available	Article 8	- fixed-term, renewal for fixed-term	- max. 4 years; - one renewal max. 2 years	Article 3(b)	- fixed-term, renewal for fixed-term	- max. 4 years; - renewal max. 2 years
'Article 2(b) temporary staff' engaged to meet temporary needs	Article 8	- fixed-term, renewal for fixed-term	- max. 4 years; - one renewal max. 2 years	Article 3(b)	- fixed-term, renewal for fixed-term	- task duration; max. 4 years; - one renewal max. 2 years
'Article 2(b) temporary staff' engaged in managerial positions or advisory functions	- no special provision	- no special provision	- no special provision	Articles 6 and 7	- fixed-term	- max. 4 years; - one renewal max. 2 years
'Article 2(c) temporary staff'	Article 8	- indefinite	- no restrictions	Article 4	- indefinite	- no restrictions
'Article 2(d) temporary staff'	Article 8	- fixed-term, renewal for fixed-term	- max. 4 years; - one renewal max. 2 years	Article 5	- no rules	- no rules
'Article 2(d) temporary staff' engaged in managerial positions or advisory functions	- no special provision	- no special provision	- no special provision	Articles 6 and 7	- fixed-term	- max. 4 years; - one renewal max. 2 years

3.2.2.2. Contract staff

Like temporary staff, contract staff too are divided into different types named after the provision which defines them. There are 'Article 3a contract staff' and 'Article 3b contract staff', the latter also referred to as 'contract staff for auxiliary tasks'.[267] Although both types belong to the same category of non-permanent staff, there are many differences between them. As explained in chapter 1 of this study, these differences concern tasks these staff may be used for, contract duration, selection procedure as well as staff grading. As far as the tasks are concerned, in the European Commission, 'Article 3a contract staff' may only be used for the performance of manual and administrative support service tasks, while 'Article 3b contract staff' may

[267] *EU Conditions of Employment of Other Servants*, Articles 3a(1) and 3b.

perform other duties as well. The 'Article 3b contract staff' may also be engaged for time-limited replacement of permanent or temporary staff serving in the function group AST and, exceptionally, also such staff serving in the function group AD and occupying highly specialized posts. The 'Article 3b contract staff' may, however, never replace staff in management positions.[268] There is no limit as to the number of contract staff who may be appointed by the Commission at any given time.[269]

One of the most significant differences between 'Article 3a contract staff' and 'Article 3b contract staff' lies in the possible duration of their appointments. While 'Article 3a contract staff' start with fixed-term appointment up to five years but may eventually, after a few renewals, end up with appointment of indefinite duration, 'Article 3b contract staff' may only be employed for a fixed-term period of maximum duration of three years, including all renewals.[270] Details especially with regard to possible contract duration and renewals of 'Article 3a contract staff' are rather complex. This is even more so under the *Commission Decision on Contract Staff* when compared to the *EU Conditions of Employment of Other Servants*. Because of this complexity, these details have been put in a table below.

Table 16: Types and duration of appointments of the European Commission contract staff

Staff category	Under *EU Conditions of Employment of Other Servants*			Under Commission decision		
	Provision	***Type***	***Duration***	***Provision***	***Type***	***Duration***
'Article 3a contract staff' in function group I	Article 85	- fixed-term; - third or fourth renewal indefinite (max. 10 years on fixed-term)	- initial min. 3 months – max. 5 years; - one renewal max. 5 years but min. 6 months with initial; - possibly second renewal when max. 10 years on fixed-term; - last renewal for indefinite	Article 6	- fixed-term; - three renewals fixed-term; - fourth renewal indefinite	- initial min. 3 months – max. 5 years; - three renewals min. 3 months – max. 5 years each; unless 10 years exceeded – than third renewal indefinite - fourth renewal, when the first four periods min. 3 years, for indefinite

[268] Ibid., Articles 3a(1) and 3b.

[269] Recall that EU entities other than institutions, e.g. agencies, entities situated inside or outside the EU and representations and delegations of EU institutions, are more limited. The maximum number of 'Article 3a contract staff' in these institutions may be seventy-five per cent. - Ibid., Article 3a(2).

[270] Ibid., Articles 85 and 88; and *Commission Decision on Contract Staff*, Articles 6 and 9.

'Article 3a contract staff' in function groups II - IV	Article 85	- fixed-term; - third renewal indefinite	- initial min. 3 m – max. 5 years; - one renewal max. 5 years but min. 9 m with initial; - third renewal indefinite	Article 6	- fixed-term; - one renewal fixed-term; - second renewal indefinite	- initial min. 3 months – max. 5 years; - one renewal min. 6 months – max. 5 years; - second renewal, if the first two periods min. 3 years, for indefinite
'Article 3b contract staff' in function groups I and II	Article 88	- fixed-term; - renewals fixed-term	- max. 3 years, incl. all renewals	Article 9	- fixed-term; - renewals fixed-term	- initial min. 3 months; - first renewal min. 3 months; - further renewals min. 1 years - last renewal may be less than 3 months if total of 3 years for all reached - in total max. 3 years
'Article 3b contract staff' in function groups III and IV	Article 88	- fixed-term; - renewals fixed-term	- max. 3 years, incl. all renewals	Article 9	- fixed-term; - renewals fixed-term	- initial min. 3 months; - first renewal min. 3 months; - further renewals min. 1 years - last renewal may be less than 3 months if total of 3 years for all reached OR if shorter task duration - in total max. 3 years

If a person has served as 'Article 3a contract staff', his employment does not count towards the maximum set for the period under Article 3b. Similarly, periods used under Article 3b are not counted for the purposes of Article 3a.[271] This means that a person may serve as contract staff member for a period longer than the maximum limit set for each sub-group of contract staff. However, for the Commission staff, the overall time limitation of six years set in the *Commission Decision on the Maximum Duration for the Recourse to Non-permanent Staff in the Commission Services* applies.

[271] *EU Conditions of Employment of Other Servants*, Articles 85(1) and 88.

As mentioned earlier, this six-year limitation is calculated over a period of 12 years.[272] It applies only to 'Article 3b contract staff' but not to 'Article 3a contract staff', since the latter may eventually serve on indefinite appointments.

3.2.2.3. Local staff

Article 120 of the *EU Condition of Employment of Other Servants* stipulates:

> *Subject to the provisions of this Title, the conditions of employment of local staff, in particular:*
>
> *(a) the manner of their engagement and termination of their contract,*
>
> *(b) their leave, and*
>
> *(c) their remuneration*
>
> *shall be determined by each institution in accordance with current rules and practice in the place where they are to perform their duties.*

For local staff employed in third countries, the European Commission has made such determination in its *Framework Rules Laying Down the Conditions of Employment of Local Staff of the Commission of the European Communities Serving in Non-member Countries*. These rules were adopted in 1989, entered into force in 1990 and remain so until now. On their basis, specific conditions of employment were adopted for each specific place, i.e. third country in which local staff are engaged by the Commission.[273] Specific conditions of employment thus reflect the Commission framework rules but also the local employment law. It appears that besides the mentioned framework rules for local staff serving in third countries, there is no other Commission decision which would set out conditions of employment of other local staff.

As noted previously, the precise relationship between the EU rules and local law has been clarified by the ECJ which has recognized a wide discretion of the EU Administration in establishing conditions of employment of local staff but required respect for its existing internal rules as well as rules and practices of the relevant country.[274]

With regard to the duration of appointment of local staff serving in third countries, the *Commission Framework Rules on Local Staff* stipulate that contracts may be concluded for fixed-term or indefinite period but do not elaborate on this issue further.[275] They do state that fixed-term contracts end, in principle, upon the expiry of the term and that indefinite contracts may be at any time terminated by providing a notice upon the expiry of a relevant period of notice.[276]

---

[272] *Commission Decision on the Maximum Duration for the Recourse to Non-permanent Staff in the Commission Services*, Articles 1(2), 2 and 3(1).

[273] *Commission Framework Rules on Local Staff*, introductory section, paras. 1 and 2.

[274] For more details see above, chapter 1, section 3.1.2.3.

[275] *Commission Framework Rules on Local Staff*, Article 3(1).

[276] Ibid., Article 18.

3.2.2.4. Seconded national experts

Seconded national experts are not EU statutory staff since their engagement in the EU institutions occurs not pursuant to the *EU Staff Regulations* or *EU Conditions of Employment of Other Servants* but pursuant to other legal instruments adopted by each EU institution. In case of the European Commission, it is regulated by the *Commission Decision on Secondment*. According to the most recent version of the *Commission Decision on Secondment*, seconded national experts may be engaged at the Commission for a period of minimum six months and maximum two years. This initial period may, however, be extended one or more times.[277] In principle, the total period of secondment should not exceed four years but:

> *Exceptionally, at the request of the DG concerned and where the interests of the service warrant it, the Director-General [for Human Resources and Security] may authorise one or more extensions of the secondment for a maximum of two more years at the end of the four-year period.*[278]

Secondment may also take place another time, after a break of at least six years from the last secondment or other employment with the Commission which followed after that secondment. The break of six years is, however, not required if the previous secondment was shorter than four years and if the new secondment is not for a period exceeding four years when counted together with the period of the previous secondment. Of course, such secondment may be extended after the expiry of these four years for additional two years mentioned above, like any other secondment.[279]

Thus, at the European Commission, secondment always occurs for a fixed-term. There is, however, no fixed-term contract concluded between the European Commission and the seconded national expert. Pursuant to the *Commission Decision on Secondment*, each secondment is effected by an exchange of letters between the Director-General for Human Resources and Security and the employer of the seconded national expert.[280]

3.2.3. Permanent, fixed-term and indefinite appointments

To facilitate better overview of the rather complex system existing in the European Commission in respect of types of appointment used for the employment of its staff, this part summarizes which type of appointment may be used for which category

---

[277] *Commission Decision on Secondment*, Article 4(1), first paragraph.

[278] Ibid., Article 4(1), first paragraph. This exceptional prolongation beyond four years has been introduced in 2008. Before that time, seconded national experts must have left the Commission after four years of service. – See *Commission Decision on Secondment of 2006*, Article 4(1) and *Commission Decision Concerning the Amendment of Decision C(2002) 1559 of 30 April 2002 Amended by Decision C(2003)406 of 31 January Laying Down Rules on the Secondment of National Experts to the Commission, C(2004) 577*, Article 4(1).

[279] *Commission Decision on Secondment*, Article 4(3).

[280] Ibid., Article 3(4).

or subcategory of staff and for what maximum duration. It also provides information on the existing legal framework for extending and renewing non-permanent appointments.

From the point of view of contract duration, there are three main types of appointment in the European Commission: permanent, fixed-term and indefinite. Permanent appointments are granted to those who serve in established posts and spend their entire career at the Commission. Permanent appointments last thus, in principle, until retirement.

Fixed-term appointments are granted to Commission staff serving in the following categories: 'Article 2(a) temporary staff' – up to six years in total; 'Article 2(b) temporary staff' engaged when reserve lists are not available or are insufficient – up to max. 4 years in total; 'Article 2(b) temporary staff' engaged when a specialist is needed and no temporary post is available or to meet temporary needs – up to six years in total; 'Article 2(d) temporary staff' - up to six years in total; 'Article 3a contract staff' in function group I – initial contract and three renewals or two renewals if the previous employment longer than ten years in total – up to ten years in total; 'Article 3a contract staff' in function groups II-IV – initial contract and first renewal – up to ten years in total; 'Article 3b contract staff' – up to three years in total; local staff serving in third countries – specific rules may depend on local rules and practices; seconded national experts – up to 6 years in total; with another possible secondment after a break of six years. Indefinite appointments are granted to Commission staff engaged under the following staff categories: 'Article 2(c) temporary staff'; 'Article 3a contract staff' in function group I – fourth renewal of the contract, or the third renewal if the previous employment was longer than 10 years in total; 'Article 3a contract staff' in function groups II-IV – second renewal; local staff - specific rules may depend on local rules and practices. For the sake of clarity, the above information is repeated in the table below.

Table 17: Types and maximum duration of appointments in the European Commission

Staff category	Permanent appointment	Fixed-term appointment	Indefinite appointment
Officials	X		
Article 2(a) temporary staff		X max. 6 years	
Article 2(b) temporary staff engaged when reserve lists are not available or are insufficient		X max. 4 years	
Article 2(b) temporary staff engaged when a specialist is needed and no temporary post is available or to meet temporary needs		X max. 6 years	
Article 2(c) temporary staff			X
Article 2(d) temporary staff		X max. 6 years	
Article 3a contract staff in function group I		X max. 10 years	X
Article 3a contract staff in function groups II - IV		X max. 10 years	X
Article 3b contract staff		X max. 3 years	
Local staff serving in third countries		X no maximum but may be set by local rules and/or practices	X
Seconded national officials		X max. 6 years	

As in the UN, so too in the EU, fixed-term appointments last, in principle, until the date set out in the contract, while indefinite appointments last until they are terminated. Termination of indefinite appointments may occur at any time by providing a notice to the other party.

The EU Administration possesses wide discretion in deciding whether and for how long it concludes a non-permanent contract. It also enjoys broad discretion in deciding on extension and renewal of fixed-term contracts. Such actions are always optional, even when conditions set out in the individual contract and/or in the *EU*

Conditions of Employment of Other Servants are met.[281] Staff serving on fixed-term basis have thus no legal right to contract renewal and must expect that, as a rule, their employment will end upon the expiry of the fixed date.[282] The situation may, of course, be different if the authority authorized to conclude contracts limits its own discretion, for example by introducing a special system designed to ensure transparency in the procedures to be used for contract renewals.[283]

There is one notable exception to the rule that staff may not expect extension or renewal of their fixed-term contract. It concerns situations in which staff may rely on the principle of the protection of legitimate expectations. Such principle was, similar to the UN principle of legal expectancy, developed by the judiciary and is considered to constitute one of the fundamental principles of EU law.[284] The right to rely on the principle of the protection of legitimate expectations belongs to 'any individual who is in a situation in which it appears that the Administration's conduct has led him to entertain reasonable expectations'.[285] A number of conditions must, however, be met. They have been developed over the years in the jurisprudence and summarized in the 2009 judgment in *Wenning*.[286]

The first condition relates to the existence of assurances by the EU Administration to the person who wishes to invoke the principle. The assurances claimed must, however, be sound. A mere recommendation, for example, made by a superior official with regard to the extension of a contract of fixed-term duration for an additional period, has not been considered to be an assurance.[287] The assurances must also be precise, unconditional and consistent and must come from authorized and reliable sources.[288] Hence, the silence of a relevant authority following a request for confirmation of a certain right cannot be considered to be a precise assurance.[289] Neither can an uncertain contractual situation created by an ambiguous amendment of the contract be regarded as such.[290]

---

281 *Cocchi et Hainz v. Commission, Case T-330/00 and T-114/01*, para. 83 and *Pyres v. Commission, Case T-7/01*, para. 39.

282 *Wenning v. Europol, Case F-114/07*, para. 142.

283 Ibid., paras. 144-147.

284 For example, Ibid., para. 175.

285 *Mavridis v. Parliament, Case 289/81*, para. 21.

286 *Wenning v. Europol, Case F-114/07*.

287 Ibid., para. 176.

288 Ibid., para. 175.

289 *Jean-Louis Chomel v. Commission of the European Communities, Case T-123/89, ECR [1990], p. II-131*, paras. 26-27.

290 *European Agency for Reconstruction (EAR) v. Georgios Karatzoglou, Case C-213/06 P, ECR [2007], p. I-6733*, paras. 31-38. In this case, the initial temporary contract of Mr. Karatzoglou was later extended for an indefinite period but the contract extension included a possibility of termination of the appointment under certain specified circumstances. The new contract of the applicant also confusingly mentioned certain provisions from the initial contract and from the *EU Conditions of Employment of Other Servants*. A year later the applicant's appointment was terminated through a notice of termination. The applicant claimed that the termination was illegal because the specific circumstances mentioned in his new contract had not taken place. He claimed, *inter alia*, that he had had legitimate expectations that his contract would only be terminated when the mentioned specific circumstances occurred, especially on the basis of a provision of the initial contract mentioned in the new contract. The Court

The second condition to be met for the principle of protection of legitimate expectations to apply involves the rise of a legitimate expectation in the mind of the person to whom the assurances were addressed. The rise of the expectation must, at the same time, be a result of the assurances given.[291]

The third and last condition requires that the assurances be in conformity with the applicable standards and law.[292] For example, assurances not to apply EU law cannot be regarded as valid.[293] Similarly, it is not possible to oppose the application of a new legislative provision by relying on the principle of protection of legitimate expectations.[294] As far as the employment relationship between an EU institution and an individual is concerned, the assurances must always comply with the provisions of the *EU Staff Regulations* or the *EU Conditions of Employment of Other Servants*.[295]

If the above three conditions are not met, EU staff cannot successfully invoke the principle of the protection of legitimate expectations and the EU Administration can exercise its broad discretion and decide autonomously whether to extend or renew an individual fixed-term contract. Pursuant to the settled case law, the Administration does not even need to provide reasons for its decision. The relevant statements of the Court of First Instance in *Pyres* deserve full citation:

> *... despite the general reference in Article 11 of the Conditions of Employment to Articles 11 to 26 of the Staff Regulations concerning the rights and obligations of officials, the situation of a member of the temporary staff differs from that of an official so as to exclude the application by analogy of Article 25 of the Staff Regulations relating to the obligation to state the grounds for any decision adversely affecting an official.*[296]

With regard to the duty to state reasons for non-renewal of a fixed-term contract, the Court held:

> *[J]ust as there is no need to state the reasons for the termination of a contract of employment of a member of the temporary staff concluded for an indefinite period, the [authority empowered to conclude contracts of employment], given its very broad discretion ... is not obliged to state the reasons for the act by which it decides, in compliance with the notice periods provided for in the contract and*

---

of First Instance agreed with the applicant but the European Court of Justice, dealing with the appeal, quashed the judgment in the first instance emphasizing that the applicant had been given no precise assurances and that his contractual situation was uncertain, also due to the confusing use of certain provisions in the new contract of the applicant.- See also Ibid., paras. 9-14.

[291] *Wenning v. Europol, Case F-114/07*, para. 175.

[292] Ibid., para. 175.

[293] *Chomel v. Commission, Case T-123/89*, para. 28.

[294] *Mediavilla and others v. Commission of the European Communities and Council of the European Union, Case C-443/07 P, ECR [2008], p. I-10945*, para. 91 and *Pilar Angé Serrano and others v. European Parliament C-496/08 P*, available at http://eur-lex.europa.eu/LexUriServ/LexUriServ.do?uri=CELEX:62008J0496:EN:HTML, last visited on 30.12.2010, paras. 91-94.

[295] *Norbert Schmitt v. European Agency for Reconstruction (EAR), Case T-175/03, ECR-SC [2004], p. I-A-211, II-939*, paras. 46-47.

[296] *Pyres v. Commission, Case T-7/01*, para. 36.

> *in Article 47(1)(b) of the Conditions of Employment and, where relevant, with the internal rules adopted by the institution concerned, not to renew such a contract of employment, concluded for a fixed period, on its expiry. That is all the more true where [the authority empowered to conclude contracts of employment] decides to extend the contract of a member of the temporary staff for a shorter period than the maximum period laid down in the agreements originally entered into by the parties.*[297]

The EU Administration also enjoys broad discretion in regard to the termination of contracts concluded for an indefinite period. In principle, it may terminate such contracts at any time by providing notice of termination to the staff member concerned. Until recently, the Administration did not need to state reasons for contract termination, as was – and still is – the case with non-extension and non-renewal of fixed-term contracts. There are many cases which confirmed this approach. The case quote above, from *Pyros,* is one of them. Another notable recent case is *Karatzoglou*. In this case the Court of First Instance recalled that the decisive difference in the position of temporary staff as compared to permanent staff lay in the temporary nature of such employment. Temporary employment is intended to exist only for a limited period of time. In addition, it is governed by the terms of the employment contract. If the temporary contract itself does not impose a duty to state reasons for its termination on the basis of the period of notice, such duty does not exist.[298]

It is interesting to note that the ruling in *Karatzoglou* was adopted at a time when an appeal was pending before the same Court against a judgment of the European Union Civil Service Tribunal in *Ladgren*. In that case the European Union Civil Service Tribunal departed from the existing case law and ruled that:

> *there is no overriding reason to exclude members of the temporary staff within the meaning of the Conditions of Employment from protection against unjustified dismissal, particularly when their contract is for an indefinite period or, if it is a fixed-term contract, they are dismissed before the expiry of the term.*[299]

The Tribunal came to this conclusion by comparing the status of various categories of staff. It stressed that an employment relationship of an indefinite duration guarantees a certain degree of job security, albeit less than permanent employment. Similarly, a fixed-term employment guarantees, in the Tribunal's view, in principle that the employment will last until the end of the fixed-term period.[300] Hence, any termination of an employment of indefinite duration, or a fixed-term employment before the expiry date, must be justified. The Tribunal also referred in this context to the requirements of international labour standards on the prevention of unfair dismissal as well as corresponding provisions of the Charter of Fundamental Rights

[297] Ibid., para. 40.

[298] *Georgios Karatzoglou v. European Agency for Reconstruction, Case T-471/04, ECR-SC [2006], p. I-A-2-35, II-A-2-157*, paras. 35-36.

[299] *Landgren v. ETF, Case F-1/05*, para. 73.

[300] Ibid., para. 68.

of the European Union.[301] The main reasons for which the obligation to state reasons must be recognized were explained as follows:

> *In order to ensure a sufficient degree of protection to that effect, the persons concerned must be able to determine whether their legitimate interests have been respected or damaged and to assess whether it would be appropriate to initiate judicial proceedings, and the courts must be able to exercise their powers of review, which amounts to recognising an obligation on the part of the competent authority to state the reasons for its decisions.*[302]

The Tribunal stressed that the recognition of the obligation to state reasons for terminating contracts does not prevent the relevant authorities from enjoying broad discretion in regard to dismissal. It added that judicial review remains limited to ensuring that no manifest error or misuse of powers occurred.[303] The Tribunal's decision in this case was upheld by the Court of First Instance in an appeal brought by the defending institution.[304] It was done by the same Court (of First Instance) which ruled a year earlier in *Karatzoglou* that no reasons had to be stated for the termination of indefinite appointments. From the point of view of protecting non-career staff against unjustified separation from service, however, the latest judgment in *Landgren* must be praised as it strengthens the position of such staff against the EU Administration.

4. The UN and the EU compared

The issue of types of appointments has proven to be rather sensitive both in the UN Secretariat and in the European Commission, although it could be argued that there has been more politicization in the UN than in the EU. Great responsiveness to this issue on the part of the staff can be detected in both respective organizations. This is, of course, a natural reaction, given the fact that the type of appointment used in an individual case produces consequences for one's conditions of employment, including the sensitive issue of remuneration and, arguably even more importantly, job security. The latter, and its influence on the independence and impartiality of international civil servants, is the reason why this study pays attention to the issue of types of appointments used in the UN Secretariat and in the European Commission.

When comparing the two respective institutions, it is striking that they both had the same initial approach. Both the UN and the EU initially attached great importance to

[301] Ibid., paras. 69-72.

[302] Ibid., para. 74.

[303] Ibid., para. 75. The Tribunal also recalled that pursuant to the previous case law, the scope of the obligation to give reasons needs to be placed in the context in which the decision at issue was adopted, and assessed in relation to specific circumstances of each case, especially in relation to the content of the measure, the nature of the reasons and the interest if the addressee. – Ibid., para. 78.

[304] *European Training Foundation v. Landgren, Case T-404/06 P, ECR [2009], p. II-2841,* paras. 143-171. It took the Court almost 30 paragraphs to explain its motives for departing from the previous case law, without admitting such departure.

the need to secure the independence and impartiality of staff and gave lesser importance to other considerations. As a consequence, both the UN Secretariat and the European Commission offered career appointments to a large majority of their staff who were responsible for carrying out core tasks that the international civil service was entrusted with. At the same time, in both the UN and EU, some room was left for employing non-permanent staff. Such staff were used for meeting temporary needs, either of pre-set or of uncertain duration. Non-permanent employment was also used for accommodating national experts seconded to the respective organizations for the purposes of exchanging experiences in handling matters of common importance. Hence, both career and non-career appointments have been offered in both the UN Secretariat and the European Commission from the outset.[305]

Gradually, this initial approach has, in practice, changed in both the UN and the EU. The main reason for the modification was the extension of mandates of these organizations, not (sufficiently) followed by the adjustment of human resources management. The situation in both the UN Secretariat and the European Commission was in this respect fairly comparable, although an additional problem existed in the UN Secretariat. There, the issue of the type of appointment to be employed in an individual case was used as a tool for meeting various political needs, be they the needs of newly acceded Member States for getting their nationals on the Secretariat or the needs of socialist Member States for exercising control over their nationals employed by the Secretariat.[306] This problem was not relevant in the European Commission which was in a more comfortable position in this regard. The EU had never had to cope with a sudden accession of a number of new Member States as large as the UN. In addition, when a new country joined the EU, the organization immediately created space for allowing nationals of this country to become a part of the EU civil service, thus avoiding possible absence of representation or underrepresentation of that country in the EU staff.[307] Moreover, the EU never had a socialist country among its Member States. Although the idea of an independent international career civil service was not shared by all EU Member States since the beginning, once accepted, it was no longer (formally) challenged.

The reaction of the UN and the EU, respectively, to the problems which occurred over the years, in particular the extension of mandates and the diversity of operational needs, differed. The UN Secretariat created a number of new types of appointment with different conditions of employment, whereas the European Commission kept its contractual framework intact, making greater use of non-permanent staff provided for in the existing legal framework. The European Commission also turned to a much greater extent to external human resources. As a result, the situation in the UN Secretariat was characterized by the complexity of, and a significant inequality in, the conditions of employment of staff, while that in the European Commission entailed considerable financial and other maladministration and mismanage-

[305] See above, sections 2.1 and 3.1.

[306] See above, section 2.1.

[307] See above, chapter 2, section 3.4.1.2.2.

ment.[308] Neither the UN Secretariat nor the European Commission was thus able to give a satisfactory solution to the problems which arose with the extension of their mandates and the diversity of operational needs. They also did not offer long term answers to the problems the organizations faced. Therefore, both organizations reformed their human resources framework over the last decade. However, once again, they did so in different ways. In the UN, legally speaking, dramatic changes took place and a completely new contractual framework was set up.[309] In the EU, changes were more cosmetic, certainly as far as the types of appointment were concerned, but significant improvements took place in the area of transparency.[310] As a result of the reforms, the UN system of contracts became simpler, whereas in the EU it remained rather complex. This is interesting to note also because the UN is in many respects a more complex and diverse organization than the EU. Yet, the UN Secretariat has chosen to simplify its contractual system dramatically, whereas the European Commission has retained a relatively complicated regime with a relatively larger number of staff categories.

Going into more detail, the UN Secretariat reduced the number of types of contract used in the past from eleven to three.[311] This is an important development especially for staff who worked previously under the 200 and 300 series of the *UN Staff Rules*. These series offered fewer rights and benefits than the 100 series which served as a model for the new single set of the *UN Staff Rules* adopted during the reform. The position of all staff was thereby equalized. In addition, the reform opened the door for all staff serving on fixed-term contracts to career appointment. For a majority of staff, the conditions for obtaining such appointment were unified.[312] It is regrettable that, despite the intention of the UN Secretary-General to do so for all staff, the General Assembly decided to place staff recruited via a competitive examination in a more favourable position. It allowed them to acquire career appointment after two years of service, while five years are required for all other staff.[313] A short-term aim of this decision, namely not to disadvantage staff recruited via a competitive examination (as compared to their pre-reform status), leads, however, to retaining long term inequality among various categories of staff.

Along with the reduced number of types of appointment, another important improvement brought by the UN reform of contractual arrangements is the introduction of a precise and clear criterion for distinguishing between the various types of appointments. The decisive element is the duration of service needed. Accordingly, temporary appointments are to be granted for service duration of less than one year; fixed-term appointments for duration of more than one year; and continuing appointments for service of continuing nature or for staff with transferable skills.[314]

---

[308] See above, sections 2.1 and 3.1.

[309] See above, sections 2.2. and 2.3.1.

[310] See above, section 3.1. and introductory part to section 3.2.2.

[311] See above, section 2.3.1.

[312] See above, section 2.3.2.

[313] See above, section 2.3.2.

[314] See above, section 2.3.1.

On the other hand, it should be noted that the last mentioned type of appointment, i.e. the continuing appointment, may only be granted after five (or exceptionally two) years of service on fixed-term. At the same time, the fixed-term appointment is, formally speaking, only provided for cases in which the service needed is of prescribed duration, i.e. limited in advance. There is thus no type of appointment available for service which is from the outset clearly of permanent or at least continuing, i.e. un-prescribed, duration.[315] In practice, however, it is clear that fixed-term appointment is to be granted also when the service at issue is of un-prescribed duration. In this sense, the new fixed-term appointment is to serve, in fact, not only for employing staff performing tasks of at least one year duration but also as probationary appointments for staff who will be granted career appointments in the future. In this sense, the former probationary appointments of two years' duration have been replaced by new fixed-term appointments for five years. This *de facto* extension of probationary period is not the only, and arguably not the most important, difference between the former and the current system. Another difference is that while the former probationary appointments were converted into permanent appointments in all cases in which staff members' performance was satisfactory, under the new regime staff serving on a fixed-term appointment and thus 'on probation' have no security of conversion of their appointment into a career one, nor when their performance during the fixed-term period is satisfactory.[316] In the European Commission, however, all staff hired for career appointment serve two years' probation, followed by a continuation of their appointment in all cases in which probation has been successful.[317] This is similar to the situation in the UN Secretariat before 2009.

The absence of a type of appointment that would fit situations in which the service to be carried out is from the outset of a continuing nature is, from a legal point of view, unfortunate as it leaves a gap in the UN system. This gap could be filled by an arrangement comparable to that existing in the EU. There, permanent appointments are used in cases in which service of long-term duration is at issue, subject to probation. The same could easily be done in the UN, also under the new system where continuing appointments have replaced permanent ones – continuing appointments could be granted not only to staff who have served on fixed-term for five years but also to newly recruited staff hired for service of continuing nature. In the latter type of situation, the granting of continuing appointments would be made conditional on successful completion of a probationary period which could be five years. Under the new contractual framework, it appears that the prolongation of the probationary period was, in fact, one of the intentions of the UN Secretary-General when proposing this framework.

Another regrettable failure of the UN contractual reform is that it did not solve the problem of uncertainty in the extensions or renewals of fixed-term appointments. In the initial years of the reform, the UN Secretary-General stated that non-career staff would no longer need to fear non-renewal of their contracts because they

[315] See above, section 2.3.1.

[316] See above, section 2.3.2.

[317] See below, chapter 7, section 3.2.1.

would all be converted into continuing ones if the prescribed conditions were met.[318] Despite this promising statement, not much has changed for the UN fixed-term staff. First, not all fixed-term staff eligible for conversion of their appointment into continuing ones will actually receive it. Those staff who will not may then remain on fixed-term appointment for a relatively long period of time, precisely as it was in the past. Moreover, as in the past, there is no guarantee of extensions or renewals of fixed-term appointments, be it those not converted into continuing ones or other fixed-term appointments. While extensions and renewals are possible, even repeatedly and with no limitations, there is no job security for non-career staff in the UN Secretariat.[319] Consequently, under the new system of contractual arrangements too, non-career staff will continue to fear for their professional future, depending on unilateral decisions of the UN Administration.

The situation in the European Commission is, in this respect, more transparent and less prone to abuse. There, a large majority of fixed-term contracts may be renewed only for a limited number of times and/or limited period of time. For temporary staff, only one renewal with a set maximum duration is permitted. In case of contract staff, there is either a total duration of appointment, including all renewals, or a maximum number of renewals, including a maximum duration. Renewal of fixed-term contracts concluded with local staff is subject to national legislation.[320] An important legal safeguard against improper use of non-permanent staff is the maximum duration set for the engagement of most non-permanent staff, including engagement under various contracts.[321] In comparison, in the UN Secretariat, only engagement under a temporary appointment is time limited. After the expiry of the maximum period, the re-engagement may only occur after a break of three months which must lapse between successive contracts.[322] No such break is required for the renewal of fixed-term appointments. Even the break existing for temporary appointments, i.e. three months, is a much weaker requirement than the one in the European Commission. There, most non-permanent staff may not be engaged for more than six years in a twelve-year period.[323]

As regards unlimited appointments, i.e. indefinite appointments, the problem of contract renewal is not relevant. Indefinite appointments do not have an expiry date and last until terminated. Therefore, there are no renewals – and thus no vulnerability to abuse. Moreover, indefinite appointments are only used for two categories of European Commission staff, namely temporary staff serving in Commissioners' cabinets, i.e. political appointees, and contract staff employed only for administrative and support tasks, i.e. performing no core tasks of the EU civil service.[324] In the UN Secretariat, indefinite appointments are no longer available. This, however, also

[318] See above, section 2.3.2.
[319] See above, sections 2.3.2 and 2.4.2.
[320] See above, sections 3.2.2.1-3.2.2.4.
[321] See above, introductory part to section 3.2.2.
[322] See above, section 2.3.1.
[323] See above, introductory part to section 3.2.2.
[324] See above, sections 3.2.2.1, 3.2.2.2 and 3.2.3.

means that in the UN Secretariat problems related to contract renewal concern all non-career staff at present. Before 2009, this was an important issue 'only' for some non-career staff, although they were a large proportion of such staff.

It can, therefore, be concluded that legal safeguards against abusive use and/or renewal of non-permanent contracts are more adequate in the European Commission than in the UN Secretariat. On the other hand, the overall set up of the contractual framework, in particular with regard to the non-career appointments, is more complex and less transparent in the European Commission than in the UN Secretariat. The latter reformed its contractual framework significantly and adopted three types of appointments, the use of which depends predominantly on the expected duration of service.[325] On the contrary, the reform in the European Commission did not change much and retained both the number of categories and subcategories of non-permanent staff who may be engaged and the differences in their conditions of employment, certainly as far as the duration of the appointment is concerned. The only notable change is the abolition of the category of auxiliary staff. Despite that, however, the overall number of staff categories did not change since a new category of contract staff was introduced simultaneously with the abolition of the category of auxiliary staff. Moreover, the new category of contract staff is divided into two distinct types, differentiated by the type of tasks they may be hired for, contract duration, and some conditions of employment.[326] The complexity of the system of non-permanent appointments has thus not been removed in the EU. In addition, as recent figures show, the number of staff employed on non-permanent basis is as high as it was shortly before the launch of the reform, namely about 40 per cent of the total Commission staff.[327] Moreover, the number of permanent staff has decreased in favour of contract staff.

[325] See above, section 2.3.1.

[326] See above, sections 3.1 and 3.2.2.

[327] For figures from 1998, see Nugent, *The European Commission*, p. 166, referred to above on p. #. For figures from 2008, see *Commission's Human Resources Report 2009*, p. 30. According to the latter, officials constituted 58.9 per cent of all Commission staff serving in 2008 in all budgets, including statutory as well as non-statutory staff, i.e. officials, temporary staff, contract staff, special advisers, local agents, agents under national law contracts, service providers, interim staff and trainees.

The table below, developed on the basis of data from the Commission's most recent *Human Resources Report* of 2009, shows the evolution from 2000 till 2008:

Table 18: Number and proportion of the European Commission staff (2000-2008)

		2000		2002		2004		2006		2008	
		Number	% of 1-4	Number	% of 1-4	Number	% of 1-4	Number	% of 1-4	Number	% of 1-4
1	**Officials**	17731	81,57	18408	79,68	20012	79,72	21542	76,59	22829	74,89
2	**Temporary staff**	2423		2827		1551		1249		1889	
Subtotal 1+2		20154	92,72	21235	91,90	21563	85,90	22791	81,03	24718	81,09
3	**Auxiliary staff**	1582		1868		3007		283		0	
4	**Contract staff**	0		0		532		5051		5766	
Subtotal 3+4		1582	7,28	1868	8,10	3539	14,10	5334	18,97	5766	18,91
Total 1-4		*21736*	*100*	*23103*	*100*	*25102*	*100*	*28125*	*100*	*30484*	*100*

Source: Developed on the basis of data provided in the Commission's *Human Resources Report* of 2009.[328]

The European Commission explains that the increase in the number of contract staff must be regarded in the light of the fact that this category has replaced not only former auxiliary staff but also some other categories.[329] However, the table above clearly shows that the proportion of contract staff in the total of Commission statutory staff, except of local staff who are subject to specific regimes, has increased to the detriment of the number of officials. The proportion of officials in the total of statutory staff, except of local staff, has decreased since 2000, this even in spite of conversion of many temporary appointments in permanent ones during the reform process.

It could be argued that many Commission contract staff perform only administrative support tasks and their increase is therefore not problematic as far as providing security of tenure to the core of EU civil servants is concerned. However, unlike 'Article

[328] *Commission's Human Resources Report 2009*, Distribution of staff in activity in the Commission by staff category, on 31/12/2008, p. 30 and Evolution of the Commission's staff by staff category between 2000 and 2008, p. 32.

[329] Ibid., Section 1.3.2., pp. 32-33. 'Article 3a contract staff' have replaced, for example, staff employed under a national law contract, such as the Local Staff for Administrative and Technical Assistance, the individual experts intra-muros, a number of local agents from the representations and staff under Belgian and Luxembourgian law. – Ibid., p. 33.

3a contract staff' who may, indeed, be employed only to perform support functions, 'Article 3b contract staff' may be engaged for a whole range of other tasks as well, except managerial ones.[330] In this regard it should also be noted that the number of this 'Article 3b contract staff' is higher than the number of 'Article 3a contract staff'.[331] Moreover, one third of the 'Article 3b contract staff' serves in the highest function group IV, i.e. possessing university degree and, arguably, performing tasks at a corresponding level, not just supporting ones.[332]

It follows that the Commission's reliance on non-permanent staff has remained rather high, despite past criticism and reform promises made by the European Commission itself that it would reduce the use of such staff. Furthermore, the simplification and rationalization of the Commission staffing structure, which was also promised, has not taken place either. There are as many staff categories and sub-categories as before, if not more, at least among the statutory staff. One of the few apparent positive developments is the reduction in reliance on external, i.e. non-statutory staff. According to data provided in the Commission's *Human Resources Report* of 2009, about 13,5 per cent of all Commission contracts were concluded with external persons, including seconded national experts and trainees.[333] Service providers constituted only about six per cent of the staff employed by the Commission in 2008.[334] To recall, in the past, reliance on external staff was higher.[335]

Another, very significant, improvement in the Commission's contractual regime which occurred over the past decade is the considerable increase in transparency, both budgetary transparency and general transparency with regard to collecting and disseminating information on human resources matters. Unlike in the past, all staff are now registered in a central electronic system and data are provided to the public, for example via the internet.[336] In addition, since 2008, the Directorate-General for Human Resources and Security annually issues a comprehensive human resources report.[337] In the UN, yearly reports on the composition of the UN Secretariat have been issued for decades. The recent initiative of the European Commission to issue annual human resources reports certainly deserves praise.

Transparency in the EU is, however, not facilitated by the complexity of the contractual system itself. Certainly, each staff category, and sub-category, covers a different situation in which recourse may be made to non-permanent staff. The fact that all these situations are listed in a rather exhaustive manner is positive as

---

[330] See above, section 3.2.2.2.

[331] *Commission's Human Resources Report 2009*, p. 33.

[332] Ibid., p. 37. See also *EU Conditions of Employment of Other Servants*, Articles 80(2) and 82(2)(c).

[333] Calculated on the basis of data in *Commission's Human Resources Report 2009*, p. 30.

[334] Ibid., p. 30.

[335] See above, section 3.1.

[336] See, for example, the European Commission civil service website available at http://ec.europa.eu/civil_service/index_en.htm, last visited on 30.12.2010. On this website, many figures can be consulted, such as those on staff nationality, gender, contracts, budgetary funding etc.

[337] The first report was issued in 2008 containing data for 2007. - *Rapport Ressources Humaines 2008, Vers une Gestion Qualitative et Prévisionnelle des Effectifs et des Compétences Grâce à une Professionnalisation de la Gestion des Ressources Humaines.*

it prevents abusive and/or repetitive recourse to non-permanent staff in instances in which career staff, protected by tenure, should be employed. On the other hand, the list of possible situations that may occur is long and the definition of, at least some, categories rather broad. In addition, it is questionable whether all the differences in the maximum contract duration allowed for each separate staff category or subcategory have a rational justification.

When comparing the UN and the EU further, an important difference in the current contractual framework of these two organizations is the abolition of permanent appointments in the UN and their replacement by continuing appointments. In the EU, permanent appointments and thus a permanent civil service are still in place. From the point of view of securing independence and impartiality of staff, undoubtedly, permanent appointments score the highest since they provide best protection of staff against termination of appointment. Nonetheless, this study argues that the continuing appointments recently introduced in the UN Secretariat do not deprive staff of such protection. Even though it is possible to separate UN staff serving on continuing appointments in the interests of the good administration of the organization without their consent, the notion 'the interests of the good administration of the organization' is interpreted strictly, leaving some but not much room for considerations other than those related to the operational needs of the UN Secretariat.[338] Moreover, separation of staff based on the need to reduce staff numbers or to abolish posts was possible under UN permanent appointments, too, and it is also possible in the EU.[339] In this sense, not much has changed in the UN.

It could even be argued that the fact that continuing appointments have replaced appointments with indefinite duration improves the position of UN staff who used to hold the latter. Previously, such staff could have been separated at any time, upon a notice, even without being given a reason.[340] Under the new regime, this is not possible and the termination is more difficult. It is limited to 'the interests of the good administration of the organization' and the strict interpretation thereof.[341] In the EU, the protection of staff serving on indefinite appointment has been enhanced rather recently, too. This has happened not by change of legislation but by judicial activity. Termination of indefinite appointments has remained within the wide discretion of the EU Administration which may have a broad range of reasons for terminating an individual appointment. The discretion of the EU Administration in these cases is in this sense broader than that of the UN Administration in cases of termination of continuing appointments. The novelty in the EU is that the Administration must now always provide the reason for termination. In the past, a notice of termination was sufficient and no reasons needed to be stated.[342] In conclusion, both the UN and the EU staff serving on (former) appointments of indefinite duration are protected

---

[338] See above, section 2.4.3.

[339] For details on these legal grounds for staff separation in both the UN Secretariat and the European Commission, see below, chapter 7, sections 2.3.2 and 3.2.3.

[340] See above, section 2.2.

[341] See above, section 2.4.3.

[342] See above, section 3.2.3.

against being fired better than they had been before the contractual reforms took place in the respective organizations.

As for seconded national experts, in the UN they have remained among the staff who serve on fixed-term appointments like any other fixed-term staff and in the EU they have remained outside the statutory framework.[343] In the European Commission, a maximum duration of engagement of seconded national experts is stated in a *Commission Decision on Secondment*, including possibilities and restrictions for re-engagement.[344] In the UN Secretariat, general rules applicable to fixed-term appointments, contained in the *UN Staff Regulations* and the *UN Staff Rules*, cover seconded national experts as well. Surprisingly, there is no mention of these experts in the documents concerning the modalities of implementation of continuing appointments. In theory, this would mean that the initial fixed-term appointment of each seconded national expert could be converted to a continuing appointment if the conditions were met, just as with any other fixed-term appointment. Clearly, this should not be permitted. Seconded national experts are employed by the UN, as also by the EU, for a limited period of time and with the intention that both the organization and the employer of the person in question benefit from the exchange of experience. If seconded national experts were to stay in the UN Secretariat on a long term basis, the very purpose of secondment would be nullified. In addition, this specific type of engagement could easily be abused by 'regularizing' those who have entered the UN Secretariat under a different arrangement and different conditions than other staff, in most cases more favourable ones and with a direct support and involvement of Member States' governments, at least as far as secondment from national civil services is concerned.

5. Conclusions

Recent developments in the UN and the EU show that the traditional belief in the importance of tenure for the independent and impartial status of the international civil service was challenged and compromised in the past by other important interests, and that is again the case. In the past, different political considerations often led to disregard, and even negation, of tenure and its role in safeguarding the international status of staff. The disturbance of this status was sometimes even a deliberate intention. More recently, other, often new, interests are placed on equal footing with the traditional concerns regarding the independence and impartiality of the international civil service. This development is, arguably, supported by the belief that the independence and impartiality of staff is currently relatively safe and safeguarded by other (legal) instruments and that its protection by tenure can therefore be weakened. Most of the interests which became equal to tenure are common to both the UN Secretariat and the European Commission, though these two organizations place emphasis on different questions.

[343] See above, sections 2.3.1 and 3.2.2.5.

[344] See above, section 3.2.2.5.

In the UN Secretariat, the predominant concern seems to be over the need for greater adaptability and efficiency in human resources management, allowing for more flexible hiring, deployment and separation of staff in accordance with the operational needs of the organization. The UN Secretary-General seems to put this objective above all other considerations. Next to the introduction of mandatory mobility for almost all UN staff (suspended in the meantime), another profound demonstration of this approach can be seen in the abolition of permanent appointments and their replacement by continuing appointments.[345] Unlike the former, the latter may be terminated in the interests of the good administration of the organization without staff members' consent. If Member States did not expressly restrict the interpretation of this legal ground for staff separation, the UN Administration would have gained a free hand in separating career staff whenever it would suit its interests. When the proposals for the new contractual arrangements were being discussed, many warnings were sounded over negative consequences of removing security of tenure for the independent and impartial status of the international civil service. Unsurprisingly, these warnings mostly came from staff and their representatives and not so much, if at all, from other sources.[346] The UN Secretary-General paid no express attention to the warnings. In his numerous reports relating to the reform of contractual arrangements he never discussed the potential impact of the reform on the independent and impartial status of the UN staff. The Member States too did not deal with this issue extensively. However, the fact that they considered it important to include rather restrictive interpretation of the decisive legal ground for the termination of continuing appointments in the General Assembly resolution shows they were not indifferent. Another proof of the Member States' mindfulness of the potentially far reaching consequences of the replacement of permanent appointments with continuing ones is their repeated requests to the Secretary-General for more detailed information on the modalities of implementation of the continuing appointments and their repetitive refusals to approve the proposed modalities. This happened although repeated postponing of the adoption of the modalities inevitably meant that the approved reform of new contractual arrangements could not be fully implemented for yet another year.

The European Commission too attaches importance to flexibility in the management of human resources, though it could be argued that in the Commission this is more a theoretical than practical approach. For example, as explained in the chapter dealing with staff mobility, there are no formal incentives for mobility in the European Commission.[347] When looking at the enforcement of flexibility through a greater use of non-career rather than career appointments, it appears that the Commission is more concerned about costs than about flexibility. By hiring more non-permanent staff, especially contract staff, the European Commission clearly aims to lower expenses. This can be deduced, *inter alia*, from the decreased use of temporary staff and the still increasing recourse to contract staff.[348] While both these categories may

[345] For details on the UN mobility policy, see above chapter 5, section 2.

[346] See above, introductory part to section 2.4.

[347] See above, chapter 5, section 3.2.1.

[348] See above, section 3.2.3.

be engaged for similar purposes, sometimes even overlapping ones, for example for meeting temporary needs or for replacing absent staff, temporary staff fall under the same salary structure as permanent ones but contract staff do not. The latter have their own salary scale at lower rates. This makes the employment of contract staff less costly for the European Commission than the employment of temporary, or permanent, staff.

Undoubtedly, societies and employment patterns have changed significantly when compared to 50 or 60 years ago, the time when the EU and the UN were established. Society in general has become more dynamic and requires more and faster adjustments in a broad range of areas and on many levels. Public administration, including that at the international and European level, is no exception to this. In order to provide services efficiently, civil services had to revise and adjust many policies, including those in human resources management. One of the major challenges is to find the right balance between different interests, all of which are important for the existence of an international civil service. In this sense it could be argued that the traditional approach towards tenure and the emphasis put on its importance for securing civil servants' independent and impartial status must be adjusted to the needs of a modern and more dynamic society. It could also be argued that the independence and impartiality of international civil servants is guaranteed not just by one safeguard but by a combination of many, tenure being merely one of them. Therefore, it could be concluded that the replacement of permanent appointments by continuing appointments in the UN Secretariat does not necessarily mean death for the international civil service and that the increased recourse by the European Commission to non-career staff does not automatically lead to insufficient independence and impartiality of the EU civil service. Nonetheless, the recent changes in the UN and in the EU took place subject to conditions and restrictions which allow the above conclusion. In the UN permanent appointments have been replaced by continuing ones, subject to legal safeguards to prevent (possible) termination of appointment being used to influence staff independence and impartiality, though it is unfortunate that no such safeguards have been adopted thus far for the protection of non-career staff against refusal of contract renewal. In the EU, it is true that non-career staff may be hired in a broad range of instances. However, it is not (fully) possible in all situations, with restrictions placed in particular in relation to the core areas of the EU civil service. In addition, extension, renewal and termination of EU non-permanent appointments are in most cases subject to clear and detailed rules, including those developed by the judiciary. Last but not least, the majority of European Commission staff continue to serve on permanent basis and it is expected that the majority of staff in the UN Secretariat will either remain on current permanent appointments or will be granted continuing appointment after five years of satisfactory service, respectively.

Chapter 7

SEPARATION FROM SERVICE

1. Introduction

The importance of a thorough legal framework under which international officials may be separated from the organization they serve has long been recognized. Plantey, for example, pointed out the following:

> *One of the keys to the position occupied by international civil servants lies in determining the conditions under which their service is terminated; it is important to the international administration, just as to its staff, that appointment should be ended on regular and impartial terms without pressure from governments.*[1]

Of course, as explained in the introduction to this study, it is at present not only governments that might want to exercise pressure on international organizations in this respect. Other external but also internal sources with their own agenda, not necessarily matching that of the organization at issue, might be interested in the separation of an international official. This may be either because of the official's 'uncomfortable' positions, or in order to create room for other, more favoured, individuals. Protection against separation from the organization for improper reasons is thus of high importance to the independence and impartiality of international civil servants. They must feel that termination of their appointment, be it a career or a non-career one, occurs only on the basis of legal grounds explicitly provided for in relevant legal instruments and in accordance with established procedures, offering sufficient protection against their abuse and misuse. Without such protection, international officials become vulnerable to pressure and temptations to act in a manner that guarantees they will not lose their job, or that if they do lose it, that their potential future employers will appreciate what they have done for them while serving in the international organization.

The previous chapter discusses one of the two aspects relevant for protection against improper separation of UN and EU civil servants, namely the type of appointment used for engaging such servants. The present chapter addresses the second aspect of such protection – the reasons for which UN and EU staff may be separated from the organization and the corresponding procedures. It discusses these reasons but especially the procedures that exists in the UN Secretariat and in the European Commission at present and assesses their sufficiency for objective and impartial decision making in instances in which there are legitimate reasons for staff separation.

2. Separation from service in the UN Secretariat

As discussed in the previous chapter, a far reaching reform of contractual arrangements took place in the UN Secretariat in 2009. That chapter also dealt with the (possible) consequences of this reform for terminating new types of appointment. This chapter supplements the previous one by discussing the legal grounds available for separation of UN staff which are not specific to a certain type of appointment,

[1] Plantey, *The International Civil Service, Law and Management*, p. 170.

i.e. other than the expiry of the fixed-term not followed by an extension or prolongation of temporary or fixed-term appointments and other than termination of continuing appointments in the interests of the good administration of the organization. These two legal grounds for separation are already discussed in detail in the previous chapter. Therefore, this chapter pays attention to them only for providing an overall picture of the issue of separation of UN staff.

Before going into the specific reasons for which appointments of UN staff may end, a formal distinction between the concept of 'separation from service' and that of 'termination of appointment' needs to be noted. The latter constitutes one of the reasons for the former and is defined as 'a separation from service initiated by the Secretary-General'.[2] Reasons for termination of appointment itself, i.e. for separation initiated by the UN as employer not by the staff member concerned, are exhaustively listed in the *UN Staff Regulations* and *UN Staff Rules*. They include abolition of posts, reduction of staff, incapacity for further service reasons of health, *post anterior* discovery of facts decisive for appointment and not known at the time of appointment, unsatisfactory service, unsatisfactory conduct and the interest of the good administration of the organization.[3] Reasons for separation from service other than termination of appointment initiated by the Secretary-General depend on the decision of the staff member concerned or on the occurrence of an objective situation, such as reaching the mandatory retirement age. Besides retirement, separation from service may result from staff member's resignation, abandonment of post or death, or of the already mentioned expiration of the fixed term.[4]

Separation of UN staff was possible on most of the above mentioned grounds ever since the organization's inception. Since that time, less than a handful of amendments of the *UN Staff Regulations* and/or *UN Staff Rules* have been adopted with significant consequences for separation of staff from UN service. The most important modifications were adopted in 1952 and 1953 and in 2009. The first ones introduced, among others, the interest (of the good administration) of the UN as a reason for termination of permanent and indefinite appointments. The second important amendment occurred more than a half century later, in 2009, in the framework of the UN's contractual arrangements, discussed in more detail in the previous chapter. The following section provides a brief overview of the reasons and consequences of the mentioned adjustments for the possibilities to separate UN staff not mentioned in the previous chapter.

2.1. Brief historical overview

The provisional *UN Staff Regulations* and *UN Staff Rules* adopted upon recommendation of the UN Preparatory Commission in 1945 contained the following reasons for separation of staff: unsatisfactory service, expiry of the fixed-term period; retirement, termination of appointment due to abolition of posts or reduction of staff,

[2] *UN Staff Rules*, Rule 9.6(a).

[3] *UN Staff Regulations of 2009*, Regulation 9.3; and *UN Staff Rules*, Rule 9.6(c).

[4] *UN Staff Regulations of 2009*, Regulations 9.1-9.3; and *UN Staff Rules*, Rules 9.1-9.5.

disciplinary reasons, and resignation.[5] In 1952, when the final *UN Staff Regulations* were first promulgated, incapacity due to health reasons and, for termination of temporary appointments other than fixed-term, also the interest (of the good administration) of the United Nations were added.[6] The inclusion of the latter reason in the *UN Staff Regulations* was a result of the so-called US loyalty cases, explained later in this section, which also resulted in two amendments of the *UN Staff Regulations* a year after their adoption, in 1953.

The 1952 amendment concerned the introduction of probationary appointment as a specific type of the temporary appointment.[7] This appointment could be terminated both during the probationary period and after its expiry. Termination during the probationary period was governed by the already mentioned regulation which allowed the UN administration to terminate any temporary appointment other than a fixed-term appointment, now explicitly including probationary appointments, at any time if the administration was of the opinion that it was in the interests of the UN. The assessment of such interest was within the discretion of the UN administration.[8] Termination of a probationary appointment at the end of the probationary period fell under a separate rule.[9] It was distinct from termination during the probationary period, providing a stronger protection to the probationary staff member by requiring a proper assessment of his suitability for permanent appointment. Such assessment was the basis for the decision of the UN administration, undertaken at the end of the probationary period, to either convert it into a permanent one or to terminate it.[10]

The second amendment of the *UN Staff Regulations*, adopted in 1953, concerned the provision seting reasons for terminating permanent appointments at that time. This provision was altered in order to include three new reasons: first, not meeting the highest standards of integrity required by Article 101(3) of the *UN Charter*;

---

[5] *Report of the UN Preparatory Commission*, paras. 60 and 64-66, and pp. 97 and 100.

[6] *General Assembly Resolution 590(VI), A/RES/590(VI)*, 02.02.1952, available in the Official Document System of the United Nations, available at http://documents.un.org/, last visited on 30.12.2010 and Annex, Article IX.

[7] *General Assembly Resolution 781(VIII), A/RES/781(VIII)*, 09.12.1953, available in the Official Document System of the United Nations, available at http://documents.un.org/, last visited on 30.12.2010 and Annex.

[8] See *UN Staff Regulations of 2007*, Regulation 9.1(c) and *Chiacchia v. Secretary-General of the United Nations, UNAT Judgment No. 90 [1963]*, available at http://untreaty.un.org/UNAT/UNAT_Judgements/Judgements_E/UNAT_00090_E.pdf, last visited on 30.12.2010, para. II.

[9] See *UN Staff Rules of 2002*, Rule 104.12(a).

[10] The difference between termination of probationary appointment during and at the end of the probationary period, and their legal consequences, was explained by the UNAT in *Cooperman*. In that case the UNAT also made clear that the broad discretion of the UN Administration to terminate probationary appointment at any time under Regulation 9.1.(c) of the *UN Staff Regulations* was not restricted by Rule 104.12(a) of the *UN Staff Rules*. This means that procedural guarantees available to the probationary staff member at the end of his probation, especially the reference of the matter to the central review bodies in case of a disagreement between the relevant department/office and the OHRM on whether the probationary appointment should be terminated or converted into a permanent one, were not available in cases of termination of probationary appointment during the probationary period under Regulation 9.1(c) of the *UN Staff Regulations*. - *Cooperman, UNAT Judgment No. 93 [1965]*, para. VI and VIII.

second, posterior discovery of facts precluding appointment but not known at the time of appointment; and third, the interest of the good administration of the organization.[11] As already mentioned, this amendment of the *UN Staff Regulations* was one of the legal consequences of the so-called US loyalty cases, which caused much turbulence and discussion of high relevance to the issue of independence and impartiality of the international civil service and of the position of the UN Secretary-General as chief administrative officer.

The cases concerned a number of nationals of the United States serving in the UN Secretariat, some on permanent and some on temporary appointments. These staff were suspected to be communist spies by the US Government. When interrogated by the US Federal Grand Jury and an internal committee of the US Senate, the officials concerned invoked the privilege against self-incrimination under the Fifth Amendment of the US Constitution. The Federal Grand Jury, which concluded that many UN officials were disloyal to the US and that the situation posed a security threat to the US, recommended, among others, that all US nationals should be cleared by the US government before being employed by the UN. Subsequently, an agreement was concluded between the US government and the UN Secretary-General Trygve Lie, resulting in summary dismissal of a number of officials concerned.[12]

Officials who held temporary appointments were dismissed with no statement of reasons being provided. When the dismissals were challenged, the UNAT recognized broad powers of the Secretary-General in administrative matters but held that they were not absolute and that their exercise was subject to procedural safeguards. Although the Secretary-General enjoyed discretion to terminate temporary appointments of indefinite duration at any time, he was obliged to pay regard to the requirements of due process and, among others, to provide reasons for termination. The same applied in cases of non-renewal of temporary appointments for fixed-term if the officials at issue could have reasonably expected that their appointment would be renewed. On this basis, the UNAT rescinded some of the termination decisions.[13]

[11] *General Assembly Resolution 782(VIII) A, A/RES/782(VIII)A*, 09.12.1953, available in the Official Document System of the United Nations, available at http://documents.un.org/, last visited on 30.12.2010 and Annex.

[12] Lemoine, *The International Civil Servant: An Endangered Species*, pp. 116-119. For more details on the agreement between the US authorities and the UN Secretary-General, see also pp. 122-124.

[13] *Howrani and 4 others v. Secretary-General of the United Nations, UNAT Judgment No. 4 [1951]*, available at http://untreaty.un.org/UNAT/UNAT_Judgements/Judgements_E/UNAT_00004_E.pdf, last visited on 30.12.2010, especially pp. 16-17 and 21-22; and on merits *Howrani v. Secretary-General fo the United Nations, UNAT Judgment No. 5 [1951]*, available at http://untreaty.un.org/UNAT/UNAT_Judgements/Judgements_E/UNAT_00005_E.pdf, last visited on 30.12.2010; *Keeny v. Secretary-General of the United Nations UNAT Judgment No. 6 [1951]*, available at http://untreaty.un.org/UNAT/UNAT_Judgements/Judgements_E/UNAT_00006_E.pdf, last visited on 30.12.2010; *Picou v. Secretary-General of the United Nations, UNAT Judgment Nr. 7 [1951]*, available at http://untreaty.un.org/UNAT/UNAT_Judgements/Judgements_E/UNAT_00007_E.pdf, last visited on 30.12.2010; *Alper v. Secretary-General of the United Nations, UNAT Judgment Nr. 8 [1951]*, available at http://untreaty.un.org/UNAT/UNAT_Judgements/Judgements_E/UNAT_00008_E.pdf, last visited on 30.12.2010 and *Kehoe v. Secretary-General of the United Nations, UNAT Judgment Nr. 9 [1951]*, available at http://untreaty.un.org/UNAT/UNAT_Judgements/Judgements_E/UNAT_00009_E.pdf, last visited on 30.12.2010.

After this judgment, the Secretary-General included an additional provision in the *UN Staff Regulations* for adoption by the General Assembly at that time in order to replace the provisional regulations in force since 1945. This provision permitted termination of temporary appointments other than those for fixed-term, i.e. indefinite appointments, when such action would be, in the opinion of the Secretary-General, in the interest of the United Nations.[14] The Secretary-General subsequently terminated appointments of a number of US nationals who held indefinite appointments. This termination was upheld by the UNAT, which accepted that the new provision of the *UN Staff Regulations* conferred a broad discretion on the Secretary-General in regard termination of temporary appointments.[15]

A different legal reasoning was used for summary dismissal of officials with permanent appointments who held US nationality, were accused of disloyal conduct towards the US and refused to comply with the request of the Secretary-General to withdraw their invocation of the Fifth Amendment of the US Constitution and answer questions posed by US authorities. The reasoning was based on the opinion that the Secretary-General possessed an inherent authority to terminate the appointment of any permanent official who breached his obligations and that this authority was independent of the causes for termination of appointments provided for in the *UN Staff Regulations*.[16] The summary dismissal of the officials concerned based on this reasoning was, however, declared illegal by the UNAT. The UNAT argued that the special nature of permanent appointments required protection against its termination, save for the cases explicitly and exhaustively provided for in the *UN Staff Regulations*. According to the UNAT, the special nature of permanent appointments was a result of their function to secure the stability of the international civil service and to create a body of international civil servants freely selected by the Secretary-General. Therefore, these appointments could be terminated only for reasons and

---

[14] *General Assembly Resolution 590(VI)*, and Annex, Regulation 9.1(c). See also Lemoine, *The International Civil Servant: An Endangered Species*, p. 119.

[15] *Kaplan v. Secretary-General of the United Nations; Middleton v. Secretary-General of the United Nations; Rubin v. Secretary-General of the United Nations; Kagen-Pozner v. Secretary-General of the United Nations; Sokolow v. Secretary-General of the United Nations; Saperstein v. Secretary-General of the United Nations; Van Tassel v. Secretary-General of the United Nations; Zap, Majorie v. Secretary-General of the United Nations; Zap, Herman v. Secretary-General of the United Nations UNAT Judgments Nr. 19-27 [1953]*, available at http://untreaty.un.org/UNAT/UNAT_Judgements/Judgements_E/UNAT_00019_E.pdf; http://untreaty.un.org/UNAT/UNAT_Judgements/Judgements_E/UNAT_00020_E.pdf; http://untreaty.un.org/UNAT/UNAT_Judgements/Judgements_E/UNAT_00021_E.pdf; http://untreaty.un.org/UNAT/UNAT_Judgements/Judgements_E/UNAT_00022_E.pdf; http://untreaty.un.org/UNAT/UNAT_Judgements/Judgements_E/UNAT_00023_E.pdf, http://untreaty.un.org/UNAT/UNAT_Judgements/Judgements_E/UNAT_00024_E.pdf; http://untreaty.un.org/UNAT/UNAT_Judgements/Judgements_E/UNAT_00025_E.pdf; http://untreaty.un.org/UNAT/UNAT_Judgements/Judgements_E/UNAT_00026_E.pdf; http://untreaty.un.org/UNAT/UNAT_Judgements/Judgements_E/UNAT_00027_E.pdf, last visited on 30.12.2010, in all cases paras. 6-9. The UNAT also held that the discretion of the Secretary-General under the Regulation 9.1(c) of the *UN Staff Regulations* could not be exercised to cover improper motives or misuse of power. However, in the cases at hand no improper motives or misuse of power was proved.

[16] *Gordon, UNAT Judgment No. 29 [1953]*, paras. 3-4. See also Lemoine, *The International Civil Servant: An Endangered Species*, pp. 119-120.

under the conditions explicitly provided for. The UNAT also held that conduct of the officials at issue did not amount to unsatisfactory service or serious misconduct justifying summary dismissal, as pleaded by the UN Administration. Since only serious misconduct could lead to summary dismissal without disciplinary procedures and such procedures did not take place, the UNAT rescinded the Secretary-General's decisions and ordered him to reinstate the applicants and/or pay compensation.[17]

The whole affair generated much uneasiness and was even discussed by the Fifth Committee of the General Assembly as well as in the Assembly's plenary meeting. This discussion took place in March 1953 but ended with no clear-cut conclusions.[18] In the meantime, Trygve Lie resigned from the office and the new Secretary-General, Dag Hammarskjöld, decided to solve the problem pragmatically. He decided to settle the individual loyalty cases by paying compensation, also to those officials who he was required by the UNAT to reinstate. In order to be able to do so, the Secretary-General requested and obtained from the General Assembly an amendment of the UNAT's Statute with a provision granting the Secretary-General discretion to decide and compensate applicants in whose favour the UNAT found without taking any further action. In the same resolution, the General Assembly amended the *UN Staff Regulations* in accordance with the Secretary-General's proposal. The amended provisions spelled out a clear prohibition of political activities and conduct in public of UN staff with potentially negative reflection on the integrity, independence and impartiality required by the status of independent civil servant. They also introduced three new causes for terminating permanent appointments, mentioned above, in order to broaden the possibilities for the Secretary-General to terminate appointments of staff whose integrity, past or present, could be questioned. The discretion to terminate permanent appointments in the interest of the good administration of the organization, which would result in almost absolute power of the Secretary-General, was, however, made subject to the consent of the staff member concerned.[19]

---

[17] *Gordon v. Secretary-General of the United Nations; Svechansky v. Secretary-General of the United Nations; Harris v. Secretary-General of the United Nations;; Eldridge v. Secretary-General of the United Nations;; Glassman v. Secretary-General of the United Nations; Older v. Secretary-General of the United Nations; Bancroft v. Secretary-General of the United Nations; Elveson v. Secretary-General of the United Nations; Reed v. Secretary-General of the United Nations; Glaser v. Secretary-General of the United Nations, UNAT Judgments No. 29-38 [1953]*, available at http://untreaty.un.org/UNAT/UNAT_Judgements/Judgements_E/UNAT_00029_E.pdf; http://untreaty.un.org/UNAT/UNAT_Judgements/Judgements_E/UNAT_00030_E.pdf; http://untreaty.un.org/UNAT/UNAT_Judgements/Judgements_E/UNAT_00031_E.pdf; http://untreaty.un.org/UNAT/UNAT_Judgements/Judgements_E/UNAT_00032_E.pdf; http://untreaty.un.org/UNAT/UNAT_Judgements/Judgements_E/UNAT_00033_E.pdf; http://untreaty.un.org/UNAT/UNAT_Judgements/Judgements_E/UNAT_00034_E.pdf; http://untreaty.un.org/UNAT/UNAT_Judgements/Judgements_E/UNAT_00035_E.pdf; http://untreaty.un.org/UNAT/UNAT_Judgements/Judgements_E/UNAT_00036_E.pdf; http://untreaty.un.org/UNAT/UNAT_Judgements/Judgements_E/UNAT_00037_E.pdf; http://untreaty.un.org/UNAT/UNAT_Judgements/Judgements_E/UNAT_00038_E.pdf, last visited on 30.12.2010, in most cases paras. 5-12.

[18] See Lemoine, *The International Civil Servant: An Endangered Species*, pp. 120 and 149-151; and *General Assembly Resolution 708(VIII), A/RES/708(VIII)*, 01.04.1953, available in the Official Document System of the United Nations, available at http://documents.un.org/, last visited on 30.12.2010.

[19] *General Assembly Resolution 782(VIII) A*, and *General Assembly Resolution 782(VIII) B, A/RES/782(VIII)*

After the modifications to the *UN Staff Regulations* and the corresponding *UN Staff Rules* which took place in 1953, no significant change in the legal grounds for separation of UN staff from service occurred for more than a half of the century. It was only in 2009 that the two legal instruments were modified in this respect again. As already mentioned, this modification was a result of the overall reform of the UN contractual arrangements, introducing three types of appointment in the Secretariat: temporary, fixed-term and continuing.[20] As for the issue of separation from service, most existing legal grounds have remained unchanged. Of course, legal grounds for terminating those types of appointments which were abolished, such as probationary and indefinite appointments, were removed. The remaining legal grounds stayed unaltered. The only, though very important, exception is the interest of the good administration of the organization which, as far as termination of continuing appointments is concerned, received a clear 'principal' interpretation from the General Assembly. Details relating to this interpretation have been provided in the previous chapter.[21] The following sections explain specificities of those legal grounds for staff separation which have not been significantly altered in 2009. For the purpose of completeness, all reasons for separation from UN service are mentioned, though.

2.2. Separation from service other than termination of appointment

2.2.1. Expiration

Expiration of appointment is the principal reason for separation from UN service of staff who serve for a fixed-term. Under the current regime of contractual arrangements in the UN Secretariat, this applies to temporary appointments and to fixed-term appointments. The *UN Staff Rule 9.4* stipulates that these two types of appointment 'expire automatically and without prior notice on the expiration date specified in the letter of appointment'.[22]

Of course, no separation takes place if, as explained in more detail in the previous chapter, an individual temporary or fixed-term appointment is extended, renewed, or in case of a fixed-term appointment converted into a continuing appointment.[23]

B, 09.12.01953, available in the Official Document System of the United Nations, available at http://documents.un.org/, last visited on 30.12.2010 and their Annexes. See also Lemoine, *The International Civil Servant: An Endangered Species*, pp. 120, 131-132, 146, 149-155 and 156-161. The US government strongly disagreed with payment by the UN of any compensation to disloyal US nationals and insisted that the payments be made from a special indemnity fund and the payment not involve any US money. – *ibid.*, pp. 158-159.

[20] For details, see above, chapter 6, section 2.3.1.

[21] See above, chapter 6, section 2.3.3.

[22] *UN Staff Rules*, Rule 9.4. See also Rule 9.1(iii).

[23] See above, chapter 6, sections 2.3.1 and 2.3.2. The UN Administration is not required to ensure that a new fixed-term appointment has the same characteristics as the previous appointment. - *Sy v. Secretary-General of the United Nations, UNAT Judgment No. 1150 [2003]*, available at http://untreaty.un.org/UNAT/UNAT_Judgements/Judgements_E/UNAT_01150_E.pdf, last visited on 30.12.2010, para. VIII.

On the other hand, both temporary and fixed-term appointments may end before the expiry of the fixed term stipulated in the letter of appointment – for any of the reasons for separation of UN appointments discussed in this chapter, including termination of the appointment by the Secretary-General. Termination of temporary and fixed-term appointments may be based on the same reasons as termination of continuing appointments, with the exception of termination in the interest of the good administration of the organization for which consent of staff members serving on temporary or fixed-term appointments is required. No such consent is needed for termination of continuing appointments in the interest of the good administration of the organization.[24] This means that during the fixed term period stipulated in the letter of appointment UN non-career staff are better protected against separation from service than UN career staff.

Separation from UN service due to the expiration of appointment must be clearly distinguished from termination of appointment. As stated by the UNAT in *Belas-Gianou*, 'the expiration of ... appointment ... is not tantamount to termination and, therefore, does not involve the same procedural or substantive requirements as a termination'.[25] Indeed, separation due to expiration of the date stipulated in the letter of appointment requires no prior notice, while termination of appointment does.[26] Further, no termination indemnity is usually paid to staff separated upon expiry of the fixed-term, while termination of appointments may, depending on the reason for termination, require such payment.[27]

2.2.2. Resignation

Resignation is a separation from service upon the staff member's own initiative.[28] Unsurprisingly, each UN staff member may at any time decide to leave the UN Secretariat. In such a case, the staff member concerned must give a written notice of his resignation.[29] The notice is due three months in advance in case of a continuing appointment, 30 days in case of a fixed-term appointment and 15 days in case of a temporary appointment, unless the letter of appointment specifies a different period.[30] In general, the letter of resignation should be submitted to the Head of

---

[24] *UN Staff Regulations of 2009*, Regulations 9.1-9.3; and *UN Staff Rules*, Rules 9.2-9.3 and 9.5-9.6. For more details on termination of appointments in the interest of the good administration of the organization, see above, chapter 6, section 2.3.3 (continuing appointments) and below, sections 2.3.1 (temporary and fixed-term appointments).

[25] *Belas-Gianou, UNAT Judgment No. 707 [1995]*, para. XVI.

[26] The period of notice of termination is at least 15 days for temporary appointments and 30 days for fixed-term appointments. - *UN Staff Rules*, Rules 9.7(b) and (c) and *Administrative Instruction, Administration of Temporary Appointments*, Section 16.2.

[27] For details, see *UN Staff Regulations of 2009*, Regulation 9.3(c) and Annex III, and *UN Staff Rules*, Rule 9.8. See also *Administrative Instruction, Administration of Temporary Appointments*, Sections 16.4 and 16.5.

[28] *UN Staff Rules*, Rule 9.2(a).

[29] *UN Staff Regulations of 2009*, Regulation 9.1.

[30] *UN Staff Rules*, Rule 9.2(b). Note that the Secretary-General may accept a shorter notice. – Ibid.

Department or Office and specify the date of resignation.[31] This date must be subsequently confirmed in the letter of acceptance of resignation.[32] The resignation itself must, however, be seen as a unilateral action of the staff member who wishes to end his employment at the UN, not subject to any acceptance by the UN Administration.[33] A rejection of a resignation would not make any legal difference on the staff member's right to leave the UN; it would only '[negate] any inference of approval'.[34] The only condition the UN Administration may impose on the resigning staff member is the requirement to submit his resignation in person.[35] Any other restriction, not provided for in the letter of appointment of the staff member in question, would be illegal. Exceptionally, the UN Administration may reject the resignation if that is necessary for a certain condition preceding the resignation to be met, for example, the imposition of a disciplinary sanction on the resigning staff member, which is not surprising.[36]

A withdrawal of resignation once submitted is allowed only with the consent of the Administration.[37] When the resignation has become effective, its withdrawal must be treated as a request for re-employment.[38] Further, allegations that resignation was involuntary, i.e. forced by the Administration, must be supported by the staff member who bears burden of proof.[39]

2.2.3. Abandonment of post

The *UN Staff Regulations* themselves do not list abandonment of post as a reason for separation from UN service, but the *UN Staff Rules* do. The latter define abandonment of post as 'a separation initiated by the staff member other than by way of resignation'.[40] They also stipulate that separation resulting from abandonment of

[31] *Guidelines on Separation from Service - Resignation*, available in the Human Resources Handbook of the United Nations, available at http://www.un.org/hr_handbook/English/, last visited on 30.12.2010, p. 1. A number of persons receive a copy of the letter of resignation, among others the staff member's supervisor and administrative officer. In addition, a copy of the letter of resignation and the acceptance is forwarded to the officers responsible for the preparation of the required separation papers. – Ibid., pp. 1 and 2.

[32] Ibid., p. 1.

[33] *Case No. 1421, UNAT Judgment No. 1339 [2007]*, available at http://untreaty.un.org/UNAT/UNAT_Judgements/Judgements_E/UNAT_01339_E.pdf, last visited on 30.12.2010, para. II.

[34] *Manson v. Secretary-General of the United Nations, UNAT Judgment No. 742 [1995]*, available at http://untreaty.un.org/UNAT/UNAT_Judgements/Judgements_E/UNAT_00742_E.pdf, last visited on 30.12.2010, para. VI.

[35] *UN Staff Rules*, Rule 9.2(c). See also *Abbas v. Commissioner-General of the United Nations Relief and Works Agency for Palestine Refugees in the Near East, UNAT Judgment No. 874 [1998]*, available at http://untreaty.un.org/UNAT/UNAT_Judgements/Judgements_E/UNAT_00874_E.pdf, last visited on 30.12.2010, especially para. III.

[36] *Case No. 1421, UNAT Judgment No. 1339 [2007]*, para. II.

[37] Ibid., para. II.

[38] *Abbas, UNAT Judgment No. 874 [1998]*, para. V.

[39] Ibid., para. VII. See also *Case No. 1421, UNAT Judgment No. 1339 [2007]*, paras. III-VII.

[40] *UN Staff Rules*, Rule 9.3. In the past a separate legal ground for separation from service on grounds of abandonment of post did not exist as an explicit legal rule but was nonetheless recognized by the UNAT.

post is not termination of appointment, i.e. separation initiated by the Secretary-General.[41] This sentence re-emphasizes that separation from service is a result of action taken by the staff member, not by the UN Administration. Although a formal decision of the Assistant Secretary-General for Human Resources Management is required, it is the conduct of the staff member concerned that leads to the loss of employment.[42]

It must be noted that the intention of the staff member at issue is irrelevant; it is the conduct that is of legal relevance for establishing whether a staff member abandoned his post or not. According to the jurisprudence, abandonment of post is an objective notion.[43] In *Alam* the UNAT held that 'regardless of the Applicant's professed intent not to abandon his post, his true intent must be judged by his conduct'.[44] In that case, the UNAT was of the opinion that a series of refusals by the applicant to return to work, that followed after the Administration had ordered him to do so, constituted abandonment of post and warranted the applicant's separation from service.[45] Similarly, in *Kennedy* the UNAT ruled that the applicant's failure to report back to work by the date fixed by the Administration in its request to the applicant to resume his duties could have been treated as repudiation of contract, i.e. abandonment of post, justifying separation from service.[46] In both these cases, the applicants put forward reasons for their refusals to return to work, arguing that they did not wish to abandon their posts, but the UNAT did not accept these arguments.

Abandonment of post must be distinguished from abandonment of duties. Such an issue arose, for example, in *Sidibeh* where the UN Administration separated the applicant from service on grounds of post abandonment, while the applicant claimed that he had never assumed the post he supposedly abandoned. The UNAT

In *Dupuy* the UNAT approved the existing practice of the UN Administration to consider, under some circumstances, unauthorized absence from work as a reason for separation. It relied on a provision in one of the annexes to the *UN Staff Regulations* dealing with termination indemnity. That provision provided that such indemnity could not to be paid to staff members who abandoned their post. The UNAT concluded that the prohibition would not have any meaning if the abandonment of post was not a separate reason for termination of the appointment. - *Dupuy v. Secretary-General of the United Nations, UNAT Judgment No. 174 [1973]*, available at http://untreaty.un.org/UNAT/UNAT_Judgements/Judgements_E/UNAT_00174_E.pdf, last visited on 30.12.2010, para. VII.

[41] *UN Staff Rules*, Rules 9.3 and 9.6(b).

[42] *Administrative Instruction, Abandonment of Post, ST/AI/400, as amended by ST/AI/2005/5*, 22.12.1994, available in the Human Resources Handbook of the United Nations, available at http://www.un.org/hr_handbook/English/, last visited on 30.12.2010, para. 12.

[43] *Selamawit Makonnen v. Secretary-General of the United Nations, UNAT Judgment No. 555 [1992]*, available at http://untreaty.un.org/UNAT/UNAT_Judgements/Judgements_E/UNAT_00555_E.pdf, last visited on 30.12.2010, para. III.

[44] *Alam v. Secretary-General of the United Nations, UNAT Judgment No. 380 [1987]*, available at http://untreaty.un.org/UNAT/UNAT_Judgements/Judgements_E/UNAT_00380_E.pdf, last visited on 30.12.2010, para. VI.

[45] Ibid., para. VI.

[46] *Kennedy v. Secretary-General of the United Nations, UNAT Judgment No. 265 [1980]*, available at http://untreaty.un.org/UNAT/UNAT_Judgements/Judgements_E/UNAT_00265_E.pdf, last visited on 30.12.2010, para. X.

agreed with the applicant stating that the Administration should have qualified the conduct of the applicant – a refusal to accept a new posting – as refusal to assume his functions and treat it under the procedures available to disciplinary cases, not as abandonment of post.[47]

The distinction between failure to report for duty (i.e. abandonment of post) and failure (or refusal) to undertake assigned functions (i.e. abandonment of duties) was also made in the *Administrative Instruction, Abandonment of Post ST/AI/400* of 22 December 1994, as amended by instruction ST/AI/2005/5.[48] In line with the case law, this instruction stipulates that failure to report for duty may lead to separation from service on the basis of abandonment of post, while the refusal to undertake assigned functions may be regarded as a disciplinary matter, possibly leading to a termination of appointment for unsatisfactory service and/or other disciplinary measures.[49]

The *Administrative Instruction, Abandonment of Post ST/AI/400* specifies in detail what constitutes abandonment of post and what procedures need to be followed in such cases, thereby ensuring that separation from service occurs after proper assessment of the situation has taken place. Paragraph 4 of this instruction repeats and further specifies that abandonment of post is separation initiated by the staff member, his unilateral repudiation of the employment contract, intention of which may be deduced from the circumstances of the case, especially from the staff member's failure to report for duty. If such a failure is accompanied by absence of a proper authorization of a leave or a satisfactory proof that the absence is involuntary and caused by forces beyond the staff member's control, a presumption of intent to separate from service may be reasonably created.[50] An even stronger presumption

---

[47] *Sidibeh v. Secretary-General of the United Nations, UNAT Judgment No. 770 [1996]*, available at http://untreaty.un.org/UNAT/UNAT_Judgements/Judgements_E/UNAT_00770_E.pdf, last visited on 30.12.2010, para. V. The applicant in this case was assigned to a post in a hardship duty station, following a number of assignments in many other hardship duty stations. After unsuccessful protests against the assignment, he refused to accept it for medical reasons. – para. I. The UNAT held that by separating the applicant on grounds of post abandonment instead of starting disciplinary proceedings against him, the Administration deprived the applicant of the opportunity to defend himself by raising the medical issue. – para. V.

[48] *Administrative Instruction, Abandonment of Post*. This administrative instruction supersedes instruction ST/AI/393 of 12 April 1994.

[49] Ibid., para. 7. Disciplinary measures may also be imposed on the staff member who had abandoned his post but, in reaction to warnings, reported for duty within the specified period. In such a case, no separation from service would take place, but that does not preclude imposition of reprimand or disciplinary measures. – *ibid*, para. 8.

[50] Ibid., para. 5. In this case, the applicant invoked temporal incapacity to work for reasons of health as the reason for his absence from work. Such defense is not acceptable as the *UN Staff Rules* provide that staff unable to perform their duties or to be present at work due to sickness or injury are granted sick leave but that all sick leave must be 'approved on behalf of, and under conditions established by, the Secretary-General.' - currently *UN Staff Rules*, Rule 6.2(a). Staff requesting a certified sick leave must inform their supervisors as soon as possible of their absence due to health reasons and submit promptly a relevant medical certificate or medical report. Uncertified sick leave may be taken up to a maximum of seven days per calendar year. – Ibid., Rules 6.2(f) and (c). In *Dupuy* the UNAT held that silence, even if lasting longer, could not be seen as implying consent with a requested leave in situation in which it was contrary to the parties' declaration and intent. - *Dupuy, UNAT Judgment No.*

is created by acceptance of another (external) employment by the staff member, or even a search for it, while the staff member concerned is absent from work without a proper authorization.[51]

The procedure to be followed in cases of unauthorized absence is set out in paragraphs 9 to 12 of the administrative instruction ST/AI/400. It begins with the reporting of unauthorized absence by the supervisor to the relevant executive or administrative officer within 4 days of such absence and an attempt to contact the staff member concerned by the executive or administrative officer by any appropriate means. In case of a failure to contact the staff member concerned, a written communication requesting reporting for duty or submitting a plausible explanation for the absence is sent to the last known address of this staff member. When no medical certificate or plausible explanation for the absence is received within ten working days, another written communication is sent to the staff member concerned including, *inter alia*, a recall of previous attempts to contact the staff member, a further period of maximum ten working days for reporting for duty or for providing a medical certification or plausible explanation, and a warning that further failure to do so would be considered abandonment of post resulting in separation from service. When the warning has not been acted upon in the requested manner, a recommendation to separate the staff member concerned from service is submitted by the Director of the Staff Administration and Training Division (or Head of Office at duty stations away from Headquarters) to the Assistant Secretary-General for Human Resources Management who takes a decision to treat the conduct of the staff member concerned as repudiation of the employment contract. The date of this decision constitutes the date on which the separation from service becomes effective. The staff member concerned is notified of the decision at his last known address.[52]

---

174 [1973], para. V. Moreover, in *Selamawit Makonnen* the UNAT ruled that special leave without pay for medical reasons, as the case was, was not a right on which UN staff members could rely but rather a discretionary power of the UN Administration. Therefore, the applicant could not use his request for such leave as justification for his absence when the request had been refused by the Administration and the leave not granted. The fact that the applicant's request was based on the advice of the UN medical officer was irrelevant, even though the UNAT noted that the Administration's refusal was regrettable. However, as no discrimination or improper motives for the refusal were proved to exist, the refusal was within the discretion of the Administration and the applicant's absence unjustified. – *Selamawit Makonnen, UNAT Judgment No. 555 [1992]*, paras. IV-VIII.

[51] *Administrative Instruction, Abandonment of Post*, para. 6. The same provision explicitly stipulates that a mere sending of one's résumé while on a certified sick leave would normally not be seen as abandonment of post. The present provision of the administrative instruction is in line with the UNAT jurisprudence. In *Hilaire* the UNAT ruled that the acceptance by the applicant of another employment without an authorization from the UN Administration was inconsistent with an intention to continue applicant's service with the UN and that it amounted to the post abandonment. The applicant in that case was on a sick leave of uncertain duration but, after a few months, accepted work for a private company in New York. In addition, the applicant did not report back to work when requested by the Administration after it had found out about the applicant's acceptance of another job. - *Hilaire v. Secretary-General of the United Nations, UNAT Judgment No. 220 [1977]*, available at http://untreaty.un.org/UNAT/UNAT_Judgements/Judgements_E/UNAT_00220_E.pdf, last visited on 30.12.2010, pp. 504-505 and para. I.

[52] *Administrative Instruction, Abandonment of Post*, paras. 9-12 and 16. Additional details are provided for alleged incapacity for reasons of health and for abandonment of post following annual or special leave – paras. 14 and 15.

With regard to the date of separation from service, it should be noted that setting a retroactive date, for example the date of the actual abandonment of post, is not permitted.[53] Paragraph 12 of the administrative instruction ST/AI/400, providing that the date of the separation is the date of the decision (and thus not the first date of the staff member's unauthorized absence from work), is thus fully in line with the jurisprudence in this area.

2.2.4. Retirement

Retirement is also a reason for separation from UN service other than termination of appointment – it does not take place upon initiation by the UN Secretary-General but upon the occurrence of an event, in this case reaching the set retirement age by the staff member concerned.[54] Pursuant to the *UN Staff Regulation 9.2*, the retirement age of UN staff appointed before 1 January 1990 is 60 years and those appointed after 1 January 1990 is 62 years.[55] Upon reaching the retirement age, the staff member concerned is separated from service, i.e. he must retire.[56] The retirement is not only an obligation but also a 'legitimate expectation on the part of an official which must be upheld'.[57] It is mandatory for both the staff member and the organization and, in principle, it has no relation to the individual circumstances of the staff member concerned.

Notwithstanding the above, there is a limited possibility to extend the employment beyond the mandatory retirement age, though that possibility is, at least formally, available only in exceptional cases.[58] Similarly, a possibility exists to re-employ staff members who have already retired through a temporary contract. Details on both possible ways of retaining staff who have reached the retirement age can be found in the *Administrative Instruction, Retention in Service Beyond the Mandatory Age of*

[53] *Kennedy, UNAT Judgment No. 265 [1980]*, para. XIV.

[54] *UN Staff Rules*, Rules 9.1(vi), 9.5 and 9.6(b).

[55] *UN Staff Regulations of 2009*, Regulation 9.2. The retirement age limit of sixty-two years for staff appointed after 1 January 1990 was adopted by the UN General Assembly in 1989. - *General Assembly Resolution 44/185 A*, Part D, para. 1 and Annex. In 2001, the General Assembly requested the Secretary-General to study implications of a possible increase of the retirement age of sixty-two years also to staff appointed before 1990. - *General Assembly Resolution 55/258*, Section XII, para. 2. Eventually, it was decided not to pursue this idea and to retain the limit of sixty-years for staff appointed before 1990. The main reason for this decision was 'the need to prioritize the rejuvenation' of the UN Secretariat. - *General Assembly Resolution 57/305*, Section VII, para. 1

[56] The actual date of separation from service is the last day of the month in which the staff member reaches the retirement age. - *Guidelines on Separation from Service - Retirement*, available in the Human Resources Handbook of the United Nations, available at http://www.un.org/hr_handbook/English/, last visited on 30.12.2010, third bullet point. On the discussion on the (in)correct date of birth for the retirement purposes, see *Cunio v. Secretary-General of the International Civil Aviation Organization, UNAT Judgment No. 321 [1984]*, available at http://untreaty.un.org/UNAT/UNAT_Judgements/Judgements_E/UNAT_00321_E.pdf, last visited on 30.12.2010.

[57] Plantey, *The International Civil Service, Law and Management*, para. 554.

[58] *UN Staff Regulations of 2009*, Regulation 9.2.

Separation and Employment of Retirees ST/AI/2003/8, adopted in 2003 and amended in 2006, addressed in the following sections.[59]

2.2.4.1. Retention in service beyond the mandatory retirement age

As already mentioned, retention of staff who have reached the mandatory retirement age may, in principle, only occur in exceptional cases. This restriction is contained in Regulation 9.2 of the *UN Staff Regulations* and, for a short while, it could have been found also in the *UN Staff Rules*. The most recent version of the latter, adopted on 2 September 2010, contains no such provision, similarly as the *UN Staff Rules* applicable before 1 July 2009.[60] Nonetheless, figures show that the number of staff retained beyond mandatory retirement age is indeed relatively small.[61]

A number of conditions need to be met in order for staff to be retained beyond the retirement age. Most importantly, staff members who have reached the retirement age may be retained in UN service only if it was not possible to find their replacement in due time and only for a limited period of time not exceeding six months after the established age of retirement. In addition, any such retention must be in the interest of the United Nations and in accordance with actual needs.[62] It is the

---

[59] *Administrative Instruction, Retention in Service Beyond the Mandatory Age of Separation and Employment of Retirees, ST/AI/2003/8*, 13.11.2003, available in the Human Resources Handbook of the United Nations, available at http://www.un.org/hr_handbook/English/, last visited on 30.12.2010 and *Administrative Instruction, Retention in Service Beyond the Mandatory Age of Separation and Employment of Retirees, ST/AI/2003/8/Amend.1*, 17.03.2006, available in the Human Resources Handbook of the United Nations, available at http://www.un.org/hr_handbook/English/, last visited on 31.12.2010. The term 'retiree' is defined as 'a former staff member 55 years of age or older who, consequent upon service exceeding five years, is in receipt of a pension benefit from the United Nations Join Staff Pension Fund'. - *Employment of Retirees, Report of the Secretary-General, A/53/526*, 20.10.1998, available in the Official Document System of the United Nations, available at http://documents.un.org/, last visited on 30.12.2010, para. 4, specifying further which staff is included or excluded from the definition.

[60] *UN Staff Regulations of 2009*, Regulation 9.2; *UN Staff Rules of 2002*, Rule 109.6; *UN Staff Rules of 2009*, Rule 9.5(b) and *UN Staff Rules*, Rule 9.5.

[61] In 2010, the Secretary-General reported that during the biennium 2008-2009 only 248 persons were retained in service after having reached retirement age. This equaled to 58.645 worked days. - *Composition of the Secretariat: Gratis Personnel, Retirees and Consultants, Report of the Secretary-General, Addendum, A/65/350/Add.1*, 15.09.2010, available in the Official Document System of the United Nations, available at http://documents.un.org/, last visited on 30.12.2010, Table 5, p. 16.

[62] *Administrative Instruction, Retention in Service Beyond the Mandatory Age of Separation and Employment of Retirees*, Sections 1.1, 2.1 and 2.2. These conditions have always been required as necessary prerequisites for the retention of staff after they reached the retirement age. See, e.g. *Administrative Instruction, Retention in Service and Employment Beyond the Age of Retirement, ST/AI/213/Rev.1*, 18.07.1984, available in the Human Resources Handbook of the United Nations, available at http://www.un.org/hr_handbook/English/, last visited on 30.12.2010, paras. 2-4; and *Administrative Instruction, Retention in Service Beyond the Mandatory Age of Separation and Employment of Retirees, ST/AI/1999/5*, 27. 05.1999, available in the Human Resources Handbook of the United Nations, available at http://www.un.org/hr_handbook/English/, last visited on 30.12.2010, Sections 1.1 and 2.3. See also *Talwar v. Secretary-General of the United Nations, UNAT Judgment No. 343 [1985]*, available at http://untreaty.un.org/UNAT/UNAT_Judgements/Judgements_E/UNAT_00343_E.pdf, last visited on 30.12.2010, para. II. In the past, some flexibility was provided for language staff and staff recruited for the General Service and related categories but the 2003 administrative instruction abandoned this flexibility. - See *Administrative Instruction, Retention in Service and Employment Beyond the Age*

needs of the service which must be the basis for any decision on the extension of employment of a staff member due to retire but willing to remain in service. Such staff member's good performance record or other reasons relating to him may not be the relevant determinant for retaining this staff member in service beyond his mandatory retirement age.[63] Further, UN staff members cannot expect extension of their employment beyond the mandatory retirement age merely because other staff members have been granted such extension. As held by the UNAT in *Talwar*, any extension of an employment contract is a discretionary decision of the UN Administration, having an exceptional nature, and staff may not argue the existence of precedents in this area. This holds true even in situations in which the UN Administration has been engaged in an erroneous practice of granting extensions contrary to established conditions.[64]

The decision on retaining staff at the level of Assistant Secretary-General and above is taken by the Secretary-General himself, while the D-2 level staff fall within the competence of the Under Secretary-General, and the staff at the Professional level and D-1 level within the competence of the Assistant Secretary-General.[65] Before a decision is taken, however, a procedure set out in the administrative instruction mentioned above must be followed. The instruction requires that each department and office regularly identifies staff members who are due to retire within the coming year and takes all necessary steps to ensure that the vacancies are advertised and filled in a timely manner. Only if circumstances beyond the control of the department or office have prevented the replacement of a staff member due to retire, may the department or office request that a staff member be retained, subject to the exceptional nature of such requests and an explanation of the reasons why timely replacement has not succeeded.[66]

2.2.4.2. Employment of retired staff

The second way in which UN staff who have already retired may be called upon to continue to serve in the UN Secretariat is through re-employment of such staff.

---

of Retirement, para. 5 and *Administrative Instruction, Retention in Service Beyond the Mandatory Age of Separation and Employment of Retirees*, Section 2.2.

63 *Talwar, UNAT Judgment No. 343 [1985]*, para. III.

64 Ibid., paras. IV and VII-VIII.

65 *Administrative Instruction, Retention in Service Beyond the Mandatory Age of Separation and Employment of Retirees*, Sections 1.2, 3.4 and 3.5.

66 Ibid., Section 3. Initially the Office of Personnel Services (now the OHRM) was responsible for identifying staff members due to retire in the next 12 months. – *Administrative Instruction, Retention in Service and Employment Beyond the Age of Retirement*, para. 8. That responsibility rests now with specific departments and offices of the UN Secretariat. Also, the responsibility of the departments and offices has been increased by requiring them to take all necessary steps in order to ensure that posts that fell vacant due to the retirement are filled on time and by emphasizing that only under the circumstances beyond the control of the departments or offices of staff member due to retire may be retained in the UN service. These changes reflect some of the concerns repeatedly expressed by the UN General Assembly in recent years about the increased use of the retired staff. – See, e.g. *General Assembly Resolution 59/266*, Section XII, paras. 1 and 2; *General Assembly Resolution 61/244*, Section XVI, para. 1; *General Assembly Resolution 63/250*, Section XI, para. 3.

The administrative instruction ST/AI/2003/8 stipulates that such action is only possible when the operational requirements of the UN cannot be met by available staff. Moreover, the employment of the returnees is only possible if it is the most cost effective and operationally sound solution and if it does not adversely affect the career opportunities of regular staff.[67] A number of additional requirements have been imposed, such as a period of at least three months since the retirement during which the returnee we may not be engaged; geographical and gender balance of the hired retirees; and their medical clearance.[68] It is understood that the engagement of retirees may only take place for a limited period of time, although the administrative instruction does not explicitly provide for any maximum. It does, however, stipulate which type of contract may be used in such situations, indirectly limiting the time of the engagement of retirees.[69]

The UN Secretary-General considers the use of retirees to be both necessary as well as beneficial for the United Nations. He lists several reasons for it, among the most important ones being the need to increase available human resources on a short-term basis in order to respond to specific mandates or requests from the General Assembly, or to react to demands of peak periods in areas marked by sharp and unpredictable workload fluctuation, for example in the area of conference services. The Secretary-General furthermore stresses the short-term and rapid demand for persons who do not need to be trained, possess full knowledge of the UN system and in-depth knowledge of the subject-matter, have well established professional recognition and networks, demonstrated leadership abilities, and often the capability of being deployed on a short notice. The Secretary General also argues that hiring retired staff is advantageous in terms of cost-effectiveness.[70]

Despite all these advantages, the UN Member States remain skeptical and cautious about the extensive use of retirees, which recently seems to be taking place on a greater scale than in the past.[71] The main objections of the Member States are the

---

[67] *Administrative Instruction, Retention in Service Beyond the Mandatory Age of Separation and Employment of Retirees*, Section 5.1.

[68] Ibid., Sections 5.1-5.3.

[69] Ibid., Section 5.4.

[70] See, for example, *Employment of Retirees, Report of the Secretary-General, A/C.5/51/2*, 16.08.1996, available in the Official Document System of the United Nations, available at http://documents.un.org/, last visited on 30.12.2010, paras. 6, 9-16, and 24-28.

[71] Comparing the figures provided by the Secretary-General in his regular reports on the employment of retirees, 328 retirees were employed during the biennium 1996-1997; 342 retirees during the biennium 1998-1999; 563 retirees during the biennium 2002-2003; 491 retirees during the biennium 2004-2003; 979 during the biennium 2006-2007; and 1.035 retirees during the biennium 2008-2009. - *Employment of Retirees, Report of the Secretary-General, A/53/526*, para. 21; *Employment of Retired Former Staff, Report of the Secretary-General, A/61/257/Add.2*, 10.08.2006, available in the Official Document System of the United Nations, available at http://documents.un.org/, last visited on 30.12.2010, Figure I, p. 6; *Employment of Retirees and Retired Former Staff, and Extension of Staff Beyond the Mandatory Age of Separation, Report of the Secretary-General, A/63/310/Add.2*, 20.08.2008, available in the Official Document System of the United Nations, available at http://documents.un.org/, last visited on 30.12.2010, Figure I, p. 7; *Composition of the Secretariat: Gratis Personnel, Retirees and Consultants, Report of the Secretary-General, Addendum, A/65/350/Add.1*, Table 5, p. 16. When looking at the number of days worked by retirees, while in the biennium 2000-2001 the number was below 50.000 hours, in

negative impact that employment of retirees may have on career development and mobility of regular staff; its negative impact on the rejuvenation of the UN Secretariat; favoritism or perception of favoritism in the selection process; geographical imbalance among hired retirees; and the use of retirees in substantive and decision-making positions.[72] While understanding the reasons for hiring retired staff put forward by the Secretary-General, Member States criticize inadequate management planning of human resources that, if improved, could prevent extensive recourse to retirees especially in area with no peak demands for workforce.[73]

Some of the Member States' concerns have been addressed in the meantime. For example, while far from ideal, the geographical representation of Member States among the rehired retirees has improved.[74] Furthermore, the relevant administrative instruction explicitly requires that employment of retirees may not adversely affect career prospects of regular staff.[75] The Secretary-General also claims that the selection of all staff, including retired staff, adheres to the paramount requirement of selecting staff with highest standards of efficiency, competence and integrity, while paying due regard to geographical balance, as required by Article 101(3) of the *UN Charter*.[76]

2.2.4.3. Retirement before the mandatory age

Besides employing staff who have reached the mandatory age of separation either through their retention in service beyond that age or by their reemployment, the

the biennium 2008-2009 retirees' work amounted to almost 190.000 hours. - *Employment of Retirees and Retired Former Staff, and Extension of Staff Beyond the Mandatory Age of Separation, Report of the Secretary-General, A/63/310/Add.2*, Figure II, p. 7; and *Composition of the Secretariat: Gratis Personnel, Retirees and Consultants, Report of the Secretary-General, Addendum, A/65/350/Add.1*, Table 5, p. 16.

72 For example, *General Assembly Resolution 57/305*, Section VI, paras. 3-4; *General Assembly Resolution 59/266*, Section XII, paras. 1-2 and 4-6 ; *General Assembly Resolution 61/244*, Section XVI; *General Assembly Resolution 63/250*, Section XI, paras. 3-4. In the last mentioned resolution of 2008, the General Assembly requested the Secretary-General to include in his future reports on the subject-matter reasons for the employment of retirees as well as the analysis of such reasons. Note that in the past there was another important concern of Member States related to the employment of retirees, namely the so-called 'double-dipping'. This refers to receiving a salary or fee as well as a pension, both from the United Nations. This problem has been solved by setting time and earning limitations as well as overall annual ceiling for the employment of retirees who receive UN pension. – See, for example, *Employment of Retirees, Report of the Secretary-General, A/53/526*, para. 10.

73 *Employment of Retirees, Report of the Advisory Committee on Administrative and Budgetary Questions, A/51/475*, 08.10.1996, available in the Official Document System of the United Nations, available at http://documents.un.org/, last visited on 30.12.2010, para. 9.

74 While in the biennium 1996-1997 employed retirees represented 57 different nationalities, from which 10 nationalities amounted to 75 per cent, in the biennium 2006-2007 in total nationals of 98 Members States were hired, though still 64,5 per cent came from 11 Member States, with a dominance of the US nationals. - *Employment of Retirees, Report of the Secretary-General, A/53/526*, para. 22 and *Employment of Retirees and Retired Former Staff, and Extension of Staff Beyond the Mandatory Age of Separation, Report of the Secretary-General, A/63/310/Add.2*, para. 12.

75 *Administrative Instruction, Retention in Service Beyond the Mandatory Age of Separation and Employment of Retirees*, Section 5.1(b).

76 *Employment of Retirees and Retired Former Staff, and Extension of Staff Beyond the Mandatory Age of Separation, Report of the Secretary-General, A/63/310/Add.2*, para. 6.

UN allows for another exception to the rule of mandatory retirement, namely retirement before the mandatory age is reached. It is commonly referred to as 'early retirement' and is open to staff members of 55 years of age or older. Staff members who wish to separate from service earlier may claim an 'early retirement benefit' from the United Nations Joint Staff Pension Fund.[77]

Formally, early retirement is regarded as resignation. The staff member is required to submit the notice of such resignation in writing and in accordance with rules applicable to resignations.[78] Also, procedures to be followed by officers responsible for administering such written notice are those that apply to resignation.[79] On the other hand, the concerned staff member receives a letter of appreciation for his service at the UN, as do staff members retiring upon reaching the mandatory retirement age.[80]

2.2.5. Death

Since 2009, the *UN Staff Rules* explicitly mention death as a reason for separation from UN service.[81] Of course, death ends one's employment with the UN regardless of whether it is mentioned in the relevant legal instrument(s) or not. On the other hand, although employment ends in such cases, some benefits continue to exist or arise. They are specified in detail in relevant provisions of the *UN Staff Rules*.[82]

2.3. Termination of appointment

As already explained, termination of appointment is a separation from service initiated by the UN Secretary-General.[83] Although the jurisprudence has stated it with regard to permanent appointments, it could be argued that termination of any appointment, regardless of the type, may take place only for reasons explicitly enumerated in the *UN Staff Regulations* and under conditions set in therein.[84] The reason for termination must always be stated in the termination decision. This obligation, developed through the jurisprudence, is currently explicitly stated in Rule 9.6(c) of the *UN Staff Rules*.[85] When more reasons are available for termination

[77] *Guidelines on Early Retirement*, available in the Human Resources Handbook of the United Nations, available at http://www.un.org/hr_handbook/English/, last visited on 30.12.2010, first and second bullet points.

[78] Ibid., third bullet point.

[79] Ibid., seventh bullet point.

[80] Ibid., fourth bullet point. See also *OHRM Guidelines on Retirement*, fourth and fifth bullet points.

[81] *UN Staff Rules of 2009*, and *UN Staff Rules*, in both instances Rule 9.1(vi).

[82] *UN Staff Rules*, Rule 9.11(a)(vii). For rules on compensation in the event of death (but also injury or illness) attributable to the performance of official duties on behalf of the UN, see Appendix D.

[83] Ibid., Rule 9.6(a).

[84] *Gordon, UNAT Judgment No. 29 [1953]*, para. 2.

[85] *UN Staff Rules*, Rule 9.6(c). For the early case law requiring statement of reasons for termination of various types of appointment, see especially *Howrani, UNAT Judgment No. 4 [1951]*, pp. 21-22; *Restrepo v. Secretary-General of the United Nations, UNAT Judgment No. 131*, available at http://untreaty.un.org/UNAT/UNAT_Judgements/Judgements_E/UNAT_00131_E.pdf, last visited on 30.12.2010, para. III,

of an individual appointment, the UN Administration does not need to rely on all but may choose one or more of them. On the other hand, the UN Administration may not freely substitute one ground for another.[86] It goes without saying that all these requirements and restrictions are important safeguards against possible misuse or abuse of the existing grounds for termination of appointment by the UN Administration. Without them, the independence and impartiality of UN staff could be compromised, for reasons noted in the introductory part of this section.

With regard to the procedure, a termination of appointment by the Secretary-General must, of course, follow formal requirements provided for in *UN Staff Rules* and/or applicable administrative instructions.[87] In all cases, a written notice of termination is required. Such notice must be given at least three months in advance when the termination concerns a continuing appointment, 30 days when it concerns a fixed-term appointment and 15 days when it concerns a temporary appointment, though a different period of notice may be indicated in the letter of appointment.[88]

The importance of observing due process in termination cases was recognized in one of the first staff cases *Howrani and 4 Others* decided in 1951:

> *[W]hile it is not for the Tribunal to substitute its judgement for that of the Secretary-General with respect to the adequacy of the grounds for termination stated, it is for the Tribunal to ascertain that an affirmative finding of cause which constitutes reasonable grounds for termination has been made, and that due process has been accorded in arriving at such an affirmative finding.*[89]

Understandably, due process and its importance for staff protection has been emphasized most in cases concerning termination of permanent appointments. In *Gordon*, one of the US loyalty cases explained above, the UNAT held that conditions and procedures provided for in the *UN Staff Regulations* must be complied with.[90] In *Gillman* the UNAT furthermore stated that:

> *having in mind the very substantial rights given by the General Assembly to those individuals who hold permanent appointments in the United Nations Secretariat, the Tribunal has considered that such permanent appointments can be terminated only upon a decision which has been reached by means of a* complete,

---

and *Senghor v. Secretary-General of the United Nations, UNAT Judgment No. 169 [1973]*, available at http://untreaty.un.org/UNAT/UNAT_Judgements/Judgements_E/UNAT_00169_E.pdf, last visited on 30.12.2010, para. VI.

86 *Nelson v. Secretary-General of the United Nations, UNAT Judgment No. 157 [1972]*, available at http://untreaty.un.org/UNAT/UNAT_Judgements/Judgements_E/UNAT_00157_E.pdf, last visited on 30.12.2010, para. IV.

87 See, for example, *Howrani, UNAT Judgment No. 4 [1951]*, p. 21, para. 1. The UNAT held: 'the power of the Secretary-General to terminate staff members holding temporary-indefinite contracts is limited by the Charter, by resolutions of the General Assembly, by Staff Regulations, by Staff Rules, and by other instruments defining the rights and obligations of members of the Secretariat.'

88 *UN Staff Rules*, Rule 9.7(a)-(c) and *Administrative Instruction, Administration of Temporary Appointments*, Section 16.2.

89 *Howrani, UNAT Judgment No. 4 [1951]*, p. 21, para. 4.

90 *Gordon, UNAT Judgment No. 29 [1953]*, para. 2.

> fair and reasonable procedure *which must be carried out prior to such decision.*[91] *(emphasis added)*

The UNAT stated also that examination of each case must be based on adequate or correct information, otherwise the termination decision may be invalid.[92] This applies also in situations in which the termination decision is based on conclusions reached by another (advisory) body which conducted actual examination of the case and did it on the basis of inadequate or incorrect information.[93] In *Restrepo* the UNAT added that the examination of the case before the decision is taken must be reasonably detailed and secure adequate consideration of all relevant judgments related to the staff member concerned.[94]

The importance of due process in general, i.e. not only for termination of permanent appointments, was emphasized by the UNAT in one of its more recent cases:

> *Even a cursory examination of the Tribunal's judgements will reveal that much of its jurisprudence has been devoted to ensuring that what is generally termed as due process is safeguarded in respect of staff at all levels and locations. Concern for, and principles of, due process as a basic requirement is reflected in every system of law and constitutes a theme which runs through the whole of the United Nations system from General Assembly resolutions, Declarations and Covenants at the highest level, through the Staff Regulations and Rules which set out the standards to be observed in an international civil service, to the more particular and focused policy statements and administrative issuances which lay down the procedures to be observed within individual organizations.*[95]

In *Monteleone-Gilfillian* the UNAT stated:

> *Failure to abide by established procedures gives rise to dissatisfaction and low morale and threatens the integrity of the entire Organization. It also leads to unnecessary and costly litigation.*[96]

By way of example, the following irregularities have been considered by the UNAT to lead to the denial of due process: failure to observe the terms of an administrative instruction applicable to the case;[97] failure to follow own procedures;[98] arrival

[91] *Gillman v. Secretary-General of the United Nations, UNAT Judgment No. 98 [1966]*, available at http://untreaty.un.org/UNAT/UNAT_Judgements/Judgements_E/UNAT_00098_E.pdf, last visited on 30.12.2010, para. II.

[92] Ibid., para. IV.

[93] *Peynado v. Secretary-General of the United Nations, UNAT Judgment No. 138 [1970]*, available at http://untreaty.un.org/UNAT/UNAT_Judgements/Judgements_E/UNAT_00138_E.pdf, last visited on 30.12.2010, para. V.

[94] *Restrepo, UNAT Judgment No. 131*, para. X. See also *Mila v. Secretary-General of the United Nations, UNAT Judgment No. 184 [1974]*, available at http://untreaty.un.org/UNAT/UNAT_Judgements/Judgements_E/UNAT_00184_E.pdf, last visited on 30.12.2010, para. III.

[95] *Applicant v. Secretary-General of the United Nations, UNAT Judgment No. 1234 [2005]*, para. II.

[96] *Monteleone-Gilfillian, UNAT Judgment No. 814 [1997]*, para. VIII.

[97] *Mila, UNAT Judgment No. 184 [1974]*, para. X.

[98] *Lopes Braga, UNAT Judgment No. 1122 [2003]*, para. V. In this case, the UN Administration did not

at conclusions with factual errors or prejudice on the matter;[99] reliance on incomplete documents, e.g. an incomplete periodic report;[100] giving excessive weight to testimony of some persons, e.g. applicant's supervisors, without (sufficient) evaluation of other relevant factors;[101] failure to have recourse to an impartial medical examination in case of two medical reports with differing conclusions, one being prepared by the UN medical officer and one by the applicant's physician;[102] procedural delays;[103] using an unofficial, unpublished memorandum for establishing staff members' status without them having a prior notice of that memorandum or of its consequences;[104] and the Administration's interventions in the work of the advisory bodies.[105] Specifically for disciplinary cases, condemned procedural irregularities include, for example: application of an obsolete procedure (for suspension);[106] lack of proper delegation of authority to the official who has taken the decision;[107] failure to notify the staff member of the members of the Joint Disciplinary Committee and thereby preventing the staff member from raising an objection against any of the members;[108] failure to notify the staff member of charges against him or to specify details connected with the charges or with the relevant evidence;[109] failure to provide the staff member with opportunity to explain his position on the issues serving as basis for the decision;[110] failure to give the staff member opportunity to be mean-

comply with one of the requirements which itself established in the vacancy announcement, namely the required qualification.

[99] *Dearing v. Secretary-General of the United Nations, UNAT Judgment No. 200 [1975]*, available at http://untreaty.un.org/UNAT/UNAT_Judgements/Judgements_E/UNAT_00200_E.pdf, last visited on 30.12.2010, para. VIII.

[100] *Mila, UNAT Judgment No. 184 [1974]*, para. X.

[101] Ibid., para. X.

[102] *Dearing, UNAT Judgment No. 200 [1975]*, para. VIII.

[103] *Kioko v. Secretary-General of the United Nations, UNAT Judgment No. 456 [1989]*, available at http://untreaty.un.org/UNAT/UNAT_Judgements/Judgements_E/UNAT_00456_E.pdf, last visited on 30.12.2010, para. XIII. See also *Federchenko, UNAT Judgment No. 1153 [2003]*, para. II.

[104] *Walter, UNAT Judgment no. 390 [1987]*, paras. XVI-XIX.

[105] *Klein, UNAT Judgment No. 1031 [2001]*, para. X.

[106] *Jhuthiv v. Secretary-General of the United Nations, UNAT Judgment No. 897 [1998]*, available at http://untreaty.un.org/UNAT/UNAT_Judgements/Judgements_E/UNAT_00897_E.pdf, last visited on 30.12.2010, para. V.

[107] Ibid., para. V. The UNAT held, however, that this irregularity, while being an error in application of law, was not sufficiently substantial as to nullify the decision imposing discriminatory measures, since the applicant received all the substantive and procedural protection he had the right for. For the irregularity, the applicant was awarded compensation.

[108] *Ikegame v. Secretary-General of the United Nations, UNAT Judgment No. 1175 [2004]*, available at http://untreaty.un.org/UNAT/UNAT_Judgements/Judgements_E/UNAT_01175_E.pdf, last visited on 30.12.2010, para. XI. In this case the conclusions of the Joint Disciplinary were 'reasonable, if not inevitable' since the applicant had admitted her misconduct. Therefore, the disciplinary decision was left intact by the UNAT. For the denial of due process rights the applicant was awarded monetary compensation. – para. XIII.

[109] *Applicant v. Secretary-General of the United Nations, UNAT Judgment No. 1234 [2005]*, para. IV.

[110] *Azzu v. Secretary-General of the United Nations, UNAT Judgment No. 103 [1966]*, available at http://untreaty.un.org/UNAT/UNAT_Judgements/Judgements_E/UNAT_00103_E.pdf, last visited on 30.12.2010, para. V.

ingfully involved, and to participate, in the proceedings;[111] denial of a possibility to test the credibility of incriminating evidence;[112] modification of extension of charges not included in the notification to the staff member.[113]

Besides the need for protecting staff members whose appointments are terminated, the importance of due process lies also in the need to ensure that justice is not only done but also seen to be done. As stated by the UNAT is *Fayemiwo*:

> *... the Tribunal considers that it is part of good administration to observe the dictum that justice should not only be done but also be seen to be done.*[114]

Upon termination of an individual appointment, and subject to authorization by the Secretary-General, the staff member concerned may receive compensation equivalent to salary, post adjustment and allowances that correspond to the period of notice.[115] In addition, a termination indemnity in accordance with relevant *UN Staff Regulations* and *Staff Rules* may be applicable.[116] These payments, however, depend on the reason(s) for termination of appointment. The following sections address each of the reasons for termination of appointment in more detail.

2.3.1. The interest of good administration of the organization

Under the current regime of contractual arrangements, all three types of appointment may be terminated in the interest of good administration of the organization.[117] This reason for termination was available also before 2009 when UN contractual arrangements were reformed. It existed under the 100 series of the *UN Staff Rules*, but it was subject to the consent of the staff member concerned if the appointment at issue was permanent or fixed-term. Only former indefinite and probationary appointments could be terminated for this reason without the staff members' consent.[118] As explained in detail in the previous chapter, since 2009, termination in the interest of the good administration of the organization without the staff member's consent is permitted for continuing appointments, whereas temporary and fixed-term appointments, both being of a fixed term nature, may be terminated for this reason only with the consent of the staff member concerned. In case of termination of a continuing appointment, the interest of the good administration of the organization must be interpreted strictly. The interpretation adopted by the UN General

[111] *Applicant v. Secretary-General of the United Nations, UNAT Judgment No. 1234 [2005]*, para. IV.

[112] Ibid., para. V.

[113] Ibid., para. IV.

[114] *Fayemiwo, UNAT Judgment No. 246 [1979]*, para. XI.

[115] *UN Staff Rules*, Rule 9.7(d).

[116] See *UN Staff Regulations of 2009*, Regulation 9.3(c) and (d) and Annex III; and *UN Staff Rules*, Rule 9.8.

[117] *UN Staff Rules*, Rule 9.6(c)(vi).

[118] *UN Staff Regulations of 2007*, Regulations 9.1(a) and 9.1(c). There was a slight difference in wording used in the two provisions: 'the interest of the good administration of the Organization' used in Regulation 9.1(a) and 'the interests of the United Nations' used in Regulation 9.1(c).

Assembly as principal, and contained in the amended *UN Staff Rules*, includes only change or termination of a mandate.[119]

Since the issue of termination of continuing appointments in the interest of the good administration of the organization is addressed in detail in the previous chapter, this section pays more attention to termination of appointments for the same reason in instances in which the staff member concerned consents to it. Such termination of appointment, be it temporary, fixed-term or even continuing, is referred to as 'agreed termination'.[120]

Of course, the UN Administration and an individual staff member may always come to an agreement on the basis of which the appointment of that staff member comes to an end. Such an agreement may also come into existence by a decision of the UN Administration to terminate an appointment and the subsequent non-contention of that decision by the staff member. The consent of the staff member may thus be either express or silent, with no need to make it in a specific form. In *Bernard* the UNAT held, for example, that a written form was not necessary:

> *Whether there was such an agreement is a question of fact to be determined on the evidence which may be documentary, oral or circumstantial. The Tribunal finds no authority for the contention that the agreement not to contest the proposed termination must be in writing.*[121]

The agreement is thus binding regardless of the form, although it can, of course, be difficult to prove its existence if it is not made in writing.

Once an agreement on the termination of the appointment has been reached, it cannot be unilaterally revoked. Such an agreement is binding not only on the staff member but also on the UN Administration, as held by the UNAT in *Piracés*. In this case the UN Administration first agreed to termination in the interest of the good administration of the organization under former Regulation 9.1(a) of the *UN Staff Regulations* but later changed its decision and invoked the former Regulation 9.1(c) of the *UN Staff Regulations* that provides for the same reason but does not require the staff member's consent. This change was caused by the fact that under the latter provision the UN Administration had to pay a smaller termination indemnity. The UNAT ruled that such action was illegal since the earlier agreement was binding on both parties. The UNAT argued that the UN Administration must comply with its own arrangements taken with regard to UN staff members.[122]

---

[119] *UN Staff Rules*, Rule 9.6(d). For more details, see above, chapter 6, section 2.3.3.

[120] *Guidelines on Separation from Sevice - General Procedures*, available in the Human Resources Handbook of the United Nations, available at http://www.un.org/hr_handbook/English/, last visited on 30.12.2010, second bullet point.

[121] *Bernard, UNAT Judgment No. 244 [1979]*, para. III.

[122] *Piracés v. Secretary-General of the United Nations, UNAT Judgment No. 264 [1980]*, available at http://untreaty.un.org/UNAT/UNAT_Judgements/Judgements_E/UNAT_00264_E.pdf, last visited on 30.12.2010, para. VI.

2.3.2. Abolition of posts or reduction of staff

As in every private and public organization, also in international organizations, including the UN, it is occasionally necessary to abolish posts or reduce staff, either due to budgetary constraints or due to structural reorganization. The *UN Staff Regulations* and the *UN Staff Rules* therefore provide a possibility of termination of UN appointments on this basis.[123] According to settled case law, the UN Administration enjoys a wide discretion to...

> *... make any reductions in posts, including abolition of posts, which may be necessary in order to observe due economy while providing adequately for the service of the United Nations.*[124]

The UNAT also held that the Administration's authority in this regard was not restricted by the organization's budgetary possibilities – the availability of a certain post in the relevant budget does not oblige the Administration to fill or retain that post. The UNAT explained that the UN Administration was free but not obliged to spend the credit provided in the relevant budget and could decide to abolish a certain post even if the budget provides a coverage for it.[125] Similarly, the fact that no change occurs in the number of budgeted posts does not necessarily mean that post abolition may not be used as the appropriate legal grounds for termination of appointment in cases in which a change in orientation of the organization's activities takes place.[126]

On the other hand, when the UN Administration decides to terminate an appointment on the basis of post abolition, post abolition must be genuine. In a 1998 case *Karmel*, for example, a post had been abolished but rather soon afterwards a virtually equivalent post was created, though the name of the post changed, the job description slightly differed and the post classification was initially one grade lower. This new post was filled by another person with no advertisement and no competition and after one year upgraded to the same grade as the formerly abolished post. On the basis of these facts the UNAT concluded that the post in question was in fact not abolished and the termination of the applicant's appointment served nothing else than her replacement by another person.[127] In this case, which is a frank example of a misuse of power aimed at replacement of a staff member by a more

[123] *UN Staff Regulations of 2009*, Regulation 9.2(a)(i) and *UN Staff Rules*, Rules 9.6(c)(i) and 9.6(e)-(g).

[124] *Aubert and others v. Secretary-General of the United Nations, UNAT Judgment No. 2 [1950]*, available at http://untreaty.un.org/UNAT/UNAT_Judgements/Judgements_E/UNAT_00002_E.pdf, last visited on 30.12.2010, p. 4.

[125] Ibid., p. 4.

[126] *Quémerais v. Secretary-General of the United Nations, UNAT Judgment No. 172 [1973]*, available at http://untreaty.un.org/UNAT/UNAT_Judgements/Judgements_E/UNAT_00172_E.pdf, last visited on 30.12.2010, paras. V-VI. In this case, the UNAT recognized the right to terminate appointment of the applicant with UNICEF which discontinued its (milk conservation) activities to which the applicant had been assigned. – Ibid.

[127] *Karmel v. Secretary-General of the United Nations, UNAT Judgment No. 879 [1998]*, available at http://untreaty.un.org/UNAT/UNAT_Judgements/Judgements_E/UNAT_00879_E.pdf, last visited on 30.12.2010, para. IV.

favourable person, the UNAT expressed its deep dissatisfaction with such practices in the UN Secretariat at the time:

> *Unfortunately, the manipulations to which the Applicant was subject are becoming a habit in the UN Administration. The Tribunal notes that by this simple device, some staff members are dismissed and others are placed in their stead. It seems to be of no importance if, at the end of the process, the Organization has to pay compensation to the person unjustly removed. The Tribunal is not aware whether any action is taken against those responsible for such elementary exercise in deviousness. The Tribunal, more than once, has come across situations like the one just described.*[128]

This quote shows that the need to protect UN staff against unjustified removal from their posts is not merely hypothetical, and that it is not just a problem of the past. Also at present, the UN Administration may come under pressure – from inside or from outside – to separate a staff member so that another person may be appointed.

Termination of appointments where posts *are* genuinely abolished, or when there is a need for reduction of staff, is therefore subject to a number of conditions. First, the UN Administration must first investigate whether there are other suitable posts in which service of the staff members who are to be separated could be utilized. If such posts are available, staff members who hold continuing appointments are to be retained in preference to those who hold another type of appointment. Further, staff members recruited through competitive examinations for a career appointment serving on a two-year fixed-term appointment are to be retained in preference to those with fixed-term appointments. In addition, in all cases, due regard must be paid to the staff's competence, integrity and length of service, and in some cases also to staff nationality.[129]

It follows that the discretion of the UN Administration in terminating appointments due to post abolition or reduction of staff is not unlimited. In selecting which staff members are to be separated, the above mentioned priority rules relating to the type of appointment and to the merits of the staff under consideration must be respected.[130] Moreover, before taking any decision on terminating an appointment, the UN Administration must consider whether other posts are available in which the staff member to be separated could provide his services.[131] As stressed by the UNAT in a recent case decided in 2008, this is:

[128] Ibid., para. V.

[129] *UN Staff Rules*, Rule 9.6(e). Locally recruited staff and staff recruited specifically for service with particular programme, fund or subsidiary organ are only entitled to consideration for suitable posts within their parent organization, duty station or organ for which they were recruited. – Rule 9.6(f)-(g).

[130] *Carson v. Secretary-General of the United Nations, UNAT Judgment No. 85 [1962]*, available at http://untreaty.un.org/UNAT/UNAT_Judgements/Judgements_E/UNAT_00085_E.pdf, last visited on 30.12.2010, para. 8.

[131] See, for example, *Quémerais, UNAT Judgment No. 172 [1973]*, para. VIII.

> *an unqualified obligation on the part of the Respondent to look for a suitable, alternative post for the affected staff member. It is not a case of looking "wherever possible"; there is an unequivocal duty to search for an alternative job, although the Tribunal recognizes that, ultimately, such search may prove in vain. There is no discretion on the part of the Administration as to whether to search or not.*[132]

The consideration of the staff member concerned against other available posts must be genuine. The UN Administration may not, for example, merely state that the staff member in question could not have qualified for any post, without actually making an assessment of his merits against the requirements of the available posts. In this regard, the Administration must take two steps: first, it must in reality consider the staff member in question for other available posts; and second, it must find that staff member is not suitable for those posts. The burden of proof with regard to both conditions rests with the UN Administration. In addition, in considering staff members' merits for the purposes of termination of appointment due to the abolition of posts, no 'sweeping generalizations' are allowed. As stated by the UNAT, decisions 'taken in haste and without due care and consideration' do not meet standards required for a proper consideration of staff members' position.[133] On the other hand, the UN Administration is permitted to verify whether the staff member under consideration is able to adapt to the new position by prescribing an adaptation period.[134] Moreover, the newly offered posts should not be such as to contain employment conditions disadvantageous to those of the former employment.[135]

The importance of the above mentioned safeguards in post abolition and staff reduction cases was emphasized by the UNAT in the first staff case *Aubert and 14 others* of 1950, already referred to above:

> *The Tribunal, while convinced on these grounds of the right of the Administration, when necessity arises to effect reductions of posts and, if appropriate, to abolish either individual posts or categories of posts and substitute others more suitable for the carrying out of necessary duties in the changed circumstances, is none the less deeply impressed by the necessity of effecting such reductions or changes in a manner which minimizes the sacrifices consequently inflicted upon*

132 *Case No. 1480, UNAT Judgment No. 1409 [2008]*, available at http://untreaty.un.org/UNAT/UNAT_Judgements/Judgements_E/UNAT_01409_E.pdf, last visited on 30.12.2010, para. VI.

133 *Carson, UNAT Judgment No. 85 [1962]*, paras. 6 and 8.
- *Carson, UNAT Judgment No. 85 [1962]*, para. 8.

134 *Quémerais, UNAT Judgment No. 172 [1973]*, para. IX.

135 *Guest and Slatford v. Secretary-General of the United Nations, UNAT Judgment No. 841 [1997]*, available at http://untreaty.un.org/UNAT/UNAT_Judgements/Judgements_E/UNAT_00841_E.pdf, last visited on 30.12.2010, para. X. In this case, one applicant would have to 'resign her status as a permanent staff member, thereby forfeiting her right to compensation for involuntary separation, lose seniority to the G-5 level, relinquish her international recruitment status and pay her own travel and removal expenses. Moreover, she was given less than a day in which to accept the offer.' Similarly, the other applicant would have to resign her permanent appointment in exchange of acquiring a one-year probationary appointment. She would also have to carry her travel and moving expenses. The UNAT ruled that such offers did not meet the minimum requirements of good faith and demonstrated 'a callous disregard on the part of the Respondent for his responsibilities towards the Applicants'.

> *individual officers and which preserves as far as may be possible in the circumstances the principle of security of tenure in accordance with the contracts applicable to individual cases. The Tribunal has therefore examined the procedure actually followed in the cases under examination from this point of view. It has paid particular regard to the provisions of staff rule 104, which appears to have been made precisely in order to regulate procedure in such cases...*[136]

The former Rule 104 of the *UN Staff Rules*, referred to by the UNAT in the cited part of the judgment, contains obligations comparable to those of the present Rule 9.6(e)-(g) of the *UN Staff Rules*.

In exercising its judicial review in cases of termination of appointment due to post abolition, the UNAT examines whether the abolition of the particular post at issue and the termination of the applicant's appointment was a valid exercise of discretion enjoyed by the UN Administration in this field, and whether the Administration has fulfilled its obligation to make an effort in good faith to find another suitable position for the applicant.[137] The existence of such review constitutes an additional safeguard against misuse or abuse of authority to terminate UN staff members' appointments for reasons of post abolition or staff reduction.

2.3.3. Incapacity for health reasons

Rule 9.6 of the *UN Staff Rules* provides for a possibility to terminate appointments of a UN staff for health reasons. In its relevant part, this rule stipulates:

> *The appointment of a staff member who has not attained the mandatory age of retirement established in the Staff Regulations and Staff Rules but whose physical or mental condition or extended illness renders him or her incapacitated for further service may be terminated after exhaustion of any sick leave entitlement.*[138]

This provision is further worked out in the *Administrative Instruction on Termination of Appointment for Reasons of Health ST/AI/1999/16* of 28 December 1999, effective since 1 January 2000.[139] The concept of 'incapacity' is defined in Section 1 of this instruction:

---

[136] *Aubert and others, UNAT Judgment No. 2 [1950]*, p. 5.

[137] *Case No. 1487, UNAT Judgment No. 1425 [2009]*, available at http://untreaty.un.org/UNAT/UNAT_Judgements/Judgements_E/UNAT_01425_E.pdf, last visited on 30.12.2010, para. III. The importance of good faith in this context has been emphasized also in *Case No. 1454, UNAT Judgment No. 1389 [2008]*, available at http://untreaty.un.org/UNAT/UNAT_Judgements/Judgements_E/UNAT_01389_E.pdf, last visited on 30.12.2010, para. XIII. The UNAT stressed that the Administration is bound by this obligation of good faith towards all its staff, disregarding whether they serve under a permanent or non-permanent appointment. – Ibid.

[138] *UN Staff Rules*, Rule 9.6(i). See also Rule 9.6(c)(iii) and *UN Staff Regulations of 2009*, Regulation 9.3(a)(iii).

[139] *Administrative Instruction, Termination of Appointment for Reasons of Health, ST/AI/1999/16*, 28.12.1999, available in the Human Resources Handbook of the United Nations, available at http://www.un.org/hr_handbook/English/, last visited on 30.12.2010.

> *"incapacity" shall mean "incapacity for further service reasonably compatible with a staff member's abilities, due to injury or illness constituting an impairment to health which is likely to be permanent or of long duration".*[140]

An appointment may be terminated on this ground only when incapacity of the staff member concerned has been 'established by conclusive medical evidence that results in the award of a disability benefit under the [United Nations Joint Staff Pension Fund] Regulations'.[141] Clearly, if such evidence were not required, this reason for termination of appointment could easily be abused and lead to unjustified removal of an individual UN staff member, for example by claiming his mental incapacity to perform his duties.

The procedure to be followed in cases where incapacity for health reasons is at issue is set out in Section 3 of the present instruction. It begins with the notification of the fact that a staff member has used all his sick leave entitlement with full pay to the medical director or a designed medical officer and a consideration of the case by such director or officer. When the medical director or the designed medical officer concludes that the illness or injury of the staff member concerned is of a nature constituting an impairment to health likely to be permanent or long lasting, the medical director or the designed medical officer sends an advice to the relevant human resources officer to notify of such a conclusion the staff member concerned or, where appropriate, his family. When the staff member under consideration contests the medical conclusions, these are reviewed by an independent medical practitioner or a medical board established in the same manner as provided in case of a review of decisions on sick leave. Subsequently, the relevant human resources officer submits a request for the award of a disability benefit to the UN Staff Pension Committee. If the determination of the UN Staff Pension Committee is positive, a disability benefit is awarded to the staff member concerned in accordance with the *United Nations Join Staff Pension Fund Regulations* and the award is notified to the relevant human resources officer and the staff member. This is followed by a submission of a recommendation for the termination of the appointment by the relevant human resources officer to the Assistant Secretary-General for Human Resources Management. If approved, a notice of termination is sent to the staff member in question, including the effective date of termination.[142]

The procedure described above is in force since 1 January 2000.[143] Before that time, there was no established procedure for termination of employment for health reasons. However, the UNAT had held as far back as in 1961, in *Miss Y.*, that decisions on termination of an appointment must have been 'reached by means of a complete, fair and reasonable procedure which must [have been] carried out prior to

[140] Ibid., Section 1.

[141] Ibid., Section 2.

[142] Ibid., Sections 3 and 5. The effective date of termination of the appointment is either the date on which the staff member exhausts all his sick leave entitlements or the date of the notice. For details, see Section 5.

[143] Ibid., Section 6.

such decision.'[144] In that case, the applicant was separated from service on grounds of health, in particular for mental problems. That decision was based on an assessment by a medical doctor made relatively long before the termination decision was taken and did not contain the conclusion that the mental illness of the applicant would incapacitate her from further service with the UN.[145] The UNAT noted that due to the absence of a specific procedure for termination of appointments on this legal basis as well as for challenging the findings of medical officers, rules similar to those that applied to settlement of differences in cases of sick leave might have been appropriate.[146] In the UNAT's view, the failure to follow proper procedures in the termination of the appointment for health reasons amounted to a denial of due process.[147] The consequence in that particular case was that it was remanded for the correction of the relevant procedure (i.e. procedure for medical examination of the applicant). In addition, the applicant was compensated for the loss caused by the procedural delays.[148]

It follows that the appropriate procedures must be adhered to before a decision to terminate an appointment for health reasons is taken so that the staff member concerned is not deprived his due process rights. Since a specific procedure has in the meantime been adopted, in case of a challenge, the UNAT will assess whether the prescribed procedure has been complied with. It will also check whether the applicant was accorded due process.[149] On the other hand, when assessing a decision on termination of an appointment, the UNAT will refrain from a substantive examination of the medical opinion on which the termination decision is based. In *Coutsis* the UNAT ruled that it was not 'competent to express views on the accuracy of the diagnosis or conclusions of the medical profession'.[150] This is not surprising, and not uncommon, given the fact that judges are usually not qualified in medical science. Said that, also such judges are able to recognize irregularities in conclusions reached by (different) medical experts. Therefore, irregularities in reaching conclusions by UN medical officers may be reviewed by the UNAT. This was the case, for example, in *Ziadeh,* where the relevant medical board considered the applicant's case two times within a period of nine days, without explaining the reasons for the reassessment. Moreover, conclusions reached by the medical board in the two assessment exercises were entirely opposite, the first finding the applicant fit

[144] *Miss Y. v. Secretary-General of the United Nations, UNAT Judgment No. 83 [1961]*, available at http://untreaty.un.org/UNAT/UNAT_Judgements/Judgements_E/UNAT_00083_E.pdf, last visited on 30.12.2010, para. 7.

[145] Ibid., para. 9.

[146] Ibid., para. 8.

[147] Ibid., para. 11.

[148] Ibid., paras. 12 and 25. For the follow up, see *Miss Y. v. Secretary-General of the United Nations, UNAT Judgment No. 91 [1964]*, available at http://untreaty.un.org/UNAT/UNAT_Judgements/Judgements_E/UNAT_00091_E.pdf, last visited on 30.12.2010.

[149] See, for example, *Ziadeh v. Commissioner-General of the United Nations Relief and Works Agency for Palestine Refugees in the Near East, UNAT Judgment No. 906 [1998]*, available at http://untreaty.un.org/UNAT/UNAT_Judgements/Judgements_E/UNAT_00906_E.pdf, last visited on 30.12.2010, para. II.

[150] *Coutsis v. Secretary-General of the United Nations, UNAT Judgment No. 69 [1957]*, available at http://untreaty.un.org/UNAT/UNAT_Judgements/Judgements_E/UNAT_00069_E.pdf, last visited on 30.12.2010, para. 4. See also *Miss Y., UNAT Judgment No. 91 [1964]*, para. XII.

for service and the second finding him unfit. No explanation of the change in the conclusion and no evidence of deterioration of the applicant health in the relevant period were offered.[151] In case of a challenge, the UNAT thus checks whether the conclusions of medical assessors have been reached in accordance with due process rights and whether there is sufficient evidence in medical opinions for the conclusion of incapacity for service reached by the UN Administration, without reviewing the medical grounds themselves. However, in the absence of a proof of improper motives or procedural irregularities, the UNAT will not substitute its judgment for that of relevant medical officers.[152]

2.3.4. *Posterior* discovery of facts

One of the legal grounds available under Regulation 9.3(a) of the *UN Staff Regulations* for terminating appointments is the discovery of facts anterior to the appointment but relevant to the suitability of the staff member for it. The condition for terminating the appointment for this reason is, however, that the discovered facts would have precluded the staff member's appointment under the standards established by the *UN Charter*, for example, the requirement of integrity, had these facts been known at the time of appointment.[153] As explained in the section on historical developments regarding legal grounds for separation from UN service, this reason for termination was introduced in connection with the US loyalty cases concerning staff members with UN nationality who were accused of membership and/or collaboration with the communist party and therefore deemed disloyal to the US.[154]

Apart from the *UN Staff Regulation* mentioned above, literally repeated in the *UN Staff Rules*, there are no further specific regulations or rules providing details on the process of termination of appointment on the basis of posterior discovery of relevant facts.[155] Fortunately, there is some jurisprudence that helps to understand the matter. One of the cases in which the issue arose is a 1999 case *Moore*. In this case, the applicant had provided incorrect information during his recruitment concerning the reasons for his departure from the previous employer. That information was relevant since the previous employer was the World Health Organization ('WHO'), one of the UN system organizations, and his separation from service with the WHO was based on grounds of being unsuitable for international service. The information became known when a relevant judicial body – the Administrative Tribunal of the International Labour Organisation ('ILOAT'), competent in staff cases concerning WHO staff, ruled upon the applicant's challenge of the legality of the WHO's separation decision. Although the UN Administration did not expressly invoke the *UN Staff Regulation* allowing for termination for posterior discovery of facts in its decision to

[151] See, for example, *Ziadeh, UNAT Judgment No. 906 [1998]*, paras. II-III.

[152] See also *Sidibeh, UNAT Judgment No. 770 [1996]*, para. VI.

[153] *UN Staff Regulations of 2009*, Regulation 9.3(a)(v).

[154] See above, section 2.1.

[155] *UN Staff Rules*, Rule 9.6(c)(v).

separate the applicant, the UNAT accepted that it had done so *de facto* and that, in principle, it had been entitled to do so.[156]

In a more recent case decided in 2006, the UNAT stressed the importance of good faith on the side of the staff member in the context of *post ante* discovery of facts. In this case the applicant did not, at the time of the recruitment, disclose his one-day-arrest dating back several years, believing he was not obliged to do so. His belief was supported by several circumstances, especially by the fact that all charges against him had been dropped and his case had been sealed by the relevant court. In addition, the applicant had consulted a lawyer who had informed him that he was not obliged to report this arrest in any job application. The UNAT, therefore, held that the applicant had acted in good faith and could not have been found liable for dishonesty, although he had answered a question on his previous arrest, posed by the UN Administration during his recruitment, in the negative.[157]

2.3.5. Unsatisfactory service

Termination of appointment due to unsatisfactory service is undoubtedly a serious matter, especially when it concerns a staff member holding a career appointment. Such termination may not only have significant consequences for further professional, and perhaps even personal, life of the staff member concerned; it may also be easily abused for removal of a staff member who has become, for various reasons, 'uncomfortable'. It is therefore of utmost importance that termination for unsatisfactory service occurs under clear and detailed conditions providing sufficient protection to staff against possible misuse.

In the UN, such conditions can be found neither in the *UN Staff Regulations* nor the *UN Staff Rules*. These two legal instruments only provide that the UN Secretary-General may terminate appointments of UN staff members for unsatisfactory service. The *UN Staff Rules* do stipulate, however, that conditions for termination for this reason are to be set out by the Secretary-General.[158] This has been done by the adoption of two administrative instructions. The first, the *Administrative Instruction, Procedure to be Followed in Cases of Termination of Permanent Appointment for Unsatisfactory Service ST/AI/222* was adopted in 1974 and is still in force. It applies to termination of appointments for unsatisfactory service made on the basis of an individual proposal submitted outside the regular performance review.[159] The second relevant instruction currently in force is the *Administrative Instruction, Performance Management*

---

[156] *Moore v. Secretary-General of the United Nations, UNAT Judgment No. 923 [1999]*, available at http://untreaty.un.org/UNAT/UNAT_Judgements/Judgements_E/UNAT_00923_E.pdf, last visited on 30.12.2010, paras. II, VII and X.

[157] *Case No. 1390, UNAT Judgment No. 1306 [2006]*, available at http://untreaty.un.org/UNAT/UNAT_Judgements/Judgements_E/UNAT_01306_E.pdf, last visited on 30.12.2010, paras. III.-VII.

[158] *UN Staff Regulations of 2009*, Regulation 9.3(a)(ii) and *UN Staff Rules*, Rules 9.6(c)(ii) and (h).

[159] *Administrative Instruction, Procedure to be Followed in Cases of Termination of Permanent Appointment for Unsatisfactory Service*, *ST/AI/222*, 10.12.1974, available in the Human Resources Handbook of the United Nations, available at http://www.un.org/hr_handbook/English/, last visited on 30.12.2010, para. 1.

and Development System ST/AI/2010/5 of 2010.[160] This instruction applies when termination of an appointment is a consequence of a negative performance evaluation which, as explained in more detail in chapter 4, is conducted on a regular basis for all UN staff.[161]

Before going into the details of conditions and procedures provided for in the two administrative instructions, the concept of 'unsatisfactory services' needs to be explained first. An early definition of this concept can be found in *Gordon*, a US loyalty case of 1953:

> *The scope of the term "unsatisfactory services" is to be determined by examination of the meaning given to the word "services" in the Staff Regulations and Rules. It appears clearly that the word "services" is used in the Staff Regulations and Rules solely to designate professional behaviour within the Organization and not to cover all the obligations incumbent upon a staff member.*[162]

The UNAT also stressed a distinction between 'unsatisfactory services' on the one hand and 'misconduct' on the other, the latter being sometimes referred to as 'unsatisfactory conduct'.[163] The UNAT made it clear in *Gordon* that the term 'unsatisfactory services' relates to the quality of staff member's work and falls under Article IX of the *UN Staff Regulations* dealing with the issue of separation from service, while the term 'misconduct' falls under Article X of the *UN Staff Regulations* which deals specifically with disciplinary matters. In the UNAT's view, 'misconduct':

> *could also be either misconduct committed in the exercise of a staff member's professional duties or acts committed outside his professional activities but prohibited by provisions creating general obligations for staff members.*[164]

While both unsatisfactory service and misconduct (or unsatisfactory conduct) may lead to termination of appointments, in the case of the latter special disciplinary proceedings must take place first. Moreover, termination of appointment due to misconduct is only one possible outcome of disciplinary proceedings, other sanctions, such as written censure, degradation, fine or suspension without pay, may be adopted too.[165]

In order to establish whether an appointment may be terminated on the basis of unsatisfactory service, it is necessary to establish not only whether 'service' or 'conduct' of the staff member concerned is at issue but, if the former is the case, also whether it is 'unsatisfactory'. As explained in the chapter discussing, *inter alia*, performance evaluation, the UN Administration enjoys wide discretion in evaluating

---

[160] *Administrative Instruction, Performance Management and Development System.*

[161] See above, chapter 4, section 2.1.2.3.

[162] *Gordon, UNAT Judgment No. 29 [1953]*, para. 7.

[163] See, for example, *Reid v. Secretary-General of the United Nations, UNAT Judgment No. 210 [1976]*, available at http://untreaty.un.org/UNAT/UNAT_Judgements/Judgements_E/UNAT_00210_E.pdf, last visited on 30.12.2010.

[164] *Gordon, UNAT Judgment No. 29 [1953]*, para. 7.

[165] *UN Staff Rules*, Rule 10.2. For more details on disciplinary proceedings and measures, see below, sections 2.3.6.2 and 2.3.6.3.

the quality of staff members' work.[166] It is thus up to the Administration to judge the level of satisfaction with performance of each individual staff member, leaving relatively little scope for judicial review. In *Restrepo*, the UNAT stressed that it:

> *[did] not consider itself competent to rule on the question whether or not the Applicant's services [had been] satisfactory, since the Secretary-General's appraisal in that respect [was] final'.*[167]

On the other hand, in *Pochonet* the UNAT ruled that it:

> *[was] entitled to seek to determine whether the decision of the department concerned that the permanent appointment of the Applicant should be terminated [had been] taken in normal circumstances or in circumstances such that the decision [had] constituted an abusive exercise of the Secretary-General's power of appraisal.*[168]

In this case the UNAT had reviewed all seven periodic staff reports concerning the applicant before concluding that the reports consistently showed deterioration and professional deficiencies of the applicant.[169]

Besides discretion in judging whether performance of an individual staff member is satisfactory or not, the UN Administration also enjoys discretion in deciding whether to terminate an individual appointment for the reason of unsatisfactory service. Like the former, also the latter discretion is broad but not unlimited. The decision to terminate an appointment for unsatisfactory service may not be taken without a 'complete, fair and reasonable' procedure.[170] As already mentioned, at present details of such procedures can be found in two administrative instructions, the applicability of which depends on the situation in which the termination of appointment takes place.

To begin with the *Administrative Instruction, Procedure to be Followed in Cases of Termination of Permanent Appointment for Unsatisfactory Services ST/AI/222*, this instruction explicitly provides that in order to ensure due process requirements during the consideration of a proposal to terminate an appointment for unsatisfactory service, a joint review body has to advise the Secretary-General, which is a welcome feature in this process ensuring its objectivity and impartiality.[171] Every proposal for termination is therefore first referred to such a joint review body made up of the Vice-Chairman and four alternates of the appropriate central review body. The actual assignment from among these alternates to a particular case occurs on an

---

[166] See below, section 2.3.6.3.

[167] *Restrepo, UNAT Judgment No. 131*, para. VII.

[168] *Pochonet v. Secretary-General of the United Nations, UNAT Judgment No. 219 [1977]*, available at http://untreaty.un.org/UNAT/UNAT_Judgements/Judgements_E/UNAT_00219_E.pdf, last visited on 30.12.2010, para. V.

[169] Ibid., paras. V-VI.

[170] *Gillman, UNAT Judgment No. 98 [1966]*, para. II. See also *Restrepo, UNAT Judgment No. 131*, para. VII and *Nelson, UNAT Judgment No. 157 [1972]*, paras. VII-XV.

[171] *Administrative Instruction, Procedure to be Followed in Cases of Termination of Permanent Appointment for Unsatisfactory Service*, para. 2.

alphabetical basis. The only limitation is that half of the members of the joint review body must come from among persons who were designated to serve in the relevant central review body by staff representatives.[172] Also this requirement must be praised because of its contribution to the objectivity and impartiality of the assessment process.

The proposal to terminate an appointment for unsatisfactory service that is submitted to the joint review body must be accompanied by supporting evidence. A copy of the proposal must be provided to the staff member concerned. During the consideration of the case, the joint review body may request information from any member of the UN Secretariat. At the same time, it must give the staff member concerned a reasonable opportunity to comment on the proposal or on any related matter. The staff member in question must also be given a reasonable opportunity to request that any information which he considers relevant is obtained from specified staff members. Hearing in person of the staff member concerned is possible, but not required, depending on the decision of the joint review body. Although this body is obliged to act in a manner ensuring a fair review of the case, it is regrettable – and difficult to understand – that hearing of the staff member concerned, whose appointment may be terminated for a reason as serious as unsatisfactory service, is merely an option, not an obligation.[173]

The report adopted by the joint review body must include its considerations, conclusions and recommendations. It is transmitted to the Secretary-General through a relevant central review body. The latter may indicate its position towards the recommendations of the joint review body and, in cases of a procedural error, may also send the case back to the joint review body. The central review body itself may not reopen the case or conduct a new review. When the report of the joint review body is submitted to the Secretary-General, it is accompanied by the statement of the central review body. It could be argued that this additional review of the matter also helps to ensure the objectivity and impartiality of the assessment process. The final decision on the matter is taken by the Secretary-General. When the decision involves termination of appointment, the staff member concerned must be provided with the notice of termination and the statement of reasons, as well as considerations, conclusions and recommendations of the joint review body.[174] These are important due process guarantees that help to prevent misuse and abuse of power by the UN Administration.

Due process rights of the staff member whose appointment is to be terminated due to unsatisfactory service must, of course, also be observed in cases in which such a decision is the result of a regular performance evaluation. The *Administrative*

---

[172] Ibid., para. 3. Note that the instruction refers to the former advisory bodies, namely the Appointment and Promotion Board, the Appointment and Promotion Committee and the appropriate Working Group of the Appointment and Promotion Panel. These bodies have been superseded by central review bodies as identified in Rule 4.15 of the *UN Staff Rules*. For more details on central review bodies, see above, chapter 3, section 2.2.2.2.

[173] Ibid., paras. 4-8.

[174] Ibid., paras. 9-11.

Instruction, Performance Management and Development System ST/AI/2010/5 which applies in such cases stipulates a number of requirements in this respect. As explained in more detail in the chapter dealing with performance evaluation, UN staff members are actively involved in their performance evaluation and may rebut negative evaluation. The administrative instruction at issue sets out a detailed procedure for both the assessment of staff performance as well as rebuttals.[175] In addition, the instruction contains a section on '[i]dentifying and addressing performance shortcomings and unsatisfactory performance'.[176] This section requires the first reporting officers, i.e. staff members' supervisors, to evaluate the performance of their staff continually and to assist them proactively in remedying shortcomings, if identified. The instruction also lists possible remedial measures to be used in such cases, including counseling, transfer to more suitable functions and additional training. When shortcomings are not cured by adopted remedial measure(s) and the performance appraisal at the end of the year indicates the staff member concerned does not meet performance expectations, his appointment may be terminated. However, the termination may only take place when the remedial measure(s) adopted during the year included a performance improvement plan. Such a plan must have been initiated at least three months before the end of the performance cycle.[177] This is an important safeguard against possible misuse or abuse of power in a situation in which an individual UN staff member has difficulties to meet the required performance standard. Such staff member may not be separated from the UN service without an attempt to help him to improve his performance first.

The specific requirements on addressing underperformance in a timely manner have been introduced in the UN Secretariat only recently. The administrative instruction which preceded the *Administrative Instruction, Performance Management and Development System St/AI/2010/5* also required identification of shortcomings throughout the performance cycle as well as adoption of remedial action, including a performance improvement plan, but it did not subject the termination of appointment to it.[178] The fact that the new instruction, adopted in April 2010, does so is a positive development. It will certainly prevent a situation such as that in *Kioko* from being repeated. In this case, the applicant's appointment was terminated, while his last periodic reports did not indicate that his performance had been unsatisfactory. The decision to terminate the appointment was recommended by the Appointment and Promotion Panel, one of the bodies formerly involved in regular performance

[175] See above, chapter 4, section 2.1.2.3.

[176] *Administrative Instruction, Performance Management and Development System*, Section 10.

[177] Ibid., Section 10.1, 10.3 and 10.4. Unsatisfactory service may also be the reason for non-renewal of an appointment concluded for a fixed-term. The requirements of Section 10 of the present instruction apply also to such non-renewal. In case that the appointment at issue expires before the performance improvement plan has been completed, the appointment is renewed for the duration necessary for such completion. – Section 10.5.

[178] *Administrative Instruction, Performance Appraisal System of 2002*, see especially Sections 8 and 10.5. Note that the UNAT also stressed the importance of giving underperforming staff 'a chance to improve' before terminating appointments due to unsatisfactory performance. – For example, *Case No. 1372, UNAT Judgment No. 1290 [2006]*, available at http://untreaty.un.org/UNAT/UNAT_Judgements/Judgements_E/UNAT_01290_E.pdf, last visited on 30.12.2010, para. V.

evaluation, despite a recommendation of the relevant department that no change in the applicant's status should take place. The Panel's recommendation was accepted and the applicant separated. However, not only did the applicant's performance evaluation never indicate unsatisfactory service, the applicant also never received a notification from the Appointment and Promotion Panel or any other relevant body that termination of his appointment was being considered.[179] The UNAT ruled that such irregularities constituted:

> *a clear failure on the part of the Administration to observe a fundamental procedural protection accorded to staff members under the applicable Staff Rules and Administrative Instructions.*[180]

It should be noted that when unsatisfactory service is one of many grounds available to the administration for terminating an individual appointment, the administration may choose which reason it uses, including that of unsatisfactory service. Such a situation occurred, for example, in *Nelson* where two reasons for termination were present - unsatisfactory service and an unauthorized outside employment. The UN Administration based its termination decision on grounds of unsatisfactory service and the applicant claimed that this had not been the real motive for the termination of his employment. He believed that he had rather been punished for his outside employment without being able to defend his case in the procedures concerning misconduct. The UNAT held, however, that the UN Administration could have used any of the relevant grounds for termination of the applicant's appointment.[181]

2.3.6. Unsatisfactory conduct

Apart from unsatisfactory service, unsatisfactory conduct too may lead to termination of appointments. The *UN Staff Regulations* provide that the termination may occur:

> *[i]f the conduct of the staff member indicates that the staff member does not meet the highest standards of integrity required by Article 101, paragraph 3, of the Charter.*[182]

To recall, Article 101(3) of the *UN Charter* requires that the paramount consideration in staff employment is the necessity to ensure the highest standards of efficiency, competence and integrity.[183] This provision is repeated in the *UN Staff Regulations* as well.[184] The latter also stipulate that the concept of integrity 'includes, but is not limited to, probity, impartiality, fairness, honesty and truthfulness in all matters affecting [staff members'] work and status'.[185] The failure to observe such highest

[179] *Kioko, UNAT Judgment No. 456 [1989]*, paras. II-V.
[180] Ibid., para. VI.
[181] *Nelson, UNAT Judgment No. 157 [1972]*, para. IV.
[182] *UN Staff Regulations of 2009*, Regulation 9.3(a)(iv).
[183] *UN Charter*, Article 101(3).
[184] *UN Staff Regulations of 2009*, Regulation 1.2(b). See also Regulation 4.2.
[185] Ibid., Regulation 1.2(b).

standards of integrity may thus constitute an unsatisfactory conduct, or misconduct, leading to disciplinary proceedings and possibly termination of appointment. The *UN Staff Rules* specify in this respect that the Secretary-General may terminate appointments for disciplinary reasons in accordance with rules applicable to disciplinary proceedings.[186] Such rules are contained in Chapter X of the *UN Staff Rules* which provide the definition of misconduct, the list of disciplinary measures and the requirements of due process that need to be adhered to. The following sections discuss details of each of these issues.

Before doing so, however, it should be noted that the UN Secretary-General provides, on the basis of the resolution of the General Assembly 59/287 of 2005, an annual overview of reported disciplinary cases as well as actions taken in such cases. The most recent report A/65/180 covers the period from July 2009 until June 2010.[187] During that period, 167 disciplinary cases were reported and 100 cases completed. Most newly reported cases concerned misuse of computer-related resources. Other cases involved financial disclosure, fraud and misrepresentation, theft and misappropriation, assault, sexual exploitation and abuse, procurement irregularities and others. In the reported period, sanctions were imposed in 65 cases, of which 13 were dismissals, 16 other disciplinary measures and 36 administrative measures. In the remaining cases a decision was adopted to take no action.[188] Recall that the total number of staff serving in the UN Secretariat on 30 June 2010 was 44.134.[189]

2.3.6.1. Definitions

The definition of misconduct is provided in Rule 10.1 of the *UN Staff Rules*. This rule stipulates:

> Failure by a staff member to comply with his or her obligations *under the Charter of the United Nations, the Staff Regulations and Staff Rules or other relevant administrative issuances, or* to observe the standards of conduct expected of an international civil servant, *may amount to misconduct and may lead to the institution of a disciplinary process and the imposition of disciplinary measures for misconduct.*[190] *(emphasis added)*

Hence, misconduct may take place when a staff member fails to meet his obligations set out in various legal instruments, including but not limited to the *UN Charter*, the *UN Staff Regulations* and the *UN Staff Rules*. It may also occur when a staff member fails to observe standards of conduct which are not necessarily explicitly stated in

[186] *UN Staff Rules*, Rule 9.6(c)(iv).

[187] *Practice of the Secretary-General in Disciplinary Matters and Possible Criminal Behaviour, 1 July 2009 to 30 June 2010, Report of the Secretary-General, A/65/180*, 29.07.2010, available in the Official Document System of the United Nations, available at http://documents.un.org/, last visited on 30.12.2010. This report also provides a comparison of figures for four previous reporting periods, starting with July 2005.

[188] Ibid., paras. 44 and 45. For details on the various types of sanction, see below, section 2.3.6.3.

[189] *Composition of the Secretariat: Staff Demographics, Report of the Secretary-General, A/65/350*, para. 2.

[190] *UN Staff Rules*, Rule 10.1..

any UN legal instrument but which are expected of all international civil servants. Of course, many of the expected standards are contained in the existing legal instruments.

To begin with the *UN Charter*, as already stated, it requires the highest standards of integrity which are further defined in the *UN Staff Regulations*. The *UN Staff Regulations* themselves, accompanied by the *UN Staff Rules*, list basic values expected from international civil servants, as well as 'particular manifestations of such basic values'.[191] Article 1 of the *UN Staff Regulations* contains a number of relevant regulations in this respect. Regulation 1.1 of the *UN Staff Regulations* provides that UN staff members are international civil servants whose responsibilities are exclusively international. Upon taking up appointment at the UN Secretariat, each staff member must declare in writing his loyalty, discretion and conscience; his preparedness not to seek or accept any instructions related to the discharge of his duty, whether originating within a government or any other authority external to the UN; and his promise to act in accordance with the obligations set out in the *UN Staff Regulations* and the *UN Staff Rules*.[192] Regulations 1.2 and 1.3 of the *UN Staff Regulations* specify the UN core values, including human rights, equality of men and women, respect for all cultures, and the staff members' basic rights and obligations. The latter include: independence from governments or any other external source in performance of duties;[193] loyalty to the aims, principles and purposes of the UN;[194] obligation to ensure that personal views and convictions do not adversely affect official duties of the staff members or interests of the UN;[195] obligation to ensure that staff members' personal conduct, including participation in political activities, is in compliance with the status of international civil servants, their independence and impartiality, and that it does not result in any conflict of interests;[196] obligation

[191] *Practice of the Secretary-General in Disciplinary Matters and Possible Criminal Behaviour, 1 July 2005 to 30 June 2006, Report of the Secretary-General, A/61/206*, 31.07.2006, available in the Official Document System of the United Nations, available at http://documents.un.org/, last visited on 30.12.2010, para. 5.

[192] *UN Staff Regulations of 2009*, Regulation 1.1.

[193] Ibid., Regulation 1.2(d).

[194] Ibid., Regulation 1.2(e).

[195] Ibid., Regulation 1.2(f).

[196] Ibid., Regulation 1.2(f) and (h). See also *UN Staff Rules*, Rule 1.2(b) concerning private legal obligations of staff. In this respect, the UNAT Judgment No. 1004 in *Capote* is interesting. In that case, the applicant was summarily dismissed by the UN Administration for serious misconduct – opening of two credit card accounts on behalf of a colleague without the colleague's authorization and making false certifications on the applications for these credit cards. However, the UNAT considered that the act of the applicant did not fall within the scope of disciplinary cases under the *UN Staff Regulations*. It explained that: 'While a personal matter that reflects adversely on the Organization may be the subject of disciplinary proceedings, the Staff Regulations and Rules principally address conduct related to employment.'- *Capote v. Secretary-General of the United Nations, UNAT Judgment No. 1004 [2001]*, available at http://untreaty.un.org/UNAT/UNAT_Judgements/Judgements_E/UNAT_01004_E.pdf, last visited on 30.12.2010, para. VI. In the case at hand, the issue concerned 'purely an arrangement of some kind between colleagues regarding personal activities and personal funds' which the UN Administration had no competence over. In addition, the action of the applicant in no way affected the professional performance of either of the colleagues, had no adverse effect on the organization, on the applicant's status of international civil servant, her integrity or her independence and impartiality.

to ensure that the office or knowledge gained from the official functions are not used for personal purposes;[197] discretion in all official matters, including vis-à-vis governments;[198] obligation not to accept honours, decorations, favours, gifts or remunerations, subject to specified exceptions;[199] obligations related to avoiding conflicts of interest in discharge of official duties, including financial disclosure;[200] restrictions related to outside employment and activities;[201] obligations concerning use of UN property and assets;[202] obligation to uphold highest standards of efficiency, competence and integrity in the discharge of duties;[203] and accountability of staff members to the Secretary-General for the proper performance of duties.[204] Chapter I of the *UN Staff Rules* further elaborates on a number of above mentioned obligations. It also emphasizes prohibition of any conduct of UN staff members that would be aimed at, or result in, (undue) influence of, or interference with, proper functioning of other staff members, UN organs and bodies as well as UN Member States.[205]

In addition to the *UN Staff Regulations* and the *UN Staff Rules*, there are a number of other documents of great importance in this respect. First of all, the *Secretary-General's Bulletin, Status, Basic Rights and Duties of United Nations Staff Members*, ST/SGB/2002/13 of 1 November 2002 which contains, *inter alia*, detailed commentaries to the above mentioned *UN Staff Regulations* and *UN Staff Rules*, offering a more detailed analysis thereof.[206] Secondly, there is a document prepared by the International Civil Service Commission in 2001 and approved by the General Assembly in its resolution 56/244 under the title *Standards of Conduct for the International Civil*

– Ibid., paras. VII-VIII. In *Hzayyen*, however, the UNAT did consider a matter similar to the one in *Capote* to be 'properly meriting the interest of the employing organization'. - *Hzayyen v. United Nations Relief and Work Agency for Palestine Refugees in the Near East, UNAT Judgment No. 1020 [2001]*, available at http://untreaty.un.org/UNAT/UNAT_Judgements/Judgements_E/UNAT_01020_E.pdf, last visited on 30.12.2010, paras. VI. In this case, the applicant had stolen an ATM card and the card containing the PIN number from his colleague's desk or handbag and made a number of withdrawal transactions for the corresponding bank account. The UNAT agreed with the UN Administration that this qualified as serious misconduct and approved the decision to summarily dismiss the applicant. - *Hzayyen, UNAT Judgment No. 1020 [2001]*, paras. VI-VII.

197 *UN Staff Regulations of 2009*, Regulation 1.2(g).

198 Ibid., Regulation 1.2(i).

199 Ibid., Regulations 1.2(j)-(l). See also *UN Staff Rules*, Rules 1.2(k)-(o).

200 *UN Staff Regulations of 2009*, Regulations 1.2(m)-(n). See also *UN Staff Rules*, Rules 1.2(p)-(q).

201 *UN Staff Regulations of 2009*, Regulations 1.2(o)-(p). See also *UN Staff Rules*, Rules 1.2(r)-(t).

202 *UN Staff Regulations of 2009*, Regulations 1.2(q)-(r).

203 Ibid., Regulation 1.3. See also *UN Staff Rules of 2002*, Rules 1.3.

204 *UN Staff Regulations of 2009*, Regulation 1.3. See also *UN Staff Rules of 2002*, Rule 1.2(a).

205 *UN Staff Rules*, Rules 1.2(e)-(j).

206 *Secretary-General's Bulletin, Status, Basic Rights and Duties of United Nations Staff Members, ST/SGB/2002/13*, 01.11.2002, available in the Human Resources Handbook of the United Nations, available at http://www.un.org/hr_handbook/English/, last visited on 30.12.2010. For *Regulations Governing the Status, Basic Rights and Duties of Officials other than Secretariat Officials, and Experts on Mission*, see *Secretary-General's Bulletin, Regulations Governing the Status, Basic Rights and Duties of Officials other than Secretariat Officials, and Experts on Mission, ST/SGB/2002/9*, 18.06.2002, available in the Human Resources Handbook of the United Nations, available at http://www.un.org/hr_handbook/English/, last visited on 30.12.2010.

Service.[207] This document provides for a comprehensive set of rules applicable to all international civil servants serving under the UN common system. The *Standards* specify guiding principles for international civil servants that must be observed in all their actions and covers issues such as working relations; harassment; conflict of interest; role of the secretariat; staff management relations; relations with Member States and legislative bodies; relations with the public and with the media; use and protection of information; respect for different customs and cultures; security and safety; personal conduct; outside employment and activities; and acceptance of gifts, honours and remuneration from outside sources. Furthermore, a number of separate administrative issuances are dedicated to specific issues of possible misconduct. For example, discrimination, (sexual) harassment and abuse of authority are addressed in the *Secretary-General's Bulletin, Prohibition of Discrimination, Harassment, Including Sexual Harassment, and Abuse of Authority ST/SGB/2008/5* of 11 February 2008 (providing for definitions, general principles, procedures and monitoring) and in the *Secretary-General's Bulletin, Prevention of Workplace Harassment, Sexual Harassment and Abuse of Authority ST/SGB/2005/20* of 28 November 2005 (on mandatory online learning programme).[208] The acceptance of honours, decorations, favours, gifts and remuneration is regulated by the *Administrative Instruction, Reporting, Retaining and Disposing of Honours, Decorations, Favours, Gifts or Remuneration from Governmental and Nongovernmental Sources ST/AI/2010/1* of 14 January 2001.[209]

There is also a considerable number of additional departmental or office-specific codes on ethics-related matters (such as ethical codes, codes of conduct with ethical components or conflict of interest), various departmental or office-related rules and guidelines dealing with specific ethics-related activities (such as outside activities, acceptance of gifts, post-employment restrictions) as well as other publications, manuals and documents on ethics-related issues produced by departments, offices

[207] *General Assembly Resolution 56/244, A/RES/56/244*, 05.02.2002, available in the Official Document System of the United Nations, available at http://documents.un.org/, last visited on 30.12.2010, Section I, Part A. The *Standards of Conduct for the International Civil Service* of 2001 replaced an earlier document of 1954 carrying the same title.

[208] *Secretary-General's Bulletin, Prohibition of Discrimination, Harassment, Including Sexual Harassment, and Abuse of Authority, ST/SGB/2008/5*, 11.02.2008, available in the Human Resources Handbook of the United Nations, available at http://www.un.org/hr_handbook/English/, last visited on 30.12.2010 and *Secretary-General's Bulletin, Prevention of Workplace Harassment, Sexual Harassment and Abuse of Authority, ST/SGB/2005/20*, 28.11.2005, available in the Human Resources Handbook of the United Nations, available at http://www.un.org/hr_handbook/English/, last visited on 30.12.2010. See also *Secretary-General's Bulletin, Special Measures for Protection from Sexual Exploitation and Sexual Abuse, ST/SGB/2003/13*, 09.10.2003, available in the Human Resources Handbook of the United Nations, available at http://www.un.org/hr_handbook/English/, last visited on 30.12.2010 on Joint Harassment Prevention Boards and *Secretary-General's Bulletin, Post-Employment Restrictions, ST/SGB/2006/15*, 26.12.2006, available in the Human Resources Handbook of the United Nations, available at http://www.un.org/hr_handbook/English/, last visited on 30.12.2010 on special measures for protection from sexual location and sexual abuse.

[209] *Administrative Instruction, Reporting, Retaining and Disposing of Honours, Decorations, Favours, Gifts or Remuneration from Governmental and Non-governmental Sources, ST/AI/2010/1*, 14.01.2010, available in the Human Resources Handbook of the United Nations, available at http://www.un.org/hr_handbook/English/, last visited on 30.12.2010.

and other entities. All these documents are in place to provide guidance and advice to the UN staff on general or specific ethics-related matters.[210]

Last but not least, there is an independent Ethics Office of the United Nations, operational since 2006 and responsible for:

> *assist[ing] the Secretary-General in ensuring that all staff members observe and perform their functions consistent with the highest standards of integrity required by the Charter of the United Nations through fostering a culture of ethics, transparency and accountability.*[211]

The UN Ethics Office provides advice and guidance to individual staff, but it also develops standards, provides training and education on ethics issues, administers financial disclosure of UN staff members, and is involved in protection of staff against retaliation for reporting misconduct or cooperating in disciplinary investigations.[212] One of the first activities of the UN Ethics Office in the area of standard-setting was the development of a system-wide code of ethics for all UN staff, including staff of other UN bodies and agencies than the UN Secretariat. The work on this code commenced by the UN Ethics Office has been in the meantime taken over by the United Nations Ethics Committee, established in 2007 and comprising heads of the Ethics Offices of the separately administered UN organs and programmes as well as the UN Ethics Office.[213] A draft *Code of Ethics for United Nations Personnel* was prepared in 2008 and, after consultation with management, staff representatives and the International Civil Service Commission, submitted to the General Assembly for consideration in 2009.[214] In 2010 the General Assembly decided that it would consider the matter during its sixty-sixth session, scheduled for opening in September 2011.[215] As the UN Ethics Committee explained, this system-wide code is not meant to be legally binding; it is intended 'to be values-based and aspirational (*sic*) in nature, instead of being rules-based and disciplinary'.[216] Accordingly, the Code has been prepared as 'a short, concise statement of the core values and

---

[210] For more detailed analysis, see *Activities of the Ethics Office, Report of the Secretary-General, A/63/301*, 18.08.2008, available in the Official Document System of the United Nations, available at http://documents.un.org/, last visited on 30.12.2010, Part V.

[211] *Secretary-General's Bulletin, Ethics Office - Establishment and Terms of Reference, ST/SGB/2005/22*, 30.12.2005, available in the Human Resources Handbook of the United Nations, available at http://www.un.org/hr_handbook/English/, last visited on 30.12.2010, Section 1.2.

[212] Ibid., Section 3.1.

[213] *Secretary-General's Bulletin, United Nations System-wide Application of Ethics: Separately Administered Organs and Programmes, ST/SGB/2007/11*, 30.11.2007, available in the Human Resources Handbook of the United Nations, available at http://www.un.org/hr_handbook/English/, last visited on 30.12.2010, Section 5.

[214] *Activities of the Ethics Office, Report of the Secretary-General, A/63/301*, paras. 57; *Activities of the Ethics Office, Report of the Secretary-General, A/64/316*, 21.08.2009, available in the Official Document System of the United Nations, available at http://documents.un.org/, last visited on 30.12.2010, paras. 79-85 and 88; and *Activities of the Ethics Office, Report of the Secretary-General, A/65/343*, 01.09.2010, available in the Official Document System of the United Nations, available at http://documents.un.org/, last visited on 30.12.2010, para. 64.

[215] *General Assembly Resolution 65/247*, paras. 79-80.

[216] *Activities of the Ethics Office, Report of the Secretary-General, A/64/316*, para. 80.

principles', all of which can already be found in staff regulations and rules applicable in the UN system and providing for sanctions in case these values and principles are breached.[217] The core values contained in the *Code of Ethics for United Nations Personnel* include independence; loyalty; impartiality; integrity; accountability; and respect for human rights. The core principles relate to the issues of conflict of interest; abuse of authority; gifts, honours, favours and other benefits; UN resources; confidentiality of information; and post-employment.[218]

The long list of documents containing and repeating general ethical principles and the rights and obligations of to the UN staff members suggests that the concept of misconduct is relatively broad. It includes professional as well as personal standards and duties that international civil servants must observe. However, it should be recalled that especially with regard to professional duties of UN staff, a distinction must be kept in mind between unsatisfactory service and unsatisfactory conduct (or misconduct). As explained above in the section dealing with termination of appointment for unsatisfactory service, this concept relates to the quality of staff work, while the concept of unsatisfactory conduct (or misconduct) relates to staff members' behavior. It must be stressed, however, that unsatisfactory behavior may relate to the exercise of professional duties as well as to general obligations outside professional activities.[219] Furthermore, in *Eren, Robertson, Sellberg and Thompson* the UNAT held that:

> *There might be instances when failures in performance are of such extreme dimension as to constitute misconduct for which disciplinary measures would be reasonable.*[220]

Hence, unsatisfactory service may, under certain circumstances amount to unsatisfactory conduct (or misconduct). The UNAT did not find this to be so in the case in question, though. The applicants in that case were accused of irregularities in the UN procurement practices but the UNAT held that no damage had been caused to the UN, that the applicants acted in line with a recommendation of the Secretary-General for speedy decision-making, and that they were provided with no standards for procedures to be followed. Thus, any irregularities that might have been caused by the applicants could not have been seen as their fault.[221]

---

[217] Ibid., paras. 80-81. The Code is to apply to all UN staff and related personnel, such as 'United Nations Volunteers; personnel or employees of non-United Nations entities or individuals who have entered into a cooperative arrangement with the United Nations (including interns, international and local consultants as well as individual and corporate contractors); experts on mission, including United Nations police officers; and members of national formed police units, corrections officers, military observers and military members of national contingents serving in United Nations peacekeeping missions'. – *Activities of the Ethics Office, Report of the Secretary-General, A/64/316*, Annex.

[218] *Activities of the Ethics Office, Report of the Secretary-General, A/64/316*, Annex.

[219] *Gordon, UNAT Judgment No. 29 [1953]*, para. 7.

[220] *Eren, Robertson, Sellberg and Thompson v. Secretary-General of the United Nations, UNAT Judgment No. 744 [1995]*, available at http://untreaty.un.org/UNAT/UNAT_Judgements/Judgements_E/UNAT_00744_E.pdf, last visited on 30.12.2010, para. XVI.

[221] Ibid., paras. XVI-XX.

Similarly, in *Al Ansari, Zarra and Khalil, and Abdulhadi et al.* the UNAT made a distinction between 'willful or reckless failure to perform duties' on the one hand and 'innate inefficiency or inability' on the other. Only the former can lead to an imposition of a disciplinary sanction, while the latter should be dealt with through an administrative action. The UNAT put emphasis on staff members' culpability – the more culpable the conduct, the more likely it can be regarded as misconduct.[222] On the other hand, the UNAT has stressed that, in some circumstances, misconduct may be established even when there is no harmful intention. Mere negligence on the side of the staff member may thus suffice, too.[223]

In another interesting case, *Alok*, the UNAT ruled that severe health problems (diminished capacity and neurological illness in the case at hand) of the applicant had to be taken into account by the UN Administration when deciding whether his conduct amounted to misconduct. The Administration considered this issue but only for the purposes of possible reduction or diminution of disciplinary sanction, not in determining the existence of misconduct. The UNAT stated that if the UN Administration had done so, it could have concluded that the applicant's conduct was to be regarded as inadequate performance rather than misconduct. The UNAT characterized the failure to make such an assessment as 'an extraordinary omission' on the side of the UN Administration.[224]

A general list of actions considered to constitute misconduct can be found in *Administrative Instruction, Revised Disciplinary Measures and Procedures ST/AI/371* of 1991.[225] This list includes, but is not limited to:

(a) *Acts or omissions in conflict with the general obligations of staff members set forth in article 1 of the Staff Regulations and the rules and instructions implementing it;*

(b) *Unlawful acts (e.g. theft, fraud, possession or sale of illegal substances, smuggling) on or off United Nations premises, and whether or not the staff member was officially on duty at the time;*

[222] *Al Ansari, Zarra and Khalil, and Abdulhadi et al. v. Commissioner-General of the United Nations Relief and Works Agency for Palestine Refugees in the Near East, UNAT Judgment No. 1014 [2001]*, available at http://untreaty.un.org/UNAT/UNAT_Judgements/Judgements_E/UNAT_01014_E.pdf, last visited on 30.12.2010, para. IV.

[223] *Case No. 1395, UNAT Judgment No. 1321 [2007]*, available at http://untreaty.un.org/UNAT/UNAT_Judgements/Judgements_E/UNAT_01321_E.pdf, last visited on 30.12.2010, para. XII. Note that in case of fraud, intent must always be proved. - *Case No. 1456, UNAT Judgment No. 1391 [2008]*, available at http://untreaty.un.org/UNAT/UNAT_Judgements/Judgements_E/UNAT_01391_E.pdf, last visited on 30.12.2010, para. VII.

[224] *Alok v. Secretary-General of the United Nations, UNAT Judgment No. 1123 [2003]*, available at http://untreaty.un.org/UNAT/UNAT_Judgements/Judgements_E/UNAT_01123_E.pdf, last visited on 30.12.2010, para. VII.

[225] *Administrative Instruction, Revised Disciplinary Measures and Procedures, ST/AI/371*, 02.08.1991, available in the Human Resources Handbook of the United Nations, available at http://www.un.org/hr_handbook/English/, last visited on 30.12.2010.

(c) *Misrepresentation or false certification in connection with any United Nations claim or benefit, including failure to disclose a fact material to that claim or benefit;*

(d) *Assault upon, harassment of, or threats to other staff members;*

(e) *Misuse of United Nations equipment or files, including electronic files;*

(f) *Misuse of office; abuse of authority; breach of confidentiality; abuse of United Nations privileges and immunities,*

(g) *Acts or behaviour that would discredit the United Nations.*[226]

When a misconduct of a UN staff member reaches a sufficient degree of seriousness, it can be regarded to be a 'serious misconduct'. Such misconduct may result in distinct disciplinary procedures and sanctions when compared to a 'regular' misconduct and even without disciplinary proceedings. The notion of serious misconduct is not defined in the *UN Staff Regulations* or the *UN Staff Rules*, except for the stipulation that both sexual exploitation and sexual abuse constitute serious misconduct.[227] Of course, many guidelines are provided in the jurisprudence. In the already mentioned case *Gordon*, a US loyalty case, the UNAT held:

> *The conception of serious misconduct enabling the Secretary-General to impose summary dismissal without disciplinary procedure was introduced at the revision of the Staff Regulations to deal with* acts obviously incompatible with continued membership of the staff.
>
> *Except in cases of agreement between the person concerned and the administration, the disciplinary procedure should be dispensed with only in those cases where* the misconduct is patent *and where* the interest of the service requires immediate and final separation.[228] *(emphasis added)*

Hence, serious misconduct is a patent (i.e. obvious, manifest) misconduct which is not only clearly incompatible with continued employment with the UN but which also requires immediate separation from UN service. Consequently, there must be no doubt about the wrongful nature of the act and no doubt that continued employment of the staff member in question would harm the UN. The UNAT has also made clear that the 'seriousness' is to be measured with regard to conduct and not its consequences.[229]

Gordon illustrates a situation in which the wrongful nature of a staff member's conduct was disputed and therefore not capable of being classified as serious misconduct.

---

[226] Ibid., para. 2.

[227] *UN Staff Regulations of 2009*, Regulation 10.1(b). See also *Secretary-General's Bulletin, Prohibition of Discrimination, Harassment, Including Sexual Harassment, and Abuse of Authority*, *Secretary-General's Bulletin, Prevention of Workplace Harassment, Sexual Harassment and Abuse of Authority*, and *Secretary-General's Bulletin, Special Measures for Protection from Sexual Exploitation and Sexual Abuse*, for the prohibition of sexual harassment, sexual exploitation and sexual abuse.

[228] *Gordon, UNAT Judgment No. 29 [1953]*, para. 8.

[229] *Dilleyta v. Secretary-General of the United Nations, UNAT Judgment No. 1103 [2003]*, available at http://untreaty.un.org/UNAT/UNAT_Judgements/Judgements_E/UNAT_01103_E.pdf, last visited on 30.12.2010, para. IX.

To recall, the conduct consisted of the refusal of the applicant to answer certain questions before an internal committee of the US Senate investigating activities of US citizens employed by the UN. The applicant had invoked his constitutional right under the Fifth Amendment to the US Constitution and under US government pressure, he was summarily dismissed. Before deciding to dismiss the applicant, the Secretary-General requested an advice from the Commission of Jurists. The issue was also discussed in the General Assembly, with no decision on the matter. In addition, the Secretary-General granted termination indemnities to the dismissed staff member, an action which is prohibited in case of summary dismissal for serious misconduct. The totality of these facts led the UNAT to conclude that because of all the doubts reflected by all the steps taken in this case, the conduct of the dismissed staff member could not have been regarded as serious misconduct.[230]

In contrast to *Gordon*, in *Ying*, for example, the UNAT considered it obvious that tax fraud and incorrect certification of tax reimbursements were 'plainly covered' by the definition of serious misconduct.[231] In this case the UNAT further explained that the mere fact that the staff member was given an additional opportunity to give more explanations or provide further information did not mean that the obvious or reprehensible degree of misconduct automatically ceased to exist.[232] In a more recent case, the UNAT further clarified that:

> *The mere fact that a decision had been made earlier to refer it as a case of misconduct to the [Disciplinary Committee] to elicit the [Disciplinary Committee]'s views before deciding on the appropriate sanction, does not preclude a further review and another view being taken by the Administrator ... as long as there were facts to justify the decision. There can be no dispute that if the charges against the Applicant have been established, this is indeed a case of serious misconduct.*[233]

In establishing whether a serious misconduct has taken place, the UN Administration must also pay regard to the degree of seriousness of the conduct. In *Iddi*, for example, the applicant declared for reimbursement purposes hospital bills he had not paid. The Administration considered this action to be serious misconduct but the UNAT disagreed. It stressed that the applicant was accused just of a single attempt of improper reimbursement in many years of 'unblemished service' and the harm to the UN would only amount to 414 US dollars. It therefore considered that categorization of such conduct as serious misconduct was excessive.[234]

---

[230] *Gordon, UNAT Judgment No. 29 [1953]*, para. 9.

[231] *Ying v. Secretary-General of the United Nations, UNAT Judgment No. 424 [1988]*, available at http://untreaty.un.org/UNAT/UNAT_Judgements/Judgements_E/UNAT_00424_E.pdf, last visited on 30.12.2010, para. XII.

[232] Ibid., para. XII.

[233] *Case No. 1333, UNAT Judgment No. 1260 [2005]*, available at http://untreaty.un.org/UNAT/UNAT_Judgements/Judgements_E/UNAT_01260_E.pdf, last visited on 30.12.2010, para. VIII.

[234] *Iddi v. Secretary-General of the United Nations, UNAT Judgment No. 1011 [2001]*, available at http://untreaty.un.org/UNAT/UNAT_Judgements/Judgements_E/UNAT_01011_E.pdf, last visited on 30.12.2010, para. VI.

The decision whether in a particular case there has been misconduct or serious misconduct and what constitutes interests of the organization is made by the UN Administration which enjoys wide discretion in this regard.[235] As stated by the UNAT on several occasions:

> *the Staff Regulations vest the Secretary-General with authority to determine whether a staff member has met the required standards of conduct.*[236]

An initial burden of proof with regard to the existence of misconduct or serious misconduct rests on the UN Administration. After a *prima facie* case is made, it is up to the staff member in question to provide evidence in order rebut the *prima facie* case or to justify the conduct.[237] The UNAT has, however, emphasized that the burden of proof in disciplinary matters is heavier than in administrative matters and the UN Administration must therefore provide evidence which is convincing and not overturned by the staff member concerned.[238] On the other hand, UNAT has also ruled that disciplinary proceedings are not of a criminal nature and that the UN Administration is 'not required to prove its case beyond reasonable doubt ... only to present adequate evidence in support of its conclusions and recommendations ... to permit a reasonable inference that a violation of law had occurred'.[239] When the *prima facie* case is made by the Administration, it is for the staff member concerned to provide an adequate explanation or evidence to rebut it. If he does not succeed, a conclusion of misconduct can be reached by the Administration.[240]

With regard to the discretion of the UN Administration, it should be noted that although the UNAT consistently held that decisions on whether there had been mis-

---

[235] For discretion in cases of misconduct, see *Roy v. Secretary-General of the International Civil Aviation Organization, UNAT Judgment No. 123 [1968]*, available at http://untreaty.un.org/UNAT/UNAT_Judgements/Judgements_E/UNAT_00123_E.pdf, last visited on 30.12.2010, para. 9. For discretion in cases of serious misconduct, see *Archibald v. Secretary-General of the United Nations, UNAT Judgment No. 222 [1977]*, available at http://untreaty.un.org/UNAT/UNAT_Judgements/Judgements_E/UNAT_00222_E.pdf, last visited on 30.12.2010, paras. I and VI. In the latter case, the UNAT held that the discretion of the Secretary-General in establishing the existence of serious misconduct was not reviewable, unless there was a contention of an improper motive. The UNAT also ruled that it could not substitute the judgment of the Secretary-General in what constituted interests of the organization justifying summary dismissal, unless the decision was arbitrary, based on bias or improperly motivated. For a more recent case law on discretion of the UN Administration in this area see, for example, *Case No. 1494, UNAT Judgment No. 1428 [2008]*, available at http://untreaty.un.org/UNAT/UNAT_Judgements/Judgements_E/UNAT_01428_E.pdf, last visited on 30.12.2010, para. II.

[236] Recently, for example, in *Case No. 1478, UNAT Judgment No. 1414 [2008]*, available at http://untreaty.un.org/UNAT/UNAT_Judgements/Judgements_E/UNAT_01414_E.pdf, last visited on 30.12.2010, para. XVI.

[237] *Patel v. Secretary-General of the United Nations, UNAT Judgment No. 850 [1997]*, available at http://untreaty.un.org/UNAT/UNAT_Judgements/Judgements_E/UNAT_00850_E.pdf, last visited on 30.12.2010, para. IV. See also *Kiwanuka v. Secretary-General of the United Nations, UNAT Judgment No. 941 [1999]*, available at http://untreaty.un.org/UNAT/UNAT_Judgements/Judgements_E/UNAT_00941_E.pdf, last visited on 30.12.2010, Para. VIII.

[238] *Case No. 1499, UNAT Judgment No. 1422 [2008]*, available at http://untreaty.un.org/UNAT/UNAT_Judgements/Judgements_E/UNAT_01422_E.pdf, last visited on 30.12.2010, para. XXI.

[239] *Araim, Judgment No. 657 [1994]*, para. V.

[240] Ibid., para. V and *Dilleyta, UNAT Judgment No. 1103 [2003]*, para. VI.

conduct or serious misconduct were discretionary, in a number of cases the UNAT exercised its judicial control rather broadly. Despite declaring that it could not substitute its judgment for the one of the UN Administration in this respect, the UNAT has, in fact, done so.[241] As explicitly admitted in *Kiwanuka*, the UNAT has developed a practice of determining whether the material factual findings in a particular case were supported by evidence and whether the proven facts legally amounted to misconduct or serious misconduct. The UNAT has explained that it has the power to decide 'whether it [agreed] that the Administration, in exercising its discretion, [had], according to the written law and general principles of law, made the appropriate characterization'.[242] In addition, the UNAT has explicitly recognized its competence to 'carry out its own analysis of the facts on which the contested decision is based in order to determine whether it was erroneous'.[243] It could be argued that this is nothing less than a substantive review of the administration's discretionary decisions. This view is supported by the statement of the UNAT in one of its recent cases in which it outlined the steps it would take in considering the case:

> *It will first consider whether the facts have been established. If they have, the Tribunal will then proceed to determine whether they amount to misconduct; lastly, it will verify whether the sanction is proportionate to the offense.*[244]

The UNAT has stressed that the Administration's discretion in disciplinary matters differs from other discretionary powers, such as transferring and terminating staff members' services, since it involves a special exercise of quasi-judicial power. Therefore, the judicial review of disciplinary decisions is of a particular nature as well.[245] The UNAT's attitude towards its own competence in disciplinary matters must be praised as it helps to prevent, or to remedy, possible misuse or abuse of power by the UN Administration which could, in the absence of judicial review, be tempted to use this reason for termination of appointments in cases in which no (serious) misconduct in fact took place. The US loyalty cases, mentioned above, are an example *par excellence* of such a case.

---

[241] For example, recent cases *Case No. 1395, UNAT Judgment No. 1321 [2007]*, paras. XI-XV; *Case No. 1478, UNAT Judgment No. 1414 [2008]*, para. XIX ; or *Case No. 1499, UNAT Judgment No. 1422 [2008]*, paras. XXI-XXV.

[242] *Kiwanuka, UNAT Judgment No. 941 [1999]*, paras. VI and VII. See also *Iddi, UNAT Judgment No. 1011 [2001]*, para. III. On the arguably unclear position of the UNAT in this respect, see also Amerasinghe, *The Law of the International Civil Service, Volume II*, pp. 817-819.

[243] *Case No. 1371, UNAT Judgment No.1289 [2005]*, available at http://untreaty.un.org/UNAT/UNAT_Judgements/Judgements_E/UNAT_01289_E.pdf, last visited on 30.12.2010, para. V.

[244] *Case No. 1499, UNAT Judgment No. 1422 [2008]*, para. XX. In the subsequent paragraphs, the UNAT has examined and evaluated the lengthy evidence presented in this case and concluded that the material facts which led the Secretary-General to taking the disciplinary measure vis-à-vis the applicant were not established. – paras. XXII-XXVI.

[245] Ibid., para. XVIII. See also *Kiwanuka, UNAT Judgment No. 941 [1999]*, para. IV. With regard to serious misconduct this tendency has been present since the early years. As mentioned above, in *Gordon* the UNAT held that the invocation of the rights under the Fifth Amendment of the United States Constitution could not have been seen as serious misconduct. - *Gordon, UNAT Judgment No. 29 [1953]*, para. 9. Similarly, in *Ying* the UNAT considered it obvious that tax fraud and incorrect certification of tax reimbursements undoubtedly fell under the definition of serious misconduct. - *Ying, UNAT Judgment No. 424 [1988]*, para. XII.

2.3.6.2. Disciplinary procedures

Unsurprisingly, the adoption of a decision establishing the existence of misconduct or serious misconduct must be preceded by a procedure respecting the rights of the defense of the staff member concerned.[246] The staff member must be informed about all charges against him and must be granted opportunity to give the facts as he sees them and to explain his conduct.[247] He must also be allowed to participate in examining the evidence.[248] The reasons for the disciplinary measure must be given 'with a reasonable degree of precision and with due regard for the facts of the case as evidenced by the file'.[249]

Until 2009, the *UN Staff Rules* contained a relatively detailed set of procedures to be followed in disciplinary cases. In accordance with the requirement of Regulation 10.1 of the *UN Staff Regulations*, the *UN Staff Rules* established an administrative machinery to advise the Secretary-General in such cases. This machinery included the Joint Disciplinary Committee and the Joint Appeals Board, both composed of staff members delegated in half by the Secretary-General and in half by staff representatives and both serving in advisory capacity. Having heard the case, the Joint Disciplinary Committee in the first instance and the Joint Appeals Board in the second instance, advised the Secretary-General whether, and if so what, sanction should be imposed on the staff member guilty of misconduct. The final decision was taken by the Secretary-General who did not have to follow the recommendation of the Joint Disciplinary Committee or the Joint Appeals Board. However, in such a case the Secretary-General had to justify his decision and support it by evidence, otherwise the UNAT – which conducted judicial review of disciplinary decisions, if challenged – could find an abuse of discretion.[250]

---

[246] *Zang-Atangana v. Secretary-General of the United Nations, UNAT Judgment No. 130 [1969]*, available at http://untreaty.un.org/UNAT/UNAT_Judgements/Judgements_E/UNAT_00130_E.pdf, last visited on 30.12.2010, para. IV.

[247] *Lindblad v. Secretary-General of the United Nations, UNAT Judgment No. 183 [1974]*, available at http://untreaty.un.org/UNAT/UNAT_Judgements/Judgements_E/UNAT_00183_E.pdf, last visited on 30.12.2010, para. IV.

[248] Ibid., para. VII. In this connection the UNAT ruled in the present case that since the internal directive applicable in the case did not explicitly provide for the right to participate in the examination of the evidence, it did not give adequate protection to staff. Consequently, the staff member in question did not receive fair procedure and the disciplinary decision was found not well founded. – *ibid.*, paras. VII-VIII.

[249] *Zang-Atangana, UNAT Judgment No. 130 [1969]*, para. VI.

[250] See *UN Staff Regulations of 2007*, Articles X and XI; *UN Staff Rules of 2002*, Chapters X and XI. See also, for example, *Applicant v. Secretary-General of the United Nations, UNAT Judgment No. 1234 [2005]*, para. V. In this case the applicant was accused of tax fraud but the Joint Disciplinary Committee did not find that his conduct was intentional. The Secretary-General ignored the Committee's recommendation and summarily dismissed the applicant characterizing his conduct as serious misconduct. The UNAT found the Secretary'-General decision 'perplexing' in view of the fact that the Committee was a very specialized body with expertise in tax matters. In addition, it considered that the Secretary-General did not sufficiently justify his decision, nor did he support it by evidence. In his decision he merely stated that he disagreed with the Joint Disciplinary Committee's finding that the applicant had not intended to commit fraud against the UN and that his conduct had been inexcusable.

In 2009, this administrative machinery, handling UN disciplinary cases for decades, was abolished. The abolition occurred as part of a comprehensive reform of the system of internal justice. The reform also resulted in the abolition of the United Nations Administrative Tribunal, established in 1949, and its replacement by two new judicial instances.[251] The new 'system of administration of justice', as formally referred to, consists of the United Nations Dispute Tribunal and the United Nations Appeals Tribunal. The former deals with staff matters, including disciplinary cases, in the first instance and the latter in the second instance. The system of administration of justice includes mechanisms for 'informal resolution' of disputes between staff and the UN Administration, involving the UN ombudsman and mediation services as well as 'management evaluation'. In general, informal resolution of disputes through mediation by the ombudsman is 'encouraged', but management evaluation is obligatory and must precede the submission of the case to the United Nations Dispute Tribunal. However, the latter does not apply to disciplinary cases which may be submitted to the United Nations Dispute Tribunal directly.[252]

Of course, before a case reaches the level of the United Nations Dispute Tribunal and the United Nations Appeals Tribunal, disciplinary process must first take place in each instance of an alleged misconduct. Although the *UN Staff Regulations* and the *UN Staff Rules* no longer provide for administrative machinery in this respect, they still require a formal decision of the Secretary-General adopted after an investigation into the allegations has been conducted, followed by a disciplinary process in which due process rights of the staff member concerned have been fully respected.[253] The due process rights explicitly required by the *UN Staff Rules* include written notification of the charges against the staff member in question, an opportunity to respond to these charges and information on the right to seek legal assistance.[254] These as well as other rights are further worked out in the *Administrative Instruction,*

---

[251] See *General Assembly Resolution 61/261, A/RES/61/261*, 04.04.2007, available in the Official Document System of the United Nations, available at http://documents.un.org/, last visited on 30.12.2010; *General Assembly Resolution 62/228, A/RES/62/228*, 22.12.2007, available in the Official Document System of the United Nations, available at http://documents.un.org/, last visited on 30.12.2010; and *General Assembly Resolution 63/253*.See also *General Assembly Resolution 64/119, A/RES/64/119*, 16.12.2009, available in the Official Document System of the United Nations, available at http://documents.un.org/, last visited on 30.12.2010 and *Secretary-General's Bulletin, Transitional Measures Related to the Introduction of the New System of Administration of Justice, ST/SGB/2009/11*, 24.06.2009, available in the Human Resources Handbook of the United Nations, available at http://www.un.org/hr_handbook/English/, last visited on 30.12.2010.

[252] *UN Staff Regulations of 2009*, Article XI, and *Provisional Staff Rules, Report of the Secretary-General, A/65/202*, Chapter XI.

[253] Disciplinary procedures must be used in all cases of alleged misconduct, also in cases in which an administrative action could be employed. For example, in *Ortega, Hernandez, Canales and Garcia* the applicants, serving on fixed-term contracts, were found to be in breach of financial rules and as a consequence their contracts were not renewed. The UNAT ruled that such administrative action should only be used when it did not prejudice or damage the staff members' situation and was not detrimental to them. The non-renewal of the contract was, in the UNAT view, detrimental to the applicants as it *a priori* excluded a possibility of other sanction than separation from service, which could have been eventually used under disciplinary procedures. Such other sanction could have had a lesser effect on the applicant's situation than separation. - *Ortega, Hernandez, Canales and Garcia, UNAT Judgment No. 610 [1993]*, para. VIII.

[254] *Provisional Staff Rules, Report of the Secretary-General, A/65/202*, Rule 10.3(a).

Revised Disciplinary Measures and Procedures, ST/AI/371 of 1991 as amended in 2010 in the light of the new system of administration of justice.[255] The purpose of this instruction is to provide guidelines and directives on the application of relevant staff rules concerning disciplinary matters and to outline due process requirements which need to be adhered to in such matters.[256]

Pursuant to the instruction, each case in which there is a suspicion of misconduct begins with an investigation and fact-finding conducted by the Head of Department or Office or other responsible officer.[257] In practice, the investigation is normally conducted by the Office of Internal Oversight Services ('OIOS'), though other investigating entities may be employed as well.[258] The OIOS may conduct an investigation either on its own initiative or at the request of the Head of Department or Office. It may also receive and investigate reports of violations from individual UN staff members as well as other persons engaged in activities with the UN. The relevant procedures for investigation by the OIOS, including safeguards of due process, fairness, staff anonymity and protection of individual rights, are provided in the *Secretary-General's Bulletin, Establishment of the Office of Internal Oversight Services ST/SGB/273* of 1994 and in the OIOS *Investigations Manual*.[259] Furthermore, in the *Secretary-General's Bulletin, Protection Against Retaliation for Reporting Misconduct and for Cooperating with Duly Authorized Audits or Investigations ST/SGB/2005/21* of 2005 rules are set out for protecting those who report misconduct to the OIOS or other competent body or person, or who cooperate with an investigation.[260] This

---

[255] *Administrative Instruction, Revised Disciplinary Measures and Procedures*, and *Administrative Instruction Amending Administrative Instruction ST/AI/371, Revised Disciplinary Measures and Procedures, St/AI/371/Amend.1*, 11.05.2010, available in the Human Resources Handbook of the United Nations, available at http://www.un.org/hr_handbook/English/, last visited on 30.12.2010.

[256] *Administrative Instruction, Revised Disciplinary Measures and Procedures*, para. 1. Special administrative issuances apply to some distinct matters, such as cases of (alleged) misconduct arising from discrimination, (sexual) harassment and abuse of authority; instances of financial responsibility for gross negligence; or cases of non-compliance with private legal obligations. - *Secretary-General's Bulletin, Prohibition of Discrimination, Harassment, Including Sexual Harassment, and Abuse of Authority; Administrative Instruction, Financial Responsibility of Staff Members for Gross Negligence, ST/AI/2004/3*, 29.09.2004, available in the Human Resources Handbook of the United Nations, available at http://www.un.org/hr_handbook/English/, last visited on 30.12.2010 and *Administrative Instruction, Private Legal Obligations of Staff Members, ST/AI/2000/12*, 25.10.2000, available in the Human Resources Handbook of the United Nations, available at http://www.un.org/hr_handbook/English/, last visited on 30.12.2010. Technically speaking, the last mentioned cases (of non-compliance with private legal obligations) are not regarded as misconduct in the strict sense of the word. However, under Rule 1.2(b) of the *UN Staff Rules*, all UN staff members must comply with their private legal obligations and local laws and honour local court orders. Further, as explicitly specified in para. 2.4. of the administrative instruction ST/AI/2000/12, abuse of the UN privileges and immunities may lead to disciplinary action.

[257] *Administrative Instruction, Revised Disciplinary Measures and Procedures*, para. 2.

[258] See *Practice of the Secretary-General in Disciplinary Matters and Possible Criminal Behaviour, 1 July 2009 to 30 June 2010, Report of the Secretary-General, A/65/180*, Annex, p. 14.

[259] *Secretary-General's Bulletin, Establishment of the Office of Internal Oversight Services, ST/SGB/273*, 07.09.1994, available in the Human Resources Handbook of the United Nations, available at http://www.un.org/hr_handbook/English/, last visited on 30.12.2010, in particular Section IV, Part D; and *Office of Internal Oversight Services, Investigations Manual*, March 2009, available at http://www.un.org/Depts/oios/pages/id_manual_mar2009.pdf, last visited on 30.12.2010.

[260] *Secretary-General's Bulletin, Protection against Retaliation for Reporting Misconduct and for Cooperating*

protection is granted to all UN staff members who report misconduct or cooperate with an audit or investigation, including interns and UN volunteers.[261] It is, however, subject to the requirement of good faith. Section 2.3 of the Bulletin explicitly states that:

> *The transmission or dissemination of unsubstantiated rumours is not a protected activity. Making a report or providing information that is intentionally false or misleading constitutes misconduct and may result in disciplinary or other appropriate action.*[262]

Rumours or intentionally false accusations are thus not welcome in the UN. On the other hand, when a UN staff member truly believes there has been a breach of UN regulations and rules, he has a duty to report it and to cooperate with an audit or investigation. He is required to do so through established internal mechanisms, namely the OIOS, the Assistant Secretary-General for Human Resources Management, the relevant Head of Department or Office, or the focal point for reports of sexual exploitation and abuse, or, under certain circumstances, through external mechanisms.[263]

A complaint alleging retaliation against a staff member for reporting misconduct or for cooperating with an audit or investigation is to be reported to the Ethics Office. The Ethics Office keeps a confidential record of all complaints, conducts preliminary review of these complaints and, if it considers it appropriate, refers the matter to the OIOS for investigation. Eventually, after the investigation has been completed, the Ethics Office makes recommendations on the matter to either the Head of Department or Office, and/or Under Secretary-General for Management, Office of Ombudsman, Performance Management Board, other relevant office, or even to the Secretary-General, depending on the findings of the investigation and actions subsequently taken. If retaliation is indeed confirmed, it is in itself considered to be a misconduct leading to a disciplinary action.[264] Moreover, when a staff member claims retaliation against himself by way of a worsened performance evaluation, non-extension or termination of his appointment, or other unfavourable application of UN regulations, rules and administrative procedures, the burden of proof is on the UN Administration to show 'by clear and convincing evidence' that the

with Duly Authorized Audits or Investigations, *ST/SGB/2005/21*, 19.12.2005, available in the Human Resources Handbook of the United Nations, available at http://www.un.org/hr_handbook/English/, last visited on 30.12.2010.

[261] Ibid., Section 2.

[262] Ibid., Section 2.3. See also Sections 1.1, 1.2 and 2.1(b) where good faith is emphasized.

[263] Ibid., Sections 1.1, 1.2, 3 and 4.

[264] Ibid., Sections 5-7. The UN policy on protection against retaliation entered into force on 1 January 2006, when the Ethics Office was formally established, too. – Ibid., Section 9. In the period from mid-2009 to mid-2010, 36 complains of retaliation were received by the Ethics Office, 18 of which warranted a preliminary review. In 8 of these cases the review were completed. In 4 of the completed cases the conclusion was reached that there was no prima facie case of retaliation. In 4 other cases the requests were either withdrawn or abandoned by the complaining staff members. During the reporting period, the preliminary review was not yet completed in 10 cases. - *Activities of the Ethics Office, Report of the Secretary-General, A/65/343*, paras. 33 and 35.

application of the regulations, rules and procedures would have been the same in case the staff member in question did not report misconduct or cooperate with audit or investigation.[265]

Returning to the reported misconduct, when the investigation indicates that the allegations of misconduct are well-founded, the Head of Office reports the matter to the Assistant Secretary-General for Human Resources Management, including all known facts, existing evidence and, if warranted by the nature and gravity of the misconduct, a recommendation of an administrative leave of the staff member concerned during investigation and disciplinary proceedings in accordance with Rule 10.4 of the *UN Staff Rules*.[266] On behalf of the Secretary-General the Assistant Secretary-General decides whether the matter should be pursued and, if warranted, whether the staff member concerned should be placed on administrative leave. If the imposed administrative leave is without pay, the decision is taken by the Under-Secretary-General for Management. When the matter is not closed at this stage but pursued further, the dossier returns to the Head of Office or other responsible officer and the staff member is subsequently informed, in writing, of the allegations, of his right to defend himself and to seek legal assistance, and if warranted, of his placement on administrative leave, its reason and probable duration. He is also provided with a copy of the available documentary evidence.[267] Within the specified time or, if requested, an extended time, the staff member concerned may respond to the allegations. After the expiry of the time available for the response, the case is submitted to the Assistant Secretary-General for Human Resources Management, who may either close the case, or impose an administrative (non-disciplinary) measure, or recommend the imposition of one or more disciplinary measures. The decision on the imposition of a disciplinary measure is taken by the Under-Secretary-General for Management on behalf of the Secretary-General. The staff member concerned must be notified of a decision to impose a disciplinary measure. Surprisingly, the instruction does not require notification in cases in which disciplinary measures are not taken.[268] Decisions which do so may be challenged by a direct application to the United Nations Dispute Tribunal.[269]

It is interesting to note that, contrary to the past, at present disciplinary decisions are adopted in the UN Secretariat without involvement of a collective body that would better ensure the objectivity and impartiality of such decisions. Even though disciplinary decisions are subject to judicial review, it could be argued that the objectivity

[265] *Secretary-General's Bulletin, Protection against Retaliation for Reporting Misconduct and for Cooperating with Duly Authorized Audits or Investigations*, Section 2.2.

[266] *Administrative Instruction, Revised Disciplinary Measures and Procedures*, paras. 2-4. Paragraphs 4 and 5 specify conditions under which the placement on administrative leave make take place. The administrative leave may be with or without pay, the latter however only in exceptional circumstances. - *Provisional Staff Rules, Report of the Secretary-General, A/65/202*, Rule 10.4(c). See also, for example, *Kiwanuka, UNAT Judgment No. 941 [1999]*, paras. XI-XIII or *Case No. 1434, UNAT Judgment No. 1357 [2007]*, available at http://untreaty.un.org/UNAT/UNAT_Judgements/Judgements_E/UNAT_01357_E.pdf, last visited on 30.12.2010, paras. VI-VIII and XI.

[267] *Administrative Instruction, Revised Disciplinary Measures and Procedures*, paras. 5-6.

[268] Ibid., paras. 7-9.

[269] Ibid., para. 10.

and impartiality of the decision should be ensured already during the administrative stage of the disciplinary process, i.e. before the staff member concerned is found 'guilty' of misconduct by its employer.

2.3.6.3. Disciplinary measures

The list of disciplinary measures that may be imposed when a staff member is found to be guilty of misconduct is provided in Rule 10.2 of the *UN Staff Rules*. This list includes the following measures: written censure; loss of one or more steps in grade; deferment of eligibility for salary increment; suspension without pay; fine; deferment of eligibility for consideration for promotion; demotion with deferment of eligibility for consideration for promotion; separation from service; and dismissal. All mentioned deferments as well as suspension without pay are for a specified period. Further, separation from service may be with notice or with compensation instead of notice, and with or without termination indemnity.[270] Besides disciplinary measures, it may be also decided that an administrative, i.e. a 'non-disciplinary', measure will be imposed.[271] Such measures may take the form, for example, of written or oral reprimand and recovery of monies owed to the UN.[272] However, in case of these measures too, due process requirements must be adhered to by the UN Administration.[273]

The choice of a specific disciplinary (or administrative) measure is within the discretion of the Secretary-General or, to be more precise, the Under-Secretary-General who takes decisions on behalf of the Secretary-General. In fact, all decisions of the Secretary-General or officials who take decision on his behalf in the process of dealing with alleged misconduct are discretionary, including the decision to launch an investigation, to proceed with the disciplinary process and to impose a disciplinary measure.[274] Despite this broad discretion, however, when a disciplinary measure is

---

[270] *Provisional Staff Rules, Report of the Secretary-General, A/65/202*, Rule 10.2(a). While separation from service takes place upon expiration of the period of notice, dismissal has an immediate effect.

[271] Ibid., Rule 10.3(a).

[272] Ibid., Rule 10.2(b). Administrative leave imposed during the disciplinary process is also considered to be an administrative (i.e. non-disciplinary) measure. – Ibid.

[273] Ibid., Rule 10.3(a). See also, for example, *Case No. 1431, UNAT Judgment No. 1354 [2007]*, available at http://untreaty.un.org/UNAT/UNAT_Judgements/Judgements_E/UNAT_01354_E.pdf, last visited on 30.12.2010, para. IV. In this case, the UNAT explained that reprimand had adverse legal consequences on the staff member concerned, especially since it was kept in his personal file. The UN Administration must, therefore, 'maintain the procedural standards expected from the United Nations' and respect 'fundamental principles governing all legal orders of the modern world. Amongst those, of special importance is the principle of due process or natural justice'. – *Case No. 1431, UNAT Judgment No. 1354 [2007]*, para. IV.

[274] *Provisional Staff Rules, Report of the Secretary-General, A/65/202*, Rule 10.1(c). See also, for example, *Ying, UNAT Judgment No. 424 [1988]*, para. XV; *Kiwanuka, UNAT Judgment No. 941 [1999]*, para. IV; *Case No. 1354, UNAT Judgment No. 1271 [2005]*, available at http://untreaty.un.org/UNAT/UNAT_Judgements/Judgements_E/UNAT_01271_E.pdf, last visited on 30.12.2010, para. VI; and *Case No. 1456, UNAT Judgment No. 1391 [2008]*, para. X.

imposed, it must be proportionate to the nature and gravity of the misconduct.[275] As noted by the UNAT:

> *The proportionality principle has been used by the Tribunal as the ultimate criterion of the legality of the measure taken against the wrongdoer, especially because, according to the Tribunal and all contemporary legal systems, the measure imposed upon the staff member must correspond to the wrong done.*[276]

The imposition of a disproportionate sanction would, in the UNAT's view, amount to injustice and abuse of the Administration's discretion.[277]

3. Termination of service in the European Commission

The previous section explains that in the UN a distinction is made between the concept 'separation from service' and the concept 'termination of appointment'. While the former relates to all reasons for which an appointment of an individual staff member may end, the latter is limited to separation that takes place upon the UN Secretary-General's initiative. No such a distinction is made in the EU. There, all manners in which an individual appointment may end are covered by the concept 'termination of service'.

Reasons for which the service of EU officials may come to an end are listed in Article 47 of the *EU Staff Regulations*. This list contains seven items: resignation; compulsory resignation; retirement in the interests of the service; dismissal for incompetence; removal from post; retirement; and death. An additional reason is provided in Article 34 of the *EU Staff Regulations* dealing with probation. Unsurprisingly, EU officials on probation may be dismissed during or at the end of their probationary

[275] *Provisional Staff Rules, Report of the Secretary-General, A/65/202*, Rule 10.3(b).

[276] *Case No. 1494, UNAT Judgment No. 1428 [2008]*, para. III.

[277] For example, *Alok, UNAT Judgment No. 1123 [2003]*, para. IX. There are many cases in which the proportionality of the disciplinary sanction was at issue. In many of these cases the UNAT declared the sanction disproportionate. In *Iddi*, for example, the UNAT ruled that summary dismissal for a single small-scale fraud attempt in a long unblemished service of the applicant was disproportional. It held that an evaluation of circumstances and a scale of penalties in all cases should be in all cases, even cases of attempted thefts. - *Iddi, UNAT Judgment No. 1011 [2001]*, para. VII. In *Galindo*, the applicant, occupying a high-level post, stole a tube of toothpaste and was penalized for it by the UN Administration by demotion into a lower grade, with no possibility of promotion and no decision-making or managerial responsibilities. The UNAT held that the penalty was disproportionate, regarding the high position of the applicant and the nature of his offense, and concluding that the applicant's conduct had most probably occurred as a result of a temporary mental lapse. - *Galindo v. Secretary-General of the United Nations, UNAT Judgment No. 1151 [2003]*, available at http://untreaty.un.org/UNAT/UNAT_Judgements/Judgements_E/UNAT_01151_E.pdf, last visited on 30.12.2010, paras. IV and VIII.1. See also *Alok, UNAT Judgment No. 1123 [2003]*, para. IX. In this case, the UNAT took also account of the previous unblemished service record as well as the contribution of the applicant's health problems to his conduct. On the other hand, separation from service with compensation in lieu notice has been held as proportionate to a fraudulent conduct of the staff member who, on several occasions, claimed and accepted overtime payments for hours that she had not worked and, when confronted, lied about the number of her fraudulent actions. - *Case No. 1357, UNAT Judgment No. 1274 [2005]*, available at http://untreaty.un.org/UNAT/UNAT_Judgements/Judgements_E/UNAT_01274_E.pdf, last visited on 30.12.2010, para. VI.

period. Besides this, and despite the absence of an explicit legal provision to that effect, service of EU officials may also be terminated as a result of an agreement reached between the official concerned and the EU Administration.

As far as non-permanent staff serving in EU institutions, i.e. 'other servants', are concerned, termination of their service depends in principle on the type of contract they hold. As explained in the previous chapter of this study, an engagement concluded for a fixed-term normally ends upon the expiry of such period. Contracts for indefinite periods are terminated by giving a notice of termination on the date specified in the contract or otherwise set out in the *EU Conditions of Employment of Other Servants* or other relevant legal instrument adopted by the institution at issue.[278] Of course, both types of contracts may also end for other reasons provided in the mentioned documents, just as in the case of permanent appointments. They all are explained in this chapter.

3.1. Brief historical overview

The historical overview of the changes of the *UN Staff Regulations* regarding reasons for staff separation noted that there have been just a handful of changes in this respect. The situation is very similar in the EU where too relevant provisions have been modified just a few times. In addition, the changes in the *EU Staff Regulations* which did take place were less significant than those in the UN. Moreover, the list of reasons for termination of service provided in Article 47 of the *EU Staff Regulations* has remained intact since their first adoption in 1961. Although all but one provision relevant for termination of service have been amended one or more times, in most cases the amendments did not make significant substantive changes to the reasons for termination of service of EU officials. The one provision that has not changed since 1961 is Article 54 that concerns an honorary rank which may be given to an official whose service has ended.

The first amendment of the *EU Staff Regulations* regarding reasons and conditions for termination of service was adopted in 1972 and concerned Articles 48, 49 and 50. This amendment added a possibility to refuse the resignation of a staff member who was subject to ongoing disciplinary proceedings; added a possibility to require compulsory resignation in a post-invalidity situation; and modified the calculation of allowances due when an official is retired in the interests of the service.[279]

The second relevant amendment of the *EU Staff Regulations*, in 1985, modified Articles 50, 52 and 53. In Article 50, the amendment modified again the calculation formula for allowances due in case an official is retired in the interest of the service. The modification of Article 52 was of a greater importance as it increased the re-

[278] See above chapter 6, section 3.2.3.

[279] *Regulation No 1473/72 Amending EU Staff Regulations and Conditions of Employment of Other Servants*, Articles 15-17, amending Articles 48-50 of the *EU Staff Regulations*.

quired age for early retirement. The amendment of Article 53 related to the specification of the date of retirement occurring as a result of permanent invalidity.[280]

The third and the last amendment of the *EU Staff Regulations* of relevance to the issue of termination of service of EU officials is, unsurprisingly, the amendment of 2004 adopted as a result of the overall reform of the European Commission launched by its *White Paper* of 2000. This last amendment touched upon Articles 48-52, though changes worth mentioning related only to Article 51 concerning termination from service due to professional incompetence, Article 52 concerning retirement, and Annex IX to the *EU Staff Regulations* concerning disciplinary proceedings.[281] With regard to Article 51, the pre-2004 version of this provision was replaced by an entirely new version reflecting, as explained in more detail below, the criticism of the Committee of Independent Experts of 1999.[282] With regard to Article 52, certain flexibility in retirement of EU officials was introduced by allowing, on an exceptional basis, a possibility of retention of officials beyond the mandatory retirement age.[283] As far as Annex IX is concerned, the 2004 amendment of the *EU Staff Regulations* replaced the pre-2004 version of this Annex by a new version.[284] Most of the remaining modifications adopted in 2004 reflected facts, such as the new career structure in the Commission and did not have much substantive significance for the issue of termination of service.

The following sections explain in more detail all the reasons for termination of service in the European Commission, including applicable procedures. They also explain the background of the two most important improvements in 2004 of the possibility to terminate services for reasons of incompetence and as disciplinary action. Termination of non-permanent contracts is addressed afterwards.

3.2. Officials

3.2.1. Dismissal during or after probation

Article 34(1) of the *EU Staff Regulations* stipulates that before an official can be established, i.e. before he can be granted a permanent appointment, he must serve a probationary period of nine months. During this period and at its end the official may be dismissed if his work proves (obviously) inadequate. The threshold for dismissal during the probationary period is higher than that for dismissal at the end of the period since it may only take place when the official's performance is 'obviously inadequate'. Dismissal at the end of the probationary period only requires

[280] *Council Regulation (ECSC, EEC, Euratom) No 2799/85 of 27 September 1985 Amending the Staff Regulations of Officials and the Conditions of Employment of Other Servants of the European Communities*, OJ L 265, 08.10.1985, p. 1-10, Articles 2-4, amending Articles 50,52-53 of the *EU Staff Regulations*.

[281] *Regulation No 723/2004 Amending the EU Staff Regulations and Conditions of Employment of Other Servants*, Annex I, paras. 46-51, amending Articles 48-52 of the *EU Staff Regulations*.

[282] For details, see below, section 3.2.6.

[283] For details, see below, section 3.2.4.

[284] *Regulation No 723/2004 Amending the EU Staff Regulations and Conditions of Employment of Other Servants*, Annex I, para. 99, replacing Annex IX. For details, see below, section 3.2.7.

'inadequacy'. This difference clearly reflects the need to provide officials on probation with sufficient time to prove their merits. A premature interruption of this time is only allowed when it is 'obvious', i.e. evident, that continuation of probationary period would not lead to a different final outcome.

Dismissal *during* the probationary period must be based on a report communicated to the official concerned. The official may comment on the report in writing. The report, accompanied by the official's comments, are submitted by his immediate superior to the appointing authority which is required to consult on the case with the so-called Joint Reports Committee, established in accordance with Article 9(5) of, and Section 4 of Annex II to, the *EU Staff Regulations*. After such consultation, the appointing authority may decide to dismiss the official with one month's notice, or, exceptionally, authorize the continuation of the probationary period. When the probation is to continue, the official in question would normally be assigned to another department.[285]

Dismissal of an official *at the end* of the probationary period must also be based on a report, this time a regular one drawn up a month before the expiry of the period. When the report shows that the official's ability to perform his duties and/or his efficiency and conduct are not sufficient for permanent employment at the European Commission, the person may be either dismissed or, exceptionally, his probation may be extended. Both possible actions are taken by the appointing authority after the official has had an opportunity to comment on the report in writing and after the Joint Reports Committee has been consulted.[286] When the official is dismissed, he receives compensation, the amount depending on the length of service completed.[287] When the probationary period is extended, it may not exceed 15 months including the initial probationary period.[288] In this scenario, a second report may be drawn up at the end of the extended probationary period. Like the first end report, the second end report too may constitute the basis for the official's dismissal, too.[289]

The right of the official concern to express his view on the matter and the involvement of the Joint Reports Committee are important safeguards helping to ensure the objectivity and impartiality of the process leading to dismissal of probationary officials and to prevent its possible misuse or abuse by the EU Administration.

[285] *EU Staff Regulations*, Article 34(2). The Joint Reports Committee is consulted on actions following completion of probationary service and on the selection of staff to be affected by staff reduction. – Article 9(5). The Committee is composed of AD officials, a half of which are designated by the appointing authority and a half by the Staff Committee for a period of one year. – Annex II, Section 4, Article 10.

[286] Ibid., Article 34(3). Extension of the probationary period must be based on a report drawn up at the end of the probationary period, not on an interim report. As ruled by the European Union Civil Service Tribunal, a recommendation to extend the probationary period expressed in an interim report would not have any legal effect on the official's position. - *Cathy Sapara v. Eurojust, Case F-61/06*, available at http://eur-lex.europa.eu/LexUriServ/LexUriServ.do?uri=CELEX:62006W0061:EN:HTML, last visited on 30.12.2010, paras. 54 and 56.

[287] *EU Staff Regulations*, Article 34(5).

[288] Ibid., Article 34(4).

[289] *Peter John Krier Tither v Commission of the European Communities, Case 175/80, ECR [1981], p. 2345*, para. 12. See also *Sapara v. Eurojust, Case F-61/06*, para. 60.

3.2.2. Resignation

Unsurprisingly, also European Commission officials may leave the, in this case, EU civil service when they wish to do so. All they need to do is inform the Administration about their decision in writing and, in the absence of any other agreement, remain in the post for another three months if they serve as AD officials, or one month if they are AST officials. The relevant legal basis for resignation can be found in Article 48 of the *EU Staff Regulations* which stipulates:

> *An official who wishes to resign shall state unequivocally in writing his intention to leave the service of the institution definitively.*
>
> *The appointing authority shall take its decision confirming the resignation within one month of receiving the letter of resignation. The appointing authority may, however, refuse to accept the resignation if disciplinary proceedings against the official are in progress at the date of receipt of the letter of resignation or if such proceedings are started within the following 30 days.*
>
> *Resignation shall take effect on the date specified by the Appointing Authority; that date shall not be more than three months after the date proposed by the official in his letter of resignation in the case of officials in function group AD, and not more than one month in the case of officials in function group AST.*[290]

Hence, although resignation is a unilateral termination of employment by the official, the EU Administration is expected to formally confirm it by a decision. On the other hand, a refusal to accept resignation is only possible in cases of pending or shortly expected disciplinary proceedings against the resigning official. In any other case, refusal to accept resignation would be illegal.[291] The obvious objective of the rule allowing the Commission to refuse resignation in disciplinary cases is to ensure that officials do not circumvent their responsibility by leaving the service. However, it should be noted that the Commission is not obliged to retain a resigning official subject to disciplinary proceedings in service. It may accept such official's resignation if his departure would not prevent the start or the continuation of disciplinary proceedings or if the departure in itself would offer an alternative solution to the problem dealt with in the disciplinary proceedings.

3.2.3. Compulsory resignation

Apart from voluntary resignation, the *EU Staff Regulations* also provide for compulsory resignation which means that officials may be required to resign. Unsurprisingly,

[290] *EU Staff Regulations*, Article 48. This provision has been modified two times since its original adoption in 1961. The first modification of 1972 introduced the right of the appointing authority to refuse to accept officials' resignation in case of pending or expected disciplinary proceedings (currently to be found in the second paragraph). The second modification took place in 2004, reflecting the transformation of former staff categories (A, LA, B, C, D) into new function groups AD and AST.

[291] See, for example, *Alberto Campolongo v. High Authority of the European Coal and Steel Community, Joined cases 27-59 and 39-59, ECR [1960], English special edition, p. 391*, pp. 402-404.

this may happen only in limited, clearly defined, circumstances. They are explicitly listed in Article 49 of the *EU Staff Regulations* which stipulates the following:

> *An official may be required to resign only where he ceases to fulfill the conditions laid down in Article 28 (a), or in the cases provided for in Articles 39, 40 and 41(4) and (5) and in the second paragraph of Article 14 of Annex VIII.*[292]

There are thus six instances in which officials may be asked to leave the European Commission service on the basis of Article 49. The first instance relates to two of the conditions laid down in Article 28 (a) of the *EU Staff Regulations*, fulfillment of which is a prerequisite of any permanent appointment with the European Commission. They concern nationality and full rights as a citizen. In principle, only nationals of EU Member States may be appointed, and remain, EU officials. Exceptions are possible but they need to be authorized. Appointment and continuation in service with EU institutions are also subject to the possession of full rights as a citizen. Hence, when a Commission official loses the nationality of an EU Member State without acquiring the nationality of another EU Member State or when he loses his full rights as a citizen, he may be required to resign, though in the former case an exception may be granted.

The second legal ground for a possible compulsory resignation is to be found in Article 39 of the *EU Staff Regulations.* It concerns officials who should return to active employment with the Commission after having been temporarily seconded to another EU or non-EU institution or organization at their own request. Such officials may be required to resign if they decline for the second time to take up a post that has been offered to them upon return if the offered post corresponds to the official's grade. It should be noted, however, that here the resignation is not a necessary consequence of the refusal, it is a possibility. It is up to the appointing authority to decide whether it requires resignation or not. If it so decides, it must first consult the relevant Joint Committee established in accordance with Article 9 of, and Section 2 of Annex II to the *EU Staff Regulations*.[293]

A very similar situation exists with regard to compulsory resignation based on the third provision referred to in Article 49, namely Article 40. It deals with leave on personal grounds and provides for compulsory resignation of officials who refuse the second post offered to them upon the expiry of their leave. Again, the request

---

[292] *EU Staff Regulations*, Article 49. This provision was modified two times in past, in 1972 and in 2004. The 1972 modification added a new ground for compulsory resignation – Article 14(2) of Annex VIII. The 2004 amendment removed one ground for compulsory resignation which used to be included in Article 13 of the *EU Staff Regulations* relating to cases of an incompatible nature of the employment of an official's spouse with that of the official.

[293] Ibid., Article 39(f). EU institutions may have their own Joint Committee or Committees, or a common Joint Committee for two or more institutions. In all cases, Joint Committee are composed of a chairman appointed by the appointing authority and members and alternates appointed in equal numbers by the appointing authority and by the Staff Committee. – Annex II, Section 2, Article 2. The Joint Committees carry out functions assigned to them by the EU Staff Regulations, such as consultation in certain cases of staff separation. Moreover, they may be consulted by the appointing authority or by the Staff Committee on questions of a general nature. - Article 9(4).

to resign is within the discretion of the appointinq authority and involves a prior consultation with the Joint Committee.[294]

The fourth and the fifth legal grounds, on the basis of which the appointing authority could require an official to resign, can be found in Article 41(4) and (5) of the *EU Staff Regulations*. Article 41 is concerned with officials placed on non-active status when they become 'supernumerary' due to reduction of posts in their institution.[295] The decision on reduction of posts is taken by an appropriate budgetary authority under the budgetary procedure. On the basis of such a decision, the relevant appointing authority determines what type of posts will be affected and draws up a list of officials who will be placed on non-active status. When doing so, it must take into account officials' 'ability, efficiency, conduct in service, family circumstances and seniority'. Both decisions, i.e. the decision on post reduction and the decision on posts and officials affected, are taken after the Joint Committee has been consulted.[296]

Officials who are placed on non-active status receive an allowance for a period of time specified in Annex IV of the *EU Staff Regulations*. If during this period the official at issue in not reinstated, he will be required to resign. The appointing authority does not possess any discretion in deciding upon this resignation – Article 41(4) clearly stipulates that resignation 'shall' be required.[297] It should be emphasized, however, that compulsory resignations do not take place immediately after posts reduction. Rather, the officials affected by posts reduction are first assigned non-active status. This means that although they do stop performing their duties and lose the right to receive remuneration and to advance to a higher grade, they receive an allowance and continue to accumulate rights to a retirement pension. In addition, such officials have the right to be considered by priority for any posts in their function group and grade that fall vacant during the first two years of their non-active status.[298] Compulsory resignation becomes thus relevant only when no reinstatement has taken place before the expiry of the period during which the officials receive the allowance.

A different situation occurs under Article 41(5), pursuant to which an official may be asked to resign if he had been offered a post corresponding to his grade but has declined it without offering a good reason.[299] In such a case, compulsory resignation is an option and it is up to the appointing authority to decide whether it proceeds this way. Moreover, in this situation a compulsory resignation may also occur after the first job offer has been refused. The situations mentioned above (under Article 39 on secondment and Article 40 on leave on personal grounds) required two refusals. In

[294] Ibid., Article 40(4)(d). A purely formal acceptance of a post which is not put into effect in reality by taking up the post at the fixed date may also be regarded as a refusal to accept the post. - *Salvatore Belfiore v. Commission of the European Communities, Case 108/79, ECR [1980], p. 1769*, para. 15.

[295] *EU Staff Regulations*, Article 41(1).

[296] Ibid., Article 41(2).

[297] Ibid., Article 41(4).

[298] Ibid., Article 41(3), second paragraph.

[299] Ibid., Article 41(5).

all relevant cases, however, the offered position must be at the grade lastly occupied by the official in question. Furthermore, the Joint Committee must be consulted before any decision on compulsory resignation is adopted.

The last situation in which compulsory resignation may take place is provided for in Article 14(2) of Annex VIII to the *EU Staff Regulations* and relates to a post-invalidity situation. Article 14(2) stipulates that when the requirements for payment of invalidity allowance are no longer satisfied by an official and this official refuses a second offer for a post corresponding to his category and career bracket, he may be required to resign.[300]

To sum up, compulsory resignation may thus occur when an official ceases to possess the nationality of a EU Member State or full rights as a citizen (Article 28(2)); when an official due to return to active employment from secondment or leave on personal grounds or invalidity pension fails to accept a second post offer (Articles 39, 40, and Article 14(2) of Annex VII); and when an official on non-active status due to post reduction refuses a post offer without good reason (Article 41(5)). In addition, compulsory resignation will affect an official on non-active status due to posts reduction, if no job is found for him during a set period of time (Article 41(4)). With the exception of this last listed situation, the appointing authority enjoys discretion in deciding on compulsory resignations. Procedurally, in all cases of compulsory resignation the official concerned must be heard and the Joint Committee must be consulted, before a decision by the appointing authority is taken.[301] These two requirements help to guarantee that compulsory resignation occurs only in cases in which it is objectively justified.

3.2.4. Retirement or death

Retirement is another legal ground that compels officials to leave the EU civil service. The employment comes to end automatically upon reaching the retirement age which is 65 years in the European Commission.[302] Recognition of permanent incapacity to perform duties due to health reasons has the same consequence as reaching the mandatory retirement age.[303] In both cases, the official is retired on the last day of the month in which the situation occurred.[304]

Retirement on invalidity grounds is based on a decision of the Invalidity Committee which consists of three medical doctors, one appointed by the official concerned, one by the appointing authority of the EU institution to which this official belongs, and one by agreement between the first two doctors.[305] The proceedings of the Invalidity Committee are secret but its conclusions are, of course, communicated

[300] Ibid., Annex VIII, Article 14(2).

[301] Ibid., Article 49, second paragraph.

[302] Ibid., Article 52(a). Until 1985, the retirement age of the EU officials was 63 years. – see *Regulation No 2799/85 Amending the EU Staff Regulations and Conditions of Employment of Other Servants* .

[303] *EU Staff Regulations*, Article 53.

[304] Ibid., Articles 52(a) and 53.

[305] Ibid., Article 9(1)(b) and Annex II, Article 7.

to both the appointing authority and the official concerned. Unsurprisingly, the latter may submit to the Committee any certificate or report he receives from his own physician or any other medical practitioner he has consulted.[306] When, having considered the case, the Invalidity Committee concludes that the official concerned suffers from 'total permanent invalidity preventing him from performing the duties corresponding to a post in his career bracket', he is automatically retired.[307] Until such official reaches 63 years of age allowing for early retirement, he receives an invalidity allowance. The allowance is, however, only due as long as the official at issue remains incapacitated for work.[308] To ascertain whether that is the case, the Commission may have officials retired on grounds of invalidity periodically medically examined.[309] If the examination shows that the conditions for granting invalidity allowance are no longer met, i.e. when an official is no longer prevented from performing his duties for reasons of health, he is reinstated in a suitable vacant post or, as mentioned above, if he refuses two posts offered to him, his service is terminated through compulsory resignation.[310]

As for retirement occurring as a result of reaching 65 years of age, this too is compulsory and automatic. However, deviation from this basic rule is possible, in both directions. EU officials may retire before the mandatory retirement age has been reached and they may remain in service afterwards.

The possibility of early retirement is provided for officials of at least 63 years of age, and for the officials between 55 and 63 years of age who satisfy conditions for immediate payment of a pension.[311] Early retirement occurs solely upon request of the official and may be refused by the appointing authority on the same ground on which resignation may be rejected, i.e. ongoing or shortly expected disciplinary proceedings.[312] When an official below 63 years of age retires, he may choose to have payment of his pension deterred until he turns 63 or paid immediately. In the latter case, however, the pension is reduced in accordance with Article 9(1) of Annex VIII to the *EU Staff Regulations*, unless the retired official at issue is successful in the call for applications for early retirement without reduction of pension rights, annually

[306] Ibid., Annex II, Article 9.

[307] Ibid., Annex VIII, Article 13(1). See also Article 53. The decision to retire an official on the ground of incapacity due to health reasons may be challenged. This includes all steps that precede the retirement decision, such as the formation of the Invalidity Committee. – See, for example, *Cesare Alfieri v. European Parliament, Case 3/66, ECR [1966], p. 437*.

[308] *EU Staff Regulations*, Article 78 and Annex VIII, Articles 13(1) and 14, first paragraph.

[309] Ibid., Annex VIII, Article 15.

[310] Ibid., Article 49 and Annex VIII, Article 14, second paragraph. See also above, section 3.2.3.

[311] Ibid., Article 52(b). See also Article 77, last paragraph, which provides that age of 63 years is the pensionable age in the EU. The EU pension schemes, including requirements for immediate payment of a pension in cases of early retirement, are set out in Annex VIII to the *EU Staff Regulations*. It appears that not many officials use the possibility of earlier retirement. Spence and Stevens argue that this is due to 'substantial disincentives' to retire early and 'considerable incentives' not to retire until the mandatory age of retirement, i.e. 65 years, is reached. - Spence and Stevens, *Staff and Personnel Policy in the Commission*, p. 190.

[312] *EU Staff Regulations*, Article 52(b).

offered by the Commission to a number of officials (as well as temporary agents) pursuant to Article 9(2) of the same Annex VIII to the *EU Staff Regulations*.[313]

The possibility of remaining in service *after* the retirement age of 65 years was introduced only in 2004.[314] The Commission explained in its *White Paper* of 2000 that such flexibility was needed in order to ensure optimum use of the available human resources.[315] That said, retention of Commission officials beyond the mandatory retirement age is regarded as an exception and is subject to the interest of the service which must justify the retention in each individual case. The decision on retention beyond the retirement age is taken by the appointing authority upon request of the official concerned. And while there is no limitation on, for example, grade or type of work such official may occupy or do, the *EU Staff Regulations* prohibit retention of officials beyond the maximum age of 67. When that age is reached, the official at issue is automatically retired.[316]

Naturally, when a European Commission official dies before he reaches the retirement age, his employment ends on the date of death.

3.2.5. Retirement in the interests of the service

Apart from the possibility of retiring before the mandatory retirement age of 65, certain Commission officials may retire earlier when the interests of the service require it. As noted before in this study, such retirement is permitted in the case of senior officials, i.e. Directors and (Deputy) Directors-General.[317] Another important difference with the regular early retirement is that retirement in the interests of the service occurs upon the initiative of the EU Administration, not upon request of the official in question. Moroever, the EU Administration is not limited by any conditions or requirements in deciding to retire an official in the interests of the service other than his rank.[318] The Administration enjoys thus wide discretion under Article 50, the provision of the *EU Staff Regulations* applicable to retirement in the interests of the service.

---

[313] *Regulation No 723/2004 Amending the EU Staff Regulations and Conditions of Employment of Other Servants*, Annex VIII, Article 9; and *Commission Decision, General Implementing Provisions on the Early Retirement of Officials and Temporary Agents without Reduction of Pension Rights, C(2004)1588 final/5*, 28.04.2004, available in the Register of Commission Documents, available at http://ec.europa.eu/transparency/regdoc/registre.cfm?CL=en, last visited on 30.12.2010 and *Decision Amending the General Implementing Provisions on the Early Retirement of Officials and Temporary Agents without Reduction of Pension Rights C(2004) 1588 of 28 April 2004*, 10.08.2006, available in the Register of Commission Documents, available at http://ec.europa.eu/transparency/regdoc/registre.cfm?CL=en, last visited on 30.12.2010.

[314] *Regulation No 723/2004 Amending the EU Staff Regulations and Conditions of Employment of Other Servants*, Annex I, para. 51.

[315] *Reforming the Commission - A White Paper - Part I*, Part IV, Section IV.2.

[316] *EU Staff Regulations*, Article 52, second paragraph.

[317] Ibid., Article 50. See also above, chapter 6, section 3.2.1.

[318] *Almini v. Commission, Case 19/70*, para. 10.

This type of retirement may, however, not be invoked for personal reasons of individual officials who, for example, wish to leave the service. Officials themselves may not request to be retired in the interest of service (and to receive the benefits connected with such a retirement); if they desire to leave the EU service, they must resort to resignation. An interesting situation occurred in this respect in *Peco*, a case brought before the ECJ in 1970. Mr. Peco was a senior official at the European Commission and was appointed to a new position which he accepted. Before commencing his new duties, however, Mr. Peco applied for another post that fell vacant in the meantime but his application was not successful. Subsequently, Mr. Peco requested that his service with the European Commission was terminated as he did not feel sufficiently qualified for the new post to which he was previously appointed. Later he requested that he be retired in the interest of the service, providing the same reason. The Commission refused both his requests, considering that Mr. Peco was capable of performing his new duties. In reaction, Mr. Peco informed the Commission that he felt compelled to resign. He also requested benefits that applied to the retirement in the interest of the service. The Commission accepted Mr. Peco's resignation but refused to grant him the benefits requested.[319] The ECJ upheld the Commission decision and ruled that any arrangements relating to compulsory retirement were only applicable in the interest of the service, not in the interest of individual officials.[320]

It is interesting to note that retirement in the interests of the service does not always lead to an actual retirement of the official concerned. Such official may also be assigned to another post corresponding to his grade. This follows from the third paragraph of Article 50 which stipulates that if an official retired in the interests of the service is not assigned to another post, he will receive the same kind of allowance as that available to officials having non-active status due to the reduction of posts.[321] In *Oslizlok* the ECJ noted that a decision not to reassign an official to another post cannot follow automatically from the decision to retire the official in the interest of the service but must rather be based on appropriate considerations. Even though in case of both decisions the European Commission enjoys a wide discretion, it must examine factors relevant to either of the decisions. In addition, the official at issue must in both instances be given an opportunity to effectively defend his interests.[322] However, officials whom the institution decides to retire under Article 50 and who are under consideration for reassignment do not have any right to receive preferential treatment over other qualified officials.[323]

Last but not the least, the second paragraph of Article 50 explicitly notes that retirement in the interests of the service is not a disciplinary measure. In practice,

---

[319] *Franco Peco v. Commission of the European Communities, Case 36/69, ECR [1970], p. 361*, paras. 3-9.

[320] Ibid., paras. 23-26.

[321] *EU Staff Regulations*, Article 50, third paragraph and Annex IV.

[322] *Oslizlok v. Commission, Case 34/77*, paras. 18 and 27-30. See also *Almini v. Commission, Case 19/70*, para. 11.

[323] *Enrico Angelini v. Commission of the European Communities, Case 131/82, ECR [1983], p. 2801*, para. 14 and *Jean-Claude Renaud v. Commission of the European Communities, Case 148/82, ECR [1983], p. 2823*, para. 12. Both these cases were decided on the same day.

however, Article 50 may be used instead of a disciplinary action.[324] Considering that no conditions or requirements other than the existence of 'the interests of the service' are in place, and that 'the interests of the service' are nowhere precisely defined, it could be an easy and speedy manner of removing a senior official suspected of misconduct. Given broad discretion of the EU Administration under Article 50, there are few possibilities, if any, to prevent the use of this provision for removal of an individual official suspected of misconduct, or even for any other reason. On the other hand, it appear that such risk is considered acceptable and a consequence of the specific nature of senior appointments.

3.2.6. Dismissal for incompetence

Another legal ground for termination of service of European Commission officials, explicitly noted as *not* being a disciplinary measure, is dismissal for incompetence. Such dismissal can take place in accordance with Article 51 of the *EU Staff Regulations*, a provision which was fundamentally amended in 2004. The pre-2004 version of Article 51 was rather straightforward and stipulated the following:

> 1. *An official who proves incompetent in the performance of his duties may be dismissed.*
>
> *The appointing authority may, however, offer to classify the official in a lower grade.*
>
> 2. *Any proposal for the dismissal of an official shall set out the reasons on which it is based and shall be communicated to the official concerned. He shall be entitled to make any comments thereon which he considers relevant.*
>
> *The appointing authority shall take a reasoned decision, after following the procedure laid down in Annex IX.*[325]

It is important to note in this respect that Annex IX deals with disciplinary proceedings. The referral to this Annex in Article 52 dealing with professional incompetence demonstrates that the pre-2004 approach to staff incompetence was a punitive one. The 2004 amendment introduces a new approach. Incompetence is no longer to be regarded as misbehavior, having an inevitable negative flavor, but rather as a situation requiring special attention and help.

The old approach was criticized by the 1999 *Committee of Independent Experts* which pointed to 'the relatively widespread tendency to confuse professional incompetence with disciplinary offenses'.[326] The Committee stressed that although the same procedure of Annex IX was to be applied to both situations, the two concepts were quite different. The Committee was of the opinion that professional incompetence called for a constructive approach seeking initially a solution to the problem and not punishment. Dismissal under Article 51 should, in the Committee's view, be

[324] *EU Staff Regulations*, Article 50, second paragraph.

[325] *EU Staff Regulations of 1968*, Article 51. This provision was amended only once, in 2004.

[326] *Second Report on Reform of the Commission of 1999, Volume II*, para. 6.5.62.

used only when other efforts do not lead to improvement of the performance.[327] The Committee also emphasized that not taking action under Article 51 was not an option and pointed out that thus far such action had been taken but rarely. It acknowledged that Article 51 itself was 'far from being a model of clarity' and set out merely the measures that may be taken, which are, in addition, disproportionate and excessive.[328]

This criticism was well received by the newly appointed European Commission which proposed and obtained an amendment of Article 51, departing from the disciplinary approach to incompetence. The amended version of Article 51 abolished reference to Annex IX and replaced it by a requirement of procedure to be established by each EU institution in order to 'identify, deal with and remedy cases of incompetence in a timely and appropriate fashion'.[329] The primary responsibility to deal with staff incompetence lies thus with the EU Administration. The Administration needs to take appropriate steps and solve the problem and only when the performance of an official at issue remains unsatisfactory despite the Administration's efforts, may the appointing authority proceed with Article 51.

There are no official internal rules or procedures within the European Commission for addressing underperformance, though. This is regrettable, and rather surprising considering that it was the Commission itself that introduced the requirement for special procedures in Article 51 of the *EU Staff Regulations*. On its internet site, the European Commission states the following:

> *The Commission's annual staff appraisal monitors achievements, skills and conduct. If a member of staff finds it difficult to meet the standards required, he/she will be expected to follow a remedial coaching programme, which includes specific targets to be achieved within a certain time frame. In the worst case scenario, where underperformance persists after efforts to remedy the situation have been exhausted, a dismissal or downgrading procedure can be launched under article 51 of the Staff Regulations.* [330]

It thus seems that when an official is found underperforming, he receives special coaching before Article 51 is invoked. The latter provides for a procedure to be followed in case such coaching fails. The procedure of Article 51 begins with a proposal by the appointing authority of a measure which should be taken. That measure does not necessarily need to be dismissal since the underperforming official may also be downgraded or classified in a lower function group at the same grade or at a lower grade.[331] The proposal of the appointing authority must be communicated to the official concerned and to the Joint Advisory Committee established especially for cases

[327] Ibid., paras. 6.5.62.-6.5.63.

[328] Ibid., paras. 6.5.61. and 6.5.66.

[329] *EU Staff Regulations*, Article 51(1).

[330] The European Commission Civil Service Portal, section on Ethics and Conduct, available at http://ec.europa.eu/civil_service/admin/ethic/index_en.htm#5 , last visited on 4.11.2010.

[331] *EU Staff Regulations*, Article 51(1). The post-2004 version of Article 51 is lengthy and elaborated. The provision consists of as many as 694 words, compared to 86 words in the pre-2004 version.

of professional incompetence.[332] This Committee is a standing body appointed for three years and composed of a chairman and at least two members who are senior officials. When the case of professional incompetence concerns a non-senior official, the Committee consists of two more members from the same function group and of the same grade as the official at issue. However, when the case concerns a senior official, the standing Committee is not used. Instead, a special *ad hoc* Joint Advisory Committee is established, made up of four members of a grade which is at least equal to that of the official at issue. In all instances, half the members of the (standing or *ad hoc*) Joint Advisory Committee are designated by the Staff Committee and half by the appointing authority.[333]

Having considered the case of underperformance, the Joint Advisory Committee adopts a reasoned opinion on the matter as well as a proposal of an appropriate measure. Both the reasoned opinion and the proposal are sent to the appointing authority and the official concerned. Having heard the latter, the appointing authority then adopts a final decision which must state reasons and indicate the date on which this decision takes effect.[334] When the official in question is dismissed, he receives a dismissal allowance, as well as certain family and household allowance. The allowances are paid for up to 12 months, depending on the length of service. It is *not* paid when the official at issue resigns after the procedure for incompetence has been started, or if he is entitled to the full pension payment. When the official in question is not dismissed but downgraded or reclassified, he may request removal of the reference to this measure from his personal files after six years.[335]

During the whole process, the official at issue has the right to obtain his full personal file, to make copies of all documents related to the procedure, to prepare his defense within 15 days from the receipt of the proposal, to be assisted by any person of his choice, to submit written comments, to call witnesses and to be heard.[336] The same rights apply to the official who represents the Commission Administration.[337] As far as the substance of the assessment is concerned, according to settled case law, the (in)competence of an individual official must be evaluated against all factors included in Article 43 of the *EU Staff Regulations* concerning periodic staff reports, i.e. efficiency, ability and conduct. Moreover, the jurisprudence requires that the official's career as a whole be taken into consideration.[338]

Last but not the least, special rules exist for addressing underperformance of Commission middle management staff. When such staff are assessed as performing poorly or insufficiently in two consecutive performance reports prepared during the Commission annual Career Development Review, they are first further assessed

---

[332] Ibid., Article 51(2).

[333] Ibid., Annex II, Article 12.

[334] Ibid., Article 51(5).

[335] Ibid., Article 51(6)-(8).

[336] Ibid., Article 51(3).

[337] Ibid., Article 51(4).

[338] *Franco Vecchioli v. Commission of the European Communities, Case 101/79, ECR [1980], p. 3069*, paras. 7 and 34.

by one of 20 senior officials assisting in personnel matters. When the reassessing senior official comes to the same conclusion, i.e. that the performance of the middle manager in question does not meet the required standard, the case is referred to the Consultative Committee on Appointments. This Committee examines the case and issues an opinion in which it may recommend transfer of the middle manager in question to another post, managerial or non-managerial. The final decision is taken by the relevant Director-General who follows the opinion of the Committee and acts in agreement with the President of the Commission as well as the Commissioner for Human Resources and Security and for the portfolio Commissioner.[339]

3.2.7. Removal from post

Article 86 of the *EU Staff Regulations* provides:

> *Any failure by an official or former official to comply with his obligations under these Staff Regulations, whether intentionally or through negligence on his part, shall make him liable to disciplinary action.*[340]

The list of obligations of EU officials, as well as their rights, can be found in Title II of the *EU Staff Regulations*. This list contains, among others, an obligation to perform one's duties and conduct oneself solely with the interest of the EU in mind, with objectivity, independence and impartiality, including a prohibition of seeking or taking instructions from authorities outside one's institution and a duty of loyalty to the organization.[341] It also contains obligations relating to issues, such as acceptance of honours, decorations, favours, gifts or payments; psychological or sexual harassment; outside activities; employment of spouses; running for public office, post-employment activities and behaviour; disclosure of information; freedom of expression; publishing; rights in writings or other work, including inventions, done in the performance of duties; residence; obedience and responsibility to supervisors; compensation of damage caused; and reporting misconduct of other officials.[342] Moreover, Article 12 of the *EU Staff Regulations* contains a general obligation to 'refrain from any action or behaviour which may reflect adversely upon [the official's]

[339] *Commission Decision on Middle Management Staff*, Article 13(1)(2). In order to avoid possible problems with good performance of middle managers serving probationary period (i.e. newly appointed middle managers who have not served at least two years in a middle management post prior to their appointment), these officials are subject to a two-phase evaluation. It includes a mid-term review after first five months and a final assessment at the end of the probationary period (which is nine months). As explicitly stated by the Commission, these two evaluations are different from the regular Career Development Review which is the basis for the annual performance appraisal of all Commission staff. The objective of the specific two-phase evaluation is to 'check whether the person being assessed has the qualities needed to carry out his or her management role effectively'. – *ibid.*, Article 11(2). Details on mid-term review and final assessment of middle managers serving probationary period can be found in Article 11(3),(4) and (5).

[340] *EU Staff Regulations*, Article 86(1).

[341] Ibid., Article 11, first paragraph and Article 11a.

[342] Ibid., Articles 11, second paragraph, and 12a- 22b.

position'.[343] This is a very broad obligation clearly linked to 'the highest standard of ... integrity' required from all EU staff.[344]

A breach of any of these or other obligations contained in the *EU Staff Regulations* may, as mentioned above, lead to disciplinary action. Such action may eventually result in the imposition of a disciplinary measure, one of them being removal from the post, i.e. termination of service of the official in question.[345] Of course, any disciplinary sanctions may only be imposed after disciplinary proceedings established by the *EU Staff Regulations* and/or other relevant legal instruments have taken place, offering the official accused of a breach of his obligations an adequate opportunity to defend himself. In the *EU Staff Regulations*, such disciplinary proceedings are set out in Annex IX which was, like Article 51 on professional incompetence, fundamentally modified under the 2004 amendment of the *EU Staff Regulations*. The modifications were based on the analysis of shortcoming of the previous system conducted by the Committee of Independent Experts of 1999. These shortcomings related, *inter alia*, to lack of legal basis and appropriate rules for the beginning stages of the disciplinary procedure (its opening and the investigation); the *ad hoc* as well as too internal character of the disciplinary board; the absence of a representative of the appointing authority in the proceedings before the disciplinary board; the absence of any correlation between misconduct and disciplinary measures; and the length of the proceedings.[346] In the *White Paper, Reforming the Commission* of 2000, the Commission accepted the majority of recommendations for improvement of the existing disciplinary proceedings made by the Committee of Independent Experts.[347] Many of them have been implemented through the 2004 amendment of the *EU Staff Regulations*, the most important ones being: the merger of all provisions on disciplinary rules, procedures and measures as well as rules and proceedings covering administrative investigations into one set of rules;[348] the introduction of a legal basis for the launch of an investigation by the European Anti-Fraud Office ('OLAF') or by a relevant appointing authority;[349] the introduction of new rules on the protection of officials who report misconduct and of additional channels through which alleged wrongdoing may be reported;[350] the specification of the rights of the official concerned before the official disciplinary procedure is started;[351] the introduction of

[343] Ibid., Article 12.

[344] Ibid., Article 27, first paragraph.

[345] Ibid., Article 47(e) and Annex IX, Article 9(1)(h).

[346] *Second Report on Reform of the Commission of 1999, Volume II*, paras. 6.6.23.-6.6.34.

[347] *Reforming the Commission - A White Paper - Part I*, Chapter IV, Section IV. 5 and *Reforming the Commission - A White Paper - Part II - Action Plan*, Chapter IV, Section XX.

[348] *EU Staff Regulations*, Annex IX. Before 2004, 'disciplinary measures' were set out in Articles 86 to 89 of the *EU Staff Regulations*, while 'disciplinary procedures' were contained in Annex IX of the *EU Staff Regulations*. In addition, the disciplinary board was defined in Articles 4 to 6 of Annex II of the *EU Staff Regulations*. Currently, all these rules are contained in Annex IX. The only provision which remained in the main text of the *EU Staff Regulations* is Article 86. This provision defines the misconduct (Article 86(1)), provides a legal basis for start of investigations (Article 86(2)) and refers to Annex IX for the remaining issues (Article 86(3)).

[349] Ibid., Article 86(2).

[350] Ibid., Articles 22a, 22b and 90a.

[351] Ibid., Annex IX, Articles 1 and 2.

the standing character of the disciplinary board;[352] and the introduction of the right of the appointing authority to be represented in proceedings before the disciplinary board.[353]

Not all recommendations of the Committee of Independent Experts have, however, been taken over and/or implemented. To begin with, the Committee called for the composition of a disciplinary board which would be less internal. In the Committee's view, such composition would better guarantee the impartiality and credibility of proceedings and prevent things from being kept 'in the family'.[354] Before 2004, all members of the disciplinary board had to be officials, with the exception of the chairman, who could come from outside the institution. The chairman, however, did not possess voting rights, unless the matter under consideration was a procedural issue or votes were tied.[355] After the 2004 amendment, Annex IX of the *EU Staff Regulations* requires that 'at least one member' of the board comes from outside the institution but that one person may, again, be the chairman whose voting rights remained unchanged.[356] In the European Commission, the chairperson of the disciplinary board is indeed to be a former official or former member of the EU institutions. The deputy chairperson is an official serving at the AD15 or AD 16 level. Other members of the disciplinary board established in the Commission are officials.[357] Since no more than one member 'must' come from outside the institution, in practice the composition of the disciplinary board can be, and as evidenced by the internal Commission rules also is, exactly the same as under the previous system. With the total number of members of the disciplinary board being six in cases involving officials below senior level and four in cases involving senior officials, plus the chairman, it is hard to conclude that the board - all of whose members are officials and a chairman coming from outside the institution - has become less internal.[358] Moreover, the inter-institutional disciplinary board, also recommended by the Committee of Independent Experts of 1999 and even envisaged in the *White Paper* of 2000, does not seem to have been established.[359]

Another missed opportunity relates to the proposed 'disciplinary scale' that would lay down a correlation between the misconduct and the disciplinary measure to be imposed, ensuring, *inter alia*, that a less serious misconduct is not abused by the EU Administration to terminate appointment of an official who has become

[352] Ibid., Annex IX, Article 6(3). Pursuant to this provision, the disciplinary board is appointed for three years. However, EU institutions have a possibility to provide for a shorter period of not less than one year.

[353] Ibid., Annex IX, Article 16(2).

[354] *Second Report on Reform of the Commission of 1999, Volume II*, paras. 6.6.25 and 6.6.26.

[355] *EU Staff Regulations of 1968*, Annex II, Articles 4 and 5(1). See also *Second Report on Reform of the Commission of 1999, Volume II*, para. 6.6.26.

[356] *EU Staff Regulations*, Annex IX, Articles 5(1) and 19(1).

[357] *Commission Decision on General Implementing Provisions Concerning the Conduct of Administrative Inquiries and Disciplinary Proceedings C(2004)1588*, 28.04.2004, available in the Register of Commission Documents, available at http://ec.europa.eu/transparency/regdoc/registre.cfm?CL=en, last visited on 30.12.2010, Articles 7 and 8.

[358] *EU Staff Regulations*, Annex IX, Article 5(1).

[359] See *Reforming the Commission - A White Paper - Part I*, Chapter IV, Section IV. 5

'uncomfortable' for other reasons or whose post could be used for placement of a favoured person. Such a scale was not introduced. The new Article 10 of Annex IX of the *EU Staff Regulations* does stipulate that '[t]he severity of the disciplinary penalties imposed shall be commensurate with the seriousness of the misconduct'. In addition, the provision at hand has a list of circumstances that need to be taken into account in determining the seriousness of the misconduct.[360] Nonetheless, there is no indication of how much weight should be given to these circumstances and what effect they should have on the decision regarding the type of measure to be imposed. The new rule seems thus rather vague, not adding much predictability to the link between the misconduct and the imposed disciplinary measure. In addition, it could be argued that it does not introduce anything new as, fortunately, the European Court of Justice has long been requiring proportionality between the disciplinary measure and the circumstances of the misconduct. In *X v. ECB*, for example, the CFI ruled that the principle of proportionality needed to be applied in disciplinary cases and that the identification of the penalty to be imposed must be based on an overall assessment of all the specific facts and matters relevant in each individual case. The Court stated that because applicable law had not specified any fixed relationship between the disciplinary measures and the various types of misconduct and had not stated the extent to which aggravating or mitigating circumstances were to be taken into account in the choice of penalty, the only review of the penalty imposed that judiciary could do was testing whether it was proportionate to the matters of which the staff member was accused and whether the weight attached by the appointing authority to any aggravating or mitigating circumstances was proportionate.[361] The new version of Article 10 of Annex IX of the *EU Staff Regulations* thus does not seem to change much in comparison to the pre-2004 state of affairs. The only added value is the list of aggravating or mitigating circumstances that need to be taken into account, although at this point too it could be argued that already pursuant to the pre-2004 case law, all relevant circumstances had to be considered by the authority deciding upon the penalty in any case.

The following sections explain in more detail each step of disciplinary action which are to be taken in the European Commission.

3.2.7.1. Reporting misconduct

Any suspicion by an official of the existence of an illegal conduct or of a serious breach of obligations is to be reported to a person listed Article 22a of the *EU Staff Regulations*:

> *Any official who, in the course of or in connection with the performance of his duties, becomes aware of facts which gives rise to a presumption of the existence of possible illegal activity, including fraud or corruption, detrimental to the interests of the Communities, or of conduct relating to the discharge of professional duties which may constitute a serious failure to comply with the obligations of officials*

[360] *EU Staff Regulations*, Annex IX, Article 10.

[361] *X v. European Central Bank, Case T-333/99, ECR [2001], p. II-3021, ECR-SC p. I-A-199, II-921*, para. 221.

of the Communities shall without delay inform either his immediate superior or his Director-General or, if he considers it useful, the Secretary-General, or the persons in equivalent positions, or the European Anti-Fraud Office (OLAF) direct.

...

This paragraph shall also apply in the event of serious failure to comply with a similar obligation on the part of a Member of an institution or any other person in the service of or carrying out work for an institution.[362]

In addition, officials may also report to the President of the Commission, to the Court of Auditors, the Council, the European Parliament, or to the European Ombudsman, though reporting to these persons and institutions may only take place after the same information has previously been reported either to the own institution or to the OLAF and that institution or the OLAF have not taken an appropriate action within the announced period of time.[363]

Formally speaking, reporting of an illegal conduct or of a serious breach of obligations is not an option but an obligation of all EU officials. The only available exception relates to documents and information received in the course of legal proceedings.[364] The obligation to report wrongdoing is, however, limited in two important respects. First, the obligation relates only to illegal activities and serious failure to comply with professional obligations. A 'non-serious' wrongdoing thus does not need to be reported. Second, wrongdoing must be reported only when such information has been obtained in connection with performance or professional duties, and not, for example, in private circumstances. Both these limitations are rather surprising and difficult to explain. First of all, it is hard to understand why non-serious misconduct should escape the duty to report it when it becomes known. Moreover, it is arguable that officials who uncover such misconduct will not always be able to judge whether the conduct amounts to misconduct or to serious misconduct. Secondly, it is strange that both misconduct and even serious misconduct should remain unreported if they are discovered outside one's official duties. Rather to the contrary, it could be argued that any misconduct, and even more so a serious one, should be uncovered and addressed. A broadly defined duty to report misconduct can contribute not only to uncovering it but, clearly, also to preventing it, with direct consequences for the independence and impartiality of EU civil servants who would be less likely to act contrary to their obligations as international civil servants.

To encourage reporting of wrongdoing, but also to protect officials who honestly report it – the so-called whistleblowers, a number of provisions have been introduced in the *EU Staff Regulations* and elsewhere, aiming at such protection. Article 22a of the *EU Staff Regulations* itself provides:

---

[362] *EU Staff Regulations*, Article 22a(1).

[363] Ibid., Article 22b(1).

[364] Ibid., Article 22a(4).

> *An official shall not suffer any prejudicial effects on the part of the institution as a result of having communicated the information referred to in paragraphs 1 and 2, provided that he acted reasonably and honestly.*[365]

Further, Article 22b stipulates in its relevant part:

> *An official who further discloses information as defined in Article 22a to the President of the Commission or of the Court of Auditors or of the Council or of the European Parliament, or to the European Ombudsman, shall not suffer any prejudicial effects on the part of the institution to which he belongs…*[366]

This is subject to two conditions. The first relates to the obligation to report first to one's own hierarchy or to the OLAF before turning to another institution, explained above. The second condition requires that the reporting official must 'honestly and reasonably believe that the information disclosed, and any allegation contained in it, are substantially true'.[367] When these conditions are met, the whistleblower enjoys protection against retaliation for reporting wrongdoing, which is an important element encouraging the reporting of misconduct. The protection entails confidentiality of the whistleblower's identity and, upon his request, a facilitation of move to another post.[368] Until 2008, the whistleblower was also protected by a special provision ensuring that retaliation does not take the form of a deteriorated performance appraisal. When the whistleblower had been awarded in his career development review report at least one point less than in the preceding report, the official deciding on his appeal would be the Director-General for Human Resources and Security and for staff in his Directorate-General the Commission Secretary-General.[369] The current *Commission Decision on Article 43*, adopted in 2008, however, no longer includes such possibility, which is rather surprising.[370] As a result, there are currently no special rules in the European Commission addressing retaliation after it has taken place, only rules aimed at preventing it, noted above. Clearly, such situation is not very supportive of whistleblowing, although it can not be doubted that in many cases retaliation could amount to misconduct and therefore become subject to disciplinary action.

As for the reporting of wrongdoing itself, it must be done in writing.[371] The official who receives such a report will transmit it to the OLAF, including any evidence he knows of in relation to the accusation.[372] The OLAF then proceeds further and

[365] Ibid., Article 22a(3).

[366] Ibid., Article 22b(1).

[367] Ibid., Article 22b(1)(a).

[368] *Communication from Vice-President Kinnock to the Commission, How to Enhance Effective Application of the Whistleblowing Rules and Protection of Whistleblowers, SEC(2004)151/2*, 06.02.2004, available in the Register of Commission Documents, available at http://ec.europa.eu/transparency/regdoc/registre.cfm?CL=en, last visited on 30.12.2010, p. 2.

[369] Ibid., pp. 2, 3 and Annex and *Commission Decision on Article 43 of 2004*, Article 3(3).

[370] On the division of roles in the career development review, see *Commission Decision on Article 43*, Article 3 and in particular paragraph (3).

[371] *EU Staff Regulations*, Article 22a(1), second subparagraph.

[372] Ibid., Article 22a(2). It is not only EU officials who have the duty to report misconduct but also 'the

launches an investigation of the matter, unless the initial assessment shows that it does not fall within the competence of the OLAF, information received is not reliable, or that the suspicions are not sufficiently serious.[373]

When the conduct concerns an official serving in the European Commission and the OLAF decides not to investigate the matter, the Commission's own Investigation and Disciplinary Office ('IDOC') may still make an administrative enquiry in accordance with the *Commission Decision on General Implementing Provisions Concerning the Conduct of Administrative Inquiries and Disciplinary Proceedings C(2004)1588 final* of 2004 ('*Commission Decision on Disciplinary Proceedings*').[374] In addition, the same action may be investigated in parallel criminal proceedings conducted by national authorities of the relevant Member State. When such parallel criminal investigation takes place, the final decision by EU disciplinary authorities may only be taken after the final judgment has been delivered by the national authorities.[375]

3.2.7.2. Investigation

The relevant legal basis for launch of the investigation possibly leading to disciplinary proceedings is laid down in Article 86(2) of the *EU Staff Regulations*:

> *Where the Appointing Authority or OLAF becomes aware of evidence of failure [by an official or former official to comply with his obligations under these Staff Regulations, whether intentionally or through negligence on his part], they may launch administrative investigations to verify whether such failure has occurred.*[376]

Of course, an investigation is never conducted by *both* the appointing authority and the OLAF. The latter investigates when the alleged conduct could amount to fraud, corruption or another illegal activity as well as

---

institutions, bodies, offices and agencies' must forward to OLAF any information that relates to possible cases of illegal activities. The same obligation applies to information relating to an on-going internal investigation and/or pertinent to the fight against fraud, corruption and other illegal activities harmful to the EU financial interests. – *Regulation No 1073/1999 of the European Parliament and the Council of 25 May 1999 Concerning Investigations Conducted by the European Anti-Fraud Office (OLAF)*, OJ L 136, 31.05.1999, p. 1, Article 7(1), (2) and (3).

[373] *OLAF Manual - Operational Procedures*, May 2007, available at http://ec.europa.eu/dgs/olaf/legal/doc/manual_short.pdf, last visited on 30.12.2010, Section 2.1.2.

[374] *Commission Decision on Disciplinary Proceedings*, Chapter II.

[375] *EU Staff Regulations*, Annex IX, Article 25. See also *Jean-Paul Francois v. Commission of the European Communities, Case T-307/01, ECR [2004], p. II-1669, ECR-SC [2004], p. I-A-183, II-823*, para. 75 and *Yves Franchet et Daniel Byk v. Commission of the European Communities, Case T-48/05, ECR [2008], p. II-1585*, paras. 341-344. On duty of EU institutions to provide national authorities information on EU officials under criminal investigation, see for example *Richard Hamill v. Commission of the European Communities, Case 180/87, ECR [1988], p. 6141.*

[376] *EU Staff Regulations*, Article 86(2).

> *serious facts linked to the performance of professional activities which may constitute a breach of obligations by officials and servants of the [Union] likely to lead to disciplinary and, in appropriate cases, criminal proceedings...*[377]

The appointing authority, and in the case of the European Commission its Investigation and Disciplinary Office (IDOC), investigate all other instances of failure to comply with obligations that the (former) Commission officials, but also (former) EU 'other servants', have under the *EU Staff Regulations* or the *EU Conditions of Employment of Other Servants*, not necessarily involving 'serious facts' or an illegal activity.[378] In order to avoid the simultaneous involvement of the OLAF and the IDOC in the same matter, the IDOC is required to consult the OLAF before opening its inquiry and to make sure that the OLAF does not deal with the same case.[379]

When the investigation is conducted by the OLAF, as mentioned above, after having received an allegation of wrongdoing, it makes an assessment of the allegation and, if that appears to be well-founded, opens official investigation. In such a case, the official concerned must be 'rapidly informed' about the situation, unless such information is harmful to the investigation.[380] As explained in the *OLAF Manual – Operational Procedures* of 2007, the objective of the investigation is to collect evidence so that facts of the cases can be verified and a decision on whether irregularities have taken place can be made.[381] The investigation must be conducted independently and comply with general principles of legality and integrity, proportionality, impartiality, reasonable duration of cases, authority, immunities, professional secrecy and confidentiality.[382] The actual investigation consists of collecting relevant documents and information, meetings, interviews, as well as physical checks on premises.[383] The rights of defence of the individual under investigation must be respected. Such individual may be assisted by a legal counsel of his choice, may request to be interviewed in any EU official language, may refuse to make self-incriminating declarations, may make statements in any EU official language, may provide documents, and must receive a copy of the interview record.[384] The official concerned, however, does not have access to the OLAF files during this stage of the proceedings, only during the disciplinary proceedings, if they follow.[385] On the other hand, such official may complain to the Director-General of the OLAF about the way

---

[377] *Commission Decision of 28 April 1999 Establishing the European Anti-Fraud Office (OLAF), 1999/352/EC*, OJ L 136, 31.05.1999, p. 20, Article 2(1). See also *Regulation No 1073/1999 on OLAF Investigations*, Article 1(3), second indent. Note that OLAF conducts investigations of fraud, corruption and other illegal activities harmful to the EU which take place internally, i.e. by officials, but also by other persons inside and outside the EU institutions.

[378] *Commission Decision on Disciplinary Proceedings*, Article 2.

[379] Ibid., Article 4(2).

[380] *EU Staff Regulations*, Annex IX, Article 1. See also *OLAF Manual - Operational Procedures*, Section 3.1.1.

[381] *OLAF Manual - Operational Procedures*, Section 2.2.

[382] Ibid., Section 1.4.

[383] Ibid., Section 2.2.1.

[384] Ibid., Section 2.2.4. and 3.1.3.

[385] Ibid., Section 3.1.3.

in which the investigation is conducted, or to the EU ombudsman.[386] The *EU Staff Regulations* provide further that the official concerned must be given opportunity to comment on facts concerning him and be informed in writing when the investigation is closed with no further action to be taken.[387] The conclusions of the OLAF must be communicated to the official concerned by the appointing authority, including all directly related documents.[388]

When the alleged misconduct does not fall within the scope of competence of, or is not investigated by, the OLAF, the investigation – or the 'administrative inquiry' – is conducted by the IDOC pursuant to Chapter II of the *Commission Decision on Disciplinary Proceedings* of 2004. The administrative inquiry opens by a decision of the Director-General for Human Resources and Security, to which the IDOC is attached, taken in agreement with the Commission's Secretary-General.[389] The official under consideration is informed as soon as it becomes clear that he is involved in the matter under investigation, so long as such notification does not harm the investigation. In all cases, however, no conclusions may be reached on the matter before the official in question has been given an opportunity to express his views on the allegations and matters relate to them. The official's views must be recorded in the final report.[390]

Notification of the launch of administrative inquiry may be withheld from the official in question when absolute secrecy is needed and when recourse to the national authorities is implied. The decision not to inform the official concerned is taken by the Commission's Secretary-General in agreement with the Director-General for Human Resources and Security. In such a case too, however, disciplinary proceedings, which may follow after the administrative inquiry, may not begin before the official concerned has been given an opportunity to comment on the matter.[391]

At the end of the administrative inquiry, a report is drawn up on the basis of which the Director-General for the Human Resources and Security decides on further action. The end of the inquiry and the conclusions contained in the report must be notified to the official concerned. Upon request, he must be granted access to all documents that are in direct connection with the allegations, subject to the protection of the legitimate interests of third parties.[392] When the allegations are not confirmed, the matter is closed but the official concerned may require that such

386 Ibid., Section 3.1.4. A complaint to the Director-General of OLAF would be reviewed by an uninvolved OLAF senior agent appointed by the Director-General. The findings and, if relevant, the action taken would be communicate to the official concerned. – Ibid. The ombudsman would deal with the case if it involved maladministration by an EU institution. In that sense, every EU official or other servant may file a complaint to the Director of the OLAF against any act committed by the OLAF that adversely affects him. – *EU Staff Regulations*, Article 90a and *Regulation No 1073/1999 on OLAF Investigations*, Article 14.

387 *EU Staff Regulations*, Annex IX, Article 1.

388 Ibid., Annex IX, Article 2(2).

389 *Commission Decision on Disciplinary Proceedings*, Article 4(1).

390 Ibid., Article 4(4), first paragraph.

391 Ibid., Article 4(4), second paragraph.

392 Ibid., Article 4(6).

decision be enclosed in his personal file.[393] In all other cases, the Director-General for Human Resources and Security may decide either to issue a warning to the official concerned or to open disciplinary proceedings.[394] The decision to open disciplinary proceedings may also be based on a report by the OLAF. The Director-General for Human Resource and Security may also decide to request the OLAF to complement the report, to open an administrative inquiry, or to drop the case, depending on the OLAF's conclusions, of course.[395]

3.2.7.3. Disciplinary proceedings

The appointing authority enjoys wide discretion in deciding whether it opens disciplinary proceedings in a particular case or not. If the proceedings are opened, they may, but do not necessarily, involve the Disciplinary Board.[396] This Board would not be engaged if the penalty imposed involves a written warning or reprimand, although the official concerned must be heard also before such action is taken.[397] The official at issue must, in fact, always be heard before the appointing authority takes its decision on action subsequent to receiving the report from the OLAF or the IDOC, regardless of what type of action it is.[398]

When the decision of the appointing authority involves initiation of disciplinary proceedings including the Disciplinary Board, the Board carries out inquiries in order 'to establish disciplinary offences and to ascertain the circumstances which are necessary to determine the severity of the penalty to be imposed.'[399] As pointed out by the European Court of Justice, the Disciplinary Board is merely a consultative body but is required to conduct a completely independent inquiry, in accordance with a special procedure provided for the purpose and respecting fundamental principles related to the rights of defence of officials under consideration.[400]

Proceedings before the Disciplinary Board begin with the submission of a report by the appointing authority to the Board and to the official concerned, clearly stating relevant facts and circumstances, and hearing of the official concerned.[401] If necessary investigating officials from the OLAF are heard as well and further investigation by the Disciplinary Board is conducted.[402] Having considered the case, the

---

[393] Ibid., Article 4(4), third paragraph. The case may be reopened when new facts become known. – Ibid., fourth paragraph.

[394] *EU Staff Regulations*, Annex IX, Article 3.

[395] *Commission Decision on Disciplinary Proceedings*, Article 4(7).

[396] *EU Staff Regulations*, Annex IX, Article 3.

[397] Ibid., Annex IX, Article 11.

[398] Ibid., Annex IX, Article 3. See also *Commission Decision on Disciplinary Proceedings*, Article 5; and *Rudolf Misset v. Council of the European Communities, Case 319/85, ECR [1988], p. 1861*, para. 7 and also *Afari v. European Central Bank, Case T-11/03, ECR-SC [2004], p. I-A-65, II-267*, para. 90.

[399] *F v. Commission of the European Communities, Case 228/83, ECR [1985], p. 275*, para. 16.

[400] Ibid., para. 16. The proceedings that take place before the Disciplinary Board may be challenged before the Court. – Ibid.

[401] *EU Staff Regulations*, Annex IX, Article 16(1).

[402] Ibid., Annex IX, Articles 16(3) and 17.

Disciplinary Board delivers a reasoned opinion, stating whether the alleged facts are established and whether, and if so which, penalty should be imposed. The report is submitted to both the appointing authority and to the official concerned.[403] The appointing authority then hears the official himself and takes a decision, stating reasons and, if relevant, impose a penalty.[404] Although the decision of the appointing authority is final, the proceedings may be reopened on the own initiative of the appointing authority or upon the official's request if new relevant facts appear.[405]

During the proceedings, the official at issue may be suspended, for a specified or indefinite period.[406] On the other hand, each official under investigation must be given a possibility to exercise his defence rights, including the right to be informed (of all evidence in the files; of the suspension; of the launch and termination of the investigation; of the conclusions of the investigation report; of the decision that no case can be made against him; of the initiation of disciplinary proceedings; of the consequences of an acknowledgment of misconduct; of the reasoned opinion of the Disciplinary Board; of the final decision of the appointing authority);[407] the right to be heard by the appointing authority and by the Disciplinary Board;[408] the right to obtain his complete personal file and copies of all relevant documents;[409] the right to prepare his defence;[410] the right to be assisted by any person of his choice;[411] the

---

403 Ibid., Annex IX, Article 18(1).

404 Ibid., Annex IX, Article 22.

405 Ibid., Annex IX, Article 28. Disciplinary proceedings may also be reopened if the initial decision of the appointing authority is annulled by the court due to a formal defect in the proceedings. Pursuant to the relevant case law, the reopening of the disciplinary proceedings in such a case should not be seen as a new reference of the matter to the relevant authorities but rather as a resumption of the proceedings from the point at which the formal defect that needed to be remedied had arisen. *Henri de Compte v. European Parliament*, Case T-26/89, ECR [1991], p. II-781, para. 70.

406 Ibid., Annex IX, Articles 23 and 24. Suspension may only take place if the official at issue is accused of a serious misconduct. This is also the only condition the appointing authority is required to comply with, apart from the obligation to adequately state reasons on basis of which the seriousness of the alleged misconduct was concluded. It follows that the appointing authority does not need to explain why the suspension itself is needed. - *Bernard Connolly v. Commission of the European Communities, C-273/99 P, ECR [2001], p. I-1575*, paras. 28-29.

407 *EU Staff Regulations*, Annex IX, Articles 1, 3, 12, 14, and 18. See also, for example, *F v. Commission, Case 228/83*, para. 23; *De Compte v. Parliament, Case T-26/89*, para. 122.

408 *EU Staff Regulations*, Annex IX, Articles 3, 16 and 23. See also, for example, *August Josef Van Eick v. Commission of the European Communities, Case 35/67, ECR [1968], p. 329*, p. 344; *Misset v. Council, Case 319/85*, para. 7; and *Afari v. ECB, Case T-11/03*, para. 90.

409 *EU Staff Regulations*, Annex IX, Article 13(1). See also *R v. Commission of the European Communities, Joined cases 255 and 256/83, ECR [1985], p. 2473*, para. 17 or *De Compte v. Parliament, Case T-26/89*, para. 122.

410 *EU Staff Regulations*, Annex IX, Article 13(2). See also *M. Maurice Alvis v. Council of the European Economic Community, Case 32/62, ECR [1963], p. 49*; and *Georges Tzoanos v. Commission of the European Communities, C-191/98 P, ECR [1999], p. I-8223*, para. 34.

411 *EU Staff Regulations*, Annex IX, Articles 4 and 13 (3). See also

right to acknowledge the misconduct;[412] the right to submit observations to the disciplinary board, either orally or in writing;[413] and the right to call witnesses.[414]

The rights of EU officials who are subject to disciplinary proceedings are similar to those provided under the procedure of Article 51 which may lead to a dismissal for incompetence. Also the procedures show many similarities. In both incompetence and disciplinary cases, the appointing authority initiates and ends the proceedings by a final decision, enjoying discretion in deciding whether either of these steps is taken. Both the actual procedures for dismissal for incompetence and the disciplinary proceedings are preceded by a special procedure attempting to remedy incompetence or the investigation of the alleged misconduct, respectively. In both instances, the appointing authority is in the formal stage of the procedure assisted by bodies appointed half by the appointing authority and half by the Staff Committee (the Joint Advisory Committee for the incompetence cases and the Disciplinary Board for disciplinary cases). After having heard the official concerned, the respective bodies deliver a reasoned opinion, on the basis of which the appointing authority decides on the measure to be taken. Both instances may eventually end with the termination of the official's service (dismissal in cases of incompetence and removal from post in disciplinary cases), in both instances the decision depending on the discretion of the appointing authority.

The most noticeable difference between the two respective procedures appears to lie with the phase that precedes the official proceedings. In cases of incompetence, a constructive solution to the problem is sought first. The official concerned is assisted in attempts to improve his performance and only when no or insufficient progress is reached, may the appointing authority initiate the actual procedure for dismissal. In instances of alleged misconduct, the official concerned is directly subject to investigation aimed at a possible follow up by a disciplinary action, if the allegations prove to be founded. When the suspicions relate to a serious misconduct, the official concerned may even be immediately suspended for a specified or indefinite period. The approach and attitudes towards the official concerned from the side of the appointing authority are thus very different in the two respective situations – an outreaching approach seeking improvement in incompetence cases and a retaliatory approach seeking punishment in disciplinary ones. This appears to be the decisive improvement of the proceedings in incompetence cases, as envisaged by the *Committee of Independent Experts* in 1999.

[412] Ibid., Annex IX, Article 14. If the official acknowledges the misconduct, the case may be withdrawn from the board, a decision which is within discretion of the appointing authority. The penalty that the appointing authority may impose in such an instance, after hearing the opinion of the chairman of the Disciplinary Board, is: written warning, reprimand, deferment of advancement to a higher step for a period of between one and twenty-three months, and relegation in step.

[413] Ibid., Annex IX, Article 16(1). See also *Van Eick v. Commission, Case 35/67*, p. 343.

[414] *EU Staff Regulations*, Annex IX, Article 16(1). Note, however, that it is for the Disciplinary Board to decide whether the examination of witnesses proposed by the official at issue is needed for the case concerned. - *Van Eick v. Commission, Case 35/67*, p. 343.

3.2.7.4. Disciplinary measures

A possible result of the disciplinary proceedings is the imposition of a disciplinary measure. Such action may be taken when the misconduct is proven and the appointing authority considers that the official concerned needs to be punished. The exhaustive list of possible disciplinary measures is provided in Article 9 of Annex IX of the *EU Staff Regulations*. The list contains the following measures: a written warning; a reprimand; deferment of advancement to a higher step for a period of between 1 and 23 months; relegation in step; temporary downgrading for a period of between 15 days and one year; downgrading in the same function group; classification in a lower function group, with or without downgrading; removal from post.[415] Removal from post is thus a possible consequence of misconduct, arguably the most severe one. It can be imposed as the sole penalty but it may also be accompanied by a pension reduction or by the withholding of a certain amount from the official's invalidity allowance.[416]

The decision on the type of disciplinary measure is within the competence – and full discretion – of the appointing authority, acting on the basis of a report of the Disciplinary Board, if this Board has been involved in the proceedings.[417] The appointing authority enjoys, furthermore, discretion in choosing the type of measure, limited only by the requirement of proportionality to the seriousness of the misconduct.[418] Circumstances, which the appointing authority needs to take into account when deciding upon the measure, are listed in Article 10 of Annex IX of the *EU Staff Regulations*. They include, for example, the nature of the misconduct and the circumstances in which it took place; intention of the official; his motives; his previous conduct; but also his grade and seniority; and level of responsibility. The appointing authority should weigh and balance all the mentioned factors and pay attention to any other relevant issue.[419] No 'disciplinary scale', as proposed by the *Committee of Independent Experts* of 1999, however, appears to exist. Despite that, the existing general requirement of proportionality and of weighting and balancing of all relevant circumstances of the case should ensure that the disciplinary measure imposed on the official concerned does not go beyond the seriousness of the offense and that his offense does not serve the Administration as a disguise for such official's removal or replacement by another person for reasons unconnected to the offense.

---

[415] *EU Staff Regulations*, Annex IX, Article 9(1). Mere observations of a superior addressed to an official are not a disciplinary measure but rather an internal administrative measure (and thus cannot be challenged before the Court). - *Labeyrie v. Commission, Case 16/67*, p. 303.

[416] *EU Staff Regulations*, Annex IX, Article 9(1)(h).

[417] As mentioned above, the appointing authority may impose a written warning or a reprimand with no prior reference of the case to the Disciplinary Board. - Ibid., Annex IX, Article 11.

[418] Ibid., Annex IX, Article 10.

[419] List of circumstances to be taken into account contained in Article 10 of Annex IX is not exhaustive, as evidenced by the wording of the provision ('in particular'). Officials may not contest the sanction which is imposed on them by relying on the fact that none was imposed on another official who was also subject to disciplinary proceedings in respect of facts connected with those of the official concerned. As stated by the ECJ in *De Compte*, each disciplinary proceeding is distinct and separate and so is the decision on eventual penalties. In addition, officials may not reply on unlawful decision adopted in favour of another. - *De Compte v. Parliament, Case T-26/89*, para. 170.

The wide discretion available to the EU Administration in disciplinary matters has been consistently confirmed by the judiciary. In *Van Eick* the ECJ held that the appointing authority had discretion in evaluating the seriousness of the misconduct established by the Disciplinary Board as well as in the choice of appropriate disciplinary measure.[420] Due to this discretion, the choice of disciplinary measure is, in principle, not subject to judicial review, although obvious disproportion, manifest error or abuse of power on the side of the Administration are.[421] Moreover, there are a number of further limitations that constrain the EU Administration in the exercise of its wide discretionary powers. Apart from the requirement of proportionality between the disciplinary measure to be imposed and the misconduct, the appointing authority is also limited by the obligation to base disciplinary proceedings on clearly defined facts and to state reasons for its decisions. The importance of defining facts on which the disciplinary proceedings are based clearly was emphasized in the second *Gutmann* case, decided in 1967. In that case the ECJ ruled that basing disciplinary proceedings on 'general complaints capable of referring to an indeterminate and unverifiable number of reprehensible matters' is insufficient. Rather, the facts of each specific disciplinary proceeding must be clearly defined so that they can be distinguished from other (disciplinary or other) proceedings.[422]

The obligation to state reasons is provided for in Article 25 of the *EU Staff Regulations* generally for all decisions adversely affecting officials and in Annex IX of the *EU Staff Regulations* specifically for acts adopted in the course of disciplinary proceedings.[423] It should be noted that the reasons on which decisions of relevant authorities are based must be stated in writing and must be sufficiently precise. It is not acceptable to supplement a brief and vague statement of reasons provided in writing by further oral explanations of the allegations to the official concerned. In the first *Gutmann* case, decided in 1966, the ECJ held that such oral information does not allow the judiciary to assess the considerations which led the Administration to its action. In that case Mr. Gutmann was suspended on the basis of allegations that his relationship with the management and with his staff was inconsistent with his duties of head of a division. In the ECJ's view, such a vague statement of reasons, not containing precise indication of misconduct, was not capable of deducing the nature and gravidity of the alleged conduct and therefore not sufficient for suspension of the official (as the relevant legal provisions permit suspension only in case of an alleged serious misconduct.)[424]

The last limitation of the EU Administration in disciplinary matters is the time limits that the Administration needs to adhere to. Annex IX of the *EU Staff Regulations*

[420] *August Joseph van Eick v. Commission of the European Communities, Case 13/69, ECR [1970], p. 3*, para. 24.

[421] For example, Ibid., para. 24; *Robert de Greef v. Commission of the European Communities, Case 46/72, ECR [1973], p. 543*, paras. 45-46; *F v. Commission, Case 228/83*, para. 34; *M. v. Council of the European Communities, Joined cases 175/86 and 209/86, ECR [1988], p. 1891*, para. 9; and *De Compte v. Parliament, Case T-26/89*, para. 220.

[422] *Max Gutmann v. Commission of the EAEC, Joined cases 18 and 35/5, ECR [1967], p. 61*, p. 66.

[423] *EU Staff Regulations*, Article 25 and Annex IX, Articles 1,2, 3, 12, 22.

[424] *Max Gutmann v. Commission of the EAEC, Joined cases 18 and 35/65, ECR [1966], p. 103*. p. 116.

provides for time limits within which the Disciplinary Board should deliver its opinion as well as time limits within which the appointing authority should take the final decision.[425] Even though these time limits are, according to the case law, not mandatory in the sense that measures adopted after the expiry of these time limits would necessarily be void, the ECJ ruled that they must be regarded as part of rules of sound administration. The aim of these rules is to prevent unjustified delay in adopting the decision terminating disciplinary proceedings.[426] Therefore, the relevant authorities must act with due diligence and make sure that each procedural step in disciplinary proceedings is taken within a reasonable period of time, the length of which is to be assessed on a case-by-case basis. A failure to comply with this obligation of due diligence may lead to the liability of the institutions for damage caused by undue delays and in some cases even to the declaration of a measure adopted after the expiry of the period as void.[427] The latter would occur if it was established that the delay, especially if considerable, prevented the official concerned from defending his interests effectively and thus constituted a breach of his rights of defence; or that such delay breached the principle of protection of the person's legitimate expectations that no disciplinary measure will be imposed.[428]

3.2.7.5. Complaints and appeals

In principle, all EU internal administrative proceedings include the possibility of filing a complaint against a decision, action or failure to act, and/or to challenge it before the European Court of Justice. Title VII of the *EU Staff Regulations* provides these possibilities to all persons to whom these regulations apply. Title VII also lays down three types of actions officials may take in order to challenge administrative decisions or failures to act. First of all, the official concerned may request the relevant administrative authority (the appointing authority, the Director of the OLAF or the European Data Protection Supervisor) to take a decision relating to him.[429] Second, if such decision is not adopted or the official disagrees with it, he may file a complaint to the same authority. The complaint would have to concern 'an act adversely affecting' the official and would have to be filed within a three-month period.[430] Third, if the relevant authority fails to reply on the complaint in due time or the official disagrees with the reaction, he may appeal to the European Court of Justice.[431]

[425] *EU Staff Regulations*, Annex IX, Articles 18 and 22.

[426] *F v. Commission, Case 228/83*, para. 30.

[427] *De Compte v. Parliament, Case T-26/89*, para. 88.

[428] *Z v. European Parliament, C-270/99 P, ECR [2001], p. I-9197*, paras. 43-44.

[429] *EU Staff Regulations*, Articles 90(1), 90a, 90b and 90c.

[430] Ibid., Articles 90(2), 90a, 90b and 90c.

[431] Ibid., Articles 91. Pursuant to Article 91a, appeals concerning cases in which an EU institution is entrusted with the exercise of its powers to another institution or to an inter-institutional body are to be submitted to the institution to which the institution entrusted with the exercise of powers is responsible.

Interestingly enough, specific provisions of the *EU Staff Regulations* which deal with disciplinary cases do not contain any reference to the provisions relating to appeals. Nor do they explicitly state that decisions adopted in the course of disciplinary proceedings may be subject to appeal. Nonetheless, since many decisions in disciplinary matters have adverse effects on the official concerned, they may be challenged. In this respect it should be stressed that the sequence of the three types of action officials may take are mandatory in the sense that recourse to the judiciary is only possible after a request and/or (subsequent) complaint has been submitted to the relevant appointing authority. As explained by the ECJ, the purpose of this requirement is to facilitate and encourage an amicable settlement of disputes between officials and institutions and thereby to avoid unnecessary litigation. To achieve this, the institutions must be placed in a position allowing them to get acquainted with the objections of their officials.[432] Only when the administrative review does not satisfy the official in question, may he turn to the court.

Until 1988, all staff cases were dealt with by the European Court of Justice which used to be the only judicial body of the then European Communities. In 1988, the Court of First Instance was established in order to relieve the burden on the ECJ by taking over all staff cases.[433] The Court of First Instance was renamed and became the General Court in 2009 when the Lisbon Treaty came into effect.[434] However, already in 2004, the competence of the CFI in staff matters was delegated to the European Union Civil Service Tribunal established by the Council Decision 2004/752 as a judicial panel.[435] After the entry into force of the Lisbon Treaty, the European Union Civil Service Tribunal became a specialized court, attached to the General Court (the previous CFI). The relevant provisions on the Tribunal's jurisdiction, composition, organization and procedure are to be found in Annex I to the *Statute of the Court of Justice* and in the Tribunal's own *Rules of Procedure*.[436]

3.3. 'Other servants'

Termination of service of EU 'other servants' depends partly on the type of appointment they hold. Thus, appointments for a fixed-term end, in principle, upon the expiry of that period, and appointments for an indefinite period end upon the expiry of the period specified in the notice of termination. Nonetheless, both types of appointment may be terminated for reasons other than the expiry of the period

[432] *Jan Amesz and others v. Commission of the European Communities, Case 543/79, ECR [1982], p. 4425*, para. 26. See also *Fred Pfloeschner v. Commission of the European Communities, Case T-135/89, ECR [1990], p. II-153*, para. 17 and *Georges Weyrich v. Commission of the European Communities*, Case T-14/91, ECR [1991], p. II-235, para. 32.

[433] The Court of First Instance was established by the *Council Decision 88/591/ECSC, EEC, Euratom Establishing a Court of First Instance of the European Communities*, OJ L 144, 16.06.1993, p. 21-22 .

[434] *Treaty Establishing the European Economic Community*, Article 225a and *Consolidated Version of the Treaty on the Functioning of the European Union*, OJ C 83, 30.03.2010, p. 47, Article 257.

[435] *Council Decision No 2004/752 (EC, Euratom) of 2 November 2004 Establishing the European Union Civil Service Tribunal*, OJ L 333, 09.11.2004, p. 7-11.

[436] *ECJ Statute*, Annex I and *Rules of Prodecude of the European Union Civil Service Tribunal*, 25.07.2007, OJ L 225, 29.08.2007, p.1.

or giving of notice. In the case of temporary and contract staff, these other reasons are explicitly provided for in the *EU Conditions of Employment of Other Servants*, and in particular in Articles 47 till 50 of the *EU Conditions of Employment of Other Servants*.[437]

In the case of EU local staff, reasons for termination of service depend partly on the rules and practices existing in the place of employment, as determined by each EU institution.[438] For the local staff employed by the Commission for service in non-member countries, a number of general provisions on termination of service are provided in the *Commission Framework Rules on Local Staff Serving in Non-member Countries* of 1989, in particular in Articles 16 and 18 till 20.[439]

Before going into details of each specific reason, it should be noted that with the exception of the expiry of fixed terms, which is only relevant for contracts concluded for such periods, most of the other reasons for termination of service apply equally to all categories of other servants serving on fixed-term contracts and those engaged on contracts concluded for an indefinite period.[440] Of course, in case of a fixed-term contract, these other reasons are of relevance only before the period for which the contract has been concluded expiries.

3.3.1. Expiry of the period

The expiry of the date stated in the fixed-term contract is the most typical reason for terminating such contracts.[441] Of course, this is only the case when the contract is not renewed. As explained in detail in the previous chapter of this study, fixed-term contracts in the EU may be extended or renewed but in most cases an overall maximum duration of employment applies.[442] When the total period of employment expires, the contract in question expires. There is only one exception to this – contract staff engaged under Article 3a of the *EU Conditions of Employment of Other Servants* may, under certain conditions, eventually receive contracts of indefinite duration. For such staff serving in the European Commission in function group I, it is the fourth contract renewal that may be for indefinite period if the previous period of employment lasted for at least 3 years. For the Commission 'Article 3a contract staff' serving in function group II, III or IV, the second renewal may be for indefinite period, subject to the requirement of at least 3 years of service under the initial contract and its first renewal.[443]

---

437 *EU Conditions of Employment of Other Servants*, Articles 47-50. These provisions are included in the Title II concerning temporary staff but they apply by analogy to contract staff pursuant to Article 119.

438 Ibid., Article 120.

439 *Commission Framework Rules on Local Staff*, Articles 16 and 18-19.

440 The previous chapter explains in more detail which EU 'other servants' are granted fixed-term contract and which ones contracts of indefinite duration. – See below, chapter 6, section 3.2.3.

441 *EU Conditions of Employment of Other Servants*, Article 47(b)(i); *Commission Framework Rules on Local Staff*, Article 18(1).

442 See above, chapter 6, introductory part to section 3.2.2.

443 *Commission Decision on Contract Staff*, Article 6. See also above, chapter 6, section 3.2.2.2.

3.3.2. Termination by notice

Giving a notice of termination to the other party is a typical way of ending contracts concluded for an indefinite period. Unlike fixed-term contracts, indefinite ones have no date specifying when they should end. Both parties to the indefinite contract thus accept that the contract may be terminated at any time, subject to a prior notice. The date of termination of service is thus the last day of the period of notice provided for in the contract or a relevant legal instrument. The *EU Conditions of Employment of Other Servants* stipulate that in case of temporary and contract staff this period may not be less than one month for each completed year of employment, with a minimum of three and a maximum of ten months.[444] For the Commission local staff serving in non-member countries, according to the *Commission Framework Rules on Local Staff Serving in Non-member Countries*, the period of notice is one month when the contract is terminated by the Commission and 15 days when it is done by the staff member, unless local rules or practice require a different period of notice.[445]

The authority authorized to conclude contracts with 'other servants' enjoys wide discretion in deciding whether and when to terminate contracts of indefinite duration, subject to the above mentioned requirements related to the period of notice. It also possesses discretion to limit its powers to terminate contracts, in the interest of the staff, by including such provision in the contract. The discretion of this authority prevents the judiciary from reviewing contracts' termination, save for cases of manifest error or misuse of power.[446] In order to facilitate such review, notice of termination of a contract of indefinite duration must, since recently, contain reason(s) for termination. As explained in the previous chapter of this study, until 2006 no such requirement was in place and contracts of indefinite duration could have been terminated without stating reasons.[447] However, in 2006 the European Union Civil Service Tribunal ruled in *Landgren* that reasons for contract termination must be provided. The Tribunal stressed, however, that the duty to state reasons has no consequences for the broad discretion of the EU Administration to terminate indefinite contracts.[448] Despite this statement, it is clear that introduction of the requirement to provide reason(s) for termination of contracts of indefinite duration has significantly strengthened the position of EU staff serving on such contracts

[444] *EU Conditions of Employment of Other Servants*, Article 47(c)(i).

[445] *Commission Framework Rules on Local Staff*, Article 18(2)(b).

[446] *De Briey v. Commission, Case 25/80*, para. 16 and *Schmitt v. EAR, Case T-175/03*, para. 56. See also, for example, *Alicia Speybrouck v. European Parliament, Case T-45/90, ECR [1992], p. II-33*, paras. 90, 63-94 and 97-98; and *V v. European Parliament, Case C-18/91 P, ECR [1992], p. I-3997*, paras. 39-40. In the latter case the Court ruled that the termination of contract is not even prevented by an on-going invalidity procedure concerning the temporary agents at issue, which was relevant in the present case, since the contract termination cannot jeopardize the completion of the procedure and/or affect the rights of the agent concerned after the procedure is completed. – *V v. Parliament, Case C-18/91 P*, para. 40.

[447] *André Schertzer v. European Parliament, Case 25/68, ECR [1977], p. 1729*, para. 39. For the preceding case law not requiring statement of reasons, see, for example, *Schertzer v. Parliament, Case 25/68*, paras. 38-40 and *Pyres v. Commission, Case T-7/01*, para. 36. See also *Karatzoglou v. EAR, Case T-471/04*, paras. 35-39.

[448] *Landgren v. ETF, Case F-1/05*, paras. 73 and 75.

and increased their protection against possible misuse or abuse of power by the EU Administration.

The same applies to EU staff serving on fixed-term contracts. In the EU, such contracts may also be terminated by giving notice to the other party, similarly as it is with contracts of indefinite duration.[449] Since the European Union Civil Service Tribunal has applied its reasoning in *Landgren* also to termination of fixed-term contracts before the expiry of the period, notice of termination of a fixed-term contract must now provide a clear reason, too.[450]

That said, it must be noted that, due to the different nature of the fixed-term and indefinite contracts, there is a difference in approach towards their termination by giving notice. As explained by the European Union Civil Service Tribunal, staff members who have signed a contract of fixed duration can normally expect that their contract will last until the end of that term. Therefore, and unlike in the case of contracts of indefinite duration, the EU Administration should use the possibility to terminate fixed-term contracts before the expiry date with caution, taking into account the legitimate interests of the staff member concerned.[451] This requirement could be regarded as a safeguard against misuse or abuse of the possibility to terminate fixed-term contracts before their expiry for improper reasons. Misuse of powers is one of the reasons for which possible challenges to an early termination of a fixed-term contract would be assessed by judiciary, next to the existence of a manifest error. In cases brought before it, the Court would review whether the competent authority remained within reasonable bounds of its discretion when assessing the interests of the service and whether it took into consideration all factors which might have affected the decision, including the interests of the staff member at issue.[452] As pointed out by the CFI in *Dejaiffe*, the EU institutions have a 'duty to have regard to the welfare of [their] staff, which reflects the balance of reciprocal rights and obligations established by the Staff Regulations, and by analogy the Conditions of Employment, in the relationship between the official authority and its staff'.[453] The newly introduced obligation to state reasons for termination by notice of fixed-term contracts before the expiry date strengthens the protection of staff serving on such contracts even more.

The actual termination of fixed-term contracts based on the termination notice takes place at the end of the period specified in the contract. This period may not be shorter than one month for each year of service. At the same time, the period may

---

449 *EU Conditions of Employment of Other Servants*, Article 47(b)(ii). The *Commission Framework Rule on Local Staff Serving in Non-member Country* do not provide for a possibility to terminate contracts of such staff concluded for a fixed-term. – *Commission Framework Rules on Local Staff*, Article 18(1) and (2).

450 *Landgren v. ETF, Case F-1/05*, para. 73. But see *Pyres v. Commission, Case T-7/01*, paras. 37-38.

451 *Luc Dejaiffe v. Office for Harmonization of the Internal Market (OHIM), Case T-223/99, ECR [2000], p. I-A-277, II-1267*, para. 79.

452 Ibid., para. 51 and *Cocchi et Hainz v. Commission, Case T-330/00 and T-114/01*, para. 50.

453 *Dejaiffe v. OHIM, Case T-223/99*, para. 51.

not be shorter than one month and longer than three months, with the exception of contracts that have been renewed, in which case the maximum is six months.[454]

3.3.3. Not meeting requirements for employment

Both fixed-term and indefinite contracts of temporary and contract staff may also be terminated by the EU Administration when the staff member at issue ceases to satisfy conditions of employment with the EU institutions listed in Article 12(2)(a) of the *EU Conditions of Employment of Other Servants*. These conditions relate to the possession of nationality of one of the EU Member States and to full rights as a citizen. Thus, when the nationality of a EU Member State is lost without simultaneous acquisition of the nationality of another EU Member State and no exception for the continuation of employment is granted, or when full rights as a citizen are lost, the employment of the staff member is terminated at the end of the period of notice calculated in the same way as in the case of termination by giving notice.[455]

This reason for termination of fixed-term and indefinite contracts corresponds to that applying to permanent officials. As explained above, employment of permanent staff serving in EU institutions would also come to an end if the EU nationality or full rights as a citizen have been lost and in case of the former no exception for retention in the EU service is authorized.[456]

The *Commission Framework Rules for Local Staff Serving in Non-member Countries* do not allow termination of service on the basis of this reason. This is not surprising considering that the employment of these staff is not subject to the condition of possessing nationality of an EU Member State or full rights as a citizen, though the latter could be imposed by local rules or practices. Naturally, *local* staff serving in *non-member* countries are most likely to possess the nationality of the host country rather than the nationality of an EU Member State.[457]

3.3.4. Termination during or after probation

Similarly as permanent appointments, also non-permanent contracts may be terminated when the performance of the staff member at issue proves insufficient during the period of probation.[458] According to Articles 14 and 84 of the *EU Conditions of Employment of Other Servants* temporary staff *may be*, and contract staff whose contract is of duration at least one year *are*, required to serve a probationary period.

[454] *EU Conditions of Employment of Other Servants*, Article 47(b)(ii).

[455] Ibid., Article 47(b)(iii) and (c)(ii).

[456] *EU Staff Regulations*, Article 47 on compulsory resignation. See also above, section 3.2.3.

[457] Engagement of local staff serving in non-member countries is subject to two conditions stipulated in the *Commission Framework Rules for Local Staff Serving in Non-member Countries*, namely the suitability and physical fitness for the performance of duties. - *Commission Framework Rules on Local Staff*, Article 2.

[458] *EU Conditions of Employment of Other Servants*, Article 48(a); *Commission Decision on Contract Staff*, Article 3; and *Commission Framework Rules on Local Staff*, Article 18(1) and (2)(a). See also, for example, *Sapara v. Eurojust, Case F-61/06*.

This period is maximum six months for temporary staff and contract staff serving in function group I, and nine months for contract staff in other function groups.[459] Conditions for termination of service of temporary and contract staff on probation are similar to those that apply to permanent officials. However, there are some additional rules relating to contract staff, provided in the *Commission Decision on Contract Staff* of 2004.[460]

If during the probationary period the staff member's work appears to be 'obviously inadequate', a report is drawn up on his abilities to perform his duties, as well as on his conduct and efficiency, and is submitted to him.[461] The staff member may comment on the report in writing. Subsequently, the authority authorized to conclude contracts may decide to dismiss the agent concerned before the end of the probationary period. Such termination would take effect one month after the notice of termination has been communicated to the staff member concerned.[462] In case of contract staff, termination of service is subject to a dialogue between the probation supervisor's hierarchical superior, who must belong to function group AD, and the probationary contract staff member. On the basis of this dialogue the probation supervisor's hierarchical superior prepares an opinion for the authority authorized to conclude contracts, which takes the final decision. If the decision concerns 'Article 3a contract staff' and the probation supervisor's hierarchical supervisor agrees with the conclusions of the probationary report, the authority authorized to conclude contracts must, in addition, obtain the opinion of the Joint Reports Committee before deciding on the action to be taken.[463]

The termination of service of both temporary and contract staff at the end of the probationary period takes place without notice.[464] It is also based on a report, this time one drawn up not less than a month before the expiry of the probationary period.[465] This report, too, must be communicated to the staff member concerned who may comment on it in writing. When the report is satisfactory, the agent remains in service under the terms of contract. However, when the staff member's work has proven inadequate, his contract is terminated, unless a decision is taken to extend the probationary period. The latter is only allowed in exceptional circumstances, though.[466] As in the case of termination of service during the probationary period, when the staff member concerned belongs to contract staff, termination of service is subject to the procedure described in the previous paragraph with regard to ter-

[459] *EU Conditions of Employment of Other Servants*, Article 14, first paragraph and Article 84(1).

[460] *Commission Decision on Contract Staff*.

[461] *EU Conditions of Employment of Other Servants*, Article 14, fourth paragraph and Article 84(4).

[462] Ibid., Article 14, fourth paragraph and Article 84(4). For details on the procedure of drawing up report on a contract staff member during or at the end of his probationary period, see *Commission Decision on Contract Staff*, Article 6(3) and (5).

[463] *Commission Decision on Contract Staff*, Articles 6(3)(h) and (4).

[464] *EU Conditions of Employment of Other Servants*, Article 48(a).

[465] For details on this procedure of drawing up report on a contract staff member at the end of his probationary period, see *Commission Decision on Contract Staff*, Article 6(3) and (5).

[466] *EU Conditions of Employment of Other Servants*, Article 14, third paragraph and Article 84(3).

mination of service of such staff during the probationary period. This also applies to extension of the probationary period in such a case.[467]

The probationary period of local staff serving in non-member countries depends on local rules and practices and the type of duties to be performed.[468] Termination of employment for unsatisfactory service or for 'obvious deficiencies' that come to light during the probationary period may take place at the end of such a period. The *Commission Framework Rules for Local Staff Serving in Non-member Countries* do not provide for any further requirements. They also do not allow termination of service during the probationary period, unlike the *EU Staff Regulations* and the *EU Conditions of Employment of Other Servants* do in case of permanent officials and temporary and contract staff, respectively.[469]

3.3.5. Health reasons

When a temporary or contract staff member falls sick, he receives paid sick-leave under the same conditions as permanent officials stipulated in Article 59 of the *EU Staff Regulations*. Such payment may, however, not exceed three months or the length of time actually worked by the staff member before falling sick, whichever is longer. In any case, the payment stops when the contract which is of fixed duration expiries.[470] If at the end of the period of paid sick-leave the staff member is unable to resume work, his contract may be terminated. The termination would take place without notice and it would be accompanied by payment of an allowance specified in Article 48 of the *EU Conditions of Employment of Other Servants*.[471]

Also local staff serving in non-member countries are entitled to paid sick leave, the conditions being specified by local rules and practice with a minimum set out in the *Commission Framework Rules for Local Staff Serving in Non-member Countries*.[472] Termination of service of these staff for reasons of health is subject to the following conditions: first, the staff member concerned holds a contract of indefinite duration, not a fixed-term contract; second, the incapacity for work has lasted for more than six months calculated over a consecutive period of 12 months; third, the incapacity is not a result of an accident at work; fourth, the case is 'duly substantiated'; and fifth, termination occurs in accordance with local rules. When these conditions are met and the staff member's service is terminated, he receives compensation which depends on the type and/or length of his contract. When the incapacity for work is caused by an accident at work, however, the contract of a local staff serving in

---

467 *Commission Decision on Contract Staff*, Article 6(4).

468 *Commission Framework Rules on Local Staff*, Article 5.

469 Ibid., Article 18(1) and (2)(a).

470 *EU Conditions of Employment of Other Servants*, Article 16, second paragraph. See also *EU Staff Regulations*, Article 59.

471 *EU Conditions of Employment of Other Servants*, Article 48(b).

472 *Commission Framework Rules on Local Staff*, Article 16(1)(a).

non-member country may only be terminated in accordance with local legislation relating to accidents at work.[473]

3.3.6. Disciplinary grounds

Unsurprisingly, non-permanent contracts may be terminated on disciplinary grounds too. Article 49 of the *EU Conditions of Employment of Other Servants* provides that termination of service of temporary or contract staff may occur in 'serious cases of intentional or negligent failure of temporary staff to comply with their obligations'.[474] Similarly, Article 19 of the *Commission Framework Rules on Local Staff Serving in Non-member Countries* lists dismissal as a possible consequence of a 'duly established failure by a member of local staff to comply with his obligations, whether intentionally or through negligence or recklessness on his part'.[475]

In case of temporary and contract staff, termination of service on this ground must be preceded by a disciplinary procedure and based on a reasoned decision delivered by the relevant authority. In addition, the staff member at issue must be given the opportunity to submit his defence before the decision to terminate his contract is taken. During the proceedings, the staff member accused of misconduct may be suspended, just as in the case of permanent officials. Other rules on disciplinary proceedings contained in Annex IX of the *EU Staff Regulations* apply to proceedings involving temporary and contract staff as well.[476] The only additional requirement relates to the composition of the disciplinary board in cases in which this board deals with a contract staff member. In such instance, the disciplinary board must have two additional members from the same function group and grade as the concerned contract staff member. They are to be appointed according to an *ad hoc* procedure established by the authority authorized to conclude contracts.[477]

If the accusation of misconduct concerns a local staff member in a non-member country, dismissal must be first consulted by the head of delegation with the authority authorized to conclude contracts which must notify the Staff Committee. Moreover, the staff member under consideration must be given an opportunity to state his case. If he so requires, he must be allowed assistance by a person of his choice. The disciplinary measure taken, including dismissal, must, of course, be notified to the staff member concerned in writing.[478]

---

[473] Ibid., Article 16(1)(b).

[474] *EU Conditions of Employment of Other Servants*, Article 49(1).

[475] *Commission Framework Rules on Local Staff*, Article 19. Article 20 provides a list of actions which are considered to constitute serious misconduct justifying immediate dismissal. The list includes theft, damage to property, bodily harm and breach of the duty of confidentiality with regard to information acquired in the exercise of, or in relation to, official duties.

[476] *EU Conditions of Employment of Other Servants*, Article 49(1). For details on disciplinary proceedings under Annex IX of the *EU Staff Regulations*, see above, section 2.3.6.2.

[477] Ibid., Article 119, second paragraph.

[478] *Commission Framework Rules on Local Staff*, Article 20.

The EU Administration enjoys discretion in deciding whether it terminates the contract of a non-permanent staff member accused of misconduct by disciplinary action or whether it does so by using a possibility of termination by giving notice. The CFI ruled that doing the latter does not, in itself, mean that the Administration had committed a manifest error or misused its powers. It stressed that the large margin of discretion allows the EU Administration to make such a choice.[479]

3.3.7. False information

Disciplinary proceedings provided for in Annex IX of the *EU Staff Regulations* must be followed also when a contract is terminated due to false information deliberately provided by the staff member at the time of his engagement which becomes known later.[480] Such termination may occur in the case of temporary and contract staff when the false information in question relates to the staff member's professional ability or his fulfillment of any of the conditions set out for employment with EU institutions in Article 12 of the *EU Conditions of Employment of Other Servants*. At the same time, the false information in question must have been decisive for the engagement of the staff member concerned.[481] When these conditions are met, the contract of the temporary or contract staff member may be ended by the EU Administration. Of course, the staff member concerned must first have been heard on the matter. In addition, as already noted, before a decision to terminate the contract is taken, disciplinary proceedings must have been conducted. The temporary or contract staff member may, however, be immediately suspended, pending the conclusion of disciplinary proceedings.[482]

Termination of service on the basis of false information is not provided for local staff serving in non-member countries. The *Commission Framework Rules on Local Staff Serving in Non-member Countries* is silent on this point. However, it could be argued that in case of these staff, the matter would be directly dealt with as a disciplinary one and termination of service could occur in accordance with the provisions provided for such proceedings.

3.3.8. Retirement and death

As with permanent officials, so also temporary and contract staff, as well as local staff serving in non-member countries, must retire when they reach 65 years of age. Moreover, engagement with the European Commission ends when such staff die.[483] Neither the *EU Conditions of Employment of Other Servants* nor the *Commission Framework Rules on Local Staff Serving in Non-member Countries* provide any further

[479] *Dejaiffe v. OHIM, Case T-223/99*, para. 38.

[480] *EU Conditions of Employment of Other Servants*, Article 50(2)

[481] Ibid., Article 50(1).

[482] Ibid., Article 50.

[483] Ibid., Article 47, introductory sentence and para. (a); and *Commission Framework Rules on Local Staff*, Article 18(2)(c) and (d).

details on this matter. The former do, however, contain provisions relating to pension rights and benefits in the event of death of temporary or contract staff member.[484]

Further, the *Commission Framework Rules on Local Staff Serving in Non-member Countries* indicate the age of 65 years and death as a possible reason for termination of service only in case of staff holding contracts of indefinite duration. No such provision is made for staff serving on fixed-term contracts. This is rather surprising considering that, obviously, staff on fixed-term contracts too cannot remain employed in case of death. Moreover, the continuation of employment of such staff beyond the age of 65 could be questioned from the point of view of equality of treatment and, arguably, discrimination on the basis of age. Therefore, it appears that the absence of the relevant provision for termination of service of local staff in non-member countries who hold fixed-term contracts is just an unfortunate omission and/or poor drafting of the *Commission Framework Rules on Local Staff Serving in Non-member Countries* rather than a deliberate intention.

3.3.9. Incompetence

Surprisingly, the *EU Conditions of Employment of Other Servants* do not list incompetence as an explicit reason for termination of service of temporary and contract staff. In contrast, the *Commission Framework Rules on Local Staff Serving in Non-member Countries* do so. The latter stipulates that, without prejudice to local conditions, termination of contract of such local staff may take place with a 15-day notice issued by the authority authorized to conclude contracts. There are no further requirements for this termination.[485]

It may be recalled that the performance of temporary staff is regularly appraised through the Commission Career Development Review which applies to both permanent officials and temporary staff.[486] The *Commission Decision on Article 43* of 2008, however, does not contain any provision addressing the issue of incompetence of either permanent or temporary staff. Neither does the *Commission Decision on Contract Staff* of 2004 or the Commission decisions on reclassification of 'Article 3a contract staff'. It appears thus that service of neither temporary nor contract staff may be terminated on grounds of professional incompetence. Naturally, termination could be effected by using a different legal ground, most obviously the giving of notice. As explained above, this is possible for both staff serving on fixed-term as well as those on contracts of indefinite duration. That said, it is regrettable that incompetence is not listed as a specific reason for termination of service of temporary and contract staff. One of the consequences is that these staff are not provided (compulsory) help leading to improvement of their performance before separation. In particular staff serving on contracts of indefinite duration should be afforded such protection, alike permanent officials.

---

[484] *EU Conditions of Employment of Other Servants*, Articles 31-42 for temporary staff and Articles 103-112 for contract staff.

[485] *Commission Framework Rules on Local Staff*, Article 18(3).

[486] *Commission Decision on Article 43*, Article 1(1) and (2).

3.3.10. Post abolition and staff reduction

This legal ground for termination of service is also explicitly provided for only in the *Commission Framework Rules on Local Staff Serving in Non-member Countries*, but not mentioned the *EU Conditions of Employment of Other Servants* with regard to temporary and contract staff. The obvious reason for the absence of such a rule in the latter is the existence of the possibility to terminate services of both temporary and contract staff by giving a notice. Clearly, if the Commission needs to abolish a specific post or to reduce staff, it can simply give a notice to the staff member(s) concerned and wait until the expiry of the period of notice. A similar approach is taken in the *Commission Framework Rules on Local Staff Serving in Non-member Countries*, too. These Rules directly link post abolition and staff reduction to the termination of service by giving notice. They, however, impose an additional requirement on the authority authorized to conclude contracts, namely a requirement to consult a joint body and to adopt special and exceptional measures facilitating the departure of the staff member concerned.[487] No such requirement is in place for terminating the services of temporary and contract staff who have to leave for reason of post abolition or staff reduction.

3.4. Seconded national experts

Experts seconded to the European Commission from national civil services or other public institutions serve on the basis of an exchange of letters between the Commission Directorate-General for Human Resources and Security and the permanent representation of the Member State concerned or other relevant employer of the national expert in question.[488] The exchange of letters specifies, *inter alia*, the period of secondment, the expiry of which leads to termination of the expert's engagement with the European Commission, unless the three involved parties, i.e. the Commission, the government of the Member State concerned (or other relevant employer) and the seconded national expert, decide to extend the period of secondment.[489] Termination of secondment before the expiry of the agreed period is possible. Such termination may be based on reasons set out in Article 10 of the *Commission Decision on Secondment* of 2008, explained in more detail in this section.

First of all, secondment may end at the request of any of the three involved parties, although when the request comes from the seconded official, it is subject to the

[487] *Commission Framework Rules on Local Staff*, Article 18(6). This provision does not use the terms post abolition and staff reduction. Rather, it refers to the event of cutting back of the Commission activities in non-member countries and changes in the interests of the service.

[488] *Commission Decision on Secondment*, Article 3(4). Seconded national experts may also come from public intergovernmental organizations and, exceptionally, also from other employer. For details, see Ibid., Article 1(2).

[489] Ibid., Article 4. For more details on the period of secondment, see above, chapter 6, section 3.2.2.4.

agreement of the European Commission and the official's employer. Termination of secondment upon request is in all cases subject to three months' notice.[490]

Exceptionally, secondment may be terminated without notice. Such termination may be requested by the seconded national official himself, for both personal and professional reasons. The official needs to address his request for termination of secondment in this manner to both the European Commission and his employer who will jointly decide on it.[491] Termination without notice may also be initiated by the official's employer if his 'essential interests' require so.[492] It may also be initiated by the European Commission, subject to the condition that either the official or his employer has failed to respect their obligations under the *Commission Decision on Secondment*.[493]

The last mentioned option of terminating secondment without notice for breach of an obligation rests with the European Commission only and not with the official's employer. However, it could be argued that the official's employer who wished to terminate secondment on the basis, for instance, of breach of an obligation by the European Commission, could resort to termination for reasons of his 'essential interests'. These interests are not defined in the *Commission Decision on Secondment* and it seems that it is up to the employer to decide whether they exist and if so whether they require termination of the official's employment without notice.

The European Commission itself clearly enjoys wide discretion in deciding when to terminate secondment without notice for breach of obligation. Since the relevant provision does not provide any details on the degree of severity of the breach of obligations required for termination of secondment, the Commission may, at least formally, terminate secondment for any breach of any obligation imposed on the seconded national expert or his employer.[494] The European Commission's discretion in this respect is, however, limited to a certain extent by the requirement of 'exceptional circumstances' contained in Article 10(2)(c) of the *Commission Decision on Secondment*. Article 1(1) of the Decision allows the Commission to use the possibility of termination of secondment without notice under Article 10(2)(c) in cases in which the administrative status of the seconded national expert in question at his employer changes or is terminated.[495] For example, when the seconded national expert ceases to be a national civil servant, his secondment with the European

[490] Ibid., Article 10(1).

[491] Ibid., Article 10(2(b).

[492] Ibid., Article 10(2)(a).

[493] Ibid., Article 10(2)(c).

[494] Rights and obligations of national experts seconded to the Commission are listed in Article 7 of the *Commission Decision on Secondment* and include, for example, and as far as obligations are concerned, duty of independence, impartiality and loyalty to the European Union; duty to request authorization for outside activities; prohibition of any action or behaviour which would reflect adversely upon the official's position; prohibition of sexual or psychological harassment; prohibition to use or disclose without authorization information acquired in the exercise of official duties or in relation to it; and obligation to inform the supervisor about the intention to publish. - Ibid., Article 7.

[495] Ibid., Article 1(1), last paragraph.

Commission may be terminated, too. Again, it is up to the European Commission to decide whether it takes such action or not.

Last but not least, secondment may be temporarily suspended, with the period of suspension not being counted in the period of secondment. Suspension can take place upon the request of the official and with the agreement with his employer. When authorizing the suspension, the European Commission should specify terms and conditions for the suspension.[496]

4. The UN and the EU compared

4.1. General observations

The reasons for which UN and EU staff may be separated have not encountered many changes since the adoption of the first *UN* and *EU Staff Regulations*. In fact, there have been no changes in this regard in the EU. The few notable modifications that took place during the recent reform concerned procedural rather than substantive matters. In the UN, important changes occurred in the early 1950s, reflecting the extreme politicization of the international organization at the time. Further changes followed in 2009, as a result of the overall reform of contractual arrangements. In both instances, new reasons for separation and/or conditions for their application were introduced in the UN.[497]

When comparing the current situation in the UN Secretariat and in the European Commission, there are more similarities than differences between the two organizations' experiences, both in the general sense but also with regard to the individual reasons for staff separation. Generally speaking, the approach of both institutions towards their career and non-career staff is comparable. Most of the differences in this respect are traceable to the nature of the various types of appointments. For example, separation due to expiry of the date set in the letter of appointment or contract is not applicable to career appointments which are, by definition, of indeterminate duration and have no expiry date. Apart from such differences, however, the general approach is similar for all staff, regardless of the type of appointment. Consequently, all UN and EU civil servants may, in principle, be separated on the basis of the same reasons. In the UN Secretariat, all such reasons are contained in a single set of rules applying to all staff. In the European Commission, separate legal instruments apply to permanent officials and to non-permanent 'other servants'. In addition, separate regimes apply to various categories of 'other servants', though the position of temporary and contract staff has been unified. Also national experts seconded to the European Commission have their own set of rules.

Of course, this difference between the UN Secretariat and the European Commission is not specific to staff separation. As explained in the previous chapter of this study, in 2009 the UN reformed its contractual arrangements and unified approach towards

[496] Ibid., Article 9.

[497] See above, sections 2.1 and 3.1.

different types of staff, introducing one set of the *UN Staff Rules*. These, together with the *UN Staff Regulations*, offer one list of reasons for separation of all staff, save for the cases based on the nature of the appointment, as noted above.[498]

Besides the similarities in the general approach of the UN Secretariat and the European Commission towards all their staff, there is also a striking similarity in the reasons available for staff separation in the UN and the EU. These reasons could be divided into three groups. The first group contains reasons for which appointments end automatically due to a specific situation. This group of reasons include the expiration of the appointment; retirement; and death. The second group concerns separation initiated by the staff member concerned and includes resignation and abandonment of post. The last and the largest group of reasons are those for which the UN or the EU Administration may initiate staff separation. It includes the following reasons: giving a notice of termination; interest of the organization or service; abolition of post or staff reduction; refusal of offered post after absence; no longer meeting conditions of employment; health reasons; incompetence during probation; incompetence; disciplinary reasons; and *posterior* discovery of relevant facts. In order to facilitate a better overview of all the reasons for separation existing in the UN Secretariat and/or the European Commission, they have been arranged in the table below.

[498] See above, chapter 6, section 2.3.

Table 19: Reasons for staff separation in the UN Secretariat and the European Commission

Reason for separation	European Commission career staff	European Commission non-career staff	UN Secretariat career staff	UN Secretariat non-career staff
AUTOMATIC				
Expiration	Not applicable	- Yes, if fixed-term contract - Not applicable if indefinite contract	Not applicable	Yes
Retirement	Yes	Yes	Yes	Yes
Death	Yes	Yes	Yes	Yes
INITIATED BY STAFF				
Resignation	Yes	Yes, under termination by giving a notice	Yes	Yes
Abandonment of post	Formally not, but probably under disciplinary reasons	Formally not, but probably under disciplinary reasons	Yes	Yes
INITIATED BY ADMINISTRATION				
Interest of the good administration of organization / interests of the service	No, unless senior staff	Yes, under termination giving a notice	Yes	Yes, with staff consent
Giving a notice of termination	No	Yes	No	No
Abolition of a post or reduction of staff	Yes, under compulsory resignation	- Yes, under termination by giving a notice - a special provision for local staff serving in non-member countries	Yes	Yes
Refusal of offered post after absence	Yes	Not applicable	No	No
No longer meeting (certain) conditions of employment	Yes	Yes	No	No
Health reasons	Yes, under compulsory resignation	Yes	Yes	Yes
Incompetence during probation	Yes	Yes	Not applicable (no probation)	Not applicable (no probation)

Incompetence	Yes	Yes	Yes	Yes
Disciplinary reasons	Yes	Yes	Yes	Yes
Posterior discovery of relevant facts	Formally not, but probably for disciplinary reasons	- Yes - For local staff serving in non-member countries formally not, but probably under disciplinary reasons	Yes	Yes

The sections below provide a more detailed comparison of individual reasons for staff separation, related conditions and/or procedures, as applied in the UN Secretariat and the European Commission.

4.2. Issues with no (significant) differences

To begin with instances that show no differences between the UN Secretariat and the European Commission, in both institutions an appointment ends, of course, when a staff member dies.[499] Furthermore, in both institutions staff may resign from their post at any time, subject to the requirement of submitting a resignation in writing and to the period of notice. This applies to both career and non career staff, although there is no explicit legal ground for resignation of European Commission non-permanent staff. Nonetheless, these staff may leave the Commission at any time by giving a notice of termination, disregarding the type of contract they hold.[500] This is in effect the same as resignation. The requirement to submit resignation in writing is an important legal safeguard against possible abuse by the Administration of this legal ground for staff separation - the Administration cannot claim staff resignation unless it can prove it by written evidence of resignation. On the other hand, the Administration cannot keep a staff member in service against his will - the refusal to accept resignation is legally effective only in disciplinary cases. The only possibility the Administration has in this respect is to require that the staff member remains in service for the period of notice. There, a slight difference exists between the UN Secretariat and the European Commission. In the former, a three months period is the standard, though the Secretary-General may accept a shorter one.[501] In the European Commission, the appointment ends on the date established by the Administration based on the resigning staff member's proposal. The maximum the Administration must adhere to is three months after resignation in case of AD officials and one month in case of AST officials.[502] For European Commission non-permanent staff who, as already mentioned, may leave the service by giving a notice to

[499] See above, sections 2.2.5, 3.2.4 and 3.3.8.

[500] See above, sections 2.2.2, 3.2.2 and 3.3.2.

[501] See above, section 2.2.2.

[502] See above, section 3.2.2.

the Administration, specific notice periods apply, depending on the type of contract and length of service. The precise period is set in the contract or in a relevant legal instrument.[503] Hence, there seems to be a certain flexibility with regard to the period of notice in case of European Commission permanent staff but not so much in case of non-permanent staff. Temporary and contract staff are, in addition, subject to a longer period of notice than other EU but also all UN staff.

4.3. Issues with similarities as well as differences

A number of reasons for separation have a comparable legal regime in both the UN Secretariat and the European Commission, while showing some dissimilarities, too. Among these are the expiration of appointment; retirement; abolition of post or staff reduction; health reasons; incompetence, disciplinary reasons and posterior discovery of facts.

4.3.1. Expiration

UN and EU appointments concluded for a fixed-term period end when the term expires, requiring no prior notice.[504] There is no difference between the UN and the EU in this respect. However, the legal regimes of the two organizations with regard to staff separation by the expiration of the set date are not identical. Three remarks would be in order here.

First, in the UN Secretariat all non-career staff serve on fixed-term appointments, while in the European Commission some categories of 'other servants' are engaged for an indefinite period.[505] This means that in the UN Secretariat all non-career staff know in advance that, unless their appointments are extended or renewed, they will have to leave the UN at the set date.[506] In the European Commission, a relatively large number of non-career staff may serve for a long period of time with no expiration date. Their separation by expiration is thus not possible.

Second, one type of UN non-career appointment concluded for a fixed period, namely the UN fixed-term appointment, may be repeatedly extended or renewed without an overall time limit being imposed.[507] Consequently, UN staff holding

---

[503] See above, section 3.3.2.

[504] See above, sections 2.2.1 and 3.3.1.

[505] See above, chapter 6, sections 2.3.1 and 3.2.3. To recall, contracts of indefinite period may be granted to temporary staff serving in the Commissioners' cabinets and to the 'Article 3a contract staff'. At the end of 2008, there were 2.822 staff in the Commission serving in these two categories, although not all 'Article 3a contract staff' held indefinite contracts given the fact that the initial contract, and in some instances also first few prolongations, is for fixed-term. In comparison, there were 4.833 staff serving in the Commission at the end of 2008 with contracts of fixed-term duration during the whole period of their engagement with the Commission. - *Commission's Human Resources Report 2009*, p. 30, including footnotes 5 and 6.

[506] For more details on the extension and renewal of UN non-career appointments, see chapter 6, section 2.3.2.

[507] See above, chapter 6, section 2.3.1.

fixed-term appointment may stay in service for a long of time, similarly as the EU non-career staff serving on indefinite contracts. In the UN Secretariat the expiration of the fixed-term appointment in these cases thus does not necessarily lead to separation of staff concerned. On the contrary, in the European Commission, all fixed-term appointments have an overall time limit, except those that may be converted to appointments of indefinite duration.[508] All staff serving in the European Commission on fixed-term contracts which may not be converted into indefinite ones thus must leave the Commission upon the expiry of the maximum period.

Third, although some UN fixed-term appointments may last relatively long, unless there are other reasons explicitly specified in the *UN Staff Regulations* or in the letter of appointment justifying earlier separation, these appointments end on the expiration date. They may not be terminated by giving a notice before the expiration date. The UN Administration also cannot terminate fixed-term appointments in the interest of the good administration of the organization, unless the staff member in question agrees.[509] In contrast, the EU Administration's discretion in terminating fixed-term contracts is broad, though only with temporary and contract staff, and not with local staff serving in non-member countries. The EU Administration may end fixed-term contracts of the former at any time by giving a notice, subject to the period of notice and to the obligation to state reason(s) for termination.[510] There is thus considerably more flexibility in the European Commission than in the UN Secretariat with regard to termination of fixed-term appointments. A consequence of this flexibility is, of course, that fixed-term staff in the European Commission are less protected against losing their job than their UN colleagues.

A further, more comprehensive, analysis of the use of fixed-term appointments and/or contracts and contracts for indefinite duration in the UN Secretariat and in the European Commission, including their consequences for the staff protection against abusive separation from their organization, is offered in the previous chapter.[511]

4.3.2. Retirement

Reaching the established age is one of the reasons for which appointment of all UN and EU staff ends automatically, i.e. upon the occurrence of the situation, just as it is with the expiration of date and death. As explained above, retirement is mandatory in both organizations, though the mandatory retirement age is higher in the EU – 65 years, as opposed to 62 or 60 years in the UN, depending on whether the UN staff entered the service before or after 1990. In both organizations, staff may retire earlier, though this does not seem to apply to EU non-career staff. Similarly, in both organizations retention beyond the retirement age is possible, in both cases it being

---

[508] See above, chapter 6, section 3.2.3.

[509] See above, section 2.3.1.

[510] See above, section 3.3.2.

[511] See above, chapter 6, in particular sections 2.4.2, 3.2.3 and 4.

an exceptional and time limited matter. In the European Commission, once again, retention seems to be only possible in case of permanent officials.[512]

It is interesting to note that although the period for which staff who have reached mandatory retirement age may be retained in service is longer in the European Commission – two years as opposed to only half a year in the UN Secretariat – it is the latter that has developed an elaborate set of rules on the conditions and set up procedures for taking decisions on staff retention.[513] No such set of rules appears to exist in the European Commission, where the basic requirements for retention are contained in the *EU Staff Regulations*.[514]

The conditions and the procedure in place in the UN Secretariat seem to be more stringent than the few conditions required by the *EU Staff Regulations*, namely the exceptional nature and the maximum period of two years. In the UN Secretariat, the retention is subject to the impossibility to find a replacement for the retiring staff member in due time, circumstances beyond control, and the actual need for the staff member's service. The retention must be in the interest of the UN, not (only) the staff member concerned. Decisions on retaining staff due to retire are taken not by Heads of Departments, who are normally competent to decide on appointments, but by the Assistant Secretary-General for Human Resources Management and in case of staff serving at the D-2 level, by the Under-Secretary-General for Management.[515] No such special requirements or procedural safeguards exist in the European Commission, which is regrettable, considering that absence of rules normally creates greater vulnerability to their misuse or abuse, for example, by retaining an official backed by (and useful to) 'his' government.

Another, arguably more important, difference in the UN and the EU approach in respect of staff who have reached the retirement age is the possibility of re-employing staff who have actually retired later. This is possible in the UN Secretariat but not in the European Commission. The Commission officials who have retired may not return to work again, unless they are appointed as special advisers, which would in most cases be an unpaid activity. In the UN Secretariat, staff who have retired may return to the Secretariat after a break of three months under certain conditions, such as that UN operational requirements cannot be met by the available staff, engagement of a retiree is the best solution and there are no adverse effects on the career of the regular staff.[516] Despite many advantages of this approach for meeting operational needs of the UN Secretariat, it has been long criticized for its adverse effects on the career of regular staff members.[517] Moreover, it could be argued that the possibility of re-employment of retired staff could be misused for getting (only) favoured persons back in the Secretariat, if sufficient efforts are made by those who wish to (continue to) have such persons on board. In the end, regular turn out of staff

[512] See above, sections 2.2.4, 3.2.4 and 3.3.8.

[513] See above, section 2.2.4.1.

[514] See above, section 3.2.4.

[515] See above, section 2.2.4.1.

[516] See above, section 2.2.4.2.

[517] See above, section 2.2.4.2.

contributes not only to the work force's refreshment, much needed for ensuring its high quality, effectiveness and innovativeness. It also helps to ensure that should improper ties exist between individual staff members and extraneous sources, they will be regularly cut upon the staff members' departure from the organization.

4.3.3. Health reasons

Unsurprisingly, permanent health problems of a staff member may lead to separation in both the UN Secretariat and the European Commission. Such step may in both institutions be taken only after the maximum sick leave has been exhausted. The difference is that while in the European Commission, separation for health reasons is an automatic consequence of the recognition of officials' permanent incapacity by the Invalidity Committee, in the UN appointments of such staff 'may' be terminated by the UN Administration.[518] The word 'may' suggests that the UN Administration enjoys, at least formally, discretion in this respect. This is rather surprising as it is difficult to imagine that a staff member incapacitated to perform his duties would be forced to nonetheless do so. However, from the point of view of this study, this difference between the UN and the EU does not appear to have any significant consequences for the independence and impartiality of UN and EU staff retired for health reasons.

Similarly as with other matters, here too the *UN Staff Regulations* and the *UN Staff Rules* make no distinction among staff holding different types of appointment. In the European Commission, a different regime applies to permanent officials on the one hand and 'other servants' on the other. When the former get permanently incapacitated due to health reasons, they are 'retired' and receive invalidity allowance. Of course, when the sickness is not permanent, officials are entitled to a sick leave after which they return to work. Similar situation occurs when the invalidity is no longer the case. When a formerly incapacitated EU official is capable of performing his work again, he loses his invalidity allowance and must return to work. If he refuses to accept an offered position twice, he may be required to resign.[519] Contrary to EU officials, EU 'other servants' may be separated from service when they are sick even if their sickness is not of a permanent nature. The decisive element here is the period of sick leave. When at the end of such period the sick 'other servant' is unable to return to work, he may be separated.[520] These differences too do not seem to be of relevance to the independence and impartiality of UN and EU staff. What may be of (more) relevance are procedures to be followed when an individual staff member is to be separated for health reasons.

In order to protect such staff member against possible abuse of this legal ground for separation, a separate administrative instruction has been prepared and adopted in the UN Secretariat, setting out the procedure as well as rights of the staff

[518] See above, sections 2.3.3, 3.2.3 and 3.3.5.
[519] See above, section 3.2.3.
[520] See above, section 3.3.5.

concerned.[521] In the EU, relevant provisions can be found at different places in the *EU Staff Regulations* and their Annexes II and VIII, which is a rather confusing situation. On the other hand, the process in the European Commission seems to be simpler than in the UN Secretariat. In the European Commission, when an official exhausts his sick leave, the Invalidity Committee determines whether he is incapacitated for work and if so, automatically retired and awarded invalidity allowance.[522] In the UN Secretariat, there are many steps to be taken before such decision is adopted, involving the UN medical director, possibly a medical board, the UN Joint Staff Pension Committee, the OHRM and the Assistant Secretary-General for Human Resources Management.[523]

In both organizations, the objectivity of the process, in particular of the decision on the incapacity for further work, is ensured by the composition of the EU Invalidity Committee and the UN medical board. They both consist of a medical doctor chosen by the staff member under consideration, a doctor chosen by the Administration and one chosen by the first two. The difference is that the involvement of the UN medical board must be required by the staff member concerned disagreeing with the initial determination of the state of his health by the UN medical director. The EU Invalidity Committee is always involved, taking the initial decision itself. Further, the decision of the EU Invalidity Committee is final and has direct legal consequences for the staff member at issue. When the Invalidity Committee finds that the staff member is permanently incapacitated to work, his service with the EU is automatically terminated and he is entitled to invalidity allowance. In the UN, when the medical board finds invalidity, the case still needs to be submitted to the UN Joint Staff Pension Committee for the decision on the award of disability benefit and afterwards to the OHRM for the decision on termination of appointment.[524] In the UN, thus, the whole process is longer and more complex than in the EU, but this is, in itself, not problematic. Moreover, the fact that also UN staff are able to require their case being reviewed by a collective body, more suitable to ensure objective and impartial assessment than an individual, makes the position of UN staff retired for health reason comparable to that of EU staff. In both cases, sufficient safeguards exist against possible misuse or abuse of power by the Administration that would wish to separate an 'uncomfortable' staff member using health reasons as a disguise.

4.3.4. Incompetence

Incompetence is also a reason for separating both UN and EU staff, although, once again, there is no explicit legal ground for such separation in case of European

[521] See above, section 2.3.3.

[522] See above, section 3.2.3.

[523] See above, section 2.3.3.

[524] See above, sections 2.3.3 and 3.2.3.

Commission temporary and contract staff. Therefore, these staff could be separated for incompetence only through being given a notice of termination.[525]

It is remarkable that in both organizations at issue, incompetence was approached in the past as a disciplinary matter. During the recent reform process, however, both organizations redefined their approach in this respect and began stressing improvement of the underperforming staff rather than their immediate punishment. More work appears to have been done in the UN Secretariat in this area. The most recent UN staff evaluation system referred to as Performance Management and Development System, adopted in 2010, explicitly regulates how underperformance should be handled. Only in cases in which these efforts fail to produce a satisfactory result, may the appointment of the staff member concerned be terminated, in accordance with an administrative instruction that sets out detailed rules for termination.[526] In the EU, there is a new version of the relevant provision of the *EU Staff Regulations* concerning the procedure for termination of service for incompetence. However, unlike in the UN Secretariat, no formal rules have been adopted by the European Commission for addressing underperformance.[527] This is regrettable as it provides staff who experience difficulties with their performance level with no safeguards they could refer to when trying to prevent their (premature) separation.

As regards procedures for separation of incompetent staff, in both organizations a joint body assesses the case and recommends action to be taken to the relevant appointing authority. The staff member concerned must be in both instances informed of the proposal to separate him, of the opinion of the joint body and of the final decision of the appointing authority, including the statement of reasons. Both UN and EU staff enjoy due process rights, though it seems that the position of EU officials is better in this respect than that of their UN colleagues. EU officials have the right to obtain their full personal file, to make copies of all relevant documents, to prepare their defence, to be assisted by another person, to call witnesses, and to be heard in person. UN staff have only the right to comment on the proposal or any related matter and to request information needed from other staff members. UN staff do not have the right to be heard by the joint body, unless this body considers it appropriate. The proposal of the joint body is reviewed by another, namely the central review body, before it is submitted to the appointing authority, which is a legal safeguard ensuring greater objectivity of the process. In addition, the joint review body is obliged to endure a fair review of the case.[528] Nonetheless, the absence of the formal right to be heard is surprising and difficult to explain. Apart from this, however, it could be argued that both the UN Secretariat and the European Commission offer sufficient guarantees for the objectivity of the existing procedures that lead to separation of incompetent staff.

Another notable difference between the UN Secretariat and the European Commission is the existence of special rules on underperformance of middle

---

[525] See above, sections 2.3.5, 3.2.5, 3.3.2 and 3.3.9.

[526] See above, section 2.3.5.

[527] See above, section 3.2.5.

[528] See above, sections 2.3.5 and 3.2.5.

management staff. When European Commission staff are found to be insufficiently performing their duties, they are not separated but transferred to another, possibly non-managerial, post.[529] This seems to be a good and constructive solution to the problem of underperformance by middle management staff as their deficiencies might indeed disappear in a post more suitable to their personal competences. However, this solution is not available for the European Commission senior officials since, by their nature, senior posts always involve management duties and responsibilities. Transfer to a non-managerial post is thus only possible for middle management staff whose performance is unsatisfactory. In the UN Secretariat, no special rules for middle or senior management staff are in place. All staff whose performance is unsatisfactory and does not improve during the remedial action could be, in principle, separated. Although appropriateness of such arrangement could be disputed, it does not appear that it has any significant consequences relevant for this study.

Last but not least remark on the possibility of separation of international civil servants for incompetence concerns 'other servants' serving in the European Commission. These staff do not receive treatment comparable to that of Commission officials or UN staff. Since there is no specific legal ground for separation for incompetence of Commission temporary and contract staff, these staff may be separated simply by giving them a notice of termination.[530] This means that special procedures for dealing with incompetence, including due process rights, do not apply to the Commission temporary and contract staff. Such staff have thus no possibility of formally defending themselves when accused of incompetence. A separate legal ground for separation of local staff serving in non-member countries does exist but there, too, no conditions, requirements or procedures are provided for.[531] Formally speaking, there is thus no protection of 'other servants' serving in the European Commission against abusive separation under a disguise of their incompetence. Since recently, the seriousness of this situation has decreased to some extent by the introduction by the EU judiciary of a duty to state reasons for each termination of service of EU 'other servants' by giving a notice.[532] This duty will certainly help to prevent incompetence being used as an excuse for termination of contracts. However, it will not change anything with regard to the right of 'other servants' to be helped first. While arguably not directly relevant for the independence and impartiality of other servants, it is nonetheless worrying especially in case of staff who serve in the European Commission on indefinite contracts, i.e. in many cases for a relatively long period of time.

[529] See above, section 3.2.5.

[530] See above, section 3.3.2.

[531] See above, section 3.3.9.

[532] See abovem, chapter 6, section 3.2.3.

4.3.5. Disciplinary reasons

Unsurprisingly, disciplinary offenses may lead to staff separation in both the UN Secretariat and the European Commission. The approach of the two institutions is very similar. It entails a duty of all staff to report misconduct to their supervisors and/or relevant organs, their protection against retaliation for doing so, investigation of the allegations, disciplinary proceedings, possibility of suspension of the staff member concerned during the process, final decision by the administration, possibly including imposition of a disciplinary measure, and judicial review. It also entails broad discretion of the Administration in each of the steps to be taken during the disciplinary process, the requirement of due process and protection of the staff member concerned, and the requirement of proportionality of the imposed disciplinary measure to the offense.[533]

A number of differences between the UN Secretariat and the European Commission can be detected. To begin with more formal differences, unlike the *EU Staff Regulations*, the *UN Staff Regulations* and the *UN Staff Rules* do not contain concrete provisions on the procedures to be used in the disciplinary process. They are contained in an administrative instruction by the Secretary-General who may, however, alter this instruction at any time and with no need for approval by the UN General Assembly or other body. On the contrary, the *EU Staff Regulations* include Annex IX which sets out in relative detail the legal framework for disciplinary matters, though particulars are further specified by individual institutions in their internal decisions, such as the *Commission Decision on Disciplinary Proceedings*. Until 2009, the *UN Staff Rules* contained specific provisions on the disciplinary process, too. The situation changed in the context of the reform of the UN system of the administration of justice and both the *UN Staff Regulations* and the *UN Staff Rules* have been left only with basic provisions in this regard. On the other hand, it must be admitted that the *UN Staff Rules* do pay detailed attention to the requirement of due process in disciplinary cases.[534]

Another notable formal difference is the wealth of documents in which obligations of UN staff are repeatedly set out, defined and/or interpreted. All obligations for which Commission staff may be held responsible are contained in the *EU Staff Regulations*, though the Commission has developed an additional guide providing illustrations of rights and obligations of the Commission staff, rules for their conduct as well as consequences of breach of obligations. The situation in the European Commission appears thus to be more transparent and simpler. It is easier for staff to be acquainted with what is expected from them. In the UN Secretariat, staff seem to be overburdened by yet another instruction and/or code they need to keep in mind but which they probably just add to the pile of all the other documents without giving it a proper reading.[535]

---

[533] See above, sections 2.3.6, 3.2.7 and 3.3.6.

[534] See above, sections 2.3.6 and 3.2.7.

[535] See above, sections 2.3.6.1 and 3.2.7.1.

Although both UN and EU staff have a duty to report breach of obligations by their colleagues or supervisors, in the European Commission this duty is not absolute. It only relates to illegal conduct or a serious failure to comply with one's obligations which, moreover, have become known to the reporting staff member in relation to the performance of professional duties.[536] This is rather surprising and difficult to understand. From the point of view of this study, it is also regrettable as it does not help to uncover all situations in which EU staff act in a manner breaching their professional obligations, including those ensuring their independence and impartiality. No comparable qualification of the duty to report breach of obligation exists in the UN Secretariat. In both organizations, however, the staff member who reports misconduct is, in principle, protected against retaliation, though the condition in both the UN Secretariat and the European Commission is that the reporting was done in good faith.[537] In the European Commission, details on the manner in which protection is extended are set out in an internal communication of the former Commission Vice-President responsible for human recourses matters. It entails confidentiality of the reporting staff member's identity and facilitation of move to another post, if required by the staff member concerned.[538] This appears to be the only existing manner in which retaliation is to be prevented. There is no specific provision or document on how to deal with retaliating staff, although it is self-evident that such staff could be subject to disciplinary proceedings. This would, however, depend on the form of retaliation. In the UN Secretariat, retaliation as such, thus disregarding its form, is always considered to be misconduct.[539] A separate set of rules has been developed for dealing with retaliation, setting out the procedures and rights and obligations of both the staff concerned as well as the UN Administration. The process is administered by a special UN Ethics Office set up, among others, for this purpose.[540] The UN Secretariat thus seems to pay more attention to the issue of retaliation than the European Commission. The former has developed a specific procedure to deal with the issue, whereas the latter even abolished in 2008 the single provision it had to protect staff reporting wrongdoing against retaliation via performance appraisal.[541] The situation in the European Commission can therefore be hardly considered as being supportive of reporting of wrongdoing, which is regrettable because it does not help to uncover possible problematic behaviour of the Commission's staff.

Another difference between the UN and the EU exists in the definition of misconduct. While in the UN not only breach of an obligation contained in the *UN Charter*, *UN Staff Regulations*, *UN Staff Rules* or other legal instruments are included but also failure 'to observe the standards of conduct expected of an international civil servant' may amount to misconduct, in the EU it is only 'failure ... to comply with ...

[536] See above, section 3.2.7.1.

[537] See above, sections 2.3.6.2 and 3.2.7.1.

[538] See above, section 3.2.7.1.

[539] *Secretary-General's Bulletin, Protection against Retaliation for Reporting Misconduct and for Cooperating with Duly Authorized Audits or Investigations*, Section 1.4.

[540] See above, section 2.3.6.2.

[541] See above, section 3.2.7.1.

obligation under [the EU] Staff Regulations' that may lead to disciplinary action.[542] This difference is, however, just formal since, as explained above, the *EU Staff Regulations* do contain a general obligation for all EU staff to refrain from action or conduct that could reflect adversely upon their position as EU officials.[543] It could thus be argued that the disobedience of the highest standards required from an international civil servant may lead to disciplinary action in both organizations.

In the UN Secretariat, formal classification of conduct as misconduct would depend on the degree of seriousness of the action or behaviour in question. If such degree of seriousness were high, it could be classified as serious misconduct, possibly leading to summary dismissal of the wrongdoer. In the European Commission, there is no formal distinction between misconduct and serious misconduct. There is also no possibility of dismissing the staff member at issue summarily, without a disciplinary process. The only available disciplinary measure in the European Commission is 'removal from post', as opposed to 'separation from service' and 'dismissal' in the UN Secretariat.[544] This means European Commission staff are better protected against separation than the UN staff, the former always requiring disciplinary proceedings before the decision on removal from post takes place, disregarding the seriousness of the misconduct. The absence of the requirement to conduct proper disciplinary process in the UN Secretariat in cases of alleged serious misconduct is unfortunate as it can be easily abused, leading to immediate separation of staff members who are no longer 'wanted'. This can include reasons not always correspondent to the interest of the organization.

Another formal difference between the UN Secretariat and the European Commission with regard to the action that may be taken against a wrongdoer is the distinction between administrative and disciplinary action which exists in the UN but not in the EU. In the latter, all penalties that may be imposed are regarded as disciplinary, including warning and reprimand which are in the UN formally considered to be administrative, not disciplinary, measures. On the other hand, imposition of these two measures, i.e. warning and reprimand, may in the EU occur without the involvement of the disciplinary board which normally takes part in the disciplinary proceedings. At the same time, although warning and reprimand are not disciplinary measures in the UN, their imposition is subject to the requirement of due process which must be accorded to the staff member at issue.[545] It could be thus argued that, despite a formal difference, the factual situation regarding warning and reprimand is very similar in the both organizations, protecting the staff member from facing either administrative or disciplinary action without the opportunity to defend himself.

Another difference, which however might have a real impact on the staff found guilty of misconduct, is the possibility to impose more than one administrative and/or disciplinary measure in the UN. In the EU, each offense may lead to just one

[542] See above, sections 2.3.6.1 and 3.2.71.

[543] See above, section 3.2.7.1.

[544] See above, sections 2.3.6.3 and 3.2.7.4.

[545] See above, sections 2.3.6.3 and 3.2.7.4.

disciplinary measure.[546] The EU staff found responsible for misconduct are thus in a more favourable position than their UN colleagues. Also the involvement of the disciplinary board, a collective consultative body which exists in the EU but not in the UN, can be seen as more advantageous for EU staff when compared to the UN staff.[547] Such a consultative body, independent of the Administration, enhances the objectivity of the disciplinary process. Although the final decision rests with the Administration in both organizations, a prior assessment of the case by another body ensures greater impartiality and objectivity of the decision. At present, this is lacking in the UN Secretariat.

Full professionalization of the review of disciplinary decisions in the UN is another significant difference between the UN and the EU. In the EU, disciplinary decisions must first be challenged administratively, i.e. by a complaint addressed to the same authority which adopted the initial decision. Only when the complaint is unsuccessful, the EU staff member concerned may turn to the judiciary for further review. In the UN, this is no longer the case. The review of disciplinary decisions is done by the judiciary already in first instance, with a possibility of an appeal.[548] Appeal against judicial decision is also possible in the EU. In fact, two appeals are possible, subject to certain admissibility conditions.[549] The removal of the requirement of a prior internal administrative review of disciplinary decisions in the UN makes the UN process faster and thus more effective – it is generally known that, certainly in some cases, justice delayed is justice denied. It is self-evident that access to judicial review must be facilitated by admissibility, legal assistance and cost bearing arrangements which do not deter staff from filing an application. It seems the UN system offers reasonable guarantees in this respect by granting legal assistance to all staff members who wish to make use of it through the newly established Office of Staff Legal Assistance. The possibility of using this assistance also removes financial disincentives for filing an application since there is no need to hire a lawyer at own expense, though it is permitted. The costs for such a private lawyer would have to be borne by the staff member but they could be awarded by the judge in case of a 'manifest abuse' of the proceedings by the UN Administration.[550]

When compared to the UN system, the requirement of a prior administrative complaint in disciplinary cases existing in the EU appears less appropriate. Given the fact that in these (i.e. disciplinary) cases the EU Administration and the staff member concerned exchange their views on the matter a number of times before the decision is taken, it is rather unlikely that an administrative complaint, dealt with by the same Administration, will succeed. Therefore, it could be argued that the

---

546 See above, sections 2.3.6.3 and 3.2.7.4.

547 See above, sections 2.3.6.2 and 3.2.7.3.

548 See above, section 2.3.6.2.

549 See above, section 3.2.7.5.

550 *UN Staff Rules*, Rule 11.4(d); and the Statute of the United Nations Dispute Tribunal, Article 9.6 and the Statute of the United Nations Appeals Tribunal, Article 9.2, to be found in *General Assembly Resolution 63/253*, Annex I and II. See also *Secretary-General's Bulletin, Organization and Terms of Reference of the Office of Administration of Justice, ST/SGB/2010/3*, available in the Human Resources Handbook of the United Nations, available at http://www.un.org/hr_handbook/English/, last visited on 30.12.2010.

requirement of a prior administrative complain in disciplinary cases only prolongs the whole process. While perhaps not directly detrimental to the staff member concerned who, in the end, may resort to a judicial body for review of his case, the requirement may result in delays in bringing justice to this staff member.

4.3.6. Posterior discovery of relevant facts

This reason for staff separation is present in both the UN Secretariat and the European Commission under the same conditions – information in question was not known at the time of appointment while it would have been decisive for decision on the appointment if known. Moreover, separation must be preceded by a disciplinary process. This is not explicitly required in the UN but it is done in practice, as evidenced by the relevant case law.[551] In the EU too, disciplinary proceedings are applied in such cases. There, however, an explicit provision allowing staff separation for the reason of false information is only provided for temporary and contract staff but not for permanent or local staff serving in non-member countries.[552] However, since disciplinary proceedings are explicitly required by the *EU Conditions of Employment of Other Servants* in case of temporary and contract staff, it can be argued that such proceedings would be initiated also if permanent officials or local staff serving in non-member countries had provided false information at the time of their appointment. In any case, the applicability of disciplinary proceedings to all cases is an important legal safeguard ensuring objectivity of the process leading to staff separation as well as respect of due process rights of the staff concerned.

4.4. Issues with significant differences

4.4.1. Abandonment of post

This reason for staff separation exists only in the UN and not in the EU. If a post is abandoned in the EU, it would most probably be handled as a disciplinary matter. Although the *UN Staff Rules* as well as the relevant administrative instruction emphasize that post abandonment is deemed separation from service initiated by the staff member concerned, in the EU it would not be possible to treat it as resignation since that must be done in writing and 'unequivocally'.[553] Moreover, resignation of an EU official, as well as its equivalent – termination of a contract of an 'other servant' by giving a notice – are subject to a period of notice during which the staff member concerned must continue to perform duties.[554] Leaving the office from one day to another would thus be regarded as a violation of obligations relating to working hours, leave as well as performance of duties, for which disciplinary proceedings may be initiated.

[551] See above, section 2.3.4.

[552] See above, section 4.3.6.

[553] See above, sections 2.2.3 and 3.2.2.

[554] See above, section 3.2.2 and 3.3.2.

In the UN Secretariat, separation on the basis of abandonment of post occurs pursuant to an elaborate administrative instruction containing many safeguards against possible abuse or misuse, including due process rights for the staff member at issue. It is in line with jurisprudence which precedes this instruction and is fairly comparable with the requirements of disciplinary process.[555] It is, nonetheless, remarkable that abandonment of post has a separate legal basis in the *UN Staff Regulations* and *UN Staff Rules*.

4.4.2. Abolition of a post or reduction of staff

Abolition of a post or reduction of staff is an explicit reason for terminating all types of appointments in the UN, but not in the EU. Of course, this does not necessarily mean that EU staff may not be separated on this basis. As repeatedly mentioned, contracts of European Commission 'other servants' may be terminated at any time by giving a notice, thus also in situations in which there is a need to abolish a post or to reduce staff.[556] The only exception are local staff serving under a fixed-term contract in non-member countries, in whose case this possibility is not available. However, the *Commission Framework Rules on Local Staff Serving in Non-Member Countries* provide an explicit basis for terminating of contracts of these staff 'in the event that the Commission's activities in non-member countries being cut back or changed in the interest of service'.[557]

The situation with regard to European Commission permanent officials is a bit more complicated. First of all, Commission officials affected by staff reduction may not be separated directly – they are first placed on non-active status and continue to receive income from the Commission in the form of allowance. As explained above, the period for which the non-active status is accorded to an individual official depends on his age and length of service in the Commission. For older officials who have spent most of their career in the Commission, this period may be longer than 10 years.[558] Second, separation of staff on non-active status occurs only when they have not been placed in another post by the end of their non-active status period, or when they have declined an offered position that corresponds to their grade without a good reason during the first two years after being placed on non-active status, such staff having priority for reinstatement in any suitable new or vacant post.[559] Third, this regime only applies to situations in which staff need to be reduced but not in those in which an individual post is abolished – the relevant provision of the *EU Staff Regulations* refers only to reduction of staff. It is however unlikely that an official whose post has been abolished would have to be retained in active service without a suitable post being available for his new placement. In addition, there is no legal ground available for direct separation of such official. Last, it could be argued that

[555] See above, section 2.2.3.

[556] See above, section 3.3.2.

[557] *Commission Framework Rules on Local Staff*, Article 18(6). See also above, section 3.3.10.

[558] The precise calculation of the period of allowance can be found in *EU Staff Regulations*, Annex IV.

[559] See above, section 3.2.3.

abolition of an individual post, certainly when no new post is created, amounts to staff reduction, albeit with the smallest number possible. Hence, the legal regime applicable to staff reduction is usable also in post abolition cases, although this is not explicitly mentioned in the *EU Staff Regulations*.

A few important differences between the EU and UN regimes need to be noted. To begin with, unlike with EU officials, separation of UN staff affected by post abolition or staff reduction occurs directly after the decision on such action is taken, subject only to the period of notice of three months in case of career staff, one month in case of fixed-term staff and fifteen days in case of temporary staff, and the obligation to investigate the availability of other suitable posts for placement of affected staff.[560] The obligation to search for alternative employment within the organization is another notable difference between the UN and the EU – no such obligation exists in the European Commission, while it does in the UN Secretariat.[561] There, the initiative of finding another post appears to behove more on the affected official than on the Administration. Of course, the latter would probably search for available posts itself in order to reduce costs, i.e. allowances paid to these staff during their non-active status. However, unlike in the UN, the EU Administration has no legal obligation to do so.

It could be argued that this provision in the UN Secretariat is a consequence of less strict, and for staff less advantageous, conditions for separation in case of abolition of a post or staff reduction, as compared to EU officials. The latter are better protected than UN staff not only in case of, but also against, losing their jobs. As they remain in EU service for the period of non-active status, EU officials do not need to worry about their future income as much as UN staff who find themselves 'on the street' a few months at most after their post is abolished or the decision to reduce staff is taken. EU officials also do not need to worry about their professional future as much. By remaining in service, EU officials have a chance to find a new position and thereby to prevent separation. Two important rules, mentioned above, make the position of EU officials easier than that of UN staff. When applying to a new position in the EU civil service, EU officials on non-active status enjoy preference over all other candidates during the first two years and afterwards in preference to all external candidates. As explained in one of the previous chapters, internal candidates always have a priority before external candidates when vacant posts are filled.[562] By formally remaining in service, EU officials on non-active status are still deemed 'internal'. This gives them a bigger chance to find another post when compared to UN staff. Certainly, also in case of the latter an alternative employment must be investigated before separation from service may take place. However, this investigation takes place in a relatively short period of time, whereas in the EU the non-active status, during which alternative employment is sought, may last years.

With the exception of young EU officials serving in the Commission for a relatively short period of time, the duration for which EU officials affected by staff reduction

[560] See above, section 2.3.2.

[561] See above, section 2.3.2.

[562] See above, chapter 3, section 1.

are placed of non-active status is fairly long. For young staff, it is only a few months, but for an official of 40 years of age serving in the European Commission for 15 years, for example, non-active status is more than seven years, assuming he started to work in the Commission at the age of 25. Moreover, the older the official, the longer the period for which he is placed on non-active status, even if the period of service is the same. During this whole period, officials receive allowances replacing their regular salary. In the above example, the official at issue would receive allowance equal to 70 per cent of his salary for the most part of his non-active status period. Hence, except for very young staff, EU officials have a considerable time and space to search for alternatives within the EU civil service with fewer worries about their income and professional future than UN staff.

Compared to the situation in the European Commission, UN staff have less time to find another job before loosing income, inside or outside the UN. The period of notice, mentioned above, during which UN staff may be considered as internal candidates is short. Also the period for which termination indemnity is due in order to compensate staff for the loss of income after separation from service is not comparable to the time EU officials may spend in non-active status. The maximum period for which indemnity is paid in the UN Secretariat is 12 months in the case of staff with the length of service of 15 years or more, disregarding the age.[563] This also applies to UN career staff who are, in principle, expected to spend (a large part of) their professional lives in the UN Secretariat. It is true that the recent reform of contractual arrangements emphasized that there was no more security of tenure in the UN, also not for staff serving on continuing appointments. However, in respect of separation from service for reasons of post abolition or staff reduction, the same conditions applied before the reform of contractual arrangements, too.[564] In addition, staff serving on continuing appointments are referred to as career staff, whose separation is subject to rather strict conditions. There is thus a clear expectation that staff serving on continuing appointments will spend a long time in the UN Secretariat. Their protection in case of separation due to post abolition or staff reduction, however, does not reflect this in any way.

One of the possible consequences of this situation can be the existence of more temptation to use post abolition or staff reduction as a disguise for separation of 'uncomfortable' career staff in the UN Secretariat, more than in the European Commission. In the latter, these two reasons do not lead directly to termination of service of the staff member(s) concerned, only to their placement on non-active status. Using these reasons as a disguise for staff separation would therefore not be a very effective, and certainly not a fast, way.

As far as non-career staff are concerned, of course, these staff serve on time-limited contracts and have in principle no expectation of continuation of service after the expiry date of their contract. This is also reflected in the order of preference for retention of UN staff in cases of staff reduction. As explained above, the *UN Staff*

[563] For details on termination indemnity in the UN, see *UN Staff Rules*, Rule 9.8 and Annex III.

[564] *UN Staff Regulations of 2007*, Regulation 9.3 and Annex III. See also *UN Staff Rules of 2002*, Rule 109.1(c) and 109.4.

Rules set out a precise order in which staff with different type of appointment may be separated, depending also on other criteria, such as competence, integrity and length of service. In principle, however, career staff are retained in service in preference to non-career staff.[565] On the other hand, it must be recalled that the new fixed-term appointment is the only entry door to the UN career service.[566] A certain level of protection of staff serving on such fixed-term appointments is reflected in the obligation to investigate alternative employment in the organization in case of post abolition or staff reduction. This obligation applies equally to UN career and non-career staff. The UN approach to separation of non-career staff therefore seems stricter than in the EU. There, the Administration enjoys maximal flexibility with regard to termination of contracts of 'other servants'. It not only has no obligation to offer another position but needs to pay no allowances to 'other servants' separated due to abolition of a post or reduction of staff.[567] In case of staff serving in the European Commission on contracts of indefinite duration, this arrangement seems rather harsh, considering that many of these staff may have spent as much time in the Commission service as permanent officials. That said, from the point of view of this study, possible abuse of post abolition or staff reduction for termination of service of EU 'other servants' not really affected by it is now prevented by the already mentioned duty to state reasons for each termination by giving a notice.

The last notable difference between the UN and the EU is that there is no specific procedure for taking decisions on separation of UN staff due to abolition of posts or staff reduction. There is also no requirement to consult a joint body. In the European Commission, such procedure and requirement are provided for when affected staff are Commission permanent officials. These conditions apply to the adoption of the decision to reduce staff numbers and to that identifying precise posts and thus staff thereby affected. Further, the requirement to consult a joint body applies also to the decision to require resignation of an individual official in non-active status who has refused a new position offered to him during the first two years of his non-active status, as well as to decisions to separate local staff in non-member countries due to cutbacks.[568] The involvement of a joint body in the process of separation of staff on this basis certainly enhances objectivity and transparency of the process.

4.4.3. Interest of the organization

Most UN and EU staff may *not* be separated in 'the interest of the good administration of the organization', a phrase used in the UN, or 'the interests of the service', a phrase used in the EU. In the UN, separation of non-career staff on this ground is subject to staff consent which is unlikely to be obtained in many cases. In the EU, such separation is only possible in case of senior staff.[569] Of course, other than senior

[565] See above, section 2.3.2.

[566] See above, chapter 6, sections 2.3.1 and 2.3.2.

[567] See above, sections 3.3.2 and 3.3.10.

[568] See above, section 3.2.3.

[569] See above, section 2.3.1 and 3.2.5.

staff could always agree to separation, too. Legally speaking, such separation would, however, fall under resignation as there is no specific legal ground for separation in the interests of service for EU non-senior staff or for separation by an agreement. Differences between the UN Secretariat and the European Commission in this respect do not stop here, though. Also where separation is possible, conditions under which it may take place differ.

In the European Commission, the Administration enjoys a wide discretion in deciding whether and when to separate an individual senior official on the basis of the interests of the service. The range of reasons for such separation is very broad, limited in fact only by the prohibition of abuse or misuse of power.[570] It could be argued that a comparable situation exists in the UN Secretariat in cases of separation in the interest of the good administration of the organization with staff consent. There, too, the interest of the good administration of the organization could be interpreted broadly. However, discretion of the UN Administration is, once again, limited by the requirement of staff consent. In the only case in which no consent is needed, i.e. in case of staff serving on continuing appointments, the interest of the good administration of the organization is interpreted strictly.[571] Discretion of the UN Administration is thus limited. This applies to all staff serving on continuing appointments, with no exception for senior staff. It means that UN senior staff are better protected against separation on this ground than EU senior staff. On the other hand, EU non-senior career staff are better protected than UN non-senior career staff. While the former may never be separated in the interests of the service (without agreeing to resign themselves), the latter may, though reasons for separation in the interest of the good administration of the organization are limited by restrictive interpretation of this legal ground. Last but not least, there is no protection of most EU non-career staff. Although there is no explicit legal ground for separation of EU temporary and contract staff in the interests of the service, once again, they may be separated at any time by giving a notice of termination. This also applies to local staff serving in non-member countries on an indefinite contract but not those on fixed-term contract.[572] The latter may thus not be separated in the interests of the service.

The differences in the UN and the EU approaches are understandable. Each of them is based on a different legitimate interest. The absolute protection of EU officials is a consequence of tenure needed for the protection of these officials, their independence and impartiality. The minimal protection of EU senior officials is a result of the special, partly political, nature of EU senior posts which is generally considered to be necessary for achieving various professional, managerial and political interests. The lack of protection for EU non-permanent staff is due to the temporary nature of their engagement, needed in order to ensure flexibility in human resources management. The limited protection of UN staff serving on continuing appointments is based on the same need for flexibility but at the same time on the career nature of

[570] See above, section 3.2.5.

[571] See above, section 2.3.1. See also chapter 6, section 2.3.3.

[572] See above, section 3.3.2.

these staff and the need for their protection against separation not based on serious reasons. The emphasis on the flexibility of the UN career staff above the career nature of these staff and the need for their protection by tenure is perhaps the most striking difference between the UN and the EU in this area. While the EU recognizes that the core of the EU civil service must be protected against firing in order to ensure their independence and impartiality, the UN places the need for flexibility above this interest. In the EU, flexibility is sought rather by employment of non-career staff and by internal mobility of career staff.

4.4.4. Refusal of offered post after absence

Only in the EU is it possible to separate officials on the basis of their refusal to accept a new post they have been offered. Of course, it is only possible in a limited number of situations, namely upon return of the official in question from secondment, personal leave or sick leave. If such official refuses an offered post twice, he may be requested to resign. As noted above, the same may happen with the official who refuses an offered position while on non-active status. In this case, one refusal suffices for a request for resignation.[573]

This legal ground is not available in the UN. Neither can it be used in the EU for 'other servants'. Naturally, this is due to the availability of other grounds for staff separation for these or comparable reasons.

4.4.5. No longer meeting (certain) conditions of employment

This legal ground also exists only in the EU, for both permanent and non-permanent staff with the exception of local staff serving in non-member countries. EU staff may be separated when they lose EU nationality and do not get an exception to remain in service or when they are deprived of their full rights as a citizen.[574]

The absence of this legal ground for separation of UN staff is due to the fact that almost all countries in the world are UN members. Therefore, it is unlikely that a UN staff member will lose a nationality of a UN Member State without acquiring another's. Moreover, the possession of nationality of a UN Member State does not appear among requirements for appointment with the UN Secretariat. As for full rights as a citizen, if their loss resulted from psychological disease, separation could occur on the basis of incapacity for work for health reasons. If it were due to a serious (criminal) offence, separation could take place on disciplinary grounds. Thus, despite the absence of a specific legal ground for separation in such cases, it could take place. On the other hand, separation for the reason of losing nationality of a UN Member State is not possible. Neither would it make much sense since very few countries remain outside the UN.

573 See above, section 3.2.3.

574 See above, sections 3.2.3 and 3.3.3.

Both approaches regarding the loss of full rights as a citizen are also applicable to European Commission local staff serving in non-member countries for whom the specific legal ground for separation for this reason is not explicitly provided. Of course, it could be argued that these approaches could also be used with regard to EU officials and therefore, no special provision is needed for them either. The situation is different in relation to the nationality issue: the existence of a specific legal ground for separation of EU staff is necessary. This does not apply to local staff serving in non-member countries. They are 'local' and serve in 'non-member' countries and it is thus self-evident that the possession of EU nationality is not required for their engagement – or retention.

4.4.6. Incompetence during probation

This is yet another specific legal ground for separation of European Commission staff which can no longer be found in the UN Secretariat. The reason for this is that the probationary appointment no longer exists in the UN - it was abolished in the framework of the reform of contractual arrangements which took place in the UN in 2009.[575] The new types of appointment introduced by this reform are not subject to probation. On the other hand, if performance of a UN staff member is found unsatisfactory, the staff member may be separated in accordance with procedures that apply to termination of appointment for incompetence. Of course, the staff member at issue must first be assisted to improve his performance.[576]

In this sense, separation of European Commission staff on probation is easier. It must be based on a special report prepared either during or at the end of probationary period, depending on when the separation of a probationary staff member is sought. In either case no remedial action is required as a condition for separation.[577] In case of UN staff, separation for incompetence is always subject to such remedial action.[578]

It is interesting to note that European Commission local staff serving in non-member countries may only be separated at the end of the probationary period, not during its course.[579] The reason for this deviation of rule which applies to permanent officials but also to temporary and contract staff is unclear. It is also remarkable, and difficult to exaplain, that the procedure that applies to separation of a probationary contract staff serving in the European Commission is subject to a more complex procedure than separation of a permanent official on probation.[580]

---

575 For details on this reform, see chapter 6, section 2.3.

576 See above, section 2.3.5.

577 See above, sections 3.2.1 and 3.3.4.

578 See above, section 2.3.5.

579 See above, section 3.3.4.

580 See above, sections 3.2.1 and 3.3.4.

4.4.7. Seconded national experts

The last legal ground for separation of staff specific to the European Commission and not available in the UN Secretariat pertains to temporarily seconded national experts. As explained above, the *Commission Decision on Secondment* contains reasons for which secondment may terminate before the end of the period agreed to between the parties involved, i.e. the Commission, the seconded expert and his employer, usually the government of the EU Member State he is a national of.[581] These reasons are specific to the nature of secondment and cannot be applied to other European Commission staff.

National experts temporarily seconded to the UN Secretariat receive a fixed term appointment with a note that the situation at issue concerns secondment.[582] Neither the *UN Staff Regulations* nor the *UN Staff Rules*, however, contain a provision that would allow termination of secondment for reasons other than those applicable to regular fixed-term appointments. The only exception is a possibility to include a special provision on termination of secondment in the agreement concluded between the seconded national expert and his employer. This agreement is enclosed with the letter of appointment the seconded national expert receives upon entering the UN service.[583] However, when this agreement includes no special clause on termination of secondment, secondment may end only under the conditions applying to all other UN staff serving on fixed-term appointment.

This means that the seconded national experts serving in the UN Secretariat are better protected against termination of secondment than their colleagues in the European Commission. The former may, in principle, not be sent back to their employer on the basis of a unilateral decision of their original employer, unless such possibility is explicitly stated in the agreement between the seconded national expert and his employer. But the latter may be, subject to the condition of 'essential interests' requiring such action. These interests are not further defined or specified, leaving the employer with a wide discretion in the matter. The employer could thus, at least formally, end secondment at any time for reasons which could in practice relate to the conduct of the expert during his secondment, thereby exercising influence over the experts serving in the European Commission.

Another difference between the UN and the EU is that the EU Administration may terminate secondment unilaterally for a breach of an obligation by the seconded national expert but also by the employer, whereas the UN Administration may not.[584] Of course, a breach of an obligation may lead to termination of secondment if such a breach has been committed by the seconded national expert. Termination in this case would take place on one of the 'regular' legal grounds available for terminating fixed-term appointments. However, the *UN Staff Regulations* and the *UN Staff Rules*

---

581 See above, section 3.4.

582 *UN Staff Rules*, Rule 4.13(a) and Annex II, paragraph (c). See also above, chapter 6, section 2.3.1.

583 Ibid., Annex II, paragraph (c).

584 See above, section 3.4.

do not provide a legal ground for termination of a fixed-term appointment held by a seconded national expert for breach of obligation by the expert's employer.

Evidently, specific provisions that exist in the European Commission with regard to termination of secondment reflect its nature as a three-party agreement. However, in the UN Secretariat, where secondment occurs under the same basic principles, the seconded national expert becomes a member of the staff protected against possible pressure by rules on termination of his engagements in the UN Secretariat. These do not allow his employer to step in at any time but to wait until the fixed term of the secondment expires. Only at that point may the expert's employer exercise influence over its employee by, for example, preventing extension of secondment or renewal even if the UN Administration and the expert at issue would wished it.

5. Conclusions

The recent reforms in human resources management in the UN Secretariat and in the European Commission paid relatively little attention to issues related to possible separation of staff serving in the two institutions. With one exception, the list of legal grounds on the basis of which UN and EU staff may be separated has not changed, the exception being the abolition of the possibility to terminate appointment of UN staff during or at the end of probation, which itself was abolished. Even in this case, however, termination of appointment for incompetence may take place. The difference with the past system is that such termination must follow the general regime applicable to all UN staff. Termination is thus possible, the difference being the conditions under which it may occur.

A similar statement can be made with regard to the entire UN and also EU reform of human resources management in the area of staff separation. In both institutions there were no significant changes in the reasons for possible separation but there were some modifications of the conditions under which these reasons may be invoked. Among the most important changes that deserve repetition are, first, the improvements in procedures and due process rights that must be obeyed in disciplinary cases and, second, the abandonment of the disciplinary approach towards staff incompetence and the introduction of the requirement to try to help incompetent staff to remedy their performance before they may be separated. Both improvements took place in the UN Secretariat as well as in the European Commission, though as far as termination of service for incompetence is concerned the former seems to have done a better job than the latter. By spelling out precise remedial steps to be taken in incompetence cases, including the time frame, the new UN administrative instruction provides a better guarantee to staff in the UN Secretariat that their difficulties with meeting required standards of performance will be treated with attention and serious efforts made to solve the difficulties before their appointment can be terminated. Although the *EU Staff Regulations* require remedial action in such cases too, the European Commission has adopted no precise rules as to how this requirement is to be implemented in practice. Therefore, even though the Commission staff encountering problems with fulfilling their duties are able to invoke the general obligation of the Administration to assist them in improving their performance, they cannot refer to any precise guarantees and safeguards to be followed which would prevent that, for example, service of such staff will be terminated after only formal help has been offered.

The UN Secretariat offers higher protection to its staff in cases of possible separation in a few more instances compared to the European Commission, though it must be stressed that this applies in particular to UN and EU non-career staff. Apart from the already mentioned incompetence cases, the only other instances in which European Commission career staff enjoy lesser protection against separation than UN staff concern, first, probationary staff and, second, senior staff.

The Commission probationary staff may be separated during or at the end of their probation without the EU Administration being obliged to offer them a possibility to improve or even to assist them to do so. This is no longer possible in the UN Secretariat. As already noted, separation of UN staff who have joined the organization recently may only take place under the general regime applicable to all staff. This means that new staff may only be separated for incompetence after defined remedial action has failed to improve the situation. The position of UN staff is thus more favourable than that of EU probationary staff. However, the abolition of probationary appointment in the UN Secretariat is rather surprising – probation is a generally used human resources tool aimed at more efficient selection of staff suitable for employment in the organization from a long term perspective. Of course, it could be argued that, after the reform of the UN contractual arrangements, the situation in the UN Secretariat is of a particular nature as no career appointments are offered to staff before they have served on fixed-term appointments. All new staff will thus need to prove themselves and their suitability for career appointment before becoming eligible for it. If they do not, their fixed-term appointment will not be converted into a career one and/or not prolonged for another fixed-term period. The fixed-term appointment serves thus, in a way, as probationary appointment too. However, staff must serve on fixed-term appointments for five years before being eligible for career appointments. That is a relatively long probationary period – for both staff and the Administration which needs to keep ill-performing staff in service or apply remedial action before it may terminate their appointment. It is even probable that remedial action helps to improve performance sufficiently for not being able to separate the problem staff member but not sufficiently enough for considering him as meeting the highest standards of competence, efficiency and integrity required by the *UN Charter*. The high protection of staff who join the UN Secretariat is thus rather surprising and it remains to be seen how efficient it will prove. From the point of view of this study, however, this state of affairs does not appear to have significant consequences for the independence and impartiality of UN staff.

Also UN senior staff members enjoy better protection against separation than their EU counterparts. As explained above, European Commission senior staff may be separated in the interests of the service at any time, with virtually no restriction being placed on the EU Administration in deciding on such separation. In the UN Secretariat, separation of senior officials is not as easy. First of all, although the Under-Secretaries-General and the Assistant Secretaries-General do not fall within the scope of this study, they serve on fixed-term appointments which end, in principle upon the expiry of the date fixed in the contract. Termination of such contracts before the expiry date in the interests of the service, or – to use the UN terminology – in the interest of the good administration of the organization is not possible when the official at issue does not consent to it. No consent is required from UN senior officials holding D-2 and D-1 appointment, also considered to be senior officials. However, as it has been repeatedly stressed, the interest of the good administration of the organization has been interpreted by the UN General Assembly restrictively for cases in which it is used without staff consent. The discretion of the UN Administration is thus significantly less broad than that of the EU Administration exercising its right to terminate the service of Commission senior officials. The situation in the UN is rather surprising. Given the specific nature of senior appointments in both the UN and EU civil service, it would be understandable that UN senior staff too were subject to the possible termination of appointment whenever the interest of the organization requires it. That said, from the point of view of this study, the absence of such legal ground is a positive rather than a negative contribution to the protection of UN senior staff against separation from service, which could easily be done for improper motives rather than for the genuine interest of the UN.

Not only UN newly appointed and senior officials but also non-career staff in the UN appear to be better protected against separation compared to their EU colleagues. Since all UN non-career staff serve, under the new system of contractual arrangements, on fixed-term appointments, their engagement with the UN ends in principle upon the expiry of the term set out in the letter of appointment, save for the cases in which one of the legal grounds specified in the *UN Staff Regulations* or in the letter of appointment is present, such as misconduct, incompetence, incapacity due to health reasons, retirement, or death. An important consequence of the UN's exclusive use of fixed-term appointments for the engagement of non-career staff is that they are protected against being separated from service through the mere provision of a notice of termination. This is different in the European Commission where many staff continue to serve on contracts of indefinite duration which, due to their nature, may be terminated by each party by giving a notice to the other party. Moreover, in the European Commission even staff who serve on fixed-term contracts may be separated by receiving a notice of termination from the EU Administration, subject only to the period of notice. Unlike their UN colleagues, European Commission fixed-term staff enjoy no protection against termination which the period of engagement agreed to in the contract of employment should provide. The need for such protection has recently been emphasized by the EU judiciary, though even the EU courts could not disregard the fact that the *EU Conditions of Employment of Other Servants* do provide an explicit legal ground for termination of service before the expiry of the fixed-term by giving a notice. To better protect EU staff serving on such contracts, the EU courts have, however, introduced the requirement to provide reasons for termination. The same considerations were applied to termination of contracts of indefinite duration which, as mentioned above, provide even less protection against unilateral termination by the Administration than the fixed-term appointments. However, in the EU, the distinction between the two types of contract is, to certain extent, blurred precisely by the fact that both types of contract may be terminated at any time by providing a notice.

One more category of UN staff seems better protected against separation than their colleagues in the European Commission, namely the UN seconded national experts. Unless a specific agreement has been made between the original employer and the seconded national expert beforehand, the employer may not terminate secondment of his expert to the UN Secretariat whenever it suits him. Neither can secondment be terminated in such a way by the UN Administration. When deciding to terminate secondment, the Administration must adhere to rules applicable to any other staff member serving on fixed-term appointments. In contrast, national experts temporarily seconded to the European Commission may be called back by their employer whenever the latter considers his essential interest to be at stake. As already mentioned, the problem here is that the essential interest is not defined, giving a relatively free hand to the original employers of national experts seconded to the European Commission. Such broad discretion may result in abuse, including possible pressure employers may exercise upon their experts to serve their interests (too), not (only) those of the Commission. Of course, there might be situations in which original employers may need their experts to return but, in order to avoid possible abuse and safeguard the independence and impartiality of the seconded national experts, such situations should be clearly delineated.

When assessing UN and EU career staff, in general it must be concluded that career staff serving in the European Commission are better protected against, and in case of, separation from service than UN career staff. Even when there is need for reduction in staff numbers, European Commission permanent officials do not lose their job directly but remain in service, on a non-active status, for a relatively long period of time. Of course, higher protection of EU career staff when compared to UN career staff is partly due to the fact that the UN no longer offers permanent appointments, while the EU does. In the EU, there is no equivalent to the possibility to terminate the new type of UN career appointments, referred to as continuing appointments, in the interest of the good administration of the organization without staff members' consent which exists in the UN now. On the other hand, it remains to be seen whether, and if so how, this specific legal ground for termination of UN career appointments is implemented in practice, given its restrictive interpretation by the UN General Assembly and the availability of other legal grounds for separation for the same reasons as those included in the Assembly's principal interpretation.

Apart from the consequences of the abolition of permanent appointments in the UN Secretariat, there are other differences in procedures and conditions required for separation of staff which place European Commission staff in a better position than that enjoyed by UN staff, although they could be more or less easily applied in the UN, too. For example, UN staff to be separated for reasons of post abolition or staff reduction could be given a priority position in the UN staff selection process, at least during the period of notice or during the period for which these staff are paid termination indemnities. This would enhance chances that staff in question find another suitable position in the UN Secretariat, even if the efforts made by the Administration in this regard before the decision on separation has been taken were not successful. The extension of time for search for another suitable post that becomes vacant could help both sides. The staff member at issue would find a new job and the UN Secretariat could, for example, reduce the termination indemnity otherwise due as well as fill posts which are sometimes vacant for a relatively long period of time.

Improvements in current UN rules could also take place in the area of separation based on the reason of incapacity caused by problems of health. In particular, the involvement of the medical board should be the standard in each case, not only when the staff member concerned disputes the decision of the UN medial director. It would contribute to a more objective and less lengthy decision making process. In the UN Secretariat this process is already relatively long, including significantly more layers and players than the system in the European Commission. There, decisions on separation for incapacity for health reasons are an automatic consequence of the recognition of permanent invalidity by the Invalidity Committee.

Also involvement of a disciplinary board or a like collective body would contribute to more objectivity in the disciplinary process. It is clear that the abolition of the former Joint Disciplinary Committee, which was involved in disciplinary proceedings against UN staff until 2009 and which could be seen as equivalent of the disciplinary board existing in the EU, is a result of the decision to professionalize the UN system of internal justice. This professionalization, i.e. handling of staff complaints by professional judges, not by bodies composed of staff members, is in itself a positive development capable of contributing to an objective, independent and impartial resolution of staff cases. It is, however, questionable whether it was advisable to accompany the abolition of the former Joint Appeals Board, which dealt with complaints against disciplinary decisions before they could have been lodged before the UNAT, by the abolition of the Joint Disciplinary Committee. This Committee was involved in advising the Secretary-General on the existence of the misconduct, its possible classification as serious misconduct, as well as on the disciplinary measure(s) to be taken. At present, all these considerations and decisions are made by the UN Administration, i.e. the OHRM and its head, the Assistant Secretary-General for Human Resources Management, and in a few specific cases the Under-Secretary-General for Management. There is thus no collective consultative body to assess disciplinary cases before a decision is taken. Although UN staff subject to a disciplinary process are protected by the requirement of due process and due process rights which, in general, do not deviate from those available to their EU colleagues, the mere fact that the UN Administration takes decisions directly, without consulting a collective body involving staff representatives, is unfortunate, diminishing the objectivity and the impartiality of the decision. Even more problematic is the possibility to dismiss UN staff accused of serious misconduct without any disciplinary process. This possibility does not exist in the EU and it could be argued that it should not be available in the UN either. Each staff member accused of misconduct, or serious misconduct, should be accorded due process before a decision is taken to separate him. It is true that such decision may be challenged before the judiciary. However, so may a decision on separation for misconduct and yet, disciplinary process, without the involvement of a disciplinary board or like body, does take place. Moreover, where the staff member accused of serious misconduct needs to be immediately removed from post, he could be placed on administrative leave, like any staff member accused of misconduct.

In disciplinary matters, the UN should consider merging all the existing separate sets of rules listing staff obligations and expected conduct into one document. Such action would benefit transparency and clarity of applicable rules, while allowing for specificities necessary to address special types of misconduct, such as (sexual) harassment. The UN should also think of adopting formal rules to prevent or reduce chances for retaliation against staff who report misconduct. At present, there are clear rules on protection against retaliation once it occurs but no rules on preventing it. The European

Commission, for example, offers in this respect confidentiality and an easier transfer to another post, if requested.

Unsurprisingly, a number of recommendations for improvements can be made for the European Commission, too. There are several areas where detailed rules on procedures and conditions for application of specific reasons for separation of Commission staff are completely missing. In order to provide legal certainty and ensure the objectivity and transparency of its decisions, the European Commission should adopt rules on addressing underperformance and retaliation for reporting misconduct once it occurs, on termination of service for incompetence in case of temporary and contract staff as well as on retention of staff who have reached the mandatory retirement age.

As for underperformance, at present it appears that the sole objective of the Commission performance evaluation system, referred to as Career Development Review, is to award points relevant for staff promotion, while the actual analysis of possible shortcomings receives little or no attention. In addition, there are no specific rules that would deal with incompetence of temporary and contract staff and their possible separation for that reason. Of course, both these categories of staff may be separated by giving a notice of termination, accompanied by statement of reasons, including incompetence. However, the period of notice to which actual termination of contract is subject, may in some instances be as long as 10 months. This is undoubtedly an advantage for insufficiently performing staff but rather unreasonable for the Administration which must retain in service such staff for a relatively long period of time. Moreover, despite the possibly long period of notice for contract termination, the entire arrangement is detrimental to staff concerned as well. These staff are deprived of the mandatory assistance of the Administration in improving their performance which is due in case of permanent officials but, because incompetence does not constitute a separate legal ground for termination of service in case of temporary and contract staff, the assistance is not obligatory in case of these staff, while many of them might serve in the Commission for many years or even decades.

Other recommendations regarding European Commission staff serving on non-permanent contracts relate to the possibility of terminating both fixed-term and indefinite contracts by giving a notice of termination. As already mentioned, the fact that this is permitted also in case of staff serving on fixed-term contracts deprives them of protection by the fixed term period agreed in the contract. It also blurs to certain extent the distinction between fixed-term and indefinite contracts. The use of notice of termination in such cases should therefore be eliminated and the specific reasons for which fixed-term contracts should be allowed to end before the expiry date should be clearly and exhaustively listed in the *EU Conditions of Employment of Other Servants*. Such solution would also offer an opportunity to address other existing problems. One of them is the absence of any safeguards for temporary and contract staff in case of termination of service for reasons of staff reduction. Currently, contracts of such staff would also be terminated by giving a notice. Unlike Commission permanent officials, these staff are not placed on non-active status, which is understandable considering that it is the tenure that entails high protection against separation and non-permanent staff cannot claim tenure. However, staff members serving on fixed-term contracts have a legitimate expectation that their engagement with the Commission will last until the expiry date. If that is not possible, for reasons on the side of the EU Administration, the premature termination of fixed-term contracts should be compensated. In case of termination of contract due to staff reduction, the compensation would take the form of termination indemnity, comparable to that offered to UN staff, including non-career staff. Moreover, decisions to reduce the number of non-career staff and to terminate service of individual staff members, including both staff serving on fixed-term and on indefinite contracts, should also be taken with the involvement of a joint body, just as it is the case when decisions concern permanent staff. The involvement of such a body would enhance the objectivity and impartiality of these decisions.

The last remarks on the European Commission rules on termination of service of its staff concern disciplinary cases. As already mentioned, many improvements have taken place during the reform of the *EU Staff Regulations* and the amendment of its Annex IX dealing with disciplinary procedures. There are, however, two points that could be improved further. The first relates to the obligation to report wrongdoing. This obligation should include not only serious breaches of duties and illegal conduct but also other violations of *EU Staff Regulations*, as it is in the UN. In the end, EU staff are required to observe all their obligations and may be subject to a disciplinary process for any breach, whether serious or not.

The second suggestion concerns the manner in which disciplinary decisions may be challenged. The European Commission should consider a move in a direction similar to that taken in the UN Secretariat and abolish in disciplinary cases the requirement of mandatory complaint before an application may be made to the court. This requirement may be of importance in 'regular' administrative matters where decisions are sometimes taken with little or no involvement of the staff member concerned, or not taken where they should have been. The requirement of a prior administrative complaint in these cases may indeed prevent unnecessary litigation and enhance chances of mutual acceptable solution to the problem. This is, however, less evident and even doubtful in disciplinary cases where both the Administration and the staff member at issue take several steps and exchange views on the matter at hand several times. It is thus rather unlikely that an administrative complaint in these cases, dealt with by the same Administration as that which adopted the decision, will lead to a result acceptable to the complaining staff member.

As explained by the UNAT in the UN context, disciplinary cases are, by their special quasi-judicial nature, different from other administrative matters.[585] This is clearly applicable in the EU context as well. It is, therefore, only reasonable and appropriate to treat disciplinary cases differently from administrative cases. In the EU, this is reflected in a separate set of rules that govern the disciplinary process. It could be argued that a specific approach should be adopted also with regard to the possible review of disciplinary decisions. Such an approach could prevent unnecessary formalities and delays in the disciplinary process which is already longer than that followed in most administrative cases. The principle 'justice delayed is justice denied' is, arguably, of more pressing importance in disciplinary cases than in other, 'regular', administrative cases.

[585] For example *Case No. 1499, UNAT Judgment No. 1422 [2008]*, para. XVIII.

Conclusion

This study is about legal safeguards incorporated in human resources policies of the UN Secretariat and the European Commission regarding staff appointment, placement and separation in order to guarantee, *inter alia*, the independence and impartiality of staff. Their independence and impartiality are among core features of the concept of international civil service on which both the UN and the EU base their human resources policies. Although some specific characteristics traditionally attached to this concept, such as the necessity of full job security, might currently be under discussion, the need for the independence and impartiality of international civil servants remains as relevant and as important as it was at the time of the emergence of this concept at the beginning of the twentieth century. Without independent and impartial international civil servants, no international civil service would be capable of winning and retaining the trust and support of the organizations' constituent Member States. The proper functioning of international organizations would then be in danger. The genuine independence and impartiality of staff serving in them remains, therefore, of vital importance.

It was not the objective of this study to assess whether staff employed by the UN Secretariat and by the European Commission are in fact independent and impartial in the performance of their duties, or what the actual effect of the policies under consideration on such independence and impartiality in reality is. As these are not legal questions, they can only be assessed by other, more empirical, disciplines than law. A lawyer can, however, describe and analyze relevant policies and assess their adequacy. This is indeed what this study is about. Its objective was to make an inventory of the existing policies, explain them, compare them with policies existing in the other international organization under consideration and, last but not least, assess their sufficiency for ensuring that civil servants in the two organizations get and remain in their positions in a manner allowing them to perform their duties to the best of their ability, free from inappropriate interference and pressure from external or internal sources outside the formal hierarchical chain of command and responsibility.

When compared to the situation existing in the UN Secretariat and in the European Commission a decade ago, much has changed in their human resources policies. In the case of the UN Secretariat, many changes have occurred also during the period in which research for this study was conducted. In both organizations, most adjustments took place as part of an overall reform process and were aimed, in the first instance, at improving efficiency, flexibility and cost-effectiveness of human resources. The adjustment did not affect the basic principles on which the concept of international civil service is based. It can thus be safely stated that the concept has survived the human resources reforms in both the UN Secretariat and the European Commission. Nonetheless, it can also be established that in both organizations the emphasis of human resources management has moved towards ensuring a less costly and more flexible work force. This move is, to a certain extent, understandable. International organizations, and their human resources policies, must adjust to the ever faster changing contemporary society and its increasingly complex demands. However, the necessity to ensure that all the demands are met to the benefit of the whole (international) society in a manner free from dominance by just some of its parts should not be forgotten.

In the case of international civil service, this brings us to the issue of geographical representation that influences human resources policies in both the UN Secretariat and the European Commission. In this respect, no fundamental change has occurred in either organization. Human resources policies of both organizations are still based on the idea that each Member State should be represented among the UN and EU staff to the extent that corresponds to the Member State's status in the organization, though the manner in which such status is determined differs between the UN and the EU. In the UN Secretariat, a formula developed decades ago is still the basis for the precise calculation of the representation status of each UN Member State, despite regular criticism and repeated requests for review.[1] In comparison, the European Commission continues to maintain its previous practice of denying the existence of any formal arrangement for determining or assessing the representation status of EU Member States. The only novelty in the European Commission is the introduction of a formal rule requiring at least one national per Member State in a senior position.[2] The denial of any other formula in the European Commission is at odds with figures indicating that the representation status of each Member State depends, to a reasonable extent, on certain criteria, including the size of its population.[3] The same applies to the absence of clear rules and/or procedures according to which the principle of broad geographical balance of nationalities within the European Commission work force is (to be) achieved. Such a situation does not contribute to transparency of the system, clearly needed for ensuring that staff members placed in specific positions are appointed not because they possess the 'right' nationality but because of their merits. Even a perception of the former being the case would be harmful to the image of an independent and impartial international civil service and international civil servant.

In the UN Secretariat, the absence of any change in the formula for calculating the representation status of each Member State is rather surprising. Clear expectations to this effect can be detected in repeated requests for a review of the existing formula as well as the explanations behind these requests. They are linked to the undisputed reality of the dramatically modified mandate and composition of the UN Secretariat when compared to the time during which the formula was developed.[4] Disregarding the changed political reality in the UN since the early 1990s, when countries formerly known as socialist countries accepted the concept of an independent and impartial international civil service, the system of desirable ranges is still politically sensitive. Under this system, the principle of geographical distribution in the UN Secretariat is implemented by providing for a minimum and a maximum number of posts to be filled by nationals of each UN Member States.[5] Despite the fact that

---

[1] See above, chapter 2, section 2.2.

[2] See above, chapter 2, section 3.3.

[3] See above, chapter 2, section 3.3.1.

[4] See above, chapter 2, section 2.2.2.

[5] See above, chapter 2, section 2.2.1.

a large majority of countries fall within their desirable range, i.e. the number of their nationals serving in the UN Secretariat is adequate, the issue of geographical distribution itself as well as the representation status of (some) individual Member States are often on the UN agenda. It appears that the political sensitivity of this issue is one of the reasons behind the difficulties with possible modification of the system and/or calculation formula for desirable ranges. In the meantime, the UN Secretariat continues to search for ways in which the representation status of each and every Member State can be brought within the desirable range and, ideally, maintained there at any point in time. The Secretariat has developed a number of mechanisms to implement the principle of geographical distribution and the system of desirable ranges in its staff selection system.[6] This deserves praise as it contributes to transparency which is absent in the European Commission. Unfortunately, some of the mechanisms used by the UN Secretariat could be questioned for their inconsistency with the *UN Charter* and the corresponding provisions of the *UN Staff Regulations* because they place the principle of geographical distribution above that of merit, while both the *UN Charter* and the *UN Staff Regulations* clearly require that staff selection be primarily based on candidates' merit. An important example is the restriction of the personal scope of national competitive examinations through which most junior Professional staff are to enter the UN civil service. The *a priori* and incurable exclusion of nationals of all Member States that are within or above their desirable range clearly cannot be reconciled with the principle of merit enshrined in the *UN Charter* and the *UN Staff Regulations*. Also the continuing close cooperation with UN Member States in staff matters may amount to a breach of the principle of Member States' non-intervention, also incorporated in the *UN Charter*.[7]

The issue of geographical representation is strongly linked to recruitment procedures in the UN Secretariat and in the European Commission. While the system in the European Commission is rather straightforward, objective and relatively transparent, at least as far as permanent officials are concerned, the situation in the UN Secretariat is marked by complexity and, in some respects, subjectivity and lack of transparency. The European Commission hires its entire permanent staff through competition, with some exceptions. Such exceptions are, however, limited and defined, preventing, or at least limiting their possible abuse.[8] In addition, for one of the two existing exceptions, namely that concerning the selection of senior officials, a clear procedure has been established. It involves a number of different actors, including a collective organ, which guarantees that the selection process is objective and transparent. It is true that the final decision on appointment to each senior post leaves certain scope for discretion, but this only reflects the – in reality – partly political nature of all senior positions in the European Commission.[9]

The competition used for recruiting other Commission permanent staff is the most objective mechanism for such endeavor and its broad use therefore deserves

[6] See above, chapter 2, section 2.3.

[7] See above, chapter 2, section 4.2.2 and section 5.

[8] See above, chapter 3, section 3.2.1.

[9] See above, chapter 3, section 3.2.3. See also chapter 3, section 5.

appreciation. The procedures under which EU competitions take place are also fairly transparent and subject to control which is necessary for any process to be considered fair. Nonetheless, it must be concluded that objectivity, transparency and control are missing in the final stage of the recruitment process used in the European Commission, i.e. actual selection from the list of candidates who have passed the competition. Another unfortunate fact is that the *EU Staff Regulations* allow for recruitment of permanent officials through internal competition which is also open to non-permanent staff. This practice was criticized in the past for its danger of subjectivism and favoritism, yet it has remained in use. Besides subjectivism and favoritism, internal competitions are problematic also because non-permanent staff eligible to participate in it may have been initially hired outside any formal set of rules. Such staff can thus acquire permanent position in the European Commission through a less objective and transparent process than others. The absence of formal rules for recruitment to some categories or subcategories of non-permanent staff of the European Commission is another problematic aspect of its human resources policy. In addition, a certain unification of recruitment procedures for all, or at least most, Commission non-permanent staff would also be beneficial to easing the currently too diverse and unnecessarily confusing state of affairs.[10]

A great diversity of recruitment procedures within the UN Secretariat constitutes a significant problem there as well, together with the absence of sufficient safeguards to prevent subjectivity in individual decisions. With regard to the diversity of the existing procedures, it is not unreasonable to maintain certain specificities for the recruitment of some categories of staff, linked to the specific nature and/or mandate of these categories. Nonetheless, the current UN system is unnecessarily complex. Statements that selection, placement, promotion and mobility of almost all global staff occur under one set of rules, i.e. the *UN Staff Selection System*, do not do justice to the reality within the UN Secretariat. A number of staff categories and/or certain of the listed policies (appointment, placement, promotion, mobility) related to these categories are excluded from this system.[11] Their legal base must be searched for in other documents, and are sometimes rather difficult to find. The discovery and understanding of what procedure, instruction and guideline (still and/or no longer) applies to what staff is usually a long process. The electronic Human Resources Handbook, available on the internet site of the OHRM since a few years, is of great help, but the confusing manner of its update and the absence of search facilities diminish its value considerably.

As for as the recruitment procedures themselves, the one established by the *UN Staff Selection System* and arguably applicable to most UN staff at present contains a number of safeguards to ensure an objective and transparent process, free from possible outside interference. They include the publication of job openings and the involvement of central review bodies. On the other hand, certain features of the staff selection process require further improvement and/or reconsideration. Among them are: the limited mandate of the central review bodies and the insufficient regulation

[10] See above, chapter 3, sections 3.2.1, 3.3 and 5.

[11] See above, chapter 3, section 2.2.2.1.

of situations in which central review bodies come to negative conclusions; the abolition of the requirement to hold interviews in each case; and the extensive powers of hiring mangers not counterbalanced by adequate safeguards against the misuse of these powers or, in a less serious case scenario, against excessive subjectivity of decisions taken by these hiring managers.[12] Despite repeated calls and attempts to increase accountability of hiring managers for their decisions, a satisfactory solution seems not to have been found. And yet, hiring managers have been appointing staff by applying the *UN Staff Selection System* for years now, including staff who are (or meant to stay) with the UN Secretariat for a long time. As far as the UN competitions are concerned, an important step forward has been taken by the adoption of a comprehensive administrative instruction that finally regulates the process.[13] It is, however, regrettable that competitions are only used for the recruitment of (not even all) junior Professional staff. Given that competition is the most objective and, if adequate rules are in place, also the most transparent recruitment mechanism, it should be employed in the UN Secretariat in other situations as well.

The existing shortcomings of the *UN Staff Selection System* should be remedied also because the recruitment procedures apply not only to the appointment of many UN staff but to their promotion as well. In fact, the *UN Staff Selection System* applies to promotion of almost all UN staff, including staff appointed under a different set of rules.[14] In this context it is important to recall that, unlike their colleagues in the European Commission, UN staff have no way of being promoted other than through appointment to a vacant post.[15] Such a limited possibility of promotion makes the selection process more vulnerable to outside pressure which some staff might harness in their eagerness to climb up the career ladder. Concentrating staff selection powers in the hands of individual hiring managers is, therefore, problematic as it may be misused and lead to favouritism and nepotism. Such misuse of power is, arguably, more likely in a selection process that involves internal candidates who may be personally known to hiring managers concerned.

In the UN promotion process also the absence of a possibility to appeal against the second best performance rating that UN staff may receive during their regular performance evaluation is open to criticism. It is true, and rather surprising, that there is no formal obligation to take past performance of staff into account in the promotion / staff selection process. Nonetheless, it is self-evident that, in practice, a difference in the performance rating received may influence staff members' chances of promotion to a vacant post at a higher level. Therefore, staff should be able to challenge all performance ratings below the highest one, thereby ensuring for themselves best possible chances for such limited possibility for promotion.[16] It must be admitted that, generally speaking, chances for promotion in the UN Secretariat have recently increased with the abolition of the precedence for mobility

[12] See above, chapter 3, sections 2.2.2.2, 2.2.2.4 and 5.

[13] See above, chapter 3, section 2.2.1.

[14] See above, chapter 3, section 2.2.2.1.

[15] See above, chapter 4, section 2.1.2.

[16] See above, chapter 4, sections 2.1.2.3 and 5.

that existed in the Secretariat for some time. Candidates who apply for a vacant post in order to exercise mobility are no longer considered before those who apply in order to get promoted.[17] Promotion prospects are thus slightly improved and are more likely to take place. However, the competition for a vacant post with other internal candidates continues to be in place and all staff should therefore be able to secure chances to succeed by, among others, providing possible proof of high performance rating. Moreover, when the 2010 request of the UN General Assembly requiring simultaneous consideration of all internal and external candidates in staff selection is incorporated in the *UN Staff Selection System*, internal candidates will no longer have a formal priority above external candidates.[18] This will place internal candidates, including staff seeking promotion, in a less advantageous position when compared to the past and limit their chances for promotion once again. The only difference with the past will be that this new limitation will not relate to the priority previously given to staff mobility but to the loss of priority that staff promotion enjoyed over the consideration of external candidates. Therefore, any supportive fact, including best possible performance rating, will be of great importance for all staff seeking promotion.[19]

That said, it must be admitted that the staff selection process should be aimed at selecting the best candidate available from among both internal and external candidates. The General Assembly's request of 2010 to consider both internal and external candidates simultaneously is therefore not unreasonable and should be implemented. However, this will mean that promotion possibilities in the UN Secretariat will remain limited. One of the important consequences of such a state of affairs is that the UN promotion / staff selection process will remain more exposed to potential pressure from outside. Given the limitations, staff aspiring for promotion will remain inclined to seek support in order to increase their individual chances.

In the European Commission, promotion possibilities are considerably broader. The annual promotion exercises provide the Commission permanent staff with a certain guarantee that, as long as they perform well, they will be regularly promoted.[20] There is thus a significantly smaller incentive to seek outside support in this respect in the European Commission when compared to the UN Secretariat. Moreover, the procedures for annual promotion exercises in the Commission are clear and objective. Naturally, subjectivity cannot be prevented entirely – in the end, promotion depends on performance appraisal which, by its very nature, is an assessment made by individual supervisors. The involvement of a second assessor in the performance evaluation and the possibility of appeal, however, limit the subjectivism to a reasonable extent. The objectivity of the annual promotion exercises is also enhanced by the possibility of appeal available at that stage, complementing the possibility to appeal against the performance appraisal.[21] The criticism that could be addressed at

[17] See above, chapter 3, section 1.

[18] See above, chapter 3, section 1.

[19] See above, chapter 4, section 5.

[20] See above, chapter 4, section 3.2.1.4.2.

[21] See above, chapter 4, sections 3.2.1.3 and 3.2.1.4.

this system is that it 'over-supports' expectations of regular promotion for all those performing well. This might lead to performance evaluation being used solely for the purpose of materializing such expectations rather than for providing a genuine assessment of staff performance, including the identification and possible tackling of existing shortcomings.[22] The new performance evaluation system introduced in the UN Secretariat in 2010 appears to be better equipped in this respect. This system is based on performance evaluation at several points in time and places emphasis on the improvement of staff performance where needed.[23]

As with promotion, in the next area of human resources policies – mobility – the European Commission appears to be more successful than the UN Secretariat, too. This is to a certain extent unsurprising, given that there are no – or if so, few – hardship duty stations in which the Commission staff would need to operate and a great majority of the Commission offices are located in the same city characterized, in addition, by high standards of living. Nonetheless, this is not the only reason that the Commission's mobility policy seems more adequate than that of the UN Secretariat. The mobility policy of the European Commission makes a distinction among various categories of staff and adjusts its requirements for mobility accordingly. In this sense, the Commission's policy acknowledges the place regular mobility plays in securing the independence and impartiality of staff vulnerable to outside pressure on the performance of their duties and leaves other staff to decide for themselves whether, and if so when, they wish to move.[24] Arguably, the absence of such distinction was one of the important reasons for the failure of the mobility policy that existed for a few years in the UN Secretariat. It could even be argued that the continuing absence of such distinction leads to the same conclusion for the present mobility policy of the UN Secretariat. This policy contains too few incentives for staff to move, in particular to move to less attractive duty stations. It also in no way ensures that staff whose independence and impartiality is directly at stake by remaining in the same post for too long change their post.[25] In comparison, in the European Commission senior staff and staff serving in sensitive posts are subject to mandatory mobility.[26] On the other hand, movement of other Commission staff is not supported by any formal incentives, which is regrettable. In this sense, the situation in the UN Secretariat can be regarded as more adequate. There, promotion to the last grade level in the Professional category, the P-5 level, is conditioned by prior lateral movement. Therefore, and save for some rather limited exceptions, all UN staff who wish to reach the highest Professional grade level must have served in more than one, and in many instances, more than two other posts.[27] Unfortunately, it must be admitted that this condition will not be difficult to fulfill for staff who joined the UN Secretariat at junior levels since the year 2000. All such staff are subject to mandatory mobility and must change jobs during the first five years of their

[22] See above, chapter 4, section 5.

[23] See above, chapter 4, sections 2.1.2.3 and 5.

[24] See above, chapter 5, sections 3.2 and 5.

[25] See above, chapter 5, section 2.2.1.

[26] See above, chapter 5, sections 3.2.1-3.2.3. and 5.

[27] See above, chapter 5, sections 2.2.1.2 and 5.

service in the UN Secretariat.[28] These staff will thus always satisfy the requirement of priori lateral movement by the time they reach the middle Professional level and will not need to move again before applying for promotion to the highest P-5 level. In this context it is questionable whether these staff will be willing, or able, to move again after reaching the middle Professional level. It would not be surprising if many of them were more resistant to do so on the basis of their – in the meantime changed – personal circumstances. Many of these staff will have established families and will therefore be more attached to their location because of their partners' work and/or children's education. It could also be argued that, in many cases, such work/family life issues cease to play a role by the time UN staff reach senior level. Movement to another duty station at that level should therefore be less difficult and should be made use of. Yet, the UN senior staff are subject to no mandatory mobility requirement. This is even more surprising, and regrettable, considering the already mentioned role that regular mobility plays in securing senior staff's independence and impartiality.

Developments in the UN Secretariat in the past few years in the area of staff mobility are comparable to those relating to the type of appointments used for staff employment. In both instances, a great deal of work and discussion took place with the eventual results arguably not leading to as much overhaul as expected. It must be admitted that important differences between the two instances can be detected, in particular the fact the reform of contractual arrangements will affect the type of appointment granted to most UN staff, while the mobility policy left in practice the majority of staff without much effect. Nonetheless, it does not appear that either of the two policies have led or will lead to significant modifications of the effect these policies will have on ensuring independence and impartiality of UN staff. As already noted, the current UN mobility policy did not and currently again does not provide for sufficient safeguards that staff serving in posts that are most vulnerable to outside pressure will regularly move to other posts. Moreover, given the deficiencies of the *UN Staff Selection System* noted in previous paragraphs, movement of UN staff from one post to another, on promotion or to exercise mobility, still does not occur in a sufficiently objective and transparent manner and leaves space for subjectivism and possible favoritism.[29]

Also the reform of UN contractual arrangements has not brought much change in the way in which both career and non-career staff are protected from outside pressure. An important improvement that did take place is the reduction in the number of types of appointment used. In particular the unification of all types of appointments used for time limited service is an important step adding to the system's objectivity and transparency.[30] However, fixed-term appointments, which have been, and will remain, in use for engagement of UN staff, still do not have any maximum duration and can thus be extended or renewed for a potentially long period of time. This has not improved the position of staff serving on such appointment. As in the

[28] See above, chapter 5, section 2.2.2.

[29] See above, chapters 3, 4 and 5, in all instances section 5.

[30] See above, chapter 6, section 2.3.1.

past, such staff will continue to worry whether their employment will go on after the expiry of the fixed term stated in their letter of appointment, and if so for how long. The absence of a guarantee for the conversion of their appointment into a career one, even in case of satisfactory performance and continuing need for their service, will expose these staff to the same pressures as in the past. In order to secure employment, staff serving on a fixed-term appointment might be more vulnerable to inappropriate demands if such demands are linked to the possibility of extending or renewing their appointment. Moreover, such staff might themselves be more inclined to look for outside help to increase their chances for contract conversion or at least contract extension or renewal.[31] Of course, it would not be reasonable to set a maximum period of time for which fixed-term appointments may be concluded, including extensions and renewals, in situations where there is no guarantee of the conversion of such appointments into career ones. However, there should be a mechanism guaranteeing that staff who do not receive continuing appointments because of the limitation of the number of available posts get it later, for example in the next year. This would prevent staff being kept on fixed-term appointments for many years with no safe prospects for their future, similarly as it was under the past system of UN contractual arrangements.

With regard to the protection of career staff, not much seems to have changed in this respect either. The introduction of the possibility to separate such staff in the interest of the good administration of the organization without their consent could make a significant difference when compared to the past. However, this study argues that UN career staff are sufficiently protected against misuse of this legal ground for separation by its restrictive interpretation adopted, and emphasized, by the UN General Assembly.[32] The replacement of permanent appointments by continuing ones should, in itself, not be regarded as an end of UN career service. The new continuing appointment must be regarded in a broader context, bearing in mind conditions under which this type of appointment is to be granted and terminated. In the end, permanency in the sense known in the UN Secretariat previously is, arguably, not the only way in which staff, and their independence and impartiality, can be protected and safeguarded. It is only regrettable that some UN staff, namely those recruited through competitive examinations, have acquired an unequal – more favorable – position than their colleagues. These staff will be granted continuing appointments in all cases of satisfactory performance and already after two instead of five years that are required from all other staff. Such preferential treatment of staff concerned unnecessarily disturbs fairness and equality among UN staff. This is in particular so in view of the limitations that exist in the UN for the use of, and participation in, competitive examinations, not allowing majority of UN staff to be recruited through such examinations. The preferential treatment of staff who *are* recruited through competitive examinations also goes against one of the most important objectives of the UN reform of contractual arrangements, namely

[31] See above, chapter 6, sections 2.4.2 and 5.

[32] See above, chapter 6, sections 2.4.3 and 5.

the creation of equality of conditions of service for all staff serving in one global UN Secretariat.[33]

The simplification of the types of appointments in the UN Secretariat, which arguably is the most important improvement brought by the reform of contractual arrangements, could be taken as an example by the European Commission. In the Commission, similarly as in the past, i.e. before the overall Commission reform, there still are many different types of appointments granted to non-permanent staff, depending on the staff category to which they are appointed. It is true that, formally speaking, the European Commission gives only three types of appointment: permanent, fixed-term and indefinite. In this sense, the situation in the EU is comparable to that in the UN where too three types of appointment exist. However, in the European Commission, the specific conditions under which the fixed-term appointment is used, in particular the duration, extension, renewal and conversion of this appointment into an indefinite one, differ for staff categories, subcategories and/or function groups. This makes the situation in the European Commission rather complex, less transparent and, consequently, more open to abuse, putting non-permanent staff in a more vulnerable position.[34] It is, to a certain extent, understandable that differences exist between different categories and subcategories of Commission staff. The question is, however, whether the European Commission really needs so many categories, subcategories and/or function groups to meet its temporary needs. If the UN Secretariat, which deals with more diverse mandates than the European Commission, can manage with three rather unified types of appointments, can the European Commission not manage with a comparable number as well? Even if the answer to this question were in the negative, there is another relevant question that could be asked, namely whether there is any justification for many existing differences in the manner in which staff of each category and subcategory are recruited and in which a certain type of appointment is granted. For example, is there a real reason for not recruiting all persons available to serve in non-permanent positions in the European Commission from one database in which all these persons would be registered after having passed a certain selection process? Such databases do exist for some categories and/or subcategories. A similar system could easily be adopted for the remaining categories of staff as well. Similar unification could take place with regard to the conditions under which appointments given to each of these categories, subcategories and/or function groups are extended, renewed or converted into indefinite appointments. In this respect, an important development has taken place in EU case law that brought different type of appointments used in the EU close to each other, offering comparable protection to all staff against possible unsubstantiated separation from service. By introducing the requirement to always provide reason for non-extension or non-renewal of non-permanent appointments, the EU judiciary has significantly restricted the discretion of the EU Administration in this respect and, consequently, strengthened the position of non-permanent staff.[35]

---

[33] See above, chapter 6, sections 2.3.2 and 5. See also chapter 3, section 2.2.1.2.

[34] See above, chapter 6, sections 3.2.2 and 5.

[35] See above, chapter 6, sections 3.2.3 and 5.

As regards the use of a specific type of personnel, the seconded national experts, the situation in the UN Secretariat is very different from that in the European Commission. In the UN Secretariat, seconded national experts receive a fixed-term appointment, like other non-career staff employed for a period longer than a short term, and serve under generally the same conditions as other staff. They also receive remuneration from the UN. The most important difference between seconded national experts and other UN staff is that an agreement with the original employer of the latter must agree to the extension or renewal of their appointment at the UN Secretariat. This is, of course, due to the very nature of secondment.[36]

Contrary to the situation in the UN, national experts seconded to the European Commission do not receive a formal appointment and serve on the basis of exchange of letters between the Commission and the expert's employer. The latter continues to pay the expert's salary. Unlike in the UN, the employer of the national experts seconded to the European Commission may even require termination of the secondment before the expiry of the agreed period, be it under certain conditions. Another difference with the UN is that secondment to the European Commission is limited to an overall maximum period of time that includes possible prolongations. When this maximum period of time expires, no further extension of secondment is possible.[37]

This brief summary of the conditions under which secondment occurs in the UN Secretariat and the European Commission shows that the link between the seconded national expert and his original employer is stronger in the latter. Although also employers of national experts seconded to the UN Secretariat have an important say regarding the prolongation of their stay in the Secretariat, in principle, they may not require termination of secondment before the expiry of the agreed fixed-term period. Moreover, during that period, the original employers of the seconded national experts lose formal connection to them. In the European Commission, the connection remains in place given that the original employer continues to pay the expert's salary and may call him back when his own interests are at stake. On the other hand, the fact that secondment in the UN Secretariat has no overall time limit puts the justifiability of secondment that lasts for a long period of time into question. In the end, secondment is, by its nature, a means of temporary engagement of national experts who possess specific knowledge and/or experience needed by but not available in the international organization, as well as acquisition of international experience by these national experts which is to be subsequently used at national level. Moreover, a clear time limit for secondment, such as that existing in the European Commission, makes the stay of the national experts more predictable and thus also more transparent.[38]

With regard to the last issue dealt with in this study, separation from service, the situation in both organizations is fairly comparable. Both have similar legal grounds for separation, often accompanied by procedures that must be followed in individual

[36] See above, chapter 6, section 2.3.1.

[37] See above, chapter 6, section 3.2.2.4.

[38] See above, chapter 6, section 5.

cases. Reforms that took place in the UN and EU did not bring many changes to the two respective systems, with the notable exception concerning separation for reasons of misconduct or incompetence.[39] These two legal grounds for separation are the most sensitive from the point of view of their possible abuse. Other sensitive legal grounds in this respect are the expiration of period for which appointments are concluded, separation in the interests of the organization, and separation based on post abolition or staff reduction. All these legal grounds are more 'suitable' for being used to threaten or to remove staff who may have become 'undesirable' because, for example, they refuse to give in to inappropriate pressure on the exercise of their duties.

In general, both the UN and the EU have many safeguards to ensure that the above mentioned legal grounds are not (easily) abused. The most elaborate are systems established for handling disciplinary matters, in both the UN and EU, though in the UN the relevant legal framework has, in 2009, been placed outside the *UN Staff Regulations*. This is regrettable as the *UN Staff Regulations* are less amenable to unilateral change by the Secretary-General than an administrative instruction, and thus provide a higher level of protection to staff. Fortunately, a number of important due process rights are contained in the *UN Staff Rules*. This compensates to a certain extent for the absence of rules in the *UN Staff Regulations*. The reform of the UN disciplinary system that occurred simultaneously, and partly also as a result of, the 2009 reform of the UN system of internal justice, also led to the abolition of the participation of a collective body in disciplinary cases. Currently, all disciplinary cases in the UN Secretariat are handled by the UN Administration (on behalf of the UN Secretary-General), with no involvement of a joint or other collective body that would – also because to the involvement of staff representatives – ensure a more objective assessment of the circumstances of each case.[40] This is better organized in the European Commission where each disciplinary case is judged by a joint body before a disciplinary decision is taken.[41] Of course, in both the UN and the EU judicial review of such decisions is possible. It could, however, be argued that recourse to the court is always a serious decision not readily taken by staff. Therefore, participation of a collective body in an earlier stage of the disciplinary proceedings would be a better way of ensuring that disciplinary decisions are free from subjectivism and that staff do not (need to) have recourse to judicial review often. On the other hand, full professionalization (meaning judicialization) of the review process of, among others, disciplinary cases is an important improvement in the new UN system of internal justice. It brings faster and more rule-based outcomes to disciplinary disputes than the former system under which disciplinary decisions were first to be reviewed by an administrative body and only in the second stage by the UN judiciary. Such a state of affairs still exists in the European Commission where disciplinary decisions must be challenged before the same administrative authority that adopted them before they become admissible for judicial review.[42] Such a system

[39] See above, chapter 7, sections 2.1, 3.1 and 5.

[40] See above, chapter 7, section 2.3.6.

[41] See above, chapter 7, section 3.2.7.3.

[42] See above, chapter 7, sections 2.3.6.2, 3.2.7.5.

clearly delays the final decision in disciplinary cases which, by their very nature, have great impact on the professional and personal situation of staff. The European Commission should therefore draw inspiration from the new developments in the UN in this respect. The same applies to the manner in which retaliation cases are handled in the two organizations. While there are no precise rules in this respect in the European Commission, the UN Secretariat has adopted a detailed system under which retaliation for reporting misconduct or for cooperation in its investigation is to be addressed.[43]

An improvement which can be seen in both organizations is a clear departure from considering incompetence as a disciplinary matter. Here too, the UN Secretariat appears to have done a better job than the European Commission. The UN's performance evaluation system with express provisions on the identification of (possible) unsatisfactory performance, accompanied by a list of remedial actions to be taken in such cases, enhances the scope for improvement in cases of unsatisfactory performance and reduces that for separation from service. The UN Secretariat has also set up a procedure for cases in which remedial action does not help and the staff member is to be separated. No such procedure exist in the European Commission, though the *EU Staff Regulations* do provide for some due process rights of the staff member concerned that must be respected. However, the procedure itself is missing. Another missing element in Commission policy is the absence of rules governing incompetence and consequent separation of non-permanent staff. In practice, such separation is possible by simply giving a notice of termination of such staff member's appointment. This means, however, that non-permanent staff deemed to be not performing well have no right to help and to remedial action before separation takes place. Moreover, due process rights available in cases of incompetence of permanent officials are not provided for non-permanent staff accused of incompetence. This applies also to non-permanent staff holding appointments of indefinite duration who may have served in the European Commission for a relatively long period of time. Such staff too may be separated in the absence of rights that would protect them against possible misuse of allegations of incompetence as a reason for separation. Clearly, such a situation cannot be regarded as appropriate.[44]

Similar criticism could be leveled over two other sensitive reasons for separation from service, namely post abolition and staff reduction, and separation before the expiry of the agreed date. With regard to the latter, it is not surprising that the European Commission non-permanent staff are less protected than the permanent staff. However, the Commission non-permanent staff are also less protected when compared with UN staff serving on non-career appointments. Since the UN no longer uses appointments of indefinite duration and fixed-term appointments may not be unilaterally terminated by the Administration without one of the reasons expressly provided for termination of appointments, UN non-career staff have a job guarantee until the expiration date clearly set out in their letter of appointment. In the European Commission, the Administration may end both fixed-term and

[43] See above, chapter 7, sections 2.3.6.2 and 5.

[44] See above, chapter 7, sections 2.3.5, 3.2.6, 3.3.9 and 5.

indefinite appointments by giving a notice of termination. The Commission non-permanent staff, regardless of the type of appointment they hold, are thus more vulnerable in this respect than their UN colleagues. Fortunately, recent developments in EU case law help to remedy this situation to a certain extent. By requiring the EU Administration to always provide a reason for separation, the judiciary has limited the scope of administrative discretion and thus increased staff protection.[45]

As regards separation for reasons of post abolition or staff reduction, the European Commission non-permanent staff enjoy not only limited but actually no protection. On the other hand, the Commission permanent staff enjoy a high level of protection, higher than UN Secretariat staff, including career staff. While Commission permanent officials may not be separated for this reason immediately and remain in the non-active (but employment) position for some time and in many cases even for a number of years, UN staff is separated relatively quickly, already after a few months after the decision on post abolition or staff reduction has been taken. Although, and unlike the European Commission, the UN Administration has an obligation to search for alternative employment of staff threatened by post abolition or staff reduction, the eventual separation when such employment is not found is rather fast. In addition, it occurs without involvement of any joint or consultative body that would guarantee objectivity of the process leading to the decision to separate individual staff members. Such body does play a role in the process of separation of the European Commission staff. The Commission offers in this respect more guarantees for the objectivity of the whole process and less scope for its abuse by individual managers than the UN Secretariat.[46]

European Commission staff are also better protected with regard to possible separation in the interest of the good administration of the organization (or interests of the service) without their consent. While in the UN in principle all staff may be separated for this reason, in the European Commission this reason is only available for senior officials. Other Commission officials may not be separated in the interests of the service, unless they consent to it. Senior officials, on the other hand, may be separated rather easily as the EU Administration enjoys broad discretion in this respect. The discretion of the EU Administration appears to be greater than that available to the UN Administration in similar cases. Although the UN reform of contractual arrangements introduced the possibility of separating career staff in the interest of the good administration of the organization without their consent, the clearly restrictive interpretation by the UN General Assembly of what the interest of the good administration of the organization include appears to limit the Administration's discretion significantly. In this sense, the position of UN senior staff is less vulnerable than that of EU senior officials. Below the senior level, the Commission staff are protected against separation to the maximum possible extent – separation for this reason is simply not possible.[47]

---

[45] See above, chapter 7, sections 2.2.1, 3.3.1 and 5.

[46] See above, chapter 7, sections 2.3.2, 3.2.3 and 5.

[47] See above, chapter 7, sections 2.3.1, 3.2.5 and 5.

The absence of distinction between senior and other staff in the UN Secretariat is rather surprising. Given the specific, partly political, nature of senior appointments, a distinction would not be regarded as unreasonable. It could even be argued that a possibility to separate senior staff in the interests of the organization could increase independence and impartiality of such staff who would be aware of it and therefore perhaps less likely to give in to inappropriate pressure in the exercise of their duties. On the other hand, it could also be argued that, like in case of all other staff, adequate protection against separation on any – including this - legal ground, increases independence and impartiality of senior staff who do not need to fear termination of their appointment for taking decisions regarded as unwelcome by internal or external sources that wish to promote their own interests rather than interests of the organization as a whole. The importance of independence and impartiality of all international civil servants, regardless of the international organization they serve, or the level they occupy, can hardly be overestimated.

Without attempting to judge whether international civil servants serving in the UN Secretariat and in the European Commission are indeed independent and impartial, this study finds that both institutions provide for a number of important legal safeguards in this respect. Many aspects of the UN and EU human resources policies concerning staff appointment, placement and separation are aimed at, or contribute to, securing staff ability to perform their duties with no regard to pressure that may be exercised upon them from outside, or from inside the organization but contrary to its normal hierarchical system. Reforms of human resources policies that took place in both the UN Secretariat and the European Commission during the last decade have improved the previous state of affairs in both institutions. They have adjusted the policies at hand in order to enable the UN Secretariat and the European Commission to react better to increasing demands of the contemporary international society for handling current as well as future challenges of a trans-boundary nature. Despite the improvements, however, the situation is ideal neither in the UN Secretariat nor in the European Commission. This study identifies a number of problems that require further attention. By comparing systems that are in place in each institution, the study also puts forwards a number of recommendations for further improvements that are based on the positive experience in the other system. If adopted, these recommendations may contribute to even stronger protection of UN and EU staff and their independence and impartiality, which is so essential to the proper functioning of any modern international organization.

SUMMARY

1. Introduction

The importance of international organizations in the contemporary world hardly needs to be emphasized. While the degree to which international organizations influence world affairs depends on the scope left to them by their Member States, their role in solving international problems has been regarded as indispensable. To ensure proper functioning, international organizations need efficient, competent and dedicated staff, who perform organizations' tasks and carry out their objectives. The importance of such staff, their quality and dedication to the international cause can hardly be disputed; they are decisive for the success or failure of each international organization. The same applies to the requirement of the independence and impartiality of staff serving in international secretariats. This requirement exists in all contemporary international organizations established by States. It aims at ensuring that staff employed by such organizations, and through the staff the organizations themselves, act in the manner beneficial to the common interests of all their Member States, not just one, or some, of them. It is commonly accepted that without independent and impartial staff, international organizations would not be able to operate properly.

Despite its vital importance, the issue of the independence and impartiality of staff serving in international secretariats has received little attention in the last two decades and largely disappeared from political and academic debates. This is despite the fact that many international organizations have gone through a thorough reform process of their human resources management, amending staff rules and regulations. In many instances, such changes took place without a close examination of their (potential) impact on the independent and impartial status of staff, focusing rather on increasing staff efficiency and on decreasing costs. At the same time, warnings that reforms, or their implementation, may have negative consequences in this area have been voiced especially by the international staff themselves.

This study assesses whether this indeed is the case. It analyzes a number of human resources policies that are currently in place in two of the most prominent contemporary international organizations, the United Nations and the European Union, and their impact on the independence and impartiality of international civil servants who work for them. The analysis is based on a detailed description of the rules in force in the UN and in the EU and their subsequent comparison. The study focuses on rules on staff appointment, placement and separation. More specifically, it analyzes and compares rules concerning the role of nationality in staff recruitment, promotion and separation; recruitment procedures; staff promotion and mobility; the type of appointment or contract used for staff engagement; and reasons and procedures under which staff may be separated from the organization. All these issues mark the entire employment cycle of staff serving in international secretariats, starting with their recruitment and ending with their separation. At the same time, each of these issues is of direct relevance not only to the quality of staff that international organizations are capable of attracting and retaining, but also to their independence and impartiality.

The study is limited to the UN proper and its Secretariat on the one hand, and to the European Commission on the other. It focuses predominantly on professional staff, who are engaged in the organizations' policy and decision making.

2. Role of nationality

Modern international organizations pay great attention to the nationality of people applying for posts in their secretariats. Constitutive instruments and/or staff regulations of all international organizations, including the UN and the EU, require that their staff be recruited on as broad a geographical basis as possible, subject to the requirement of ensuring the highest standards of quality, efficiency and integrity. The requirement to recruit the best talent available is generally referred to as the principle of merit, while the requirement of the broadest possible geographical basis for staff recruitment has become known as the principle of geographical distribution in the UN and the principle of geographical balance in the EU. This study refers to this principle to by a joint name: the principle of broad geographical representation, unless the specific UN or EU system is discussed.

The relevance of the principle of broad geographical representation in international organizations lies not only with the reflection of their international membership and the consequent ability of this principle to ensure that international organizations can profit from the richness and diversity of various cultures as well as from the best technical knowledge and competence available in any of their Member States. International composition of international secretariats also guarantees an independent and impartial approach on the part of the international civil service towards issues dealt with by international organizations. It does so by preventing the predominance of one or some Member States in international organizations, be it political or cultural. Such predominance would inevitably diminish confidence among the rest of the Member States in the organization in question.

As important as the principle of broad geographical representation is, it is not unproblematic. Problems may arise especially when nationality becomes the decisive determinant in the individual staff selection process. When posts are filled by persons possessing the desired nationality rather than by the most meritorious, the quality of staff will inevitably suffer. In addition, while the international composition of the international secretariats is of vital importance to the independence and impartiality of the international civil service, it may, at the same time, be detrimental to the independence and impartiality of individual international civil servants. If an individual needs to posses the 'right' nationality in order to be selected for a certain post in an international secretariat, the danger that such a person would rely on his ties with the country of origin in order to enhance his chances for appointment, promotion or other placement is great. Such a situation may then easily result in inappropriate connections between the person concerned and the country involved once this person obtains the desired position. Even where no such undue ties are developed in reality, a mere perception or a possibility of their existence compromises the independent and impartial status of the international civil servant.

The question is thus how the principle of broad geographical representation can be implemented in practice without compromising the independence and impartiality of individual international civil servants. There are a number of difficulties there, including the problematic nature of the relationship between this principle and that of merit; the shortage of the 'right' people (i.e. people with the required qualifications and experience) from the 'right' countries (i.e. countries whose representation should be improved in a particular international organization); and the considerable interest of Member States in getting a sufficient number of their nationals in international secretariats. The latter is based not only on Member States' belief in the importance of broad national diversity of the international civil service for the high quality, independence and impartiality of this service, but also on their conviction that a high number of their nationals in international secretariats is a matter of prestige and national interest. This is in particular the case with positions at a more senior level.

International organizations, including the UN and the EU, have been trying to reconcile the different interests in this area in various ways and with varying degrees of success. When looking at the UN and the EU, both organizations have the same starting point with regard to the relationship between the principle of geographical representation and that of merit, but differ in the manner of its practical application in the staff selection process. While the UN Secretariat has developed a system known as system of desirable ranges, where national quotas are calculated in great detail for each individual Member State pursuant to an agreed formula, the European Commission has adopted no such mechanism, at least not formally. The Commission believes that any national quotas would be inappropriate and even contrary to the EU Staff Regulations. This is an interesting view, considering that the relevant provision of the EU Staff Regulations is almost identical to that in the UN Charter and the UN Staff Regulations, used as the legal basis for the system of desirable ranges in the UN Secretariat.

Notwithstanding the European Commission's formal position, this study joins those who argue that de facto national quotas do exist in the Commission, as evidenced by staff figures. The study also argues that national quotas should not necessarily be regarded as illegal in the EU, though their implementation may. While an assessment of de facto national quotas has never been done by the EU judiciary, the ECJ has declared illegal some practices that were employed in the European Commission in the past for achieving balanced representation of all nationalities. This includes, for example, linguistic and other nationality related eligibility requirements for vacant posts. A number of other mechanisms and practices were, however, accepted by the ECJ as justified and continue to be used at present. This includes competitions restricted to nationals of newly acceding Member States and direct appointment of external candidates with the desirable nationality into senior posts (referred to as 'parachutage'). This study argues that a series of measures adopted under the framework of the last Commission reform have eliminated the use of practices which had undue influence on staff appointment based on nationality considerations.

Among most important examples is the involvement of Commission cabinet staff with strong national links in the appointment of senior officials.

In the UN Secretariat, a strict and sometimes rather extreme adherence to the system of desirable ranges has led to the adoption of many formal measures aimed at combating the non-representation and under-representation of countries not reaching the minimum figure of their desirable range. Most of these measures and practices are still in use, including those related to the national competitive recruitment examinations (NCRE), human resources action plans and senior officials' compacts, staff selection system, electronic staffing system, cooperation with Member States, and institutionalized outreach. This study argues that some of these measures and practices are, or could be, incompatible with the UN Charter and UN Staff Regulations because they place the principle of geographical distribution above that of merit. In particular the involvement of UN Member States in staff appointment and the exclusion of a large number of potential candidates from participation in national competitive recruitment examinations solely on the grounds that their country is adequately represented among the UN staff at present give cause for concern. The study also argues that the UN should stop accentuating the geographical representation status of every individual country at every given moment, especially when considering that a great majority of Member States have been adequately represented in the UN Secretariat for years. Rather, the UN should address the real problem in this area, namely the fact that the current system of desirable ranges no longer reflects the reality of UN human resources and the massive change in the composition and role of a great majority of the UN staff that has taken place during the last two decades. Apart from the political problems existing in the UN, this appears to be an issue deserving, but lacking, sufficient attention by both the UN Secretariat and Member States. Flexibility and a longer-term approach are perhaps something the UN Secretariat could learn from the European Commission. On the other hand, the European Commission should be more open on the existing, albeit less formal, arrangements concerning the implementation of the principle of geographical balance in practice. The present Commission's secrecy may lead to perhaps unsubstantiated suspicions with regard to the real state of affairs as well as methods used to address nationality considerations in the European Commission.

That said, perhaps the most challenging question in both organizations is how they cope with Member States' interest in, and pressure over, individual staff appointments. There, procedures for appointment and placement of staff are of vital importance. Chapters 3 to 5 explain the details of such procedures, including those that apply to recruitment of external candidates (chapter 3) and promotion (chapter 4) and mobility of internal candidates (chapter 5).

3. Recruitment

Recruitment constitutes one of the three modes of staff appointment to specific posts, next to promotion and transfer of internal candidates. Procedures used for all three modes of appointment are of great importance to this study. Precise, objective and transparent procedures, precluding subjectivism and favoritism, must be in place in international organizations in order to prevent that their staff selection process is directly or indirectly influenced by Member States or other subjects with stakes in the organizations' work, and therefore possibly interested in compromising the independence and impartiality of international civil servants for their own benefit. An adequate procedural framework for staff appointment must thus be in place in such organizations ensuring that both the officials involved in the staff selection process as well as officials subject to it are sufficiently protected from outside pressures.

In both the UN Secretariat and the European Commission, procedures for staff recruitment are more elaborate than they used to be in the past. The UN Secretariat has taken several important steps forward in this respect, adopting a number of new administrative issuances. The most notable examples are the instructions on the NCRE, on staff selection and on temporary posts, covering the recruitment process of most UN staff. By placing this process in a legal framework, the UN Secretariat has enhanced its transparency and facilitated greater objectivity of the recruitment process. The European Commission too shows progress on this front. Detailed rules, often more detailed than in the UN Secretariat, are in place for each method of recruitment. This includes rules relating to senior officials, bringing thereby more transparency into the process, characterized by considerable secrecy and overriding political concerns in the past.

There are many features in the respective UN and EU recruitment procedures ensuring their objectivity and transparency. Apart from the existence of relevant formal legal instruments, they include the use of competitions, the obligation to publish vacancy announcements, the involvement of collective bodies and in many instances, of staff representatives in the process, especially in the EU, and the possibility of review, including judicial review.

Nonetheless, it appears that the current state of affairs is ideal in neither organization. In the UN Secretariat, one of the most worrying concerns is that many staff serve in career posts without having passed a competition which is generally considered to be the most objective recruitment method for the international civil service, and possibly even without having gone through any tests that would assess their expertise and suitability for the service with the UN Secretariat. Another concern is the broad discretion of UN hiring managers in staff selection and the lack of competence of the only collective organs involved, central review bodies, to review the selection process substantively. Where competitions are held, no staff representatives are involved. Moreover, involvement of human resources management is not a matter of course, although the possibility of including them in the competition boards exists. This applies to both the UN Secretariat and the European Commission. It is also regrettable that, in both organizations, the final selection for appointment from a roster or reserve list lacks transparency. It often depends considerably on direct or indirect personal links with the official responsible for making the choice. For senior posts in both organizations, political considerations play a role even though the posts in question are formally considered to be career jobs. In the UN Secretariat, in addition, the limited involvement of the Senior Review Group, which advises the UN Secretary-General on appointments to senior posts, reduces transparency and objectivity of the process, placing, once again, most power in the hands of UN hiring managers. The difference is striking especially when comparing the UN Senior Review Group to the European Commission's Consultative Committee on Appointments. Last but not least, the relatively large number of relevant legal instruments regulating the UN recruitment process is rather confusing and diminishes transparency of the recruitment system for outside candidates. It also leads to an impression that a piecemeal approach continues to be present in the UN human resources management. Some consolidation of legal instruments would therefore be advisable.

The recruitment system in the European Commission is less complex in this regard, reflecting the fact that most permanent posts are filled by using a sole recruitment method, namely competition. Separate rules apply only to senior posts and possibly to posts requiring specialized knowledge. On the other hand, there are also a number of different regimes for different categories and even subcategories of non-permanent staff. Also here a single set of rules would better serve transparency for outside candidates who are often not familiar with the complexities of the overall human resources framework of the organization in question. Even more worrying in the European Commission is, however, that some staff are selected without a proper selection process. For some staff categories, rules are very general and lack necessary detail, and for others they are even non-existent. It is perhaps understandable, and even endorsed by the judiciary, for staff serving in private cabinets of individual Commissioners. However, such a state of affairs does not promote transparency in the Commission recruitment process. In fact, many of these staff, recruited without a formal and transparent selection process, eventually remain in the European Commission after their posting in a cabinet ends, often becoming (highly placed) permanent officials. This is possible when such non-permanent staff pass internal competition. Also the fact that some non-permanent staff are permitted to participate in internal competitions has been criticized in the past. The European Commission had taken note of this criticism and promised discontinuation of internal competition, but the possibility of organizing them, including for such staff, has been retained in the EU Staff Regulations and is still used in practice. This study argues that this situation is unfortunate and should be changed.

4. Promotion

The relevance of the UN and EU promotion policies to this study is twofold. First, promotion is a way of filling vacant posts in the UN Secretariat and in the European Commission. Without addressing it, the picture on the appointment processes in the two organizations would be incomplete. Second, adequate promotion prospects are a prerequisite without which no international organization would succeed not only in attracting and retaining the best staff possible, but also in securing their independence and impartiality. It can hardly be disputed that the independence and impartiality of staff serving in international secretariats would be compromised if these staff were compelled, or even just tempted, to reach out to certain individuals or institutions in order to enhance their promotion chances because they are otherwise objectively too limited or because the procedural framework for promotion does not guarantee a fair and transparent process but, rather, leaves room to subjectivity and favouritism.

As in the past, also at present a considerable difference exists in the possibilities for promotion available to UN and EU civil servants. In the UN, the only way in which staff can achieve promotion is by being appointed to a vacant post at a higher level. Without such a vacant post, no promotion can take place. This study argues that such policy does not provide adequate promotion possibilities for all UN staff - an overwhelming majority of UN staff experience few promotions during their whole career, just two or three, while no other reward mechanisms are in place, save for regular salary increase. While the lack of promotion opportunities in the UN Secretariat was recognized already some time ago, no effective change has taken place.

The position of European Commission staff appears to be more adequate in this respect. There, as long as officials perform well, they have a de facto guarantee of promotion, sooner or later. Such promotion takes place during an annual exercise when EU officials reach the promotion threshold established for each such exercise in line with budgetary possibilities of the relevant EU institution. Apart from this, EU permanent officials can, similarly to UN staff, also be promoted through appointment to a vacant post classified at one level higher than their current post. Although this occurs in practice only for posts at the managerial level, such promotion further extends promotion opportunities of EU officials. Moreover, Commission officials who do not qualify, aspire for, or succeed in being promoted into the managerial level may also be promoted several times. This is possible as promotion has been partly decoupled from managerial functions. In the past, no Commission official could be promoted above a relatively low grade without necessarily accepting corresponding management functions. At the same time, the number of management functions was inevitably limited by the size and responsibilities of the Commission as a whole, inevitably halting the careers of a large majority of officials at a lower level. Due to the unchanged pyramidal structure of the EU and UN civil services, the limited number of management functions is of course still the case in both the European Commission and in the UN Secretariat. However, the European Commission has found a solution to this limitation by allowing promotion not linked to an appointment to a managerial function. As a result, European Commission officials are promoted regularly, either through annual promotion exercises or through appointment to a vacant post at a higher level. Another way of promotion is available to officials serving in the Assistant function group (AST) and to contract staff. The former can be promoted by appointment in the Administrator function group (AD) and latter by reclassification to a higher level.

Besides broadening promotion opportunities, the European Commission has also established a detailed set of rules according to which promotion takes place in all possible instances. They provide for procedures to be followed; rights and obligations of both officials and the Administration; involvement, composition and competences of committees or advisory bodies; as well as possibilities of review of decisions taken at several stages of the process. While the discretion of the EU Administration in promotion matters is broad, it is limited by a number of requirements and basic principles the EU Administration needs to keep in mind. This helps to ensure that promotion process is as transparent, objective and free from subjectivism as possible.

The foregoing illustrates that the situation in the European Commission has improved as compared to the past. However, problems remain. Arguably the most important problem is the fact that promotion via annual promotion exercises appears, in practice, to be commonly regarded as a right of all officials. It is broadly expected that, sooner or later, all Commission officials are to be promoted to the next grade. This must be consciously or subconsciously considered by all involved persons, including those who conduct performance evaluation. If so, the performance evaluation loses its value by not necessarily and fully reflecting the real quality of work of European Commission officials. Rather, it is used as a tool for ensuring regular promotion of all staff. Although from the point of view of ensuring the independence and impartiality of staff this does not appear problematic, the effect of the system on staff performance could be seriously questioned.

In comparison, the UN Secretariat still needs to find a way in which effective promotion opportunities will be provided for all staff so that they do not seek out possibilities of influence on their career prospects by external sources, such as governments that would attempt to influence promotion decisions. The existing annual salary increases, resulting from satisfactory performance, can compensate stagnation at the same career level only to some, and arguably limited, extent.

This study argues that in both the UN Secretariat and the European Commission promotion needs to have a better linkage to staff merit than is the case at present. It is true that both the UN Secretariat and the European Commission claim that promotion of their respective staff occurs solely on the basis of merit. However, this could be disputed for both organizations: In the UN Secretariat, this is because there are other criteria that must be taken into account when a specific post is being filled, such as the need to ensure equitable geographical distribution at all levels. And the same applies for the European Commission, where promotion of senior officials to a higher grade partly depends on factors, such as the need to ensure geographical and gender balance at all levels. Furthermore, in the European Commission, eligibility of all staff for promotion is also determined by taking into account their seniority, both de jure and de facto. It could be argued that if staff promotion is linked solely to their merits, staff will have no option but to perform well. It will also eliminate the incentive to seek external help to advance their chances of climbing higher on the career ladder. Although it appears that in both the UN Secretariat and the European Commission possibilities for such influences from outside have been limited by the adoption and enforcement of more precise and transparent rules, where there is a will, there is a way. This study argues that no chances should be taken.

5. Mobility

Staff transfer (or mobility) is the last method through which vacant posts may be filled both in the UN Secretariat and in the European Commission. It comprises a broad range of possible moves, including not only those within the same organizational unit but also those involving a change in duty station.

Regular mobility of staff is important for individual professional development, providing the staff members with an opportunity to acquire new knowledge and/or skills they can then use to the benefit of the organization they serve in. At the same time, mobility allows international secretariats to deploy their human resources in a flexible manner, thereby responding effectively to the needs of the day. In addition, regular mobility also helps to ensure that no individual staff member 'owns' the post he holds and that his decisions and work are open to scrutiny by his successor. This enhances the chances that each staff member's performance is of the highest possible quality and free of nepotism.

While this study argues that the greater the mobility among staff of an international organization, the better, it also argues that a good mobility policy must be flexible and reflect the internal diversity of the organization and its functions. Regular movement of all staff seems neither necessary nor advisable – it is extremely complex and burdensome for both the staff and the organization in question, with benefits that do not correspond to the burden. A distinction is therefore needed between different types of functions with precise identification of posts subject to regular mobility, either due to the nature and/or due to the level of the function. Staff in posts in areas or at levels that are vulnerable to risks of undue influence should be protected by regular and mandatory mobility facilitated by an objective, clear and transparent, substantive as well as procedural legal framework.

On this basis it seems that the European Commission mobility scheme more adequately responds to the needs of both the staff and the organization than the scheme formerly and currently in place in the UN Secretariat. The latter introduced in 2002 mandatory mobility for, in principle, all staff. The main intention was to create a mobility culture in the UN Secretariat. Despite such an understandable reason, the rigidity of the UN policy led to many problems, frustration of both the staff and the Administration and, eventually, to the overall failure of the policy in 2008. Arguably, one of the main reasons was the absence of proper differentiation between various types of posts with no clear identification of posts which would or could be excused from mandatory mobility. In addition, the great internal diversity of the organization itself, its mandates and locations of duty stations, was not sufficiently reflected in the policy. Many related problems, such as work and family life issues, remained unresolved or inadequately resolved when the policy was implemented.

While the UN Administration has, at least for the time being, departed from the failed mandatory mobility policy, it has not (yet) developed a new policy. At present, mobility is no more than 'encouraged' for all but junior Professional staff, with no real incentives that would contribute to the development of the mobility culture sought by the UN Secretary-General. In addition, any distinction between various types of posts (with the exception of junior Professional posts), which was arguably one of the reasons for the failure of the former mandatory policy in the UN Secretariat, is still absent. In that respect, there is thus no protection in place for the independent and impartial exercise of functions related to posts more vulnerable to outside pressures or to misuse. For such posts, regular mobility is essential, but lacking.

The European Commission mobility policy is more of a success - many staff members appear to move gladly to another post from time to time. There seem to be two main reasons for this. First, the policy clearly defines which posts are subject to mandatory movement, obliging only staff members who occupy sensitive or managerial posts to move regularly. The rationale of such policy is easier for the staff to accept and thus easier to implement. The second important reason is the presence of many possibilities to move within the institution with a large number of relatively diverse job opportunities, while remaining in the same or a similar location. Certainly, the fact that a change of post has no or only a limited influence on staff members' personal and family lives contributes greatly to their readiness to move.

Despite the relative success of the Commission mobility policy, this study argues that in case of staff members who are subject to voluntary policy the success is due to the staff perception of positive effects of regular change of jobs on their personal development, rather than due to the incentives the Commission policy provides for. In fact, the European Commission mobility policy contains fewer incentives to mobility than the UN policy. While in the UN Secretariat at least one incentive exists, namely the requirement of prior lateral movement before staff become eligible for promotion to higher levels, in the European Commission there are no incentives and no link to career development or promotion. This is regrettable. With good incentives, arguably (even) more staff would be prepared to move in both organizations.

The European Commission mobility policy appears to be not only more successful than the UN policy, but also more amenable to ensuring independence and impartiality of the Commission senior officials. Unlike in the past, all senior officials move regularly now, although certain flexibility has remained. The question is only whether the existing flexibility is justified for managers when it is not available to staff occupying sensitive posts. This study argues that regular movement of managers, dealing with matters of high importance, vulnerable to inappropriate outside interference, is at least as necessary as movement of staff in sensitive posts.

As far as procedures are concerned, the situation in the UN Secretariat is more adequate than that in the European Commission for the majority of their staff. The total absence of formal rules for staff transfer in the European Commission below the managerial level is disappointing. Although staff members move at the same career level, a process of selection for a specific job takes place each time mobility is exercised. Each selection should thus occur under objective, clear and transparent procedures in order to avoid (any appearance of) undue influences in the process. Procedures developed in the UN Secretariat provide, from that point of view, a more adequate legal framework for implementing staff mobility. Regrettably, the transparency of this framework is reduced by the multiplicity of administrative issuances that apply – and sometimes overlap – to different UN staff. This study also argues that central review bodies should be included in the selection process initiated for the purpose of exercising staff mobility. Involvement of these, or alike, bodies would enhance objectivity, impartiality and transparency of the selection process. This conclusion stands for both the UN Secretariat and the European Commission.

6. Type of appointment

Most international organizations, including the UN and the EU, use various types of appointment or contract for engaging their staff, with only a certain proportion of staff members who may expect to spend most of their career in the (same) organization. The main reason for this is the need for flexibility which exists in international organizations just as it does in national public administrations and in the private sphere, though the extent of such flexibility may differ. The question arising in this respect is whether the use of (certain types of) non-career appointments and contracts in international organizations does not compromise independence and impartiality of their staff. Indeed, it is a commonly shared opinion that the use of non-career appointments and contracts may lead not only to many persons with high professional expertise staying away from an organization incapable of offering, or willing to offer, reasonable security of employment, but that it may also result in fear of losing employment, inevitably adversely affecting international civil servants' independent and impartial performance of their duties. It is therefore of utmost importance that the contractual set up in international organizations ensures that the employment of non-career staff does not have such negative effects.

When comparing the situation in the UN Secretariat and in the European Commission, they both had the same initial approach, attaching great importance to the need to secure the independence and impartiality of staff and giving lesser importance to other considerations. As a consequence, both the UN Secretariat and the European Commission offered career appointments to a large majority of their staff who were responsible for carrying out core tasks that the international civil service was entrusted with. At the same time, in both institutions, some room was left for employing non-permanent staff used for meeting temporary needs, either of pre-set or of uncertain duration. Non-permanent employment was also used for accommodating national experts seconded to the respective organizations for the purposes of exchanging experiences in handling matters of common importance.

Gradually, this initial approach has, in practice, changed in both the UN and the EU. The main reason for the modification was the extension of mandates of these organizations, not (sufficiently) followed by the adjustment of human resources management. The reaction to this, and other, problems adopted by the two institutions over the years, differed. The UN Secretariat created a number of new types of appointment with different conditions of employment, whereas the European Commission kept its contractual framework intact, making greater use of non-permanent staff provided for in the existing legal framework. The European Commission also turned to a much greater extent to external human resources. As a result, the situation in the UN Secretariat was characterized by the complexity of, and a significant inequality in, the conditions of employment of staff, while that in the European Commission entailed considerable financial and other maladministration and mismanagement. Neither the UN Secretariat nor the European Commission was thus able to give a satisfactory solution to the problems which arose with the extension of their mandates and the diversity of operational needs. They also did not offer long term answers to the problems the organizations faced. Therefore, both organizations reformed their human resources framework over the last decade. However, once again, they did so in different ways. In the UN, legally speaking, dramatic changes took place and a completely new contractual framework was set up in 2009. In the EU, changes were more cosmetic, certainly as far as the types of appointment were concerned, but significant improvements took place in the area of transparency. As a result of the reforms, the UN system of contracts became simpler, whereas in the EU it remained rather complex. This is interesting to note also because the UN is in many respects a more complex and diverse organization than the EU. Yet, the UN Secretariat has chosen to simplify its contractual system dramatically, whereas the European Commission has retained a relatively complicated regime with a relatively larger number of staff categories.

Recent developments in the UN and the EU show that the traditional belief in the importance of tenure for the independent and impartial status of the international civil service was challenged and compromised in the past by other important interests, and that is again the case. At present, other, often new, interests are placed on equal footing with the traditional concerns regarding the independence and impartiality of the international civil service. This development is, arguably, supported by the belief that the independence and impartiality of staff is currently relatively safe and safeguarded by other (legal) instruments and that its protection by tenure can therefore be weakened. Most of the interests which became equal to tenure are common to both the UN Secretariat and the European Commission, though these two organizations place emphasis on different questions.

In the UN Secretariat, the predominant concern seems to be over the need for greater adaptability and efficiency in human resources management, allowing for more flexible hiring, deployment and separation of staff in accordance with the operational needs of the organization. The UN Secretary-General seems to put this objective above all other considerations. Next to the introduction of mandatory mobility for almost all UN staff (suspended in the meantime), another profound demonstration of this approach is the abolition of permanent appointments and their replacement by continuing appointments. Unlike the former, the latter may be terminated in the interests of the good administration of the organization without staff members' consent. If Member States did not expressly restrict the interpretation of this legal ground for staff separation, the UN Administration would have gained a free hand in separating career staff whenever it would suit its interests.

The European Commission too attaches importance to flexibility in the management of human resources, though it could be argued that in the Commission this is more a theoretical than practical approach. When looking at the enforcement of flexibility through a greater use of non-career rather than career appointments, it appears that the Commission is more concerned about costs than about flexibility. By hiring more non-permanent staff, especially contract staff, the European Commission clearly aims to lower expenses. This can be deduced, inter alia, from the decreased use of temporary staff and the still increasing recourse to contract staff. While both these categories may be engaged for similar, sometimes even overlapping, purposes, temporary staff fall under the same salary structure as permanent ones but contract staff do not. The latter have their own salary scale at lower rates. This makes the employment of contract staff less costly for the European Commission than the employment of temporary, or permanent, staff.

This study agrees that significant changes of the society and of employment patterns of the last 50 or 60 years require many adjustments on the side of public administration, including that at the international and European level and including the traditional approach towards tenure and the emphasis put on its importance for securing civil servants' independent and impartial status. The study also agrees that the independence and impartiality of international civil servants is guaranteed not just by one safeguard but by a combination of many, tenure being merely one of them. Therefore, the study argues that the replacement of permanent appointments by continuing appointments in the UN Secretariat does not necessarily mean death for the international civil service, and that the increased recourse by the European Commission to non-career staff does not automatically lead to insufficient independence and impartiality of the EU civil service. This is because of the conditions and restrictions subject to which the recent changes in the UN and in the EU took place. In the UN, permanent appointments have been replaced by continuing ones, subject to legal safeguards to prevent (possible) termination of appointment being used to influence staff independence and impartiality, though it is unfortunate that no such safeguards have been adopted thus far for the protection of non-career staff against refusal of contract renewal. In the EU, even though non-career staff may be hired in a broad range of instances, it is not (fully) possible in all situations and restrictions exist in particular in relation to the core areas of the EU civil service. In addition, extension, renewal and termination of EU non-permanent appointments are in most cases subject to clear and detailed rules, including those developed by the judiciary. Last but not least, the majority of European Commission staff continue to serve on permanent basis and it is expected that the majority of staff in the UN Secretariat will either remain on current permanent appointments or will be granted continuing appointment, respectively.

7. Separation from service

The importance of a thorough legal framework under which international civil servants may be separated from the organization they serve has long been recognized. As it has already been mentioned, solid, long-term opportunities to build a career and an adequate protection against losing the employment are necessary for attracting and retaining persons of high quality for service in international organizations. Adequately regulated separation policies also prevent international civil servants from paying regard, in the exercise of their international responsibilities, to interests of those whose goodwill they need in order to keep their job, or of those who could become their future employers in case of losing their current jobs. Without sufficient protection against separation from service on grounds unrelated to the interests of the organization or satisfactory performance and conduct of staff, and without procedures for separation offering sufficient protection against their abuse and misuse, the independence and impartiality of international civil servants would be compromised.

The recent reforms in human resources management in the UN Secretariat and in the European Commission paid relatively little attention to issues related to possible separation of staff serving in the two institutions. With one narrow exception in the UN, the list of legal grounds on the basis of which UN and EU staff may be separated has not changed. The few modifications that did take place in the two institutions concern the conditions under which reasons for separation of staff may be invoked. Among the most important changes are the improvements in procedures and due process rights that must be obeyed in disciplinary cases, and the abandonment of the disciplinary approach towards staff incompetence and the introduction of the requirement to try to help incompetent staff to remedy their performance before they may be separated. Both improvements took place in the UN Secretariat as well as in the European Commission, though as far as termination of service for incompetence is concerned the former seems to have done a better job than the latter. By spelling out precise remedial steps to be taken in incompetence cases, including the time frame, the new UN administrative instruction provides a better guarantee to staff in the UN Secretariat that their difficulties with meeting required standards of performance will be treated with attention and serious efforts made to solve the difficulties before their appointment can be terminated. Although the EU Staff Regulations require remedial action in such cases too, the European Commission has adopted no precise rules as to how this requirement is to be implemented in practice. Moreover, EU non-career staff enjoys no protection in cases of incompetence and may be separated at any time simply by giving a notice.

The UN Secretariat offers higher protection to its staff in cases of possible separation in a few more instances compared to the European Commission, including non-career staff, probationary and senior staff. As for non-career staff, in the UN all such staff serve since the adoption of the new system of contractual arrangements on fixed-term appointments. Consequently, employment of all UN non-career staff ends in principle upon the expiry of the term set out in the letter of appointment, save for the cases in which one of the legal grounds specified in the UN Staff Regulations or in the letter of appointment is present, such as misconduct, incompetence, incapacity due to health reasons, retirement, or death. In the European Commission, many non-career staff members continue to serve on contracts of indefinite duration which, due to their nature, may be terminated by each party by giving a notice to the other party. Moreover, also EU staff members who serve on fixed-term contracts may be separated by receiving a notice of termination from the EU Administration, subject only to the period of notice. Unlike their UN colleagues, European Commission fixed-term staff enjoy thus no protection against termination which the period of engagement agreed to in the contract of employment should provide. The need for such protection has recently been emphasized by the EU judiciary, though even the EU courts could not disregard the fact that the EU Conditions of Employment of Other Servants do provide an explicit legal ground for termination of service before the expiry of the fixed-term by giving a notice. To better protect EU staff serving on such contracts, the EU courts have, however, introduced the requirement to provide reasons for termination. The same considerations were applied to termination of contracts of indefinite duration.

From among the career staff, lesser protection than in the UN is offered to EU probationary and senior officials. In the European Commission, staff on probation may be separated during or at the end of the probation without the EU Administration being obliged to offer them a possibility to improve or even to assist them to do so. This is no longer possible in the UN Secretariat where newly appointed staff may only be separated for incompetence after defined remedial action has failed to improve the situation. With regard to senior staff, the EU senior officials members may be separated in the interests of the service at any time, with virtually no restriction being placed on the EU Administration in this regard, while separation of UN senior officials is not as easy. Although termination of their appointment may occur in the interest of the good administration of the organization without their consent, the interest of the good administration of the organization has been interpreted by the UN General Assembly restrictively.

Save for these two instances (of probationary and senior staff), in all other instances career staff serving in the European Commission are better protected against, and in case of, separation from service when compared to UN career staff. For example, there is no equivalent in the EU to the possibility to terminate the new type of UN career appointments, referred to as continuing appointments, in the interest of the good administration of the organization without staff members' consent, which exists in the UN now, though conditions for its use in the UN have been limited to a certain extent by the principal interpretation of this legal ground by the General Assembly. Furthermore, even when there is need for reduction in staff numbers, European Commission permanent officials do not lose their job directly but remain in service, on a non-active status, for a relatively long period of time, whereas UN staff is separately relatively quickly.

This study identifies a number of areas in which improvements could take place in both the UN and the EU policies. For the UN, it argues, for example, that a disciplinary board or a like collective body should be involved in each disciplinary process initiated against an UN staff member, just as it is in the EU. Although UN staff members subject to a disciplinary process are protected by the requirement of due process and due process rights which, in general, do not deviate from those available to their EU colleagues, the mere fact that the UN Administration takes disciplinary decisions directly, without consulting a collective body involving staff representatives, is unfortunate, diminishing the objectivity and the impartiality of the decision. Even more problematic is the possibility to dismiss UN staff accused of serious misconduct without any disciplinary process. This possibility does not exist in the EU and it could be argued that it should not be available in the UN either. Each staff member accused of misconduct, or serious misconduct, should be accorded due process before a decision is taken to separate him.

In the European Commission, there are several areas where detailed rules on procedures and conditions for application of specific reasons for separation of Commission staff are completely missing. In order to provide legal certainty and ensure the objectivity and transparency of its decisions, the European Commission should, for example, adopt rules on addressing underperformance and retaliation for reporting misconduct, as well as on termination of service for incompetence in case of temporary and contract staff. Another suggestion for possible improvement in the European Commission concerns possible challenges of disciplinary decisions. The study suggests that the European Commission considers a move in a direction similar to that taken in the UN Secretariat, abolishing in disciplinary cases the requirement of mandatory complaint before an application may be made to the court. While this requirement may be of importance in 'regular' administrative matters, it is unlikely that in disciplinary cases, which involve a number of instances of exchange of views between the staff member concerned and the Administration, an administrative complaint will lead to a result acceptable to the complaining staff member. In the end, the complaint is to be decided upon by the same Administration that took the challenged decision. This study argues that such state of affairs may unnecessarily delays justice in matters which, due to their nature, are of high importance and sensitivity and should, therefore, be resolved promptly.

8. Conclusion

This study is about legal safeguards incorporated in human resources policies of the UN Secretariat and the European Commission regarding staff appointment, placement and separation in order to guarantee, inter alia, the independence and impartiality of staff. They belong to core features of the concept of international civil service on which both the UN and the EU base their human resources policies. Although some specific characteristics traditionally attached to this concept, such as the necessity of full job security, might currently be under discussion, the need for the independence and impartiality of international civil servants remains as relevant and as important as it was at the time of the emergence of this concept at the beginning of the twentieth century. Without independent and impartial international civil servants, no international civil service would be capable of winning and retaining the trust and support of the organizations' constituent Member States. The proper functioning of international organizations would then be in danger. The genuine independence and impartiality of staff serving in them remains, therefore, of vital importance.

It was not the objective of this study to assess whether staff employed by the UN Secretariat and by the European Commission are in fact independent and impartial in the performance of their duties, or what the actual effect of the policies under consideration on such independence and impartiality in reality is. The objective was rather to make an inventory of the existing policies, explain them, compare them with policies existing in the other international organization under consideration and, last but not least, assess their sufficiency for ensuring that civil servants in the two organizations get and remain in their positions in a manner allowing them to perform their duties to the best of their ability, free from inappropriate interference and outside pressures.

When compared to the situation existing in the UN Secretariat and in the European Commission a decade ago, much has changed in their human resources policies. In both organizations, most adjustments took place as part of an overall reform process and were aimed, in the first instance, at improving efficiency, flexibility and cost-effectiveness of human resources. The adjustment did not affect the basic principles on which the concept of international civil service is based. It can thus be safely stated that the concept has survived the human resources reforms in both the UN Secretariat and the European Commission. Nonetheless, it can also be established that in both organizations the emphasis of human resources management has moved towards ensuring a less costly and more flexible work force. This move is, to a certain extent, understandable. International organizations, and their human resources policies, must adjust to the ever faster changing contemporary society and its increasingly complex demands. However, the necessity to ensure that all the demands are met to the benefit of the whole (international) society in a manner free from dominance by just some of its parts should not be forgotten.

This study finds that both the UN Secretariat and the European Commission provide for a number of important legal safeguards in this respect. Many aspects of the UN and EU human resources policies concerning staff appointment, placement and separation are aimed at, or contribute to, securing staff independence and impartiality. Reforms of human resources policies that took place in the UN Secretariat and the European Commission during the last decade have improved the previous state of affairs in both institutions, adjusting the policies at hand in order to enable them to react better to increasing demands of the contemporary international society. Despite the improvements, however, this study argues that the situation is ideal neither in the UN Secretariat nor in the European Commission. It identifies a number of problems that require further attention and puts forward a number of recommendations. If adopted, they may contribute to even stronger protection of UN and EU staff and their independence and impartiality, which is so essential to the proper functioning of any modern international organization.

SAMENVATTING

1. Introductie

Internationale organisaties zijn vandaag de dag niet meer uit de samenleving weg te denken. Hoewel de mate waarin internationale organisaties de wereldpolitiek kunnen beïnvloeden afhankelijk is van de ruimte die de lidstaten hun beschikbaar stellen, wordt hun rol bij het oplossen van internationale problemen als onmisbaar beschouwd. Om een goede werking te kunnen garanderen, hebben internationale organisaties behoefte aan een efficiënte, competente en toegewijde ambtelijke staf die uitvoering geeft aan de taken en doelstellingen van haar organisatie. Het belang van een dergelijke staf, haar kwaliteit en toewijding aan de internationale zaak kan moeilijk worden betwist; zij is zonder enige twijfel bepalend voor het succes of falen van elke internationale organisatie. Hetzelfde geldt voor de onafhankelijkheid en onpartijdigheid van die staf. Vandaar dat dit vereiste in alle hedendaagse internationale organisaties is vastgelegd door haar lidstaten. Dit vereiste dient erop toe te zien dat ambtenaren in dienst van deze organisaties, en daardoor de organisaties zelf, handelen op een wijze die gunstig is voor de gemeenschappelijke belangen van al hun lidstaten en niet slechts één, of een aantal, van hen. Het is een algemeen aanvaard gegeven dat zonder een onafhankelijke en onpartijdige ambtelijke staf, internationale organisaties niet in staat zijn om goed te functioneren.

Ondanks het vitale belang, heeft het vraagstuk van de onafhankelijkheid en onpartijdigheid van het ambtelijke apparaat werkzaam bij internationale organisaties, de laatste twee decennia, nauwelijks enige aandacht gekregen en is het onderwerp nagenoeg verdwenen uit politieke en academische debatten. Dit ondanks het feit dat veel internationale organisaties in het recente verleden grondige hervormingen hebben doorgevoerd in hun personeelsbeleid die hebben geleid tot belangrijke wijzigingen in hun ambtenarenstatuten. In veel gevallen hebben deze wijzigingen plaatsgevonden zonder onderzoek naar hun (potentiële) impact op de onafhankelijkheid en onpartijdigheid van het ambtelijke apparaat; daarentegen spitsten de wijzigingen zich veeleer toe op het vergroten van de efficiëntie van het personeel en op het verminderen van de kosten. Tegelijkertijd waarschuwden vooral de internationale ambtenaren zelf dat deze hervormingen negatieve gevolgen kunnen hebben op hun onafhankelijke en onpartijdige functioneren.

Deze studie gaat na of dit inderdaad het geval is. Het analyseert een specifiek aantal onderwerpen van het vigerende personeelsbeleid in twee van de meest prominente hedendaagse internationale organisaties, de Verenigde Naties (VN) en de Europese Unie (EU) en hun impact op de onafhankelijkheid en onpartijdigheid van VN en EU ambtenaren. De analyse is gebaseerd op een gedetailleerde beschrijving en vergelijking van de relevante regelgeving van de twee organisaties. Deze studie richt zich derhalve primair op het beleid en regelgeving betreffende de aanstelling, plaatsing en ontslag van VN en EU ambtenaren. Meer in het bijzonder analyseert en vergelijkt het de regels met betrekking tot de rol van nationaliteit in de werving, promotie en ontslag van ambtenaren; wervings- en selectieprocedures; promotie en mobiliteit;

de aanstellingsvormen en gronden en procedures met betrekking tot ontslag. Deze stappen markeren de gehele werknemerscyclus van internationale ambtenaren, te beginnen met de werving en eindigend met de ontbinding van het dienstverband. Tegelijkertijd, elk van de hierboven genoemde onderwerpen is van direct belang; niet alleen op de kwaliteit van het personeel dat internationale organisaties weten aan te trekken en te behouden, maar ook op hun onafhankelijkheid en onpartijdigheid.

Dit onderzoek beperkt zich tot het VN-secretariaat enerzijds en de Europese Commissie anderzijds. Het richt zich voornamelijk op hoger (niet ondersteunend) ambtelijk personeel betrokken bij de beleids- en besluitvorming van deze twee organisaties.

2. De rol van nationaliteit

Hedendaagse internationale organisaties besteden veel aandacht aan de nationaliteit van kandidaten voor een functie bij hun ambtelijk apparaat. Alle internationale organisaties, inclusief de VN en de EU, vereisen middels hun constitutieve instrumenten en/of ambtenarenstatuten dat de werving van hun ambtelijke apparaat op basis van zo breed mogelijke geografische spreiding plaatsvindt, mits aan het vereiste van de hoogste standaard van kwaliteit, efficiency en integriteit van het aan te werven personeel wordt voldaan. De verplichting om het best beschikbare talent te werven wordt algemeen aangeduid als het 'principe van verdienste', terwijl het vereiste van een zo breed mogelijke geografische basis voor de werving van internationale ambtenaren bekend staat als het 'principe van geografische spreiding' in de VN en het 'principe van geografisch evenwicht' in de EU. In deze studie wordt dit principe aangeduid onder de gezamenlijke noemer: 'het principe van brede geografische vertegenwoordiging', tenzij het specifieke VN- of EU-systeem wordt besproken.

Het principe van brede geografische vertegenwoordiging bij de werving van personeel wordt van belang geacht omdat het ervoor zorgt dat internationale organisaties kunnen profiteren van de pluriformiteit en diversiteit van verschillende culturen en van de beste technische kennis en competentie die in alle bij die organisaties aangesloten lidstaten beschikbaar is. De internationale samenstelling van het ambtelijke apparaat staat ook garant voor een onafhankelijke en onpartijdige benadering van internationale vraagstukken door deze staf en als zodanig van de organisatie. Het voorkomt dat belangen van politieke of culturele aard van één of enkele lidstaten in internationale organisaties domineren. Een dergelijke onbalans zou onvermijdelijk leiden in een afnemend vertrouwen tussen de rest van de lidstaten en de internationale organisatie in kwestie.

Hoewel het belang van een brede geografische vertegenwoordiging groot is, is het vervullen ervan in de praktijk erg complex. Problemen kunnen zich vooral voordoen in die situaties waarin nationaliteit de beslissende factor wordt om een individuele kandidaat te selecteren. Wanneer vacatures worden vervuld door nieuw geworven personeel die bovenal zijn geselecteerd op basis van hun gewenste nationaliteit in plaats van hun verdienstelijkheid, zal de kwaliteit van de internationale ambtelijke staf (en dus van de organisatie) hier onvermijdelijk onder lijden. Bovendien, terwijl de internationale samenstelling van de ambtelijke staf van vitaal belang is voor het onafhankelijk en onpartijdig functioneren van die staf als geheel, kan het, tegelijkertijd ten koste gaan van de onafhankelijkheid en onpartijdigheid van individuele internationale ambtenaren. In dit verband moet een duidelijk onderscheid worden gemaakt tussen enerzijds de internationale ambtelijke staf als een orgaan van ambtenaren en anderzijds de individuele internationale ambtenaren als zodanig. Het potentiële probleem ligt primair bij de laatste categorie. Als een individu over de 'juiste' nationaliteit dient te beschikken om te worden geselecteerd voor een bepaalde functie bij een internationale organisatie, bestaat het gevaar dat een dergelijke kandidaat zich beroept op zijn banden met het land van herkomst om zo zijn kansen op benoeming, promotie of overplaatsing te vergroten. Een dergelijke situatie kan relatief gezien gemakkelijk leiden tot ongepaste relaties tussen betrokkene en het betreffende land van herkomst zodra deze persoon de gewenste positie verkrijgt. Zelfs indien dergelijke relaties zich in werkelijkheid niet zouden voordoen is de schijn op het ontstaan ervan voldoende om de onpartijdigheid van de internationale ambtelijke staf in diskrediet te brengen.

De vraag is dus op welke wijze het principe van een brede geografische vertegenwoordiging in de praktijk kan worden geïmplementeerd, zonder afbreuk te doen aan de onafhankelijkheid en onpartijdigheid van de individuele internationale ambtenaren. Hier doen zich verschillende problemen voor waaronder het problematische karakter van de relatie tussen dit principe en het principe van verdienste; het gebrek van de 'juiste' mensen uit de 'juiste' landen; en de grote belangstelling van de lidstaten bij de selectie van internationale staf. Dit laatste wordt niet alleen ingegeven vanuit het belang dat lidstaten hebben bij een brede internationale samenstelling van de staf teneinde een hoge kwaliteit, onafhankelijkheid en onpartijdigheid te kunnen waarborgen, maar ook op hun overtuiging dat het hebben van een groot aantal van hun onderdanen in internationale secretariaten een kwestie is van prestige en van nationaal belang. Dit fenomeen doet zich vooral voor bij hoge posities.

Internationale organisaties, waaronder de VN en de EU, hebben allen op eigen wijze en met wisselend succes getracht om de verschillende belangen op dit gebied met elkaar te verzoenen. Zowel de VN als de EU delen hetzelfde uitgangspunt met betrekking tot de relatie tussen het principe van de geografische vertegenwoordiging en die van verdienste; echter de wijze waarop beide organisaties hieraan in hun selectieprocedures uitvoering geven verschilt. Het VN-secretariaat heeft een systeem ontwikkeld dat bekend staat als systeem van 'desirable ranges', waarbij per lidstaat een gedetailleerd quotum is berekend op basis van de financiële bijdrage van de betreffende lidstaat aan de VN begroting, het aantal inwoners van het desbetreffende land en het lidmaatschap van de VN als zodanig. De Europese Commissie kent een dergelijk mechanisme niet, althans niet formeel. De Commissie is van mening dat nationale quota ongepast zijn en zelfs in strijd zijn met het *EU Ambtenarenstatuut*. Dit vormt een interessant gegeven, aangezien de relevante bepalingen in het *EU Ambtenarenstatuut* nagenoeg identiek zijn aan die van het *VN Handvest* en het *VN Ambtenarenstatuut*, die op haar beurt weer de rechtsgrondslag vormen voor het systeem van 'desirable ranges' in het VN-secretariaat.

Ondanks het formele standpunt van de Europese Commissie, voegt deze studie zich bij degenen die beweren dat er feitelijk weldegelijk nationale quota bestaan in de Commissie, zoals ook blijkt uit de personeelsstatistieken. Deze studie stelt ook dat nationale quota niet noodzakelijkerwijs als clandestien dienen te worden beschouwd in de EU, hoewel de uitvoering dit wel kan zijn. Hoewel de *de facto* nationale quota nooit beoordeeld zijn door de EU rechterlijke macht, heeft het Europese Hof van Justitie een aantal maatregelen illegaal verklaard die door de Europese Commissie werden uitgevoerd teneinde een evenwichtige vertegenwoordiging van alle nationaliteiten te bewerkstelligen. Deze maatregelen hadden o.m. betrekking op taalkundige en andere nationaliteit gerelateerde voorwaarden om in aanmerking te komen voor vacante posten. Een aantal andere maatregelen en praktijken werden door het Europese Hof van Justitie echter aanvaard en worden diensovereenkomstig tot op de dag van vandaag toegepast. Dit geldt ook voor het beperken van open competities (de zogenaamde '*concoursen*') tot de onderdanen van de nieuw toegetreden lidstaten en de directe benoeming van externe kandidaten met de gewenste nationaliteit in hogere functies (aangeduid als '*parachutage*'). Deze studie stelt dat een reeks maatregelen, vastgesteld in het kader van de laatste hervorming van de Europese Commissie, het gebruik van praktijken die ongewenste invloeden hebben op de aanstelling van personeel op grond van nationaliteit heeft geëlimineerd. Eén van de belangrijkste voorbeelden in deze is wel het beëindigen van de betrokkenheid van de staf van de privé kabinetten van de EU Commissarissen bij de benoeming van hoge ambtenaren.

In het VN-secretariaat, heeft het tot het extreme toe vasthouden aan het systeem van de 'diserable ranges' geleid tot het aannemen van een groot aantal formele maatregelen ter bestrijding van niet-vertegenwoordiging en/of ondervertegenwoordiging van ambtelijk personeel afkomstig uit lidstaten die niet aan de 'desirable ranges' voldeden. De meeste van deze maatregelen en praktijken zijn vandaag de dag nog steeds in gebruik, waaronder die met betrekking tot de nationale competitieve wervingsexamens (NCRE), human resources actieplannen, individuele werkplannen voor hooggeplaatste ambtenaren, selectie van personeel, elektronisch personeel systeem, samenwerking met de lidstaten en geformaliseerde personeelswervingscampagnes. Deze studie stelt dat een aantal van deze maatregelen en praktijken onverenigbaar zijn of zouden kunnen zijn met het VN-Handvest en het VN-statuut, omdat ze het principe van geografische spreiding boven die van verdienste stellen. In het bijzonder doet zich dit voor bij de betrokkenheid van de VN-lidstaten in de personeelsbenoeming en de uitsluiting van een groot aantal potentiële kandidaten van deelname aan nationale competitieve wervingsexamens, uitsluitend op grond van het feit dat hun land reeds voldoende in de VN is vertegenwoordigd. Deze studie stelt ook dat de VN het belang van de geografische vertegenwoordiging van elk individueel land op elk moment, dient te beëindigen, zeker wanneer men bedenkt dat de overgrote meerderheid van de lidstaten al jarenlang adequaat zijn vertegenwoordigd in het VN-secretariaat. Daarentegen dient de VN dient het echte probleem op dit gebied aan te pakken, namelijk het feit dat het huidige systeem van de 'desirable ranges' niet meer overeenkomt met de realiteit van het VN-personeelsbestand en de enorme verandering die de laatste twee decennia hierin hebben plaatsgevonden. Afgezien van de politieke problemen waar de VN momenteel mee kampt, lijkt deze kwestie zondermeer de aandacht te behoeven van de VN-secretariaat en haar lidstaten; aandacht die het ten enen male ontbreekt.

Flexibiliteit en een lange termijn aanpak zijn typische onderwerpen waar het VN-secretariaat lering zou kunnen trekken bij de aanpak van de Europese Commissie. Aan de andere kant dient de Europese Commissie meer openheid te betrachten in de bestaande, zij het minder formele, regelingen met betrekking tot de toepassing van het beginsel van geografisch evenwicht in de praktijk. De huidige geheimhouding van de Commissie kan leiden tot ongefundeerde vermoedens met betrekking tot de werkelijke stand van zaken en methoden die worden gebruikt om dit principe in de Europese Commissie te implementeren.

Dat gezegd hebbende, misschien wel de meest uitdagende vraag is hoe beide organisaties omgaan met de belangen van de lidstaten in, en de druk die zij uitoefenen op, individuele stafbenoemingen. Juist op dit punt zijn, procedures voor de benoeming en de plaatsing van het personeel van vitaal belang. De hoofdstukken 3 tot en met 5 beschrijft in detail dergelijke procedures, inclusief procedures welke van toepassing zijn op de werving van externe kandidaten (hoofdstuk 3), promotie (hoofdstuk 4) en de mobiliteit van interne kandidaten (hoofdstuk 5).

3. Werving

Werving is één van de drie manieren waarop de benoeming van personeel voor specifieke functies plaatsvindt, naast promotie en de overplaatsing van interne kandidaten. De voor benoeming geldende procedures die in alle drie de modi van de benoeming van toepassing zijn, zijn van groot belang voor deze studie. Nauwkeurige, objectieve en transparante procedures, die willekeur en vriendjespolitiek tegenaan, dienen van toepassing te zijn in internationale organisaties, om te voorkomen dat hun personeelsselectieprocedures direct of indirect beïnvloed worden door de lidstaten dan wel door andere individuen of entiteiten/groepen die belang hebben bij het werk dat deze organisaties uitvoeren. Een adequaat (procedureel) kader voor de aanstelling van personeel is derhalve noodzakelijk en dient er voor te zorgen dat zowel de ambtenaren die betrokken zijn bij het personeelsselectieproces en de personen op wie dit selectieproces betrekking heeft voldoende beschermd zijn tegen druk van buitenaf.

In zowel het VN-secretariaat en de Europese Commissie, zijn de procedures met betrekking tot de werving van het personeel uitgebreider dan vroeger het geval was. Het VN-secretariaat heeft in dit verband verschillende belangrijke stappen voorwaarts gezet tot vaststelling van een aantal nieuwe regels en procedures met betrekking tot de werving en selectie van personeel. Noemenswaardig zijn in dit verband: de administratieve instructie betreffende de nationale competitieve wervingsexamens ('NCRE'); de instructie betreffende het stafselectiesysteem; en de instructie betreffende tijdelijke posten, die in totaal de werving van het overgrote deel van het VN-personeel dekken. Door dit proces in een wettelijk kader te plaatsen heeft het VN-secretariaat haar transparantie in deze verstrekt hetgeen bijdraagt aan een grotere objectiviteit van het wervingsproces. Ook de Europese Commissie toont in dit verband vooruitgang. Gedetailleerde regels, vaak gedetailleerder dan die bij het VN-secretariaat, zijn van toepassing op alle wervingsmethoden. Dit geldt ook voor regels met betrekking tot benoemingen van hoge posities waardoor meer transparantie in het proces ontstaat; een proces dat in het verleden primair gekenmerkt werd door geheimhouding en politieke overwegingen.

Objectiviteit en transparantie van VN- als de EU wervings- en selectieprocedures wordt gegarandeerd door een aantal waarborgen, inclusief – naast de bovengenoemde vaststelling van de relevante juridische kaders – het werken met competities, de verplichting tot het publiceren van vacatures, de betrokkenheid van een collectief orgaan en in veel gevallen de betrokkenheid van personeelsvertegenwoordigers in het proces, primair in de EU en beroepsmogelijkheden inclusief rechterlijke toetsing.

Toch blijkt dat de huidige situatie in beide organisaties nog niet optimaal is. Eén van de verontrustende problemen in het VN-secretariaat betreft het feit dat veel personeel met een vaste aanstelling niet heeft hoeven deelnemen aan een competitie of aan welke vorm van een test dan ook, die moet uitwijzen of de betreffende kandidaat op basis van zijn kennis en ervaring geschikt is voor dienst bij het VN-secretariaat. Dit terwijl competities gezien worden als de meest objectieve wervingsprocedure voor de internationale civiele dienst.

Een andere zorg betreft de ruime discretionaire (beslissings)bevoegdheid van VN-personeelsmanagers in de selectie van personeel en het gebrek aan bevoegdheden van de centrale beroepsinstanties teneinde het selectieproces inhoudelijk te evalueren. Daar waar competities worden gehouden zijn stafvertegenwoordigers niet betrokken. Bovendien is de betrokkenheid van het human resources management niet vanzelfsprekend, hoewel de mogelijkheid om deze in het bestuur dat toeziet op de competitie weldegelijk aanwezig is. Dit geldt voor zowel het VN-secretariaat als de Europese Commissie. Het is betreurenswaardig dat, in beide organisaties, de definitieve selectie voor benoeming op basis van de testresultaten van de competitie of van degenen die op een reservelijst worden geplaatst iedere vorm van transparantie missen. De uiteindelijke keuze hangt vaak af van de persoonlijke banden met de ambtenaar die verantwoordelijk is voor het maken van de keuze. Voor hoge posities spelen politieke overwegingen in beide organisaties een rol, ook al gaat het om banen die, formeel gezien, niet door politieke benoemingen vervuld worden. In het VN-secretariaat vermindert de beperkte betrokkenheid van de 'Senior Review Group', die de VN Secretaris-generaal adviseert over benoemingen voor hoge posities, transparantie en objectiviteit van het proces en plaatst de meeste macht wederom in handen van de 'hiring managers'. Het verschil is vooral opvallend als de VN-Senior Review Group vergeleken wordt met het raadgevende comité voor benoemingen van de Europese Commissie. Het relatief grote aantal relevante juridische instrumenten die het VN-wervingsproces omkleden is nogal verwarrend en vermindert de transparantie van dit proces. Het lijkt ook de indruk te wekken dat een versnipperde aanpak nog steeds in het VN-human resources management aanwezig is. Consolidatie van de juridische instrumenten die het wervingsproces omkleden is dan ook wenselijk.

Het wervings- en selectiesysteem in de Europese Commissie is in dit opzicht minder complex. Dit als gevolg van het feit dat de meeste permanente posities in de Europese commissie ingevuld worden door één en dezelfde wervings- en selectiemethode, namelijk via open competities. Afzonderlijke regels gelden alleen voor hoge posities en/of voor posities die zeer gespecialiseerde kennis vereisen. De werving en selectie van niet-permanent personeel vindt daarentegen plaats op basis van een aantal verschillende stelsels die gelden voor verschillende categorieën en zelfs subcategorieën van niet-permanent personeel. Ook hier zou een eenduidig wervings- en selectieregiem de transparantie ten goede komen voor externe kandidaten. Deze kandidaten zijn vaak niet bekend met de complexiteit van het totale 'human resource framework' van de organisatie in kwestie.

Nog verontrustender in de Europese Commissie is echter dat sommige niet-permanente stafleden worden aangenomen zonder enige formele selectie. Voor sommige personeelscategorieën zijn wervings- en selectieprocedures zeer algemeen en missen noodzakelijke details, terwijl voor anderen ze zelfs helemaal niet aanwezig zijn. Voor personeel werkzaam in de privékabinetten van de Eurocommissarissen is dit wellicht begrijpelijk – hetgeen zelfs wordt ondersteund door de rechterlijke macht. Echter, een dergelijke gang van zaken is niet bevorderlijk voor de transparantie van het wervingsproces. Het is immers zo dat veel van deze personeelsleden, die zonder formele en transparante selectieprocedures zijn aangenomen, werkzaam blijven bij de Europese Commissie nadat hun aanstelling in het privékabinet eindigt. Ze krijgen vaak een vaste aanstelling en/of bekleden hooggeplaatste posities. Dit is mogelijk nadat deze niet-permanente personeelsleden hebben deelgenomen aan, en zijn geslaagd voor, een interne competitie. Het feit dat niet-permanente stafleden überhaupt kunnen deelnemen aan zulke competities is vanuit het verleden reeds meermaals bekritiseerd. De Europese Commissie heeft kennis genomen van deze kritiek en beloofde deelname aan interne competities voor niet-permanent personeel te staken. Echter, deze specifieke mogelijkheid is ook na de herziening van het EU Personeelsstatuut behouden gebleven en wordt tot op de dag van vandaag nog steeds gebruikt. Deze studie stelt dat deze gang van zaken ongewenst is en dient te worden herzien.

4. Promotie

Het VN en EU promotie beleid is om twee redenen voor deze studie relevant. Ten eerste is promotie een manier van het vervullen van vacatures in zowel het VN-secretariaat als de Europese Commissie. Zonder het te behandelen, zou het beeld over de wervings- en selectieprocedures in deze twee organisaties incompleet zijn. Ten tweede zijn adequate promotieperspectieven een absolute voorwaarde voor internationale organisaties om het beste personeel aan te trekken en te behouden. Bovendien zouden ze er niet in slagen om onafhankelijkheid en onpartijdigheid van hun personeel veilig te stellen. Het kan immers moeilijk worden betwist dat de onafhankelijkheid en onpartijdigheid van internationale ambtenaren aangetast zou worden indien zij in de verleiding komen om bepaalde personen of instellingen te benaderen om hun promotiekansen te vergroten, omdat ze anders te beperkt zijn of omdat de relevante procedures geen garantie bieden op een eerlijk en transparant promotieproces.

Heden ten dage bestaan er nog steeds aanzienlijke verschillen tussen promotiemogelijkheden voor VN- en EU-ambtenaren. De enige manier waarop VN personeel promotie kan bereiken is door te worden benoemd in een vacante post op een hoger niveau. Zonder de aanwezigheid van een dergelijke vacature, kan er geen promotie plaatsvinden. Deze studie stelt dat een dergelijk beleid geen adequate promotiemogelijkheden biedt voor al het VN personeel; de overgrote meerderheid van het VN-personeel krijgt slechts een enkele promotie gedurende zijn of haar gehele carrière bij de VN. Eveneens kent de VN geen andere beloningsmechanismen, behalve de reguliere loonsverhogingen. Terwijl het gebrek aan promotiekansen in het VN-secretariaat al enige tijd vastgesteld is, heeft er tot op heden geen effectieve verandering op dit gebied plaatsgevonden.

De positie van het personeel van Europese Commissie lijkt op dit punt meer adequaat. Zolang ambtenaren naar behoren presteren hebben zij een *de facto* garantie op promotie. Een dergelijke promotie vindt plaats tijdens een jaarlijks promotieproces waarin de het presteren van de betreffende ambtenaar wordt beoordeeld. Indien hij een promotiedrempel bereikt die vastgesteld wordt in overeenstemming met de budgettaire mogelijkheden van de betrokken EU-instelling komt de betreffende ambtenaar in aanmerking voor promotie. Daarnaast kunnen EU-ambtenaren - net als VN-personeel - promotie krijgen door middel van een benoeming in een vacante post die op één niveau hoger gekwalificeerd is. Hoewel dit in de praktijk alleen voorkomt voor managementfuncties, vergroot het verder de promotiekansen van EU-ambtenaren. Het gevolg van dit promotiebeleid van de Europese Commissie is dat ook EU ambtenaren die niet in aanmerking komen voor een managementfunctie, er niet naar streven, of erin slagen, om een dergelijke leidinggevende functie te vervullen, nog altijd wel meerdere keren promotie kunnen maken in hun carrière. Dit is mogelijk omdat promotie gedeeltelijk losgekoppeld is van het uitoefenen van een leidinggevende functie. Dit was in het verleden anders. Toen kon geen enkele ambtenaar van de Europese Commissie promotie krijgen boven het bereiken van een bepaalde rang, die in hiërarchische structuur van de organisatie als relatief laag beschouwd kon worden, zonder een managementfunctie te accepteren. Tegelijkertijd werd het aantal managementfuncties onvermijdelijk beperkt door de grootte en verantwoordelijkheden van de Europese Commissie als geheel. Dit bracht onvermijdelijk een einde aan de verdere carrière van een grote meerderheid van de ambtenaren met een functie op een relatief laag niveau. Als gevolg van de onveranderde piramidale structuur van de EU en de VN publieke dienst is het beperkte aantal managementfuncties natuurlijk nog steeds het geval in zowel de Europese Commissie en in het VN secretariaat. Toch heeft de Europese Commissie een oplossing gevonden voor deze beperking door promotie los te koppelen van managementfuncties. Als gevolg daarvan krijgen de ambtenaren van de Europese Commissie regelmatig promotie, hetzij door middel van het jaarlijkse promotieproces of door aanstelling in een vacante post op een hoger niveau. Een andere manier van promotie is beschikbaar voor ambtenaren in de assistent-functiegroep (AST) en voor niet-permanent personeel in de categorie 'contractant'. De eerste kunnen promotie krijgen door een aanstelling in de administrator-functiegroep (AD) en de laatste door herclassificatie naar een hoger niveau.

Naast het vergroten van promotiekansen, heeft de Europese Commissie tevens gedetailleerde regels vastgesteld op basis waarvan elk bovengenoemde type van promotie plaats vindt. De regels voorzien in procedures; rechten en plichten van de ambtenaren en van de administratie, de betrokkenheid, de samenstelling en bevoegdheden van betrokken commissies of adviesorganen; en beroepsmogelijkheden in verschillende stadia van het proces. Hoewel de discretionaire bevoegdheid van de EU-Administratie in promotie zaken breed is, wordt het beperkt door een aantal vereisten en principes waarmee de EU-Administratie rekening moet houden. Dit dient er mede voor te zorgen dat het promotieproces zo transparant, objectief en vrij van subjectivisme mogelijk is.

Het voorgaande illustreert dat de situatie in de Europese Commissie is verbeterd ten opzichte van het verleden. Desondanks blijven zich een aantal problemen voordoen. Misschien wel het belangrijkste probleem is dat promotie die plaats vindt via het jaarlijkse promotieproces in de praktijk te vaak beschouwd lijkt te worden als een gegeven recht van alle ambtenaren. Het wordt alom verwacht dat, vroeg of laat, alle Commissie ambtenaren promotie maken naar de volgende rang. Het kan in de praktijk niet anders worden uitgelegd dan dat dit gegeven bewust of onbewust door alle betrokken in het proces in ogenschouw wordt genomen, inclusief degenen die verantwoordelijk zijn voor de uitvoering van de beoordeling van de door de betreffende ambtenaar geleverde prestaties. Indien dit inderdaad het geval is, verliest de prestatie-evaluatie haar waarde omdat het niet noodzakelijkerwijs en volledig de echte kwaliteit van het werk van de ambtenaren weerspiegelt. In plaats daarvan wordt de prestatie-evaluatie gebruikt als een instrument om de reguliere promotie van alle ambtenaren te bevorderen. Hoewel dit niet problematisch lijkt te zijn uit het oogpunt van het waarborgen van de onafhankelijkheid en onpartijdigheid van internationale ambtenaren, kan de effectiviteit van een dergelijk systeem van prestatie-evaluaties ernstig in twijfel worden getrokken.

Wat het VN-secretariaat betreft, moet het nog een manier vinden waarop effectieve promotiekansen voor haar internationale ambtenaren kunnen worden gecreëerd, zodat zij niet in de verleiding komen om op een onverantwoorde wijze hun carrière trachten te bevorderen; bijvoorbeeld door het benaderen van externe bronnen, zoals overheden, teneinde promotiebesluiten te beïnvloeden. De reguliere salarisverhogingen voor geleverde goede prestaties kunnen stagnatie op hetzelfde niveau slechts in beperkte mate compenseren. Deze studie stelt dat, zowel in het VN-secretariaat als in de Europese Commissie, er een betere koppeling dient te worden gelegd tussen het verstrekken van een promotie en de geleverde prestaties. Hoewel zowel het VN-secretariaat als de Europese Commissie beweren dat promotie van hun ambtenaren uitsluitend plaatsvindt op basis van geleverde prestaties, kan deze stelling voor beide organisaties worden betwist. In het VN-secretariaat omdat er ook andere criteria zijn die in acht moeten worden genomen bij het vervullen van een specifieke vacante post, waaronder de noodzaak een billijke geografische vertegenwoordiging te garanderen op alle niveaus. Hetzelfde geldt ook voor de Europese Commissie, waar promotie van ambtenaren tot senior posities mede afhankelijk is van meerdere factoren, zoals de noodzaak om geografische en gender-evenwicht op alle niveaus te garanderen. Bovendien wordt in de Europese Commissie het in aanmerking komen voor de promotie medebepaald door senioriteit, zowel *de jure* als *de facto*. Er kan gesteld worden dat indien promotie uitsluitend gebaseerd zou worden op geleverde prestaties, het personeel niets anders rest dan goed te presteren. Zo zou iedere verleiding om externe hulp aan te boren worden geëlimineerd. Het lijkt dat zowel in het VN-secretariaat als in de Europese Commissie de mogelijkheden voor dergelijke invloeden van buitenaf recentelijk zijn ingeperkt door het vaststellen en de toepassing van vastomlijnde en transparante regels. Deze studie stelt echter dat voor een onafhankelijk en onpartijdig functionerende internationale ambtelijke staf alle onvolkomenheden in deze moeten worden uitgesloten, temeer daar de druk op internationale ambtenaren groot is en de persoonlijke belangen eveneens groot kunnen zijn. Er geldt immers nog steeds het credo: 'waar een wil is, is een weg'.

5. Arbeidsmobiliteit

Overplaatsing van personeel is de laatste manier waarop vacatures, zowel bij het VN-secretariaat als bij Europese Commissie vervult kunnen worden. Het omvat een brede waaier van overplaatsingsvormen, niet alleen overplaatsing binnen dezelfde eenheid, maar ook overplaatsingen die verandering van standplaats met zich meebrengen.

Het regelmatig switchen van posten is belangrijk voor de individuele professionele ontwikkeling waardoor medewerkers de gelegenheid geboden wordt om nieuwe kennis en/of vaardigheden te ontwikkelen, die vervolgens ten gunste komen aan de organisatie die zij dienen. Bovendien biedt interne arbeidsmobiliteit de internationale secretariaten de mogelijkheid om hun arbeidspotentieel op een flexibele manier in te zetten, waadoor adequaat kan worden gereageerd op de behoeften van de dag. Daarnaast draagt het regelmatig wisselen van posten binnen de organisatie ook bij aan te voorkomen dat individuele personeelsleden de post die zij bekleden 'bezitten' en zo voorkomen dat hun beslissingen en werkzaamheden open staan voor kritisch onderzoek door hun opvolger. Arbeidsmobiliteit vergroot de kans dat de prestatie van elk personeelslid van de hoogst mogelijke kwaliteit is en vrij van subjectiviteit.

Hoewel deze studie stelt dat hoe groter de interne arbeidsmobiliteit onder het personeel van een organisatie hoe beter, betoogt het ook dat een goed mobiliteitsbeleid flexibel moet zijn en de diversiteit binnen de organisatie en haar functies moet weerspiegelen. Regelmatige overplaatsing van al het personeel lijkt nog noodzakelijk noch wenselijk, het is uiterst complex en belastend voor zowel het personeel als de organisatie in kwestie, terwijl de voordelen niet in verhouding staan tot de belasting. Er dient daarom onderscheid gemaakt te worden tussen de verschillende soorten functies inclusief een precieze aanduiding van posten die, als gevolg van de aard of het niveau van de functie, onderworpen dienen te zijn aan regelmatige overplaatsing. Personeel in functies of op niveaus die kwetsbaar zijn voor risico's van ongewenste interne en/of externe beïnvloeding, moeten worden beschermd door regelmatige en verplichte overplaatsing, gefaciliteerd door een zowel inhoudelijk als procedureel objectief, helder en transparant wettelijk kader.

De mobiliteitsregeling van de Europese Commissie lijkt beter te voldoen aan zowel de behoeften van het personeel en de organisatie dan die van het VN-secretariaat. Het VN-secretariaat introduceerde in 2002 verplichte arbeidsmobiliteit, voor in beginsel al het personeel, met als belangrijkste doel een mobiliteitscultuur te creëren. Ondanks deze begrijpelijke reden, leidde de starheid van het VN-beleid tot veel problemen en frustratie bij zowel het personeel als de Commissie in de hoedanigheid als werkgever, en uiteindelijk tot de totale mislukking van het beleid. Eén van de belangrijkste redenen van deze mislukking was ongetwijfeld het ontbreken van een adequaat onderscheid tussen de verschillende soorten functies zonder duidelijke identificatie van de posten die zouden of konden worden vrijgesteld van de verplichte arbeidsmobiliteit. Daarnaast kwam de grote interne diversiteit van de organisatie, haar mandaten en haar diverse standplaatsen niet voldoende tot uiting in het beleid. Daarnaast bleven, ten tijde van de implementatie van het beleid, werk- en gezinsproblemen die het gevolg waren van de verplichte arbeidsmobiliteit onopgelost of onvoldoende opgelost.

Terwijl de Commissie in de hoedanigheid als werkgever het mislukte verplichte arbeidsmobiliteitsbeleid heeft verlaten, of althans voor dit moment, heeft zij op dit terrein nog geen nieuw beleid ontwikkeld. Op dit moment wordt de interne arbeidsmobiliteit van al het personeel slechts aangemoedigd, met uitzondering van junior personeel, zonder echte stimulansen die daadwerkelijk bijdragen aan de ontwikkeling van een mobiliteitscultuur waarnaar de Secretaris-generaal van de VN naar op zoek is. Daarnaast ontbreekt nog steeds elk onderscheid tussen de verschillende soorten functies (met uitzondering van de junior functies), hetgeen aantoonbaar één van de redenen van het mislukken van het voormalige verplichte beleid binnen het VN-secretariaat is. In dat opzicht is er dus geen bescherming aanwezig voor de onafhankelijke en onpartijdige uitoefening van functies die kwetsbaar zijn voor ambtsmisbruik of druk van buitenaf. Voor dergelijke functies is regelmatige overplaatsing essentieel. Desondanks ontbreekt het hier ten enen male aan.

Het arbeidsmobiliteitsbeleid van de Europese Commissie is succesvoller; veel personeelsleden lijken van tijd tot tijd graag naar een andere functie over te stappen. Daar lijken twee belangrijke redenen voor te zijn. In de eerste plaats bepaalt het beleid duidelijk welke functies onderworpen zijn aan verplichte overplaatsing, waarbij alleen personeelsleden die gevoelige of leidinggevende functies bekleden verplicht worden om regelmatig van functie te wisselen. De reden van een dergelijk beleid is door het personeel eenvoudiger te accepteren en daardoor gemakkelijker te implementeren. De tweede belangrijke reden is de aanwezigheid van de vele functiemogelijkheden binnen de organisatie en standplaats. Het feit dat een verandering van functie geen of slechts beperkte invloed heeft op het privé- c.q. gezinsleven, draagt in grote mate bij aan hun bereidheid tot interne arbeidsmobiliteit.

Ondanks het relatieve succes van het arbeidsmobiliteitsbeleid van de Europese Commissie, stelt deze studie dat in het geval van personeelsleden die onderworpen zijn aan een vrijwillig beleid, het succes te danken is aan hun perceptie dat regelmatige verandering van werk een positief effect heeft op hun persoonlijke ontwikkeling, in plaats van de prikkels waarvoor het beleid van de Commissie in voorziet. In feite bevat het mobiliteitsbeleid van de Europese Unie minder prikkels tot interne arbeidsmobiliteit dan het beleid van de VN. Terwijl binnen het VN-secretariaat tenminste één stimulans bestaat, namelijk het vereiste van verplaatsing voordat men in aanmerking komt voor promotie naar een hogere functie, kent de Europese Commissie geen prikkels en geen link naar loopbaanontwikkeling en promotie. Dat is jammer. Met goede prikkels zouden in beide organisaties misschien (nog) meer personeelsleden bereid zijn om regelmatig over te stappen naar een andere post of functie.

Het arbeidsmobiliteitsbeleid van de Europese Commissie lijkt niet alleen succesvoller te zijn dan dat van de VN, maar ook meer ontvankelijk voor het waarborgen van de onafhankelijkheid en onpartijdigheid van ambtenaren die hoge posities bekleden. In tegenstelling tot het verleden stappen dergelijke hoge ambtenaren werkzaam bij de Europese Commissie nu met een zekere regelmaat over naar andere functies binnen de organisatie hoewel enige flexibiliteit aangaande de 'verplichte' arbeidsmobiliteit behouden is gebleven. De vraag is alleen of deze flexibiliteit gerechtvaardigd aangezien deze flexibiliteit niet beschikbaar is voor ander (lager geplaatst) personeel op zgn. gevoelige functies. Deze studie stelt dat het regelmatig overstappen van functies door leidinggevenden die tijdens de uitvoering van hun werkzaamheden te maken hebben met zaken van groot belang en daardoor kwetsbaar zijn voor ongepaste bemoeiing van buitenaf, tenminste even noodzakelijk met regelmaat van functie dienen te wisselen als het (lager geplaatste) personeel in gevoelige functies.

Wat betreft procedures is de situatie in het VN-secretariaat adequater dan die in de Europese Commissie, tenminste met betrekking tot het grootste deel van het personeel. De totale afwezigheid in de Europese Commissie van formele regels voor arbeidsmobiliteit van personeel onder het niveau van leidinggevenden, is teleurstellend. Hoewel de betrokken ambtenaren van functie wisselen op vergelijkbaar niveau, vindt er voorafgaand altijd een selectieproces plaats. Ook een dergelijke selectie moet gebeuren op basis van objectieve, duidelijke en transparante procedures om elke schijn van ongewenste invloeden in het proces te vermijden.

Vanuit dat gezichtspunt bezien, hebben de procedures ontwikkeld bij het VN-secretariaat een adequater juridisch kader voor de uitvoering van arbeidsmobiliteit. Helaas wordt de transparantie van dit kader ondermijnd door de veelheid van interne administratieve regelingen die van toepassing zijn – en elkaar soms zelfs overlappen – op verschillend VN-personeel. Deze studie stelt ook dat in de selectieprocedure, die opgesteld is met het doel arbeidsmobiliteit uit te voeren, 'central review bodies' moeten worden opgenomen. Betrokkenheid van deze, of soortgelijke, organen zou de objectiviteit, onpartijdigheid en transparantie van het selectieproces vergroten. Deze conclusie geldt voor zowel het VN-secretariaat als de Europese Commissie.

6. Aard van de aanstelling

De meeste internationale organisaties, waaronder de VN en de EU, maken gebruik van verschillende soorten arbeidsovereenkomsten van hun personeel. De belangrijkste reden hiervoor is de behoefte aan flexibiliteit van zowel internationale organisaties als de betreffende medewerkers, hoewel de mate van flexibiliteit kan verschillen. De vraag die in dit verband rijst is of de onafhankelijkheid en onpartijdigheid van internationale ambtenaren niet in gevaar komt door het gebruik van (bepaalde soorten van) niet-permanente aanstellingen. Het is een algemeen geaccepteerd gegeven dat niet-permanente aanstellingen er toe kunnen leiden dat mensen met een hoge professionele deskundigheid wegblijven bij een organisatie die niet in staat, of niet bereid, is redelijke vormen van werkzekerheid te bieden.

Het kan ook leiden tot angst voor verlies van werkgelegenheid waardoor onvermijdelijk schade berokkend wordt aan de onafhankelijke en onpartijdige uitoefening van taken door internationale ambtenaren. Het is daarom van het grootste belang dat de contractuele structuur in internationale organisaties er voor zorgt dat dergelijke negatieve effecten bij de tewerkstelling van niet-permanent personeel niet voordoet.

Bij het vergelijken van de situatie in het VN-secretariaat met die in de Europese Commissie, hebben beide aanvankelijk dezelfde benadering gekozen, waarin groot belang werd toegekend aan de behoefte om onafhankelijkheid en onpartijdigheid van het personeel te verzekeren en minder belang aan andere overwegingen. Als gevolg hiervan boden zowel het VN-secretariaat als de Europese Unie permanente aanstellingen aan een groot deel van haar ambtenaren die verantwoordelijk waren voor de uitoefening van de kerntaken die aan de internationale publieke dienst waren toevertrouwd. Tegelijkertijd bleef in beide instanties enige ruimte voor het aanstellen van niet-permanent personeel om aan tijdelijke behoeften te voldoen, hetzij voor bepaalde hetzij voor onbepaalde duur. Tijdelijke aanstellingen werden ook gebruikt voor het onderbrengen van uitgezonden nationale ambtenaren bij de betreffende organisaties met het oog op het uitwisselen van ervaringen.

Geleidelijk is deze aanvankelijke benadering in de praktijk, zowel bij de VN als bij de EU, komen te wijzigen. De belangrijkste reden voor deze wijziging was de uitbreiding van de mandaten van deze organisaties, die niet (voldoende) werd gevolgd door de aanpassing van het personeelsbeleid. De reactie die op deze, en andere, problemen volgde, verschilde in de loop der jaren bij de twee organisaties. Het VN-secretariaat creëerde een aantal nieuwe type aanstellingen met verschillende voorwaarden, terwijl de Europese Commissie daarentegen haar contractuele structuur in tact liet en meer gebruik maakte van tijdelijk personeel, hoewel dit laatste feitelijk niet passend was conform haar beleid. De Europese Commissie maakte ook in veel grotere mate gebruik van externe staf. Vanwege de grote mate van diversiteit van type aanstellingen werd de situatie bij het VN-secretariaat gekenmerkt door een hoge mate van complexiteit, en significante ongelijkheid, in de arbeidsvoorwaarden van de internationale ambtelijke staf, terwijl e.e.a. in de Europese Commissie leidde tot financiële wanorde. Noch het VN-secretariaat noch de Europese Commissie kon dus een bevredigende oplossing vinden voor de problemen die waren ontstaan met de uitbreiding van hun mandaten en de diversiteit van hun operationele behoeften. Zij boden ook geen lange termijn antwoorden voor de problemen waarmee de organisaties hadden te kampen. Daarom hervormden beide organisaties de afgelopen 10 jaar hun 'human resource framework'. Beide organisaties deden dit echter wederom op verschillende wijze. In de VN vonden, juridisch gesproken, verregaande veranderingen plaats en werd in 2009 een compleet nieuw 'human resource framework' opgezet.

In de EU waren het meer cosmetische veranderingen, zeker wat betreft de verschillende type aanstellingen. Echter aanzienlijke verbeteringen vonden plaats op het gebied van transparante procesvoering. Als gevolg van de hervormingen werd de contractuele structuur van het VN 'human resource framework' eenvoudiger, terwijl het in de EU vrij complex bleef. Dit is een interessant gegeven aangezien de VN in veel opzichten een meer complexe en gevarieerde organisatie is dan de EU. Toch heeft het VN-secretariaat er voor gekozen haar contractuele structuur drastisch te hervormen, terwijl de Europese Commissie een relatief ingewikkelde structuur met een relatief groter aantal aanstellingstypes heeft behouden.

Recente ontwikkelingen in zowel de VN en de EU laten zien dat het traditionele geloof in het belang van permanente aanstellingen voor de onafhankelijke en onpartijdige status van internationale ambtenaren, net als in het verleden, ook heden ten dage nog steeds relevant is. Ook nu worden andere, vaak nieuwe, belangen op gelijke hoogte geplaatst met de traditionele bezorgdheid over de onafhankelijkheid en onpartijdigheid van de internationale publieke dienst. Deze ontwikkeling wordt mogelijk ondersteund door de overtuiging dat de onafhankelijkheid en onpartijdigheid van internationale ambtenaren relatief veilig en gewaarborgd is door andere (juridische) instrumenten en dat de bescherming door permanente aanstellingen derhalve kan worden verzwakt. Hoewel beide organisaties eenzelfde ontwikkeling doormaken leggen ze op andere accenten de nadruk.

De belangrijkste zorg bij het VN-secretariaat lijkt de behoefte aan grotere flexibiliteit en efficiency van het personeel te zijn, waardoor flexibelere inhuur, ontplooiing en ontslag van personeel overeenkomstig de operationele doelen van de organisatie mogelijk is. Naast de introductie van verplichte mobiliteit voor bijna alle VN ambtenaren (inmiddels is deze regeling buitenwerking gesteld) is de afschaffing van permanente aanstellingen en de vervanging hiervan door zgn. doorlopende aanstellingen hier een bewijs van. Dergelijke doorlopende aanstellingen kunnen, in tegenstelling tot de permanente aanstellingen, zonder instemming van het personeel worden beëindigd in het belang van een goed bestuur van de organisatie. Indien de VN lidstaten niet uitdrukkelijk de interpretatie van deze wettelijke grond voor ontslag van personeel hadden beperkt, zou de VN, in hoedanigheid als werkgever, de vrije hand hebben gehad in het ontbinden van dergelijke arbeidsovereenkomsten.

Ook de Europese Commissie hecht in haar personeelsbeleid belang aan flexibiliteit, al zou kunnen worden betoogd dat dit in de Commissie meer theorie dan praktijk is. Kijkend naar de verwezenlijking van de noodzakelijk geachte flexibiliteit door een groter gebruik te maken van niet-permanente aanstellingen in plaats van permanente aanstellingen, lijkt het er op dat de Commissie bezorgder is over de kosten dan over de flexibiliteit. Door het in toenemende mate inhuren van niet-permanent personeel, in het bijzonder contractueel personeel, wil de Europese Commissie duidelijk een verlaging van de kosten realiseren. Dit kan onder meer worden afgeleid uit het verminderd gebruik van 'tijdelijk' personeel en de aanzienlijke toename van contractueel personeel. Terwijl beide vormen van niet-permanent personeel kunnen worden gebruikt voor dezelfde functies, valt 'tijdelijk' personeel onder dezelfde salarisstructuur als het permanente personeel terwijl het contractuele personeel dit niet doet. Deze laatste categorie heeft haar eigen salarisopbouw met lagere tarieven. Dat maakt het in dienst nemen van contractueel personeel minder duur voor de Europese Commissie dan de aanstelling van 'tijdelijk' of permanent personeel.

Deze studie stelt dat de significante veranderingen die zich de afgelopen 50-60 jaar zowel in de maatschappij als in de arbeidsverhoudingen hebben voorgedaan, haar reflectie dient te hebben op het openbaar bestuur, zowel op internationaal als op Europees niveau met in achtneming van het belang van permanente aanstellingen teneinde de onafhankelijke en onpartijdige status van internationale ambtenaren te kunnen waarborgen. Deze studie stelt dan ook dat de onafhankelijkheid en onpartijdigheid van internationale ambtenaren niet alleen gegarandeerd wordt door één waarborg, maar door een combinatie van vele; permanente aanstellingen is er slechts één van. Daarom stelt deze studie dat de vervanging van permanente aanstellingen door doorlopende aanstellingen bij het VN-secretariaat niet noodzakelijkerwijs het 'einde' van de internationale publieke dienst hoeft te betekenen en dat de toegenomen toevlucht van de Europese Commissie tot niet-permanent personeel niet automatisch leidt tot onvoldoende onafhankelijkheid en onpartijdigheid van Europese ambtenaren. Dit komt door de voorwaarden en beperkingen waaronder de recente veranderingen in de VN en EU hebben plaatsgevonden. In de VN zijn permanente aanstellingen vervangen door doorlopende aanstellingen met inachtneming van wettelijke waarborgen om te voorkomen dat (mogelijke) beëindiging van een aanstelling wordt gebruikt om de onafhankelijkheid en onpartijdigheid van het personeel te beïnvloeden. Het is echter betreurenswaardig dat dergelijke waarborgen niet zijn van toepassing zijn op de bescherming van niet-permanent personeel tegen de weigering van contractvernieuwing.

Hoewel in de EU, niet-permanent personeel in veel gevallen kan worden ingehuurd bestaan er ook restricties. Het is namelijk niet mogelijk dergelijk niet-permanent personeel in te zetten voor taken die worden gerekend tot de kerntaken van de publieke sector van de EU. Daarnaast is uitbreiding, vernieuwing en beëindiging van niet-permanente aanstellingen bij de Europese Unie in de meeste gevallen afhankelijk van duidelijke en gedetailleerde regels, met inbegrip van waarborgen ontwikkelt door de rechterlijke macht. Wel het laatst genoemd, maar daarom niet minder belangrijk, de meerderheid van het personeel bij de Europese Commissie werkt op basis van permanente aanstellingen en de verwachting is dat de meerderheid van het personeel bij het VN-secretariaat de huidige permanente aanstellingen behoud dan wel werkzaam zal worden op basis van doorlopende aanstellingen.

7. Ontbinding van het dienstverband

Het belang van een gedegen juridisch kader op basis waarvan internationale ambtenaren kunnen worden ontslagen bij de organisatie waar zij werken, is reeds lang erkend. Zoals reeds eerder genoemd, zijn goede perspectieven op het gebied van carrière ontwikkeling noodzakelijk evenals een adequate bescherming tegen verlies van werk noodzakelijk, voor het aantrekken en behouden van kwalitatief hoogwaardig personeel in dienst van internationale organisaties. Een adequaat gereguleerd ontslagbeleid voorkomt ook dat internationale ambtenaren vatbaar worden voor de belangen van degenen van wiens goodwill zij afhankelijk zijn om hun baan te behouden of van degenen die mogelijkerwijs hun toekomstige werkgever zou kunnen worden in geval van verlies van hun huidige baan. Zonder voldoende bescherming tegen ontslag op gronden die geen verband houden met de belangen van de organisatie als zodanig of met de prestaties en het gedrag van het personeel, en zonder procedures voor ontslag die voldoende bescherming bieden tegen misbruik en verkeerd gebruik van ontslagprocedures, zou de onafhankelijkheid en onpartijdigheid van internationale ambtenaren in gevaar worden gebracht.

Het is dan ook bevreemdend dat in de recente hervormingen van het personeelsbeleid bij zowel het VN-secretariaat als bij de Europese Commissie relatief weinig aandacht is geschonken aan mogelijke kwesties die verband houden met ontbinding van het dienstverband van hun ambtenaren. Op een kleine uitzondering na is de lijst van juridische gronden op basis waarvan het dienstverband van VN en EU ambtenaren ontbonden kan worden ongewijzigd gebleven. De weinige aanpassingen die bij de twee instanties hebben plaatsgevonden hadden betrekking op de voorwaarden waaronder redenen voor ontbinding van het dienstverband kunnen worden ingeroepen. Tot de belangrijkste veranderingen behoren: de verbeteringen die zijn doorgevoerd in de ontslagprocedures, het recht op een eerlijk proces in tuchtzaken, het loslaten van de disciplinaire aanpak bij onbekwaamheid van personeel en de invoering van het vereiste om onbekwaam personeel te helpen hun prestaties te verbeteren voordat tot ontslag mag worden overgegaan. Voornoemde verbeteringen vonden zowel bij het VN-secretariaat als bij de Europese Commissie plaats, hoewel ten aanzien van de beëindiging van het dienstverband door onbekwaamheid, het VN-secretariaat beter werk lijkt te hebben geleverd dan de Europese Commissie. Door expliciet en nauwkeurige de corrigerende stappen te vermelden, inclusief daaraan gekoppelde termijnen, die in gevallen van onbekwaamheid moeten worden genomen, geeft de nieuwe administratieve instructie van de VN haar personeel betere garanties dat hun problemen om te voldoen aan de vereiste standaard van prestatie met aandacht zullen worden behandeld en dat inspanningen vanuit werkgeverszijde worden verricht teneinde de geconstateerde problemen op te lossen alvorens sprake kan zijn van beëindiging van het dienstverband.

Hoewel het EU Ambtenarenstatuut in dergelijke gevallen ook corrigerende acties vereist, heeft de Europese Commissie geen precieze regels over hoe dit vereiste in de praktijk moet worden uitgevoerd. Bovendien geniet het niet-permanente personeel van de EU geen bescherming in geval van onbekwaamheid en kan het op elk moment ontslagen worden, enkel door een formele aanzegging van ontslag.

Het VN-secretariaat geeft in vergelijking met de EU haar personeel in een aantal situaties betere bescherming bij de ontbinding van het dienstverband. Dit geldt voor zowel niet-permanent personeel, ambtenaren met een proeftijd en ambtenaren in hoge posities. Wat betreft het niet-permanent personeel, al deze stafleden werken sinds de invoering van de nieuwe contractuele structuur op basis van contracten voor bepaalde tijd. Als gevolg daarvan eindigt elk dienstverband van het niet-permanent VN-personeel in principe na het verstrijken van de termijn vermeld in de aanstellingsbrief, met uitzondering van die gevallen waarin het gaat om één van de wettelijke gronden tot beëindiging van het dienstverband zoals vermeld in de *VN Ambtenarenstatuut* of in de aanstellingsbrief, zoals wangedrag, onbekwaamheid, ongeschiktheid wegens gezondheidsredenen, pensionering of overlijden. In de Europese Commissie blijven veel niet-permanente stafleden werken op basis van contracten voor onbepaalde tijd, die door hun aard door beide partijen kunnen worden beëindigd door een kennisgeving aan de andere partij. Bovendien kan ook EU-personeel met een aanstelling voor bepaalde tijd ontslagen worden door een kennisgeving van beëindiging door de EU Administratie. In tegenstelling tot hun collega's bij de VN geniet het EU-personeel met niet-permanente aanstellingen geen bescherming tegen ontbinding van hun dienstverband tijdens de in de aanstellingsbrief overeengekomen arbeidsduur. De behoefte aan een dergelijke bescherming werd onlangs benadrukt door de rechterlijke macht van de EU, ook al konden de rechtbanken van de EU niet voorbijgaan aan het feit dat de *EU Regeling voor Andere Personeelsleden* voorzien in een wettelijke grondslag voor beëindiging van het dienstverband voordat de vastgestelde termijn is verstreken door een kennisgeving. Om het niet permanente personeel bij de EU beter te beschermen, hebben de EU rechtbanken de verplichting ingevoerd om in de kennisgeving de redenen van ontbinding op te nemen. Dezelfde verplichting is van toepassing op de beëindiging van beide typen niet-permanente aanstellingen, te weten: aanstellingen voor bepaalde en onbepaalde tijd.

Binnen de categorie permanent personeel wordt aan EU ambtenaren met een proeftijd en aan ambtenaren die hoge posten bekleden, minder bescherming geboden dan aan het personeel bij de VN. In de EU kunnen ambtenaren in de proeftijd worden ontslagen tijdens of aan het einde van deze proeftijd, zonder dat de EU Administratie verplicht is hen de gelegenheid te bieden zich te verbeteren of hen hierbij hulp aan te bieden. Een dergelijke handelwijze is niet meer mogelijk bij het VN-secretariaat, waar nieuw benoemd personeel alleen mag worden ontslagen vanwege onbekwaamheid nadat bepaalde acties ter verbetering niet tot het gewenste resultaat hebben geleid. Ambtenaren die hoge posities bekleden, kunnen in de EU op elk moment worden ontslagen in het belang van de dienst, waarbij feitelijk geen beperkingen worden opgelegd aan de EU Administratie. Ontslag van ambtenaren die in de VN daarentegen hoge posities bekleden is niet zo gemakkelijk. Hoewel de aanstelling van deze ambtenaren in het belang van behoorlijk bestuur zonder hun toestemming kan worden beëindigd, is het belang van behoorlijk bestuur van de organisatie door de Algemene Vergadering van de VN restrictief geïnterpreteerd.

Behoudens in deze twee gevallen (ambtenaren met een proeftijd en ambtenaren die hoge posten bekleden) is in alle andere gevallen permanent personeel in dienst van de EU beter beschermd tegen en bij ontbinding van hun dienstverband dan VN permanent personeel. Zo is er bijvoorbeeld in de EU geen equivalent voor de ontbinding van het nieuwe type VN aanstelling, aangeduid als doorlopende aanstelling, in het belang van behoorlijk bestuur zonder instemming van het betreffende personeelslid. Bovendien, ook wanneer er behoefte bestaat aan vermindering van het personeelsbestand, verliezen ambtenaren in permanente dienst bij de EU niet direct hun baan, maar blijven - op non-actief - gedurende een relatief lange tijd in dienst, terwijl VN-ambtenaren daarentegen relatief snel worden ontslagen.

Deze studie doet diverse verbeteringsvoorstellen. Voor de VN betoogt zij bijvoorbeeld dat een tuchtcommissie, of een soortgelijk collectief orgaan, betrokken dient te worden bij elke tuchtprocedure geïnitieerd tegen een VN-staflid, net zo als dit het geval is in de EU. Hoewel VN-stafleden onderworpen aan een tuchtprocedure, beschermd zijn door het totaal aan regels en gedragingen volgens welke een rechtszaak moet verlopen, waarbij het recht van de aangeklaagde wordt geëerbiedigd. Deze procesregels wijken in het algemeen niet af van de regels welke van toepassing zijn op hun EU-collega's echter het feit dat de VN Administratie direct disciplinaire beslissingen neemt zonder raadpleging van een collectief orgaan met personeelsvertegenwoordigers doet afbreuk aan de objectiviteit en de onpartijdigheid van dergelijke beslissingen. De mogelijkheid om een VN-staflid te ontslaan wegens beschuldigingen van ernstig wangedrag zonder tuchtrechterlijk proces is zo niet nog problematischer. Deze mogelijkheid bestaat niet bij de EU en er kan worden aangevoerd dat deze ook in de VN niet beschikbaar zou moeten zijn. Elk staflid dat beschuldigd wordt van wangedrag of ernstig wangedrag, zou een eerlijk proces moeten krijgen met ruimte ter verdediging, alvorens een beslissing tot ontslag kan worden genomen.

In de Europese Commissie, zijn er verschillende terreinen waar gedetailleerde regels voor procedures en voorwaarden voor de toepassing van specifieke redenen voor ontbinding van het dienstverband totaal ontbreken. Teneinde de rechtszekerheid van het personeel in kwestie te kunnen waarborgen en om te zorgen voor objectieve en transparante beslissingen, zou de EU o.a. regels dienen aan te nemen om: onderprestatie van personeel aan te pakken, om staf die wangedrag aan de orde stelt te beschermen, als ook voor ontslag wegens onbekwaamheid in geval van tijdelijk en contractueel personeel. Een andere suggestie voor mogelijke verbetering in de EU heeft betrekking op mogelijk beroep tegen disciplinaire beslissingen. Deze studie stelt voor dat de EU stappen overweegt, vergelijkbaar met die zijn genomen door het VN-secretariaat, om in tuchtzaken de eis van het verplicht indienen van een administratieve klacht voordat er een beroep kan worden ingediend bij de rechtbank af te schaffen. Hoewel dit vereiste bij 'gewone' administratieve zaken van belang kan zijn is het echter onwaarschijnlijk dat de administratieve klacht in een tuchtzaak, die over het algemeen gekenschetst wordt door een uitwisseling van standpunten tussen het betrokken personeelslid en de werkgever, leidt tot een acceptabel resultaat voor de klagende medewerker, aangezien over de klacht wordt beslist door hetzelfde orgaan als die de gewraakte beslissing heeft genomen. Deze studie stelt dat een dergelijke gang van zaken het recht onnodig vertraagt in zaken die van groot belang en te allen tijde zeer gevoelig zijn en daarom naar de mening van de auteur zonder onnodige vertraging zouden moeten worden opgelost.

8. Conclusie

Deze studie richt zich op de juridische waarborgen in het personeelsbeleid van het VN-secretariaat en de Europese Commissie voor het onafhankelijk en onpartijdig kunnen functioneren van diens internationale ambtenaren. In het bijzonder wordt in deze studie gekeken naar de aanstelling en plaatsing van internationale ambtenaren en de ontbinding van hun dienstverband. Het waarborgen van een onafhankelijk en onpartijdig functionerende internationale publieke dienst is één van de, zo niet het belangrijkste uitgangspunt, waarop zowel de VN als de EU hun personeelsbeleid baseren. Hoewel sommige specifieke items van oudsher verbonden met het concept van een onpartijdig en onafhankelijk functionerende internationale publieke dienst momenteel ter discussie staan, zoals bijvoorbeeld het belang van werkzekerheid, blijft de noodzaak voor het onafhankelijk en onpartijdig kunnen functioneren van internationale ambtenaren net zo relevant en belangrijk als het was op het moment van ontstaan van dit concept in het begin van de 20e eeuw. Zonder een onafhankelijk en onpartijdig functionerend internationaal ambtelijk apparaat geen enkele internationale publieke dienst in staat zijn om het vertrouwen en de steun te winnen en te behouden van de lidstaten die onderdeel uitmaken van de betreffende internationale organisatie. De goede werking van de internationale organisatie zou dan zondermeer in gevaar zijn. Een goed en adequaat functionerende en daadwerkelijk onafhankelijke en onpartijdige staf blijft dan ook tot op de dag van vandaag van vitaal belang.

Het doel van deze studie is niet om te beoordelen of het personeel in dienst van het VN-secretariaat en de Europese Commissie feitelijk onafhankelijk en onpartijdig functioneert noch om het effect van het beleid met betrekking tot deze onderwerpen te bepalen. Het doel was veeleer om een grondige inventarisatie uit te voeren naar het complexe vigerende beleid op dit onderwerp, het te verklaren en te vergelijken met relevant beleid in een andere internationale organisatie. Last but not least, te beoordelen of het beleid in beginsel toereikend c.q. voldoende waarborgen biedt om er voor te zorgen dat internationale ambtenaren werkzaam in één van beide organisaties een positie bij de organisatie krijgen respectievelijk behouden op een manier die hen in staat stelt hun taken naar beste vermogen te vervullen, zonder ongepaste inmenging en druk van buitenaf.

Zowel het VN-secretariaat als de Europese Commissie hebben het afgelopen decennium veel veranderingen doorgevoerd in hun personeelsbeleid. In beide organisaties vonden de meeste wijzigingen plaats als onderdeel van een algeheel hervormingsproces die primair was gericht op het verbeteren van de efficiëntie, flexibiliteit en kosteneffectiviteit van het ambtelijk apparaat. De aanpassingen hadden geen effect op de grondbeginselen waarop het concept van de internationale publieke dienst is gebaseerd. Er kan dus worden gesteld dat het concept van een onpartijdig en onafhankelijk opererende internationale ambtelijke staf de hervormingen in het personeelsbeleid heeft overleefd, zowel bij het VN-secretariaat als bij de Europese Commissie. Desalniettemin dient te worden vastgesteld dat in beide organisaties de nadruk in het personeelsbeleid meer is komen te liggen op het waarborgen van een goedkoper en flexibeler ambtelijk apparaat. Deze wijziging in prioriteitstelling is, tot op zekere hoogte, begrijpelijk. Internationale organisaties dienen zich, net als het door haar te voeren personeelsbeleid, aan te passen aan de steeds sneller veranderende hedendaagse samenleving en haar toenemende complexere eisen. Echter, de noodzaak om ervoor te zorgen dat de eisen voldoen aan het algemeen belang van de internationale samenleving, op een wijze vrij van iedere vorm van partijdigheid mag niet worden vergeten.

Deze studie stelt vast dat zowel het personeelsbeleid van het VN-secretariaat als de Europese Commissie over een aantal belangrijke juridische waarborgen beschikken die bijdragen aan het onafhankelijk en onpartijdig functioneren van hun internationale ambtenaren. De hervormingen die de afgelopen 10 jaar in het personeelsbeleid hebben plaatsgevonden bij zowel het VN-secretariaat als de Europese Commissie hebben ertoe geleid dat zij beter kunnen inspelen op de toenemende eisen die de hedendaagse samenleving stelt aan het functioneren van internationale organisaties. Ondanks voornoemde verbeteringen stelt deze studie dat de situatie nog bij het VN-secretariaat noch bij de Europese Commissie ideaal is. In deze studie worden derhalve concrete aanbevelingen gedaan ter verbetering van bepaalde beleidsonderdelen. Indien deze aanbevelingen worden geïmplementeerd, dragen zij bij aan een verdere verbetering van het onafhankelijk en onpartijdig kunnen functioneren van het VN- en EU-ambtelijke apparaat. Dit laatste is een absolute voorwaarde voor een goede werking van elke moderne internationale organisatie en het vertrouwen in deze organisaties door de internationale samenleving.

BIBLIOGRAPHY

BOOKS

Amerasinghe, C. F., *The Law of the International Civil Service, Volume I,* Claredon Press, Oxford, 1994

Amerasinghe, C. F., *The Law of the International Civil Service, Volume II,* Clarendon Press, Oxford, 1988

Archer, C., *International Organizations,* Routledge, London / New York, 2001

Beigbeder, Y., *Threats to the International Civil Service: Past Presures and New Trends,* Pinter Publishers Limited, London, 1988

Bodiguel, J.-L., *Les Fonctions Publiques dans l'Europe Des Douze,* Librairie Général de Driot et de Jurisprudence, Paris, 1994

Cini, M., *The European Commission, Leadership, Organisation and Culture in the EU Administration,* Manchester University Press, Manchester / New York, 1996

Claude, I. L., Jr., *Swords Into Plowshares,* Random House, Inc.&Random House of Canada Limited, New York / Toronto, 1971

Coombes, D., *Politics and Bureaucracy in the European Community, A Portrait of the Commission of the E.E.C.,* George Allen and Unwin Ltd., London, 1970

Coombes, D., *Towards a European Civil Service,* Chatham House, London, 1968

Dinan, D., *Ever Closer Union. An Introduction to European Integration,* Palgrave, Basingstoke, 1999

Emadi-Coffin, B., *Rethinking International Organizations, Deregulation and Global Governance,* Routledge, London / New York, 2002

Endo, K., *The Presidency of the European Commission under Jacques Delors, The Politics of Shared Leadership,* Macmillan Press and St. Martin's Press in association with St Antony's College, Oxofrd, Basingstok / New York, 1999

Franck, T. M., Renninger, J. P. and Tikhomirov, V. B., *An Attitude Survey: Diplomat's View on the United Nations System,* UNITAR, New York, 1982

Grant, C., *Delors: Inside the House that Jack Built,* Nicholas Brealy Publishing, London, 1994

Hammarskjöld, D., *The International Civil Servant in Law and in Fact,* Oxford University Press, Oxford, 1961

Hooghe, L., *The European Commission and the Integration of Europe, Images of Governance,* Cambridge University Press, Cambridge, 2001

Klabbers, J., *An Introduction to International Institutional Law,* Cambridge University Press, Cambridge, 2002

Langrod, G., *The International Civil Service, Its Origins, Its Nature, Its Evolution,* A. W. Sythoff & Oceana Publications, Inc., Leyden / New York, 1963

Lemoine, J., *The International Civil Servant: An Endangered Species,* Kluwer Law International, The Hague / London / Boston, 1995

Martinez, M. M. M., *National Sovereignty and International Organizations,* Kluwer Law International, The Hague / Boston / London, 1996

Meron, T., *Status and Independence of the International Civil Servant,* Sijthoff & Noordhoff, Alphen aan den Rijn, 1980

Meron, T., *The United Nations Secretariat,* Lexington Books, Lexington, Toronto, 1977

Mouritzen, H., *The International Civil Service, A study of Bureaucracy: International Organizations,* Dartmouth, Aldershot / Brookfield / Hong Kong / Singapore / Sydney, 1990

Nugent, N., *The European Commission,* Palgrave, Houndmills / Basingstoke / Hampshire / New York, 2001

Page, E. C., *People Who Run Europe,* Clarendon Press, Oxford, 1997

Plantey, A., *The International Civil Service, Law and Management,* MASSON Publishing USA, Inc., New York / Paris / Barcelona / Milan / Mexico City / Rio de Janeiro, 1981

Reymond, H. and Mailick, S., *International Personnel Policies and Practices,* Praeger Publishers, New York, 1985

Sands, P. and Klein, P., *Bowlett's Law of International Institutions,* Sweet & Maxwell, London, 2001

Sarooshi, D., *International Organizations and Their Exercise of Sovereign Powers,* Oxford University Press, Oxford, 2005

Schermers, H. G. and Blokker, N. M., *International Institutional Law, Unity within Diversity,* Martinus Nijhoff Publishers, Boston / Leiden, 2003

Shapero, A., *Managing Professional People: Understanding Creative Performance,* The Free Press, New York, 1985

Stevens, A. and Stevens, H., *Brussels Bureaucrats? The Administration of the European Union,* PALGRAVE, Houndmills / New York, 2001

Weber, M., *The Theory of Social and Economis Organization, Edited with an Introdcution by Talcott Parsons,* The Free Press, A division of Macmillan Publishing Co., Inc., Collier Macmillan Publishers, New York / London, 1964

Weiss, T. G., *International Bureaucracy, An Analysis of the Operation of Functional and Global International Secretariats,* Lexington Books, D.C. Health and Company, Massachusetts / Toronto / London, 1975

White, L. D., *Introduction to the Study of Public Administration,* MacMillan, New York, 1958

EDITED BOOKS

Cooker, C. D. (ed.), *Accountability, Investigation and Due Process in International Organizations*, Martinus Nijhoff Publishers, Leiden / Boston, 2005

Dimitrakopoulos, D. G. (ed.), *The Changing European Commission*, Manchester University Press, Manchester / New York, 2004

Graham, N. A. and Jordan, R. S. (eds.), *The International Civil Service, Changing Role and Concepts*, Pergamon Press (published in cooperation with UNITAR), New York / Oxford / Toronto / Sydney / Frankfurt / Paris, 1980

Kassim, H., Menon, A., Peters, B. G. and Wright, V. (eds.), *The National Co-ordination of EU Policy, The European Level*, Oxford University Press, Oxford, 2001

Nugent, N. (ed.), *At the Heart of the Union, Studies of the European Commission*, Macmillan Press Ltd, Houndmills / Basingstoke / Hampshire / London, 1997

Spence, D. and Edwads, G. (eds.), *The European Commission*, John Harper Publishing, London, 2006

BOOK SECTIONS

Ali, A., *The International Civil Service: The Idea and the Reality*, in: C. De Cooker (ed.), International Administration, Law and Management Pratices in International Organizations, Martinus Nijhoff Publishers, Dordrecht / Boston / London, 1990, pp. INT.ADMIN I.1/3-20

Bertrand, M., *The Recruitment Policy of the United Nations Staff*, in: C. De Cooker (ed.), International Administration, Law and Management Practices in International Organizations, Martinus Nijhoff Publishers, Dordrecht / Boston / London, 1990, pp. INT.ADMIN II.2/1-9

Göttelmann and Münch, *Article 101*, in: B. Simma (ed.), The Charter of th United Nations, A Commentary, Oxford University Press, Oxford, 2002, pp. 1252-1276

Kassim, H. and Peters, B. G., *Co-ordinating National Action in Brussels - a Comparative Perspective*, in: H. Kassim, A. Menon, B. G. Peters and V. Wright (eds.), The National Co-ordination of EU Policy, The European Level, Oxford University Press, Oxford, 2001, pp. 297-339

McDonald, M., *Identities in the European Commission*, in: N. Nugent (ed.), At the Heart of the Union, Studies of the European Commission, Macmillan Press Ltd, Houndmills / Basingstoke / Hampshire / London, 1997, pp. 49-70

Spence, D., *Staff and Personnel Policy in the Commission*, in: G. Edwards and D. Spence (eds.), The European Commission, Longman, London, 1997, pp. 97-114

Spence, D. and Stevens, A., *Staff and Personnel Policy in the Commission*, in: D. Spence and G. Edwards (eds.), The European Commission, John Harper Publishing, London, 2006, pp. 173-208

Stevens, H. and Stevens, A., *The Internal Reform of the Commission*, in: D. Spence and G. Edwards (eds.), The European Commission, John Harper Publishing, London, 2006, pp. 454-480

JOURNAL ARTICLES

Barnes, R., *Tenure and Independence in the United Nations International Civil Service*, in: New York University Journal of International Law and Politics, Vol. 14, pp. 767-782

Bulkeley, J. R., *Depoliticizing United Nations Recruitment: Establishing a Genuinly International Civil Service*, in: New York University Journal of International Law and Politics, Vol. 22, Nr. 4, pp. 749-792

Cameron, H., *Establishment of the European Union Civil Service Tribunal*, in: The Law and Practice of International Courts and Tribunals, Vol. 5, Nr. 2, pp. 273-283

Coull, J. and Lewis, C., *The Impact of the Staff Regulations in Making the Commission a More Modern and Efficient Oragnization: an Insider's Perspective*, in: Eipascope, Vol. 2003, Nr. 3, pp. 2-9

Goodrich, L. M., *Geographical Distribution of the Staff of the UN Secretariat*, in: International Organization, 1962, pp. 465-482

Jonah, J. O. C., *Independence and Integrity of the International Civil Service: The Role of the Executive Heads and the Role of States*, in: New York University Journal of International Law and Politics, Vol. 14, pp. 841-859

Lengyel, P., *Some Trends in the International Civil Service*, in: International Organization, 1959, pp. 520-537

Meron, T., *Charter Powers of the United Nation's Secretary-General with regard to the Secretariat and the Role of General Assembly Resolutions*, in: Heidelberg Journal of International Law, Vol. 42, pp. 731-779

Meron, T., *Editorial Comment: "Exclusive Preserves" and the New Soviet Policy towards the UN Secretariat*, in: American Journal of International Law, Vol. 85, pp. 322-329

Meron, T., *The Role of the Executive Heads*, in: New York University Journal of International Law and Politics, Vol. 14, pp. 861-869

Meron, T., *Staff of the United nations Secretariat: Problems and Directions*, in: The American Journal of International Law, Vol. 70, pp. 659-693

Miron, D., *Tenure, Fixed-Term Appointments and Secondment in the United Nations*, in: New York University Journal of International Law and Politics, Vol. 14, pp. 783-798

Swift, R. N., *Personnel Problems and the United Nations Secretariat*, in: International Organization, 1956, pp. 228-247

Szasz, P. C., *The Role of the U.N. Secretary-General: Some Legal Aspects*, in: New York University Journal of International Law and Politics, Vol. 24, pp. 161-198

ELECTRONIC ARTICLES

Amann, D. M., *Impartiality Deficit and International Criminal Judging*, 2006, avaiable in the Social Science Research Network, available at http://ssrn.com/paper=955431, last visited on 30.12.2010

Egeberg, M., *The European Commission - The Evolving EU Executive*, ARENA Working Papers WP 02/30, 2002, available at http://www.sv.uio.no/arena/english/research/publications/arena-publications/workingpapers/working-papers2002/wp02_30.htm, last visited on 30.12.2010

Egeberg, M., *Organising Institutional Autonomy in a Political Context: Enduring Tensions in the European Commission's Development*, ARENA Working Papers WP 02/2004, 2004, available at http://www.sv.uio.no/arena/english/research/publications/arena-publications/workingpapers/working-papers2004/wp04_2.pdf, last visited on 30.12.2010

Georgakakis, D. and De Lassalle, M., *Who Are the Directors-General? European Construction and Administrative Careers in the Commission*, Paper based on EU-CONSENT WORKSHOP The Commission and the European Civil Service, Paris, 21-22.6.2006 (Deliverable No. '17'), 2007, available at http://www.eu-consent.net/library/deliverables/D17_Team7_georgakakis-delassalle.pdf, last visited on 30.12.2010

Hooghe, L., *Consociationists or Weberians? Top Commission Officials on Nationality*, ARENA Working Paper WP 98/20, 1998, available at http://www.sv.uio.no/arena/english/research/publications/arena-publications/workingpapers/working-papers1998/wp98_20.htm, last visited on 30.12.2010

Kassim, H. and Menon, A., *European Integration since the 1990s: Member States and the European Commission*, ARENA Working Papers WP 6/04, 2004, available at http://www.sv.uio.no/arena/english/research/publications/arena-publications/workingpapers/working-papers2004/wp04_6.pdf, last visited on 30.12.2010

Schon-Quinlivan, E., *Administrative Reform in the European Commission: From Rethoric to Re-legitimisation*, Paper based on EU-CONSENT WORKSHOP The Commission and the European Civil Service, Paris, 21-22.6.2006 (Deliverable No. '17'), 2006, available at http://www.eu-consent.net/library/deliverables/D17_Team7_Schon1.pdf, last visited on 30.12.2010

Trondal, J., *An Institutional Perspective on Representation. Ambiguous Representation in the European Commission*, European Integration Online Papers (EIoP) Vol. 10, No. 4, 2006, available at http://eiop.or.at/eiop/texte/2006-004a.htm, last visited on 30.12.2010

Wass, D., *Loyality, Neutrality and Commitment in a Career Civil Service*, EGPA Leuven Conference paper, 1985, 1985, available at http://ipac.coleurop.be/ipac20/ipac.jsp?session=1312621X119B4.179112&profile=brugge&uri=link=3100006~!20462~!3100001~!3100002&aspect=power&menu=search&ri=1&source=~!horizon&term=Loyality%2C+neutrality+and+commitment+in+a+career+civil+service+%2F&index=TITLE#focus, last visited on 30.12.2010

NEWSPAPER ARTICLES

Barroso Urges Reshuffle of Top EU Officials in: EurActiv Network, 21.01.2010

Brand, C., *Hague Vows to Increase UK's EU Influence*, in: European Voice, 01.07.2010

Britain's Costly Disdain, in: The Economists, 3.11.2007

King, T., *Staff Reforms that Failed to Make the Grade*, in: EuropeanVoice.com, 26.07.2007

Pop, V., *New EU Exam to Axe Dreaded Quiz on Union Trivia*, in: euobserver.com, 03.03.2010

Pop, V., *Sweden Continues Attack on US Appointment*, in: euobserver.com, 23.02.2010

Rettman, A., *EU Parliament to Arm-Twist Ashton on Appointments*, in: euobserver.com, 01.09.2010

Rettman, A., *MEPs Drop Idea of Soft Quotas for EU Diplomatic Staff*, in: euobserver.com, 19.10.2010

Rettman, A., *Old Boys Club Dominates EU Diplomacy*, in: euobserver.com, 25.08.2010

Rettman, A., *Sweden Complains about EU Appointment to US*, in: euobserver.com, 22.02.2010

Willis, A., *UK Sets Out Plan To Regain Influence in EU*, in: euobserver.com, 02.07.2010

DOCUMENTS OF, OR RELATED TO, THE UNITED NATIONS

TREATIES

Charter of the United Nations, 26.06.1945, available at http://www.un.org/aboutun/charter/index.html, last visited on 30.12.2010

RESOLUTIONS OF THE GENERAL ASSEMBLY

General Assembly Resolution 13(I), A/RES/13(I), 13.02.1946, available in the Official Document System of the United Nations, available at http://documents.un.org/, last visited on 30.12.2010

General Assembly Resolution 31/26, A/RES/31/26, 29.11.1976, available in the Official Document System of the United Nations, available at http://documents.un.org/, last visited on 30.12.2010

General Assembly Resolution 33/143, A/RES/33/143, 20.12.1978, available in the Official Document System of the United Nations, available at http://documents.un.org/, last visited on 30.12.2010

General Assembly Resolution 34/219, A/RES/34/219, 20.12.1979, available in the Official Document System of the United Nations, available at http://documents.un.org/, last visited on 30.12.2010

General Assembly Resolution 35/210, A/RES/35/210, 17.12.1980, available in the Official Document System of the United Nations, available at http://documents.un.org/, last visited on 30.12.2010

General Assembly Resolution 37/235, A/RES/37/235, 21.12.1982, available in the Official Document System of the United Nations, available at http://documents.un.org/, last visited on 30.12.2010

General Assembly Resolution 39/245, A/RES/39/245, 18.12.1984, available in the Official Document System of the United Nations, available at http://documents.un.org/, last visited on 30.12.2010

General Assembly Resolution 40/258, A/RES/40/258, 18.12.1985, available in the Official Document System of the United Nations, available at http://documents.un.org/, last visited on 30.12.2010

General Assembly Resolution 41/206B, A/RES/41/206B, 11.12.1986, available in the Official Document System of the United Nations, available at http://documents.un.org/, last visited on 30.12.2010

General Assembly Resolution 42/220A, A/RES/42/220A, 21.12.1987, available in the Official Document System of the United Nations, available at http://documents.un.org/, last visited on 30.12.2010

General Assembly Resolution 44/185 A, 18.12.1989, available in the Official Document System of the United Nations, available at http://documents.un.org/, last visited on 30.12.2010

General Assembly Resolution 47/226, A/RES/47/226, 08.04.1993, available in the Official Document System of the United Nations, available at http://documents.un.org/, last visited on 30.12.2010

General Assembly Resolution 49/222, A/RES/49/222, 15.02.1995, available in the Official Document System of the United Nations, available at http://documents.un.org/, last visited on 30.12.2010

General Assembly Resolution 49/223, A/RES/49/223, 23.12.2010, available in the Official Document System of the United Nations, available at http://documents.un.org/, last visited on 30.12.2010

General Assembly Resolution 51/226B, A/RES/51/226B, 03.04.1997, available in the Official Document System of the United Nations, available at http://documents.un.org/, last visited on 30.12.2010

General Assembly Resolution 52/12B, A/RES/52/12B, 19.12.1997, available in the Official Document System of the United Nations, available at http://documents.un.org/, last visited on 30.12.2010

General Assembly Resolution 53/221, A/RES/53/221, 03.04.1997, available in the Official Document System of the United Nations, available at http://documents.un.org/, last visited on 30.12.2010

General Assembly Resolution 53/221, A/RES/53/221, 07.04.1999, available in the Official Document System of the United Nations, available at http://documents.un.org/, last visited on 30.12.2010

General Assembly Resolution 55/258, A/RES/55/258, 14.06.2001, available in the Official Document System of the United Nations, available at http://documents.un.org/, last visited on 30.12.2010

General Assembly Resolution 56/244, A/RES/56/244, 05.02.2002, available in the Official Document System of the United Nations, available at http://documents.un.org/, last visited on 30.12.2010

General Assembly Resolution 57/305, A/RES/57/305, 15.04.2003, available in the Official Document System of the United Nations, available at http://documents.un.org/, last visited on 30.12.2010

General Assembly Resolution 59/266, A/RES/59/266, 22.12.2004, available in the Official Document System of the United Nations, available at http://documents.un.org/, last visited on 30.12.2010

General Assembly Resolution 61/159, A/RES/61/159, 19.12.2006, available in the Official Document System of the United Nations, available at http://documents.un.org/, last visited on 30.12.2010

General Assembly Resolution 61/244, A/RES/61/244, 22.12.2006, available in the Official Document System of the United Nations, available at http://documents.un.org/, last visited on 30.12.2010

General Assembly Resolution 61/261, A/RES/61/261, 04.04.2007, available in the Official Document System of the United Nations, available at http://documents.un.org/, last visited on 30.12.2010

General Assembly Resolution 62/228, A/RES/62/228, 22.12.2007, available in the Official Document System of the United Nations, available at http://documents.un.org/, last visited on 30.12.2010

General Assembly Resolution 63/250, A/RES/63/250, 24.12.2008, available in the Official Document System of the United Nations, available at http://documents.un.org/, last visited on 30.12.2010

General Assembly Resolution 63/253, A/RES/63/253, 24.12.2008, available in the Official Document System of the United Nations, available at http://documents.un.org/, last visited on 30.12.2010

General Assembly Resolution 64/119, A/RES/64/119, 16.12.2009, available in the Official Document System of the United Nations, available at http://documents.un.org/, last visited on 30.12.2010

General Assembly Resolution 65/247, A/RES/65/247, 24.12.2010, available in the Official Document System of the United Nations, available at http://documents.un.org/, last visited on 30.12.2010

General Assembly Resolution 153(II), A/RES/153(III), 15.11.1947, available in the Official Document System of the United Nations, available at http://documents.un.org/, last visited on 30.12.2010

General Assembly Resolution 297(IV), A/RES/297(IV), 22.11.1949, available in the Official Document System of the United Nations, available at http://documents.un.org/, last visited on 30.12.2010

General Assembly Resolution 590(VI), A/RES/590(VI), 02.02.1952, available in the Official Document System of the United Nations, available at http://documents.un.org/, last visited on 30.12.2010

General Assembly Resolution 708(VIII), A/RES/708(VIII), 01.04.1953, available in the Official Document System of the United Nations, available at http://documents.un.org/, last visited on 30.12.2010

General Assembly Resolution 781(VIII), A/RES/781(VIII), 09.12.1953, available in the Official Document System of the United Nations, available at http://documents.un.org/, last visited on 30.12.2010

General Assembly Resolution 782(VIII) A, A/RES/782(VIII)A, 09.12.1953, available in the Official Document System of the United Nations, available at http://documents.un.org/, last visited on 30.12.2010

General Assembly Resolution 782(VIII) B, A/RES/782(VIII)B, 09.12.01953, available in the Official Document System of the United Nations, available at http://documents.un.org/, last visited on 30.12.2010

General Assembly Resolution 1294(XIII), A/RES/1294(XIII), 5.12.1958, available in the Official Document System of the United Nations, available at http://documents.un.org/, last visited on 30.12.2010

General Assembly Resolution 1436(XIV), A/RES/1436(XIV), 5.12.1959, available in the Official Document System of the United Nations, available at http://documents.un.org/, last visited on 30.12.2010

General Assembly Resolution 1559(XV), A/RES/1559(XV), 18.12.1960, available in the Official Document System of the United Nations, available at http://documents.un.org/, last visited on 30.12.2010

General Assembly Resolution 1852 (XVII), A/RES/1852(XVII), 19.12.1962, available in the Official Document System of the United Nations, available at http://documents.un.org/, last visited on 30.12.2010

General Assembly Resolution 1928(XVIII), A/RES/1928(XVIII), 11.12.1963, available in the Official Document System of the United Nations, available at http://documents.un.org/, last visited on 30.12.2010

General Assembly Resolution 2241(XXI), A/RES/2241(XXI), 20.12.1966, available in the Official Document System of the United Nations, available at http://documents.un.org/, last visited on 30.12.2010

General Assembly Resolution 2359 (XXII), A/RES/2359(XXII), 19.12.1967, available in the Official Document System of the United Nations, available at http://documents.un.org/, last visited on 30.12.2010

General Assembly Resolution 2480(XXIII), A/RES/2480(XXIII), 21.12.1968, available in the Official Document System of the United Nations, available at http://documents.un.org/, last visited on 30.12.2010

General Assembly Resolution 2539(XXIV), A/RES/2539(XXIV), 11.12.1969, available in the Official Document System of the United Nations, available at http://documents.un.org/, last visited on 30.12.2010

General Assembly Resolution 2736(XXV), A/RES/2736(XXV), 17.12.1970, available in the Official Document System of the United Nations, available at http://documents.un.org/, last visited on 30.12.2010

General Assembly Resolution 3042(XXVII), A/RES/3042(XXVII), available in the Official Document System of the United Nations, available at http://documents.un.org/, last visited on 30.12.2010

General Assembly Resolution 3417(XXX), A/RES/3417(XXX), 8.12.1975, available in the Official Document System of the United Nations, available at http://documents.un.org/, last visited on 30.12.2010

GENERAL DOCUMENTS

International Civil Service Commission, Statute and Rules of Procedure, ICSC/1/Rev.1, May 1975, March 1987, available at http://icsc.un.org/resources/pdfs/statute/english.pdf, last visited on 30.12.2010

Office of Internal Oversight Services, Investigations Manual, March 2009, available at http://www.un.org/Depts/oios/pages/id_manual_mar2009.pdf, last visited on 30.12.2010

OLAF Manual - Operational Procedures, May 2007, available at http://ec.europa.eu/dgs/olaf/legal/doc/manual_short.pdf, last visited on 30.12.2010

Senior Review Group, Rules of Procedure, 31.07.2008, available at http://www.un.org/hr_handbook/English/sourcedocuments_/topics_/appointment2adv/appointment2adv.doc#ICTaskToolsAdvisoryBodies, last visited on 30.12.2010

Staff Regulations of the United Nations, ST/SG/2007/4, 01.01.2007, available in the Human Resources Handbook of the United Nations, available at http://www.un.org/hr_handbook/English/, last visited on 30.12.2010

Staff Regulations of the United Nations, ST/SGB/2009/6, 27.05.2009, available in the Human Resources Handbook of the United Nations, available at http://www.un.org/hr_handbook/English/, last visited on 30.12.2010

Staff Rules of the United Nations, ST/SGB/2010/6, 02.09.2010, available in the Human Resources Handbook of the United Nations, available at http://www.un.org/hr_handbook/English/, last visited on 30.12.2010

Staff Rules of the United Nations, 100 Series, ST/SGB/2009/7, 16.06.2009, available in the Human Resources Handbook of the United Nations, available at http://www.un.org/hr_handbook/English/, last visited on 30.12.2010

Staff Rules of the United Nations, 100 Series, consolidated text, ST/SGB/2002/1, 01.01.2002, as last amended by ST/SGB/2008/1, available in the Human Resources Handbook of the United Nations, available at http://www.un.org/hr_handbook/English/, last visited on 30.12.2010

Staff Rules of the United Nations, 200 Series, ST/SGB/2002/2, 01.01.2002, as amended by ST/SGB/2008/2 of 01.01.2008, ST/SGB/2007/2 of 01.01.2007, ST/SGB/2006/2 of 01.01.2006, ST/SGB/2005/2 of 01.01.2005, ST/SGB/2004/2 of 01.01.2004 and ST/SGB/2003/2 of 01.01.2003, available in the Human Resources Handbook of the United Nations, available at http://www.un.org/hr_handbook/English/, last visited on 30.12.2010

The Common Classification of Occupational Groups, April 1994, available at http://icsc.un.org/resources/pdfs/ppd/ccog/ccogi_ii.pdf, last visited on 30.12.2010

United Nations Common System of Salaries, Allowances and Benefits, January 2009, available at http://icsc.un.org/resources/pdfs/sal/sabeng09.pdf, last visited on 30.12.2010

ADMINISTRATIVE INSTRUCTIONS

Administrative Instruction Amending Administrative Instruction ST/AI/371, Revised Disciplinary Measures and Procedures, St/AI/371/Amend.1, 11.05.2010, available in the Human Resources Handbook of the United Nations, available at http://www.un.org/hr_handbook/English/, last visited on 30.12.2010

Administrative Instruction, Abandonment of Post, ST/AI/400, as amended by ST/AI/2005/5, 22.12.1994, available in the Human Resources Handbook of the United Nations, available at http://www.un.org/hr_handbook/English/, last visited on 30.12.2010

Administrative Instruction, Administration of Temporary Appointments, ST/AI/2010/4, 27.04.2010, available in the Human Resources Handbook of the United Nations, available at http://www.un.org/hr_handbook/English/, last visited on 30.12.2010

Administrative Instruction, Appointment, Extension and Conversion of Contractual Status of Staff in the General Service, Security Service and Manual Workers Categories, ST/AI/274, 30.06.1980, available in the Human Resources Handbook of the United Nations, available at http://www.un.org/hr_handbook/English/,

Administrative Instruction, Competitive Examination for Recruitment to the Professional Category of Staff Members from Other Categories, ST/AI/2003/7, 30.10.2003, as amended by ST/AI/2005/9 of 01.08.2005, available in the Human Resources Handbook of the United Nations, available at http://www.un.org/hr_handbook/English/, last visited on 30.12.2010

Administrative Instruction, Competitive Examination for Recruitment to the Professional Category of Staff Members from Other Categories ST/AI/2010/7, 01.06.2010, available in the Human Resources Handbook of the United Nations, available at http://www.un.org/hr_handbook/English/, last visited on 30.12.2010

Administrative Instruction, Competitive Examinations for Recruitment and Placement in Posts Requiring Specific Language Skills in the Professional Category, ST/AI/1998/7, 23.03.1998, available in the Human Resources Handbook of the United Nations, available at http://www.un.org/hr_handbook/English/, last visited on 30.12.2010

Administrative Instruction, Conditions under which Individuals May Take National Competitive Recruitment Examinations, ST/AI/2010/8, 01.06.2010, available in the Human Resources Handbook of the United Nations, available at http://www.un.org/hr_handbook/English/, last visited on 30.12.2010

Administrative Instruction, Consultants and Individual Contractors, consolidated text, ST/AI/1999/7, as last amended by ST/AI/1999/7/Amend.1, 25.08.1999, available in the Human Resources Handbook of the United Nations, available at http://www.un.org/hr_handbook/English/, last visited on 30.12.2010

Administrative Instruction, Consultants and Participants in Advisory Meetings, ST/AI/296, 19.11.1982, available in the Human Resources Handbook of the United Nations, available at http://www.un.org/hr_handbook/English/, last visited on 30.12.2010

Administrative Instruction, Financial Responsibility of Staff Members for Gross Negligence, ST/AI/2004/3, 29.09.2004, available in the Human Resources Handbook of the United Nations, available at http://www.un.org/hr_handbook/English/, last visited on 30.12.2010

Administrative Instruction, Gratis Personnel, ST/AI/1999/6, 28.5.1999, available in the Human Resources Handbook of the United Nations, available at http://www.un.org/hr_handbook/English/, last visited on 30.12.2010

Administrative Instruction, Institutional or Corporate Contractors, ST/AI/327, 23.01.1985, available in the Human Resources Handbook of the United Nations, available at http://www.un.org/hr_handbook/English/, last visited on 30.12.2010

Administrative Instruction, Managed Reassignment Programme, ST/AI/2007/2, 23.05.2007, available in the Human Resources Handbook of the United Nations, available at http://www.un.org/hr_handbook/English/, last visited on 30.12.2010

Administrative Instruction, Managed Reassignment Programme for Junior Professional Staff, ST/AI/2001/7, 28.08.2001, available in the Human Resources Handbook of the United Nations, available at http://www.un.org/hr_handbook/English/, last visited on 30.12.2010

Administrative Instruction, Movement of Staff from the Field Service Category to the Professional Category, 15.11.1993, available in the Human Resources Handbook of the United Nations, available at http://www.un.org/hr_handbook/English/, last visited on 30.12.2010

Administrative Instruction, Non-reimbursable Loans of Personnel Services from Sources External to the United Nations Common System, ST/AI/231/Rev.1, 23.1.1991, available in the Human Resources Handbook of the United Nations, available at http://www.un.org/hr_handbook/English/, last visited on 30.12.2010

Administrative Instruction, Performance Appraisal System, ST/AI/2002/3, 20.03.2002, available in the Human Resources Handbook of the United Nations, available at http://www.un.org/hr_handbook/English/, last visited on 30.12.2010

Administrative Instruction, Performance Management and Development System, ST/AI/2010/5, 30.04.2010, available in the Human Resources Handbook of the United Nations, available at http://www.un.org/hr_handbook/English/, last visited on 30.12.2010

Administrative Instruction, Placement and Promotion, ST/AI/390, 15.11.1993, available in the Human Resources Handbook of the United Nations, available at http://www.un.org/hr_handbook/English/, last visited on 30.12.2010

Administrative Instruction, Private Legal Obligations of Staff Members, ST/AI/2000/12, 25.10.2000, available in the Human Resources Handbook of the United Nations, available at http://www.un.org/hr_handbook/English/, last visited on 30.12.2010

Administrative Instruction, Procedure to be Followed in Cases of Termination of Permanent Appointment for Unsatisfactory Service, ST/AI/222, 10.12.1974, available in the Human Resources Handbook of the United Nations, available at http://www.un.org/hr_handbook/English/, last visited on 30.12.2010

Administrative Instruction, Reporting, Retaining and Disposing of Honours, Decorations, Favours, Gifts or Remuneration from Governmental and Non-governmental Sources, ST/AI/2010/1, 14.01.2010, available in the Human Resources Handbook of the United Nations, available at http://www.un.org/hr_handbook/English/, last visited on 30.12.2010

Administrative Instruction, Retention in Service and Employment Beyond the Age of Retirement, ST/AI/213/Rev.1, 18.07.1984, available in the Human Resources Handbook of the United Nations, available at http://www.un.org/hr_handbook/English/, last visited on 30.12.2010

Administrative Instruction, Retention in Service Beyond the Mandatory Age of Separation and Employment of Retirees, ST/AI/1999/5, 27. 05.1999, available in the Human Resources Handbook of the United Nations, available at http://www.un.org/hr_handbook/English/, last visited on 30.12.2010

Administrative Instruction, Retention in Service Beyond the Mandatory Age of Separation and Employment of Retirees, ST/AI/2003/8, 13.11.2003, available in the Human Resources Handbook of the United Nations, available at http://www.un.org/hr_handbook/English/, last visited on 30.12.2010

Administrative Instruction, Retention in Service Beyond the Mandatory Age of Separation and Employment of Retirees, ST/AI/2003/8/Amend.1, 17.03.2006, available in the Human Resources Handbook of the United Nations, available at http://www.un.org/hr_handbook/English/, last visited on 31.12.2010

Administrative Instruction, Revised Disciplinary Measures and Procedures, ST/AI/371, 02.08.1991, available in the Human Resources Handbook of the United Nations, available at http://www.un.org/hr_handbook/English/, last visited on 30.12.2010

Administrative Instruction, Special Conditions for Recruitment or Placement of Candidates Successful in a Competitive Examination for Posts Requiring Special Language Skills, ST/AI/2000/1, 12.01.2000, as amended by ST/AI/2003/1, available in the Human Resources Handbook of the United Nations, available at http://www.un.org/hr_handbook/English/, last visited on 30.12.2010

Administrative Instruction, Staff Selection System, ST/AI/2002/4, 23.04.2002, available in the Human Resources Handbook of the United Nations, available at http://www.un.org/hr_handbook/English/, last visited on 30.12.2010

Administrative Instruction, Staff Selection System, ST/AI/2006/3, 15.11.2006, available in the Human Resources Handbook of the United Nations, available at http://www.un.org/hr_handbook/English/, last visited on 30.12.2010

Administrative Instruction, Staff Selection System, ST/AI/2010/3, 21.04.2010, available in the Human Resources Handbook of the United Nations, available at http://www.un.org/hr_handbook/English/, last visited on 30.12.2010

Administrative Instruction, Staff Selection System, ST/AI/2006/3/Rev.1, 11.01.2010, available in the Human Resources Handbook of the United Nations, available at http://www.un.org/hr_handbook/English/, last visited on 30.12.2010

Administrative Instruction, System for the Classification of Posts, ST/AI/1998/9, 6.10.1998, available in the Human Resources Handbook of the United Nations, available at http://www.un.org/hr_handbook/English/, last visited on 30.12.2010

Administrative Instruction, Technical Co-operation Personnel and OPAS Officers, ST/AI/297, 19.11.1982, available in the Human Resources Handbook of the United Nations, available at http://www.un.org/hr_handbook/English/, last visited on 30.12.2010

Administrative Instruction, Technical Co-operation Personnel and OPAS Officers, Addendum, ST/AI/297/Add.1, 7.12.1995, available in the Human Resources Handbook of the United Nations, available at http://www.un.org/hr_handbook/English/, last visited on 30.12.2010

Administrative Instruction, Temporary Staff and Individual Contractors, ST/AI/295, 19.11.1982, available in the Human Resources Handbook of the United Nations, available at http://www.un.org/hr_handbook/English/, last visited on 30.12.2010

Administrative Instruction, Termination of Appointment for Reasons of Health, ST/AI/1999/16, 28.12.1999, available in the Human Resources Handbook of the United Nations, available at http://www.un.org/hr_handbook/English/, last visited on 30.12.2010

Administrative Instruction, United Nations Internship Programme, ST/AI/2000/9, 19.09.2000, consolidated text as last amended by ST/AI/2005/11 effective on 01.09.2005, available in the Human Resources

SECRETARY-GENERAL'S BULLETINS

Secretary-General's Bulletin, Central Review Bodies, ST/SGB/2002/6, 23.04.2002, available in the Human Resources Handbook of the United Nations, available at http://www.un.org/hr_handbook/English/, last visited on 30.12.2010

Secretary General's Bulletin, Consideration for Conversion to Permanent Appointment of Staff Members of the Secretariat Eligible to be Considered by 30 June 2009, ST/SGB/2009/10, 23.06.2009, available in the Human Resources Handbook of the United Nations, available at http://www.un.org/hr_handbook/English/, last visited on 30.12.2010

Secretary-General's Bulletin, Establishment of the Office of Internal Oversight Services, ST/SGB/273, 07.09.1994, available in the Human Resources Handbook of the United Nations, available at http://www.un.org/hr_handbook/English/, last visited on 30.12.2010

Secretary-General's Bulletin, Introduction of a New Staff Selection System, ST/SGB/2002/5, 23.4.2002, available in the Human Resources Handbook of the United Nations, available at http://www.un.org/hr_handbook/English/, last visited on 30.12.2010

Secretary-General's Bulletin, Management Performance Board, ST/SGB/2010/4, 15.04.2010, available in the Human Resources Handbook of the United Nations, available at http://www.un.org/hr_handbook/English/, last visited on 30.12.2010

Secretary-General's Bulletin, National Competitive Examinations, ST/SGB/210, 22.01.1985, available in the Human Resources Handbook of the United Nations, available at http://www.un.org/hr_handbook/English/, last visited on 30.12.2010

Secretary-General's Bulletin, Organization of the Office of Human Resources Management, ST/SGB/2004/8, 07.04.2004, available in the Human Resources Handbook of the United Nations, available at http://www.un.org/hr_handbook/English/, last visited on 30.12.2010

Secretary-General's Bulletin, Placement and Promotion, ST/SGB/267, 15.11.1993, available in the Human Resources Handbook of the United Nations, available at http://www.un.org/hr_handbook/English/, last visited on 30.12.2010

Secretary-General's Bulletin, Policies for Obtaining the Services of Individuals on behalf of the Organization, ST/SGB/177, 19.11.1982, available in the Human Resources Handbook of the United Nations, available at http://www.un.org/hr_handbook/English/, last visited on 30.12.2010

Secretary-General's Bulletin, Post-Employment Restrictions, ST/SGB/2006/15, 26.12.2006, available in the Human Resources Handbook of the United Nations, available at http://www.un.org/hr_handbook/English/, last visited on 30.12.2010

Secretary-General's Bulletin, Prevention of Workplace Harassment, Sexual Harassment and Abuse of Authority, ST/SGB/2005/20, 28.11.2005, available in the Human Resources Handbook of the United Nations, available at http://www.un.org/hr_handbook/English/, last visited on 30.12.2010

Secretary-General's Bulletin, Prohibition of Discrimination, Harassment, Including Sexual Harassment, and Abuse of Authority, ST/SGB/2008/5, 11.02.2008, available in the Human Resources Handbook of the United Nations, available at http://www.un.org/hr_handbook/English/, last visited on 30.12.2010

Secretary-General's Bulletin, Protection against Retaliation for Reporting Misconduct and for Cooperating with Duly Authorized Audits or Investigations, ST/SGB/2005/21, 19.12.2005, available in the Human Resources Handbook of the United Nations, available at http://www.un.org/hr_handbook/English/, last visited on 30.12.2010

Secretary-General's Bulletin, Regulations Governing the Status, Basic Rights and Duties of Officials other than Secretariat Officials, and Experts on Mission, ST/SGB/2002/9, 18.06.2002, available in the Human Resources Handbook of the United Nations, available at http://www.un.org/hr_handbook/English/, last visited on 30.12.2010

Secretary-General's Bulletin, Senior Review Group, ST/SGB/2009/2, 01.01.2009, available in the Human Resources Handbook of the United Nations, available at http://www.un.org/hr_handbook/English/, last visited on 30.12.2010

Secretary-General's Bulletin, Special Measures for Protection from Sexual Exploitation and Sexual Abuse, ST/SGB/2003/13, 09.10.2003, available in the Human Resources Handbook of the United Nations, available at http://www.un.org/hr_handbook/English/, last visited on 30.12.2010

Secretary-General's Bulletin, Status, Basic Rights and Duties of United Nations Staff Members, ST/SGB/2002/13, 01.11.2002, available in the Human Resources Handbook of the United Nations, available at http://www.un.org/hr_handbook/English/, last visited on 30.12.2010

Secretary-General's Bulletin, The Financial Situation of the Organization, ST/SGB/222, 22.12.1986, available in the Human Resources Handbook of the United Nations, available at http://www.un.org/hr_handbook/English/, last visited on 30.12.2010

Secretary-General's Bulletin, Transitional Measures Related to the Introduction of the New System of Administration of Justice, ST/SGB/2009/11, 24.06.2009, available in the Human Resources Handbook of the United Nations, available at http://www.un.org/hr_handbook/English/, last visited on 30.12.2010

Secretary-General's Bulletin, United Nations System-wide Application of Ethics: Separately Administered Organs and Programmes, ST/SGB/2007/11, 30.11.2007, available in the Human Resources Handbook of the United Nations, available at http://www.un.org/hr_handbook/English/, last visited on 30.12.2010

Secretary-General's Bulletin, Use of "When Actually Employed" Contracts for Special Representatives, Envoys and Other Special High-level Positions, ST/SGB/283, 29.8.1996, available in the Human Resources Handbook of the United Nations, available at http://www.un.org/hr_handbook/English/, last visited on 30.12.2010

Secretary-General's Bulletin, Ethics Office - Establishment and Terms of Reference, ST/SGB/2005/22, 30.12.2005, available in the Human Resources Handbook of the United Nations, available at http://www.un.org/hr_handbook/English/, last visited on 30.12.2010

Secretary-General's Bulletin, Field Central Review Bodies, ST/SGB/2009/5, 01.05.2009, available in the Human Resources Handbook of the United Nations, available at http://www.un.org/hr_handbook/English/, last visited on 30.12.2010

Secretary-General's Bulletin, Management Performance Board, ST/SGB/2005/13, 05.05.2005, available in the Human Resources Handbook of the United Nations, available at http://www.un.org/hr_handbook/English/, last visited on 30.12.2010

Secretary-General's Bulletin, Organization and Terms of Reference of the Office of Administration of Justice, ST/SGB/2010/3, available in the Human Resources Handbook of the United Nations, available at http://www.un.org/hr_handbook/English/, last visited on 30.12.2010

DOCUMENTS OF THE OFFICE OF HUMAN RESOURCES MANAGEMENT

2009 National Competitive Recruitment Examination (P-1/P-2), 2008, available at http://www.un.org/Depts/OHRM/examin/2009e.doc, last visited on 30.12.2010

2010 Competitive Examinations for Russian-language Translators/Precis-writers (Russian main language), Notice, 2010, available at http://www.un.org/Depts/OHRM/examin/languageexam.htm, last visited on 30.12.2010

2010 National Competitive Recruitment Examinations (P-2), 2010, available at http://www.un.org/Depts/OHRM/examin/2010e.pdf, last visited on 30.12.2010

Evaluation and Selection Guidelines for Action by Programme Case Officers and Heads of Department under ST/AI/2006/3/Rev1, available in the Human Resources Handbook of the United Nations, available at http://www.un.org/hr_handbook/English/, last visited on 30.12.2010

G to P Roster: Guidelines, available in the Human Resources Handbook of the United Nations, available at http://www.un.org/hr_handbook/English/, last visited on 30.12.2010

Guidelines for Programme Case Officers on Building Vacancy Announcements and Evaluation Criteria under ST/AI/2006/3/Rev1, available in the Human Resources Handbook of the United Nations, available at http://www.un.org/hr_handbook/English/, last visited on 30.12.2010

Guidelines on Early Retirement, available in the Human Resources Handbook of the United Nations, available at http://www.un.org/hr_handbook/English/, last visited on 30.12.2010

Guidelines on Separation from Sevice - General Procedures, available in the Human Resources Handbook of the United Nations, available at http://www.un.org/hr_handbook/English/, last visited on 30.12.2010

Guidelines on Separation from Service - Resignation, available in the Human Resources Handbook of the United Nations, available at http://www.un.org/hr_handbook/English/, last visited on 30.12.2010

Guidelines on Separation from Service - Retirement, available in the Human Resources Handbook of the United Nations, available at http://www.un.org/hr_handbook/English/, last visited on 30.12.2010

NCRE Frequently Asked Questions, available in the Human Resources Handbook of the United Nations, available at http://www.un.org/hr_handbook/English/, last visited on 30.12.2010

Roster Management Guidelines, 16.09.2005, available in the Human Resources Handbook of the United Nations, available at http://www.un.org/hr_handbook/English/, last visited on 30.12.2010

REPORTS

A More Secure World: Our Shared Responsibility, Report of the High-level Panel on Threats, Challenges and Change, A/59/565, 02.12.2004, available in the Offical

Document System of the United Nations, available at http://documents.un.org/, last visited on 30.12.2010

Activities of the Ethics Office, Report of the Secretary-General, A/63/301, 18.08.2008, available in the Official Document System of the United Nations, available at http://documents.un.org/, last visited on 30.12.2010

Activities of the Ethics Office, Report of the Secretary-General, A/64/316, 21.08.2009, available in the Official Document System of the United Nations, available at http://documents.un.org/, last visited on 30.12.2010

Activities of the Ethics Office, Report of the Secretary-General, A/65/343, 01.09.2010, available in the Official Document System of the United Nations, available at http://documents.un.org/, last visited on 30.12.2010

Composition of the Secretariat, Report of the Secretary-General, A/53/375, 11.09.1998, available in the Official Document System of the United Nations, available at http://documents.un.org/, last visited on 30.12.2010

Composition of the Secretariat, Report of the Secretary-General, A/60/310, 29.08.2005, available in the Official Document System of the United Nations, available at http://documents.un.org/, last visited on 30.12.2010

Composition of the Secretariat, Report of the Secretary-General, A/62/315, 31.08.2007, available in the Official Document System of the United Nations, available at http://documents.un.org/, last visited on 30.12.2010

Composition of the Secretariat, Report of the Secretary-General, A/63/310, 29.09.2008, available in the Official Document System of the United Nations, available at http://documents.un.org/, last visited on 30.12.2010

Composition of the Secretariat, Report of the Secretary-General, A/64/352, 15.09.2009, available in the Official Document System of the United Nations, available at http://documents.un.org/, last visited on 30.12.2010

Composition of the Secretariat: Gratis Personnel, Retirees and Consultants, Report of the Secretary-General, Addendum, A/65/350/Add.1, 15.09.2010, available in the Official Document System of the United Nations, available at http://documents.un.org/, last visited on 30.12.2010

Composition of the Secretariat: Staff Demographics, Report of the Secretary-General, A/65/350, 08.09.2010, available in the Official Document System of the United Nations, available at http://documents.un.org/, last visited on 30.12.2010

Comprehensive Assessment of the System of Geographical Distribution and Assessment of the Issues Relating to Possible Changes in the Number of Posts Subject to the System of Geographical Distribution, Report of the Secretary-General, A/59/724, 04.03.2005, available in the Official Document System of the United Nations, available at http://documents.un.org/, last visited on 30.12.2010

Comprehensive Report on the Staffing of Field Missions, Including the Use of 300 and 100 Series Appointments, Report of the Secretary-General, A/59/291, 23.08.2004, available in the Official Document System of the United Nations, available at http://documents.un.org/, last visited on 30.12.2010

Consultants and Individual Contractors, Report of the Secretary-General, A/63/310/ Add.3, 21.08.2008, available in the Official Document System of the United Nations, available at http://documents.un.org/, last visited on 30.12.2010

Delegation of Authority for the Management of Human and Financial Resources in the United Nations Secretariat, Report of the Joint Inspection Unit, JIU/REP/2000/6, 2000, available in the Official Document System of the United Nations, available at http://documents.un.org/, last visited on 30.12.2010

Detailed Proposals for Streamlining United Nations Contractual Arrangements, Report of the Secretary-General, A/62/274, 17.08.2007, available in the Official Document System of the United Nations, available at http://documents.un.org/, last visited on 30.12.2010

Detailed Proposals for Streamlining United Nations Contractual Arrangements: A Way Forward, Report of the Secretary-General, A/63/298, 15.08. 2008, available in the Official Document System of the United Nations, available at http://documents.un.org/, last visited on 30.12.2010

Employment of Retired Former Staff, Report of the Secretary-General, A/61/257/ Add.2, 10.08.2006, available in the Official Document System of the United Nations, available at http://documents.un.org/, last visited on 30.12.2010

Employment of Retirees and Retired Former Staff, and Extension of Staff Beyond the Mandatory Age of Separation, Report of the Secretary-General, A/63/310/Add.2, 20.08.2008, available in the Official Document System of the United Nations, available at http://documents.un.org/, last visited on 30.12.2010

Employment of Retirees, Report of the Advisory Committee on Administrative and Budgetary Questions, A/51/475, 08.10.1996, available in the Official Document System of the United Nations, available at http://documents.un.org/, last visited on 30.12.2010

Employment of Retirees, Report of the Secretary-General, A/C.5/51/2, 16.08.1996, available in the Official Document System of the United Nations, available at http://documents.un.org/, last visited on 30.12.2010

Employment of Retirees, Report of the Secretary-General, A/53/526, 20.10.1998, available in the Official Document System of the United Nations, available at http://documents.un.org/, last visited on 30.12.2010

Gratis Personnel Provided by Governments and Other Entities, Report of the Secretary-General, A/59/716, 28.02.2005, available in the Official Document System of the United Nations, available at http://documents.un.org/, last visited on 30.12.2010

Human Resources Management Reform, Accountability and Responsibility, Personnel Practices and Policies and Management Irregularities, Report of the Advisory Committee on Administrative and Budgetary Questions, A/55/499, 19.10.2000, available in the Official Document System of the United Nations, available at http:// documents.un.org/, last visited on 30.12.2010

Human Resources Management, Report of the Advisory Committee on Administrative and Budgetary Questions, A/63/526, 07.11.2008, available in the Official Document

System of the United Nations, available at http://documents.un.org/, last visited on 30.12.2010

Human Resources Management, Report of the Advisory Committee on Administrative and Budgetary Questions, A/64/518, 06.11.2009, available in the Official Document System of the United Nations, available at http://documents.un.org/, last visited on 30.12.2010

Human Resources Management, Report of the Advisory Committee on Administrative and Budgetary Questions, A/65/537, 22.10.2010, available in the Official Document System of the United Nations, available at http://documents.un.org/, last visited on 30.12.2010

Human Resources Management, Report of the Fifth Committee, A/64/550, 03.12.2010, available in the Official Document System of the United Nations, available at http://documents.un.org/, last visited on 30.12.2010

Human Resources Management Policies, Report of the Secretary-General, A/49/445, 29.09.1994, available in the Official Document System of the United Nations, available at http://documents.un.org/, last visited on 30.12.2010

Human Resources Management Reform, Report of the Secretary-General, A/53/414, 13.10.1998, available in the Official Document System of the United Nations, available at http://documents.un.org/, last visited on 30.12.2010

Human Resources Management Reform, Report of the Secretary-General, A/55/253, 01.08.2000, available in the Official Document System of the United Nations, available at http://documents.un.org/, last visited on 30.12.2010

Human Resources Management Reform, Report of the Secretary-General, A/57/293, 08.08.2002, available in the Official Document System of the United Nations, available at http://documents.un.org/, last visited on 30.12.2010

Human Resources Management Reform, Report of the Secretary-General, A/59/263, 13.08.2004, available in the Official Document System of the United Nations, available at http://documents.un.org/, last visited on 30.12.2010

Human Resources Management Reform, Report of the Secretary-General, A/61/228, 07.08.2006, available in the Official Document System of the United Nations, available at http://documents.un.org/, last visited on 30.12.2010

Human Resources Management Reform, Report of the Secretary-General, A/63/282, 14.08.2008, available in the Official Document System of the United Nations, available at http://documents.un.org/, last visited on 30.12.2010

Human Resources Management Reform, Report of the Secretary-General, Addendum, Contractual Arrangements, A/59/263/Add.1, 09.09.2004, available in the Official Document System of the United Nations, available at http://documents.un.org/, last visited on 30.12.2010

Human Resources Management Reform, Report of the Secretary-General, Corrigendum, A/61/228/Corr.1, available in the Official Document System of the United Nations, available at http://documents.un.org/, last visited on 30.12.2010

Human Resources Management Reform: Comprehensive Assessment of the System of Geographical Distribution and Assessment of the Issues Relating to Possible Changes in the Number of Posts Subject to the System of Geographical Distribution, Report of the Secretary-General, A/65/305/Add.2, 02.09.2010, available in the Official Document System of the United Nations, available at http://documents.un.org/, last visited on 30.12.2010

Human Resources Management Reform: Contractual Arrangements and Harmonization of Conditions of Service, Report of the Secretary-General, A/65/305/Add.1, 07.09.2010, available in the Official Document System of the United Nations, available at http://documents.un.org/, last visited on 30.12.2010

Human Resources Management Reform: Recruitment and Staffing, Report of the Secretary-General, A/61/822, 27.03.2007, available in the Official Document System of the United Nations, available at http://documents.un.org/, last visited on 30.12.2010

Human Resources Management Reform: The Talent Management Tool, Inspira, Report of the Secretary-General, A/65/305/Add.3, 02.09.2010, available in the Official Document System of the United Nations, available at http://documents.un.org/, last visited on 30.12.2010

Human Resources Management Reform: Young Professionals Programme, Report of the Secretary-General, A/65/305/Add.4, 02.09.2010, available in the Official Document System of the United Nations, available at http://documents.un.org/, last visited on 30.12.2010

Impact of the Human Resources Management Reform, Report of the Office of Internal Oversight Services, A/59/253, 24.09.2004, available in the Official Document System of the United Nations, available at http://documents.un.org/, last visited on 30.12.2010

Implementation of Continuing Appointments, Report of the Secretary-General, A/64/267, 07.08.2009, available in the Official Document System of the United Nations, available at http://documents.un.org/, last visited on 30.12.2010

Implementation of the Mobility Policy, Report of the Secretary-General, A/62/215, 08.08.2007, available in the Official Document System of the United Nations, available at http://documents.un.org/, last visited on 30.12.2010

Implementation of the Mobility Policy, Report of the Secretary-General, A/63/208, 01.08.2008, available in the Official Document System of the United Nations, available at http://documents.un.org/, last visited on 30.12.2010

Improvement of Equitable Geographical Representation in the United Nations Secretariat, Report of the Secretary-General, A/59/264, 13.04.2004, available in the Official Document System of the United Nations, available at http://documents.un.org/, last visited on 30.12.2010

In Larger Freedom: Towards Development, Security and Human Rights for All, Report of the Secretary-General, A/59/2005, 21.03.2005, available in the Official Document System of the United Nations, available at http://documents.un.org/, last visited on 30.12.2010

In-depth Evaluation of the Office of Human Resources Management, Report of the Office of Internal Oversight Services, A/63/221, 22.09.2008, available in the Official Document System of the United Nations, available at http://documents.un.org/, last visited on 30.12.2010

Inspection of the Application of United Nations Recruitment, Placement, and Promotion Policies, Part II – Placement and Promotions, Report of the Joint Inspection Unit, JIU/REP/96/6, 1996, available in the Official Document System of the United Nations, available at http://documents.un.org/, last visited on 30.12.2010

Investing in People, Report of the Secretary-General, A/61/255, 09.08.2006, available in the Official Document System of the United Nations, available at http://documents.un.org/, last visited on 30.12.2010

Investing in People, Report of the Secretary-General, Addendum, Reforming the Field Service Category: Investing in Meeting the Human Resources Requirements of United Nations Peace Operations in the Twenty-First Century, A/61/255/Add.1, 22.08.2006, available in the Official Document System of the United Nations, available at http://documents.un.org/, last visited on 30.12.2010

Investing in the United Nations: For a Stronger Organization Worldwide, Report of the Secretary-General, A/60/692, 07.03.2006, available in the Official Document System of the United Nations, available at http://documents.un.org/, last visited on 30.12.2010

Management Performance Board, Report of the Secretary-General, A/61/319, 09.09.2006, available in the Official Document System of the United Nations, available at http://documents.un.org/, last visited on 30.12.2010

Measures to Address the Imbalance in the Geographical Distribution of the Staff in the Office of the United Nations High Commissioner for Human Rights, Report of the Secretary-General, A/61/823, 28.03.2007, available in the Official Document System of the United Nations, available at http://documents.un.org/, last visited on 30.12.2010

Measures to Improve the Balance in the Geographical Distribution of the Staff in the Office of the United Nations High Commissioner for Human Rights, Report of the Secretary-General, A/62/823, 28.03.2007, available in the Official Document System of the United Nations, available at http://documents.un.org/, last visited on 30.12.2010

Measures to Improve the Balance in the Geographical Distribution of the Staff in the Office of the United Nations High Commissioner for Human Rights, Report of the Secretary-General, A/63/204, 31.07.2008, available in the Official Document System of the United Nations, available at http://documents.un.org/, last visited on 30.12.2010

Measures to Strengthen Accountability at the United Nations, Report of the Secretary-General, A/60/312, 30.08.2005, available in the Official Document System of the United Nations, available at http://documents.un.org/, last visited on 30.12.2010

National Professional Officers, Report of the Secretary-General, A/62/762, 25.03.2008, available in the Official Document System of the United Nations, available at http://documents.un.org/, last visited on 30.12.2010

Official Records, General Assembly, Sixty-fourth Session, 67th Plenary Meeting A/64/PV.67, 22.12.2009, available in the Official Document System of the United Nations, available at http://documents.un.org, last visited on 30.12.2010

Official Records, Fifth Committee, Summary Record of the 18th Meeting of 14 November 2008, A/C.5/63/SR.18, 20.01.2009, available in the Official Document System of the United Nations, available at http://documents.un.org/, last visited on 30.12.2010

Official Records, Summary Record of the 14 meeting of 1 November 2006, A/C.5/61/SR.14, 01.11.2006, available in the Official Document System of the United Nations, available at http://documents.un.org/, last visited on 30.12.2010

Official Records, Summary Record of the 17 Meeting, A/C.5/60/SR.17, 01.11.2005, available in the Official Document System of the United Nations, available at http://documents.un.org/, last visited on 30.12.2010

Overview of Human Resources Management Reform, Report of the Secretary-General, A/65/305, 02.09.2010, available in the Official Document System of the United Nations, available at http://documents.un.org/, last visited on 30.12.2010

Personnel Questions, Composition of the Secretariat, Alternative Options for Desirable Ranges for the Geographical Distribution of Staff in the Professional Category and Above, Report of the Secretary-General, A/C.5/46/2, 27.08.1991, available in the Official Document System of the United Nations, available at http://documents.un.org/, last visited on 30.12.2010

Personnel Questions: Other Personnel Questions, Secondment from Government Service, Report of the Secretary-General, A/C.5/46/9, 23.09.1991, available in the Official Document System of the United Nations, available at http://documents.un.org/, last visited on 30.12.2010

Practice of the Secretary-General in Disciplinary Matters and Possible Criminal Behaviour, 1 July 2005 to 30 June 2006, Report of the Secretary-General, A/61/206, 31.07.2006, available in the Official Document System of the United Nations, available at http://documents.un.org/, last visited on 30.12.2010

Practice of the Secretary-General in Disciplinary Matters and Possible Criminal Behaviour, 1 July 2009 to 30 June 2010, Report of the Secretary-General, A/65/180, 29.07.2010, available in the Official Document System of the United Nations, available at http://documents.un.org/, last visited on 30.12.2010

Provisional Staff Rules, Report of the Secretary-General, A/64/230, 05.08.2009, available in the Official Document System of the United Nations, available at http://documents.un.org/, last visited on 30.12.2010

Provisional Staff Rules, Report of the Secretary-General, A/65/202, 20.08.2010, available in the Official Document System of the United Nations, available at http://documents.un.org/, last visited on 30.12.2010

Reform and Renewal in the United Nations: Progress Report of the Secretary-General on the Implementation of the General Assembly Resolution 41/213, A/42/234, 23.04.1987, available in the Official Document System of the United Nations, available at http://documents.un.org/, last visited on 30.12.2010

Renewing The United Nations: A Programme for Reform, Report of the Secretary-General, A/51/950, 14.07.1997, available in the Official Document System of the United Nations, available at http://documents.un.org/, last visited on 30.12.2010

Report of the Group of High Intergovernmental Experts to Review the Efficiency of the Administrative and Financial Functioning of the United Nations, A/41/49, available in the Official Document System of the United Nations, available at http://documents.un.org/, last visited on 30.12.2010

Report of the International Civil Service Commission for the Year 1994, 05.08.1994, available in the Official Document System of the United Nations, available at http://documents.un.org/, last visited on 30.12.2010

Report of the International Civil Service Commission for the Year 2010, A/65/30, August 2010, available in the Official Document System of the United Nations, available at http://documents.un.org/, last visited on 30.12.2010

Report of the Preparatory Commission of the United Nations, PC/20, 23.12.1945, available in the Official Document System of the United Nations, available at http://documents.un.org/, last visited on 30.12.2010

Results-based Management in the United Nations in the Context of the Reform Process, Report of the Joint Inspection Unit, JIU/REP/2006/6, 2006, available in the Official Document System of the United Nations, available at http://documents.un.org/, last visited on 30.12.2010

Review of the National Competitive Recruitment Examination as a Recruitment Tool, Report of the Joint Inspection Unit, JIU/REP/2007/9, 2007, available in the Official Document System of the United Nations, available at http://documents.un.org/, last visited on 30.12.2010

Senior-Level Appointments in the United Nations, Its Programmes and Funds, Report of the Joint Inspection Unit, JIU/REP/2000/3, 2000, available in the Official Document System of the United Nations, available at http://documents.un.org/, last visited on 30.12.2010

Staff Mobility in the United Nations, Note by the Secretary-General, Addendum, Comments of the Secretary-General on the Report of the Joint Inspection Unit, A/61/806/Add.1, 02.04.2007, available in the Official Document System of the United Nations, available at http://documents.un.org/, last visited on 30.12.2010

Staff Mobility in the United Nations, Report of the Joint Inspection Unit, JIU/REP/2006/7, 2006, available in the Official Document System of the United Nations, available at http://documents.un.org/, last visited on 30.12.2010

Strengthening of the United Nations: An Agenda for Further Change, Report of the Secretary-General, A/57/387, 09.09.2002, available in the Official Document System of the United Nations, available at http://documents.un.org/, last visited on 30.12.2010

The Use of Consultants in the United Nations, Report of the Joint Inspection Unit, JIU/REP/2000/2, 2000, available in the Official Document System of the United Nations, available at http://documents.un.org/, last visited on 30.12.2010

Towards a Compact, Appendices to the Report of Final Proposals by the Four Nations Initiative on Governance and Management of the UN, September 2007, available at http://www.the4ni.org/images/stories/documents/towards%20a%20compact%20-%20appendices.pdf, last visited on 30.12.2010

Towards a Compact, Proposals for Improved Governance and Management of the United Nations Secretariat, Report of Final Proposals by the Four Nations Initiative on Governance and Management of the UN, September 2007, available at http://www.the4ni.org/images/stories/documents/towards%20a%20compact%20-%20final%20report%20by%20the%204ni.pdf, last visited on 30.12.2010

Toward a New System of Performance Appraisal in the United Nations Secretariat: Requirements for Successful Implementation, Report of the Joint Inspection Unit, JIU/REP/94/5, June 1994, available in the Official Document System of the United Nations, available at http://documents.un.org/, last visited on 30.12.2010

PRESS RELEASES

Budget Committee Takes up Reports on Staff Rules for New Contractual Arrangements, Secretariat Make-up, Ethics Office, Disciplinary Matters, Continuing Contracts, Press Release, GA/AB/3931, 17.11.2009, available at http://www.un.org/News/Press/docs/2009/gaab3931.doc.htm, last visited on 30.12.2010

General Assembly Calls for Urgent Implementation of Proposals to Assist Survivors of 1994 Rwandan Genocide, including Medical Care, Skills Training, Victim Support, Press Release, GA/10908, 22.12.2009, available at http://www.un.org/News/Press/docs//2009/ga10908.doc.htm, last visited on 30.12.2010

CASE LAW

Abbas v. Commissioner-General of the United Nations Relief and Works Agency for Palestine Refugees in the Near East, UNAT Judgment No. 874 [1998], available at http://untreaty.un.org/UNAT/UNAT_Judgements/Judgements_E/UNAT_00874_E.pdf, last visited on 30.12.2010

Abebe v. Secretary-General of the United Nations, UNAT Judgment No. 1169 [2004], available at http://untreaty.un.org/UNAT/UNAT_Judgements/Judgements_E/UNAT_01169_E.pdf, last visited on 30.12.2010

Adler v. Secretary-General of the United Nations, UNAT Judgment No. 267 [1980], available at http://untreaty.un.org/UNAT/UNAT_Judgements/Judgements_E/UNAT_00267_E.pdf, last visited on 30.12.2010

Al-Abed v. Secretary-General of the United Nations, UNAT Judgment No. 128 [1969], available at http://untreaty.un.org/UNAT/UNAT_Judgements/Judgements_E/UNAT_00128_E.pdf, last visited on 30.12.2010

Al-Fahoum v. Secretary-General of the United Nations, UNAT Judgment No. 1018 [2001], available at http://untreaty.un.org/UNAT/UNAT_Judgements/Judgements_E/UNAT_01018_E.pdf, last visited on 30.12.2010

Al Ansari, Zarra and Khalil, and Abdulhadi et al. v. Commissioner-General of the United Nations Relief and Works Agency for Palestine Refugees in the Near East, UNAT Judgment No. 1014 [2001], available at http://untreaty.un.org/UNAT/UNAT_Judgements/Judgements_E/UNAT_01014_E.pdf, last visited on 30.12.2010

Alam v. Secretary-General of the United Nations, UNAT Judgment No. 380 [1987], available at http://untreaty.un.org/UNAT/UNAT_Judgements/Judgements_E/UNAT_00380_E.pdf, last visited on 30.12.2010

Alba et al and Fernandez-Amon et al v. Secretary-General of the United Nations, UNAT Judgment No. 712 [1995], available at http://untreaty.un.org/UNAT/UNAT_Judgements/Judgements_E/UNAT_00712_E.pdf, last visited on 30.12.2010

Alok v. Secretary-General of the United Nations, UNAT Judgment No. 1123 [2003], available at http://untreaty.un.org/UNAT/UNAT_Judgements/Judgements_E/UNAT_01123_E.pdf, last visited on 30.12.2010

Alper v. Secretary-General of the United Nations, UNAT Judgment Nr. 8 [1951], available at http://untreaty.un.org/UNAT/UNAT_Judgements/Judgements_E/UNAT_00008_E.pdf, last visited on 30.12.2010

Anderson Bieler v. Secretary-General of the United Nations, UNAT Judgment No. 765 [1996], available at http://untreaty.un.org/UNAT/UNAT_Judgements/Judgements_E/UNAT_00765_E.pdf, last visited on 30.12.2010

Anderson v. Secretary-General of the United Nations, UNAT Judgment No. 457 [1989], available at http://untreaty.un.org/UNAT/UNAT_Judgements/Judgements_E/UNAT_00457_E.pdf, last visited on 30.12.2010

Applicant v. Secretary-General of the United Nations, UNAT Judgment No. 1234 [2005], available at http://untreaty.un.org/UNAT/UNAT_Judgements/Judgements_E/UNAT_01234_E.pdf, last visited on 30.12.2010

Araim v. Secretary-General of the United Nations, Judgment No. 657 [1994], available at http://untreaty.un.org/UNAT/UNAT_Judgements/Judgements_E/UNAT_00657_E.pdf, last visited on 30.12.2010

Archibald v. Secretary-General of the United Nations, UNAT Judgment No. 222 [1977], available at http://untreaty.un.org/UNAT/UNAT_Judgements/Judgements_E/UNAT_00222_E.pdf, last visited on 30.12.2010

Aubert and others v. Secretary-General of the United Nations, UNAT Judgment No. 2 [1950], available at http://untreaty.un.org/UNAT/UNAT_Judgements/Judgements_E/UNAT_00002_E.pdf, last visited on 30.12.2010

Azzu v. Secretary-General of the United Nations, UNAT Judgment No. 103 [1966], available at http://untreaty.un.org/UNAT/UNAT_Judgements/Judgements_E/UNAT_00103_E.pdf, last visited on 30.12.2010

Balogun v. Secretary-General of the United Nations, UNAT Judgment No. 852 [1997], available at http://untreaty.un.org/UNAT/UNAT_Judgements/Judgements_F/UNAT_00852_E.pdf, last visited on 30.12.2010

Belas-Gianou v. Secretary-General of the United Nations, UNAT Judgment No. 707 [1995], available at http://untreaty.un.org/UNAT/UNAT_Judgements/Judgements_E/UNAT_00707_E.pdf, last visited on 30.12.2010

Bernard v. Secretary-General of the United Nations, UNAT Judgment No. 244 [1979], available at http://untreaty.un.org/UNAT/UNAT_Judgements/Judgements_E/UNAT_00244_E.pdf, last visited on 30.12.2010

Bhattacharyya v. Secretary-General of the United Nations, UNAT Judgment No. 142 [1971], available at http://untreaty.un.org/UNAT/UNAT_Judgements/Judgements_E/UNAT_00142_E.pdf, last visited on 30.12.2010

Boelen v. Secretary-General of the United Nations, UNAT Judgment No. 261 [1980], available at http://untreaty.un.org/UNAT/UNAT_Judgements/Judgements_E/UNAT_00261_E.pdf, last visited on 30.12.2010

Bonder v. Secretary-General of the United Nations, UNAT Judgment No. 1052 [2002], available at http://untreaty.un.org/UNAT/UNAT_Judgements/Judgements_E/UNAT_01052_E.pdf, last visited on 30.12.2010

Capio v. Secretary-General of the United Nations, UNAT Judgment No. 266 [1980], available at http://untreaty.un.org/UNAT/UNAT_Judgements/Judgements_E/UNAT_00266_E.pdf, last visited on 30.12.2010

Capote v. Secretary-General of the United Nations, UNAT Judgment No. 1004 [2001], available at http://untreaty.un.org/UNAT/UNAT_Judgements/Judgements_E/UNAT_01004_E.pdf, last visited on 30.12.2010

Carson v. Secretary-General of the United Nations, UNAT Judgment No. 85 [1962], available at http://untreaty.un.org/UNAT/UNAT_Judgements/Judgements_E/UNAT_00085_E.pdf, last visited on 30.12.2010

Case No. 1309, UNAT Judgment No. 1258 [2005], available at http://untreaty.un.org/UNAT/UNAT_Judgements/Judgements_E/UNAT_01258_E.pdf, last visited on 30.12.2010

Case No. 1333, UNAT Judgment No. 1260 [2005], available at http://untreaty.un.org/UNAT/UNAT_Judgements/Judgements_E/UNAT_01260_E.pdf, last visited on 30.12.2010

Case No. 1354, UNAT Judgment No. 1271 [2005], available at http://untreaty.un.org/UNAT/UNAT_Judgements/Judgements_E/UNAT_01271_E.pdf, last visited on 30.12.2010

Case No. 1355, UNAT Judgment No. 1272 [2005], available at http://untreaty.un.org/UNAT/UNAT_Judgements/Judgements_E/UNAT_01272_E.pdf, last visited on 30.12.2010

Case No. 1357, UNAT Judgment No. 1274 [2005], available at http://untreaty.un.org/UNAT/UNAT_Judgements/Judgements_E/UNAT_01274_E.pdf, last visited on 30.12.2010

Case No. 1358, UNAT Judgment No. 1275 [2005], available at http://untreaty.un.org/UNAT/UNAT_Judgements/Judgements_E/UNAT_01275_E.pdf, last visited on 30.12.2010

Case No. 1360, UNAT Judgment No. 1277, available at http://untreaty.un.org/UNAT/UNAT_Judgements/Judgements_E/UNAT_01277_E.pdf, last visited on 30.12.2010

Case No. 1371, UNAT Judgment No.1289 [2005], available at http://untreaty.un.org/UNAT/UNAT_Judgements/Judgements_E/UNAT_01289_E.pdf, last visited on 30.12.2010

Case No. 1372, UNAT Judgment No. 1290 [2006], available at http://untreaty.un.org/UNAT/UNAT_Judgements/Judgements_E/UNAT_01290_E.pdf, last visited on 30.12.2010

Case No. 1379, UNAT Judgment No. 1297 [2006], available at http://untreaty.un.org/UNAT/UNAT_Judgements/Judgements_E/UNAT_01297_E.pdf, last visited on 30.12.2010

Case No. 1386, UNAT Judgment No. 1302 [2006], available at http://untreaty.un.org/UNAT/UNAT_Judgements/Judgements_E/UNAT_01302_E.pdf, last visited on 30.12.2010

Case No. 1387, UNAT Judgment No. 1303 [2006], available at http://untreaty.un.org/UNAT/UNAT_Judgements/Judgements_E/UNAT_01303_E.pdf, last visited on 30.12.2010

Case No. 1389, UNAT Judgment No. 1305 [2006], available at http://untreaty.un.org/UNAT/UNAT_Judgements/Judgements_E/UNAT_01305_E.pdf, last visited on 30.12.2010

Case No. 1390, UNAT Judgment No. 1306 [2006], available at http://untreaty.un.org/UNAT/UNAT_Judgements/Judgements_E/UNAT_01306_E.pdf, last visited on 30.12.2010

Case No. 1392, UNAT Judgment No. 1285 [2006], available at http://untreaty.un.org/UNAT/UNAT_Judgements/Judgements_E/UNAT_01285_E.pdf, last visited on 30.12.2010

Case No. 1395, UNAT Judgment No. 1321 [2007], available at http://untreaty.un.org/UNAT/UNAT_Judgements/Judgements_E/UNAT_01321_E.pdf, last visited on 30.12.2010

Case No. 1398, UNAT Judgment No. 1324 [2007], available at http://untreaty.un.org/UNAT/UNAT_Judgements/Judgements_E/UNAT_01324_E.pdf, last visited on 30.12.2010

Case No. 1402, UNAT Judgment No. 1326 [2007], available at http://untreaty.un.org/UNAT/UNAT_Judgements/Judgements_E/UNAT_01326_E.pdf, last visited on 30.12.2010

Case No. 1403, UNAT Judgment No. 1327 [2007], available at http://untreaty.un.org/UNAT/UNAT_Judgements/Judgements_E/UNAT_01327_E.pdf, last visited on 30.12.2010

Case No. 1408, UNAT Judgment No. 1331 [2007], available at http://untreaty.un.org/UNAT/UNAT_Judgements/Judgements_E/UNAT_01331_E.pdf, last visited on 30.12.2010

Case No. 1414, UNAT Judgment No. 1315 [2006], available at http://untreaty.un.org/UNAT/UNAT_Judgements/Judgements_E/UNAT_01315_E.pdf, last visited on 30.12.2010

Case No. 1415, UNAT Judgment No. 1313 [2006], available at http://untreaty.un.org/UNAT/UNAT_Judgements/Judgements_E/UNAT_01313_E.pdf, last visited on 30.12.2010

Case No. 1421, UNAT Judgment No. 1339 [2007], available at http://untreaty.un.org/UNAT/UNAT_Judgements/Judgements_E/UNAT_01339_E.pdf, last visited on 30.12.2010

Case No. 1431, UNAT Judgment No. 1354 [2007], available at http://untreaty.un.org/UNAT/UNAT_Judgements/Judgements_E/UNAT_01354_E.pdf, last visited on 30.12.2010

Case No. 1434, UNAT Judgment No. 1357 [2007], available at http://untreaty.un.org/UNAT/UNAT_Judgements/Judgements_E/UNAT_01357_E.pdf, last visited on 30.12.2010

Case No. 1447, UNAT Judgment No. 1369 [2007], available at http://untreaty.un.org/UNAT/UNAT_Judgements/Judgements_E/UNAT_01369_E.pdf, last visited on 30.12.2010

Case No. 1449, UNAT Judgment No. 1371 [2007], available at http://untreaty.un.org/UNAT/UNAT_Judgements/Judgements_E/UNAT_01371_E.pdf, last visited on 30.12.2010

Case No. 1454, UNAT Judgment No. 1389 [2008], available at http://untreaty.un.org/UNAT/UNAT_Judgements/Judgements_E/UNAT_01389_E.pdf, last visited on 30.12.2010

Case No. 1455, UNAT Judgment No. 1390 [2008], available at http://untreaty.un.org/UNAT/UNAT_Judgements/Judgements_E/UNAT_01390_E.pdf, last visited on 30.12.2010

Case No. 1456, UNAT Judgment No. 1391 [2008], available at http://untreaty.un.org/UNAT/UNAT_Judgements/Judgements_E/UNAT_01391_E.pdf, last visited on 30.12.2010

Case No. 1457, UNAT Judgment No. 1392 [2008], available at http://untreaty.un.org/UNAT/UNAT_Judgements/Judgements_E/UNAT_01392_E.pdf, last visited on 30.12.2010

Case No. 1470, UNAT Judgment No. 1402 [2008], available at http://untreaty.un.org/UNAT/UNAT_Judgements/Judgements_E/UNAT_01402_E.pdf, last visited on 30.12.2010

Case No. 1475, UNAT Judgment No. 1405 [2008], available at http://untreaty.un.org/UNAT/UNAT_Judgements/Judgements_E/UNAT_01405_E.pdf, last visited on 30.12.2010

Case No. 1477, UNAT Judgment No. 1407 [2008], available at http://untreaty.un.org/UNAT/UNAT_Judgements/Judgements_E/UNAT_01407_E.pdf, last visited on 30.12.2010

Case No. 1478, UNAT Judgment No. 1414 [2008], available at http://untreaty.un.org/UNAT/UNAT_Judgements/Judgements_E/UNAT_01414_E.pdf, last visited on 30.12.2010

Case No. 1479, UNAT Judgment No. 1408 [2008], available at http://untreaty.un.org/UNAT/UNAT_Judgements/Judgements_E/UNAT_01408_E.pdf, last visited on 30.12.2010

Case No. 1480, UNAT Judgment No. 1409 [2008], available at http://untreaty.un.org/UNAT/UNAT_Judgements/Judgements_E/UNAT_01409_E.pdf, last visited on 30.12.2010

Case No. 1487, UNAT Judgment No. 1425 [2009], available at http://untreaty.un.org/UNAT/UNAT_Judgements/Judgements_E/UNAT_01425_E.pdf, last visited on 30.12.2010

Case No. 1494, UNAT Judgment No. 1428 [2008], available at http://untreaty.un.org/UNAT/UNAT_Judgements/Judgements_E/UNAT_01428_E.pdf, last visited on 30.12.2010

Case No. 1498, UNAT Judgment No. 1430 [2008], available at http://untreaty.un.org/UNAT/UNAT_Judgements/Judgements_E/UNAT_01430_E.pdf, last visited on 30.12.2010

Case No. 1499, UNAT Judgment No. 1422 [2008], available at http://untreaty.un.org/UNAT/UNAT_Judgements/Judgements_E/UNAT_01422_E.pdf, last visited on 30.12.2010

Case No. 1500, UNAT Judgment No. 1423 [2008], available at http://untreaty.un.org/UNAT/UNAT_Judgements/Judgements_E/UNAT_01423_E.pdf, last visited on 30.12.2010

Chiacchia v. Secretary-General of the United Nations, UNAT Judgment No. 90 [1963], available at http://untreaty.un.org/UNAT/UNAT_Judgements/Judgements_E/UNAT_00090_E.pdf, last visited on 30.12.2010

Choudhury and Ramchandani v. Secretary-General of the United Nations, UNAT Judgment No. 870 [1998], available at http://untreaty.un.org/UNAT/UNAT_Judgements/Judgements_E/UNAT_00870_E.pdf, last visited on 30.12.2010

Cooperman v. Secretary-General of the United Nations, UNAT Judgment No. 93 [1965], available at http://untreaty.un.org/UNAT/UNAT_Judgements/Judgements_E/UNAT_00093_E.pdf, last visited on 30.12.2010

Coutsis v. Secretary-General of the United Nations, UNAT Judgment No. 69 [1957], available at http://untreaty.un.org/UNAT/UNAT_Judgements/Judgements_E/UNAT_00069_E.pdf, last visited on 30.12.2010

Crawford v. Secretary-General of the United Nations, UNAT Judgment No. 18 [1953], available at http://untreaty.un.org/UNAT/UNAT_Judgements/Judgements_E/UNAT_00018_E.pdf, last visited on 30.12.2010

Cunio v. Secretary-General of the International Civil Aviation Organization, UNAT Judgment No. 321 [1984], available at http://untreaty.un.org/UNAT/UNAT_Judgements/Judgements_E/UNAT_00321_E.pdf, last visited on 30.12.2010

Dale v. Secretary General of the International Civil Aviation Organization, UNAT Judgment No. 132 [1969], available at http://untreaty.un.org/UNAT/UNAT_Judgements/Judgements_E/UNAT_00132_E.pdf, last visited on 30.12.2010

Dauchy v. Secretary-General of the United Nations, UNAT Judgment No. 492 [1990], available at http://untreaty.un.org/UNAT/UNAT_Judgements/Judgements_E/UNAT_00492_E.pdf, last visited on 30.12.2010

De Pojidaeff v. Secretary-General of the United Nations, UNAT Judgment No. 17 [1952], available at http://untreaty.un.org/UNAT/UNAT_Judgements/Judgements_E/UNAT_00017_E.pdf, last visited on 30.12.2010

Dearing v. Secretary-General of the United Nations, UNAT Judgment No. 200 [1975], available at http://untreaty.un.org/UNAT/UNAT_Judgements/Judgements_E/UNAT_00200_E.pdf, last visited on 30.12.2010

Detière v. Secretary-General of the Civil Aviation Organization, UNAT Judgment No. 136 [1970], available at http://untreaty.un.org/UNAT/UNAT_Judgements/Judgements_E/UNAT_00136_E.pdf, last visited on 30.12.2010

Dilleyta v. Secretary-General of the United Nations, UNAT Judgment No. 1103 [2003], available at http://untreaty.un.org/UNAT/UNAT_Judgements/Judgements_E/UNAT_01103_E.pdf, last visited on 30.12.2010

Dupuy v. Secretary General of the United Nations, UNAT Judgment No. 174 [1973], available at http://untreaty.un.org/UNAT/UNAT_Judgements/Judgements_E/UNAT_00174_E.pdf, last visited on 30.12.2010

El-Naggar v. Secretary-General of the United Nations, UNAT Judgment No. 205 [1975], available at http://untreaty.un.org/UNAT/UNAT_Judgements/Judgements_E/UNAT_00205_E.pdf, last visited on 30.12.2010

El-Sharkawi v. Secretary-General of the United Nations, UNAT Judgment No. 795 [1996], available at http://untreaty.un.org/UNAT/UNAT_Judgements/Judgements_E/UNAT_00795_E.pdf, last visited on 30.12.2010

Eren, Robertson, Sellberg and Thompson v. Secretary-General of the United Nations, UNAT Judgment No. 744 [1995], available at http://untreaty.un.org/UNAT/UNAT_Judgements/Judgements_E/UNAT_00744_E.pdf, last visited on 30.12.2010

Estabial v. Secretary-General of the United Nations, UNAT Judgment No. 310 [1983], available at http://untreaty.un.org/UNAT/UNAT_Judgements/Judgements_E/UNAT_00310_E.pdf, last visited on 30.12.2010

Fayemiwo v. Secretary-General of the United Nations, UNAT Judgment No. 246 [1979], available at http://untreaty.un.org/UNAT/UNAT_Judgements/Judgements_E/UNAT_00246_E.pdf, last visited on 30.12.2010

Federchenko v. Secretary-General of the United Nations, UNAT Judgment No. 1153 [2003], available at http://untreaty.un.org/UNAT/UNAT_Judgements/Judgements_E/UNAT_01156_E.pdf, last visited on 30.12.2010

Furst v. Secretary-General of the United Nations, UNAT Judgment No. 241 [1979], available at http://untreaty.un.org/UNAT/UNAT_Judgements/Judgements_E/UNAT_00241_E.pdf, last visited on 30.12.2010

Galindo v. Secretary-General of the United Nations, UNAT Judgment No. 1151 [2003], available at http://untreaty.un.org/UNAT/UNAT_Judgements/Judgements_E/UNAT_01151_E.pdf, last visited on 30.12.2010

Gillman v. Secretary-General of the United Nations, UNAT Judgment No. 98 [1966], available at http://untreaty.un.org/UNAT/UNAT_Judgements/Judgements_E/UNAT_00098_E.pdf, last visited on 30.12.2010

Gomez v. Secretary-General of the United Nations, UNAT Judgment No. 342 [1985], available at http://untreaty.un.org/UNAT/UNAT_Judgements/Judgements_E/UNAT_00342_E.pdf, last visited on 30.12.2010

Gordon v. Secretary-General of the United Nations, UNAT Judgment No. 29 [1953], available at http://untreaty.un.org/UNAT/UNAT_Judgements/Judgements_E/UNAT_00029_E.pdf, last visited on 30.12.2010

Gordon v. Secretary-General of the United Nations; Svechansky v. Secretary-General of the United Nations; Harris v. Secretary-General of the United Nations;; Eldridge v. Secretary-General of the United Nations;; Glassman v. Secretary-General of the United Nations; Older v. Secretary-General of the United Nations; Bancroft v. Secretary-General of the United Nations; Elveson v. Secretary-General of the United Nations; Reed v. Secretary-General of the United Nations; Glaser v. Secretary-General of the United Nations, UNAT Judgments No. 29-38 [1953], available at http://untreaty.un.org/UNAT/UNAT_Judgements/Judgements_E/UNAT_00029_E.pdf; http://untreaty.un.org/UNAT/UNAT_Judgements/Judgements_E/UNAT_00030_E.pdf; http://untreaty.un.org/UNAT/UNAT_Judgements/Judgements_E/UNAT_00031_E.pdf; http://untreaty.un.org/UNAT/UNAT_Judgements/Judgements_E/UNAT_00032_E.pdf; http://untreaty.un.org/UNAT/UNAT_Judgements/Judgements_E/UNAT_00033_E.pdf; http://untreaty.un.org/UNAT/UNAT_Judgements/Judgements_E/UNAT_00034_E.pdf; http://untreaty.un.org/UNAT/UNAT_Judgements/Judgements_E/UNAT_00035_E.pdf; http://untreaty.un.org/UNAT/UNAT_Judgements/Judgements_E/UNAT_00036_E.pdf; http://untreaty.un.org/UNAT/UNAT_Judgements/Judgements_E/UNAT_00037_E.pdf; http://untreaty.un.org/UNAT/UNAT_Judgements/Judgements_E/UNAT_00038_E.pdf, last visited on 30.12.2010

Grinblat v. Secretary-General of the United Nations, UNAT Judgment No. 671 [1994], available at http://untreaty.un.org/UNAT/UNAT_Judgements/Judgements_E/UNAT_00671_E.pdf, last visited on 30.12.2010

Guest and Slatford v. Secretary-General of the United Nations, UNAT Judgment No. 841 [1997], available at http://untreaty.un.org/UNAT/UNAT_Judgements/Judgements_E/UNAT_00841_E.pdf, last visited on 30.12.2010

Gurun v. Secretary-General of the United Nations, UNAT Judgment No. 851 [1997], available at http://untreaty.un.org/UNAT/UNAT_Judgements/Judgements_E/UNAT_00851_E.pdf, last visited on 30.12.2010

Handelsman v. Secretary-General of the United Nations, UNAT Judgment No. 885 [1998], available at http://untreaty.un.org/UNAT/UNAT_Judgements/Judgements_E/UNAT_00885_E.pdf, last visited on 30.12.2010

Higgins v. Secretary-General of the Inter-Governmental Maritime Consultative Organization, UNAT Judgment No. 92 [1964], available at http://untreaty.un.org/UNAT/UNAT_Judgements/Judgements_E/UNAT_00092_E.pdf, last visited on 30.12.2010

Hilaire v. Secretary-General of the United Nations, UNAT Judgment No. 220 [1977], available at http://untreaty.un.org/UNAT/UNAT_Judgements/Judgements_E/UNAT_00220_E.pdf, last visited on 30.12.2010

Ho v. Secretary-General of the United Nations, UNAT Judgment No. 122 [1968], available at http://untreaty.un.org/UNAT/UNAT_Judgements/Judgements_E/UNAT_00122_E.pdf, last visited on 30.12.2010

Howrani and 4 others v. Secretary-General of the United Nations, UNAT Judgment No. 4 [1951], available at http://untreaty.un.org/UNAT/UNAT_Judgements/Judgements_E/UNAT_00004_E.pdf, last visited on 30.12.2010

Howrani v. Secretary-General fo the United Nations, UNAT Judgment No. 5 [1951], available at http://untreaty.un.org/UNAT/UNAT_Judgements/Judgements_E/UNAT_00005_E.pdf, last visited on 30.12.2010

Hzayyen v. United Nations Relief and Work Agency for Palestine Refugees in the Near East, UNAT Judgment No. 1020 [2001], available at http://untreaty.un.org/UNAT/UNAT_Judgements/Judgements_E/UNAT_01020_E.pdf, last visited on 30.12.2010

Ibañez v. Secretary-General of the United Nations, UNAT Judgment No. 223 [1977], available at http://untreaty.un.org/UNAT/UNAT_Judgements/Judgements_E/UNAT_00223_E.pdf, last visited on 30.12.2010

Iddi v. Secretary-General of the United Nations, UNAT Judgment No. 1011 [2001], available at http://untreaty.un.org/UNAT/UNAT_Judgements/Judgements_E/UNAT_01011_E.pdf, last visited on 30.12.2010

Ikegame v. Secretary General of the United Nations, UNAT Judgment No. 1175 [2004], available at http://untreaty.un.org/UNAT/UNAT_Judgements/Judgements_E/UNAT_01175_E.pdf, last visited on 30.12.2010

Jabbour v. Secretary-General of the United Nations, UNAT Judgment No. 305 [1983], available at http://untreaty.un.org/UNAT/UNAT_Judgements/Judgements_E/UNAT_00305_E.pdf, last visited on 30.12.2010

Jhuthiv v. Secretary-General of the United Nations, UNAT Judgment No. 897 [1998], available at http://untreaty.un.org/UNAT/UNAT_Judgements/Judgements_E/UNAT_00897_E.pdf, last visited on 30.12.2010

Kahale v. Secretary-General of the United Nations, UNAT Judgment No. 165 [1972], available at http://untreaty.un.org/UNAT/UNAT_Judgements/Judgements_E/UNAT_00165_E.pdf, last visited on 30.12.2010

Kaplan v. Secretary-General of the United Nations; Middleton v. Secretary-General of the United Nations; Rubin v. Secretary-General of the United Nations; Kagen-Pozner v. Secretary-General of the United Nations; Sokolow v. Secretary-General of the United Nations; Saperstein v. Secretary-General of the United Nations; Van Tassel v. Secretary-General of the United Nations; Zap, Majorie v. Secretary-General of the United Nations; Zap, Herman v. Secretary-General of the United Nations UNAT Judgments Nr. 19-27 [1953], available at http://untreaty.un.org/UNAT/UNAT_Judgements/Judgements_E/UNAT_00019_E.pdf; http://untreaty.un.org/UNAT/UNAT_Judgements/Judgements_E/UNAT_00020_E.pdf; http://untreaty.un.org/UNAT/UNAT_Judgements/Judgements_E/UNAT_00021_E.pdf; http://untreaty.un.org/UNAT/UNAT_Judgements/Judgements_E/UNAT_00022_E.pdf; http://untreaty.un.org/UNAT/UNAT_Judgements/Judgements_E/UNAT_00023_E.pdf; http://untreaty.un.org/UNAT/UNAT_Judgements/Judgements_E/UNAT_00024_E.pdf; http://untreaty.un.org/UNAT/UNAT_Judgements/Judgements_E/UNAT_00025_E.pdf; http://untreaty.un.org/UNAT/UNAT_Judgements/Judgements_E/UNAT_00026_E.pdf; http://untreaty.un.org/UNAT/UNAT_Judgements/Judgements_E/UNAT_00027_E.pdf, last visited on 30.12.2010

Karmel v. Secretary-General of the United Nations, UNAT Judgment No. 879 [1998], available at http://untreaty.un.org/UNAT/UNAT_Judgements/Judgements_E/UNAT_00879_E.pdf, last visited on 30.12.2010

Karmoul v. Secretary-General of the United Nations, UNAT Judgment No. 791 [1996], available at http://untreaty.un.org/UNAT/UNAT_Judgements/Judgements_E/UNAT_00791_E.pdf, last visited on 30.12.2010

Keeny v. Secretary-General of the United Nations UNAT Judgment No. 6 [1951], available at http://untreaty.un.org/UNAT/UNAT_Judgements/Judgements_E/UNAT_00006_E.pdf, last visited on 30.12.2010

Kehoe v. Secretary-General of the United Nations, UNAT Judgment Nr. 9 [1951], available at http://untreaty.un.org/UNAT/UNAT_Judgements/Judgements_E/UNAT_00009_E.pdf, last visited on 30.12.2010

Kennedy v. Secretary-General of the United Nations, UNAT Judgment No. 265 [1980], available at http://untreaty.un.org/UNAT/UNAT_Judgements/Judgements_E/UNAT_00265_E.pdf, last visited on 30.12.2010

Khan v. Secretary-General of the United Nations, UNAT Judgment No. 848 [1997], available at http://untreaty.un.org/UNAT/UNAT_Judgements/Judgements_E/UNAT_00848_E.pdf, last visited on 30.12.2010

Khawaja v. Secretary-General of the United Nations, UNAT Judgment No. 930 [1999], available at http://untreaty.un.org/UNAT/UNAT_Judgements/Judgements_E/UNAT_00930_E.pdf, last visited on 30.12.2010

Kioko v. Secretary-General of the United Nations, UNAT Judgment No. 456 [1989], available at http://untreaty.un.org/UNAT/UNAT_Judgements/Judgements_E/UNAT_00456_E.pdf, last visited on 30.12.2010

Kiwanuka v. Secretary-General of the United Nations, UNAT Judgment No. 941 [1999], available at http://untreaty.un.org/UNAT/UNAT_Judgements/Judgements_E/UNAT_00941_E.pdf, last visited on 30.12.2010

Klein v. Secretary-General of the United Nations, UNAT Judgment No. 1031 [2001], available at http://untreaty.un.org/UNAT/UNAT_Judgements/Judgements_E/UNAT_01031_E.pdf, last visited on 30.12.2010

Knight et al v. Secretary-General of the United Nations, UNAT Judgment No. 722 [1995], available at http://untreaty.un.org/UNAT/UNAT_Judgements/Judgements_E/UNAT_00722_E.pdf, last visited on 30.12.2010

Levcik v. Secretary-General of the United Nations, UNAT Judgment No. 192 [1974], available at http://untreaty.un.org/UNAT/UNAT_Judgements/Judgements_E/UNAT_00192_E.pdf, last visited on 30.12.2010

Lindblad v. Secretary-General of the United Nations, UNAT Judgment No. 183 [1974], available at http://untreaty.un.org/UNAT/UNAT_Judgements/Judgements_E/UNAT_00183_E.pdf, last visited on 30.12.2010

Lopes Braga v. Secretary-General of the United Nations, UNAT Judgment No. 1122 [2003], available at http://untreaty.un.org/UNAT/UNAT_Judgements/Judgements_E/UNAT_01122_E.pdf, last visited on 30.12.2010

Manson v. Secretary-General of the United Nations, UNAT Judgment No. 742 [1995], available at http://untreaty.un.org/UNAT/UNAT_Judgements/Judgements_E/UNAT_00742_E.pdf, last visited on 30.12.2010

Mendez v. Secretary-General of the United Nations, UNAT Judgment No. 268 [1981], available at http://untreaty.un.org/UNAT/UNAT_Judgements/Judgements_E/UNAT_00268_E.pdf, last visited on 30.12.2010

Mila v. Secretary-General of the United Nations, UNAT Judgment No. 184 [1974], available at http://untreaty.un.org/UNAT/UNAT_Judgements/Judgements_E/UNAT_00184_E.pdf, last visited on 30.12.2010

Miss Y. v. Secretary-General of the United Nations, UNAT Judgment No. 83 [1961], available at http://untreaty.un.org/UNAT/UNAT_Judgements/Judgements_E/UNAT_00083_E.pdf, last visited on 30.12.2010

Miss Y. v. Secretary-General of the United Nations, UNAT Judgment No. 91 [1964], available at http://untreaty.un.org/UNAT/UNAT_Judgements/Judgements_E/UNAT_00091_E.pdf, last visited on 30.12.2010

Mizuno v. Secretary-General of the United Nations, UNAT Judgment No. 415 [1988], available at http://untreaty.un.org/UNAT/UNAT_Judgements/Judgements_E/UNAT_00415_E.pdf, last visited on 30.12.2010

Monteleone-Gilfillian v. Secretary-General of the United Nations, UNAT Judgment No. 814 [1997], available at http://untreaty.un.org/UNAT/UNAT_Judgements/Judgements_E/UNAT_00814_E.pdf, last visited on 30.12.2010

Moore v. Secretary-General of the United Nations, UNAT Judgment No. 923 [1999], available at http://untreaty.un.org/UNAT/UNAT_Judgements/Judgements_E/UNAT_00923_E.pdf, last visited on 30.12.2010

Moser v. Secretary-General of the United Nations, UNAT Judgment No. 388 [1987], available at http://untreaty.un.org/UNAT/UNAT_Judgements/Judgements_E/UNAT_00388_E.pdf, last visited on 30.12.2010

Nelson v. Secretary-General of the United Nations, UNAT Judgment No. 157 [1972], available at http://untreaty.un.org/UNAT/UNAT_Judgements/Judgements_E/UNAT_00157_E.pdf, last visited on 30.12.2010

Noll-Wagenfeld v. Secretary-General of the United Nations, UNAT Judgment No. 636 [1994], available at http://untreaty.un.org/UNAT/UNAT_Judgements/Judgements_E/UNAT_00636_E.pdf, last visited on 30.12.2010

Ortega, Hernandez, Canales and Garcia v. Secretary-General of the United Nations, UNAT Judgment No. 610 [1993], available at http://untreaty.un.org/UNAT/UNAT_Judgements/Judgements_E/UNAT_00610_E.pdf, last visited on 30.12.2010

Patel v. Secretary-General of the United Nations, UNAT Judgment No. 850 [1997], available at http://untreaty.un.org/UNAT/UNAT_Judgements/Judgements_E/UNAT_00850_E.pdf, last visited on 30.12.2010

Pereyra v. Secretary-General of the United Nations, UNAT Judgment No. 647 [1994], available at http://untreaty.un.org/UNAT/UNAT_Judgements/Judgements_E/UNAT_00647_E.pdf, last visited on 30.12.2010

Peynado v. Secretary-General of the United Nations, UNAT Judgment No. 138 [1970], available at http://untreaty.un.org/UNAT/UNAT_Judgements/Judgements_E/UNAT_00138_E.pdf, last visited on 30.12.2010

Picou v. Secretary-General of the United Nations, UNAT Judgment Nr. 7 [1951], available at http://untreaty.un.org/UNAT/UNAT_Judgements/Judgements_E/UNAT_00007_E.pdf, last visited on 30.12.2010

Piracés v. Secretary-General of the United Nations, UNAT Judgment No. 264 [1980], available at http://untreaty.un.org/UNAT/UNAT_Judgements/Judgements_E/UNAT_00264_E.pdf, last visited on 30.12.2010

Pochonet v. Secretary-General of the United Nations, UNAT Judgment No. 219 [1977], available at http://untreaty.un.org/UNAT/UNAT_Judgements/Judgements_E/UNAT_00219_E.pdf, last visited on 30.12.2010

Quémerais v. Secretary-General of the United Nations, UNAT Judgment No. 172 [1973], available at http://untreaty.un.org/UNAT/UNAT_Judgements/Judgements_E/UNAT_00172_E.pdf, last visited on 30.12.2010

Rau v. Secretary-General of the United Nations, UNAT Judgment No. 101 [1966], available at http://untreaty.un.org/UNAT/UNAT_Judgements/Judgements_E/UNAT_00101_E.pdf, last visited on 30.12.2010

Reid v. Secretary-General of the United Nations, UNAT Judgment No. 210 [1976], available at http://untreaty.un.org/UNAT/UNAT_Judgements/Judgements_E/UNAT_00210_E.pdf, last visited on 30.12.2010

Restrepo v. Secretary-General of the United Nations, UNAT Judgment No. 131, available at http://untreaty.un.org/UNAT/UNAT_Judgements/Judgements_E/UNAT_00131_E.pdf, last visited on 30.12.2010

Roy v. Secretary-General of the International Civil Aviation Organization, UNAT Judgment No. 123 [1968], available at http://untreaty.un.org/UNAT/UNAT_Judgements/Judgements_E/UNAT_00123_E.pdf, last visited on 30.12.2010

Safavi v. Secretary-General of the United Nations, UNAT Judgment No. 465 [1989], available at http://untreaty.un.org/UNAT/UNAT_Judgements/Judgements_E/UNAT_00465_E.pdf, last visited on 30.12.2010

Salama v. Secretary-General of the United Nations, UNAT Judgment No. 936 [1999], available at http://untreaty.un.org/UNAT/UNAT_Judgements/Judgements_E/UNAT_00936_E.pdf, last visited on 30.12.2010

Salinas v. Secretary-General of the United Nations, UNAT Judgment No. 530 [1991], available at http://untreaty.un.org/UNAT/UNAT_Judgements/Judgements_E/UNAT_00530_E.pdf, last visited on 30.12.2010

Seaforth v. Secretary-General of the United Nations, UNAT Judgment No. 1163 [2003], available at http://untreaty.un.org/UNAT/UNAT_Judgements/Judgements_E/UNAT_01163_E.pdf, last visited on 30.12.2010

Selamawit Makonnen v. Secretary-General of the United Nations, UNAT Judgment No. 555 [1992], available at http://untreaty.un.org/UNAT/UNAT_Judgements/Judgements_E/UNAT_00555_E.pdf, last visited on 30.12.2010

Senghor v. Secretary-General of the United Nations, UNAT Judgment No. 169 [1973], available at http://untreaty.un.org/UNAT/UNAT_Judgements/Judgements_E/UNAT_00169_E.pdf, last visited on 30.12.2010

Seraphides v. Secretary-General of the United Nations, UNAT Judgment No. 140 [1971], available at http://untreaty.un.org/UNAT/UNAT_Judgements/Judgements_E/UNAT_00140_E.pdf, last visited on 30.12.2010

Shahrour v. Commissioner-General of the United nations Relief and Works Agency for Palestine Refugees in the Near East, UNAT Judgment No. 939 [1999], available at http://untreaty.un.org/UNAT/UNAT_Judgements/Judgements_E/UNAT_00939_E.pdf, last visited on 30.12.2010

Sidibeh v. Secretary-General of the United Nations, UNAT Judgment No. 770 [1996], available at http://untreaty.un.org/UNAT/UNAT_Judgements/Judgements_E/UNAT_00770_E.pdf, last visited on 30.12.2010

Sikand v. Secretary-General of the United Nations, UNAT Judgment No. 95 [1965], available at http://untreaty.un.org/UNAT/UNAT_Judgements/Judgements_E/UNAT_00095_E.pdf, last visited on 30.12.2010

Stepczynski v. Secretary-General of the United Nations, UNAT Judgment No. 774 [1996], available at http://untreaty.un.org/UNAT/UNAT_Judgements/Judgements_E/UNAT_00774_E.pdf, last visited on 30.12.2010

Sy v. Secretary-General of the United Nations, UNAT Judgment No. 1150 [2003], available at http://untreaty.un.org/UNAT/UNAT_Judgements/Judgements_E/UNAT_01150_E.pdf, last visited on 30.12.2010

Talwar v. Secretary-General of the United Nations, UNAT Judgment No. 343 [1985], available at http://untreaty.un.org/UNAT/UNAT_Judgements/Judgements_E/UNAT_00343_E.pdf, last visited on 30.12.2010

Tortel v. Secretary-General of the United Nations, UNAT Judgment No. 444 [1989], available at http://untreaty.un.org/UNAT/UNAT_Judgements/Judgements_E/UNAT_00444_E.pdf, last visited on 30.12.2010

Upadhya v. Secretary-General of the United Nations, UNAT Judgment No. 537 [1991], available at http://untreaty.un.org/UNAT/UNAT_Judgements/Judgements_E/UNAT_00537_E.pdf, last visited on 30.12.2010

Uspensky v. Secretary-General of the United Nations, UNAT Judgment No. 1040 [2001], available at http://untreaty.un.org/UNAT/UNAT_Judgements/Judgements_E/UNAT_01040_E.pdf, last visited on 30.12.2010

Walter v. Secretary-General of the United Nations, UNAT Jugment no. 390 [1987], available at http://untreaty.un.org/UNAT/UNAT_Judgements/Judgements_E/UNAT_00390_E.pdf, last visited on 30.12.2010

Warner v. Secretary-General of the United Nations, UNAT Judgment No. 418 [1988], available at http://untreaty.un.org/UNAT/UNAT_Judgements/Judgements_E/UNAT_00418_E.pdf, last visited on 30.12.2010

Williamson v. Secretary-General of the United Nations, UNAT Judgment No. 362 [1986], available at http://untreaty.un.org/UNAT/UNAT_Judgements/Judgements_E/UNAT_00362_E.pdf, last visited on 30.12.2010

Ying v. Secretary-General of the United Nations, UNAT Judgment No. 424 [1988], available at http://untreaty.un.org/UNAT/UNAT_Judgements/Judgements_E/UNAT_00424_E.pdf, last visited on 30.12.2010

Zafari v. Commissioner-General of the United Nations Relief and Works Agency for Palestine Refugees in the Near East, UNAT Judgment No. 461 [1989], available at http://untreaty.un.org/UNAT/UNAT_Judgements/Judgements_E/UNAT_00461_E.pdf, last visited on 30.12.2010

Zang-Atangana v. Secretary-General of the United Nations, UNAT Judgment No. 130 [1969], available at http://untreaty.un.org/UNAT/UNAT_Judgements/Judgements_E/UNAT_00130_E.pdf, last visited on 30.12.2010

Ziadeh v. Commissioner-General of the United Nations Relief and Works Agency for Palestine Refugees in the Near East, UNAT Judgment No. 906 [1998], available at http://untreaty.un.org/UNAT/UNAT_Judgements/Judgements_E/UNAT_00906_E.pdf, last visited on 30.12.2010

MISCELLANEOUS

A Guide to a Career with the United Nations, available at http://esa.un.org/techcoop/associateexperts/APPLICANTS/Guide_to_employment/unpan000153.pdf, last visited on 30.12.2010

A Picture of the UN Staff, 2005, available at http://www.unspecial.org/StaffPictures/report_p2a.html, last visited on 30.12.2010

Draft Decision Submitted by the Chairman of the Committee following Informal Consultations, Provisional Staff Rules, A/C.5/64/L.9, 02.12.2009, available in the

Official Document System of the United Nations, available at http://documents.un.org/, last visited on 30.12.2010

Handbook of the United Nations, available at http://www.un.org/hr_handbook/English/, last visited on 30.12.2010

Jonah, J. O. C., *Can the United Nations Survive Without a Vital International Civil Service?, A talk to an AFICS (NY) luncheon*, 04.12.2002, available at http://www.un-staff.org/index.php?option=com_content&task=view&id=83&Itemid=8, last visited on 17.03.2009

Personnel Statistics 2006, United Nations System, Chief Executives Board for Coordination, High-Level Committee on Management, CEB/2007/HR/15, 15.10.2007, available at http://www.unsceb.org/ceb/stats/hr/ps/years/2006, last visited on 30.12.2010

Preliminary Position of the Group of 77 and China on Actions Contained in the Report of the Secretary-General: Renewing the United Nations: A Programme for Reform (A/51/950), 29.10.1997, available at http://www.g77.org/doc/reform2.htm, last visited on 30.12.2010

Repertory of Practice of United Nations Organs, available at http://www.un.org/law/repertory/, last visited on 30.12.2010

Views of the Staff Representatives of the United Nations Secretariat, A/C.5/63/3/Add.2, 11.10.2006, available in the Official Document System of the United Nations, available at http://documents.un.org/, last visited on 30.12.2010

Views of the Staff Representatives of the United Nations Secretariat: Staff Union (New York), Field Staff Union (Brindisi) and Staff Coordinating Council (United Nations Office in Geneva), Addendum, A/C.5/63/3/Add.2, 15.10.2008, available in the Official Document System of the United Nations, available at http://documents.un.org/, last visited on 30.12.2010

DOCUMENTS OF, OR RELATED TO, THE EUROPEAN UNION

TREATIES

Consolidated Version of the Treaty on the Functioning of the European Union, OJ C 83, 30.03.2010, p. 47,

Treaty Establishing the European Atomic Energy Community, 25.03.1957, available at http://eur-lex.europa.eu/en/treaties/index.htm#founding, last visited on 30.12.2010

Treaty Establishing the European Economic Community, 25.03.1957, available at http://eur-lex.europa.eu/en/treaties/index.htm#founding, last visited on 30.12.2010

COUNCIL REGULATIONS AND DECISIONS

Council Decision 88/591/ECSC, EEC, Euratom Establishing a Court of First Instance of the European Communities, OJ L 144, 16.06.1993, p. 21-22

Council Decision No 2004/752 (EC, Euratom) of 2 November 2004 Establishing the European Union Civil Service Tribunal, OJ L 333, 09.11.2004, p. 7-11

Council Regulation (EC) No 626/95 of 20 March 1995 Introducing Special and Temporary Measures Applicable to the Recruitment of Officials of the European Communities as a Result of the Accession of Austria, Finland and Sweden, OJ L 66, 24.03.1995, p. 1

Council Regulation (EC, EURATOM) No 723/2004 of 22 March 2004 Amending the Staff Regulations of Officials of the European Communities and the Conditions of Employment of Other Servants of the European Communities, OJ L 124, 27.04.2004, p. 1-118

Council Regulation (ECSC, EEC, Euratom) No 2615/76 of 21 October 1976 Amending Regulation (EEC, Euratom, ECSC) No 259/68 as Regards the Conditions of Employment of Other Servants of the European Communities, OJ L 299, 29.10.1976, p. 1 - 3

Council Regulation (ECSC, EEC, Euratom) No 2799/85 of 27 September 1985 Amending the Staff Regulations of Officials and the Conditions of Employment of Other Servants of the European Communities, OJ L 265, 08.10.1985, p. 1-10

Council Regulation (ECSC, EEC, Euratom) No 3517/85 of 12 December 1985 Introducing Special and Temporary Measures Applicable to the Recruitment of Officials of the European Communities as a Result of the Accession of Spain and Portugal, OJ L 335, 13.12.1985, p. 55

Council Regulation (ECSC/EEC/Euratom) No 662/82 of 22 March 1982 Introducing Special and Temporary Measures Applicable to the Recruitment of Officials of the European Communities in Consequence of the Accession of the Hellenic Republic to the Communities, OJ L 78, 24.03.1982, p. 1

Protocol on the Statute of the Court of Justice annexed to the Treaty on European Union, to the Treaty Establishing the European Community and to the Treaty Establishing the European Atomic Energy Community, in accordance with Article 7 of the Treaty of Nice, amending the Treaty on European Union, the Treaties establishing the European Communities and certain related acts, signed at Nice on 26 February 2001 (OJ C 80 of 10 March 2001), as amended by Council Decision of 15 July 2003 (OJ L 188 of 26 July 2003, p. 1), by Article 13(2) of the Act concerning the conditions of accession of 16 April 2003 (OJ L 236 of 23 September 2003, p. 37), Council Decisions of 19 and 26 April 2004 (OJ L 132 of 29 April 2004, pp 1 and 5, and OJ L 194 of 2 June 2004, p. 3 (corrigendum)), Council Decision of 2 November 2004 establishing the European Union Civil Service Tribunal (OJ L 333 of 9 November 2004, p. 7 and OJ L 103 of 20 April 2007, p. 54), by Council Decision of 3 October 2005 (OJ L 266 of 11 October 2005, p. 60), by Article 11 of the Act concerning the conditions of accession of 25 April 2005 (OJ L 157 of 21 June 2005, p. 203) and by Council Decision of 20 December 2007 (OJ L 24 of 29 January 2008, p. 42)

Regulation No 31 (EEC), 11 (EAEC), Laying down the Staff Regulations of Officials and the Conditions of Employment of Other Servants of the European Economic Community and the European Atomic Energy Community, First Part: Staff Regulations of Officials, OJ 45, 14.06.1962, p. 1385, subsequently amended, available at http://eur-lex.europa.eu/LexUriServ/LexUriServ.do?uri=CONSLEG:1962R0031:20100101:EN:PDF (consolidated unofficial version), last visited on 30.12.2010

Regulation No 31 (EEC), 11 (EAEC), Laying down the Staff Regulations of Officials and the Conditions of Employment of Other Servants of the European Economic Community and the European Atomic Energy Community, Second Part: Conditions of Employment of Other Servants, OJ 45, 14.06.1962, p. 1442, subsequently amended, available at http://eur-lex.europa.eu/LexUriServ/LexUriServ.do?uri=CONSLEG:1962R0031:20100101:EN:PDF (consolidated unofficial version), last visited on 30.12.2010

Regulation (EEC, Euroatom, ECSC) No 259/68 of the Council of 29 February 1968 laying down the Staff Regulations of Officials and the Conditions of Employment of Other Servants of the European Communities and Instituting Special Measures Temporarily Applicable to Officials of the Commission, OJ L 56, 04.03.1968 - Special Edition 1968, 1 December 1972

Regulation (Euratom, ECSC, EEC) No 1473/72 of the Council of 30 June 1972 Amending Regulation (EEC, Euratom, ECSC) No 259/68 Laying Down the Staff Regulations of Officials and the Conditions of Employment of Other Servants of the European Communities, OJ L 160, 16.07.1972, p. 1-16, English special edition: Series I Chapter 1972(III), p. 703

Regulation (Euratom, ECSC, EEC) No 2530/72 of the Council of 4 December 1972 Introducing Special and Temporary Measures Applicable to the Recruitment of Officials of the European Communities in Consequence of the Accession of New Member States, and for the Termination of Service of Officials of Those Communities, OJ L 272, 05.12.1972, p. 1-5

Regulation No 31 (EEC), 11 (EAEC), Laying down the Staff Regulations of Officials and the Conditions of Employment of Other Servants of the European Economic Community and the European Atomic Energy Community, 18.12.1961, OJ 45, 14.06.1962 - Special Edition 1959-62, November 1972

Regulation No 1073/1999 of the European Parliament and the Council of 25 May 1999 Concerning Investigations Conducted by the European Anti-Fraud Office (OLAF), OJ L 136, 31.05.1999, p. 1

Staff Regulations of Officials and Conditions of Employment of Other Servants of the European Communities, consolidated version, February 1998

Rules of Prodecude of the European Union Civil Service Tribunal, 25.07.2007, OJ L 225, 29.08.2007, p.1

COMMISSION DECISIONS AND OTHER DOCUMENTS

Code of Conduct for Commissioners, SEC(2004)1487/2, available in the Register of Commission Documents, available at http://ec.europa.eu/transparency/regdoc/registre.cfm?CL=en, last visited on 30.12.2010

Decision of the Director-General for Human Resources and Security on the Exercise of the Powers Conferred on the Appointment Authority and the Authority Responsible for Concluding Contracts of Employment, 03.02.2010,

Collection and Use of Expertise by the Commission, Principles and Guidelines - "Improving the Knowledge Base for Better Policies", COM(2002) 713 final, available in the Register of Commission Documents, available at http://ec.europa.eu/transparency/regdoc/registre.cfm?CL=en, last visited on 30.12.2010

Commission Decision Amending Decision C(2007)5730 of 30 November on the Exercise of Powers Conferred by the Staff Regulations on the Appointing Authority and by the Conditions of Employment of Other Servants on teh Authority Responsible for Concluding Contracts of Employment, C(2009)3074 final, 29.04.2009, available in the Register of Commission Documents, available at http://ec.europa.eu/transparency/regdoc/recherche.cfm?CL=en, last visited on 30.12.2010

Commission Decision Amending Decision C(2007)5730 of 30 November on the Exercise of Powers Conferred by the Staff Regulations on the Appointing Authority and by the Conditions of Employment of Other Servants on teh Authority Responsible for Concluding Contracts of Employment, C(2010)184 final, 19.01.2010, available in the Register of Commission Documents, available at http://ec.europa.eu/transparency/regdoc/recherche.cfm?CL=en, last visited on 30.12.2010

Commission Decision Amending Decision C(2007) 5730 of 30 November on the Exercise of Powers Conferred by the Staff Regulations on the Appointing Authority and by the Conditions of Employment of Other Servants on teh Authority Responsible for Concluding Contracts of Employment, C(2008) 5085, 10.09.2008, available in the Register of Commission Documents, available at http://ec.europa.eu/transparency/regdoc/registre.cfm?CL=en, last visited on 30.12.2010

Commission Decision C(2004)1313 of 7 April 2004 on General Implementing Provisions on the Procedures Governing the Engagement and the Use of Contract Staff at the Commission, as amended by Commission Decision C(2004)2862 of 27 February 2004, Commission Decision C(2004)4952 of 17 December 2004, and Commission Decision C(2005)5411 of 16 December 2005, available in the Register of Commission Documents, available at http://ec.europa.eu/transparency/regdoc/registre.cfm?CL=en, last visited on 30.12.2010

Commission Decision C(2006)2033 Laying Down Rules on the Secondment of National Experts to the Commission, C(2006)2033, 01.06.2006, available at http://ec.europa.eu/reform/human_resources/regime_end_2006_en.pdf, last visited on 30.12.2010

Commission Decision Concerning the Amendment of Decision C(2002) 1559 of 30 April 2002 Amended by Decision C(2003)406 of 31 January Laying Down Rules on the Secondment of National Experts to the Commission, C(2004) 577, 27.02.2004, available in the Register of Commission Documents, available at http://ec.europa.eu/transparency/regdoc/registre.cfm?CL=en, last visited on 30.12.2010

Commission Decision Laying Down Rules on the Secondment to the Commission of National Experts and National Expert in Professional Training, C(2008) 6866 final, 12.11.2008, available in the Register of Commission Documents, available at http://ec.europa.eu/transparency/regdoc/registre.cfm?CL=en, last visited on 30.12.2010

Commission Decision Laying Down the General Provisions for Implementing Article 45a of the Staff Regulations, C(2007) 5694, 20.11.2007, available in the Register of Commission Documents, available at http://ec.europa.eu/transparency/regdoc/registre.cfm?CL=en, last visited on 30.12.2010

Commission Decision of 28 April 1999 Establishing the European Anti-Fraud Office (OLAF), 1999/352/EC, OJ L 136, 31.05.1999, p. 20,

Commission Decision on a New Policy for the Engagement and Use of Temporary Agents, C(2004)1597, Informations Administratives No 74-2004 of 23.4.2004, 28.4.2004, available at http://europa.eu/epso/documents/decision_new_policy_for_at_en.pdf, last visited on 30.12.2010

Commission Decision on General Implementing Provisions Concerning the Conduct of Administrative Inquiries and Disciplinary Proceedings C(2004)1588, 28.04.2004, available in the Register of Commission Documents, available at http://ec.europa.eu/transparency/regdoc/registre.cfm?CL=en, last visited on 30.12.2010

Commission Decision on General Implementing Provisions Concerning the Criteria Applicable to Classification in Grade and Step in Appointment or Engagement, C(2004)1313, Informations Administratives No 55-2004 of 4.6.2004, 7.4.2004, available at http://europa.eu/epso/documents/decision_on_classification_en.pdf, last visited on 30.12.2010

Commission Decision on General Provisions for Implementing Article 43 of the Staff Regulations, 23.12.2004, available in the Register of Commission Documents, available at http://ec.europa.eu/transparency/regdoc/registre.cfm?CL=en, last visited on 30.12.2010

Commission Decision on General Provisions for Implementing Article 43 of the Staff Regulations, C(2008) 3026, 18.06.2008, available in the Register of Commission Documents, available at http://ec.europa.eu/transparency/regdoc/registre.cfm?CL=en, last visited on 30.12.2010

Commission Decision on General Provisions for Implementing Article 45 of the Staff Regulations, C(2008) 3028, 18.06.2008, available in the Register of Commission Documents, available at http://ec.europa.eu/transparency/regdoc/registre.cfm?CL=en, last visited on 30.12.2010

Commission Decision on General Provisions for Implementing Article 87(3) of the Conditions of Employment of Other Servants of the European Communities, C(2007)3714, 01.08.2007, available in the Register of Commission Documents available at http://ec.europa.eu/transparency/regdoc/registre.cfm?CL=en, last visited on 30.12.2010

Commission Decision on General Provisions for Implementing Article 87(3) of the Conditions of Employment of Other Servants of the European Communities, C(2008)3933, 29.07.2008, available in the Register of Commission Documents, available at http://ec.europa.eu/transparency/regdoc/registre.cfm?CL=en, last visited on 30.12.2010

Commission Decision on Middle Management Staff, Consolidated Version, C(2008) 5028/2, 09.09.2008, available in the Register of Commission Documents, available at http://ec.europa.eu/transparency/regdoc/registre.cfm?CL=en, last visited on 30.12.2010

Commission Decision on the Exercise of Powers Conferred by the Staff Regulations on the Appointing Authority and by the Conditions of Employment of Other Servants on the Authority Responsible for Concluding Contracts of Employment, C(2007)5730, 30.11.2007, available in the Register of Commission Documents, available at http://ec.europa.eu/transparency/regdoc/recherche.cfm?CL=en, last visited on 30.12.2010

Commission Decision on the Maximum Duration for the Recourse to Non-permanent Staff in the Commission Services, C(2004)1597, Informations Administratives No 75-2004 of 24.6.2004, 26.4.2004, available at http://europa.eu/epso/documents/regle_des_six_ans_en.pdf, last visited on 30.12.2010

Commission Decision, General Implementing Provisions on the Early Retirement of Officials and Temporary Agents without Reduction of Pension Rights, C(2004)1588 final/5, 28.04.2004, available in the Register of Commission Documents, available at http://ec.europa.eu/transparency/regdoc/registre.cfm?CL=en, last visited on 30.12.2010

Communication from Vice-President KINNOCK to the Commission, Guidelines on Mobility, SEC(2002)146, 05.02.2002, available in the Register of Commission Documents, available at http://ec.europa.eu/transparency/regdoc/rep/2/2002/EN/2-2002-146-EN-1-0.Pdf, last visited on 30.12.2010

Communication from Vice-President Kinnock to the Commission, How to Enhance Effective Application of the Whistleblowing Rules and Protection of Whistleblowers, SEC(2004)151/2, 06.02.2004, available in the Register of Commission Documents, available at http://ec.europa.eu/transparency/regdoc/registre.cfm?CL=en, last visited on 30.12.2010

Communication Relative au Recruitement de Fonctionnaires de la Commission des Nouveaux Etats Membres, Communication de M. Kinnock, C(2003)436/5, 14.02.2003, available at http://ec.europa.eu/reform/pdf/sec_2003_0436_en.pdf, last visited on 15.01.2008

Compilation Document on Senior Officials Policy, SEC(2004) 1352/2, 25.10.2004, available in the Register of Commission Documents, available at http://ec.europa.eu/transparency/regdoc/registre.cfm?CL=en, last visited on 30.12.2010

Decision Amending the General Implementing Provisions on the Early Retirement of Officials and Temporary Agents without Reduction of Pension Rights C(2004) 1588 of 28 April 2004, 10.08.2006, available in the Register of Commission Documents, available at http://ec.europa.eu/transparency/regdoc/registre.cfm?CL=en, last visited on 30.12.2010

General Rules Governing Open Competitions, 2009/C 47 A/01, 26.02.2009, available at http://eur-lex.europa.eu/LexUriServ/LexUriServ.do?uri=OJ:C:2009:047A:0001:0017:EN:PDF, last visited on 30.12.2010

Framework Rules Laying Down the Conditions of Employment of Local Staff of the Commission of the European Communities Serving in Non-member Countries, 21.11.1989, available in the Register of Commission Documents, available at http://ec.europa.eu/transparency/regdoc/registre.cfm?CL=en, last visited on 30.12.2010

Notice of Internal Competition, Heads of Unit AD12 (COM/INT/EU27/09/AD12), No 29-2009, 20.04.2009, available at http://www.cc.cec/guide/publications/infoadm/2009/ia09029_en.html, last visited on 07.05.2010

Notice of Vacancy, Seconded National Experts, available at http://www.mof.gov.cy/mof/papd/papd.nsf/all/C5D7B9006BE32327C225770E0038D474/$file/EN%20rectificatif%2029.pdf?openelement, last visited on 30.12.2010

Promotion of Commission Senior Officials, Principles and Procedure, SEC(2007)605, 04.05.2007, available in the Register of Commission Documents, available at http://ec.europa.eu/transparency/regdoc/registre.cfm?CL=en, last visited on 30.12.2010

Proposal for a Council Regulation Amending the Staff Regulations of Officials and the Conditions of Employment of Other Servants of the European Communities, COM(2002) 213 final 24.04.2002, OJ C 291E , 26.11.2002, p. 33-135,

Recruitment of Senior Managers from the New Member States - Implementation Measures, Communication from Vice-President Kinnock in Agreement with the President, SEC(2004)0252, available at http://ec.europa.eu/reform/pdf/sec_2004_0252_en.pdf, last visited on 15.01.2008

Rules Governing the Composition of the Members' Cabinets and the Spokespersons, SEC(2008) 2602, 08.10.2008, available in the Register of Commission Documents, available at http://ec.europa.eu/transparency/regdoc/registre.cfm?CL=en, last visited on 30.12.2010

Rules Governing the Official Traineeships Scheme of the European Commission, Commission Decision C(2005)458, 02.03.2005, available at http://ec.europa.eu/stages/rules/rules_en.pdf, last visited on 30.12.2010

Rules of Procedure of the Commission, C(2000) 3614, 08.12.2010, OJ L 308, 08.12.2000, p. 26, as amended by Commission Decision 2010/138/EU of 24.02.2010, OJ L 55, 05.03.2010, p. 60,

Rules on Special Advisers to the Commission, C(2007) 6655, 19.12.2007, available at http://ec.europa.eu/civil_service/about/who/sa_en.htm, last visited on 30.12.2010

Selection of Temporary Staff for the Directorate-General Regional Policy, Vacancy Announcement, COM/TA/REGIO/10/01, available at http://ec.europa.eu/dgs/regional_policy/communication/doc/vacancy_1001_en.pdf, last visited on 30.12.2010

REPORTS

An Administration at the Service of Half a Billion Europeans, Staff Reforms at the European Commission, State of Play: Spring 2002, available at http://ec.europa.eu/reform/2002/documents/staff_reform_2002_en.pdf, last visited on 30.12.2010

First Report on Allegations Regarding Fraud, Mismanagement and Nepotism in the European Commission, 15.03.1999, available at http://www.europarl.europa.eu/experts/pdf/reporten.pdf, last visited on 30.12.2010

Human Resources Report 2009, Towards a Qualitative and Forward-looking Management of Staff and Competencies Through the Professionalisation of Human Resources Management, unpublished, acquired at the Directorate-General for Human Resources and Security of the European Commission

Rapport Ressources Humaines 2008, Vers une Gestion Qualitative et Prévisionnelle des Effectifs et des Compétences Grâce à une Professionnalisation de la Gestion des Ressources Humaines, unpublished, acquired at the Directorate-General for Human Resources and Security of the European Commission

*Reforming the Commission - A White Paper - Part I, /*COM/2000/0200 final*/*, 01.03.2000, available at http://eur-lex.europa.eu/LexUriServ/LexUriServ.do?uri=CELEX:52000DC0200(01):EN:HTML, last visited on 30.12.2010

*Reforming the Commission - A White Paper - Part II - Action Plan, /*COM/2000/0200 final*/*, 1.3.2000, available at http://eur-lex.europa.eu/LexUriServ/LexUriServ.do?uri=CELEX:52000DC0200(02):EN:HTML, last visited on 30.12.2010

Report from the Commission to the European Parliament and the Council - Follow-up Report on the European Parliament Resolution on 2000 Discharge for the General Budget, COM/2002/0696 final, 10.12.2002, available at http://eur-lex.europa.eu/LexUriServ/LexUriServ.do?uri=COM:2002:0696:FIN:EN:PDF, last visited on 30.12.2010

Second Report on Reform of the Commission, Analysis of Current practice and proposals for Tackling Mismanagement, Irregularities and Fraud, Volume I, 10.09.1999, available at http://www.europarl.europa.eu/experts/pdf/rep2-1en.pdf, last visited on 30.12.2010

Second Report on Reform of the Commission, Analysis of Current Practice and Proposals for Tackling Mismanagement, Irregularities and Fraud, Volume II, 10.09.1999, available at http://www.europarl.europa.eu/experts/pdf/rep2-2en.pdf, last visited on 30.12.2010

PRESS RELEASES

Better, Faster, Stronger: Launch of New Selection Procedure for EU Officials, Press Release, IP/10/262, 11.03.2010, available at http://europa.eu/rapid/pressReleasesAction.do?reference=IP/10/262&format=HTML&aged=1&language=EN&guiLanguage=en, last visited on 30.12.2010

Commission Adopts Mobility Package for Directors-General, Directors and Principal Advisers, Press Release, IP/06/1610, 22.11.2006, available at http://europa.eu/rapid/

pressReleasesAction.do?reference=IP/06/1610&format=HTML&aged=0&language=EN&guiLanguage=en, last visited on 30.12.2010

Commission Reshuffles Senior Managers, Press Release, IP/08/1881, 03.12.2008, available at http://europa.eu/rapid/pressReleasesAction.do?reference=IP/08/1881&format=HTML&aged=0&language=EN&guiLanguage=en, last visited on 30.12.2010

Commissioners Meet Prodi's Targets for Better Gender Balance and Multinational Mix in Cabinets, Press Release, IP/99/703, 28.09.1999, available at http://europa.eu/rapid/pressReleasesAction.do?reference=IP/99/703&format=HTML&aged=0&language=EN&guiLanuage=en, last visited on 30.12.2010

EEAS: Joint Press Statement by Parliament Rapporteurs, Press Release, 20101019IPR88330, 19.10.2010, available at http://www.europarl.europa.eu/pdfs/news/expert/infopress/20101019IPR88330/20101019IPR88330_en.pdf, last visited on 30.12.2010

EEAS: Staff Rules to Ensure Geographical and Gender Balance, Press Release, 20101018IPR87689, 18.10.2010, available at http://www.europarl.europa.eu/pdfs/news/expert/infopress/20101018IPR87689/20101018IPR87689_en.pdf, last visited on 30.12.2010

EU Diplomatic Service: Accountability and Balanced Recruitment, Press Release, 20101020IPR88408, 20.10.2010, available at http://www.europarl.europa.eu/pdfs/news/expert/infopress/20101020IPR88408/20101020IPR88408_en.pdf, last visited on 30.12.2010

European Commission Announces Next Steps in Implementing New Senior Staff Policy, Press Release, IP/02/124, 23.01.2002, available at http://europa.eu/rapid/pressReleasesAction.do?reference=IP/02/124&format=HTML&aged=0&language=EN&guiLanguage=en, last visited on 30.12.2010

Mr. Niel Kinnock, Vice President of the European Commission, Press Statement, Brussels, 29 September 1999, SPEECH/99/118, 29.09.1999, available at http://europa.eu/rapid/pressReleasesAction.do?reference=SPEECH/99/118&format=HTML&aged=1&language=EN&guiLanguage=en, last visited on 30.12.2010

New Faces in Top Management Posts: Commission Reshuffles its Directors General and Deputy Directors General Teams, Press Release, IP/05/1399, 09.11.2005, available at http://europa.eu/rapid/pressReleasesAction.do?reference=IP/05/1399&format=HTML&aged=1&language=EN&guiLanguage=fr, last visited on 30.12.2010

CASE LAW

Adam P.H. Blomefield v. Commission of the European Communities, Case 190/82, ECR [1983], p. 3981

Afari v. European Central Bank, Case T-11/03, ECR-SC [2004], p. I-A-65, II-267

Alicia Speybrouck v. European Parliament, Case T-45/90, ECR [1992], p. II-33

Alain de Briey v. Commission of the European Communities, Case 25/80, ECR [1981], p. 637

Alberto Campolongo v. High Authority of the European Coal and Steel Community, Joined cases 27-59 and 39-59, ECR [1960], English special edition, p. 391

Alberto Toronjo Benitez v. Commission of the European Communities, Case F-33/07, available at http://curia.europa.eu/jurisp/cgi-bin/form.pl?lang=en&Submit=Rechercher&alldocs=alldocs&docj=docj&docop=docop&docor=docor&docjo=docjo&numaff=F-33/07&datefs=&datefe=&nomusuel=&domaine=&mots=&resmax=100, last visited on 30.12.2010

Alessandro Albani and others v. Commission of the European Communities, Case T-35/89, ECR [1990], p. II-395

Ana Fernandes Ferreira de Freitas v Commission of the European Communities, Case T-2/90, ECR [1991], p. II-103

André Bonnet v. Court of Justice of the European Communities, Case T-406/04, ECR-SC [2006], p. I-A-2-213, II-A-2-1097

Andre Huybrechts v. Commission of the European Communities, Case 306/85, ECR [1987], p. 629

André Huybrechts v. Commission of the European Communities, Case 21/68, ECR [1969], p. 85

André Schertzer v. European Parliament, Case 25/68, ECR [1977], p. 1729

Andreas Reinarz v. Commission of the European Communities, Case 17/68, ECR [1969], p. 61

Andreas Reinarz v. Commission of the European Communities, Case 55/70, ECR [1971], p. 379

Andrée Anselme, née Heirwegh and Roger Constant v. Commission of the European Communities, Case 255/78, ECR [1979], p. 2323

Androniki Vlachou v. Court of Auditors of the European Communities, Case 135/87, ECR [1988], p. 2901

Anna-Maria Campogrande and others v. Commission of the European Communities, Joined cases 112, 144 and 145-73, ECR [1974], p. 957

Anna Bonino v. Commission of the European Communities, Case 233/85, ECR [1987], p. 739

Anna Guglielmi v. European Parliament, Case 268/80, ECR [1981], p. 2295

Antonio Giannini v. Commission of the European Communities, Case 265/81, ECR [1982], p. 3865

Antonio Marcato v. Commission of the European Communities, Case 44-71, ECR [1972], p. 427

Aristides Vlachos v. Court of Justice of the European Communities, Joined cases 20 and 21/83, ECR [1984], p. 4149

Armelle Detti v. Court of Justice of the European Communities, Case 144/82, ECR [1983], p. 2421

August Josef Van Eick v. Commission of the European Communities, Case 35/67, ECR [1968], p. 329

August Joseph van Eick v. Commission of the European Communities, Case 13/69, ECR [1970], p. 3

Augusta Agneessens and others v. Commission of the European Communities, Case 122/77, ECR [1978], p. 2085

Bernard Connolly v. Commission of the European Communities, C-273/99 P, ECR [2001], p. I-1575

Bernard Michel v. European Parliament, Case 195/80, ECR [1981], p. 2861

Bernhard Schloh v. Council of the European Communities, Case 85/82, ECR [1983], p. 2105

Berthold Küster v. European Parliament, Case 22/75, ECR [1975], p. 1267

Berthold Küster v. European Parliament, Case 123/75, ECR [1976], p. 1701

Betriebsrat der Vertretung der Europäischen Kommission in Österreich v. European Communities, Commission of the European Communities, Case C-165/01, ECR [2003], p. I-07683, last visited on 08.09.2010

Brigitte Bataille and others v. European Parliament, Case T-56/89, ECR [1990], p. II-597

Calvin E. Williams v. Court of Auditors of the European Communities, Case T-33/91, ECR [1992], p. II-2499

Canzio Almini v. Commission of the European Communities, Case 19/70, ECR [1971], p. 623

Carmen Jiménez v. Office for Harmonisation in the Internal Market (Trade Marks and Designs) (OHIM), Case T-200/97, ECR-SC [1999], p. I-A-19; II-73

Cathy Sapara v. Eurojust, Case F-61/06, available at http://eur-lex.europa.eu/LexUriServ/LexUriServ.do?uri=CELEX:62006W0061:EN:HTML, last visited on 30.12.2010

Chantal Hectors v. European Parliament, Case T-181/01, ECR-SC [2003[, p. I-A-19, II-103

Charlotte von Bonkewitz-Lindner v. European Parliament, Case T-33/90, ECR [1991], p. II-1251

Cesare Alfieri v. European Parliament, Case 35/64, ECR [1965], p. 261

Cesare Alfieri v. European Parliament, Case 3/66, ECR [1966], p. 437

Christiane Hoffmann v. Commission of the European Communities, Case 280/81, ECR [1983], p. 889

Claude Lassalle v. European Parliament, Case 15/63, ECR [1964], p. 36

Claudette van Belle v. Council of the European Communities, Case 176/73, ECR [1974], p. 1361

Claudia Delloye and others v. Commission of the European Communities, Case T-44/92, ECR [1993], p. II-221

Constantin Verros v. European Parliament, Case 306/81, ECR [1983], p. 1755

Cornelis Henrick Fabius v. Commission of the European Communities, Case 39/83, ECR [1984], p. 627

Cornelis Volger v. European Parliament, Case T-52/90, ECR [1992], p. II-121

Daniele Grassi v. Council of the European Communities, Case 188/73, ECR [1974], p. 1099

Daniele Grassi v. Council of the European Communities, Joined cases 6/79 and 97/79, ECR [1980], p. 2141

David Lipman v. Commission of the European Communities, Case 143/82, ECR [1983], p. 1301

Detlef Brüggemann v. Economic and Social Committee of the European Communities, Case 248/86, ECR [1987], p. 3946

Dierk Booss and Robert Caspar Fischer v. Commission of the European Communities, Case T-58/91, ECR [1993], p. II-147

Dietrich Kurrer v. Council of the European Communities, Case 33/67, ECR [1968], p. 127

Dimitrios Coussios v. Commission of the European Communities, Case C-119/94 P, ECR [1995], p. I-1439,

Domenico Morina v. European Parliament, Case 11/65, ECR [1965], p. 1017

Donal Gordon v. Commission of the European Communities, Case C-198/07 P, ECR [2008], p. I-10701

Dorothea Kobor, née Sonne, v. Commission of the European Communities, Case 112/78, ECR [1979], p. 1573

Edward Patrick Latham v. Commission of the European Communities, Case T-63/89, ECR [1991], p. II-19

Enrico Angelini v. Commission of the European Communities, Case 131/82, ECR [1983], p. 2801

Enrico M. Salerno, Xavier Authié and Giuseppe Massangioli v. Commission of the European Communities, Joined cases 4, 19 and 28/78, ECR [1978], p. 2403

Eoghan O'Hannrachain v. European Parliament, Case C-121/01 P, ECR [2003], p. I-05539

Erik Dan Frederiksen v. European Parliament, Case T-169/89, ECR [1991], p. II-1403

Erik van der Stijl and Geoffrey Cullington v. Commission of the European Communities, Joined cases 341/85, 251, 258, 259, 262 and 266/86, 222 and 232/87, ECR [1989], p. 511

Erik van der Stijl v. Commission of the European Communities, Case 128/84, ECR [1985], p. 3281

Ernest Ley v. Commission of the EEC, Joined cases 12/64 and 29/64, ECR [1965], p. 10

European Agency for Reconstruction (EAR) v. Georgios Karatzoglou, Case C-213/06 P, ECR [2007], p. I-6733

European Parliament v. Pierre Richard, Case C-174/99 P, ECR [2000], p. I-6189

European Training Foundation v. Landgren, Case T-404/06 P, ECR [2009], p. II-2841

Eva Rittweger v. Commission of the European Communities, Case 21/70, ECR [1971], p. 7

F v. Commission of the European Communities, Case 228/83, ECR [1985], p. 275

Fausta Deshormes, née La Valle v. Commission of the European Communities, Case 17/78, ECR [1979], p. 189

Fernando Carbajo Ferrero v. European Parliament, Case C-304/97 P, ECR [1999], p. I-1749

Francesco Bonu v. Council of the European Communities, Case 89/79, ECR [1980], p. 553

Francine Deboeck v. Commission of the European Communities, Case 90/74, ECR [1975], p. 1123

Franco Colussi v. European Parliament, Case 298/81, ECR [1983], p. 1131

Franco Peco v. Commission of the European Communities, Case 36/69, ECR [1970], p. 361

Franco Vecchioli v. Commission of the European Communities, Case 101/79, ECR [1980], p. 3069

Fred Pfloeschner v. Commission of the European Communities, Case T-135/89, ECR [1990], p. II-153

Friedrich Asmussen and others v. Commission and Council of the European Communities, Case 50/74, ECR [1975], p. 1003

Fritz-August Bode v. Commission of the European Communities, Joined cases 45 and 49-70, ECR [1971], p. 465

G. B. C. Echternach and A. Moritz v. Minister van Onderwijs en Wetenschappen, Joined cases 389/87 and 390/87, ECR [1989], p. 723

Georges Caravelis v. European Parliament, Case T-182/99, ECR [2001], p. II-1313, ECR-SC [2001], IA-113, II-523

Georges Caravelis v. European Parliament, Case T-197/02, ECR-SC [2004], p. I-A-33, II-133

Georges Kolivas v. Commission of the European Communities, Case 40/86, ECR [1987], p. 2643

Georges Marcopoulos v. Court of Justice of the European Communities, Joined cases T-32/89 and T-39/89, ECR [1990], p. II-281

Georges Tzoanos v. Commission of the European Communities, C-191/98 P, ECR [1999], p. I-8223

Georgios Karatzoglou v. European Agency for Reconstruction, Case T-471/04, ECR-SC [2006], p. I-A-2-35, II-A-2-157

Gertrud Rauch v. Commission of the EEC, Case 16/64, ECR [1965], p. 135

Giovanni Barbi v. Commission of the European Communities, Case T-73/89, ECR [1990], p. II-619

Giovanni Barbi v. Commission of the European Communities, Case T-68/91, ECR [1992], p. II-2127

Gijsbertus van Reenen v. Commission of the European Communities, Case 189/73, ECR [1975], p. 445

Giovanni Sergio and others v. Commission of the European Communities, Joined cases 64, 71 to 73 and 78/86, ECR [1988], p. 1399

Giuliano Marenco and others v. Commission of the European Communities, Joined cases 81 to 88/74, ECR [1975], p. 1247

Gloria Pérez-Mínguez Casariego v. Commission of the European Communities, Case T-1/90, ECR [1991], p. II-143

Gregoris Evangelos Kalavros v. Court of Justice of the European Communities, Joined cases T-160/89 and T-161/89, ECR [1990], p. II-871

Guido van Hecken v. Economic and Social Committee, Case T-158/89, ECR [1991], p. II-1341

Harald List v. Commission of the European Communities, Case 263/81, ECR [1983], p. 103

Hartmut Schwiering v. Court of Auditors of the European Communities, Case 142/85, ECR [1986], p. 3177

Heinz-Jörg Moritz v. Commission of the European Communities, Case T-20/89, ECR [1990], p. II-769

Helen Mc Avoy v. European Parliament, Case T-45/91, ECR [1993], p. II-83

Hélène Martin v. Commission of the European Communities, Case 24/78, ECR [1979], p. 603

Helmut Müllers v. Economic and Social Committee of the European Communities, Case C-81/88, ECR [1990], p. I-249

Henri Brasseur v. European Parliament, Case 88/71, ECR [1972], p. 499

Henri Labeyrie v. Commission of the European Communities, Case 16/67, ECR [1968], p. 293

Henri Maurissen v. Court of Auditors of the European Communities, Case 417/85, ECR [1987], p. 551

Hermanus Adams and others v. Commission of the European Communities, Case 294/84, ECR [1986], p. 977

Hugues Desmedt v. Commission of the European Communities, Case 105/80, ECR [1981], p. 1701

Ingfried Hochbaum v. Commission of the European Communities, Case T-38/89, ECR [1990], p. II-43

Iñigo Valverde Mordt v. Court of Justice of the European Communities, Case T-156/89, ECR [1991], p. II-407

J. Mulcahy v. Commission of the European Communities, Case 110/77, ECR [1978], p. 1287

Jack Hanning v. European Parliament, Case T-37/89, ECR [1990], p. II-463

Jan Amesz and others v. Commission of the European Communities, Case 543/79, ECR [1982], p. 4425

Jan Eliza de Wind v. Commission of the European Communities, Case 62/75, ECR [1976], p. 1167

Jacques Hinderyckx v. Council of the European Union, Case F-57/06, available at http://curia.europa.eu/jurisp/cgi-bin/form.pl?lang=en&Submit=Rechercher&alldocs=alldocs&docj=docj&docop=docop&docor=docor&docjo=docjo&numaff=F-57/06&datefs=&datefe=&nomusuel=&domaine=&mots=&resmax=100, last visited on 30.12.2010

Jean-Claude Renaud v. Commission of the European Communities, Case 148/82, ECR [1983], p. 2823

Jean-Jacques Geist v. Commission of the European Communities, Case 61/76, ECR [1977], p. 1419

Jean-Louis Burban v. European Parliament, Case T-133/89, ECR [1990], p. II-245

Jean-Louis Burban v. European Parliament, Case C-255/90 P, ECR [1992], p. I-2253

Jean-Louis Chomel v. Commission of the European Communities, Case T-123/89, ECR [1990], p. II-131

Jean-Paul Francois v. Commission of the European Communities, Case T-307/01, ECR [2004], p. II-1669, ECR-SC [2004], p. I-A-183, II-823

Jeannette Fux v. Commission of the European Communities, Case 26/68, ECR [1969], p. 145

John Szemerey v. Commission of the European Communities, Case 178/78, ECR [1979], p. 2855

José Luis Buendía Sierra v. Commission of the European Communities, Case T-311/04, ECR [2006], p. II-4137, ECR-SC [2006], p. I-A-2-221, II-A-2-1135

Jozef Oslizlok v. Commission of the European Communities, Case 34/77, ECR [1978], p. 1099

Juan Jaenicke Cendoya v. Commission of the European Communities, Case 108/88, ECR [1989], p. 2711

Kuno Ditterich v. Commission of the European Communities, Case 207/81, ECR [1983], p. 1359

Kurt Weighardt v. Commission of the EAEC, Case 11/64, ECR [1965], p. 285

Lars Bo Rasmussen v. Commission of the European Communities, Case 173/84, ECR [1986], p. 197

Lars Bo Rasmussen v. Commission of the European Communities, Case C-398/93 P, ECR [1994], p. I-4043

Luc Dejaiffe v. Office for Harmonization of the Internal Market (OHIM), Case T-223/99, ECR [2000], p. I-A-277, II-1267

Luigi de Pascale v. Commission of the European Economic Community, Case 97/63, European Court Reports, English special edition, p. 515

M. Goffredo Raponi v. Commission of the European Economic Community, Case 27/63, European Court Reports, English special edition, p. 129

M. Maurice Alvis v. Council of the European Economic Community, Case 32/62, ECR [1963], p. 49

M. v. Council of the European Communities, Joined cases 175/86 and 209/86, ECR [1988], p. 1891

Magdalena Allgayer née Parzinger v. European Parliament, Case 74/77, ECR [1978], p. 977

Malcolm Bevan v. Commission of the European Communities, Case 140/87, ECR [1989], p. 701

Manlio Serio v. Commission of the EAEC, Case 62/65, ECR [1966], p. 561

Manlio Serio v. Commission of the European Communities, Case 115/73, ECR [1974], p. 341

Mareile Tziovas, née Aldinger, and Gabriella Schettini, née Virgili, v. European Parliament, Joined cases 23 and 24/87, ECR [1988], p. 4395

María del Carmen de la Cruz v. European Agency for Safety and Health at Work (OSHA), Case F-32/06, available at http://curia.europa.eu/jurisp/cgi-bin/form.pl?lang=en&Submit=Rechercher&alldocs=alldocs&docj=docj&docop=docop&docor=docor&docjo=docjo&numaff=F-32/06&datefs=&datefe=&nomusuel=&domaine=&mots=&resmax=100, last visited on 30.12.2010

Maria Grazia Celant and others v. Commission of the European Communities, Joined cases 118 to 123/82, ECR [1983], p. 2995

Marie Hélène Ruske v. Commission of the European Communities, Case 67/81, ECR [1982], p. 661

Mario Costacurta v. Commission of the European Communities, Case 31/75, ECR [1975], p. 1563

Mario Paulo Tenreiro v. Commission of the European Communities, Case T-216/03, ECR-SC [2004], p. I-A-245, II-1087

Martial Ott and others v. Commission of the European Communities, Case T-250/06 P, available at http://curia.europa.eu/jurisp/cgi-bin/form.pl?lang=en&Submit=Rechercher&alldocs=alldocs&docj=docj&docop=docop&docor=docor&docjo=docjo&numaff=T-250/06%20P&datefs=&datefe=&nomusuel=&domaine=&mots=&resmax=100,, last visited on 30.12.2010

Mathilde Becker and Josyane Starquit v. European Parliament, Case C-41/88 and C-178/88, ECR [1989], p. 3807

Max Gutmann v. Commission of the EAEC, Joined cases 18 and 35/65, ECR [1966], p. 103

Max Gutmann v. Commission of the EAEC, Joined cases 18 and 35/5, ECR [1967], p. 61

Mediavilla and others v. Commission of the European Communities and Council of the European Union, Case C-443/07 P, ECR [2008], p. I-10945

Miguel Vicente-Nuñez v. Commission of the European Communities, Case T-294/02, ECR-SC [2004], p. I-A-283, II-1279

Mrs X. v. Commission of the European Communities, Joined cases T-89/91, T-21/92 and T-89/92, ECR [1993], p. II-1235

Nelly Kohler v. Court of Auditors of the European Communities, Joined cases 316/82 and 40/83, ECR [1984], p. 641

Neophytos Neophytou v. Commission of the European Communities, Case F-22/05, ECR-SC [2006], p. I-A-1-159, II-A-1-617

Norbert Schmitt v. European Agency for Reconstruction (EAR), Case T-175/03, ECR-SC [2004], p. I-A-211, II-939

Norman Pyres v. Commission of the European Communities, Case T-7/01, ECR-SC [2003], p. IA-37, II-239

Onno Plug v. Commission of the European Communities, Case 191/81, ECR [1982], p. 4229

Oreste Montalto v. Council of the European Union, Case T-116/03, ECR-SC [2004], p. I-A-339, II-1541

Pachtitis v. Commission, Case F-35/08, available at http://curia.europa.eu/jurisp/cgi-bin/form.pl?lang=en&Submit=Rechercher&alldocs=alldocs&docj=docj&docop=docop&docor=docor&docjo=docjo&numaff=F-35/08&datefs=&datefe=&nomusuel=&domaine=&mots=&resmax=100, last visited on 30.12.2010, available at http://curia.europa.eu/jurisp/cgi-bin/form.pl?lang=en&Submit=Rechercher&alldocs=alldocs&docj=docj&docop=docop&docor=docor&docjo=docjo&numaff=F-35/08&datefs=&datefe=&nomusuel=&domaine=&mots=&resmax=100, last visited on 30.12.2010

Patricia Belardinelli and others v. Court of Justice of the European Communities, Case 225/87, ECR [1989], p. 2353

Peter John Krier Tither v Commission of the European Communities, Case 175/80, ECR [1981], p. 2345,

Petros Kotzonis v. Economic and Social Committee, Case T-586/93, ECR [1995], p. II-665, ECR-SC [1995], p. I-A-61, II-203

Pia Landgren v. European Training Foundation, Case F-1/05, ECR-SC [2006], p. I-A-1-123, II-A-1-459

Pierre Gratreau v. Commission of the European Communities, Joint cases 156/79 and 51/80, ECR [1980], p. 3943

Pilar Angé Serrano and others v. European Parliament C-496/08 P, available at http://eur-lex.europa.eu/LexUriServ/LexUriServ.do?uri=CELEX:62008J0496:EN:HTML, last visited on 30.12.2010

Prodromos Mavridis v. Commission of the European Communities, Case T-97/02, ECR-SC [2004], p. I-A-9, II-45

R v. Commission of the European Communities, Joined cases 255 and 256/83, ECR [1985], p. 2473

Ralph Loebisch v. Council of the European Communities, Case 14/79, ECR [1979], p. 3679

Rainer Wenning v. European Police Office (Europol), Case F-114/07, available at http://curia.europa.eu/jurisp/cgi-bin/form.pl?lang=en&Submit=Rechercher&alldocs=alldocs&docj=docj&docop=docop&docor=docor&docjo=docjo&numaff=F-114/07&datefs=&datefe=&nomusuel=&domaine=&mots=&resmax=100, last visited on 30.12.2010

Richard Hamill v. Commission of the European Communities, Case 180/87, ECR [1988], p. 6141

Richard Schönherr v.Richard Schönherr v Economic and Social Committee Economic and Social Committee, Case T-25/90, ECR [1992], p. II-63

Risto Suvikas v. Council of the European Union, Case F-6/07, available at http://curia.europa.eu/jurisp/cgi-bin/form.pl?lang=en&Submit=Rechercher&alldocs=alldocs&docj=docj&docop=docop&docor=docor&docjo=docjo&numaff=F-6/07&datefs=&datefe=&nomusuel=&domaine=&mots=&resmax=100, last visited on 30.12.2010

Robert Adam and others v Commission of the European Communities, Joined cases 80 to 83/81 and 182 to 185/82, ECR [1984], p. 3411

Robert de Greef v. Commission of the European Communities, Case 46/72, ECR [1973], p. 543

Roberto Vitari v. European Training Foundation, Case C-126/99, ECR [2000], p. I-09425

Rudolf Misset v. Council of the European Communities, Case 319/85, ECR [1988], p. 1861

Rudy Verzyck v. Commission of the European Communities, Case 225/82, ECR [1983], p. 1991

Salvatore Belfiore v. Commission of the European Communities, Case 108/79, ECR [1980], p. 1769

Salvatore Ragusa v. Commission of the European Communities, Case 282/81, ECR [1983], p. 1245

Santo Picciolo v. European Parliament, Case 111/83, ECR [1984], p. 2323

Sorani and others v. Commission of the European Communities, Case 293/84, ECR [1986], p. 967

Stefano Cocchi et Evi Hainz v. Commission of the European Communities, Case T-330/00 and T-114/01, ECR-SC [2002], p. I-A-193, II-987

Sven-Ole Mogensen and others v. Commission of the European Communities, Case 10/82, ECR [1983], p. 2397

Thérèse Marie-Louise Vandevyvere v. European Parliament, Case 23/64, ECR [1965], p. 157

Tony Robinson v. European Parliament, Case T-328/01, ECR-SC [2004], p. I-A-5, II-23

V v. European Parliament, Case C-18/91 P, ECR [1992], p. I-3997

V. R. v. Commission of the European Communities, Case 75/85, ECR [1986], p. 2775

Vassilios Kotsonis v. Council of the European Communities, Case 246/84, ECR [1986], p. 3989

Vassilis Mavridis v. European Parliament, Case 289/81, ECR [1983], p. 1731

Vincenzo Gallone v. Council of the European Communities, Case T-132/89, ECR [1990], p. II-549

Vincenzo Le Voci v. Council of the European Union, Case T-371/03, ECR-SC [2005], p. I-A-209, II-957

Vivien Prais v. Council of the European Communities, Case 130/75, ECR [1976], p. 1589

Willy Orlandi v. Commission of the European Communities, Case 117/78, ECR [1979], p. 1613

Willy Seghers v. Council of the European Communities, Case T-69/92, ECR [1993], p. II-651

Wolfdietrich Zoder v. European Parliament, Case T-30/90, ECR [1991], p. II-207,

X v. European Central Bank, Case T-333/99, ECR [2001], p. II-3021, ECR-SC p. I-A-199, II-921

Xavier Authié v. Commission of the European Communities, Case 34/80, ECR [1981], p. 665

Yves Franchet et Daniel Byk v. Commission of the European Communities, Case T-48/05, ECR [2008], p. II-1585

Z v. European Parliament, C-270/99 P, ECR [2001], p. I-9197

MISCELLANEOUS

Distribution of Officials and Temporary Agents by Directorate General and Nationality (All Budgets), 01.02.2010, available at http://ec.europa.eu/civil_service/docs/bs_dg_nat_en.pdf, last visited on 05.03.2010

Distribution of Officials and Temporary Agents by Genders, Nationalities, Function Groups and Grades (All Budgets), 01.02.2010, available at http://ec.europa.eu/civil_service/docs/bs_sexe_nat_grade_en.pdf, last visited on 05.03.2010

Distribution of Staff by Statutory Links and DGs, 01.03.2010, available at http://ec.europa.eu/civil service/docs/bs_fonct_ext_dg_en.pdf, last visited on 05.03.2010

Guide to Open Competitions, 2010/C 184 A/01, 08.07.2010, available at http://eur-lex.europa.eu/LexUriServ/LexUriServ.do?uri=OJ:C:2010:184A:0001:0014:EN:PDF, last visited on 30.12.2010

New Admінission Tests - The Re-designed Computer-Based Testing (CBT), 29.01.2010, available at http://europa.eu/discover/news/news15_en.htm, last visited on 10.03.2010

New Selection Procedures - Your Questions Answered, 20.01.2010, available at http://europa.eu/discover/news/news14_en.htm, last visited on 10.03.2010

Reforming the Commission, An Administration at the Service of Half a Billion Europeans, 15.10.2010, 22.05.2006, available at http://ec.europa.eu/reform/2002/index_en.htm

Reserve Lists: Administrators (A-A-AD)*, 2010, available at http://europa.eu/epso/success/list/admin/index_en.htm, last visited on 10.03.2010

Selection Procedure, 2010, available at http://europa.eu/epso/discover/selection_proced/selection/index_en.htm, last visited on 10.03.2010

The Slovak Voice in Brussels, How to Make It Louder and More Coherent, Report of the Slovak Governance Institute, July 2007, available at http://www.governance.sk/assets/files/publikacie/slovak%20voice%20in%20brussels%20web.pdf, last visited on 30.12.2010

Union Syndicale, *Activity Report of the Executive Committee for the 2004-2007 Mandate*, 16.04.2007, available at http://www.unionsyndicale.eu/usb/usb_070923_04.pdf, last visited on 30.12.2010

Union Syndicale, *Assessment and Careers "From VERY BAD to EVEN WORSE"*, 08-09, 23.03.2009, available at http://www.unionsyndicale.eu/public/t_090420_03.pdf, last visited on 30.12.2010

Union Syndicale, *The Career ReDucer Has Arrived*, 16-09, 26.05.2009, available at http://www.unionsyndicale.eu/public/t_090601_08.pdf, last visited on 30.12.2010

Union Syndicale, *Demolition of the European Public Service: After the Newly Imposed REC, We Are Now Faced with the "Modernisation" of Human Resources*, 18.07.2008, available at http://www.uslux.eu/articles.php?lng=en&pg=374, last visited on 30.12.2010

MISCELLANEOUS DOCUMENTS OF OTHER INTERNATIONAL ORGANIZATIONS

FAO Reform: A Vision for the Twenty-first Century, C 2005/INF/19, October 2005, available at ftp://ftp.fao.org/docrep/fao/meeting/009/j6285e.pdf, last visited on 30.12.2010

International Labour Office, Staff Regulations, January 2010, available at http://www.ilo.org/public/english/bureau/pers/staffreg/downloads/staff_reg_2010-compilation-en.pdf, last visited on 30.12.2010

Peace Treaty of Versailles, 28.06.1919 available in the The World War I Document Archive, available at http://net.lib.byu.edu/~rdh7/wwi/versailles.html, last visited on 30.12.2010

Report of the Committee of Enquiry into the Organization of the Secretariat, International Labour Office and the Registry of the Permanent Court of International Justice (Committee of Thirteen), A.16.1930, 11th Assembly, 4th Committee, Annex 8, 28.06.1930

The Future of the World Trade Organization, Addressing Institutional Challenges in the New Millenium, Report by the Consultative Board to the Director-General Supachai Panitchpakdi, 2004, available at http://www.wto.org/english/thewto_e/10anniv_e/future_wto_e.pdf, last visited on 30.12.2010

CURRICULUM VITAE

Iveta Alexovičová was born on 27 November 1973, in Bardejov, Slovakia. She obtained her Master degree in law from Comenius University in Bratislava, Slovakia in 1997, following a five-year full-time study. In 2004, Iveta graduated *cum laude* from the postgraduate Master programme in Comparative, European and International Law *Magister Iuris Communis* at Maastricht University. In 2006, following her thesis defence, Iveta was granted the postgraduate academic title JUDr. (doctor of law) by the Charle's University in Prague, Czech Republic.

Since 2011, Iveta Alexovičová works as a lecturer at the Department of International and European Law, Faculty of Law, Maastricht University, teaching several courses on international trade law, public international law and European law. In addition, Iveta is a member of the international faculty of the China – EU School of Law in Beijing, China. She is also a fellow of the Institute for Globalisation and International Regulation and a member of the *Ius Commune* Research School. Iveta's previous working experience includes public civil service in Slovakia and legal consultancy in the private sector, first in Slovakia and later in the Netherlands (1997-2003). From 2004 to 2010 Iveta conducted research towards her PhD at the Law Faculty of Maastricht University, in combination with part-time lecturing and coaching award-winning teams in several international law moot court competitions. She has also participated in various capacity building activities in the Netherlands as well as abroad.